T0271067

'Vast in scope and unparalleled in the depth of its contributions, this new edition of the Routledge Companion is an indispensable up-to-date source for aspiring and established accounting historians, and all those interested in this vibrant and foundational sub-discipline of accounting'.

Rob Bryer, Emeritus Professor of Accounting Warwick Business School, Warwick University, UK

THE ROUTLEDGE COMPANION TO ACCOUNTING HISTORY

The Routledge Companion to Accounting History presents a single-volume synthesis of research in this expanding field, exploring and analysing accounting from ancient civilisations to the modern day.

No longer perceived as the narrow study of how a mysterious technique was used in the past, the scope of accounting history has widened substantially. This revised and updated volume moves beyond the history of accounting technologies, accounting theories and practices, and the accountants who applied them. Expert contributors from around the world explore the interfaces between accounting and the economy, society, culture and the polity. Accounting history is shown to offer important insights into such disparate phenomena as the evolution of capitalism, control of labour, gender and family relationships, racial exploitation, the operation of religious organisations, and the functioning of the state.

Illuminating the foundation and development of accounting systems, this updated, classic book opens the field to a new generation of accounting scholars and historians around the world.

John Richard Edwards is Professor of Accounting at Cardiff University, UK.

Stephen P. Walker is Professor of Accounting at the University of Edinburgh, UK.

ROUTLEDGE COMPANIONS IN BUSINESS, MANAGEMENT AND ACCOUNTING

Routledge Companions in Business, Management and Accounting are prestige reference works providing an overview of a whole subject area or sub-discipline. These books survey the state of the discipline including emerging and cutting-edge areas. Providing a comprehensive, up to date, definitive work of reference, Routledge Companions can be cited as an authoritative source on the subject.

A key aspect of these Routledge Companions is their international scope and relevance. Edited by an array of highly regarded scholars, these volumes also benefit from teams of contributors which reflect an international range of perspectives.

Individually, Routledge Companions in Business, Management and Accounting provide an impactful one-stop-shop resource for each theme covered. Collectively, they represent a comprehensive learning and research resource for researchers, postgraduate students and practitioners.

Published titles in this series include

The Routledge Companion to Career Studies
Edited by Hugh Gunz, Mila Lazarova and Wolfgang Mayrhofer

The Routledge Companion to Nonprofit Management
Edited by Stefan Toepler and Helmut Anheier

The Routledge Companion to Inclusive Leadership
Edited by Joan Marques

The Routledge Companion to Accounting History, Second edition
Edited by John Richard Edwards and Stephen P. Walker

The Routledge Companion to Managing Digital Outsourcing
Edited by Erik Beulen and Pieter Ribbers

For more information about this series, please visit: www.routledge.com/Routledge-Companions-in-Business-Management-and-Accounting/book-series/RCBMA

THE ROUTLEDGE COMPANION TO ACCOUNTING HISTORY

Second edition

Edited by John Richard Edwards and Stephen P. Walker

LONDON AND NEW YORK

Second edition published 2020
by Routledge
2 Park Square, Milton Park, Abingdon, Oxon OX14 4RN

and by Routledge
605 Third Avenue, New York, NY 10017

First issued in paperback 2021

Routledge is an imprint of the Taylor & Francis Group, an informa business

Publisher's Note
The publisher has gone to great lengths to ensure the quality of this reprint but points out that some imperfections in the original copies may be apparent.

First edition published by Routledge 2008

British Library Cataloguing-in-Publication Data
A catalogue record for this book is available from the British Library

Library of Congress Cataloging-in-Publication Data
A catalog record has been requested for this book

Typeset in Bembo
by Swales & Willis, Exeter, Devon, UK

ISBN 13: 978-0-8153-7586-9 (hbk)
ISBN 13: 978-1-03-223664-3 (pbk)

DOI: 9781351238885

CONTENTS

ILLUSTRATIONS

Figure

Tables

CONTRIBUTORS

Marcia Annisette is a Professor of Accounting at the Schulich School of Business, York University. She is co-editor in chief of *Accounting Organizations and Society*. Her major research interest is in the social organisation of the accountancy profession and she has published studies on professional accountancy in Trinidad and Tobago, England, Ireland and Canada.

Ignace De Beelde is Professor of Auditing at Ghent University. He has written on accounting and auditing including the history of accounting and the development of the accounting profession in Belgium. His history publications include articles in *Accounting, Organizations and Society*, *Accounting, Business & Financial History*, *Accounting History* and *Accounting Historians Journal*.

Chiara Bottausci is a Lecturer in Accounting at the University of Bristol. She recently received her doctorate in accounting at HEC Paris. Chiara has written on the sociology of translation and its contributions to accounting research. Her current research focuses on performance management systems and the role of accounting in processes of market making.

Gordon Boyce is Associate Professor in Social and Environmental Accounting at La Trobe University, Melbourne. His research utilises critical and interpretive perspectives on accounting and accountability, with a particular focus on understanding accounting's functioning in its socio-political context. He is interested in the implications for sustainability, public administration, professionalism, the public interest and education.

Salvador Carmona is Professor of Accounting and Management Control at IE Business School, Madrid. His research interests include accounting history, accounting and religion, and the design and functioning of cost accounting practices in non-competitive environments. He is a past-President of the Academy of Accounting Historians and the European Accounting Association.

Roy Chandler is a Chartered Accountant and Professor in Accounting at Cardiff Business School. He has published on varied aspects of auditing and accounting history as well as more contemporaneous issues in corporate governance. His work has appeared in both professional and academic journals.

Frank L. Clarke was Emeritus Professor at the University of Newcastle and Honorary Professor of Accounting at the University of Sydney when he died in 2020. He was a former editor of *Abacus* and the author of books and articles addressing issues relating to financial reporting. Books include (with Graeme Dean): *Indecent Disclosure: Gilding the Corporate Lily* (2007) and (with Dean and Mathew Egan) *The Unaccountable & Ungovernable Corporation* (2014).

Philip Colquhoun is a Senior Learning Designer for the CA Program at Chartered Accountants Australia and New Zealand. He was previously Senior Lecturer in the School of Accounting and Commercial Law at Victoria University of Wellington. His research on local government accounting and auditing has been published in *Accounting History* and *Accounting History Review.*

David J. Cooper is Emeritus Professor at the University of Alberta and part-time Professor at the University of Edinburgh. He has written nine books and over 90 articles. He is a joint editor at *Accounting, Organizations and Society* and founding editor of *Critical Perspectives on Accounting*. He currently researches performance measurement systems and the global regulation of accounting.

Graeme W. Dean is an Emeritus Professor at the University of Sydney and during 1994–2008 was the sole editor of *Abacus*. He has published several books on the role of accounting in corporate failures and financial dilemmas including (with Frank Clarke and Kyle Oliver) *Corporate Collapse* (1997, 2003). He has also authored over 70 refereed articles.

Alisdair Dobie is Professor of Accounting at Edge Hill University. He has published on monastic accounting and administration and on medieval ethics, including his book *Accounting at Durham Cathedral Priory: Management and Control of a Major Ecclesiastical Corporation 1083–1539* (2015). He is a co-ordinator of the Edge Hill University multi-disciplinary research group *Monastic Lancashire.*

John Richard Edwards is a part-time Research Professor at the Cardiff Business School. He has published articles on various episodes in accounting history in a range of professional and academic journals. Books include *A History of Corporate Financial Reporting in Britain* (2019) and (jointly) *The Priesthood of Industry* (1998), *A History of Management Accounting* (2013).

Mahmoud Ezzamel is Research Professor, Cardiff Business School. His research interests include accounting history, particularly in the ancient world, accounting and religion, the interface between accounting and social theory, accounting in the public sector, corporate governance, and more recently accounting regulation and the accounting profession in China.

Richard Fleischman is Professor Emeritus of Accounting at John Carroll University. He has published extensively on British industrial revolution cost accounting, US standard costing, and slavery accounting. He is a Life Member of the Academy of Accounting Historians and a recipient of its Hourglass Award.

Dale L. Flesher is Professor of Accountancy and Associate Dean at the University of Mississippi and holder of the Roland & Sheryl Burns Chair in Accountancy. He is a past-President of the Academy of Accounting Historians. He has authored 50 books and over 400 journal articles. He has specialised in railroad accounting, organisational histories and biographies.

Carolyn Fowler is an Associate Professor in the School of Accounting and Commercial Law, Victoria University Wellington. Her research focuses on the accounting profession and education, accounting history, strategy and management accounting, and the use of information technology in accounting. She is currently Joint Editor of *Accounting History*.

Warwick Funnell is Professor of Accounting and Public Sector Accountability at the University of Kent. He has published widely on the history of public sector accounting. Recent books include *Accounting by the First Public Company* (2015), *A History of British National Audit* (2017) and *The Italian and Iberian Influence in Accounting History* (2018).

Sonja Gallhofer is Professor of Accounting, Governance and Accountability in the Adam Smith Business School at the University of Glasgow. A major focus of her research is the exploration of the possibilities for more enabling and emancipatory accounting, corporate governance and corporate social responsibility practices.

Jim Haslam is Professor of Accounting, Governance and Society at Sheffield University Management School. He has published numerous articles which contribute to the critical, historical and social analysis of accounting. He was previously employed at Aston, Essex, Waikato, Heriot-Watt, Dundee, Durham and Newcastle universities, the University College of North Wales and the London School of Economics.

Lisa Jack is Professor of Accounting at University of Portsmouth. She carries out interdisciplinary research on the food industry and accounting, and won the Coleman Prize awarded by the Business History Association in 2005 for her thesis 'The Persistence of Post-War Accounting Practices in UK Agriculture'.

Barbara E. Kemmerer retired in 2007 as an Associate Professor of Management at Eastern Illinois University. She has published on the gender of the accounting workforce, diversity in the workforce, job stress and job complexity.

Rihab Khalifa is a Professor in Accounting, Vice Dean of the College of Business and Economics, and the founding Director of the Emirates Institute for Learning Outcomes Assessment, at the United Arab Emirates University. Rihab's research has concerned gender issues in accounting, and audit and governance as fields of professional practice.

Eksa Kilfoyle is a Chartered Accountant and Associate Professor in Accounting at Monash University. Her research examines how institutional, social and political contexts shape individual responses to accounting systems and processes, and how in turn individuals shape accounting systems and processes in organisations.

Linda M. Kirkham is a former Professor of Accounting at The Robert Gordon University, Aberdeen. She has written extensively on the accounting profession, gender and accounting history. Her publications include a number of key articles examining the interface of accounting history and gender processes.

Margaret Lamb is Associate Director of the Lazarus Center for Career Development at Smith College. Previously she was Reader in Accounting at Warwick Business School. She has published on the history of taxation and accounting, the public administration of taxation, interdisciplinary approaches to tax research and scholarship, and UK and international financial reporting.

Thomas A. Lee is Emeritus Professor of Accountancy at the University of Alabama. His research includes financial reporting as well as accounting history. He was President of the

Academy of Accounting Historians (1999) and received a Life-time Achievement Award from the British Accounting Association (2005).

Josephine Maltby was Professor of Accounting and Finance at Sheffield University Management School at the time of her untimely death in 2017. Her research interests were in accounting, finance and business history. She published on corporate governance, financial reporting, corporate social reporting, and on women as investors and wealth managers during the nineteenth and twentieth centuries.

Lachlan McDonald-Kerr is a Lecturer at the La Trobe Business School, Melbourne. He holds a PhD in accounting and researches critical, social and environmental accounting and accountability, and related areas. He is a Chartered Accountant (CAANZ), Certified Practicing Accountant (CPA Australia) and Certified Fraud Examiner (CFE).

Sam McKinstry was formerly Professor of Accounting at the University of the West of Scotland. He has published extensively in the accounting and business history literature. His books on the arts include: *Rowand Anderson: The Premier Architect of Scotland* (Thomas Ross Prize, 1997) and *'Greek' Thomson* (American Institute of Architects' Prize, 2000, with Gavin Stamp).

Tom McLean is Associate Professor of Accounting at Durham University Business School. His main research interests lie in British management accounting history of the nineteenth century.

Cheryl Susan McWatters holds the Father Edgar Thivierge Chair in Business History and is Professor of Accounting at the University of Ottawa. Her research adopts transdisciplinary approaches to accounting history, management control and operations management. She is currently editor of *Accounting History Review* and president of the Association pour l'histoire du management et des organisations.

Christopher J. Napier is Professor of Accounting at Royal Holloway University of London. After qualifying as a Chartered Accountant, he taught at the London School of Economics and the University of Southampton. He has served as a member of the Council of the Institute of Chartered Accountants in England and Wales.

Ciarán Ó. hÓgartaigh is President of NUI Galway. He has published widely on financial reporting and accounting history in, for example, *Accounting, Organizations and Society* and *Critical Perspectives on Accounting*. He previously held accounting faculty positions in Ireland and New Zealand and was a Fulbright Fellow at Northeastern University, Boston in 2000–1.

Lynne Oats is Professor of Taxation and Accounting, University of Exeter Business School. She has published widely in the accounting and taxation fields. Her research interests centre on taxation policy and practice in both historical and contemporary settings, including social, institutional and international dimensions.

David Oldroyd is a Professor of Accounting at Newcastle University. His historical work has followed three main strands: 1) estate management practice in the North-east of England during the eighteenth century; 2) plantation management in the Caribbean and American South during the transition from slavery to a free economy; and 3) health and the poor in Victorian cities.

Chris Poullaos is Honorary Associate Professor of Accounting at the University of Sydney. His work on the history of the accounting profession in Australia, Britain, Canada, South Africa and the Philippines has appeared in *Accounting, Organizations and Society, Abacus, Accounting, Auditing & Accountability Journal* and *Critical Perspectives on Accounting.*

Gary J. Previts is Professor of Accountancy at Case Western Reserve University. His interests include the development of accounting thought, institutions, regulation and public policy. He has published in many academic and professional journals. He is co-author of *A History of Accountancy in the United States* (1998) and developer of the Accounting History Research Database.

Carlos Ramirez is Professor of Accounting at ESSEC Business School. His research focuses on the history and sociology of the accounting profession, and accounting and auditing standard setting. His work has been published in accounting journals (*Accounting, Organizations and Society, Accounting Business & Financial History, Accounting, Auditing & Accountability Journal*) and management journals (*Organization, Journal of Management Studies*).

Alan J. Richardson is Professor Emeritus, York University, Canada. Most recently he held the Odette Research Chair, University of Windsor. He has published on the regulation of practice rights and standard-setting processes. He is on the editorial board of eight journals including *Accounting, Organizations and Society, Contemporary Accounting Research* and *Journal of Professions and Organization.*

Keith Robson is Professor of Accounting at HEC Paris. He has published extensively on performance measurement systems, socio-political studies of accounting regulation, the profession, audit firms and professionalization, and auditing methodologies in journals such as *Accounting, Organizations and Society, Contemporary Accounting Research, Critical Perspectives on Accounting, Human Relations* and *Organization.* He is currently Co-Editor-in-Chief of *Accounting, Organizations and Society.*

Greg Stoner is Professor of Accounting in the Adam Smith Business School of the University of Glasgow. He has published on the history and uses of technologies in accounting, accounting education, including Pacioli as an early writer and educationalist on accounting, and the history and development of the accounting profession. He is editor of *Accounting Education.*

Steven Toms is currently Professor of Accounting and Finance at the University of Leeds. He is a former editor of the journal *Business History.* His research has examined the financial aspects of business history, including the relationship between business organisations and the development of accounting.

Stephen P. Walker is Professor of Accounting at the University of Edinburgh. He is a former editor of *Accounting Historians Journal* and *Accounting History Review,* a past-President of the Academy of Accounting Historians and a recipient of the Academy's Hourglass Award. His research focuses on the history of the accountancy profession, accounting and gender, and histories of accounting and society.

Charles W. Wootton retired in 2013 as Professor of Accountancy at Eastern Illinois University. He has published on gender and the accounting workforce, the development of machine accounting, early financial reporting in the US, and auditor concentration among large public accounting firms.

ACKNOWLEDGEMENTS

Thanks are due to Jacqueline Curthoys, formerly Business and Management Editor at Routledge, for planting the seed of this project. We appreciated the ongoing support of other Routledge staff during the various stages to publication of the *Companion*. The comments of academic referees helped refine our proposals for the first and second editions and were much appreciated.

We owe a special debt of gratitude to our contributors for their enthusiastic participation in this challenging enterprise. A number of the authors who contributed to the original volume were unable to revise their chapters for the second edition due to retirement or other commitments. Josephine Maltby agreed to update her chapter but passed away shortly thereafter, to the considerable regret of the accounting and business history communities. We welcome and thank the several new 'Routledge Companions' who generously agreed to revise the chapters of those who were unavailable, or undertook to write new chapters for this edition.

Some authors were confronted with sparse, emergent literatures where the identification of themes and trends was difficult. Others committed themselves to remits of almost unmanageable proportions – topics which were not easily subjected to synthetic treatment, particularly when authoritarian editors imposed tight word limits. The extent to which the authors succeeded not only in providing syntheses but also writing stimulating and insightful chapters which identify opportunities for others is evidence of the committed scholarship which has firmly established history in the canon of accounting research. We hope that authors have found this exercise personally rewarding, if not in the financial sense.

It seems appropriate that we pay tribute to the generations of accounting historians before us who made the case for the academic study of a discipline hitherto assumed to concern the present rather than the past. It is testament to their achievements that Chapter 1 of this book does not bear the legitimating title 'Why study accounting history?'

As ever, it is those closest to us, Liz and Sandie, who bear the heaviest burden of our marriage to accounting history as well as to them.

INTRODUCTION

Synthesis and engagement

John Richard Edwards and Stephen P. Walker

If for many history is boring and all about dead people, why produce a *Companion* to the history of a discipline that is widely perceived as a mind-numbing activity performed by the living dead – cold, colourless number crunchers? In this volume we hope to show that accounting history is much more than describing the content of crumbling ledgers, the scrutiny of faded balance sheets and charting impenetrable methods for recording transactions in the past. While we don't promise to excite readers with historical tales of lust, debauchery and murder, we do hope to reveal the manner in which the seemingly innocuous practice of accounting has pervaded human existence in numerous and fascinating ways.

As a process of information gathering, inscription, processing and dissemination, and as a basis for decision-making, accounting has impacted on lived experiences in the diverse arenas in which it has been practised throughout history. Sometimes its presence is conspicuous, as in large corporations, financial institutions and government organisations. In other places its operation is shrouded and its effects almost imperceptible. But present it invariably is – not only in the realms of capital markets, financial management and accountability structures but also in the pursuit of economic and social policy, the control of labour in organisations, the management of family relationships, the destruction of indigenous peoples, and the pursuit of military campaigns. It even features in religious belief systems, literature, art and architecture. Accounting has been implicated in key transitional events such as the emergence of capitalism and the industrial revolution. Further, those who practise accounting and the organisations that employ, regulate and represent them have amassed considerable power and significance in the modern age. It is the search for the presences, roles and impacts of accounting and accountants in manifold times and locations which excite those who research accounting history.

Why a *Companion to Accounting History*

The aims of the *Routledge Companion* are to offer an introduction to the shifting arenas that attract the attention of accounting historians, relate the findings of their research and address the controversies which energise debate in the field. The *Routledge Companion* is not intended to offer a metahistory but a comprehensive overview of the current state of historical knowledge in accounting.

Accounting historians operate in an environment where the production of general histories of their subject is not encouraged. An emphasis by university funding bodies and promotion panels on publication through the medium of refereed academic journals tends towards the production of detailed investigations of specific and manageable subjects. Although specialist and particular histories are generally considered to require the most intellectual labour, they are also the histories which are read the least. Textbooks and popular histories attract larger audiences but tend to command less academic respect. Readers may be assured that we have no intention of excessively popularising a serious academic subject by preparing a book on 'awesome accountants', 'barmy bookkeepers', 'calamitous cash flows' or 'devilish depreciation'. However, we do perceive the need for a greater engagement with accounting history and recognise the potential of synthesis in achieving it. The production of a convenient vehicle for surveying and communicating the results of accounting history research to a wider audience and inspiring others to enter the field is desirable if the subject is to be dislodged from its status as a narrow specialism on the outer fringes of the history universe, a minor descendant on the economics and business branch of the history family tree. Catching the attention and engaging with a wider audience is also likely to prove beneficial to accounting historians who have been charged with exhibiting an unhealthy tendency to introversion (Walker 2005; Guthrie and Parker 2006).

This call for greater engagement has parallels with other maturing subdisciplines of history. In the 1980s labour historians discussed whether synthesis was necessary due to the 'truncated state of the field – rich in its findings, unclear as to larger meanings' (quoted in Schatz 1984). Diplomatic historians have discussed whether the greater infusion of theory in their subject would act as a palliative to its 'subdisciplinary fragmentation' (Leffler 1995). Some social historians have suggested that importations such as the 'cultural turn' have increased particularism and the consequent desirability of synthesis (Stearns 2003). Other social historians have critically explored whether grand and partial narratives are a fruitful way of integrating their splintering discipline given that its vitality rests largely on constantly extending the field (van der Linden 2003).

More broadly, there have also been demands for syntheses in American history with a view to making sense of the findings of the fragmented and increasingly remote 'new' (social and cultural) histories that have proliferated in recent times. This raised pedagogical issues such as how to address 'overspecialisation' without descending to superficiality (Curtin 1984). It was argued, controversially, that assimilation and crystallisation were necessary to restore history to its rightful place in the intellectual culture of the American nation and fulfil its role in informing political discourse. This was not only deemed to be conducive to raising the profile of the discipline and its practitioners; it was the historian's 'civic service' to interact with the wider public (Bender 1986, 1987). While we do not make such claims for accounting history, the need to showcase the enormous contribution to knowledge made by accounting historians as the discipline has blossomed in recent decades is apparent. It is true that the state of knowledge varies significantly across the subject areas featuring in this volume, but the advance of research in accounting history is such that the time appears ripe for ventures beyond particularity.

Indeed, attempts have already been made in this direction. During the 1990s reference books appeared on accounting history. Most notably Chambers' (1995) *An Accounting Thesaurus: 500 Years of Accounting* was published, a work described by one reviewer as a 'filing cabinet full of apt and well-ordered quotations' on accounting (Baxter 1996).

Chatfield and Vangermeersch (1996) produced *The History of Accounting: An International Encyclopedia*. Also indicative of attempts to make sense of the field has been the appearance of multi-volume collections of some of the most significant academic articles published on accounting history (Edwards 2000; Fleischman 2006). Summary histories of core subjects such as financial accounting and management accounting have appeared as separate volumes (Edwards 1989, 2019; Boyns and Edwards 2013) or within edited handbooks (Chapman et al. 2007). However single-volume works of a synthetic character that address the numerous other themes in the widening field of accounting history research are not to be found.

There are other benefits of syntheses. While they may encourage excessive generalisation and 'open the way to erroneous and vacuous statements' (Monkkonen 1986) they can also be a route to the identification of emergent and overarching themes, fresh interpretations, future possibilities, the posing of new research questions and the facilitation of theory development. The object of synthesis may be to attempt to survey a field, identify or reformulate essential themes. The *Routledge Companion* does not aspire to the latter lofty form of holism. It is not an attempt to present a grand or metanarrative from a particular philosophical perspective (Fulbrook 2002: 58–62). Rather, it begins the task of 'relating parts to a whole' (Bender 1987) by presenting in a single place segmented syntheses of extant work in 29 subject areas of accounting history. Collectively, the chapters provide a comprehensive and critical survey of the current scope of accounting history research. The contribution which we believe the *Routledge Companion* makes is encapsulated in the following statement about the virtues of syntheses:

> They give specialists a sense of what historians in other subfields are writing. Syntheses provide a quick overview of a discipline, note important starting points and useful bibliographies. Syntheses can make comprehensible the research agendas of narrow specializations. They can set narrowly focused work in appropriate contexts and can identify materials and issues critical to our understanding of the past. Syntheses may even acquaint a larger reading public with issues in historical research, although contributions of this type are rare.
>
> *(Monkkonen 1986)*

Like other aspects of the historical research process synthesis involves questions of selection, interpretation and representation. Accordingly, synthesis is biased and, in various respects, its achievement is illusory (Painter 1987). Any attempt at universality and totalisation is problematical (Ryn 2000). The content of the *Routledge Companion* is inevitably partial in its reliance on history as performed and conveyed by accounting and other historians. Numerous untold histories of accounting remain silent, and will remain so until researched and articulated by historians. The *Routledge Companion* is also biased in that the editors' selection defines and privileges certain themes. The choice of authors conditions the emphases and standpoints which inform individual contributions. The *Routledge Companion* presents a series of narratives penned by 44 authors and joint-authors, each offering their own interpretations of the extant histories produced in their specialist fields. There is no pretension that these are definitive or complete accounts. Indeed, if the experience of the recent decades is at all indicative of what may happen in the future, the contours of accounting history knowledge will be substantially different within a relatively short time frame. Fresh syntheses will be required as agendas shift and new controversies redirect the attention of accounting historians. Indeed, for this second edition of the *Routledge*

Companion we commissioned new chapters on subjects where research activity has increased in recent years, namely accounting histories of agriculture and mercantilism. The authors featuring in the volume were given an assignment aligned to our objective of engagement. They were requested to provide a balanced overview of current knowledge, identify issues, discuss relevant debates and reflect on research opportunities.

A review of the contents of previous single-volume edited works on accounting history in the English language illustrates the need to produce a work which reveals to a wider audience the broadening scope and contribution of accounting history. Richard Brown's landmark *A History of Accounting and Accountants* of 1905 comprised two parts. Chapters on the 'History of Accounting' were concerned with the technical, embracing Numeration, Ancient Systems of Accounting, Early Forms of Accounts, History of Auditing and two chapters on the History of Bookkeeping. There followed ten chapters on the 'History of Accountants' which explored the origins and progress of accounting practitioners in locations such as Italy, Scotland, England and Wales, the British colonies and the USA. Half a century later appeared Littleton and Yamey's (1956) *Studies in the History of Accounting*. This work had the history of double-entry bookkeeping at its heart. It offered a chronologically organized volume of chapters primarily on record keeping (before and after double entry), from classical antiquity to the nineteenth century.

By the end of the twentieth century the inclusion of sections on local government, cost and management accounting, and accounting theory in Parker and Yamey's (1994) *Accounting History: Some British Contributions* revealed movement beyond the hitherto dominant focus of accounting history on bookkeeping and financial accounting. The inclusion of a final section on 'Accounting in Context' signalled the then recent extension of the subject beyond its traditional boundaries. When compared with these important works the contents of the *Routledge Companion* indicate the new ground which accounting history has covered in a relatively short time. The inclusion of sections on institutions, economy, society and culture, polity, and discussion of the discipline itself, illustrate the transformational effects of greater interfacing with a range of knowledge fields. Moreover, readers of chapters in sections which resonate more strongly with traditional foci of accounting history – technologies, and theory and practice – will discern how new ways of conducting and interpreting the history of accounting as technique have emerged in recent years.

Design of the *Companion*

The design of a work intended to provide a synthesis of accounting history research could be approached in a number of ways. A chronological emphasis with chapters exploring developments from the earliest accountings in ancient civilisations through to the electronic accounting in the modern age would be an obvious way of organising a work on history. Another possibility would be to commission a set of accounting histories of individual nations organised by continent. This might also reveal sensitivity to calls for the greater inclusivity of histories and historical traditions beyond the Anglophone world which has featured large in the literature and institutions of the discipline. It might also satisfy an audience of academic accountants interested in the historical background to the complexities of achieving accounting harmonisation in the age of globalisation. However, the approach decided upon for the *Routledge Companion* is thematic, one that is sensitive to chronology and geographical coverage but also indicative of the established and emerging subjects of accounting history research.

This emphasis is in accord with our priority of engagement with those considering researching accounting history, with scholars of the past and present of accounting, and those hailing from the diverse other disciplines with which accounting is increasingly seen to interact (Walker 2005, 2011; McWatters 2014, 2017). We particularly want to convey to the academic community, within and beyond accounting, the extent to which accounting history has advanced beyond a narrow concern with accounting as technique, a calculative method found predominantly in the realm of business. In an age when interdisciplinary engagement is high on the agenda, it is especially hoped that economic, social, cultural, literary, political and even military historians will discover points of connection between their own interests and the history of accounting through the themes explored in the *Routledge Companion*. In the past many scholars operating in such disciplines have found accounting 'too devious and contrived a subject to be penetrated by the historian without special grounding in the art' (Stacey 1954: xv). The content of the *Routledge Companion* will hopefully illustrate that accounting is not so mysterious, particularly where it interfaces with numerous other fields of history.

Our emphasis on engagement also extended to the manner in which we suggested authors approached their chapters and formulated organizing principles. While we indicated the importance of providing essential historical signposts and the inclusion of key literature for the guidance of those new to the subject, we also encouraged a focus on the discursive – a reflection on issues and debates, and consideration of research potentialities. Many of the contributors to the *Routledge Companion* took seriously our call to discuss their theme on as broad a geographical canvas as possible. That said the emphasis in most chapters is on reviewing extant knowledge as conveyed in the language which has long dominated the accounting history literature – English.

The chapters reveal the various motivations behind accounting history research and the different perspectival paradigms employed in the literature. Some scholars of accounting history have as their objective to understand symbols and calculations in their contemporary contexts or to uncover accounting relics in a search for the origins of a technique, concept or institution that features prominently in the accounting present. Other accounting historians seek to inform contemporary accounting policy-making by offering insights into the emergence of a modern-day issue, revealing how a similar problem was addressed in the past or merely to remind us that such issues endure or are incapable of resolution. Some use historical accounting data as the empirical basis for hypothesis testing or advancing a theory. Motivations for accounting history research also include the further exploration of issues and controversies raging in accounting history and evaluating an assertion about accounting made by a historian operating in another sub-field. Increasingly it is recognised that history may be deployed as part of the critical analysis of the accounting present or as a powerful way of exposing accounting in processes of oppression, exclusion or emancipation. As some of the chapters in the *Routledge Companion* illustrate, histories can be employed to draw into the accounting agenda groups hitherto largely invisible to it, such as the poor, women and ethnic minorities.

Structure of the *Companion*

Given that each chapter begins with a brief overview, it is not our intention here to detail the content of every contribution. But a few words about the structure of the *Routledge Companion* and some dominant themes are appropriate. The first four parts might be described as essentially *intra*disciplinary in character. In Part I 'The discipline' the authors of the chapters explain the growth of accounting history research, discuss the emergence and current state of disciplinary institutions, chart changes in the subjects studied, identify the practitioners of accounting history, the methods they employ and the outlets in which their work appears. Of particular importance to the development of the discipline has been a vibrant discourse on accounting historiography. This has had a significant impact on research in the subject areas which feature in later chapters.

Part II concerns 'Technologies'. Here the contributing authors provide contextualised insights into the varied and changing calculative techniques and devices employed for the measurement, representation and communication of financial (and other) data. They also discuss the mechanisms for holding persons accountable in diverse settings through ancient, classical, medieval and modern times. Accounting technologies are revealed as central to the functioning of governments, estates, traders, households and global corporations. At the chronological centre of this part lies enduring debates about the emergence of double-entry bookkeeping.

Part III explores the historical development of 'Theory and practice' in the core subjects of financial accounting, management accounting and auditing. The chapters discuss the frustrated search for a comprehensive theory of accounting, the relationship between accounting theory and practice, continuity and change in accounting practices, and consider the socio-economic motivations and impacts of those practices. It is in the history of managerial accounting that the search for motivations and impacts has been particularly intense. Controversy has been fuelled by the import of a range of theoretical perspectives, new methodologies and the investigation of a range of empirical sites. These controversies have been of significance beyond the pursuit of histories of management accounting. The concern with identifying motives for implementation has also encouraged polarised debate in the history of auditing, a practice increasingly understood as an almost omnipresent feature of modernity (Power 1997).

Part IV on 'Institutions' focuses on those who perform accounting functions, the organisations in which they are employed and educated, and by whom they are regulated. It is here that the sociologies of occupations, identity and socialisation meet accounting history. The chapters in this part reveal the complex histories of the professionalisation of accountants, their shifting work jurisdictions, the emergence and advancing power of accounting firms, the history of vocational preparation and pedagogical practice in accounting, and the development of the regulatory frameworks within which accounting is performed.

In Parts V, VI and VII attention shifts to histories that explore the interfaces of accounting with the economy, society and culture, and politics. These parts are especially indicative of the *inter*disciplinary panorama and widening scope of accounting history research. The chapters in Part V discuss histories of accounting which relate to the 'Economy'. Here the role of accounting in the histories of key sectors such as agriculture and railroads are explored. These industries were the location of significant developments in accounting. This part contains chapters on the role of accounting in the operation of economic systems, namely mercantilism and capitalism. The latter connects with the observation that 'accounting is fundamentally implicated in all stages of the development of capitalism'. Part V of the volume on 'Economy' also contains a chapter that focuses on the visibility of accounting at the macroeconomic level – in the national accounting regimens of liberal democracies and totalitarian states. Accounting becomes most controversial and its economic effects most visible when it is implicated in scandal, when auditing fails or accountants are accused of sharp practice or outright criminality. A chapter which reviews histories of corporate reporting scandals closes Part V.

'Society and culture' is the subject of Part VI. The opening chapters on gender, race, and colonialism and indigenous peoples contain two dominant features: first the exclusion of women and ethnic groups from the accounting profession; and second, the manner in which accounting and those who practise it are implicated in the construction and maintenance of unequal distributions of power, and in the exploitation, discrimination and management of particular populations. The first three chapters of Part VI emphasise exclusion, repression and oppression. The fourth offers a corrective in its relating historical instances where accounting displayed the potential to mobilise and challenge when deployed in emancipatory projects. The subsequent chapters on religion and the creative arts examine some of the linkages between accounting and culture. The application of accounting in religious organisations and its presence in religious texts is revealed as an important theme in accounting history, one that identifies new sites for exploring the development of accounting practices and the conceptual foundations of the craft. The breadth of accounting presences is also evident in the last chapter of Part VI, which reviews the significance of historical representations of accounting and accountants in architecture, literature, fine art, the graphic arts and film.

The final part of the *Routledge Companion* on 'Polity' contains chapters on the role of accounting in the government, protection and financing of states. The opening chapter of Part VII shows how central and local governments and their agencies have been major locations for the institution of accountability relationships, debates over appropriate accounting techniques and the use of accounting for purposes of social control. The penultimate chapter illuminates the centrality of accounting to successful military interventions, legislative control of the military, and the importance of war to the development of core accounting practices such as costing. The concluding chapter emphasises the importance of taxation to the fabric and maintenance of political systems and explores some of the areas where the histories of accounting and taxation interrelate.

Through these themed chapters it is expected that readers will gain historical insights into the many places in which accounting has featured, the diverse reasons for its introduction, the identity of those who have performed it, the forms it has taken, the purposes to which it has been put, and the effects it has had on those subjected to it. The authors show how the study of many of these accounting phenomena has been illuminated by the application of theory. They also reveal the way in which accountings, like other forms of text, offer historical pathways into the economic, social, cultural and political realms.

Over 60 years ago the eminent US accountant Sidney Davidson, when reviewing Littleton and Yamey (1956) *Studies in the History of Accounting*, confessed that

> I began this volume with some reluctance, for essays on accounting history are frequently dull and uninspired. As I read on I felt that this volume had come closer than most to living up to its extravagant publisher's blurb that 'this book makes fascinating reading'
>
> *(Davidson 1957)*

Our ambition is that readers of the *Routledge Companion* will arrive at the same conclusion.

References

Baxter, W.T. (1996) Review of *An Accounting Thesaurus: 500 Years of Accounting*, *Accounting and Business Research*, 26 (4): 358.

Bender, T. (1986) Wholes and parts: the need for synthesis in American history, *Journal of American History*, 73 (1): 120–36.

Bender, T. (1987) Wholes and parts: continuing the conversation, *Journal of American History*, 74 (1): 123–30.

Boyns, T. and Edwards, J.R. (2013) *A History of Management Accounting. The British Experience* (London: Routledge).

Chambers, R.J. (1995) *An Accounting Thesaurus: 500 Years of Accounting* (Oxford: Pergamon Press).

Chapman, C.S., Hopwood, A.G. and Shields, M.D. (eds) (2007) *Handbook of Management Accounting Research* (Amsterdam: Elsevier).

Chatfield, M. and Vangermeersch, R. (1996) *The History of Accounting: An International Encyclopedia* (New York: Garland).

Curtin, P.D. (1984) Depth, span, and relevance, *American Historical Review*, 89 (1): 1–9.

Davidson, S. (1957) Review of studies in the history of accounting, *Economica*, 24 (94): 176–77.

Edwards, J.R. (1989) *A History of Financial Accounting* (London: Routledge).

Edwards, J.R. (ed.) (2000) *The History of Accounting. Critical Perspectives on Business and Management* (London: Routledge).

Edwards, J.R. (2019) *A History of Corporate Financial Reporting in Britain* (London: Routledge).

Fleischman, R.K. (ed.) (2006) *Accounting History* (London: Sage Publications).

Fulbrook, M. (2002) *Historical Theory* (London: Routledge).

Guthrie, J. and Parker, L. (2006) The coming out of accounting research specialisms, *Accounting, Auditing & Accountability Journal*, 19 (1): 5–16.

Leffler, M.P. (1995) New approaches, old interpretations, and prospective reconfigurations, *Diplomatic History*, 19 (2): 172–96.

Littleton, A.C. and Yamey, B.S. (1956) Preface, in A.C. Littleton and B.S. Yamey (eds) *Studies in the History of Accounting*, pp. v–viii (London: Sweet & Maxwell).

McWatters, C.S. (2014) Historical accounts, conversations and contexts, *Accounting History Review*, 24 (1): 1–5.

McWatters, C.S. (2017) Historians but not necessarily so, *Accounting History Review*, 27 (3): 219–21.

Monkkonen, E.H. (1986) The dangers of synthesis, *American Historical Review*, 91 (5): 1146–57.

Painter, N.I. (1987) Bias and synthesis in history, *Journal of American History*, 74 (1): 109–12.

Parker, R.H. and Yamey, B.S. (eds) (1994) *Accounting History. Some British Contributions* (Oxford: Clarendon Press).

Power, M. (1997) *The Audit Society. Rituals of Verification* (Oxford: Oxford University Press).

Ryn, C.G. (2000) History as synthesis, *Humanitas*, 13 (1): 89–102.

Schatz, R.W. (1984) Labor historians, labor economics, and the question of synthesis, *Journal of American History*, 71 (1): 93–100.

Stacey, N.A.H. (1954) *English Accountancy: A Study in Social and Economic History* (London: Gee and Company).

Stearns, P.N. (2003) Social history present and future, *Journal of Social History*, 37 (1): 9–19.

van der Linden, M. (2003) Gaining ground, *Journal of Social History*, 37 (1): 69–75.

Walker, S.P. (2005) Accounting in history, *Accounting Historians Journal*, 33 (2): 233–59.

Walker, S.P. (2011) Editorial, *Accounting History Review*, 21 (1): 1–5.

PART I

The discipline

1
STRUCTURES, TERRITORIES AND TRIBES

Stephen P. Walker

Overview

The aim of this chapter is to explore the development and current status of accounting history as a sub-discipline. The terrain of accounting history is mapped by surveying the institutions which characterise and legitimate its pursuit. In particular, the chapter examines the emergence of disciplinary organisations for accounting historians, the increasing number of conferences on the subject, the growth in accounting history publications and the pedagogical claims advanced by advocates of accounting history education. The principal intellectual currents which have run through these disciplinary structures are explored in Chapter 2 and the development of the subject areas of accounting research which they have helped to sustain are reviewed in Chapter 3.

It is shown that progress in some areas of disciplinary endeavour (such as establishing specialist journals and conferences) has been more marked than in others (such as creating enduring and inclusive organisations and integrating accounting history into the curriculum). The chapter begins by discussing the expansion of accounting history research, locating its disciplinary territory and exploring some of the features which define the 'academic tribe' of accounting historians (Becher and Trowler 2001: 23–4).

The growth of accounting history

According to Becher and Trowler (2001: 14):

> Disciplinary growth can be measured by the number and types of departments in universities, the change and increase in types of HE courses, the proliferation of disciplinary associations, the explosion in the number of journals and articles published and the multiplication of recognized research topics and research clusters.

Similarly, Clark (1996) suggests that the growth of a discipline may be discerned by tracking the expansion of the institutions surrounding it. In particular, the growth of academic departments and units, degree programmes and courses, disciplinary associations, disciplinary journals, the existence of recognised research topics and related research clusters. While one would be hard pressed to identify university departments of accounting history and degree programmes on the subject, courses on various aspects of the history of accounting do feature. Further, various organisations represent the practitioners of accounting history, several specialist journals exist and operate in traditional and web-based formats, and an increasing number of articles on accounting history are published in specialist and general accounting journals. There is also an increasing plurality of research themes and some research centres have been established (Walker 2006).

Although its advocates frequently relate the pedagogical and practical utility of knowledge of the subject, accounting history is not a field of study which grew in response to societal or professional calls for its inclusion in the curriculum. The growth of accounting history is more usefully interpreted as a response to various developments in higher education in recent decades. These include massification and the attendant expansion of academic knowledge, the increasing fragmentation of disciplines and the career-enhancing potential of academic specialisation in the context of the 'research imperative' (Blau 1973: 190–8; Clark 1987: 197–210, 1996; Metzger 1987; Henkel 2000: 29–145). A Marxist interpretation of this scene perceives the proliferation of accounting histories as a consequence of the commodification of history and historians under advanced capitalism. This interpretation perceives the expansion of histories as the production of self-referential signifiers in the interest of capital (Cooper and Puxty 1996).

More conventionally, the growth in accounting history research is explicable as both reactive and substantive. It is reactive in that the expansion of the sub-discipline represents a response to the increased demand for accounting labour and the consequential growth of vocationally relevant higher education in accounting and business. Educational expansion has been serviced by a rapid increase in the numbers of university staff teaching accounting. In the UK, for example, the number of accounting academics more than doubled in the 20 years to 2004 (Brown et al. 2007). Those who instruct the student population have been increasingly urged to comply with the institutional priority of pursuing research and publication (Gray and Helliar 1994; Whittington 1995; Wallace 1997; Beattie and Goodacre 2004). Accounting history represents one research specialism which attracted increasing numbers of accounting academics (Matthews 2017). However, the expansion of accounting history has also been substantive, or knowledge-led (Metzger 1987). Its growth illustrates the extension of the accounting research agenda beyond its technical core. This broadening in the scope of academic accounting has been attended by the dignification of a number of specialisms and the advancing status of the interdisciplinary study of the discipline, including its history (Elzinga 1987).

Characterising the accounting history tribe and locating its territory

The fragmentation of academic disciplines into research sub-disciplines and specialisms is certainly not unique to accounting. The discipline of history has not only witnessed the emergence of economic, social and cultural history but, in recent decades, the further splintering of each sub-discipline (Eley 1979; Marwick 1989: 72–141; Jordanova 2000: 34–46; Vincent 2001: 133–67). However, it would be wrong to perceive the growth of accounting history as a manifestation of subject dispersion and the emergence of new specialisms in the discipline of history. Accounting history emanates from the broadening terrain of accounting. The pathways to academic careers in accounting history are diverse but are predominantly characterised by undergraduate, postgraduate and/or professional education in accounting rather than history, though on occasion, both. Thus from an early stage disciplinary associations and various authors in accounting history have felt obliged to instruct entrants to the field on the historical research methodologies which are absent from an accounting education (Gaffikin 1981; Parker and Graves 1989; Fleischman et al. 2003).

The disciplinary habitation of accounting historians in accounting rather than history is also indicated by other institutional factors. The great majority of accounting historians reside in the accounting and finance departments of business schools and everyday interaction tends to be with colleagues in these fields. Its practitioners tend to identify themselves as operating in the discipline of accounting but belong to a research community that specialises in history. The instructional mission of accounting historians is grounded in accounting rather than history and the sustainability of the specialist courses they offer depends on attracting students following accounting rather than history programmes. In the absence of departments of accounting history the institutional focus of its practitioners is the research conference, the accounting history association and sometimes the research unit. Examples of the latter have included the Accounting and Business History Research Unit at Cardiff University, which commenced in 1988, and the *Centro de Estudos de História da Contabilidade* (Accounting History Research Centre) of the Portuguese Association of Accountants which was formed in 1996 (de Serra Faria 2008).

The institutional and disciplinary locus in accounting rather than history is confirmed by an examination of the research environment. In the UK Research Assessment Exercise accounting history fell within the orbit of the sub-panel on accounting and finance as opposed to history (RAE 2002, 2009). In the more recent Research Excellence Framework, along with accounting and finance, it falls within the scope of the sub-panel on Business and Management Studies. In the assessment of 2014 the sub-panel specifically identified accounting history as an area within accounting and finance where 'substantial scholarship' is demonstrated (REF 2015). Further, the publication media favoured by accounting historians are conditioned by those which confer greatest esteem in accounting – articles in high ranking journals tend to be the vehicle for the communication of new knowledge in accounting history rather than the monograph favoured by historians.

In addition to their career tracks being located in the disciplinary structures of accounting rather than history, accounting historians as a whole tend not to engage with the wider history community. Relationships with near neighbours, such as business historians, are often explored (Johnson 1975; Boyns and Edwards 1990; Fridenson 2007) and accounting historians have a presence in the journals of that sub-field. However, while there are notable exceptions, they seldom publish in history journals and often appear disinclined to embark on research collaborations with historians (Walker 2005). Despite its undoubted potential to do so, accounting history has not impacted on the historical mainstream in the way that, for example, women's history has. It does not feature in history textbooks, fire debates in the greater history literature or induce questions in the sister discipline about the nature and pursuit of history. On the occasions when historians, popular or professional, venture into the world of accounting, their outputs are often critiqued for insufficient engagement with the research produced by accounting historians and questions are raised about why such works seldom emanate from those best placed to author them (Carnegie and Napier 2013; Vollmers 2015).

Given the general lack of interdisciplinary communication between accounting and other historians, it is not surprising that perceptions of the scope and character of accounting history appear to differ according to whether the stance is internal or external to the craft. For accounting historians the potential scope of their subject is multidisciplinary and vast, and embraces research based on data which may be documentary or oral, qualitative or quantitative. For historians, accounting history is more likely perceived as a progeny of business history, a specialism which focuses on mysterious calculative techniques manifested in sources such as invoices, ledgers and balance sheets.

It would be wrong to suggest that the boundaries between accounting and other historians are closed. There are undoubtedly cross-disciplinary influences which suggest that accounting history is a 'hybrid field' (Dogan 1997). However, the communication is substantially unidirectional and involves more borrowing than lending. Accounting historians import methodologies and historiographical discourses from history and its sub-disciplines. Accounting history increasingly draws on standards in history when establishing and reinforcing the benchmarks of quality research in its own domain. These attributes are generally considered to emanate from comprehensive evidence gathering (accounting historians as auditors have an affinity with historians on this matter; Napier 2002; Walker 2004), contextualisation, thorough literature review, analytical rather than descriptive writing, high quality narrative and addressing the 'so what' question. Whereas accounting historians have frequently been compelled to legitimate their research by illustrating its relevance to modern day accounting issues and policy making, as in history, good accounting history is increasingly recognised as meritorious when it advances understandings and encourages debate about the past.

Accounting history is thus best understood as a sub-field of accounting which also draws inspiration from other disciplines. It embraces various specialisms based on configurations relating to subject areas (such as management accounting, financial accounting, accounting institutions), theoretical approaches (such as Marxist, Foucauldian, economic rationalist), interdisciplinary influences (various sub-disciplines of history, and other disciplines such as economics, politics, sociology), methodologies and use of sources (oral, archival), and sectoral, spatial and/or temporal foci. Each of these arenas may contain sub-specialisms that represent compound delineations such as the history of cost accounting in the modern period, the sociological history of the accountancy profession, archival studies of financial accounting practice, or Marxist interpretations of the development of financial accounting. As the contents of this volume attest, the research field is extraordinarily broad, offering scope for investigating historical phenomena across the corpus of accounting and accountability subjects.

The research themes which occupy accounting historians are sensitive to a range of influences. These are internal to the sub-discipline, as in the discourses generated by research findings and seeking answers to enduring questions. Influences are also external in the form of themes emerging in the contemporary academic discipline of accounting (such as international accounting, corporate social and sustainability reporting); the professional and institutional environment (regulation, organisations, ethics); and discourses and shifting themes in related disciplines such as history, management and sociology. Accounting history is a field where fresh methodological and theoretical approaches, new ways of seeing older debates, and the discovery of unexplored arenas for the practice of accounting in historical contexts are usually greeted with enthusiasm.

The practitioners of accounting history are predominantly male (Carnegie et al. 2003; de Serra Faria 2008; Matthews 2017), operate in diverse national and cultural contexts and are socialised in various traditions of accounting and historical research. Compare, for example, the position of the accounting historian in the US with his counterpart in Italy. The former operates in an academic environment where capital markets research dominates and career-building rests heavily on the achievement of publication in the most prestigious generalist accounting journals. The latter, by contrast, benefits from an institutional context where the state explicitly recognises accounting history as a legitimate specialism and where publication in its specialist journals contributes to career progression (Fleischman and Radcliffe 2005; Antonelli and D'Alessio 2014).

This range of situational contingencies together with the unbounded research field suggests that accounting historians operate in a divergent and potentially conflictual sub-discipline, especially when the purview extends beyond the local. Indeed, there have been heated contests over the merits of 'old' and 'new' accounting history, and cultural clashes over access to research journals and the perceived Anglo-American *zeitgeist* in the institutions of the craft (Carmona 2004; see also Chapter 2). At the same time accounting historians can display a capacity for commonality borne of the unifying effects of challenges to the legitimacy of their discipline in the modern business school, the unfairly low ranking of their specialist journals and the exclusion of their work from certain eminent accounting journals, a common concern for the advance of the discipline, and the quest for its greater recognition in the wider realm of history.

Accounting historians are an academic tribe whose identity is increasingly reinforced at numerous specialist conferences. They are a research community which canonises those heroic figures who blaze trails by conferring awards and producing league tables of influential contributors (Carmona 2006; Matthews 2017). While such analyses can give visibility to challenges confronting the tribe, a number of its members have displayed an introverted concern with publication patterns, citation analyses and rates of co-authorship. It is not entirely clear whether this represents a healthy attempt to plot shifting disciplinary territories and explore the potential for new research themes, or is a symptom of the existence of too many specialist accounting history journals or, more worryingly, of intellectual exhaustion.

Accounting history is a sub-discipline in which identities are often constructed around the individual's approach to historical research (archival v. armchair theorising), writing history (description v. theorised analysis), or adherence to a theoretical perspective. These distinctions are abstracted as identifiers such as 'old' and 'new' accounting historian, a distinction based not on the age of the practitioner but her/his approach to historical research (Carnegie and Napier 1996). The potency of such labels has recently diminished somewhat amid calls for greater plurality, tolerance and a focus on what unites rather than divides accounting historians (see Chapter 2).

Disciplinary associations

Given that accounting history is not institutionalised in academic departments and research centres in the subject are few in number, organisations for practitioners beyond the university are of particular importance for sustaining communication and fostering collective identity. The development of disciplinary associations in accounting history is now considered.

The Academy of Accounting Historians

The foremost international disciplinary association in accounting history is the Academy of Accounting Historians, formed in 1973. The origins of the Academy are usually traced to 1968 when the American Accounting Association established a Committee on Accounting History chaired by Stephen Zeff of Tulane University. The remit of the Committee was to:

> [p]ropose objectives for research in accounting history, develop guidelines for the teaching of accounting history in undergraduate and graduate courses, and provide a forum … through which those interested in the teaching or research of accounting history can hear papers and exchange ideas.
>
> *(American Accounting Association 1970)*

The Committee observed that the recent pursuit of accounting knowledge beyond the technical had encouraged increased interest in the history of accounting. However, the subject was not as advanced as the histories of other disciplines. The Committee stated forcibly that:

> [h]istorical research is a continuing and necessary element in the overall research effort of scholars in an academic discipline. Accounting is at once professional and academic, and its history is no less relevant than medical history is to medicine, legal history is to law, economic history is to economics, and architectural history is to architecture.
>
> *(American Accounting Association 1970)*

The Committee on Accounting History considered that the objects of accounting history research were to understand the development of accounting thought, practice and institutions, and argued that such knowledge would assist the formulation of solutions to modern day accounting problems. The Committee was keen to encourage research in accounting history, particularly that which engaged business and economic historians. Further, recognising that identifying archival materials was a constraint, it provided a comprehensive review of sources for accounting history research. The Committee also observed the absence of an organisation for accounting historians and the need for a vehicle to communicate the results of research on the subject. It suggested that 'roundtables on accounting history' should be convened at gatherings of the American Accounting Association.

The fact that the American Accounting Association did not act on the report of the Committee on Accounting History inspired a small group of accounting professors to form an Academy of Accounting Historians (Coffman et al. 1989). The key meeting took place in Quebec on 15 August 1973. Gary J. Previts was elected President. The object of the new organisation was 'to encourage research, publication, teaching and personal interchanges in all phases of accounting history and its interrelation with business and economic history including the environment within which they developed' (*Accounting Historians Notebook*: Fall 1978).

Although the Academy was perceived as an organisation that would embrace researchers throughout the world, its founders and early office holders were American. The Academy was incorporated in Alabama, its research centres were established in Georgia and Mississippi, its journal editors were American, its meetings and conferences were focused in the US, and its members were primarily US resident. The individual and institutional membership of the Academy reached a high point of 913 in 1995 but fell to 709 in 2006. The declining membership primarily reflected a number of threats to accounting history research in the US (Fleischman and Radcliffe 2005). Hence, while in 1986 the ratio of US individual members to non-US individual members was 3.2:1, in 2006 it was 1.3:1. In response to the shifting composition of its membership, the Academy sought to internationalise its activities and office bearers (Coffman et al. 2014). A succession of four non-US presidents were elected during 2006–2009. However, the decline in membership did not abate and stood at 380 by 2015.

Following a number of strategic reviews and divided opinion on whether the organisation should be internationally or US-focused, in 2015 the members authorised the officers to pursue a merger with the American Accounting Association, with whom a memorandum of understanding had been signed in 2008. In 2017 the Academy was formally constituted as a special interest section of the American Accounting Association.

In accord with its original objectives the work of the Academy of Accounting Historians has centred on publication, research and education. The most important initiatives of the Academy have been in publication. It has performed valuable service as a vehicle for communication between accounting historians and the dissemination of their work. Most significantly it inaugurated *The Accounting Historians Journal* (see below). It also commenced a working paper series in 1974 which published 80 articles until its discontinuance in 1991. An accounting history monograph series was introduced in 1976 as was the reproduction of key works in an Accounting History Classics series (until 1991).

The Academy has also encouraged research through its committee work on accounting history bibliography and the identification of archives. Given that limited awareness of relevant methodology has often been perceived as an impediment to the pursuit of historical research by accounting academics, the activities of the Accounting History Research Methodology Committee during the 1980s was particularly important (Parker and Graves 1989; Previts et al. 1990; Fleischman et al. 2003). The Academy also sponsored research institutions such as the Accounting History Research Center opened in 1982 at Georgia State University (and closed in 2005), and the Tax History Research Center at the University of Mississippi in 1987. The Academy convenes an annual research conference in the US and has co-sponsored World Congresses of Accounting Historians. A seminar series attempted to reveal the relevance of history to accounting practitioners and its significance to understanding contemporary issues. The Academy has also attempted to attract new researchers and encourage doctoral study by offering graduate stipends, grants, scholarships and manuscript awards (such as the Richard G. Vangermeersch Award from 1988 and the Schoenfeld Scholarship from 2008).

The third major area of Academy activity has been in accounting history education. From the early 1980s much attention was devoted to integrating history into the university accounting curriculum (Coffman et al. 1989, 1998). This subject is discussed later in the chapter.

The international committee of accounting historians

The formation of the Academy of Accounting Historians was not the first attempt to establish an international organisation for accounting historians. In October 1970 the First International Symposium of Accounting Historians was held in Brussels. The event was organised by the *Collège National des Experts Comptables de Belgique* (Coffman et al. 1989). The prime mover and Secretary-General of the Symposium was Ernest Stevelinck, a leading accounting historian and member of the Council of the *Collège National* (Dunlop 1970). The Symposium was attended by representatives of various national accounting organisations. Stevelinck argued that national committees on accounting history should be set up and their activities co-ordinated by an international committee. He also suggested establishing a multilingual journal on accounting history as well as a number of bibliographical ventures.

A working party was instituted during the First International Symposium. It was resolved that Stevelinck would chair a study group on accounting history under the auspices of the *Collège National* and the formation of national accounting history committees would be encouraged. From this agenda emerged the International Committee of Accounting Historians, based at the *Collège National* with Stevelinck as Secretary-General. Its object was to provide a means of communication between national accounting history groups. It would alert members to the appearance of accounting history articles, encourage the inclusion of accounting history in the curriculum, publish a bulletin, and inaugurate a programme of quinquennial international congresses on accounting history (*Accountant* 8 April 1971: 451).

It was envisaged that the International Committee would embrace a broad range of interested researchers including academic and practitioner accountants, historians, and archivists. However, little appears to have come of this organisation. Although references can be found to Stevelinck as President of the Belgium National Committee of Accounting Historians and Secretary of the International Committee of Accounting Historians during the 1980s (see *Accounting Historians Notebook* 1983, also 1987), neither organisation appears to have existed for long. The apparent failure of the International Committee resulted in the Academy of Accounting Historians assuming the mantle of the foremost disciplinary association in the field, though its credentials as an international organisation were questionable given its US-centrism.

Although an enduring and active International Committee of Accounting Historians did not materialise, the initiatives taken at the First International Symposium of Accounting Historians in 1970 did result in a programme of world congresses of accounting historians and the formation of a number of national accounting history committees.

National committees of accounting historians

In December 1970, on returning from the First International Symposium, Professor Robert H. Parker suggested to the Institute of Chartered Accountants of Scotland (ICAS) that an accounting history committee for Scotland be established. The Scottish Committee on Accounting History, comprising academics, practitioners and archivists, held its first meeting in December 1971. Its object was 'to promote the study of accounting history and to establish and maintain contact with accounting historians and with other committees on accounting history throughout the world'. The Accounting History Committee of ICAS continued until 2002 when its functions were rolled into the Research Committee of the Institute. The Committee performed valuable work in bibliographical compilation, locating and preserving archives, managing the antiquarian book collection of its sponsoring institute, and supporting research projects and publication, primarily on Scottish subjects including biographical and institutional studies on the history of the accountancy profession.

In 1971 the formation of a British Committee on Accounting History was also mooted. However, the early establishment of a separate committee for Scotland ensured that this venture was organised as the Accounting History Committee in England and Wales. The inaugural meeting of this Committee took place in March 1972. Its objects were to promote the study of accounting history in England and Wales, encourage communication among those interested in the subject (especially with business and economic historians), hold conferences and deposit articles on accounting history in the Library of the Institute of Chartered Accountants in England and Wales (ICAEW). Much of the early work of the Committee concerned the identification and preservation of business records, which it pursued with the Business Archives Council.

In 1974 the Accounting History Committee in England and Wales was re-constituted as The Accounting History Society. The objects of the Society were as follows:

a) to provide a forum for those interested in the subject;
b) to improve facilities for research into accounting history;
c) to encourage the publication of relevant material;
d) to promote the preservation and recording of primary sources material; and
e) to co-operate with others interested in the same or related fields of study.

(Accounting History *1976: 3)*

The Accounting History Society was proactive in fostering links with its counterpart in Scotland, the Business Archives Council, the Academy of Accounting Historians and economic historians (*Accounting History* 1977, Vol. 2 (2): 1). A major task was organising the Third International Congress of Accounting Historians in London, 1980, to coincide with the centenary of the formation of the ICAEW (Parker 1981). However, the Society languished following the discontinuance of its journal, *Accounting History*, in 1986 and by 1994 was described as extant 'but comatose' (Mumford 1994). In 2018 an Accounting History Special Interest Group of the British Accounting and Finance Association was launched with the aim of encouraging research and enhancing teaching in the subject.

The Accounting History Special Interest Group (AHSIG) of the Accounting and Finance Association of Australia and New Zealand also originated from the First International Symposium of Accounting Historians in Brussels in 1970. Louis Goldberg of the University of Melbourne had attended the Symposium and subsequently communicated with Ernest Stevelinck about the prospect of establishing a national committee for Australia (Goldberg 1987: 207). The Accounting History Committee was formed as a sub-group of the Accounting Association of Australia and New Zealand in 1973 (Goldberg 1987: 208). The objects of the Committee were the promotion of accounting history research and teaching, communication with accounting historians overseas, the identification and archiving of records and the compilation of a bibliography of sources (*Accounting History Newsletter* 1980: 1). By 1980 there were over 50 members of the Committee and a newsletter was produced. In 1985 the Committee became the Accounting History Section of the Accounting Association of Australia and New Zealand and, subsequently, the Accounting History Special Interest Group. Although the progress of the Group has been frustrated by the geographical dispersal of its small membership (Goldberg 1987: 212–13), which currently numbers about 40, the accounting history community in Australasia is influential on the international scene both in relation to research activity and disciplinary institutions.

A number of other national accounting history committees have a less direct lineage to the First International Symposium of Accounting Historians in 1970.

In the early 1970s the Japan Accounting Association had established a temporary study group on the History of Accounting Development in Japan to mark the centenary of the adoption of western bookkeeping there in 1873 (Nishikawa 1975). A more enduring organisation, the Accounting History Association, Japan, was formed in 1982. The objective of the Association is to promote research on accounting history through conferences and a journal. Membership in 2016 stood at 176. The Association is perceived as an important vehicle for researchers entering the field. Accounting history research in China was long discouraged by political and cultural factors. However, economic reforms from the late 1970s created an environment more conducive to the formation of an accounting history research group of the Chinese Society of Accountants in 1988. During the mid-1990s the group was reconstituted as an Accounting History Committee (Lu and Aiken 2003).

In Italy the *Società Italiana di Storia Della Ragioneria* (SISR) (Italian Society of Accounting History), which currently boasts 224 members, was formally constituted at the Fourth World Congress of Accounting Historians at Pisa in August 1984. Its objectives are to promote accounting history through research, publication and conferences. In addition to its programme of conferences and workshops and publishing a journal (see below), the Society organises classes for graduate students such that future accounting academics in Italy are acquainted with historical research (Antonelli and D'Alessio 2014).

In 1978 it was reported that an *Institut National des Historiens Comptables de France* (National Institute of Accounting Historians of France) had been established under the presidency of Yves Cleon. The Institute published a biannual bulletin from 1978 to 1982 but it subsequently disappeared. At the end of the 1980s a history of accounting study group was formed by *l'Ordre des Experts Comptables* (Parker et al. 1997) and in 1990 an accounting history workshop was convened at the annual conference of the *Association Française de Comptabilité* (AFA). Accounting historians in France feature significantly in the *Association d'Histoire du Management et des Organisations* (Association for the History of Management and Organisations), which was constituted in 2013 as a cross-disciplinary venture.

In Spain there exists a *Comisión de Historia de la Contabilidad* (Commission of Accounting History) of the *Asociacion Española de Contabilidad y Auditoria* (AECA) (Spanish Association of Accounting and Management) (The Commission of Accounting History of AECA 2006). The Commission was formed in 1992 under the presidency of Esteban Hernández Esteve. Its objects are to encourage interest in accounting, business and management history, particularly in Spain, Portugal and Latin America; provide a medium of communication; promote publication in the subject; and seek the preservation of archival material (Commission of Accounting History 2006). Since 1996 the Commission has presented an annual award for contributions to accounting history in an Iberian language. It also publishes works on Spanish accounting history and in 2004 commenced an online journal, *De Computis*. The Commission had 96 members in 2006 but this fell to 29 by 2018 as the regime for assessing the performance of accounting academics in Spain became less favourable to accounting historians.

Disciplinary publication

Scale of publication

The 1990s have been described by some accounting historians as a glorious decade for their discipline (Carmona and Zan 2002; Fleischman and Radcliffe 2005). The increasing volume of publications on accounting history during this 'golden age' is the principal reason for this view.

Matthews' (2017) analysis of the annual bibliographies of English language publications in accounting history (as compiled by Malcolm Anderson for *Accounting, Business & Financial History*, subsequently *Accounting History Review*) indicates the considerable expansion of the field during the later decades of the twentieth century. In the years 1970–9, 149 articles on accounting history were published. This increased to 805 in the years 1990–9 and 1013 in 2000–9 (also Parker 1980; Edwards 2004; also Gaffikin 1981). There are, however, signs of marginal decline in the 2010s.

Studies of the content of more generalist accounting journals also reveal a marked increase in the publication of accounting history papers. For example, 143 (14.2 per cent) of the articles appearing in *Accounting, Organizations and Society*, 1976–2005, were identified as 'historical' (Napier 2006). Matthews (2017) indicates that almost 20 per cent of accounting history articles published between 1989 and 2015 appeared in interdisciplinary accounting journals, namely *Accounting, Auditing & Accountability Journal*, *Accounting, Organizations and Society* and *Critical Perspectives on Accounting*. It is in these generalist outlets, especially *Accounting, Organizations and Society*, that the most influential papers in accounting history have been published (Bisman 2011). A number of these journals have produced special issues on the subject. British accounting historians in particular have featured significantly in rankings of the most productive researchers in leading accounting and finance journals during the 1990s and 2000s (Chan et al. 2006, 2014).

Some shifting patterns are discernible in relation to publication media. In the context of the contemporary research imperative the practitioners of accounting history are now more inclined to produce outputs for academic journals. Hence, there has been a relative decline in the number of books on accounting history (Matthews 2017). Short articles on accounting history produced for professional audiences also appear to have become less common of late. The decline of the latter two forms of output has implications for the broader dissemination of accounting history research, its popularisation and impact (Edwards 2004, and Chapter 3).

Specialist journals

There are three Anglophone specialist journals in accounting history: *Accounting Historians Journal*, *Accounting History Review* (formerly *Accounting, Business & Financial History*) and *Accounting History*. The eldest of these is *Accounting Historians Journal*, which traces its origins to 1974. In that year the Academy of Accounting Historians produced a vehicle for short articles and news, *Accounting Historian*. This was superseded in 1977 by a research journal, *Accounting Historians Journal*, and (in 1978) by a newsletter, *Accounting Historians Notebook* in which short articles continued to appear. The policy of *Accounting Historians Journal* has been to publish research on 'the development of accounting thought and practice, including but not limited to research that provides an historical perspective on contemporary accounting issues'. However, neither this statement nor the US location of the journal should be taken as an indicator of a narrow conceptual or spatial focus. Although the journal was long produced by the Academy of Accounting Historians in the US and in 2017 (with the Academy's new status as one of its sections) became one of the journals of the American Accounting Association, its contributors and scope are international (Badua et al. 2003).

The launch of *Accounting History* (1976–86) was an attempt to provide impetus to the Accounting History Society (in England and Wales) referred to earlier. During its early existence this bi-annual refereed journal and newsletter (edited by J. Freer and temporarily by G. A. Lee and P. Boys) did attract interest and new members to the Society. However the effect was short-lived. By 1980, a dearth of submissions was reported and in 1981 only one issue was produced. The last numbers of *Accounting History* appeared in December 1986 when the editor lamented that insufficient submissions prevented publication. While its production was erratic, a number of the 37 articles that appeared in *Accounting History* represented valuable contributions to the literature (Boys and Freer 1992).

Although the journal of the Accounting History Society folded in 1986, a new British-based medium, produced by a commercial publisher, emerged in 1990: *Accounting, Business & Financial History (ABFH)*. *ABFH* aimed to explore: 'the inter-relationship between accounting practices, financial markets and economic development, the influence of accounting on business decision-making and the environmental and social influences on the business and financial world'. The journal had a particular focus on histories that explained modern structures and practices and assisted in the search for solutions to modern-day accounting problems. The journal was especially famed for its special issues on the histories of accounting in countries such as France, Italy, Spain, Germany, the US, China and Japan (Anderson 2002). With a view to broadening its scope beyond the interfaces between accounting, business and finance, and in response to suggestions of introversion in the field, *ABFH* was relaunched as *Accounting History Review* in 2011 (Walker 2011; McWatters 2014).

In 1980 an *Accounting History Newsletter* was established by the Accounting History Committee of the Accounting Association of Australia and New Zealand to circulate items of interest among members. In 1989 the *Newsletter* was supplanted by a biannual journal, *Accounting History* edited by Robert W. Gibson. The journal title had been passed from the Accounting History Society (in England and Wales). In 1995 Garry Carnegie became editor of *Accounting History* (Carnegie and Wolnizer 1996) and in 1996 an international editorial board was appointed. *Accounting History* thereby became the third specialist journal in the field (Carnegie 2017). Its objects are to:

> [p]ublish high quality historical papers. These could be concerned with exploring the advent and development of accounting bodies, conventions, ideas, practices and rules. They should attempt to identify the individuals and also the local, time-specific environmental factors which affected accounting, and should endeavour to assess accounting's impact on organisational and social functioning.

There are also a number of journals which are not primarily orientated to English-speaking audiences. The Accounting History Association, Japan, has produced the *Yearbook of the Accounting History Association* since its inception in 1982. The *Yearbook* is a medium for the publication of papers presented at the preceding annual conference of the Association. The journal primarily (but not exclusively) reports the results of research conducted by Japanese authors.

In 2001 appeared the first volume of the journal of the *Società Italiana di Storia Della Ragioneria* (SISR) (Italian Society of Accounting History), the biannual *Contabilità e Cultura Aziendale* (2006). The journal primarily contains the work of Italian authors. It encourages contributions on the history of accounting and the interface of accounting and economics, histories of firms and the accounting profession as well as reviews of literature on accounting history research themes, descriptive pieces on archival sources, interviews and book reviews.

In December 2004 the first issue of *De Computis. Revista Española de Historia de la Contabilidad* (Spanish Journal of Accounting History 2006) was published. This e-journal is produced by the Commission of Accounting History of AECA. It appears biannually, is free of charge and seeks to publish high quality, peer-reviewed contributions in Spanish and other major languages. Abstracts of articles are provided in Spanish and English. In addition to research papers the journal contains reports on conferences, abstracts of doctoral theses, book reviews, news on archives and other notices. The appearance of *De Computis* is explained by the Commission of Accounting History as a response to the need for a Spanish accounting history journal given the limited number of local publication outlets in a 'publish or perish' environment and the difficulties encountered by Spanish authors in securing publication in English language journals.

The expansion of e-journals has provided opportunities for other (national) communities of accounting historians to launch their own publications. In 2010 the *Institut de Researches Historiques du Septentrion* at the University of Lille commenced publication of *Comptabilité(s)*:

Revue d'histoire des comptabilités. A themed issue of this open-access journal on accounting history is produced annually. One year later the Turkish association of accounting and finance academics launched the biannual *Accounting and Financial History Research Journal* with a view to providing a publication medium for its expanding community of accounting historians operating outside the Anglo-American tradition. Further, in 2017, appeared *Research in Accounting History*, the journal of the International Centre for Accounting History Research, China Accounting Museum, at Shanghai Lixin University of Accounting and Finance.

Analyses of the content of the principal specialist journals point to the dominance of authors from Anglo-American institutions, a focus on Anglo-American subjects in the modern period, limited engagement with other history literatures and high rates of self-citation (see Chapter 3; Anderson 2002; Carmona 2004; Carnegie and Potter 2000; Walker 2005; Bisman 2011). That said, studies of more recent publication patterns in accounting history indicate some movement in subject and temporal coverage and the increasing receptivity of specialist journals to the work of scholars operating in continental Europe (Matamoros and Gutiérrez-Hidalgo 2010; Antonelli and D'Alessio 2014; Matthews 2017).

Other disciplinary publications

Important books and monographs on particular areas of accounting history will be discussed in later chapters of this volume. Early general histories of accounting in English and other languages are discussed in Chapter 2 (also Parker and Yamey 1994: 1–6). Here we need simply mention general works such as Brown's (1905) *A History of Accounting and Accountants*, Woolf's (1912) *A Short History of Accountants and Accountancy*, Green's (1930) *History and Survey of Accountancy*, Murray's (1930) *Chapters in the History of Bookkeeping, Accounting and Commercial Arithmetic* and Littleton's (1933) *Accounting Evolution to 1900.*

During the 1970s other general histories were produced by O. Ten Have, *The History of Accountancy* (1976) and M. Chatfield, *A History of Accounting Thought* (1977). Such works have been less common in recent decades. While Chatfield and Vangermeersch (1996) attempted *The History of Accounting* in encyclopaedic format, few present-day authors have displayed the bravado necessary to write general histories of accounting. That said, some have ventured into histories of major sub-fields. Examples include Previts, Walton and Wolnizer's four volume *A Global History of Accounting, Financial Reporting and Public Policy* (2010–2012), which offers a comprehensive survey of accounting and financial reporting in major economies, and Boyns and Edwards (2013) *A History of Management Accounting*, which tracks the British experience since the Middle Ages.

While research in accounting history in recent decades has improved in scope and quality, it is also clear that considerable spatial and temporal territory remains unexplored (see also Chapters 2 and 3). Debates on fundamental aspects of the history of accounting are ongoing. In this progressive context the publication of collections of papers indicative of the current state of knowledge is more common than the production of metahistories of accounting. Indeed, there is an established tradition of such works. Early examples include Littleton and Yamey's *Studies in the History of Accounting* (1956) and Garner and Hughes' *Readings on Accounting Development* (1978). The state of subsequent scholarship is apparent from the contents of edited volumes such as Parker and Yamey's *Accounting History: Some British Contributions* (1994), Edwards' *The History of Accounting, Critical Perspectives on Business and Management* (2000) and Fleischman's *Accounting History* (2006).

An important resource for accounting historians is the hundreds of books published from the mid-1970s, first by Arno Press and later by Garland Publishing under the editorship of Richard Brief. These series include reprints of major works and articles on accounting, reproductions of original documents, doctoral theses and new monographs on accounting history. The Arno Series commenced in 1976 with 29 volumes on 'The History of Accounting'. Other works were published under the series titles 'The Development of Contemporary Accounting Thought' (1978) and 'Dimensions of Accounting Theory and Practice' (1980). Garland subsequently published numerous books under the themes of 'Accountancy in Transition' (1982), 'Accounting History and the Development of the Profession' (1984), 'Accounting Thought and Practice through the Years' (1986), 'Foundations of Accounting' (1988), 'Accounting History and Thought' (1990), and 'New Works in Accounting History' (1991–2000). Although less voluminous than predecessor series, important works have also appeared since 2000 in the JAI: Elsevier (later Emerald) series 'Studies in the Development of Accounting Thought', and since 2001 in the Routledge series 'New Works in Accounting History'.

Disciplinary conferences

The principal events in the accounting history calendar are the World Congresses of Accounting Historians, inaugurated by the First International Symposium of Accounting Historians in Brussels in 1970 (Richardson 2008). Subsequent world congresses were held in Atlanta (1976), London (1980), Pisa (1984), Sydney (1988), Kyoto (1992), Kingston (1996), Madrid (2000), Melbourne (2002), St Louis and Oxford (2004), Nantes (2006), Istanbul (2008), Newcastle upon Tyne (2012) and Pescara (2016). In addition, the Academy of Accounting Historians has held annual research conferences in the US since 1992, often preceding the gatherings of the American Accounting Association. An annual conference at Cardiff Business School, later aligned to *Accounting, Business & Financial History*, commenced in 1989 and continued until 2011. The Accounting History Association, Japan, has held annual conferences since its formation in 1982. An international biennial conference associated with *Accounting History* commenced in 1999 and has been convened in Melbourne, Osaka, Siena, Braga, Banff (Canada), Wellington, Seville, Ballarat, Verona and Paris. Since 2003 *Accounting History* has organised a series of emerging scholars' colloquia. An accounting history symposium has also preceded the annual Accounting and Finance Association of Australia and New Zealand conference since 2008.

In Europe, the Italian Society of Accounting History has organised biennial national conferences since 1991. It also convened special international conferences on Luca Pacioli from 1994, workshops for graduate researchers from 1996, and an International Seminar on Accounting History from 2015. Following an initiative by the President of the *Association Française de Comptabilité*, a series of annual conferences on accounting and management history commenced in France in 1995 (Boyns and Nikitin 2001). With the formation of the *Association d'Histoire du Management et des Organisations* in 2013 the conference focused on the history of management and organisations. The Commission on Accounting History in Spain has arranged workshops and conferences since 1992. The 13th annual International Research Seminar on Accounting History at University of Pablo de Olivade was convened in 2018. The Accounting History Committee in China instituted a triennial conference. International accounting history conferences have occasionally been held for practitioners in the Balkans and Middle East and in Central and South America. Despite these advances, it is evident that several parts of the globe continue to remain largely outside such activity.

In addition to these specialist events accounting history sessions also feature at national and international conferences on accounting, particularly those focusing on interdisciplinary perspectives on accounting.

Education in the discipline

It was suggested earlier that although the growth of accounting history may be partly understood as a response to the expansion of accounting education, this was not attended by societal demands that the subject itself should be included in the curriculum (Clark 1996). Accounting historians are primarily engaged in teaching modern-day accounting techniques and regulations and have had to campaign hard for the introduction of research-led courses in their sub-discipline. Where it does feature, accounting history tends to be taught as a specialist module in the later stages of an undergraduate degree or as a component of graduate programmes.

In a period when research was less dominant on the academic agenda, the first priority of many accounting historians and their disciplinary associations was to pursue the integration of the subject in the accounting curriculum. In 1970 the Committee on Accounting History of the American Accounting Association lamented the absence of historical instruction in accounting programmes and supported the development of graduate-level courses on the subject. Indeed, one of the Committee's leading members, Richard H. Homburger (1958), had been a forceful advocate of the integration of history in the accounting curriculum as early as the 1950s.

During the 1970s establishing a course in accounting history was perceived as a tangible manifestation of the 'arrival' of the subject in universities (Previts 1977). From 1984 the Accounting History Education Committee of the Academy of Accounting Historians sought to facilitate this by assembling and disseminating materials for integration in accounting courses (Coffman et al. 1989). The Academy's Syllabi Project of 1994 focused on encouraging accounting doctoral students to include a historical component in their dissertations, as well as collecting accounting history syllabi and materials for teaching. The Academy also supports an award for Innovation in Accounting History Education.

The integration of accounting history in the curriculum has proved difficult to achieve given that the content of accounting programmes is heavily determined by the need for students to be instructed in the expanding technical and regulatory requirements of the craft, as enforced by professional accreditation, and where the value of historical study is often questioned in the modern business school. However, periodic calls from accounting organisations and professional firms, particularly in the US, for more broadly educated accounting graduates have given cause for optimism even though the rhetoric has seldom become manifest in a requirement for instruction in accounting history (Coffman et al. 1993; Richardson 2008; Bisman 2009). In those UK schools where there exists a resident expert there may be scope in the latter stages of degree schemes for the inclusion of an offering in accounting history. Here the emphasis has tended to be on instituting separate accounting history modules as opposed to integrating the subject into mainstream accounting courses. In Japan accounting history is taught in some undergraduate and graduate programmes.

Accounting historians have tended to make the case for the inclusion of accounting history in teaching programmes by emphasising its capacity to enhance practical and theoretical understandings of accounting, increased awareness of the issues surrounding the rules and techniques applied in the modern day, and its potential for contextualising student knowledge of accounting (Flegm 1991). Other commentators have emphasised that attempts to legitimate accounting history in the curriculum should be based not only on its capacity for knowledge enhancement but also on the intellectual and personal skills which the study of history nurtures (Walker 2002).

A number of US authors have related their experiences of teaching accounting history either as a separate module or when integrated in mainstream accounting courses. These authors have also discussed the impediments to the inclusion of the subject in the curriculum, the use of historical materials in teaching, the stage of the programme at which the subject is best introduced and the teaching methods most effectively deployed (Homburger 1958; Peragello 1974; Wichita State University 1978; Bloom and Collins 1988; Armernic and Elitzur 1992; Coffman et al. 1993; Vruwink and Deines 2002; Williams and Schwartz 2002). Some commentators have explored the extent to which the subject is actually taught and the findings have been somewhat disappointing (Slocum and Sriram 2001; van Fleet and Wren 2006). As Richardson (2008) concludes:

> The ultimate test of an academic discipline is its ability to offer courses in its own area. The number of accounting history courses currently offered at the undergraduate level is small. These courses are more likely to be offered in Europe, Australia/New Zealand and in the southern USA.

Conclusions

Becher and Trowler (2001: 41) suggest that the existence of an identifiable academic discipline is indicated by its separate organisational structures, particularly in the form of academic departments. While some of its practitioners have coalesced around university and cross-university research units, the primary affiliation of the majority of accounting historians is the department of accounting and finance and the business school. The emergence of departments of accounting history remains a distant prospect. Becher and Trowler also refer to the emergence of a 'free-standing international community' with its own associations and specialist journals. Judged by these criteria, accounting history has a more convincing claim to disciplinary status.

Accounting history is best understood as an expanding and maturing sub-discipline of accounting. It is a sub-discipline which embraces a number of specialisms and diverse research traditions. These features, together with the receptivity of its practitioners to fresh methodological and theoretical insights, ensure that the status of accounting history as a separate sub-discipline is seldom questioned, particularly when compared with the experience of its close neighbour, business history (Gourvish 1995). Indeed, accounting history displays increasing signs of 'free-standing' autonomy from the parent discipline of accounting. Guthrie and Parker (2006) assert that the advance and academic maturation of accounting history has been attended by diminishing engagement with the wider accounting community, a development contrary to the spirit of interdisciplinarity that encouraged the expansion of this and other sub-fields of accounting from the 1980s.

The fact that accounting historians increasingly congregate at their own specialist conferences and publish in journals devoted to their specialism are indeed signs of greater autonomy and introversion, but they are also indicative of a confident sub-discipline whose practitioners have fought hard to legitimate their presence within a home subject area which emphasises its contemporaneity. Complaints about the increasing autonomy of sub-disciplines are not only levelled at accounting historians. In the discipline of history it is perceived that, while the 'fashionable breeze of specialization' (Gardiner 1988) has extended the scope of knowledge fragmentation, it has also tended towards disorientation. As illustrated in the Introduction to the *Companion*, calls have been made for specialists in various sub-disciplines of history to reconnect with each other, reveal the significance of their findings to empirical and epistemological debates of wider concern in the parent discipline, and revisit synthesis. This *Companion* represents a partial response to this call by attempting to present insights into the current state of accounting history knowledge in a single volume.

The expanding sub-discipline of accounting history is not without its problems. There remain marked micro and macro-spatial variations in the dignification of the craft. Advancing esteem in a number of European sites contrasts with the bleaker prospect for accounting history in the US. The 'Anglo-American hegemony' in the disciplinary associations and publication media of accounting history remains a source of frustration among scholars operating in languages and cultures other than English. In a context where recruitment and career progression in accounting is increasingly dependent on publication in the highest ranking journals (Gendron 2008, 2015), accounting historians are concerned about the potentially atrophic effect of the comparatively low standing of their specialist outlets in journal ranking lists and the limited receptivity of the most eminent accounting journals to their work (Hoepner and Unerman 2012; Sangster 2015). The potency of such lists is such that impetus in accounting history research varies according to the ranking of specialist journals in different jurisdictions. Also of concern is the limited extent to which the accounting history journals are the repository of influential contributions that drive the research agenda.

Concern has been expressed about a research focus that emphasises the history of accounting in the industrial and post-industrial ages and on organisations that inhabit the economic sphere. There is a need for new controversies to emerge, akin to those that ignited the 'roaring nineties' (Walker 2008), and a 'rethinking and resituating of issues' (Gaffikin 2011). Despite some spatial advances, the accounting history tribe contains few members in Central and South America, Africa and much of Asia (Sy and Tinker 2005, 2006). It also displays limited interdisciplinary engagement with the wider community of historians beyond its immediate neighbours. The extent to which the results of accounting history scholarship have penetrated the accounting curriculum and resulted in an array of courses that ignite the interest of future generations of accounting practitioners and researchers is a source of disappointment. But as the contributions which feature in this volume show, accounting history is a sub-discipline where considerable advances in knowledge continue to be made, advances which have enriched understandings of accounting, history and the increasing range of other disciplines from which it draws inspiration.

Key works

American Accounting Association (1970) *Committee on Accounting History*. This report is something of a foundational document in accounting history. Its attempts to legitimate the discipline and identify research subject-matter and sources have enduring relevance.

Carmona (2004) offers an important exposition of the need to embrace a wider community of scholars in accounting history research.

Coffman et al. (1989, 1998, 2014) chart the history of the Academy of Accounting Historians, the principal disciplinary association in accounting history.

Fleischman and Radcliffe (2005) review the 'golden decade' of accounting history and is a potent expression of concerns about the future of the discipline in the US.

Acknowledgment

I am grateful to the following for their insights into the development of disciplinary associations in accounting history: Richard P. Brief, Garry Carnegie, John R. Edwards, Takehisa Hashimoto, Michael Mumford, Masayoshi Noguchi, Robert H. Parker and Gary Previts.

References

The Accountant (1970–1).

Accounting History (1976–86).

Accounting History Newsletter (1980).

Accounting Historians Notebook (various).

American Accounting Association (1970) Committee on Accounting History, *Accounting Review*, 45 (Supplement): 53–64.

Anderson, M. (2002) An analysis of the first ten volumes of research in accounting, business and financial history, *Accounting, Business & Financial History*, 12 (1): 1–24.

Antonelli, V. and D'Alessio, R. (2014) Accounting history as a local discipline: the case of the Italian-speaking literature (1869–2008), *Accounting Historians Journal*, 41 (1): 79–112.

Armernic, J. and Elitzur, R. (1992) Using annual reports in teaching. Letting the past benefit the present, *Accounting Historians Journal*, 19 (1): 29–50.

Badua, F.A., Previts, G.J. and Vasarhelyi, M.A. (2003) The Accounting Historians Journal index: employing the accounting research database to profile and support research, in R.K. Fleischman, V. S. Radcliffe, and P.A. Shoemaker (eds) *Doing Accounting History*, pp. 203–16 (Oxford: Elsevier).

Beattie, V. and Goodacre, A. (2004) Publishing patterns within the UK accounting and finance academic community, *British Accounting Review*, 36 (1): 7–44.

Becher, T. and Trowler, P.R. (2001) *Academic Tribes and Territories. Intellectual Enquiry and the Culture of Disciplines* (Buckingham: SRHE/Open University Press).

Bisman, J. (2009) Making accounting historians, *Accounting Historians Journal*, 26 (1): 135–62.

Bisman, J. (2011) Cite and seek: Exploring accounting history through citation analysis of the specialist accounting history journals, 1996 to 2008, *Accounting History*, 16 (2): 161–83.

Blau, P.M. (1973) *The Organization of Academic Work* (New York: John Wiley & Sons).

Bloom, R. and Collins, M. (1988) Motivating students with an historical perspective in financial accounting courses, *Journal of Accounting Education*, 6 (1): 103–15.

Boyns, T. and Edwards, J.R. (1990) Editorial, *Accounting, Business & Financial History*, 1 (1): 1–4.

Boyns, T. and Edwards, J.R. (2013) *A History of Management Accounting. The British Experience* (London: Routledge).

Boyns, T. and Nikitin, M. (2001) Introduction, *Accounting, Business & Financial History*, 11 (1): 1–6.

Boys, P. and Freer, J. (eds) (1992) *Accounting History 1976–1986* (London and New York: Garland).

Brown, R. (ed.) (1905) *A History of Accounting and Accountants* (Edinburgh: T. C. and E. C. Jack).

Brown, R., Jones, M. and Steele, T. (2007) Still flickering at the margins of existence? Publishing patterns and themes in accounting and finance research over the last two decades, *British Accounting Review*, 39 (2): 125–51.

Carmona, S. (2004) Accounting history research and its diffusion in an international context, *Accounting History*, 9 (3): 7–23.

Carmona, S. (2006) Performance reviews, the impact of accounting research, and the role of publication forms, *Advances in Accounting*, 22: 241–67.

Carmona, S. and Zan, L. (2002) Mapping variety in the history of accounting and management practices, *European Accounting Review*, 11 (2): 291–304.

Carnegie, G.D. (2017) Contributing to the international accounting history movement: integrated forums of discourse, *Accounting History*, 22 (4): 488–509.

Carnegie, G.D., McWatters, C.S. and Potter, B.N. (2003) The development of the specialist accounting history literature in the English language. An analysis by gender, *Accounting, Auditing & Accountability Journal*, 16 (2): 186–207.

Carnegie, G.D. and Napier, C.J. (1996) Critical and interpretive histories: insights into accounting's present and future through its past, *Accounting, Auditing & Accountability Journal*, 9 (3): 7–39.

Carnegie, G.D. and Napier, C.J. (2013) Popular accounting history: evidence from post-Enron stories, *Accounting Historians Journal*, 40 (2): 1–20.

Carnegie, G.D. and Potter, B.N. (2000) Publishing patterns in specialist accounting history journals in the English language, 1996–1999, *Accounting Historians Journal*, 27 (2): 177–98.

Carnegie, G.D. and Wolnizer, P.W. (eds) (1996) *Accounting History Newsletter, 1980–1989 and Accounting History, 1989–1994: A Tribute to Robert William Gibson* (New York: Garland).

Chan, K.C., Chang, H.-C., Tong, J.T. and Zhang, F. (2014) A long-term assessment of research productivity in accounting and finance departments in UK: 1991–2010, *Managerial Finance*, 40 (4): 416–31.

Chan, K.C., Chen, C.R. and Cheng, L.T.W. (2006) A ranking of accounting research output in the European region, *Accounting and Business Research*, 36 (1): 3–17.

Chatfield, M. (1977) *A History of Accounting Thought* (Huntington, NY: R.E Krieger).

Chatfield, M. and Vangermeersch, R. (1996) *The History of Accounting: An International Encyclopedia* (New York: Garland).

Clark, B.R. (1987) *The Academic Life. Small Worlds, Different Worlds* (Princeton, NJ: The Carnegie Foundation for the Advancement of Teaching).

Clark, B.R. (1996) Substantive growth and innovative organization: new categories for higher education research, *Higher Education*, 32 (4): 417–30.

Coffman, E.N., Lazdowski, Y.J. and Previts, G.J. (2014) A history of the Academy of Accounting Historians 1999–2013, *Accounting Historians Journal*, 41 (2): 1–73.

Coffman, E.N., Roberts, A.R. and Previts, G.J. (1989) A history of the Academy of Accounting Historians 1973–1988, *Accounting Historians Journal*, 16 (2): 155–206.

Coffman, E.N., Roberts, A.R. and Previts, G.J. (1998) A history of the Academy of Accounting Historians 1989–1998, *Accounting Historians Journal*, 25 (2): 167–210.

Coffman, E.N., Tondkar, R.H. and Previts, G.J. (1993) Integrating accounting history into financial accounting courses, *Issues in Accounting Education*, 8 (1): 18–39.

Contabilità e Cultura Aziendale. Available HTTP: www.cca.unisi.it (accessed 15 October 2006).

Cooper, C. and Puxty, A. (1996) On the proliferation of accounting (his)tories, *Critical Perspectives on Accounting*, 7 (3): 285–313.

De Computis. Revista Española de Historia de la Contabilidad. Available HTTP: www.decomputis.org (accessed 15 October 2006).

de Serra Faria, A.R.S. (2008) An analysis of accounting history research in Portugal: 1990–2004, *Accounting History*, 13 (3): 353–82.

Dogan, M. (1997) The new social sciences: cracks in the disciplinary walls, *International Social Science Journal*, 49 (3): 429–43.

Dunlop, A.B.G. (1970) Accounting history: exhibition and first international symposium, *Accountant's Magazine*, 73 (November): 552–56.

Edwards, J.R. (ed.) (2000) *The History of Accounting, Critical Perspectives on Business and Management* (London: Routledge).

Edwards, J.R. (2004) Some problems and challenges in accounting history research. Paper presented at the 10th World Congress of Accounting Historians, St. Louis and Oxford, August.

Eley, G. (1979) Some recent tendencies in social histories, in G.G. Iggers and H.T. Parker (eds) *International Handbook of Historical Studies: Contemporary Research and Theory*, pp. 55–70 (Westport, CT: Greenwood Press).

Elzinga, A. (1987) Internal and external regulatives in research and higher education systems, in R. Premfors (ed.) *Disciplinary Perspectives on Higher Education and Research*, Report No. 37 (Stockholm: University of Stockholm).

Esteve, E.H. (2006) The Commission of Accounting History of AECA, *De Computis-Revista Española de Historia de la Contabilidad*, 3 (4): 183–96.

Flegm, E.H. (1991) The relevance of history in accounting education: some observations, *Journal of Accounting Education*, 9 (2): 355–63.

Fleischman, R.K. (ed.) (2006) *Accounting History* (London: Sage).

Fleischman, R.K. and Radcliffe, V.S. (2005) The roaring nineties: accounting history comes of age, *Accounting Historians Journal*, 32 (1): 61–109.

Fleischman, R.K., Radcliffe, V.S. and Shoemaker, P.A. (eds) (2003) *Doing Accounting History* (Oxford: JAI Elsevier).

Fridenson, P. (2007) The bilateral relationship between accounting history and business history: a French perspective, *Accounting, Business & Financial History*, 17 (3): 375–80.

Gaffikin, M. (2011) What is (accounting) history? *Accounting History*, 16 (3): 235–51.
Gaffikin, M.J.R. (1981) Toward a taxonomy of historical research in accounting, *Accounting History*, 5 (1&2): 22–62.
Gardiner, J. (1988) Introduction, in J. Gardiner (ed.) *What is History Today?* pp. 1–3 (Basingstoke: Macmillan Education Ltd).
Garner, S.P. and Hughes, M. (1978) *Readings in Accounting Development* (New York: Arno Press).
Gendron, Y. (2008) Constituting the academic performer: the spectre of superficiality and stagnation in academia, *European Accounting Review*, 17 (1): 97–127.
Gendron, Y. (2015) Accounting academia and the threat of the paying-off mentality, *Critical Perspectives on Accounting*, 26: 168–76.
Goldberg, L. (1987) *Dynamics of an Entity: The History of the Accounting Association of Australia and New Zealand* (Accounting Association of Australia and New Zealand).
Gourvish, T. (1995) Business history: in defence of the empirical approach? *Accounting, Business & Financial History*, 5 (1): 3–16.
Gray, R. and Helliar, C. (1994) UK accounting academics and publication: an exploration of observable variables associated with publication output, *British Accounting Review*, 26 (3): 235–54.
Green, W.L. (1930) *History and Survey of Accountancy* (New York: Standard Text).
Guthrie, J. and Parker, L. (2006) The coming out of accounting research specialisms, *Accounting, Auditing & Accountability Journal*, 19 (1): 5–16.
Have, O. Ten (1976) *The History of Accountancy* (Palo Alto, CA: Bay Books).
Henkel, M. (2000) *Academic Identities and Policy Change in Higher Education* (London: Jessica Kingsley).
Hoepner, A.G. F. and Unerman, J. (2012) Explicit and implicit subject bias in the *ABS Journal Quality Guide, Accounting Education*, 21 (1): 3–15.
Homburger, R.H. (1958) Study of history-gateway to perspective, *Accounting Review*, 33 (3): 501–3.
Johnson, H.T. (1975) The role of accounting history in the study of modern business enterprise, *Accounting Review*, 50 (3): 444–50.
Jordanova, L. (2000) *History in Practice* (London: Arnold).
Littleton, A.C. (1933) *Accounting Evolution to 1900* (New York: Institute Publishing Co.).
Littleton, A.C. and Yamey, B.S. (eds) (1956) *Studies in the History of Accounting* (London: Sweet and Maxwell).
Lu, W. and Aiken, M. (2003) Accounting history: Chinese contributions and challenges, *Accounting, Business & Financial History*, 13 (1): 1–3.
Marwick, A. (1989) *The Nature of History* (Basingstoke: Macmillan).
Matamoros, J. B-S. and Gutiérrez-Hidalgo, F. (2010) Patterns of accounting history literature: movements at the beginning of the 21st century, *Accounting Historians Journal*, 37 (2): 123–44.
Matthews, D. (2017) Publications in accounting history: a long-run statistical survey, *Accounting Historians Journal*, 44 (2): 69–98.
McWatters, C.S. (2014) Editorial. Historical accounts, conversations and contexts, *Accounting History Review*, 24 (1): 1–5.
Metzger, W.P. (1987) The academic profession in the United States, in B.R. Clark (ed.) *The Academic Profession. National, Disciplinary, and Institutional Settings*, pp. 123–208 (Berkeley, CA: University of California Press).
Mumford, M. (1994) Book review of accounting history 1976–1986, *Accounting, Business & Financial History*, 4 (3): 462–64.
Murray, D. (1930) *Chapters in the History of Bookkeeping, Accountancy and Commercial Arithmetic* (Glasgow: Jackson Wylie & Co).
Napier, C.J. (2002) The historian as auditor: facts, judgments as evidence, *Accounting Historians Journal*, 29 (2): 131–55.
Napier, C.J. (2006) Accounts of change: 30 years of historical accounting research, *Accounting, Organizations and Society*, 31 (4/5): 445–507.
Nishikawa, K. (1975) Historical studies in recent years in Japan, *Accounting Historian*, 2 (3): 1, 7.
Parker, L.D. and Graves, F. (eds) (1989) *Methodology and Method in History: A Bibliography* (New York: Garland).
Parker, R.H. (ed.) (1980) *Bibliographies for Accounting Historians* (New York: Arno Press).
Parker, R.H. (1981) The third international congress of accounting historians, *Journal of European Economic History*, 10 (3): 743–54.

Parker, R.H., Lemarchand, Y. and Boyns, T. (1997) Introduction, *Accounting, Business & Financial History*, 7 (3): 251–57.

Parker, R.H. and Yamey, B.S. (eds) (1994) *Accounting History. Some British Contributions* (Oxford: Clarendon Press).

Peragello, E. (1974) Challenges facing teachers of accounting history, *Accounting Historians Journal*, 1 (2): 1, 3.

Previts, G.J. (1977) Pawing over the past, *Accounting History*, 2 (1): 34–8.

Previts, G.J., Parker, L.D. and Coffman, E.N. (1990) Accounting history: definition and relevance, *Abacus*, 26 (1): 1–16.

Previts, G.J., Walton, P. and Wolnizer, P. (2010–2012) *A Global History of Accounting, Financial Reporting and Public Policy, Volumes 1–4* (Bingley: Emerald Group Publishing).

RAE (2002) RAE 2001 – Overview reports from the panels. Available HTTP: www.hero.ac.uk/rae/overview (accessed 15 October 2006).

RAE (2009) RAE 2008 – Sub Panel 35 – Accounting and Finance. Subject Overview Reports. Available HTTP: www.rae.ac.uk/pubs/2009/ov/

REF (2015) Research Excellence Framework 2014. Overview Report by Panel C and sub-panels 16 to 26. Available HTTP: www.ref.ac.uk/2014/media/ref/content/expanel/member/Main%20Panel%20C%20overview%20report.pdf (accessed 24 July 2018).

Richardson, A.J. (2008) Strategies in the development of accounting history as an academic discipline, *Accounting History*, 13 (3): 247–80.

Sangster, A. (2015) You cannot judge a book by its cover: the problems with journal rankings, *Accounting Education*, 24 (3): 175–86.

Slocum, E.L. and Sriram, R.S. (2001) Accounting history: a survey of academic interest in the U.S., *Accounting Historians Journal*, 28 (1): 111–30.

Sy, A. and Tinker, T. (2005) Archival research and the lost worlds of accounting, *Accounting History*, 10 (1): 47–69.

Sy, A. and Tinker, T. (2006) Bury Pacioli in Africa: a bookkeeper's reification of accountancy, *Abacus*, 42 (1): 105–27.

Van Fleet, D.D. and Wren, D.A. (2006) Accounting history in today's business schools, *Accounting Historians Notebook*, 29 (1): 10–20.

Vincent, J. (2001) *An Intelligent Person's Guide to History* (London: Duckbacks).

Vollmers, G. (2015) A reexamination of Alan Sangster's review of Jacob Soll's "The Reckoning: Financial Accountability and the Rise and Fall of Nations", *Accounting Historians Journal*, 42 (2): 141–47.

Vruwink, D.R. and Deines, D. (2002) The case for teaching accounting history with accounting theory in the undergraduate curriculum, *Accounting Historians Notebook*, 24 (1): 15, 22–4.

Walker, S.P. (2002) Legitimating history in the accounting curriculum, *Accounting Historians Notebook*, 24 (1): 12–5.

Walker, S.P. (2004) The search for clues in accounting history, in C. Humphrey and B. Lee (eds) *Real-Life Guide to Accounting Research*, pp. 5–21 (Oxford: Elsevier).

Walker, S.P. (2005) Accounting in history, *Accounting Historians Journal*, 33 (2): 233–59.

Walker, S.P. (2006) Current trends in accounting history, *Irish Accounting Review*, 13 (1): 107–21.

Walker, S.P. (2008) Innovation, convergence and argument without end in accounting history, *Accounting, Auditing & Accountability Journal*, 21 (2): 296–322.

Walker, S.P. (2011) Editorial, *Accounting History Review*, 21 (1): 1–5.

Wallace, R.S.O. (1997) The development of accounting research in the UK, in T.E. Cooke and C. W. Nobes (eds) *The Development of Accounting in an International Context. A Festschrift in Honour of R. H. Parker*, pp. 218–54 (London: Routledge).

Whittington, G. (1995) Is accounting becoming too interesting? Sir Julian Hodge Accounting Lectures, University of Wales, Aberystwyth.

Wichita State University (1978) On the present and future importance of accounting history, *Accounting Historians Journal*, 5 (2): 63–5.

Williams, S.V. and Schwartz, B.N. (2002) Accounting history in undergraduate introductory financial accounting courses: an exploratory study, *Journal of Education for Business*, 77 (4): 198–203.

Woolf, A.H. (1912) *A Short History of Accountants and Accountancy* (London: Gee).

2

HISTORIOGRAPHY

Christopher J. Napier

Overview

The word 'historiography' is understood by historians in two senses (Munslow 2006). The first sense relates to the body of literature about a particular period, location or topic. For example, 'the historiography of the causes of World War One' could simply refer to all the writings that address the causes of that conflict. However, even within this sense, historiography implies a structured and critical analysis of a body of literature, rather than a mere list. Most of the chapters in this book are historiographies in this sense. The other understanding of historiography is that it is the analysis of how history is, and has been, written. According to this understanding, accounting historiography examines how and why accounting has been written about as an object of historical study, how historical writings on accounting have developed, and the main topics and themes of accounting history.

Historians of accounting have commented extensively on how historical accounting research may be undertaken and written up, and why such research is valuable. Carnegie (2014) reviewed 62 contributions to the accounting historiography literature published between 1983 and 2012. Historiographical writing, such as the review of historiography in qualitative accounting research by Carnegie and Napier (2017), and the critical assessment of 'postmodern' accounting historiography by Tyson and Oldroyd (2017), is still emerging. The latter contribution shows that long-standing debates, particularly that between the so-called 'traditional' and 'new' accounting history, continue to rumble on.

This chapter concentrates on the development of accounting history as a body of knowledge and reviews issues relating to the historical craft, such as the nature of evidence, how the accounting historian draws conclusions from evidence, the role of theory in historical accounting research, and how accounting history is communicated – the centrality of narrative and the possibility of other modes of history-writing. Although historical accounting research has at times been antiquarian, with an interest in collecting examples of old accounting materials, much recent accounting history adopts an interpretive and critical attitude to understanding the past. Accounting historians may be classified in terms of their underlying theoretical perspective, with different historians advocating the relevance of a range of economic and social theories to understand accounting's past, how accounting affects organisations and society, and change processes within accounting. Accounting historians continue to investigate both ideas and methods within accounting itself and the impact of accounting in broader contexts. The focus of enquiry includes both primary archival material and secondary sources.

Defining accounting history

Since the 1970s, there have been several attempts to clarify the nature and purposes of accounting history. These include the American Accounting Association's Committee on Accounting History (1970), the survey of historical accounting research in the 1990s presented by Fleischman and Radcliffe (2005), and the present author's review of historical accounting research published in the leading journal *Accounting, Organizations and Society* (Napier 2006). More recent discussions include the attempt of Gaffikin (2011) to make accounting historians more aware of developments in general history and the endorsement of accounting history as a research programme by Gomes et al. (2011). Many of the central contributions were summarised by Carnegie (2014: 715), who noted 'the advent of new accounting history' as constituting 'a key development in the accounting historiography literature'. The emergence of the 'new accounting history' (Miller et al. 1991) led Stewart (1992) to give the label 'traditional accounting history' to the large body of historical accounting research that did not apply ideas of political economy or social theories to the study of accounting's history. As Tyson and Oldroyd (2017) show, the debate between traditional and new accounting history continues to stimulate thought about how and why historical accounting research should be undertaken.

Traditional and new histories

The earliest use of the term 'new accounting history' appears to be by Johnson (1986: 75), who compares it with 'the "new" economic history that has engaged many outstanding economists during the 1960s and 1970s'. Johnson was referring to the explicit application of economic theory, particularly the notion of transaction costs, to historical accounting research, for which Johnson was a particular proponent, as discussed later in this chapter. However, the use of 'new accounting history' as the title of an issue of the journal *Accounting, Organizations and Society* in 1991 devoted to interpretive and critical studies in accounting history has meant that Johnson's earlier use of the term has become overshadowed.

The new accounting history was described in this issue as 'a loose assemblage of often quite disparate research questions and issues' (Miller et al. 1991: 396), characterised by an intensive use of social theory to define research questions and provide a structure for understanding and interpreting the research results. Historical research in accounting adopting this approach had been appearing since the early 1980s, with Tinker (1980) opening up the debate through his use of ideas from political economy to study accounting over a period of 46 years in an iron ore company in Sierra Leone.

The debate between the 'traditional' and 'new' historians has emphasised historiographic questions. What is the role of theory in historical accounting research, and which theories are likely to prove most cogent? What counts as a significant research question, as evidence, as reasoning? Is narrative the main way in which histories are communicated, or is there space for a 'counter-narrative' (Funnell 1998a)? How does the historian cope with the absence of written or even oral evidence? If early accounting historians did not reflect on these issues, more recent historians have had to ask themselves questions such as these, even if their actual practice as historians remains close to 'tradition'.

A different categorisation

Instead of the 'traditional'/'new' dichotomy, it may be more helpful to separate historical accounting research into two other strands. The first of these may be called simply 'history of accounting'. Here, the researcher's objective is to understand accounting as a set of procedures or practices. Researching the 'history of accounting' will probably involve the study of original accounting records, or secondary literature such as books and professional journals documenting how accounting was actually undertaken in the past. Researchers may seek to explain as well as describe the phenomena of past accounting: they might use a theoretical framework to help pose and answer questions as to why accounting took the form that it did, why individuals and organisations adopted particular methods and rejected others, and why accounting ideas emerged and changed at particular points in time. Theoretical explanations could be based in economics (for example, that a particular accounting method provided reliable information at lowest cost) or in sociology (for example, that an emerging accounting idea was influenced by new discourses within a specific society). The important point is that accounting is the 'dependent variable' in such studies – accounting is explained in terms of other variables or factors.

Research within the 'history of accounting' strand may focus on technical matters such as the details of accounting practices and the form and content of accounting records, but such research is likely to go beyond simple description in order to develop understandings. For example, 'history of accounting' research could be motivated by a desire to understand how current accounting ideas and methods have developed. This strand of research sometimes appeals to a notion of 'evolution' (American Accounting Association 1970), implying for some researchers that modern-day accounting practices and ideas are evidence of progress. However, a study of accounting's past could also suggest that today's practices are contingent rather than necessary (Napier 2001).

The other strand is 'socio-historical accounting research', where the researcher is primarily concerned with how accounting impacts on specific individuals and organisations, and more broadly on society. This strand shares characteristics with historical sociology (the study of past events using methods and theories drawn from sociology or social theory). Much of the 'new' accounting history emerging in the late 1980s and early 1990s showed the clear influence of theorists such as Marx, Weber, Foucault, Habermas, Derrida, Latour and Giddens, as well as sociological ideas such as institutional theory, feminist/gender theory and social constructivism. This strand often used an examination of past events (which could be quite recent) to gain insight into current situations. A common view of socio-historical accounting research is that accounting plays deep and complex roles in modern society that need to be excavated and revealed in order to gain an adequate understanding of how individuals are controlled, restricted and in some cases enabled through the use of records and calculations.

The two strands of historical accounting research should be mutually supportive, if we accept that accounting is shaped by its environment but also feeds back into shaping the world in which it operates. For example, the development of standard costing in the years around 1900 may be documented by reference to contemporary writings by accountants and engineers (Epstein and Epstein 1974), or explained as a specific case of the rational pursuit of profit by businesspeople (Johnson and Kaplan 1987: ch. 3). In these approaches, the researcher seeks to understand and explain the emergence and adoption of a specific accounting method as a consequence of external environmental factors. A 'new' accounting history of standard costing could also seek to explain the emergence of the method, but now by reference to new ideas about the administration of society centring on attempts to make individuals, in society and in specific organisations, 'visible' and 'calculable' (Miller and O'Leary 1987). In this explanation, standard costing is not just a form of measurement but actually acts on people in the organisation to affect and change their behaviours. It can also inspire the use of similar types of calculation for controlling and modifying the behaviour of individuals in other social settings. The object of research is an understanding, not just of an accounting method, but more significantly of the impact of that method on broader social ideas and practices. In socio-historical accounting research, accounting is an 'explanatory variable' that helps us gain insight into a phenomenon of interest.

The development of accounting history

European beginnings

In his comprehensive international survey of nineteenth- and early twentieth-century accounting researchers, Mattessich (2003) provides a list of early contributors to the literature of accounting history, bringing out the extent to which Italian and, to a lesser extent, German scholars dominated the field until an English-language literature began to emerge around 1900. Mattessich also indicates the continuing significance of a range of national traditions of historical accounting research, with important work in countries such as France, Belgium, the Netherlands and Spain within Europe and an emerging interest in accounting history in Japan. There are also significant national traditions of accounting history in Turkey (Coskun and Gungormus 2015) and Russia (Kuter et al. 2011).

The 'Italian school' of accounting history has been explored in depth by Zan (1994; see also Maran and Leoni 2019), who documents the way in which scholarly writers on accounting theory and practice from the nineteenth century tended to support their theoretical analyses by interpreting or reinterpreting the development of accounting ideas and methods. For example, Giovanni Cerboni, a leading member of the 'Tuscan school' of accounting theorists, and advocate of *logismografia* as a 'scientific' method for 'representing administrative facts' (Zan 1994: 281), underpinned his theoretical expositions (for example, Cerboni 1886) with a chronological survey of Italian writings on bookkeeping and accounting, and surviving Italian accounting records (Cerboni 1889). This trend was to continue into the twentieth century, with central Italian textbooks such as Besta's *La Ragioneria* (1922) containing chapters on such historical topics as early Italian double-entry treatises and records, and other accounting approaches such as the 'cameralist' system used by governmental bodies (see Näsi et al. 2014, for more details).

An early German contributor to the accounting history literature was Ernst Jäger, who was typical of early historians of accounting in concentrating on the development of double-entry bookkeeping (Jäger 1874), with much reference to early Italian and French sources. A greater focus on accounting's development in Germany itself was offered by Penndorf (1913), drawing on archival materials and treatises. Early accounting historians were often bibliophiles, fascinated with reading, and in some cases collecting, early books on bookkeeping, accounting and commercial practices. An important collector was Karl Kheil, whose books were ultimately acquired by the Institute of Chartered Accountants in England and Wales (Yamey et al. 1963: v). Kheil had translated the first printed book on double-entry bookkeeping, Luca Pacioli's *Tractatus de Computis et Scripturis* (part of his *Summa de Arithmetica*) of 1494, into German (Kheil 1896); there had been an earlier German translation by Jäger (1876). Kheil's book was translated into Spanish (Kheil 1902) by Fernando López y López under the grand title *Historia de la Contabilidad* ('History of Accounting'), representing one of the earliest contributions to Spanish accounting historiography (González Ferrando 2006).

This interest in early writings on bookkeeping has been one of the more significant and persistent historiographic trends, and translations of books such as Pacioli's continue to emerge. The quincentenary of the publication of Pacioli's *Summa* stimulated renewed interest in this first and highly symbolic accounting textbook (see for example, Hernández-Esteve 1994 for a discussion of translations, including his own). Pacioli's name has been regularly mobilised by accounting writers wanting to lend the authority of history to their arguments (Carnegie and Napier 1996: 9–11).

English-language contributions

The bibliographic theme is also present in one of the earliest English-language histories, Benjamin Foster's *The Origin and Progress of Book-keeping* (Foster 1852). This is an annotated list of mainly British and American books on accounting published before 1850. Previts and Merino (1998: 80) describe this book as 'a unique and historical reference point', as it identifies a wide range of early English-language writings on accounting. Other early English-language histories demonstrate another important historiographic trend: an interest in accountants – the people involved in preparing and increasingly auditing accounts – as well as accounting as a practice. An early example of this type of history was Beresford Worthington's *Professional Accountants* (1895), and the most important was Richard Brown's *A History of Accounting and Accountants* (1905). This book, compiled by the Secretary of the Society of Accountants of Edinburgh to mark the 50th anniversary of the Society's Royal Charter, was at the same time a celebration of the professional status of chartered accountants in Scotland and propaganda for the idea that the accountancy profession should be regarded as equal in status to more established occupational groupings such as medicine and law, on the basis of accounting's deep historical roots. Hence the book emphasises the early origins of accountancy practice in ancient and classical periods as well as more current forms of accounting. Another early English-language general history was Woolf's *A Short History of Accountants and Accountancy* (1912).

Although accounting was established as a component of university business education in many European countries by the early years of the twentieth century (Zambon 1996), university-level accounting education was slower to emerge in the UK (Napier 1996) and USA (Previts and Merino 1998: 150). One of the earliest full professors of accounting in the USA, Henry Rand Hatfield, appealed to accounting's early origins and long history as a justification for its inclusion on the university curriculum (Hatfield 1924; see also Zeff 2000), and his arguments were aided by an emerging interest among social and economic historians in the role of accounting in business development. The German economic historian Werner Sombart expressed his views on this in his compendious *Der Moderne Kapitalismus* (1919). The links between calculation and economic success drawn by Sombart had previously been noted by other scholars, for example Max Weber (Miller and Napier 1993: 635). Contemporary accounting historians, however, found that Sombart's emphasis on double-entry bookkeeping resonated with their own bibliographic interests in double-entry treatises stemming from Pacioli's initial work. In *Accounting Evolution to 1900*, undoubtedly the most influential English-language work on accounting history of the first half of the twentieth century, A. C. Littleton (1933) drew heavily on double-entry bookkeeping treatises to narrate a story of progress.

Littleton was aware that accounting could have an impact on the social and economic environment in which it operated, but put more stress on the external factors that stimulated accounting to change and develop. He suggested that there were various preconditions for the emergence of a systematic bookkeeping: writing, arithmetic, private property, money, credit, commerce and capital. These preconditions seem to fit double-entry particularly well, since it is a written, monetarised method of recording commercial transactions (frequently based on credit rather than cash exchange), and it emerges alongside modern capitalist economies. As Miller and Napier (1993) note, the tendency to equate systematic accounting with double-entry bookkeeping had historiographic significance, because it encouraged researchers to focus their attention on double-entry records (or, given the scarcity of surviving accounting documents, on double-entry treatises), at the expense of other forms of systematic record-keeping and accounting (such as the charge and discharge system used on medieval manors and in a wide range of 'stewardship' contexts until comparatively recently – Baxter 1980). Littleton's work also tended to induce a 'periodisation' in the thinking of accounting historians, with accounting appearing to emerge as a systematic activity with the Italian renaissance and the coming of double-entry, the industrial revolution creating a need for more sophisticated records of cost for manufacturers, and the emergence of the modern corporation stimulating a demand for professional accountants to act as auditors and business consultants (Carnegie and Napier 1996: 12).

By the 1930s and 1940s, accounting's past and historical development were attracting interest from economists and from economic and social historians as well as from accounting scholars. A key contributor to the more traditional accounting history literature over several decades was the economist Basil Yamey, one of many accounting historians to be fascinated by old books (Yamey 1978). His critique of the 'Sombart Thesis' on the importance of double-entry bookkeeping to the rise of capitalism (Yamey 1949) was based on a study of early bookkeeping treatises in several languages. Yamey spent most of his career at the London School of Economics (LSE), where early accounting scholars such as Ronald Edwards (1937) had shown an interest in accounting history. After the Second World War, when the LSE became one of the most important centres of accounting education and research in the UK (Napier 2011), historical research continued to be of great interest to teachers such as Baxter (1956), Solomons (1952) and Edey (1956).

With Littleton, Yamey edited *Studies in the History of Accounting* (Littleton and Yamey 1956), a collection of both reprinted material and specially commissioned articles covering a wide geographical and chronological spread. Chapters such as those by De Ste. Croix on Greek and Roman accounting, de Roover on bookkeeping in medieval Italy, Jackson on British bookkeeping treatises, Pollins on early railway accounting, Edey and Panitpakdi on the law relating to company accounting, and Nishikawa on early use of double-entry in Japan, have remained classics of the literature. The collection, however, reflects preoccupations of many accounting historians of the time in being international until around 1600, largely Anglocentric thereafter, with a focus on double-entry bookkeeping and little attention given to costing and management accounting, or to the accountancy profession.

Developing a discipline

Similar biases may be observed in a range of general and more specific histories emerging in the 1950s and 1960s. The substantial accounting history offered by the Italian scholar Melis (1950) concentrates on the period before 1840, with emphasis being placed on accounting in the ancient world, a description of medieval and early renaissance Italian records (mainly double-entry), a review of treatises after Pacioli with little reference to practice, and a hurried coverage of more modern developments. Melis did not neglect cost accounting, but exemplified it using double-entry accounts. A general history written in French by Vlaemminck (1956), a Belgian scholar, attempts to be comprehensive by beginning in the ancient world and finishing with modern management accounting (the final part of the book is titled 'accounting in the age of the scientific organisation'), though again with an emphasis on double-entry practice before 1500 and double-entry theory after that date. Outside Europe, a pioneering history of cost accounting by Garner (1954) described the emergence of ideas and methods relating to the measurement of production cost in the period up to 1925, with a particular emphasis on the writings of accountants and engineers. Again, descriptions in articles and textbooks of actual or potential accounting methods are allowed to stand in for reference to original business records.

By the mid-1960s, Parker (1965) was able to compile a bibliography of 231 accounting history items, ranging from book-length general histories (in a range of languages) to short papers and notes, covering a wide range of topics, and almost all written in English. By far the most prolific author in Parker's list was Yamey, with 19 entries (Raymond de Roover had seven entries, Littleton six, while most authors had one or at most two entries). Early Italian accounting features strongly, as does mercantile accounting from England and Scotland. On the other hand, few items reflect interest in accounting after about 1850, in particular themes such as costing, accounting by companies and auditing. With the growth in accounting as an academic discipline in many countries during the 1950s and 1960s, historical accounting research was to expand alongside other research approaches, and the establishment of new academic journals provided a wider range of outlets for scholars.

As well as experiencing a growth in publication opportunities, accounting history began to benefit from institutional interest. In 1968, the American Accounting Association set up a Committee on Accounting History. The committee defined accounting history as 'the study of the evolution in accounting thought, practices, and institutions in response to changes in the environment and societal needs', noting that accounting history 'also considers the effect that this evolution has worked on the environment' (American Accounting Association 1970: 53). An understanding of how accounting had changed in the past was thought to provide an appreciation of generic change processes in accounting.

Further institutional developments stimulated historical accounting research. As discussed in Chapter 1, in 1970, an International Congress of Accounting Historians took place in Brussels, organised by Ernest Stevelinck, a professional accountant and bibliophile who had been responsible for the first translation of Pacioli's *Tractatus* into French. Stevelinck had ambitious plans for international collaboration, and built on his personal links with scholars and amateurs in many countries to encourage historical research. In the USA, the Academy of Accounting Historians was established in 1974 and began to publish a newsletter, which from 1977 became the *Accounting Historians Journal*, published twice a year. An Accounting History Society had been set up in 1972 in Britain, and other national bodies were to follow. Yet by the mid-1970s, historical accounting research was a fringe activity, with a small number of dedicated researchers and a rather larger group who combined an interest in accounting history with research addressing more contemporary issues, working in the context of a 'mainstream' of accounting researchers who had no interest in, and indeed strong theoretical and methodological objections to, historical accounting research.

Reaching maturity

By the 1970s, a desire to understand change processes in accounting led various researchers to examine historical accounting research for insights. Goldberg, an Australian academic accountant with a strong interest in accounting history, provided both an intellectual and a methodological justification for studying accounting from a historical perspective, suggesting that this would:

> give us appreciation of how our current practices and problems came into being … It should provide tools of thought for solving problems, not only by showing us how our predecessors solved or failed to solve some of their problems but also through its requirement for painstaking, meticulous accuracy in the examination of material.
>
> *(Goldberg 1974: 410)*

However, to the emerging generation of researchers imbued with a desire to understand accounting not just as a technical but also as a social phenomenon, this type of history was regarded as 'partial, uncritical, atheoretical and intellectually isolated' (Hopwood 1985: 366). A new, more theoretically grounded style of accounting history was called for.

One obvious theoretical foundation for accounting history was economics, and the emerging transaction cost economics that was also beginning to influence research into the choice of accounting policies and procedures in modern organisations began to appear in historical writing (Johnson 1981, 1983). Earlier historical researchers had tended to overlook the modern corporation as a site for accounting, but economists were identifying a central role for accounting in such organisations, to provide the co-ordination that in a market setting was achieved through the price mechanism. Accounting numbers could be seen as economically useful within a complex organisation for tracing costs to products, not only for control purposes (for example, helping to reveal waste) but also as a crucial input into the determination of prices for businesses that were no longer price takers in competitive economies but often price makers in situations of monopoly or oligopoly. Economic theory provided uses for accounting information not just within the organisation but also externally in a world where corporate ownership was rapidly becoming divorced from control. Accounting could be used to monitor managers and both prevent them from acting against the interests of owners (and indeed other external stakeholders) and, more positively, provide the basis for performance-based incentive plans. Within such a conceptual framework for the modern corporation, accounting could be regarded as a technology of economic calculation, but certainly not a neutral technology. If some commentators (for example, Watts and Zimmerman 1983) tended to view conflicts over accounting policy choice and audit as unproblematic workings-out of economic processes, other researchers were beginning to regard such conflicts as amenable to understanding and analysis through a range of social and political theories that saw the conflicts as anything but unproblematic.

Marxist perspectives on accounting history

A particular example of theory based on social conflict is Marxism. Within the historical accounting literature, early advocates for a Marxist accounting history were Tinker and Neimark (1987, 1988). These writers argue that the transaction cost economics view of the role of accounting emphasises the concept of 'economic efficiency', so observed accounting practices are theorised as the least-cost solutions to technical problems of co-ordination and management. Tinker and Neimark criticise this view on three main grounds. Firstly, they suggest that the basic concept of 'efficiency' is ideological rather than socially neutral; secondly, they identify a circularity of reasoning (only efficient methods are assumed to survive, so the methods that survive must by definition be efficient); and thirdly they note that transactions cost explanations tend to take the 'human' dimension out of the analysis (Tinker and Neimark 1988: 57). By contrast, it is suggested that the modern business organisation must be studied as a principal site of social conflict, not only between capital and labour but also between different groups, including ethnic and gender groups. From this perspective, entities such as the State are seen not as neutral legislators and enforcers of contracts, but as allied with capital against labour, consumers and other sectors of society.

A Marxist influence may be identified in historical accounting research that makes use of the concept of the 'labour process' (Armstrong 1985, 1987), where cost accounting and budgeting-based control systems are viewed as mechanisms for controlling labour, and financial reporting is theorised as a process for allocating surplus value among different 'fractions of capital'. The Marxist approach has been taken furthest by Bryer (2005, 2006), who has suggested that changing 'modes of production', most particularly the transition from feudalism through mercantilism to capitalism as exemplified by the British Industrial Revolution, can be associated with changes in modes of accounting.

Marxist approaches to historical accounting research emphasise important factors that the more traditional histories of accounting had tended to downplay if not ignore: the ways in which accounting calculations in themselves promote particular kinds of social order and inhibit others, the roles of accounting in establishing relationships of control and in empowering some while disempowering others, and the central role of the state. These were all factors identified by Anthony Hopwood (1981) as crucial for a critical understanding of a rapidly changing accounting domain. Hopwood was editor of a relatively new journal, *Accounting, Organizations and Society* (first published in 1976), whose primary area of interest was the social and organisational impact of accounting. Hopwood himself was enthusiastic about history, and the journal was to become a central advocate of 'socio-historical accounting research'. Although the theoretical perspectives adopted by researchers ranged widely, there were two main inspirations: Marx and the French theorist Michel Foucault.

Foucault and historical accounting research

Foucault appealed to some accounting historians because he saw what appeared to be technical practices (such as accounting) as fundamentally based in 'discourse' – in language as practised at a social level. Accounting is not just about measuring phenomena such as 'income' or 'cost', or keeping track of resources. Accounting is used to construct categories or concepts, such as the 'standard cost' and the 'efficient worker', which themselves are mobilised in organisations and societies. Foucault stressed the intimate association between power and knowledge: those who have power are able to define what counts as knowledge (for example, what is measured, recorded and reported), while the knowledge thus produced can be used not just for blatant coercion (as a Marxist would probably suggest) but in more subtle and personal ways. Indeed, in some situations accounting may even 'empower' individuals, enabling them to act in ways that would previously not have been conceivable. For example, the use of standard costs based on the time-and-motion studies encouraged by 'scientific management' could be seen as a bid on the part of capital to extract greater productivity and hence more surplus value from workers, but could also be interpreted as making workers more aware of their repetitive actions and thus potentially reducing effort.

The Foucauldian research programme in socio-historical accounting research has been one of the central aspects of the 'new accounting history'. It has concentrated on how accounting makes 'visible' various activities of human life and behaviour, using concepts such as the 'calculable man' (Foucault 1977: 193) to interpret accounting methods such as standard costing as helping to construct the worker as a 'governable person' (Miller and O'Leary 1987). This approach tends to view standard costing as part of a discourse of government emerging at the end of the nineteenth century, as the state (and organisations in general) seeks to achieve a more detailed form of administration over the lives of citizens. Foucault's concept of 'governmentality', which he defined as 'the ensemble formed by institutions, procedures, analyses and reflections, calculations, and tactics that allow the exercise of … power that has the population as its target' (Foucault 2007: 108) has, as McKinlay and Pezet (2010) have observed, been a central element of critical accounting history. Foucauldian researchers have also made methodological claims about how historical research in accounting should be undertaken (for example, Miller and Napier 1993; Kearins and Hooper 2002).

An early review of Foucauldian historical accounting research was provided by Napier (1989), as the main example of a research approach labelled 'contextualising accounting'. This paper was one of several contributions designed to influence the growing research literature in accounting history. This literature was encouraged by the creation of new academic accounting journals, some specialising in historical research and others, though more general in their scope, willing to publish historical work. At the same time, first Arno Press and later Garland Publishing were reprinting many original accounting works and compilations of articles published in hard to access sources. Expansion of the literature of accounting history was coupled with greater theoretical and methodological rigour, something that most (though not all) contributors to a developing stream of historiographical writing within accounting history were keen to advocate.

Historiographies of accounting history

A survey of early historiographical contributions was undertaken by Oldroyd (1999), and, as already noted, Carnegie (2014) has reviewed work in accounting historiography up to 2012, so only the main writings are mentioned here. Previts et al. (1990) propose a range of broad subjects for research: biography, institutional history, development of accounting thought, general history of accounting, critical histories, data bases (including bibliographies) and historiography itself. They advocate a typical social science research model, beginning with problem or hypothesis formulation, applying rigorous methods to clearly identified and evaluated data, and drawing conclusions in terms of the objective of the research. Merino and Mayper (1993) see a key role of historical accounting research as being the provision of a critical commentary on 'archival/empirical' research using historical accounting data sets, to ensure that such research fully takes into account institutional and social factors that could be relevant in providing a more 'plausible story' of events being examined. Carnegie and Napier (1996) call for what they label 'critical and interpretive histories', and suggest a range of topics and approaches in which such critical and interpretive histories could be of interest. Some of these – examining surviving business records of firms, biography, institutional history, public sector accounting – are areas of research that have long been central to historical accounting research. Others, such as prosopography (the collective biography of a group of well-defined individuals, for example, the founders of a professional body), were less common within accounting history. Carnegie and Napier (1996) strongly supported the use of alternative research methods, in particular oral history (see also Hammond and Sikka 1996), and called for comparative international accounting history (see also Carnegie and Napier 2002).

More recently, despite concerns expressed by Fleischman and Tyson (1997) that archival researchers in accounting history were an 'endangered species', there has been growing realisation that historical accounting research must at the same time be firmly grounded in archival evidence and have a clear theoretical perspective to provide a coherent philosophical basis and a rigorous structure. This does not imply that all historical research in accounting needs to use archival material directly – it is quite appropriate, for example, for researchers to make use of the labours of others in locating, extracting and transcribing primary materials (whether these are accounting records or original literature relevant to accounting), so long as they are conscious that 'examination of original accounting documents is crucial in giving our theories and generalisations some empirical content' (Napier 1989: 240). However, as a call for 'confluence' between the traditional and new streams of accounting history put it: 'it is not enough, and it may be quite wasteful, for authors to simply present historical materials without a sense of how they illuminate broader developments of accountancy in the field' (Fleischman and Radcliffe 2003: 22).

Carnegie and Napier (2012) revisited their earlier programmatic paper (Carnegie and Napier 1996). They noted that some of the themes that they had suggested as areas of interest for accounting historians had proved fruitful, in particular the move towards accounting histories of public sector entities, examinations of accounting as an occupational category (where histories of the accounting profession were increasingly 'critical of the "traditional" professional project, emphasising class, race and gender as important factors' – Carnegie and Napier 2012: 348), and the use of surviving accounting records, where researchers were increasingly moving beyond a concentration on business firms and were embracing a wider range of settings in which accounting was important. A curious international schism has emerged, with historical accounting research flourishing in the UK and Australasia, and in many continental European countries, but declining in the USA (Matthews 2017). This decline had already been identified by Fleischman and Radcliffe (2005). They saw threats from a dominant econometric orientation in accounting research, where statistical analysis of large data sets is carried out with little consciousness of the contexts within which the data emerged. Much historical accounting research is more like case study work, capable of generating insights but less easily generalised than statistical analysis of large samples. The challenge for historical accounting research is to continue to offer insights, firmly grounded in evidence and at the same time theoretically rich. Hence, in the next section, the broader philosophical and methodological issues of accounting history are considered.

Theories, methods and evidence

What counts as accounting

How does theory help the accounting historian? Are there specific issues relating to how the historian should go about the process of research? How can researchers convince themselves of the validity of their conclusions, and how can they go about convincing others? Despite their disagreements over which theory is likely to be most helpful in providing a foundation for understanding accounting's history, there has been wide agreement on methodological issues. Methodological disputes have tended to focus on the scope of accounting history, and on the presentation of historical arguments. Miller and Napier (1993: 631) refused to offer a definition of accounting: 'There is no "essence" to accounting, and no invariant object to which the name "accounting" can be attached'. This reflected both the wide range of activities described at different points in time as 'accounting' and/or undertaken by individuals and organisations describing themselves as 'accountants', and also the dramatic expansion in such activities since the 1960s. It also left open the scope of research into 'accounting' – Miller and Napier (1993) advocated a wider view that could potentially encompass any form of record-keeping, rendering of account, or use of structured and systematic information in the context of personal and organisational management. Subsequent scholars have qualified Miller and Napier's refusal to provide a concrete definition of accounting. Neu (2000b: 270) defined accounting as 'numerical, monetarised calculations and techniques … which mediate the relations between individuals, groups, and institutions as well as the accountability relationships that result from these social relations', while Carmona, Ezzamel and Gutiérrez (2004: 34) have suggested that 'accounting is a constructor of economic value, and this "essence" is invariant across time and space'.

Although 'history of accounting' tends to limit its attention to records of transactions and activities expressed in monetary form, or used for purposes such as planning and controlling individual and organisational activities (for example, inventory records used to control against waste of physical resources), 'socio-historical accounting research' has cast its net much wider. Napier (2006) has suggested that two of the key characteristics of the new accounting history are 'broadening conceptions of accounting' and 'widening arenas for accounting'. Not only do researchers resist any limitation as to what counts as accounting but also see accounting operating in a wide range of contexts, going beyond an emphasis on business to encompass government, individuals, the household and estate, trade unions, the academy and other potential sites for research. The roles of accounting have been explored in a wide range of contexts, from the oppression of native peoples (for example, Neu 2000a) to the Holocaust (Funnell 1998b). Researchers show how particular types of accounting procedure and record, used in precise ways, not just facilitated but actually made possible particular actions within society. However, a danger of socio-historical accounting research is that practitioners do not probe into the details of the accounting that they claim is affecting organisations and society. Walker (2008: 308) observes that readers of such studies will often ask: 'Where is the accounting? How did it operate as a social practice?' This is particularly an issue if the practices under investigation were not actually identified as 'accounting' at the time they were in use.

From this perspective, a clear theoretical position on the factors that affect accounting ideas and practices that are observed within the archive, and on how these ideas and practices can influence individual, social and organisational phenomena, is important, whether this position is derived from neo-classical economics, the ideas of Marx or Foucault, or some other source. Theory can help the researcher to clarify, even to identify, promising research questions, by suggesting influences, relationships and mechanisms. For example, a neo-classical economics perspective would prompt the researcher to consider the likely costs and benefits that would arise from the adoption of a particular accounting method in preference to an alternative method (such as double-entry bookkeeping rather than charge/discharge accounting), and would consider on whom the respective costs and benefits might fall. A more interpretive theory might inspire the researcher to examine contemporary discourses in which particular accounting methods were promoted, in order to locate a specific accounting choice or change against a wider conceptual background (Napier 1998: 696).

An important insight into the nature of theory in historical accounting research comes from the work of Llewellyn (2003), who suggests that 'theory' is not a monolithic concept but needs to be understood as operating at different levels. These range from 'grand theories about everything', through more specific theories about how organisational practices operate in context, to conceptual frameworks that help to provide understandings and explanations of the behaviour of individuals and groups. Indeed, 'theories' can be as simple as systems of differentiation that provide classifications or taxonomies, or metaphorical re-descriptions of phenomena that draw out useful images and provide novel ways of thinking. Llewellyn (2003) suggests that accounting historians have tended to use more simple theoretical frameworks, although the rise of new accounting history has encouraged more attention to 'higher' levels of theorisation. Llewellyn (2003: 697) sees 'desires for more theoretical input into history' but suggests that leading accounting historiographers are willing to 'leave the appropriate level of theorisation open and dependent on the problem under consideration'.

Issues with evidence

In principle, theory can also inform attitudes to research method and to the validity of evidence. Llewellyn (2003: 697) argues that 'traditionally, historians have focused on the credibility of their sources of evidence'. Among accounting historians there is little sense of the sort of 'deconstructive' history that may be associated with contemporary historiographers such as Keith Jenkins (1991, 2003), although many accounting historians are sympathetic to views that multiple histories are possible and that evidential traces of the past are neither neutral nor objective (Napier 2002). Historians of accounting are well aware of the practical problems in accessing archival evidence (Fleischman and Tyson 2003; Walker 2004), which include the need to identify documents of possible interest from often scanty catalogue references and the physical challenge of deciphering old handwriting. They are also conscious of the difficulties that come from interpreting items out of their original context, and are aware that the survival of particular records is the outcome of a combination of deliberate selection (and suppression) and pure chance.

It is certainly possible to debate the meaning and significance of particular surviving traces of the past, and there is a constant danger of on the one hand becoming fascinated by the source evidence while losing sight of the broader context, and on the other hand of reaching broad and possibly erroneous conclusions on the basis of inadequate evidence. Arnold and McCartney (2003) provide an interesting case study of how historians of nineteenth-century British railway accounting frequently either relied uncritically on earlier secondary literature or misinterpreted primary sources, and they challenge both 'traditional' and 'new' accounting historians for poor use of evidence. A major source of revisionism in historical research more generally is the discovery of new sources of evidence, perhaps previously overlooked or not considered important, but revisionism can also come from new interpretations of existing evidence.

A current challenge to historical accounting research is how to research periods and places in respect of which written records have not survived. Sy and Tinker (2005: 63) have criticised what they perceive as a fetishism of archives by accounting historians: 'Under the shadow of Archivalism, too much history has been sidetracked into a cul-de-sac of sterile empiricism'. They note that accounting historians have largely ignored accounting in pre-colonial Africa, despite extensive evidence of sophisticated economic and social activity that could reasonably be expected to require some form of accounting. Much of this accounting was likely to be oral, hence no permanent writings or other artefacts could be expected to survive. Annisette (2006) explores the problems of researching accounting history in the absence of written records by examining the Yoruba *esusu*, a form of mutual finance not unlike a modern credit union. She notes that, in some contexts, this type of arrangement may have been chosen precisely because it was not permanently documented, and thus fell outside more formal social and economic relationships. The challenge for accounting historians in this type of situation is to be aware how far they can use whatever evidence of practices and procedures still survives as a basis for conclusions about accounting. Descriptions in secondary sources of behaviour that may appear to be accounting to an accounting historian might not be good proxies for any actual accounting activities. On the other hand, researchers with little accounting knowledge may use information from accounting records in a naïve manner, and may not provide helpful descriptions of the accounts themselves.

Although there has been growing interest in the use of oral history methods as a way of enabling 'voices from below' to be heard (Napier 2006: 459), the main sources of evidence for accounting historians remain surviving records and other documents. Combining different types of evidence can be fruitful. A good example of this is the history of auditing in the UK by Matthews (2006). This makes use of documentary sources, including the archives of professional associations, company reports, contemporary books and journals, and histories of accountancy firms, alongside a postal questionnaire designed to generate systematic data on the experiences of auditors working as long ago as the 1920s, and an extensive set of interviews. Matthews provides an explanation of changes in the prevalence of general audit approaches and specific audit techniques (such as statistical sampling) by referring to the internalisation of control that was not only economically feasible but operationally necessary for businesses as they became larger, and to the changing costs faced by auditors as junior audit staff became more expensive to employ while computers permitted mechanisation and automation of basic audit processes.

Methods for using evidence

Finding historical evidence of accounting is only part of the process of historical accounting research. If communication of the evidence is to go beyond simple transcription of archives, then the researcher needs to impose some structure on the material. Using the categories proposed by Munslow (2006), most accounting historians would see themselves as either 'reconstructionists' or 'constructionists'. That is, they believe that the past is real and that the role of the historian is to uncover the facts – what actually happened – and then to communicate them. 'Reconstructionists' believe that the facts, including structures and relationships between events, are 'there' independently of historians' interpretations, while 'constructionists' suggest that interpretations of the facts are imposed by the historian. Interpretations may be more or less cogent and convincing, but no single interpretation is likely to be possible for all but the most simplistic historical facts. Also, interpretations are always conditional not only on the evidence available at any point in time but also on ideas and concepts that are taken for granted by the researcher.

A particular issue in historical accounting research is whether causal relationships are independent of interpretations. It has been suggested (Keenan 1998: 662) that 'historical explanation is a necessary, constitutive feature of historical research', to such an extent that research into the past that either does not seek to explain or fails to explain is not worthy of being described as 'historical'. One type of explanation particularly common in historical research is causal, but causal explanations may operate at different levels of generality. At one extreme is the view that historical explanation involves showing that a specific event may be subsumed under some 'law-like generalisation' (Hempel 1942). In practice, a historian may merely sketch out such a general explanation, but in principle, it ought to be possible to identify the general historical law that explains the event. Napier (2006: 452) suggests that accounting histories grounded in neo-classical economics come closest to providing such general historical explanations.

At the other extreme, specific events may be explained in terms of specific contingencies, with no implication that the events exhibit any sort of regularity. Although the events are not reduced to instances of some general historical mechanism, the research may gain significance from being seen as a case of some broader phenomenon. Higher-level concepts may be used to provide some structure to individual episodes. For example, although the story of the development of the accountancy profession is different in each country (Poullaos and Sian 2010), some common themes, such as the desire to 'close' the profession to outsiders (whether seen as a way of maintaining control over the quality of professional work or as a method of reducing competition), and the advancing of claims to uphold certain values, are frequently observed. The historian does not merely uncover relevant evidence but shows how a particular case reflects features in common with other cases while presenting its own unique features, and explains why such similarities and differences have occurred.

Accounting historians working from a Foucauldian viewpoint are particularly loath to offer simple and broad explanations of historical events. The approach labelled 'genealogies of calculation' by Miller and Napier (1993) eschews the notion that different historical events have underlying common structures. Instead, researchers are encouraged to look for the 'accounting constellation', a 'very particular field of relations which existed between certain institutions, economic and administrative processes, bodies of knowledge, systems of norms and measurements, and classification techniques' (Burchell et al. 1985: 400). The idea of the accounting constellation suggests certain recurring aspects that may or may not help researchers to interpret a specific situation, and it locates accounting at the centre of a complex 'network of intersecting practices, processes and institutions' (Burchell et al. 1985: 400). In particular, researchers are directed to consider the meanings that actors (human and institutional) give to their calculations. These meanings, and the accounting constellations themselves, change through time, allowing for a phenomenon, such as 'audit quality', to be examined through the changes in the accounting constellation that imbue the phenomenon with different uses and meanings (Toh 2016).

Methodologically, researchers are encouraged to withhold their preconceptions about particular situations and events, rather than viewing them through a lens consisting of current concepts and values (Kearins and Hooper 2002). Although Foucauldian history is often described as a 'history of the present' in that it attempts to cast light on current concerns by tracing the emergence of contingencies and conditions that have made the present possible, it is also a 'history of the present' in that the historian tries to avoid judging the past with the benefit of hindsight – the past is treated as its own present.

Other historians using a Foucauldian approach have developed structures to help understand the events and episodes that they document. An influential approach, though one that the author denied should be regarded as a formal model of accounting change, was offered by Miller (1991). He noted that demands for change in methods of accounting and other economic calculations could arise because of the way in which particular issues were 'problematised'. That is, underlying difficulties could be expressed in certain ways rather than others, and this 'problematisation' allowed certain processes and procedures to appear as plausible solutions while others would not emerge. Miller also noted that specific methods of accounting and economic calculation could find themselves bound up with particular 'programmes', for example a national quest for economic growth or a belief in scientific management. However, the relationship between a method and a programme is contingent. There is a need for 'translation', a process of reinterpretation of ideas and practices that makes the relationship begin to appear necessary rather than contingent. Finally, Miller made use of Latour's metaphor of 'action at a distance' to help understand how accounting and related calculations provide the ability to exercise power – they make visible what was previously not visible and allow different actors to 'capture' information in ways that allow them to achieve objectives that previously may have been literally inconceivable.

Narratives and explanations

Although accounting historians may offer explicit structural explanations and understandings of the events and phenomena that they have researched, more often the structure of any explanation is implicit in the way in which the historians present their histories. Historical studies in accounting usually convey some sense of the passing of time as the event under scrutiny unfolds. This conceptualisation of time as something that 'passes' (Quattrone 2005) is often associated with an assumption that history presents a 'story' that it is the responsibility of the historian to discern and narrate. 'Reconstructionist' accounting historians are thus aiming to reconstruct the 'story of accounting history'. Although 'constructionist' historians will deny that there is a unique story to find, they are increasingly aware of the central role of narrative in human life (Funnell 1998a; Llewellyn 1999).

Napier (1989: 241) suggested that 'the sign of a good historian' is that they 'tell a good story'. This expression can be understood in different ways – that the story is 'good', 'because it is true to the sources, because it is elegantly written, or because it inculcates desirable beliefs and practices' (Napier 2017: 46). A major feature of historiographical writing in accounting in recent years has been a growing self-consciousness about how accounting historians communicate their histories. The social science model advocated by Previts et al. (1990) often led to the writing of papers in which theory and narrative were not integrated, and accounting historians have been more likely to allow the theoretical contribution of their work to emerge subtly from a well-structured narrative.

Historical accounting researchers have referred to literary theory to understand different forms of narrative (see for example Napier 2001), and have suggested that many historical episodes can be narrated using a range of broad narrative structures. Funnell (1998a) has gone so far as to suggest the use of 'counter-narrative' as an alternative way of telling accounting history, though it is not always clear how far this term refers simply to telling different stories as opposed to telling stories using different forms of communication. Parker (1999) has noted the rise in oral history, yet most historians 'read' such histories in printed form rather than 'hearing' them, with all the additional nuances that speech can communicate beyond bare words. Indeed, the term 'oral history', which to the general historian implies a personal testimony available in a public depository, may not strictly apply to semi-structured interviews undertaken under conditions of anonymity (Carnegie and Napier 2013). Parker has also mentioned the possibility of visual histories of accounting (an initial attempt at such a history has been offered by Graves et al. 1996), and notes that even recordings of interviews that underpin oral history omit a visual dimension. If one of the methodological challenges facing accounting history is how to research accounting in cultures that have not left written records, another is how to narrate accounting's past in new and more sophisticated ways.

Conclusion

Historical accounting research has developed to address many new themes, going well beyond the traditional subject matter of the development of systematic record-keeping of economic transactions by businesses. The strand identified in this chapter as 'history of accounting' has explored accounting ideas, practices and methods in broader settings, while the strand identified as 'socio-historical accounting research' has investigated how accounting (in a broad sense) affected society in the distant and recent past, helping us to understand how accounting changes and itself may act as an engine of social, economic and political change.

Carmona (2004) and Walker (2005) have pointed out that much historical research in accounting has focused on developments in predominantly English-speaking countries, and on events since the 1870s (including the roles of accounting in the large industrial organisation, the growth of the accounting profession, and the contribution of financial reporting, auditing and governance to the modern corporation and its relationships with key stakeholders). Walker notes that important areas for historical accounting research exist outside the 'Anglo-Saxon' (or 'Anglo-Celtic') regions, not only in Continental Europe but also in Asia, Africa and Latin America. Also, little is known about accounting in rural, pre-industrial settings (at least in comparison with our knowledge of industrial and corporate accounting). Walker points out that accounting historians are often unaware of research using accounting records within 'mainstream' historical research.

However, accounting history has made a salutary contribution to broadening the range and depth of accounting research, by providing an interdisciplinary perspective that has acted as an important counterbalance to a research discipline that has often been dominated by econometrics and behavioural psychology. If such approaches tend to dehumanise the basically human activity of giving an account, then historical research returns the human aspect of accounting firmly to the centre, not only in specifically human-oriented histories such as biographical studies but also through balanced consideration of the importance of human agency as well as structure in the development of accounting. The existence of accounting history has allowed for significant debates within the more interpretive and critical accounting research community to be mounted (for example, the discussion 'Accounting and Praxis: Marx after Foucault' in *Critical Perspectives on Accounting*, March 1994 and the debate over 'Critical Accounting History' in the same journal, December 1998).

The writing of accounting history has emerged from an interest in uncovering origins of accounting within the ancient world, a desire to document early records and treatises on double-entry bookkeeping to celebrate the role of Italy in providing accounting to the modern world, and a fascination with old and curious books, to form a coherent and significant element of accounting's knowledge base. In doing so, costs have been incurred: accounting history has become specialised, and interested non-specialists (exemplified by individuals such as Ernest Stevelinck) are less prevalent among the ranks of accounting historians than they were in the 1970s. However, accounting historians have a more rigorous conception of historiographical issues, such as evidence, the role of theory, the nature of historical explanation, and the significance of narrative to the communication of history. The gaps in historical accounting research identified by commentators such as Walker (2005) and Carnegie and Napier (2012) may be celebrated as opportunities for encouraging new national and international traditions of historical accounting research to emerge, rather than as reasons for regret.

Key works

Carnegie (2014) reviews over 60 contributions to the historiographical literature in accounting.

Carnegie and Napier (1996) advocate theoretically based historical research in accounting and identify a range of innovative research approaches.

Fleischman and Radcliffe (2003) argue that the 'traditional'/'new' distinctions in accounting history are no longer helpful and call for a synthesis in research methods and theoretical perspectives.

Miller et al. (1991) set out the agenda for the 'new' accounting history, reflecting some of the main theoretical approaches adopted in that literature.

Napier (2006) reviews the development of accounting history since the 1970s and suggests possible future directions.

References

American Accounting Association. (1970) Report of the committee on accounting history, *Accounting Review*, 45 (supplement): 53–64.

Annisette, M. (2006) People and periods untouched by accounting history: an ancient Yoruba practice, *Accounting History*, 11 (4): 399–417.

Armstrong, P. (1985) Changing management control strategies: the role of competition between accountancy and other organisational professions, *Accounting, Organizations and Society*, 10 (2): 129–48.

Armstrong, P. (1987) The rise of accounting controls in British capitalist enterprises, *Accounting, Organizations and Society*, 12 (5): 415–36.

Arnold, A.J. and McCartney, S. (2003) 'It may be earlier than you think': evidence, myths and informed debate in accounting history, *Critical Perspectives on Accounting*, 14 (3): 227–53.

Baxter, W.T. (1956) Accounting in colonial America, in A.C. Littleton and B.S. Yamey (eds.) *Studies in the History of Accounting*, pp. 272–87 (London: Sweet & Maxwell).

Baxter, W.T. (1980) The account charge and discharge, *Accounting Historians Journal*, 7 (1): 69–71.

Besta, F. (1922) *La Ragioneria* 2nd edn. (Milan: Vallardi).

Brown, R. (ed.) (1905) *A History of Accounting and Accountants* (Edinburgh: T. C. & E. C. Jack).

Bryer, R.A. (2005) A Marxist accounting history of the British industrial revolution: a review of evidence and suggestions for research, *Accounting, Organizations and Society*, 30 (1): 25–65.

Bryer, R.A. (2006) The genesis of the capitalist farmer: towards a Marxist accounting history of the origins of the English agricultural revolution, *Critical Perspectives on Accounting*, 17 (4): 367–97.

Burchell, S., Clubb, C. and Hopwood, A. (1985) Accounting in its social context: towards a history of value added in the United Kingdom, *Accounting, Organizations and Society*, 10 (4): 381–413.

Carmona, S. (2004) Accounting history research and its diffusion in an international context, *Accounting History*, 9 (3): 7–23.

Carmona, S., Ezzamel, M., and Gutiérrez, F. (2004) Accounting history research: traditional and new accounting history perspectives, *De Computis: Revista Española de Historia de la Contabilidad*, 1: 24–53.

Carnegie, G.D. (2014) Historiography for accounting: methodological contributions, contributors and thought patterns from 1983 to 2012, *Accounting, Auditing & Accountability Journal*, 27 (4): 715–55.

Carnegie, G.D. and Napier, C.J. (1996) Critical and interpretive histories: understanding accounting's present and future through its past, *Accounting, Auditing & Accountability Journal*, 9 (3): 7–39.

Carnegie, G.D. and Napier, C.J. (2002) Exploring comparative international accounting history, *Accounting, Auditing & Accountability Journal*, 15 (5): 689–718.

Carnegie, G.D. and Napier, C.J. (2012) Accounting's past, present and future: the unifying power of history, *Accounting, Auditing & Accountability Journal*, 25 (2): 328–69.

Carnegie, G.D. and Napier, C.J. (2013) Popular accounting history: evidence from post-Enron stories, *Accounting Historians Journal*, 40 (2): 1–19.

Carnegie, G.D. and Napier, C.J. (2017), Historiography in accounting research, in Z. Hoque, L. D. Parker, M.A. Covaleski and K. Haynes (eds.) *The Routledge Companion to Qualitative Accounting Research Methods*, pp. 72–91 (Abingdon: Routledge).

Cerboni, G. (1886) *La Ragioneria Scientifica e le sue Relazioni con le Discipline Amministative e Sociali* (Rome: Loeschner).

Cerboni, G. (1889) *Elenco Cronologico delle Opere di Computisteria e Ragioneria Venute alla Luce in Italia dal 1202 al 1888* (Rome: Tipografia Nazionale).

Coskun, A. and Gungormus, A.H. (2015) Exploring the accounting history research in Turkey: publishing patterns of academicians, *Mediterranean Journal of Social Science*, 6 (4): 323–32.
Edey, H.C. (1956) Company accounting in the nineteenth and twentieth centuries, *Accountants Journal*, 48 (4): 95–6. (5) 127–9.
Edey, H.C. and Panitpakdi, P. (1956), British company accounting and the law 1844–1900, in A. C. Littleton and B.S. Yamey (eds.) *Studies in the History of Accounting*, pp. 356–79 (London: Sweet & Maxwell).
Edwards, R.S. (1937) Some notes on the early literature and development of cost accounting in Great Britain, *The Accountant* (7 August): 193–5; (14 August): 225–31; (21 August): 253–5; (28 August): 283–7; (4 September): 313–6; (11 September): 343–44.
Epstein, M.J. and Epstein, J.B. (1974) An annotated bibliography of scientific management and standard costing to 1920, *Abacus*, 10 (2): 165–74.
Fleischman, R.K. and Radcliffe, V.S. (2003), Divergent streams of accounting history: a review and call for confluence, in R.K. Fleischman, V.S. Radcliffe and P.A. Shoemaker (eds.) *Doing Accounting History: Contributions to the Development of Accounting Thought*, pp. 1–29 (Kidlington, Oxford: Elsevier).
Fleischman, R.K. and Radcliffe, V.S. (2005) The roaring nineties: accounting history comes of age, *Accounting Historians Journal*, 32 (1): 61–109.
Fleischman. R.K. and Tyson, T.N. (1997) Archival researchers: an endangered species? *Accounting Historians Journal*, 24 (2): 91–109.
Fleischman, R.K. and Tyson, T.N. (2003), Archival research methodology, in R.K. Fleischman, V. S. Radcliffe and P.A. Shoemaker (eds.) *Doing Accounting History: Contributions to the Development of Accounting Thought*, pp. 31–47 (Kidlington, Oxford: Elsevier).
Foster, B.F. (1852) *The Origin and Progress of Bookkeeping* (London: C. H. Law).
Foucault, M. (1977) *Discipline and Punish: The Birth of the Prison*, trans. A. Sheridan (London: Allen Lane).
Foucault, M. (2007) *Security, Territory, Population. Lectures at the Collège de France 1977–1978* trans. G. Burchell (Basingstoke: Palgrave Macmillan).
Funnell, W. (1998a) The narrative and its place in the new accounting history: the rise of the counter-narrative, *Accounting, Auditing & Accountability Journal*, 11 (2): 142–62.
Funnell, W. (1998b) Accounting in the service of the Holocaust, *Critical Perspectives on Accounting*, 9 (4): 435–64.
Gaffikin, M. (2011) What is (accounting) history? *Accounting History*, 16 (3): 235–51.
Garner, S.P. (1954) *The Evolution of Cost Accounting to 1925* (Tuscaloosa: University of Alabama Press).
Goldberg, L. (1974) The future of the past in accounting, *Accountant's Magazine*, 68 (820): 405–10.
Gomes, D., Carnegie, G.D., Napier, C.J., Parker, L.D. and West, B. (2011) Does accounting history matter? *Accounting History*, 16 (4): 389–402.
González Ferrando, J.M. (2006) Balbuceos y primeros pasos de la historia de la contabilidad en España, *De Computis: Revista Española de Historia de la Contabilidad*, 5: 39–64.
Graves, O.F., Flesher, D.L. and Jordan, R.E. (1996) Pictures and the bottom line: the television epistemology of US annual reports, *Accounting, Organizations and Society*, 21 (1): 57–88.
Hammond, T. and Sikka, P. (1996) Radicalising accounting history: the potential of oral history, *Accounting, Auditing & Accountability Journal*, 9 (3): 79–97.
Hatfield, H.R. (1924) An historical defense of bookkeeping, *Journal of Accountancy*, 37 (4): 241–53.
Hempel, C.G. (1942) The function of general laws in history, *Journal of Philosophy*, 39 (2): 35–48.
Hernández-Esteve, E. (1994) Comments on some obscure or ambiguous points of the treatise *De Computis et Scripturis* by Luca Pacioli, *Accounting Historians Journal*, 21 (1): 17–80.
Hopwood, A.G. (1981), Commentary on "The study of accounting history" [by R. H. Parker], in M. Bromwich and A.G. Hopwood (eds.) *Essays in British Accounting Research*, pp. 294–6 (London: Pitman).
Hopwood, A.G. (1985) The tale of a committee that never reported: disagreements on intertwining accounting with the social, *Accounting, Organisations and Society*, 10 (3): 361–77.
Jäger, E.L. (1874) *Beiträge zur Geschichte der Doppelbuchhaltung* (Stuttgart: Kröner).
Jäger, E.L. (1876) *Lucas Paccioli und Simon Stevin, nebst einigen jüngeren Schriftstellern über Buchhaltung. Skizzen zur Geschichte der kaufmännischen, staatlichen und landwirtschaftlichen Buchführung* (Stuttgart: Kröner).
Jenkins, K. (1991) *Re-thinking History* (London: Routledge).
Jenkins, K. (2003) *Refiguring History: New Thoughts on an Old Discipline* (London: Routledge).

Johnson, H.T. (1981) Toward a new understanding of nineteenth-century cost accounting, *Accounting Review*, 56 (3): 510–8.

Johnson, H.T. (1983) The search for gain in markets and firms: a review of the historical emergence of management accounting systems, *Accounting, Organizations and Society*, 8 (2/3): 139–46.

Johnson, H.T. (1986), The organizational awakening in management accounting history, in M. Bromwich and A.G. Hopwood (eds.) *Research and Current Issues in Management Accounting*, pp. 67–77 (London: Pitman).

Johnson, H.T. and Kaplan, R.S. (1987) *Relevance Lost: The Rise and Fall of Management Accounting* (Boston: Harvard Business School Press).

Kearins, K. and Hooper, K. (2002) Genealogical method and analysis, *Accounting, Auditing & Accountability Journal*, 15 (5): 733–57.

Keenan, M.G. (1998) A defence of 'traditional' accounting history research methodology, *Critical Perspectives on Accounting*, 9 (6): 641–66.

Kheil, K.P. (1896) *Über einige ältere Bearbeitungen zur Geschichte des Buchhaltungs von Luca Pacioli – Ein Beitrage zur Geschichte der Buchhaltung* (Prague: Bursik & Kohout).

Kheil, K.P. (1902) *Historia de la Contabilidad* (Alicante: Moscat y Oñate).

Kuter, M.I., Gurskaya, M.M., Kuznetsov, A.V. and Kuter, K.M.A. (2011) New stage of studying of accounting history in Russia, *International Accounting*, 4 (1): 49–63.

Littleton, A.C. (1933) *Accounting Evolution to 1900* (New York: American Institute Publishing Co.).

Littleton, A.C. and Yamey, B.S. (1956) *Studies in the History of Accounting* (London: Sweet & Maxwell).

Llewellyn, S. (1999) Narratives in accounting and management research, *Accounting, Auditing & Accountability Journal*, 12 (2): 220–36.

Llewellyn, S. (2003) What counts as 'theory' in qualitative management and accounting research? Introducing five levels of theorising, *Accounting, Auditing & Accountability Journal*, 16 (4): 662–708.

Maran, L. and Leoni, G. (2019) The contribution of the Italian literature to the international accounting history literature, *Accounting History*, 24 (1): 5–39.

Mattessich, R. (2003) Accounting research and researchers of the nineteenth century and the beginning of the twentieth century: an international survey of authors, ideas and publications, *Accounting, Business & Financial History*, 13 (2): 125–70.

Matthews, D. (2006) *A History of Auditing: The Changing Audit Process in Britain from the Nineteenth Century to the Present Day* (London: Routledge).

Matthews, D. (2017) Publications in accounting history: a long-run statistical survey, *Accounting Historians Journal*, 44 (2): 69–98.

McKinlay, A. and Pezet, E. (2010) Accounting for foucault, *Critical Perspectives on Accounting*, 21 (6): 486–95.

Melis, F. (1950) *Storia della Ragioneria* (Bologna: Zuffi).

Merino, B.D. and Mayper, A.G. (1993) Accounting history and empirical research, *Accounting Historians Journal*, 20 (2): 237–67.

Miller, P. (1991) Accounting innovation beyond the enterprise: problematizing investment decisions and programming economic growth, *Accounting, Organizations and Society*, 16 (8): 733–62.

Miller, P., Hopper, T. and Laughlin, R. (1991) The new accounting history: an introduction, *Accounting, Organizations and Society*, 16 (5/6): 395–403.

Miller, P. and Napier, C. (1993) Genealogies of calculation, *Accounting, Organizations and Society*, 18 (7/8): 631–47.

Miller, P. and O'Leary, T. (1987) Accounting and the construction of the governable person, *Accounting, Organizations and Society*, 12 (3): 235–65.

Munslow, A. (2006) *Deconstructing History*, 2nd edn. (London: Routledge).

Napier, C.J. (1989) Research directions in accounting history, *British Accounting Review*, 21 (3): 237–54.

Napier, C.J. (1996) Accounting and the absence of a business economics tradition in the United Kingdom, *European Accounting Review*, 5 (3): 449–81.

Napier, C.J. (1998) Giving an account of accounting history: a reply to Keenan, *Critical Perspectives on Accounting*, 9 (6): 685–700.

Napier, C.J. (2001) Accounting history and accounting progress, *Accounting History*, 6 (2): 7–31.

Napier, C.J. (2002) The historian as auditor: facts, judgments and evidence, *Accounting Historians Journal*, 29 (2): 131–55.

Napier, C.J. (2006) Accounts of change: 30 years of historical accounting research, *Accounting, Organizations and Society*, 31 (4/5): 445–507.

Napier, C.J. (2011) Accounting at the London School of Economics: opportunity lost? *Accounting History*, 16 (2): 185–205.

Napier, C.J. (2017) The good fraud: accounting, finance and banking in a 1930s English novel, *Contabilità e Cultura Aziendale*, 17 (2): 43–70.

Näsi, S., Saccon, C., Wüstemann, S. and Walton, P. (2014), European accounting theory: evolution and evaluation, in C. van Mourik and P. Walton (eds.) *The Routledge Companion to Accounting, Reporting and Regulation*, pp. 72–92 (Abingdon: Routledge).

Neu, D. (2000a) 'Presents' for the 'Indians': land, colonialism and accounting in Canada, *Accounting, Organizations and Society*, 25 (2): 162–84.

Neu, D. (2000b) Accounting and accountability relations: colonisation, genocide and Canada's first nations, *Accounting, Auditing & Accountability Journal*, 13 (3): 268–88.

Oldroyd, D. (1999) Historiography, causality and positioning: an unsystematic view of accounting history, *Accounting Historians Journal*, 26 (1): 83–102.

Parker, L.D. (1999) Historiography for the new millennium: adventures in accounting and management, *Accounting History*, 4 (2): 11–42.

Parker, R.H. (1965) Accounting history: a select bibliography, *Abacus*, 1 (1): 62–84.

Penndorf, B. (1913) *Geschichte der Buchhaltung in Deutschland* (Leipzig: Gloeckner).

Poullaos, C. and Sian, S. (eds.) (2010) *Accounting and Empire: The British Legacy of Professional Organisation* (Abingdon: Routledge).

Previts, G.J. and Merino, B.D. (1998) *A History of Accountancy in the United States: The Cultural Significance of Accounting* (Columbus: Ohio State University Press).

Previts, G.J., Parker, L.D. and Coffman, E.N. (1990) An accounting historiography: subject matter and methodology, *Abacus*, 26 (2): 136–58.

Quattrone, P. (2005) Is time spent, passed or counted? The missing link between time and accounting history, *Accounting Historians Journal*, 32 (1): 185–218.

Solomons, D. (1952), The historical development of costing, in D. Solomons (ed.) *Studies in Costing*, pp. 1–52 (London: Sweet & Maxwell).

Sombart, W. (1919) *Der Moderne Kapitalismus* (Munich and Leipzig: Duncker & Humblot).

Stewart, R.E. (1992) Pluralizing our past: Foucault in accounting history, *Accounting, Auditing & Accountability Journal*, 5 (2): 57–73.

Sy, A. and Tinker, T. (2005) Archival research and the lost worlds of accounting, *Accounting History*, 10 (1): 47–69.

Tinker, A.M. (1980) Towards a political economy of accounting: an empirical illustration of the Cambridge controversies, *Accounting, Organizations and Society*, 5 (1): 147–60.

Tinker, T. and Neimark, M. (1987) The role of annual reports in gender and class contradictions at General Motors: 1917–1976, *Accounting, Organizations and Society*, 12 (1): 71–88.

Tinker, T. and Neimark, M. (1988) The struggle over meaning in accounting and corporate research: a comparative evaluation of conservative and critical historiography, *Accounting, Auditing & Accountability Journal*, 1 (1): 55–74.

Toh, D. (2016) The changing constellations of audit quality. PhD Thesis, The London School of Economics and Political Science. Available on-line at: http://etheses.lse.ac.uk/3426/.

Tyson, T.N. and Oldroyd, D. (2017) The debate between postmodernism and historiography: an accounting historian's manifesto, *Accounting History*, 22 (1): 29–43.

Vlaemminck, J.-H. (1956) *Histoire et Doctrines de la Comptabilité* (Brussels: Éditions du Treurenberg).

Walker, S.P. (2004), The search for clues in accounting history', in C. Humphrey and B. Lee (eds.) *The Real Life Guide to Accounting Research: A Behind-the-Scenes View of Using Qualitative Research Methods*, pp. 3–21 (Kidlington, Oxford: Elsevier).

Walker, S.P. (2005) Accounting in history, *Accounting Historians Journal*, 32 (2): 233–59.

Walker, S.P. (2008) Innovation, convergence and argument without end in accounting history, *Accounting, Auditing & Accountability Journal*, 21 (2): 296–322.

Watts, R.L. and Zimmerman, J.L. (1983) Agency problems, auditing and the theory of the firm: some evidence, *Journal of Law and Economics*, 26 (3): 613–33.

Woolf, A.H. (1912) *A Short History of Accountants and Accountancy* (London: Gee).

Worthington, B. (1895) *Professional Accountants: An Historical Sketch* (London: Gee).

Yamey, B.S. (1949) Scientific bookkeeping and the rise of capitalism, *Economic History Review*, Ser. II. 1 (2/3): 99–113.

Yamey, B.S. (1978) *Essays on the History of Accounting* (New York: Arno Press).

Yamey, B.S., Edey, H.C. and Thomson, H.W. (1963) *Accounting in England and Scotland: 1543–1800. Double Entry in Exposition and Practice* (London: Sweet & Maxwell).

Zambon, S. (1996) Accounting and business economics traditions: a missing European connection? *European Accounting Review*, 5 (3): 401–11.

Zan, L. (1994) Toward a history of accounting histories: perspectives from the Italian tradition, *European Accounting Review*, 3 (2): 255–307.

Zeff, S.A. (2000) *Henry Rand Hatfield: Humanist, Scholar, and Accounting Educator* (Greenwich, CT: JAI Press).

3
SUBJECTS, SOURCES AND DISSEMINATION

John Richard Edwards

Overview

This chapter starts by demonstrating the growth and increasing diversity of accounting history research with the role of interdisciplinarity in that process recognised. Concerns about the restricted coverage of historical studies in time and place are rehearsed, and the role of special journal issues in addressing these deficiencies, and in guiding the future direction of historical research, is recognised. Sources of evidence used to conduct accounting history research are discussed and the potential and limitations of written and oral sources are explored. Patterns of dissemination of research are analysed and possible explanations for an apparent decline in the role of generalist journals in that process are considered. Encouragement provided by editors of critical journals for innovation in the application of methodologies capable of providing meaningful interpretations of accounting's past is acknowledged. The decision of the accounting history community to privilege articles over books and monographs is criticised and use of the popular press to disseminate research findings and connect with policy makers is encouraged.

Subjects

There exist several resources that enable researchers to discover the titles of most previously published English-language material in the field of accounting history. The first three of Parker's (1980b: 'Introduction') bibliographies 'of secondary material on all aspects of accounting history' cover publications to 1980 while Parker (1988) extends coverage to 1987. Since their initial publication, *Accounting History Review* (formerly *Accounting, Business & Financial History*) (1990) and *Accounting History* (1996) have produced annual lists of publications. There exists a plethora of historiographical articles that focus on publishing patterns in academic journals, including analysis and discussion of the subjects studied.

The categorisation of accounting history in terms of subjects studied has become, in my estimation, an increasingly difficult and unsatisfactory exercise. When Robert H. Parker produced his first bibliography it was possible to capture 94 percent of published items under 15 subject-based headings. I adopted Parker's taxonomy when preparing the corresponding chapter for inclusion in the first edition of the *Companion*, though this involved adding six new categories. More importantly, the proportion of studies falling outside any of the identified categories had grown and this trend has continued since 2009. Part of the reason is the significant broadening of what counts as accounting history. Whereas most studies up to the late 1980s focused on what Napier (see Chapter 2) labels the 'history of accounting' (i.e., the study of accounting as a set of procedures or practices), the decades that followed have seen the rise of 'socio-historical accounting research', which focuses on how accounting impacts on individuals, organisations and society in general.

Central to this blossoming of the research agenda has been the focus on interdisciplinarity (Baskerville et al. 2017; Carnegie and Napier 2012: 330) under the initial impetus provided by the Interdisciplinary Perspectives on Accounting Conference first held in Manchester in 1985. The engagement with both scholars and theories from other disciplines liberated accounting historians from studies which were, in Hopwood's (1985: 366) estimation, 'partial, uncritical, atheoretical and intellectually isolated'.[1] Carnegie and Napier (1996) provide an excellent example of the way in which 'New accounting history' (Miller et al. 1991) radicalised the study of accounting's past. Their 1996 paper in *AAAJ* identified the study of surviving accounting records of firms as one of eight promising areas for further study. Sixteen years later, they admit not to have anticipated the extent to which new ways of viewing accounting's past 'permitted extending the study of surviving accounting records into a diversity of social settings, such as the family home, the place of worship, the school, the prison and the asylum' (Carnegie and Napier 2012: 336). In a similar vein, Walker (2011: 2) has noted 'the venturing of accounting historians into the territories of social, diplomatic, political, architectural, literary, military, gender, ethnic, theology and art history'. The outcome, in Guthrie and Parker's (2006: 7) estimation, has been that accounting history 'matured from an almost unitary economic and historiographically unsophisticated discourse, into a vibrant and interdisciplinary, multi-paradigmatic scholarly literature embracing vigorous and largely productive introspection and debate'.

Despite the difficulty of classifying the study of accounting history by subject area, it is possible to make some general comments concerning the direction of accounting research. Cost and management accounting continues to be a thriving area of study (see Chapter 9) and the site for much of the debate concerning different ways of understanding accounting's past (Walker 2008: 299). It is a subject where provocative and scholarly papers enhanced interest in an established area of research. Three papers, all published in *Accounting, Organizations and Society*, stand out: Loft's (1986) investigation of cost accounting in Britain during and immediately after World War I; Hopwood's call (1987: 207) for studies of 'accounting in motion' within its organisational context; and Hoskin and Macve's research (1988) into the connection between West Point and the Springfield Armory. It was also, within this three-year period, that Johnson and Kaplan's *Relevance Lost* (1987) appeared and further stimulated debate. The significance of these publications can be inferred from Carmona's (2006: 246, 257) citation-based study that ranks all four within the top five 'most influential works' in accounting history.

Among the themes focused on by 'new' accounting historians, three, in particular, have featured prominently in the columns of *Accounting, Organizations and Society* (Napier 2006: 446). Publications on 'Accounting, power and knowledge' draw heavily on the work of Foucault in 'attempts to identify (or construct) networks of people, principles and practices ("accounting constellations") and to show how accounting can be "caught" in such networks' (Napier 2006: 446, 462). Major contributions include Hoskin and Macve (1986, 1988), Loft (1986) and Miller and O'Leary (1987). The second theme identified by Napier (2006: 464) is 'The accountant and the allure of professionalization'. Here Willmott (1986) was 'one of the earliest writers to attempt to get beyond the official histories of professional accountancy bodies in the UK in order to apply ideas from the sociology of the professions' (Napier 2006: 464). The third theme provides new understandings of accounting's role in presenting the economic. Much of this work is Marxist-oriented with Rob Bryer its most active proponent.

It is also possible to cite two recent studies which provide evidence of subject areas that have proved popular with researchers and those which appear to have been neglected.[2] An examination of the content of a single journal, in this instance *Accounting History*, is not necessarily representative of the broader picture, but Fowler and Keeper (2016) do provide some useful indications of publication trends and of the difficulties in deriving precise classifications of available material. They employ a 10 subject-based analysis for the second decade of that journal's publication for comparison with that constructed by Williams and Wines (2006) for the period 1996–2005. Studies of surviving business records and business history show significant decline as a proportion of total publications whereas work on public sector accounting is revealed to have enjoyed a noticeable rise. The major discontinuity, however, is the introduction of a new 'broad and diverse' category entitled 'social institutions' which accounted for no less than 30 or 16.6 percent of the publications during the period 1996–2005 (Fowler and Keeper 2016: 405). Matthews (2017: 80) also acknowledges the difficulty of achieving a subject-driven classification of published articles with 18.3 percent of publications over the period 1989–2015 despatched to an 'Other' category. He also draws attention to the fact that auditing, tax, insolvency and consultancy tend to receive little coverage which, in his estimation, seems rather peculiar given their prominent role, historically as well as today, in the work of professional accountants (Matthews 2017: 82).

Countries and periods

Starting in the early 1990s, a series of studies expressed anxiety with domination of the literature by authors working at Anglo-Saxon universities addressing events in Anglo-Saxon countries during the nineteenth and twentieth centuries (Parker 1993: 106; Carmona and Zan 2002; Sánchez-Matamoros and Gutiérrez-Hidalgo 2010, 2011; Jones and Oldroyd 2015: 118). Jones and Oldroyd's (2015: 119) recent review of publishing patterns caused them to conclude that, in some respects, 'little has changed since 1990'. They explore the nature and depth of the problem by analysing submissions to the 2012 World Congress of Accounting Historians and comparing their findings with the content of the special issue of *British Accounting Review*, which they co-edited, entitled 'Widening the accounting history debate'. Of the 119 papers presented at the Congress, just 50 were authored by '*Anglo Saxon* affiliates' (Jones and Oldroyd 2015: 119). Second and fourth among the 23 countries represented at the conference were Turkish researchers with 20 papers and Italian with 14.5. The fact that these weightings are unlikely to be reflected in subsequent publications in English-language academic journals might be inferred from Jones and Oldroyd's experience with the *British Accounting Review*'s special issue drawn from papers presented at the Congress. Twenty-nine submissions included five from the UK and the US, of which four were accepted, eight from Turkey (one accepted), three from Italy (none accepted), two from Japan (one accepted) and 11 papers from other non-Anglo-Saxon countries around the world which were all rejected (Jones and Oldroyd 2015: 120).

The international community of authors and the countries studied is nevertheless more diverse than it once was. Sánchez Matamoros and Gutiérrez-Hidalgo (2010, 137, 141) found that, out of 385 authors published in the three accounting history journals between 2000 and 2008, 20 percent were scholars from Italy, France, Portugal and Spain, compared to an equivalent figure constructed by Carnegie and Potter (2000: 184), for the 1990s, of 9.2 percent. Fowler and Keeper (2016, 390) similarly conclude that 'Increases in the number of authors from different countries, researching on an increasingly diverse range of topics, countries and time-periods are evident'.

A recent review of countries studied (Matthews 2017: 83–4) compares findings for the period up to 1980 with that since 1989. It shows that the UK, as a site for investigation, has accounted for over 40 percent of published articles through time and, in conjunction with the US, supplied the basis for over three-quarters of all historical studies in the earlier period. The amount of space devoted to US and Italian studies declined, post-1989, to about 60 percent of previous levels. In the former case this is probably due to the diminished status of accounting history as a subject of study in that country (Fleischman and Radcliffe 2005); in the latter case because accounting historians in general are now rather less preoccupied with the role of Italy in the emergence of double-entry bookkeeping. Much of the growth of interest has occurred in other English-speaking countries (Australia, Canada and New Zealand) and in Western Europe (France, Holland, Portugal and Spain). Vast areas of the world – including Africa, China, Eastern Europe, India, Russia, Scandinavia and South America – remain almost entirely undisturbed. The extent to which this might be attributed to a lack of interest in accounting history or the absence of an incentive to publish in English-language journals is unknown. Accounting historians competent in the English language are sometimes pilloried for ignoring events in many parts of the globe but, given their modest numbers and the fact that there are plenty of local issues which remain under-studied, if studied at all, such criticisms appear to this writer difficult to justify, particularly given the threat from university administrators to 'publish [quickly] or perish'.

Table 3.1 shows that the twentieth century was the period most studied both before 1980 and after 1989, accounting, overall, for about 40 percent of the total. Coverage of the nineteenth century, however, has increased significantly at the expense of all earlier epochs. There are many explanations for this which include the decrease in the attention devoted to early bookkeeping, on the one hand, and, on the other, the popularity of studying the rise of cost and management accounting during the British industrial revolution and the emergence of professional accountants and their organisational bodies in the nineteenth century. The outcome is that 80.2 percent of all published articles post-1989, leaving aside those incapable of temporal classification, are located in the nineteenth and twentieth centuries.

Table 3.1 Publishing patterns by period studied

	1899–1980	*1989–2015*
	%	%
Ancient	4.5	3.4
Medieval	16.3	4.4
Sixteenth-eighteenth centuries	21.3	11.9
Nineteenth century	20.3	37.9
Twentieth century	37.5	42.3
Total	100.0	100.0
N	284	715

Source: Derived from Matthews (2017: table 5).

The role of special issues in encouraging the investigation of new subjects, times and places is considered next.

Special issues

Special issues serve two main purposes. First, to encourage research into new or emerging fields of study and, second, 'to stimulate new research and illuminate path-breaking directions on more developed themes that may not have been otherwise initiated' (Carnegie 2012: 216). The role of special issues in encouraging researchers to pursue greater diversity in terms of subjects, periods and places studied is, in principle, welcomed, but the idea that 'Special issues provide editors with the ability to guide the literature in distinct ways' is, potentially, a little worrying (Bisman 2012: 21). It cannot always be the case that journal editors know what is best for the future of their subject or always behave in an entirely disinterested manner.

The first generalist journal to devote an issue to accounting history was *ABR*,[3] in 1980, to mark the centenary of the Institute of Chartered Accountants in England and Wales (ICAEW) (Table 3.2). According to its editor: 'If this issue has a message it is that accounting history is a much wider subject than was generally realised. There is something of value here for everyone' (Parker 1980a: ii). The growing historical content of *AOS* in the second half of the 1980s (Napier 2006: 447) received a further fillip from the 1991 special issue on 'The new accounting history' (Miller et al. 1991). In 1996, *AAAJ* published its first number devoted to historical studies, entitled 'Accounting history into the twenty-first century' and, in the same year, *CPA* contributed to these initiatives through an issue appropriately labelled 'Critical accounting history'. The distinctive contribution of the special section of *EAR* in 2002 was to encourage accounting historians to broaden their coverage of time and space. Altogether, generalist journals published 11 numbers devoted wholly or partly to the study of accounting history between 1980 and 2002, but just one since. Two specialist accounting history journals – *AHR/ABFH* and *AH* – have contributed 34 special issues; 24 of which have appeared in print since 2003.

Table 3.2 Special issues on accounting history – title, journal, year and volume

Special history issue, *ABR*, 1980, 10(37A)
The new accounting history, *AOS*, 1991, 16(5/6)
Feminist perspectives on accounting research, *AOS*, 1992, 17(3/4)*
Accounting, calculation and institutions: historical studies, *AOS*, 1993, 18(7/8)*
Business history through accounting records, *ABFH*, 1993, 3(3)
From clay tokens to *Fukushiki-Boki*: record keeping over ten millennia, *ABFH*, 1994, 4(1)
Management accounting and empirical investigation, *ABFH*, 1995, 5(1)
Accounting history into the twenty-first century, *AAAJ*, 1996, 9(3)
Critical accounting history, *CPA*, 1996, 9(6)
Recent studies in French accounting history, *ABFH*, 1997, 7(3)
Regulation, *AH*, 1998, 3(1)
Organising the accounting profession in Asia, *AAAJ*, 1999, 12(3)
Histories of accounting professionalism, *ABFH*, 1999, 9(1)
US accounting history and historiography, *ABFH*, 2000, 10(2)

(*Continued*)

Table 3.2 (Cont.)

Accounting and indigenous peoples, *AAAJ*, 2000, 13(3)
Accounting in crises, *AH*, 2000, 5(2)
Recent research in accounting, business and management history by French authors, *ABFH*, 2001, 11(1)
Studies in Japanese accounting history, *ABFH*, 2001, 11(3)
Mapping variety in the history of accounting and management, *EAR*, 2002, 11(2)*
International accounting history special issue, *ABR*, 2002, 32(2)
Studying accountancy's emergent occupational structures, *AOS*, 2002, 27(4/5)*
Accounting history: Chinese contributions and challenges, *ABFH*, 2003, 13(1)
Mechanisation and computers in banking, *ABFH*, 2004, 14(3)
Historical perspectives on accounting and audit failure, *AH*, 2005, 10(3)
Accounting history in the German language arena, *ABFH*, 2005, 15(3)
Accounting and religion: A historical perspective, *AH*, 2006, 11(2)
Women, accounting and investment, *ABFH*, 2006, 16(2)
International perspectives on race and gender in accounting's past, *AH*, 2007, 12(3)
Italian accounting history, *ABFH*, 2007, 17(1)
Studies of Irish accounting history, *ABFH*, 2008, 18(1)
Accounting in other places, accounting by other peoples, *AH*, 2009, 14(1/2)
Perspectives and reflections on accounting's past in Europe, *AH*, 2009, 14(4)
Accounting and management history: Some French examples, *ABFH*, 2009, 19(2)
Accounting and the military, *AH*, 2010, 15(2)
Histories of accounting research, *AH*, 2011, 16(2)
Accounting and the state, *AH*, 2012, 17(3/4)
Accounting and accountability in local government, *AH*, 2013, 18(4)
The emergence of accounting as a global profession, *AH*, 2014, 19(1/2)
Accounting and the First World War, *AHR*, 2014, 24(2/3)
Innovation in accounting thought and practice, *AH*, 2015, 20(3)
Widening the accounting history debate: Papers from the thirteenth World Congress of Accounting Historians, *BAR*, 2015, 47(2)
The history of accounting in hospitals, *AHR*, 2015, 25(3)
Accounting's past in sport, *AH*, 2016, 21(1)
Accounting and charities, *AH*, 2016, 21(2/3)
Histories of accounting and agriculture, *AHR*, 2016, 26(2)*
Accounting's history in diverse settings, *AH*, 2017, 22(3)

* Special section

Sources

Having discussed the changing subjects which accounting historians investigate, we now turn to an overview of the sources they deploy.

Archival evidence

The historian (accounting or otherwise) aims to use evidence to craft a coherent and probable picture of what has happened in the past. Table 3.3 lists and classifies sources of historical evidence. According to its compilers (Fleischman et al. 1996: 61): 'Most important for accounting history is communicative evidence, usually taking the form of written documents'.

Table 3.3 Evidences of history

Natural evidence
Past landscapes
Natural objects
Human remains
Alterations of natural objects (tilled fields, cleared forests, etc.)
Processive evidence
Language, customs, institutions
Tools, other artefacts
Communicative evidence
Written
Chronicles, annals, biographies, genealogies
Memoirs, diaries, letters, newspapers
Literature, public documents, business records
Inscriptions
Oral
Ballads, anecdotes, tapes, sagas
Recordings (tapes, disks)
Works of art
Portraits, other paintings, sculpture, coins, medals
Films, videotapes, music

Source: Fleischman et al. (1996: 61).

The question of what counts as 'adequate' evidence is studied by Napier (2002) with the process through which evidence is transformed into written history set out in Figure 3.1.

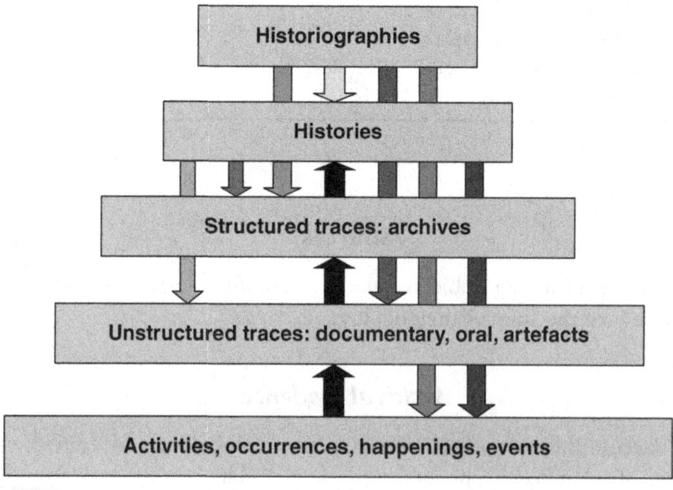

Figure 3.1 The process of historical research

Source: Napier (2002: 137; see p.138 for a full explanation of the significance of the arrows in the above diagram).

Communicative evidence has long been considered the principal foundation for historical research, enabling investigators to make the discoveries from which their stories can be constructed. The use of archival material is of course problematic. Quite apart from the question of what counts as evidence, there are the following further problems: (i) only a fraction of the evidence initially available continues to survive; (ii) that which does survive may not be in useable form for a number of possible reasons (e.g., the material may be machine-readable but the equipment required for that purpose may be unavailable); (iii) surviving data may be non-representative of the past (e.g., accounting archives tend to concentrate on large companies and to exclude the small); and (iv) the meaning of what has been written down can be interpreted in different ways.

Critical historians often criticise the traditional historians' use of archival evidence (e.g., Miller and Napier 1993). Some are equally concerned with a lack of ambition on the part of traditional researchers and argue they should do better:

> The traditional interpretive historian benefits from exposure to methodological choices which can facilitate greater rigour in the accessing and interpretation of primary sources and can lift the ensuing analysis above the level of naive antiquarian narrative.
>
> *(Parker 1997: 131)*

Under fire from critical historians, Fleishman and Tyson's (1997: 91) concern that archival-oriented researchers might be 'an endangered species' underestimated the latter's resilience. Also, their characterisation of archivists as the 'drones whose only job is to provide grist for the paradigmatic mills' caricatures historians of both persuasions (Fleischman and Tyson 1997: 103). Fleischman and Tyson's thoughtful vindication of archival research elicits several inconsistencies in the criticisms levelled by critical historians at the traditional, which include allegations that the former does not make the perceived mistake of searching for origins. Others agree. In Zan's estimation (2004: 182), the search by Hoskin and Macve (1994) for the 'genesis of managerialism' is associated with the assumption of a 'linear view of history' of which traditional historians are so often accused. Fleischman and Tyson (1997: 105) also raise the following interesting question: 'by what standard is it more acceptable to write an interpretive piece without doing archival research than it is to report the results of archival research without accompanying interpretation?' The answer that the former displays scholarship and intellect and the latter merely hard work has a degree of validity, but it is one that disregards the essential archaeological contribution of the archival researcher.

The limitation of archival records as representations of the past is one of the criticisms directed at traditional accounting historians by some critical writers (Fleischman and Tyson 1997: 97–100). But, of course, critical historians also use discoveries as the evidential basis for their own work. Perhaps this was not so evident in earlier times when practitioners of the new accounting history had a stock of prior discoveries to re-interpret (Willmott 1986; Hopwood 1987; Miller and O'Leary 1987; Bryer 1991; Hopper and Armstrong 1991). But some critical historians were immersed in archival research from the outset (e.g., Hoskin and Macve 1986, 1988; Loft 1986), while others (such as Bryer 2006) more recently turned to original records as the basis for theorising accounting's past.

Fleischman and Tyson (2003) staunchly defend the archival orientation of the so-called traditional researchers, but they also devote space to rehearsing some of the challenges associated with archival research and in advising researchers how they might best prepare themselves for that labour (see also Walker 2004). Johnson (2000) describes and analyses the hazards associated with archival research in her case study of the bookkeeping records of a company well-represented in the accounting history literature. Johnson (2000: 129) discovered that 'the process of understanding, interpreting, and validating the record keeping' of E. I. DuPont de Nemours & Co., 'led to a number of misleading, confusing, and time-consuming issues which had to be resolved'. Her experience elicited the following warning to archival researchers who:

> [m]ust understand that they are able to rely on secondary sources, when they exist, only as long as they remain circumspect when depending on the secondary interpretation of primary sources, and that even the primary sources themselves may lead the researcher astray.
>
> *(Johnson 2000: 129; see also Arnold and McCartney 2003)*

Sy and Tinker (2005: 63) launch a scathing attack on accounting historians of all persuasions for their commitment to written, primary sources which encourages 'sterile empiricism'. They believe that, released from such constraint, the potential of historical research would be much enhanced. They demonstrate how it might be possible to escape from dead-end intellectualism 'by sketching a Post-Kuhnian panorama in terms of a Non-Eurocentric, social, gendered, environmental, public interest and labour orientation' (Sy and Tinker 2005: 47). Hammond and Sikka (1996: abstract) also express concern that 'Much of the historical research in accounting continues to mimic idealized scientific methods in which written and official evidence is privileged'.

Oral history

Hammond (2003: 85) believes that enriched understandings of the past require 'examining new documentary sources, including "oral history" (talking to people about their experiences)'. More specifically, in collaboration with Sikka, she 'calls for the use of oral histories so that those marginalized and neglected by conventional history can be given a voice and problematize the narratives of "progress" dominating accounting history research' (Hammond and Sikka 1996: abstract). Fleischman and Tyson (2003: 32) agree that archival materials (narrowly defined) suffer from 'failure to represent the suppressed voices of the past – the poor, the illiterate, women, the economically powerless for whom accounting records were not an available avenue of expression'. Returning to Hammond and Sikka (1996: 91):

> Without oral history, the role of accountancy practices and firms in colonizing organizations (Armstrong, 1987), influencing unemployment, divestment (Bryer and Brignall, 1986), crime (Mitchell et al., 1996) and industrial disputes (Berry et al., 1985), remains ill understood.

Oral history is privileged as 'giving greater insight into the "why" and "how" of events' (Burrows 1999: 100). The material collected may be about the interviewee or about people or events of which they are knowledgeable. Collins and Bloom (1991: 23) see the role of oral history as 'an historical methodology, [which] can be used as a research tool to supplement and clarify the written record or provide a record where no written record exists'. Or it might be undertaken to preserve evidence for future use. For example, a project funded by the Institute of Chartered Accountants of Scotland (ICAS) had as its purpose to record the life histories of influential figures in the Scottish accounting profession that might otherwise have been lost (Walker 2005: iii). Collins and Bloom (1991) provide guidance on the process of gathering oral testimony and, to illustrate its potential, explain how oral history could be used to study the evolution of accounting standards.

Initially, fears were expressed concerning the validity of oral history as an evidential base, and a literature developed to address allegations that it was 'too soft and subject to bias' (Hammond 2003: 85). Such reservations were put into context, though not resolved, by growing recognition of the fact that '*all* histories are selective and biased' (Hammond 2003: 85). In Hammond's judgement, traditional researchers rarely acknowledge this reality, and she welcomes a 'literature on the use of oral history [which] grapples with questions of validity and authority without contending that a purely scientific and unbiased approach is possible' (Hammond 2003: 85). Indeed, proponents of oral history consider one of its strengths to be forthright recognition of its limitations: 'acknowledgement of the lack of objectivity is, in fact, key to the contribution of oral history' because, what the researcher strives to discover, 'must be based on the interviewees' own interpretation of their experiences' (Hammond 2003: 86).

Hammond (2003) is also well-placed to explain the potentials and pitfalls of the oral history methodology (see also, Hammond and Sikka 1996: 86–91; Matthews and Pirie 2001: chapter 1) based on her extensive, pioneering research into the histories of African-American accountants and of women in accounting. In a witty and erudite essay, Goldberg (1997) provides further discussion of the hazards of oral history, questioning the oral history contained in two studies of Australian accounting institutions (Burrows 1996; Linn 1996). Although favourably disposed towards historical research, Goldberg (1997: 113) was sufficiently aroused to conclude: 'while both histories are well-written, how much of what they include about other people can I believe accords with perceived experiences of those people themselves?' Such a criticism is not exclusive to oral history, of course, but the importance of taking steps to ensure, as far as possible, the accuracy of 'facts' reported is well made.

Examples of oral history research

It was not until relatively recently that much use was made of oral testimony in the construction of accounting's history (Collins and Bloom 1991). An early example occurred when Zeff (1972) collected material for *Forging Accounting Principles in Five Countries*. While acknowledging the valuable role of committee minutes, internal reports, correspondence and other publicly available material, Zeff (1980: 14, emphasis added) observed: 'these documents will seldom yield useful insights into the *real factors* that influenced the course of standard-setting. It becomes necessary to conduct interviews with the principal policy makers and others who were close observers of the standard-setting process'. Later in the 1970s, Mumford conducted a series of interviews of leading accountants, and 12 that took place between 1979 and 1984 formed the basis for a paper on 'Chartered accountants as business managers' (Mumford 1991). The practical problem of getting tapes transcribed slowed this project, however, and it was not until 16 years later that arrangements were made for the results to made publicly available thanks to a research grant from the Institute of Chartered Accountants of Scotland (Mumford 2007).

The growing amount of oral history-based research is to be welcomed, even if much of it continues to contain stories of the great and the good rather than the marginalised 'voices from below' (Napier 2006: 459–60). Matthews and Pirie (2001) explain how they tackled the thorny problem of who to interview when collecting material for their study of the

British auditing profession. The initial plan was to compile a random selection of interviewees from the ICAEW's list of members, but this was abandoned in favour of the 'purposeful' sample recommended by Hammond and Sikka (1996: 88) in the endeavour to capture the 'key figures' (Matthews and Pirie 2001: 2) as well as to ensure adequate coverage of other voices.

Matthews and Pirie (2001) also discuss dispiriting issues which can arise following the collection of oral evidence. Several of the interviewees displayed misgivings over the publication of extracts from their interviews having seen the transcribed version. Most participants eventually acquiesced but seven, of 77, withdrew their permission altogether. Four of these were retired partners from the then Big Six: 'One, an ex-Coopers and Lybrand partner, refused despite giving a charming and informative interview at the end of which he stated that he had no objection to almost all of what he said being ascribed to him' (Matthews and Pirie 2001: 9).

Pictures as archival resources

Pictorial sources are increasingly used to improve our understanding of accounting's past. A pioneering contribution is Yamey's (1989) *Art and Accounting* which examines the many roles that the appearance of an account book signified in paintings and other art between the fifteenth and nineteenth centuries. Turning to the content of published accounts, McKinstry (1996) explains the use of design and designers by Burton plc, revealing that, from 1984, the firm's annual report was transformed into a corporate communications tool. A significant increase in 'face work' is evident from Campbell et al.'s (2009) study of 14 companies for the years 1989 to 2003. Davison (2011) examines the role of paratext in framing the annual report, drawing attention to the increased use of images as evidence of growing attention to paratextual presentation and the perceptions of stakeholders. Walker (2015) studies how images of accounting were used as part of a US state-directed attempt to protect and advance a threatened way of life in the 1930s and 1940s. A more general study of the potential of photographs as an archival source is provided by Parker (2009; see also Davison 2013) who explores the methodological dimensions and potential of photo-elicitation, particularly as a historical research tool for critical accounting and management historians.

Dissemination

Fleischman and Radcliffe (2005: 61–2), in their celebration of the 'expansion and maturation' of accounting history research during the 'roaring nineties', consider its 'coming of age' to be signalled by the growth of publishing opportunities. The role of accounting journals in the dissemination of accounting history research is considered in this section where attention is also drawn to other publication outlets which might be better exploited.

Specialist accounting journals

The first English-language journal devoted to the publication of articles on accounting history was titled *Accounting History*. It was launched by the Accounting History Society in England and Wales in 1976 but discontinued ten years later due to lack of submissions. In Australia, in 1980, Robert W. Gibson launched the *Accounting History Newsletter* which

Table 3.4 Journals publishing accounting history articles 1989–2015

	No.	*%*
AHR/ABFH	385	15.6
AH	364	14.7
AHJ	323	13.1
AAAJ	165	6.7
AOS	160	6.5
CPA	153	6.2
EAR	89	3.6
Abacus	86	3.5
ABR	80	3.2
BH	53	2.1
BHR	50	2.0
FAM	22	0.9
MAR	19	0.8
Others	525	21.1
Total	2,474	100.0

Source: Extracted from Matthews (2017: 77).

ran until 1989 and, following renaming as *Accounting History*, continued through to 1994. The three specialist accounting history journals, today, are the US-based *AHJ*, launched 1977, the British-based *AHR* (initially *ABFH*), launched in 1990, and *AH*, new series, founded in Australia in 1996.

The appearance of specialist accounting history journals provided a major boost for the publication of historical material. Between 1970 and 1980, 161 articles were published in refereed journals, of which 28 appeared in *ABR* (17.4 percent), 16 in *Abacus* (9.9 percent), 15 in *TAR* (9.3 percent) and 9 in *JAR* (5.6 percent) (Matthews 2017: 76). *AHJ* accounted for 37 (23 percent) of the articles published over that same time period. The dominant role played by specialist journals over the later period 1989–2015 – accounting for 43.4 percent of all published articles – is revealed in Table 3.4. The part played by generalist accounting journals in projecting accounting history as a respected subject for study is further examined in the next sub-section.

Generalist accounting journals

Generalist accounting journals have contributed significantly to the expansion of what counts as accounting history but by no means all continue to participate signficantly in that process. According to Fleischman and Radcliffe (2005: 62), 'certain flagship U.S. accounting journals were once willing to publish quality history articles', but this is no longer the case. In the 1960s and 1970s, *JAR* published a number of historical works, but there was then a void until 1989 (when it published a three-page comment by Scorgie), and nothing since.[4] Another elite journal, *TAR*, published accounting history articles most years through to the 1980s but, since then, only a handful (Matthews 2017: 78) including, most recently Sangster (2016, 2018). The publication of historical material in generalist journals therefore depends on editorial policy, and it is for this reason that accounting history owes a debt to editors who opened the door to the discipline early on. Examples include Parker at *ABR* and Murray Wells at *Abacus*. The publication culture which they helped develop has been important in making accounting history a respected area of study. *ABR* and *Abacus* remain receptive to historical work and have been joined by some of the more recently launched critical journals.

In an editorial accompanying the first issue of *AOS*, Anthony Hopwood attacked the 'all too often' perception of accounting as 'a rather static and purely technical phenomenon' (Hopwood 1976: 1). Sometime later, Hopwood (1987) launched a withering attack on prior historical research on the grounds that it adopted 'a rather technical perspective delineating the residues of the accounting past rather than more actively probing the underlying processes and forces at work' (Hopwood 1987: 207). Hopwood advocated an examination of accounting over time through a consideration of the preconditions for change, the process of change and its organisational consequences. His critique of prior research naturally went down poorly with many traditional historians, but his support for 'new accounting history' encouraged much greater diversity in historical methodology and an upsurge of interest in accounting history as a legitimate subject for study.

In their inaugural editorial, Guthrie and Parker (1988: 3) asserted that *AAAJ* would 'offer a unique mix of research topics and traditions which have been marginalised by more traditional journals' including 'critical and historical perspectives of current issues and problems in accounting and auditing'. They also encouraged innovative theoretical approaches and the deployment of new methodologies. In a similar vein, the research areas within which *CPA* invites submissions include 'Studies of accounting's *historical role*, as a means of "remembering" the subject's social and conflictual character'.

Although the three specialist accounting history journals carry a much larger number of history publications than do the generalist journals listed in Table 3.4, taken together, citation analysis indicates that it is the latter that have more influence on the accounting history community (Anderson 2002; Carmona 2006; Bisman 2011). Bisman (2011) carried out an analysis of citations appearing in 546 articles published over the 13-year period from 1996 to 2008 in the specialist accounting history journals. It was discovered that this data set contained 6,108 references to research publications in 64 separate journals. After deleting journals cited infrequently, their number was reduced to 27 but still accounted for 5,750 (94.1 percent) of all citations.

The level of citation of generalist journals (Table 3.5) appears, at first sight, remarkable given the much larger number of history articles published in the specialist journals. *AOS* is comfortably the most cited journal and the next three generalist journals in the list all have more citations than *AH*. A similar situation exists in the case of *AHJ* once self-citations are removed. The inevitable conclusion is that publications in generalist journals are more highly regarded by the accounting community than those in specialist journals. One influential factor in the hegemony of generalist journals, however, is that papers appearing in specialist journals might previously have sought homes in generalist journals which are cited to connect with the initially intended audience. Why might authors choose to target generalist journals? One simple explanation in the case of the British-based researcher is that specialist journals are given a rating of 2 by the Academic Journal Guide (AJG)[5] whereas the generalist journals listed in Table 3.5 are graded 3, 4 or 4*.

Whatever the motivation for authors aspiring to publish in specialist or generalist journals, the inescapable message conveyed by Table 3.5 is that it is the latter that has the stronger impact on the diffusion of accounting history research (Carmona 2006: 262; Sánchez-Matamoros and Gutiárrez-Hidalgo 2011: 332). It is therefore interesting and relevant to study the apparent willingness of generalist journals to publish historical material, and this is the subject of Table 3.6.

Table 3.5 Citations by specialist accounting history journals

	AHJ	*ABFH*	*AH*	*Total*	*%*
AOS	419	256	465	1,140	19.8
AAJ	207	88	219	514	8.9
TAR	210	85	98	393	6.8
ABR	118	112	116	346	6.0
CPA	152	29	122	303	5.3
Abacus	119	76	89	284	4.9
*B&EH**	127	269	134	530	9.2
AHJ	366	121	198	685	11.9
ABFH	212	181	151	544	9.5
AH	114	47	175	336	5.8
Other	240	248	187	675	11.7
Total	2,284	1,512	1,954	5,750	100.0

Source: Derived from Bisman (2011: 166–167, 169).

* This heading covers six business and economic history journals.

Table 3.6 Publications in English-language journals*

	Number of publications			*% of grand total*	
Journals	*1998–2002*	*2012–2016*	*% change*	*1998–2002*	*2012–2016*
AHJ	65	43	−33.8	15.0	12.8
ABFH/AHR	90	62	−31.1	20.8	18.5
AH	53	106	100.0	12.2	31.6
All history	208	211	1.4	48.0	63.0
Critical					
AAAJ	38	42	10.5	8.8	12.5
AOS	46	19	−58.7	10.6	5.7
CPA	39	27	−30.8	9.0	8.1
Total	123	88	−28.5	28.4	26.3
Other generalist					
Abacus	30	11	−63.3	6.9	3.3
ABR	21	8	−61.9	4.8	2.4
BAR	16	14	−12.5	3.7	4.2
EAR	35	3	−91.4	8.1	0.9
Total	102	36	−64.7	23.6	10.7
All generalist	225	124	−44.9	52.0	37.0
Grand total	433	335	−22.6	100.0	100.0

* Table 3.5 is based on the annual listings of accounting history publications contained in *AH* and *AHR/ABFH* for two five-year time periods. The assessment of what counts as an historical article in generalist accounting journals, by those responsible for compiling the annual lists, is accepted and contains no bias given that the compilers were the same in both time periods.

Journals listed in Table 3.6 are divided into three categories: history journals, critical journals and other generalist journals. The number of publications in history journals is consistent for both study periods – 1998–2002 and 2012–2016 – with major increases in the number of articles published in *AH* (which comprised four issues a year in the latter period compared with two earlier on) matching reductions of about one-third in each of the other outlets. The number of papers published in the critical journals declined by 28.5 percent. Those in *AAAJ* actually rose by 10.5 percent whereas publications in *AOS* – the source of many of the papers most cited by the accounting history community – fell sharply from 46 to 19. The decline in visibility of accounting history papers in the 'Other generalist' category is even more dramatic – falling by almost two-thirds from 102 publications in 1998–2002 to just 36 in 2012–2016. Whereas generalist journals accounted for 52 percent of history publications in the earlier period, they contributed just 37 percent in the latter.

It is difficult to imagine why these major changes should have occurred although I am sure that many in the accounting history community have opinions on this issue. The drop in the publication rate in generalist journals is even more dramatic if one accepts the hypothesis that scholars are likely to have become *more* incentivised to publish in such journals, over time, given the higher status attributed to them by some research funding regimes. One possible explanation is that the level of scholarship within the accounting history community is declining. Another is that some generalist journals, at least, have become less receptive to historical studies. As noted above, publishing patterns in elite US journals radically altered with the movement towards empirical accounting research that began in the 1960s, and the subsequent positivists' agency-information research programme. Both normative researchers and historians were casualties of that 'revolution' (Beaver 1989). There is the possibility that changes in publication criteria among qualitative generalist journals is affecting the acceptability of historical studies.

The editors of the critical journal, *AAAJ*, recently used part of a reflective essay for the purpose of 'Confronting theoretical engorgement' (Guthrie and Parker 2017: 9). Drawing on their experience as editors and authors, they concluded that too many reviewers have become obsessed with theory, 'contending that a paper is inadequately theorised, arguing for better integration of theory throughout findings exposition, or declaring the study to be insufficiently theoretically problematised' (Guthrie and Parker 2017: 9). They describe such statements as having become 'the *lingua franca* of the contemporary accounting research community' (Guthrie and Parker 2017: 9). Such criticism, they continue, 'ignores the value of interpretive research that inductively generates theory, such as field-based case study, ethnography, grounded theory, historical archival research in the business and accounting history traditions' (Guthrie and Parker 2017: 10).

Books and monographs

During the 1970s publishing houses recognised the opportunity to make money from reprinting books of interest to accounting historians. Scholar Books' 'Accounting classic series' (1975), initiated and seen through by Robert ('Bob') Sterling, comprised 13 texts. A more substantial initiative got underway the following year with Richard P. Brief of Stern School, New York University, serving as the main facilitator between the academic community and, successively, Arno Press and Garland Publishing. Those publishing houses printed approximately 370 books on accounting history between 1976 and the end of the century. It was a phenomenal project which made available early bookkeeping texts that would otherwise have been extremely difficult to access, such as Edward Hatton's *The Merchant's Magazine* (first published 1695),[6] reprints of accounting classics such as Dicksee's *Auditing* (first published 1892), anthologies of extracts from government reports such as Edwards' (1986) *Legal Regulation of British Company Accounts 1836–1900*, collections of articles on particular topics or by well-known authors, and completely new contributions to the literature such as Hein's (1978) *The British Companies Acts and the Practice of Accountancy 1844–1962*. Since 2000 the Routledge New Works in Accounting History series has supplied a further 34 book-length contributions for use by the accounting history community.

As the contents of Chapters 1 and 2 of this *Companion* demonstrate, books on accounting history have proved their worth in the development of the discipline. Carmona (2006) provides statistical confirmation of their significance for the diffusion of knowledge through the application of citation analysis to the accounting history literature of the 1990s. Whereas journal articles received 3,724 citations or 21 percent of the total, other sources of accounting history literature, mainly books and research monographs, received 13,985 citations or 79 percent of the total. Carmona (2006: 256) further reveals that 11 out of the 27 'most influential works' were published as books. He concludes: 'books and research monographs constitute key venues for the dissemination of accounting knowledge' (Carmona 2006: 256).

Despite their importance, Edwards' (2004) analysis of accounting history publications, 1998–2002, reveals that only 2.8 percent of these were books. Indeed, 8 of the 11 influential books identified by Carmona (2006) were published before 1980 and none of them after 1990. The modus operandi of research assessment projects, today labelled the Research Excellence Framework, which date from 1986,[7] is certainly responsible for the emphasis on journal articles in the UK. While a wide range of eligible outputs are identified for submission to research assessment panels and guidance notes suggest that output media is less significant than the quality of the research it contains, no one really attaches much weight to these assertions. For accountancy, the first type of output usually identified is 'refereed articles' and this is what university administrators encourage accounting faculty to publish.

This effective bias against books is at variance with the state of affairs in the sister discipline of history. Indeed, within university history departments in Britain, the book rather than the portfolio of articles is judged to be the appropriate vehicle for communicating the results of sustained historical scholarship. A relevant book also becomes, as Carmona (2006) demonstrates, the source of initial reference for new researchers, and it is of course the purpose of the *Companion* to help satisfy their needs. Parker (1999) also makes the case for book-length accounting history publications when calling for a 'return to the "grand tour" literary narrative' capable of 'offering a longer term, broader scope macro-scope view of the past' (Parker 1999: 24).[8]

Popularising research findings

Carnegie and Napier (2012: 351) are convinced that accounting historians can make useful contributions to policy debates:

> An understanding of the factors implicated in past change events may allow historians to evaluate current proposals for accounting reform and even to advance their own recommendations (Gomes et al. 2011). For example, recent debates over such notions as fair value would undoubtedly have been more informed had participants had a clearer idea of the origins and development of fair value as a term and as a concept.

In a similar vein Gomes et al. (2011: 392) argue that we should strive to 'demonstrate the contemporary relevance/implications of accounting history scholarship'. And there are signs that some academics take these urgings seriously. For example, accounting historians have actively contributed to the ICAEW's Information for Better Markets Conference, held annually in London, which is attended by an audience of leading practitioners and policy makers as well as academics from a range of international institutions. Zeff (2013) – The objectives of financial reporting: a historical survey and analysis – was initially presented to the 2012 Conference which focused on the question of 'Who is financial reporting for?' Two years later a paper by Nobes (2015) – Accounting for capital: the evolution of an idea – was read at the annual Conference devoted to the theme: 'Capital: reporting, regulation and resource allocation'.

The importance of disseminating research findings to a non-specialist readership and generating impactful research is increasingly recognised by research funding bodies and research assessment agencies. The UK government-financed Economic and Social Research Council (ESRC), for example, attaches great importance to 'public engagement' through appropriate initiatives capable of bringing together researchers and the general public. For this reason, researchers, although initially publishing their findings in academic journals, should seek wider circularisation of their work through books, newspapers and professional journals. In so doing, the practical significance of their discoveries can be explored,

An episode in accounting's history from the 1960s demonstrates the practical significance of placing accounting findings in the public domain. During the latter part of that decade there occurred a series of *causes célèbres* that called into question the utility of published financial reports. The game-changing event was Edward Stamp's (Stamp 1969b; see also 1969a) letter to *The Times* which is evidence to support the idea that it is not so much what you say but where you say it. A few years earlier the Australian academic, Ray Chambers, had published an article in *Abacus* complaining that, under existing GAAP, it was possible to come up with a 'million sets of mutually exclusive rules, each giving a true and fair view of the company's state of affairs and its profits!' (Chambers 1965: 16). He continued: 'Where there are so many possible rules there are in effect no rules' (Chambers 1965: 16). Published in an academic journal, Chambers' paper attracted no more than a ripple of attention whereas Stamp's intervention, broadcast in the British establishment's favourite newspaper, *The Times*, fuelled a debate that soon afterwards led to the creation of the Accounting Standards Steering Committee and the publication of accounting standards in the endeavour to improve financial reporting practices.

Despite the importance of wider dissemination, the results of accounting history research seldom feature prominently in professional journals or other popular media. Indeed, Beattie and Goodacre (2004: 25) observe a general decline in publications by academics in Britain's professional accounting journals. This clearly places a significant limitation on the profile of accounting history beyond the academic community.

Conclusions

This chapter focuses on the growth of accounting history as an academic pursuit. The subject areas studied are expanding, with the last 30 years witnessing diversity in the methods used to gather data and interpret the meaning of accounting's discovered past. The community of accounting historians is well served in terms of publication outlets; there are three specialist journals and many generalist journals that are open to their work. The editors of critical and interdisciplinary accounting journals have played a key role in expanding the methodological horizons of accounting historians.

There are continuing concerns about the Anglo-Saxon dominance of the discipline, though less so than when the *Companion* was first published in 2009. Authors in English-language journals tend to focus on the accounting histories of their own countries post-1800. This is a highly restricted orientation in terms of time and place. There is no doubt that many of those whose first language is not English are at a significant disadvantage when targeting English language journals as outlets for their work (Fleischman and Schuele 2009). Things continue to improve, however, with international conferences providing just one forum where ideas for trans-national collaboration can emerge and develop. Also, special issues of academic journals have been successfully employed to help widen the scope of the subject and the geographical focus of historical studies.

Although accounting history, as an area of study, is in a fairly healthy state (Baskerville et al. 2017: 404–5), there are signs that the momentum provided by theoretical and methodological innovations in the 1990s has not been entirely sustained. Table 3.6 indicates a significant reduction in the number of published research papers over the period 2012–2016 as compared with 14 years earlier. Perhaps even more worrying is the fact that the same timescale reveals a disproportionate reduction in the number of papers published in generalist journals. This concern is heightened by the knowledge that generalist journals are more highly rated by funding bodies and, indeed, by the accounting community itself when its outputs are the subject of citation analysis.

Accounting historians have traditionally relied heavily on communicative evidences in the written form. There has been healthy discussion of the potential and pitfalls of archival sources for the work of both traditional and critical historians. Methodological debate has demonstrated how oral history can be employed not only 'to supplement and verify other forms of history' but also 'to problematize and contradict the traditional stories of accounting' and 'give sustained visibility to the lived experiences of the wide variety of communities affected by accounting' (Hammond and Sikka 1996: 80–1).

The existing subject matter of accounting history is enormous as revealed by the themes featuring in this *Companion*. Overall, the depth of coverage of these research areas varies; some are long-established others are relatively new. Accounting history research is thriving in many countries, but the scope for further development is great. The potential arenas for research are vast and the number of accounting historians meagre by comparison. As the remaining chapters in this *Companion* reveal, there is reason for the accounting community to believe that progress has been made, but there remains much to be done.

Key works

Carmona (2006) offers a broad-based study of the accounting history literature published during the 1990s. The authors and the coverage of their research are profiled and criticised.

Fleischman and Tyson (2003) offer a useful introduction to the pursuit of accounting history research based on archival sources. The chapter is a practical guide to locating primary materials.

Hammond and Sikka (1996) criticises written evidence because it privileges major personalities and ignores ordinary people whose lives and experiences can be better captured and understood through oral history.

Matthews (2017) profiles the history of publications in accounting history from the early days of the twentieth century through to 2015.

Walker (2006) examines the changing frontiers of accounting history and the challenges facing the discipline including limited interdisciplinary engagement and Anglo-Saxon dominance of research agendas.

Appendix: Journal Abbreviations

Abacus	*Abacus*
Accounting and Business Research	*ABR*
Accounting, Business & Financial History	*ABFH*
Accounting Historians Journal	*AHJ*
Accounting History	*AH*
Accounting History Review	*AHR*
Accounting, Auditing & Accountability Journal	*AAAJ*
Accounting, Organizations and Society	*AOS*
British Accounting Review	*BAR*
Business History	*BH*
Business History Review	*BHR*
Critical Perspectives on Accounting	*CPA*
European Accounting Review	*EAR*
Financial Accountability & Management	*FAM*
Journal of Accounting Research	*JAR*
Management Accounting Research	*MAR*
The Accounting Review	*TAR*

Notes

1 Carnegie and Napier (2012: 330) suggest that this was not an entirely fair assessment of the prior contribution of accounting historians, but there is no doubt that Hopwood's comments produced a fundamental reappraisal of the state of the craft and encouraged the development of theories and methods capable of 'taking the study of accounting beyond work that had hitherto been dominated by economics'.
2 See also Walker (2008) and Carnegie and Napier (2012).
3 A list of journals together with abbreviations appears in the Appendix.
4 Papers which use historical data, such as Basu's (2003) study of income smoothing in early nineteenth-century railroads, but make no attempt to place the discussion within either the contemporary context or other relevant historical literature, would fall only within a very wide definition of accounting history.
5 The AJG supplies a guide to the range and quality of journals in which business and management academics publish their research, where 1 is the lowest rating and 4* the highest.
6 Today, many pre-1800 publications can be accessed through the following websites: Early English Books Online and Eighteenth Century Collections Online.
7 The main purpose of these reviews is to enable the higher education funding bodies to distribute public funds for conducting research based on research quality.
8 Duke and Coffman (1993) offer helpful advice on writing accounting or business histories of this type.

References

Anderson, M. (2002) An analysis of the first ten volumes of research in *Accounting, Business & Financial History*, *Accounting, Business & Financial History*, 12 (1): 1–24.

Arnold, A.J. and McCartney, S. (2003) 'It may be earlier than you think': evidence, myths and informed debate in accounting history, *Critical Perspectives on Accounting*, 14 (3): 227–53.

Baskerville, R., Carrera, N., Gomes, D., Lai, A. and Parker, L. (2017) Accounting historians engaging with scholars inside and outside accounting: issues, opportunities and obstacles, *Accounting History*, 22 (4): 403–24.

Basu, S. (2003) Discussion of enforceable accounting rules and income measurement by early 20th-century railroads, *Journal of Accounting Research*, 41 (2): 433–44.

Beattie, V. and Goodacre, A. (2004) Publishing patterns within the UK accounting and finance academic community, *British Accounting Review*, 36 (1): 7–44.

Beaver, W.H. (1989) *Financial Reporting: An Accounting Revolution* (Englewood Cliffs, NJ: Prentice-Hall).

Bisman, J.E. (2011) Cite and seek: exploring accounting history through citation analysis of the specialist accounting history journals, 1996 to 2008, *Accounting History*, 16 (2): 161–83.

Bisman, J.E. (2012) Surveying the landscape: the first 15 years of *Accounting History* as an international journal, *Accounting History*, 17 (1): 5–34.

Bryer, R.A. (1991) Accounting for the 'railway mania' of 1845 – a great railway swindle? *Accounting Organizations and Society*, 16 (5/6): 439–86.

Bryer, R.A. (2006) The genesis of the capitalist farmer: towards a Marxist accounting history of the origins of the English agricultural revolution, *Critical Perspectives on Accounting*, 17 (4): 367–97.

Burrows, G.H. (1996) *The Foundation: A History of the Australian Accounting Research Foundation 1966–1991* (Melbourne: Australian Accounting Research Foundation).

Burrows, G.H. (1999) A response to Lou Goldberg's concerns about oral history, *Accounting History*, 4 (1): 99–106.

Campbell, D., McPhail, K. and Slack, R. (2009) Face work in annual reports. A study of the management of encounter through annual reports, informed by Levinas and Bauman, *Accounting, Auditing & Accountability Journal*, 22 (6): 907–32.

Carmona, S. (2006) Performance reviews, the impact of accounting research, and the role of publication forms, *Advances in Accounting*, 22: 241–67.

Carmona, S. and Zan, L. (2002) Mapping variety in the history of accounting and management practices, *European Accounting Review*, 11 (2): 291–304.

Carnegie, G.D. (2012) The special issue: *AAAJ* and research innovation, *Accounting, Auditing & Accountability Journal*, 25 (2): 216–27.

Carnegie, G.D. and Napier, C.J. (1996) Critical and interpretive histories: understanding accounting's present and future through its past, *Accounting, Auditing & Accountability Journal*, 9 (3): 7–39.

Carnegie, G.D. and Napier, C.J. (2012) Accounting's past, present and future: The unifying power of history, *Accounting, Auditing & Accountability Journal*, 25 (2): 328–69.

Carnegie, G.D. and Potter, B.N. (2000) Publishing patterns in specialist accounting history journals in the English language, 1996–1999, *Accounting, Historians Journal*, 27 (2): 177–98.

Chambers, R.J. (1965) Financial information and the securities market, *Abacus*, 1 (1): 3–30.

Collins, M. and Bloom, R. (1991) The role of oral history in accounting, *Accounting, Auditing & Accountability Journal*, 4 (4): 23–31.

Davison, J. (2011) Paratextual framing of the annual report: liminal literary conventions and visual devices, *Critical Perspectives on Accounting*, 22: 118–34.

Davison, J. (2013) Visual perspective, in: L. Jack, J. Davison and R. Craig (eds) *Routledge Companion to Accounting Communication*, pp. 58–75 (Abingdon: Routledge).

Dicksee, L.R. (1892) *Auditing: A Practical Manual for Auditors* (London: Gee).

Duke, M. and Coffman, E.N. (1993) Writing an accounting or business history: notes toward a methodology, *Accounting Historians Journal*, 20 (2): 217–35.

Edwards, J.R. (ed) (1986) *Legal Regulation of British Company Accounts 1836–1900* (New York: Garland Publishing).

Edwards, J.R. (2004) Some problems and challenges in accounting history research. Paper presented at Tenth World Congress of Accounting Historians, St. Louis, MO and Oxford, MS, 1–5 August.

Fleischman, R.K., Mills, P.A. and Tyson, T.N. (1996) A theoretical primer for evaluating and conducting historical research in accounting, *Accounting History*, 1 (1): 55–75.

Fleischman, R.K. and Radcliffe, V.S. (2005) The roaring nineties: accounting history comes of age, *Accounting Historians Journal*, 32 (1): 61–109.

Fleischman, R.K. and Schuele, K. (2009) Co-authorship in accounting history: advantages and pitfalls, *Accounting, Business & Financial History*, 19 (3): 287–303.

Fleischman, R.K. and Tyson, T.N. (1997) Archival researchers: an endangered species, *Accounting Historians Journal*, 24 (2): 91–109.

Fleischman, R.K. and Tyson, T.N. (2003) Archival research methodology, In R.K. Fleischman, V.S. Radcliffe and P.A. Shoemaker (eds) *Doing Accounting History: Contributions to the Development of Accounting Thought*, pp. 31–47 (Amsterdam: JAI).

Fowler, C.J. and Keeper, T. (2016) Twenty years of accounting history, 1996–2015: evidence of the changing faces of accounting history research, *Accounting History*, 20 (4): 389–418.

Goldberg, L. (1997) Comment: send three and fourpence: some reflections on oral – and other – history, *Accounting History*, 2 (1): 107–14.

Gomes, D., Carnegie, G.D., Napier, C.J., Parker, L.D. and West, B. (2011) Does accounting history matter? *Accounting History*, 16 (4): 389–402.

Guthrie, J. and Parker, L.D. (1988) Editorial, *Accounting, Auditing & Accountability Journal*, 1 (1): 3–5.

Guthrie, J. and Parker, L.D. (2006) Editorial: the coming out of accounting research specialisms, *Accounting, Auditing & Accountability Journal*, 19 (1): 5–16.

Guthrie, J. and Parker, L.D. (2017) Reflections and projections: 30 years of the interdisciplinary accounting, auditing and accountability search for a fairer society, *Accounting, Auditing & Accountability Journal*, 30 (1): 2–17.

Hammond, T. and Sikka, P. (1996) Radicalizing accounting history: the potential of oral history, *Accounting, Auditing & Accountability Journal*, 9 (3): 79–97.

Hammond, T.D. (2003) Histories outside the mainstream: oral history and non-traditional approaches, in: R.K. Fleischman, V.S. Radcliffe and P.A. Shoemaker (eds) *Doing Accounting History: Contributions to the Development of Accounting Thought*, pp. 81–96 (Amsterdam: JAI).

Hatton, E. (1695) *The Merchant's Magazine: Or, Tradesman's Treasury* (London: C. Coningsby).

Hein, L.W. (1978) *The British Companies Acts and the Practice of Accountancy 1844–1962* (New York: Arno Press).

Hopper, T. and Armstrong, P. (1991) Cost accounting, controlling labour and the rise of conglomerates, *Accounting, Organizations and Society*, 16 (5/6): 405–38.

Hopwood, A.G. (1976) Editorial: The path ahead, *Accounting, Organizations and Society*, 1 (1): 1–4.

Hopwood, A.G. (1985) The tale of a committee that never reported: disagreements on intertwining accounting with the social, *Accounting, Organizations and Society*, 10 (4): 361–77.

Hopwood, A.G. (1987) The archaeology of accounting systems, *Accounting, Organizations and Society*, 12 (3): 207–34.

Hoskin, K.W. and Macve, R.H. (1986) Accounting and the examination: a genealogy of disciplinary power, *Accounting, Organizations and Society*, 11 (2): 105–36.

Hoskin, K.W. and Macve, R.H. (1988) The genesis of accountability: The West Point connections, *Accounting, Organizations and Society*, 13 (1): 37–73.

Hoskin, K.W. and Macve, R.H. (1994) Reappraising the genesis of managerialism: a re-examination of the role of accounting at Springfield Amory, 1815–1845, *Accounting, Auditing & Accountability Journal*, 7 (2): 4–29.

Johnson, H.T. and Kaplan, R. (1987) *Relevance Lost: The Rise and Fall of Management Accounting* (Boston: Harvard Business School Press).

Johnson, R.T. (2000) In search of E. I. duPont de Nemours & Company: the perils of archival research, *Accounting, Business & Financial History*, 10 (2): 129–68.

Jones, M.J. and Oldroyd, D. (2015) The 'internationalisation' of accounting history publishing, *British Accounting Review*, 47 (2): 117–23.

Linn, R. (1996) *Power, Progress and Profit: A History of the Australian Accounting Profession* (Melbourne: Australian Society of Certified Practising Accountants).

Loft, A. (1986) Towards a critical understanding of accounting. The case of cost accounting in the UK, 1914–1925, *Accounting, Organizations and Society*, 11 (2): 137–69.

Matthews, D. (2017) Publications in accounting history: a long-run statistical survey, *Accounting Historians Journal*, 44 (2): 69–98.

Matthews, D. and Pirie, J. (2001) *The Auditors Talk. An Oral History of a Profession from the 1920s to the Present Day* (New York: Garland Publishing).

McKinstry, S. (1996) Designing the annual reports of Burton plc from 1930 to 1994, *Accounting, Organizations and Society*, 21 (1): 89–111.

Miller, P., Hopper, T. and Laughlin, R. (1991) The new accounting history: an introduction, *Accounting, Organizations and Society*, 16 (5/6): 395–403.

Miller, P. and Napier, C. (1993) Genealogies of calculation, *Accounting, Organizations and Society*, 18 (7/8): 631–47.

Miller, P. and O'Leary, T. (1987) Accounting and the construction of the governable person, *Accounting, Organizations and Society*, 12 (3): 235–65.

Mumford, M.J. (1991) Chartered accountants as business managers: an oral history perspective, *Accounting, Business & Financial History*, 1 (2): 123–40.

Mumford, M.J. (2007) *Their Own Accounts. Views of Prominent 20th Century Accountants* (Edinburgh: Institute of Chartered Accountants of Scotland).

Napier, C.J. (2002) The historian as auditor: facts, judgments and evidence, *Accounting Historians Journal*, 29 (2): 131–55.

Napier, C.J. (2006) Accounts of change: 30 years of historical accounting research, *Accounting, Organizations and Society*, 31 (4/5): 445–507.

Nobes, C.W. (2015) Accounting for capital: the evolution of an idea, *Accounting and Business Research*, 45 (4): 413–41.

Parker, L. (2009) Photo-elicitation: an ethno-historical accounting and management research prospect, *Accounting, Auditing & Accountability Journal*, 22 (7): 1111–29.

Parker, L.D. (1997) Informing historical research in accounting and management: traditions, philosophies and opportunities, *Accounting Historians Journal*, 24 (2): 111–49.

Parker, L.D. (1999) Historiography for the new millennium: adventures in accounting and management, *Accounting History*, 4 (2): 11–42.

Parker, R.H. (1980a) Editorial, special accounting history issue, *Accounting and Business Research*, 10 (37A): ii.

Parker, R. H. (ed) (1980b) *Bibliographies for Accounting Historians* (New York: Arno Press).

Parker, R.H. (1988) Select bibliography of works on the history of accounting 1981–1987, *Accounting Historians Journal*, 15 (2): 1–81.

Parker, R.H. (1993) The scope of accounting history: a note, *Abacus*, 29 (1): 106–10.

Sánchez-Matamoros, J.B. and Gutiérrez-Hidalgo, F.G. (2010) Patterns of accounting history literature: movements at the beginning of the 21st century, *Accounting Historians Journal*, 37 (2): 123–44.

Sánchez-Matamoros, J.B. and Gutiárrez-Hidalgo, F.G. (2011) Publishing patterns of accounting history research in generalist journals: lessons from the past, *Accounting History*, 16 (3): 331–42.

Sangster, A. (2016) The genesis of double entry bookkeeping, *Accounting Review*, 91 (1): 299–315.

Sangster, A. (2018) Pacioli's lens: god, humanism, Euclid, and the rhetoric of double entry, *Accounting Review*, 93 (2): 299–314.

Scorgie, M.E. (1989) The role of negative numbers in the development of double entry bookkeeping. A comment, *Journal of Accounting Research*, 27 (2): 316–18.

Stamp, E. (1969a) The public accountant and the public interest, *Journal of Business Finance*, 1 (1): 32–42.

Stamp, E. (1969b) Auditing and auditors, *Times Digital Archives* issue no. 57662: 25.

Sy, A. and Tinker, T. (2005) Archival research and the lost worlds of accounting, *Accounting History*, 10 (1): 47–69.

Walker, S.P. (2004) The search for clues in accounting history, in: C. Humphrey and B. Lee (eds) *The Real Life Guide to Accounting Research: A Behind-the-Scenes View of Using Qualitative Research Methods*, pp. 3–21 (Kidlington, Oxford: Elsevier).

Walker, S.P. (ed.) (2005) *Giving an Account. Life Histories of Four CAs* (Edinburgh: Institute of Chartered Accountants of Scotland).

Walker, S.P. (2006) Current trends in accounting history, *Irish Accounting Review*, 13: 107–21.

Walker, S.P. (2008) Innovation, convergence and argument without end in accounting history, *Accounting, Auditing & Accountability Journal*, 21 (2): 296–322.

Walker, S.P. (2011) Editorial, *Accounting History Review*, 21 (1): 1–5.

Walker, S.P. (2015) Accounting and preserving the American way of life, *Contemporary Accounting Research*, 32 (4): 1676–713.

Williams, B. and Wines, G. (2006) The first 10 years of *Accounting History* as an international refereed journal: 1996–2005, *Accounting History*, 11 (4): 419–45.

Willmott, H. (1986) Organising the profession: a theoretical and historical examination of the development of the major accountancy bodies in the UK, *Accounting, Organizations and Society*, 11 (6): 555–80.

Yamey, B.S. (1989) *Art and Accounting* (New Haven & London: Yale University Press).

Zan, L. (2004) Writing accounting and management history. Insights from unorthodox music historiography, *Accounting Historians Journal*, 31 (2): 171–92.

Zeff, S.A. (1972) *Forging Accounting Principles in Five Countries: A History and an Analysis of Trends* (Champaign, IL: Stipes Publishing).

Zeff, S.A. (1980) The promise of historical research in accounting: some personal experiences, in: R. D. Nair and T.H. Williams (eds) *Perspectives on Research*, pp. 13–25 (Madison: University of Wisconsin).

Zeff, S.A. (2013) The objectives of financial reporting: a historical survey and analysis, *Accounting and Business Research*, 43 (4): 262–327.

PART II

Technologies

4
ANCIENT ACCOUNTING

Salvador Carmona and Mahmoud Ezzamel

Overview

This chapter provides an overview of prior research on ancient accounting derived from both the accounting and non-accounting disciplines. In so doing, it highlights remarkably rich insights into a variety of ancient accounting practices, the contexts within which they emerged, and the applications to which they have been put. The review of the literature demonstrates that accounting played a key role in facilitating the functioning of ancient states and economies, helping to regulate and coordinate activities conducted at various levels in ancient societies. Further, the review points to the capacity of ancient accounting to intervene in the domain of state activities, religious institutions, private business and the household. Far from being a rudimentary and crude technology, this chapter shows how these ancient accounting practices exhibited a complex and rich variety of valuing and recording techniques.

Providing a comprehensive review of the diverse literature on ancient accounting is beyond the scope of one chapter; hence the focus is on Mesopotamia and ancient Egypt as well as emerging research on Persia. This excludes the important literature on other early civilisations (e.g., Greece: De Ste. Croix 1956 and Costouros 1978; China: Fu 1971; India: Scorgie 1990; Rome: Oldroyd 1995), some of which is covered in Chapter 5 of this volume. By restricting our attention to Mesopotamia and ancient Egypt, we examine ancient accounting in two civilisations that co-existed during similar historical eras yet exhibited significantly different socio-political and economic contexts.

The next section outlines key challenges facing researchers in the field. Some of these challenges are specific to the nature of the accounting materials that the literature draws upon, whereas others relate to the contexts of remote history. The chapter then summarises the main findings of the extant literature on the technical and social attributes of ancient accounting, and the domains covered by accounting; specifically, the state/royal domain, private business and the household. A summary section pulls together the key arguments of the chapter and suggests possible avenues for future research.

Challenges

In undertaking research on ancient accounting, it is important to ask two key questions. What problems does one encounter in researching ancient history compared to other historical eras? What measures does one take to deal with these problems? The significance of these challenges depends largely on the views that a researcher holds of accounting. If accounting is conceptualised as a set of neutral, technical tools that are virtually divorced from social, economic and historical contexts, then the challenges would be significantly reduced. However, a view that we adopt is of accounting as an assemblage of socially and historically embedded technologies of calculation, and reporting demands an appreciation of ancient socio-political and economic contexts, rendering the study of ancient accounting highly challenging (Miller 1998). The challenges we wish to emphasise here are by no means exhaustive (Vollmers 2003) but have particularly bedevilled our own research into the area; these are: what constitutes primary sources, material lacunae, translation, and theorising ancient accounting material.

Primary sources

For much accounting history research, the archive represents the key primary data source, and the quality of the archive and the archivist are key determinants of the quality of published work. An archive is usually understood to be located in a well-known space like a library. In the case of remote civilisations, such as those of Mesopotamia and ancient Egypt, our concept of an 'archive', if we are to invoke one at all, has to be much broader; indeed, some may prefer instead to speak of historical material rather than an 'archive'. This is because ancient historical material is widely dispersed, maybe all over the world. An additional source of complexity comes from the varying surfaces on which ancient texts are inscribed. In their study of ancient accounting in Africa, Sy and Tinker (2006) show that bones were used to record prime numbers. In the case of ancient Egypt, historical material is inscribed upon the surfaces of stones (walls of temples and monuments), ostraca (shreds of pottery) and papyri. Specifically, literary, legal and commercial matters were inscribed onto papyri and ostraca, whereas monumental and religious texts were mainly inscribed on stone. Any serious attempt to study the emergence and functioning of ancient accounting would require careful consultation of most of these sources. Consequently, we argue that the ancient 'archive' is rather complex, in many cases inaccessible except to experts in ancient history, and accounting researchers have little option but to be selective. The question of course is: how selective? This is an issue that we deal with later.

Lacunae

There are considerable gaps in the ancient material that has survived. This creates an unwanted problem of discontinuity that bedevils any attempt to forge an account of ancient history. Many of the texts on seemingly 'permanent' and virtually indestructible writing surfaces such as building stones have been lost forever because of acts of nature (e.g., floods), acts by the ancients themselves (reuse of stone in new buildings, revenge acts to erase the deeds of previous rulers) or acts by contemporary people (e.g., use of material for modern buildings, poor preservation, vandalism). This means that only a fraction, sometimes a very small one, of the original material has survived. Given this considerable loss, the question of *how selective* a researcher could be becomes almost simple to answer: examine virtually everything you can lay your hands on! This comment is made in acknowledgement of the precious but sparse amount of original material that has reached us. This problem is even more acute because much of the surviving material has been damaged, sometimes quite considerably, at times rendering a text almost meaningless. Indeed, the problem of data lacunae is so serious that, at times, the researcher has to make assumptions concerning missing/damaged inscriptions based on the patterns of previous texts, sometimes reaching to other historical episodes because of the lack of comparable texts from the same era.

The choice is either that we attempt to forge accounts of such histories, no matter how incomplete, or do nothing. Finley (1992: 25) has lamented ancient historians who rely on anecdotes, calling for 'abandoning the anecdotal technique of dredging up an example or two as if that constituted proof'. While we would endorse Finley's suggestion when evidence is plentiful, we would disagree if all that is available as evidence is of an anecdotal nature. However, historical researchers are aware that evidence is rarely well preserved and complete and is usually messy and deficient. Consequently, even small fragments of evidence can reveal much, and the careful researcher should highlight their source's limitations and any consequential implications for the findings from the study, but without shying away from using anecdotes.

Translation

A significant number, but by no means all, of the texts containing accounting entries from Mesopotamia and ancient Egypt have been transliterated and then translated into modern European languages. For those texts not yet translated into contemporary languages, the only way to access them is to learn to decipher ancient languages (see Vollmers 2003). In addition to this, there is the daunting problem of translating a text from the remote past into the present, with all that this entails in terms of finding suitable equivalent contemporary terms to those the ancients have used. To what extent, for example, can we sensibly describe 'exchange of goods for a price' as equivalent to 'market exchange'? How legitimate is it for us to speak of an ancient economy as a means of describing the creation, accumulation and distribution of ancient 'wealth'? Are we entitled to use terms such as 'tax' to represent levies imposed by the ancient state on its subjects? Can we indeed speak of 'accounting' practices and techniques in the remote past? Given how controversial the use of the term 'government' is even today (Rose and Miller 1992), can we legitimately speak of government in the ancient world?

Even more importantly, there is major concern with the constitutive power of language and its effect on forging a picture of the remote past; contemporary researchers may not be reproducing the past but, instead, creating it via the language they employ. Previts and Bricker (1994) use the notion of 'presentmindness' to refer to this concern by intimating that the use of present-day notions to write about institutions and practices of the past brings about understandings that could be different from those held by our ancestors. For example, current understandings of accountability differ from those of ancient people (see Carmona and Ezzamel 2007; Ezzamel and Hoskin 2002). Consequently, an unproblematic use of such notion in writing on ancient accounting history would mistakenly suggest that contemporary practices of accountability and those of the ancient world are very similar. Although these concerns are well taken, we suggest that there is scope for accounting historians to carefully adapt notions such as the 'state', the 'economy', 'markets', 'monies of account' to the ancient world as long as the limitations are acknowledged. We recognise that this is a controversial area and that there is considerable debate on the extent to which such terms can be extended beyond the specific contexts in which they were first developed. Much depends on how strict one wishes to be in delineating the conditions that have to be satisfied in order for the use of a term to be deemed acceptable. For example, the term 'state' can readily be applied to virtually all ancient societies if it is taken to imply only three conditions – a geographical area with a population and a visible authority – and this applies to country states as well as city-states (for views on this debate, see Eisenstadt 1969; Ball 1995; Gills 1995; Warburton 1997; but see Bourdieu's 2014 critique of this definition).

On 'economy', Janssen (1975: 39) warns that 'the distance between ancient Egyptian and modern European economics is so wide that it is useful to stress and perhaps even overstress it in order to avoid a too modern conception of economic life in ancient Egypt'. Similarly, Finley argues at some length that the ancients did not have a concept similar to the notion of what we now understand as 'the economy':

> [The ancients] in fact lacked the concept of an 'economy', and *a fortiori*, they lacked the conceptual elements which together constitute what we call 'the economy'. Of course, they farmed, traded, manufactured, mined, taxed, coined, deposited and loaned money, made profits or failed in their enterprises. And they discussed these activities in their talk and their writing. What they did not do, however, was to combine these particular activities conceptually into a unit, in Parsonian terms into 'a differentiated sub-system'.
>
> *(Finley 1992: 21)*

There is every reason to believe that the ancients did not develop a conceptual construct similar to what we now call 'the economy', and care should be exercised when interpreting ancient practices so that they are not laboured by meanings the ancients would not have recognised. Reasonable apprehension, however, should not hamper efforts to study ancient economic and social practices, even though they may not correspond to conceptual categories that we now employ. There is also no reason why the word 'economy' and similar terms could not be used in an ancient context, as long as they are bracketed and their meanings are differentiated from those circulating in modern economies. Hence, we need to move away from such misplaced concern with what constitutes historical 'proof' (ibid.: 25) and acknowledge that there is no such a thing as a concrete history 'out there' to be captured in its reality, but rather accept that in writing history we 'construct history' (Ezzamel and Willmott 2004). In the context of our chapter, what we offer is our own account of these ancient histories via our own reconstruction of how previous researchers constructed these histories.

Similarly, we wish to address the extent to which 'markets' existed and functioned in the civilisations of the ancient Near East. Briefly, two schools of thought exist, one denying this possibility and the other affirming the existence (and indeed importance) of markets, even though proponents of the latter view would concede that these markets did not exhibit all the characteristics associated with the modern notion of market.

Polanyi (1957) is perhaps the most influential writer of the school challenging the existence of markets in these societies. Commenting on trading in the time of Hammurabi, he stated, 'Babylonia, as a matter of fact, possessed neither market places nor a functioning market system of any description' (ibid.: 16). Other researchers attested to the existence of places for markets in Mesopotamia, but either insisted on the absence of a market economy (Oppenheim 1964), or spoke of a possible notion of a market price but then surmised that it might have been fixed by the government and not by trade in the market (Leemans 1960). For this school, even when places existed for markets, they were confined spaces where few items were exchanged and in a manner that did not contribute appreciably to the livelihood of producers and sellers (Dalton 1971).

Polanyi (1977: 125) refined his thoughts further by developing the notion of 'market elements' in order to emphasise the institutional characteristics that constitute the market. These elements comprise:

> [a] site, physically present or available goods, a supply crowd, a demand crowd, custom or law, and, equivalencies … Whenever the market elements combine to form a supply – demand–price mechanism, we speak of price-making markets. Otherwise, the meeting of supply and demand crowds, carrying on exchange at fixed equivalencies, forms a non-price-making market. Short of this we should not speak of markets, but merely of the various combinations of the market elements the exchange situation happens to represent.

For Polanyi, ports of trade and the provisioning at the gates of towns in what he terms 'redistributive oriental economies' exhibit market elements, but none of them are proper markets, because there is no supply–demand–price interaction. Given these refinements to Polanyi's thoughts, it can be stated that at the very least local markets existed in both ancient Egypt (Janssen 1975) and Mesopotamia (Renger 1984), although whether these local markets ever developed to become 'markets proper' by meeting Polanyi's criteria is unlikely.

It is within this understanding that we seek to approach our attempt to contextualise ancient accounting practices. Such contextualisation will hopefully enable us to come closer to the meaning given by our ancestors to activities that present-day terminology can only describe superficially.

Theorising

There is considerable debate in the literature concerning how ancient accounting material can be theorised. For example, Silver (1985), Kemp (1989) and Warburton (1997) have each invoked rational economic ideas in interpreting ancient Egyptian records, in the belief that the ancient Egyptians displayed many of the rational attributes ascribed by modern economic theories to humans. In contrast, Polanyi (1977) and many of his followers (e.g., Dalton 1971) have suggested that ancient civilisations should be studied using a lens different from that of modern economic analysis; he emphasises the desirability of using economic anthropology as the appropriate means of studying ancient economies. To clarify, traditional economic thinking views humans, ancient and contemporary, as engaged in essentially economising behaviour. Such behaviour is based on the assumption that an efficient market allocation system exists and operates in a manner that motivates people to act accordingly. In contrast, economic anthropology starts from the position that human desire for material gain leads them to take actions aimed at achieving this aim, but such actions are constrained by the context of their specific culture. As we shall see below, allocation mechanisms different from market distribution and reciprocity play a significant role in ancient societies This alternative approach has found favour with a number of ancient historians (e.g., for ancient Egypt, see Bleiberg 1996; Janssen 1975).

It is clear from the above that the debate on the forces that are assumed to underpin the behaviour of ancient peoples is far from resolved. The accounting literature we review below is suggestive of this theoretical diversity. Our own preference is for sensitive theorising of the ancient historical material within its specific socio-political, economic and cultural settings, rather than approaching the study of ancient accounting with a predetermined grand theoretical framing.

The technical attributes of ancient accounting: accounting, counting and duality

Most of the literature covering this theme relates to the work of Mattessich (1987, 1989, 1991, 1994, 2000) drawing on the path-breaking research of Schmandt-Besserat (1977, 1978, 1979, 1980, 1981a, 1981b, 1983, 1984, 1986a, 1986b, 1992, 1997) on counting and accounting in Mesopotamia. Schmandt-Besserat's work demonstrates that token accounting was invented before both abstract counting and writing. Motivated by Wittgenstein's search for symbolic representation, Mattessich (1987) forges a link between Mesopotamian token accounting and the correspondence theory of representation. Following the lead of Schmandt-Besserat (1992), he notes that an envelope of tokens (sealed clay envelopes that contained the actual tokens inside and impressions of the same tokens on the outside surface) could have functioned as a personal account of a steward or debtor as well as an inventory of his investments. Simple tokens were used for such items as grain and cattle (with tokens of different shapes assigned to different commodity accounts), whereas more incised and perforated tokens recorded services and manufactured items. Mattessich stresses the dual significance of these tokens, being both a set of individual assets in their detail and a representation of equity in their totality. This early accounting was capable of monitoring obligations and levies from stewards and tax payers and recording actual payments in kind by debtors. He then argues that not only does every piece of commercial reality (such as a jar of oil) correspond to a specific token but also the relations (such as property rights) had proper correspondence through the location of certain tokens in a particular aggregate. Hence, input–output relations were exhibited not in the actual transfer of commodities but also in their representations.

Accounting and modes of counting

One of Mattessich's key concerns was to differentiate between types of counting and to revisit the argument that Mesopotamian accounting was based on the input–output principle. Mattessich (1991) distinguishes between three modes of counting:

1. Counting by one-to-one matching. This entailed a one-to-one correspondence between a sign and the item or object being counted, via markings, pebbles, or sticks, where the sign was repeated for every additional unit of an item or object.
2. Concrete counting by tokens. Tokens used for specific counting were either simple or complex. Simple, plain clay tokens dating from 8000 BC were used for concrete counting of objects. From around 3250 BC these tokens were deposited inside hollow clay envelopes, or bullae, after the tokens were impressed on the surface of the bullae but before they were sealed. Hence, it was possible at a glance to identify the token contents of a bulla by simply 'reading' the impressions made on its surface. This presented one of the earliest known accounting 'systems'. Each type of token signified either a particular object or number of items of the same object, so that every token sign was entwined exclusively with a specific object. Complex tokens exhibited a greater range of shapes and markings, and were typically perforated so that they could be strung together. While counting in the abstract sense was not yet known, Schmandt-Besserat contends that the notion of cardinality was already implied in this concrete counting:

> The hypothesis that from the beginning of the token system groups of counters were no longer the mere representation of one unit ('and one more') but expressed a cardinal number is based on my argument that certain tokens stood for sets (x = n). I posit, for example, that tetrahedrons, which occur in two distinct subtypes 'small' and 'large' … represent two different units of the same commodity.
>
> *(Schmandt-Besserat 1992: 189)*

3. Abstract counting. Here the number becomes totally detached from the object, so that a given number (numeral) can be used to designate the *same quantity* of different objects; for example, the number '3' could be placed before the word for sheep and also before the word for apple to designate three sheep and three apples.

Mattessich (1989, 1991, 1994), following Schmandt-Besserat, argues that every type of simple or complex token represented a specific type of account, whereas a sphere/bulla/envelope with tokens deposited inside it and a sealed string of tokens were equivalent to a personal account about stewards or debtors with accompanying lists of inventories. Thus, the total sum of tokens inside an envelope or on a string represented the equity that a creditor lent to a debtor. Mattessich argues that this is similar to a 'superaccount' or a balance sheet, and that the aggregation of the tokens had a dual meaning: in its details it revealed individual assets, and in its totality it revealed an equity interest or part of it. In ancient Egypt (see Ezzamel and Hoskin 2002: 335; Ezzamel 2009: 355), counting referred to tallying or reckoning items (individuals, objects) so that they could be sub-aggregated. Moreover, accounting had several features: a *practice* of entering in a visible format a record; an account involved *signs* which both *name* and *count* the items and activities recorded; and, finally, the practice of producing an account was always a form of *valuing*. Therefore, accounting was invested in writing which outperformed oral accounts.

Duality and the input–output principle

Mattessich contends that, contrary to today's familiar understanding, the foundations of accounting were not based on double entry but on the logical form of a transaction. He considers economic events, such as sales, as the *empirical* manifestation of this logic with the journal entries as well as matrices, algebraic equations, or vectors constituting the *conceptual* manifestation of this logic. Mattessich applies this understanding to the Mesopotamian accounting evidence, arguing that 'Since the ancient people of the Middle East exploited the *transfer of clay tokens from one location to another* to represent various economic transactions, there can be little doubt that *an input–output structure dominated those early accounting systems*' (1991: 38, original emphasis). Mattessich suggests that any attempt to treat the above point as trivial is misguided, since the transfer of objects from one place to another exhibits this duality:

> [t]his objection fails to grasp the essential point: the objection refers only to empirical structures and events and misses *the crucial idea of duplicating the input–output of actual commodities through the input–output of tokens by means of which conceptual representation of this duality becomes possible.*
>
> *(ibid.: 38, original emphasis)*

Mattessich then develops the notions of physical duality and social duality as applied to Mesopotamian accounting. For him, physical duality relates to the physical aspects of the 'output of a commodity from one place, and its input into another' (ibid.). Hence, physical duality expresses a one-to-one correspondence between a physical economic transaction as an empirical event and some representational scheme such as Mesopotamian token accounting. In contrast, social duality arises from the fact that every asset belongs to someone and hence it is simultaneously an equity or part of it. This social duality therefore relates to activities, such as owning, lending or borrowing, which are economic transactions that become represented by accounting transactions through recording, with these activities sharing a social character. Mattessich (1991) distinguishes between two types of social duality based on social and legal differences, debt claims (financial-legal relations between two persons) and ownership claims (legal or quasi-legal relations between a person and an object) which, in addition to the physical duality already mentioned, gives accounting three dualities. These two types of social duality, Mattessich (1991: 41) argues, were evident in Mesopotamian accounting: 'by 3250 B.C. – the time when the sealed clay envelopes and string systems emerged – accounting had already incorporated ownership claims as well as stewardship or debt relations'.

Mattessich (1991, 1994) was further interested in demonstrating the theoretical link between ancient Mesopotamian accounting and modern accounting via recourse to two sets of argument. First, he examined the underlying technical characteristics of both types of accounting, as evident in the input–output principle and the duality argument. This line of thinking was elaborated further by inserting terms such as 'credit' and 'debit' into Mattessich's (1994: 19) interpretations of the tokens, such that inputting tokens into an envelope was considered equivalent to a debit entry, while output of a token from an envelope was treated as a credit entry. Similarly, impressing token shapes on the outside of envelopes was taken as equivalent to a credit entry in an equity account, whereas inserting tokens into the envelopes was treated as a debit entry in an asset account. He also identified what he saw as the control features of these early accountings: empirical control and tautological control. He treated empirical control as tantamount to taking actual inventory (e.g., counting assets such as sheep) in a particular location and comparing it with tokens for the same object deposited in the appropriate envelope for that location to verify that the two are the same and, if not, identifying the discrepancy. Tautological control involved, according to Mattessich, counting the tokens inside an envelope and comparing that with the impressions on the outside surface of that same envelope.

The second approach Mattessich takes to enhance the similarity of Mesopotamian accounting to modern accounting emphasises the double-entry nature of both systems and proposes that the origin of modern accounting may indeed lie in the invention of the clay tokens. He contends that the use of tokens to record the transfer of physical objects from one location to another represents 'double', 'entry' and 'recording' (Mattessich 1994: 19–20), because it involves the simultaneous recording of the two aspects of input and output in different places in the system (structural characteristic). For example, the indentations of the tokens impressed on the outside surface of the envelope 'are the mirror pictures and true counter-entries (credit entries) on the equity side of this prehistoric record-keeping system' (Mattessich 1991: 44), and also because it combines both empirical control and tautological control. This double-entry recording, however, should not be confused with 'double-entry *bookkeeping*' in the modern sense 'where a tautological control checks whether the *monetary* values were entered equally on both sides' (Mattessich 1994: 20, original emphasis). Nevertheless, Mattessich argues that the basic logical structure of this ancient double-entry recording is virtually identical to that of the modern double-entry system (Mattessich 1991: 43).

The social attributes of ancient accounting: accounting, writing and money

Ezzamel and Hoskin (2002) extend Mattessich's findings by adopting a social perspective on ancient accounting. Drawing on a theoretical framing that integrates Foucault's work on practices and Derrida's ideas on the logic of the supplement, they analyse an extensive amount of evidence drawn from Mesopotamia and Ancient Egypt. Although Ezzamel and Hoskin argue that the technical aspects of ancient accounting were distinctly different from those featured in double-entry bookkeeping, they suggest that such ancient accounting was sufficiently complex to yield important theoretical insights.

Ezzamel and Hoskin argue that writing emerged as a supplement to accounting, while money emerged as a double supplement to both accounting and writing. Yet accounting itself became a supplement to prior ways of numbering and valuing, and so accounting was part of a play of supplements. In ancient history, accounting simultaneously named and counted objects as commodities, and in so doing it conferred a precise (denominated) value upon them: a value reproducing recontextualised actions, as items could, beyond the here and now, be called up, checked and demanded in precisely the amount denominated. Consequently, accounting, writing and money, as supplementary technologies, enact new power and knowledge relations which produce a transformation in the forms that power and knowledge can take.

After re-examining the role played by accounting in making possible the genesis of counting and writing, Ezzamel and Hoskin point to the theoretical complexity of accounting's role as the supplement that produces further supplements. In this respect, they suggest that the invention of accounting, writing and money made it possible to enter a world of 'transactionality', which in turn represented a double break: (1) a break *from* a world in which equivalence and value reciprocity are meaningless because of the absence of money; (2) a break *into* a world where equivalence and value reciprocity are always enacted through supplementarity.

Accounting for what? On the domains of activities covered by accounting

In this section, we synthesise the literature that has examined the types of activities in which accounting intervened as a technology of measuring, 'valuing' and recording. These activities turned out to be quite varied. To embed the evidence in its wider contexts, we organise our review around the activities that witnessed the emergence of accounting practices in ancient societies, ranging from those that belong to the state to transactions involving barter or semi-barter exchange.

Accounting for the state or royal domain

Investigations addressing accounting for the royal domain come primarily from ancient Egypt and, to a lesser extent, from Mesopotamia. Prior research covers several important activities in ancient history, such as taxation, construction projects/workshops, bakeries, the royal palaces and the temples.

Taxation

In an economy as highly centralised as that of ancient Egypt, the importance of taxation looms large. While the genesis of levying and collecting tax goes back to pre-dynastic Egypt

(5500–3100 BC; see Davies and Friedman 1998), work on ancient Egyptian taxation in the accounting literature has so far focused on the Middle Kingdom (2030–1640 BC) and beyond. Ezzamel (2002b) examined a tax-assessor's journal covering the end of the Twelfth (1991–1778 BC) and the beginning of the Thirteenth Dynasty (1778–1625 BC). The papyrus is badly damaged and thus it contains no information on tax calculations, but it shows details of the steps taken by the scribe to assess tax. Initially, the land to be taxed was surveyed and the tax crop was measured. The tax scribe was accompanied by several others, each entrusted with a specific responsibility: the clerk of land (the custodian of the regulations of land registry); the envoy of the steward (who took internal measures of both land and crop on behalf of the steward); the stretcher of the cord, and the holder of the cords (who both took measures of the standing crop). Ezzamel also reviews additional evidence pertaining to the levying and collection of tax from the Twelfth Dynasty, where specific individuals were charged with the responsibility for collecting given amounts of tax (wheat, corn, barley, bread, ducks and geese) levied as dues on the Pharaoh's subjects.

Further research on the functioning of taxation in ancient Egypt has examined the cycle of taxation 'which involves the definition of taxable entities, the estimation, final assessment, collection, transportation and storage of taxes' (Ezzamel 2002a: 17), with specific accounting procedures for each of these stages. Tax subjects were the temples, state officials (who were taxed only in exceptional circumstances), Khato-lands (lands earmarked to supply revenues to the Crown) and ordinary people. For example, in the case of Khato-lands, exact measures were determined for each plot assigned to a given individual, in addition to a precise assessment of tax due. Tax was assessed in capacity measures. The evidence suggests that harvest tax assessment was a function of two variables: the area of land and its quality (fertility), with tax liability being the product of multiplying land area by the appropriate tax bracket for that type of land. Ezzamel then examines how the remaining parts of the cycle of taxation were carried out and discusses a case of tax defalcation that continued undetected for nine years.

In Mesopotamia, taxation played an important role in the economies of Sumerian city-states. The excise of tax was based on coercion and performed by the royal palace and the temple. As argued by several commentators (e.g., Schmandt-Besserat 1992), the royal palace relied on taxes to engage in public construction projects on a major scale (e.g., dams), invest in public buildings and strengthen state bureaucracy. On the other hand, the temples provided regular offerings to the gods and made their provision by designated individuals compulsory, leading some commentators to view these offerings as obligatory taxes (Beale 1978: 310).

The deployment of taxation exerted an important influence on accounting practices in Mesopotamian city-states (Rivero Menéndez 2000). According to Schmandt-Besserat (1994), the large number of bureaucrats employed by the state enabled increasing sophistication of accounting practices employing complex clay tablets, envelopes, bullae and cylinders. The aim of these refined accounting instruments was twofold: (1) to make possible a precise tracking of transactions taking place in Sumerian cities, in particular those affecting agricultural goods, food, textiles, or perfumes; and (2) to keep a record of unpaid taxes.

Royal construction projects/workshops

The most detailed evidence available from ancient Egypt comes from the Middle Kingdom, and from the reign of Senusret III (Twelfth Dynasty). This era witnessed a major expansion in administrative titles and practices, and also crucially in recordkeeping. Ezzamel (2004) examined some of this evidence within the context of ancient work organisation. His analysis shows how detailed daily attendance lists were kept for royal projects, including names, titles, days spent by each workman on project work, days of absence, days in transit (between projects) and total days, payroll or provision allocations per day, tasks (work targets) allocated to workmen converted into equivalent man-days, work completed and work remaining. Workshop accounts included details of items delivered to be worked on converted in their diversity into a single common denominator as money of account (*deben*, a precise weight measure), amount of work completed and the remainder. Ezzamel argues that this evidence reveals a full system of ancient human accountability at work based on division of labour, allocation of predetermined work targets, and regular reporting on actual and completed work. The evidence also suggests that a finely tuned reward structure (in the form of fixed provisions) was used, which reflected the rank of every category of worker, hierarchical position, or responsibility. Ezzamel, however, notes:

> The notion of time emphasised in these practices was not 'timed labour', the concept associated with industrial capitalism, but rather was much closer to 'task orientation' … In this emphasis, concern was focused upon ensuring that a particular task was completed, rather than being obsessed with meeting time targets, such as those enshrined in modern time-and-motion studies.
>
> *(ibid.: 530–1)*

Bakeries

Ezzamel (1997) used pictorial evidence as well as several accounts to forge a preliminary depiction of accounting for the bakeries of ancient Egypt (with similar conclusions applying to breweries). He constructed a cycle of ancient accountability that began with input of grain transferred from the granaries to the bakery, as well as the detailed accounting for the baking process. Such process was scrutinised carefully by scribes to determine precise allowances for natural loss in baking, use of weight conversion rates to calculate the number of loaves of a given weight/size expected from a given input of flour, use of a dilution (baking/cooking) ratio to control for the precise proportions of water and flour in making the dough, equivalent weight of baked bread transferred from the bakery to the storehouse, and a final comparison of output (numbers of breads of given weights and dilution actually produced) against expected output from the input of grain. The accounts also traced targets and actual output per individual baker every day. The system of accounting used entailed weighing, pure counting, a measure of quantity equivalence, a quality adjustment (the baking ratio), predetermined natural loss in baking, predetermined targets of output, measures of actual output, and calculation and reporting of variances between targets and actual achievements.

One may wonder at so much detailed accounting of the activities of a bakery. As in much of this work, the context is typically sparsely examined because contextual evidence is usually lacking. However, some contextualising of the activities of the bakery examined by Ezzamel (1997) is now possible. Bread in ancient Egypt had a great symbolic significance; it was endowed with life-giving and sustaining power symbolism; it was the very stuff of life (Wilkinson 1994). Moreover, the bakery examined by Ezzamel (1997) was an army bakery, dating to the reign of Seti I (1303–1290 BC) who waged major military campaigns outside Egypt. In this respect, Ezzamel argues that the proliferation of the above detailed accounting practices for the bakery may have been underpinned by an incentive to ensure the careful monitoring of regular army supplies of bread (and beer).

The royal palaces

Sparse evidence remains from records kept for the royal palaces in ancient Egypt. The most complete evidence dates to the Middle Kingdom, ancient Egypt, in the form of summary accounts of a royal visit to Thebes from the Thirteenth Dynasty (Ezzamel 2002b). The royal entourage included the Pharaoh, his family, immediate dependants, the Vizier (similar to Prime Minister in a ruling monarchy), high officials, and courtiers covering the treasury, the priesthood and the military. The papyri include: (1) statements of account covering provisions, special deliveries, remainders, balances and surplus; (2) orders of provisions earmarked for specific individuals; (3) expenditure on valuable commodities such as lists of offerings; and (4) official reports and documents detailing specific items received in the presence of witnesses.

The accounts reveal an intricate web of redistribution that co-ordinated the inflows and outflows of commodities. On a daily basis, the scribes kept a recurrent balance of bread as a safety-net in case supplies fell short of requirements; whereas for fresh and perishable goods such as vegetables, supply exactly matched requirements. In a similar vein, the accounts were kept daily, with separate columns for each type of commodity. Finally, special requirements for a particular day were accounted for via a new entry called 'due today' to trace this special requirement.

Ezzamel argues that these daily summary accounts established and reproduced social order by observing a sequence for the entries that reflected social status and power. Furthermore, the precisely determined rations of provisions reinforced dependency relations reflected in the social and political status of the recipient. Yet, they linked sources of revenues and provisions to specific institutions which reflected the dependency of the state on these institutions. Mandeville (2014) examined the monthly payment system to royal workmen at Thebes and observed seasonal fluctuations in the delivery schedule, the frequency of payments, the classes of workmen found listed in the ration texts, and the amounts of grain that they individually received. Mandeville also observed that the scribes used a specialised vocabulary in reporting grain shipments to the village of Deir el-Medina.

Vollmers (1996, 2009) investigated accounting and organisational procedures enforced in Persepolis (509–494 BC) by the Persian Empire to control food provided to royal personnel and workers. Vollmers shows that bookkeeping became instrumental in the control and distribution of food and consisted of large tablets that resemble ledger accounts, written acknowledgments of transactions, labels and accounting balances to attest to amounts remaining in inventory. Taking an inventory was an essential part of control because records of receipts and disbursements were suspect without the assurance of beginning and ending inventory. Namazi and Taak (2017) also focused on the same observation period to examine the inventory system used by the state in its internal transactions as well as with private citizens. They show that it contained short- and long-term inventory accounts, end-of-year inventory recording and auditing, and transfer of balances to the following year.

Accounting for the activities of the temples

Death is perhaps the most significant single event in the experience of any human society, and this is particularly true in ancient Egypt. It is not surprising therefore that, among surviving evidence, several fascinating papyri and inscriptions on stone relate to temple activities and the preservation of the cult of dead Pharaohs and important officials. Ezzamel (2005) examines a set of documents from the Old Kingdom relating to the temple of King Néferirkarê-Kakai (Fifth Dynasty).

Jobs were performed by phyles (gangs). The available papyri contain lists of attendance and allocation of work duties on a daily basis, along with daily and monthly accounts detailing collection of goods and their distribution, and inventory lists of equipment and various other items. In the case of inventory lists, a grid structure was used whereby items are grouped in specific categories that are organised under a hierarchy of three levels of classification. At the end of its period of work (usually two months), the departing phyle (a Greek term widely used to describe an ancient Egyptian work team) delivered the equipment to the stores and the scribe noted the exact state of each item of equipment and the repairs required. Red and black inks was used to differentiate the entries and the columns of the inventory list and to enhance visibility. Lines were drawn by the inspectors to indicate completion of their work. The departing phyle and the incoming phyle separately reported about the state of the equipment they were leaving behind or receiving. The temple income accounts again used a grid structure and black and red inks to record, on a daily basis, deliveries by name of porter and source, the remainder, and the place to which they were sent as provisions.

In the case of inventory lists, recording items by using a combination of black and red inks in a tabular format (*organising/recording visibility*), and the enumeration of quantities of items and the classification taxonomy used for families of items (*technical visibility*), made it easy for the scribe to signal damaged items as well as the nature of the damage. Apart from legitimising the role of the scribes, this made it possible both to trace responsibility for damage to the appropriate (departing) phyle and to plan the repairs in time for the arrival of the new phyle. In the monthly income accounts of the temple, the scribes could trace a delivery to its exact amount and original source with such *dependency visibility* enshrined into accounting entries. Using a grid system and the judicious combination of black and red inks the scribe could differentiate between amounts due as revenue, actual quantities delivered and balance remaining. Ezzamel argues that accounting played a key role in determining the precise allocations of provisions for every member of temple staff and in recording the delivery of these provisions.

Further evidence on accounting for the temple comes from the Middle Kingdom in the form of ten contracts intended to be executed after the death of a high-ranking official. In that study, Ezzamel (2002b) shows how accounting practices underpinned the contractual arrangements of the dead that were finalised in their lifetimes. The intervention of accounting was not simply restricted to the writing of a will; it also involved determining the precise amounts of offerings to be made of each type of commodity after death. Rather than being enforced by law, these contracts were sanctioned by social norms as well as incentives built into the contracts to motivate the priests entrusted with their execution to ensure that the measured giving on behalf of the dead was observed.

Accounting for the private domain

In this section, we examine the literature on accounting for the private domain in both Mesopotamia and ancient Egypt. Because Mesopotamia was a much less centralised economy compared to ancient Egypt, more material on accounting for the private domain is available.

Accounting for private business

Mattessich (1998a, 1998b) builds on the work of Niessen et al. (1993) to examine the role of Mesopotamian accounting in the private domain. Different types of cuneiform tablets emerged during the third millennium BC; three types seemingly performing auxiliary tasks, even though they include some numbers, and the fourth type, with columns and partitions (including entries identified by Niessen et al. as debits and credits), being the accounts of archaic bookkeeping. On these larger tablets, the reverse (credit/discharge) side typically contains the sum of the numbers entered on the obverse (debit/charge) side. Mattessich (1998a: 5–6) argues that many of these later tablets still retained the kind of double-entry recording system identified in earlier token accounting. Unlike the token system, though, this was not a closed, or self-contained system, as not all the discharges are matched to the charges and hence it has to be seen in conjunction with other recordings.

In commenting on the clay tablets of the fourth millennium BC, Niessen et al. (1993: 35) note how the level of detail varied according to the administrative level. Almost without exception, however, these tablets simply list numbers or quantities of items or commodities, without any reference to their purpose or context. These archaic tablets also 'document early types of information processing which led to "theoretical" amounts in the form of future calculations, debit postings, standardised obligation, and similar nonempirical accounting procedures' (ibid.). Such development of 'theoretical' amounts led Mattessich (1998a: 10–11) to invoke the modern term 'budgetary procedures' when discussing these developments.

Niessen et al. (1993) provide more detailed and intriguing accounting entries relating to a number of activities, including the administrative activities of Kushim, presumed to be an official responsible for a storage facility containing the basic ingredients (malt and cracked barley or barley groats) for the production of beer (Kushim could alternatively be an institution – the meaning rendered is not exact). The tablets recording these activities specified the amounts of the product, its quality, location, or connected responsibility for a given period of time. As barley left the granaries of Kushim for processing, the quantities were added up, with each entry quoting the title of the official, thereby locating responsibility for the allocated barley with that official, and both Kushim and the official signed the tablet. In these tablets, quantities of barley were differentiated by type between barley groats or malt. The individual quantities of groats and malt were aggregated and then combined to produce a grand total. Finally, the actual beer produced was recorded as were the names of the persons who received the beer, with a *possibility* that labour time required for beer production was also measured (ibid.: 46).

The accounting contents of the tablets became more meaningful with the evolution of writing, as language-related specifications began to be added to the entries to clarify the function of records and their relationships (ibid.: 47). Some tablets from the early dynastic III period (2500–2300 BC) detail bread baking while others included entries for bread and beer rations and the ingredients required to make them. Such tablets tended to begin by listing the names of individuals with the largest rations followed by those with smaller rations. At the end of the tablet, the amounts of bread and beer are totalled by type and the grand total for the flour and barley used was also recorded. These tablets were dated by day, and the scribes showed how the amount of flour corresponded exactly to the amount used in producing the bread, and the same applied to barley and beer. Niessen et al. (1993: 49) suggest that 'Perhaps the most important accounting operation introduced during the third millennium B.C. was the balancing of theoretical debits postings with real production'. The evidence reveals that deficits in one year, arising from shortage of actual amounts compared to theoretical amounts, were carried forward to the following year and were liable to later reimbursement.

Niessen et al. (1993: 49) argue that, by 2100 BC (Ur III), accounting for theoretical (expected) and actual performance reached its most developed form. From then onwards, the entries record labour performance along with theoretical credits and duties. The balance of expected and actual labour performance was recorded at regular intervals for the foremen of the state-controlled labour force, using an accounting period of a 12-month year, with each month being 30 days long. Balances were carried forward to next periods; most frequently these balances were deficits (overdrawn) as expected performance seems to have been 'fixed as the maximum of what a foreman could reasonably demand of his workers' (ibid.: 49). Such balancing entries were underpinned by some measure of standardisation of performance and a value equivalence system:

> A precondition for the feasibility of such global balancing of all expected and real performances was the standardization and calculability of the expected performances, as well as a means of comparing all performances ... Although we are often only able to trace the performance standards and value equivalences through calculation of account entries, there can be no doubt of the existence of explicitly formulated norms which were strictly adhered to. They can be reconstructed from conversions of labor performances and products into equivalent products specific to the respective centre of the economic organization.
>
> *(ibid.: 49–51)*

The organisation of the accounting texts of this era can be illustrated by reference to a more complete account of female labour (ibid.: 52–4). The top left-hand of the obverse side of the tablet contains entries for the debit balance carried forward from the previous period and the expected (theoretical) performance for the current period, with the aggregate of these two items clearly written. The lower part of the left-hand and the whole of the right-hand of the obverse side have entries showing credits as amount of delivered flour, converted into female workdays, and other labour performance by the female labour force. The reverse side contains other credit entries, the aggregation of all performed labour as credit, and the final balance to be carried forward to the next period. In commenting on how these remaining balances were traced, Niessen et al. state:

> From other texts, we know what drastic consequences such continuous control of deficits meant for the foreman and his household. Apparently, the debts had to be settled at all costs. The death of a foreman in debt resulted in confiscation of his possessions as compensation for the state.
>
> *(ibid.: 54)*

Further evidence from the administration of fields attests to the use of length measures to calculate areas in order to determine the amount of grain required to sow a field. Figures on the obverse of a tablet typically represented the grain needed to sow the field area detailed on the reverse of the tablet, and these tended to be accompanied by entries of the name or title related to the activity/field, and it appears that grain seeds came from central granaries (ibid.: 55–9). Other field administrative texts dealing with domestic matters contain entries on field cultivation, expenditures, yield and current rights of disposition, amounts of grain required to plough and sow a given field, and fodder for the oxen used (ibid.: 64–8).

There is a significant amount of evidence concerning the distribution of rations and organisation of labour, especially as we move to the Old Sumerian era (2450 BC). The archaic evidence shows names of workmen and entries of rations, equivalent to 0.8 litres of grain per workman daily. This ration applied irrespective of the workman's employment; it approximated the minimum level of subsistence and remained virtually unchanged throughout the third millennium BC (ibid.: 70–4). Workmen were organised into gangs of ten each plus a foreman (similar to ancient Egypt), and their rations were delivered through a chief supervisor.

It is not until the Old Sumerian period that we encounter evidence of calculation of expected work performance for each task, for example the amount of barley a labourer had to harvest. Levels of expected performance varied according to the sex and age of the labourer. Accounts of a grain processing workshop reveal detailed measures of control at work for 36 female labourers. Here, each day of the month, for several months, raw and finished products were recorded, with finished products converted into the standard value unit of barley. The entries also show in the total balance the labour time of the millers to an exactness of 1/6th of a work-day. The balance showed the difference between raw materials and labour force required to work them expressed in labourer days at the end of an accounting period against actual data on production delivered and the work performed, and any deficits had to be cleared directly (ibid.: 83–4).

The final set of accounts discussed by Niessen et al. relate to animal husbandry during the archaic and Old Sumerian periods. Before the twenty-fifth century BC, texts record the compilation of flocks differentiated by type and sex and amounts of 'dairy fat' (ibid.: 92–5). They comment: 'The modalities by which the processing of animal products was organized complied with the centralized structure of the administration of livestock herds itself' (ibid.: 93).

In the Old Sumerian period, cheese delivery quotas for herdsmen in charge were recorded, using jars with standardised liquid capacity as measures (these were the traditional measures used for grain), in contrast to archaic times when cheese was counted in discrete units (ibid.: 96–7). Cattle breeding was also accounted for, and the authors cite a document which calculated annual production of 'dairy fat' and cheese for four cows over ten years. This document does not appear to be a record of actual activities, but rather a theoretical calculation of expected production of consecutive generations of cows. The text assumes a cow mortality rate of zero, calving at regular intervals and cows producing the same amount of milk irrespective of age. Further, it assumes annual reproduction of cattle at the rate of one calf for every two adult cows, in addition to fixed amounts of 'dairy fat' and cheese per cow per year. The total amount of 'dairy fat' and cheese production over the ten-year period was calculated and converted into a value equivalence expressed in silver. An exchange rate of 10 sila of dairy fat or 150 sila of cheese for one shekel of silver was used. Reviewing this evidence, Niessen et al. suggest that the text represents a trial or model calculation of hypothetical herd growth.

In their examination of accounting practices in ancient Egypt, Ezzamel and Hoskin (2002) analysed transactions that involved a breakdown of the 'cost' of each of the various items that made a bigger item, say the legs, head-board and the body of a bed, along with the 'cost' of decorating each part. The evidence stops short of explaining what these breakdowns were used for. Perhaps it was the seller's way of justifying the full price of the complete item (a bed in this case). Some other transactions revealed the payment for a share of an object (an ox): 'My share in the ox which he bought, makes 2½ *deben*. My share in the sheep … which he bought, makes 1 *deben*' (Janssen 1975: 532, cited in Ezzamel and Hoskin 2002: 356). The ability to make the ownership of an item divisible into smaller shares opened up the possibility, through the use of money of account, of sharing an expensive item among several owners.

Accounting for the household

Ezzamel (2002c) analysed a set of business letters and accounts belonging to a farmer's household from the Middle Kingdom – the only surviving evidence of household and farm accounts from the history of ancient Egypt. The household part of the letters and accounts deals with a new set of provisions for every member of the household, which had been reduced substantially following a drop in the level of the Nile. Not only did the rations ensure the matching of what the head of the family provided for consumption with the needs of every member of the family, they also reflected and reproduced the standing in which each member was held. The second part of the letters and accounts relates specifically to farm activities charged to a farmer's agent while he was absent from his farm, including cultivation of own land, renting and cultivating additional land, managing the herd and their fodder, a list of some agricultural produce, and private debt and its collection. As in evidence examined earlier, a variety of accounting measures were employed. Reasonably homogeneous items (for example, bundles of flax) were simply counted and recorded as identities, as the counted items in themselves carried implicit values through which equivalence within a given category of items could be observed. Where items were not homogenous, equivalence was secured via the specification of precise weights/volume or via the use of more direct monies of account, such as the *deben* (a weight measure) or the *khar* (a capacity measure). These monies of account exhibited a strong measure of internal consistency, as any of them could be easily inter-translated into another money of account. Such accounting intervention made possible a process of accountability at a distance, helping the absent farmer not only monitor the performance of his agent but equally importantly inform himself of what was going on in his household.

In the fourth millennium BC, Mesopotamian scribes assigned tokens of different shapes to different commodity accounts. Simple tokens were used for such items as grain and cattle whereas more incised and perforated tokens recorded services and manufactured items. The tokens represented sheep and were signed by the shepherd Ziqarru; this form of accountability was vested in an enumeration of different types of sheep:

21 ewes that lamb 6 female lambs
8 rams
4 male lambs
6 she-goats that kid 1 he-goat
3 female kids

The entries were recorded in the tablets at the moment of the transaction. According to Rivero Menéndez (2000: 283), it was customary to call the scribe to the temple, palace, or private domain to record commercial transactions, irrespective of their volume. Written accounts of transactions were signed by the transacting parties, witnesses and the scribe (Keister 1963: 371; Chatfield 1977: 5), and such records were eventually used to resolve legal disputes (Basu and Waymire 2006). From the archaic period onwards, the name of the debtor was identified through his seal on the envelope (Schmandt-Besserat 1978). The following tablet, recording a lease of cattle, illustrates the level of detail when recording such transactions, stating dates, naming and counting items of cattle, stating the names of accountable individuals, stipulating precise sanctions in cases of failure, and listing witnesses (Finkelstein 1968: 31):

92 ewes
20 rams
22 breeding lambs
24 [spring(?)] lambs
33 she-goats
4 male goats
27 kids
Total: 158 sheep; total: 64 goats,

Which Sinšamuh has entrusted to Dadā the shepherd.

He [i.e., Dadā] assumes liability [therefore] and will replace any lost [animals].

Should Nidnatum, his [i.e., Dadā's] shepherd boy, absent himself, he [i.e., Nidnatum] will bear responsibility for any [consequent] loss, [and] Dadā will measure out 5 *kōr* of barley.

Three witnesses; date; Samsuiluna year 1 (?), fourth month, 16th day.

Janssen (1975) collated the prices of many commodities in ancient Egypt, covering a period of approximately 150 years, in the necropolis village of Deir El-Medina during the New Kingdom, but his main concern was with documenting and comparing prices rather than with accounting transactions *per se*. Ezzamel and Hoskin (2002) examined the development of monies of account in ancient Egypt. Importantly, they explored how money and accounting were used by the ancient scribes to constitute value reciprocity. Two types of exchange were noted.

The first type is a record of one person exchanging one item (say, a wooden stela) for another (say, a chest). In this case, and in an economy where exchange typically emphasised a strong element of economic reciprocity (see examples below), it may be reasonably assumed that the items exchanged were thought to be of the same value by both parties:

1. What draughtsman Neferehotep gave to Haremwia.
2. One wooden stela of Nofreteroy, may she live, which he gave to me.
3. One chest in exchange for it. (I) decorated two coffins for him.
4. On the riverbank (?) and he made one bed for me.

(Janssen 1975: 510, cited in Ezzamel and Hoskin 2002: 352)

The second, and most frequent, type of exchange involved valuation of items in terms of money of account. Entries for both types of transactions were made by the scribe who acted as a witness, stating the date of exchange, the names of parties to the exchange, and an enumeration and valuation of the items:

Year 5, third month of the summer season, day 20. Given to Hay by the chief policeman Nebsmen: I head of cattle, makes 120 *deben*. Given to him [i.e., Nebsmen]: 2 pots of fat, makes 60 *deben*; 5 mss-shirts of smooth fabric, makes 25 *deben*; 1 dress of Upper-Egyptian cloth, makes 20 *deben*; 1 hide, makes 15 *deben*.

(Černý 1954: 907, cited in Ezzamel and Hoskin 2002: 352)

In the above transaction, the debit side (the head of cattle received and valued at 120 *deben*) is equated to the credit side involving the giving of several items (60 + 25 + 20 + 15) = 120 *deben*.

Although the entry does not add up the sums to demonstrate economic equivalence of the values of the goods exchanged to both parties to the transactions, this value equivalence was typically observed, and other entries emphasised such equality (Ezzamel and Hoskin 2002: 353).

Conclusion

Our survey has revealed a remarkably broad arena in which ancient accounting practices intervened. The arena ranged from the state and its various institutions, such as palaces, taxation, state workshops and the manufactories, through religious institutions, in particular large temples which played a key role in ancient economies as well in the spiritual domain, to private activities that included barter or semi-barter exchange, private businesses and the household. In all these domains, the role of ancient accounting loomed large.

Concerning the role of accounting in state institutions, accounting functioned both as a means of ensuring that regular monitoring of progress on state projects could be carried out, appropriate provisions for the palace and its dependencies could be secured, tax levies could be assessed, collected and transferred to state coffers, and appropriate lines of accountability could be established. In all these activities, a measure of expectation by the state from its subjects and institutions was inscribed through accounting-based targets. Equally important, our review suggests that a measure of the responsibility of the state towards its subjects was affirmed via the intervention of accounting, in the sense of determining precise rations or wages to be paid to individuals. Apparently, this arrangement was designed to secure the sustenance of individuals and their families, and a means of ensuring that these rations/wages were delivered on time and in the amounts stipulated. A measure of reciprocity, not entirely underpinned by some form of ancient economic reasoning, was at play here. For, in this game of reciprocity, it was not always a 'measure-for-measure' metric that was evidently in use. Payments for tasks performed for the state, as far as we can tell, were not determined based on some modern notion of marginal productivity of human labour, or determined by the forces of supply of and demand for human effort in a kind of labour market. Rather, the state took as its responsibility the payment of what was deemed to be, at the lowest level of the hierarchy, sufficient rations that ensured the survival of the population, but also with clear recognition of rank with rations rising significantly for higher ranks.

The temples of the ancient world were not only spiritual institutions but also significant economic institutions. Accounting for temple activities identified work targets, monitored work progress and dealt with payment to appropriate individuals in the form of rations or wages. Moreover, accounting traced the inflow and outflow of goods and foodstuffs provided by other institutions to the temples for the upkeep of priests and other personnel working at temples. Readers are referred to Chapter 25 for additional evidence and analysis of accounting in this domain.

Concerning the private domain, ancient accounting played a major role in coordinating and facilitating many private activities, including accounting for private businesses, for the household, and for barter and semi-barter exchange. In these activities, surviving records traced accountability to the appropriate agents and reported on their performance, allowing for an ancient system of monitoring at a distance to function. In the case of exchange, a system of equivalence between the goods given and received from another party was established, by which economic reciprocity was observed in a calculus underpinned by the use of monies of accounting and the recording of the transactions by vigilant scribes. In these transactions, as indeed in all the domains where accounting intervened, each accounting entry was assigned to a precise date of the week, month, season and year, as well as frequently providing an indication of the place where the activities recorded took place. This system, therefore, not only vested accountability in the relevant agents but also qualified such accountability by time and location. There remains, however, much more historical evidence to be examined in these, and indeed novel, domains. Moreover, other researchers employing different theoretical lenses may emphasise other aspects of the roles of ancient accounting than has hitherto been revealed.

The literature has also attempted to tease out some of the technical attributes of ancient accounting systems, notably the work of Mattessich, by examining properties such as duality and input-output relations, and in the process arguing for some time-invariant attributes of accounting. Others have sought to provide theoretical insights about accounting by exploring its role as a constructor of value, reciprocity and equivalence (see Ezzamel and Hoskin 2002). Ezzamel (2009, 2012) argued that accounting functioned as a performative ritual that constructed coherence and order in the cosmos, on earth and in the netherworld. In spite of their merits, these efforts represent an embryonic stage in theorising accounting. Using material from ancient Egypt, Ezzamel (2012: 418) briefly explores several possibilities for the further theorisation of accounting: accounting as a performative ritual; accounting as a myth; accounting as a sign; accounting as a signifier; accounting as a time ordering device; accounting as a spatial ordering device; accounting as violence; and accounting as an archive and cultural memory. More sustained in-depth studies of these themes using ancient accounting archives can contribute significantly to the theorisation of accounting.

Given the remoteness of the historical eras covered by the literature reviewed here, and the special challenges facing researchers working in that field, we made a number of points concerning these challenges in order to sensitise the reader to the nature of the evidence that the literature has drawn upon. We have prefaced the chapter with a discussion of some of these challenges borne out of our own research experience. Other researchers are bound to emphasise other issues, explore other settings (e.g., non-Western spaces, Africa; see Sy and Tinker 2006). For us, the most salient challenges are: what counts as primary sources; how to deal with considerable lacunae in ancient records; the problems of interpreting translations of ancient texts into contemporary languages; and the difficulty of using contemporary theories to frame and theorise ancient accounting material. Although we acknowledge that these are very serious issues, we argue that a judicious approach that combines honesty in acknowledging the limitations of research, coupled with sensitivity and understanding of ancient contexts, and a careful approach to theorising, would go a long way towards confronting these constraints.

Our argument is that the extant literature has provided some remarkable insights, but there is still much more to do. The research challenges we have identified call for a more concerted effort by accounting historians to progress the field. Rather than being a cause for researchers to shy away from conducting research on ancient accounting, we believe the challenges provide an exciting prospect for an intellectually stimulating research agenda. We lament the lack of attention accorded by accounting historians to the study of ancient accounting, and contend that there is much to gain if accounting historians were to devote some of their time and expertise to a careful and systematic study of ancient times.

Key works

Carmona and Ezzamel (2007) trace the notion of accountability and provide an updated review of ancient accounting practices in Mesopotamia and ancient Egypt.

Ezzamel and Hoskin (2002), in contrast to the dominant, technical approach to ancient accounting, adopt a wider social perspective to illustrate the potentials of ancient accounting for advancing the theorisation of accounting.

Mattessich (2000) is a collection of articles previously published by the author in scholarly journals. It is an essential reference for those interested in the technical aspects of ancient accounting and its implications for accounting theory.

Niessen et al. (1993) is a must for those interested in examining ancient accounting practices in the Near East, either from a technical or social perspective.

Schmandt-Besserat (1992) constitutes an essential reference for those concerned with investigating the emergence of accounting and writing.

References

Ball, T. (1995) *Reappraising Political Theory: Revisionist Studies in the History of Political Thought* (Oxford: Oxford University Press).

Basu, S. and Waymire, G.B. (2006) Recordkeeping and human evolution, *Accounting Horizons*, 20 (3): 201–229.

Beale, T.W. (1978) Beveled rim bowls and their implications for change and economic organization in the later fourth millennium B.C., *Journal of Business Eastern Studies*, 37 (4): 289–313.

Bleiberg, E. (1996) *The Official Gift in Ancient Egypt* (Norman, OK: University of Oklahoma Press).

Bourdieu, P. (2014) *On the State* (Cambridge: Polity Press).

Carmona, S. and Ezzamel, M. (2007) Accounting and accountability in ancient civilizations: Mesopotamia and ancient Egypt, *Accounting, Auditing & Accountability Journal*, 20 (2): 177–209.

Černý, J. (1954) Prices and wages in Egypt in the Ramesside period, *Journal of World History*, 1: 903–921.

Chatfield, M. (1977) *A History of Accounting Thought* (Huntington, NY: Robert E. Krieger).

Costouros, G.J. (1978) Development of an accounting system in ancient Athens as a response to socio-economic changes, *Accounting Historians Journal*, 4 (1): 37–54.

Dalton, G. (ed.) (1971) *Primitive Archaic and Modern Economies: Essays of Karl Polanyi* (Boston: Beacon Press).

Davies, V. and Friedman, R. (1998) *Egypt Uncovered* (New York: Stewart, Tabori & Chang).

De Ste. Croix, G.E.M. (1956) Greek and Roman accounting, in Littleton, A.C., Yamey, B.S. (eds.) *Studies in the History of Accounting*, pp. 14–74 (London: Sweet & Maxwell).

Eisenstadt, S.N. (1969) *The Political Systems of Empire: The Rise and Fall of the Historical Bureaucratic Societies* (New York: Free Press).

Ezzamel, M. (1997) Accounting, control and accountability: preliminary evidence from ancient Egypt, *Critical Perspectives on Accounting*, 8 (6): 563–601.

Ezzamel, M. (2002a) Accounting working for the state: tax assessment and collection during the New Kingdom, ancient Egypt, *Accounting and Business Research*, 32 (1): 17–39.

Ezzamel, M. (2002b) Accounting and redistribution: the palace and mortuary cult in the Middle Kingdom, ancient Egypt, *Accounting Historians Journal*, 29 (1): 61–103.

Ezzamel, M. (2002c) Accounting for private estates and the household in the twentieth century B.C. Middle Kingdom, ancient Egypt, *Abacus*, 38 (2): 235–262.

Ezzamel, M. (2004) Work organization in the Middle Kingdom: ancient Egypt, *Organization*, 11 (4): 497–537.

Ezzamel, M. (2005) Accounting for the practices of funerary temples: the intertwining of the sacred and the profane, *Accounting and Business Research*, 35 (1): 29–51.

Ezzamel, M. (2009) Order and accounting as a performative ritual: evidence from ancient Egypt, *Accounting, Organizations and Society*, 34 (3): 348–380.

Ezzamel, M. (2012) *Accounting and Order* (Oxon: Routledge).

Ezzamel, M. and Hoskin, K. (2002) Retheorizing accounting, writing and money with evidence from Mesopotamia and ancient Egypt, *Critical Perspectives on Accounting*, 13 (3): 333–367.

Ezzamel, M. and Willmott, H. (2004) Rethinking strategy: contemporary perspectives and debates, *European Management Review*, 1 (1): 43–48.

Finkelstein, J.J. (1968) An old Babylonian herding contract and Genesis 31: 38f., *Journal of the American Oriental Society*, 88 (1): 30–36.

Finley, M.I. (1992) *The Ancient Economy* (Harmondsworth: Penguin Books).

Fu, P. (1971) Governmental accounting in China during the Chou dynasty (1122–256 BC), *Journal of Accounting Research*, 9 (1): 40–51.

Gills, B.K. (1995) Capital and power in the processes of world history, in Sanderson, S. (ed.) *Civilizations and World Systems*, pp. 136–162 (Walnut Creek, CA: Altamira Press).

Janssen, J.J. (1975) *Commodity Prices from the Ramessid Period* (Leiden: E. J. Brill).

Keister, O.R. (1963) Commercial record-keeping in ancient Mesopotamia, *Accounting Review*, 38 (2): 371–376.

Kemp, B. (1989) *Ancient Egypt: Anatomy of a Civilization* (London: Routledge).

Leemans, W.F. (1960). *Foreign Trade in the Old Babylonian Period as Revealed by Texts from Southern Mesopotamia*. Available HTTP: <https://doi.org/10.7767/zrgra.1962.79.1.344>.

Mandeville, R. (2014) *Wage Accounting in Deir el-Medina* (Warsaw: Abercromby Press).

Mattessich, R. (1987) Prehistoric accounting and the problem of representation: on recent archaeological evidence of the middle-east from 8000 B.C. to 3000 B.C., *Accounting Historians Journal*, 14 (2): 72–91.

Mattessich, R. (1989) Accounting and the input-output principle in the ancient and prehistoric world, *Abacus*, 25 (2): 74–84.

Mattessich, R. (1991) Counting, accounting, and the input-output principle: recent archaeological evidence revising our view on the evolution of early record keeping, in Graves, O.F. (ed.) *The Costing Heritage: Studies in Honour of S. Paul Garner, Monograph No. 6*, pp. 25–49 (Harrisonburg, VA: Academy of Accounting Historians).

Mattessich, R. (1994) Archaeology of accounting and Schmandt-Besserat's contribution, *Accounting, Business & Financial History*, 4 (1): 5–28.

Mattessich, R. (1998a) Recent insights into Mesopotamian accounting of the 3rd millennium B.C. – successor to token accounting, *Accounting Historians Journal*, 25 (1): 1–27.

Mattessich, R. (1998b) Follow-up to: 'Recent insights into Mesopotamian accounting of the 3rd millennium B.C.': correction to table 1, *Accounting Historians Journal*, 25 (2): 147–149.

Mattessich, R. (2000) *The Beginnings of Accounting and Accounting Thought* (New York: Garland).

Miller, P. (1998) The margins of accounting, *European Accounting Review*, 7 (4): 605–621.

Namazi, M. and Taak, F. (2017) Accounting and bookkeeping content analysis of the Achaemenid clay-tablets in Iran, Shiraz University working paper series.

Niessen, H.J., Damerow, P. and Englund, R.K. (1993) *Archaic Bookkeeping*, translated by P. Larsen (Chicago, IL: The University of Chicago Press).

Oldroyd, D. (1995) The role of accounting in public expenditure and monetary policy in the first century AD Roman empire, *Accounting Historians Journal*, 22 (2): 117–129.

Oppenheim, A.L. (1964) *Ancient Mesopotamia: Portrait of a Dead Civilization* (Chicago, IL: The University of Chicago Press).

Polanyi, K. (1957) Trade and market, in Polanyi, K., Arsenberg, C.M., Pearson, H.W. (eds.) *Trade and Market in the Early Empires: Economies in History and Theory*, pp. 12–38 (New York: Free Press).

Polanyi, K. (1977) *The Livelihood of Man* (New York: Academic Press).

Previts, G. and Bricker, R. (1994) Fact and theory in accounting history: present mindedness and capital market research, *Contemporary Accounting Research*, 10 (2): 625–641.

Renger, J. (1984) Patterns of non-institutional trade and non-commercial exchange in ancient Mesopotamia at the beginning of the second millennium B.C., in Archi, A. (ed.) *Circulation of Goods in Non-Palatial Context in the Ancient Near East*, pp. 31–123 (Rome: Edizioni Dell'Ateneo).

Rivero Menéndez, M.R. (2000) *La Formación de los Registros Contables en Mesopotamia* (Madrid: Dimasoft).

Rose, N. and Miller, P. (1992) Political power beyond the state: problematics of government, *British Journal of Sociology*, 43 (2): 173–205.

Schmandt-Besserat, D. (1977) An archaic recording system and the origin of writing, *Syro-Mesopotamian Studies*, 1 (2): 1–32.

Schmandt-Besserat, D. (1978) The earliest precursor of writing, *Scientific American*, 238 (6): 50–58.
Schmandt-Besserat, D. (1979) Reckoning before writing, *Archaeology*, 32 (3): 23–31.
Schmandt-Besserat, D. (1980) The envelopes that bear the first writing, *Technology and Culture*, 21 (3): 357–385.
Schmandt-Besserat, D. (1981a) Tablets and tokens: a re-examination of the so-called 'Numerical Tablets', *Visible Language*, 15 (3): 321–344.
Schmandt-Besserat, D. (1981b) Decipherment of the earliest tablets, *Science*, 211 (4479): 283–285.
Schmandt-Besserat, D. (1983) Tokens and counting, *Biblical Archaeologist*, 46: 117–120.
Schmandt-Besserat, D. (1984) Before numerals, *Visible Language*, 15 (1): 48–59.
Schmandt-Besserat, D. (1986a) The origins of writing – an archaeologist's perspective, *Written Communication*, 3 (1): 31–45.
Schmandt-Besserat, D. (1986b) The precursor to numerals and writing, *Archaeology*, 39 (6): 32–38.
Schmandt-Besserat, D. (1992) *Before Writing Vol. I: From Counting to Cuneiform* (Austin, TX: University of Texas Press).
Schmandt-Besserat, D. (1994) Forerunners of writing, in Harmut, G. (ed.) *Schrift und Schriftlichkeit*, pp. 264–268 (Berlin: Walter de Gruyter).
Schmandt-Besserat, D. (1997) *The History of Counting* (New York: Morrow Junior Books).
Scorgie, M. (1990) Indian imitation of invention of cash-book and algebraic double-entry, *Abacus*, 26 (1): 63–70.
Silver, M. (1985) *Economic Structures of the Ancient Near East* (Totowa, NJ: Barnes and Noble).
Sy, A. and Tinker, T. (2006) Bury Pacioli in Africa: a bookkeeper's reification of accountancy, *Abacus*, 42 (1): 105–127.
Vollmers, G.L. (1996) The Persepolis fortification texts: accounting and control in ancient Persia from 509 to 494 BC, *Accounting Enquiries*, 6 (1): 1–43.
Vollmers, G.L. (2003) Accounting historiography using ancient sources: problems and rewards, in Fleischman, R.K., Radcliffe, V.S., Shoemaker, P.A. (eds.) *Doing Accounting History*, pp. 49–62 (Oxford: Elsevier).
Vollmers, G.L. (2009) Accounting and control in the Persepolis fortification tablets, *Accounting Historians Journal*, 36 (2): 93–111.
Warburton, D.A. (1997) *State and Economy in Ancient Egypt* (Fribourg: University Press Fribourg).
Wilkinson, R.D. (1994) *Symbol and Magic in Egyptian Art* (London: Thames & Hudson).

5
BOOKKEEPING

Alisdair Dobie and David Oldroyd[1]

Overview

The chapter analyses key themes and debates in the history of bookkeeping within a broadly chronological arrangement, starting with Classical Greece and Rome and continuing with sections on the Roman legacy, West and East, developments in the Islamic world, medieval charge and discharge accounting, mercantile accounting, the origins of double-entry, early industry and the Victorian expansion during the nineteenth century. The aim of the chapter is to embed developments in bookkeeping practice within their social and economic contexts. Tracking rights and obligations, holding agents accountable, conveying information at a distance, dealing with complexity and acting as a legal record are identified as the recurrent functions of bookkeeping throughout its history. Changes in practice were prompted by a diverse range of factors, including economic opportunity, political and religious pressure, conquest, educational developments and the influence of significant individuals.

Since the original version of the chapter was published in 2009 there has been a resurgence of interest in the history of bookkeeping practice, including volumes appealing to a wider, non-specialist audience as well as academics (e.g. Gleeson-White 2012; Soll 2014). The history of bookkeeping is huge, and to give the chapter focus the *modus operandi* is to concentrate mainly on Western Europe with particular reference to Italy and the British Isles. Italian practice is significant because of the dual legacy of the Classical world and the Renaissance. Britain too is important because of the links forged through trade and colonisation, and especially its close connections with North America. However, the complexity of trade relations, the continuation of Roman traditions under the Byzantine emperors until 1453 and the conquest of much of the former Roman Empire by Islam mean that bookkeeping developments within the Middle East and beyond are of necessary concern to accounting historians. The relative neglect of the East by Western historians has been censured (Frankopan 1988; Goody 2002), and although space restricts what can be covered, a key expansion of this chapter is to move beyond the existing Western Euro-focus to include significant developments in Eastern Europe and the Middle East.

Unfortunately, space constraints prevent a fuller examination of a number of geographic areas with important bookkeeping histories, including South America before the arrival of Europeans, Russia, the Persian Empire, China, India, Japan and a range of other Asian, European and African cultures. In China, for example, the history of accounting is said to extend back 6,000 years. During the Western Zhou period (1100–771 BC) it is claimed that accounting reached 'a peak of sophistication unknown elsewhere in the world'. Under the Tand dynasty (AD 618–907) the *Bi-Bu* auditing system was developed. Government accounting was refined during the Song dynasty (960–1279) (Lu and Aiken 2003, 2004); and the *Lóngmén Zhàng* system has been claimed to be an early example of commercial double-entry bookkeeping, although this view has been challenged (Lin 1992; Peng and Brown 2015; Yuan and Macve 2017).

Introduction

The nature of the study of bookkeeping history is a contentious area. On the one hand, it is portrayed as the subject of antiquarian interest to 'the traditionalist' historians who 'decontextualise accounting' by fruitlessly focusing on its 'mechanical, procedural and technical aspects' (Johnson 1986: 67; Hopwood 1987: 207–9). On the other, there is an emerging consensus among accounting historians that technical practices such as bookkeeping can play a crucial role in shaping beliefs. Thus, Ezzamel and Hoskin (2002), approaching the origins of recording systems in antiquity from a Foucauldian perspective (see Chapter 4 for further discussion), argue that the invention of token accounting in ancient Mesopotamia was significant not just because it facilitated economic exchanges, but because it encouraged people to see the world around them in terms of quantifiable outcomes. Miller and Napier (1993: 633) likewise portray accounting as part of the 'disparate and variable' assemblage of calculative practices that help create order in society. Such views are not confined to Foucauldians. As discussed in Chapter 17, Bryer (2000), an avowed Marxist, argues that the main significance of bookkeeping lies in its ability to bend the mentality of agents to the will of the principal by rendering them accountable for their actions. Notwithstanding this, the ability of agents to use accounting forms to 'manage' principals should not be underestimated (Lee 2006).

It follows that while there may be some truth in the idea that the history of bookkeeping ends with the triumph of double-entry over other forms owing to the globalisation of Western practice, the reality of the situation is more nuanced. If one regards bookkeeping as a social artefact that encapsulates people's attitudes and beliefs (Gray 1988), what lies behind the figures will have different connotations in cultures with differing bookkeeping histories (e.g. Gao and Handley-Schachler 2010).

Before embarking on any history of 'bookkeeping', it is advisable to consider what is meant by the term. Certainly, it does not just encompass bound books of account. The recording of transactions has utilised a variety of other media, such as scrolls, indentures, tally sticks, potsherds, wax, wooden or clay tablets, inscriptions and computers: essentially all media for the compilation and transcription of accounting data, which in the modern era constitute the basis of an organisation's internal management accounts and external reports to stakeholders.

To review writings on the history of 2,500 years of bookkeeping in a single chapter is a challenge. There is a danger that issues may become distorted through their juxtaposition in such a piece, and many historians prefer to analyse specific contexts. Taking a 'bird's eye view', however, was defended by Yamey (1981: 128), and followed by Baladouni (1989) and Lee (1990) as a means of developing a coherent theory of accounting history.

As described in Chapter 4, the invention of a form of bookkeeping using clay tokens in the early agricultural societies of the eastern Mediterranean and Iraq represented a huge cognitive leap for mankind. According to Soll (2014), the strengths and weaknesses of bookkeeping have been central to the success and decline of nation states throughout history. Bookkeeping has been described as a 'foundation stone of culture' (Mattessich 2000: 74), and this is perhaps as true of today as it is of its origins in antiquity.

Classical Greece and Rome

This section follows De Ste. Croix's (1956) classic exposition of Greek and Roman accounting in discussing the two societies as a unity, although whether such an approach is entirely defensible is a moot point (Cohen 2002: 3). Greek and Roman civilisation was at its height for several hundred years and embraced many different races and cultures, but De Ste. Croix (1956: 33) observed remarkable consistency in bookkeeping practice over this period with little in the way of 'important general advances'. The major difference relates to the status of accounts in law, which seem to have carried less sway as legal evidence in Athens in the fourth century BC compared to Rome in the first (ibid.: 28). The most noteworthy technical advance of Greek and Roman bookkeeping compared to earlier civilisations, such as that of the Egyptians, lay in the adoption of coinage, which allowed the Greeks and Romans to employ a monetary unit of measurement although 'they often failed to do so' (ibid.: 21–2). Typically, their books of account tracked receipts, payments, goods, debtors and creditors (ibid.: 42). However, according to De Ste. Croix (ibid.: 34–8), there was no distinction between capital and revenue expenditure, little conception of separating the costs of activities and no evidence of double-entry. In exceptional cases, transactions were recorded in columns in bilateral format.

Much of the discussion regarding the supposed lack of sophistication in Greek and Roman bookkeeping centres on the level of economic enterprise in society. Finley (1992), in particular, imputed a lack of interest in economic matters, which he believed was reflected in the rudimentary nature of their accounts (Macve 2002: 455). Economic enterprise was allegedly impeded by the structure of society, in particular by the heavy reliance on slaves for economic activities allied to a reluctance to exploit fellow citizens (ibid.: 454). Wealth was important in Graeco-Roman society because it reflected a citizen's status, but wealth was acquired first and foremost as a result of family and political connections, not through entrepreneurship (Macve 2002: 460). De Ste. Croix (1956: 15, 34) maintained that bookkeeping practices not only reflected a lack of economic endeavour in society, they actually prevented the Greeks and Romans from advancing economically. Hence, he argued that the confusion of capital and revenue in the books would have made profit calculations impossible and prevented the state from taxing income (ibid.: 38). While supporting De Ste. Croix's main theme – the rudimentary nature of the accounts – Macve (1994: 67; 2002: 460) disagreed that this impeded economic development. Instead, he hypothesised that the primitive nature of the bookkeeping reflected the 'limited [economic] opportunities and choices that were generally available in antiquity' (Macve 1994: 67).

However, Most's (1979: 10) observation that manufacturing industry and trade flourished on a large scale in the Roman Empire is supported by archaeological findings (Greene 1990: 169–71). Conquest played a major part in this, as it provided a valuable source of booty that directly impinged on the stocks of bullion in the Roman treasury (Howgego 1992: 4), as well as creating new economic opportunities for merchants. Roman financiers, for instance, had a large stake in Julius Caesar's second expedition to Britain (54 BC), contributing ships to the invasion fleet in exchange for a share of the anticipated plunder and future trading opportunities (Grant 1969: 125). Trade ties between Britain and Rome increased significantly during the 90 years leading up to the Claudian invasion (AD 43) that brought 'a mass of fresh merchants, speculators and prospectors in the wake of the armies' (Frere 1974: 320).

The creation through conquest of a common market from the Danube to North Africa and from Spain to the Caspian Sea, supported by a uniform medium of exchange, produced unparalleled opportunities for trade. Indeed, the extent of the economic connections and the range of situations in which bookkeeping was deployed seriously challenge the rather negative interpretation of Greek and Roman bookkeeping presented by De Ste. Croix, Finley and Macve. Rathbone (1994: 17), for example, takes exception to the idea that the sole purpose of Roman accounts was 'to act as a check against carelessness or dishonesty on the part of subordinates'. His work on the Appianus estate in Roman Egypt in the third century AD, reveals an interlocking and centrally controlled system of accounting over a dispersed range of activities that went far beyond tracking rights and obligations to encompass cost control and performance measurement.

Control of costs was also identified as a key concern of Cato the Elder (2004: II) in his second-century BC textbook on agriculture and estate management (Bryer 2019: 131–3). Cato's instructions for estate owners included comparing the 'results attained' to the 'program of work' which the master 'had laid out' for the overseer on his last visit. Thus, the accounts were not solely a check on the overseer's honesty; or from his point of view, the means by which he could prove himself trustworthy to the master given he was probably a slave (Puyou and Quattrone 2018). Estate accounts also served to hold the stewards accountable for production as was the case on the Appianus estate (Bryer 2019: 120–1). Rathbone (1994: 55) conceded that the Appianus operations may have been 'the exception which proves the rule'; and another rare survival of a Roman estate account-book, the *Kellis agricultural account-book*, also from Egypt, appears more focused on tracking inventory and the obligations of tenants than in monitoring performance, notwithstanding this was a smaller enterprise (Kehoe 1999).

The Kellis account-book is particularly interesting from a technical bookkeeping point of view as it is the most comprehensive accounting document to survive from the Roman world in wooden tablet form. According to Puyou and Quattrone (2018), the layout of the document is significant as it reflected a formulaic, rhetorical approach to the grouping and presentation of transactions, which they maintain would have imbued the accounts with a sense of authority in Roman society.

The existence of the Mediterranean Sea was vital to the development of Classical society, including bookkeeping practice:

> It is in fact the major feature of the sea's destiny that it should be locked inside the largest group of landmasses on the globe, the 'gigantic linked continent' of Europe-Asia-Africa, a sort of planet in itself, where goods and people circulated from earliest times … This was where the crucial exchanges took place.
>
> *(Braudel 2002: 25)*

From a bookkeeping perspective, the continuous flow of goods throughout this natural waterway necessitated systems that were capable both of tracking the various exchanges taking place over wide distances and dealing with the complexities of the contractual arrangements. The simplest case in ancient Rome was when the ship-owner and merchant were one and the same. However, ships could be hired to third parties or owned in partnership, and sometimes carried multiple consignments for different merchants. On occasion, the management of the vessel was entrusted to agents; in other cases, it was managed directly. The number of possible permutations bears witness to the flexibility of the bookkeeping procedures, with records kept 'at each step' of the voyage on behalf of the 'owners, shippers and their representatives on board' (Minaud 2006: 6).

Public accountability too was affected by the geography of the region. As well as economic goods, 'cultural goods' circulated throughout the Mediterranean, 'mingling ideas and beliefs' (Braudel 2002: 307). Rome was still in its infancy when the concept of the Greek city state (*polis*) was at its most developed, and the fledgling republic was inevitably influenced by the political institutions of its more mature neighbour. Despite the political differences between the various cities, the Greeks and Romans shared a common conception of the polis that went beyond the notion of a 'defined territory' or a particular form of government to embrace the idea of citizens 'acting in concert' (Finley 1975: 56). It was a society in which the elite were expected to perform public service, and to apply large portions of their wealth for the benefit of the community for which they were accountable (Finley 1992: 150–3). This is particularly relevant to the development of bookkeeping, as many of the accounts that have survived or are referred to in the contemporary literature were of a public nature.

Indeed, the highly developed notion of public accountability in Greek and Roman society is evident from the physical form of the accounts, which were often inscribed on the walls of public buildings to endow them with a sense of permanence as well as high visibility. In most cases these accounts comprised simple lists of receipts and payments in chronological order. According to De Ste. Croix (1956: 26), their layout was 'clumsy and confusing'; usually the information was not tabulated, and expenditure was neither collated nor summarised. Instead it was shown in 'minute detail' (ibid.: 25). However, to criticise the bookkeeping for the lack of information in summary form would be unreasonable as the prime purpose of these documents was to render a full record of the financial accountability of officials' stewardship. What is significant about these inscriptions, as far as the bookkeeping is concerned, is that they prove both that the information was recorded and that it could be retrieved, in some cases several years after the event, signifying the existence of public archives.

Bookkeeping was also deployed in the administration of the Roman Empire. Much public finance was conducted at a distance because of the dispersed locations of the provinces, and local officials were obliged to keep detailed records of tax revenues and expenditures. This was a requirement of law and a necessary precaution against charges of corruption. Launching prosecutions in the law courts was an established method of gaining renown for young political aspirants in Athens and Rome (Grant 1969: 27; Finley 1992: 150–1). Cicero was involved in cases where the lack of detail in officials' accounting records was a major issue (De Ste. Croix 1956: 43–5), and the fact that bookkeeping could be used as a weapon in the courts illustrates its importance as legal evidence.

Tax assessments too required systematic information gathering procedures, the most famous example being the census in Luke's Gospel (2, i–v). Provincial censuses of land, property and population formed the basis of direct taxation levies throughout the Roman Empire (Duncan-Jones 1990: 187–93). The provisioning of the army on campaign likewise required bookkeeping. The best example of the survival of written documents in the Empire, outside Egypt, comes from the fort of Vindolanda in today's northern England. These include a number of accounts prepared by clerks who were responsible 'for looking after the storage and issue of supplies and recording carefully what was taken in and what was dispensed' (Bowman and Thomas 1974: 30). Records were also kept to control payments to the troops (De Ste. Croix 1956: 39). Finally, bookkeeping was used to record the flows of bullion and obsolete coin into the Roman Treasury and, from there, to the Imperial Mint. As such, it was one of a range of measures employed to safeguard the stocks of precious metals (Oldroyd 1995: 121–2).

The salient characteristic of bookkeeping practice in the Classical world is its versatility in dealing with a wide range of situations. It was deployed in tracking the rights and obligations of private property owners and the state, holding estate stewards accountable for production, ensuring their trustworthiness, conveying information at a distance in relation to trade, agriculture and public administration, dealing with the complexity of contractual arrangements and acting as a legal record enforceable in court.

Legacy of the Roman Empire in the West[2]

The 400 years following the collapse of Roman authority in the West in the fifth century are commonly referred to as the 'Dark Ages' because of the lack of surviving documentary evidence, including accounts. This was a turbulent period marked by the migration of Germanic tribes into Roman territory and the conquest of much of the eastern and southern Empire by Islamic armies. In the West, a new Frankish empire was established which at its height encompassed France, Germany and northern Italy.

However, the lack of documentary evidence does not mean that records never existed and one of the most important documents to survive relates to bookkeeping practice. The *Capitulare de Villis* comprises a series of written instructions for the management of estates, inspired by the Frankish emperor Charlemagne towards the end of the eighth century.[3] Its existence reflects the importance of land both as a source of Crown revenue and a basis of political authority in the new post-Roman Europe (Latouche 1967: 180–1; Martindale 1983: 160, 165). Essentially, two types of accounting can be distinguished (see Loyn and Percival 1975: 68–73 for the full text). The first is a kind of charge and discharge account whereby the steward was held accountable for the difference between the income of his district and his payments in goods or money (clauses 63, 20, 30–1, 44, 55). These accounts were subject to audit (clause 28). The second type, which is evident in the requirement for the steward to submit an account at Christmas-time of the estate's produce for the year, classified by type (clause 62), is more in the nature of a survey, known as a *polyptyque*, of possessions and revenues. The juxtaposition of estate survey and charge and discharge statements in the *Capitulare de Villis* indicates that they shared a common aim of enabling the centre to exercise control at a distance over dispersed resources.

According to Latouche (1967: 179–80), these arrangements were initiated by Charlemagne as a control measure against 'sharp practices' that had crept into the administration of the royal estates. Hence, the emperor rebuked estate stewards for not having submitted proper returns (clause 44). The inclusion of information concerning the gross product of the estate indicates that the records could also have been used for planning next year's output, as seems to have been the case at the abbey of Saint-Germain-des-Près (ibid.: 192).

It is difficult to tell the extent to which the *Capitulare de Villis* was an innovation as opposed to the formulation of established practice. The *Capitulare* is pre-dated by a seventh-century *polyptyque* from the abbey of St Martin of Tours (Wallace-Hadrill 1983: 125). The chance survival of this document – fragments of it were used to make a bookbinding – suggests that such returns were not necessarily retained on a permanent basis and implies the existence of others which may not have survived.

The collapse of the Roman Empire in the West did not necessarily result in an end to Roman bookkeeping practice, and it is pertinent to question whether the *Capitulare de Villis* was influenced by Roman methods. After all, one of the main aims of Roman accounting seems to have been to expose any losses due to the dishonesty or negligence of officials (De Ste. Croix 1956: 38), which is consistent with the spirit of the *Capitulare de Villis*. It is possible that Roman estate practices never fully died out. There was continuity, for example, in late Roman field division, agricultural techniques and manorial organisation; and authors have commented on the ready integration of the incoming Germanic peoples into Gallo-Roman country life (Latouche 1967: 102; Boussard 1968: 10–12; Geary 1988: 96; James 1988: 189–91). The church too played a key role in preserving Roman ideas. According to Loyn (1991: 233, 283):

> [t]here is much more than mere abstraction to the generalization that in the church appeared the true heir of Rome … In face of at times most savage difficulties the Gallic bishops kept alive the spirit of Roman administration.

Bishops took the place of Roman officials as the 'characteristic social leader' in the towns of Gaul in the fifth century and tended to be drawn from the old aristocratic senatorial class (Geary 1988: 33–4).

Reference material too existed in the form of preserved Classical texts. The Carolingian court, and the monasteries associated with it, made a concerted attempt from the late eighth century to preserve Classical knowledge through the collection and copying of ancient material from Italy (Reynolds 1983: xxi–xxv; Bischoff 1994: 94–5). Columella's *On Agriculture* and Pliny the Elder's *Natural History* were copied at this time. Like the *Capitulare de Villis*, their writings describe large estates that were dependent on stewards for their management, with Columella's text containing more information about stewardship accounting. A copy of Pliny existed in the court library at Aachen at around the time the *Capitulare de Villis* was compiled, and the same is likely of Columella given the provenance of the copies known to be in circulation.

While continuity between Roman and Carolingian bookkeeping practice is a possibility, subsequent links with English estates in the tenth and eleventh centuries are clearer. The Carolingian practice of surveying estates was preserved by the church in the ninth century and transmitted to England in the tenth via the Benedictine reform movement (Campbell 1986: 164). English monastic reform depended on European houses, which provided models for both spiritual living and the efficient estate management necessary to support new foundations. Corroboration that the European practice of surveying estates was disseminated to England at this time exists in the form of surviving documents from the tenth and eleventh centuries, showing English monasteries surveying their estates and compiling lists of stocks, treasures and sources of income in the manner of the Carolingian *polyptyque* (Campbell 1986: 165–6, 173; Loyn 1986: 6).

The adoption of European estate practice in England in the tenth century raises the question of whether this included charge and discharge accounting as well as estate surveys, as the two appear linked under the Carolingians, and also later in England in the thirteenth and fourteenth centuries (Harvey 1984: 18–19). No examples of charge and discharge accounts relating to estates have survived prior to the thirteenth century, although this lacuna probably reflects the vagaries of record survival which favoured the preservation of surveys over charge and discharge accounts. Estate surveys were intended for use on an ongoing basis, and thus tended to be copied into cartularies or registers more readily than other manorial records (ibid.: 15).

Wickham (2005: 267) disagrees, observing that the *Capitulare de Villis* was 'normative, not descriptive', and that it is likely that registration of the payment of dues to estates was carried out orally or through 'non-written recording methods' such as tallies until the 'thirteenth century when accounts begin again'. However, given the size and scope of royal, church and noble estates in the intervening 400 years, this interpretation of events could only work a) if the level of literacy was too low and b) if estates were rentiers, solving the management control problem by leasing. Otherwise, there would have been no means of tracking inventories, payments and receipts of goods and money, the obligations of stewards or assessing their honesty and diligence at a distance (Miller and Oldroyd 2018). The existence of estate surveys during this period and the role of the church in estate management militates against a lack of literacy (Oldroyd 1997). The rentier explanation is interesting as the movement away from renting to direct management is, as we shall see, advanced as an explanation for the emergence of charge and discharge accounting in England in the thirteenth century. But it is unfounded as an explanation for the absence of stewardship accounts in the Carolingian period. Whilst the *Capitulare de Villis* was undoubtedly normative, it would have served no useful purpose unless the method of production it described was employed in practice, which was not predominantly leasing.

Roman heritage in the East

There is a danger that using the term 'Roman Empire' encourages a conception of a monolithic, enduring and unchanging institution. This was not the case. For example, by the fourth century AD, the political and economic centre of gravity of the Empire had shifted eastwards with a new capital established in the Greek city of Byzantium on the Bosporus, first renamed 'New Rome' and later Constantinople. Likewise, the focus on the economic structures and bureaucratic methods of the richly documented 'Golden Age' of Rome before the crises of the third century AD can lead to the erroneous assumption that these functioned in their entirety until the final 'fall' to the Ottomans in 1453. Similarly, the categorisation of the surviving eastern portion of the Roman Empire as 'Byzantine' has tended perhaps to mask both the continuity and development of Roman forms of accounting occurring. During this period of over a thousand years, the Byzantines traded with their neighbours, both to the west and the east, and thus were in a position to influence, and be influenced by, developments in Italian mercantile accounting and Islamic accounting.

The fiscal and economic management of the Byzantine Empire varied enormously over its existence. Its alleged wealth has been well documented. The emperor Anastasios (491–518) generated and retained huge surpluses: it is said that on his death the treasury contained 320,000 pounds of gold (Laiou 2002: 12). Manuel I Komnenos (1143–1180) is reputed to have expended on a single expedition to Italy, 8 tons of gold comprising 2.16 million gold coins (Laiou 2002: 3). Such surpluses certainly contributed to the territorial renaissance of the Empire under Anastasios' successors in the sixth century when under the Emperor Justinian (527–565), the generals Bellisarius and Narses extended the Empire's boundaries to include mainland Italy, Sicily, North Africa and Southern Spain as well as Egypt, Syria, Asia Minor, Greece and the Balkans. This territorial extension did not endure long. Syria (636), Palestine (641), Egypt (641), North Africa (705), Sicily (902) and Spain (714) fell before the onslaught of Islamic armies who also were successful in modern day Iraq and Iran and made advances into the Indus valley and beyond (Saunders 1980: xiii–xv). Later Asia Minor was more gradually acquired by the Seljuks and Ottomans. By the late fourteenth century, the remnant of the Empire was 'a tiny and disjointed state' (Laiou 2009: 827).

Accounting practices in the Byzantine Empire have been somewhat neglected. As Baker (2013) observes, no paper on Byzantine accounting had then been published in any of the specialised accounting history journals. It would be easy to assume that just as the Byzantines continued to call themselves 'Romans', even though Greek eventually replaced Latin as the language of government and people, so too Roman bookkeeping practices endured. It seems likely that Byzantine officials, estate owners and merchants initially continued Roman forms of bookkeeping. However, the succession of shocks which the Empire suffered, in particular the loss of so much of its territory (Egypt had been the bread basket of the Empire) and the ongoing need to raise huge sums for on-going military campaigns and diplomacy would have encouraged and necessitated reviews of revenue raising processes and recording systems (Haldon 2005: 28). The three volume *Economic History of Byzantium* edited by Laiou (2002) contains no chapter specifically on accounting or record keeping but does include references to accounting by government, estate owners and the church.

In terms of government accounting, the sixth century saw three bodies responsible for the administration of government revenues: the *praetorian prefectures* calculated, collected and transported land taxes; the *sacred largesses* oversaw the mining of precious metals and the minting of coins; and, the *private fisc* supervised rent collection from lands owned by the emperor (Haldon 2005: 43–5). Extremely detailed tax records were maintained (Baker 2013). The preparation of new assessments was necessary in North Africa in the sixth century as previous Roman records had been destroyed during the Vandal invasions (Procopius 1916, vol. 2: 277–9). Such tax records survive and have been published (Bagnall et al. 2011). Loss of land, population and revenue threatened the Empire with bankruptcy on occasion. Cost-cutting and borrowing averted this, and Treadgold (1997) has even managed to identify sufficient data to draft a series of state budgets from the fourth to the fourteenth centuries. Accounts survive from 911 and 949 for two campaigns in Crete. The former entailed payment of 28,300 sailors and 6,037 infantry and cavalry at a total cost of 234,732 nomismata (Oikonomides 2002: 1015). Manuals dealing with the collection of taxes were prepared and available for the use of government officials (ibid.: 975).

Estate accounting was relevant to emperors, nobility and the church, who depended on stewards owing to the scale and geographical dispersion of their properties (Morrisson and Sodini 2002: 182). Returns included rents and profits of direct land management using labour dues and paid labour (Lefort 2002: 240–1). Estate management, accounting and investment have been descried as 'sophisticated' in the eleventh century (Laiou and Morrisson 2010: 104, 239). The *Geoponika*, which deals with agricultural practices, specified that the steward should render accounts (Lefort 2002: 294). In 1073 a property is detailed as generating 307 nomismata, requiring 7 nomismata for the payment of expenses, thus yielding a net income of 300 nomismata. An early twelfth-century letter claims that accountants know how to boost revenues, decrease expenses and generate wealth (ibid.: 295). Nobles and officials also maintained household accounts and a late sixth-century account survives of the bread, meat, oil and wine supplied by the patrician Athanasius to his retinue (Hunt and Edgar 1934: 543–7).

The second council of Nicaea (787) mandated the employment of a steward for bishoprics and monasteries (Lefort 2002: 285). Sometimes *typika*, the foundation charters of monasteries, detailed financial arrangements for the support of the houses: the generation of surpluses was considered desirable to allow the house to offer hospitality. The *typikon* of the monastery of the Theotokos Evergetis (founded c.1050) mentions the need for the appointment of a *docheiarios* (treasurer) to record all income and expenditure in detail (Jordan and Morris 2012: 190–7). Monastic financial misconduct was considered to be a serious risk, and four levels of accountability were prescribed at the monastery of Pakourianos (Kaplan 1994: 105, 115–16; Thomas 1994: 255; Armstrong 2007: 316). Inventories (*brebia*) of real estate and moveable goods were also maintained. An example dating from the fifth or sixth century lists altar vessels, cloth, books and other furnishings (Hunt and Edgar 1932: 433; A. Harvey 1994: 126). The extent to which tax matters, instructions for the deliveries of goods and authorisations for payments were recorded in writing by monastic houses can be seen in the number of eighth-century papyri which survive from the Monastery of Apollo at Bawit (Clackson 2008).

Developments in the Islamic world

Islamic accounting can be said to have had its inception rooted in the teachings of the Prophet Muhammad (c.571–632). It is a vast potential arena extending geographically from Spain, across Africa, the Middle East and beyond and covering a plethora of states, dynasties and political, religious, commercial and agricultural institutions which have developed, flourished and declined over the centuries since Muhammad preached. For the historian, the period between 800 and 1200, which has been described as 'one of the most brilliant civilizations in the history of humanity' (Saunders 1980: 187), was one when trade flourished (Arabic coins even made their way to Scandinavia); Greek science and philosophy was translated into Arabic; paper manufacture was learnt from the Chinese; Sanskrit writings were explored and translated; and al-Khwarizmi utilised Hindu mathematical achievement to develop the science of algebra (ibid.). Indeed, many Classical texts such as the first century *Oikonomikos Logos* (*Management of the Estate*) have survived because of Arabic translations (Swain 2016).

Muhammad preached in Mecca and Medina and worked as a merchant. The Qur'an provides ethical guidance on the conduct of economic activities: condemning usury, advocating 'trading by mutual consent', and commanding the giving of 'good measure and fair weight' (Lewis 1979: 124–5). The Mecca of Muhammad's day appears to have experienced social tension between a growing mercantile economy and more traditional values, and the Qur'an is explicit on the need to care for the unfortunate (Watt 1978: 33–4). The *hadith* (sayings) of Muhammad praise industriousness and trade: 'The best of gain is from honourable trade'. They state that it is a Muslim duty to seek lawful gain and to be honest and truthful, that Muslim merchants will join the martyrs on the day of judgement, and that merchants are 'God's trusted servants on earth', notwithstanding markets are described also as the worst things in cities (Lewis 1979: 126–30). The importance of recording debts and contracts including the date of settlement is stated in *Surah* (chapter) 2.282–3 of the Qur'an (Zaid 2004). The reference is interesting from a bookkeeping perspective on several counts. First, it shows bookkeeping fulfilling its traditional role of tracking rights and obligations. The fact that the instruction to record transactions has the authority of scripture suggests this was no random directive, but perceived as necessary for the general well-being of society. The instruction to find a scribe to do the writing is also interesting as it assumes that traders were likely to be illiterate and indicates the existence of a professional class of record-keepers that they could draw on.

After Muhammad's death, the swift conquests of the armies of Islam required administrative mechanisms for the collection of taxes, and existing local arrangements continued in force (Sijpesteijn and Clackson 2009: 104). The inhabitants of the conquered territories were surprised to find that the taxes payable to their new rulers were less onerous than those formerly payable to Byzantium (Lewis 1977: 58; Vaglieri 1978: 62). Local administrations were permitted to continue and amirs (governors) were appointed by the caliph to superintend financial matters. Taxes were remitted to the treasury which paid the soldiers. From the eighth century there survive records relating to tax: demands, appeals, arrears, lists of taxpayers and receipts (Lewis 1979: 130–3; Sijpesteijn and Clackson 2009). Inventories were compiled which reveal that, on the death of Harun al-Rashid in 809, for example, his stores included robes, spices, jewels, furnishings and armour (Lewis 1979 140–1). From the ninth century lists of expenses, leases and debt instruments also survive. Papyri of the ninth century show land taxes in Egypt raised to boost falling revenues. Ahmad ibn al-Mudabbir, a financial administrator, was sent from Baghdad to Egypt in 861 to impose a whole new raft of taxes (Lewis 1978: 177). His successor, Ibn Tulun, increased land-tax revenue from 800,000 dinars to 4,300,000 dinars by extending cultivation and inducing higher agricultural yields (ibid.: 183). The central government in Baghdad was faced with a mismatch of revenue and expenditure which the Abbasid vizier, Ali ibn Isa, addressed by imposing an economy programme on the court (von Grunebaum 1953: 161; Sourdel 1977: 135). Government bureaucracies from an early period evidently maintained detailed accounting records and were the subject of intellectual consideration, such as the vizier Nizam al-Mulk's *Treatise on Government* dating from around 1092 (ibid.: 203).

State accounting manuals produced by the Ilkhanids in the fourteenth century explained government accounting systems, which included day-books, income and expense ledgers, and tax records. These treatises were following in the tradition of earlier Muslim scholars who had documented government accounting practices from as early as 768 (Zaid 2004). The Ilkhanate was a province of the Mongol Empire which completed its defeat of the Abbasids with the sack of Baghdad in 1258 and the killing of the Caliph and his family. The Abbasids had dominated the Muslim world since the eighth century. The final book in the sequence, the *Risale-i Felekiyye*, is notable not least because it sets out the *Merdiven* method of bookkeeping using *siyakat* script, adopted subsequently by the Ottomans (Sensoy and Güvemli 2015). *Merdiven* (literally 'stair' or 'ladder') bookkeeping was so named because it recorded transactions in descending level of detail from the general to the specific, the one above the other. *Siyakat* script was a specialised, condensed form of writing and numbering that had to be learnt. It was useful both for its precision and for keeping information confidential as outsiders would find it hard to read. *Siyakat* contained elements of Persian and Arabic script and was utilised in countries as far afield as Hungary and Mughal India (Napier 2009). The *Merdiven* method seems to have been invented by the Abbasids. It formed the backbone of the financial administration of the Ottoman Empire until 1879 when it was replaced by double-entry. At various times during its long lifespan the system was adapted to deal with different situations such as government administrative reform, the establishment of *cash waqfs* (a type of charitable foundation) to fund private business, or industrial enterprise (Demirhan et al. 2012; Güvemli 2012; Toraman et al. 2012). It follows that in terms of longevity, *Merdiven* bookkeeping rivals double-entry. The utilisation and development of the *Merdiven* system and *Siyakat* script by different peoples over many centuries illustrates how bookkeeping practice can transcend particular times and societies and 'assume the status of conventional wisdom', particularly once a method is set down in textual form for others to follow (Jones and Oldroyd 2015: 121), a theme we shall return to in relation to Luca Pacioli's *Summa*.

Enlightened rulers in the Muslim world attempted to facilitate trade to generate further revenues by means of constructing caravanserais where merchants could stay for three days without charge. As early as the ninth century banking facilities had developed sufficiently for a merchant 'to draw a cheque in Baghdad and cash it in Morocco' (Lewis 1977: 91). The Seljuk sultans also offered a form of state insurance to those transporting goods whereby merchandise lost to bandits was indemnified by payments from the state. In 1336 the Seljuk state was said to have annual revenues of 27 million dinars and Turkey at this date was known as a land of legendary wealth and treasures (Turan 1978: 258–62). Their Ottoman successors continued to support caravanserai and also benefited from this prosperity. It is alleged that only in the seventeenth century did government start to find receipts inadequate for expenditure. By the eighteenth century the financial administration of the state comprised 25 bureaux staffed by trained officials (Inalcik 1976: 52–3; Itzkowitz 1980: 47, 56).

All the above factors argue for the existence of detailed and developed accounting records in the Islamic world from the seventh century onwards. The problem is that few documents have survived outside the Ottoman Empire, partly owing to the ravages of war (Napier 2009). There is also the question of what previous generations would have considered worth preserving. In the statist cultures of the Middle East (Demirhan et al. 2012), this is more likely to have been governmental records than ones pertaining to private business, notwithstanding Zaid argues (2004) such records must have existed. The challenge for accounting historians is to uncover more of what does exist, ideally working in collaboration with scholars with the necessary palaeographic skills.[4]

Medieval charge and discharge accounts[5]

The focus of this section is on medieval charge and discharge accounting and agency relationships. Governmental accounts are not considered, although their form was similar and mention must be made here of the magnificent English Exchequer pipe-roll series which extends back to the reign of Henry I (1100–35) and the operation of which is explained in the *Dialogus de Scaccario*, written between 1177 and 1179 (Fitz Nigel 1983). It is likely that influences passed between government, the church and landowners as the great royal offices were filled by magnates who were concerned with the orderly running and exploitation of their own estates as well as the administration of the king's business.[6]

The form of a 'typical' medieval account has been described many times (Noke 1981: 141–5; Harvey 1984: 25–40; Bailey 2002: 97–116; Boyns and Edwards 2013: 57–8). Widely known as the charge and discharge account, its purpose was to enable a person entrusted with the management of a property, manor or office to render an account of their stewardship. These written accounts were examined orally at the audit and amendments made as necessary (Bailey 2002: 102–3).

Medieval landowners frequently owned estates scattered throughout the country, perhaps the result of deliberate royal policy (Stenton 1971: 627–8). For example, although half of the manors held by the Bishop of Winchester were located within Hampshire, the remainder were spread throughout Berkshire, Buckinghamshire, Oxfordshire, Somerset, Surrey and Wiltshire (Page 2002: 6). Even when a magnate was close at hand, other responsibilities and the sheer size of estates necessitated the delegation of managerial powers.

An individual manor or group of manors might be made the overall responsibility of an official known as a reeve, steward or bailiff (Denholm-Young 1963: 32–85). The manor might comprise land occupied and exploited by tenants in exchange for agreed rents (which might be payable in kind, in money or in labour services), and land known as 'demesne' which was managed directly for the benefit of the lord and worked either by tenants who owed labour dues or by paid labour. The lord's reeve would be responsible for implementing decisions as to which crops should be grown, for the gathering of the harvest, and its safe storage for sale or consumption by the lord's household. Thus, the reeve would account to his lord for all rents and dues owed by those living on the estate, and for the income and expenses of managing the demesne (Poole 1970: 36–7, 56–7).

The account was perceived in terms of the personal responsibility of the reeve to the lord of the manor. It normally began with 'the charge': the income which was due to the lord. From this was deducted the 'discharge': all allowances and expenses which the reeve was entitled to claim or incur, which usually left a balance deliverable to the lord. On the dorse (reverse side) of the account might be found an inventory giving particulars of grain, livestock, or other goods and utensils (Kirk 1892: ix–x). A full account would normally be presented once a year after the gathering in of the harvest, with an interim view of the account given part way through the year in order to discuss the income received to date and the expectations for the full year (Bailey 2002: 103). The accounts were usually presented in Latin: the term for the charge (*oneratio*) and discharge (*exoneracio*) account being *compotus* and the inventory was referred to as the *status* or *inventarium*.

Harvey (1984: 25–40; 1994) has analysed the forms of written manorial accounts and identified three broad phases in their development: an early phase (c.1200–1270) with diverse formats; a second period (c.1270–1380) which shows standardisation and great detail; and a final phase (c.1380–1530) in which the accounts are less detailed. The early phase is characterised by a wide variety of formats and a lack of sub-headings, beyond those of receipts and expenditure. By the second phase the accounts have become much more detailed, the use of sub-headings and sub-totals for different categories of income and expense had expanded greatly, and there is much greater comparability between the accounts of different estates and institutions. In phase three, the accounts become more divergent in form and often much shorter (see Bailey 2002: 116–50 for examples).

Both Harvey (1984, 1994) and Bailey (2002) explain these transitions in terms of the changing patterns of estate exploitation. Until the thirteenth century, the bulk of income was received in the form of fixed rents, even the demesne being farmed out. In the thirteenth century, however, there occurred a movement towards the reclaiming of the demesne and its direct management, possibly a response to general economic growth. Commodity prices were rising whereas customary rents were fixed, and landlords perceived direct management as a means of increasing their income. In place of the fixed rent, landlords now received income from the sale of a variety of crops and livestock and incurred a multiplicity of types of expense related to the direct exploitation of the land (Miller and Hatcher 1980: 198–239). Accounts in the second phase became more detailed to reflect these changes. Subsequently, this movement was reversed and land was returned from direct management to leasing. Phase three accounts are diverse as this process was spread over a long period and varied greatly from estate to estate, some estates still needing to account for the variety entailed by direct management, others having the much simpler accounts of rentiers (McKisack 1971: 341; Dobson 1973: 272; Duby 1976: 261).

Turning to the standardisation of accounts in the second phase, this may be seen as a reflection of the diffusion and adoption of improvements in business practice. For example, advances in accounting at the Royal Exchequer served as a model for others (Oschinsky 1971: 214). Royal methods appear to have been introduced and continued at a number of ecclesiastical estates when they were administered by a royal official during a vacancy (Hall 1903: xi–xii; Salter 1922: 80; Graham 1929: 253). Jones (2008) highlights the role magnates connected to the Exchequer played as change-agents in the dissemination of charge and discharge accounting firstly to church estates and subsequently to lay ones. The systems in use at the Royal Exchequer were documented in 1177–9 by Richard Fitz Nigel (1983), Bishop of London, in his *Dialogus de Scaccario*. This was followed from the mid-thirteenth century onwards by estate management manuals (such as Walter of Henley's) and accounting treatises which described procedures and gave examples of accounts

(Oschinsky 1971: 235–57). From Beaulieu Abbey survives a formulary written in 1269–70, with an introduction giving rules for preparing accounts followed by a set of specimen accounts to be used as a guide for accounting and auditing in future years (Hockey 1975). Accounting was taught at universities, certainly from the second half of the fourteenth century onwards (Richardson 1941: 260). Additionally, pressure on ecclesiastical estates to prepare written accounts came from the papacy (Knowles 1956: 57–8; Dobie 2008), and on both ecclesiastical and lay estates from developments in legal practice which required well laid out accounts in order to be considered convincing evidence (Oschinsky 1971: 72; Bailey 2002: 19; Dobie 2008).

Thus far the manorial account has been considered in isolation, but a manor was likely to be one of many on a great estate which would also have other departments that would be required to prepare accounts. Thus, at Durham Cathedral Priory, in addition to manorial and livestock accounts, there survive accounts from a range of office bearers or obedientiaries such as the bursar and cellarer, the heads of dependent cells, and the proctors charged with administering more distant possessions in Scotland. Selections from these accounts have been published and it is possible to trace transactions from the discharge section of one account into the charge of another – an example of the dual nature of a transaction being reflected within a single-entry system of accounts (Fowler 1898–1900; Dobie 2015).

The accounts were of course the outcome of a whole series of underlying vouchers and records. As well as the formal *compoti* and *status* mentioned earlier, accounting records also included rent-rolls, summaries and bad debt listings (Dobie 2015). Wooden tallies and small written indentures were widely used to record the transfer of money from one agent to another, again reflecting the dual nature of financial transactions (Clanchy 1979: 95–6; Baxter 1994). Surveys summarised all the revenues due to a lord (Clanchy 1979: 72–3).[7] Other accounting records included lists of debtors and creditors (Lomas and Piper 1989; Bailey 2002: 152–3).

Although the prime purpose of the accounts was to attest the stewardship of officials, the totals from individual accounts were on occasion summarised and combined with the totals from other accounts to yield a picture of overall financial position. Thus, at Norwich Cathedral Priory, the *Status Obedientiariorum* (the earliest extant dates from 1345) combined the totals from the accounts of the individual obedientiaries to arrive at the total receipts, total expenditure and surplus or deficit for each year (Saunders 1930: 17). Stone (1962: 25) traces the development of a *proficium* (profit or gain) figure at Norwich Cathedral Priory from the second half of the thirteenth century. Expenditure on capital items such as the building of a new grange was excluded from the calculation, which was also adjusted for goods transferred elsewhere on the estates (Stone 1962: 28; Postles 1994: 118).

Bookkeeping on medieval estates therefore demonstrates a variety of forms which emerged in response to changing economic conditions and opportunities. It attracted the attention of learned men who taught at the universities and wrote treatises explaining current best practice, which aided both the diffusion of more complex bookkeeping techniques and their standardisation. Such a movement was also encouraged by papal bulls demanding that accounts be prepared and audited for ecclesiastical offices, and by the increasing ability of creditors to enforce their claims in court, provided they could supply written accounting evidence.

Mercantile accounting: literature and practice

The factors which encouraged landlords to take land back into direct management – a growing population leading to both rising demand and rising prices for agricultural foodstuffs (Duby 1976: 260; Harvey 1984, 1994; Bailey 2002) – also underlie the expansion of trade which occurred throughout Europe as the Middle Ages progressed (Bernard 1972: 274–5; Russell 1972: 36; Jones 1997: 152–3). Two centuries of relative prosperity (c.1050–1250) were followed by a century and a half of disruption marked by the Black Death, financial crises and political unrest (Trevor-Roper 1965: 161–75). The overall trend, however, was one of economic growth in which an urban class of merchants grew rich and influential. Families such as the Medici in Florence, whose fortune was founded in banking, became powerful rulers in their own right (De Roover 1966: 5; Bernard 1972: 289–302). The fifteenth and sixteenth centuries were an age of discovery of new worlds in the West, and a new seaborne trading route to the East, both of which had a profound impact on European trade and investment (Clough and Cole 1952: 108–33).

Producing goods for markets provided cash incomes for landlords which could be spent on imported luxury items. The interrelatedness and interdependence of a large number of factors emerging in parallel is evident. A money economy surfaced against a background of sustained population growth, growth in towns and trade, a reduction in transaction costs, improvements in transport and distribution networks, supplies of silver for coinage, reliable coinage, increasing literacy and numeracy, systems of reckoning and recording, recognised weights and measures, and a legal process for the enforcement of credit over time (Bolton 2004: 7). These developments enabled and accompanied a revival in trade, while at the same time requiring more sophisticated accounting systems to track and provide evidence of increasingly complex networks of transactions.

Internationally, economic activity was at its most advanced in Italy between the twelfth and fifteenth centuries (Bernard 1972: 291); great banking houses such as the Medici developed that were capable of transferring credit over the whole of Europe (De Roover 1966: 2–3). It is widely agreed today that double-entry bookkeeping emerged among the flourishing city states of Italy in the thirteenth and fourteenth centuries (Edwards 1989: 48–9; Mills 1994: 82). Most of the surviving examples of account-books exhibiting double-entry elements are post 1290 (De Roover 1956; Edwards 1989: 49–50; Lee 1977, 1994). Fra Luca Pacioli's *Summa de Arithmetica, Geometrica, Proportioni et Proportionalita*, published in 1494, claims that the double-entry system he was describing (in the chapter entitled *De Computis et Scripturis*) had been used in Venice for more than 200 years (Galassi 1996). This would date its origin there to the late-thirteenth century.

Born in 1445, Pacioli is often perceived as the father of double-entry bookkeeping and modern accounting (Hatfield 1968: 3). Certainly, *De Computis* was the first published work on double-entry bookkeeping. However, an earlier work written in 1458, but not published until 1573, by Benedetto Cotrugli (*Della Mercatura et del Mercante Perfecto*), also included an account of double-entry bookkeeping, and stated that a merchant should have three books: ledger, journal and memorial (a type of day book for collecting information prior to processing); and that the ledger should be closed off annually and a trial balance drawn up (Yamey 1994a: 43–7; Kojima 1995: 69). It has since been suggested that Pacioli's treatise is a combination of different works written at different times (Hernández-Esteve 1994a: 65–78; 1994b: 68), although this is contested by Yamey (1994b) and Sangster (2018). Pacioli stated that the objective of bookkeeping is 'to give the trader without delay information as to his assets and liabilities' (Brown 1968: 111–12). His work gave practical guidance to merchants, providing examples on how to open a new set of accounts, starting with an inventory of assets and liabilities, and citing the initial double-entry for the opening of the books that is still taught to students today: debit cash and credit capital (Geüsbeek 1974: 33–5, 43). According to Sangster (2018: 309), Pacioli's treatise was not simply a set of rules which described 'how to do double entry', but an axiomatic exposition of 'how double entry works'.

The main importance of Pacioli's work probably lies not so much in its originality as in its influence in disseminating knowledge of the double-entry method throughout Europe. It is significant that the work's publication coincided with the advent of the printing press, which made new ideas more accessible (Thompson 1991; Mills 1994: 90–3; Sangster et al. 2011). This was the heyday of the Italian Renaissance, when Italian influence in art, music, philosophy, science, technology and warfare was at its height. New learning spread northwards from Italy through France, Germany, the Low Countries and England. As a result, not only did Pacioli's *De Computis* attract considerable attention in his native Italy (Taylor 1956: 180–1), it was also widely reproduced elsewhere: 'All of the accounting books published during the sixteenth century in other European countries, particularly in Germany, the Netherlands, and England, presented descriptions of bookkeeping similar to that of Pacioli' (Galassi 1996: 445). Authors borrowed freely from each other often without acknowledgement (Yamey 1979).

The first book in English on bookkeeping was Oldcastle's *A Profitable Treatyce* published in 1543, of which no copy is known to have survived (Coomber 1956: 206). It was used and acknowledged by Mellis in his *A Briefe Instruction and Maner How to Keep Bookes of Accompts After the Order of Debitor and Creditor*, published in 1588. Both works were almost literal translations of Pacioli, notwithstanding the omission of certain sections of the earlier work (Yamey et al. 1963: 155–9; Chatfield 1977: 56). Ympyn's translation of his *Nieuwe Instructie* of 1543 into English in 1547 as *A Notable and Very Excellente Woorke, Expressing and Declaring the Maner and Forme How to Kepe a Boke of Accomptes or Reconynges*, moved beyond Pacioli by including a set of illustrative accounts and by incorporating a balance account into the ledger to record all of the closing balances prior to opening up a new ledger (Yamey et al. 1963: 159–161; Chatfield 1996b: 616). Peele's *The Maner and Fourme How to Kepe a Perfect Reconyng* followed in 1553. Important innovations included a general rule which could be applied to assist in the categorisation of transactions: 'To make the thinges Receivyd, or the receiver, Debter to the things delivered, or to the deliverer' (quoted in Chatfield 1996a: 455). Peele's second and larger work, *The Pathe Waye to Perfectnes*, was published in 1569 and owed much to another English author, Weddington, who published two years earlier. The *Pathe Waye* took the form of a dialogue between teacher and student. In both his works, Peele supplied examples of journal entries to which a bookkeeper in doubt could refer (Yamey et al. 1963: 162–3; Chatfield 1996a: 455). According to Jackson (1956: 288), 'The history of the teaching of bookkeeping until almost the end of the nineteenth century consists … of the evolution of methods of explaining how to find which accounts to debit and credit'. Notable exceptions include John Clark who developed an algebraic approach to the teaching of bookkeeping (Edwards 2014) and John Dodson who employed deductive logic (Edwards 2015).

These books of instruction contain a common core of recommendations. The accounting books to be maintained comprised as a minimum the ledger, journal and memorial, although the memorial was sometimes referred to as a 'waste book' (Yamey et al. 1963: 12; Mepham 1988: 176–98). From the memorial, which acted as a memory aid, transactions were formalised (and overseas currencies converted into a single currency) as debits and credits in the journal, from which postings were made to the ledger. Merchants might be engaged in an inherently complex trading environment involving credit sales and purchases, loans, interest, bills of exchange and foreign currency losses/gains, and so examples of many types of transaction are provided in these texts and the use of references and cross-references described. Balancing off the ledger is also explained, although such an activity appears to have been conducted infrequently early on, mainly occurring when a partnership was concluded or a ledger was full (Brown 1968: 106; Mepham 1988: 199).

There was instruction too about writing letters which provided merchants with a means of controlling their operations at a distance and was recognised by contemporary authors as part of the accounting process (Oldroyd 1998). Ympyn, Weddington and Peele all listed the copy letter-book among the merchant's account books (Yamey et al. 1963: 21, 25, 44), and a series of letter writing manuals such as *The Merchants' Avizo* of 1589 provided examples of business letters (Jeacle and Brown 2006: 30). Weddington in particular referred to the need for correspondence with factors, which would include abstracts of accounts and source data for the memorial in order to manage a merchant's affairs properly (Yamey et al. 1963: 48–9, 97). Finally, although the focus of these texts was on tracking exchanges and establishing accountability, there is some evidence of consideration given to the use of accounting for costing and decision-making purposes. For example, John Collins, in *The Perfect Method of Merchants Accompts Demonstrated* of 1697, detailed the application of double-entry bookkeeping to the internal transfers of raw materials from a stock account to a process account (Boyns et al. 1997; Boyns and Edwards 2013: 123).

The steadily increasing number of books published on double-entry bookkeeping undoubtedly was a factor in the dissemination of knowledge of the technique. A 'small and intermittent trickle' became by the eighteenth century a 'steady and widening stream' (Yamey et al. 1963: vii; Edwards 2011). The popularity of such books can be seen by the number of editions published, although this could be more definitely assessed were details of the size of print-runs known. Webster's volume, first published in 1717, appeared in at least 13 editions. John Mair's *Bookkeeping Methodized* of 1736 was reissued in over 20 versions, with a further eight editions of his new 1773 title appearing in print by 1807 (Yamey et al. 1963: 213–14; Mepham 1988: 78–9). Books focusing on individual sectors were also produced. Thus in Germany and Denmark, Albrecht Daniel Thaer (1752–1828) and Carl Frederik Gyllembourg (1767–1815) both published works which sought to establish double-entry bookkeeping systems for agricultural enterprises (Lampe and Sharp 2017).

How common it was in practice for the knowledge available in texts to be applied is another matter. In Italy, examples of the early use and later adoption of double-entry extended to religious organisations involved in business practices such as the *Monte de Pieta*, which extended small loans to needy residents. The *Monte* established in Bologna in 1473 was using double-entry bookkeeping from at least the second half of the sixteenth century onwards (Orelli et al. 2013). In Castile, legislation of 1549 required merchants and bankers to maintain double-entry records. Later in 1755 a Spanish trading company, *Real Compania de Comercio de Barcelona a Indias*, included in its constitution a provision that it should use double-entry bookkeeping and in 1761 Portugal mandated double-entry bookkeeping for the higher levels of the royal treasury. In the colonies single-entry bookkeeping was still permitted as officials there did not have the necessary experience to introduce double-entry bookkeeping systems (Rodrigues and Sangster 2013). The Kingdom of Sardinia has also been identified as a state which had an accounting system based upon double-entry bookkeeping in the early nineteenth century (Coronella et al. 2013).

On the other hand, Ramsey (1956: 186) agrees with Ympyn that the extant accounts of sixteenth-century English merchants were generally 'grosly, obscurely and lewdely kept'. Single-entry accounting seems to have remained the norm in Britain even among large organisations until at least the nineteenth century (Hoskin and Macve 1986).

This situation was not unique to Britain. Tuition in double-entry remained patchy in Italy in Pacioli's lifetime and, even though it had been known about for 200 years, most merchants continued not to employ it (Sangster 2018). Bookkeeping practice in North-Western Europe tended to follow the conventions of the Hanseatic League, a mercantile confederation of market towns and ports on the northern coast of Europe, which at its height exercised considerable economic and political power. Hanseatic merchants favoured single-entry systems where the purpose was confined to tracking debtors, creditors and inventory, holding agents accountable, and the concept of capital had little meaning (Robertson and Funnell 2014: 53–6). Charge and discharge accounting remained popular in France in the eighteenth century in certain industries (Lemarchand 1994). The Dutch East India Company, following in the Hanseatic tradition, resisted the adoption of double-entry, as did the Whitin Machine Company in the US until 1918 (Macve 1996: 29).

In answer to the question of why the rate of adoption of double-entry bookkeeping was so slow, Edwards (1989: 56–7) concluded that the absence of strong demand from business is the most likely explanation, rather than ignorance or lack of expertise on the part of the merchants. Firms of merchants in England in the sixteenth and seventeenth centuries generally comprised loose associations of individuals who would band together for particular ventures, sharing the proceeds of the completed undertaking between them (Winchester 1955: 212–13). Because mercantile business was venture-based, the notion of periodic profit measurement as a means of calculating dividends did not apply. Similarly, there was no need to calculate profit for tax purposes, as income tax was not conceived in Britain until the end of the eighteenth century. In these circumstances it is unsurprising that the distinctions between capital and revenue items, and between business and personal expenditure were not sharply defined, and that the ability of double-entry bookkeeping to measure periodic profits on a routine basis was not exploited. Much diversity has been observed in the treatment of fixed assets, stock valuation, and bad and doubtful debts, and there is little evidence of the practical application of the accruals concept (Yamey 1962: 32–7; Yamey et al. 1963: 193–201).[8]

Merchants required accounts that were capable of eliminating errors, preventing fraud, agreeing probate, tracking debtors, creditors, cash and inventory, dividing proceeds between partners, holding agents to account, and providing evidence in courts of law. Hence, the prime purpose of account books was to safeguard the merchant's property entitlements. The enduring popularity of single-entry systems suggests this end could be achieved without recourse to double-entry.

Explaining the origins of double-entry bookkeeping

Pinpointing the origins of double-entry bookkeeping is particularly important given the alleged connections discussed in Chapter 17 between double-entry and the rise of capitalism. Two key questions arise: why did double-entry appear in Italy in the thirteenth century; and why in the nineteenth century did its use apparently become widespread in the UK? The first of these questions is considered in this section and the second in the section entitled 'Victorian expansion'.

The emergence of double-entry systems in Italy from the thirteenth century onwards may have resulted from a process of 'trial and error' which eventually recognised that every transaction had two aspects. If a sale was made, either cash was received or the business had a debtor to monitor. Both features had to be written down for the books to show a correct record (Lee 1975: 7–8). It may be that a system of cross-checking was done between the cash book and the debtors book: the accounting records of Giovanni Farolfi from 1299–1300 feature such cross-references (De Roover 1956: 119; Lee 1977). The duality of transactions was also evident from manorial accounts in which the discharge section of one account comprised the charge of another. Likewise, Chapter 4 of the *Companion* has described how the notion of recording systems that were capable of representing the physical as well as the social realities of transactions may have existed as early as the Neolithic. Another possibility is that double-entry evolved out of charge and discharge accounting. Although the systems of charge and discharge and double-entry bookkeeping may be perceived as distinct, numerous examples of hybrid systems containing elements of both charge and discharge and double-entry bookkeeping can be found, such as that used in 1759–60 on the Mackworth Estate (Neath) where the traditional accountability of charge and discharge statements was combined with the maintenance of a ledger based on double-entry principles (Boyns and Edwards 2013: 47–9; see also King 2010).

However, double-entry bookkeeping goes much further in its classification of transactions into *nominal* (revenue and expenses), *personal* (debtors/creditors) or *real* (other assets/liabilities) accounts than any of its known antecedents (Galassi 1996). Indeed, its very distinctiveness allied to its sudden appearance in one part of Europe militates against an evolutionary explanation of its development, unless there are many sets of earlier records that have been lost. The earliest example containing double-entry elements identified so far relates to 1211, whereas by 1299 one is able to observe a fully developed system in operation in the branch accounts of the Florentine merchants, Giovanni Farolfi and Company. Lee (1977: 87), who described these books, subscribes to the idea 'of the gradual acceptance and application' by merchants of the underlying 'concepts' of double-entry between 1211 and 1300. However, there is nothing gradual about such a radical departure occurring within the space of 90 years when viewed against the history of bookkeeping as a whole. Charge and discharge accounting is an example of a system that predominated on English estates from at least the thirteenth to the nineteenth centuries. The double-entry system employed by the Farolfi family in 1299–1300 was very similar to the one described by Pacioli 200 years later, which in turn has remained largely unchanged through to the modern day (Lee 1977; Galassi 1996: 447).

Given this tendency on the part of practitioners to follow established methods, which helps explain why double-entry did not sweep the board despite its apparent advantages,[9] one searches for a catalyst in the thirteenth century to account for the sudden change. Hoskin and Macve (1986; see also Macve 1996), approaching the issue from a Foucauldian perspective, ground the origins of double-entry in educational advances that occurred in medieval universities from the eleventh century, which affected the layout of written texts among other matters.[10] Textual innovations in the Middle Ages included alphabetical ordering, subject indexing, subdividing material into sections, cross-referencing and commentary, all of which are relevant to a double-entry ledger. However, these developments were not confined to Italy or to the thirteenth century. Indeed, changes to the university curriculum, allied to religious pressure at the end of the fifteenth century 'to re-emphasize a belief in order sanctified by God' (Thompson 1991: 584; see also Dean et al. 2016), possibly provide a more convincing explanation of why Pacioli, a professor of mathematics, was motivated to write his *Summa*, than why double-entry was originally conceived.

Edwards (1989: 50–1) offers the increasing complexity of the business environment in Italy as another explanation for double-entry, particularly the increase in credit transactions.

However, as observed earlier, merchants proved able to carry on their trade involving credit, loans, interest, negotiable instruments and foreign currencies through to the Victorian era without recourse to double-entry, suggesting that a functionalist explanation of its origins will not alone suffice.

Hence, one seeks other external factors that would account for the emergence of double-entry bookkeeping in thirteenth-century Italy, an obvious one being contact between Italian merchants and other cultures where proto-double-entry systems were already in use. Such an explanation is certainly possible. Extensive trade was conducted between Italy and the eastern Mediterranean during the medieval period, and perhaps new mercantile practices were observed and imitated or exchanged in both directions. The trading networks of Jewish merchants too may have acted as avenues for the dissemination of bookkeeping ideas (Napier 2009). Zaid (2000, 2001) and Nobes (2001) have debated the possibility and extent of influences from the medieval Islamic world. The protagonists are at least able to agree that 'several features of pre-double-entry accounting were used in the Muslim world before they were used in the West' (ibid.: 212).

The thirteenth century witnessed the creation of the great Mongol Empire ruled by Genghis Khan and his descendants, which at its height stretched from China to the fringes of Western Europe, creating 'a huge free-trade area' and bringing 'Christendom, as never before, into touch with the great, old civilizations of the East' (Trevor-Roper 1965: 177, 180): 'The great, orderly, tolerant Mongol Empire crossed and re-crossed by continual caravans, provided one of the most effective means for the diffusion of culture and technology', the most famous examples being gunpowder and printing, which were transmitted from China to Europe around this time (ibid.: 178–9). The same might have been true of bookkeeping. The chapter has highlighted the link between the Mongolian Ilkhanate, the Abbasids and the Ottoman Empire. The history of Chinese bookkeeping covers several thousand years (Lin 2003; Lu and Aiken 2003, 2004). This same is true of India, whence claims Lall Nigam (1986) double-entry originated.

However, such claims remain unproven. Nobes (1987) disputes the Indian connection on the grounds of a lack of documentary evidence. Likewise, an original and ongoing investigation of Chinese business archives has found no evidence to date to support the claim that an indigenous, Chinese form of double-entry bookkeeping developed from the mid-fourteenth century on. The study by Hoskin et al. (2016) controls for the possibility of Western influence by focusing on records predating the mid-nineteenth century when China was forced to accept Western incursion following the Opium Wars. One of the main differences identified is that the double-entry expounded by Pacioli was a 'self-contained' system which expressed all transactions in monetary terms, which was not the case in China (Yuan and Macve 2017: 417). There the books of account were supplemented by abacus calculations that were not recorded. It follows that although the dissemination of bookkeeping practice from the East remains a possibility, double-entry in its developed form appears 'unique' (Chatfield 1977: 34). Thus, a number of factors, none of which individually explain the phenomenon satisfactorily, may have contributed to the origins of double-entry.

Early industry

Some of the earliest examples of industrial accounting in Britain relate to landed estates. This is not surprising given that the landed estate was the largest, wealthiest and most clearly defined type of business organisation at the dawn of the Industrial Revolution (Pollard

1965: 25, 29–30). Moreover, British landowners enjoyed a relative advantage over many of their continental counterparts, in that the law entitled them to the coal, ironstone, lead and other mineral deposits under their land, with no social disapprobation attaching to the economic exploitation of their properties (Habakkuk 1953: 96, 99). The availability of timber from their estates for the production of charcoal was another incentive encouraging some landowners to diversify into iron production in the late sixteenth century (King 2010). Indeed, the early development of industry on estates, together with the major part played by landowners as investors in other enterprises, such as canal and railway companies, favours the notion of the dissemination of estate management practice to other sectors of the British economy (Napier 1997).

As far as bookkeeping was concerned, charge and discharge accounts prepared by individual stewards persisted as the dominant form of accounting on estates throughout the eighteenth and nineteenth centuries (Napier 1991, 1997), and were used to record industrial activities on estates (James 1955: xliv; Hatcher 1993: 303). These could be in bilateral format and, in certain instances, part of a full double-entry system (King 2010). According to Hatcher (ibid.), charge and discharge persisted as the only form of bookkeeping in many collieries until the 1670s. Generally, however, the system proved incapable of dealing with the full complexities of the trading operations, and a range of other types of report containing a common 'core of vital data on costs, output, and sales' was needed to address the shortfall (ibid.: 304). For example, 'coalpit' and 'sinking books' were used to analyse output, sales and production costs on the Willoughbys' estate at Wollaton in the sixteenth century, as supplements to the traditional charge and discharge statements (Lee 1991: 70). Likewise, the ledger of John Wheeler's Staffordshire ironworks from 1689 contains memoranda production accounts for each of the furnaces (King 2010).

Diversification in the types of records kept was a prominent feature of eighteenth-century estates in the north-east of England where a range of different reports was prepared in addition to the charge and discharge statements. For example, schedules of output were used to verify payments to and from subcontractors and lessees; stocks of goods and materials were listed and quantified; payments to workmen were dealt with through pay-bills which priced their daily output at the agreed rates; and the profitability of particular activities was calculated. The number of parties that were involved in the operations is quite striking and included stewards, lessees, partners, shareholders, labourers, agents and tenants, in addition to a host of different kinds of subcontractor. The method used to regulate these relationships was legally enforceable contracts supported by accounting to monitor compliance and, if necessary, seek redress in court. Bookkeeping was thus used throughout the estate operations to quantify and track the various exchanges taking place, and without it the various participants would have been unable to trade (Oldroyd 2007: 81, 102).

The main method of bookkeeping employed by these estates was the bilateral recording of cash receipts and payments, with adjustments for opening and closing debtors, creditors and stocks if the intention was to calculate profit. Bilateral cash accounting seems to have been commonplace on eighteenth-century landed estates. For example, it was the method recommended in Charles Snell's *Accompts for Landed-Men* (1711), and Edward Laurence's *The Duty and Office of a Land Steward* (1731). Other guides such as Thomas Richards' *The Gentleman's Auditor* (1707) and Roger North's *The Gentleman Accomptant* (1714) advocated the use of double-entry.[11] However, the relative advantage of the bilateral method over double-entry lay in its simplicity, which allowed it to be applied to all of the trading situations described, without requiring specialist bookkeeping knowledge (Oldroyd 2007: 46, 60).

If the need to protect property rights was the prime motivator of the bookkeeping arrangements on estates, detailed costing records were maintained as well to help plan the operations and inform investment decisions (ibid.: 107). This was true also of other early industrial enterprises where, in certain instances, the financial and management record-keeping systems were kept separately, and in others they were integrated. A review of 25 British firms between 1760 and 1850 revealed that 'costing activities were rarely reported in financial accounting records' (Fleischman and Parker 1991). By way of contrast, 'an integrated system of financial/management accounting' was uncovered in the iron-making industry in Sheffield c.1690 (Edwards and Boyns 1992).

Management accounting practice is considered in Chapter 9. However, it is worth stressing in the context of a chapter on bookkeeping that the distinction which exists today between 'financial' and 'management' accounting procedures was rarely relevant prior to the mid-nineteenth century. In the first place, the boundaries over who was responsible for collating and reporting different types of information were more fluid in the absence of defined engineering and accountancy professions. In the second, the division between external and internal reporting did not apply to most industrial enterprises, which were privately owned either by individuals or limited numbers of partners.

Returning to estates, the business interests of landowners were often varied and dispersed. The Earl of Balcarres, for example, owned coal and cannel mines in Scotland in addition to plantations in Jamaica (Oldroyd 2007: 105). No matter how conscientious proprietors were in visiting their properties, they would need a management system that was capable of controlling the operations at a distance and, in this respect, chief stewards played a vital role. These were highly remunerated full-time officials who operated through a central estate office normally situated in the landowner's main residence. It was through this office that accounting returns from all the various activities were channelled (Mingay 1967: 18–19).

Although the chief stewards were responsible for determining the bookkeeping arrangements, they were not primarily bookkeepers. According to Spring (1963: 100), stewards tended to be the sons of tenant farmers, yeomen, land agents, builders, surveyors and mining engineers: 'In a word they were the sons of practical men, often familiar from youth with the varied business of land management'. Pollard (1965: 29) maintained that stewards, in the north of England especially, were renowned for their industrial, commercial and financial acumen. Thus, John Hardy, a chief steward in the West Riding of Yorkshire, advised his master on a variety of matters, including taxation, investment in canal and iron companies, as well as mineral exploitation and textile production on the estate (Beckett 1986: 143). In the north-east of England, where the main business of many estates was coalmining, it was commonplace to employ viewers (mining engineers) as stewards. Chief stewards were highly remunerated. Hardy, whose tenure stretched for 30 years (1773–1803), received £80 a year in addition to a favourable lease of Barnby Hall with extensive farmlands. Personal wealth was desirable in the case of a steward as it conferred the social status needed to command the respect of tenants (Mingay 1967: 7–12; Martin 1979: 17).

Although stewards were not specialist bookkeepers, they needed to acquire a knowledge of bookkeeping. Various sources of guidance were available to them in addition to the printed handbooks mentioned previously. For example, Charles Snell described himself in his text as a 'teacher of writing and accompts at the free writing-school in Foster Lane with whom young gentlemen may board', which indicates the availability of external tuition. In most cases, however, the knowledge would have been acquired internally, with stewards either replicating the practice of their predecessors or following exemplars. Boyns and Edwards (1996) highlighted the role of proprietors and their agents in the 'dissemination of accounting techniques' in Welsh industry in the eighteenth and nineteenth centuries (see also Boyns and Edwards 2013: 34). Bookkeeping exemplars have survived on the Bowes estates in County Durham relating to the lead and salt operations. Family dynasties of stewards were common on these estates, and the marked similarity in the layout and presentation of the account-books over several generations of stewards confirms that they learnt from each other (Oldroyd 2007: 60–1).

Victorian expansion

The nineteenth century is, for the UK, the time when double-entry bookkeeping allegedly assumed the hegemony which it continues to claim today (Yamey 1956: 11; Hoskin and Macve 1986). Two factors supported this change: first, the widening gulf between investors and managers in a period of increasing industrialisation, which necessitated a transformation in business financial reporting practices; second, the increasing professionalisation of accountancy, which resulted in the adoption and diffusion through training and teaching of uniform accounting methods. This section will focus on the first of these developments as the effects of professionalisation are considered in Chapter 11.

At the outset, however, it should be acknowledged that the archives which have survived, and on which the research findings reported in this section have been based, tend to be from larger companies. In contrast, most businesses in existence in the mid-1800s were small (More 1997: 105–6; Boyce and Ville 2002: 148): 'most industrial labour continued to be carried out in homes and small workshops until the late Victorian period' (Morgan 1999: 48). Many of the individuals keeping the books probably would have been family members, and household accounting 'featured prominently in the everyday life and culture of the middle-class family' (Walker 1998: 485). Household management books extolled the virtues of maintaining accounts to ensure that insolvency, waste and fraud were avoided. It is unlikely that these accounts comprised a full set of double-entry records, but instead might have included a cash book listing receipts and expenditure, lists of credit transactions and their subsequent settlement, and inventories of goods (ibid.: 493), representing little development in the techniques employed.

Company accounts, however, tell a different story. In the nineteenth century, the Industrial Revolution, expansion of transport networks and growing markets created an increasing demand for capital. This demand was matched by an increase in the number of companies aiming to attract funds from debt and equity investors who were concerned to protect and monitor their investments.[12] An increasing number of companies began to use double-entry bookkeeping, and even mentioned the use of double-entry specifically in their articles of association or equivalent (Lemarchand 2016). Shareholder and creditor concerns were further strengthened by the high profile frauds and bankruptcies which occurred frequently during the nineteenth century. George Hudson, the 'Railway King', was obliged to move abroad to escape lawsuits arising from alleged frauds, including doctoring the books, amounting to a total of £598,785 (Glynn 1994: 331). In 1878, the City of Glasgow Bank collapsed. Its insolvency had been concealed and dividends continued to be paid by a deliberate policy of overvaluing assets (about £7 million of bad debts were treated as though they were good debts), and by falsifying figures submitted in government returns (French 1985: 10, 15). Such instances increased the demand for credible financial statements based on reliable accounting records.

Government was not necessarily keen to intervene, however, and a conflict can be seen between the forces of *laissez-faire* and those attempting to regulate and control. On the one hand, the nature of the accounting systems and information published by companies was regarded as a matter to be negotiated between the shareholders and the directors. Thus, Poulett Thomson, a minister at the Board of Trade, could say in 1837: 'It is by the Government not meddling with capital that this country has been able to obtain a superiority over every other country' (quoted in Glynn 1994: 330). On the other hand, the power of individual shareholders to influence such matters was seen as limited because of the widening gap between directors and shareholders (Littleton 1933: 206).

Consequently, some limited intervention did take place, although it was not until the Companies Act of 1928 that, for the generality of companies, any attempt was made to prescribe the form and content of the balance sheet (Edey 1968: 141–2). The Joint Stock Companies Act of 1844 had made accounting compulsory: companies were to keep books of account and to present 'full and fair' balance sheets to members at general meetings, which balance sheets were to be reported on by appointed auditors. However, little detail was given, the books of account were not described, and the contents and the format of the balance sheet were not laid down. Even these limited conditions were removed from the Joint Stock Companies Act of 1856, although the non-mandatory model articles of association specified the use of double-entry, a provision that was dropped from the model articles attached to the consolidating act of 1862 (Edey and Panitpakdi 1956). As Edey (1968: 137) has stated, the entire period between 1855 and 1900 is 'marked by a complete absence of statutory regulation in matters relating to accounting and audit for companies incorporated under the general company law, the only exceptions being those carrying on a few special classes of business' which were, nevertheless, of considerable economic significance (Parker 1990).

Although the government was hesitant to intervene in the affairs of companies in general, it did intercede in the affairs of public bodies and of specific industries such as the railways, banks, life assurance and gas on the grounds of public interest (Parker 1990). The 1835 Municipal Corporation Act was a watershed in extending the accountability of local authorities (Edwards 1992), and in 1867 all parishes were obliged to adopt double-entry as the old method of receipts and expenditure statements ignored outstanding liabilities (Jones 1994: 400). Local government had on occasion moved in advance of this: in 1785 the City of Bristol adopted a double-entry system (Jones 1994: 399) but, even as late as 1907, it could only be said that double-entry bookkeeping was employed by 'almost all local authorities' (Coombs and Edwards 1993: 41; 1994: 176).

A major factor prompting the adoption of double-entry systems by companies was the need to calculate dividends. Lenders required assurance that the security of their capital would be maintained, and so companies needed to be able to identify clearly the profits available for distribution. The Companies Acts of 1855–56 included a provision within the model articles that no dividend should be paid except out of profits (Edey and Panitpakdi 1956: 362). Accounts were therefore needed that were capable of enabling capital to be maintained. Double-entry bookkeeping, with its distinction between nominal, real and capital accounts, was ideal for that purpose.

Thus, the need to produce financial statements to protect the interests of lenders and investors necessitated the maintenance of appropriate records which recognised expenses fully and distinguished between capital and revenue items. The increasing emphasis during the nineteenth century on regular year-end reporting was significant in elevating the status of published financial statements. At the start of the period, financial statements were very much a residual product of the bookkeeping system, whereas by 1900 and, increasingly thereafter, it was the form and requirements of the annual financial statements which informed and drove the bookkeeping system and led to the increasing adoption of double-entry methods.

Conclusion

Although this account of bookkeeping practice spans some 2,500 years, a number of common threads emerge. The most important one is the role bookkeeping has played in safeguarding property entitlements, without which trade would have been impossible. Funnell (2001) considers the association between accounting, justice and property, arguing that the protection of property rights, for which accounting is vital, lies at the heart of capitalist law-codes as the ultimate end of justice. What he is essentially referring to, therefore, is bookkeeping, for it is this which tracks the rights and obligations attaching to property and provides the necessary legal evidence for claims to be enforced in court. The chapter has observed bookkeeping fulfilling these functions from Classical times onwards, showing that the triangular relationship subsisting between accounting, justice and property rights is not confined to capitalist societies.

The second theme is the role that distance from events has played in creating agency relationships, which in turn necessitated bookkeeping systems that were capable of holding agents accountable. This was as true on medieval estates as on those of the nineteenth century, or in the operations of sixteenth-century merchants, or those of Victorian joint-stock companies where the desire to protect the interests of shareholders provided an impetus for better record keeping. Thus, the chapter has observed bookkeeping continuously adapting to a variety of modes of organisational control in order to fulfil these two related functions. This leads to the final theme, which is the relationship between bookkeeping and complexity.

Throughout its history, bookkeeping has been effectively deployed in a range of contractual situations, modes of operation or business environments. However, there is a paradox, as the adaptability displayed by bookkeeping seems to have stemmed from its simplicity throughout most of its history. The range of situations in which bookkeeping was utilised in Roman society is a case in point. For most of the 2,500 years reviewed in this chapter, cash accounting supported by supplementary schedules of assets and liabilities has sufficed. Indeed, the success of single-entry recording systems long after the invention of double-entry raises a question mark over the inevitability of the latter. As Jack (1966) pointed out in her historical defence of single-entry bookkeeping, a system that was fit for purpose should not be dismissed as inferior simply because more sophisticated systems existed.

In terms of future research directions and challenges, the foregoing analysis suggests certain possibilities. For instance, how extensive were the gaps between bookkeeping instruction and practice? A lack of archival research means that accounting historians have only begun to answer this question (Yamey 1981: 128). There is still not a satisfactory explanation for the emergence of double-entry bookkeeping in Italy in the thirteenth century. What were the effects of interaction between merchants trading within and outside Europe? A worthwhile site for comparison would be the records of the merchant communities of different nationalities living side-by-side in great trading centres such as Antwerp or London. Given the intercontinental scale of trade from the Classical period onwards, there is a relative dearth of comparative studies. What were the effects of changes in bookkeeping practice in terms of economic and social development and the ways in which people viewed the world around them? Did double-entry really become commonplace in nineteenth-century Britain as is usually assumed? And what about other countries? Aside from the accounting records themselves, business correspondence and the articles of association might provide an additional source of evidence for joint-stock companies, although the latter would not help with the more numerous unincorporated organisations. The legal documents pertaining to bankruptcy proceedings might provide clues here. These are but a few suggestions in this important but still underdeveloped area of accounting history which may interest future researchers.

Key works

Bryer (2019) contains detailed information on bookkeeping practice from ancient Mesopotamia and Egypt through to the medieval period.

Chatfield (1977) is a comprehensive general history of accounting, with the first seven chapters focusing on 'the development of basic accounting methods'.

Edwards and Yamey (1994) celebrate the 500th anniversary of the publication of Pacioli's *Summa*. Their work contains articles on the history of bookkeeping from ancient times through to the nineteenth century.

Littleton and Yamey (1956) remains one of the best collections of articles on bookkeeping, covering the period from classical times to the nineteenth century.

Parker and Yamey (1994) start with ten articles dealing with the ancient world through to the development of double-entry bookkeeping.

Yamey et al. (1963) bring together commentary, analysis and extracts from original treatises on bookkeeping.

Notes

1 The authors gratefully acknowledge the helpful comments of John Richard Edwards and Richard Macve on the draft.
2 Information in this section is drawn mainly from Oldroyd (1997: 18–22).
3 The Carolingian dynasty dominated Western Europe c.750–987.
4 Scorgie's (1994) analysis of accounting fragments from the eleventh and twelfth centuries originally stored in the Old Cairo Genizah suggests there may be other records accounting historians are currently unaware of.
5 The information in this section is drawn mainly from Dobie (2008).
6 A wealth of accounting material survives from medieval England from ecclesiastical institutions (Kitchin 1892; Fowler 1898–1900; Saunders 1930; Smith 1943; Greatrex 1984; Page 1996, 1999; Harvey 2002), manorial and lay household accounts (Clanchy 1979: 72; Woolgar 1992–93: 6) and government records (Hunter 1844: Foreword).
7 On a macro level, the Domesday Book (1085–6), which contains a detailed survey of all the manors of England with the exception of the northern counties, has been claimed to be a working accounting document used in the raising of revenue (Godfrey and Hooper 1996; Oldroyd 1997; McDonald 2005).
8 Conversely, Boyns and Edwards (2013: 56–61, 115–20) cite plenty of evidence of the early use of accruals accounting by industrial companies, and for its application in the case of estate activities where charge and discharge was in use.
9 The advantages of double-entry over single-entry are elucidated by Yamey (1956: 7–8).
10 Hoskin and Macve (1986) also advance educational changes as the catalyst for double-entry's growing acceptance in the nineteenth century.
11 Boyns and Edwards (2013: ch. 3) contains a study of the estate and farm accounting literature including a rehearsal of the occupations of some authors and a classification of their texts as double-entry, charge and discharge, and cash book based.
12 The advantages of double-entry bookkeeping in reducing the scope for errors and omissions and the difficulties of ensuring a complete representation of all assets and liabilities with single-entry methods were realised before the nineteenth century. In 1784, when the Forth and Clyde Navigation appointed a new accountant, Richard Smellie, it was specifically to post up the books of account using the principles of double-entry, with the aim of giving the proprietors a clear and distinct view of the application of the money (Forrester 1994: 302–3). Smellie's new approach uncovered numerous errors and inaccuracies which resulted in £1,223 being reclaimed from his predecessor.

References

Armstrong, P. (2007) Monasteries old and new: the nature of the evidence, in M. Mullett (ed.) *Founders and Refounders of Byzantine Monasteries*, pp. 315–43 (Belfast: Belfast Byzantine Enterprises, Institute of Byzantine Studies Queen's University Belfast).

Bagnall, R.S., Keenan, J.G. and MacCoul, L.S.B. (eds.) (2011) *A Sixth-Century Tax Register from the Hermopolite Nome* (Durham, NC: American Society of Papyrologists).

Bailey, M. (2002) *The English Manor C.1200–1500* (Manchester: Manchester University Press).

Baker, C.R. (2013) Administrative and accounting practises in the Byzantine Empire, *Accounting History*, 18 (2): 211–27.

Baladouni, V. (1989) A paradigm for the analysis of accounting history, in R.H. Tondkar and E.N. Coffman (eds.) *Working Paper 66, Working Paper Series 4*, pp. 95–109 (Alabama: Academy of Accounting Historians).

Baxter, W.T. (1994) Early accounting: the tally and the checker-board, in R.H. Parker and B.S. Yamey (eds.) *Accounting History: Some British Contributions*, pp. 197–235 (Oxford: Clarendon Press).

Beckett, J.V. (1986) *The Aristocracy in England 1660–1914* (Oxford: Basil Blackwell).

Bernard, J. (1972) Trade and finance in the Middle Ages 900–500, in C.M. Cipolla (ed.) *The Fontana Economic History of Europe: The Middle Ages*, pp. 274–338 (Glasgow: Collins).

Bischoff, B. (1994) *Manuscripts and Libraries in the Age of Charlemagne* (Cambridge: Cambridge University Press).

Bolton, J. (2004) What is money? What is a money economy? when did a money economy emerge in medieval England? in D. Wood (ed.) *Medieval Money Matters*, pp. 1–15 (Oxford: Oxbow Books).

Boussard, J. (1968) *The Civilisation of Charlemagne* (London: Weidenfeld & Nicolson).

Bowman, A.K. and Thomas, J.D. (1974) *The Vindolanda Writing Tablets* (Newcastle upon Tyne: Frank Graham).

Boyce, G. and Ville, S. (2002) *The Development of Modern Business* (Basingstoke: Palgrave).

Boyns, T. and Edwards, J.R. (1996) Change agents and the dissemination of accounting technology: Wales' basic industries, c.1750–1870, *Accounting History*, 1 (1): 11–34.

Boyns, T. and Edwards, J.R. (2013) *A History of Management Accounting: The British Experience* (London and New York: Routledge).

Boyns, T., Edwards, J.R. and Nikitin, M. (1997) The development of industrial accounting in Britain and France before 1880: a comparative study of accounting literature and practice, *European Accounting Review*, 6 (3): 393–437.

Braudel, F. (2002) *The Mediterranean in the Ancient World* (Harmondsworth: Penguin).

Brown, R. (1968) *A History of Accounting and Accountants* (London: Frank Cass).

Bryer, R.A. (2000) The history of accounting and the transition to capitalism in England. Part one: theory, *Accounting, Organizations and Society*, 25 (2): 131–62.

Bryer, R.A. (2019) *Accounting for History in Marx's Capital: The Missing Link* (Lanham, MD: Lexington).

Campbell, J. (1986) *Essays in Anglo-Saxon History* (London: Hambledon Press).

Cato, M.P. (2004) *The Project Gutenberg eBook of Roman Farm Management, by Marcus Porcius Cato.* HTTP: <www.gutenberg.org/ebooks/12140>.

Chatfield, M. (1977) *A History of Accounting Thought* (Huntington, NY: Robert E. Krieger).

Chatfield, M. (1996a) Peele, James, in M. Chatfield and R. Vangermeersch (eds.) *The History of Accounting: An International Encyclopedia*, pp. 455–6 (New York: Garland).

Chatfield, M. (1996b) Ympyn, Jan, in M. Chatfield and R. Vangermeersch (eds.) *The History of Accounting: An International Encyclopedia*, p. 616 (New York: Garland).

Clackson, S.J. (ed.) (2008) *It Is Our Father Who Writes: Orders from the Monastery of Apollo at Bawit* (Cincinnati, OH: American Society of Papyrologists).

Clanchy, M.T. (1979) *From Memory to Written Record: England 1066–1307* (London: Edward Arnold).

Clough, S.B. and Cole, C.W. (1952) *Economic History of Europe* (Boston, MA: D.C. Heath).

Cohen, E.E. (2002) Introduction, in P. Cartledge, E.E. Cohen and L. Foxhall (eds.) *Money, Labour and Land: Approaches to the Economics of Ancient Greece*, pp. 1–7 (London: Routledge).

Coomber, R.R. (1956) Hugh Oldcastle and John Mellis, in A.C. Littleton and B.S. Yamey (eds.) *Studies in the History of Accounting*, pp. 206–14 (London: Sweet & Maxwell).

Coombs, H.M. and Edwards, J.R. (1993) The accountability of municipal corporations, *Abacus*, 29 (1): 26–52.

Coombs, H.M. and Edwards, J.R. (1994) Record keeping in municipal corporations: a triumph for double entry bookkeeping, *Accounting, Business & Financial History*, 4 (1): 163–80.

Coronella, S., Lombrano, A. and Zanin, L. (2013) State accounting innovations in pre-unification Italy, *Accounting History Review*, 23 (1): 1–21.

De Roover, R. (1956) The development of accounting prior to Luca Pacioli according to the account books of medieval merchants, in A.C. Littleton and B.S. Yamey (eds.) *Studies in the History of Accounting*, pp. 114–74 (London: Sweet & Maxwell).

De Roover, R. (1966) *The Rise and Decline of the Medici Bank* (New York: Norton Library).

De Ste. Croix, G.E.M. (1956) Greek and Roman accounting, in A.C. Littleton and B.S. Yamey (eds.) *Studies in the History of Accounting*, pp. 14–74 (London: Sweet & Maxwell).

Dean, G., Clarke, F. and Capalbo, F. (2016) Pacioli's double entry: part of an intellectual and social movement, *Accounting History Review*, 26 (1): 5–24.

Demirhan, D., Susmus, T. and Gonen, S. (2012) Cash waqfs and their accounting applications at the end of the 18th century in the Ottoman Empire, Paper presented at Twelfth World Congress of Accounting Historians, Newcastle upon Tyne.

Denholm-Young, N. (1963) *Seignorial Administration in England* (London: Frank Cass).

Dobie, A. (2008) The development of financial management and control in monastic houses and estates in England c.1200–1540, *Accounting, Business & Financial History*, 18 (2): 141–59.

Dobie, A. (2015) *Accounting at Durham Cathedral Priory: Management and Control of a Major Ecclesiastical Corporation, 1083–1539* (Basingstoke: Palgrave Macmillan).

Dobson, R.B. (1973) *Durham Priory 1400–1450* (Cambridge: Cambridge University Press).

Duby, G. (1976) *Rural Economy and Country Life in the Medieval West* (Columbia, SC: University of South Carolina Press).

Duncan-Jones, R. (1990) *Structure and Scale in the Roman Economy* (Cambridge: Cambridge University Press).

Edey, H.C. (1968) Company accounting in the nineteenth and twentieth centuries, in M. Chatfield (ed.) *Contemporary Studies in the Evolution of Accounting Thought*, pp. 135–43 (Belmont, CA: Dickinson).

Edey, H.C. and Panitpakdi, P. (1956) British company accounting and the law 1844–1900, in A.C. Littleton and B.S. Yamey (eds.) *Studies in the History of Accounting*, pp. 356–79 (London: Sweet & Maxwell).

Edwards, J.R. (1989) *A History of Financial Accounting* (London: Routledge).

Edwards, J.R. (1992) Companies, corporations and accounting change, 1835–1933: a comparative study, *Accounting and Business Research*, 23 (89): 59–73.

Edwards, J.R. (2011) Accounting education in Britain during the early modern period, *Accounting History Review*, 21 (1): 37–67.

Edwards, J.R. (2014) 'Different from what has hitherto appeared on this subject', John Clark, writing master and accomptant, 1738, *Abacus*, 50 (2): 227–44.

Edwards, J.R. (2015) The method of book-keeping, deduced from clear principles, *Accounting and Business Research*, 45 (2): 256–77.

Edwards, J.R. and Boyns, T. (1992) Industrial organization and accounting innovation: charcoal ironmaking in England 1690–1783, *Management Accounting Research*, 3 (2): 151–69.

Edwards, J.R. and Yamey, B.S. (eds.) (1994) From clay tokens to Fukushiki-Boki: record keeping over ten millennia, Special Issue of *Accounting, Business & Financial History*, 4 (1).

Ezzamel, M. and Hoskin, K. (2002) Retheorizing accounting, writing and money with evidence from Mesopotamia and Ancient Egypt, *Critical Perspectives on Accounting*, 13 (3): 333–67.

Finley, M.I. (1975) *The Ancient Greeks* (Harmondsworth: Penguin).

Finley, M.I. (1992) *The Ancient Economy* (Harmondsworth: Penguin).

Fitz Nigel, R. (1983) *Dialogus de Scaccario* (Oxford: Clarendon Press).

Fleischman, R.K. and Parker, L.D. (1991) British entrepreneurs and pre-industrial revolution evidence of cost management, *Accounting Review*, 66 (2): 361–75.

Forrester, D.A.R. (1994) Early canal company accounts: financial and accounting aspects of the Forth and Clyde Navigation, 1768–1816, in R.H. Parker and B.S. Yamey (eds.) *Accounting History: Some British Contributions*, pp. 297–326 (Oxford: Clarendon Press).

Fowler, J.T. (ed.) (1898–1900) *Extracts from the Account-Rolls of the Abbey of Durham, from the Original MSS*, 3 Vols (Durham: Surtees Society, 99, 100, 103).

Frankopan, P. (1988) *The Silk Roads: A New History of the World* (London: Bloomsbury).

French, E.A. (1985) *Unlimited Liability: The Case of the City of Glasgow Bank* (London: Certified Accountant Publications).

Frere, S. (1974) *Britannia: A History of Roman Britain* (London: Cardinal).

Funnell, W. (2001) Accounting for justice: entitlement, want and the Irish famine of 1845–7, *Accounting Historians Journal*, 28 (2): 187–206.

Galassi, G. (1996) Pacioli, Luca, in M. Chatfield and R. Vangermeersch (eds.) *The History of Accounting: An International Encyclopedia*, pp. 445–7 (New York: Garland).

Gao, S. and Handley-Schachler, M. (2010) The influences of Confucianism, Feng Shui and Buddhism in Chinese accounting history, *Accounting, Business & Financial History*, 13 (1): 41–68.

Geary, P.J. (1988) *Before France and Germany* (New York: Oxford University Press).

Geüsbeek, J.B. (1974) *Ancient Double-Entry Bookkeeping* (Houston, TX: Scholars Book).

Gleeson-White, J. (2012) *Double Entry: How the Merchants of Venice Created Modern Finance* (London: Norton).

Glynn, J.J. (1994) The development of British railway accounting 1800–1911, in R.H. Parker and B.S. Yamey (eds.) *Accounting History: Some British Contributions*, pp. 327–42 (Oxford: Clarendon Press).

Godfrey, A. and Hooper, K. (1996) Accountability and decision-making in feudal England: Domesday Book revisited, *Accounting History*, 1 (1): 35–54.

Goody, J. (2002) *The East in the West* (Cambridge: Cambridge University Press).

Graham, R. (1929) *English Ecclesiastical Studies* (London: SPCK).

Grant, M. (1969) *Julius Caesar* (London: Weidenfeld & Nicolson).

Gray, S.J. (1988) Towards a theory of cultural influence on the development of accounting systems internationally, *Abacus*, 24: 1–15.

Greatrex, J. (ed.) (1984) *Account Rolls of the Obedientiaries of Peterborough* (Wellingborough: Northamptonshire Record Society, 33).

Greene, K. (1990) *The Archaeology of the Roman Economy* (Berkeley, CA: University of California Press).

Güvemli, B. (2012) Industrialization and investment cost calculations in the Ottoman Empire in the mid-19th century, Paper presented at Twelfth World Congress of Accounting Historians, Newcastle upon Tyne.

Habakkuk, J. (1953) Economic functions of English landowners in the seventeenth and eighteenth centuries, *Explorations in Entrepreneurial History*, 6: 92–102.

Haldon, J.F. (2005) Economy and administration: how did the empire work? in M. Maas (ed.) *The Cambridge Companion to the Age of Justinian*, pp. 28–50 (Cambridge: Cambridge University Press).

Hall, H. (ed.) (1903) *The Pipe Roll of the Bishopric of Winchester for the Fourth Year of the Pontificate of Peter des Roches, 1208–1209* (London: King & Son).

Harvey, A. (1994) Land taxation and trade in the eleventh-century monastic economy: the case of evergetis, in M. Mullet and A. Kirby (eds.) *The Theotokos Evergetis and Eleventh-Century Monasticism*, pp. 124–36 (Belfast: Belfast Byzantine Enterprises).

Harvey, B. (2002) *The Obedientiaries of Westminster Abbey and Their Financial Records* (Woodbridge: Boydell Press).

Harvey, P.D.A. (1984) *Manorial Records*, British Record Association, Archives and the User, No. 5 (Gloucester: Alan Sutton).

Harvey, P.D.A. (1994) Manorial accounts, in R.H. Parker and B.S. Yamey (eds.) *Accounting History: Some British Contributions*, pp. 91–115 (Oxford: Clarendon Press).

Hatcher, J. (1993) *The History of the British Coal Industry, Vol. 1: Before 1700* (Oxford: Clarendon Press).

Hatfield, H.R. (1968) An historical defence of bookkeeping, in M. Chatfield (ed.) *Contemporary Studies in the Evolution of Accounting Thought*, pp. 1–11 (Belmont, CA: Dickinson).

Hernández-Esteve, E. (1994a) Comments on some obscure or ambiguous points of the treatise De Computis et Scripturis by Luca Pacioli, *Accounting Historians Journal*, 21 (1): 17–80.

Hernández-Esteve, E. (1994b) Luca Pacioli's treatise De Computis et Scripturis: a composite or a unified work? *Accounting, Business & Financial History*, 4 (1): 67–82.

Hockey, S.F. (ed.) (1975) *The Account-Book of Beaulieu Abbey* (London: Royal Historical Society).

Hopwood, A.G. (1987) The archaeology of accounting systems, *Accounting, Organizations and Society*, 12 (3): 207–34.

Hoskin, K.W., Ma, D. and Macve, R.H. (2016) Rational evolution or socially constructed counter-myth? cross-cultural perceptions of the development of Chinese commercial accounting up to c.1850 and its significance, LSE/Birmingham University working paper.

Hoskin, K.W. and Macve, R.H. (1986) Accounting and the examination: a genealogy of disciplinary power, *Accounting, Organizations and Society*, 11 (2): 105–36.
Howgego, C. (1992) The supply and use of money in the Roman world 200 B.C. to A.D. 300, *Journal of Roman Studies*, 82: 1–31.
Hunt, A.S. and Edgar, C.C. (1932) *Select Papyri: Private Documents* (Cambridge: Harvard University Press).
Hunt, A.S. and Edgar, C.C. (1934) *Select Papyri: Public Documents* (Cambridge: Harvard University Press).
Hunter, J. (ed.) (1844) *The Great Rolls of the Pipe for the Second, Third, and Fourth Years of the Reign of King Henry the Second, A.D. 1155, 1156, 1157, 1158* (London: Spottiswoode).
Inalcik, H. (1976) The rise of the Ottoman Empire, in M.A. Cook (ed.) *A History of the Ottoman Empire to 1730*, pp. 10–53 (Cambridge: Cambridge University Press).
Itzkowitz, N. (1980) *Ottoman Empire and Islamic Tradition* (Chicago, IL: University of Chicago Press).
Jack, S.M. (1966) An historical defence of single entry book-keeping, *Abacus*, 2 (2): 137–58.
Jackson, J.G.C. (1956) The history of methods of exposition of double-entry book-keeping in England, in A.C. Littleton and B.S. Yamey (eds.) *Studies in the History of Accounting*, pp. 206–14 (London: Sweet & Maxwell).
James, E. (1988) *The Franks* (Oxford: Basil Blackwell).
James, M.E. (1955) *Estate Accounts of the Earls of Northumberland 1562–1637* (Durham: Surtees Society, 163).
Jeacle, I. and Brown, T. (2006) The construction of the credible: epistolary transformations and the origins of the business letter, *Accounting, Business & Financial History*, 16 (1): 27–43.
Johnson, H.T. (1986) The organizational awakening in management accounting history, in M. Bromwich and A.G. Hopwood (eds.) *Research and Current Issues in Management Accounting*, pp. 67–77 (London: Pitman).
Jones, M.J. (2008) The role of change agents and imitation in the diffusion of an idea: charge and discharge accounting, *Accounting and Business Research*, 38 (5): 355–71.
Jones, M.J. and Oldroyd, D. (2015) The 'internationalisation' of accounting history publishing', *British Accounting Review*, 47 (2): 117–23.
Jones, P. (1997) *The Italian City-State: From Commune to Signoria* (Oxford: Clarendon Press).
Jones, R.H. (1994) Accounting in English local government from the Middle Ages to c.1835, in R.H. Parker and B.S. Yamey (eds.) *Accounting History: Some British Contributions*, pp. 377–406 (Oxford: Clarendon Press).
Jordan, R.H. and Morris, R. (eds.) (2012) *The Hypotyposis of the Monastery of the Theotokos Evergetis, Constantinople (11th–12th Centuries)* (Farnham: Ashgate).
Kaplan, M. (1994) The Evergetis *Hypotyposis* and the management of monastic estates in the eleventh century, in M. Mullet and A. Kirby (eds.) *The Theotokos Evergetis and Eleventh-Century Monasticism*, pp. 103–23 (Belfast: Belfast Byzantine Enterprises).
Kehoe, D. (1999) Tenancy and oasis agriculture on an Egyptian estate of the 4th c. A.D, *Journal of Roman Archaeology*, 12: 745–51.
King, P.W. (2010) Management, finance, and cost control in the Midlands charcoal iron industry, *Accounting, Business & Financial History*, 20 (3): 385–412.
Kirk, R.E.G. (ed.) (1892) *Accounts of the Obedientars of Abingdon Abbey* (Camden Society, New Series, 51).
Kitchin, G.W. (ed.) (1892) *Compotus Rolls of the Obedientiaries of St. Swithun's Priory, Winchester* (London: Simpkin).
Knowles, D. (1956) *The Religious Orders in England: Vol. I* (Cambridge: Cambridge University Press).
Kojima, O. (1995) *Accounting History* (Osaka: Offset).
Laiou, A.E. (2002). Political history: an outline, in A.E. Laiou (ed.) *The Economic History of Byzantium*, Vol. 1, pp. 9–28 (Washington, DC: Dumbarton Oaks).
Laiou, A.E. (2009) The Palaiologoi and the world around them (1261–1400), in I. Shepard (ed.) *The Cambridge History of the Byzantine Empire*, pp. 803–33 (Cambridge: Cambridge University Press).
Laiou, A.E. and Morrisson, C. (2010) *The Byzantine Economy* (Cambridge: Cambridge University Press).
Lall Nigam, B.M. (1986) Bahi-Khata: the pre-Pacioli Indian double-entry system of bookkeeping, *Abacus*, 22 (2): 148–61.
Lampe, M. and Sharp, P.R. (2017) A quest for useful knowledge: the early development of agricultural accounting in Denmark and Northern Germany, *Accounting History Review*, 27 (1): 73–99.
Latouche, R. (1967) *The Birth of Western Economy: Economic Aspects of the Dark Ages* (London: Methuen).

Lee, G.A. (1975) *Modern Financial Accounting* (London: Nelson).

Lee, G.A. (1977) The coming of age of double entry: the Giovanni Farolfi ledger of 1299–1300, *Accounting Historians Journal*, 4 (2): 79–95.

Lee, G.A. (1991) Colliery accounting in sixteenth-century England: the Willoughbys of Wollaton, Nottinghamshire, in O.F. Graves (ed.) *The Costing Heritage: Studies in Honor of S. Paul Garner*, pp. 50–73 (Harrisonburg,VA: Academy of Accounting Historians).

Lee, G.A. (1994) The oldest European account book: a Florentine bank ledger of 1211, in R.H. Parker and B.S. Yamey (eds.) *Accounting History: Some British Contributions*, pp. 116–38 (Oxford: Clarendon Press).

Lee, T.A. (1990) A systematic view of the history of the world of accounting, *Accounting, Business & Financial History*, 1 (1): 73–107.

Lee, T.A. (2006) The war of the sidewardly mobile corporate financial report, *Critical Perspectives on Accounting*, 17 (4): 419–55.

Lefort, J. (2002). The rural economy, seventh-twelfth centuries, in A.E. Laiou (ed.) *The Economic History of Byzantium*, Vol. 1, pp. 225–310 (Washington, DC: Dumbarton Oaks).

Lemarchand, Y. (1994) Double entry versus charge and discharge accounting in eighteenth-century France, *Accounting, Business & Financial History*, 4 (1): 119–45.

Lemarchand, Y. (2016) Revisiting the birth of industrial accounting in France, a return to the actors involved, *Accounting History Review*, 26 (3): 351–71.

Lewis, B. (1977) *The Arabs in History* (London: Hutchinson).

Lewis, B. (1978). Egypt and Syria, in P.M. Holt, A.K.S. Lambton and B. Lewis (eds.) *The Cambridge History of Islam*, Vol. 1A, pp. 175–230 (Cambridge: Cambridge University Press).

Lewis, B. (ed. and trans.) (1979) *Islam from the Prophet Muhammad to the Capture of Constantinople, Vol. 2: Religion and Society* (London: Macmillan).

Lin, Z.J. (1992) Chinese double-entry bookkeeping before the nineteenth century, *Accounting Historians Journal*, 19 (2): 103–22.

Lin, Z.J. (2003) Chinese bookkeeping systems: a study of accounting adaptation and change, *Accounting, Business & Financial History*, 13 (1): 83–98.

Littleton, A.C. (1933) *Accounting Evolution to 1900* (New York: American Institute Publishing).

Littleton, A.C. and Yamey, B.S. (eds) (1956) *Studies in the History of Accounting* (London: Sweet & Maxwell).

Lomas, R.A. and Piper, A.J. (eds) (1989) *Durham Cathedral Priory Rentals* (Durham: Surtees Society, 197).

Loyn, H.R. (1986) Progress in Anglo-Saxon monetary history, in M.A.S. Blackburn (ed.) *Anglo-Saxon Monetary History, Essays in Memory of Michael Dolley*, pp. 1–10 (Leicester: Leicester University Press).

Loyn, H.R. (1991) *Anglo-Saxon England and the Norman Conquest* (London: Longman).

Loyn, H.R. and Percival, J. (1975) *The Reign of Charlemagne: Documents on Carolingian Government and Administration* (London: Edward Arnold).

Lu, W. and Aiken, M. (2003) Accounting history: Chinese contributions and challenges, *Accounting, Business & Financial History*, 13 (1): 1–3.

Lu, W. and Aiken, M. (2004) Origins and evolution of Chinese writing systems and preliminary counting relationships, *Accounting History*, 9 (3): 25–51.

Macve, R.H. (1994) Some glosses on Greek and Roman accounting, in R.H. Parker and B.S. Yamey (eds.) *Accounting History: Some British Contributions*, pp. 57–87 (Oxford: Clarendon Press).

Macve, R.H. (1996) Pacioli's legacy, in T.A. Lee, R. Bishop and R.H. Parker (eds.) *Accounting History from the Renaissance to the Present*, pp. 3–30 (New York: Garland).

Macve, R.H. (2002) Insights to be gained from the study of ancient accounting history: some reflections on the new edition of Finley's The Ancient Economy, *European Accounting Review*, 11 (2): 453–71.

Martin, J. (1979) Estate stewards and their work in Glamorgan, 1660–1760: a regional study of estate management, *Morgannwg*, 23: 9–28.

Martindale, J. (1983) The kingdom of Aquitaine and the dissolution of the Carolingian fisc, *Francia*, 11: 131–91.

Mattessich, R. (2000) *The Beginnings of Accounting and Accounting Thought* (New York: Garland).

McDonald, J. (2005) Using William the Conqueror's accounting record to assess manorial efficiency, *Accounting History*, 10 (2): 125–45.

McKisack, M. (1971) *The Fourteenth Century* (Oxford: Clarendon Press).

Mepham, M.J. (1988) *Accounting in Eighteenth Century Scotland* (New York: Garland).

Miller, A.D. and Oldroyd, D. (2018) Does stewardship still have a role? *Accounting Historians Journal*, 45 (1): 69–82.

Miller, E. and Hatcher, J. (1980) *Medieval England: Rural Society and Economic Change 1086–1348* (London: Longman).

Miller, P. and Napier, C. (1993) Genealogies of calculation, *Accounting, Organizations and Society*, 18 (7/8): 631–47.

Mills, G.T. (1994) Early accounting in northern Italy: the role of commercial development and the printing press in the expansion of double-entry from Genoa, Florence and Venice, *Accounting Historians Journal*, 21 (1): 81–96.

Minaud, G. (2006) Accounting and maritime trade in ancient Rome, Paper presented at Eleventh World Congress of Accounting Historians, Nantes.

Mingay, G.E. (1967) The eighteenth century land steward, in E.L. Jones and G.E. Mingay (eds.) *Land, Labour and Population in the Industrial Revolution: Essays Presented to J. D. Chambers*, pp. 6–12 (London: Edward Arnold).

More, C. (1997) *The Industrial Age: Economy and Society in Britain 1750–1995* (Harlow: Pearson).

Morgan, K. (1999) *The Birth of Industrial Britain: Economic Change 1750–1850* (Harlow: Addison Wesley Longman).

Morrisson, C. and Sodini, J.P. (2002). The sixth-century economy, in A.E. Laiou (ed.) *The Economic History of Byzantium*, Vol. 1, pp. 171–220 (Washington, DC: Dumbarton Oaks).

Most, K. (1979) The accounts of ancient Rome, in E.N. Coffman (ed.) *Working Paper 3, Working Paper Series 1*, pp. 22–31 (Alabama: Academy of Accounting Historians).

Napier, C.J. (1991) Aristocratic accounting: the Bute estate in Glamorgan 1814–1880, *Accounting and Business Research*, 21 (82): 163–74.

Napier, C.J. (1997) The British aristocracy, capital and income, and nineteenth century company accounting, Paper presented at Fifth Interdisciplinary Perspectives on Accounting Conference, Manchester.

Napier, C.J. (2009) Defining Islamic accounting: current issues, past roots, *Accounting History*, 14 (1-2): 121–44.

Nobes, C.W. (1987) The pre-Pacioli Indian double-entry system of bookkeeping: a comment, *Abacus*, 23 (2): 182–4.

Nobes, C.W. (2001) Were Islamic records precursors to accounting books based on the Italian method? a comment, *Accounting Historians Journal*, 28 (2): 207–14.

Noke, C. (1981) Accounting for bailiffship in thirteenth century England, *Accounting and Business Research*, 11 (42): 137–51.

Oikonomides, N. (2002). The role of the Byzantine state in the economy, in A.E. Laiou (ed.) *The Economic History of Byzantium*, Vol. 3, pp. 973–1058 (Washington, DC: Dumbarton Oaks).

Oldroyd, D. (1995) The role of accounting in public expenditure and monetary policy in the first century AD Roman Empire, *Accounting Historians Journal*, 22 (2): 117–29.

Oldroyd, D. (1997) Accounting in Anglo-Saxon England: context and evidence, *Accounting History*, 2 (1): 7–23.

Oldroyd, D. (1998) John Johnson's letters: the accounting role of Tudor merchants' correspondence, *Accounting Historians Journal*, 25 (1): 57–72.

Oldroyd, D. (2007) *Estates, Enterprise and Investment at the Dawn of the Industrial Revolution: Estate Management and Accounting in the North-East of England c.1700–1780* (Aldershot: Ashgate).

Orelli, R.L., del Sordo, C. and Fornasari, M.A. (2013) Credit and accounting in early modern Italy: the case of the Monte di Pietà in Bologna, *Accounting History Review*, 23 (3): 273–93.

Oschinsky, D. (1971) *Walter of Henley and Other Treatises on Estate Management and Accounting* (Oxford: Clarendon Press).

Page, M. (ed.) (1996) *The Pipe Roll of the Bishopric of Winchester 1301–2* (Winchester: Hampshire County Council).

Page, M. (ed.) (1999) *The Pipe Roll of the Bishopric of Winchester 1409–10* (Winchester: Hampshire County Council).

Page, M. (2002) *The Medieval Bishops of Winchester: Estate, Archive and Administration* (Hampshire Record Office, Hampshire Papers, 24).

Parker, R.H. (1990) Regulating British corporate financial reporting in the late nineteenth century, *Accounting, Business & Financial History*, 1 (1): 51–71.

Parker, R.H. and Yamey, B.S. (eds.) (1994) *Accounting History. Some British Contributions* (Oxford: Clarendon Press).

Peng, L. and Brown, A. (2015) The milieu of accountability of early companies in the Qing dynasty: evidence from the Shanghai-based print media, *Accounting History Review*, 25 (1): 1–26.

Pollard, S. (1965) *The Genesis of Modern Management* (London: Edward Arnold).

Poole, A.L. (1970) *From Domesday Book to Magna Carta* (Oxford: Clarendon Press).

Postles, D. (1994) The perception of profit before the leasing of demesnes, in R.H. Parker and B. S. Yamey (eds.) *Accounting History: Some British Contributions*, pp. 116–38 (Oxford: Clarendon Press).

Procopius. (1916) *History of the Wars*, 5 Vols translated by H.B. Dewing (Cambridge: Harvard University Press).

Puyou, F. and Quattrone, P. (2018) The visual and material dimensions of legitimacy: accounting and the search for socie-ties, *Organization Studies*, 39 (5/6): 721–46.

Ramsey, G.D. (1956) Some Tudor merchant accounts, in A.C. Littleton and B.S. Yamey (eds.) *Studies in the History of Accounting*, pp. 185–201 (London: Sweet & Maxwell).

Rathbone, D. (1994) Accounting on a large estate in Roman Egypt, in R.H. Parker and B.S. Yamey (eds.) *Accounting History: Some British Contributions*, pp. 13–56 (Oxford: Clarendon Press).

Reynolds, L.D. (ed.) (1983) *Texts and Transmission: A Survey of the Latin Classics* (Oxford: Clarendon Press).

Richardson, H.G. (1941) Business training in medieval Oxford, *American Historical Review*, 46 (2): 259–80.

Robertson, J. and Funnell, W. (2014) *Accounting by the First Public Company: The Pursuit of Supremacy* (London and New York: Routledge).

Rodrigues, L. and Sangster, A. (2013) The role of the state in the development of accounting in the Portuguese-Brazilian Empire, 1750–1822, *Accounting History Review*, 23 (2): 161–85.

Russell, J.C. (1972) Population in Europe 500–1500, in C.M. Cipolla (ed.) *The Fontana Economic History of Europe: The Middle Ages*, pp. 25–70 (Glasgow: Collins).

Salter, H. (1922) The death of Henry of Blois, Bishop of Winchester, *English Historical Review*, 37: 79–80.

Sangster, A. (2018) Pacioli's lens: god, humanism, Euclid, and the rhetoric of double entry, *Accounting Review*, 93 (2): 299–314.

Sangster, A., Stoner, G.N. and McCarthy, P. (2011) In defense of Pacioli, *Accounting Historians Journal*, 38 (2): 105–24.

Saunders, H.W. (1930) *An Introduction to the Obedientiary and Manor Rolls of Norwich Cathedral Priory* (Norwich: Jarrold).

Saunders, J.J. (1980) *A History of Medieval Islam* (London: Routledge).

Scorgie, M.E. (1994) Accounting fragments stored in the Old Cairo Genizah, *Accounting, Business & Financial History*, 4 (1): 29–42.

Sensoy, F. and Güvemli, O. (2015) The state accounting doctrine book of the Middle East in the 14th century: Risale-i Felekiyye and its place in accounting culture, *British Accounting Review*, 47 (2): 159–76.

Sijpesteijn, P. and Clackson, S. (2009) A mid-eighth-century trilingual tax demand related to the monastery of Apa Apollo at Bawir, in A. Boud'hors, J. Clackson and C. Louis (eds.) *Monastic Estates in Late Antique and Early Islamic Egypt*, pp. 102–23 (Cincinnati, OH: American Society of Papyrologists).

Smith, R.A.L. (1943) *Canterbury Cathedral Priory: A Study in Monastic Administration* (Cambridge: Cambridge University Press).

Soll, J. (2014) *The Reckoning: Financial Accountability and the Making and Breaking of Nations* (London: Allen Lane).

Sourdel, D. (1977). The Abbasid caliphate, in P.M. Holt, A.K.S. Lambton and B. Lewis (eds.) *The Cambridge History of Islam*, Vol. 1a, pp. 104–39 (Cambridge: Cambridge University Press).

Spring, D. (1963) *The English Landed Estate in the Nineteenth Century: Its Administration* (Baltimore, MD: Johns Hopkins Press).

Stenton, F. (1971) *Anglo-Saxon England* (Oxford: Oxford University Press).

Stone, E. (1962) Profit-and-loss accountancy at Norwich Cathedral Priory, *Transactions of the Royal Historical Society*, Fifth Series, 12: 25–48.

Swain, S. (2016) *Economy, Family and Society from Rome to Islam: A Critical Edition, English Translation, and Study of Bryson's Management of the Estate* (Cambridge: Cambridge University Press).

Taylor, R.E. (1956) Luca Pacioli, in A.C. Littleton and B.S. Yamey (eds.) *Studies in the History of Accounting*, pp. 175–84 (London: Sweet & Maxwell).

Thomas, J.P. (1994) Documentary evidence from the Byzantine monastic *Typika* for the history of the Evergentine reform movement, in M. Mullet and A. Kirby (eds.) *The Theotokos Evergetis and Eleventh-Century Monasticism*, pp. 246–73 (Belfast: Belfast Byzantine Enterprises).

Thompson, G. (1991) Is accounting rhetorical? methodology, Luca Pacioli and printing, *Accounting, Organizations and Society*, 16 (5/6): 572–99.

Toraman, C., Ata, A. and Akdemir, Y. (2012) The state accounting organization, accounting practices and reform of mid-17th century in the Ottoman Empire, Paper presented at Twelfth World Congress of Accounting Historians, Newcastle upon Tyne.

Treadgold, W. (1997) *A History of the Byzantine State and Society* (Stanford, CA: Stanford University Press).

Trevor-Roper, H. (1965) *The Rise of Christian Europe* (London: Thames & Hudson).

Turan, O. (1978). Anatolia in the period of the Seljuks and the Beyliks, in P.M. Holt, A.K.S. Lambton and B. Lewis (eds.) *The Cambridge History of Islam*, Vol. 1A, pp. 231–62 (Cambridge: Cambridge University Press).

Vaglieri, L.V. (1978). The patriarchal and ummayad caliphates, in P.M. Holt, A.K.S. Lambton and B. Lewis (eds.) *The Cambridge History of Islam*, Vol. 1A, pp. 57–103 (Cambridge: Cambridge University Press).

von Grunebaum, G.E. (1953) *Medieval Islam* (Chicago, IL: University of Chicago Press).

Walker, S.P. (1998) How to secure your husband's esteem: accounting and private patriarchy in the British middle class household during the nineteenth century, *Accounting, Organizations and Society*, 23 (5/6): 485–514.

Wallace-Hadrill, J.M. (1983) *The Frankish Church* (Oxford: Clarendon Press).

Watt, W.M. (1978) Muhammad, in P.M. Holt, A.K.S. Lambton and B. Lewis (eds.) *The Cambridge History of Islam*, Vol. 1A, pp. 30–56 (Cambridge: Cambridge University Press).

Wickham, C. (2005) *Framing the Early Middle Ages: Europe and the Mediterranean 400-800* (Oxford: Oxford University Press).

Winchester, B. (1955) *Tudor Family Portrait* (London: Jonathan Cape).

Woolgar, C.M. (ed.) (1992–93) *Household Accounts from Medieval England* (British Academy, Oxford: Records of Social and Economic History, New Series, 17–18).

Yamey, B.S. (1956) Introduction, in A.C. Littleton and B.S. Yamey (eds.) *Studies in the History of Accounting*, pp. 1–13 (London: Sweet & Maxwell).

Yamey, B.S. (1962) Some topics in the history of financial accounting in England 1500–1900, in W.T. Baxter and S. Davidson (eds.) *Studies in Accounting Theory*, pp. 11–34 (London: Sweet & Maxwell).

Yamey, B.S. (1979) Oldcastle, Peele and Mellis: a case of plagiarism in the sixteenth century, *Accounting and Business Research*, 9 (35): 209–16.

Yamey, B.S. (1981) Some reflections on the writing of a general history of accounting, *Accounting and Business Research*, 11 (42): 127–35.

Yamey, B.S. (1994a) Benedetto Cotrugli on bookkeeping (1458), *Accounting, Business & Financial History*, 4 (1): 43–50.

Yamey, B.S. (1994b) *Luca Pacioli: Exposition of Double Entry Bookkeeping*, English translation by Antonia von Gebsattel with introduction and commentary by Basil Yamey (Venice: Albrizzi Editore).

Yamey, B.S., Edey, H.C. and Thomson, H.W. (1963) *Accounting in England and Scotland: 1543–1800, Double Entry in Exposition and Practice* (London: Sweet & Maxwell).

Yuan, W. and Macve, R.H. (2017) The development of Chinese accounting and bookkeeping before 1850: insights from the Tŏng Tài Shēng business account books (1798–1850), *Accounting and Business Research*, 47 (4): 401–30.

Zaid, O.A. (2000) Were Islamic records precursors to accounting books based on the Italian method? *Accounting Historians Journal*, 27 (1): 73–90.

Zaid, O.A. (2001) Were Islamic records precursors to accounting books based on the Italian method? a response, *Accounting Historians Journal*, 28 (2): 215–18.

Zaid, O.A. (2004) Accounting systems and recording procedures in the early Islamic state, *Accounting Historians Journal*, 31 (2): 149–70.

6

MECHANISATION, COMPUTERISATION AND INFORMATION SYSTEMS

Greg Stoner, Charles W. Wootton and Barbara E. Kemmerer

Overview

This chapter examines the effects of technical innovations in record keeping on accounting and the nature of accounting work. There is no clear-cut periodisation of the changes in technologies but, for convenience, changes are dealt with in four overlapping eras. The first era covers the period of increasing mechanical-aided record keeping from the mid-nineteenth century until about 1930. The second period looks at the changes from the Second World War until the early 1970s arising from the early introduction of digital computing into the business sphere. The last three decades of the century, when computing became established as the prime mode of business record keeping and the personal computer (PC) revolution took place, represents the third era. This epoch blends into the final era when the combination of the Internet and highly integrated systems changes the nature of business operations as well as the record keeping of which accounting is a part.

One of the reasons for a lack of clear periodisation is that not all businesses, or all accounting practices, changed at the same rate or in the same ways. There were clear sectorial differences in all periods, in several dimensions, as well as geographical differences in part influenced by levels of economic development. In this context, the periods discussed are mainly from the developed Anglo-Saxon and European perspective. Additionally, various degrees of delay and inertia operated with the result that, even in the later, more technically advanced periods, some organisations continued to use systems from earlier eras though possibly for good (economic) reasons. Indeed it is likely that even today there are small organisations using little technology, and some not keeping accounting records at all.

The chronological study of accounting technologies is then shown to be central to the transformation of the ways in which accounting and accountants operated. Beyond these first order changes, the technological changes have, partly through lowered processing costs and increased process and communication speeds, facilitated growth in the scale of business operations and led to more information for decision making and control. It is clear that the technical changes discussed in this chapter have created opportunities and threats for accounting firms and for accountants, both within public practice and the commercial or public sectors. Some of these changes are explored, including the effects of a lack of 'paper trail' on the audit process, the opportunities for accounting firms to broaden their scope of business consultancy, the deskilling and feminisation of bookkeeping, and threats from new technologies.

The chapter concludes with a review and reflections on the further development of information systems in accounting and their impact.

Introduction

> The scope of AIS [Accounting Information Systems] has expanded throughout history with the role of accountants, and as a consequence technological development has shaped how accountants perform their work.
>
> *(Rosati and Paulsson 2018: 13)*

This chapter is concerned with that history, and in particular of accounting and the mechanical and computing technologies that have shaped it, in effect, over the last two centuries. The changing nature of what is seen as accounting makes any tracing of its history problematic and, as modelled by Mauldin and Ruchala (1999), it is important, in the context of what accounting has become, to consider a range of cognitive and organisational issues as well as the technical to have a sound perspective on that history. In the related field of general information systems research Hassan (2018: 17) notes that:

> IS historical studies require a balance that combines social organizational concerns with technological concerns, and ideally addresses questions about some major historical event.

Reflecting the content of the existing literature, the focus of this chapter is principally on technical change although some broader, organisational and social concerns will be addressed.

The mechanical accounting era

The background to mechanical accounting

Until the late nineteenth century, accounting was a manual process. Generally, at least in the West, transactions were entered by hand into large bound journals or day books and then posted by hand to bound ledgers. As the closing process could be time-consuming not all businesses closed their accounts or produced financial statements on an annual basis. As Yates (1985: 144) points out, owners were usually involved in their companies' day-to-day operations and had direct knowledge of their financial conditions.

With the emergence of new, large and geographically diverse corporations with management more separated from ownership, the demand for information accelerated. Chandler notes (1977: 19) that, for these large companies to succeed, an increased flow of information to both managers and owners was necessary. As this demand increased, the first major innovations in information processing also occurred (Yates 1991).

The first mechanical devices

De Wit et al. (2002: 69–70) point out that machines are often introduced with one purpose in mind, but their functions normally expand. This was the case with the typewriter which, invented to aid the writing process (e.g. E. Remington & Sons typewriter in 1873, Bliven 1954: 42–56), became the predecessor of the bookkeeping machine as businesses found it useful in preparing invoices and reports, especially if they used pre-printed forms containing standard information (Yates 1991: 122). To aid this process businesses standardised reporting and document preparation practices and, with this greater uniformity, the analysis of information became easier (Yates 1994: 32). With typewriters, prepared forms, carbon paper and standardised reporting, the cost of information processing noticeably dropped (Page 1906).

In 1891, with the introduction of the 'book-typewriter', a typewriter modified to accept bound books and generate multiple carbon copies, an accountant could enter a transaction directly in a bound journal or ledger and create multiple copies of invoices (Moore 1932: 57).

One of the first successful commercially used calculators in Europe was the Thomas Arithmometer, developed in France in the 1820s and generally available from the 1850s. So successful was the Arithmometer, along with other European designed machines (e.g. the Odhner in 1873 and the Brunsviga in 1892), that they were used (with improvements) for nearly a century (Cortada 1993: 27–8). However, in the USA, the Thomas Arithmometer was little adopted early on, and most computations continued to be performed manually until the turn of the nineteenth century.

In the late 1880s, Dorr Eugene Felt developed a key-driven calculating machine called the 'Comptometer' (Turck 1921: 75) which could add, subtract, multiply and divide. During the same period, William S. Burroughs introduced a recording/adding machine that provided a record of transactions. These machines had an immediate effect on accounting. Addition was such a major part of accounting that George Seward (1904: 607), writing in the *Engineering Magazine*, estimated that 95 per cent of accounting work in a factory could be attributed to that task. Given the increased speed and accuracy with which accounts could be totalled using these machines, preparation of trial balances became more common and the determination of unit costs, and data analysis generally, became a simpler process. Whereas, previously, many companies did not analyse financial/managerial data because of the time involved, this drawback no longer applied (Galloway 1919: 83).

The introduction of the Arithmometer and the Comptometer relegated many office practices to routine operations. Until the late nineteenth century office clerks were often considered the 'predecessors of modern middle management' (Cooper and Taylor 2000: 561), with the collection and computation functions related to financial data handled by an accountant/bookkeeper considered skilled tasks. As the processing of information became more routine, repetitive and mechanised, the tasks and the people performing the task became 'deskilled', and with deskilling came lower wages (Cooper and Taylor 2000: 556–8). As the cost of processing information fell dramatically it became more cost effective to meet the demand for more information, and companies began to hire women for these roles as they were paid substantially less than the men they replaced.

More early innovations in information processing

From bound volumes to loose leaf

As the size of companies increased and the number of transactions multiplied, the deficiencies of bound books became more apparent, and towards the end of the nineteenth century these were gradually replaced by loose leaf accounting systems. Early versions include those developed by the Baker-Vawter Company in the USA in 1896, and at about the same time by Andreas Tengwall in Sweden, which was distributed by the Krag Manufacturing Company in the USA (Wootton and Wolk 2000: 87–9).

Some businesses and accountants were reluctant to adopt loose leaf systems and in some countries bound volumes were required by regulation (see Chapter 5). Security of records was a major concern. In publications such as *The Accountant*, articles and letters were published on the merits and weaknesses of loose leaf systems. A common criticism was that, since pages could be easily removed from the volume, it would encourage dishonesty which in turn would be harder to detect. Those in favour of change, by way of contrast, cited the new systems' greater flexibility and efficiency (Dicksee 1911: 652–7). This debate, and how to overcome the systems' weaknesses (Aspray 1917: 311–13), continued into the early 1920s. One feature of the system that received considerable attention in *The Accountant* was the use of slips for postings (Price 1902: 9–18); instead of posting the ledger from the journal, the preparation of the slip (sales invoice, bank deposit slip) served as the original entry from which the ledger was posted (Leading article 1902: 1069–72). Over time, the systems' advantages slowly began to be recognised. For example, the Post Office Savings Bank in Britain evaluated the loose leaf system in 1908–10 but rejected it because of security concerns. Not until 1925 did it finally adopt a card-based ledger (Campbell-Kelly 1998: 23–9).

Tabulating, billing and duplex adding machines

During the early twentieth century another major mechanical innovation gained ground – the tabulating machine. The tabulator was the computation element of a three-part tabulating system – the others being the card punch machine and the card sorter. In companies where vast amounts of data were processed, the tabulator quickly found acceptance. Railroads recognised its utility for freight accounting, for example the New York Central processed more than four million waybills using a Hollerith tabulator in 1897 (Norberg 1990: 762). Railroads also discovered that they could replace an expensive accountant with a clerk or bookkeeper to handle data entry. Recognising the economic value of tabulators to their users, manufacturers normally refused to sell the machines but would instead lease them, guaranteeing continuous cash inflow.

Another useful innovation was the billing machine which combined typewriter and adding machine, allowing a bookkeeping clerk to prepare an invoice and post the transaction to the ledger at the same time. It was claimed that the Elliott-Fischer billing machine, at $325, was cost effective given that a billing machine operated by a single clerk could often replace two accountants.

The 'duplex' adder was another innovative aid to the accounting process. These had two adding wheels and could transfer amounts between the wheels, allowing them to perform two operations at once. For example, they could record both cost and retail price at the same time and keep track of the payroll of individual departments while determining the total payroll. The Burroughs Company offered a duplex, from 1910, that could record employees' earnings on individual payroll envelopes while it recorded the payroll sheet (Lewis 1914: 179–88).

Growing acceptance of mechanical accounting

As the capabilities of bookkeeping machines rose, their use gained growing acceptance in Europe as well as in the USA. Early on tabulator usage was restricted to a few large insurance companies and railroads. By 1920, the market for tabulating machines was international and users included large manufacturers and retail firms. In the USA companies including Marshall Field and Eastman-Kodak used tabulators in cost and sales analysis and inventory control (Strom 1992: 181–2) and the textile industry became a leader in the use of the tabulators in payroll, stock control, dispatching and standard costing (Norberg 1990: 772–3).

In Europe, the tabulator also found widespread application. Rotterdamsche Bankvereeniging (Robaver Bank) installed a Hollerith system to handle its giro department (de Wit and van den Ende 2000: 97). By 1923 the Prudential Assurance Company (UK) had in operation a Powers Tabulating System including 35 tabulators, 24 sorters and 100 card punches (Campbell-Kelly 1992: 131). Prudential also acquired the British rights to manufacture and distribute the Powers machine throughout the British Empire. At one time, its punch card machine held nearly 50 per cent of the British market (ibid.). Also both Société Générale and Banque Générale du Nord achieved significant cost efficiencies by utilising bookkeeping and calculating machines (Bonin 2004: 266–7). This mechanisation of bank accounting reduced jobs and costs and led to increased centralisation of record processing activities (ibid.: 269).

From the 1920s the cost of business machines fell. For example, the Victor Adding Machine Company introduced a machine costing half the price of comparable machines (Darby 1968: 29) and, in competition with the widely used Comptometer, companies began to market electric calculators such as the Monroe Calculating Machine Company's Model K electric calculators (Martin 1925: 250–1). With lower costs, most large businesses and many small ones employed some form of mechanical accounting to record information and to reduce the manual aspects of accounting by 1930.

Mechanisation changed the nature of the tasks required of a bookkeeper, which came to be perceived as more repetitive and menial and less managerial. The resultant feminisation of the workforce increased and was further relegated to the status of bookkeeping as a technical trade while accounting was evolving into a profession (see Chapter 11). This transition was encouraged by the ability to pay women lower wages and by a shortage of white middle-class males. From comprising only 1 per cent of the bookkeeping workforce in the USA in 1870, women accounted for 63 per cent of the bookkeeping workforce by 1930. The established professions, at this time, remained male dominated (Perks 1993: 11). In contrast to bookkeeping, in 1930 only 9 per cent of accountants were women, and this percentage did not notably change until the early 1960s (Wootton and Kemmerer 2000: 172).[1]

The general acceptance of mechanical accounting that had occurred by the Second World War was not without controversy. In 1949, a report was issued by the Mechanised Accounting Sub-Committee of the Taxation and Financial Relations Committee of the Institute of Chartered Accountants in England and Wales. The report stated that, while mechanised accounting seemed to be nothing more than a change in the way information was processed, in reality mechanisation sometimes resulted in the loss of documentation without a 'compensating' increase in the information required for an audit (ICAEW 1949: 14). The Report also emphasised that the company and the auditor should work together at all stages of mechanisation – from the selection of machines to the determination of records to be mechanised. The Report set out steps that a company might take to make the examination of mechanised records easier and it reminded the auditor to exploit the potential of mechanisation as an aid to the audit process.

Transition from mechanical to computerised accounting

The first computers and transition of accounting processes

For nearly 30 years following the general acceptance of mechanical accounting in the early decades of the twentieth century, few radical innovations occurred in processing accounting information. Computers and the increasing scale of businesses were the next catalyst of change. Charles Babbage is considered the inventor of the (analogue) computer in the early nineteenth century. Alan Turing invented the principle of the modern electronic computer in 1936, but his design was not developed until after 1945 (Copeland 2017). The Second World War acted as a catalyst to the development of the first fully functioning electronic digital computer, COLOSSUS, by British Intelligence: a huge 'main-frame' computer which came into operation in December 1943 (Shurkin 1984: 140–3). Similarly, in the USA, there was a push to develop a machine that could process vast amounts of mathematical information resulting in the creation of ENIAC.

The effects of computers on accounting was to become significant, but was far from instantaneous or universal. For a further two decades mechanical and computerised systems were being developed and used. Further, in sharp contrast to early predictions that around ten large computers would satisfy the USA's entire business needs (Sanders 1968: 28), the need to efficiently process financial information became a catalyst in the expansion of the computer's use. By the mid-1960s, studies found that nearly 50 per cent of a computer's time was used to process accounting-related information (Li 1968: 12). As computerisation became more universal, use of mechanical systems began to decline.

Early years of business computerisation

> J Lyons & Co were amongst the world's leaders in office management systems … As they grew rapidly in size in the early part of [the 20th] century … they had to deal on the accounting side with an enormous number of very small individual transactions.
>
> *(Hendry 1987: 74)*

In 1947, Lyons – in particular John Simmons – recognised the potential of electronic machines to process business data and, in conjunction with a team from the University of Cambridge, worked on developing a computer that could handle accounting tasks (Hendry 1987: 75; Ferry 2003: 34–70). The computer, LEO, which stood for Lyons electronic office, was commissioned in 1953 and was soon processing payrolls for a range of companies including the Ford Motor Company (Ferry 2003: 111, 149). Two years later LEO became 'the heart of [Lyon's] ordering and distribution system' (ibid.: 129) and was so successful that Lyons set up a separate company (Leo Computers Ltd) to exploit its commercial potential. LEO and its successors were recognised as 'ground-breaking' machines (ibid.: 166). However, its development and marketing required vast amounts of capital at a time when teashops were in decline. In 1963, Leo Computers merged with English Electric. Although LEO III was comparable (maybe superior) to the IBM System 360, the introduction of the 360 and IBM's vast resources hastened the demise of LEO, which ceased production in 1967 (ibid.: 184–95). Despite justification of the use of LEO to save clerk labour, Haddy (1958: 164) notes that Lyons employed more staff after installation than before, as the 'amount of work done has greatly increased'.

The General Electric Company purchased a Universal Automatic Computer (UNIVAC) to process business information at its Appliance Division just three years after Remington Rand's first UNIVAC Computer was used at the US Bureau of the Census in 1951 (Li 1968: 5). Arthur Andersen & Co. had recommended the UNIVAC to General Electric as part of an accounting system it was installing (Spacek 1989: 176–7), an early example of the involvement of an accounting practice in computer consultancy, and a key element in their practice development (ibid.: 197). However, at this time, the computer's future in accounting did not seem particularly bright: according to Spacek, Learson (head of sales at IBM) stated that 'there was no future in the accounting field for computers' shortly after the GE installation (ibid.: 136–7).

In 1953, a significant breakthrough occurred when IBM introduced its 650 Magnetic Drum Data Processing Machine. Included in the accounting functions were payroll processing, actuarial computations, customer billing and branch store accounting (650 applications n.d.). The first IBM 650 was installed in the controller's department of the John Hancock Life Insurance Company in Boston (650 chronology n.d.), and nearly 2,000 were retailed by 1962 (IBM 650 n.d.). In 1957 the IBM 650 was first used in Europe, led by the Dutch Land Cultivation Company's purchase (de Wit et al. 2002: 65).

In 1956, IBM announced its 305 RAMAC and 650 RAMAC (Random Access Method of Accounting and Control) computers, claiming they would revolutionise office procedures. More specifically, given their random access memory (RAM), accounting could be a 'continuous' process with data entered and retrieved nearly instantaneously. The RAMAC remote feature allowed accountants in other offices to check sales figures and determine the level of current inventories (650 RAMAC announcement n.d.).

In Germany, for example, computers were also finding greater use in accounting. Heinz Nixdorf founded the Heinz Nixdorf Company and, by the mid-1960s, had sold 5,000 small computers specially designed to perform daily accounting functions. The company's success in Germany encouraged the Victor Comptometer Corporation to sign a marketing agreement which allowed it to sell (under the Victor name) the computer in the USA and Canada. An advantage enjoyed by the Victor Comptometer Corporation was that its computers were priced significantly lower than the larger IBM mainframes (Darby 1968: 217–19).

Hybrid accounting technologies in the decline of mechanical accounting systems

In 1962 IBM introduced the hybrid electronic/mechanical 6400 Magnetic Ledger Accounting Machine. Through the use of magnetic tape enhanced cards, the 6400 combined electronic storage with visible text and could handle billings, inventory, accounts receivables, payroll and general accounting (New: the IBM alpha-numeric magnetic ledger card 1963: 5). Both Friden's 6010 (Friden 6010 electronic computer 1963: 14) and General Electric's GE-225 (Computer progress at General Electric 1963: 26) had similar features. However, their cost was significant at $4,000 to $10,000 per month (Announcing the GE-215 1963: 10–11).

Also in 1962, the Bank of America implemented its ERMA (Electronic Recording Machine Accounting) system. This was a historic attempt to change the ways cheques were processed, recorded and chequing accounts updated. Instead of the customer's name, as had been used for a century, the system used a magnetic ink character recognition (MICR) account number printed on the cheques to facilitate their sorting and processing. The MICR system soon became a standard in the banking sector both in the USA and elsewhere. By 1962, ERMA was handling more than 2.3 million of the Bank of America's cheque accounts, resulting in the elimination of 2,332 jobs for proof and transit operators and bookkeepers (McKenney et al. 1997: 332–5). MICR cheque systems have evolved and are still in use, but other elements of the mechanical accounting systems soon became uneconomic compared to the emerging computer-based systems.

Widespread electronic data processing and computerised accounting

Electronic data processing (EDP) and the computerised accounting systems

This section covers the last three decades of the twentieth century, the period during which the use of computers became almost ubiquitous in the processing of transaction data and in the maintenance of accounting records. By the early 1970s, the cost of a computer had dropped significantly. For example an IBM System/3 minicomputer could be rented for around $1,000 a month (Ceruzzi 1998: 158), although many organisations were still using mainframe computers for EDP purposes during this period.

In the three years following its launch in 1983, IBM sold 100,000 System/36 minicomputers (IBM System/36 n.d.). These and other 'mini' computers became an ideal substitute for expensive mainframe computers for smaller businesses. The variety of systems in use varied substantially. Many organisations used bespoke or adapted systems, although standardised/packaged systems were more prevalent towards the end of the period (Hirschheim and Klein 2011).

The advantages of computers lay in areas involved with the processing of large volumes of data. In accounting, therefore, sales, purchasing and/or payroll systems, depending on the nature of the business, along with their associated payments and receipts transactions, were most commonly computerised, at least in the initial phase. The use of general (nominal) ledger-based EDP systems also became more prevalent, although in many cases these were largely separate from the operational/transaction and report generation systems (Rosati and Paulsson 2018).

Personal computers, lower costs and new software

Personal computers began to be available in the mid-1970s and became a major influence on business computing and accounting at the start of the 1980s. IBM entered the market with the IBM 5100 Portable Computer range which, though barely 'portable', were at least movable (IBM 5100 portable computer n.d.). IBM marketed towards business and accounting uses, with the inclusion of application software encompassing billing, inventory control, accounts receivables, sales analysis (IBM 5110 n.d.) and, later, payroll and general ledger accounting (IBM 5120 applications n.d.; IBM 5120 c.1980).

However, the most successful family of micro-systems in the late 1970s were CP/M operating system-based PCs of many makes (Bresnahan and Greenstein 1999). The CP/M Osborne 1 of 1981 is also widely credited as the first really portable, or at least 'luggable', PC. It was in use at Peat, Marwick, Mitchell & Co. (now KMPG) in London in c.1982.[2] Apple systems eventually ranked second towards the end of the period (ibid.: 13). It was in these environments that the spreadsheet revolution that has had such a major effect on accounting ever since, took place: Visicalc on Apples in 1979 and Supercalc on CP/M in 1980 (Mattessich and Galassi 2000).

IBM introduced their PC in 1981, with a US price of around $1,600, making the computer attractive to smaller businesses (The IBM PC's debut n.d.). The PC (IBM and compatible computers) was to become the dominant PC platform in business use for several decades, fuelled in many respects by the availability of spreadsheet software. Supercalc running under DOS (Disk Operating System) in 1982 was an immediate success, with more than 100,000 copies sold in the first year. Three years later, the more powerful and faster spreadsheet, Lotus 1–2–3, package was introduced. Costing just $495, more than 800,000 copies were sold in 18 months (Campbell-Kelly and Aspray 2004: 134). Lotus dominated the spreadsheet market into the early 1990s. However, ultimately Microsoft's Excel (which had started on the Mac platform) took control of that market (Campbell-Kelly 2001: 131), helped by the move of PCs from DOS to Windows.

The availability of a spreadsheet package made the emerging PC more attractive to users, especially accountants, as their relatively low operating costs enabled then to break away from the control of corporate information technology (IT) departments.

By the late 1980s the computer had secured its place in processing accounting information, PCs were in widespread use across organisations utilising accounting data (sometimes accessing central systems data) in decision support systems of various types, and the spreadsheet and PC had become the ubiquitous tool of the accountant.

Systems integration: the beginnings

In the mid/late 1990s, the integration of separate operational and accounting cycle systems and also between PC and central systems became more common (Rosati and Paulsson 2018), developing the notion of more complete AIS. Also integrated production-focused MRP (Manufacturing Resource Planning) systems, which had their roots in the database developments of the late 1960s and 1970s, became more important, more visible and more closely aligned with accounting functions (Jacobs and Weston 2007). These innovations combined with the PC revolution set the scene for the Internet era and more functional organisational information systems. By the late 1980s specialised accounting software packages (for mainframe, mini and PCs) had become common for both the corporation and the accounting firm. For the corporation, software could handle the payroll, accounts payable, fixed assets, personnel and capital project analysis. For accounting firms, software packages were available for depreciation schedules, tax preparation, records management, not-for-profit organisations, work scheduling, management reports and client billings (All we provide is the best accounting software 1982: 23). On the audit side, audit software soon became available for accounting firms that had not developed their own EDP audit programmes. Combining the PC and dial-ups, accounting firms could access vast tax and accounting research service centres.

Accounting, information systems and the Internet

Introduction: nature and antecedents

The transition from the type of computerised accounting discussed in the last section and the next phase is far from clear cut. The variety of systems in use and pathways to change were diverse. Even within the more technically developed territories, individual company differences were significant both within and between different sectors and sizes of organisations. AIS as a field of practice and research has its roots in the early days of business computer systems, and by the mid-1980s was being seen as a specific and separate, if ill-defined, field (Murthy: 2016; Weber: 2016).[3] However, from the 1990s onwards, there are two linked technical issues that have had a major effect on the shape, nature and power of accounting: communication technologies, particularly those of the Internet; and the increased integration and complexity of organisational information systems. Though to an extent these are separate issues, they are inherently linked, as the communication systems provide the operational capacity to integrate systems not just within a local environment but also (potentially) globally. The globalisation of business, of the profession and of information and systems technologies that provides the competitive impetus for many of the changes and developments discussed in this section, are likely to determine the 'future history' of accounting.

The Internet and world wide web

Though the terms are often used interchangeably, the Internet and the World Wide Web (WWW) are quite different things. The Internet is the underlying communication system and the WWW is an application that runs on top of the net in order to provide a particular human friendly interface. Though the origins of the Internet are typically traced to the US military Advanced Research Projects Agency Network (APRANET) of the 1960s and 1970s, commercial uses of the net were rare until the introduction and standardisation of Electronic Data Interchange (EDI) as a means of transferring transaction data or instigating transactions between typically large organisations in the mid-1980s. By 1988 'Nearly one-third of [US] business firm[s] are either EDI users, or planning to implement EDI within two years' (Ferguson et al. 1990: 91; Slesinger 1992) and use of EDI and the Internet increased internationally into the 1990s. In many cases the use of EDI was driven by the need to streamline processes in order to meet the needs of the 'just-in-time' or lean process of production and distribution (Fedorowicz 2002), and of the more global economy this entailed, both of which the Internet made possible.

The growth of the Internet was also fuelled, after 1991, by the establishment of the WWW, which, invented by Tim Berners-Lee, added a Hypertext interface to the Internet that used HTLM[4] to define and display information and URLs[5] to provide the links of the web. Used initially to provide information, the Dot-Com boom, or bubble, of the late 1990s turned the WWW into a major element of the commercial landscape, providing the universal platform for what was to become known as Business-2-Customer E-Commerce.

Both the use of EDI and the transaction interfaces of the WWW had significant effects on business transaction records and the way they were maintained, and therefore on accounting. Both of these changes meant that transaction data was input, not by employees of the company, but by outsiders: in the case of EDI, by people or systems in counterparty organisations; in the case of the WWW, by customers. The result of these developments was the further divorce of accounting from bookkeeping and the processes of record maintenance, and shifts in the locus of control.

In addition to the processing changes it was during this period that technological change reached beyond the traditional transaction processing, auditing and report production processes of accounting, to the ways in which accounting information was communicated to external users of accounting data. Around the turn of the millennium eXtensible Business Reporting Language (XBRL) was introduced as a new standardised and regulated way of providing computer readable financial statement data across the WWW. XBRL has since become an optional or required form of account filing standards in at least 10 major jurisdictions. XBRL does not change the fundamental financial data, but is a faster and more reliable form of electronic communication of regulated data. In addition to standard XBRL, the XBRL consortium has also introduced XBRL General Ledger (XBRL/GL), which is a definition for a standardised WWW-based transactional reporting system to provide data at least at the level of general ledger transactions that can be used in more detailed accounting.[6] There are additional iXBRL (inline XBRL) standards and requirements, for example for tax reporting purposes in the UK.

There is little published historical work on XBRL, but there is potential interest in the historical analysis of why and how it came about, and how the consortium is run and maintained.

Information systems and integration: enterprise systems

Unlike the very public and well-known (if not well-understood) developments in communications, especially the Internet and the WWW, the process of integration of organisational information systems, including AIS and enterprise information systems, has achieved much less attention. In many respects this is as true within many accounting arenas as in the wider social conscious and understanding, particularly within the accounting academy.[7] The lack of popular appreciation of this is largely understandable as the processing of transactions is not of inherent interest, even though the 'public' are increasingly an integral part of the transaction processing systems, for example through their unwitting role as primary 'bookkeeping clerks' in their Web-buying activities. It is arguably the rise of 'information systems' and the integration that this has entailed that has had the most significant impact on accounting, albeit exacerbated by the opportunities offered by the widening and globalisation of communication technologies.

The increasing integration of earlier accounting and business-related transaction and information systems continued and accelerated throughout this period, in particular the development and widespread implementation of Enterprise Resource Planning (ERP) systems. ERP are enterprise-wide integrated transaction processing and decision information systems that have at their core the transaction and accounting systems of an organisation, including complex costing and management accounting functions, and evolved from earlier MRP systems (Jacobs and Weston 2007). From an accounting perspective ERPs were, and still are, one of the most significant system developments of any time as they envelop almost the entire accounting process. Further, their foundation within database technologies allows, and business demands require, the implementation of rich data models that could not realistically be handled with the conventional double-entry model of accounting or AISs. The result is systems that have widespread effects on the work of accountants, particularly management accountants (Grabski et al. 2009, 2011). The history of the development of ERP systems, along with other Enterprise Systems such as Customer Relationship Management (CRM), Supply Chain Management (SCM) and Business Intelligence (BI) systems are outlined in Romero and Vernadat (2016), and the impact of such systems on accountants and accounting are discussed in, for example, Ballantine and Galliers (2018) and Appelbaum et al. (2017).

Implications for accounting and accountants

The changing role of accountants in industry

The role and work of accountants and others involved with accounting systems over time has changed substantially. The separation of record keeping from accounting continued, and more of the bookkeeping, that was once considered part of the esoteric knowledge of accounting that helped to create and preserve the professional status of accountants (Edwards et al. 2007), became routine, and a lot more was automated as systems became more integrated. With fully integrated AISs there was, for example, no more posting of sub-system (or day book) balances to the general ledger. In the more advanced systems many aspects of costing and allocation or apportionment (such as depreciation charges) were also automated, moving the intellectual and skilled work of accounting even more towards the preparation of financial reports, and even aspects of this were being more fully automated. However, in some other respects the role of accounting was increasing, at least in some organisations, as accounting and transaction data was becoming more in demand for a variety of types of decision support systems. In some contexts this was a 'two edged sword' as, although more data was required, accountants had to understand more complex data models and the underlying technology to be able to retrieve it. In addition, just as accountants gained independence from IT departments through the use of spreadsheets, other users were potentially able to bypass accounting expertise and information gate keepers.

The new technologies, especially advances during the third period (c.1970–2000), were potentially leading to further re- and de- skilling of the accounting and recordkeeping work force, with further female genderisation of the lower ranks of accounting work Roslender (1996). In addition to this deskilling, or redefining of the boundaries of what counted as the professional accountants' work, a new threat to status was getting stronger: the threat from computer or information systems professionals. In this context the institutional and professional histories of the different disciplines become important and there is a need to look beyond functional analysis of the power and importance of the different roles (Murray and Knights 1990). Though this issue was primarily a concern for accountants in business, accountants in practice were also under some potential threat from computer audit specialists.

The effects of IT and systems changes in the most recent period have witnessed a continuation of the issues that arose earlier, but have intensified. The accelerated pace of change was, and is, fuelled by greater pressure on managerial efficiency and processing, that is the result of heightened global competition arising from better communication and systems technologies, and facilitated by the increased pace of information technology developments. There is also recent evidence that the long separated roles of financial and management accounting are converging under the influence of systems that are more attuned to forward looking (including fair values) alongside the adoption of more strategic (less control) focused management accounting (Taipaleenmäki and Ikäheimo 2013).

Technology in practice and audit

With growing reliance on computers for accounting information, companies and accounting firms were faced with the problem of incompatibility with the traditional audit function. Concerns arose in the initial period of computerisation, for example Touche Ross reported in 1956 that with clients installing computers the way an audit was conducted would have to 'radically' change (Collard 1983: 123). The earlier mechanical accounting changes had much less effect, as there were still hard documents that could be inspected. As transactions were increasingly entered directly into the computer system visual inspections became impossible. The important audit issue became how to audit a computer-based accounting system. Some advocates favoured auditing 'through the computer' while others favoured auditing 'around the computer' (Monteverde 1966: 92–7). There was, however, consensus that major changes had to occur in the audit process itself. With this in mind, accounting firms, accounting educators and companies devoted significant resources to developing new programmes, concepts, and methods for auditing a computer-based accounting system.

The new audit systems involved employing staff within audit with appropriate computer expertise (Davis et al. 1983: 305–6), requiring the recruitment of suitably skilled individuals and/or providing existing accounting staff with appropriate computer training. Further, for each audit there needed to be a recognition of the various systems in use and an appreciation of the differences and effects of computers on audit risk and a more nuanced appreciation of management's attitudes toward controls in order for them to 'obtain a sufficient understanding of a client's internal control system' (Konrath 1999: 208, 236, 332–40). It was also important for an audit firm 'to make the machines work for you' (Monteverde 1966: 95–7), that is, to use the computer's speed and efficiency in the audit process itself. Audit tests that were impossible through manual or mechanical means could be performed in minutes or seconds with the computer.

Although the computer created the necessity to change audit practice it achieved widespread acceptance at major accounting firms, largely by speeding up the audit process (Allen and McDermott 1993: 124) and by using tax packages to divert effort away from computation and towards tax planning.

Increased use of computers within the economy, and within accounting practice, also provided accounting firms with the opportunity to develop a new source of revenue. By 1970, all major accounting firms had established management consultancy departments, and these departments' growth and profit margins, over the decades which followed, facilitated continued rapid expansion given that a monopoly of large audit clients had already been achieved. For instance, at Price, Waterhouse & Co. in the UK, the Management Consultancy Services department's billings expanded at the rate of 15 to 20 per cent per year 'throughout the mid-to-late seventies' (Jones 1995: 295). The emergence of management consultancy departments also had a major effect on hiring practices and education requirements. Traditionally, in the USA, for example, firms hired accounting majors and expected them to become CPAs. However, in the management consultancy area, where a key requirement was that personnel possessed a strong computer background, firms began to hire non-accountants and in many firms management consultancy departments became dominated by non-CPAs (Allen and McDermott 1993: 132–3).

Continuous audit has become a major area for research in the audit field, though this has a long history of use in some cases, for example AT&T Bell Laboratories' use goes back to the late-1980s (see for example Aquino et al. 2008; Alles et al. 2018). Similarly business intelligence and data analytics, including big data, have recently become more prominent in audit research and professional consciousness and it appears that many audits now use these tools (Alles 2015; Cao et al. 2015).

Accounting education

The effect of changing technologies on accountants has been significant. As early as 1957 Hammond was urging that:

> The accounting faculty, as a faculty, should combine an excellent understanding of business, sound logical training, and knowledge of business data. On this base the accounting faculty should undertake the leadership in E.D.P.M. [Electronic Document Processing and Management] systems as such in schools of business administration.
>
> *(Hammond 1957: 579)*

By the 1970s it was becoming clear that accounting educators should respond to rapid developments in processing information and provide courses on information systems and

EDP. Yet, by 1972, in only 14 per cent of business schools accredited by the American Association of Collegiate Schools of Business (AACSB) were accounting majors required to study Accounting Systems (AS) and only 5 per cent required students to take both AS and EDP (Schroeder 1972). In the UK, from the inception of the Batchelor of Accountancy (BAcc) degree at the University of Glasgow in 1968, computing courses were part of the curriculum (Stoner et al. 2018). The inclusion of computers, information systems or AIS in the curriculum of accounting programmes is not, however, universal, and its absence is currently moving towards crisis-point in at least some jurisdictions (Boritz and Stoner 2014).

Review and reflections

Hassan (2018: 24) ends his discussion in 'Taking IS research seriously' as follows:

> we have not yet missed the opportunity to build our historical tradition, but that opportunity needs to be grasped with an understanding and approach that take[s] full advantage of insights from one of humanity's oldest disciplines – history.

To a considerable extent this statement is also true in relating to the history of mechanisation, computerisation and the development of information systems in accounting and their impact.

The remainder of this section focuses separately on a number of different themes.

Defining the field

In many respects within this chapter a relatively narrow boundary has necessarily been drawn: one that looks to the processes of record keeping within organisations, the work of bookkeeping and accounting, the audit environment and, to a limited extent, accounting as a profession. Having taken this fairly constrained perspective it is, however, not entirely clear where accounting stops and information systems, of various flavours, start. This is a criticism of the two most closely related fields: see, for example, Hassan (2018) and Markus (2011) on Management Information Systems and Weber (2016) and Murthy (2016) in relation to AIS.

However, there is positive potential in both of these critical perspectives, in that they make suggestions for improvement, largely based on clarity of approach and methods, and in Hassan (2018) the call for well-theorised historical approaches. This message is also relevant in the area of research covered here, where much is at best lightly theorised. There is clearly space in the literature for research that looks to the systems of accounting and recording in relation to broader notions and systems of accounting and/or accountability.

These issues notwithstanding, there is relatively little within this field that has been explicitly written as history of systems in accounting. An observation supported by Spraakman and Quinn's (2018) analysis of over 440 accounting history papers from the three principal accounting history journals, which does not identify any themes related to systems or technologies of accounting,[8] and identifies only one paper concerned with AIS – though even that paper (Badua and Watkins 2011) is referenced only in relation to methodology. Similarly, Matthews (2017), which covers a much broader database, does not identify any aspect of the history of the technologies of accounting systems as significant.

Much of what is reported here is a reinterpretation of near contemporary research, reports or other documentation. On the positive side it is clear that there is a wealth of such research, much of it case based, on how systems in an accounting context work or are changed or redesigned. Though this research is not in itself historical it could, with care and caution, provide a basis for detailed investigation of the phenomena with which they are concerned. They could provide data for research either at a period of time in a wider context or, by using a series of case type studies, over periods of time. In part that is the approach taken in this chapter.

Technology in accounting

As in many fields early technological change in bookkeeping and recording technology tended to be relatively simple: e.g. the replacement of simple processes with a specific tool (e.g. the calculator). As time progresses the changes tend to become more complex, with technologies replacing multiple processes, tools or steps: as does a ledger machine. Later, technologies progress towards automating ranges of activities in organised ways, for example the accounting within an integrated ledger system. Along the way further complexity is added by facilitating customisation and multiple variations, for example as ERP installations were designed to meet multiple information needs.

In the case of the accounting and recording systems discussed in this chapter we see changes being typically motivated by a combination of increasing demands for information, required in increasingly competitive and more global environments, and reductions in the costs of processing. These savings frequently being achieved via the reduction of labour costs: either via time saving or labour substitution.

Mauldin and Ruchala (1999) discuss enterprise systems, such as ERP as a complex combination of technological, organizational and cognitive factors in relation to task characteristics, and propose a meta-theory and model to help understand and research systems in their organisational settings.

The changing nature of accounting

Rosati and Paulsson (2018: 13) highlight how technological changes are implicated in the growth of complexity of IS and, following the analysis of Reneau and Grabski (1987), how the operation of accounting based systems effect most decision makers in an organisation.

The changes in technology identified have been seen to have effects on the nature of accounting work and the characteristics of those who undertake the work. For example, we see different, often lower level (or less valued), skills being required to complete the process orientated work of bookkeeping and record management. In parallel we see accounting associated more with the less routine, and invariably more valued, work. Within this situation there appears to be significant evidence, at least in the earlier years of mechanisation and computers, that the less valued roles are more likely to be associated with female labour, which at the time was significantly cheaper. This genderisation of the bookkeeping and record management processes may also be seen in the accounting field, for example it is a possible cause of the widespread gender gap in the accounting profession (as in many other fields of work).

Alongside these changes we see technology being associated with more widespread aspects of the nature of what is seen as accounting. For example the rise in consultancy within accounting practices, the shared systems responsibilities for and within ERP systems, and in the boundaries of what audit work is considered to be accounting, or at least within the domain of accountants.

Educational requirements

The discussions above show the changing nature of accounting, and above all the increasing interconnectivity and growing immediacy of the work of accountants, and of the nature of the tasks and understandings required within the field. This chapter has only lightly touched on this. However, communication between systems and technical professionals and accountants is clearly an important aspect in the efficient operation and redesign of business information processes, as is critical interpretation and analysis.

It is unclear from the extant historical research to what extent accountants' abilities in these spheres have helped or hindered the role of accountants or the progress of technological change. Research in the accounting education sphere identifies this as an area of known difficulty (see for example Boritz and Stoner 2014). This potential educational deficiency, and the role of the professions in engendering appropriate development of these competencies, raises important research questions that might well be illuminated through historical research.

Looking to the past to understand the future

The acceleration of change in technologies that is evident from the historical record, together with technology predictions, indicates that the pace and extent of change is with us to stay. Good historical research has the potential to help us better understand the past in order to cope with predicted future changes.

In this context there are many potential research topics in this field. The examples below are just a few of those that seem most promising, and for many of these it would be potentially interesting from a socio-economic perspective to consider the role of the 'accounting profession' either in the form of the professional accounting bodies or the major accounting firms in fostering or hindering specific systems developments or implementations.

- The penetration and success of artificial intelligent systems (in accounting and decision making) within business, practice or public sectors, including ethical, social, labour and economic implications.
- Machine learning in the selection of (accounting) information used to inform decisions and determine actions.
- Continuous audit and the effects of whole population audits (rather than sample audit methodologies) on audit process, judgments and perceived risks and fees.
- The degree of implementation of ERP systems in, particularly small, organisations that might have little inherent economic incentives for doing so.
- XBRL and XBRL/SL, establishment, development and regulation.
- The international diffusion of accounting and audit technologies, and reasons for adoption/success in differing environments.
- Opportunities for accountants to be instrumental in the greater provision of detailed and near real-time information in a variety of environments that are not already well served.
- Cybersecurity of accounting, and other, data and the accountants' and auditors' responsibilities.
- Behavioural effects of (new) more onerous data protection legislation.

There are many gaps in our historical understanding in this field of study and there are many areas that have been researched where more interpretative or more critical research could further illuminate work that has already been published, much of which is predominantly descriptive rather than theoretically informed.

Key works

Appelbaum et al. (2017) cover many aspects of the emerging technologies in the IS field and the implications they have for accounting and accountants, including continuous audit and assurance.

Boritz and Stoner (2014) outline educational, training and competency issues that have implications for the interpretation of historical research on accountants' understanding of or reaction to systems' change.

Hassan (2018) takes a critical look at the history of Information Systems and IS research, discusses the historiography of the field and provides details of several studies in the area.

Hirschheim and Klein (2011) provide a detailed history of IS from the perspectives of education and research as well as the technologies and applications.

Weber (2016), Murthy (2016) and Moffitt et al. (2016) in the 30th anniversary edition of the American Accounting Association *Journal of Information Systems* provide an interesting and in parts critical discussion of the history of research in AIS and associated areas.

Notes

1 Feminisation of the workforce of clerks and bookkeepers in Britain over a similar time period is studied by Kirkham and Loft (1993).
2 Personal experience of Greg Stoner, joint author.
3 The American Accounting Association launching its *Journal of Information Systems* in 1986.
4 Hypertext Mark-up Language, a coding that defines how text and other information is defined and to be displayed.
5 Uniform Resource Locator, in effect the internet address of a resource.
6 See www.xbrl.org/and www.xbrl.org/the-standard/what/global-ledger/.
7 See for example the discussion on technology in Boritz and Stoner (2014).
8 And given that the authors have an interests in systems in accounting, they might have been expected to identify such themes if there was relevant literature.

References

650 applications (n.d.) Available HTTP: <www-03.ibm.com/ibm/history/exhibits/650/650_ap1.html>.

650 chronology (n.d.) Available HTTP: <www-03.ibm.com/ibm/history/exhibits/650/650_ch1.html>.

650 RAMAC announcement (n.d.) Available HTTP: <www-03.ibm.com/ibm/history/exhibits/650/650_pr2.html>.

All we provide is the best accounting software. (1982) *Journal of Accountancy*, 153 (6): 23.

Allen, D.G. and McDermott, K. (1993) *Accounting for Success. A History of Price Waterhouse in America1890–1990* (Boston, MA: Harvard Business School Press).

Alles, M., Brennan, G., Kogan, A and Vasarhelyi, M.A. (2018) Continuous monitoring of business process controls: a pilot implementation of a continuous auditing system at siemens, in D.Y. Chan, V. Chiu and M.A. Vasarhelyi (eds.) *Continuous Auditing*, pp. 219–46 (Bingley and England: Emerald Publishing).

Alles, M.G. (2015) Drivers of the use and facilitators and obstacles of the evolution of big data by the audit profession, *Accounting Horizons*, 29 (2): 439–49.

Announcing the GE-215. (1963) *Journal of Accountancy*, 115 (4): 10–11.

Appelbaum, D., Kogan, A., Vasarhelyi, M. and Yan, Z. (2017) Impact of business analytics and enterprise systems on managerial accounting, *International Journal of Accounting Information Systems*, 25 (C): 29–44.

Aquino, C.E. de, Silva, W.L. da and Vasarhelyi, M.A. (2008) Moving toward continuous auditing: establishing audit priority areas can lead to a more effective continuous audit process, *Internal Auditor*, August: 27.

Aspray, N. (1917) Loose-leaf books, *Accountant*, 57 (2237): 311–13.

Badua, F.A. and Watkins, A.L. (2011) Too young to have a history? Using data analysis techniques to reveal trends and shifts in the brief history of accounting information systems, *Accounting Historians Journal*, 38 (2): 75–103.

Ballantine, J. and Galliers, R.D. (2018) New developments in information technology: a call for action, in M. Quinn and E. Strauss (eds.) *Routledge Companion to Accounting Information Systems*, pp. 292–301 (London: Routledge).

Bliven, Jr., B. (1954) *The Wonderful Writing Machine* (New York: Random House).

Bonin, H. (2004) The development of accounting machines in French banks from the 1920s to the 1960s, *Accounting, Business & Financial History*, 14 (3): 257–76.

Boritz, J.E. and Stoner, G.N. (2014) Technology in accounting education, in R.M.S. Wilson (ed.) *Routledge Companion to Accounting Education*, pp. 247–75 (London: Routledge).

Bresnahan, T.F. and Greenstein, S. (1999) Technological competition and the structure of the computer industry, *Journal of Industrial Economics*, 47 (1): 1–40.

Campbell-Kelly, M. (1992) Large-scale data processing in the Prudential, 1850–1930, *Accounting, Business & Financial History*, 2 (2): 117–39.

Campbell-Kelly, M. (1998) Data processing and technological change: the Post Office Savings Bank, 1861–1930, *Technology and Culture*, 39 (1): 1–32.

Campbell-Kelly, M. (2001) Not only Microsoft: the maturing of the personal computer software industry, 1982–1995, *Business History Review*, 75 (1): 103–45.

Campbell-Kelly, M. and Aspray, W. (2004) *Computer: A History of the Information Machine* (Boulder, CO: Westview Press).

Cao, M., Chychyla, R. and Stewart, T. (2015) Big data analytics in financial statement audits, *Accounting Horizons*, 29 (2): 423–29.

Ceruzzi, P.E. (1998) *A History of Modern Computing* (Cambridge, MA: MIT Press).

Chandler Jr., A.D. (1977) *The Visible Hand: The Managerial Revolution in American Business* (Cambridge, MA: Harvard University Press).

Collard, E.A. (1983) *Stories About 125 Years at Touche Ross* (Canada: Touche Ross).

Computer progress at General Electric. (1963) *Journal of Accountancy*, 115 (2): 26.

Cooper, C. and Taylor, P. (2000) From Taylorism to Ms Taylor: the transformation of the accounting craft, *Accounting, Organizations and Society*, 25 (6): 555–78.

Copeland, B.J. (2017) The modern history of computing, in *The Stanford Encyclopedia of Philosophy*. Available HTTP: <https://plato.stanford.edu/archives/win2017/entries/computing-history/>.

Cortada, J.W. (1993) *Before the Computer* (Princeton, NJ: Princeton University Press).

Darby, E. (1968) *It All Adds Up: The Growth of Victor Comptometer Corporation* (Chicago, IL: Victor Comptometer Corporation).

Davis, G.B., Adams, D.L. and Schaller, C.A. (1983) *Auditing & EDP*, 2nd edn. (New York: American Institute of Certified Public Accountants).

de Wit, O. and van den Ende, J. (2000) The emergence of a new regime: business management and office mechanisation in the Dutch financial sector in the 1920s, *Business History*, 42 (2): 87–118.

de Wit, O., van den Ende, J., Schot, J. and van Oost, E. (2002) Office technologies in the Netherlands, 1880–1980, *Technology and Culture*, 43 (1): 50–72.

Dicksee, L.R. (1911) Loose-leaf systems, *Accountant*, 44 (1927): 652–57.

Edwards, J.R., Anderson, M. and Chandler, R. (2007) Claiming a jurisdiction for the 'public accountant' in England prior to organisational fusion, *Accounting, Organizations and Society*, 32 (1/2): 61–100.

Fedorowicz, J. (2002) Discussion of: Adoption of just-in-time and electronic data interchange systems and perceptions of cost management systems effectiveness, *International Journal of Accounting Information Systems*, 3 (1): 63–68.

Ferguson, D.M., Hill, N.C. and Hansen. J.V. (1990) Electronic data interchange: foundations and survey evidence on current use, *Journal of Information Systems*, 4 (2): 81–91.

Ferry, G. (2003) *A Computer Called LEO* (London: Fourth Estate).

Friden 6010 electronic computer. (1963) *Journal of Accountancy*, 116 (11): 14.

Galloway, L. (1919) *Office Management its Principles and Practice* (New York: Ronald Press).

Grabski, S. Leech, S. and Sangster, A. (2009) *Management Accounting in Enterprise Resource Planning Systems* (Oxford: CIMA/Elsevier).

Grabski, S.V., Leech, S.A. and Schmidt, P.J. (2011) A review of ERP research: a future agenda for accounting information systems, *Journal of Information Systems*, 25 (1): 37–78.

Haddy, P. (1958) Some thoughts on automation in a British office, *Journal of Industrial Economics*, 6 (2): 161–70.

Hammond, W.R. (1957) Electronic data processing and the accounting faculty, *Accounting Review*, 32 (4): 576–79.

Hassan, N.R. (2018) Taking IS history seriously, in R.D. Galliers and M-K. Stein (eds.) *Routledge Companion to Management Information Systems*, pp. 3–29 (Abingdon and New York: Routledge).

Hendry, J. (1987) The teashop computer manufacturer: J. Lyons, Leo and the potential and limits of high-tech diversification, *Business History*, 29 (1): 73–102.

Hirschheim, R. and Klein, H.K. (2011) Tracing the history of the information systems field, in R. D. Galliers and W.L. Currie (eds.) *The Oxford Handbook of Management Information Systems: Critical Perspectives and New Directions*, pp. 16–61 (Oxford: Oxford University Press).

IBM 5100. portable computer (n.d.) Available HTTP: <www-03.ibm.com/ibm/history/exhibits/pc/pc_2.html>.

IBM 5110 (n.d.) Available HTTP: <www-03.ibm.com/ibm/history/exhibits/pc/pc_4.html>.

IBM 5120. applications (n.d.) Available HTTP: <www-03.ibm.com/ibm/history/exhibits/pc/pc_7.html>.

IBM 5120. (c.1980) Available HTTP: <www-03.ibm.com/ibm/history/exhibits/pc/pc_6.html>.

IBM 650 (n.d.) Available HTTP: <www-03.ibm.com/ibm/history/exhibits/650/650_intro.html>.

IBM System/36 (n.d.) Available HTTP: <www-03.ibm.com/ibm/history/exhibits/rochester/roches-ter_4018.html>.

ICAEW. (1949) *Mechanised Accounting and the Auditor* (London: Institute of Chartered Accountants in England and Wales).

Jacobs, F.R., and Weston Jr., F.C. (2007) Enterprise resource planning (ERP) – a brief history, *Journal of Operations Management*, 25 (2): 357–63.

Jones, E. (1995) *True and Fair. A History of Price Waterhouse* (London: Hamish Hamilton).

Kirkham, L.M. and Loft, A. (1993) Gender and the construction of the professional accountant, *Accounting, Organizations and Society*, 18 (6): 507–58.

Konrath, L.F. (1999) *Auditing Concepts and Applications: A Risk Analysis Approach* (Cincinnati, OH: South-Western College Publishing).

Lewis, E.S. (1914) *Efficient Cost Keeping* (Detroit, TX: Burroughs Adding Machine Company).

Leading article (1902) 'Slip' or 'card' bookkeeping. *Accountant*, 28 (1455): 1069–72.

Li, D.H. (1968) *Accounting Computers Management Information Systems* (New York: McGraw-Hill).

Markus, M.L. (2011) Historical reflections on the practice of information management and implications for the field of MIS, in R.D. Galliers and W.L. Currie (eds.) *Oxford Handbook of Management Information Systems: Critical Perspectives and New Directions*, pp. 4–15 (Oxford: Oxford University Press).

Martin, E. (1925) *The Calculating Machines: Their History and Development*, trans. P. A. Kidwell and M. R. Williams (Germany: Johannes Meyer).

Mattessich, R. and Galassi, G. (2000) History of the spreadsheet: from matrix accounting to budget simulation and computerization, in AECA (ed.) *Accounting and History: Selected Papers from the 8th Congress of Accounting Historians*, pp. 203–32 (Madrid: Asociación Española de Contabilidad y Administración).

Matthews, D. (2017) Publications in accounting history: a long-run statistical survey, *Accounting Historians Journal*, 44 (2): 69–98.

Mauldin, E.G. and Ruchala, L.V. (1999) Towards a meta-theory of accounting information systems, *Accounting, Organizations and Society*, 24 (4): 317–31.

McKenney, J.L., Mason, R.O. and Copeland, D.G. (1997) Bank of America: the crest and trough of technological leadership, *MIS Quarterly*, 21 (3): 321–53.

Moffitt, K.C., Richardson, V.J., Snow, N.M., Weisner, M.M. and Wood, D.A. (2016) Perspectives on past and future AIS research as the *Journal of Information Systems* turns thirty, *Journal of Information Systems*, 30 (3): 157–71.

Monteverde, R.J. (1966) Audits of electronically produced records, in J.M. Palen (ed.) *Encyclopedia of Auditing Techniques*, Vol. 1: pp. 75–116 (Englewood Cliffs, NJ: Prentice-Hall).

Moore, P. (1932) *Business Machines* (London: Longmans, Green).

Murray, F. and Knights, D. (1990) Inter-managerial competition and capital accumulation: IT specialists, accountants and executive control, *Critical Perspectives on Accounting*, 1 (2): 167–89.

Murthy U.S. (2016) Researching at the intersection of accounting and information technology: a call for action, *Journal of Information Systems*, 30 (2): 159–67.

New: the IBM alpha-numeric magnetic ledger card. (1963) *Journal of Accountancy*, 116 (6): 5.

Norberg, A.L. (1990) High-technology calculation in the early 20th century: punched card machinery in business and government, *Technology and Culture*, 31 (4): 753–79.

Page, E.D. (1906) The new science of business: making an office efficient, *World's Work*, 12 (June): 7682–84.

Perks, R.W. (1993) *Accounting and Society* (London: Chapman & Hall).

Price, E.E. (1902) Ledger posting on the slip system, *Accountant*, 28 (1422): 256–66.

Reneau, J.H. and Grabski, S.V. (1987) A review of research in computer-human interaction and individual differences within a model for research in accounting information systems, *Journal of Information Systems*, 2 (1): 33–53.

Romero, D. and Vernadat, F. (2016) Enterprise information systems state of the art: past, present and future trends, *Computers in Industry*, 9: 3–13.

Rosati, P. and Paulsson, V. (2018) Development of accounting information systems over time, in M. Quinn and E. Strauss (eds.) *Routledge Companion to Accounting Information Systems*, pp. 13–22 (London: Routledge).

Roslender, R. (1996) Critical accounting and the labour of accountants, *Critical Perspectives on Accounting*, 7 (4): 461–84.

Sanders, D.H. (1968) *Computers in Business* (New York: McGraw-Hill).

Schroeder, J.G. (1972) Systems and electronic data processing courses in the accounting curriculum, *Accounting Review*, 47 (2): 387–89.

Seward, G.H. (1904) Mechanical aids in factory-office economy, *Engineering Magazine*, 27: 605–25.

Shurkin, J. (1984) *Engines of the Mind* (New York: W.W. Norton).

Slesinger, G. (1992) Electronic data interchange: how to make it work, *Journal of Corporate Accounting and Finance*, 4 (2): 3–10.

Spacek, L. (1989) *The Growth of Arthur Andersen & Co. 1928–1973: An Oral History* (New York: Garland Publishing).

Spraakman, G.P. and Quinn, M. (2018) Accounting history research topics—an analysis of leading journals, 2006–2015, *Accounting Historians Journal*, 45 (1): 101–14.

Stoner, G., Kininmonth, K and Stoner, A. (2018) *Celebrating 50 Years of the BAcc: 1968–2018* (University of Glasgow: Adam Smith Business School).

Strom, S.H. (1992) *Beyond the Typewriter: Gender, Class, and the Origins of Modern American Office Work* (Urbana, IL: University of Illinois Press).

The IBM PC's debut (n.d.) Available HTTP: <www-03.ibm.com/ibm/history/exhibits/pc25/pc25_intro.html>.

Taipaleenmäki, J. and Ikäheimo, S. (2013) On the convergence of management accounting and financial accounting – the role of information technology in accounting change, *International Journal of Accounting Information Systems*, 14 (4): 321–48.

Turck, J.A.V. (1921) *Origin of Modern Calculating Machines* (Chicago, IL: Western Society of Engineers).

Weber, R. (2016) Thirty years of the *Journal of Information Systems*: reflections of a prodigal son, *Journal of Information Systems*, 30 (1): 137–46.

Wootton, C.W. and Kemmerer, B.E. (2000) The changing genderization of the accounting workforce in the US, 1930–90, *Accounting, Business & Financial History*, 10 (2): 169–90.

Wootton, C.W. and Wolk, C.M. (2000) The evolution and acceptance of the loose-leaf accounting system, 1885–1935, *Technology and Culture*, 41 (1): 80–98.

Yates, J. (1985) Internal communication systems in American business structures: a framework to aid appraisal, *American Archivist*, 48 (2): 141–58.

Yates, J. (1991) Investing in information: supply and demand forces in the use of information in American firms, 1850–1920, in P. Temin (ed.) *Inside the Business Enterprise*, pp. 117–59 (Chicago. IL: University of Chicago Press).

Yates, J. (1994) Evolving information use in firms, 1850–1920, in L. Bud-Frierman (ed.) *Information Acumen*, pp. 26–50 (London: Routledge).

PART III

Theory and practice

7
FINANCIAL ACCOUNTING THEORY

Thomas A. Lee

Overview

This chapter outlines and reviews the history of financial accounting theory (FAT) in the English-speaking world. Its principal objectives are to identify significant contributions to the development of FAT and assess their success in changing accounting practice. The narrative is written in the context of financial accounting practice, public accountancy, and academic accounting research. The chapter begins with a statement on the meaning of FAT and its connection to financial accounting practice. The initial history of FAT extends from the late nineteenth century (with theories of double-entry bookkeeping) to the middle of the twentieth century (with individual theories on specific financial accounting practice issues). The continuing history, which extends from the mid-twentieth century to the present day, considers individual and institutional attempts to produce a general statement of FAT. The impact of conceptual framework projects is considered, as are theoretical contributions by academic researchers in the name of science. The chapter concludes with an assessment of the history of FAT and its impact on practice. The overall conclusion is that the long-running project to find a universal FAT has failed, despite individual theoretical contributions that, from time to time, have produced practice changes. More generally, the search for FAT appears to have served a political role for practitioners and academic researchers seeking professional legitimacy and reputation. The question for the future in these circumstances is whether there is merit in continuing to search for a universal FAT to rationalise, explain, and predict financial accounting practice.

Definitions and restrictions

It is necessary to contain this review within manageable proportions by means of definitions and topic boundaries. These are pragmatic and subjective restrictions that determine the shape of the chapter, recognising that it is not a complete history of FAT. For example, there are various histories of specific topics relating to FAT and these are referenced but not covered in detail in this review (e.g. Wells 1976; Tweedie and Whittington 1984; Cushing 1989; Storey and Storey 1998; Zeff 2013). In effect, this means there are two restrictions on chapter content. The first restriction concerns the meaning of FAT, i.e. what is a theoretical statement about financial accounting. The second restriction deals with the meaning of financial accounting, i.e. what is financial accounting practice for the purposes of this history.

In this chapter, the term theory means any linguistic statement of belief about the function of financial accounting, expressed in logical argument, and intended to rationalise, explain, or predict financial accounting practice. Theoretical statements can be deductive (i.e. starting from a normative and general position about practice and arguing to a specific theoretical conclusion testable by empirical observation) or inductive (i.e. starting from specific empirical observations of practice and arguing to a generalised theoretical conclusion or explanation). All theoretical statements in this chapter are perceived as arguing to conclusions that assist in understanding the nature, role, and impact of financial accounting information. Such definitions are made in order to permit this history of FAT to be as broad as possible while containing different approaches to theorising over time.

The term financial accounting in this chapter connotes the accounting information (and processes of producing such information) disclosed in corporate financial reports. Most statements of FAT implicitly or explicitly acknowledge this restriction and, as later sections of this chapter demonstrate, anomalies and problems in corporate financial reporting are typical triggers for theoretical contributions to the financial accounting literature. With respect to the latter, the FAT in this chapter is that of the English-speaking world and, more specifically, of the UK and the US. Justification for this restriction is grounded in the argument that the UK and the US have led thinking about global accounting standards and practices – particularly those of the International Accounting Standards Board (IASB) whose standards are expected to be consistent with those of the US Financial Accounting Standards Board (FASB 2002a).

An additional caveat concerns the specific contributions to FAT cited in this review. Because of space limitations and the size of the literature, it has been possible only to select those writings that appear to have been important influences in the history of FAT. Many of these writings have been cited or debated in the literature as seminal works.

Preview

In his classic text on the social role of professions, Abbott (1988: 325) observed that 'surely accounting is today more socially important than medicine'. Despite this positive and independent support for the potential of financial accounting, its current state is perceived by accounting historians to be in crisis. For example, West (2003: 193) argued that the authority of the public accountancy profession is unjustified so long as its body of knowledge lacks a robust framework and is dependent on an increasing number of accounting rules. Lee (2013: 144) claimed these rules generate meaningless accounting numbers that create an economic hazard with respect to accountability and decision-making. Dyckman and Zeff (2015: 522) predicted the current accounting research system was unlikely to generate change in practice in the foreseeable future. Inanga and Schneider (2005: 245) argued such research was irrelevant to the information needs of accountancy practitioners and report users because there was no universal FAT with which to test and evaluate practice. They believed this failure was due to the separation of researchers and practitioners as evidenced by the lack of research content in classroom instruction and practice standards. If true, these arguments indict accounting research generally and FAT specifically, because each function has a long history and considerable economic resources have been devoted to them. This chapter addresses the above criticisms by reviewing the history of FAT and its impact on practice.

The historical analyses relating to FAT in the following sections cover the period from the end of the nineteenth century to the present day. They examine individual and institutional contributions to FAT and reveal an evolutionary pattern. Initial contributions came from accounting practitioners largely concerned with resolving practice issues to improve financial accounting as an exercise in stewardship and accountability. Gradually, however, academic researchers joined practitioners in an expanded and joint effort to confront practice problems by reference to theory. Despite this co-operative effort, there remained a lack of resolution of practice problems. This led to accountancy associations becoming involved with FAT as they attempted to exercise control and authority over financial accounting and reporting practice, respond to public criticism, and avoid government regulation. In turn, individual applications of a theoretical approach to financial accounting issues expanded into comprehensive statements of FAT. These theories were typically normative and increasingly focused on the decision-usefulness model of satisfying information needs of investors and others. Further developments led to theoretical statements presented by accounting standard-setters as conceptual frameworks intended to justify financial accounting principles and practices. Despite this attention to FAT, however, established practice problems remained unresolved and new problems emerged. The normative focus was eventually proscribed as unscientific by academic accounting researchers and replaced by empirical and statistically driven observations of financial accounting practices. Perhaps unsurprisingly, because these 'scientific' studies offered no resolution of practice issues, the problems of practice persisted. The consequence of this was that attempts to produce FAT to resolve practical problems gradually disappeared from the accounting research literature. Today, all that remains of FAT in the relevant literature are conceptual frameworks intended to support principles-based standards and occasional ad hoc attempts at theory based on a philosophy of pragmatism. In addition, doubts have emerged in the research literature about the validity and worth of 'scientific' observations of accounting practices. Thus, the arguments and conclusions of researchers such as West, Lee, Dyckman and Zeff, and Inanga and Schneider, appear reasonable. The following sections attempt to provide a more detailed review to validate their positions.

The following historical review is divided into three approximate time periods. The first from circa 1881 to 1940 includes the first individual attempts to theorise about financial accounting problems. The second period from 1941 to 1970 covers the classical or golden age of normative FAT. The third period from 1971 to the present day is one in which public accountancy institutions responded to practice deficiencies and criticisms with conceptual frameworks to improve accounting standards, and academic researchers abandoned the normative approach to FAT in favour of more 'scientifically based' research.

Initial attempts at theory: 1881 to 1940

The expansion of trading and monetary systems of the European Renaissance evolved into complex and continuous commercial activity in the seventeenth, eighteenth, and nineteenth centuries (Edwards 2019: *passim*; Lee 2013: 145–52). Technological changes in manufacturing created by innovations of the Industrial Revolution, the introduction and expansion of capital markets, and the evolution of capital-intensive business enterprises contributed to accounting-related functions such as financial reporting and auditing that, in turn, became part of corporate regulation and business legislation designed to make corporate managers accountable to shareholders. Unsurprisingly, public accountants from the mid-nineteenth century onwards organised collectively to create associations to defend their economic and social interests in such matters. However, reporting scandals and accounting frauds were frequent (see Chapter 20 for discussion of such issues) and much was left initially to lawyers and judges in court cases to determine appropriate accounting practice (e.g. as with profits available for dividend payments). Public accountancy associations appeared reluctant to interfere in these matters although, from time to time, leading practitioners communicated their concerns about specific financial accounting issues. Practitioner articles began to appear in an emerging accounting literature, e.g. *The Accountant* from 1874.

Initial UK contributions

The process by which public accountants began to articulate what now is described as FAT started in the nineteenth century when double-entry bookkeeping was adopted as their core body of knowledge (Macve 1996: 23). This was particularly the case in the UK where public accountancy developed earlier than elsewhere in the English-speaking world and where, for example, Pixley (1881: 78) concluded that knowledge and experience of bookkeeping was one of the most important qualifications for an auditor.

Other writers elaborated on this theme. George Lisle (1900) began his *Accounting in Theory and Practice* with a theoretical discussion on double-entry bookkeeping to facilitate a permanent record of business transactions and their impact on the wealth of the business owner, thus implicitly emphasising the proprietary theory of accounting. Lisle followed his theoretical exposition with a section on practical bookkeeping that explained the use of specific accounting records. But he also addressed individual accounting topics from a theoretical perspective. For example, he defined profit in terms of an economic theory allowing for the replacement of capital (ibid.: 48). Lisle explored accounting concepts more specifically in a later article on foreign exchange conversion in which he enunciated the need to represent assets and liabilities at market rates quoted at the balance sheet date (Lisle 1903). He also examined average conversion rates and his theoretical exposition is comparable to contemporary statements of principle in this area (e.g. IASB 2004).

Somewhat earlier than Lisle, Edwin Guthrie, identified by Kitchen and Parker (1980: 22) as a pioneer of accounting thought, looked beyond double-entry bookkeeping to the production of financial statements such as the balance sheet and the need for consistency of accounting treatment and disclosure over time and between entities (Guthrie 1882). His arguments on reporting consistency are similar to those of policy-makers responsible for contemporary conceptual frameworks used by accounting standard-setters (e.g. Schipper 2003: 62–3).

Other British writers in the late nineteenth century began to explore theoretical accounting issues. For example, Lawrence R. Dicksee, described by Brief (1980: 1) as 'the father of modern accounting', wrote articles in the early 1890s in which he applied 'logical imagination' and 'first principles' to emerging issues (ibid.: 2). For example, in 1893, Dicksee examined the form and content of financial statements and addressed issues that continue to be of theoretical and practical significance today, e.g. charging interest on capital against profit and defining assets for accounting purposes (Dicksee 1893). In 1895, in a series of public lectures, Dicksee (1895) tackled a subject that had been introduced earlier by Ernest Cooper (1888), a leading public accountancy practitioner of his time, and which remains central to FAT, i.e. the nature and purpose of periodic profit. Dicksee (1895: 40) repeated Cooper's question: 'What is profit of a company?' and addressed issues such as unrealised operating and non-operating profits, undisclosed liabilities, and depreciation of fixed assets. In 1903, Dicksee (1903a) reviewed the purpose of financial statements and emphasised that, despite their subjective nature, accounting numbers needed to be reliable for their effective use. Dicksee was one of the earliest proponents of FAT, although he never used such a term in his writings. In his emphasis on income, he appears to have been an early advocate of a theoretical focus on entity income.

Other leading British public accountancy practitioners of this period with contributions to FAT include Richard Brown in the UK and Arthur L. Dickinson in the US and the UK. Brown did much to develop the early Scottish public accountancy profession. In 1904, in *The Accountant's Magazine*, the journal he founded and edited from 1897, Brown (1904: 146) wrote about financial statements based on the now familiar theoretical accounting notion of economic substance being of greater importance than legal form, and of the 'theory of accounts'. He also explained how financial statements could be stated in percentage form in order to assist users to compare periods and entities – an early example of the financial statement user approach to FAT.

Dickinson was a partner in Price, Waterhouse & Co., first in the US and then in the UK, who did much to develop US institutionalised public accountancy. He was the engagement partner in the audit of the United States Steel Corporation from 1902 when it commenced publishing consolidated financial statements. Dickinson was credited with this initiative, which had its origins in practices devised in the early 1890s (DeMond 1951: 60). Although there are some reservations concerning the validity of this claim, there is no doubt that Dickinson worked with the Corporation's comptroller and wrote about consolidated accounting in 1906 when it was in its infancy as a reporting technique (Dickinson 1906). His work can be argued as an early contribution to entity theory in financial accounting – in this respect, concerned with identifying the income and financial position of a group of companies defined for this purpose as a single economic entity.

The previously mentioned contributions to FAT have certain characteristics. For example, they were the writings of practitioners and teachers dealing with practice problems. Each writing had a theoretical component although they were not written explicitly as theoretical pieces. In particular, they reflected a focus away from double-entry bookkeeping to growing problems associated with financial statements for public disclosure as part of an exercise to make corporate managers accountable to shareholders and other stakeholders. They therefore contained ideas that remain relevant to FAT today. And they all reflected an inductive approach to theorising, i.e. a practitioner drawing on practical observations and experience to theorise.

Ad hoc contributions such as those above began to develop in a number of ways in the early 1900s. First, and occasionally, practitioner writers extended their thoughts into book-length treatises. For example, Dicksee published books on accounting issues with a theoretical content, i.e. depreciation (Dicksee 1903b) and goodwill (Dicksee and Tillyard 1906). Second, practitioner contributions became part of long-standing and persistent debates in the literature, e.g. accounting for the depreciation of fixed assets in relation to determining profit for dividend purposes (Brief 1976). Such debates began to inform thinking about income and capital in accounting beyond the existing contributions of lawyers and judges and, in turn, extended into a wider discussion in the early decades of the twentieth century on the nature of income, capital, and capital maintenance (Lee 1983). These later contributions to FAT included topics such as income realisation, financial and physical capital maintenance, operating and holding gains, and price and price-level changes – all matters theorised about in the era of normative accounting thought 1941–70 (e.g. Chambers 1966). Third, inputs to these debates began to involve academics and practitioners and, consequently, arguments became more explicitly theoretical. This was a period that started in the early 1900s and continued into the 1940s. Much of the writing was US in origin although there were occasional contributions from the UK.

Initial US contributions

One of the earliest US contributions to FAT was *The Philosophy of Accounts* by Charles E. Sprague (Sprague 1907). This book adopted the earlier focus of George Lisle and was an explanation of the theory and practice of double-entry bookkeeping with an added emphasis on the balance sheet, assets and liabilities, and, particularly, income as the periodic change in capital. Sprague's further concern was with the distinction between entity and proprietary theory (i.e. whether financial accounting is about the business entity or the owner's capital in it). He rejected the entity theory in favour of the proprietary alternative as he did not regard owner's capital as a liability. His bookkeeping framework therefore focused on profit as the periodic change in proprietorship rather than as a measure of entity performance.

Sprague's contribution to FAT was followed in 1909 by Henry R. Hatfield's *Modern Accounting* (Hatfield 1909/1927). This book was revised several years later as *Accounting* (Hatfield 1909/1927) and the latter is used in this and later sections. *Accounting* was arguably the first comprehensive attempt to explain financial accounting from a theoretical perspective. It used an inductive process of observing practice and contained real-world illustrations. Each chapter ended with an annotated bibliography of other writings. (Hatfield 1909/1927: 6) advocated a proprietary approach to accounting and started with the general nature of the balance sheet before moving on to a more detailed discussion of assets and valuations, intangible assets, depreciation, capital, and liabilities. He then examined the nature of profit and related this to matters such as dividends and capital losses. Surpluses, reserves, and sinking funds were also analysed. As a proprietary theorist, Hatfield regarded liabilities as negative assets. His approach was analytical and critical as well as explanatory, and he asked and discussed basic theoretical questions that remain unresolved today. For example, 'Does the balance sheet record costs or exhibit values?' (ibid.: 25) and 'When are profits realized?' (ibid.: 251). He was particularly critical of the inability of lawyers and judges in early court cases to understand the nature of accounting capital (ibid.: 274).

Hatfield was an explicit proponent of historical cost accounting (HCA). This was not the case with a contemporary, William A. Paton, who can be regarded as the father of modern FAT. Educated as an economist, Paton (1922) revolutionised FAT in his *Accounting Theory: With Special Reference to the Corporate Enterprise*. He rejected the proprietary accounting model of Sprague and Hatfield, and stated theory by focusing on accounting for a specific economic unit, the corporate business enterprise. This was an entity theory of accounting that recognised shareholders separately from creditors, and was contrary to the then existing economic theories of property rights. The principal accounting focus ceased to be double-entry bookkeeping and, instead, became accounting information as a guide to effective entity management of capital. Paton addressed the issue of current valuation in accounting and his model for financial accounting was based on the value-based information needs of corporate managers rather than proprietors. He argued at length about the limitations of HCA and the need for replacement costs and price-level adjustments to permit corporate management to maintain physical capital without having to raise additional financial capital.

This was a theory that recognised total income as a combination of operating, holding, and financial gains and losses, i.e. an all-inclusive concept of income.

Accounting Theory used practice only to illustrate theory. It ended with a chapter familiar to today's researchers of normative theory, i.e. the postulates or basic premises or assumptions of accounting (later developed in Moonitz 1961). Accounting issues of the twenty-first century such as revenue recognition, capital maintenance and the monetary unit, and goodwill were discussed by Paton and he linked the idea of judging managerial efficiency with reported income. *Accounting Theory* could have been written in the 1960s and 1970s but its impact at the time of writing was negligible. It was several decades before accounting standard-setters began to reflect Paton's ideas in their prescriptions (Chambers 1963). The accounting model propounded by Sprague and Hatfield had more contemporary impact presumably because it reflected existing and therefore familiar practice. That of Paton did not and he appears to have succumbed to the practical dominance of the HCA model by the end of the 1930s in his co-authorship of Paton and Littleton (1940) (see Zeff 2018).

Paton's arguments about income, capital, and the monetary unit were developed further by Henry W. Sweeney, a professor of accounting and law who later practised as a public accountant. He adapted his doctoral dissertation to produce *Stabilized Accounting* in 1927 with publication in 1936 (Sweeney 1936; see Clarke 1976). *Stabilized Accounting* brought together theoretical ideas from accounting and economics to reveal the problems in financial accounting practice caused by monetary units that fluctuate in value over time. Sweeney was influenced by German and Dutch thinkers and his work provided a theoretical basis for later institutional attempts to mandate price-level accounting using a monetary unit of constant purchasing power (e.g. Jones 1956). Sweeney criticised the use in practice of different monetary units in a single set of financial statements, and advocated a uniform unit for accounting. More specifically, in order to maintain proprietary capital in real purchasing power terms, he argued for the application of replacement costs to non-monetary assets and purchasing power adjustments to monetary assets and liabilities – thus introducing to FAT the ideas of realised and unrealised holding gains and losses, coupled with realised and unrealised monetary gains and losses that became part of current cost accounting in the 1970s and 1980s (see e.g. Tweedie and Whittington 1984: 60–189).

US contributions post Paton and Sweeney

If Paton and Sweeney provided the first comprehensive statements of FAT built on economic and accounting concepts, Canning (1929) produced a framework of economic theory with which to explain and discuss financial accounting. John B. Canning was a professor of economics with responsibility for accounting education and wrote *The Economics of Accountancy* as a means of educating economists about accounting practice by focusing on valuation and income. The book had little immediate impact on accountants but gradually influenced later accounting theorists concerned with integrating economic concepts into FAT. Canning's importance lies in his drawing attention to deficiencies in financial accounting. This was particularly true with respect to accounting for income, the central theme of *The Economics of Accountancy*.

Canning criticised accountants such as Hatfield for lacking a theory of income. Canning perceived accounting income, as then reported, to be no more than a residue of various accounting practices applied to the production of the balance sheet under the proprietary approach. In contrast, financial position according to Canning was a statement of prospect and future cash flows, and he advocated an entity approach to such accounting. The value of capital in an ideal world was, for him, discounted net future cash flow. He decried accountants' lack of a concept of value and what he termed the 'mongrel origins' of accounting numbers in balance sheets (i.e. a mix of various accounting bases) (Canning 1929: 319). Canning defined assets in terms of 'future service in money' (ibid.: 187) and advocated direct valuation on this basis where possible and indirect valuation where reasonable forecasting was not possible. In this respect, the single greatest influence on Canning's thinking was provided by the contemporary economist Irving Fisher (1906). The importance of Canning's theory was its identification of economic notions inherent in accounting practices such as the calculation of income and capital – particularly the idea of future benefits or services as the basis for valuing assets and therefore determining income. He was, however, somewhat ambiguous in his support of valuation bases other than historical cost.

The contributions of Paton and Canning were published in times of increasing public criticism of corporate financial reporting quality – particularly in the US (Carey 1969). This eventually led to institutional action involving corporate regulators and public accountants (e.g. the Securities Act 1933). However, there was no attempt by public accountancy associations to produce a coherent statement of FAT. In 1929, for example, despite the American Society of Certified Public Accountants' (ASCPA 1929) criticism of the inadequacies of professional associations in relation to FAT, the American Institute of Accountants (AIA) limited its efforts to a definitional statement of *Accounting Terminology* (AIA 1931). Unsurprisingly, in response, Greer (1932) called for a council of accounting research to improve institutional efforts.

Theories by individuals, however, continued to appear. Scott (1931), for example, wrote *The Cultural Significance of Accounts* not so much as a new theory of accounting but more as a historical review of the evolution of financial accounting as a cultural and social practice. Scott's work was based on a study of economic organisation and control through time. It was therefore the first major study of accounting in an explicit social context and can be related to the institutional, organisational, and social literature of accounting today (as in research journals such as *Accounting, Organizations and Society*, *Accounting, Auditing & Accountability Journal*, and *Critical Perspectives on Accounting*). Using a historical lens, Scott examined the rise and fall of market control in economic activity, blaming its disintegration on market factors such as size, complexity, instability, technological change, regulation, and law. He criticised traditional economic value theory and studied changes in corporate management and accountability. Scott concluded that the decline of control in economic markets required reassessment of the growing importance and role of accounting information in economic activity. He argued that better use of accounting information permitted business enterprises to adapt to changing economic circumstances. He believed accounting was an important means of mediating conflicts of interest in business and providing 'justice' (Scott 1931: 202; see also West 2003: 193). Scott concluded that, if accounting information was to supplant the market as the principal tool of economic organisation, then FAT was needed to supplant market theory as the means of understanding economic theory. Despite its debatable analyses of economic theory and practice, Scott's perception of FAT as a primary cultural influence was the precursor to later critical theories about accounting's influence in society (e.g. as in Hopwood 1983; Roslender 1992). It is also consistent with Williams' (2017: 84–5) argument that accounting is about accountability, fairness, and justice.

Unlike Scott, his contemporary Kenneth MacNeal was not an academic. He worked as a public accountancy practitioner and used his practice experience to write *Truth in Accounting* in 1939 as a repost to what he perceived to be the neglect by public accountants of unrealised gains when calculating periodic income. MacNeal (1939: vii) argued that the majority of audited financial statements were untrue and misleading due to unsound accounting principles. His analysis started with three fables on the misleading nature of reported accounting information before explaining the deception in terms of lack of market values and unrealised gains, inclusion of unrealised losses, and exclusion of non-recurrent realised gains and losses from periodic income. MacNeal (ibid.: 82–3) criticised accounting principles designed for a past proprietary age instead of an era of corporate businesses often marked by a separation of shareholders and managers and a consequent need for the accountability of the latter to the former. His book was a theoretical argument for using net realisable values as the basis for financial accounting reports. MacNeal concluded by linking HCA to the decline in the reputation of public accountancy, and argued the need for public accountants to admit the irrelevance of HCA (ibid.: 323–4). MacNeal was an early example of a writer associating failure in FAT with professional reputation and status. His text was also the beginning of a long line of critical research about professionalism in public accountancy (see West 2003; Lee 2006a, 2013). It was also the precursor for a later persistent stream of theoretical argument for the use of net realisable values in financial accounting (e.g. Chambers 1966; Sterling 1970).

Stephen Gilman was a public accountancy practitioner and educator who published *Accounting Concepts of Profit* in 1939 (Gilman 1939). This was not a book of original FAT. Instead, Gilman emphasised the prevailing trend in financial accounting away from the balance sheet to the income statement (i.e. from proprietary to entity theory). He concentrated on the flexibility associated with the calculation of income (particularly through topics such as inventory adjustment), a matter of increasing criticism in practice over the previous two decades that eventually led to the introduction of mandatory accounting standards.

US institutional theories

Institutional involvement with FAT began to emerge at the end of the 1930s as a result of public criticism of financial accounting practice. First, the American Accounting Association (AAA) stated 20 basic accounting propositions related to costs and values, income, and capital and surplus (AAA 1936). This was not a complete FAT, rather a theoretical review of certain financial accounting practices using a deductive approach. The statement reinforced the accounting convention of conservatism and the historical cost principle, and advocated an all-inclusive concept of income (differentiating between operating and non-operating gains and losses). The 1936 AAA statement was explicitly expanded into a larger work by Paton and Littleton (1940). The latter can be argued as the first institutional attempt at producing a fully integrated FAT and is certainly the first conceptual framework for accounting standards (ibid.: ix). The monograph used an inductive approach to FAT and provided, in chapter 2, a conceptual explanation of HCA based on notions such as business entity, going concern, historical cost, and matching. These ideas were expanded by Paton and Littleton in separate chapters explaining cost, revenue, income, and surplus. The principal objective of financial accounting was seen as periodically reporting on managerial performance in terms of its 'effort' (costs) and 'accomplishment' (revenue) (ibid.: 14–15). The thinking behind this focus was a need for a recognition and acceptance by corporate management of a responsibility to be accountable to shareholders. Although practitioners and academics at this time were not convinced by the entity approach of Paton and Littleton, the importance of their study is demonstrated by the fact that many of its basic ideas remain in conceptual frameworks and accounting standards today. Indeed, Zeff (2018: 64) concluded that Paton was the major influence on matters such as cost, revenue, income, and surplus, with Littleton providing the basis for these ideas in terms of the matching principle to produce objective and verifiable historic cost data.

The 1936 statement of the AAA also evoked a practitioner response from the AIA because of its recommendation of all-inclusive income. Funded by a leading public accountancy firm, three academics (including Hatfield) were asked by the AIA to review accounting practice. They wrote *A Statement of Accounting Principles* in 1938 (Sanders et al., 1938). The *Statement* was published by the AIA and drew criticism from academics because it accepted existing practice. It also emphasised the subjectivity of accounting because of the need for personal judgement. Many of the basic ideas in the *Statement* were also in Paton and Littleton (1940) (e.g. the information needs of management, historical cost, and going concern). However, it introduced to the accounting literature the notion of generally accepted accounting principles, not as matters of law but from consensus in practice, speech, and writing (Sanders et al., 1938: 5). In combination, the 1936 and 1940 statements of the AAA and the 1938 statement of the AIA can be argued to be the origins of later institutional statements. In particular, Paton and Littleton (1940) brought legitimacy and authority to HCA theory in the US and elsewhere, and it remains an active publication of the AAA. By 1939, the AIA had created a research function within its accounting standards activities.

In the UK, there were few significant developments in the 1930s with respect to FAT. However, two attempts to bring together academics and practitioners to discuss theory and practice are noteworthy (Edwards 2019: 309–11). In 1935, the Society of Incorporated Accountants and Auditors created the first British research committee whose most significant achievement was the launch, in 1948, of the first British journal devoted to FAT and related practice issues (*Accounting Research*). In 1936, academics at the London School of Economics created the Accounting Research Association to influence practice change. Neither development appears to have had any long-term impact in terms of FAT but reflected contemporary concern in the UK about the need for co-operation between accounting researchers and practitioners.

Classical financial accounting theory: 1941 to 1970

The Second World War affected activity associated with FAT in different ways. In the UK in 1942, for example, the Institute of Chartered Accountants in England and Wales (ICAEW) created a research committee to publish guidance on financial accounting practice. However, it would be several decades before it and other UK bodies published statements on FAT. In the US, on the other hand, the War postponed until 1947 an AIA initiative to study business income. The inflationary effects of the War resurrected the initiative and papers were written by economists (Alexander et al., 1950) and debated by the AIA Study Group on Business Income (1952). Alexander and his co-authors revealed a spectrum of economic ideas applicable to accounting for business income (i.e. real and monetary, operating and holding, and realised and accrued gains and losses; and general and specific price-level changes). The Study Group examined the meaning of income from economic, legal, and accounting standpoints before reviewing several accepted accounting assumptions or principles seen in previous theoretical studies (e.g. the monetary unit, realisation, going concern, matching, and historical cost). Specific accounting income issues were discussed including the stability of the monetary unit and the all-inclusive concept of income. The Study Group (1952: 107) came to the conclusion there was a need for greater uniformity in financial accounting practice but that no single system could meet all the needs of financial statement users.

The 1952 Study Group report reflects the primacy of entity income in FAT at this time and a growing debate about the conservatism of accounting thought and practice in periods of dynamic economics. In particular, the debate concerned the questionable relevance of the historical cost and realisation conventions that dominated practice. The exclusion of unrealised gains and monetary gains and losses from reported business income was to become a central issue addressed by writers of the classical or so-called golden age of theorising from 1941 to 1970 (Nelson 1973: 4). Even professional accountancy associations became involved. For example, in 1949, the ICAEW published a guidance statement on general price-level accounting, and in the US in 1956 the AAA produced a similar study (Jones 1956).

Individual academic contributions on both sides of the debate increased significantly after the Second World War. For example, in the US, William J. Vatter published his *Fund Theory of Accounting* (Vatter 1947). Vatter explicitly recognised the speculative nature of his theory, in which he argued for a package of financial statements based on a balance sheet decomposed into funds or business activities (i.e. operating, investing, financing, and capital). These statements were intended to describe periodic movements in these funds. Conventional notions such as periodic income would not be reported although the financial statement user could construct such an accounting number from reported flows. Vatter based his arguments on what he regarded as inadequacies of the proprietary and entity theories of accounting, and attempts by theorists to meet the needs of specific user groups such as investors. Although it was not well received or followed up because of its arbitrary classifications and user unfriendliness, Vatter's fund theory was a precursor to later financial accounting theories based on funds and cash flows (see Lee 1986), and should be recognised as innovative in seeking to satisfy multiple user needs.

Ananias C. Littleton was a considerable influence on US accountancy for several decades and published books and articles on FAT. Littleton believed theory and practice were a single subject of financial accounting and it is unsurprising to find that *Structure of Accounting Theory* (Littleton 1953) defended HCA by means of the inductive approach to theory (i.e. observing practices and drawing concepts and principles from the observations). 'Experience, let it be noted, is not the same as experiment' (ibid.: 185). He argued that the best way to advance financial accounting was to allow practitioners to develop and evolve practices and then, by observation of these practical experiences, derive the principles on which they were based. 'Good experience becomes accepted practice' (ibid.: 186). Littleton argued that reported accounting numbers require to be based on objective evidence thereby validating the continued use of historical costs. Income was the 'centre of gravity' of accounting (ibid.: 18). Financial statements should assist users to evaluate managerial performance. They were therefore not valuation statements because values were transient and subjective. As Littleton (ibid.: 34) concluded, the purpose of accounting was to permit 'calculated judgment' of business enterprise success.

Structure of Accounting Theory provided many legacies. It explicitly emphasised a general-purpose approach to financial reporting with a stewardship objective (ibid.: 15) – an objective that had been implicit in most previous attempts at FAT. Littleton used the inductive approach to theorise and presented FAT within a framework of objectives, concepts, and principles. He gave considerable comfort to practitioners wedded to the historical cost, income-orientated system of financial reporting. In fact, his book could be used today to justify contemporary HCA practice. However, Littleton (1953) can be viewed also in a different way. It is consistent with the philosophy of a later theoretical approach, positive accounting theory (PAT), in that it perceives the role of the theorist as observing, explaining, and predicting actual practices rather than prescribing alternative practices (Watts and Zimmerman 1986: 2).

Laying down classical theory

As the previous sections indicate, there were many attempts to articulate FAT prior to the mid-1950s. Their origins lay in practitioner explanations of bookkeeping theory that evolved into commentaries about financial statements and their basic elements. Practitioners were joined by academic researchers and the theorising became more formal, although the subject-matter tended to be specific problems from practice rather than overall systems of reporting. The preference of early theorists was for inductive studies based on observations of practice, and for proprietary rather than entity theory. Gradually, however, FAT was influenced by economic thinking and, because of the importance of income concepts in economic theory, the focus in FAT became periodic income and problems associated with it (e.g. pricing and valuation). The meaning of accounting numbers based on historical costs was challenged and defended, and seminal works on FAT were published and recognised as such (e.g. Sprague 1907; Hatfield 1909/1927; Paton 1922; Canning 1929; Sweeney 1936; Gilman 1939; MacNeal 1939; Paton and Littleton 1940; Littleton 1953). Professional accountancy bodies in the US began to examine theoretical aspects of financial accounting practice.

Hatfield, Paton, Canning, Littleton, and MacNeal became the intellectual basis for study by a community of financial accounting theorists in the 1950s and 1960s. Their work was frequently cited, predominantly by academics intent on changing financial accounting practice. More specifically, the studies of Paton and Littleton (1940) and Littleton (1953) provided a conventional model with which to construct a theory to justify existing practice. The new theorists, however, were arguing for an alternative FAT. This was particularly true of Raymond J. Chambers, an Australian professor.

Chambers advocated continuously contemporary accounting, a reporting system based on net realisable values in which financial position was central and income a derivative as in the proprietary approach to FAT. The development of Chambers' theory was influenced by personal and practical experience of price regulation, teaching management, concern about inductive reasoning from practice by previous theorists, lack of methodology in prior theories, and increasing evidence of the unreliability of reported accounting numbers. Chambers developed a deductive theory of financial accounting using ideas from disciplines such as communication, economics, management, mathematics, measurement, organisational behaviour, and philosophy. His initial thesis appeared in Chambers (1955) with four fundamental concepts, i.e. entities, rational management, monetary statements, and accounting as a service function. He developed these ideas in various papers using normative thinking within a deductive framework. For example, in Chambers (1962), theory was explained in terms of actors and their decisions and actions in a market economy (including exchange, money, credit, and price), the need for and qualities of information for these decisions and actions (including relevance, neutrality, correspondence, consistency, and objectivity), and the business entity and its financial position (monetary and non-monetary based on net realisable values) and changes therein (realised and unrealised). The full theory appeared as *Accounting, Evaluation and Economic Behaviour* (Chambers 1966).

The long-term importance of Chambers in the history of FAT was not so much the specifics of his theory (e.g. the reporting relevance of net realisable values). It had more to do with his methodology for theorising (e.g. the context, structure, and relationships of a theory and its application to practice). The deductive work of Chambers was a direct challenge to the dominant inductive approach and pragmatism of prior researchers such as Paton and Littleton. His legacy is seen in later FAT (including conceptual frameworks), and in practice embodied in the increasing attention to financial position and the use of net realisable value to operationalise fair value accounting (e.g. see Georgiou and Jack 2011).

Building on classical theory tradition

Other classical contributions to FAT in the 1960s were predominantly US in origin and included Edwards and Bell (1961), Moonitz (1961), Staubus (1961), Sprouse and Moonitz (1962), Grady (1965), Mattessich (1964), AAA (1966), Ijiri (1967), Thomas (1969), and Sterling (1970). They each reveal a formal theoretical structure and follow a deductive approach and normative prescription.

Edwards and Bell (1961) was written by Edgar O. Edwards and Philip W. Bell, both US professors of economics. Based on an economic theory of the firm under conditions of uncertainty, Edwards and Bell developed a concept of business income they argued to be useful to internal management, investors, creditors, and others, and also for taxation purposes. They related measurement of business activity to current values and to general price-level changes, and advocated calculating income on short-term assets on a net realisable value basis and long-term assets using replacement costs. Edwards and Bell applied their recommendations to inventory and depreciable fixed assets, distinguishing between operating and holding gains and losses, and real and fictitious gains and losses due to general price-level adjustments. In order to maintain capital, holding gains were not regarded as distributable or taxable income. Edwards and Bell (1961) was a normative proprietary theory of income using multiple current valuation bases but lacked the theoretical superstructure of studies such as Chambers (1966). However, it influenced the current cost accounting (CCA) debate of the 1970s in its argument for mixed values and the separation of operating and holding income (see Tweedie and Whittington 1984: *passim*). The study failed to explore FAT in relation to financial position and ignored the problem of aggregating different current values.

The American Institute of Certified Public Accountants (AICPA) in the late 1950s decided to explore the basic foundations of financial accounting in order to determine the broad principles upon which practice was based at that time and from which practice improvements could be made. It did so in two studies. Moonitz (1961) explored the foundations (or postulates) of accounting and Sprouse and Moonitz (1962) focused on accounting principles (the broad guidelines to help formulate specific practice rules). These studies fell within the definition of FAT and both evoked a critical reaction from practitioners and academic researchers. However, Moonitz's postulates were unremarkable and most had been included in previous studies, e.g. exchange, entity, periodicity, unit of account, continuity, and consistency. They therefore can be argued to frame financial accounting in relatively uncontroversial truths. The most serious criticism was directed at Sprouse and Moonitz (1962) with its primary focus on financial position before income and use of a mixture of historical costs, current values, and price-level adjustments. The recommended move from HCA to an all-inclusive income-orientated reporting based on mixed valuations was apparently seen as too radical.

Derived from his doctoral dissertation on revenue accounting, Staubus' (1961) *A Theory of Accounting for Investors* was an attempt to introduce an explicit objective for financial reporting (i.e. satisfying investors' decisions). This created the related qualitative characteristic of reported information (i.e. decision-usefulness). Staubus analysed investor and manager decisions and, by relating them to reporting characteristics such as relevance and reliability, argued for measurements indicative of changes in future cash flows. These ideas can be traced to later institutional theorising by bodies such as the AICPA and the FASB in the US. They also signalled the start of de-emphasising stewardship and accountability as the main financial reporting objectives.

Further work on the postulates and principles studies was shelved by the AICPA, although some features re-emerged in later conceptual frameworks and specific accounting standards of the FASB and other similar bodies. In addition, effectively as an antidote to the studies by Moonitz and Sprouse, the AICPA produced *Inventory of Generally Accepted Accounting Principles for Business Enterprises* (Grady 1965). This was a deliberate attempt to encapsulate conventional practice in a theoretical framework of the basic concepts needed to support HCA. Grady (1965) placed considerable emphasis on several notions: of government 'reserving the economic area primarily for development by the people' (ibid.: 25), that 'diversity in accounting among independent business entities is a basic fact of life' (ibid.: 33), that 'conservatism is an essential quality in the performance of the auditing function' (ibid.: 35), and of disclosure as material if it 'would be likely to influence or "make a difference" in the judgment and conduct of a reasonable person' (ibid.: 40). These were not notions addressed in Moonitz (1961) and Sprouse and Moonitz (1962). Indeed, Grady (1965: 43–4) identified the postulates of Moonitz (1961) that he had ignored when constructing his own framework, i.e. those postulates which effectively supported principles associated with the use of current values. FAT, at least from an institutional public accountancy perspective in the US in the 1960s, was therefore a theory that supported HCA (see Zeff 2007).

While the AICPA was attempting to formulate a statement of conventional FAT, academic researchers continued to produce individual theories reflecting the multi-disciplinary approach seen in the work of Chambers (1966). Richard V. Mattessich, for example, is an Austrian accountant who became a Canadian professor of accounting. He is also an engineer and economist and this background is reflected in *Accounting and Analytical Methods* (Mattessich 1964), a quantitative-analytical explanation of financial accounting from ex post and ex ante positions. Mattessich brought ideas from logic, economics, sociology, decision theory, and measurement to his analysis of income and capital. He advocated use of a mixed system of current values. In particular, he emphasised the idea of accounting for 'real and financial objects' (ibid.: 36), i.e. distinguishing between physical and social realities, a subject he continued to develop in the 1990s as part of a debate on accounting for economic reality (Mattessich 1991; see also Lee 2006b).

Yuji Ijiri was a Japanese-born mathematician who pursued his academic career in the US. He brought mathematical rigour to *The Foundations of Accounting Measurements* (Ijiri 1967). This was FAT based on the mathematical axioms of control, value, and exchange. Ijiri argued for HCA, using double-entry bookkeeping as the only logical means of providing reliable and objective accounting information. He argued against the use of current values as these were inconsistent with his axioms. His arguments reflected the information needs of both internal management and external users of financial statements. As with Mattessich, Ijiri made use of measurement and decision theories. Also as with Mattessich, Ijiri covered ideas that were part of a continuing debate concerning improvements to financial reporting. He focused on accounting as a function concerned with phenomena or 'principles' represented by phenomena or 'surrogates' in a linguistic form and therefore with issues of representation, language, and measurement (Ijiri 1967: 3–28). Ijiri (1981) extended his case for HCA in less complex terms than his 1967 work.

A Canadian accounting researcher, Arthur L. Thomas, explored the specific FAT issue of the allocation of accounting data in the form of accruals, prepayments, depreciation, and amortisation (Thomas 1969). His conclusion was that these arithmetical calculations were arbitrary, incorrigible, pervasive, and unjustifiable in accounting practice. They could either continue to be accepted by practitioners as part of conventional practice or be replaced by accounting measurements that avoided allocation (e.g. net realisable values and cash flows). Thomas' ideas are found in contemporary research by Chambers (see above) and Sterling (see below) in the 1960s and 1970s, and in later research in the 1970s and 1980s by cash flow accounting advocates in the UK (e.g. Lee 1986). Thomas (1974) later clarified and extended his arguments on the arbitrariness and incorrigibility of accounting allocations.

Sterling (1970) initially appeared as a doctoral dissertation in 1962. Robert R. Sterling was a US economist and philosopher of science. He brought this background to his study of accounting in the 1960s and his career was devoted to criticising the meaninglessness of HCA and advocating an alternative reporting system based on net realisable values. Sterling (1970) gathered together his initial ideas on FAT, and did so by examining income from the perspective of four competing theoretical models, i.e. economic (evolving from Fisher 1906), accounting (historical cost-realisation), market value, and Boulding's constant (adopting a constant value to avoid arbitrary choice). He examined each of these alternatives in terms of two principal characteristics – verity (i.e. representational faithfulness or reliability) and relevance (i.e. to decisions). Sterling's arguments were made in the context of a simple business model of a wheat trader under conditions of certainty and uncertainty. He concluded that current market price alone 'relates all the extant alternatives' (Sterling 1970: 339). Sterling later developed his theory in a number of studies, most notably in Sterling (1979) in which he argued decision relevance as the primary qualitative characteristic of financial accounting (Sterling 1979: 85) and identified a flaw in most previous and later FAT, i.e. they described decision makers rather than decisions and therefore lacked sufficient underlying detail to determine accounting numbers relevant to their decisions.

End of classical theorising

By the late 1960s, FAT had a chaotic flavour. Theorists such as Littleton, Grady, and Ijiri argued for HCA. Chambers, Thomas, and Sterling advocated net realisable values. Edwards and Bell, and Staubus were primarily concerned with mixed values. Sprouse and Moonitz, and Mattessich also desired a range of current values in financial reports. A further study by the AAA (1966) gave another theoretical alternative, i.e. HCA supplemented by current cost accounting (defined in terms of replacement costs, realisable values, and price indices). AAA (1966) was a report arguing for general-purpose financial statements to satisfy the decision needs of a variety of report user groups. Stewardship continued to be recognised as a secondary reporting aim and four basic standards were recommended. The latter were to become the cornerstones of later conceptual frameworks of accounting standard-setters, i.e. decision relevance, verifiability, freedom from bias, and quantifiability (AAA 1966: 7).

The incoherence of this situation was reviewed by an AAA committee in 1977, a decade after its 1966 *Statement of Basic Accounting Theory* (AAA 1977). The review was US-centric and based on the work of Paton (1922) and Hatfield 1909/1927 in its 1927 reissue, Canning (1929), Sweeney (1936), Gilman (1939), MacNeal (1939), Paton and Littleton (1940), Alexander et al. (1950), Littleton (1953), Edwards and Bell (1961), Moonitz (1961), Sprouse and Moonitz (1962), and Ijiri (1975). It therefore focused primarily on theories relating to historical costs, replacement costs, and mixed current values. With the exception of MacNeal, the net realisable value argument was ignored. The AAA committee believed the lack of a generally accepted FAT was due to the difficulty of relating theories to practice, coping with arbitrary accounting allocations, the subjectivity of normative argument, interpreting user behaviour, cost-benefit considerations, and information overload (AAA 1977: 31–9). Events of the next three decades did little to change this perception.

Conceptual frameworks and scientific theory: 1971 to 2018

There have been four developments in FAT during this period. First, with the exception of a handful of academic researchers, classical normative theory has largely disappeared from the relevant literature generally and from financial accounting instruction specifically. Second, the cause of this decline can be attributed to the emergence of empirical finance-based accounting research generally, and PAT research particularly. Third, despite the disappearance of normative theory in research and teaching, it appeared in the literature of accounting standard-setters in their conceptual frameworks. Fourth, a succession of financial reporting scandals has contributed to accounting standard-setters using conceptual frameworks to produce principles-based standards. Each of these developments is explained below.

Fall of normative research

For those accounting theorists continuing to argue normatively, the 1970s and 1980s resulted in a diminishing contribution to the accounting literature, particularly in the US. For example, Chambers advocated continuously contemporary accounting theory into the 1980s (see Chambers and Dean 1986), and Sterling argued for net realisable value accounting into the 1990s (see Lee and Wolnizer 1997). The reason for this overall decline in normative FAT was the reaction by economics-trained researchers to normative theorising (e.g. Demski 1973). Normative theorists such as Chambers and Sterling found leading accounting research journals closed to classical FAT and, instead, favouring the new 'science' of economics-based accounting empiricism (largely connected to PAT) (Edwards et al. 2013).

There were exceptions to this general trend. For example, in the 1970s, as a result of high rates of inflation and associated government concern, accounting researchers debated practical alternatives to HCA, e.g. current purchasing power accounting and CCA (Tweedie and Whittington 1984: 60–258). There were many individual contributions to this debate. For example, Baxter (1975) proposed an income theory based on Bonbright's insurance concept of value to the owner, the maximum loss from permanent deprivation of an asset. This theory used a mixture of replacement cost, economic value, net realisable value, and indexed historical cost, and produced operating and holding gains and losses as well as monetary gains and losses for reporting purposes. The initial argument for such a system was made a decade before by Solomons (1966). Variants of value to the owner were adopted by accounting standard-setters in the UK and the US for a short period in the early 1980s as a mandatory supplement to HCA (e.g. Accounting Standards Committee, FASB 1979; ASC 1980). The change in practice, however, was brief – in part because the general rate of inflation diminished and the additional accounting numbers created confusion for report users, and also because there was no formal theoretical framework in place with which to judge the relevance of a system of mixed values such as CCA (Tweedie and Whittington 1984: 329–31).

A further exception to the decline of normative theorising was the development of cash flow accounting (CFA) and reporting theory from the early 1970s – particularly in the UK. CFA arguments eventually led to mandatory CFA standards in the US in 1987 and the UK in 1991. The main motivation for suggesting change from an accrual and allocation-based system of financial accounting to a cash-based one was a debate in the UK in the late 1960s about the lack of uniformity, incompleteness, and meaningless of HCA. Thomas A. Lee (1986) is a British researcher who argued for a theory of CFA in two steps, i.e. as an articulating system, first, of statements of actual and forecast cash flows and, second, of statements of realised and unrealised flows, and financial position based on net realisable values as potential cash flows. Lee's arguments were entity-based and used reporting characteristics such as decision relevance and informational reliability. Gerald H. Lawson (1997) is also a British researcher who advocated reports of actual and forecast cash flows but in combination with the market value of enterprise capital in order to assist internal management and external investors to assess enterprise performance. Lawson's arguments took FAT into the macro-economic areas of dividend policy, inflation, and taxation. As a contribution to reviewing conceptual frameworks based on the balance sheet approach to financial reporting advocated by the FASB and the ISAB, Dichev (2017) argued for an alternative income approach based on decomposing periodic income into operating cash flow and associated accrual (i.e. non-cash net asset periodic changes) components. Dichev (2017) therefore represented a rare return to normative thinking with respect to FAT.

Rise of scientific theory

Arguably the most damaging influence on classical FAT was the emergence in the late 1960s and early 1970s of empirical financial accounting research. This research stream started with studies such as Ball and Brown (1968) and was based on economic theories relating to efficient markets, capital asset pricing, economic agency, and market regulation. The various strands of research were merged into PAT by Watts and Zimmerman (1986). PAT attempted to explain and predict accounting practice in specific circumstances, and was an off-shoot of neo-liberal positive economics based on a *laissez faire* regime of free capital markets and minimal government regulation. It was intended to assist accountants, auditors, and standard-setters to assess the consequences of their accounting choices. In particular, it observed the behaviour of accountants, auditors, and financial report users with respect to specific accounting disclosures and practices. PAT was claimed by its advocates to be scientific because of the apparent statistical objectivity of its empirical observations. It was also stated not to be intended to change accounting practice. Its impact can be seen in terms of the increase of empirical studies and decrease of normative studies in leading accounting research journals since the 1980s. Indeed, PAT theorists condemned normative theory as lacking empirical validity (Watts and Zimmerman 1986: 4–5) and fulfilling a political role of providing excuses for accounting practice failures or prescriptions (ibid.: 344–5).

Sterling (1990: 129–30) concluded that PAT was not FAT. In his opinion, it did not examine accounting practices or financial statements. Instead, it observed the behaviour of those individuals associated with these practices and statements. Mouck (1992: 54) categorised PAT as rhetoric to disseminate the political ideology of *laissez faire*. Even proponents of PAT in the form of capital market researchers admitted its inability to explain anomalies in empirical results about market efficiency (Beaver 2002: 456–7), its use of 'contextual accounting arguments' instead of a general theory (ibid.: 462), the need for better understanding of accounting report users (ibid.: 465), and a lack of understanding of the nature of earnings management (ibid.: 468). However, despite its limitations as a theory, PAT in its various forms proved influential in removing classical normative research from leading accounting research journals.

A more specific consequence of PAT affected the accounting research community. Journal editorial boards and academic associations in the US were persistently dominated by researchers with doctorates from a small number of élite universities working in networked relationships (see, e.g. Lee 1995; Williams and Rodgers 1995; Lohmann and Eulerich 2017). Recently, Lohmann and Eulerich (2017: 22) predicted that accounting researchers from a small number of élite universities in the US would perpetuate and even increase the domination of positive, neoclassical economics over normative, conceptual studies of FAT into the foreseeable future.

Despite these reservations about the impact of PAT, a research stream related to capital markets was associated with the search for a generally acceptable FAT. James A. Ohlson (e.g. 1995, 2006), a US researcher, described FAT based on HCA and attempted to minimise its inherent problems of allocation and valuation. Ohlson's theory used an accounting income number inclusive of all gains and losses associated with changes in the book value of capital (i.e. the clean surplus). Ohlson defined the price of equity as the sum of an entity's reported book value and the present value of its expected abnormal income stream. He defined the latter as the difference between total income on a modified cash basis and the required rate of return on the beginning-of-period book value of capital. Modified cash income was the periodic change in cash-related net assets at book value plus the net dividend (i.e. dividend payments minus any capital issued). Ohlson's model attempted to provide a theoretical prescription of accounting numbers based on conventional HCA practice within a variant of the capital asset pricing model. The theory was controversial as it remained rooted in the proprietary approach related to income calculation and depended on allocated historical costs.

Rise of conceptual frameworks

At a time when financial accounting researchers turned away from normative theory to promote empirical economic studies of financial accounting, the public accountancy profession in the US and the UK became involved in normative theorising in the form of conceptual frameworks designed to provide an intellectual basis for mandatory accounting standards. This was first seen in two conceptual studies in the US by the AICPA (1970, 1971). It gathered momentum when the AICPA's Wheat Committee recommended the creation of the FASB in 1972 to produce accounting standards independent of public accountancy bodies. From then on, a series of studies associated with conceptual frameworks was generated. Each study emphasised a conceptual approach relating to the decision use of financial statements by investors and creditors.

The Trueblood Committee was formed in 1972 by the AICPA and reported a year later (AICPA 1973). Although explicitly focused on the objectives of financial reporting, Trueblood provided a blueprint for later conceptual frameworks. It advocated the provision of information useful for decisions relating to investment and lending, service to other users relying on financial statements, and assessments associated with earning power, accountability, and prediction. The study also examined the basic elements and characteristics of reported financial statements. In this respect, the Trueblood Committee appears to have been influenced by prior normative theorising of individual researchers.

The theoretical framework for accounting standards pioneered by Trueblood centred on financial reporting objectives, financial statement elements, and accounting information qualities or characteristics. These issues were also addressed in the UK in the Accounting Standards Steering Committee's (ASSC 1975) *The Corporate Report* which reviewed the objectives and concepts of financial reporting in the context of making business enterprises more publicly accountable. As with the Trueblood report, it advocated a report user approach but recommended accounting based on price-level-adjusted HCA. In the same year, the Sandilands Committee (Inflation Accounting Committee 1975), created by the UK government in 1974 to consider whether and how corporate financial statements should account for changing prices, also argued for a user approach and looked at various reporting characteristics previously examined in individual works of FAT. It advocated a value to the business approach using current values. Again, these studies appear to have been influenced by prior ideas introduced by individual researchers of FAT.

In the US, the FASB (1976) began a long-term project to produce a complete conceptual framework. It published a statement on reporting objectives in 1978 (FASB 1978) followed between 1980 and 2000 by supporting statements to guide practice (i.e. on qualitative characteristics, elements of financial statements, and recognition and measurement). In combination, these statements provided the foundation for the current FASB conceptual framework. All were based on the decision-usefulness approach, the entity approach to income derived from a statement of assets and liabilities, normative and deductive reasoning, and previous individual studies of FAT. The user approach was emphasised in an AICPA review by the Jenkins Committee (AICPA 1999). A similar project in the UK began in 1991 (see Arnold et al., 1991) and culminated in a conceptual framework produced by the Accounting Standards Board (ASB 1999). The ASB's framework was not influenced greatly by a prior Institute of Chartered Accountants of Scotland (ICAS) study arguing for reports of cash flows and net realisable values as a means of portraying economic reality defined in terms of economic substance not legal form (McMonnies 1988).

Scandal and principle

The most recent position with respect to conceptual frameworks and FAT is associated with financial and corporate scandals such as Cendant, Enron, and WorldCom in the US, and BCCI and Maxwell Communications in the UK in the 1990s (see Chapter 20 for details). In 2002, the FASB (2002b) announced its intention to use its conceptual framework to produce principles-based accounting standards, i.e. to explicitly associate standards with theoretical notions such as the qualitative characteristics of decision relevance and reliability. This approach was endorsed by the Securities Exchange Commission (SEC 2003) and effectively became a global project when the FASB and the IASB agreed in 2002 to harmonise their conceptual frameworks and accounting standards (FASB 2002a). Bullen and Crook (2006) reviewed the FASB–IASB initiative and predicted it would not unduly change ideas, emphases, and approaches in existing frameworks. For example, the proprietary approach to the calculation of income would be retained (ibid.: 9).

The joint FASB–IASB conceptual framework project had a protracted and fractured history. Work on it began in 2004, produced initial joint statements on reporting objectives and qualitative characteristics in 2010, was suspended also in 2010, and resumed in 2012 (for the IASB) and in 2014 (for the FASB). The final completed framework was published by the IASB in 2018 (IASB 2018). The FASB project remains incomplete. IASB (2018) used the notion of decision-usefulness and focused on assets and liabilities as the primary elements from which periodic income and cash flows derive. The IASB subsumed stewardship into the decision-usefulness objective, despite this approach being misaligned with economic theory and property rights as well as historical evidence of decision-useful data not being a realistic substitute for stewardship data (Miller and Oldroyd 2018). The IASB permitted the use of a mix of measurement bases including HCA and fair values. It did not resolve long-standing concerns about the conflict between accounting primarily for stocks or flows (e.g. Financial Accounting Standards Committee, FASC 2012).

Baker (2017) researched a history of the conceptual framework and its predecessors of pre-classical and classical FAT to demonstrate that proponents of FAT through the decades prior to the conceptual framework influenced its contemporary content. Also, the reporting objectives and qualitative characteristics of conceptual frameworks such as IASB (2018) inspired a series of critical studies concerning the topic of accounting for economic reality. The conceptual mandate prescribed for accountants to account and represent faithfully the economic substance or so-called reality of assets and liabilities generated a number of research studies focused on the meaning of such reality in the context of corporate business and financial reporting – more specifically, the ontology and epistemology of economic reality (see, e.g. Lee 2006b; Mattessich 2009; Moore 2009). The subjectiveness of the social constructions forming the main elements of reported financial statements should be a primary concern for future researchers of FAT.

Whether ideas prescribed in conceptual frameworks and drawn from previous individual and institutional studies of FAT have had or will result in significant change to accounting practice is doubtful. A leading standard-setter in the US revealed the decision-usefulness approach would be practised by the FASB in terms of the reporting objectives of comparability and consistency (Schipper 2003: 62). In other words, despite more than a century of searching for a universal FAT, the fundamental reporting framework remained an income statement and balance sheet based predominantly on accrued and allocated historical costs applied consistently. It is therefore not unreasonable to support the conclusion reached by Hines (1991) and others that the historical role of the conceptual framework has not been to provide a theoretical basis to examine and improve financial accounting practice but, instead, to be a political tool of public accountants in their goal to achieve professional legitimacy as an occupational grouping. In these circumstances, conceptual frameworks are therefore seen as a means by which professional associations of public accountants demonstrate the collective professionalism of their members by revealing the existence of an apparently intellectual body of knowledge to support their reporting practices (West 2003).

A UK accounting researcher has recently advocated a return to classical, normative research of FAT. Rutherford (2010, 2013) argued that, far from being unscientific, classical FAT was based on philosophical pragmatism providing legitimacy as a rigorous, systematic and empirically grounded means of acquiring knowledge of relevance to the production of accounting numbers for financial reporting. Norreklit et al. (2010) produced this pragmatic approach to FAT when advocating a normative accounting model based on four constituent dimensions of the reality of human behaviour (i.e. values, facts, possibilities, and communication) and the twin reporting attributes of correspondence and coherence.

Conclusion and the future

FAT has a history covering 130 years in the English-speaking world. It began with accountancy practitioners expressing concern about emerging issues in practice and continued with practitioners attempting to address these problems by reference to theoretical notions. Thus, by the end of the nineteenth century and the beginning of the twentieth century, practitioners were shaping FAT before giving way to ideas and arguments from academic researchers. By the mid-twentieth century, the latter were producing versions of FAT in apparent competition with one another. Deductive reasoning replaced inductive processes. Purely accounting notions were supplemented and then driven by ideas from related disciplines such as economics.

In the early years of the history of FAT, the inductive approach meant practical applications became the subject of later theoretical definitions and explanations. Occasionally, and particularly in more recent times, deductive arguments contributed to changes in practice, e.g. CCA in the early 1980s and CFA since the 1980s. Only CFA, however, established a permanent position in practice. Thus, if FAT exists to improve practice, it does not appear to have done much after more than a century of individual and institutional effort.

Despite the continuous increase in regulated corporate disclosure requirements, the primary financial reporting focus in the practices of the late nineteenth century remains that of 2018, i.e. a package of accounting numbers representing income and financial position based on historical costs, supplemented from time to time by fair values. The underlying theoretical emphasis has changed from a proprietary perspective concentrating on the financial position of shareholders to an entity perspective focusing on corporate enterprise income or earnings. Paradoxically, within the context of FAT appearing in conceptual frameworks, the IASB (2018) adopts financial position (i.e. assets and liabilities) as the accounting basis to derive income. With conceptual frameworks more generally over time, the explicit emphasis has been the user of financial statements requiring relevant and reliable accounting information for decisions. This has meant decision-usefulness has supplanted stewardship as the principal reporting objective and quality, with an underlying questionable assumption that stewardship is satisfied by the provision of decision-useful information. However, a practical means of satisfying the information needs of decision-makers remains elusive when so little is known about these needs in practice. Declaring decision-usefulness as the primary reporting objective is a hollow gesture in such circumstances (see Williams and Ravenscroft 2017).

So what can be concluded from this review of the history of FAT? First, it appears to have involved a continuous, sustained, and long-term search to improve the quality of financial reporting. Second, this search has involved practitioners and academic researchers using inductive then deductive reasoning, and then back to induction. Third, no version of FAT has won out over others and, in the so-called golden age of FAT, theorists effectively competed with one another without changing practice. Fourth, despite their lack of influence on practice, individual accounting theorists gained considerable reputations and their theories came to be regarded as classics. Fifth, accounting standard-setters introduced FAT through conceptual frameworks and standards and, therefore, indirectly related theory to practice. In this way, although FAT has not resulted in general laws applicable to accounting practice, it has seen the introduction of cash flows and fair values to financial statements. Finally, despite considerable cost and effort over many decades, FAT has not been used by accountancy practitioners to do what theories are intended to do, i.e. predict practice, produce testable hypotheses, and guide problem-solving.

This last point is a considerable concern. Accountants appear to use FAT to demonstrate collectively and politically their professional status to a wider world of corporate managers, users, and regulators. FAT appears occasionally in the classroom but only as a separate topic from practice and typically at the end of a degree course before employment. Thus, future practitioners do not learn in depth about FAT as a basis for their intended practice. It is therefore doubtful if problems arising in practice can ever be thought through from theoretical principles by individual practitioners. In other words, the contributions to FAT of researchers such as Hatfield, Paton, Chambers, and Sterling have had marginal impact on the general state of practice and education. This is not a healthy position to be in after more than a century of continuous effort directed at FAT. As Cushing (1989: 36–7) concluded 'double-entry bookkeeping has been remarkably resilient' and 'accounting standard-setting has precipitated a crisis in the accounting discipline'.

What then of the future for FAT? The history described in this chapter suggests there have been two types of theories and theorists. The first type relates to individual attempts to rationalise, explain, and predict accounting practice. These evolved from inductive studies of practice to become normative prescriptions that became academically competitive and eventually proscribed as unscientific, then to be supplanted by statistical observations of conventional practice. The result of this aspect of FAT history has been an overall lack of success in challenging conventional practice issues. A question for the future is whether further normative or empirical FAT studies will result in significant change to practice conventions. This review suggests a negative answer unless there is fundamental commitment by accountancy practitioners, corporate managers, academic researchers, and government regulators to such change. In the case of academic accounting research, Dyckman and Zeff (2015) usefully produced a detailed plan of action.

The second type of accounting theory and theorist is found in conceptual frameworks intended to support and therefore perpetuate conventional practice. A question here for the future is whether more tinkering with these frameworks is likely to significantly change conventional practice. Again, the answer appears to be negative unless there is a commitment to change from the aforementioned stakeholders. All these suggest that FAT as the basis for improving accounting practice may not be a viable project. Rather, FAT appears to be a will-o'-the-wisp attracting and seducing accountants away from their primary task of finding accounting numbers that report users can trust to reflect managerial compliance and accountability (Williams 2017: 84). The principal challenge for accountants, therefore, is deciding whether or not financial accounting is a practical function that has a credible basis in theory. If it does not, then continuing to spend considerable cost and effort merely to enhance the reputation and social status of accountancy academics and practitioners seems a very dubious process that brings the legitimacy of the accountancy profession as a profession into question (West 2003; Lee 2013).

Key works

Baker (2017) studies the history of conceptual frameworks to demonstrate and evidence the influence of earlier normative contributions to FAT.

Cushing (1989) uses Kuhn's model of the evolution of scientific thought to explore the development of FAT.

Edwards (2015) provides a history of the development of FAT in the UK.

Previts and Flesher (2015) provide a comprehensive history of the development of financial reporting (including FAT) in the US.

Dyckman and Zeff (2015) review the history of the failed FAT research effort in the English-speaking world and provide an action plan in response.

References

AAA. (1936) *A Tentative Statement of Accounting Principles Underlying Corporate Financial Statements* (New York: AAA).

AAA. (1966) *A Statement of Basic Accounting Theory* (Evanston, IL: AAA).

AAA. (1977) *Statement on Accounting Theory and Theory Acceptance* (Evanston, IL: AAA).

Abbott, A. (1988) *The System of Professions: An Essay on the Division of Labor* (London: University of Chicago Press).

AIA. (1931) *Accounting Terminology* (New York: AIA).

AICPA. (1970) *Basic Concepts and Accounting Principles Underlying Financial Statements of Business Enterprises Statement of Accounting Principles Board 4* (New York: AICPA).

AICPA. (1971) *Establishing Financial Accounting Standards* (New York: AICPA).

AICPA. (1973) *Objectives of Financial Statements* (New York: AICPA).

AICPA. (1999) *Report of the Special Committee on Financial Reporting* (New York: AICPA).

Alexander, S.S., Bronfenbrenner, M., Fabricant, S. and Warburton, C. (1950) *Five Monographs on Business Income* (New York: AIA).

Arnold, J., Boyle, P., Carey, A., Cooper, M. and Wild, K. (1991) *The Future Shape of Financial Reports* (London: ICAEW and ICAS).

ASB. (1999) *Statement of Principles for Financial Reporting* (London: ASB).

ASC. (1980) *Current Cost Accounting, Statement of Standard Accounting Practice 16* (London: ASC).

ASCPA. (1929) Report of Committee on Technical Affairs, *Certified Public Accountant*, September: 293.

ASSC. (1975) *The Corporate Report* (London: ICAEW).

Baker, C.R. (2017) The influence of accounting theory on the FASB conceptual framework, *Accounting Historians Journal*, 44 (2): 109–24.

Ball, R. and Brown, P. (1968) An empirical evaluation of accounting income numbers, *Journal of Accounting Research*, 6 (2): 159–78.

Baxter, W.T. (1975) *Accounting Values and Inflation* (New York: McGraw Hill).

Beaver, W.H. (2002) Perspectives on recent capital market research, *Accounting Review*, 77 (2): 453–74.

Brief, R.P. (1976) *The Late Nineteenth Century Debate over Depreciation, Capital, and Income* (New York: Arno Press).

Brief, R.P. (1980) *Dicksee's Contribution to Accounting Theory and Practice* (New York: Arno Press).

Brown, R. (1904) The form of revenue accounts and balance sheets, and the use of percentages in connection therewith, *Accountant's Magazine*, 8 (73): 145–64.

Bullen, H.G. and Crook, K. (2006) *A New Conceptual Framework Project* (Norwalk, CT: FASB).

Canning, J.B. (1929) *Economics of Accountancy: A Critical Analysis of Accounting Theory* (New York: Ronald Press).

Carey, J. (1969) The origins of modern financial accounting, *Journal of Accountancy*, 128 (3): 35–48.

Chambers, R.J. (1955) Blueprint for a theory of accounting, *Accounting Research*, 6 (1): 17–25.

Chambers, R.J. (1962) *Towards a General Theory of Accounting, Australian Society of Accountants Annual Lecture* (Adelaide: University of Adelaide).

Chambers, R.J. (1963) Book review, *Accounting Review*, 38 (4): 448–49.

Chambers, R.J. (1966) *Accounting, Evaluation, and Economic Behaviour* (Englewood Cliffs, NJ: Prentice Hall).
Chambers, R.J. and Dean, G.W. (1986) *Chambers on Accounting* (New York: Garland Publishing).
Clarke, F.L. (1976) A closer look at Sweeney's stabilized accounting proposals, *Accounting and Business Research*, 6 (24): 264–75.
Cooper, E. (1888) What is profit of a company? *Accountant*, 14 (727): 740–46.
Cushing, B.E. (1989) A Kuhnian interpretation of the historical evolution of accounting, *Accounting Historians Journal*, 16 (2): 1–41.
DeMond, C.W. (1951) *Price, Waterhouse & Co in America: A History of A Public Accounting Firm* (New York: Comet Press for Price, Waterhouse & Company).
Demski, J.S. (1973) The general impossibility of normative accounting standards, *Accounting Review*, 48 (4): 718–23.
Dichev, I.D. (2017) On the conceptual foundation of financial reporting, *Accounting and Business Research*, 47 (6): 617–32.
Dickinson, A.L. (1906) Notes on some problems relating to the accounts of holding companies, *Journal of Accountancy*, 1 (6): 487–91.
Dicksee, L.R. (1893) Form of accounts and balance sheets, *Accountant*, 19 (988–9): 954–9, 973–81.
Dicksee, L.R. (1895) Profits available for dividends, in L.R. Dicksee (ed.) *Four Lectures Delivered to the Institute of Chartered Accountants in England and Wales during the Years 1894 and 1895*, pp. 33–59 (London: Gee).
Dicksee, L.R. (1903a) The nature and limitations of accounts, *Accountant*, 29 (1478): 469–74.
Dicksee, L.R. (1903b) *Depreciation, Reserves, and Reserve Funds* (London: Gee).
Dicksee, L.R. and Tillyard, F. (1906) *Goodwill and its Treatment in Accounts* (London: Gee).
Dyckman, T.R. and Zeff, S.A. (2015) Accounting research: past, present and future, *Abacus*, 51 (4): 511–24.
Edwards, E.O. and Bell, P.W. (1961) *The Theory and Measurement of Business Income* (Berkeley, CA: University of California Press).
Edwards, J.R. (2015) History of financial accounting theory in Britain, in S. Jones (ed.) *The Routledge Companion to Financial Accounting*, pp. 12–38 (Abingdon: Routledge).
Edwards, J.R. (2019) *A History of Corporate Financial Reporting in Britain* (London: Routledge).
Edwards, J.R., Dean, G., Clarke, F. and Wolnizer, P. (2013) Accounting academic elites: the tale of ARIA, *Accounting, Organizations and Society*, 38 (5): 365–81.
FASB. (1976) *Scope and Limitations of Conceptual Framework Project* (Stamford, CT: FASB).
FASB. (1978) *Objectives of Financial Reporting of Business Enterprises, Statement of Financial Accounting Concepts 1* (Stamford, CT: FASB).
FASB. (1979) *Financial Reporting and Changing prices, Statement of Financial Accounting Standards 33* (Stamford, CT: FASB).
FASB. (2002a) *The Norwalk Agreement* (Norwalk, CT: FASB).
FASB. (2002b) *Proposal for a Principles-Based Approach to US Standard Setting* (Norwalk, CT: FASB).
FASC. (2012) Some conceptual tensions in financial reporting, *Accounting Horizons*, 26 (1): 125–33.
Fisher, I. (1906) *The Nature of Capital and Income* (New York: Macmillan).
Georgiou, O. and Jack, L. (2011) In pursuit of legitimacy: a history behind fair value accounting, *British Accounting Review*, 43 (3): 311–23.
Gilman, S. (1939) *Accounting Concepts of Profit* (New York: Ronald Press).
Grady, P. (1965) *Inventory of Generally Accepted Accounting Principles for Business Enterprises, Accounting Research Study 7* (New York: AICPA).
Greer, H.C. (1932) A council on accounting research, *Accounting Review*, 7 (3): 176–81.
Guthrie, E. (1882) The want of uniformity in accounts, *Accountant*, 8 (412): 8–13.
Hatfield, H.R. (1909/1927) *Modern Accounting: Its Principles and Some of its Problems* (New York: D. Appleton).
Hines, R.D. (1991) The FASB's conceptual framework, financial accounting and the maintenance of the social world, *Accounting, Organizations and Society*, 16 (4): 313–31.
Hopwood, A.G. (1983) On trying to study accounting in the contexts in which it operates, *Accounting, Organizations and Society*, 8 (2/3): 287–305.
IASB. (2004) *The Effects of Changes in Foreign Exchange Rates, International Accounting Standard 21* (London: IASB).
IASB. (2018) *Conceptual Framework for Financial Reporting* (London: IASB).

Ijiri, Y. (1967) *The Foundations of Accounting Measurement* (Englewood Cliffs, NJ: Prentice-Hall).
Ijiri, Y. (1975) *Theory of Accounting Measurement, Studies in Accounting Research 10* (Sarasota, FL: AAA).
Ijiri, Y. (1981) *Historical Cost Accounting and its Rationality, Research Monograph 1* (Vancouver, BC: Canadian Certified General Accountants' Research Foundation).
Inanga, E.L. and Schneider, W.B. (2005) The failure of accounting research to improve accounting practice: a problem of theory and lack of communication, *Critical Perspectives on Accounting*, 16 (3): 227–48.
Inflation Accounting Committee. (1975) *Inflation Accounting* (London: HMSO).
Jones, R. (1956) *Effects of Price Level Changes on Business Income, Capital, and Taxes* (Columbus, OH: AAA).
Kitchen, J. and Parker, R.H. (1980) *Accounting Thought and Education: Six English Pioneers* (London: ICAEW).
Lawson, G.H. (1997) *Aspects of the Economic Implications of Accounting* (New York: Garland Publishing).
Lee, T.A. (1983) The early debate on financial and physical capital, *Accounting Historians Journal*, 10 (1): 25–50.
Lee, T.A. (1986) *Towards a Theory and Practice of Cash Flow Accounting* (New York: Garland Publishing).
Lee, T.A. (1995) Shaping the US academic research profession: the American Accounting Association and the social construction of a professional elite, *Critical Perspectives on Accounting*, 6 (3): 241–61.
Lee, T.A. (2006a) The war of the sidewardly mobile corporate financial report, *Critical Perspectives on Accounting*, 17 (4): 419–55.
Lee, T.A. (2006b) The FASB and accounting for economic reality, *Accounting in the Public Interest*, 6: 1–21.
Lee, T.A. (2013) Reflections on the origins of modern accounting, *Accounting History*, 18 (2): 141–61.
Lee, T.A. and Wolnizer, P.W. (1997) *The Quest for a Science of Accounting: An Anthology of the Research of Robert R Sterling* (New York: Garland Publishing).
Lisle, G. (1900) *Accounting in Theory and Practice* (Edinburgh: William Green).
Lisle, G. (1903) Foreign currencies and their treatment in home accounts, in G. Lisle (ed.) *Encyclopaedia of Accounting*, vol. 3. pp. 88–96 (Edinburgh: William Green).
Littleton, A.C. (1953) *Structure of Accounting Theory* (Sarasota, FL: AAA).
Lohmann, C. and Eulerich, M. (2017) Publication trends and the network of publishing institutions in accounting: data on *The Accounting Review*, 1926-2014, *Accounting History Review*, 27 (1): 1–25.
MacNeal, K.F. (1939) *Truth in Accounting* (Philadelphia, PA: University of Philadelphia Press).
Macve, R.H. (1996) Pacioli's legacy, in T.A. Lee, A.G. Bishop and R.H. Parker (eds.) *Accounting History from the Renaissance to the Present: A Remembrance of Luca Pacioli*, pp. 3–30 (New York,: NY: Garland Publishing).
Mattessich, R.V. (1964) *Accounting and Analytical Methods* (Homewood, IL: Richard D. Irwin).
Mattessich, R.V. (1991) Social reality and the measurement of its phenomena, *Advances in Accounting*, 8: 3–17.
Mattessich, R.V. (2009) FASB and social reality – an alternative realistic view, *Accounting in the Public Interest*, 9: 39–64.
McMonnies, P. (1988) *Making Corporate Reports Valuable* (Edinburgh: ICAS).
Miller, A.D. and Oldroyd, D. (2018) Does stewardship still have a role? *Accounting Historians Journal*, 45 (1): 69–82.
Moonitz, M. (1961) *The Basic Postulates of Accounting, Accounting Research Study 1* (New York: AICPA).
Moore, L. (2009) Economic 'reality' and the myth of the bottom line, *Accounting Horizons*, 23 (3): 327–40.
Mouck, T. (1992) The rhetoric of science and the rhetoric of revolt in the 'story' of positive accounting theory, *Accounting, Auditing & Accountability Journal*, 5 (4): 35–56.
Nelson, C.L. (1973) A priori research in accounting, in N. Dopuch and L. Revsine (eds.) *Accounting Research 1960-1970: A Critical Evaluation*, pp. 3–19 (Urbana-Champagne: University of Illinois).
Norreklit, H., Norreklit, L. and Mitchell, F. (2010) Towards a paradigmatic foundation for accounting practice, *Accounting, Auditing and Accountability Journal*, 23 (6): 733–58.
Ohlson, J.A. (1995) Earnings, book values, and dividends in security valuation, *Contemporary Research in Accounting*, 11 (2): 661–87.
Ohlson, J.A. (2006) A practical model of earnings measurement, *Accounting Review*, 81 (1): 271–79.
Paton, W.A. (1922) *Accounting Theory, with Special Reference to the Corporate Enterprise* (New York: Ronald Press).

Paton, W.A. and Littleton, A.C. (1940) *An Introduction to Corporate Accounting Standards* (Evanston, IL: AAA).
Pixley, F.W. (1881) *Auditors: Their Duties and Responsibilities* (London: Effingham Wilson).
Previts, G.J. and Flesher, D.L. (2015) Financial accounting and reporting in the United States of America – 1820 to 2010: toward sunshine from shadows, in S. Jones (ed.) *Routledge Companion to Financial Accounting*, pp. 39–90 (Abingdon, Oxon: Routledge).
Roslender, R. (1992) *Sociological Perspectives on Modern Accounting* (London: Routledge).
Rutherford, B.A. (2010) The social science turn in UK financial accounting research: a philosophical and sociological analysis, *Accounting and Business Research*, 40 (2): 149–71.
Rutherford, B.A. (2013) A pragmatist defence of classical financial accounting research, *Abacus*, 49 (2): 197–218.
Sanders, T.H., Hatfield, H.R. and Moore, U. (1938) *A Statement of Accounting Principles* (New York: AIA).
Schipper, K. (2003) Principles-based accounting standards, *Accounting Horizons*, 17 (1): 61–72.
Scott, DR. (1931) *The Cultural Significance of Accounts* (New York: Henry Holt).
SEC. (2003) *Study Pursuant to Section 108(d) of the Sarbanes-Oxley Act of 2002 on the Adoption by the United States Financial Reporting System of a Principles-based Accounting System* (Washington, DC: SEC).
Solomons, D. (1966) Economic and accounting concepts of cost and value, in M. Backer (ed.) *Modern Accounting Theory*, pp. 117–40 (Englewood Cliffs, NJ: Prentice Hall).
Sprague, C.E. (1907) *The Philosophy of Accounts* (New York: Ronald Press).
Sprouse, R.T. and Moonitz, M. (1962) *A Tentative Set of Broad Accounting Principles for Business Enterprises, Accounting Research Study 3* (New York: AICPA).
Staubus, G.J. (1961) *A Theory for Accounting for Investors* (Berkeley, CA: University of California Press).
Sterling, R.R. (1970) *Theory of the Measurement of Enterprise Income* (Lawrence, KS: University Press of Kansas).
Sterling, R.R. (1979) *Toward a Science of Accounting* (Houston, TX: Scholars Book Company).
Sterling, R.R. (1990) Positive accounting: an assessment, *Abacus*, 26 (2): 97–135.
Storey, R.K. and Storey, S. (1998) *The Framework of Financial Accounting Concepts and Standards* (Stamford, CT: FASB).
Study Group on Business Income. (1952) *Changing Concepts of Business Income* (New York: AIA).
Sweeney, H.W. (1936) *Stabilized Accounting* (New York: Harper).
Thomas, A.L. (1969) *The Allocation Problem in Financial Accounting Theory* Studies in Accounting Research No. 3 (Sarasota, FL: American Accounting Association).
Thomas, A.L. (1974) *The Allocation Problem: Part 2*. Studies in Accounting Research No. 9 (Sarasota, FL: American Accounting Association).
Tweedie, D.P. and Whittington, G. (1984) *The Debate on Inflation Accounting* (Cambridge: Cambridge University Press).
Vatter, W. (1947) *The Fund Theory of Accounting and its Implications for Financial Reports* (Chicago, IL: University of Chicago Press).
Watts, R.L. and Zimmerman, J.L. (1986) *Positive Accounting Theory* (Englewood Cliffs, NJ: Prentice-Hall).
Wells, M.C. (1976) A revolution in accounting thought? *Accounting Review*, 51 (3): 471–82.
West, B.P. (2003) *Professionalism and Accounting Rules* (Abingdon: Routledge).
Williams, P.F. (2017) Jumping on the wrong bus: reflections on a long, strange journey, *Critical Perspectives on Accounting*, 49: 76–85.
Williams, P.F. and Ravenscroft, S.P. (2017) Rethinking decision usefulness, *Contemporary Accounting Research*, 32 (2): 763–88.
Williams, P.F. and Rodgers, J.L. (1995) The *Accounting Review* and the production of accounting knowledge, *Critical Perspectives on Accounting*, 6 (3): 263–87.
Zeff, S.A. (2007) The SEC rules historical cost accounting: 1934 to the 1970s, *Accounting and Business Research*, Special Issue, 37: 49–62.
Zeff, S.A. (2013) The objectives of financial reporting: a historical survey and analysis, *Accounting and Business Research*, 43 (4): 262–327.
Zeff, S.A. (2018) An introduction to *Corporate Accounting Standards*: detecting Paton and Littleton's influence, *Accounting Historians Journal*, 45 (1): 45–67.

8
FINANCIAL ACCOUNTING PRACTICE

Ciarán Ó hÓgartaigh

Overview

Hopwood (2000: 763) remarks that:

> [t]he institutional and social aspects of financial accounting are still relatively unexplored. Compared with our insights into the economic theory of income calculation and the economic determinants and consequences of modes of corporate financial reporting, our knowledge of how forms of financial accounting emerge from, sustain and modify wider institutional and social structures is modest.

One of the reasons Hopwood offers (2000: 764) for this *lacuna* in accounting research is that 'insufficient attention [is] given to the actual practices of financial accounting'. This view of the history of accounting – and of accounting practice in particular – is increasingly prevalent (e.g. Burchell et al. 1980; Cooper and Sherer 1984; Tinker 1985): 'the technical practices of accounting must be understood, not as the expression of some transcendental rationality, but as reflection and reinforcement of social, political, and economic relationships' (Bryer 1993: 649).

Recognising that accounting is 'constitutive as well as reflective' (Napier 2006: 455), this chapter focuses specifically on the main issues and changes in financial accounting practice, as distinct from – but shaped by – financial accounting theory (Chapter 7) and regulation (Chapter 14). On that basis, the chapter will set out the context and the content (and historical discontents) of financial accounting practice. The chapter will conclude with brief observations on continuity with change in financial statements since the mid-nineteenth century.[1]

The context of financial accounting practice

Agency theory

Defined conventionally, financial accounting has been widely characterised as an instrument of agency, a means of providing information to (primarily) external users.[2] Within the accounting history literature, the existence and expansion of financial accounting has often been attributed to agency problems (e.g. De Roover 1938; Yamey 1960; Watts and Zimmerman 1983), through providing a mechanism for monitoring the actions of the agent (e.g. management) by the principal (e.g. shareholders and other users). This chapter employs agency theory as a useful lens through which to observe the contours of change in financial accounting practice.[3] First, it limits the landscape by delineating the boundaries of several centuries of practice. Given that Chapter 5 deals in detail with bookkeeping, this chapter will begin by briefly exploring the relevant literature on the origins of final accounts and the preparation of certain forms of balance sheet, particularly in the late eighteenth and early nineteenth centuries. Second, an appropriately nuanced perspective of the landscape shaped by agency problems recognises that the essence of the principal-agent relationship is not constant but is one whose contours shift with changes in the relative importance of stakeholders and in the structures of capital markets.[4] Previts and Bricker (1994) and Bricker and Chandar (1998, 2000), for example, caution that conventional characterisations of historical principal-agent relationships are sometimes overly embedded in today's context. As reporting entities are financed in different ways and as societal expectations change, the composition of principals shifts, as does the motivation of agents.

Hence, while 'in the typical pre-industrial organization profit measurement was often not a priority' (Edwards 2019: 63), the increasing capital-intensiveness of commercial enterprise during and after the industrial revolution arguably (Sombart 1924; Yamey 1964; Bryer 2000a, 2000b; Napier 2006) nurtured the need for – and was facilitated by – improved accounting procedures. The demand for capital led to the expansion of new forms of industrial organisation, including partnerships and the joint stock and limited liability company, and a consequent need to measure and record profits to be divided between the partners and/or the investors. The emergence of the industrial organisation – and the corporate *persona* – also marked a transition from a proprietorship view of the firm to the entity view. This led to a significant shift in the practice of profit calculation, from a valuation approach to a matching approach leading to the widespread adoption of historical cost valuation (Hendriksen 1977; Edwards 2019). Later, the increasing complexity of forms of organisation and finance prompted the emergence of the concept of 'substance over form', manifest in accounting practices such as consolidated accounting.

New forms of business organisation extended the distance between principal and agent, rendering more acute the need for increased statutory protection of shareholders and other providers of finance (Storrar and Pratt 2000). Financial accounting and periodic reporting were employed as mechanisms for monitoring management. In the UK legislation from 1844 onwards initially required and subsequently shaped periodic reporting to shareholders (and others) through financial statements (e.g. Gilmore and Willmott 1992; Arnold and Matthews 2002; Napier 2010; Edwards 2019: chs 8 and 10). The impact and implications of these nineteenth- and twentieth-century legislative changes for financial accounting practice will be examined in this chapter.

While macro- and micro-economic failures gave an impetus to legislative change, company law was perceived as increasingly inadequate in responding to, and reflecting, the complexity faced by the modern corporation. As a consequence in the UK, the Accounting Standards Steering Committee (later renamed the Accounting Standards Committee – ASC) was formed in 1969 and, in the US, the Financial Accounting Standards Board (FASB) in 1973. These issued accounting standards which increasingly codified, in particular, the meaning of the 'true and fair view' and 'generally accepted accounting principles' (GAAP). Towards the end of the twentieth century, the globalisation of capital markets had their most significant impact in accounting terms with the formation of the International Accounting Standards Board (IASB) and the drive to develop a set of global accounting standards which would be acceptable internationally, particularly in the US (Cooke and Nobes 1997; Zeff 2002; Kirsch 2012; Previts and Flesher 2015; see also Chapter 14).

These international trends in standard-setting and accounting practice are explored generally in Nobes (2015) and, locally, in a series of texts edited by Previts, Walton and Wolnizer examining some case-by-country developments in that regard in Europe (Previts et al. 2010), the Americas (Previts et al. 2011a), Asia and Oceania (Previts et al. 2011b) and Eurasia, Middle East and Africa (Previts et al. 2012).

Financial accounting practice prior to the industrial revolution

Early forms of financial accounting, which may be seen as serving a management accounting purpose (see Chapter 9), migrated into (external) financial reporting on the formation of the limited liability company and the obligation on directors to 'inform outside financial supporters of the states of the financial affairs of their companies from time to time' (Chambers 1987: 98). These tendencies in calculation revealed the basic financial information needs of owner-managers – position and performance – which were, through financial reporting, transmitted to external stakeholders and, through regulation and other influences, transfigured over time.

While, in the fifteenth and sixteenth centuries most overseas trade was undertaken by 'merchants operating entirely on their own account, or with one or two partners, who were often related to them by blood or marriage' (Clay 1984: 191), the joint stock company emerged as a means of financing overseas exploration and trade in the mid-sixteenth century. The capital base of such trade was extended, representing a transfer of capital from the land to trade. It also extended the distance between those managing and financing those activities. While this did not yet give rise to a pervasive practice of financial accounting, it rendered necessary an increased accountability (Winjum 1971).

A case in point is the East India Company (EIC), a chartered company whose accounting practices are studied in some detail by Bryer (2000b) and others (for example, Baladouni 1981; Keay 1991; Edwards 2019: 56–9). As it evolved, the EIC was increasingly financed by the merchant 'élite' and the 'generality' of investors. The EIC represented an opportunity for the élite to acquire commodities cheap to sell dear on their own account. For the generality, the EIC was simply a form of investment (Keay 1991). Baladouni (1981: 69) suggests that the accounting of the EIC does not constitute evidence of a widespread 'practice'. However, Bryer (2000b: 345) claims that it is indicative of a 'calculative mentality' and a function of an 'escalating conflict of interest between the generality and the merchant élite'. As a 'case study' of the development of accounting in the EIC from 1600 to 1657, Bryer describes two sets of accounts arising from the establishment of the *Lawes or Standing Orders of the East India Company* in 1621. These comprised the *Accompts Proper*, providing a summary of the Company's capital, and the *Accompts Currant*, detailing the movements on capital during the year. The EIC also produced 'financial statements' which were headed 'The Success of the Second Joynt Stock Briefly Valued'; the first surviving example was produced around 1640.

While Baladouni (1986: 28) suggests that the 'financial statements' of the EIC are not balance sheets and seem 'to be a product of an uncertain conceptual framework', the second surviving financial statement of the EIC, headed 'The Ballance of Estate of the 3d Joint Stock taken to the fine of April 1641 continued and encludinge the Crispiana', comprises debit[or] and creditor balances. Yamey (1970: 73–4) describes the underlying technology of these accounts as precursors to 'what today we would call a balance sheet, a statement of the sources and uses of an entity's capital'. Early accounting reports such as those of the EIC may arguably be viewed as part of the lineage of more contemporary financial accounting practice even though the gait and guise of its accounting ancestors is markedly different. In particular, we can here trace the outline if not fill out the canvass of modern financial accounting practice through the realisation of a need for the disclosure of a statement of position and financial flows.

The joint stock company became a vessel for financing endeavours such as overseas trade (e.g. the EIC), mining (e.g. Mines Royal and the Mineral and Battery Works) and public utilities (e.g. the New River Company). This form of incorporation led to the emergence of several corporate characteristics which are precursors of contemporary structures. For example, by 1630 the investors in the EIC began to invest on a time basis rather than in particular ventures 'marking the transition from adventurers jointly financing the stock of goods to investors holding shares in a company' (Edwards 2019: 21). By 1657, this concept was extended to the 'non-terminable stock'.

The industrial revolution and beyond

The late eighteenth and early nineteenth centuries saw increasing competition for capital among joint stock companies, fed by and feeding the industrial revolution (Davies 1952). A 'search for industrial accounting records' by Jones (1985: 8) reveals examples of the emergence of financial accounting by industrial companies in the context of 'Welsh industrial development, decay and redevelopment' between 1700 and 1830. While material on the early industrial context is relatively underexplored, Jones (1985) provides some detailed discussion on the development of accountability and reporting practices by Welsh industrial companies during this period.

In the US, railroads gave an impetus to the development of financial markets and, in turn, financial reporting and a wider range of publicly available financial information (the latter well-documented by, for example, Thompson 2013). Railroads crisscross the course and discourse of financial accounting practice reflecting the extent to which they laid the sleepers of that practice particularly in areas such as fixed assets and accruals. They are generally viewed as pioneers in the development of US financial accounting practices (see Chapter 18). Previts and Merino (1998) attribute this to the different geographic as well as financial stretch of railroads *vis-à-vis*, for example, textiles (which constituted an important element of the industrial revolution). In the UK, in response to regulations, railway companies published standardised or uniform financial statements from 1868, a requirement which extended, for example, to life assurance companies (1870), gas companies (1871) and electric lighting companies (1882) with the objective of improving investor protection through increased comparability (Edwards 2019: ch. 11).

The development of the limited liability company and accompanying legislation, which initially required a balance sheet but not an income statement, privileged the balance sheet as 'the primary financial statement'. While the income statement became a matter of public record, with the growth of the railways in the nineteenth century (Napier 2010: 247–9; Thompson 2013) and the need for the railways to report their performance to the providers of finance, in a world where firms operating in most industrial sectors were externally financed largely through bank lending, ability to pay as represented in the balance sheet remained a primary focus (Edey and Panitpakdi 1956).

The origins of the balance sheet – as information for creditors and an indication of ability to pay – shaped the valuation practices stitched into its fabric: 'essentially, asset valuation and income determination were based on an incomplete application of the going concern convention tempered by conservatism' (Storey 1959: 272). Early balance sheets were representations of the investment of the owner (Winjum 1970; Hendriksen 1977), being essentially at historical cost.

Accrual accounting became a cornerstone of accounting practice as 'operating continuity' (Bryer 1993; Chatfield 1996c: 24), going concern and income measurement gained in importance in the nineteenth century. Matching of revenues and expenses is at the heart of accrual accounting and this became increasingly significant with the advent of the limited liability company, the need for 'periodic reckonings as a prelude to dividend payments' and investors' eyes on the bottom-line (Chatfield 1996c). Edwards (2019: 99) finds evidence of the use of 'partial accruals accounting' by railway companies in the mid-nineteenth century and comments that, elsewhere, accrual accounting was in widespread use at the time. While noting considerable variation in practice, Edwards (2019: ch. 6) also identifies 'stages' of accounting development whereby, between 1840 and the early 1900s, first the railways and then public utilities were more generally making a transition towards 'full' accruals accounting. Coombs and Edwards (1996: 53–59) find similar trends in the accounting practices of UK municipal corporations in the latter half of the nineteenth century. In the US, accounting objections to cash-based tax laws in favour of the use of accrual accounting for tax purposes (Previts and Merino 1998: 181) suggest a widespread use of the latter by the beginning of the twentieth century. This in turn 'facilitated accounting obtaining an institutional status in society' (Takatera and Sawabe 2000: 790).

While the 'constitutive', 'disciplinary' influences of cost and management accounting have been actively explored throughout this and later periods (e.g. Hoskin and Macve 1986; Miller and O'Leary 1987), less critical attention has been paid to the manner in which financial accounting practices shaped the managerial and societal behaviour. Nonetheless, the late nineteenth century marked the 'birth' of modern financial accounting, 'founded on the principles of cost-based accrual accounting and independent professional audits' (Bryer 1993: 649–50). In a series of well-argued papers focusing on the underlying ideology of accounting, Bryer (2012, 2013a, 2013b) argues inter alia that (2013b: 273) 'capitalism only appeared in America by around 1900, after more than two decades of intense conflict between "capital and labour", and became established by the 1920s. This is the critical turning point in American business history'. A counterpoint to Bryer's theses in this regard is offered by Oldroyd et al. (2015).

Developments in the corporate form and tensions between stakeholders had profound implications for financial accounting practice. Echoing Yamey's (1970) invocation of agency problems as an impetus for accounting change in the late nineteenth century, Chandler (1977: 10) describes the emergence of the modern corporation in the US thus: 'Ownership became widely scattered. The stockholders did not have the influence, knowledge, experience, or commitment to take part in the high command'. Bryer (1993, 2013a, 2013b) challenges this unnuanced agency explanation of the development of 'modern financial reporting', arguing (1993: 650) that 'an alternative explanation is suggested by Marx's view that the age of individual capitalists was rapidly closing, and the age of collective capitalism dawning'.

This period was marked by a *laissez-faire*[5] approach to accounting regulation. Several authors (e.g. Brief 1966; Chatfield 1977; Yamey 1977; Previts and Bricker 1994; Previts and Merino 1998) as a consequence suggest as Edwards (1989: 109–10) concludes:

> [i]n these circumstances, management was free to choose, and in fact chose, the set of accounting principles and practices that had the highest utility, given the goals the organization was trying to achieve and the non-regulatory constraints under which it operated. One of these constraints was the requirement for shareholders and creditors to believe the content of published financial statements … The fact is that assets and profits were probably both under- and overstated at different times and in different places. This was a result of both error and systematic bias … The main causes of error and bias were the failure systematically (a) to distinguish between capital and revenue expenditure and (b) to allocate the original cost of fixed assets to expense.

Although the reporting of a profit and loss account was not legally required in the UK until 1928, there is evidence that business entities, at least those operating on a relatively large scale, calculated profits (Edwards and Baber 1979; Edwards 2019: ch. 4) or produced a profit and loss account for shareholders prior to the late nineteenth century (Edey and Panitpakdi 1956; Yamey 1960). Chatfield (1996b: 63) argues that, from the 1920s onwards in the US, 'when stock [share] sales became the chief external source of funds, and stockholders became the primary readers of financial statements, the income statement became the more meaningful report'.

These trends have been traced to changes in the nature and context of the reporting entity over this period. First, the 'transition from venture to going concern' (Chatfield 1977: 98) marked the corresponding shift from the proprietorship view of the firm – which saw assets as the personal possessions of the owner – to the entity basis – which sees assets and liabilities as an integral part of the body corporate (Yamey 1964; Edwards 2019). The entity, and its assets and liabilities, had the potential to exist beyond the current owners and the assets and liabilities were not intended to be realised separately from the entity itself. The extension of the life of the corporation beyond the single venture and, more significantly, beyond the single reporting period gave rise to the problem of allocating the effects of transactions between consecutive accounting periods: Littleton (1933) and Thomas (1969, 1974) correctly characterise this 'allocation problem', arising from the need for 'periodic reporting', as the enduring challenge of financial accounting.

Second, the emergence of a 'corporate personality' separate and distinct from the owners (or indeed the managers) of the firm established its existence in space as well as in time: owners could (and would) come and go and the firm would continue in existence. Agency issues were, therefore, exacerbated as the involvement and interest of owners became increasingly distant and short term. While management accounting was generally *of* management *for* management, financial accounting developed as information *of* management *for* others, bringing with it the need for monitoring through market, contractual and/or regulatory means.

Third, in practical terms, managers were motivated by the link between dividend distributions and realised profits. There was less motivation for asset revaluation in profit terms as unrealised profits were in practice not distributable. While there was no explicit legal prohibition on the payment of dividends out of unrealised profits, it was an increasing characteristic of articles of association (Weiner 1928; Yamey 1962). Finally, cost-based valuation and its increased 'reliability' *vis-à-vis* non-transaction-based valuations was also appealing to the newly professionalised accounting cadre of the late nineteenth century (Cowan 1965; Richard 2004; Edwards 2016, 2019).

The twentieth-century context

Focusing on the US, Hendriksen comments (1977: 52) that:

> [t]he historical development of the corporation during the latter part of the 19th century and the early 20th century gave rise to new institutions and new relationships which were in turn to influence the development of accounting thought. Of these new developments, the more important include the development of the holding company as a common form of organisation, the formation of the New York Stock Exchange (NYSE), and the investment in American corporations by foreign investors and American investment abroad.

Also in Britain, these characteristics suffused the accounting context of the twentieth century, which was marked by increased levels of regulation and globalisation, accompanied by a growing emphasis on disclosure and on statements which reported the financial affairs of the economic – as well as the legal – entity (Edwards 2019: ch. 12). Further, an increase in mandatory forms of financial reporting was consistent with an ebb and flow of obligatory and voluntary disclosure, marked at the end of the twentieth century by a high tide of regulation. In particular, in the early 1970s, a new era of accounting standard-setting was introduced which is reflected in the structure of the discussion in this section.

The increased complexity of the organisational form meant that methods of group accounting (increasingly framed as consolidated financial statements), which were published voluntarily early on, became a more substantive part of the fabric of financial reporting as the century progressed. New forms of financial statements also emerged, such as the funds flow statement (which came and went), the cash flow statement, the statement of changes in equity and the value added statement. In the latter decades of the century, new largely unregulated forms of accounting – such as social and environmental accounting – reflected a broader conceptualisation of accountability and stewardship. Underlying all of these changes was – and is – the prevalence and persistence of the balance sheet and income statement as the primary forms of financial reporting.

The presentation of a profit and loss account to shareholders was not legally required in Britain until the Companies Act 1928 but 'was by no means unknown prior to that date' (Edwards 1989: 129). Similarly in the US, 'while income statements had long been included in the annual reports of railroads, the industrial trusts of the late 1800s and the very early 1900s rarely included income statements' (Vangermeersch 1996a: 317), but, in a context of increased equity financing, were thereafter increasingly evident in practice. In the US, publication of the income statement was required by the Securities and Exchange Commission (SEC) from 1935, having been recommended in 1917 in *Uniform Accounting* (Vangermeersch 1996a).

Earnings and trends in earnings – as represented in the income statement – were 'of cardinal importance to investors' in their assessment of the reporting entity (American Institute of Accountants 1931: 3). Indeed, Vangermeersch (1979: 64) comments that the disclosure of earnings per share (EPS) was 'apparently a common practice in annual reports' between 1923 and 1959 (cf. Hendriksen 1977: 537). Previts and Merino (1998: 81) trace the beginnings of the disclosure of numbers such as EPS to the development of geographically dispersed sources of finance, and its subsequent importance reflects the increasing hegemony of capital markets in the twentieth century. Buckmaster (1992), invoking agency theory, traces the beginnings of earnings manipulation to the same circumstances.

The increased globalisation of financial structures and the growing dominion of equity markets gave weight to a shifting emphasis from the balance sheet (and ability to pay) to the income statement (and earnings capacity). The shift in focus from the balance sheet (and stewardship) to the income statement (and decision-making) was also reflected in preparer behaviour and a consequent movement in regulatory focus from 'secret reserves' in the early part of the century to 'earnings management' in the latter decades.

Twentieth-century practice prior to 1970

At the beginning of the twentieth century, the NYSE in particular mediated requirements with regard to the publication and presentation of financial statements in the US. In 1900, it was agreed that all companies listed on the exchange would make statements of their 'financial condition and operating results' available to their stockholders; a requirement expanded to 'an annual financial report' in 1926 (Greidinger 1950). The principle of 'full disclosure' was also at the heart of the financial reporting reforms introduced by the SEC in the 1930s (May 1932; Moyer 1955; Previts and Merino 1998). With regard to the foundations of standard-setting in the US, as the basis for guiding accounting practice, Persson and Napier (2015: 104) comment:

> [t]he events that transpired at the AICPA in the 1960s irrevocably altered the accounting standard-setting process in the US. Whereas the AICPA had previously exercised an important role in the promulgation of financial accounting standards, the failure of the AICPA's postulates and principles approach contributed to the establishment of the Financial Accounting Standards Board (FASB) in the late 1960s. FASB took over the standard-setting function, abandoned the postulates and principles mode of research as a basis for accounting regulation, and laid the groundwork for the conceptual framework project in the 1970s and 1980s.
>
> *(Zeff 1999)*

In the UK, 1900 marked, 'after a long period of "non-interference" in accounting matters, a decisive step towards the detailed regulation with which we are now familiar' (Edey and Panitpakdi 1956: 356).[6] The Companies Act 1900 (re)introduced the requirement for an external audit for registered companies. Although it did not contain an explicit requirement for companies to prepare and make public a balance sheet, that requirement was implicitly contained in section 23, which placed a duty on auditors to report to shareholders on every balance sheet laid before the company. The Companies Act 1907 added the requirement to prepare and publish a balance sheet – but not a profit and loss account – and also introduced the 'minimum disclosure' principle (a tendency extended in 1928, 1948, 1967 and 1976) requiring a minimum level of disclosure which the directors 'are at liberty to exceed' (Edwards 1981: 3, 2019: chs 8 and 10). From the beginning of the twentieth century, stock exchange requirements stipulated that quoted companies make their financial statements available to shareholders.

The holding company, the economic entity and consolidated financial statements

The development of the holding company gave rise to the need in practice for group accounts, presenting the performance and position of the group as a whole as well as that of the holding company, further reflecting the trend towards supplementary disclosure (Edwards and Webb 1984). Peloubet (1955) traces the first US consolidated accounts to 1886, although he comments that they were not in 'common usage' until the first decade of the twentieth century. Greidinger (1950) and Hendriksen (1977) credit the more widespread promulgation of consolidated financial statements to the initiative of the US Steel Corporation in 1901: 'it has also been hailed as the first really modern type of annual report which attempted to provide adequate financial information to stockholders' (Hendriksen 1977: 53).

Bircher (1988: 5) finds a 'relatively low' rate of adoption of consolidated accounting in the UK prior to the Companies Act 1948. Edwards and Webb (1984) find evidence for the use of consolidated accounts in the UK before the First World War although the most publicised early application of the technique was by ICI (then Nobel Industries) in the early 1920s and Dunlop in the early 1930s (Kitchen 1972; Parker 1977). Commenting that the 'preparation of an aggregate statement of assets and liabilities for the group' was 'apparently the [group] reporting method favoured by British accountants in the early 1920s', Edwards and Webb (1984: 47) conclude that 'experimentation' with the introduction of consolidated accounts in the UK began in 1910, 'but that the pace of adoption was slow' and certainly slower than in the US. They posit several reasons for this, including the fact that (ibid.: 44) 'during this period secret reserves, as a means of fostering financial stability, were highly regarded'.

From 'secret reserves' to 'earnings manipulation'

Clare (1945), Hawkins (1963) and Previts and Bricker (1994) also associate the early twentieth century with a culture of secrecy in the US and a characterisation of corporate publicity as conducting business with 'glass pockets' (Chandler and Tedlow 1985). In the first decade of the twentieth century, much of the financing for corporate growth was provided through 'money trusts', which were the subject of several public hearings, including the Pujo Committee 'Money Trust' Hearings. The money trusts were closely associated with a series of mergers between 1898 and 1903, termed by Sobel (1965) the 'Morganisation of America'. One consequence of this trend, according to Previts and Merino (1998: 222), was that 'financial capitalists, not accountants, led the drive for consolidated statements' in the US. Another was the prevalence of 'secret reserves' (Joplin 1914; Marriner 1980; Lister 1981; Edwards and Boyns 1994). The development of these practices provoked much debate in the US (e.g. Montgomery 1912; Paton and Stevenson 1918) even prior to the publication in 1917 of *Uniform Accounting*. *Uniform Accounting* was a symptom of an increasing propensity to view uniformity – or consistency – as a cure-all for the ills of accounting practice (Merino and Coe 1978; Chatfield 1996a).

The Stock Market Crash of 1929, the subsequent passing of the Securities Acts 1933 and 1934, and the consequent establishment of the SEC, changed the face of accounting practice in the US. By the end of the 1930s, the income statement had become the 'focal point' of US accounting practice, based on the widely held view that investors were interested in 'future income' as well as an acceptance of the 'entity concept' of the firm (Husband 1938; Previts and Merino 1998: 278, 283; Moore 2017). This development also reflected the growing primacy of equity markets – and of shareholders – as providers of finance, which Chatfield (1996b) partly attributes to the retreat from commercial lending in the US as a result of the collapse of inventory prices in 1920–1 and 'mass marketing of stock issues' in the 1920s.

Once again, however, the history of financial accounting practice was marked by an exogenous change prompted by accounting failures (see Chapter 20). In the US, the McKesson-Robbins case reflected 'certain fundamental weaknesses in the preparation of financial statements by large corporations' (Bennett 1939: 14). Similarly, in the UK, *Rex v. Kyslant* – the Royal Mail case – of 1931 (Davies and Bourn 1972) prompted a voluntary 'general raising of financial reporting standards during the 1930s' (Edwards 2019: 162). In both the UK and the US, several companies appeared to take a lead in pushing forward the boundaries of disclosure, including for example Unilever (Camfferman and Zeff 2003) and US Steel (Greidinger 1950; Hendriksen 1977).

Levels of inflation in the real economy during the Second World War saw certain firms mount challenges to conventional practices. US Steel attempted unsuccessfully to value its plant at depreciated replacement cost (Previts and Merino 1998). In the same period, Chrysler adopted accelerated depreciation which, it argued, approximated replacement cost (May 1949). However, this did not shake the resolve of the SEC or the Committee on Accounting Procedure that income be presented as 'an accurate historical record' (SEC 1945). An increasing level of debate regarding income measurement and the development of normative theories of accounting contributed to criticism of the Committee on Accounting Procedure, particularly on the grounds that its accounting standards drew inordinately on existing practice (Spacek 1956; Briloff 1964; Chambers 1973).

In the UK, while a series of 29 non-mandatory Recommendations issued by the Institute of Chartered Accountants in England and Wales (ICAEW) between 1942 and 1969 are thought to have significantly improved financial reporting practices (Zeff 1972), they were effectively *laissez-faire* and proved acceptable to preparers largely because of their flexibility; a position reflected in the debate in 1968 on the ills of financial accounting practice between Professor Edward Stamp and Sir Ronald Leach, then President of the ICAEW (Stamp and Marley 1970; Leach 1981; Singleton-Green 1990). This debate in part represented a discourse between theoretically grounded accounting principles and the pragmatism of the profession. In both jurisdictions, the interplays of theory and practice signified the hegemony of accounting practice and served as a signal to contemporary and future standard setters of the wisdom of an evolutionary development of financial reporting (see Accounting Standards Board (ASB) 1990). As a consequence, accounting practice did not change radically in this period and, to the extent that change did occur, it was again largely though not exclusively as a necessity arising from accounting and corporate failure.

The 1960s was a decade of considerable economic growth globally. The failure in the US to narrow the options permitted by accounting standards and, therefore, to limit earnings manipulation and diverse accounting practices was exposed particularly in the context of accounting for mergers and consolidations (Kripke 1970; Briloff and Engler 1979). Lenders also voiced concerns that the balance sheet – with its emphasis on conservative valuations – did not give a basis for the estimation of future cash flows and that financial statements in general – with the flexibility embedded in permissible accounting practice – did not allow for comparability (Laeri 1966).

Similarly, in the UK, the GEC-AEI takeover battle (1968) revealed another symptom of the ills of flexibility in accounting practice, as more conservative valuations of AEI assets after the takeover transformed a forecast profit of £10 million into a reported loss of £4.5 million, with much of the discrepancy attributable to differing applications of GAAP. Further evidence of the imprecision of UK GAAP followed in 1969 with revelations surrounding Rolls-Royce and the Leasco-Pergamon affair (Tweedie and Whittington 1984; Whittington 1989; Napier and Noke 1992). As in the US, public concern was fuelled by press comment (see Stamp and Marley 1970; Stamp 1984) and, in both jurisdictions, concerns led to the establishment of new accounting standard-setting infrastructures which shaped accounting practice from the 1970s onwards.

Financial accounting practice in the 'new era' of standard setting post 1970

After a period of 'complacency' concerning accounting practice (Napier and Noke 1992) and precipitated by public pressure (Edwards 2019: ch. 18), the ASC was formed in the UK in 1969[7] and the FASB in the US in 1973. There followed a 'new era' in accounting standard setting which saw an increased emphasis on the provision of accounting information for decision-making (Leach 1981; Olson 1982; Street 1996; Persson and Napier 2015). A period of codification also followed which once again extended the scope of disclosure without radically altering the fundamental shape of financial statements (Power 1990).

Other forms of financial statements

One of the extensions to disclosure related to segment reporting. The preparation of consolidated financial statements resulted in the aggregation in financial statements of elements of financial performance and position which had differing risk profiles. Given that mergers and acquisition were often motivated by a desire for diversification, consolidated financial statements masked that diversity by reporting a single consolidated balance sheet and income statement. As a consequence, the need for better analysis of these conglomerations led to a desire for disaggregated data and the reporting of segment information (see, for example, Mautz 1967a, 1967b, 1967c; Sommer 1967; Schachner 1968). These disclosures had existed in Sweden since the Swedish Stock Incorporation Act of 1944 and were first required in the UK by the Companies Act 1967 (Walker 1968). The requirement for segmental reporting in registration statements in the US was first promulgated by the SEC in 1969 and extended to all annual reports filed with the SEC in 1974 (Hendriksen 1977).

Likewise, the statement of sources and applications of funds (or 'funds flow statement') came into common use in the US (Käfer and Zimmerman 1967; Roberts and Gabhart 1972), Germany (Haller and Jakoby 1995), Japan (Nissan et al. 1995) and elsewhere, before being required by regulation, for example, in the US in 1969 and in the UK in 1976, and being introduced as an option in France in 1982 (Boussard and Colasse 1992). Käfer and Zimmerman (1967: 89), reviewing the early development of funds flow statements, describe the statement as a 'supplement to the two traditional financial statements', representing a link between the opening and closing balance sheets and, in particular, identifying working capital as a key flow in the business. However, the failure of the funds flow statement to alert readers to large financial failures such as Penn Central (1969), WT Grant (1976) and, later, Coloroll (1990), highlighted the statement's limitations (Smith 1992) and, on the basis that cash is a better representation of financial health, led to the development of the cash flow statement as a 'primary financial statement' (ASB 1991) framed as a 'radical change in financial reporting' (ASB 1996a: para. 4).

The fragile persistence of historical cost and asset valuation practices

The boundaries of accounting practice – and the choices between revolutionary and evolutionary change – were also tested in the discussions regarding inflation accounting which were played out again when general price changes had significant single-period economic effects in the 1970s. In 1979 when inflation in the US reached 13%, the FASB issued Statement of Financial Accounting Standards (SFAS) 33 requiring supplemental price-level adjusted and current cost disclosures (replacing its earlier replacement cost approach) until it was rescinded in

1986 as inflation rates declined. Inflation rates in the UK resulted in efforts to introduce inflation-adjusted accounting, through Provisional Statement on Standard Accounting Practice 7 and, subsequently, current cost accounting through Statement on Standard Accounting Practice (SSAP) 16 (Sandilands 1975; Stamp and Mason 1977). Hanson (1989) provides *inter alia* a useful survey of the number of companies producing 'price-level statements' between 1977 and 1988: the percentage of such firms peaked at 95% in 1981, falling to 3% in 1987 as inflation abated. Pong and Whittington (1996: 51) conclude:

> [t]he dramatic collapse in support for CCA [Current Cost Accounting] demonstrates that, however compelling the theoretical case for a particular accounting practice or reform, it will not be followed, in the absence of legal compulsion, if preparers of accounts do not regard it as being in their economic interests.

The limited life of these accounting practices, as well as their supplemental nature, did not therefore mark a substantive change in financial reporting practice, but did further reflect a trend towards the extension of disclosures as a means of mitigating the limitations of prevailing recognition and measurement practices.

Globalisation and accounting practice

The increased globalisation of the world economy – and of capital markets in particular – from the 1960s onwards shaped developments in financial accounting practice. This initially manifested itself in the desire by the European Union (EU) to facilitate free movement of capital within the EU and led to early efforts at international harmonisation of accounting practices by way of European Directives (Defliese 1981). In an attempt to enhance international comparability, a particular legacy of the Fourth EC Directive was standardisation of the format of financial statements of member states, introduced in the UK for example by the Companies Act 1981. This was the culmination of a debate on a standardised presentation that ebbed and flowed since the formation of the limited liability company in the UK and whose trackbed had been laid by the railway companies over a century earlier (Edwards 2019: ch. 11).

The Fourth Directive was a product of compromise, particularly as it allowed options in asset valuation and as the interpretation of 'the true and fair view' enshrined in the Directive varied across jurisdictions. This facilitated the consensus which gave it life in the short term but also sowed the seeds of its failure (Freedman and Power 1992). However, the diversity of European accounting traditions signified in the Directive broadened the canvas of European accounting practices (Mueller et al. 1997; Nobes and Parker 2006).

Historically, different European countries placed contrasting emphases on different 'users' of financial statements – in agency terms, different 'principals' – for example, the state sector in France, financial institutions in Germany and the public good in Scandinavia. This generated a variety of accounting practices including, for example, the *Plan Comptable* in France, differing valuation and reserve accounting practices in Germany, and the more sophisticated accounting technologies of Scandinavian companies such as Skandia and Nokia (Walton 2006). While there is archival evidence of corporate social reporting in the financial statements of, for example, US Steel (Hogner 1982) and the UK steel company Hadfields (Maltby 2004), globalising entities such as Skandia and Nokia brought with them local reporting traditions which reflected a wider set of value choices than those of capital markets, and validated a wider set of users of financial statements than shareholders. The history and implications of these reporting practices are considered in, for example, Hogner (1982), Lewis et al. (1984), Guthrie and Parker (1989, 1990), Carroll (1999) and Maltby (2004).

Throughout the twentieth century, in particular in the US and in the UK, capital markets played an increasingly important role in providing finance. More frequent (quarterly) periodic reporting placed increased demands on financial accounting and provided further impetus for earnings management (e.g. Healy and Wahlen 1999; Dechow and Skinner 2000), creative accounting (Griffiths 1986; Smith 1992) and 'exceptional innovation' in financial reporting in the UK and elsewhere (Tweedie and Whittington 1990: 87). These demands were fed in the late twentieth century by the 'irrational exuberance' (Greenspan 1996; Shiller 2000) associated with technology stocks, accompanied by increasingly aggressive incidences of revenue recognition. Other practices peculiar to particular sectors also emerged within, for example, financial services and exploration. Many of these sectoral practices may be traced through historical seams (see in banking, e.g. Capie and Billings 2001; and in exploration and mining, e.g. Edwards and Boyns 1994). Moreover, many of the accounting practices developed historically in these sectors – such as mark-to-market accounting in banking – spilled over into other sectors – such as energy trading – with differing and sometimes detrimental consequences (Baker and Hayes 2004; Eichenwald 2005; Stewart 2006; Haswell and Evans 2018).

Earnings management and the 'relevance' of financial accounting

Healy and Wahlen (1999), in a review of the earnings management literature, conclude that while such financial accounting practices were (and are) motivated by capital market, contractual and regulatory considerations, the extant research provides little evidence of the extent and scope of earnings management in the latter half of the twentieth century. The chronicle of financial accounting suggests that such practices are not new: Edwards (2019: 147) contends that 'Accounting history is littered with examples of financial information used a means of deception'. Dicksee (1927) discusses 'window dressing' and Samson et al. (2003) provide specific, firm-level historical examples of creative accounting (see also Chapter 20).

The turn of the millennium also saw discussion regarding the relevance of financial accounting practice to ordinary shareholders (Lev and Zarowin 1999; Levitt and Dwyer 2002) with arguments supporting the decision-usefulness of financial accounting information (e.g. Francis et al. 2002) drawing sustenance from the extended disclosures in financial statements, consistent with historical trends.

Whereas the income statement – and the presentation of financial performance – was perceived as a vital element of financial accounting throughout the twentieth century, income measurement – linked to valuation – was and is one of the intractable problems in financial accounting theory and practice (Sweeney 1936; Solomons 1961; Hendriksen 1977; Georgiou and Jack 2011; Edwards 2016). While the completed cycles of early trading ventures rendered the calculation of profit relatively easy, if unsophisticated, the need to allocate revenues and expenses between accounting periods and to value assets and liabilities at the end of an accounting period raised problems – Thomas' 'allocation problem' – which continue to the present day (Lee 1979; Tweedie and Whittington 1990).

The implications of these controversies and 'discontents' for the recognition and measurement of the elements of financial statements – assets and liabilities in particular – are explored in the next section.

The contents and historical discontents of financial accounting practice

Property, plant and equipment

Issues in practice regarding the treatment of property, plant and equipment extend from, in the railway age, the recognition/capitalisation of repairs, renewals and maintenance costs (Pollins 1956; Glynn 1984; Edwards 2019: ch. 14) to the capitalisation of borrowing costs (discussed in the context of the nineteenth century by Ladelle 1890; Brief 1969). However, the 'pervasive' problem in the practice of accounting for property, plant and equipment is the question of valuation (Tweedie and Whittington 1990). Brief (1966: 3) asserts that 'Historically, permanent enterprise [such as railroads and utilities] practiced some form of cash accounting and determined profit by matching receipts and disbursements', and that the:

> [s]hortcomings [of this approach] became apparent at an early date and some railroads began periodically to record depreciation in the accounts. However, the attempt to record regular provisions for depreciation did not persist over time, and most railroads began to practice replacement cost accounting, which is a modification of strict cash accounting.
>
> *(Brief 1966: 4)*

Capital investment by the railroad companies and other capital-intensive enterprises exposed the soft underbelly of unadjusted historical cost accounting (Pollins 1956; Brief 1966; Kitchen 1979; Glynn 1984). Dicksee (1902: 180–1) was critical of the absence of a depreciation charge: assets should be valued 'as a going concern', meaning 'at such value as they would stand in the books if proper depreciation had been provided for' (see also Brief 1966; Kitchen 1980). The perpetual life of the corporate entity also ruled out the use of exit values as fixed assets were to be used in the business and not sold at a profit: 'there being no intention to sell such assets, fluctuations in their market prices could not be considered gains or losses. Long-term assets should be valued at acquisition cost less depreciation' (Chatfield 1996c: 256). Edwards (1989: 122–4) characterises this period as 'the coming of age' of depreciation. While depreciation was not statutorily required, in the face of increasing criticism regarding inflated profits and inadequate retentions against future acquisitions of fixed assets, 'the practice of charging depreciation gained in popularity' in the early twentieth century (Edwards 1989: 124).

While a consistent cause of debate, historical cost has proved, in practice, an unshakeable foundation for financial reporting in the US (Walker 1992; Zeff 2007), whereas in the UK, inflation levels in the 1950s and 1960s encouraged British companies to 'experiment' with a 'variety of *ad hoc* adjustments designed to take account of changing prices' (Edwards 1989: 252; see also Noguchi and Edwards 2004). More recently, on the issue of Financial Reporting Standard (FRS) 15 entitled *Tangible Fixed Assets*, the ASB noted that 'in the past, companies have taken advantage of the alternative accounting rules in the Companies Act, 1985 to revalue selected tangible fixed assets (usually properties) as and when it has suited them to do so' (ASB 1999). In a further, contemporary indication of the hegemony of practice over theory, FRS 15 did not require the recognition of fixed assets at a revalued amount (unless there was impairment) but, where a policy of remeasurement was adopted, carrying values should be kept up to date.

Financial fixed assets

In the case of financial fixed assets, Edwards (1989: 135–6) comments that iron and steel was one of the first industries in the UK where companies invested in the shares of other companies and that, in the early decades of the twentieth century, 'trade investments' were reported 'at cost', 'at cost less amount written off', 'at under cost' and 'at cost less depreciation'. The separate disclosure of shares in and amounts due to and from subsidiaries was first required in the UK by the Companies Act 1928. Vangermeersch (1979: 8, 72), in his survey of US reporting practices since 1861, finds that 'there have been many valuation bases for marketable securities', including cost, 'cost or less', market value, lower of cost or market value, estimated realisable value and 'market value or less'. A logical extension of the valuation of assets on a 'going concern' basis was that financial fixed assets – intended for realisation – be valued at realisable values. The history of the use of current values in accounting – particularly with respect to marketable financial instruments but also in times of inflation accounting – is explored in, for example, Boer (1966) and Tweedie and Whittington (1984). More recently, fair value accounting (FVA) 'has entered certain accounting standards [e.g. SFAS 115 (1993) and SFAS 133 (1998) in the US and IAS 39 (1998) and IFRS 9 (2009) in international standards] as a response to needs, on a standard-by-standard basis rather than as a result of a formal amendment to conceptual frameworks' (van Zijl and Whittington 2006: 122).

Edwards (2019: ch. 16) provides a comprehensive history of accounting for changing prices in Britain. This more recent history is discussed by Haswell and Evans (2018). Drawing on documentary evidence, they examine 'how well regulators, political actors, and other commentators may have understood the use, misuse, effects and consequences of FVA at the time of Enron, and to examine how this collective understanding (or lack thereof) has influenced later accounting policy' (Haswell and Evans 2018: 25).

Intangible assets

Yang (1927: 19) argues that, when balance sheets were primarily used by financial institutions to assess ability to pay and collateral, intangible assets were 'ordinarily looked upon with considerable disfavour, particularly by bankers, because they have been subject to manipulations of value to such a degree that they have become more or less a nuisance'. While there is evidence of capitalisation and amortisation of patents in the early twentieth century (Montgomery 1912; Yang 1927; Vangermeersch 1979), the capitalisation of research and development costs remained a matter of contention (Bierman and Dukes 1975; Hope and Gray 1982; Gray 1986). Following the introduction of regulations, in the US (SFAS 2 *Accounting for Research and Development Costs*, 1974) such expenditures were written off as incurred while, in the UK (through SSAP 13 *Accounting for Research and Development*, 1977), development costs could be capitalised if they met specified criteria.

Problems regarding the elusive and inexclusive nature of intangibles materialised early on, particularly in the case of goodwill where, in the fifteenth and sixteenth centuries, 'the sale of goodwill ran afoul of then-existing "restraint of trade" doctrines' (Hughes 1996: 281). However, in partnerships, the transferability of goodwill on the death or retirement of a partner led to nineteenth-century discussion regarding its valuation (Veblen 1908; Hughes 1996). The increasingly corporate focus of accounting – and rising number of mergers and acquisitions – drew attention away from goodwill in partnerships and towards the recognition and measurement of purchased goodwill in corporate financial statements (Cooper 2007).

In the US, different accounting treatments of goodwill 'proliferated' prior to 1929 and 'its financial-statement presentation was also a matter of some flexibility' (Hughes 1996: 282). Following the Stock Market Crash of 1929, conservatism intervened, and all treatments other than the recording of goodwill at cost disappeared and immediate write-off was viewed as good practice (Hughes 1996). In 1944, Accounting Research Bulletin (ARB) 24 *Accounting for Intangible Assets* drew two distinctions: one between purchased intangibles (which could be capitalised) and non-purchased intangibles (where the related expenditures were to be written off); the other between purchased intangible assets with a limited life and those with a permanent life. ARB 24 gave equal weight to permanent retention and systematic write-off of purchased goodwill and discouraged discretionary write-offs (Committee on Accounting Procedure 1944). ARB 43 – issued in 1953 – indicated a preference for systematic amortisation. By 1970, this requirement was further refined by the Accounting Principles Board (APB) in APB 17 *Intangible Assets* (1970), which required the amortisation of purchased goodwill over a period not exceeding 40 years.

Around the same time in the UK, Lee (1971, 1973, 1974) reviewed the accounting treatment of goodwill by 66 companies. Characterising the treatment of goodwill as 'will o' the wisp accounting' (Lee 1971), he found a wide variety of accounting practices including capitalisation with and without amortisation and write-off to reserves. This dichotomy in accounting treatments – capitalisation or write-off to reserves – continued into the 1980s in the UK and was preserved by the ASC's first standard on the subject, SSAP 22 *Accounting for Goodwill.* Write-off to reserves was permitted probably because it was favoured business practice at the time (Tonkin and Skerratt 1991) – writing off goodwill in this manner by-passed the income statement and left reported earnings and EPS unaffected. The permitted flexibility reflected the ASC's declining authority following, for example, its failure to devise a system of price-level accounting that garnered sufficient support from government, professional accountants and the business community (Pong and Whittington 1996). More recently, the capitalisation of purchased goodwill has been the trend in international accounting standards with annual impairment reviews replacing amortisation (international accounting standards on intangible assets, 1998, 2004), a treatment proposed by Montgomery (1912) at the beginning of the twentieth century.

Current assets

It has been argued that, prior to the emergence of the corporate entity and the consequent development of the need for periodic reporting, inventories were measured in quantity not value (Vangermeersch 1996b) or, indeed, were not measured at all given that their measurement remained irrelevant to the merchant who monitored profit or loss on a venture-by-venture basis (De Roover 1956). However, there is growing evidence that inventory was often the subject of financial measurement although methods of recognition varied considerably before, during and after the industrial revolution (Fleischman and Parker 1990).

The adoption of the practice of valuing inventories at the lower of cost or market value, as enunciated by Montgomery (1912), is attributed to a variety of factors (which are not mutually exclusive). Storey (1959: 235) suggests that, while the valuation of fixed assets was set down by legislation, 'the law [in the US] apparently made no stipulation as to the valuation of current floating assets'. He believes that the valuation of inventories at the 'lower of cost or market' was the logical extension of the going concern concept. Parker (1965) suggests that the adoption of the lower of cost or market in the UK was a product of an accounting profession which expanded, during the nineteenth century, on the back of liquidation and bankruptcy work at a time of falling prices. By the second decade of the twentieth century, the practice of valuing inventories at the lower of cost and market value appears to have been widely accepted (Gilman 1939; Littleton 1941), although Edwards (1989: 137) remarks that it was 'not uncommon' before the First World War to value inventories 'well below cost' to create secret reserves and, one might imagine, help smooth reported profit. This treatment 'came under attack' by the issuance of Inland Revenue guidance in 1919 that inventory be valued at the lower of cost or market price.

Methods of calculating cost varied and were undoubtedly influenced by developments in cost accounting. 'Base stock', whereby the reporting entity would specify a portion of its inventory as the minimum required for the business to continue in operation, 'apparently originated in Britain during the nineteenth century … mainly in the metals trades and the textile industry' but was phased out by taxation and legal pronouncements in the UK (1919) and the US (1919 and 1930) (Chatfield 1996d: 68). The last-in first-out (LIFO) method emerged in the US in the 1930s, largely for tax reasons; its use was sanctioned by the 1938 Revenue Act (Davis and Strawser 1996) and continued to be used on a 'widespread' basis (Davis 1982; Lee and Hsieh 1985). In contrast, the tax authorities in the UK disallowed the use of LIFO accounting and FIFO or average cost became the normal practice and was institutionalised by the ASC in SSAP 9 *Stocks and Long-term Contracts*.

The practice of accounting for receivables and the recognition of provisions for bad debts sometimes also followed conservative principles. While there is some evidence of accounting for bad debts in early accounts:

> [a]fter 1850, pressures for consistency in bad debt accounting came from three sources: the companies acts, the courts and the accounting profession. The Companies Act of 1855–6 contained a model balance sheet, which included a space for 'debts considered doubtful and bad'. This suggests that the preferred practice, if not the common practice, favoured making provision for doubtful accounts.
>
> *(Chatfield 1996e: 58–9)*

The judgement at the heart of doubtful debt calculations left considerable scope for variety in practice. The recognition of write-offs for taxation purposes, in the early twentieth century, 'did most to standardise the accounting treatment of bad debts' (Chatfield 1996e: 59).

Liabilities

With the increasing complexity of business transactions and the changing nature of business financing, the recognition and measurement of liabilities in financial statements posed commensurate challenges in practice. The overstatement of liabilities through the creation of secret reserves (Arnold 1996; Edwards 2019: chs 9 and 13), and over-enthusiastic applications of conservatism to asset valuation (Sterling 1967; Hendriksen 1977) was subtly mitigated by regulatory change throughout the twentieth century. In the US, consistent with the notion that the conservative recognition of provisions was a cushion against uncertainty, a practice emerged during the Second World War of recognising special contingency reserves (ARB 13, 1942). ARB 28 (1947), which outlawed the utilisation of such reserves in determining net income, marked the beginning of a series of accounting regulations reining in the overzealous recognition of contingencies (ARB 50, 1958; SFAS 5, 1975; SFAS 105, 1990). Turning to the UK, when issuing FRS 12, the ASB (1996b, Appendix VII, para. 3) noted that:

> [i]n the absence of an accounting standard on provisions the practice has grown up of aggregating liabilities with expected liabilities of future years, and sometimes even with expected expenditures related to ongoing operations, in one large provision, often reported as an exceptional item.[8]

Over time, accruals, liabilities and other obligations became the insecure territory in which contrasting conceptualisations of income and the balance sheet were pragmatically played out in practice. Hendriksen (1977: 446) comments disapprovingly that 'traditionally ... the recording of liabilities has been closely interrelated to the matching of expenses and related revenue' (the income approach) as opposed to recognition and measurement which would 'permit economic and financial interpretation' (the balance sheet or 'liability' approach). The matching concept shaped recognition practices with respect to provisions generally as well as in specific instances, before a renewed focus on the balance sheet shifted the emphasis towards a 'liability' approach.

For example, while Vangermeersch (1979: 63, 97) finds some evidence that deferred taxation was recognised in the US from the early 1960s, with a majority of the companies in his sample employing the deferred method, Johnson (1996) argues that the preferred accounting for deferred taxation varied depending on the balance of emphases placed by the regulators on the income statement compared with the balance sheet. Between 1967 and 1987, APB 11 – emphasising the income statement and the matching concept – required 'the deferred method of comprehensive interperiod tax allocation ... resulting in virtual permanent deferrals of reversing differences' (Johnson 1996: 190). A revision in 1987 (further revised in 1992) of this accounting treatment required the use of the liability method, with an asset and liability orientation for the financial reporting of income taxes in 1987 and 1992 (SFAS 96 and 109). A similar approach, described as 'pragmatic' by Edwards (1989: 249), was adopted in the UK. The short-lived SSAP 11 (1975) allowed for the use of either the deferral or liability methods before SSAP 15 (1978) required the liability method with partial provision, amended to full provision by the ASB in FRS 19 (2000), reflecting trends towards international harmonisation.

The accounting treatment of pensions is also a site for conflict between recognising pension obligations in the balance sheet and matching (smoothing) pension costs in the income statement (Hendriksen 1977: 478–9). Baker (1964: 52) writes that, in the US, 'by and large the very early industrial plans recognised pension costs on a pay-as-you-go basis or cash disbursement basis', as 'continuing pension payments were predicated upon the financial ability of the company to maintain such payments'. However, in the early 1920s, 'using actuarial procedures some companies made financial provisions through balance sheet reserves, some made financial provisions through the facilities of an insurance company, still others used the pension trust to reduce the financial outlay of growing pension requirements'. These variations in practice were reflected in ARB 47 (1956) and, to a certain extent, shaped the development of SFAS 87 (1985) on accounting for pensions. Street (1996: 88) concludes that SFAS 87 clearly reveals the impact of compromise resulting from special interest intervention and resulted in 'earlier but gradual recognition of significant liabilities ... Other compromises (e.g. smoothing rules) further softened the impact'.

Likewise in the UK, the ASC (1988: para. 16), while noting that 'many companies have, until now, simply charged the contributions payable to the pension scheme as the pension cost in each accounting period', required recognition of 'the cost of providing pensions on a systematic and rational basis over the period which benefits from the employees' services'. This was based on the matching concept and, with some exceptions, smoothed variations in pension costs over the average expected service lives of employees. More recent amendments by the ASB and the IASB reflect the shifting emphasis between the income statement and the balance sheet approaches by controversially requiring the recognition of pension assets and liabilities, an approach which moved away from income smoothing and introduced more volatility to both the balance sheet and the income statement (Federation des Experts Comptables Européens 2001). In that regard, the recognition of pension liabilities is an example of the accrued history between the 'liability' and 'matching' approaches, between principle and practice, between the regulator and the regulated: an enduring discontent made new by its context.

Conclusion

The content of financial accounting practice was shaped by, and in turn shaped, its context. From an agency perspective, the development of the corporate form and the need for finance to sustain the reporting entity led to the representation of financial position as a primary focus of mid-nineteenth-century financial statements. In turn, the emergence and importance of equity markets as a form of business finance in the late nineteenth, early twentieth centuries led to an increasing focus on the income statement whose publication was required by regulation in the UK and the US from the third decade of the twentieth century.

A number of authors have mapped the changes in financial statements (e.g. Edwards 1981; Lee 1994; Arnold and Matthews 2002) and in annual reports more generally (e.g. Clagett and Hirasuna 1988; Graves et al. 1996; McKinstry 1996). Change is evident in these representations of the reporting entity throughout the twentieth century. The reasons for such changes are manifold, although they often result from efforts by financial accounting practice to respond to or compensate for accounting and business failure either voluntarily (for example, after the Royal Mail case) or through legislation. The hegemony of practice at times constrained regulatory change, at times provided an impetus for innovation. Conversely, changes in practice, while often codified or constrained by statute, were not limited to legislation but were also influenced by economic and political events. For example, value added reporting in the UK is attributed by Burchell et al. (1985: 400) to an 'accounting constellation', a 'very particular' variety of factors which existed at the time. It has been argued that changes in reporting practices are, hence, also signifiers of change in society, whether through the development of social and environmental reporting or the design-intensification of annual reports (McKinstry 1996; Graves et al. 1996). These frontiers and frontlines of financial accounting practice, these contested territories, these times of transition, represent opportunities for further research into the appearances and 'disappearances' (Pong and Mitchell 2005) of financial accounting practice.

However, notwithstanding the sifting of accounting practice throughout the modern era and consistent with Edwards' (2019) characterisation of financial accounting practice as a chronicle of 'continuity with change', the extent to which such practices that existed prior to the industrial revolution represent a *mappa mundi* of contemporary financial statements – the balance sheet and income statement – is also worthy of further exploration. The balance sheet and income statement formed the basic edifice of financial statements. The increasing complexity of business relationships and structures did not alter this basic shape but did stretch and ultimately extend the boundaries of financial reporting through additional disclosures, voluntary and involuntary.

The income statement supplemented and then, to a certain extent, supplanted the balance sheet as the principal financial report. Statements such as the funds flow statement and the value added statement appeared and then disappeared (Burchell et al. 1985; Pong and Mitchell 2005). The appearance of the cash flow statement was a response to the perceived limitations of the balance sheet and income statement (Lee 1981). The steady extension of disclosures of information regarding, for example, business segments, the nature of earnings, financial instruments and risk reflected the increasing complexity of business and businesses. They extended the financial accounting house but left its frame intact. Throughout this period, there is evidence at times of an entrenched continuity, evidence of financial accounting practice struggling to represent an increasingly complex world while clinging to principles such as prudence and historical cost which have formed the back-bone of financial reporting since the nineteenth century (Bryer 1993; Edwards 2019).

Consequently, financial accounting practice has, through its history, struggled to accommodate uncertainty between its (balance) sheets. Furthermore, in agency terms, the asymmetrical contest in both information and intention between the providers of finance and managers continued to test the reliability of financial statements in the form of 'secret reserves', 'earnings management' and 'creative accounting'. Many of the challenges posed by the growing complexity of business have been without resolution and without revolution: the accounting revolution has been, in Lee's words (1979: 299), 'as if on a spinning wheel'.

Hence, financial accounting practice, as a setting for iterative change, is a creature of its past. Coming full circle once more, in the special issue of *Accounting, Organizations and Society* cited at the beginning of this chapter (Hopwood 2000), McSweeney (2000: 784–5) argues that periodic reporting means that 'financial reports are not mere records, not the equivalent of pointing. They are descriptions of the past made before all that is essential for such accounts has happened … the end of a financial accounting story is in the future'. As with financial statements themselves, the story of financial accounting practice – rooted in the past – remains to be played out in the future.

Key works

Bryer (2012, 2013a, 2013b) provides a provocative perspective on the ideological origins of accounting theory and practice in the US, a discussion which is continued and contested in Oldroyd et al. (2015).

Edwards (2019) provides an accessible, mainstream history of financial accounting in Britain, giving particular attention to corporate financial reporting since the beginning of the railway age.

Hopwood (2000) argues for the importance of research that can provide more adequate insights into the wider institutional and social positioning of financial accounting.

Napier (2006) reviews financial reporting themes in the 'new accounting history' (see Chapter 2) and their contribution to understanding the processes of change within accounting.

Acknowledgements

I am grateful to Rachel Baskerville, Peter Clarke, Nora Munhuu, Brendan O'Dwyer, Philip O'Regan, Keith Warnock, Geoff Whittington and, in particular, the late Margaret Ó hÓgartaigh RIP for their contributions to the development of this chapter.

Notes

1 Given the broad canvas represented by financial accounting practice, the chapter will focus in particular on its contrasting history in the US and the UK. The undoubtedly significant and rich histories of financial accounting in other contexts, for example, Continental Europe and Japan, can be found in Walton (2006) and Cooke and Kikuya (1992) respectively.

2 For detailed studies of the objectives, users and uses of financial reports, see Cascino et al. (2013) and Zeff (2013).

3 For an alternative, political economy perspective, see the many works of Rob Bryer including Bryer (2017).

4 The invocation of agency theory as an explanation of the motivations of the various actors in financial accounting is not without its critics. Mills (1993: 802) argues that agency theory is 'flawed' by the '"economic fallacy" – granting economic activities a privileged position over other forms of human behaviour'. Other critics, such as Barzun and Graff (1977: 43), express concern regarding 'the habit of reading into the past our own modern ideas and intentions'. These admonitions are less a call to disregard agency theory but more evocative of different and multi-faceted characterisations of agency: see, for example, discussions of the 'rhetorical agency' (Carruthers and Espeland 1991), the 'surveillant agency' of accounts (Hopper and Macintosh 1993) and the discussions in new accounting history which bring 'into its exposition new actors' (Napier 2006: 456).

5 Reid (1987: 29) challenges this view by reviewing a number of legal cases involving 'judicial intervention in accounting behaviour', which saw 'the birth of many ideas which are basic to accounting today'. Her conclusion, drawing on Littleton (1933: 221), that the courts were not 'formulating new principles' but rather that 'it is more probable that principles which it was customary for auditors to apply in their professional engagements were being given public and legal sanction' suggests an institutionalisation rather than a rebuttal of *laissez-faire*.

6 Edey and Panitpakdi's conclusions relate to the general regulatory context. Parker (1990: 51) finds that financial accounting practices of companies in major British industrial sectors, such as railways, public utilities and financial institutions, were in fact regulated prior to 1900 and argues that the reason for such regulation 'was not primarily to protect investors but in order to control monopoly, privilege and safety'.

7 Hanson (1989) provides a wide-ranging summary of developments in financial reporting between 1969 (the formation of the ASC) and 1989 (the advent of the ASB), based on Tonkin and Skerratt's surveys of UK Reporting Practices.

8 Empirical evidence of 'big bath' accounting in the 1980s can be found in, for example, Griffiths (1986), Elliott and Shaw (1988) and Smith (1992).

References

American Institute of Accountants. (1931) *Resumé of Special Report of the Accounting Procedures Committee of the American Institute of Accountants* (New York: AICPA).

Arnold, A.J. (1996) Should historians trust late nineteenth century financial statements? *Business History*, 38 (2): 40–54.

Arnold, A.J. and Matthews, D.R. (2002) Corporate financial disclosures in the UK, 1920–1950: the effects of legislative change and managerial discretion, *Accounting and Business Research*, 32 (1): 3–16.

ASB. (1990) *Statement of Aims* (London: ASB).

ASB. (1991) *FRS 1 Cash Flow Statements* (London: ASB).

ASB. (1996a) *FRS 1 Cash Flow Statements (Revised)* (London: ASB).

ASB. (1996b) *FRS 12 Provisions, Contingent Liabilities and Contingent Assets* (London: ASB).

ASB. (1999) *Press Notice: Tangible Fixed Assets – New Accounting Standard Published*, ASB PN 132, 18 February (London: ASB).

ASC. (1988) *SSAP 24 Accounting for Pension Costs* (London: ASC).

Baker, C.R. and Hayes, R. (2004) Reflecting form over substance: the case of Enron Corp., *Critical Perspectives on Accounting*, 15 (6/7): 767–85.

Baker, R.E. (1964) The pension cost problem, *Accounting Review*, 39 (1): 52–62.

Baladouni, V. (1981) The accounting records of the East India Company, *Accounting Historians Journal*, 8 (1): 67–69.

Baladouni, V. (1986) Financial reporting in the early years of the East India Company, *Accounting Historians Journal*, 13 (1): 19–30.

Barzun, J. and Graff, H.F. (1977) *The Modern Researcher* (Boston: Houghton Mifflin).
Bennett, J. (1939) *Transcript of Conference with John bennett, Attorney-General of New York state, the American Institute of Certified Public Accountants and the New York Society of CPAs, January 6* (New York: AICPA).
Bierman, H. and Dukes, R.E. (1975) Accounting for research and development costs, *Journal of Accountancy*, 139 (4): 48–56.
Bircher, P. (1988) The adoption of consolidated accounting in Great Britain, *Accounting and Business Research*, 19 (73): 3–13.
Boer, G. (1966) Replacement cost; a historical look, *Accounting Review*, 41 (1): 92–97.
Boussard, D. and Colasse, B. (1992) Funds-flow accounting and cash-flow accounting in France, *European Accounting Review*, 1 (2): 229–54.
Bricker, R. and Chandar, N. (1998) On applying agency theory in historical accounting research, *Business and Economic History*, 27 (2): 486–500.
Bricker, R. and Chandar, N. (2000) Where Berle and Means went wrong: a reassessment of capital market agency and financial reporting, *Accounting, Organizations and Society*, 25 (6): 529–54.
Brief, R.P. (1966) The origin and evolution of eighteenth century asset accounting, *Business History Review*, 40 (1): 1–23.
Brief, R.P. (1969) A late nineteenth century contribution to the theory of depreciation, *Journal of Accounting Research*, 5 (1): 27–38.
Briloff, A.J. (1964) Needed: a revolution in the determination and application of accounting principles, *Accounting Review*, 39 (1): 12–14.
Briloff, A.J. and Engler, C. (1979) Accountancy and the merger movement: a symbiotic relationship, *Journal of Corporation Law*, 5 (1): 81–104.
Bryer, R.A. (1993) The late nineteenth century revolution in financial reporting: accounting for the rise of investor or managerial capitalism, *Accounting, Organizations and Society*, 18 (7/8): 649–90.
Bryer, R.A. (2000a) The history of accounting and the transition to capitalism in England. Part one: theory, *Accounting, Organizations and Society*, 25 (2): 131–62.
Bryer, R.A. (2000b) The history of accounting and the transition to capitalism in England. Part two: evidence, *Accounting, Organizations and Society*, 25 (4/5): 327–81.
Bryer, R.A. (2012) Americanism and financial accounting theory – Part 1: was America born capitalist? *Critical Perspectives on Accounting*, 23 (7/8): 511–55.
Bryer, R.A. (2013a) Americanism and financial accounting theory – Part 2: the 'modern business enterprise', America's transition to capitalism, and the genesis of management accounting, *Critical Perspectives on Accounting*, 24 (4/5): 273–318.
Bryer, R.A. (2013b) Americanism and financial accounting theory – Part 3: Adam Smith, the rise and fall of socialism, and Irving Fisher's theory of accounting, *Critical Perspectives on Accounting*, 24 (7/8): 572–615.
Bryer, R.A. (2017) *Accounting for Value in Marx's Capital: The Invisible Hand* (Lanham, MD: Lexington Books).
Buckmaster, D.A. (1992) Income smoothing in accounting and business literature prior to 1954, *Accounting Historians Journal*, 19 (4): 147–73.
Burchell, S., Clubb, C., Hopwood, A.G. and Hughes, J. (1980) The roles of accounting in organizations and society, *Accounting, Organizations and Society*, 5 (1): 5–27.
Burchell, S.C., Clubb, C. and Hopwood, A.G. (1985) Accounting in its social context: towards a history of value added in the United Kingdom, *Accounting, Organizations and Society*, 10 (4): 381–413.
Camfferman, K. and Zeff, S.A. (2003) The apotheosis of company accounting: Unilever's financial reporting innovations from the 1920s to the 1940s, *Accounting, Business & Financial History*, 13 (2): 171–206.
Capie, F. and Billings, M. (2001) Accounting issues and the measurement of profits – English banks 1920–68, *Accounting, Business & Financial History*, 11 (2): 225–51.
Carroll, A.B. (1999) Corporate social responsibility, *Business & Society*, 38 (3): 268–96.
Carruthers, B.G. and Espeland, W.N. (1991) Accounting for rationality: double-entry bookkeeping and the rhetoric of economic rationality, *American Journal of Sociology*, 97 (1): 31–69.
Cascino, S., Clatworthy, M., García Osma, B., Gassen, J., Imam, S. and Jeanjean, T. (2013) *The Use of Information by Capital Providers* (Edinburgh: Research Committee of the ICAS and European Financial Reporting Advisory Group).
Chambers, R.J. (1973) Accounting principles or accounting politics, *Journal of Accountancy*, 135 (5): 48–52.

Chambers, R.J. (1987) Accounting education for the twenty-first century, *Abacus*, 23 (2): 97–106.

Chandler, A.D. (1977) *The Visible Hand: The Managerial Revolution in American Business* (Cambridge, MA and London: Belknap Press).

Chandler, A.D. and Tedlow, R. (1985) *The Coming of Managerial Capitalism: A Casebook* (Homewood, IL: Richard D. Irwin).

Chatfield, M. (1977) *A History of Accounting Thought* (Huntington, NY: Robert E. Krieger).

Chatfield, M. (1996a) Comparability, in M. Chatfield and R. Vangermeersch (eds.) *The History of Accounting: An International Encyclopaedia*, pp. 139–44 (New York: Garland).

Chatfield, M. (1996b) Balance sheet, in M. Chatfield and R. Vangermeersch (eds.) *The History of Accounting: An International Encyclopaedia*, pp. 60–64 (New York: Garland).

Chatfield, M. (1996c) Accrual accounting, in M. Chatfield and R. Vangermeersch (eds.) *The History of Accounting: An International Encyclopaedia*, pp. 23–24 (New York: Garland).

Chatfield, M. (1996d) Base stock method, in M. Chatfield and R. Vangermeersch (eds.) *The History of Accounting: An International Encyclopaedia*, p. 68 (New York: Garland).

Chatfield, M. (1996e) Bad debts, in M. Chatfield and R. Vangermeersch (eds.) *The History of Accounting: An International Encyclopaedia*, pp. 58–59 (New York: Garland).

Clagett, L. and Hirasuna, D. (1988) *A Historical Review of Annual Report Design* (New York: Cooper-Hewitt Museum, The Smithsonian Institution's National Museum of Design).

Clare, R.S. (1945) Evolution of corporate reports, *Journal of Accountancy*, 79 (1): 39–51.

Clay, C.G.A. (1984) *Economic Expansion and Social Change: England 1500–1700* (Cambridge: Cambridge University Press).

Committee on Accounting Procedure. (1944) *Accounting Research Bulletin No. 24: Accounting for Intangible Assets* (New York: AICPA).

Cooke, T.E. and Kikuya, M. (1992) *Japanese Reporting in Its Environmental Context* (London: ICAEW).

Cooke, T.E. and Nobes, C.W. (1997) *The Development of Accounting in an International Context: A Festschrift in Honour of R. H. Parker* (London: Routledge).

Coombs, H.M. and Edwards, J.R. (1996) *Accounting Innovation – Municipal Corporations 1835–1935* (New York: Garland).

Cooper, D.J. and Sherer, M.J. (1984) The value of corporate accounting: argument for a political economy of accounting, *Accounting, Organizations and Society*, 9 (3): 207–32.

Cooper, J. (2007) Debating accounting principles and policies: the case of goodwill, 1880–1921, *Accounting, Business & Financial History*, 17 (2): 241–64.

Cowan, T.K. (1965) A resources theory of accounting, *Accounting Review*, 40 (1): 12–21.

Davies, K.G. (1952) Joint stock investment in the later seventeenth century, *Economic History Review*, 4 (3): 283–301.

Davies, P.M. and Bourn, A.M. (1972) Lord Kyslant and the Royal Mail, *Business History*, 14 (2): 102–23.

Davis, H.Z. (1982) History of LIFO, *Accounting Historians Journal*, 9 (1): 1–23.

Davis, H.Z. and Strawser, J.A. (1996) Last-in, first-out, in M. Chatfield and R. Vangermeersch (eds.) *The History of Accounting: An International Encyclopaedia*, pp. 367–69 (New York: Garland).

de Roover, R. (1938) Characteristics of bookkeeping before Paciolo, *Accounting Review*, 13 (2): 144–50.

de Roover, R. (1956) The development of accounting prior to Luca Pacioli according to the account-books of medieval merchants, in A.C. Littleton and B.S. Yamey (eds.) *Studies in the History of Accounting*, pp. 114–74 (London: Sweet & Maxwell).

Dechow, P.M. and Skinner, D.J. (2000) Earnings management: reconciling the views of accounting academics, practitioners, and regulators, *Accounting Horizons*, 14 (2): 235–50.

Defliese, P.L. (1981) British accounting standards in a world setting, in R. Leach and E. Stamp (eds.) *British Accounting Standards: The First Ten Years*, pp. 105–18 (Cambridge: Woodhead-Faulkner).

Dicksee, L.R. (1902) *Auditing*, 5th edn (London: Gee).

Dicksee, L.R. (1927) *Published Balance Sheets and Window Dressing* (London: Gee).

Edey, H.C. and Panitpakdi, P. (1956) British company accounting and the law 1844–1900, in A. C. Littleton and B.S. Yamey (eds.) *Studies in the History of Accounting*, pp. 356–79 (London: Sweet & Maxwell).

Edwards, J.R. (1981) *Company Legislation and Changing Patterns of Disclosure in British Company Accounts 1900–1940* (London: ICAEW).

Edwards, J.R. (1989) *A History of Financial Accounting* (London: Routledge).

Edwards, J.R. (2016) Asset valuation, profit measurement and path dependence in Britain to 1800, *British Accounting Review*, 48 (1): 87–101.

Edwards, J.R. (2019) *A History of Corporate Financial Reporting in Britain* (London: Routledge).

Edwards, J.R. and Baber, C. (1979) Dowlais Iron Company: accounting policies and procedures for profit measurement and reporting purposes, *Accounting and Business Research*, 9 (34): 139–51.

Edwards, J.R. and Boyns, T. (1994) Accounting practice and business finance, case studies from the iron and coal industry 1865–1914, *Journal of Business Finance & Accounting*, 21 (4): 1151–78.

Edwards, J.R. and Webb, K.M. (1984) The development of group accounting in the United Kingdom to 1933, *Accounting Historians Journal*, 11 (1): 31–61.

Eichenwald, K. (2005) *A Conspiracy of Fools* (New York: Random House).

Elliott, J.A. and Shaw, W.H. (1988) Write offs as accounting procedures to manage perceptions, *Journal of Accounting Research*, 26 (Supplement): 91–117.

Federation des Experts Comptables Européens. (2001) *How European Companies are Applying IAS 19 (Revised) in the First Year of Application* (Bruxelles: FEE).

Fleischman, R.K. and Parker, L.D. (1990) Managerial accounting early in the British industrial revolution: the Carron Company, a case study, *Accounting & Business Research*, 20 (79): 211–21.

Francis, J., Schipper, K. and Vincent, L. (2002) Earnings announcements and competing information, *Journal of Accounting & Economics*, 33 (3): 313–44.

Freedman, J. and Power, M. (1992) Law and accounting: transition and transformation, in J. Freedman and M. Power (eds.) *Law and Accountancy – Conflict and Cooperation in the 1990s*, pp. 1–23 (London: Paul Chapman).

Georgiou, O. and Jack, L. (2011) In pursuit of legitimacy: a history behind fair value accounting, *British Accounting Review*, 43 (4): 311–23.

Gilman, S. (1939) *The Accounting Concept of Profit* (New York: Ronald Press).

Gilmore, C. and Willmott, H. (1992) Company law and financial reporting: a sociological history of the UK experience, in M. Bromwich and A. Hopwood (eds.) *Accounting and the Law*, pp. 159–90 (London: Prentice Hall).

Glynn, J.J. (1984) The development of British railway accounting: 1800–1911, *Accounting Historians Journal*, 11 (1): 103–18.

Graves, O.F., Flesher, D.L. and Jordan, R.E. (1996) Pictures and the bottom line: the television epistemology of US annual reports, *Accounting, Organizations and Society*, 21 (1): 57–88.

Gray, R.H. (1986) *Accounting for R&D: A Review of Experiences with SSAP 13* (London: ICAEW).

Greenspan, A. (1996) The challenge of central banking in a democratic society, remarks by Chairman Alan Greenspan at the annual dinner and Francis Boyer lecture of the American Enterprise Institute for Public Policy Research, Washington, DC, December 5.

Greidinger, B.B. (1950) *Preparation and Certification of Financial Statements* (New York: Ronald Press).

Griffiths, I. (1986) *Creative Accounting: How to Make Your Profits What You Want Them to Be* (London: Unwin).

Guthrie, J. and Parker, L.D. (1989) Corporate social reporting: a rebuttal of legitimacy theory, *Accounting and Business Research*, 19 (76): 343–52.

Guthrie, J. and Parker, L.D. (1990) Comparative social disclosure practice: a comparative international analysis, *Advances in Public Interest Accounting*, 3: 159–75.

Haller, A. and Jakoby, S. (1995) Funds flow reporting in Germany: a conceptual and empirical state of the art, *European Accounting Review*, 4 (3): 515–34.

Hanson, J.D. (1989) Developments in financial reporting practice over the last twenty years, in D.J. Tonkin and L.C.L. Skerratt (eds.) *Financial Reporting 1988–89: A Survey of UK Reporting Practice*, pp. 3–66 (London: ICAEW).

Haswell, S. and Evans, E. (2018) Enron, fair value accounting, and financial crises: a concise history, *Accounting, Auditing & Accountability Journal*, 31 (1): 25–50.

Hawkins, D.F. (1963) The development of modern financial reporting practices among American manufacturing corporations, *Business History Review*, 37 (3): 135–68.

Healy, P. and Wahlen, J. (1999) A review of the earnings management literature and its implications for standard setting, *Accounting Horizons*, 13 (4): 365–84.

Hendriksen, E.S. (1977) *Accounting Theory* (Homewood, IL: Richard D. Irwin).

Hogner, R.H. (1982) Corporate social reporting: eight decades of development in US Steel, *Research in Corporate Performance and Policy*, 4: 243–50.

Hope, T. and Gray, R.H. (1982) Power and policy making: the development of an R&D standard, *Journal of Business Finance & Accounting*, 9 (4): 531–58.

Hopper, T. and Macintosh, N. (1993) Management accounting as disciplinary practice: the case of ITT under Harold Geneen, *Management Accounting Research*, 4 (2): 181–216.

Hopwood, A.G. (2000) Understanding financial accounting practice, *Accounting, Organizations and Society*, 25 (8): 763–66.

Hoskin, K.W. and Macve, R.H. (1986) Accounting and the examination: a genealogy of disciplinary power, *Accounting, Organizations and Society*, 11 (2): 105–36.

Hughes, H.P. (1996) Goodwill, in M. Chatfield and R. Vangermeersch (eds.) *The History of Accounting: An International Encyclopaedia*, pp. 281–83 (New York: Garland).

Husband, G.R. (1938) The corporate entity fiction and accounting theory, *Accounting Review*, 13 (3): 241–53.

Johnson, R.T. (1996) Deferred income tax accounting, in M. Chatfield and R. Vangermeersch (eds.) *The History of Accounting: An International Encyclopaedia*, pp. 190–93 (New York: Garland).

Jones, H. (1985) *Accounting, Costing and Cost estimation, Welsh Industry: 1700–1830* (Cardiff: University of Wales Press).

Joplin, J.P. (1914) Secret reserves, *Journal of Accountancy*, 18 (6): 407–17.

Käfer, K. and Zimmerman, V.K. (1967) Notes on the evolution of the statement of sources and applications of funds, *International Journal of Accounting*, 2 (2): 89–121.

Keay, J. (1991) *The Honourable Company: A History of the English East India Company* (London: Harper Collins).

Kirsch, R.J. (2012) The evolution of the relationship between the US Financial Accounting Standards Board and the International Accounting Standard Setters:1973–2008, *Accounting Historians Journal*, 39 (1): 1–51.

Kitchen, J. (1972) The accounts of British holding company groups: development and attitudes to disclosure in the early years, *Accounting and Business Research*, 2 (6): 114–36.

Kitchen, J. (1979) Fixed asset values: ideas on depreciation 1892–1914, *Accounting and Business Research*, 9 (36): 281–91.

Kitchen, J. (1980) Lawrence Dicksee, depreciation and the double account system, in H.C. Edey and B. S. Yamey (eds.) *Debits, Credits, Finance and Profits*, pp. 109–30 (London: Sweet & Maxwell).

Kripke, H. (1970) Conglomerates and the moment of truth in accounting, *St. John's Law Review*, 44 (Special Issue): 791–97.

Ladelle, O.G. (1890) The calculation of depreciation, *Accountant*, 16 (834): 659–60.

Laeri, J.H. (1966) Statement in quotes, *Journal of Accountancy*, 121 (3): 57–58.

Leach, R.G. (1981) The birth of British accounting standards, in R.G. Leach and E. Stamp (eds.) *British Accounting Standards in the First 10 Years*, pp. 3–11 (Cambridge: Woodhead-Faulkner).

Lee, C. and Hsieh, D. (1985) Choice of inventory accounting methods: comparative analyses of alternative hypotheses, *Journal of Accounting Research*, 23 (2): 468–85.

Lee, T.A. (1971) Goodwill. An example of will o' the wisp accounting, *Accounting and Business Research*, 11 (43): 318–28.

Lee, T.A. (1973) Accounting for goodwill, *Accounting and Business Research*, 13 (50): 175–96.

Lee, T.A. (1974) Accounting for and disclosure of business combinations, *Journal of Business Finance & Accounting*, 1 (1): 1–33.

Lee, T.A. (1979) The evolution and revolution of financial accounting practice: a review article, *Accounting and Business Research*, 19 (75): 292–99.

Lee, T.A. (1981) Cash flow accounting and corporate financial reporting, in M. Bromwich and A.G. Hopwood (eds.) *Essays in British Accounting Research*, pp. 63–78 (London: Pitman).

Lee, T.A. (1994) The changing form of the corporate annual report, *Accounting Historians Journal*, 21 (1): 215–34.

Lev, A. and Zarowin, P. (1999) The boundaries of financial reporting and how to extend them, *Journal of Accounting Research*, 37 (2): 353–85.

Levitt, A. and Dwyer, P. (2002) *Take on the Street: What Wall Street and Corporate America Don't Want You to Know. What You Can Do to Fight Back* (New York: Pantheon).

Lewis, N., Parker, L. and Sutcliffe, P. (1984) Financial reporting to employees: the pattern of development 1919 to 1979, *Accounting, Organizations and Society*, 9 (3/4): 275–89.

Lister, R. (1981) Company financial statements as source material for business historians: observations on the underlying conceptual framework, *Business History*, 23 (2): 223–39.

Littleton, A.C. (1933) *Accounting Evolution to 1900* (New York: American Institute Publishing Company).

Littleton, A.C. (1941) A genealogy of cost and market, *Accounting Review*, 16 (2): 141–66.
Maltby, J. (2004) Hadfields Ltd: its annual general meetings 1903–1939 and their relevance for contemporary corporate social reporting, *British Accounting Review*, 36 (4): 415–38.
Marriner, S. (1980) Company financial statements as source material for business historians, *Business History*, 22 (2): 203–35.
Mautz, R.K. (1967a) Identification of the conglomerate company, *Financial Executive*, 4 (7): 18–26.
Mautz, R.K. (1967b) Conglomerate reporting and data reliability, *Financial Executive*, 4 (9): 25–35.
Mautz, R.K. (1967c) Bases for more detailed reporting by diversified companies, *Financial Executive*, 4 (11): 52–60.
May, G.O. (1932) Influence of the depression on the practice of accountancy, *Journal of Accountancy*, 52 (5): 336–50.
May, G.O. (1949) *Business Income and Price Levels: An Accounting Study* (New York: AICPA).
McKinstry, S. (1996) Designing the annual reports of Burton plc from 1930 to 1994, *Accounting, Organizations and Society*, 21 (1): 89–111.
McSweeney, B. (2000) Looking forward to the past, *Accounting, Organizations and Society*, 25 (8): 767–86.
Merino, B.D. and Coe, T. (1978) Uniformity in accounting: a historical perspective, *Journal of Accountancy*, 146 (2): 62–69.
Miller, P. and O'Leary, T. (1987) Accounting and the construction of the governable person, *Accounting, Organizations and Society*, 12 (3): 235–65.
Mills, P.A. (1993) Accounting history as social science: a cautionary note, *Accounting, Organizations and Society*, 18 (7/8): 801–03.
Montgomery, R.H. (1912) *Auditing: Theory and Practice* (New York: Ronald Press).
Moore, L. (2017) Carving nature at its joints: the entity concept in an entangled society, *Accounting Historians Journal*, 44 (2): 125–38.
Moyer, C.A. (1955) Trends in presentation of financial statement and reports, in M. Backer (ed.) *Handbook of Modern Accounting Theory*, pp. 425–52 (New York: Prentice-Hall).
Mueller, G.H., Gernon, H. and Meek, G.K. (1997) *Accounting: An International Perspective*, 4th edn (Chicago, IL: Richard D. Irwin).
Napier, C.J. (2006) Accounts of change: 30 years of historical accounting research, *Accounting, Organizations and Society*, 31 (4/5): 445–507.
Napier, C.J. (2010) The history of financial reporting in the in United Kingdom, in G. Previts, P. Walton and P. Wolnizer (eds.) *A Global History of Accounting, Financial Reporting and Public Policy: Europe*, pp. 243–73 (Bingley: Emerald).
Napier, C.J. and Noke, C. (1992) Accounting and the law: an historical overview of an uneasy relationship, in M. Bromwich and A.G. Hopwood (eds.) *Accounting and the Law*, pp. 30–54 (Hemel Hempstead: Prentice-Hall).
Nissan, S., Kamata, N. and Okata, R. (1995) Cash reporting in Japan, *International Journal of Accounting*, 30 (2): 168–80.
Nobes, C. (2015) International differences in IFRS adoptions and IFRS practices, in S. Jones (ed.) *The Routledge Handbook to Accounting Theory*, pp. 167–96 (London: Routledge).
Nobes, C. and Parker, R.H. (2006) *Comparative International Accounting*, 9th edn (London: Pearson).
Noguchi, M. and Edwards, J.R. (2004) Accounting principles, internal conflict and the state: the case of the ICAEW, 1948–1966, *Abacus*, 40 (3): 280–320.
Oldroyd, D., Tyson, T.N. and Fleischman, R.K. (2015) American ideology, socialism and financial accounting theory: a counter view, *Critical Perspectives on Accounting*, 27: 209–18.
Olson, W.E. (1982) *The Accounting Profession: Years of Trial: 1969–1980* (New York: AICPA).
Parker, R.H. (1965) Lower of cost and market in Britain and the United States: an historical survey, *Abacus*, 1 (2): 156–72.
Parker, R.H. (1977) Explaining national differences in consolidated accounts, *Accounting and Business Research*, 6 (22): 203–07.
Parker, R.H. (1990) Regulating British corporate financial reporting in the late nineteenth century, *Accounting, Business & Financial History*, 1 (1): 51–71.
Paton, W.A. and Stevenson, R. (1918) *Principles of Accounting*, 3rd edn (New York: Macmillan).
Peloubet, M.E. (1955) The historical background of accounting, in M. Backer (ed.) *Handbook of Modern Accounting Theory*, pp. 5–39 (New York: Prentice-Hall).
Persson, M.E. and Napier, C.J. (2015) R.J. Chambers and the AICPA's postulates and principles controversy: a case of vicarious action, *Accounting Historians Journal*, 42 (2): 103–34.

Pollins, H. (1956) Aspects of railway accounting before 1868, in A.C. Littleton and B.S. Yamey (eds.) *Studies in the History of Accounting*, pp. 332–55 (London: Sweet & Maxwell).

Pong, C.M. and Mitchell, F. (2005) Accounting for a disappearance: a contribution to the history of the value added statement in the UK, *Accounting Historians Journal*, 32 (2): 173–99.

Pong, C.M. and Whittington, G. (1996) The withdrawal of current cost accounting in the United Kingdom: a study of the Accounting Standards Committee, *Abacus*, 32 (1): 30–53.

Power, M. (1990) The horizons of financial reporting, in M. Power (ed.) *Brand and Goodwill Strategies*, pp. 1–8 (Cambridge: Woodhead Faulkner).

Previts, G.J. and Bricker, R. (1994) Fact and theory in accounting history: presentmindedness and capital markets research, *Contemporary Accounting Research*, 10 (2): 625–41.

Previts, G.J. and Flesher, D.L. (2015) Financial accounting and reporting in the United States of America, 1820–2010: toward sunshine from shadows, in S. Jones (ed.) *The Routledge Handbook to Accounting Theory*, pp. 39–90 (Abingdon, Oxon: Routledge).

Previts, G.J. and Merino, B.D. (1998) *A History of Accountancy in the United States: The Cultural Significance of Accounting* (Columbus, OH: Ohio State University Press).

Previts, G.J., Walton, P. and Wolnizer, P. (eds) (2010) *A Global History of Accounting, Financial Reporting and Public Policy: Europe* (Bingley, UK: Emerald Group Publishing).

Previts, G.J., Walton, P. and Wolnizer, P. (eds) (2011a) *A Global History of Accounting, Financial Reporting and Public Policy: Americas* (Bingley, UK: Emerald Group Publishing).

Previts, G.J., Walton, P. and Wolnizer, P. (eds) (2011b) *A Global History of Accounting, Financial Reporting and Public Policy: Asia and Oceania* (Bingley, UK: Emerald Group Publishing).

Previts, G.J., Walton, P. and Wolnizer, P. (eds) (2012) *A Global History of Accounting, Financial Reporting and Public Policy: Eurasia, Middle East and Africa* (Bingley, UK: Emerald Group Publishing).

Reid, J.M. (1987) Judicial intervention in accounting behavior: a reevaluation of the nineteenth century experience, *Journal of Accounting and Public Policy*, 6 (1): 9–34.

Richard, J. (2004) The secret past of fair value: lessons from history applied to the French case, *Accounting in Europe*, 1: 95–107.

Roberts, A.C. and Gabhart, D.R.L. (1972) Statement of funds: a glimpse of the future? *Journal of Accountancy*, 133 (4): 54–59.

Samson, W.D., Flesher, D.L. and Previts, G.J. (2003) Quality of earnings: The case of the mobile and Ohio railroad in the 19th century, *Issues in Accounting Education*, 18 (4): 335–57.

Sandilands, F.E.P. (1975) *Inflation Accounting: Report of the Inflation Accounting Committee* (London: HMSO).

Schachner, L. (1968) Accountability under industrial diversification, *Accounting Review*, 43 (2): 304–26.

SEC. (1945) *Accounting Series Release No. 53*, November 16, New York.

Shiller, R.E. (2000) *Irrational Exuberance* (Princeton, NJ: Princeton University Press).

Singleton-Green, B. (1990) The rise and fall of the ASC, *Accountancy*, 122 (1164): 84–85.

Smith, T.E. (1992) *Accounting for Growth: Stripping the Camouflage from Company Accounts* (London: Century Business).

Sobel, R. (1965) *The Big Board. A History of the New York Stock Market* (New York: Free Press).

Solomons, D. (1961) Economic and accounting concepts of income, *Accounting Review*, 39 (2): 374–83.

Sombart, W. (1924) *Der Moderne Kapitalismus* (Munich: Duncker & Humblot).

Sommer, A.A. (1967) Conglomerate disclosure: friend or foe? *Journal of Accountancy*, 123 (5): 61–67.

Spacek, L. (1956) *Are Industrial Common Stocks Selling at Fictitious Earnings? Address before Financial Analysts of Philadelphia* (Chicago, IL: Arthur Andersen Library).

Stamp, E. (1984) *Selected Papers on Accounting, Auditing and Professional Problems* (New York: Garland Publishing).

Stamp, E. and Marley, C. (1970) *Accounting Principles and the City Code: The Case for Reform* (London: Butterworths).

Stamp, E. and Mason, A.K. (1977) Current cost accounting: British panacea or quagmire, *Journal of Accountancy*, 143 (4): 66–73.

Sterling, R.R. (1967) Conservatism: the fundamental principle of valuation in traditional accounting, *Abacus*, 3 (4): 109–32.

Stewart, B. (2006) The real reasons Enron failed, *Journal of Applied Corporate Finance*, 18 (20): 116–99.

Storey, R.K. (1959) Revenue realization, going concern and the measurement of income, *Accounting Review*, 34 (2): 232–39.

Storrar, A.C. and Pratt, K.C. (2000) Accountability vs Privacy, 1944–1907: the coming of the private company, *Accounting, Business & Financial History*, 10 (3): 259–91.

Street, D.L. (1996) A recent history of financial reporting in the UK and US, in T.A. Lee, A. Bishop and R.H. Parker (eds.) *Accounting History from the Renaissance to the Present – A Remembrance of Luca Pacioli*, pp. 71–118 (New York: Garland).

Sweeney, H.W. (1936) *Stabilized Accounting* (New York: Harper & Row).

Takatera, S. and Sawabe, N. (2000) Time and space in income accounting, *Accounting Organizations and Society*, 25 (8): 787–98.

Thomas, A.L. (1969) *The Allocation Problem in Financial Accounting Theory*, Studies in Accounting Research No. 3 (Sarasota, FL: American Accounting Association).

Thomas, A.L. (1974) *The Allocation Problem: Part 2*, Studies in Accounting Research No. 9 (Sarasota, FL: FL: American Accounting Association).

Thompson, J.E. (2013) Railroad investing and the importance of financial accounting information in 1880s America, *Accounting Historians Journal*, 40 (2): 55–89.

Tinker, A.M. (1985) *Paper Prophets: A Social Critique of Accounting* (Eastbourne: Holt, Rinehart & Winston).

Tonkin, D.J. and Skerratt, L.C.L. (1991) *Financial Reporting: A Survey of UK Reporting Practice* (London: ICAEW).

Tweedie, D.P. and Whittington, G. (1984) *The Debate on Inflation Accounting* (Cambridge: Cambridge University Press).

Tweedie, D.P. and Whittington, G. (1990) Financial reporting: current problems and their implications for systematic reform, *Accounting and Business Research*, 21 (81): 87–102.

van Zijl, T. and Whittington, G. (2006) Deprival value and fair value: a reinterpretation and a reconciliation, *Accounting and Business Research*, 36 (2): 121–30.

Vangermeersch, R. (1979) *Financial Reporting Techniques in 20 Industrial Companies since 1861* (Gainesville: University Presses of Florida).

Vangermeersch, R. (1996a) Income statement/income account, in M. Chatfield and R. Vangermeersch (eds.) *The History of Accounting: An International Encyclopaedia*, pp. 315–18 (New York: Garland).

Vangermeersch, R. (1996b) Inventory valuation, in M. Chatfield and R. Vangermeersch (eds.) *The History of Accounting: An International Encyclopaedia*, pp. 346–47 (New York: Garland).

Veblen, T. (1908) On the nature of capital: investment, intangible assets, and the pecuniary magnate, *Quarterly Journal of Economics*, 23 (1): 104–36.

Walker, R.G. (1968) Disclosure by diversified companies, *Abacus*, 4 (1): 27–38.

Walker, R.G. (1992) The SEC's ban on upward asset revaluations and the disclosure of current values, *Abacus*, 28 (1): 3–35.

Walton, P. (2006) *Accounting in Europe* (London: Taylor & Francis).

Watts, R.L. and Zimmerman, J.L. (1983) Agency problems, auditing, and the theory of the firm: some evidence, *Journal of Law and Economics*, 26 (4): 613–34.

Weiner, J.L. (1928) Theory of Anglo-American dividend law: the English cases, *Columbia Law Review*, 28 (8): 1046–60.

Whittington, G. (1989) Accounting standard setting in the UK after 20 years: a critique of the Dearing and Solomons Reports, *Accounting and Business Research*, 19 (75): 195–205.

Winjum, J.O. (1970) Accounting in its age of stagnation, *Accounting Review*, 45 (4): 743–61.

Winjum, J.O. (1971) Accounting and the rise of capitalism: an accountant's view, *Journal of Accounting Research*, 9 (2): 333–50.

Yamey, B.S. (1960) The development of company accounting conventions, *Three Banks Review*, 47: 3–18.

Yamey, B.S. (1962) The case law relating to company dividends, in W.T. Baxter and S. Davidson (eds.) *Studies in Accounting History*, pp. 428–42 (Homewood, IL: Irwin).

Yamey, B.S. (1964) Accounting and the rise of capitalism: further notes on a theme by Sombart, *Journal of Accounting Research*, 2 (2): 117–36.

Yamey, B.S. (1970) Closing the ledger, Simon Stevin, and the balance sheet, *Accounting and Business Research*, 1 (1): 71–77.

Yamey, B.S. (1977) Some topics in the history of financial accounting in England, 1500–1900, in W.T. Baxter and S. Davidson (eds.) *Studies in Accounting*, pp. 11–34 (London: ICAEW).

Yang, J.M. (1927) *Goodwill and Other Intangibles: Their Significance and Treatment in Accounts* (New York: Ronald Press).

Zeff, S.A. (1972) *Forging Accounting Principles in Four Countries: A History and an Analysis of Trends* (Springfield, IL: Stipes Publishing).

Zeff, S.A. (1999) The evolution of the conceptual framework for business enterprises in the United States, *Accounting Historians Journal*, 26 (2): 89–131.

Zeff, S.A. (2002) 'Political' lobbying on proposed standards: a challenge to the IASB, *Accounting Horizons*, 16 (1): 43–54.

Zeff, S.A. (2007) The SEC rules historical cost accounting: 1934 to the 1970s, *Accounting and Business Research*, (Special Issue), 37: 49–62.

Zeff, S.A. (2013) The objectives of financial reporting: a historical survey and analysis, *Accounting and Business Research*, 43 (4): 262–327.

9

MANAGEMENT ACCOUNTING

Theory and practice

Richard Fleischman and Tom McLean

Overview

The term 'management accounting' lacks a clear, universally accepted definition. This chapter uses the term to encompass the related activities of 'cost recording, costing, cost accounting, managerial accounting and management accounting' (Boyns and Edwards 1997: 22). The historical literature discussed in this chapter indicates these activities have not been confined to the work of accountants but have also been undertaken by diverse groups including engineers, managers and entrepreneurs.

Mainstream accounting history journals have been dominated by the Anglo-Saxon world until relatively recently. However, building upon the pioneering efforts of a few individuals such as Tito Antoni (Antonelli 2017), and encouragement from leading scholars (e.g. Carmona and Zan 2002; Carmona 2004; Zan 2004b), a new cadre of researcher has widened the geographical scope of the management accounting history literature. For example, the *Handbook of Management Accounting Research* (Chapman et al. 2007) includes individual chapters on management accounting history not only in the UK (Boyns and Edwards) and the US (Fleischman and Tyson) but also in France, Italy, Portugal and Spain (Carmona); China (Chow et al.); German-speaking countries (Ewert and Wagenhofer); the Nordic countries (Näsi and Rohde); and Japan (Okano and Suzuki). Some members of the new cadre of researchers have chosen to publish in their native tongues, resulting in a substantial knowledge loss to the traditional mainstream literature. Nevertheless, this chapter seeks to recognise the wide geographical representation of the history of management accounting practice and, also, a variety of theoretical perspectives, in its examination of management accounting through to contemporary times.

This chapter parallels Garner's (1954) topical approach and it is organised into seven further sections: theoretical frameworks, pioneering studies in management accounting history, the search for origins, debates in management accounting history, time-honoured themes, contemporary management accounting history and the conclusion.

Theoretical frameworks

Loft (1995) noted a range of theoretical frameworks employed by management accounting historians. Traditionalists tended to base their work on published literature and adopt an evolutionary perspective that saw management accounting in terms of ongoing technical improvement over time (e.g. Edwards 1937). Neoclassical revisionists set their archive-based company and industry case studies within contextual frameworks but continue to work within a paradigm that tends to stress the techniques of management accounting as used in pursuit of organisational efficiency and profit (e.g. Edwards 1989; Fleischman and Parker 1991). Building upon Hopwood's (1987) criticisms of a focus on techniques, Miller et al. (1991) used the term 'new accounting history' to encompass critical approaches to the writing of management accounting history, including: the Foucauldian power-knowledge framework that argues that management accounting is a device that makes the workforce visible and calculable, thereby enabling managers to control and discipline labour; the genealogical approach that focuses on 'the outcomes of the past rather than the origins of the present' (Miller and Napier 1993: 631); and Marxist analysis (Bryer 2005). Napier (2001) noted that, working from a sociological basis, new historians emphasise theory, generalisation and societal critiques rather than the particulars of accounting history. There has been extensive debate between neoclassical revisionists and 'new' accounting historians (Sánchez-Matamoros and Hidalgo 2011: 338). In their recent manifesto, Tyson and Oldroyd (2017: 35) examined three debates between accounting historians in which they 'believe certain authors crossed the line between politically committed history and social/political advocacy'.

The 'new realist economic rationalism' (Boyns and Edwards 2013: 4) posits that the drive for efficiency and profit underlies the development of management accounting, but it also acknowledges the potential influence of social, institutional and other factors. Setting a wider context, Luft (2007: 269; see also Chapter 2) provides an analysis of 'theoretical debates in historical research and their relevance to management accounting studies'.

Pioneering studies in management accounting history

Prior to the late 1980s, academic analysis of the history of management accounting was sporadic, limited and confined largely to the European context. Pioneering studies provided evidence of industrial accounting prior to the publication of Pacioli's *Summa* in 1494, in, for example, the cloth manufacturing operations of the Medicis, the Florentine ruling family (De Roover 1941) and the accounts of Christopher Plantin, a Flemish printer (Elder 1937). Other Italian textile operations were studied with particular reference to production cost control – the Datinis in Prato (Brun 1930), the Bracci in Arezzo (Melis 1950) and Francisco del Bene & Co. (Sapori 1932).

Moving forward in time, Scheuermann (1929) described the accounting for the Fugger mining and smelting operations in Germany between 1548–1655. British industrial costing was explored in relation to decision making and planning in the late seventeenth-century Newmills Cloth Manufactory (Marshall 1980); production planning in the early eighteenth-century Crowley ironworks (Flinn 1957, 1962); and in a treatise (Dodson 1759) on a system described (Edwards 1937; Solomons 1952) as an early example of batch costing in shoemaking. Other notable early/mid-twentieth-century studies of costing history included Littleton (1933), Yamey (1949) and Garner (1954).

Significant developments in the study of management accounting history occurred in the late 1980s. In their book *Relevance Lost*, Johnson and Kaplan (1987) argued that management accounting information was used to enable the management of decentralised US companies of the late nineteenth-early twentieth centuries. Furthermore, they contended that, in the 1980s, a period of economic crisis and rising international competition, US managers operated businesses by using management accounting systems that were outdated and not fit for purpose. This indictment of US managerial accounting was quickly seconded by a chorus of well-known theorists (Berliner and Brimson 1988; Cooper and Kaplan 1988; Bromwich and Bhimani 1989; Sakuri 1989; Shank and Govindarajan 1989). Although the Johnson and Kaplan thesis was subjected to heavy criticism (e.g. Fleischman 2009: 212–4), it had a significant impact in moving the study of 'accounting's *history* centre-stage' (Ezzamel et al. 1990: 157). Research into management accounting's history was also much aided and stimulated by Hopwood's (1987) 'The archaeology of accounting systems', which recognised that most early studies had been principally technical in nature. Hopwood's call for historical research that probed more deeply into the forces underlying management accounting systems has been answered by subsequent generations of scholars.

Antecedents of management accounting may be found in the ancient worlds of China (Chow et al. 2007), Egypt and the Middle East (see Chapter 4), and classical Greece and Rome (see Chapter 5). Given the ongoing academic interest in the matter, particularly when related to practice and theory that have direct links to the present world, this chapter turns next to the search for the origins of management accounting.

The search for origins

Iberian roots

Within recent decades, a rich literature on Spanish management accounting history has developed. Although a particular focus has been placed on costing developments in a number of Spanish royal factories, practices on the estates of ecclesiastical institutions have also been researched. Fatjó (1991, 2001) and Llopis et al. (2002) related how, at the Spanish Monastery of Guadalupe between 1507–1784, an accounting system was devised and employed to aid decision making in the management of lands and other business operations (see also Chapter 25). In their study of large rural estates in Catalonia, 1850–1950, Planas and Saguer (2005) noted the lack of a Spanish literature on agrarian accountancy until the twentieth century. They stated that the accounting records of the secular estates that they studied had few parallels with those of earlier ecclesiastical estates, given changes in administrative methods and social relationships. Moreover, they noted that this secular estate accounting bore little resemblance to modern accounting systems elsewhere, given the absence of double-entry bookkeeping. Nevertheless, Planas and Saguer (2005: 178) concluded that it 'seems reasonable to associate the existence of accounting records with good estate management practice'.

In industry, the Royal Soap Factory of Seville received a governmental monopoly in the late fourteenth century. The main focus of accounting there, in the sixteenth and seventeenth centuries, was the intricate calculation of production costs to determine a 'just price' for soap. Performance standards for raw materials and labour went into its determination. Outside experts were called in to observe testing procedures for these standards. Factory costs, including capacity considerations and opportunity costs, were also factored in (Carmona and Donoso 2004; Carmona 2007).

Carmona and Gómez (2002) studied the Royal Textile Mill of Guadalajara, 1717–1744, and found that cost accounting technology was used to control raw material usage and waste as well as labour and management productivity. In contrast to the findings of Fleischman et al. (1995) that material standards typically predate labour standards, evidence at the textile mill suggested the reverse. One interesting feature was the utilisation of standards to compare the efficiency of native Spanish workers with that of imported Dutch labour.

Núñez (2002) wrote of the accounting associated with the Crown's gunpowder monopoly plied in the Spanish colony of Mexico (New Spain) during the seventeenth century. Accounting was necessary to track a very sensitive commodity through various stages of production. The system not only regulated the flow of work but provided for rewards and punishments to operatives and managers based on their relative efficiencies.

It is clear that the cost accounting advances in evidence at the royal factories rivalled the British Industrial Revolution (BIR) innovations in terms of technical sophistication. The showcase for eighteenth-century Spanish industrial accounting was the Royal Tobacco Factory of Seville. Gutiérrez (1993) revealed costing practices which included production standards for the control of raw materials and labour (Carmona et al. 1997, 1998; Alvarez et al. 2002) while Gutiérrez and Romero (2007) examined the implication of costing in quality-related decisions. Gutiérrez et al. (2005) expanded the study of Spanish industrialisation to encompass 13 large and medium-sized firms for the period 1760–1800, and confirmed parallels with the UK-related findings of Fleischman and Parker (1991, 1997). The authors found that cost accounting methods varied as a function of product and ownership structure. Factories run by the Spanish government in monopolistic environments tended to be more successful than those operating under certain market conditions (Carmona 2007). By contrast, in later history, Macías (2002a, 2002b) has shown that privatisation had the opposite effect as far as managerial accounting was concerned. For example, when the tobacco monopoly was leased to the Bank of Spain in 1887, the use of cost data for decision making and the monitoring of managerial performance increased. Ultimately, the 'imposing presence of the Spanish state in all spheres of life kept privately owned firms relatively small and unsophisticated, so there are few surviving records of cost management systems' (Carmona 2007: 933). However, Guillén (2005) noted that, in an attempt to break the printing monopoly in Castile that was held by Plantin's Flemish workshop, in 1732 a Spanish printer presented a costing analysis to the King of Spain to demonstrate that he could maintain quality standards while lowering prices.

Sánchez-Matamoros and Hidalgo (2012) employed a Foucauldian governmentality framework in analysing the roles of accounting in the implementation of the Spanish Ordinances of the Mints in 1730. They found that accounting was used managerially to deal with 'three main issues: production control, the management of expenses and the registration of official documentation' (Sánchez-Matamoros and Hidalgo 2012: 363). Accounting was an essential element in developing tight control over the production of gold and silver coins and, thus, supported the government's monetary policy.

A study of the Silk Factory Company in Portugal has seconded the claim made by Spanish scholars that purposeful cost accounting on the Iberian Peninsula predated the BIR and escalated the pace of innovation and the expansion of enterprises in which change took place. Matos Carvalho et al. (2007: 83) have pointed out that in the period 1745–1747, while the Silk Factory Company was still under private ownership, albeit enjoying a governmental monopoly, not only was double-entry bookkeeping and the integration of its costing and financial accounts present, but a job-order costing system was operational that 'allocated overhead costs to products, allowed for direct materials shrinkage … [and evinced] elements of a rudimentary standard raw material costing system'. Alas, studies of Portuguese cost and management accounting history remain scarce (Faria 2008).

The British experience

In a significant addition to the literature, *A History of Management Accounting: The British Experience*, Boyns and Edwards (2013: 4) adopted a perspective of 'new realist economic rationalism' in which economic factors predominate but non-economic factors also exert influence over management accounting. They argued that the history of British management accounting should not be seen in terms of a 'rise and fall' (Johnson and Kaplan 1987) but in terms of continuity and change (Boyns and Edwards 2013: 277).

Scorgie (1997) discussed the use of performance standards in pre-industrial England, while other features of management accounting may be observed on medieval ecclesiastical estates (Dobie 2011, 2015), manorial estates (Oldroyd and Dobie 2009), for purposes of Crown budgeting in the Tudor era (Bisman 2012), in decision making (Freaar 1994) and in the measurement and management of human performance (McLean 2009) in early seventeenth-century farming (see also Chapter 15). Merchants adopted double-entry bookkeeping (DEB) in the seventeenth and eighteenth centuries and contemporary authors thought that a 'compelling reason for adopting DEB was to enable businessmen to better manage their financial affairs' (Boyns and Edwards 2013: 95). Pre BIR evidence of industrial accounting has been examined in the contexts of, for example, the copper, iron, charcoal-making and coal mining industries (Jones 1985; Edwards et al. 1990; Edwards and Boyns 1992; Oldroyd 2007; King 2010). Such industrial accounting employed 'techniques designed to enable the businessman to plan for the future, choose between alternatives, control costs and enhance profit' (Boyns and Edwards 2013: 125).

Mid-twentieth-century authors argued that there was a shortfall in management accounting in the BIR (Solomons 1952; Johnson and Kaplan 1987) due to the prevailing high profit margins (Edwards 1937; Pollard 1965; Hudson 1977; Parker 1986) and a lack of accounting infrastructure (Stacey 1954; Yamey 1960; Parker 1986). However, Fleischman and Parker (1991) and Edwards (1989), argued that it was counter-intuitive that BIR entrepreneurs would fail to appreciate the value of cost accounting to their nascent enterprises. This optimism has been validated by the exposition of a contemporary literature (Boyns and Edwards 2013: 140–2) and a wealth of archive-based studies of BIR enterprises which have found evidence of management accounting in business planning, control and decision making in, for example, iron making (Boyns and Edwards 1997), shipbuilding (McLean 1995) and coal mining (Brackenborough et al. 2001; Fleischman and Macve 2002; Lloyd Jones 2010). However, management accounting also played a role in social change. Toms and Shepherd (2017) demonstrated that accounting, and specifically knowledge of cost behaviour, played a part in the struggle to regulate working hours and the use of child labour during the BIR. Richardson (2008: 124) reveal how a 'cost-based logic' was used by Rowland Hill in 1837 to illustrate the potential of postal services reform. Robson (2006) and Funnell et al. (2014) examined the role of accounting in voluntary hospitals during the late nineteenth-early twentieth centuries.

The BIR has provided the setting for methodological debate between management accounting historians. Fleischman et al. (1996) and Fleischman and Radcliffe (2003) suggested that the insights furnished by researchers representing rival worldviews (see Fleischman et al. 1995; Bryer 2005) could contribute additively and synergistically (Fleischman and Macve 2002) to our understanding of vital historical periods such as the BIR. In an ambitious research project (Bryer et al. 2007), Fleischman, an economic-rationalist, was joined by Bryer, a Marxist historian, and Macve, a Foucauldian, in an investigation of the Carron Company archive. While there was consensus that the accounting methodology at Carron was impressive for its time, ultimately the joint Carron project failed as the team split its findings into separate statements (Bryer 2006; Fleischman and Macve 2007). Ding and McKinstry (2012) extended the methodological range and scope of BIR research by using a systems/contingency model to explore the use of management accounting, including standard costing and budgetary control, in papermaking in Scotland, 1779–1965.

It may be noted that, despite its economic significance, the BIR 'did not represent a major discontinuity [in management accounting]'. Rather, in the estimation of Boyns and Edwards (2013: 163–6), it signalled an important phase in the evolution of cost calculation practices from the previous era through to developments in the post-1870 period.

French cost accounting theory and practice

While the BIR featured a significant volume of costing activity over a wide range of industries and firms in the absence of much by way of a theoretical literature, corresponding developments in France were quite the opposite (Boyns et al. 1997). Focused mainly in the 1820s, there was a spate of French writings at a time when indigenous industrial enterprises were relatively small and family owned. Hence, adoptions of the innovations suggested were correspondingly few. Nevertheless, Lemarchand (2016) has examined the actors involved in the development and diffusion of French industrial accounting.

Payen (1817) related accounting systems at a carriage manufactory and a glue factory that resembled job-order and process-costing methods respectively, though he did not label them as such (Garner 1954). Payen is also credited with insights into the areas of transfer pricing, cost allocation and the integration of cost and financial records (Garner 1954; Holzer and Rogers 1990). De Cazaux (1824), although he dealt primarily with agricultural accounting, had a better sense than Payen of input factors in costing individual transformation processes (Holzer and Rogers 1990) and was an early theorist on budgeting (Solomons 1952). Godard (1827), who embodied both theory and practice, was the owner/manager of the Baccarat Chrystalworks and the author of a managerial accounting classic, *Traité Générale et Sommaire de la Comptabilité Commerciale*. Advances at Baccarat (Nikitin 1996) included rigorous quality control procedures, sensitivity analyses, the allocation of acquisition and installation costs over multiple periods, and an awareness of fixed and variable costs. Simon (1830) anticipated Johnson and Kaplan's arguments that there should be no period costs and that expenses such as rent, administrative salaries and taxes should be allocated as overhead to productive processes (Garner 1954; Holzer and Rogers 1990). Moussalli et al. (2009: 355) noted that the literature on French cost accounting theory was ahead of French practice, but argued that 'the early French industrial sector may have used the methods described by Payen well before 1817'.

Nikitin (1990) studied a number of other French industrial firms operating at approximately the same time as the theoretical outpouring. Saint-Gobain, a glass works, had implemented double-entry bookkeeping by 1820, and by 1880 had developed a full-costing system that included transfer pricing, depreciation and the allocation of overhead cost to activity centres. Founded in the 1820s, the Decazeville iron works operated a disciplinary regime to control labour that was sufficiently impressive to cause Hoskin and Macve (1988: 64) to link it to events at the Springfield Armory. Boyns, et al. (1997) also found evidence that, by the late 1830s, managers of French enterprises were analysing the causes of cost variations.

Italian developments

Cinquini et al. (2008: 15) noted that management accounting 'developed later in Italy than in Anglo-Saxon countries' for reasons including late industrial development and protectionist economic policies. Nevertheless, in respect of the nineteenth and early twentieth centuries, researchers such as Antonelli et al. (2002) analysed the rise of cost accounting in Italy; Mussari and Magliacani (2007: 87) demonstrated 'the role of accounting in the management control process' in an agricultural context; and Mura and Emmanuel (2010: 380) examined scholarly debates on transfer pricing from the first half of the nineteenth century through to the first half of the twentieth century and noted that 'Italian scholars were aware of many of the issues that exist today'.

Antonelli et al. (2017: 278) examined the industrial accounting system of the Royal Silk Factory of San Leucio for the period 1802–1826 'from a very broad perspective, covering the social, institutional, organisational and accounting aspects'. The Royal Silk Factory was a hybrid organisation, built upon elements of both capitalism and socialism and, *inter alia*, it 'had a threefold form of control on labour' based on social controls within the community, surveillance in the workplace and a system of labour accounting that 'enabled the General Superintendent to monitor each individual [worker's] performance' (ibid.: 291–2).

In their study of the development of cost accounting in Italy, c.1800 to c.1940, Antonelli et al. (2009: 465) note that the relationship between cost accounting theory and practice 'is not well understood'. Their study of this relationship sheds light on 'diffusionist' and 'multiple origins' theories of cost accounting's genesis. They concluded that the multiple origins thesis may be more relevant to the nineteenth century but diffusion became increasingly important in the twentieth century, given the greater level of contact that existed with other countries and their firms and ideas. More broadly, Maran and Leoni (2019) provide an analysis of Italian contributions to the accounting history literature.

American events

Chandler (1977), the noted economic historian, made a strong case for the US transcontinental railroads of the mid-nineteenth century as the first corporations of a modern type. He argued that railroad accounting signalled the emergence of accounting from bookkeeping. Early US railroad accounting (see Chapter 18) has subsequently been studied extensively by Heier (e.g. 2000); Flesher, Previts and Samson (e.g. Flesher et al. 2003; Samson et al. 2006); and Hoskin and Macve (2007); while for UK railways, Arnold and McCartney (e.g. 2002, 2004) have written prolifically.

The Springfield Armory has provided the setting for contrasting analyses of management accounting history. Foucauldian scholars Hoskin and Macve (1988, 1994, 1996, 2000) dated the genesis of modern management from events that transpired at the Springfield Armory during the 1830s and 1840s. According to Hoskin and Macve, post-1840 productivity improvements were attributable to the 'invention' of managerialism, which they defined as managers' ability to enforce accounting norms and exert discipline over labour. However, Tyson's (1990, 1993, 2000) examination of the Springfield Armory archives revealed that a comprehensive piece-rate regime was in evidence as early as 1815. As an economic-rationalist, he concluded that economic factors (falling prices, skilled-labour surpluses, technological improvements, etc.) better explain management's desire and ability to reduce piece rates and significantly increase productivity after 1841. Toms and Fleischman re-examined the cases of both the Springfield Armory and the British firm of Boulton and Watt; in each case, they found that 'the management of internal-contractual relationships and a preoccupation with efficiency rather than profit or control through surveillance were the dominant explanations of accounting change' (Toms and Fleischman 2015: 19).

Further debate has taken place over another contender for honours as the birth place of sophisticated US cost accounting – the New England textile industry (Johnson 1972). Cost accounting information, broadly interpreted, was first used in the US in a managerial manner in the New England textile industry of the early nineteenth century (Tyson 1992, 1998; Fleischman and Tyson 1998, 2007). Prior to that time, most businesses were small and entrepreneurial, and owners were hands-on managers. Large-scale textile manufacturing in New England reflected the transition from mercantile to industrial accounting. The New England mills were large, integrated and professionally managed. Cost accounting information included comparative costing between different mills, time periods and product lines. Comparative cost data were used in a number of managerial ways: make or buy decisions, comparisons of mill efficiency, and price-cost comparisons.

These and other traditional interpretations of early nineteenth-century New England mill costing were countered by Hoskin and Macve (1996), who argued that the cost reports were based on arbitrary allocations and were clearly suboptimal, thus lacking managerial utility. Only at Springfield Armory, they countered, could managers discipline workers, hold them accountable to empirically based standards and improve labour productivity. Tyson (1998) acknowledged that formal ledger-based cost reports did result from simple averaging and allocations and that labour norms were never established in the New England mills. Nevertheless, mill owners and managers clearly made do with sub-optimal information to make important and ongoing business decisions. In a recent study of cost accounting practices in US cloth mills in the 1820s, Gervais and Quinn (2016: 191) argued that, while 'these practices were indeed institutionalised … a merchant mindset on costs and profits was engrained within them', indicating the Industrial Revolution was a period of continuity in cost accounting rather than a dramatic break point.

Debates in management accounting history

The theory/practice schism

The schism in management accountancy's past has featured a dichotomy between the volume and erudition of a period's managerial accounting literature, on the one hand, and the prevalence of advocated methodologies within industrial enterprises, on the other. At least two formative epochs have been misevaluated by historians who have drawn conclusions about management accounting in practice from the theoretical literature.

The first of these epochs concerns the BIR. Pollard's (1965: 248) oft-quoted claim that 'the practice of using accounts as direct aids to management was not one of the achievements of the British industrial revolution' led to a consensus of learned opinion, until c.1990, that cost accounting was in a nascent state during the BIR. However, there were several pre-1980 studies of individual BIR firms that inspired later researchers to look more deeply into the period. Most significant were Roll's book (1930) on Boulton & Watt, McKendrick's article (1970) on Wedgwood and Stone's investigation (1973) of the Charlton cotton mills. The large-scale rehabilitation of BIR costing was initially undertaken by Edwards, Boyns and Newell (Edwards 1989; Edwards and Newell 1991; Boyns and Edwards 1996a, 1996b, 1997) and, working independently, Fleischman and Parker (1990, 1991, 1992, 1997). Ultimately, Pollard's claim was laid to rest.

The second epoch of theory/practice schism involves the scientific management era of pre-World War I America. By virtue of the vast outpouring of theoretical literature authored by luminaries such as Garcke and Fells (1887), Norton (1889), Church (1901), Taylor (1903, 1911, 1912), Emerson (1914), Gantt (1916) and Harrison (1918–1919, 1930), many accounting historians considered this epoch the dawning of modern managerial accounting. However, the query suggested by the schism is, to what degree was this theoretical bonanza reflected in actual practice? Fleischman (2000) compiled a list of US businesses identified (Hoxie 1920; Nelson 1974; Epstein 1978) in the Taylor archives as firms that embraced scientific management. Instead of numbering in the hundreds as one might expect, the result was a rather meagre 80.

So why is it that accounting historians have been misguided? The venerated cost accounting historians of earlier times, rather that undertaking archival research into BIR records, took it for granted that since nobody was writing about industrial costing, there was nothing to write about. Even Pollard (1965), who did a substantial amount of archival investigation, tended to ignore the best evidence, examining letter books rather than production reports. It was much the same for the scientific management era but in reverse. Since so much was being written about time-and-motion studies, standard costing and variance analysis, it was easy to assume that these innovations were widely embraced into practice. Great names representing each of the prevailing paradigms in managerial accounting history – Johnson and Kaplan (1987) for economic rationalism, Miller and O'Leary (1987) for Foucauldianism and Hopper and Armstrong (1991) for Marxism – assumed prevalent standard costing in the US although subsequent researchers failed to find widespread evidence of its utilisation until after World War II. These scholars, like those who wrote the early BIR histories, had bigger fish to fry in their broad surveys than to concentrate upon a single component.

Of course, schisms between theory and practice, where they exist, are unlikely to last for ever. Lampe and Sharp (2017: 73) noted that the work of late eighteenth- and early nineteenth-century German and Danish writers highlighting 'the use of double-entry accounting for scientific and efficiency purposes [and] the calculation of economic returns' in agriculture laid the foundations for nineteenth-century developments in accounting practice which supported the 'rapid modernisation and success of Danish agriculture'.

Sharing information

Early cost accounting historians suggested that the dictates of competitive advantage militated against the dissemination of costing innovations during the BIR (Edwards 1937; Garner 1954; Urwick and Brech 1964; Wells 1977, 1978). Secrecy was offered as an explanation for the absence of a theoretical literature: since any public disclosure of costing and pricing could lead to competitive disadvantage, cost accounting methodology could only have been passed by word of mouth (Garner 1954; Chatfield 1977). The debate continues, as evidenced by the differing views of the co-authors in the Carron study mounted by Bryer et al. (2007).

Boyns and Edwards (2007) pointed out that the movement of individuals around the country could serve as a catalyst for the dissemination of ideas. Two examples offered as proof were the activities of Smeaton, perhaps the second most famous BIR engineer behind Watt and its most prominent consultant, who seemed to pop up everywhere (Fleischman and Parker 1997), and the coal-mining 'viewers' who went from mine to mine performing a number of managerial functions including cost accounting (Oldroyd 1996; Fleischman and Macve 2002). McKinstry and Ding (2015) examined linkages between quantity surveyors and accountants in the building of Glasgow University, in the mid-nineteenth century, and analysed its implications for management accounting change and the development of hybridised financial control. For the period c.1890–1960, Kininmonth and McKinstry (2007: 387) offered a counter view on the role of secrecy when arguing that the British multinational thread-makers J. & P. Coats' management accounting systems 'incorporated high levels of secrecy, highly valued in the UK textile industry, probably because of the family orientation of its shareholdings'.

Spraakman and Margret (2005) provided evidence of the dissemination of management accounting practices from London counting houses to the British North American fur trade during the late eighteenth and early nineteenth centuries. Vent and Milne (1997: 77) noted that Australian 'cost accounting practices continued to evolve from and improve upon methods previously developed in Britain'. Vent (1991) also examined the activities of Bewick, Moreing & Co., a British firm of professional mine managers and consulting engineers, who operated in like fashion to the viewers in Britain a century before. The dissemination of the various costing and measurement techniques that comprise scientific management indicates that secrecy was not a high priority. In 1910, John Jensen, on behalf of the Australian Defence Department, visited a number of leading US and Canadian manufacturers (e.g. Underwood, Colt, Remington, and a number of armouries including Springfield). Foreman (2001: 31) observed that he brought back Taylorite practices that became 'significantly modified' to conform to the control requirements and environment of the Australian government's munitions factories.

Antonelli et al. (2008: 62) reported that the Italian firm Ansaldo sent directors to the US and Germany in the 1910s to study scientific management. Destinations included such business giants as Ford, Bethlehem Steel and Krupp. Agostino Rocca, an engineer who 'had a clear understanding of financial and management accounting, which he had developed abroad' (ibid.: 72), became Ansaldo's Chief Executive Officer and, in 1935, he established a central office for the organisation of new plants, the *Organizzazione nuovi impianti*, which unsuccessfully promoted studies and programs based on Taylorite methods.

In the aftermath of World War II (1948), the Anglo-American Council on Productivity was established under the auspices of the Marshall Plan. US experts visited Britain as consultants and British missions to the US were undertaken to learn first-hand of US scientific management techniques. However, no great explosion of scientific management techniques eventuated for a variety of economic, cultural and political reasons, but also because the methods touted by the Americans were already well known in Britain (Boyns and Edwards 2007; Fleischman et al. 2007). In 1954, Palle Hansen, founder of the Copenhagen Business School, was chosen by the Danish Ministry of Trade's Productivity Committee to lead a delegation on a six-week tour of the US (Näsi and Rohde 2007). The next year, the recently founded Japanese Productivity Center organised a similar study tour. Perhaps the most significant story line here was the participation of Taiichi Ohno, years later the architect of Toyota's meteoric rise to greatness.

Díaz et al. (2009) conducted a study of the literature in order to examine the evolution of cost accounting in Spain, 1900–1978. They noted that the official standardisation of Spanish cost accounting occurred in 1978 and was much affected by other European influences, particularly French and German, and by US thought. Lemarchand (2016) noted the diffusion of double-entry bookkeeping and industrial accounting between the countries of Europe and the regions of France in the eighteenth and nineteenth centuries. Bessire and Baker (2005) presented a critical analysis of the French *tableau de bord* and the US balanced scorecard, while Pezet (2009) questioned the specifically French nature of *tableau de bord* and noted US influences on their development.

In addressing the 'sharing information' debate, it is useful to look beyond dissemination practices noted above and to consider how information may be shared within companies. Chandar et al. (2012) examined the American Telephone and Telegraph Company (AT&T) during the 1920s and noted that firm-wide 'conferences were extensively used to disseminate knowledge about new management accounting techniques and graphical communication throughout the firm' (ibid.: 56). They concluded that this had the beneficial effect of 'reducing the uncertainty associated with internal informational asymmetries that frequently arise in enterprises of great scale, scope and complexity' (ibid.: 35).

Scientific management

It was not until the late nineteenth century that an English-language costing literature appeared in significant volume. In particular, the engineering profession and its journal literature on the development of scientific management launched cost accounting into the modern era. Sowell (1973: 524) wrote how 'the industrial engineer, rather than the cost accountant, recognised the need for a revolution in the industrial order and initiated ideas that grew into predetermined cost techniques'. The contribution of the engineering profession and a host of individual commentators to the development of scientific management theory in the US is well documented (Garner 1954; Sowell 1973; Epstein 1978; Wells 1978; Fleischman 1996, 2000).

In the discussion that follows, there will appear frequent mention of standard costing as the *sine qua non* of scientific management. However, the term 'standard' has been used to signify a wide range of different approaches to costing. Fleischman and Parker (1991), for example, used the term for BIR enterprises that based standards on historical experience, sometimes only the preceding year's results, and then compared those 'standards' to the current period's actuals. Labour standards at Boulton & Watt were based on time-and-motion studies but were badly rounded and infrequently amended (Fleischman et al. 1995). The standard costing theory of the scientific management movement described here was at a much higher level of sophistication and science, with engineers determining optimal work routines and standards of efficiency. What was most innovative at this point in time was the advent of variance analysis techniques.

Early UK theorists (Garcke and Fells 1887; Norton 1889) also had significant insights on the subject. Garcke and Fells' (1887) classic, *Factory Accounts, Their Principles and Practice*, is often regarded as the first truly authoritative contribution to cost accounting literature, although a case can be made for BIR theorist Hamilton (1777) for his insights on return-on-investment (ROI) and Babbage (1835) for his differentiation between fixed and variable costs. Garcke and Fells suggested the value of establishing norms of cost wherein the person best acquainted with a particular process should estimate a probable cost in terms of wages and materials. They, as well as Mann (1903a, 1903b), argued for the allocation of overhead based on direct labour (hours or cost) and this became typical practice for decades. Nicholson (1909), meanwhile, made the case for machine hours. Church (1901), although critical of Taylor, did not differ substantively in his discussion of engineered standards and their utilisation in predetermining costs and comparing estimates with actual results (Sowell 1973). He argued that product and period costs (shop and establishment) could be applied to products using a variety of allocation bases, thereby presaging activity-based costing (ABC). He urged the establishment of production centres to facilitate these applications (Johnson and Kaplan 1987; Fleischman 1996). Norton (1889) and Dicksee (1911) spoke to the idea of having each processing department operate as a separate profit centre, with the development of transfer pricing to allow for the flow of costs throughout an enterprise. Solomons (1952) credited Whitmore (1908) with detailing a standard costing system based on the ideas of Taylor and Church, though he made original contributions in his own right in handling idle time and material use variations (Parker 1969; Sowell 1973). Emerson (1914) distinguished a new method of ascertaining costs contemporarily coming into vogue in large plants wherein costs were determined in advance of manufacturing.

Continental European theorists were heard during the Age of Taylor, although not on the subject of scientific management. Holzer and Rogers (1990) cautioned historians not to ignore French contributions that were concerned with integrating cost accounting within DEB. Léautey and Guilbault (1889) emphasised the accuracy of the *prix de revient* and its overhead component. Croizé and Croizé (1907) made important distinctions between period and product costs (Holzer and Rogers 1990). In Germany, meanwhile, Ballewski (1877) considered cost behaviours at different output levels, and Tolkmitt (1894) analysed the role of costing in management decision making (Coenenberg and Schoenfeld 1990). Schmalenbach (1899), early in his illustrious career, wrote of the dichotomy between fixed and variable costs and the appropriate exclusion of the former for purposes of cost estimation and pricing policy (Schweitzer 1992). Fayol, the managing director of a French mining company, has been identified alongside Taylor as the embodiment of the classical management model (Parker and Lewis 1995), although Parker (2016) stresses the diversity of Fayol's ideas along with their international and theoretical influence.

Yet it was Frederick Taylor, as the premier populariser and consultant on scientific management in its early years, who stamped the age with his imprimatur. A concentration on his ideas is not intended in any way to marginalise the systematising efforts of his collaborators or competitors, such as Barth, Emerson, Gantt, Gilbreth and Thompson, all of whom shared many of the same basic ideas. Taylor (1911) generalised scientific management to mean:

1. the deployment of science in management to replace rules of thumb;
2. harmony in industrial relations rather than discord;
3. cooperation in the productive process rather than individualism;
4. maximisation of output rather than restriction ('soldiering'); and
5. the development of each worker to maximum efficiency and, hence, economic well-being.

Taylor's industrial philosophy extended to such issues as machine layout and design, tool standardisation and tool-room reorganisation, standard purchasing and stores methodology, and functional foremanship (a proliferation of supervisors each with a specialised expertise). However, method-study, stopwatch-based time study and incentive wage schemes were the central features of the emerging theory of scientific management (Taylor 1903, 1911). Taylor believed that the determination of incentive wages, based upon scientific time study and motivational considerations, could provide solutions to many, if not all, labour problems (Nelson 1975). However, in respect of Britain, Smith and Boyns (2005: 210) noted that scientific management that featured an emphasis on the use of piecework led to 'seriously problematic outcomes for industrial relations and performance in the manufacturing sector [particularly] in the three decades following the Second World War'. Edwards (2010) provided a detailed case study of the introduction and use of job analysis on the London, Midland and Scottish Railway.

Other industrial philosophies were germinated that deserve mention as components of the scientific management movement. After 1918, 'the development of rationalization movements … was widespread in Europe' (Antonelli et al. 2008: 56). Fordism featured mass production techniques and the payment of high wages to labour. Fordism was embraced in post-Revolution Russia, favoured by Lenin and inculcated into the early five-year plans.

Bedaux, born in France but an early émigré to the US, functioned as an industrial consultant in the 1920s and 1930s, although his worldwide enterprise was founded pre-World War I. He disagreed with Taylor's approach to time study and his Bedaux system was founded upon a scientific investigation of the relationship between a prescribed amount of work, the fatigue that it produced and the time required for recovery. Based on these factors, an optimum rate of work and a standard time for any activity (expressed in Bedaux points) would be established. Bedaux's system was immensely popular with businessmen and a British study concluded that a 50 per cent increase in productivity could be achieved by companies embracing the method. However, the hatred aroused among labour, which saw it as an ultimate 'speeding' device, led to numerous violent strikes in Britain and the US. Consequently, Bedauxism suffered an ignominious death (Levant and Nikitin 2006) and the social Utopian concepts attributed to his work have been exposed as a myth (Levant and Nikitin 2009).

Budgeting: governments and business

In China, cost accounting had its genesis as a function of government budgeting and control rather than private-sector enterprise (Fu 1971; Guo 1988; Lin 1992, 2003). Similarly, there is ample evidence to suggest that, during the 1920s, budgeting was a lesson conveyed from government to business in the US (see Chapter 27; Gilman 1922). In 1921, J. O. McKinsey, a Chicago certified public accountant (CPA) published a series of nine articles in *Administration* which provided a cogent rationale for business budgeting, followed by an in-depth development of a master budget. He also described the importance of the budget committee and internal lines of authority and responsibility for effective budgetary control (McKinsey 1922; Marquette and Fleischman 1992). By the early 1930s, production budgeting had become well established. Rudimentary flexible budgets were introduced into the management literature by Maynard (1928) and Drucker (1929). Like government, business had learned that 'there can be no effective control of … costs unless there is a proper classification of accounts' (Rogers 1932: 196), with costs recorded by line item linked to the department that incurred them. Financial institutions contributed to the evolutionary process by according superior credit ratings to businesses that had instituted budgeting (Theiss 1937). From these beginnings, budgeting theorists began a decades-long process of formulating the psychological parameters of effective budgeting and the processes by which budgets could be most effectively constructed within business enterprises.

In pre-World War II Japan, 'special companies' such as airlines 'operated mainly in areas critical to the achievement of [the country's] national policy goals, in particular economic growth and expansion/defence of the empire' (Noguchi and Boyns 2012). In these companies, budgets served to legitimise 'receipt of subsidies from the state' (ibid.: 444). In 1938, Japan Air Transport was reorganised and became Japan Airways (JA), a semi-nationalised concern. Between 1938 and 1941:

> [t]he budget system at JA increasingly came to be used as a tool to control and coordinate operations in accordance with a pre-determined business plan [but …] when JA came under the direct control of the military with the start of the Pacific War, the role of budgets seem to have been pushed into the background.
>
> *(ibid.: 444–5)*

Thus, Noguchi and Boyns (ibid.: 445) demonstrate 'that the coercive power of the state … can vary over time'.

Standard costing and budgeting around the world

The dissemination of scientific management was significantly aided by an international movement to spread the gospel. The First International Congress in Scientific Management was held in Prague in 1924. This event led to the establishment of national associations in several European nations to popularise and disseminate the new methodologies.

Fleischman et al. (2008) found that standard costing followed an evolutionary progression in Britain from World War I through to the 1940s and 1950s and, as such, was not as much in arrears of US developments as had been popularly believed (Boyns 1998). The British pattern differs from findings in the US where standard costing developed slowly until the end of World War II and then underwent a substantial boom at least in quantitative, if not qualitative, terms. As in the US, the literature suggests that knowledge of scientific methods came to Britain earlier than their widespread introduction into practice (Garner 1954). Standard costing was mentioned frequently in the 1920s in *The Cost Accountant*. Boyns (1998, 2003) studied the archives of the Manchester firm Hans Renold Ltd. and found that standard costing emerged there in the 1910s following a consulting engagement by Church. Likewise, budgetary control was in evidence there as well as at Austin Motors in the 1920s.

In a response to Chandler (1990), Kininmonth and McKinstry (2007: 367) researched thread-makers J. & P. Coats Ltd, c.1890–1960, one of the UK's 'largest and most successful multinational companies' and one where 'family members remained dominant on the board throughout most of the period studied' (ibid.: 369). Rather than employing the divisional organisational form, Coats achieved success via a series of subsidiaries and an extensive committee structure backed, *inter alia*, by management accounting controls on capital expenditure and cash, plus, from the 1930s, a formal budgeting system. Furthermore, in the mid-1930s, Coats engaged US expertise to help in the installation of a standard costing system.

In their study of shipbuilding, engineering and metals industries in the west of Scotland, c.1900–1960, Fleming et al. (2000) found that scientific management, standard costing and budgetary control were not in use because of factors related to the dominance of engineers over accountants, difficult labour relations and the bespoke nature of contracts undertaken. McLean and Tyson's (2006) study of the post-World War II Sunderland shipbuilding industry found that, in a major firm, the introduction of new technology, in the form of welding, stimulated modernisation and reorganisation and the consequent adoption of scientific management and standard costs. However, these new techniques were used for the calculation of piece-work rates rather than for management control. McLean and Tyson also found that the use of engineering information for planning and control purposes and the continuing dominance of the craft administration of the ship construction process inhibited the development of scientific management and standard costing in the shipbuilding industry. Although the concept of the governable worker is often linked to the disciplinary practice of standard costing, Edwards (2018: 36) demonstrates that, in the British government's military establishments from the 1850s onwards, accounting 'played a key role in the formulation of disciplinary practices designed to construct a governable labour force some decades before' the advent of standard costing. Standard costing and budgeting were important elements in the management accounting systems adopted by newly nationalised industries in the UK in the 1950s (Boyns and Edwards 2013: 239–40), although 'standard costing was a disaster' in the National Coal Board due mainly to frequent changes in standards (Berry et al. 1985).

The pattern in France more closely resembled the US experience. Standard costing was known in the 1920s, albeit not seen much in practice until the late 1950s or early

1960s (Carmona 2007). A few French firms, such as the car maker Renault, were in the vanguard at much earlier points in time (Bhimani 1993, 1994). In general, budgeting had an earlier genesis in France than did standard costing (Berland 1998, 2001; Berland and Boyns 2002).

Turning to Italy, Antonelli et al. (2006) found that, in the 1880s, the pottery giant Manifattura Ginori used comparisons of actual output and predetermined standards as a basis for bonuses and punishments, although these standards were probably not scientifically determined. An Italian organisation, ENIOS, was established in the 1920s to popularise and diffuse scientific management principles. However, the take-up was limited due to 'political and socio-cultural factors' (Antonelli et al. 2008: 73).

Näsi and Rohde (2007) report that scientific management gained a 'foothold' in the Nordic countries from early in the twentieth century. Ideas on standard and direct costing and budgetary control were introduced from the US in the 1950s and Kari Lukka (e.g. Lukka 1988) has made a substantial contribution to the exploration of the behavioural aspects of budgeting.

Japan presents an interesting case. Okano and Suzuki (2007) identified Mitsubishi Electric, Toyobo and Fukusuke as early developers of scientific management but as a version that was adapted to Japan's cultural environment. Taylorism made substantial inroads during the 1930s as its emphasis on efficiency was viewed as a means to promote recovery from the Great Depression. Standard costing was also promoted during the1930s among governmental suppliers of war materiel as the militarists anticipated the road to World War II. Okano and Suzuki (2007) also reported that standard costing during the 1930s did not work well because of volatile price fluctuations and the nation's tax laws that did not accept standard costing for inventory valuation.

In the case of Australia, we have seen an example of the very early introduction of scientific management as a result of Jensen's efforts. However, progress was only made in governmentally run factories, so far as we know. Presumably private industry was too small to consider Taylorite innovations worthwhile. This pattern of adoption might also explain the situation in Spain where clear antecedents of scientific management were evident in the royal factories of an earlier time but had passed from the scene by the twentieth century. More perplexing is the absence of discussion of scientific management in German-speaking countries (Ewert and Wagenhofer 2007). Of course, the Germanic industrial scene in the 1930s was totally directed by the Hitlerian regime, which did not see standard costing as relevant to its war preparations. Given the meteoric recovery of German industrial capacity following the war, however, it might be expected that standard costing played a role.

Direct vs. absorption costing

The 1950s and 1960s witnessed a theoretical battle royal between traditionalists defending absorption or full costing and 'progressives' advancing the cause of direct (variable/marginal) costing. Direct costing first appeared in popular parlance in a *NACA* [National Association of Cost Accountants] *Bulletin* article by Harris (1965), but it was not until the aftermath of World War II that numerous articles began to appear there and in its British counterpart, *The Cost Accountant*, in which the pros and cons of direct costing were argued. The US literature on this topic, which continued for several decades, has been collected in Marple (1965); the British literature has been reviewed by Dugdale and Jones (2003, 2005) and Baxter (2005).

Defenders of the orthodoxy argued that absorption costing was necessary as fixed factory overhead became an increasingly substantial component of product cost and, hence, inventory valuations. They felt that absorption costing provided better information for stockholders and the public at large. Also, it was argued, the analysis of cost into its fixed and variable components was not always a realistic proposition (Greer 1965: 151; Ludwig 1965) and that direct costing would lead to perilously low pricing. Dugdale and Jones identified support from non-academic sources for absorption costing in Britain. The Inland Revenue opposed direct costing because it felt that it would result in the loss of short-term tax revenues but, in the Duple Motor Bodies case (1961), it was told it could not force a taxpayer to use absorption costing. Nevertheless, the Inland Revenue continued to press its argument strongly. The accounting profession, through Recommendation 10 issued by the Institute of Chartered Accountants in England and Wales, favoured absorption costing for external reporting purposes for the sake of consistency with past practice. Finally, trade associations, such as the printers, trying to effectuate uniform accounting among their memberships (Walker and Mitchell 1997), perceived absorption costing as the path of least resistance.

Given the perceived inaccuracies arising from the apportionment of fixed overheads between products (Luenstroth 1965), advocacy of direct costing was particularly strong among academicians. It was argued that, since all costs tend to be variable in the long term, direct costing was appropriate for long-term pricing and planning policy decisions (National Association of Accountants 1957; Dugdale and Jones 2005). Furthermore, direct costing was perceived as better suited than absorption costing for such control tools as flexible budgeting, standard costing, cost-volume-profit calculations and breakeven analysis.

In the 1950s and 1960s, the UK and US cost accounting professional organisations took opposite positions in the absorption costing v direct costing debate. The Institute of Cost and Works Accountants supported direct costing while the National Association of Accountants (1957), successor to the NACA, opted for absorption costing in its Research Series No. 23. In due course, standard-setting bodies on both sides of the Atlantic (the US Committee on Accounting Procedure and the UK Accounting Standards Steering Committee) made absorption costing mandatory for financial reporting.

In the Germanic countries, a system similar to direct costing was developed independently in the mid-1950s and early 1960s by Plaut, a management consultant, and Kilger, an academic. *Grenzplankostenrechnung* was a 'widely used cost accounting system for cost planning and control purposes' (Ewert and Wagenhofer 2007: 1065). Its major features were the separation of variable ('relevant') costs from fixed costs for decision-making purposes and the use of a variety of cost drivers and cost centres in tracking relevant costs through the production process. In many ways it may be seen as a forerunner of ABC. As with so many other cost accounting innovations, the Nordic countries seem to have followed in the footsteps of Germany, although Näsi and Rohde (2007) traced the originating spark of variable costing to the influence of the London School of Economics. As US costing literature began to supplant German as the most influential in Nordic countries in the mid-1950s, a full-blown debate between full and variable costing emerged. Näsi and Rohde (2007) provide figures reflecting a vastly greater acceptance of variable costing in Norway than anything that occurred in the US or the UK: all Norwegian companies used full costing in 1948, but 45 per cent had adopted variable costing by 1963. By 1975, two-thirds of all companies in the country were using the latter method. By 1960, direct costing was also adopted widely in France given its relative simplicity compared to the existing methods (Levant and Zimnovitch 2013).

Time-honoured themes

The integration of costing records

A time-honoured theme has been the dating of the integration of the costing and financial records within the context of DEB. Examples of DEB implementation were fairly universal by the eighteenth century with the possible exception of Japan where Kimizuka (1992) and Okano and Suzuki (2007) claim it was not in evidence until the 1870s, following the Meiji Restoration. The larger question is, when did the integration of the costing and financial records occur? Iberia is an interesting case. Carmona (2007) felt that integration came late to Spain while Matos Carvalho et al. (2007), in a study of Portuguese cost accounting, found integration at the Silk Factory Company in the eighteenth century. Integration in France appeared in the immediate post-Napoleonic period, particularly evidenced at Godard's Baccarat Chrystalworks. However, early factories operating under royal patent were not as successful in achieving cost accounting innovation in France as they were in Spain. After the Napoleonic era, French cost accounting improved markedly, helped in large part by integration (Nikitin 1990, 1996; Boyns et al. 1997). Manifattura Ginari, the Italian pottery concern, had DEB in place by the early 1900s (Antonelli et al. 2006) but, although there are surviving costing records, the authors are unable to state definitively whether they were integrated with the financial accounts.

Integration has been an important focus in the BIR rehabilitation project. Drawing on Jones (1985), Edwards (1989) reported the integration of the costing records at the huge Cyfarthfa iron enterprise in the 1780s. Bryer (2006) and Fleischman and Macve (2007) found evidence of integration at Carron from its foundation in 1760, overlooked by Campbell (1961) and Fleischman and Parker (1990) in earlier investigations. In a study of the shipbuilding industry, 1818–1917, McLean (1995: 142) noted an evolution from mercantile-based integrated accounting through to 'systems of contract accounting and costing incorporating financial and cost accounting sub-systems [given the need] to provide information for pricing decisions in a competitive environment during a period of technological and organisational change'. Boyns and Edwards (2016: 187) examined the advent of double-entry-based costing in an engineering firm, 1856–1863, and found it to be developed by practitioners 'in the absence of instruction from a relevant literature'. However, the British literature did begin to develop shortly afterwards (e.g. Garcke and Fells 1887; Plumpton 1895; Burton 1900).

Levant and Nikitin (2012) note that the integration of cost and financial accounting was regarded as natural in France until the 1940s, when State imposition of a standardised system of financial accounting led to separation into two systems. An attempt to reintroduce integration by means of the *système croisé* failed because of insufficient support.

Cost accountancy and war

The impact of war and preparations for armed conflict on the development of cost accounting have been mixed (see also Chapter 28). Serious attention has been accorded to the Venice Arsenal during the sixteenth and seventeenth centuries; the US in the nineteenth and twentieth centuries; and to the impacts of World War I and World War II.

Zan (2004a) and Zambon and Zan (2007) explored the Venice Arsenal archives for the period 1580–1679 and Carmona (2007) summarised the cost accounting advances found in this research. One innovation was a form of budgeting for planning and control purposes, with the involvement not only of accountants and supervisors but also the participation of shop floor 'gang bosses'. Other features of accounting at the Arsenal were the control of waste and the articulation of a system of rewards and punishments for operatives and foremen based ostensibly on expected performance. However, as Zan and Carmona both cautioned, the events at the Venice Arsenal, as well as at other governmental installations of this type, should be evaluated in the context of an organisation committed to public welfare rather than profit-seeking.

Turning to the US, the Springfield Armory story has been noted already in this chapter as it is featured in debates over the origins of purposeful managerial accounting. If the events at Springfield augured cost accounting advance at military facilities, the difficulties of innovation were highlighted in the attempt by the US government to install Taylorite systems, particularly time-and-motion studies, at arsenals and other locations in the immediate pre-World War I era. There were labour disruptions in response to these efforts, particularly at the Naval Shipyard at Mare Island and at the Watertown Arsenal. The strike at Watertown in 1911 was so severe that the US Congress passed legislation prohibiting time study in governmental shipyards and arsenals, a prohibition that lasted from 1915 to 1949 (Fleischman and Marquette 2003).

There has been conflicting evidence with respect to the impact of war on cost accounting practice. The most famous study is that of Loft (1986), who wrote of significant advances in the UK during World War I. The improvement was magnified in Loft's estimation by her perception that the UK's costing expertise was effectively at ground zero in the pre-war milieu. Loft concurred with Chandler's (1984) view that the prevalence of family firms, coupled with the power of British trade unions, had forestalled interest in innovative management techniques, such as cost accounting systems. However, neither Loft's perception of the bankruptcy of British costing before the war (cf. Boyns 1993; Boyns and Edwards 2007), nor the developments she felt occurred during the war, are agreed upon universally (cf. Marriner 1980; Fleischman and Tyson 2000; Boyns and Edwards 2007).

A similar lack of consistency in respect of the World War I effect on costing is evident in McWatters and Foreman's (2005) comparative study of meat-packing concerns in Australia and Canada. Here, and in earlier work (Foreman and Tyson 1998; Foreman 2001), the war decade in Australia saw the advent of scientific management only in governmental factories and industrial enterprises of significant size. Meanwhile, in Canada, the verdict was that the effect of the war on accounting was minimal. Quinn and Jackson (2014: 191) examined the impact of World War I on management accounting at Ireland's Guinness brewery and found that, while the war was a driver of change, in essence 'existing practices guided the creation/adaptation of [new] routines'. Fleischman and Tyson (2000) found no discernible costing innovations in the US as a result of World War I. In their examination of the Italian Ministry of War and Ministry of Munitions during World War 1, Antonelli et al. (2014: 155–6) noted that 'state accounts were constructed in ways which concealed the detailed costs of war and thereby shrouded dubious contracting arrangements in which embezzlement and bribery featured', and they concluded that budget data and processes 'were used to legitimate decisions and policy making in the area of managing war resources'.

Noguchi et al. (2015: 204) examined World War II relationships between accounting control and the Japanese military at Mitsubishi's Nagoya Engine Factory (NEF) and found that, as the military and the NEF interacted, 'their relationships became more cooperative and specific cost accounting features employed at the NEF came to be integrated into the military's unified rules'. There is general agreement among all observers that the industrial environment of World War II (Hoyt 1943; Caminez 1944) had a negative impact on standard costing in the US (Stempf 1943). Kohler and Cooper (1945: 306) concluded their

41-page survey of World War II accounting in the *Accounting Review* by observing that 'accounting practice suffered perceptibly and even degenerated as the result of the war', a finding that was confirmed by a later micro-level investigation of the Sperry Corporation (Fleischman and Marquette 2003).

Uniform cost accounting

Kallapur and Krishnan (2009) examined the long history of management accounting in India. Relevant here is their discovery that the British East India Company – established in 1600 and which functioned until 1850 as not just a company but an imperial power in itself – employed 'uniform accounting systems for comparability' and managerial purposes (ibid.: 1400). Much of the research into the advent of uniform cost accounting is from a later genre.

Segelod and Carlsson (2010: 359) argue that the emergence of uniform cost accounting principles in Sweden in the early twentieth century 'was closely associated with the development of new methods of standardized mass production and [US-influenced] engineers … not, as previously assumed, German cost accounting'. An early initiative in the US featured the efforts of Harvey Chase to inspire uniform municipal accounting. This was carried forward in the municipal research bureau movement and its journal, *National Municipal Review*, but without much in the way of concrete results. A multitude of trade associations, established during the 1920s, tried to effect industry-wide uniformity in costing practices. During the Great Depression, the US government attempted standardisation across virtually every industry in the hope of minimising unfair competition that might impair recovery efforts. Despite the weightiness of these efforts, very little was achieved.

Rather more success was evident in the UK in the private sector with uniform costing efforts in the printing industry (Walker and Mitchell 1996, 1997, 1998). Edwards et al. (2003: 25) studied uniform costing initiatives in the British steel industry, based on a cooperative venture between the British Iron and Steel Federation and various governmental regulatory agencies, commencing in 1935 and lasting for some 35 years. It was found to be a difficult arrangement as the companies on occasion refused 'to supply neutral accounting numbers to help the government reach decisions'. However, in the post-World War II nationalisation of industries such as coal, railroading and electricity, uniform accounting was demanded by the regulatory agencies.

Similarly, a standardised cost accounting methodology was imposed in countries where the government closely controlled the economy. On the road to war in Japan, the adoption of cost accounting standards was demanded by the government for all munitions suppliers (Okano and Suzuki 2007: 1124). With regard to Italy, Cinquini et al. (2016) employed a genealogical perspective in examining the uniform costing system initiative developed by the Fascist government and the Confederation of Industry during World War II. In the post-World War II era, the Chinese government established uniform accounting rules for 'state-owned enterprises' (Chow et al. 2007).

The rise of the US mega-corporation and ROI

A series of events of profound importance coexisted chronologically with the evolution of scientific management in the US. These produced the rise of the decentralised mega-corporation. Two firms that have received extensive study from Chandler (1962, 1977, Chandler and Salisbury 1971) and Johnson and Kaplan (Johnson 1980a, 1980b; Kaplan 1983; Johnson and Kaplan 1987) are DuPont and General Motors (GM). Certainly, there were huge enterprises that predated these two, such as Carnegie Steel, Standard Oil and the American Tobacco Company, but what differentiated DuPont and GM was the appearance of a managerial hierarchy that made a multidivisional structure feasible. Earlier industrial giants tended to be highly centralised, depending on an omnipotent CEO of the calibre of Carnegie, Rockefeller or Duke. Drawing upon Williamson (1970), Johnson and Kaplan (1987: 98) explained:

> Multidivisional organizations arose to supplant these markets [labour and capital] by internalizing the multi-activity operations of several integrated firms to earn higher asset returns than the market could elicit from the same firms if they operated independently.

Nowhere in the immense scrutiny of DuPont and GM was there mention of standard costing, time-and-motion studies, or the scientific development of work routines, although Pierre DuPont was impressed by the raw material and labour cost controls central to the Taylorite system (Johnson 1980a). Furthermore, Alfred Sloan (1964), long-time chief executive of GM and architect of its managerial structure, made no mention in his autobiography of scientific management being practised there.

The story of the DuPont Powder Company, founded in 1903, tells of the transition from a single to a multi-activity firm. As the organisation became increasingly diversified during World War I and beyond, it became necessary to devise a management accounting system to control the value chain and to harmonise departmental performance with ownership interests. DuPont was the first major industrial firm in the US to be decentralised, although it continued to manifest certain centralised features that characterised nineteenth-century enterprises. A number of innovative managerial accounting methods were devised to control the organisation. The most ingenious and famous was the adoption of an elaborate return-on-investment (ROI) measure developed by Donaldson Brown. ROI was used primarily to make decisions about alternative uses of capital rather than in its more familiar role as a mechanism to evaluate managerial performance (Flesher and Previts 2007). This focus on capital investment decisions was a new development that came with diversification. Chandler pointed out that Brown's ROI formula was also used for more routine analyses of each mill's performance, the locating of inefficiencies and the adjustment of plans and processes when appropriate. DuPont was also heavily involved in business forecasting for inventory control and central purchasing. In this regard, it stands as an early example of a demand-pull manufacturing environment, a forerunner of the just-in-time approach.

By 1918, Pierre DuPont had taken control of GM and brought in Brown to implement DuPont's accounting and financial control structures. Brown's ROI formula was used prominently, but more traditionally to evaluate divisional and managerial performance than at DuPont where the focus was on capital investment decisions. The art of forecasting was well developed at GM. Brown moved the organisation forward from decision making based on past and present performance to conditions anticipated in the future. GM was a pathfinder in introducing a number of accounting and managerial methods common in today's world, including flexible budgeting, market-based transfer pricing and divisional autonomy.

The management accounting/financial reporting interface

A major component of Johnson and Kaplan's (1987) indictment of US managerial accounting was its domination by financial reporting. An important cause of this domination is the requirement that inventory be reported using absorption costing despite the greater value of direct costing for managerial decision making.

The attempt in 1933 to establish industrial codes for most US industries caused cost accountants and the NACA's leadership to envision a golden age for cost accountants, but these dreams were soon dashed (Fleischman and Tyson 1999). The Securities Acts of 1933 and 1934 mandated audited financial statements for all publicly traded firms, guaranteeing a high-profile role for public accountants. The impact of the Securities and Exchange Commission (SEC) on the US accounting profession has been incalculable. The Securities Acts formalised the audit process, limited its practice to CPAs and glamorised that part of the profession. In essence, SEC audit regulations helped enforce a CPA-based career path for ambitious accountants.

The US experience has been replicated over time in France, China and the UK. Carmona (2007) referenced Zimnovitch (1997) who observed the delay of standard costing's advent in France until the 1950s and 1960s, because French accountants, struggling to attain professional status, stonewalled its implementation as it was perceived to be a non-accounting method. For China, meanwhile, Chow et al. (2007) labelled management research and education as introductory, lacking in theorisation and viewed as supplemental to financial accounting (Wang and Zhang 2000). The story of UK struggles has been detailed by Boyns and Edwards (2007: 980–4).

In many parts of the world, cultural and historical developments have combined to forestall the intertwining of the two branches of the profession. This is best reflected in the role of the 'controller'. Okano and Suzuki (2007) commented that, in Japan, greater effort is given to the improvement of managerial accounting rather than financial reporting. In Japanese industrial enterprises generally, controllers are responsible only for the financial statements while tasks related to planning and control are relegated to lower organisational levels and personnel where greater expertise might well reside.

By contrast, in the Germanic countries, and probably among the Nordic nations, there has been a conscious effort historically to avoid integration (Ewert and Wagenhofer 2007). In Germany, the educational system is dichotomised into financial reporting and what is called 'controlling'. German students have the option to major in 'control' as distinct from accounting. The functions of the controller differ markedly from what is typical in the US. Stoeffel (1995) compared German and US controllers and found that the majority of US controllers were responsible for financial accounting, cost accounting, financial planning, financial reporting and tax planning. Meanwhile, German controllers were more engaged in operational planning, strategic planning and capital budgeting. Ewert and Wagenhofer (2007) concluded that while, historically, a characteristic trait of German management accounting has been to divorce itself from financial accounting, the two branches are becoming increasingly reconciled in the contemporary world.

The professionalisation of management accounting

While there has been a substantial volume of work done on the professionalisation of public accountancy (see Chapter 11), there has been less carried out on similar processes for management accountants. In the British context, the limited but developing literature on the professionalisation of management accounting in the new industries of the Second BIR of the late nineteenth and early twentieth centuries explores the continuing importance of engineers, rather than accountants, in the costing function of a diverse range of industries such as: vehicle making (McKinstry 1999); chemicals (Matthews et al. 2003); metal, engine-powered shipbuilding (McLean 2013); electrical engineering (McLean et al. 2015); and electricity supply (McLean and McGovern 2017). Loft (1986, 1990) portrayed the growing influence of accountants in her study of the formation of the Institute of Cost and Works Accountants in the UK in 1919, a professional body which evolved into the present-day Chartered Institute of Management Accountants (CIMA) and the Association of International Certified Professional Accountants, CIMA's joint venture with the American Institute of Certified Public Accountants (AICPA).

Fleischman and Tyson (2000) explored struggles for dominance between engineers and cost accountants in the US. The National Association of Cost Accountants was established in 1919 (Carey 1969). It evolved into the Institute of Management Accountants which, along with the industry section of the AICPA, is the professional organisation for management accountants who, in a sense, dominate the accounting scene in the US. As Sorensen (2009: 1271) points out: 'in 2005, 85 per cent of the [US] accountancy profession works inside [business] organizations as accounting professionals and 15 per cent of the profession works externally and performs public accounting services. In other words, most accountants are management accountants'.

Anderson (1996) related the early history of the Australian Institute of Cost Accountants, founded in 1921. This professional body grew out of the events of World War I and was modelled after the US and UK organisations founded two years earlier. However, growth in membership was slow, given a limited use of costing in the country and the lack of a professional journal until 1936. Verma (2015) explored the genesis of the Institute of Cost and Works Accountants of India during the period 1954–1959 and noted the political, economic, social and imperial factors underlying its establishment.

Coenenberg and Schoenfeld (1990) examined the development of management accounting in Germany, and Heinzelmann (2016) compared the development of the profession of management accounting in the UK and German-speaking countries. German accountants formed their first professional society in 1931. However, within two years, Hitler had risen to power and perverted the organisation to his purposes. Cost accountancy was forced to serve the public interest as interpreted by the Third Reich. That meant that practitioners were instructed to undertake such heinous assignments as costing slave labour in the concentration camps and determining the cost-efficient way to gas Jewish and other prisoners (Funnell 1998; Lippman and Wilson 2007). In 1937, the German government mandated the *Uniform Chart of Accounts*, the Goering Plan, which identified the purpose of accounting as pricing and unit valuation. After the fall of the Nazi regime, the common chart of accounts became voluntary, although practically all German firms continued to adhere to it (see also Chapter 19).

Challenges remain despite the increasing professionalisation of management accounting internationally. There has been a growth in the numbers and influence of women in the profession of management accounting, but it is still thought necessary to provide 'advice and insights from senior female management accountants around the world' (CIMA 2010: 1) about breaking the glass ceiling. While seen to be of increasing importance, the ethical dimension of management accounting is 'not … well addressed in the literature' (Bampton and Cowton 2013: 557). Moreover, while CIMA (2017) has published advice on *Global Management Accounting Principles*, Hopper et al. (2009) note the relative paucity of management accounting in less developed countries.

Contemporary management accounting history

After World War II, accounting information came to be seen as increasingly relevant for managerial planning, control and decision-making activities (e.g. Schmalenbach 1948; Simon et al. 1954; Demski 1967; Dopuch et al. 1967; Parker 1969; Scapens 1991; Schweitzer 1992). This contemporary growth of interest among theorists and practitioners of the discipline is worthy of scrutiny in relation to the debates and themes of this chapter's historical study of management accounting.

The integration of costing records and the management accounting/financial reporting interface continue to be live issues. In a paper that spans the period from c.1860 to the early twenty-first century, Brandau et al. (2017: 82) noted that the contemporary German practice of 'a partial integration of financial and management accounting ... is not only shaped by its current environment, but also its historical path'. However, they warned that 'a further abandonment of the German management accounting techniques, and a reliance on the IFRS [International Financial Reporting Standards], may risk losing the benefits of detailed, technical, operational knowledge as the basis for management control'. Despite this threat, Schäffer and Binder (2008: 34) found that 'controlling' has become an established academic 'discipline of business administration in German-speaking countries'.

MacDonald and Richardson (2011: 365) researched the schism between management accounting education and practice in North America during the period 1967–1997 and found that 'education lags practice and the length of the lag has increased since the early 1980s'. Sorensen (2009: 1271) noted that, in the US, the contemporary environment and the 'knowledge, skills and abilities required for doing management accounting [are changing] at blistering rates'. The theory/practice schism has also been addressed by Dimitru et al. (2011) who found that Romanian research journals tend to be focused on traditional costing and management accounting topics. However, Ihantola (2010: 156) noted that research findings in the 'behavioural, social and organizational aspects of budgeting ... were already to be found in the newest Finnish textbooks' in the 1990s. Jansen (2018: 1486) argued that interventionist researchers can help to bridge the gap between management accounting theory and practice by using 'existing theoretical knowledge in shaping interventions that aim to solve a practical problem'.

In terms of the professionalisation of management accounting, Kurunmäki (2004) examined hybridisation in Finnish health care during the 1990s and noted the growing acquisition of management accounting expertise by medical professionals. Issues of this nature also feature in the contemporary history of management accounting in the UK. In the immediate aftermath of World War II, the UK's Labour government created the National Health Service (NHS) and, also, brought industries such as coal mining, railways and the supply of gas and electricity into public ownership as nationalised organisations. In the 1980s and 1990s, nationalised industries were returned to private ownership under the Thatcher government's privatisation programme and there have been on-going changes in the NHS. These arenas of contemporary history have proven to be fertile ground for management accounting research.

Gebreiter (2016) examined the role of costing in the administrative functions of the NHS during the two decades following its foundation in 1948 and noted that prevailing mentalities precluded its application in the area of clinical medicine. Robson (2003) also analysed accounting change in the NHS, noting the shift in 1956 from uniform accounting to the production of departmental information. However, in considering accounting and managerial reforms in the NHS between 1958 and 1974, Robson (2007: 445) noted:

'Accounting practitioners and senior civil servants appeared to be content to adjust existing accounting practices rather than embrace major change'.

Under the influence of Conservative governments of the 1980s and 1990s, the concept of internal markets was introduced. Then, beginning in 1997, under a New Labour government, the NHS introduced 'a new system focused on regulation via inspection, performance measurement and comparisons between hospitals' aligned with 'a business-focused attitude and co-operative relationships between clinicians, managers and accountants' (Conrad and Uslu 2011: 46).

In a study of an 'Area' of the nationalised National Coal Board (NCB), Berry et al. (1985: 24) found that many 'of the themes that have emerged from our observations emphasise the significance of tradition and culture for an understanding of management control in the NCB'. History weighed heavily in the coal mining industry and the long-established approaches, skills and methods of engineers and colliery managers were dominant: 'it was deliberate [policy] that [management] accounting and financial control should not intrude into the management of the Area'.

Mueller and Carter (2007: 181) noted that economists and engineers were the dominant professional groupings in the UK's nationalised electricity supply industry but argued that post privatisation 'economists were joined by management accountants in what amounted to a hybridisation of economics and management accounting … and there was an interpenetration of accounting and economics into the sphere of engineering'.

In the broader context, McCartney and Stittle (2017: 1) presented a detailed analysis of cost data in the privatised railway industry and concluded that 'rail privatisation has resulted in considerable additional costs: it was a major public policy error'.

Issues related to hybridisation have also been studied in the UK private sector (e.g. Miller et al. 2008), while Pong and Mitchell (2006) have continued the direct v absorption costing debate in their examination of manufacturing companies, 1988–2002. Pong and Mitchell (2006: 131) found that 'stock [inventory] remains a substantial variable in profit measurement' and argued for continuing research.

In China, the government has played an important role in the development of accounting in recent decades (Lu et al. 2009). The survey of Chinese management accounting by Chow et al. (2007) centred almost entirely on post-1949 events following the establishment of the People's Republic of China – a time when the industrial economy was comprised largely of state-owned enterprises which operated under uniform accounting systems. Accounting, both financial and managerial, was used as a governmental tool for central planning, budgeting started from handed-down targets rather than forecasting, and responsibility accounting was imposed at the group rather than the individual level. From the government's perspective, management accounting was clearly secondary to financial reporting. However, O'Connor et al. (2004: 370) reported that Chinese state-owned enterprises 'increased their use of management accounting/controls' in the 1990s as a result of the government's economic reforms.

The story of Japanese management accounting is fascinating, given the dichotomy between myth and reality. Buzzwords associated with post-World War II Japanese management such as *kanban* (just-in time), *kaizen* (continuous improvement) and target costing imply managerial innovation and sophistication. Okano and Suzuki (2007) dispelled much of this as mythical, thus re-enforcing the work of Scarbrough et al. (1991) who surveyed a large number of Japanese firms and found that most used traditional cost accounting methods, such as single cost systems, payback and accounting rate of return for analysing investment opportunities, ROI and residual income for evaluating managers, and standard costing.

Okano and Suzuki (2007) also noted the post-World War II influence of western management gurus on Japan's reconstruction and attainment of global competitiveness (Cooper 1995). Burrows and Chenhall (2012: 139) argued, in particular, that the target costing concept had 'North American rather than Japanese origins and can be conservatively dated to the late 1940s and probably back at least to World War II'. In addition to providing a 'traditional historical overview of the development of Japanese management accounting' (Black 2017: 388), Okano's (2015) *History of Management Accounting in Japan: Institutional & Cultural Significance of Accounting* examined target costing and organisational learning at Toyota and provided a case study of the application of contemporary Japanese approaches to management accounting to the European context. Takeda and Boyns (2014: 345) examined the development of management accounting in Japan's Kyocera Corporation, 1959–2013, noting that its 'management accounting system is embedded within a holistic management philosophy and the corporate culture which emanates therefrom' and that management's success depended upon the ability 'to harness latent cultural beliefs'.

McLaren et al. (2016) provided case analyses of three New Zealand firms to 'configure and explain the life (from birth to death) of a management accounting system (MAS)'. The MASs considered, based on the concept of Economic Value Added (EVA^{TM}), were introduced during the 1990s but were abandoned after 12–15 years as 'the result of a progressive accumulation of factors that related to the three companies' troublesome experience with EVA over a considerable period of time and changes in their circumstances' (ibid.: 354).

The contemporary world offers many research challenges and opportunities for management accounting historians. Fleischman and Tyson (2007) noted that post-1970 America has been marked by continual change and innovation, multi-tasking flexibility, customer-focused creativity, and the need for continual cost reduction. They argued that traditional, labour-based standard costing systems were simply not designed to handle such an environment of constant change, flexible relationships and continuous innovation. However, a start has been made in responding to those challenges both in the US and elsewhere. In the US context, Sorensen (2009: 1271) noted that in:

> [t]he past two decades management accountants have moved from data accumulators, financial reporters, data analysts, decision-supporters and business advisers to business partners. Top level management accountants are now emerging as members of the most important business decision-making groups guiding major organizational, operational and strategic choices.

Management accounting theory and practice have been developed (Chapman et al. 2007, 2009; Bhimani et al. 2015), and new systems made available: for example, ABC, the Balanced Scorecard and non-financial performance measures, and management accounting for quality and just-in-time. These developments have happened at 'blistering rates' (Sorensen 2009: 1271) and critical analysis by management accounting historians will help to deepen our understanding.

Many of the contemporary developments in management accounting could not have taken place without recent changes in information technology. While 'mechanical accounting' (Wootton and Kemmerer 2007) and early computing (Chandar et al. 2012; Boyns and Edwards 2013) have been studied (see also Chapter 6), the impacts of digitisation (Bhimani 2007), social media and big data (Arnaboldi et al. 2017) on management accounting remain to be placed in full historical perspective.

Scapens (2006: 1) reviewed changes in management accounting research over the previous 35 years and argued that 'to make sense of the diversity in management accounting practices we need to understand the complex mish-mash of inter-related influences which shape practices in individual organisations'. Surely, management accounting historians have an important role to play in developing our understanding of contemporary practices and concepts.

Conclusion

Stimulated by Johnson and Kaplan (1987) and Hopwood (1987), historians of management accounting have moved beyond the confines of early, pioneering studies and have brought their discipline to the centre stage of accounting's history (Ezzamel et al. 1990: 157) since the early 1990s. New, critical approaches (Miller et al. 1991) to the analysis and writing of history have challenged the dominance of archive-based studies that build narratives of the technical development of management accounting in the pursuit of profit (e.g. Edwards 1989; Fleischman and Parker 1991), leading to ongoing theoretical debate (Sánchez-Matamoros and Hidalgo 2011; Boyns and Edwards 2013; Tyson and Oldroyd 2017).

Since 2000 in particular, the discipline of management accounting history has been in decline in the US (Matthews 2017) while histories from beyond the Anglo-Saxon world have been brought to wider attention. However, we still know relatively little about developments in many parts of the world, including South and Central America, Africa, and many regions of Asia and, also, opportunities remain for further international comparisons of management accounting's continuities and changes throughout history.

The search for the origins of management accounting continues to attract researchers, particularly from Iberia, France and Italy as well as from the UK and the US, although recent additions to the US literature are rather limited in number. Since the early 1990s, researchers have engaged in a series of lively debates on management accounting history, including, for example, 'the theory/practice schism' and 'sharing information', while continuing to address time-honoured themes such as the integration of costing records and the professionalisation of management accounting. Management accounting histories have ranged over wide time periods, but much work remains to be done for epochs both before and after the Industrial Revolution. Contemporary management accounting history is a growing focus of attention, offering opportunities for research into a period of rapid and pervasive economic, social, technological and organisational change, and for collaborative research between academics and practitioners.

Key works

Boyns and Edwards (2013) examine British management accounting history.

Chapman et al. (2007; 2009) contain collections of contemporary and historical chapters on many aspects of management accounting.

Edwards (ed.) (2000), volume III, reprints 17 of the most cited articles on cost and management accounting in accounting historiography.

Fleischman (ed.) (2006) contains a number of highly regarded articles on cost and management accounting, especially in volume 1, part 2 (the great debates) and volume 2, part 3 (US scientific management).

Johnson and Kaplan (1987) is a book about the history of managerial accounting that helped to move the discipline of accounting history centre-stage.

References

Alvarez, M.J., Gutiérrez, F., and Romero, D. (2002) Accounting and quality control in the Royal Tobacco Factory of Seville, 1744–1790: an historical perspective, *Accounting Business & Financial History*, 12 (2): 253–74.

Anderson, R.H. (1996) A history of the Australian Institute of Cost Accountants: a progress report 1921–1939, in G.D. Carnegie and P.W. Wolnizer (eds) *Accounting History Newsletter 1980–1989 and Accounting History 1989–1994*, pp. 169–86 (New York and London: Garland).

Antonelli, V. (2017) Tito Antoni and the internationalization of accounting history scholarship, *Accounting Historians Journal*, 44 (1): 109–11.

Antonelli, V., Boyns, T., and Cerbioni, F. (2006) Multiple origins of accounting? An early Italian example of the development of accounting for managerial purposes, *European Accounting Review*, 15 (3): 367–401.

Antonelli, V., Boyns, T., and Cerbioni, F. (2008) The development of accounting in Europe in the era of scientific management: the Italian engineering conglomerate, Ansaldo, c.1918–c.1940, *Accounting Historians Journal*, 35 (1): 49–81.

Antonelli, V., Boyns, T., and Cerbioni, F. (2009) The development of cost accounting in Italy, c.1800–c.1940, *Accounting History*, 14 (4): 465–507.

Antonelli, V., Cerbioni, F., and Parbonetti, A. (2002) The rise of cost accounting: evidence from Italy, *Accounting, Business & Financial History*, 12 (3): 461–86.

Antonelli, V., D'Alessio, R., and Rossi, R. (2014) Budgetary practices in the Ministry of War and the Ministry of Munitions in Italy, 1915–1918, *Accounting History Review*, 24 (2–3): 139–60.

Antonelli, V., D'Alessio, R., Rossi, R., and Cafaro, E.M. (2017) Accounting in hybrid forms of capitalist/socialist enterprises: a multiple interpretative approach to the Royal Factory of Silk of San Leucio, 1802–1826, *Accounting History*, 22 (3): 274–300.

Arnaboldi, M., Busco, C., and Cuganesan, S. (2017) Accounting, accountability and big data: revolution or hype? *Accounting, Auditing & Accountability Journal*, 30 (4): 762–76.

Arnold, A.J. and McCartney, S. (2002) The beginnings of accounting for capital consumption: disclosure practices in the British railway industry, 1830–55, *Accounting and Business Research*, 32 (4): 195–208.

Arnold, A.J. and McCartney, S. (2004) Were they ever 'productive to the capitalist'? Rates of return on Britain's railways, 1830–55, *Journal of European Economic History*, 33 (2): 383–410.

Babbage, C. (1835) *On the Economy of Machinery and Manufactures*, 4th edn (London: Charles Knight).

Ballewski, D. (1877) *Die Calculation von Maschinenfabriken* (Magdeburg).

Bampton, R. and Cowton, C.J. (2013) Taking stock of accounting ethics scholarship: a review of the journal literature, *Journal of Business Ethics*, 114 (3): 549–63.

Baxter, W.T. (2005) Direct versus absorption costing: a comment, *Accounting, Business & Financial History*, 15 (1): 89–91.

Berland, N. (1998) The availability of information and the accumulation of experience as motors for the diffusion of budgetary control: the French experience from the 1920s to the 1960s, *Accounting, Business & Financial History*, 8 (3): 303–29.

Berland, N. (2001) Environmental turbulence and the functions of budgetary control, *Accounting, Business & Financial History*, 11 (1): 59–77.

Berland, N. and Boyns, T. (2002) The development of budgetary control in France and Britain from the 1920s to the 1960s: a comparison, *European Accounting Review*, 11 (2): 329–56.

Berliner, C. and Brimson, J.A. (eds) (1988) *Cost Management in Today's Advanced Manufacturing: The CAM-1 Conceptual Design*, (Boston: Harvard Business School Press).

Berry, A.J., Capps, T., Cooper, D., Ferguson, P., Hopper, T., and Lowe, E.A. (1985) Management control in an area of the NCB: rationales of accounting practices in a public enterprise, *Accounting, Organizations and Society*, 10 (1): 3–28.

Bessire, D. and Baker, R. (2005) The French *Tableau de Bord* and the American Balanced Scorecard: a critical analysis, *Critical Perspectives on Accounting*, 16: 645–64.

Bhimani, A. (1993) Indeterminacy and the specificity of accounting change: Renault 1898–1938, *Accounting, Organizations and Society*, 18 (1): 1–39.

Bhimani, A. (1994) Accounting and the emergence of the 'economic man', *Accounting, Organizations and Society*, 19 (8): 637–74.

Bhimani, A. (2007) Management accounting and digitization, in A. Bhimani (ed) *Contemporary Issues in Management Accounting*, pp. 69–91 (Oxford: Oxford University Press).

Bhimani, A., Horngren, C.T., Datar, S.M., and Rajan, M. (2015) *Management and Cost Accounting*, 6th edn (London: Pearson).
Bisman, J.E. (2012) Budgeting for famine in Tudor England, 1527–1528, *Accounting History Review*, 22 (2): 105–26.
Black, W.H. (2017) Book review: Okano, H., 2015 *History of Management Accounting in Japan: Institutional & Cultural Significance of Accounting* (Bingley: Emerald Publishing).
Boyns, T. (1993) Cost accounting in the south Wales coal industry, c.1870–1913, *Accounting, Business & Financial History*, 3 (3): 327–52.
Boyns, T. (1998) Budgets and budgetary control in British businesses to c.1945, *Accounting, Business & Financial History*, 8 (3): 261–301.
Boyns, T. (2003) In memoriam: Alexander Hamilton Church's system of 'scientific machine rates' at Hans Renold Ltd., c.1901–c.1920, *Accounting Historians Journal*, 30 (1): 3–44.
Boyns, T. and Edwards, J.R. (1996a) Change agents and the dissemination of accounting technology: Wales' basic industries, c.1750–c.1870, *Accounting History*, 1 (1): 9–34.
Boyns, T. and Edwards, J.R. (1996b) The development of accounting in mid-nineteenth century Britain: a non-disciplinary view, *Accounting, Auditing & Accountability Journal*, 9 (3): 40–60.
Boyns, T. and Edwards, J.R. (1997) Cost and management accounting in early Victorian Britain: a Chandleresque analysis? *Management Accounting Research*, 8 (1): 19–46.
Boyns, T. and Edwards, J.R. (2007) The development of cost and management accounting in Britain, in C.S. Chapman, A.G. Hopwood, and M.D. Shields (eds) *Handbook of Management Accounting Research*, pp. 987–1052 (Oxford: Elsevier).
Boyns, T. and Edwards, J.R. (2013) *A History of Management Accounting, The British Experience* (London and New York: Routledge).
Boyns, T. and Edwards, J.R. (2016) The advent of double-entry-based costing practices in the British engineering industry: Ransomes of Ipswich, 1856–1863, *Accounting History Review*, 26 (3): 171–90.
Boyns, T., Edwards, J.R., and Nikitin, M. (1997) *The Birth of Industrial Accounting in France and Britain* (New York: Garland).
Brackenborough, S., McLean, T., and Oldroyd, D. (2001) The emergence of discounted cash flow analysis in the Tyneside coal industry, c.1700–1820, *British Accounting Review*, 33 (2): 137–55.
Brandau, M., Endenich, C., Luther, R., and Trapp, R. (2017) Separation – integration – and now …? A historical perspective on the relationship between German management accounting and financial accounting, *Accounting History*, 22 (1): 67–91.
Bromwich, M. and Bhimani, A. (1989) *Management Accounting: Evolution not Revolution* (London: Chartered Institute of Management Accountants).
Brun, R. (1930) A fourteenth-century merchant in Italy, *Journal of Economic and Business History*, 2 (3): 451–66.
Bryer, R.A. (2005) A Marxist accounting history of the British industrial revolution: a review of the evidence and suggestions for research, *Accounting, Organizations and Society*, 30 (1): 25–65.
Bryer, R.A. (2006) Capitalist accountability and the British industrial revolution: the Carron Company, 1759-circa 1850, *Accounting, Organizations and Society*, 31 (8): 687–734.
Bryer, R.A., Fleischman, R.K., and Macve, R.H. (2007) Smith, Marx, or Foucault in understanding the early British industrial revolution? Paper presented at Seventeenth Accounting, Business & Financial History Conference, Cardiff Business School, 14–15 September.
Burrows, G. and Chenhall, R.H. (2012) Target costing: first and second comings, *Accounting History Review*, 22 (2): 127–42.
Burton, F.G. (1900) *Engineers' and Shipbuilders' Accounts*, 2nd edn (London: Technical Publishing).
Caminez, D.B. (1944) Controlling costs with physical unit budgets, *NACA Year Book*, 25: 143–69.
Campbell, R.H. (1961) *Carron Company* (Edinburgh and London: Oliver & Boyd).
Carey, J.L. (1969) *The Rise of the Accounting Profession* (New York: AICPA).
Carmona, E. and Gómez, D. (2002) Early cost management practices, state ownership and market competition: the case of the Royal Textile Mill of Guadalajara, 1714–1744, *Accounting, Business & Financial History*, 12 (3): 231–51.
Carmona, S. (2004) Accounting history research and its diffusion in an international context, *Accounting History*, 9 (3): 7–23.
Carmona, S. (2007) The history of management accounting in France, Italy, Portugal, and Spain, in C.S. Chapman, A.G. Hopwood, and M.D. Shields (eds) *Handbook of Management Accounting Research*, pp. 923–40 (Oxford: Elsevier).

Carmona, S. and Donoso, R. (2004) Cost accounting in early regulated markets: the case of the Royal Soap Factory of Seville (1525–1692), *Journal of Accounting and Public Policy*, 23 (2): 129–57.

Carmona, S., Ezzamel, M., and Gutiérrez, F. (1997) Control and cost accounting practices in the Spanish Royal Tobacco Factory, *Accounting, Organizations and Society*, 22 (5): 411–46.

Carmona, S., Ezzamel, M., and Gutiérrez, F. (1998) Towards an institutional analysis of accounting change in the Royal Tobacco factory of Seville, *Accounting Historians Journal*, 25 (1): 115–47.

Carmona, S. and Zan, L. (2002) Mapping variety in the history of accounting and management practices, *European Accounting Review*, 11 (2): 291–304.

Chandar, N., Collier, D., and Miranti, P. (2012) Graph standardization and management accounting at AT&T during the 1920s, *Accounting History*, 17 (1): 35–62.

Chandler, A.D. (1962) *Strategy and Structure* (Cambridge, MA: MIT Press).

Chandler, A.D. (1977) *The Visible Hand: The Managerial Revolution in American Business* (Cambridge, MA and London: Belknap Press).

Chandler, A.D. (1984) The emergence of managerial capitalism, *Business History Review*, 58 (4): 473–503.

Chandler, A.D. (1990) *Scale and Scope: The Dynamics of Industrial Capitalism* (Cambridge, MA and London: Belknap Press).

Chandler, A.D. and Salisbury, S. (1971) *Pierre DuPont and the Making of the Modern Corporation* (New York, NY: Harper & Row).

Chapman, C.S., Hopwood, A.G., and Shields, M.D. (eds) (2007, 2009) *Handbook of Management Accounting Research* Vols 1–3 (Oxford: Elsevier).

Chatfield, M. (1977) *A History of Accounting Thought* (Huntington, NY: Robert E. Krieger).

Chow, C.W., Duh, R.R., and Xiao, J.Z. (2007) Management accounting practices in the People's Republic of China, in C.S. Chapman, A.G. Hopwood, and M.D. Shields (eds) *Handbook of Management Accounting Research*, pp. 941–86 (Oxford: Elsevier).

Church, A.H. (1901) The proper distribution of establishment charges, *Engineering Magazine*, 21: 508–17, 725–34, 904–12. 22: 31–40, 231–40, 367–76.

CIMA (2010) *Breaking Glass, Strategies for Tomorrow's Leaders* (London: CIMA).

CIMA (2017) *Global Management Accounting Principles* (London: CIMA).

Cinquini, L., Giannetti, R., and Tenucci, A. (2016) The making of uniform costing in a war economy: the case of the *Uniconti* Commission in Fascist Italy, *Accounting History*, 21 (4): 445–71.

Cinquini, L., Marelli, A., and Tenucci, A. (2008) An analysis of publishing patterns in accounting history research in Italy, 1990–2004, *Accounting Historians Journal*, 35 (1): 1–48.

Coenenberg, A.G. and Schoenfeld, H.M.W. (1990) The development of managerial accounting in Germany: a historical analysis, *Accounting Historians Journal*, 17 (2): 95–112.

Conrad, L. and Uslu, P.G. (2011) Investigation of the impact of 'Payment by Results' on performance measurement and management in NHS Trusts, *Management Accounting Research*, 22 (1): 46–55.

Cooper, R. (1995) *When Lean Enterprises Collide* (Boston: Harvard Business School Press).

Cooper, R. and Kaplan, R.S. (1988) Measure costs right: make the right decisions, *Harvard Business Review*, 88 (5): 96–103.

Croizé, A. and Croizé, H. (1907) *De l'Inventaire Commercial* (Paris: Librairie Comptable Pigier).

De Cazaux, L.F.G. (1824) *De la Comptabilité dans une Enterprise Industrielle et Spécialement dans une Exploitation Rurale* (Toulouse: J. M. Douladoure).

De Roover, R. (1941) A Florentine firm of cloth manufacturers, *Speculum*, 16 (1): 3–33.

Demski, J.S. (1967) An accounting system structured on a linear programming model, *Accounting Review*, 42 (4): 701–12.

Díaz, D.C., Hernández-Esteve, E., Caparrós, M.J.M., and Toledano, D.S. (2009) 20th century publications on cost accounting by Spanish authors previous to the Standardization Act (1900–1978), *Accounting Historians Journal*, 36 (2): 139–79.

Dicksee, L.R. (1911) *Advanced Accounting* (London: Gee).

Dimitru, M., Calu, D.A., and Gorgan, C. (2011) A historical approach of change in management accounting topics published in Romania, *Accounting and Management Information Systems*, 10 (3): 375–96.

Ding, Y.Y. and McKinstry, S. (2012) Paper trails: the development of management accounting at Alex. Cowan & Sons Ltd. Penicuik, 1779–1965, *Accounting History*, 18 (1): 99–119.

Dobie, A. (2011) A review of the granators' accounts of Durham Cathedral Priory 1294–1433: an early example of process accounting? *Accounting History Review*, 21 (1): 7–35.

Dobie, A. (2015) *Accounting at Durham Cathedral Priory: Management and Control of a Major Ecclesiastical Corporation, 1083–1539* (Basingstoke: Palgrave Macmillan).
Dodson, J. (1759) *The Accountant or the Method of Book-keeping* (London: J. Norse).
Dopuch, N., Birnberg, J.G., and Demski, J.S. (1967) An analysis of standard cost variance analysis, *Accounting Review*, 42 (3): 526–36.
Drucker, A.P.R. (1929) Budgeting and the sales quota, *Accounting Review*, 4 (1): 75–80.
Dugdale, D. and Jones, T.C. (2003) Battles in the costing war: UK debates, 1950–75, *Accounting, Business & Financial History*, 13 (3): 305–38.
Dugdale, D. and Jones, T.C. (2005) Direct versus absorption costing: a reply, *Accounting, Business & Financial History*, 15 (1): 93–95.
Edwards, J.R. (1989) Industrial cost accounting development in Britain to 1830: a review article, *Accounting and Business Research*, 19 (76): 305–17.
Edwards, J.R. (ed) (2000) *The History of Accounting. Critical Perspectives on Business and Management* (London and New York: Routledge).
Edwards, J.R. (2018) Towards constructing the governable worker in nineteenth-century Britain, *Critical Perspectives on Accounting*, 50: 36–55.
Edwards, J.R. and Boyns, T. (1992) Industrial organization and accounting innovation: charcoal iron-making in England 1690–1783, *Management Accounting Research*, 3 (2): 151–69.
Edwards, J.R., Boyns, T., and Matthews, M. (2003) Cost, pricing and politics in the British steel industry, 1918–1967, *Management Accounting Research*, 14 (2): 25–49.
Edwards, J.R., Hammersley, G., and Newell, E. (1990) Cost accounting at Keswick, England, c.1598–1615: the German connection, *Accounting Historians Journal*, 17 (1): 61–80.
Edwards, J.R. and Newell, E. (1991) The development of industrial cost and management accounting before 1850: a survey of the evidence, *Business History*, 33 (1): 35–57.
Edwards, R. (2010) Job analysis on the LMS: mechanisation and modernisation c.1930–c.1939, *Accounting, Business & Financial History*, 17 (1): 91–105.
Edwards, R.S. (1937) Some notes on the early literature and development of cost accounting in Great Britain, *Accountant*, 97: 193–5, 225–31, 253–5, 283–7.
Elder, F. (1937) Cost accounting in the sixteenth century, *Accounting Review*, 12 (3): 226–37.
Emerson, H. (1914) *Efficiencies as a Basis for Operation and Wages*, 4th edn (New York: Engineering Magazine Co.).
Epstein, M.J. (1978) *The Effect of Scientific Management on the Development of Standard Costing* (New York: Arno Press).
Ewert, R. and Wagenhofer, A. (2007) Management accounting theory and practice in German-speaking countries, in C.S. Chapman, A.G. Hopwood, and M.D. Shields (eds) *Handbook of Management Accounting Research*, pp. 1053–87 (Oxford: Elsevier).
Ezzamel, M., Hoskin, K., and Macve, R. (1990) Managing it all by numbers: a review of Johnson and Kaplan's 'Relevance Lost', *Accounting and Business Research*, 20 (78): 153–66.
Faria, A.R.S. (2008) An analysis of accounting history research in Portugal: 1990–2004, *Accounting History*, 13 (3): 353–82.
Fatjó, P. (1991) Organización y gestión de una hacienda eclesiástica en la Cataluña de XVII: la cathedral de Barcelona, *Revista de Historia Económica*, XVII (1): 89–118.
Fatjó, P. (2001) La contabilidad du una institución eclesiásticas desde la perspectiva del historiador económico, *XI Congresso de la Asociación Española de Contabilidad y Administración de Empresas* (Madrid: AECA).
Fleischman, R.K. (1996) A history of management accounting through the 1960s, in T.A. Lee, A. Bishop, and R.H. Parker (eds) *Accounting History from the Renaissance to the Present*, pp. 119–42 (New York: Garland).
Fleischman, R.K. (2000) Completing the triangle: taylorism and the paradigms, *Accounting, Auditing & Accountability Journal*, 13 (5): 597–623.
Fleischman, R.K. (ed) (2006) *Accounting History* (London: Sage).
Fleischman, R.K. (2009) Management accounting: theory and practice, in J.R. Edwards and S.P. Walker (eds) *The Routledge Companion to Accounting History*, pp. 189–223 (London: Routledge).
Fleischman, R.K., Boyns, T., and Tyson, T.N. (2008) The search for standard costing in the United States and Britain, *Abacus*, 44 (4): 341–76.
Fleischman, R.K., Hoskin, K.W., and Macve, R.H. (1995) The Boulton & Watt case: the crux of alternative approaches to accounting history? *Accounting and Business Research*, 25 (99): 162–76.

Fleischman, R.K., Kalbers, L.P., and Parker, L.D. (1996) Expanding the dialogue: industrial revolution costing historiography, *Critical Perspectives on Accounting*, 7 (3): 315–37.

Fleischman, R.K. and Macve, R.H. (2002) Coals from Newcastle: alternative histories of cost and management accounting in the northeast coal mining during the British industrial revolution, *Accounting and Business Research*, 32 (3): 133–52.

Fleischman, R.K. and Macve, R.H. (2007) Carron Company, non-Marxist perspectives: responses to Bryer. Paper presented at Fifth Accounting History Conference, Banff, 9–11 August.

Fleischman, R.K. and Marquette, R.P. (2003) The impact of World War II on cost accounting at the Sperry Corporation, *Accounting Historians Journal*, 30 (2): 67–104.

Fleischman, R.K. and Parker, L.D. (1990) Management accounting early in the British industrial revolution: the Carron Company, a case study, *Accounting and Business Research*, 20 (79): 211–21.

Fleischman, R.K. and Parker, L.D. (1991) British entrepreneurs and pre-industrial revolution evidence of cost management, *Accounting Review*, 66 (2): 361–75.

Fleischman, R.K. and Parker, L.D. (1992) The cost accounting environment in the British industrial revolution iron industry, *Accounting, Business & Financial History*, 2 (2): 141–60.

Fleischman, R.K. and Parker, L.D. (1997) *What is Past is Prologue: Cost Accounting in the British Industrial Revolution, 1760–1850* (New York: Garland).

Fleischman, R.K. and Radcliffe, V.S. (2003) Divergent streams of accounting history: a review and call for confluence, in R.K. Fleischman, V.S. Radcliffe, and P.A. Shoemaker (eds) *Doing Accounting History*, pp. 1–29 (Amsterdam: JAI).

Fleischman, R.K. and Tyson, T.N. (1998) The evolution of standard costing in the UK and US: from decision making to control, *Abacus*, 34 (1): 92–119.

Fleischman, R.K. and Tyson, T.N. (1999) Opportunity lost? Chances for cost accountants professionalization under the National Recovery Act of 1933, *Accounting, Business & Financial History*, 9 (1): 51–75.

Fleischman, R.K. and Tyson, T.N. (2000) Parallels between US and UK cost accountancy in the World War I era, *Accounting, Business & Financial History*, 10 (2): 191–212.

Fleischman, R.K. and Tyson, T.N. (2007) The history of management accounting in the U.S., in C.S. Chapman, A.G. Hopwood, and M.D. Shields (eds) *Handbook of Management Accounting Research*, pp. 1089–107 (Oxford: Elsevier).

Fleming, A.I.M., McKinstry, S., and Wallace, K. (2000) Cost accounting in the shipbuilding, engineering and metals industries of the west of Scotland, 'The workshop of the empire', c.1900–1960, *Accounting and Business Research*, 30 (3): 195–211.

Flesher, D.L. and Previts, G.J. (2007) Donaldson Brown (1885–1965): twentieth-century financial management innovator. Paper presented at Business History Conference, Cleveland, 31 May-2 June.

Flesher, D.L., Samson, W.D., and Previts, G.J. (2003) Accounting, economic development, and financial reporting: the case of three pre-Civil War US railroads, *Accounting History*, 8 (2): 61–77.

Flinn, M.W. (ed) (1957) *The Law Book of the Crowley Ironworks* (Durham: Andrews).

Flinn, M.W. (1962) *Men of Iron: The Crowleys in the Early Iron Industry* (Edinburgh: Edinburgh University Press).

Foreman, P. (2001) The transfer of accounting technology: a study of the Commonwealth of Australia government factories, 1910–1916, *Accounting History*, 6 (1): 31–59.

Foreman, P. and Tyson, T.N. (1998) Accounting, accountability and cost efficiency at the Commonwealth of Australia clothing factory, 1911–1918, *Accounting History*, 3 (2): 7–36.

Freaar, J. (1994) Robert Loder, Jacobean management accountant, *Abacus*, 6: 25–38.

Fu, P.Y. (1971) Government accounting in China during the Chou dynasty (1122–256 BC), *Journal of Accounting Research*, 9 (1): 40–51.

Funnell, W., Holden, A., and Oldroyd, D. (2014) Costing in the Newcastle Infirmary, 1840–1888, *Accounting, Auditing & Accountability Journal*, 27 (3): 465–88.

Funnell, W.N. (1998) Accounting in the service of the Holocaust, *Critical Perspectives on Accounting*, 9 (4): 435–64.

Gantt, H.L. (1916) Production and sales, *Engineering Magazine*, 50: 593–600.

Garcke, F. and Fells, J.M. (1887) *Factory Accounts, their Principles and Practice* (London: Crosby, Lockwood).

Garner, S.P. (1954) *Evolution of Cost Accounting to 1925* (University, AL: University of Alabama Press).

Gebreiter, F. (2016) 'Comparing the incomparable': hospital costing and the art of medicine in post-war Britain, *British Accounting Review*, 48 (2): 257–68.

Gervais, P. and Quinn, M. (2016) Costing in the early Industrial Revolution: gradual change to cost calculations at US cloth mills in the 1820s, *Accounting History Review*, 26 (3): 191–217.

Gilman, S. (1922) Discussion, *NACA Year Book*, 3: 263–66.

Godard, M. (1827) *Traité Général et Sommaire de la Comptabilité Commerciale* (Paris: Hachette).

Greer, H.C. (1965) Alternatives to direct costing, in R.P. Marple (ed) *National Association of Accountants on Direct Costing*, pp. 147–58 (New York: Ronald Press).

Guillén, J.M. (2005) The Bordázar memorandum: cost calculation in Spanish printing during the 18th century, *Accounting Historians Journal*, 32 (2): 81–103.

Guo, D. (1988) The historical contribution of Chinese accounting, in A.T. Craswell (ed) *Collected Papers of the Fifth World Congress of Accounting Historians*, pp. 1–8 (Sydney: University of Sydney).

Gutiérrez, F. (1993) 'Distribución Espacial y Cambio Contable: El Caso de la Real Fábrica de Tabacos de Sevilla en el Siglo XVIII', unpublished thesis, University of Seville.

Gutiérrez, F., Larrinaga, C., and Núñez, M. (2005) Pre-industrial revolution evidence of cost and management accounting in Spain, *Accounting Historians Journal*, 32 (1): 111–48.

Gutiérrez, F. and Romero, D. (2007) The 1770s, a lively decade for quality control: the case of the Royal Tobacco Factory of Seville, *Accounting History*, 12 (4): 393–415.

Hamilton, R. (1777) *An Introduction to Merchandise* (Edinburgh: privately printed).

Harris, J.N. (1965) What did we earn last month? in R.P. Marple (ed) *National Association of Accountants on Direct Costing*, pp. 17–40 (New York: Ronald Press).

Harrison, G.C. (1918–19) Cost accounting to aid production, *Industrial Management*, 56 (4): 273–82, (5): 391–8, (6): 456–63, 57 (1): 49–55, (2): 131–8, (3): 218–24, (4): 314–7, (5): 400–3, (6): 483–7.

Harrison, G.C. (1930) *Standard Costs: Installation, Operation and Use* (New York: Ronald Press).

Heier, J.R. (2000) The foundations of modern cost management: the life and work of Albert Fink, *Accounting, Business & Financial History*, 10 (2): 213–43.

Heinzelmann, R. (2016) Comparing professions in UK and German-speaking management accounting, *Accounting in Europe*, 13 (1): 103–20.

Holzer, H.P. and Rogers, W. (1990) The origins and developments of French costing systems, *Accounting Historians Journal*, 17 (2): 57–71.

Hopper, T., Tsamenyi, M., and Uddin, S. (2009) Management accounting in less developed countries: what is known and needs known, *Accounting, Auditing & Accountability Journal*, 22 (3): 469–514.

Hopper, T.M. and Armstrong, P. (1991) Cost accounting, controlling labour and the rise of conglomerates, *Accounting, Organizations and Society*, 16 (5/6): 405–38.

Hopwood, A.G. (1987) The archaeology of accounting systems, *Accounting, Organizations and Society*, 12 (3): 207–34.

Hoskin, K.W. and Macve, R.H. (1988) The genesis of accountability: the West Point connections, *Accounting, Organizations and Society*, 13 (1): 37–73.

Hoskin, K.W. and Macve, R.H. (1994) Reappraising the genesis of managerialism: a re-examination of the role of accounting at the Springfield Armory, 1815–1845, *Accounting, Auditing & Accountability Journal*, 7 (2): 4–29.

Hoskin, K.W. and Macve, R.H. (1996) The Lawrence Manufacturing Company: a note on early cost accounting in US textile mills, *Accounting, Business & Financial History*, 6 (3): 337–61.

Hoskin, K.W. and Macve, R.H. (2000) Knowing more as knowing less? Alternative histories of cost and management accounting in the U.S. and the U.K., *Accounting Historians Journal*, 27 (1): 91–149.

Hoskin, K.W. and Macve, R.H. (2007) The Pennsylvania Railroad, 1849 and the 'Invention of Management', working paper.

Hoxie, R.F. (1920) *Scientific Management and Labor* (New York: D. Appleton).

Hoyt, F.F. (1943) Cost control in wartime, *NACA Year Book*, 24: 81–97.

Hudson, P. (1977) Some aspects of nineteenth-century accounting development in the West Riding textile industry, *Accounting History*, 2 (2): 4–22.

Ihantola, E-M. (2010) An historical analysis of budgetary thought in Finnish specialist business journals from c.1950 to c.2000, *Accounting, Business & Financial History*, 20 (2): 135–61.

Jansen, E.P. (2018) Bridging the gap between theory and practice in management accounting: reviewing the literature to shape interventions, *Accounting, Auditing & Accountability Journal*, 31 (5): 1486–509.

Johnson, H.T. (1972) Early cost accounting for internal management control: lyman Mills in the 1850s, *Business History Review*, 46 (4): 466–74.

Johnson, H.T. (1980a) Management accounting in an early integrated industrial: E.I. DuPont de Nemours Powder Co., 1903–1912, in H.T. Johnson (ed) *System and Profits*, pp. 184–204 (New York: Arno Press).

Johnson, H.T. (1980b) Management accounting in an early multidivisional organization: general Motors in the 1920s, in H.T. Johnson (ed)*System and Profits*, pp. 490–517 (New York: Arno Press).

Johnson, H.T. and Kaplan, R.S. (1987) *Relevance Lost: The Rise and Fall of Management Accounting* (Boston: Harvard Business School Press).

Jones, H. (1985) *Accounting, Costing and Cost Estimation, Welsh Industry: 1700–1830* (Cardiff: University of Wales Press).

Kallapur, S. and Krishnan, R. (2009) Management Accounting in India, in C.S. Chapman, A. G. Hopwood, and M.D. Shields (eds) *Handbook of Management Accounting Research*, Vol. 3, pp. 1399–410 (Oxford: Elsevier).

Kaplan, R.S. (1983) Measuring manufacturing performance: a new challenge for managerial accounting research, *Accounting Review*, 58 (4): 686–705.

Kimizuka, Y. (1992) Cost accounting in the Meiji era (1868–1912), *Sakushin Business Review*, 1: 13–42.

King, P.W. (2010) Management, finance, and cost control in the Midlands charcoal industry, *Accounting, Business & Financial History*, 20 (3): 385–412.

Kininmonth, K.W. and McKinstry, S. (2007) Stitching it up: accounting and financial control at J&P Coats Ltd, c1890–1960, *Accounting History*, 12 (4): 367–91.

Kohler, E.L. and Cooper, W.W. (1945) Costs, prices and profits: accounting in the war program, *Accounting Review*, 20 (3): 267–308.

Kurunmäki, L. (2004) A hybrid profession – the acquisition of management accounting expertise by medical professionals, *Accounting, Organizations and Society*, 29 (3–4): 327–47.

Lampe, M. and Sharp, P. (2017) A quest for useful knowledge: the early development of agricultural accounting in Denmark and Northern Germany, *Accounting History Review*, 27 (1): 73–99.

Léautey, E. and Guilbault, A. (1889) *La Science des Comptes Mise à la Portée de tous* (Paris: Librairie Comptable et Administrative).

Lemarchand, Y. (2016) Revisiting the birth of industrial accounting in France, a return to the actors involved, *Accounting History Review*, 26 (3): 351–71.

Levant, Y. and Nikitin, M. (2006) Should Charles Eugène Bedaux be revisited?? Paper presented at Eighteenth Accounting, Business & Financial History Conference, Cardiff Business School, 14–15 September.

Levant, Y. and Nikitin, M. (2009) Charles Eugène Bedaux (1886–1944): 'cost killer' or Utopian socialist? *Accounting, Business & Financial History*, 19 (2): 167–87.

Levant, Y. and Nikitin, M. (2012) Can cost and financial accounting be fully re-integrated? The role of the French state in the separation of accounting systems and the failed attempt of the *système croisé* to re-integrate them, *Accounting History*, 17 (3–4): 437–61.

Levant, Y. and Zimnovitch, H. (2013) Contemporary evolutions in costing methods: understanding these trends through the use of equivalence methods in France, *Accounting History*, 18 (1): 51–75.

Lin, Z.J. (1992) Chinese double-entry bookkeeping before the nineteenth century, *Accounting Historians Journal*, 19 (2): 103–22.

Lin, Z.J. (2003) Chinese bookkeeping systems: a study of accounting adaptation and change, *Accounting, Business & Financial History*, 13 (1): 83–98.

Lippman, E.J. and Wilson, P.A. (2007) The culpability of accounting in perpetuating the Holocaust, *Accounting History*, 12 (3): 283–303.

Littleton, A.C. (1933) *Accounting Evolution to 1900* (New York: American Institute Publishing Co.).

Llopis, E., Fidalgo, E., and Méndez, T. (2002) The 'Hojas de Ganado' of the Monastery of Guadalupe, 1597–1784: an accounting instrument for fundamental economic decisions, *Accounting, Business & Financial History*, 12 (2): 203–29.

Lloyd Jones, B. (2010) Was the nineteenth-century Denbighshire coalfield a worthwhile investment? An analysis of the investors and their returns, *Accounting, Business & Financial History*, 20 (2): 231–61.

Loft, A. (1986) Towards a critical understanding of accounting: the case of accounting in the UK, 1914–1925, *Accounting, Organizations and Society*, 11 (2): 137–69.

Loft, A. (1990) *Coming into the Light* (New York: CIMA).

Loft, A. (1995) The history of management accounting: relevance found, in D. Ashton, T. Hopper, and R.W. Scapens (eds) *Issues in Management Accounting*, pp. 17–38 (London and New York: Prentice Hall).

Lu, W., Ji, X-d, and Aiken, M. (2009) Governmental influences in the development of Chinese accounting during the modern era, *Accounting, Business & Financial History*, 19 (3): 305–26.

Ludwig, J.W. (1965) Inaccuracies of direct costing, in R.P. Marple (ed) *National Association of Accountants on Direct Costing*, pp. 167–79 (New York: Ronald Press).

Luenstroth, H.W. (1965) The case for direct costing, in R.P. Marple (ed) *National Association of Accountants on Direct Costing*, pp. 95–112 (New York: Ronald Press).

Luft, J. (2007) Historical theorizing in management accounting research, in C.S. Chapman, A. G. Hopwood, and M.D. Shields (eds) *Handbook of Management Accounting Research*, pp. 269–84 (Oxford: Elsevier).

Lukka, K. (1988) Budgetary biasing in organizations: theoretical frameworks and empirical evidence, *Accounting, Organizations and Society*, 13 (3): 281–301.

MacDonald, L.D. and Richardson, A.J. (2011) Does academic management accounting practice lag? A cliometric study, *Accounting History*, 16 (4): 365–88.

Macías, M. (2002a) Ownership structure and accountability: the case of the privatization of the Spanish tobacco monopoly, 1887–96, *Accounting, Business & Financial History*, 12 (2): 317–45.

Macías, M. (2002b) Privatization and management accounting systems change: the case of the 19th century Spanish tobacco monopoly, *Accounting Historians Journal*, 29 (2): 31–57.

Mann, J. (1903a) Cost records or factory accounts, in *Encyclopaedia of Accounting*, (London: William Green).

Mann, J. (1903b) Oncosts, in *Encyclopaedia of Accounting* (London: William Green).

Maran, L. and Leoni, G. (2019) The contribution of the Italian literature to the international accounting history literature, *Accounting History*, 24 (1): 5–39.

Marple, R.P. (ed) (1965) *National Association of Accountants on Direct Costing* (New York: Ronald Press).

Marquette, R.P. and Fleischman, R.K. (1992) Government/business synergy: early American innovation in budgeting and cost accounting, *Accounting Historians Journal*, 19 (2): 123–45.

Marriner, S. (1980) The Ministry of Munitions 1915–1919 and government accounting procedures, *Accounting and Business Research*, 10 (37A): 130–42.

Marshall, G. (1980) *Presbyteries and Profits* (Oxford: Clarendon Press).

Matos Carvalho, J., Lima Rodrigues, L., and Craig, R. (2007) Early cost accounting practices and private ownership: the Silk Factory Company of Portugal, 1745–1747, *Accounting Historians Journal*, 34 (1): 57–89.

Matthews, D. (2017) Publications in accounting history: a long-run statistical survey, *Accounting Historians Journal*, 44 (2): 69–98.

Matthews, M., Boyns, T., and Edwards, J.R. (2003) Chandlerian image or mirror image? Managerial and accounting control in the chemical industry: the case of Albright & Wilson, c.1892–c.1923, *Business History*, 45 (4): 24–52.

Maynard, H.W. (1928) What the standard costs and the flexible budget are doing for the reduction of costs in the manufacturing department, *NACA Year Book*, 9: 300–08.

McCartney, S. and Stittle, J. (2017) 'A very costly industry': the cost of Britain's privatised railway, *Critical Perspectives on Accounting*, 49: 1–17.

McKendrick, N. (1970) Josiah Wedgwood and cost accounting in the industrial revolution, *Economic History Review*, 23 (1): 45–67.

McKinsey, J.O. (1922) *Budgetary Control* (New York: Ronald Press).

McKinstry, S. (1999) Engineering culture and accounting development at Albion Motors, 1900–1970, *Accounting, Business & Financial History*, 9 (2): 203–23.

McKinstry, S. and Ding, Y.Y. (2015) 'Hybridised' financial control in the Victorian construction industry: George Gilbert Scott's rebuilding of Glasgow University, 1864–1872, *Accounting History*, 20 (2): 206–27.

McLaren, J., Appleyard, T., and Mitchell, F. (2016) The rise and fall of management accounting systems: a case study investigation of EVA™, *British Accounting Review*, 48 (3): 341–58.

McLean, T. (1995) Contract costing and accounting in the Sunderland shipbuilding industry, 1818–1917, *Accounting, Business & Financial History*, 5 (1): 109–45.

McLean, T. (2009) The measurement and management of human performance in seventeenth century English farming: the case of Henry Best, *Accounting Forum*, 33 (1): 62–73.

McLean, T. (2013) Cost engineering and costing in Hawthorn Leslie Shipbuilders, 1886–1915, *British Accounting Review*, 45 (4): 284–96.

McLean, T. and McGovern, T. (2017) Costing for strategy development and analysis in an emerging industry: the Newcastle upon Tyne Electric Supply Company, 1889–1914, *British Accounting Review*, 49 (3): 294–315.

McLean, T., McGovern, T., and Davie, S. (2015) Management accounting, engineering and the management of company growth: Clarke Chapman, 1864–1914, *British Accounting Review*, 47 (2): 177–90.

McLean, T. and Tyson, T. (2006) Standard costs, standard costing and the introduction of scientific management and new technology into the post-Second World War Sunderland shipbuilding industry, *Accounting, Business & Financial History*, 16 (3): 389–417.

McWatters, C.S. and Foreman, P. (2005) Reaction to World War I constraints to normal trade: the meat-packing industry in Canada and Australia, *Accounting History*, 10 (2): 67–102.

Melis, F. (1950) *Storia Della Ragioneria* (Bologna: Dott, Cesare Zuffi).

Miller, P., Hopper, T., and Laughlin, R. (1991) The new accounting history: an introduction, *Accounting, Organizations and Society*, 12 (3): 235–65.

Miller, P., Kurunmäki, L., and O'Leary, T. (2008) Accounting hybrids and the management of risk, *Accounting, Organizations and Society*, 13 (7–8): 942–67.

Miller, P and Napier, C. (1993) Genealogies of calculation, *Accounting, Organizations and Society*, 18 (7–8): 631–47.

Miller, P. and O'Leary, T. (1987) Accounting and the construction of the governable person, *Accounting, Organizations and Society*, 12 (3): 235–65.

Moussalli, S.D., Flesher, D.L., and Lemarchand, Y. (2009) Pierre Boucher and the 1803 edition of La science des négocians: accounting in the Republic, *Accounting, Business & Financial History*, 19 (3): 353–64.

Mueller, F. and Carter, C. (2007) 'We are all managers now': managerialism and professional engineering in UK electricity utilities, *Accounting, Organizations and Society*, 32 (1–2): 181–95.

Mura, A. and Emmanuel, C. (2010) Transfer pricing: early Italian contributions, *Accounting, Business & Financial History*, 20 (3): 365–83.

Mussari, R. and Magliacani, M. (2007) Agricultural accounting in the nineteenth and early twentieth centuries: the case of the noble Rucellia family farm in Campi, *Accounting, Business & Financial History*, 17 (1): 87–103.

Napier, C.J. (2001) Accounting history and accounting progress, *Accounting History*, 6 (2): 7–31.

Näsi, S. and Rohde, C. (2007) Development of cost and management accounting ideas in the Nordic countries, in C.S. Chapman, A.G. Hopwood, and M.D. Shields (eds) *Handbook of Management Accounting Research*, pp. 1109–37 (Oxford: Elsevier).

National Association of Accountants (1957) NAA research series no. 23: direct costing (New York: National Association of Accountants).

Nelson, D. (1974) Scientific management, systematic management, and labor, 1880–1915, *Business History Review*, 48 (4): 479–500.

Nelson, D. (1975) *Frederick W. Taylor and the Rise of Scientific Management* (Madison, WI: University of Wisconsin Press).

Nicholson, J.L. (1909) *Factory Organisation and Costs* (New York: Kohl Technical Publishing Co.).

Nikitin, M. (1990) Setting up an industrial accounting system at Saint-Gobain (1820–1880), *Accounting Historians Journal*, 17 (2): 73–93.

Nikitin, M. (1996) The birth of industrial accounting in France: the role of Pierre-Antoine Godard-Desmarest (1767–1850) as strategist, industrialist, and accountant at the Baccarat Chrystalworks, *Accounting, Business & Financial History*, 6 (1): 93–110.

Noguchi, M. and Boyns, T. (2012) The development of budgets and their use for purposes of control in Japanese aviation, 1928–1945: the role of the state, *Accounting, Auditing & Accountability Journal*, 25 (3): 416–51.

Noguchi, M., Nakamura, T., and Shimizu, Y. (2015) Accounting control and interorganisational relations with the military under the wartime regime: the case of Mitsubishi Heavy Industry's Nagoya Engine Factory, *British Accounting Review*, 47 (2): 204–23.

Norton, G.P. (1889) *Textile Manufacturers' Bookkeeping for the Counting House, Mill and Warehouse* (London: Simpkin, Marshall, Hamilton & Kent).

Núñez, T.M. (2002) Organizational change and accounting: the gunpowder monopoly in New Spain, 1757–87, *Accounting, Business & Financial History*, 12 (2): 275–315.

O'Connor, N.G., Chow, C.W., and Wu, A. (2004) The adoption of 'Western' management accounting/controls in China's state-owned enterprises during economic transition, *Accounting, Organizations and Society*, 29 (3–4): 349–75.

Okano, H. (2015) *History of Management Accounting in Japan: Institutional & Cultural Significance of Accounting* (Bingley: Emerald Publishing Group).

Okano, H. and Suzuki, T. (2007) A history of Japanese management accounting, in C.S. Chapman, A. G. Hopwood, and M.D. Shields (eds) *Handbook of Management Accounting Research*, pp. 1139–57 (Oxford: Elsevier).

Oldroyd, D. (1996) The costing records of George Bowes and the grand allies in the north-east coal trade in the eighteenth century: their type and significance, *Accounting, Business & Financial History*, 9 (2): 175–201.

Oldroyd, D. (2007) *Estates, Enterprise and Investment at the Dawn of the Industrial Revolution: Estate Management and Accounting in the North-East of England c. 1700–1780* (Aldershot: Ashgate).

Oldroyd, D. and Dobie, A. (2009) Bookkeeping, in J.R. Edwards and S.P. Walker (eds) *The Routledge Companion to Accounting History*, pp. 95–119 (London: Routledge).

Parker, L.D. (2016) The global Fayol: contemporary management and accounting traces, *Enterprises et Histoire*, 2 (83): 51–63.

Parker, L.D. and Lewis, N.R. (1995) Classical management control in contemporary management and accounting: the persistence of Taylor and Fayol's world, *Accounting, Business & Financial History*, 5 (2): 211–35.

Parker, R.H. (1969) *Management Accounting: An Historical Perspective* (New York: Augustus Kelley).

Parker, R.H. (1986) *The Development of the Accountancy Profession in Britain in the Early Twentieth Century* (San Antonio, TX: Academy of Accounting Historians).

Payen, A. (1817) *Essai sur la Tenue des Livres d'un Manufacturer* (Paris: Chez A. Johanneau).

Pezet, A. (2009) The history of the French tableau de bord (1875–1975): evidence from the archives, *Accounting, Business & Financial History*, 19 (2): 103–25.

Planas, J. and Saguer, E. (2005) Accounting records of large rural estates and the dynamics of agriculture in Catalonia (Spain), 1850–1950, *Accounting, Business & Financial History*, 15 (2): 171–85.

Plumpton, T. (1895) Manufacturing costs as applied to shipbuilding, *Accountant*, 21 September: 758–60; 28 September: 773–75.

Pollard, S. (1965) *The Genesis of Modern Management* (Cambridge, MA: Harvard University Press).

Pong, C. and Mitchell, F. (2006) Full costing versus variable costing: does the choice still matter? An empirical exploration of UK manufacturing companies 1988–2002, *British Accounting Review*, 38 (2): 131–48.

Quinn, M. and Jackson, W.J. (2014) Accounting for war risk costs: management accounting change at Guinness during the First World War, *Accounting History Review*, 24 (2–3): 191–209.

Richardson, A. (2008) Organizational founding, strategic renewal, and the role of accounting: management accounting concepts in the formation of the 'Penny Post', *Journal of Management Accounting Research*, 20 (special issue): 107–27.

Robson, N. (2003) From voluntary to state control and the emergence of the department in UK hospital accounting, *Accounting, Business & Financial History*, 13 (2): 99–123.

Robson, N. (2006) The road to uniformity: accounting change in UK voluntary hospitals, *Accounting & Business Research*, 36 (4): 271–88.

Robson, N. (2007) Adapting not adopting: 1958–74, accounting and managerial 'reform' in the early NHS, *Accounting, Business & Financial History*, 17 (3): 445–67.

Rogers, D.M. (1932) Development of the modern business budget, *Journal of Accountancy*, 53 (3): 186–205.

Roll, E. (1930) *An Early Experiment in Industrial Organization* (New York: Augustus Kelley).

Sakuri, M. (1989) Target costing and how to use it, *Journal of Cost Management*, 3 (2): 39–50.

Samson, W.D., Flesher, D.L., and Previts, G.J. (2006) Corporate governance and external and internal controls: the case of the Baltimore and Ohio Railroad, circa 1831, *Issues in Accounting Education*, 21 (1): 45–62.

Sánchez-Matamoros, J.B. and Hidalgo, F.G. (2011) Publishing patterns of accounting history research in generalist journals: lessons from the past, *Accounting History*, 16 (3): 331–42.

Sánchez-Matamoros, J.B. and Hidalgo, F.G. (2012) Accounting for the production of coins: the enactment and implementation of the Spanish Ordinances of the Mints, 1730, *Accounting History*, 17 (3–4): 351–67.

Sapori, A. (1932) *Una Compagnia di Calimala ai Primi del Trecento* (Florence: Olschki).
Scapens, R.W. (1991) *Management Accounting: A Review of Recent Developments* (London: Macmillan).
Scapens, R.W. (2006) Understanding management accounting practices: a personal journey, *British Accounting Review*, 38 (1): 1–30.
Scarbrough, P., Nanni, A.J., and Sakurai, M. (1991) Japanese management accounting practices and the effects of assembly and process automation, *Management Accounting Research*, 2 (1): 27–46.
Schäffer, U. and Binder, C. (2008) 'Controlling' as an academic discipline: the development of management accounting and management control research in German-speaking countries between 1970 and 2003, *Accounting History*, 13 (1): 33–74.
Scheuermann, L. (1929) *Die Fugger als Montanindustrielle in Tirol und Karnten* (Munich: Duncker & Humbolt).
Schmalenbach, E. (1899) Buchfuehrung und Kalkulation in Fabrikgeschäft, *Deutsche Metallindustriezeitung*, 15.
Schmalenbach, E. (1948) *Pretiale Wirschaftslenkung* (Bremen-Horn: W. Dorn).
Schweitzer, M. (1992) Eugèn Schmalenbach as the founder of cost accounting in the German-speaking world, in A. Tsuji (ed) *Collected Papers of the Sixth World Congress of Accounting Historians*, Vol. II, pp. 393–418 (Japan: Accounting History Association).
Scorgie, M.E. (1997) Progenitors of modern management accounting concepts and mensurations in pre-industrial England, *Accounting, Business & Financial History*, 7 (1): 31–59.
Segelod, E. and Carlsson, L. (2010) The emergence of uniform principles of cost accounting in Sweden 1900–36, *Accounting, Business & Financial History*, 20 (3): 327–63.
Shank, J.K. and Govindarajan, V. (1989) *Strategic Cost Analysis: The Evolution from Managerial to Strategic Accounting* (Homewood, IL: Irwin).
Simon, F.N. (1830) *Méthode Complète de Tenue des Livres* (Châtillon sur Seine: Cornillac).
Simon, H.A., Guetzkow, H., Kozmetsky, G., and Tyndall, G. (1954) *Centralization vs. Decentralization in Organizing the Controller's Department* (New York: Controllership Foundation).
Sloan, A.P. (1964) *My Years at General Motor* (Garden City, NY: Doubleday).
Smith, I. and Boyns, T. (2005) Scientific management and the pursuit of control in Britain to c. 1960, *Accounting, Business & Financial History*, 15 (2): 187–216.
Solomons, D. (1952) *Studies in Costing* (London: Sweet & Maxwell).
Sorensen, J.E. (2009) Management Accountants in the United States: practitioner and academic views of recent developments, in S.C. Chapman, A.G. Hopwood, and M.D. Shields (eds) *Handbook of Management Accounting Research*, pp. 1271–96 (Oxford: Elsevier).
Sowell, E.M. (1973) *The Evolution of the Theories and Techniques of Standard Costs* (Tuscaloosa, AL: University of Alabama Press).
Spraakman, G. and Margret, J (2005) The transfer of management accounting practices from London counting houses to the British north American fur trade, *Accounting, Business & Financial History*, 15 (2): 101–19.
Stacey, N.A.H. (1954) *English Accountancy 1800–1954* (London: Gee).
Stempf, V.H. (1943) War contracts, costs, and profits, *Journal of Accountancy*, 75 (6): 496–509.
Stoeffel, K. (1995) *Controllership im Internationalen Vergleich* (Wiesbaden: Gabler).
Stone, W.E. (1973) An early English cotton mill cost accounting system: Charlton Mills, 1810–1889, *Accounting and Business Research*, 4 (17): 71–78.
Takeda, H. and Boyns, T. (2014) Management, accounting and philosophy: the development of management accounting at Kyocera, 1959–2013, *Accounting, Auditing & Accountability Journal*, 27 (2): 317–56.
Taylor, F.W. (1903) *Shop Management* (New York: Harper).
Taylor, F.W. (1911) *The Principles of Scientific Management* (New York: Harper).
Taylor, F.W. (1912) *Scientific Management* (New York: Harper).
Theiss, E.L. (1937) The beginnings of business budgeting, *Accounting Review*, 12 (1): 43–55.
Tolkmitt, H. (1894) *Grundriss der Fabrik-Geschaeftsfuehrung* (Leipzig: Verlag von G. A. Gloeckner).
Toms, S. and Fleischman, R.K. (2015) Accounting fundamentals and accounting change: Boulton & Watt and the Springfield Armory, *Accounting, Organizations and Society*, 41 (1): 1–20.
Toms, S. and Shepherd, A. (2017) Accounting and social conflict: profit and regulated working time in the British industrial revolution, *Critical Perspectives on Accounting*, 49: 57–75.
Tyson, T.N. (1990) Accounting for labor in the early nineteenth century: the U.S. arms making experience, *Accounting Historians Journal*, 17 (1): 47–59.

Tyson, T.N. (1992) The nature and environment of cost management among early 19th century U.S. textile manufacturers, *Accounting Historians Journal*, 19 (1): 1–24.

Tyson, T.N. (1993) Keeping the record straight: foucauldian revisionism and 19th century cost accounting history, *Accounting, Auditing & Accountability Journal*, 6 (2): 4–16.

Tyson, T.N. (1998) Mercantilism, management accounting or managerialism? Cost accounting in early 19th century US textile mill, *Accounting, Business & Financial History*, 8 (2): 211–29.

Tyson, T.N. (2000) Accounting history and the emperor's new clothes: a response to 'knowing more or knowing less'? *Accounting Historians Journal*, 27 (1): 159–71.

Tyson, T.N. and Oldroyd, D. (2017) The debate between postmodernism and historiography: an accounting historian's manifesto, *Accounting History*, 22 (1): 29–43.

Urwick, L. and Brech, E.F.L. (1964) *The Making of Scientific Management* (London: Sir Isaac Pitman).

Vent, G.A. (1991) The standardization of the Bewick, Moreing & Co. cost accounts, *Accounting History*, 2 (2): 65–79.

Vent, G.A. and Milne, R.A. (1997) Cost accounting practices at precious metal mines: a comparative study, 1869–1905, *Accounting History*, 2 (2): 77–104.

Verma, S. (2015) Political, economic, social and imperial influences on the establishment of the Institute of Cost and Works Accountants in India post independence, *Critical Perspectives on Accounting*, 31: 5–22.

Walker, S.P. and Mitchell, F. (1996) Propaganda, attitude change and uniform costing in the British printing industry, 1913–1939, *Accounting, Auditing & Accountability Journal*, 9 (3): 98–126.

Walker, S.P. and Mitchell, F. (eds) (1997) *Trade Associations and Uniform Costing in the British Printing Industry, 1900–1963* (New York & London: Garland).

Walker, S.P. and Mitchell, F. (1998) Labor and costing: the employees' dilemma, *Accounting Historians Journal*, 25 (2): 35–62.

Wang, L.Y. and Zhang, R. (2000) The management value of accounting information – past, present and future of management accounting, *Finance and Accounting*, 2: 20–23.

Wells, M.C. (1977) Some influences on the development of cost accounting, *Accounting Historians Journal*, 4 (2): 47–61.

Wells, M.C. (1978) *Accounting for Common Costs* (Urbana, IL: Center for International Education and Research in Accounting).

Whitmore, J. (1908) Shoe factory cost accounts, *Journal of Accountancy*, 4 (1): 12–25.

Williamson, O.E. (1970) *Corporate Control and Business Behavior: An Inquiry into the Effects of Organization Form on Enterprise Behavior* (Englewood Cliffs, NJ: Prentice-Hall).

Wootton, C.W. and Kemmerer, B.E. (2007) The emergence of mechanical accounting in the U.S., 1880–1930, *Accounting Historians Journal*, 34 (1): 91–124.

Yamey, B.S. (1949) Scientific bookkeeping and the rise of capitalism, *Economic History Review*, 1 (2/3): 99–113.

Yamey, B.S. (1960) The development of company accounting conventions, *Three Banks Review*, 47 (September): 3–18.

Zambon, S. and Zan, L. (2007) Controlling expenditure, or the slow emergence of costing at the Venice Arsenal, 1586–1633, *Accounting, Business & Financial History*, 17 (1): 105–28.

Zan, L. (2004a) Accounting and management discourse in proto-industrial settings: the Venice Arsenal in the turn of the 16th century, *Accounting and Business Research*, 34 (2): 145–75.

Zan, L. (2004b) Writing accounting and management history. Insights from unorthodox music historiography, *Accounting Historians Journal*, 31 (2): 171–92.

Zimnovitch, H. (1997) Les calculs du prix de revient dans la seconde industrialisation en France, unpublished dissertation, Poitiers University.

10
AUDITING

Josephine Maltby and Roy Chandler[1]

Overview

There are numerous reasons for companies[2] to undergo an audit. Watts and Zimmerman (1983: 614) famously characterise it as a mechanism to enable managers to add credibility to their position as stewards or to confirm the reliability of information issued to investors. Others argue that audit is not market-driven: companies undergo audit when it suits their needs, for instance as a means of avoiding stringent regulation of their financial reports or to obtain professional advice. Historical evidence provides an opportunity to study the adoption of audit in a variety of different legal and economic environments.

Closely linked with this is the question of the role of audit within corporate governance. Is the auditor's primary responsibility that of defender of the shareholders' interests or as adviser to the directors; are the two roles complementary or competing? This has implications for audit objectives – should the audit be primarily directed at statement verification, or fraud detection, or at preventing error and misstatement? The desired audit objective also has an impact on audit technique – the relative importance of testing the substance of transactions versus the testing of accounting controls, the use of sampling and the emphasis on risk in planning audit work. These are issues which began to be debated during the nineteenth century as investors took an increasing interest in financial statements and auditors' reports. These same issues continue to be controversial.

In the late twentieth century, the audit of public sector bodies, including local and national government, education authorities and the health service, was centralised and intensified with the aim of economising on resources and promoting efficiency and effectiveness. Commentators suggested that there was an inherent tension between a public sector ethic of delivering services and an audit approach derived from private enterprise. The history of public sector audit provides a useful insight into the extent of the changes wrought in the 1980s and the factors behind those changes.

Auditing practices are converging worldwide because of the demands of globalised markets. This convergence and the economic changes in Eastern Europe, China and other emerging economies have led to the development of professional accounting bodies which are heavily influenced by UK/US models. Growing research interest in aspects of the development of auditing in different environments, especially those that do not follow the Anglo-American pattern, offers a critical perspective on the forces underlying change and the prospects for success.

In addition, the audit 'explosion' has seen approaches, technologies and skills honed in, or based on, the audit of financial statements being applied in many other contexts. The growth of 'assurance services' provides audit firms with new income streams and researchers with a potentially rich source of material.

Introduction

A recurring theme in academic accounting journals of the late twentieth/early twenty-first centuries is that of a major expansion in writing about accounting history.[3] Work on the history of audit is part of that expansion, as is evident from the dates of the majority of the pieces cited below. This chapter will attempt to identify the major themes and controversies that have emerged in writing about audit history during this busy period, and suggest future directions that research might take. The view given here is inevitably a partial one; what follows is intended to help stimulate further discussion and research activity.

The chapter does not offer a detailed chronological study of audit – although key events are briefly outlined below – neither does it attempt to be comprehensive in its coverage of relevant themes. It begins by reviewing work on the reasons for the growth of both the audit function and the accounting profession and, in particular, the links between audit and the development of corporate governance. The chapter gives an overview of literature on the history of audit objectives and audit techniques, with particular attention to the continuing argument about auditors' responsibility for the detection of fraud. Much of the above (like most historical writing about audit) has dealt with the private sector and the UK. The later sections of the chapter address the history of audit in the public and non-profit sectors and the research on audit outside of the Anglo-American sphere.

Before 'The Roaring Nineties' (Fleischman and Radcliffe 2005), when accounting history was a field that attracted less academic attention, a number of publications nevertheless studied topics in audit history.[4] Examples include Moyer's (1951) concern with the diffusion of audit techniques, Brown (1962) with changes in audit objectives and practices, Jones (1981) with the role of audit in the growth of the accounting profession and Watts and Zimmerman (1983) with audit as evidence of the validity of agency theory. A common feature is that they were inspired by what Moyer (1951: 8) calls 'auditing as we have come to know it' – that is, the professional audit of limited companies and the associated arguments about what shareholders, managers and a variety of other stakeholders expect the auditor to do. These are all themes which subsequently recur in various forms in writing about audit – indeed they are among the most popular topics in subsequent historical writing.

Miller and Napier (1993: 631), writing about the 'genealogies of calculation', warn against the '*a priori* limiting of the field of study to accounting as it currently exists'. In some of the early papers cited above, the *a priori* temptation is strongly apparent – that of framing audit as having always been, or always having tried to be, the activity of that name in the late twentieth/early twenty-first centuries. The papers by Moyer and Brown, for instance, are both about the development of audit, and both are written from the perspective that history is valuable because it enables modern practitioners to chart the course of future events from what has happened in the past. Moyer (1951: 3) hopes that a study of early developments 'may lead to a better understanding of what is happening in the present and offer clues to what future trends may be'. Brown (1962: 703) is more confident in regarding auditing as following a predictable trajectory: 'In most professions it is rather difficult to predict the future, but there are some significant trends revealed by the history of auditing which should carry forward into succeeding years'.

When Humphrey et al. entitled their 1992 paper 'The audit expectations gap – plus ca change, plus c'est la meme chose?' and Chandler and Edwards (1996) called theirs 'Recurring issues in auditing: back to the future?' they were arguably taking the same perspective as Brown and Moyer, with the difference that they saw unsatisfactory stasis whereas the earlier writers had looked towards a future of improvement. This is not to deny that there are points of comparison between audit practice in the nineteenth, twentieth and twenty-first centuries – but it is to suggest that historians should be prepared to recognise differences as well as similarities. It can be argued that there is a need to see audit in the nineteenth century as other than the twenty-first, and attend to 'the different meanings that have been attached to practices at different moments in time' (Miller and Napier 1993: 632). It also carries with it the possibility that historians will have a better understanding of accounting and auditing change if they stop looking for what Miller and Napier call 'immobile forms that appear to move without difficulty across time and space' and attend to 'the piecemeal fashion in which ... technologies have been invented and assembled' (ibid.). The history of audit in times and places other than the UK and the end of the nineteenth century deserves exploration in pursuit of that possibility.

Audit chronology

There is evidence for auditing, in the sense of a review of accounts being rendered, from Babylonian times onwards (Edwards 1989: 23–31). In England, manorial and government accounts were the subject of a highly developed system of public audits (see below), and audit was rapidly introduced to joint-stock companies (as discussed below for the East India Company in the seventeenth century). The late eighteenth and nineteenth centuries saw the growth of the joint-stock company – most importantly at first the formation of canal, utility and railway companies. The Acts of Parliament instituting these often called for shareholder audits (Matthews et al. 1998: 35), but, as discussed below, there was a steady transition to professional audit. Mid-nineteenth-century legislation first made the audit of joint-stock companies compulsory (Joint Stock Companies Act 1844) then, after the introduction of limited liability, put both reporting and audit on a voluntary basis (Joint Stock Companies Act 1856) (Edwards 2019: 79–80). It was not until 1900 that audit was again mandatory for the generality of joint-stock companies, and only with the 1947 Companies Act were companies required to appoint a professionally qualified accountant as auditor. Despite this apparently slow growth in regulatory requirements, demand for professional audits became a crucial factor in the growth of accountants' occupational groupings in Great Britain.

Reasons why companies undergo audit

One of the most frequently cited pieces of work on the origins of audit – Watts and Zimmerman (1983) – puts forward the thesis that audit arose as a solution to the problem created by the separation of ownership and control. They cite Jensen and Meckling's identification of audit as 'one type of monitoring activity that increases the value of the firm' (Watts and Zimmerman 1983: 613), that will therefore be welcomed by both main parties – principals and agents, here owners and managers. Owners want the audit because it confirms the reliability of information being provided to them; managers because it confirms their trustworthiness as stewards. In support of their argument, Watts and Zimmerman (ibid.: 614) point to the existence of audit as 'part of the efficient technology for organising firms' which existed from the fourteenth century onwards, as firms' legal status altered from merchant guilds to joint stock companies to limited liability companies (ibid.: 618–26). It is an explanation which suggests that legal and regulatory interventions are unnecessary because market demand will elicit a supply of suitably independent auditors at a fair price.

Their argument has substantial advantages since it explains the persistence of the activity over a long period – auditors' faculty of being 'invulnerable to their own failure' (Power 1994a: 7; see also Chapter 20): whatever the shortcomings of the individual audit, the provision of the service remains desirable because it reduces the risks inherent in agency relationships. It also suggests that there is no need for 'government fiat' (Watts and Zimmerman 1983: 613) in the form of legislation, or for professional regulation. Audit services, Watts and Zimmerman argue, alter in response to market conditions. The transition from shareholder to professional auditors in the mid-nineteenth century, they contend, is an example of the work of market forces, due to an expansion either in the demand for audit (because of the increase in the number of limited companies) or in the supply of auditors (because accounting firms had grown in response to a new demand for insolvency services). Audit anticipated legislative provisions? It did not follow them. The agency model therefore enjoys considerable popularity – see for instance Lee (1993: 23), Nikkinen and Petri (2004) on audit fees and agency theory, or the Institute of Chartered Accountants in England and Wales' (ICAEW 2005: 8) *Audit Quality: Agency Theory and the Role of Audit*, which summarises audit history by stating that 'the modern audit function has evolved over centuries, apparently in response to agency issues'.

A number of objections have been raised to the agency theorists' explanation for the rise of audit, which suggest that the motives for audit are more complex than Watts and Zimmerman believe, and that audit needs to be understood as an activity changing within, and shaping, a changing environment, rather than as 'static and purely technocratic' (Hopwood 1977: 277).

One major objection relates to the terms of the contracts under which agency relations operate. Watts and Zimmerman (1983) argue that the need to maintain a reputation for acting independently was, and remains, a crucial asset for auditors who wish to protect their credibility and thus their value in the market. Armstrong (1991: 1), in his 'attempt to re-think the theory of agency', points out that the agency theoretical explanation of audit 'immediately raises the question of how the independence of third party monitors [auditors] is to be guaranteed, particularly when these are normally engaged by agents [management] rather than principals [shareholders]' (ibid.: 12). In Armstrong's words (ibid.: 13) 'monitors are agents too'. Auditors' agency duties concern oversight and review rather than control of resources, but their function for owners is as much a delegated one as that of managers. If 'both managers and monitors are agents … the analysis of how independence in monitors might be secured leads to an infinite regress within the present paradigm of agency theory' (ibid.). Although the auditing profession is likely to benefit from being viewed as independent, it may, he points out, be in the interests of individual auditors *not* to act independently, and it is possible for the auditor to decouple reputation from behaviour (ibid.). If there is no foundation to Watts and Zimmerman's assumption that individual auditors will see themselves as contractually obliged to act independently, agency theory is in trouble. Armstrong proposes instead a 'radical agency theory' which bases relationships between agents and principals not on contract but on 'seeking and allocating trust' (ibid.: 20) – and hence on the mechanisms for creating and identifying a *reputation* for trustworthiness. Armstrong's account touches on a number of issues in audit history: the role of the auditor within corporate governance, the continuing debate about auditor independence, and the increasing importance of audit as a management tool within organisations.

The paradox of Watts and Zimmerman's paper is that, in offering a *history* of audit, it ignores the possibility of historical change. They trace the recurrence of audit from the fourteenth century to the beginning of the twentieth, in what they describe as 'early English business corporations' (Watts and Zimmerman 1983: 615) and subsequently in joint-stock and limited companies. Underlying their history is the assumption that the members and the managers of guilds, merchant adventurers and railway companies all had the same expectations and incentives, and thus that both the agency relationship and the audit passed fundamentally unchanged from the middle ages to the end of Queen Victoria's reign. Napier (2006: 449) criticises this approach when he refers to accounting research that treats the subject as 'a phenomenon of the present' and the textbooks that:

> [d]iscuss different aspects of the … discipline … in terms of the recognised rules and practices of the day, with little or no suggestion that these might have been different at some earlier time (and therefore by implication might be different again in the future).

Mennicken (2006: 22), writing about the introduction of Anglo-American auditing techniques to post-Soviet Russia, describes the import of auditing textbooks which treat audit as an 'a-contextual, universal and homogeneous activity' that can fit seamlessly into any setting. This description could equally be applied to Watts and Zimmerman's conception of audit.

A variety of writers challenge Watts and Zimmerman from different perspectives such as the context in which audit took place and the possibility of understanding audit as a product of political, legal and social as well as economic factors. Some of this work is discussed in the following sections of the chapter, looking first at audit and corporate governance.

Audit and corporate governance

An analysis of the function of audit in corporate governance needs to assign the auditor a role within the governance structure: is the audit conducted primarily for the benefit of shareholders or for that of managers, or can the auditor hold the ring between the two? Agency theory suggests that the last is the case – the manager gains assured reputation and the shareholder has the value of information confirmed. But historical studies have suggested that audit can be understood as a service principally to *one* of these groups, and that the demand for audit comes from this understanding among contemporaries.

An early instance is given in Bryer's study (2000) of the East India Company at the beginning of the seventeenth century. He charts the dissatisfaction of the 'generality' of investors with the small, elite mercantile group of governors. The resulting 'revolution' in the Company 'abolished its feudal directorate and replaced them by modern managers, specialised wage workers accountable to a social capital' (ibid.: 328). As the number of investors increased, 'the generality' demanded more frequent and accurate information about the performance of their capital. The audit was part of a seizure of power by the investors, because it was part of their campaign to be given more frequent and reliable information than they believed the Company was prepared to volunteer to them. The nature of the audit and the character of the auditor's position also changed from one of ex ante approval of expenditure by unpaid members taken from the generality of the shareholders, to a verification of the financial reports after the event undertaken by a paid individual who no longer needed to be a shareholder (Dobija 2018).

The Lancashire cotton mills, the 'Oldham Limiteds' of the late nineteenth century, operating on the principle of one shareholder, one vote, had widely dispersed share ownerships, amateur shareholder auditors and intense investor involvement in their governance. Quarterly cash accounts with detailed information about performance were discussed at general meetings and reported in local newspapers. Toms (2002) treats this as part of the continuing process of socialisation of capital which Bryer discerns in the East India Company – except that, in the Oldhams, socialisation was conducted via co-operation rather than capitalism. Toms (2002: 81) describes the amateur audit, together with cash-based accounting, as 'imposed' by shareholders as a means of carrying out socialisation. 'Socialized capital ... demanded accurate accounting information (and got it) ... through cash based accounting and amateur audit'. After the cotton slump, at the end of the century, financial cliques bought out the local shareholders, building up large blocks of investment. It was at this stage that amateurs were replaced by professional auditors. For Toms, the change of ownership marks a turning-point in the use of audit in these companies. The new owners amended the companies' articles from 'one shareholder, one vote' to 'one share, one vote', effectively giving themselves block votes, and excluded mill managers from boards of directors. These owners could monitor performance via financial controls such as the review of bank balances and the authorisation of expenditure; unlike the former dispersed owners, they placed 'little reliance ... on the publication or auditing of financial statements' (ibid.: 77).

A number of historians, like Toms, contribute to a view of nineteenth-century audit as a weak discipline on directors. Jones (1995) looks at the recommendations by witnesses to various committees on company law between the 1830s and the 1890s in Great Britain to assess the level of support for mandatory auditing. He concludes that witnesses, in general, favoured mandatory audit over compulsory financial reporting as a means of control. Jones (1995: 181) suggests that this preference existed despite the fact that the scope of audit was 'quite restricted' and 'there was little sense of the auditor as an independent third party'. Audit was preferable to a requirement for financial reports because the latter entailed the disclosure of information to competitors; thus there was a 'trade-off' between audit and reporting (ibid.: 182).[5] A similar point is made by Collier (1996) about the rise of the audit committee in the US following the McKesson & Robbins fraud of the late 1930s, when he suggests that, both there and later in the UK, this innovation occurred less because of audit committees' effectiveness than as 'an attempt to avoid legislative solutions to deficiencies in corporate governance' (ibid.: 135).

The development of audit is inextricably linked to the growth of the accounting – and the auditing – profession.[6] Self-promotion as skilled, reliable and independent auditors was crucial to the profession in establishing its jurisdiction over an area that was contested between accountants, lawyers and amateur shareholder auditors.[7] Matthews et al. (1998: 35) stress the importance of auditing in Britain – 'the basis of the accountancy profession's future growth' from the early nineteenth century onwards. They emphasise that, although insolvency was a major activity in the early years of accounting firms' formation, it was audit that took firms into the 'upper echelons' (ibid.: 36). Audit was remarkably effective at giving some accounting firms a leading position that they maintained for more than a century. The table of 'top auditors 1891–1995' contained in Matthews et al. (1998: 46–7) shows that four of the five leading audit firms in 1995 (Coopers & Lybrand, KPMG, Price Waterhouse, Ernst & Young) had predecessors in the top ten in 1891.

Maltby (1999) explores the extent to which the nineteenth-century auditing profession depicted itself as the ally of directors and large shareholders, *against* small (and feckless) speculators. This promoted the profession's strategy for establishing its area of jurisdiction, as did the view of informative financial reports as unnecessary and possibly damaging – the directors knew what was going on, and would communicate to shareholders that which was in the company's and their own interests to disclose. The professional accountant could portray himself as a 'sort of guide, philosopher and friend' as one contributor to *The Accountant* put it (quoted ibid.: 43), providing expert knowledge for directors, rather than as the representative of the interests of the mass of shareholders. Popp (2000) confirms this view of the auditor-director relationship in the audit reports sent to Mintons Ltd between 1876 and 1900. The reports 'did focus on the veracity of … the financial statements' but 'very frequently far exceeded this brief and contained detailed discussion of and recommendations concerning production strategy' (ibid.: 357), apparently with the aim of improving the company's profitability in a period of severe financial difficulties. Popp (ibid.) concludes that the reports 'were used as a vehicle for expanding the role to be played by auditors'.

The evolution of the concept of auditor independence in the US context is examined by Nouri and Lombardi (2009) through their analysis of the various editions of a leading textbook, Montgomery's *Auditing*, from 1905 through to the late twentieth century. They reveal that although the notion of objectivity as a 'state of mind' was recognised and valued from the first, the word 'independence' made its first appearance in the 1934 edition. It is not surprising that given the growth in regulations over auditor independence and ethical matters, later editions contain much more material and discussion on these issues.

A similar approach is taken by Roberts (2010) who looks at the treatment of independence and other ethical issues in *The Journal of Accountancy* during the 1930s – a particularly turbulent time for the US profession. The decade started with the profession contending with the aftermath of the 1929 Wall Street Crash and ended with the more profession-centric McKesson & Robbins scandal. Roberts also notes that matters of independence and ethics were considered to be a 'state of mind' – or principles-based approach – at the start of the 1930s. Over the next decade the arguments used in editorials and elsewhere in the *Journal* appear designed to deflect attention and the risk of greater government regulation away from the profession and onto its clients by prescribing a more rules-based approach.

Napier (1998: 117) draws on the changing role of the auditor when discussing the contemporary arguments for and against limiting auditors' liability for negligence. He traces a movement in the nineteenth century from a view of the company as 'a collectivity model of the interests of shareholders, with directors and auditors being elected from the mass of shareholders' (ibid.: 117) to a 'business company' where 'the auditor "intermediates" between shareholders and directors *whose interests are not necessarily aligned with those of the shareholders*' (ibid.: emphasis added). Here there is a similar path to that outlined above – from Bryer's and Toms' auditors as representatives of socialised capital to the auditors as allies and advisers of the directors – and it makes up a strand in the 'running debate' about the objectives of the audit, discussed below, which drew in the accounting and legal professions as well as shareholders.

The collectivity model places auditors on a par with directors and hence confines their liability to that of directors. In cases such as the Kingston Cotton Mill (1896), an action brought by the official receiver on behalf of the failed mill, 'judges were reluctant to impose on auditors a duty of care more onerous than that imposed on (non-executive) directors' (Napier 1998: 125). Judges were, arguably, slower than accountants to move to the business company model in which the auditor would not necessarily stand as a representative of shareholder interests. Napier, writing before the Companies Act 2006 enabled accountants to set a contractual limit on their liability, warned that auditors' attempts to move in that direction reflected 'a trend away from regarding auditing as a profession' (ibid.: 126).

The argument about limitation of liability continues. Opponents of extended liability claim that a system that imposed more detailed regulation (i.e. extension of auditors' liabilities to third parties) would reduce the scope for auditors to apply professional judgement and would also open them up to 'opportunistic' behaviour by dissatisfied investors who could treat them as a form of insurance (Grout et al. 1994: 343). The Grout argument is of interest as evidence of the extent to which auditors have been decoupled from shareholders by some commentators. In the same vein, O'Sullivan (1993: 417) warns that increased auditor liability would encourage investors to place too much reliance on the audit report. Others argue that there seems to be little value in the audit function if only clients can sue those auditors who perform negligently. Support for this latter view can be found in the judgement of Lord Denning in *Candler v. Crane Christmas* ([1951] 2 KB 164) (emphasis added):

> [t]o whom do these professional people owe this duty [to take care]? They owe the duty, of course, to their employer or client; *and also I think to any third person to whom they themselves show the accounts, or to whom they know their employer is going to show the accounts*, so as to induce him to invest money or take some other action on them.

The argument about auditors' liability that went on through the nineteenth and twentieth centuries and beyond was a continuation of the dispute about the place of the auditor within corporate governance that had begun in the Victorian era. It linked with new situations and expectations – a change in the composition of the shareholder population, more detailed financial reporting regulation, the move of accounting firms to limited liability partnerships, for instance – but in Napier's words (1998: 126), it took shape 'against the shadows and residues of the past'.

Audit objectives and audit techniques

The early development of audit objectives

Jones (2009) shows that from the beginning of the twelve century medieval administrative and accounting systems in Britain drew on a battery of internal control mechanisms, including accountability, supervision and audit. Oschinsky's (1971) collection of texts on medieval estate management and accounting includes reference to internal controls including the division of duties.

There are frequent references in the medieval accounting literature of the thirteenth and fourteenth centuries to the manorial audit. It was an oral examination, a structured process designed to challenge the fairness of the accounts rendered and to arrive at an agreed value. Harvey (1994: 101) describes an audit of the mid-thirteenth century as 'virtually a dialogue, a debate between local official and auditors'. The auditors frequently annotated and amended the accounts presented to them, adding to the cash liability of the local official if expenses were disallowed or output was below fixed minimum returns (ibid.: 104).

Harvey's description is supported by texts such as the *Husbandry* of 1300, which includes a manual of audit procedures. The audit began with an oath by the accountant 'that he will render true accounts' (Oschinsky 1971: c1, 419). The auditor should proceed by investigating the corn account (c2, 419) working out the desirable yield (c3-c9) so that any shortages could be charged against the accountant, then the stock account, including cattle, sheep, poultry, pigs, the output from the dairy, and cash income including rents in cash and in kind, and finally proceeds from sales of wood, stock, dairy products and wool. The auditor was then told:

> After the account has been heard compare how the figures differ from the particulars, and if they show any deficiencies in cash, corn or stock, or any other items commute all of them into cash: to charge the accountant with these deficiencies must be your first duty before you can total the account.
>
> *(Oschinsky 1971: c40, 435)*

As a result, accounts of this period show:

> [w]hat happened at the audit: we see what the local official claimed, what was queried or disallowed by the auditors, and very often why, for revealing notes and comments may be added to explain the alterations made on the account [such as] – 'In future so much will not be allowed' … 'This has been sworn to at the audit'.
>
> *(Harvey 1994: 101)*

The audit was an integral part of estate management. The auditors were engaged in making sure that the official rendering account was not merely telling the truth but was thereby producing an acceptable yield.[8] Hoskin and Macve (1986: 122) describe manorial accounting as 'rudimentary indeed', but the audit was part of a managerial system structured to convert measures of agricultural production into cash values that could be recovered from officials.

The medieval case is of particular interest because there is substantial documentary evidence of the techniques employed by manorial auditors of the period, both in the various treatises on audit which have survived (see Oschinsky 1971 for a collection of short texts) and in manuscript accounts with auditors' amendments (as discussed by Harvey 1994). But the early modern period, and indeed the nineteenth century until the accession of the professional auditor, has not been studied for evidence of audit objectives and audit techniques. Bryer, as discussed above, refers to the importance of the East India Company auditors as investor representatives, but the nature of the work they carried out is not part of his analysis. Forrester (1994) notes the recurring concern among shareholders and managers of the Forth and Clyde Navigation that the accounts should be audited, but he does not quote evidence of the type of work involved.

The auditor and fraud in the nineteenth century

Brown (1962: 696), in an early contribution to the history of audit techniques, identified possible audit objectives as detection of fraud and/or clerical error, and 'determination of fairness of reported financial position'. According to his summary, audit verification in pursuit of these objectives could be either 'detailed' or 'testing', and the importance of internal controls, 'not recognized' from ancient times until 1905, progressively attracted 'slight recognition … awakening of interest … substantial emphasis' in the course of the twentieth century (ibid.). Brown matched the move to the audit of internal control with a change in audit emphasis from detecting fraud to identifying misstatement. He was confident that this process would continue as 'the modern audit … has shifted from a review of past operations to a review of the system of internal control' (ibid.: 703, quoting Nielsen 1960).

Brown sees audit techniques as following an orderly progression based on a shared professional understanding of their objectives. He links advances in audit with a development in client systems that began with the emergence of internal control – an 'order and method' – in the mid-nineteenth century (ibid.: 697). But subsequent research has suggested that audit objectives changed in a much less orderly fashion, and that their relationships with techniques and with client internal controls were less direct and consequential.

In 1849, a Select Committee (1849: i, xvii) set up by the House of Lords 'with a view of providing for a more effectual audit of [railway] accounts' (the Monteagle Committee) stated that an independent public audit would be 'indispensable' in ensuring the reliability of their published accounts. The Committee further stated that the auditor's duties should be limited to 'verification [of the accounts], to the comparison of the entries with the vouchers, and to the investigation of the authorities under which payments are made, and their legality' (ibid.: xv). But the auditor must not 'acquire any power whatever to interfere in the internal administration of the company as a commercial enterprise' (ibid.). It is not clear from the evidence whether the Committee was setting out its requirements on the basis of existing practice or was designing a programme of work to eliminate existing shortcomings.[9] Odlyzko (2011) suggests that the crisis following the railway mania started a revolution in shareholder attitudes towards accounting (and audit), with greater recognition being given to the need for more professionalism in both disciplines, although it took time for this to be generally accepted even by those who stood to gain from such advances.

There was a running debate throughout the latter part of the nineteenth century, contemporaneously with the growth of professional audit, about the extent to which the auditor could be held responsible for the detection of fraud. Chandler et al. (1993) describe it as a 'continuing and fluctuating theme', with a shift in emphasis between responsibility for statement verification and fraud detection, rather than the steady progress which Brown identified from fraud detection in the mid-nineteenth century to opining on fairness by the early twentieth century. The disagreement about audit responsibility was a major part of the audit expectations gap, which Teo and Cobbin (2005) recognise within the accounting profession, as well as between auditors and users of accounts. They quote Dicksee's 1892 *Auditing* text, which remarked that some auditors:

> [c]laim an auditor's duty is confined to a comparison of the Balance Sheet with the books, while others assert that it is the auditor's duty to trace every transaction back to its source. Between those two extremes every shade of opinion may be found and among others the opinion of most practical men.
>
> *(Teo and Cobbin 2005: 42)*

The recurrent nineteenth-century argument about the auditor and fraud has attracted considerable attention (e.g. Humphrey et al. 1992; Chandler 1997; Chandler and Fry 2005). The moral drawn tends to resemble that of Chandler and Edwards (1996: 5–6) that 'the essential problems which troubled the auditing profession at its birth remain unresolved and recur through its maturity'. Teo and Cobbin (2005: 53, 54) describe the situation within the profession at the end of the nineteenth century as 'precarious' with an 'abject lack of guidance' about responsibility. But the profession has survived this continuing crisis without decisive clarification of its responsibility. Research has concentrated on the judicial battles of the late-nineteenth century and the discussion within the profession (e.g. in journals, as reviewed by Teo and Cobbin 2005); it has paid less attention to what the profession had to gain from downplaying its responsibility for fraud.

Relevant here is the work of Power (1992: 58) on a subsequent episode in the history of audit techniques which has attracted less attention – the emergence in the 1930s of what he describes as 'a discourse of sampling'. He argues that the *use* of selective audit testing preceded by 30 or so years its *discussion* in professional texts such as those of Montgomery or Dicksee, and consequently that the installation in textbooks of scientific sampling was intended 'to rationalise practices that had been in place for some years and to invest auditing with a new scientific authority' (ibid.: 37). Power's paper is of interest for a number of reasons. He is directing research attention to the development of audit in the early twentieth century, which has attracted far less concern than the late nineteenth century, and he is making the important point that historical writing needs to avoid assuming 'a historically neutral concept of auditing' (ibid.: 38). The 'neutral' characterisation of audit is liable to view it as a process whose objectives are given, so that changes in technique are evolutionary stages leading to a more perfect exercise of the craft. Power challenges this stance by suggesting that the discourse of sampling was intended to justify and to rationalise techniques which had already proved to be cost-saving, and to reinforce the image of accountants as part of a scientific profession.

This idea offers another perspective on the argument about the auditor's responsibility for fraud detection – that the recurrent debate did not represent a failure by the profession in the nineteenth century to come to an agreement with the users of accounts. Rather, it needs to be understood in its context, as the outcome of the professional orientation towards the interests of social capital – the mission of the accountant to be seen as the 'guide, philosopher and friend' of management and large insider investors (Maltby 1999). The development of the professional auditor's role in the late nineteenth century can be understood as a social process rather than a project aimed at aligning nineteenth-century audit with a timeless 'best practice'. A comment by A. E. (1883) in a leading article in *The Accountant* is particularly telling in this context:

> A *true* audit ... goes far beyond the checking of vouchers, items and balances. It means going behind the scenes, searching out the causes by which the effects have been created, the discovery of managerial errors, and the suggesting of remedies.
>
> A true auditor is in the confidence of his client. The latter almost invariably consults him on matters far removed from the simple question of the balance-sheet and profit and loss. The power we thus hold is great; it should be used with intelligence and earnestness, and not abused, as is the case where work is done in a perfunctory manner, without real interest in our client's welfare.

It is instructive to compare this mission statement with the Monteagle Committee's 1849 recommendations for the duties of the auditor, quoted above, which focused on verification and vouchers, and stipulated that he should not 'interfere' in the running of the company. The late nineteenth-century orientation of the audit away from fraud detection reflected the developing idea of the auditor as an ally of management (the singular 'client' in the extract above) rather than of small outsider investors. But note also the warning against auditors concentrating only on increasing their income – this would be a lesson that needed to relearned frequently over the coming years.

Robson et al. (2007) develop the idea of the continuing process of professional legitimation – the extension of the field of professional jurisdiction. They perceive it at work in the continuing development of risk-based methods of auditing, which reduce audit time (and hence costs) and can be presented as a business advisory function rather than merely audit testing:

> New business risk audit techniques, and their associated discourses and rationales, can be seen as being intertwined with the status accountants and auditors perceive of themselves and their craft, and with their identity as auditors or, rather, as 'business advisers'.
> *(ibid.: 431)*

They conclude (ibid.: 430) that business risk audit:

> [o]ffered to the audit industry and the profession a new form of rationality and legitimacy for the audit task. It occluded the distinction between audit and business (or value-adding) services in a seeming harmony of interest between auditor and corporate management.

Their analysis is consonant with the interpretation offered by Maltby (1999) and Power (1992) of audit techniques being developed in line with the interests of the audit profession rather than in the service of a timeless notion of best audit practice. From this viewpoint, the argument within the profession about fraud detection may be attributed to divided views about the way forward for the profession. Was the audit client the shareholder, who was served by fraud detection, or the corporate manager who would pay for business advice? The comments by Robson et al. suggest that this dichotomy persists, and is a major contributor to the audit expectations gap.

The function of auditing of course is not confined to the private sector, although for many years academic research tended to focus on that arena. Indeed, the early history of auditing shows that a great deal of effort was expended in developing systems of accountability and audit for governmental expenditure. Research into public sector auditing is further reviewed in the next section.

Audit in the public sector

In one of her Reith Lectures, part of a series titled 'A Question of Trust', O'Neill (2002) attacked the extent to which audit in the public sector had subverted previous relations of trust:

> The idea of audit has been exported from its original financial context to cover ever more detailed scrutiny of non-financial processes and systems … This audit explosion, as Michael Power has so aptly called it, has often displaced or marginalised older systems of accountability.

O'Neill is voicing here a widely held view that public sector audit was a product of the 1980s, part of a 'proliferation' (Power 1994a) which also included the arrival of environmental audit, value for money audit and many others. Power's prolific writing on audit (Power 1994a, 1994b, 1997, 2000a, 2000b, 2003) has promoted the idea of public sector audit as colonisation of 'older systems' by private sector practices. According to Power, the explosion of audit has introduced alien values into the public sector, promoted by a 'rhetoric of accountability' which has imposed a model of financial accountability on a disparate collection of activities and outcomes. The mere fact of undergoing audit, under this new dispensation, confers legitimacy, replacing trustworthiness with submission to inspection. The intrusion of audit, according to Power, leads to a preoccupation with 'making things auditable' by producing quantifiable results, however inappropriate these are to the organisations or activities under inspection.

There is nevertheless scope for this view to be challenged on the basis of the historical development of public sector audit. The fundamental question is how far it is valid to regard audit as a new activity which is necessarily inimical to the objectives of the public sector. Jones and Pendlebury (2000: 233) claim that government audit is 'the oldest aspect of the auditing profession'. Yet public sector audit has not been the subject of as much historical research as corporate audit, although there are a number of relevant studies of various periods and in various contexts.

Descriptions of early government audit do not suggest that it was introduced as a reflection of commercial audit practices. Hoskin and Macve (1986: 113) note that accounting and auditing change took place in 'the administrative arena before ... the merchant world'. The *Dialogus de Scaccario* (1177–9) provides an overview of the internal control and audit methods of the Royal Treasury, giving evidence of concern with systems and of confrontational dialogues between the accountant and the auditor.[10] Exchequer audit was a powerful practice, part of what Hoskin and Macve term an 'examinatorial discourse'. Jones (2008, 2009, 2010) reveals a great deal about how early forms of accounting, audit and division of duties were established in order for the King of England to exercise remote control over the estates he owned but could not personally supervise.

The history of public sector audit between the Middle Ages and the nineteenth century, even more than that of corporate audit, has been neglected by accounting historians: the early modern period has not so far attracted attention. Studies by Funnell (1994, 2004) deal with the resurgence of government audit in the early Victorian period. Funnell points to the importance of government audit as part of the reforms undertaken by Gladstone's government, and to their continuing significance in saving taxpayers' money:

> The purpose of writing this paper is to identify the origins of economy as a concern of modern central government auditors by recognising the irresistible influence ... of the belief that Gladstone, Graham and Trevelyan had in the virtue of economy.
>
> *(Funnell 2004: 28)*

Funnell (2004: 27) suggests that public sector audit's 'arid technicalities' ensured its neglect by government reformers until crisis made it a matter for urgent attention; it may be that the same has been true of historical research in the area.

Work by Coombs and Edwards (1990, 2004) has covered the growth of the local authority audit, again a relatively neglected area despite its long history. They focus on the nineteenth-century development of audit, when there was an urgent need to adapt and to reform practices in response to the pressures of very rapid urban growth. Audit grew in response, in a piecemeal fashion and with various clashes between new and existing structures. The auditor regularly challenged expenditure on the grounds of value for money as well as compliance with regulations.[11] A further complication was the continuing tussle between three groups – the elected ratepayer auditors, government-appointed district auditors, and professional accountants – for auditing municipal corporations. Arguments about democratic representation, efficiency and technical expertise suffused a 'strenuously contested power struggle between vested interests' (Coombs and Edwards 2004: 80) that continued from the early nineteenth century to the 1930s. When the municipal corporations were dissolved in 1974, 202 had moved to professional audit, 119 to district audit and 21 still had elected auditors (ibid.: 82).

The Westminster-style of administration of public finance was exported to the British colonies. Bunn and Gilchrist (2013) examine the early years of the third colony established in Australia, the Swan River Colony. They describe the weaknesses in the system of checks and balances over public finances in the colony brought about through lack of clear direction from central government in London and the paucity of personnel to carry out separate functions. In spite of the potential for loss through misappropriation, Bunn and Gilchrist find no evidence that such loss occurred. This they attribute to the careful appointment to key posts of individuals with the personal qualities of honour and loyalty.

Given space constraints and the endeavour to supply a coherent narrative, this chapter has focused principally on the UK. However, a growing body of research examines the history of audit in other countries, some of which closely follow the Anglo-American model while other work reflects quite different conditions and cultures. Some of this research is reviewed in the next section.

International aspects of auditing

The widely accepted model in writing about audit outside Great Britain is that practices which originated in Great Britain were transmitted overseas, firstly to the US and subsequently to the Empire/Commonwealth, to Europe and finally to the developing world and to the former Communist countries of Eastern Europe and Asia.

The US

Moyer (1951: 3) states that 'The first audits in America were of course patterned after the British general model' because of the influence of British auditors retained by British investors. The pattern of US and British work diverged at the end of the nineteenth century, according to Moyer, because 'bookkeeper audits' on the British model, with 'endless checking of postings' were too expensive for the US. Moyer (1951: 7) ascribes the growth of sampling and systems in the US to the profession's need to demonstrate value for money. Flesher et al. (2005) contest Moyer's premise that US practice derived from UK corporate audit. They suggest that audit activity had begun in the seventeenth century with the companies financing settlers, and continued through the colonial period, with a government auditor appointed by Congress in 1789 (ibid.: 22–6). In the nineteenth century, the growth of the road, canal and railway companies produced a demand for accounting and audit which generated 'a pool of talent' (ibid.: 36) for the new profession. Feeney (2013: 3) provides examples of early railway audits although he certainly exaggerates when he claims that early in the nineteenth century 'the concept of an external audit just did not exist'. Nevertheless, it was not until 1898 that the first auditor's report on a US railway company was published. For much of the twentieth century US railroad companies appear to have been exempt from the sort of regulations that were mandating other companies not only to publish financial statement but also to have them audited. As the century wore on, much as happened elsewhere and in other industries, railroad companies increasingly opted voluntarily to publish audited financial statements.

One problem which, although not unique to the US, was certainly felt more keenly there than elsewhere, was the pressure placed on audit firm employees because so many clients had the same year end, December 31. To cope with the workload, through the first half of the twentieth century, audit firms would recruit armies of temporary audit clerks. The American Institute of Accountants (AIA) championed a more satisfactory solution by encouraging corporations to select their natural business year rather than the calendar year as their accounting period. Doron (2013) credits the AIA with taking a leading role in setting up the Natural Business Year Council. It was claimed that spreading the workload more evenly over the year would improve the quality of audits. To some extent the campaign was successful as a number of corporations did change their year ends. Audit firms also began to develop more formalised interim audit procedures. However, it was not until the 1960s that US firms no longer used temporary audit staff.

Perhaps some of the most interesting research about the development of audit internationally focuses on issues that arise when new practices are introduced to existing structures and norms. Some of the varied instances of this phenomenon are discussed below.

Germany

Evans (2003) and Quick (2005) trace the history of the German auditing profession and point to significant differences between the Anglo-American and German regimes: the long-established limited liability partnerships in Germany, the specialisation of audit firms and the low level of auditor liability. They stress the extent to which these features are embedded in the history of corporate governance in Germany – the key role played by banks as both shareholders and investors thereby reducing the separation of ownership from control. Evans (2003: 56) quotes a German lawyer who commented in 1930 that 'the "auditors" of the English law have to fulfil a large part of the functions of the German supervisory board'. Gietzmann and Quick (1998: 81), in their discussion of proposed changes in auditor liability in the European Union, make the point that audit is embedded in a 'model of corporate governance' and that one feature of audit cannot sensibly be changed without considering the corporate governance system as a whole. This is an issue that recurs in other studies of international change.

France

Praquin (2012) charts the growth of limited liability companies in France from the early nineteenth century to the middle of the twentieth. The development of the audit function was fraught with confusion about the exact nature and purpose of the audit – was it simply to verify the profit figure from which dividends could be paid, or was it also appropriate for auditors to comment on operational matters within the company (effectively to interfere in the management)? Praquin casts doubt on both the independence and competence of auditors. These key audit qualities were neither defined in the statutory regulations nor through jurisprudence. It was not until the mid-1930s that legislation was introduced to modernise the conception of the audit function. Fournès Dattin (2014) uses two case studies of French companies whose auditors in the late nineteenth and early twentieth centuries were quite clearly more concerned with maintaining good relations with management rather than acting as guardians of the shareholders' interests. In a later paper, Fournès Dattin (2017a) again illustrates her analysis of developments within the French profession using these two major companies. She describes the resistance felt by men of business to the idea of outside auditors who may be critical of management. Against this sort of attitude, French accountants had to battle to achieve the professional kudos that their British counterparts had enjoyed for many years. It would be late in the twentieth century before some parity was obtained.

Fournès Dattin returns to the subject of independence when considering whether European Union proposals to introduce mandatory auditor rotation would be likely to assist French auditors in achieving greater independence from management (Fournès Dattin 2017b). On balance, she concludes that such a move would not be effective since France, unlike many other countries, already has an effective auditor rotation regime as well as a ban on non-audit services and a system of joint audits.

Scandinavia

Holm (2014) examines how the regulatory regime over the auditing profession developed in Denmark. Although, as elsewhere, the practice of some form of audit had been carried out for centuries, it was not until the early years of the twentieth century that regulations were proposed to cover the competence and effectiveness of corporate auditing. Initially these were resisted by a senior government minister who later became embroiled in a massive fraud for which he was convicted and jailed. A system of dual auditors (which required one of the two to be a state authorised auditor) was introduced and remained in place until 2005. Holm traces the regulatory response to fraud cases and the evolution of enhanced auditor responsibilities in relation to fraud through legislation, case law and the findings of professional disciplinary tribunals.

Öhman and Wallerstedt (2012) trace developments in the rise of the auditing profession in Sweden, noting that progressive steps were often taken only after scandals and crises had prompted action (as in Denmark and elsewhere). Although there is evidence that voluntary audits were performed from the seventeenth century onwards, as in Britain, company auditing really only began to be significant from the middle of the nineteenth century. In the absence of criteria over independence and competence, however, it remains doubtful whether this activity was very effective. Öhman and Wallerstedt report that most Swedish companies were being voluntarily audited by the end of the nineteenth century. They also note the existence of a legal requirement that auditors examine the management's administration of the company. The Swedish auditing profession developed through the twentieth century mirroring in many ways changes that had been introduced in the British professional bodies, for example, making the occupation a full-time one and requiring adequate education and training. Such steps must have improved the quality of Swedish practitioners but were not sufficient a safeguard to unmask the Ivar Kreuger fraud (it was Kreuger's suicide in 1932 which initiated a full investigation). When it was discovered that the auditor was an employee of Kreuger's and had signed the audit report without having done any audit work, there was an outcry. The Swedish professional body woke to the need for a more explicit code of ethics and rules began to be issued from 1933. More importantly, the Swedish authorities took tighter control of the licensing of audit practitioners. The protected market that Swedish auditors had enjoyed for much of the twentieth century began to be eroded when the small company audit exemption was introduced in 2010. This forced Swedish audit firms to become more commercial. Despite this changed environment, Broberg et al. (2018) nevertheless find from their survey of Swedish auditors that generally a sense of professional identity has not been eclipsed by loyalty to the firm they work for. They also find that auditors from the Big Four audit firms are more likely to be commercially driven, perhaps reflecting the greater emphasis on commercialism ingrained in the culture of those firms.

Japan

Matsumoto and Previts (2010) explore how the concept of the audit of corporate financial statements has evolved in a fundamentally different way in Japan. At the end of the nineteenth century regulations in the form of a Commercial Code (CC) were introduced to establish company auditors, but these individuals were closely linked to the companies that they audited since most corporate finance was provided by a relatively small group of investors. The needs of these investors centred on both accounting and operational issues which the CC auditor was expected to address. There was at the time no active stock market demanding the provision of reliable financial information to prospective investors. Despite the flaws in this system revealed by a number of corporate scandals, regulatory change was slow in coming. It was not until the middle of the twentieth century that Japan introduced a Western-style external audit – the Securities and Exchange Law (SEL) audit. Both forms of audit (CC and SEL) operated side by side giving rise to a 'dual system' of audit.

China

Lu et al. (2009) look at the difficulties caused by the simultaneous arrivals of corporate audit and of new corporate structures under different regimes in China during the twentieth century. As China has become a global economic player it has moved towards the Western model of accounting and in some respects auditing too, although it retains some unique features. For example, Lu et al. consider that if there has been any regulatory capture over the discipline of accounting it has been by government bureaucrats rather than accounting practitioners.

Tang et al. (1999) focus on the problems of introducing audit to the newly privatised state-owned enterprises during the 1980s and 1990s. They point to a shortage of audit staff, a mismatch between the commercial state-owned enterprises and the governmental auditors, and the change in the role of audit, from monitoring compliance with rules to verification of statements. Changes in regulation are found to be ineffectual if they do not address the network of structures and expectations that already exist.

Eastern Europe

Sucher and Zelenka (1998) outline the problems caused in the Czech Republic by the rapid transition to a market economy. Audit prior to 'marketisation' had taken the form of internal managerial 'revision' or of state control, in either case aimed at ensuring compliance with regulations. The adjustment to an audit based on systems review and an opinion on truth and fairness was problematical, partly because of the shortage of staff with relevant training, and partly because of clients' expectations of audit. They quote an auditor's comment that '[Czech companies] see the objective of the audit as the tax return' (ibid.: 739), and note that audit continues to be associated with regulatory inspection (ibid.: 740).

Similar issues are raised in papers by Bychkova (1996) and Mennicken (2006) about the development of audit in Russia after the collapse of the Soviet Union. Here again, audit is based on a tradition of state inspection and control (Bychkova 1996: 78–83). The arrival of an audit regime based on international standards demands the development of a new profession and client understanding of, and demand for, a new mode of audit. Mennicken (2006: 1) suggests that new audit regulations have not necessarily arisen in response to investor demand, but rather as part of a drive towards modernisation and globalisation: a means of 'integrating the Russian economy into the international marketplace'. The absence of stable regulatory institutions means that there is no framework within which audit activity can be anchored. She concludes that 'the Russian auditing profession has emerged on the basis of highly rationalised and idealised imaginations of market-oriented development that are not tailored to the context of Russia's transitional economy' (ibid.: 27).

Case studies can be an effective means of highlighting interesting developments especially if they can be shown to have had some lasting effects or legacy. Some examples are provided in the next section.

Case studies

Heier and Leach-López (2010) tell the story of a mill in the US that was the victim of a fraud committed by a trusted individual on secondment from the company's auditors. They claim that an indirect effect of the revelation of this fraud in the late 1930s brought about renewed and improved institutional concerns with matters such as auditor independence, the need for greater supervision of an audit firm's employees and a greater awareness that client management should accept its responsibility for the accuracy of its financial statements even if it is buying in help from its audit firm.

In the Hudson's Bay Company, audit arrangements were first put in place in 1866 even though the company had been in operation since 1670 (Spraakman 2011). The familiar dual auditor system was established with one auditor representing the interests of the shareholders and another looking after the interests of the management. In the first three years, the auditors prepared as well as audited the financial statements. Thereafter, although the establishment of an audit was brought about by shareholder pressure, only the management's auditor was left in place and he only acted as auditor, no longer taking part in the accounts preparation. That this individual happened to be William Quilter, one of the most respected practitioners in Victorian Britain, probably allayed any concern on the part of the shareholders.

The dangers of auditors being too close to those whose statements they audit are shown in the case of the Scottish brewer, R. D. Sharp Ltd (Sangster and Gibb 2017). In this case the auditor, a chartered accountant, who happened also to be an investor in the business, appears to have allowed quite blatant manipulations of the measurement of accounting profit while hiding behind cleverly crafted words that seem designed to protect him (in the manner of the Royal Mail case – see Chapters 8 and 20) from liability should the worst happen.

A lack of independence and what we would now call 'professional scepticism' is demonstrated in a case involving a Victorian auditor connected with one of the most notorious financial scandals of the age, the collapse of the London and General Bank and the Liberator Building Society. Although a good deal has been written about the individual at the heart of the fraud, Jabez Balfour, rather less is known about his acolytes and the external auditors who allowed the publication of balance sheets that they knew to be misleading. Chandler and Macniven (2014) report how the failure of the auditors, who were chartered accountants, brought discredit to the whole profession. 'What is the value of an audit?' was a popular headline during the debate about the scandal. That one of the auditors was a spiritualist who believed in the ability of a medium to communicate with the souls of dead relatives received almost no attention, perhaps because his beliefs were shared by many others at the time.

Antonelli et al. (2017) produce what they claim is the first English language case of auditing in an Italian private company, the Leopolda Railroad Company. Following the design of Robert Stephenson, work began in 1841 and when it was finished seven years later, the line ran from Livorno to Florence. Antonelli et al. unearth some interesting facts about the appointment of the auditor, a post which was often contested, the details of the audit work actually performed, the errors that the auditors found and their suggestions for improvements in running the company. In the 15-year period examined, the company's auditors' reports varied in length from 19 to 55 pages. Their reports had a standard heading but that was as far as uniformity went – each year's report was a unique specimen.

One of the less well-known cases of audit failure occurring right at the end of the twentieth century is examined by Agostini and Favero (2017). They dissect the machinations of the CEO of Sunbeam, an Arthur Andersen audit client. The authors coin the term 'creative auditing' to denote actions by auditors which, even if they are legal, are not considered ethical and which amount effectively to colluding with management. One facet of the Sunbeam case which is particularly noteworthy, once the accounting manipulations had been discovered, is the 'scapegoating' of the CEO rather than the auditors, as is usually the case. However, Sunbeam was just one of a long list of Andersen clients found to have produced misleading financial statements.

Conclusion and directions for further research

This chapter, in a necessarily brief and selective survey of historical work on auditing, has attempted to do two things. One is to draw attention to the main elements of historical writing to date, and the other to provoke further inquiry.

Humphrey (2008), writing about the same time as the publication of the first edition of this book, set out an agenda for the future direction of auditing research and, even though more than ten years have now elapsed, many of his ideas retain currency. He decried the domination of quantitative research papers based on US data in what are regarded as the leading accounting journals. He urged researchers to become more involved in qualitative research into, for example, the political nature of standard-setting (auditing as well as accounting) and to question the grounds on which standard-setters claimed legitimacy. While acknowledging the difficulties of obtaining inside information about the true nature of audit practice, he suggested that more could be done by researchers to get into the mechanics of actual auditing procedures and approaches, perhaps using the reports of the disciplinary processes (and, one could add, published law reports where the question of auditor negligence is being contested) and using case studies as a way of better informing those outside the audit firms.

Another of the major gaps in knowledge is that we know very little about the shareholder audits of joint-stock and limited companies during the middle of the nineteenth century, and hence little about the expectations that were brought to bear on the first professional corporate auditors. In addition, and perhaps more curiously, there is very little research into audit from the early twentieth century until its end.[12] The scandals that occurred in the last decade of the twentieth century and the first decade of the twenty-first (BCCI, Enron and the Global Financial Crisis 2007–8) have attracted a great deal of interest (see, for instance, O'Connell 2004; Carnegie and Napier 2010; and *Accounting, Organizations and Society* 2009, 34 (6/7)). Nevertheless, this period in time offers many opportunities for further research.

The development of audit and the legal and professional controversies of the mid- to late nineteenth centuries, as they appeared in the press and in textbooks, have been thoroughly researched. However, little is known about the nature of the work undertaken, as distinct from the debate about it. Subject to the limitations of existing material, there is a strong case for attempting further research to enrich our knowledge of actual audit practice.

Another major area that deserves further investigation is that of public sector audit. Power's writing on the subject (e.g. Power 1994a) is part of a large literature about its potentially disruptive arrival at the end of the twentieth century. Little work has been done about its earlier presence and impact, although existing studies (e.g. Coombs and Edwards 1990) suggest that it played an important, though contested, part in government from a much earlier date.

Auditing is an activity that appears capable of resisting severe challenges. In 2001 the collapse of Enron and the complicity of its auditors in misleading the public were claimed to have had a catastrophic effect on the reputation of both auditors and audit (O'Connell 2004; Carnegie and Napier 2010). During the Global Financial Crisis, a rather glib and perhaps complacent comment was made to the effect that the 'auditing profession was having a good crisis' insomuch as most of the criticism at that stage was aimed at the bankers. That began to change in the UK with the parliamentary investigations into the role of auditors in the banking crisis (House of Lords 2011) and the EU initiatives aimed at further strengthening auditor independence (see ICAEW 2016). Serious questioning of the value of the audit function and the conduct of the Big Four continues (see Brooks 2018). An examination of how the professional bodies and the large accounting firms responded to the crisis and subsequent criticism of the structure of the audit market and the independence of auditors would be a fruitful area for future research.

One of the abiding challenges for historians, in whatever context, is to understand and to explain why auditors, in the aftermath of a financial scandal, have so often been made the scapegoats (for one explanation, see Guénin-Paracini and Gendron 2010) and, paradoxically, how the auditing profession, despite a lengthy history of 'audit failure', continues to display such extraordinary resilience.

Herda and Herda (2016) lament the lack of positive news stories on auditors and auditing. They suggest that, whereas conventional auditing text books emphasise past cases where auditors got it wrong, more should be done to make students and the public aware of the audit success stories. We rarely hear of such cases but, one imagines, there must be many of them. The problem is that auditors do not tend to blow their own trumpets and in many cases could not even if they wanted to for fear of breaching duties of client confidentiality. How are we, as researchers, to get the inside story? Fewer accounting academics these days have any direct experience of auditing and, therefore, may lack the credentials and contacts to convince audit firms that it is safe to let them peer inside the 'black box' of auditing. Without such cooperation from practitioners, making the auditor into a 'hero', should they hypothesise that to be the case, is another challenge for the next generation of researchers.

Key works

Chandler and Edwards (1996) is a useful introduction to the growing literature on late-Victorian audit. It reviews the existence, from the late nineteenth century onwards, of controversies about problems of audit independence, the expectations gap, reporting and regulation.

Fournès Dattin (2014, 2017a, 2017b) presents an insight into the evolution of company auditing in France. At a time when the effect of EU regulations over auditor independence is being felt most keenly, it is enlightening to see how the French approach to auditing has developed.

Jones (2008, 2009, 2010) examines the details of the accountability and audit arrangements of the medieval system of the governance of Britain, with particular emphasis on the financial management and controls exercised over the Kingdom.

Mennicken (2006) studies the significance of the introduction of international audit practice as part of a wider economic and social change being attempted within Russia. The paper is particularly interesting as a basis for discussing initiatives for globalising audit practices.

Napier (1998) discusses the close relationships between audit and law and between audit and corporate governance, and the need to understand the auditor's role within changing systems of corporate governance.

Watts and Zimmerman (1983) introduced the widely cited argument that audit has arisen as a voluntary response to agency problems in firms rather than because of legislative requirements.

Notes

1 Josephine Maltby sadly passed away in 2017 before she could revise this chapter. It is a great honour for me to be invited by the editors to update Jo's work. I have kept the same structure and much of the content of the original piece while trying to reflect more recent additions to the literature. I hope that I have done so in a way that does not detract from Jo's intelligent and insightful style of writing.
2 This chapter focuses principally on the modern corporate audit although there is some discussion of prior developments on manorial estates, as is also the case in Chapter 5.
3 See, for instance, Fleischman and Radcliffe (2005) and Chapters 1–3 of this book.
4 See Lee (1989) for an overview of the prior, sparse writing on the history of audit.
5 Jones' discussion does not examine the witnesses' occupations. These may have had an impact on their support for audit, to the extent that the advocates of audit were suppliers, rather than users, of information.
6 See also Chapter 12 on the importance of audit for the development of the accounting profession.
7 See Edwards et al. (2007) on the 'jurisdictional battle' waged by the professional against, for instance, the shareholder auditor in the mid-nineteenth century, and Sikka and Willmott (1995) on the relationship between professional jurisdiction and independence.
8 See Harvey (1994: 101–5) for a detailed exposition of the managerial function of the audit.
9 Bryer points out (1991: 459) that railway audits were described during the mania of 1845 as 'the greatest farce possible … arithmetical rather than judicial' and 'a mere child's play'.
10 See Baxter (1994, esp. 223–8) for a description of the highly ritualised process of the audit.
11 See, for instance, Coombs and Edwards (1990: 161, 168) on clashes between district auditors and first poor law unions and later town councils on this matter.
12 One rare study is that by Matthews (2005) of the audit failures which preceded the collapse of London and County Securities Bank in 1973.

References

A.E. (1883) Accountants: their duties and responsibilities, *The Accountant*, January 6: 5–6.

Agostini, M. and Favero, G. (2017) Accounting fraud, business failure and creative auditing: a microanalysis of the strange case of the Sunbeam Corporation, *Accounting History*, 22 (4): 472–87.

Antonelli, V., D'Alessio, R. and Cafaro, E.M. (2017) Auditing practices from a historical perspective: the case study of an Italian railroad company in the mid-19th century, *Accounting Historians Journal*, 44 (1): 17–34.

Armstrong, P. (1991) Contradiction and social dynamics in the capitalist agency relationship, *Accounting, Organizations and Society*, 16 (1): 1–25.

Baxter, W.T. (1994) Early accounting: the tally and the checker-board, in R.H. Parker and B.S. Yamey (eds) *Accounting History. Some British Contributions*, pp. 197–235 (Oxford: Clarendon Press).

Broberg, P., Umans, T., Skog, P. and Theodorsson, E. (2018) Auditors' professional and organizational identities and commercialization in audit firms, *Accounting, Auditing & Accountability Journal*, 31 (2): 374–99.

Brooks, R. (2018) *Bean Counters: The Triumph of the Accountants and How They Broke Capitalism* (London: Atlantic Books).

Brown, R.G. (1962) Changing audit objectives and techniques, *Accounting Review*, 37 (4): 696–703.

Bryer, R.A. (1991) Accounting for the 'railway mania' of 1845 – a great railway swindle? *Accounting, Organizations and Society*, 16 (5/6): 439–86.

Bryer, R.A. (2000) The history of accounting and the transition to capitalism in England. Part two: evidence, *Accounting, Organizations and Society*, 25 (4/5): 327–81.

Bunn, M. and Gilchrist, D.J. (2013) 'A few good men': public sector audit in the Swan River Colony, 1828–1835, *Accounting History*, 18 (2): 193–209.

Bychkova, S. (1996) The development and status of auditing in Russia, *European Accounting Review*, 5 (1): 77–90.

Carnegie, G.D. and Napier, C.J. (2010) Traditional accountants and business professionals: portraying the accounting profession after Enron, *Accounting, Organizations and Society*, 35 (3): 360–76.

Chandler, R.A. (1997) Judicial views on auditing from the nineteenth century, *Accounting History*, 2 (1): 61–80.

Chandler, R.A. and Edwards, J.R. (1996) Recurring issues in auditing: back to the future? *Accounting, Auditing & Accountability Journal*, 9 (2): 4–29.

Chandler, R. A. and Fry, N. (2005) Audit failure, litigation, and insurance in early twentieth century Britain, *Accounting History*, 10 (3): 13–38.

Chandler, R.A., Edwards, J.R. and Anderson, M. (1993) Changing perceptions of the role of the company auditor, 1840–1940, *Accounting and Business Research*, 23 (92): 443–59.

Chandler, R.A. and Macniven, L. (2014) The unusual tale of an auditing spiritualist, *Accounting History*, 19 (3): 333–49.

Collier, P. (1996) The rise of the audit committee in UK companies: a curious phenomenon? *Accounting, Business & Financial History*, 6 (2): 121–40.

Coombs, H.M. and Edwards, J.R. (1990) The evolution of the district audit, *Financial Accountability and Management*, 6 (3): 153–76.

Coombs, H.M. and Edwards, J.R. (2004) The audit of municipal corporations – a quest for professional dominance, *Managerial Auditing Journal*, 19 (1): 68–83.

Dobija, D. (2018) The early evolution of corporate control and auditing: the English East India Company (1600–1640), *Accounting, Auditing & Accountability Journal*, 31 (1): 214–36.

Doron, M.E. (2013) The American Institute of Accountants and the professionalization of auditing: the campaign to end temporary audit staff and promote the natural business year, 1923–1960, *Accounting History*, 18 (2): 257–69.

Edwards, J.R. (1989) *A History of Financial Accounting* (London: Routledge).

Edwards, J.R. (2019) *A History of Corporate Financial Reporting in Britain* (London: Routledge).

Edwards, J.R., Anderson, M. and Chandler, R. (2007) Claiming a jurisdiction for the 'public accountant' in England prior to organisational fusion, *Accounting, Organizations and Society*, 32 (1/2): 65–104.

Evans, L. (2003) Auditing and audit firms in Germany before 1931, *Accounting Historians Journal*, 30 (1): 28–65.

Feeney, K. (2013) Railroad audits: some arrived ahead of schedule, *Accounting Historians Journal*, 40 (1): 1–30.

Fleischman, R.K. and Radcliffe, V.S. (2005) The roaring nineties: accounting history comes of age, *Accounting Historians Journal*, 32 (1): 61–110.

Flesher, D.L., Previts, G.J. and Samson, W.D. (2005) Auditing in the United States: a historical perspective, *Abacus*, 41 (1): 21–39.

Forrester, D.A.R. (1994) Early canal company accounts: financial and accounting aspects of the Forth and Clyde Navigation, 1768–1816, in R.H. Parker and B.S. Yamey (eds) *Accounting History. Some British Contributions*, pp. 297–326 (Oxford: Clarendon Press).

Fournès Dattin, C. (2014) The practice of statutory auditing in France (1867–1935): the case of *Pont-à-Mousson* and *Saint-Gobain* companies, *Accounting History*, 19 (3): 351–68.

Fournès Dattin, C. (2017a) The emergence of statutory auditing in France and the recurring issues of independence and competence, 1867–1966, *Accounting History*, 22 (2): 193–213.

Fournès Dattin, C. (2017b) Developments in France regarding the mandatory rotation of auditors: do they enhance auditors' independence? *Accounting History*, 22 (1): 44–66.

Funnell, W. (1994) Independence and the state auditor in Britain: a constitutional keystone or a case of reified imagery? *Abacus*, 30 (2): 175–95.

Funnell, W. (2004) Victorian parsimony and the early champions of modern public sector audit, *Accounting History*, 9 (1): 25–60.

Gietzmann, M.B. and Quick, R. (1998) Capping auditor liability: the German experience, *Accounting, Organizations and Society*, 23 (1): 81–103.

Grout, P., Jewitt, I., Pong, C. and Whittington, G. (1994) 'Auditor professional judgement': implications for regulation and the law, *Economic Policy*, 9 (2): 308–51.

Guénin-Paracini, H. and Gendron, Y. (2010) Auditors as modern pharmakoi: legitimacy paradoxes and the production of economic order, *Critical Perspectives on Accounting*, 21 (2): 134–58.

Harvey, P.D.A. (1994) Manorial accounts, in R.H. Parker and B.S. Yamey (eds) *Accounting History. Some British Contributions*, pp. 91–115 (Oxford: Clarendon Press).

Heier, J.R. and Leach-López, M.A. (2010) Development of modern auditing standards: the strange case of Raymond Marien and the fraud at Interstate Hosiery Mills, 1934–1937, *Accounting Historians Journal*, 37 (2): 67–93.

Herda, D.N. and Herda, J.N. (2016) Take the good with the bad: a Girardian recommendation for auditing pedagogy, *Accounting Historians Journal*, 43 (1): 158–63.

Holm, C. (2014) Civil and common law influences on the Danish auditor's responsibilities in relation to fraud, *Accounting History Review*, 24 (1): 7–26.

Hopwood, A.G. (1977) Editorial, *Accounting, Organizations and Society*, 2 (4): 277–8.

Hoskin, K.W. and Macve, R.H. (1986) Accounting and the examination: a genealogy of disciplinary power, *Accounting, Organizations and Society*, 11 (2): 105–36.

House of Lords. (2011) *Economic Affairs Committee – Second Report – Auditors: Market Concentration and their Role*. Available HTTP: <https://publications.parliament.uk/pa/ld201011/ldselect/ldeconaf/119/11902.htm#evidence>.

Humphrey, C. (2008) Auditing research: a review across the disciplinary divide, *Accounting, Auditing & Accountability Journal*, 21 (2): 170–203.

Humphrey, C., Moizer, P. and Turley, S. (1992) The audit expectations gap – plus ça change, plus c'est la même chose? *Critical Perspectives on Accounting*, 3 (2): 137–61.

ICAEW. (2005) *Audit Quality: Agency Theory and the Role of Audit* (London: ICAEW).

ICAEW. (2016) *Implementation of European Audit Reforms*. Available HTTP: <www.icaew.com/technical/ethics/auditor-independence/implementation-of-european-audit-reforms>.

Jones, E. (1981) *Accountancy and the British Economy 1840–1980: The Evolution of Ernst & Whinney* (London: Batsford).

Jones, M.J. (2008) Internal control, accountability and corporate governance: medieval and modern Britain compared, *Accounting, Auditing & Accountability Journal*, 21 (7): 1052–75.

Jones, M.J. (2009) Origins of medieval Exchequer accounting, *Accounting, Business & Financial History*, 19 (3): 259–85.

Jones, M.J. (2010) Sources of power and infrastructural conditions in medieval governmental accounting, *Accounting, Organizations and Society*, 35 (1): 81–94.

Jones, R. and Pendlebury, M. (2000) *Public Sector Accounting*, 5th edn (Harlow: Pearson).

Jones, S. (1995) A cross-sectional analysis of recommendations for company financial disclosure and auditing by nineteenth-century parliamentary witnesses, *Accounting, Business & Financial History*, 5 (2): 159–86.

Lee, T.A. (1989) *The Evolution of Audit Thought and Practice* (London: Taylor & Francis).

Lee, T.A. (1993) *Corporate Audit Theory* (London: Chapman & Hall).

Lu, W., Ji, X-d. and Aiken, M. (2009) Governmental influences in the development of Chinese accounting during the modern era, *Accounting, Business & Financial History*, 19 (3): 305–26.

Maltby, J. (1999) 'A sort of guide, philosopher and friend': the rise of the professional auditor in Britain, *Accounting, Business & Financial History*, 9 (1): 29–50.

Matsumoto, Y. and Previts, G.J. (2010) The dual audit system for joint stock companies in Japan, *Accounting, Business & Financial History*, 20 (3): 317–26.

Matthews, D. (2005) London and County Securities: a case study in audit and regulatory failure, *Accounting, Auditing & Accountability Journal*, 18 (4): 518–36.

Matthews, D., Anderson, M. and Edwards, J.R. (1998) *The Priesthood of Industry: The Rise of the Professional Accountant in British Management* (Oxford: Oxford University Press).

Mennicken, A. (2006) Changing rationalities of government: the rise of audit professionalism in post-Soviet Russia. Paper presented at Eighth Interdisciplinary Perspectives on Accounting Conference, Cardiff, 10–12 July.

Miller, P. and Napier, C.J. (1993) Genealogies of calculation, *Accounting, Organizations and Society*, 18 (7/8): 631–47.

Moyer, C.A. (1951) Early developments in American auditing, *Accounting Review*, 26 (1): 3–8.

Napier, C.J. (1998) Intersections of law and accountancy: unlimited auditor liability in the United Kingdom, *Accounting, Organizations and Society*, 23 (1): 105–28.

Napier, C.J. (2006) Accounts of change: 30 years of historical accounting research, *Accounting, Organizations and Society*, 31 (4/5): 445–507.

Nielsen, O. (1960) New challenges in accounting, *Accounting Review*, 35 (4): 583–9.

Nikkinen, J. and Petri, S. (2004) Does agency theory provide a general framework for audit pricing? *International Journal of Auditing*, 8 (3): 253–62.

Nouri, H. and Lombardi, D. (2009) Auditors' independence: an analysis of Montgomery's auditing textbooks in the 20th Century, *Accounting Historians Journal*, 36 (1): 81–112.

O'Connell, B.T. (2004) Enron. Con: 'he that filches from me my good name … makes me poor indeed', *Critical Perspectives on Accounting*, 15 (6/7): 733–49.

Odlyzko, A. (2011) The collapse of the railway mania, the development of capital markets, and the forgotten role of Robert Lucas Nash, *Accounting History Review*, 21 (3): 309–45.

Öhman, P. and Wallerstedt, E. (2012) Audit regulation and the development of the auditing profession: the case of Sweden, *Accounting History*, 17 (2): 241–57.

O'Neill, O. (2002) A question of trust, Reith lectures, Available HTTP: <www.bbc.co.uk/radio4/reith2002/lecture3.shtml> (accessed 17 September 2018).

Oschinsky, D. (1971) *Walter of Henley and Other Treatises on Estate Management and Accounting* (Oxford: Clarendon Press).

O'Sullivan, N. (1993) Auditors' liability: its role in the corporate governance debate, *Accounting and Business Research*, 23 (91A): 412–20.

Popp, A. (2000) Specialty production, personal capitalism and auditors' reports: Mintons Ltd, c.1870–1900, *Accounting, Business & Financial History*, 10 (3): 347–69.

Power, M. (1994a) *The Audit Explosion* (London: Demos).

Power, M. (1994b) The audit society, in A.G. Hopwood and P. Miller (eds) *Accounting as Social and Institutional Practice*, pp. 299–316 (Cambridge: Cambridge University Press).

Power, M. (1997) *The Audit Society: Rituals of Verification* (Oxford: Oxford University Press).

Power, M. (2000a) Editorial – exploring the audit society, *International Journal of Auditing*, 4 (1): 1.

Power, M. (2000b) The audit society: second thoughts, *International Journal of Auditing*, 4 (1): 111–19.

Power, M. (2003) Evaluating the audit explosion, *Law & Policy*, 25 (3): 185–202.

Power, M.K. (1992) From common sense to expertise: reflections on the prehistory of audit sampling, *Accounting, Organizations and Society*, 17 (1): 37–62.

Praquin, N. (2012) Commercial legislation and the emergence of corporate auditing in France, 1856–1935, *Accounting History Review*, 22 (2): 161–89.

Quick, R. (2005) The formation and early development of German audit firms, *Accounting, Business & Financial History*, 15 (3): 317–43.

Roberts, D.H. (2010) Changing legitimacy narratives about professional ethics and independence in the 1930's journal of accountancy, *Accounting Historians Journal*, 37 (2): 95–122.

Robson, K., Humphrey, C., Khalifa, R. and Jones, J. (2007) Transforming audit technologies: business risk audit methodologies and the audit field, *Accounting, Organizations and Society*, 32 (4/5): 409–38.

Sangster, A. and Gibb, F. (2017) Earnings management, ultra vires borrowing, and auditing of a Scottish brewery 1884–1927, *Accounting Historians Journal*, 44 (2): 1–15.

Select Committee on the amending of railways acts as to the audit of accounts. (1849) House of Lords, third report, BPP 1849, x, 469.

Sikka, P. and Willmott, H. (1995) The power of 'independence': defending and extending the jurisdiction of accounting in the United Kingdom, *Accounting, Organizations and Society*, 20 (6): 547–81.

Spraakman, G.F. (2011) The first external auditors of the Hudson's Bay Company, 1866, *Accounting Historians Journal*, 38 (1): 57–80.

Sucher, P. and Zelenka, I. (1998) The development of the role of the audit in the Czech Republic, *European Accounting Review*, 7 (4): 723–51.

Tang, Q., Chow, C.W. and Lau, A. (1999) Auditing of state-owned enterprises in China: historic development, current practice and emerging issues, *International Journal of Accounting*, 34 (2): 173–87.

Teo, E. and Cobbin, P. (2005) A revisitation of the 'audit expectations gap': judicial and practitioner views on the role of the auditor in late-Victorian England, *Accounting History*, 10 (2): 35–66.

Toms, J.S. (2002) The rise of modern accounting and the fall of the public company: the Lancashire cotton mills 1870–1914, *Accounting, Organizations and Society*, 27 (1/2): 61–84.

Watts, R.L. and Zimmerman, J.L. (1983) Agency problems, auditing, and the theory of the firm: some evidence, *Journal of Law and Economics*, 26 (4): 613–34.

PART IV

Institutions

11
PROFESSIONALISATION

Chris Poullaos and Carlos Ramirez

Overview

In Chapter 3 professionalisation was identified as an important research area in accounting history. The aim of this chapter is to examine the major themes and findings of the academic research published in this area since the early 1980s. The chapter tracks the geographical spread of professional organisation. It shows that professionalisation processes are diverse. England and Scotland were pioneers in a professionalisation movement that was exported in the late nineteenth and early twentieth centuries via the relays of empire and international capital. Professional organisation outside of the Anglo-American world would assume a different pattern, most notably in continental Europe. More recently, processes of regional integration and globalisation have contributed to a further transformation of the profession's structure and identity. The chapter also evidences that the construction of this identity, envisaged as the outcome of professionalisation endeavours, is intimately connected with the broader social context within which it occurs. In this respect histories of professionalisation fall squarely within the 'new' accounting history and the tradition of socio-historical accounting research discussed in Chapter 2. This chapter provides an overview of the motivations, elements and outcomes of professionalisation at various times and places, and discusses the key institutions (within the occupation and outside it) involved in initiating, supporting, opposing and otherwise shaping professionalisation processes. We touch upon the following themes:

- the meaning and significance of 'profession', 'professionalisation' and the importance of organisation;
- explanations for the 'success' or 'failure' of particular professionalisation endeavours;
- internal divisions and competition within the occupation and rivalry with other occupations;
- the role of symbols, credentials and designations;
- relationships between the profession and the institutions of state and market;
- professionalisation and social structure;
- imperialism, globalisation and professionalisation.

Introduction

From the second half of the nineteenth century strenuous efforts were made to organise the occupation of accountancy as a profession with a view to participating, to a greater or lesser degree, in the enhanced wealth, social status and power of ancient professions such as physicians and lawyers. From this perspective professionalisation refers to actions and processes undertaken to achieve the status of professional and to subsequently maintain and enhance that status through professionalism. These processes take time and they change over time.

The professionalisation of accountancy is usually presented as having its origin in the Anglo-American world. The first modern professional accountants emerged in Scotland, their formal organisations becoming visible in the 1850s. Accountants in England and Wales followed in the 1870s and Ireland in the 1880s. By the end of the twentieth century a British accountancy arena had emerged. By then, Britain was the major imperial power and self-governing settler communities had become established in Canada, Australia and elsewhere. As well as being a significant industrial and trading nation, Britain was also a major supplier of international finance. British accountants followed British capital across the empire and beyond. Some settled where capital had led them and became important contributors to local accountancy professions which, although modelled on British exemplars, developed their own momentum and history. By around 1910 an imperial accountancy arena was starting to emerge. Also, by this time an American accountancy profession had become established with its own distinctive trajectory.

Even though the bulk of the historiography published in English on the professionalisation of accountants concerns what could be loosely defined as the Anglo-American world (i.e. countries that at some point in their history were under the rule or influence of Britain or the United States), the production of histories of the profession in 'non-Anglo-American countries' has gained momentum. Continental Europe (including the former colonial powers of France, Belgium and the Netherlands), Latin America, the ex-republics of the USSR including Russia, China and Japan, are no longer *terrae incognitae* to the English-speaking readership. As well as filling a gap in historical knowledge accounts of the development of the profession in these non-Anglophone sites serve to highlight the perils of making generalisations based on Anglo-American experiences. They show that professionalisation processes are not univocal but that they amalgamate elements that may vary, sometimes greatly, from one country to another and from one historical period to another.

This variety may contrast with recent tendencies towards uniformisation in the world of accounting, especially its regulation. Regional integration and globalisation present new challenges to the historian of the professionalisation of accountants. Contrary to the phase from the late nineteenth to the early twentieth century that saw the spread of professional accounting from a centre located in the British Isles to North America and the peripheries of the empire, the late twentieth and early twenty-first centuries have witnessed the transformation of the profession beyond the traditional limits of the Anglo-American world (Samsonova-Taddei and Humphrey 2014). It has also been marked by the advancing power (as discussed in Chapter 12) of global accounting firms. This has implications for the role of the national professional organisation in the global age.

One might wonder whether the advent of the global firm (Cooper and Robson 2006) constitutes a new age of professionalism. Once the dust has settled on accounting entering the era of globalisation, historians will be able to resolve the debate on the significance of the global firm for the history of the accountancy profession. In the meantime, the rise of this type of firm sheds light on the fact that although it may be possible to set a date for the official birth of a profession, it is more difficult to define its subsequent evolution and to determine whether this represents continuity or a (series of) rebirth(s) (Ramirez 2009b). In other words, historians of the profession have to decide whether the 'animal' they study is a mammal (at least those of the placental kind) that looks more or less the same throughout its life, or whether it is like an insect that undergoes several metamorphoses during its existence.

In this chapter we will focus on those episodes which saw the ascension of an occupation to the status of a profession. We will also refer to episodes that represent a substantial inflexion in the history of a profession towards adopting (or failing to adopt) a transformed identity. We will return to the changes in accounting professionalism during the modern era of the global firm in the conclusion to the chapter. Before presenting a detailed analysis of the professionalisation of accountants in diverse countries, we address the epistemological issues that confront the researcher in this area.

Studying the history of accountancy as a profession

Writing a history of professionalisation means coming to terms with the definition of what a profession is. This is a tricky issue, especially if one considers the potential for the metamorphosis or evolution of a profession with its multiple rebirths and transformations. What seems well-established is that 'profession' is not a definitive status that is reached by fulfilling a series of predefined criteria or traits (Wilenski 1964). Our conception of professions owes much to the work of the sociologists and sociological historians (Habenstein 1963; Millerson 1964; Rueschemeyer 1964, 1983; Johnson 1972; Roth 1974; Klegon 1978; Saks 1983; Macdonald 1995) who, from the 1970s onwards, criticised those functionalist theories of professions that identified a common pathway to professional status and envisioned this as something natural and desirable.

'Critical' scholars analysed professions as the outcome of a hard-fought struggle by status and rent-seeking aspirants whose right to professional status was sometimes far from obvious. Analyses of claims to be recognised as a profession and the collective action that was necessary to achieve that end became the focus of sociologists of professions (Larson 1977). Without being constrained by an overarching definition of 'profession' or a fixed endpoint of the professionalisation process (see Freidson 1983; Collins 1990; Walker 2004a), scholarly work could concentrate on efforts to construct occupational identities and to then 'keep up a continual effort to maintain and if possible enhance the position of the group' (Macdonald 1995: 188). Efforts to close the market for professional services through establishing entry barriers, often sanctioned by the state, came to be defined as a 'professional project'.[1]

In the accounting literature a paper by Willmott (1986) was a marker for the introduction of the aforementioned sociological insights to the study of the accountancy profession. His contribution was part of the movement to study accounting in its social context (Burchell et al. 1980). Analyses of accounting professionalisation produced since have, in contrast to 'official' histories commissioned by professional organisations (such as Brown 1905; Garrett 1961; Collard 1980) and others sympathetic to accountants' endeavours (such as Stacey 1954), tended to be sceptical of claims of altruistic service and functional contribution that emanated from the accountancy profession itself.

Yet, thirty years after Willmott's contribution was published, and in spite of some criticism (Matthews 2017), there has been little change in the choice of concepts that are used to study the professional projects of accountants. Neo-Weberianism, and in particular the concept of closure, remains a principal instrument in the theoretical toolbox of the historian of the accountancy profession. Abbott's (1988) interactionist approach has also been influential. The works that have been published since the first edition of the *Routledge Companion* seem to confirm this tendency (for instance, Edwards and Walker 2008;

O'Regan 2008; Anderson and Walker 2009, Lee 2010a; Sian 2011; Verhoef 2014; Coronella et al. 2015), although Foucauldian (McKinstry 2014) and, more recently, Bourdieusian theories (Spence and Brivot 2011; Poullaos 2016) have also featured along with the exploration of more specific notions such as boundary work (Annisette 2017). Recent explorations have contributed to a finer-grained understanding of accountants' professional projects. They go hand in hand with a broadening of the sources of archival investigation to include censuses (that are scrutinised to analyse the occupational and social structure of the accountants' community)[2] and the breaking down of professionalisation stories into 'sub-plots' that embrace topics such as gender (Edwards and Walker 2007, 2008; Lee 2007; Walker 2011; Roberts 2013) and race (Hammond et al. 2009, 2012; Poullaos 2009), or the specific role played by individuals (Lee 2009, 2015) or collective actors, such as accountants working in industry (Noguchi and Edwards 2008) or small practitioners (Ramirez 2009a).

As stated earlier, this chapter mainly deals with early episodes of professionalisation and considers professional associations as the main vehicle for the achievement of accountants' professional projects. Insights into the role of other actors in professional projects such as firms may be found in Chapter 12. Exclusionary processes operating on the basis of race and gender are given separate treatment in Chapters 21 and 22. Details that supplement those provided in the present chapter are also touched on in Chapter 13 (which broaches forms of occupational preparation and knowledge) and Chapter 14 (which addresses regulatory issues in accounting).

The review of histories of the professionalisation of accountancy is arranged on a broadly geographical and chronological basis. The intention is to convey the idea of a spreading of the professional phenomenon around the world.

Britain

Scotland (to 1914)

The incorporation by royal charter of the Society of Accountants in Edinburgh (SAE) in 1854, the Institute of Accountants and Actuaries in Glasgow (IAAG) in 1855 and the Society of Accountants in Aberdeen (SAA) in 1867 provide convenient markers of professional organisation. What has been learnt about the pioneering efforts of the Scots?[3] The move to formal organisation was prompted by a 'massive … threat to the *whole insolvency practice* of Scottish accountants' emanating from English merchants (Walker 1995: 292, *original emphasis*). The founders of the Scottish bodies were elite accountants with close links to the legal profession and the higher strata of Scottish society (Walker 1988; Lee 2011a). Formal organisation was crucial as a means of mobilising allies and other resources, building group identity and putting arguments in relevant fora, public and private. Also involved was a more general desire to maintain dominance of lucrative markets.

While authors such as Lee (2010a, 2011a, 2011b) have revealed the practice of social closure in the incorporation of the Scottish professional bodies and forms of pre-organisation structuration of the occupational community, the interplay of diverse ingredients in the professionalisation process (economic class and social status, collective mobility and market control, social and professional closure) are evident. The Scottish pattern of professionalisation also displayed other features that were replicated elsewhere in Britain and abroad. One was the delineation of the range of 'professional' work to ensure close alignment with the values of societal elites. Another was the establishment of demanding examinations and tests of 'character'. These helped to establish market (and social) reputation and were implicated in efforts to control the numbers entering accountancy. An associated development was the realisation that reputation could be impounded in designations like 'chartered accountant' and 'CA' (Walker 1991; Chandler 2017). Consequently, exclusive access to such symbolic capital was defended vigorously against the efforts of other determined (and often excluded) accountants and their newly formed professional bodies who could organise examinations easily enough but found the other advantages of the chartered bodies harder to replicate.

Fragmentation of the occupation has been widely remarked upon both in the Scottish case and elsewhere in the Anglo-American world. In both the defence of bankruptcy work in the 1850s (Lee 2011a) and the protracted defence of 'CA' up to 1914, the Scottish chartered bodies drew upon prevailing professional and broader societal ideologies. Major targets of the accountants' discursive barrages were various arms of the state, the legal profession, the business community and members of other social elites. The Scots were also pioneers in 'equating public practice with *professional* accountancy' (Walker 1995: 286), a strategy imported into England and then exported abroad, creating even further fragmentation of the accountancy community. Co-operation among the chartered bodies to deal with external threats went hand in hand with disputes between and within them.

The relationship between professionalisation and social mobility has also been explored (Walker 1988). Lee (2004: 27) argues that the SAE, IAAG and SAA 'coped with the economics of a growing market for their services by increasingly recruiting men from lower middle class and working class backgrounds while maintaining social respectability with leaderships almost exclusively of upper class and upper middle class origins'. Analysis of recruitment to the SAE to 1914 shows how complex the relationship could be. The relative newness of (organised) accountancy and other contextual factors enhanced its potential to be a vehicle for upward social mobility (Lee 2011b).

By the time of the SAE's fiftieth anniversary, the Scottish chartered bodies had not only 'developed expanding, high standing professional organisations, they had also gained domination of the practice of their vocation, secured judgements which provided legal protection for the source of that dominance and, witnessed the demoralization and ineffectiveness of their competitors' (Walker 1991: 281). The following 100 years have not been studied by academics in the same detail. Although McKinstry (2014) contended that the Institute of Chartered Accountants in Scotland developed a 'discourse of superiority', analyses of the Scots' professionalising endeavours after 1914 see them as another player in the British professional arena.

England and Wales, and Ireland

The professionalisation dynamics behind the formation of the predecessors of the Institute of Chartered Accountants in England and Wales (ICAEW), namely, the Incorporated Society of Liverpool Accountants (1870), the Institute of Accountants in London (1870), the Manchester Institute of Accountants (1871) and the Institute of Accountants in Sheffield (1877) are discussed by Walker (2004a).[4] Pre-organisation communities of accountants in England are discussed in Edwards et al. 2007 and Edwards 2010. O'Regan (2008) provides an account of the formation in 1888 of the Institute of Chartered Accountants in Ireland (ICAI), which was formed on an all-island basis by a group of prominent public accountants.

In England the key event in professional organisation was changes to insolvency administration. Ironically, the Scottish model of bankruptcy was imported into England and Wales in 1869 setting in motion competition between accountants and lawyers and efforts to create shelters *from* the market (Freidson 1994) and to protect professional elites. As Walker notes (2004a: 127), in Liverpool:

> [t]he organisation of accountants … was instigated by lawyers anxious to establish a medium for negotiating the boundaries of bankruptcy work with local accountants. In London, Manchester and Sheffield (and partly in Liverpool) organisation concerned the protection of established accountants from interlopers and was actualised by erecting market shelters and the imposition of exclusionary closure.

Formal organisation facilitated all these processes in a context where there were no legal barriers to entry. Contrary to Abbott (1988), disturbances and work on the one hand and structures and organisation on the other could not meaningfully be untangled or prioritised. Neither could the drive to capture jurisdiction be unpicked from 'status protection, exclusion and differentiation' in the face of intense *intra*-professional rivalry (Walker 2004a: 152). Furthermore, the accountants seeking a market shelter were protecting their elite status rather than conspiring to achieve collective upward mobility *per se*.

The bedding-in of organisations can be awkward, as shown in Anderson et al.'s (2005) analysis of the ICAEW from its incorporation by royal charter in 1880 to the turn of the twentieth century. Its leadership went down the exclusionary closure/credentialism path by constructing the 'well-qualified' chartered accountant, in image if not always in outcome. Constructive elements included, among others, tough exams, an extended period of articles involving payment of a premium to a master, and tests of financial probity. These may have helped to establish the ICAEW's reputation, but they also prompted criticisms from unsuccessful applicants. For example, the examinations were deemed to be too hard, the difficulty or assessment of examinations varied over time and some masters were more interested in cheap labour than imparting training. The exam requirement became particularly problematic when a new non-examination route was introduced in 1893 to attract eminent non-member practitioners with sizable audit clients. It is not entirely clear how these tensions were managed,[5] but the resulting fracas illustrates the difficulties of jointly managing internal and external relations in the early days of a professional project. A similar story of the tumultuous early history of competing professional bodies is offered by O'Regan (2013) in his study of the formation by Irish accountants of a local branch of the English-based Society of Incorporated Accountants and Auditors (which was a rival of the ICAEW until it merged with it in 1957).

Relevant publications since the first edition of the *Routledge Companion* have tended to underscore the complexities of the professionalisation process in Britain and the challenges of maintaining professionalism. The problematic adherence to altruism, for example, has been examined by Walker (2017) in his study of the profession during the First World War. Recent scholars have also examined the official establishment of professional bodies from a broader perspective in order to reinforce the social rather than institutional character of the history of professionalisation. The examination of the occupation in pre-organisation periods (Edwards 2010; Edwards and Anderson 2011) reveals the profession before its professionalisation. The exploitation of censuses and biographical data has been utilised to detail the social complexion of the community of accountants before and after the establishment of professional bodies (Edwards and Walker 2007; Anderson and Walker

2009). The investigation of these sources has brought to the fore the existence of outliers (Lee 2009, 2015) or populations that did not fit easily in the mainstream accounts of professionalisation, such as women (Walker 2011) or accountants working in industry (Noguchi and Edwards 2004, 2008).

Subsequent episodes in the history of the professionalisation of accountants in Britain and Ireland

A significant body of research into professionalisation has used 'Britain' or 'the UK' or 'the British Isles' as its geographic unit of analysis. Macdonald (1985), for example, seeks to explain the failure of British and Irish accountants (up to 1954) to achieve registration – a means of achieving a legal monopoly 'at the upper end of a range of exclusionary devices' (ibid.: 543). The analysis offers a range of explanatory factors:

- tension between liberalism and closure;
- endemic quarrelling between large numbers of professional bodies as to relative status and access to work within varying locales;
- variations in accounting knowledge needed to service different types of clients;
- the perception by elite accountants that their position in the accountancy hierarchy would be threatened by a common register;
- the difficulty of proving that registration was in 'the public interest' – that there was societal demand for registration or that non-registration would result in societal damage;
- the evolution of 'adequate' closure for the accountancy elite, e.g. via investment in designations or other means.

Macdonald's conclusion (ibid.: 554) offers a synoptic view of three time/path dependent strategies of market control, namely: the careful building up of professional organisations with reputations for competence, probity and respectability; the amalgamation of those organisations while maintaining reputability; and the piecemeal achievement of control by obtaining the statutory restriction of accountancy functions to members of the senior professional bodies for an increasing number and range of organisations. Willmott's (1986) analysis of the same period identifies factors behind the merger of the ICAEW and the Society of Incorporated Accountants and Auditors (SIAA) in 1957. These include the breakdown of previous efforts to unify the profession, the avoidance of disputation over post-war competition for accounting labour, and the problem of dealing with partnerships between their respective members.

Walker and Shackleton's (1995) examination of a smaller stretch of time (1930–57) highlights the dramatic expansion of the state's planning and central coordination role during wartime, in which accountants were acknowledged to have played a significant part. One result was the emergence of a corporatist state in which accountants could potentially move from 'mere' pressure group status to becoming part of the governing apparatus – if they could become unified. But they could not. At one stage their response was to propose something that looked like registration, thereby alienating business and key state actors. Past experience had rendered the Scots, the Irish and some second-tier accountants suspicious of the intentions of the ICAEW. The cost and works accountants and municipal treasurers resented being excluded on the grounds that they were not public accountants. The accountants could not even agree (in 1946) on what a 'public accountant' was. Nevertheless the arduous negotiations between segments of the occupation and the state did encourage the Scots to merge in 1951 (as the Institute of Chartered Accountants of Scotland). They also contributed to the merger of the ICAEW and the SIAA in 1957. Walker and Shackleton detect a slowly emerging momentum towards amalgamation, supported by the Board of Trade, the objective being to reduce the problems arising from the multiplicity of accountants' voices.

The profession's leaders were again disappointed during the 1960s when they tried to erect a 'ring fence' around existing associations via legislation to: 'restrict the right to practice accountancy to members of the unified profession, restrict audit and certain tax work to chartered public accountants, and to prohibit the formation of further organisations of public accountants' (Walker and Shackleton 1998: 44). This involved achieving consensus between the leaders of first, second and third tier accounting bodies, gaining the support of their members, and convincing the Board of Trade and politicians. Although the first condition was met the others were not in a context where corporatism and the public sector were being wound back and a long held suspicion of 'monopolisation' re-emerged. Overall, closing off the British profession through political/legal means has proved to be a mountain too high to climb. Later attempts to merge sections of the profession, such as the chartered accountants in Britain, have also failed (Lee 2010b).

The Institute of Cost and Works Accountants (ICWA, formed in 1919, now the Chartered Institute of Management Accountants) and the Corporate Treasurers and Accountants' Institute (CTAI, 1885, now the Chartered Institute of Public Finance Accountants) were not originally formed to provide their members with access to public practice. To date the ICWA and the CTAI have received limited scholarly attention compared to bodies with historical roots in public accountancy. The major examination of the ICWA's formation was authored by Loft (1986). What was the objective of the ICWA's professional project? Achieving a status equal to that of the chartered accountants, apparently, but to what end? Applicants from 'the industrial community' felt 'the need of a body which would cater for an entirely works outlook upon costing instead of the hitherto professional auditors view' (ibid.: 155). Presumably they did not want their field to be constructed by chartered accountants. But what was the danger in that? Some interviewees in Loft's study reported that they gained a sense of *identity* from joining. But, is this an outcome or an objective? Possibly the ICWA wanted its members to have 'the same status and monetary awards as the chartered accountants' (ibid.: 157). But it is not evident that a payment mechanism along these lines existed. The question about the ICWA's objectives remains open and there is limited knowledge of the process through which its project evolved to the point that it 'had' to be included inside the proposed ring fence by 1966.

It may be too soon to examine in historical perspective shifts in British professional project(s) over the decades characterised by the rise of neo-liberalism. Nevertheless, a steady stream of papers analysing in a more sociological light contemporary events have provided some interesting insights. For example the state-profession relationship has been, and is still, undergoing dramatic change. Cooper et al. (1996) highlight the role of British state agents, conscious of the contribution of accountancy to the national interest, in promoting the British professional project *into the rest of Europe* (ibid.: 602; see also Robson et al. 1994; Sikka and Willmott 1995).

Accountancy bodies were authorised under the Financial Services Act 1986 to arrange inspection of their members' practices on behalf of government (Radcliffe et al. 1994; Robson et al. 1994). In an era of hyper-liberalism accountants became both the watchers and the watched (Ramirez 2013). At the same time their dealings with clients were 'commercialised', a process involving the loosening of 'professional' constraints (Hanlon

1994, 1996, 1997; Willmott and Sikka 1997). These evolutions have also entailed a straining of the relations between the different categories of members of professional bodies. Smaller practitioners for instance may feel estranged from their institutes, which they perceive as primarily serving the interests of the bigger firms (Ramirez 2009a).

The imperial arena

Accountancy as a modern profession was born in the country that established an empire that extended worldwide by the end of the nineteenth century. With the spread of the metropolis' commercial culture and the flows of physical and human capital circulating within the empire, it was to be expected that the pattern of organisation of the profession in Britain would determine its development in the territories of the empire, either because this form of organisation was imported by settlers or because local accountants decided themselves to establish their own associations, sometimes competing with the British ones. Relations between the centre and the periphery, which were highlighted by Cooper and Robson (2006) as an important avenue for future research on the accountancy profession, have been widely addressed in an abundant historiography (see Poullaos and Sian 2010), which stresses the importation of, and reaction to, the British professional organisation by local populations. These episodes reveal the responses of the metropolitan centre to the importation of professional agendas and the operation of racism that accompanied imperial domination (Poullaos 2009). In some parts of the empire relations with the centre could be fraught. Canada and South Africa for instance saw the emergence of strong local accounting organisations with vested economic interests and strategies to resist attempts by the parent body to spread its authority. In other outposts such as Nigeria (Wallace 1992; Uche 2002), Trinidad and Tobago (Annisette 1999, 2000) and Kenya (Sian 2011), British immigrants first set up lucrative practices and further tried to build a local professional organisation that encompassed local practitioners. Whatever the path followed to professionalisation and the local cultural, social and economic particularities of peripheral states, professionalisation processes were all marked by a conception of educational requirements, ethical standards, and constitution and governance of professional institutions that can be described as representing the legacy of British culture.

Canada

In recent years the history of the professionalisation of accountants in Canada has been enriched by a series of contributions that have enhanced our knowledge of themes such as:

- The acquisition/creation of 'CA' as a by-product of incorporation by statute. (Institutes of CAs had been established in Quebec, Ontario, Manitoba, Nova Scotia, British Columbia, Alberta and Saskatchewan by 1908).
- The spread of professional accountancy from the east to the west of the country as part of the 'settling' or 'development' of a large territory in a series of separate but connected provincial professional projects.
- The complications arising from a federal political structure.
- The arduous construction of a national accountancy arena.
- Ethnic division – the French factor.
- Tensions between British and Canadian accountants.
- The supplanting of British by American influence; and the travails and opportunities of having a major, then a super, and then a hyper-power as a neighbour.

As with research on Britain and Ireland, so in Canada, the availability of electronically available census material has enabled a better understanding of the connections between the social physiognomy of a population of accountants and the process of professionalisation (Edwards and Walker 2008). The endeavours to grasp the details of this process go hand in hand with the development of new theoretical explanations, beyond classical neo-Weberian social closure. Given the fragmentation of the accountant community in Canada and the contentious relations between its different components, it is not surprising that recent studies have explored boundary work (Annisette 2017), Bourdieusian approaches to linguistic capital (Spence and Brivot 2011) and symbolic violence (Poullaos 2016).[6]

Richardson's (1987: 610) analysis of the period 1879–1979 provides an overview of professionalisation as the ultimate outcome of a competition between accountants' associations marked by an escalating commitment to professional standards and symbolism. More detailed analysis of different episodes in the period covered by Richardson either highlights the efforts to achieve an official status for the profession or the persistence of divisions within the profession. The work by Richardson (1989a) and MacDonald and Richardson (2004) on occupational licensing in Ontario (beginning with the formation of a Public Accountants' Council (PAC) – a state agency – in 1950) moves into the first direction. The formation of the PAC required that suspicion about the CAs excluding non-CAs from public practice be overcome. This was a corporatist period *at the provincial level* suggesting a 'need' for an accountants' organisation to be available for integration into the provincial governing apparatus, while amalgamations and negotiations within the accountancy community helped to defuse internal tensions within the occupation. Unlike their British counterparts, the Ontario accountants got their ring fence. The PAC was empowered to grant or refuse licences to engage in public practice, speak for the profession, exercise disciplinary powers and prosecute offenders. The ICAO (Institute of Chartered Accountants of Ontario) appointed eight of the PAC's fifteen council members, its public practice rival – the Certified Public Accountants Association of Ontario (CPAA) – appointed five, while the remaining two were elected by licensees other than members of the ICAO and CPAA. The PAC slowly worked towards a situation of having to deal with only one body (the ICAO), establishing it as the sole or main port of entry to public practice while gradually raising entry standards, thereby achieving what the ICAO's founders could only have dreamed of: a body with both exclusive access to 'CA' *and* a more or less exclusive occupational licence, enforceable by law.

Poullaos (2016) examines the struggle between Canadian accountants and their British confreres that took place in the beginning of the twentieth century and which ended with the local professionals resisting the attempts of the British chartered accountants to push them down the professional status hierarchy. This fight helped to unify Canadian accountants and raised the possibility that colonial profession-state axes elsewhere in the British Empire could assert their autonomy.

In Britain, tests of 'character' – the personal attributes of the accountant – were used as ascriptive barriers to entry and to align the social status of members with those of their clients and other social elites. Richardson's (1989b) analysis suggests that a variant of these tendencies applied to Canada in the period 1880–1930. Accountancy was not open to all social groups, did not represent the diversity of social interests in the population and was 'significantly linked with other sectoral elites' (ibid.: 18). Neu and Saleem (1996) used published ethical codes to analyse the ICAO's handling of 'character issues' from its incorporation in 1883 to 1993. At first 'character' was an admission criterion and there was no published code. By 1961, however, forty behavioural injunctions were in print. More generally, published codes effaced both internal divisions between members and contradictions between self-interest and public interest, while locating ICAO members among other high-status professions – at least discursively. The 1973 revision constructed a mythical past for the ICAO and its members as having always been responsible to the public, even as the publication of detailed ethical codes marked a loss of faith on the part of ICAO leaders in the 'character' of its own members. Similarly, from the 1980s onwards, in the wake of corporate scandals, escalating litigation and the overt commercialisation of practitioner-client relations, 'independence' and 'objectivity' became – again discursively – the cornerstone of the Canadian profession from its very beginnings even though the terms were rarely used before the 1920s (Everett et al. 2005). The authors' also note the replacement of the religion-based character discourse by a secular scientific discourse favouring independence and objectivity, a point also made about America (Preston et al. 1995), and Australia and New Zealand (Velayutham 2003).

Other contributions focus on the divisions that pre-existed, subsisted and/or were created within the profession. Richardson (2002), for instance, explored relations between Canadian financial and management accountants from 1926 to 1986. The two groupings are seen as competing for jurisdiction over firms' accounting processes and the uses to which their outputs are put. As in Britain, the financial accountants were the established professional elite and the management accountants' search for legitimacy was severely hampered by the former's professional dominance. Divisions existed also within professional bodies between an English-speaking elite and French-speaking accountants, or between more established professionals and professionals from recently immigrated ethnic minorities (Annisette 2017). In the case of the Association of Accountants in Montreal (AAM), Spence and Brivot (2011) remark that the organisation possessed a 'distinctive' cultural and linguistic habitus. They observe that for many years the AAM enacted a number of exclusion strategies to effectively limit its admittance of Francophone compatibles who possessed a different cultural and linguistic habitus. When the AAM eventually explicitly embraced Francophone members, this was in order to counter the threat of a rival accounting designation.

Australia and New Zealand

Both the *idea* of professional accountancy and British accountancy *qualifications per se* were exported from Britain to Australia (Parker 1989).[7] But neither British trained *accountants* nor British accounting *associations* were dominant players in Australian accountancy from the mid-1880s to 1914 (Carnegie and Parker 1999). By 1910 there were at least eighteen accountancy bodies around Australia, some focusing on cities, some on regions within states, some on states, while others organised nationally (ibid.: 99; see also Carnegie 1993).

Carnegie and Edwards (2001) examined the occupation prior to the formation of the Incorporated Institute of Accountants in Victoria (IIAV) in 1886, the first accounting association formed in the state of Victoria (also Carnegie 2016). Of the IIAV's forty-five founders forty-one were immigrants, but ten at most were 'accountants' at the time of arrival and only two were members of British accountancy bodies. By 1886 all forty-five founders were offering a range of services to the public and for the most part they were not sons of a pre-existing accountancy elite. The key event prompting the establishment of a professional body in Melbourne was the attempt by an SIAA[8] member to start a local branch. At least some of the IIAV's founders were approached to join, but they formed a local association instead. Possibly nationalism and the logistics of running a professional project in conjunction with the SIAA in London played a part. There were, furthermore, a growing number of public accountants in Melbourne who might join and many more clerks from whom they might want to distinguish themselves (ibid.: see also Carnegie et al. 2003).

Thereafter the IIAV and other Australian bodies played out local variations of patterns evident in Britain and Canada. A registration attempt was led by the IIAV in Victoria in the late 1890s during an economic crisis, when significant amounts of British capital was lost and the prospect of competition from British accountants was in the air (Chua and Poullaos 1998). After the attempt failed, there followed a sustained campaign by various combinations of elite Australian accountants to obtain a royal charter from the Privy Council in London in the first three decades of the twentieth century. They succeeded at the third attempt in 1928 (Chua and Poullaos 1993; Poullaos 1994). Broadly speaking, their efforts reflected a desire to be able to compete successfully with British CAs in Australia, to construct a national accountancy arena that distinguished unequivocally between practising ('public') and non-practising accountants, and to establish the former as the elite occupational grouping. The reasons for the failure of the first two charter attempts and the success of the third (1922–8) are discussed in detail in the cited sources (Poullaos 1994: ch. 9 provides an overview).

Later episodes in the history of professionalisation in Australia and New Zealand have been analysed by Carnegie and O'Connell (2012) and by Baskerville and Hay (2010). Carnegie and O'Connell's article, set in the 1960s, examines the responses of the two major professional accounting bodies (The Institute of Chartered Accountants in Australia, the body responsible for accountants in public practice, and the Australian Society of Accountants, the body responsible for members in commerce, industry and government) to a financial and regulatory crisis that necessitated the defence of the profession's legitimacy. The episode illustrates the fact that, while the history of the accounting profession has been characterised by intra-professional rivalries, these rivalries could be put aside when the power of collective action is recognised.

On the basis of an oral history study of partners in large New Zealand accounting firms in the 1980s, Baskerville and Hay (2010) explore how partners survived the turbulence of globalisation and firm affiliations and mergers. Following these transformations, the previous partnership model was replaced with a globally based, managed professional business, leading to a loss of each local firm's autonomy. The loss was unavoidable given the promised advantages of international referrals and status, and the disadvantages of being left out of international affiliations with a global firm. However, it also led to costly redundancies of partners and for some a loss of control over their careers and employment choices. Baskerville and Hay's contribution shows that changes in professional identity can emerge at later stages in the history of the profession and do not necessarily result from the institutional work of professional associations. We will come back to this point later in the chapter.

South Africa

In South Africa the SIAA, more successful there than in Australia, was heavily involved in setting up a society in the Transvaal (1904) under an ordinance which gave this body considerable authority over the organisation of public accountants. The subsequent history of the professionalisation of accountants in South Africa is that of the attempts by British accountants outside of Transvaal to gain privileges equivalent to those bestowed on the Transvaal Society of Accountants (Verhoef 2014). It was not the indigenous population or the emerging Dutch/Afrikaner population that was instrumental in pursuing social closure, but the British accountants themselves: up to the 1950s no Afrikaner or person of colour in South Africa was of any consequence to the professional rivalry that played itself out on this soil. The leadership was English-speaking and gave birth to a distinct South African professional nationalism (Verhoef 2014: 224). With the help of the state, which secured a ring fence around the profession in 1951 (Verhoef 2013), the successful closure strategies of the local accountancy societies effectively barred non-residents from the market for accountancy services (Verhoef 2014). For a later period Hammond et al. (2009) provide evidence of the continuing exclusion of the Black population from careers in the profession on the basis of race and class. Even though apartheid gave way to political freedom and firms began to hire Black South African trainees, oral histories collected from the first Black chartered accountants reveal discriminatory treatment by accounting firms that contrast with the version of history published in official professional sources (Hammond et al. 2012).

Post-colonial professionalisation

This section discusses the contrasting professional projects that have emerged in some 'former' British colonies or protectorates hard on the heels of formal decolonisation. In each case building a national profession required that local actors adapt the legacy of British patterns of organisation to the particularities of the national or regional context.

In the Caribbean the emergence of national professions was marked by the central role, not of the ICAEW but the Association of Chartered Certified Accountants (ACCA), another UK-based professional body. In Trinidad and Tobago the government played a major role in developing the economy, becoming a significant employer of accountants in the process. Accountancy rapidly emerged as a high-status occupation (Annisette 1999). In 1964 a CA social club merged with the local branch of the ACCA (dominated by Trinidadians working in the public sector) to form the Trinidad and Tobago Association of Chartered Accountants and Certified Accountants (TTACACA later incorporated as the Institute of Chartered Accountants of Trinidad and Tobago or ICATT). The formation of the Institute of Chartered Accountants of Jamaica (ICAJ) in 1965 represented a similar drive by a new government and a section of the local accountancy community to open the profession to Jamaicans. The ICAJ would 'replace all forms of colonial bodies operating on the island' (Bakre 2005: 996). These objectives were to be enacted by a national accountancy law 'which would guarantee the conduct of local examinations and also protect the interest of the Jamaican accountants against any external encroachments' (ibid.).

However, in both Jamaica and T&T, efforts to develop a profession independent of external influences were thwarted as these countries remained dependent on British and then American capital as they became increasingly integrated into an American-dominated world economy. Informal domination replaced formal empire and local accounting firms became aligned to international accountancy networks. In T&T ICATT effectively became the ACCA's 'local agents' (Annisette 2000: 647). In Jamaica the ICAJ contained an influential ACCA-trained grouping with internationalist leanings which leveraged the local power of global capital and managed to procure a clause allowing the ICAJ to seek external examination and credentials. Variations of this dynamic continued into the 1980s with similar results (Bakre 2006, 2014).

Africa was also the setting of efforts to constitute truly national professions after independence had been achieved. In Kenya the government sought to transfer control of high-level accountancy work from expatriates to Kenyans as part of its Africanisation policy

(Sian 2006, 2007). Pre-independence attempts at social closure by the Association of Accountants in East Africa (AAEA), an organisation essentially constituted by British expatriate accountants (Sian 2011), were swayed by a form of 'revolutionary usurpation' on the part of African Kenyans. The implementation of the new professional organisation was characterised by openness to all practising accountants be they Africans or members of other communities. In Nigeria the nationalist objective of setting up a local infrastructure for the production of an indigenous accountancy workforce and breaking down the dominance of expatriates came to the fore immediately after independence (Wallace 1992). The newly formed (in 1965) Institute of Chartered Accountants of Nigeria (ICAN) was handed a 'monopoly of regulating the accounting profession' (Uche 2002: 480).

The extent of the British Empire was vast and diverse and was maintained through ties that linked colonial outposts to the imperial centre. Kuwait and India offer examples of a weaker influence than the cases discussed so far. They constitute examples where local characteristics embedded in the national culture played a more prominent role in the development of the profession than overt British influence. Although Kuwait was a former British protectorate (1899–1961) the organisation of the profession after independence (the Kuwaiti Association of Accountants and Auditors was founded in 1973) was informed by Arabic laws and customs and nationalist movements (Altaher et al. 2014). In the relatively neglected case of India (Verma and Gray 2006; Sidhu and West 2014; Verma 2015), the rise of the Institute of Chartered Accountants of India replicated British conceptions of professional accountancy but also reflected that unique feature of Indian culture – the organisation of society in castes. The over-representation of the Brahman upper caste endowed the profession with high status but also contributed to the reproduction of social inequality.

British influence in the development of the profession could also be supplanted by the rise of new global powers. In Ethiopia, for instance, the ACCA seized the opportunity provided by British economic influence to take control of the training and certification processes of the Ethiopian Professional Association of Accountants and Auditors (Mihret et al. 2012). But here, as elsewhere, British ways of practising and organising the accountancy profession has increasingly coexisted or been gradually replaced by, American influence (Mihret et al. 2014).

The United States of America

In our analysis of the development of professional accounting in Anglo-American countries we single out the case of the United States as, by 1880, it had long since asserted its independence from Britain. Although America was a destination for both British capital and accountants (Lee 1997, 2001, 2002a, 2002b, 2004), there was much less British influence in American affairs via diplomatic channels than was the case, for instance, in the 'self-governing' Canada and Australia. The most sustained analysis of the American accountancy community to 1940 is by Miranti (1990; also Miranti 1986, 1988). The remarks below will be based on his work and focused on the period from 1800 to 1906, the aim being to illustrate differences between American accountancy projects and those discussed previously.

The major elements of accountancy professionalisation projects in America have been identified in the research literature, albeit in less detail than for Britain. Between 1874 and 1889, thirteen societies were formed 'with identities related to accounting activities' (Previts and Merino 1998: 136).[9] The Institute of Accountants and Book-keepers of New York (hereafter 'NYIA', formed in 1882) offered an examination-based accountancy qualification to both public and salaried accountants more than a decade before any state-recognised credential had been established (ibid.: 135–7). For present purposes, the NYIA is of interest as the vehicle through which leading American accountants, such as Charles Waldo Haskins and Charles E. Sprague, expressed views at odds with those emanating from the American Association of Public Accountants (AAPA – formed in 1886, incorporated in 1887), a body influenced by resident British CAs.

The AAPA was formed ostensibly as a national body for public accountants. It had the potential to be part of a network of practitioners capable of serving clients with interests across the nation – a role for formal organisation not previously highlighted. The AAPA also appealed to American accountants whose clients 'had developed strong connections with British business interests' (ibid.: 34) and to those in accountancy and business circles concerned about the wave of non-British immigrants to America. This point was not highlighted elsewhere as a reason for preferring one professionalisation model over another. But there was little in the way of national accountancy regulation and most accountants lacked clients with national reach. Consequently, instead of attracting recruits from across the country the AAPA found itself struggling with the NYIA.

One issue dividing the AAPA and the NYIA was quasi-epistemological. Was accounting an art or a science? American-born accountants felt that accountancy should be developed along 'scientific' lines in contrast to their British counterparts who stressed the necessity of 'the virtue, experience, and steady judgment of the seasoned accountant' (ibid.: 39; Kimball 1992; McMillan 1999; Persson et al. 2018). These attributes would be acquired during a long apprenticeship, taking us to the second area of difference: vocational preparation. In spite of the scepticism of some British CAs, the institutionalisation of college/university instruction as an essential part of professional training came about much earlier in America than in Britain or Australia. One implication was that the NYIA and AAPA fought for recognition from the bodies regulating the granting of degrees.

A third source of conflict was the challenges to American identity created by mass immigration. Charles Waldo Haskins responded with a strident form of anti-British patriotism while Charles E. Sprague and others allegedly harboured lingering resentment of British support for the Confederates in the Civil War. Sprague and Hopkins had served in the Union army. Haskins, furthermore, had married into the Havermeyer family, which was probably well aware of English/German imperial rivalry and was anti-imperialist in any case. It did not help that American and British imperial rivalries were manifesting in Latin America and the Pacific during the 1890s. Further, leading figures in the NYIA were of Irish descent. For them 'the great famine of 1842 and the suppression of the revolutionary Fenian Brotherhood' (Miranti 1990: 45) were within living memory.

The mood of such people was not helped by the market success of chartered accountants. 'CA' was recognised as a significant contributing factor taking us to a fourth point: competition over designations. The NYIA stiffened its examinations, developed its own designation and tried (unsuccessfully) to claim for itself 'CA' – 'certified accountant'. A subsequent bitter public controversy made division within the occupation highly visible, damaging the prospects of profession-led accountancy regulation. One result was that the New York licensing law of 1896 – the outcome of a process where the NYIA and AAPA put up competing bills – 'merely provided legal protection to a special title of professional competency' (ibid.: 47) rather than legal exclusion of competitors. The title was 'CPA' – 'certified *public* accountant'.

As the New York law became the model for other states, tensions between British and American accountants spilled over state borders (ibid.: 48–60). State CPA associations were formed to organise those who had passed CPA examinations. One of these, the New York State Society of CPAS (NYSSCPA), became a new vehicle for the opposition of Haskins, Sprague and others to the AAPA.

In the late 1890s the merger boom created a new crop of national business entities, creating potential for the parallel formation of national accountancy practices and state accounting associations seeking local licensing legislation. The national accountancy firms were, however, vulnerable to the efforts of local accountants to keep them out by tapping into intense preferences for local autonomy. In this context, competition between the AAPA and the NYSSCPA (and CPAs in other states) made the process of forming national practices and regulatory networks tortuous (ibid.: 59–68). Events external to the profession resulted in a compromise whereby the AAPA became, for the time being, the national body to which the state CPA societies became affiliated, with the NYSSCPA claiming New York as its preserve.

Studies beyond the establishment of the founding institutions of public accountancy in America have considered the protection of the professional turf (see Mills and Young 1999 on the challenge posed by non-CPA public accountants), the adjustment of business practices to auditors' needs (Doron 2013) and the professionalisation of specialisms such as internal auditing (Parker and Johnson 2017). Studies on the development of ethical codes merit particular attention. Roberts (2015), for example, has discussed the role that these codes played in the socialisation of new entrants to the profession.

Further investigation of the American experience is encouraged in light of the global importance of American capital since 1945 and its role in the propagation of hegemonic power in the rampant neo-liberalism of recent decades. We know much less about American influence in overseas professionalisation projects than we do about the British. Dyball et al.'s (2006, 2007) analysis of the sudden passing in 1923 of US-style CPA legislation in the American-ruled Philippines illustrates the importance of pursuing this research agenda. The legislation is seen as an attempt by the Filipino elite, faced with a difficult American governor-general, to capture the CPA role for its own familial networks. In arriving at this suggestion Dyball et al. note that the disparate interactions analysed in previous research have involved some combination of a proactive accountancy community, a (more or less) competitive market for public accountancy services and a self-directed, modernist state. The authors cannot find evidence for the existence of these factors in the Philippines prior to 1923. The problematic grafting of American accountancy institutions overseas is also noted in Sakagami et al.'s (1999) analysis of Japanese accountancy subsequent to the creation of Japanese CPAs during the American-led occupation after the Second World War. While the Japanese Institute of CPAs was able to establish its members' social status through passing difficult examinations and a legal monopoly over external audit, their functional contribution has been challenged in the wake of corporate scandals. CPAs have not been able to sufficiently extricate themselves from the domination of the Ministry of Finance with its strong links to the *Zaibatsu*: 'It is certain that individual auditors must change their consciousness about independence. But it might also be true that we really need the reform of social relationships based on interdependence' (ibid.: 353).

The 'non-Anglo-American' world

We now turn to the cases of a series of countries that we group under the descriptor 'non-Anglo-American', that is to say countries where the professionalisation of accountants was not conditioned by the overt influence of Britain or the United States. This categorisation posits that there are common characteristics shared by professional projects in these countries, in spite of their diversity. The main characteristic is the power of the State in leading or shaping professionalisation. Another characteristic is the delayed development of financial markets and the limited historical presence of major international firms when compared to the Anglo-American world.

Continental Europe and beyond

In continental Europe the first accounting associations in the modern age were created around the same time as their British counterparts, but often they did not establish a clear distinction between practitioners, members working in industry or 'experts in accounting' more generally (Bocqueraz 2001; Ramirez 2001; Coronella et al. 2015; Evans 2018). For much of the time these associations pursued struggles on several fronts. First, to establish that accountants were deserving of the same recognition as more prestigious professions such as lawyers and physicians (Ramirez 2001). Second, to defend their turf against competitors and/or to contest new territories such as taxation (Coronella et al. 2015). Third, to try to impose their supremacy over other accountants' associations on the basis of the division of expert labour or the hierarchical distinction between credentials. In Belgium and Italy, for instance, a preferential path into the profession was organised for university graduates, reflecting the ongoing influence of the civil service model (De Beelde 2002; Coronella et al. 2015).

The outcome of these intricate internecine conflicts did not necessarily result in the acquisition of privileges for the profession (Evans 2018) which depended on the State's goodwill. Very often, it was the evolution of commercial legislation (see Praquin 2012 on France, and Ohman and Wallerstedt 2012 on Sweden) and/or the intervention of the State in the educational arena (Carrera and Carmona 2013) that prompted the bettering of the status of accountants and auditors. Thus, even though researchers of professionalisation in these countries invariably resort to the same theoretical frameworks used by students of the Anglo-American scene (essentially neo-Weberian social closure theory and Abbott's system of professions), the trajectory and outcome of professional projects can be quite different due to variations in the constellation of factors that shape the occupational arena. In a number of European countries professional associations may play a different role than in the Anglo-American world (Schäffer et al. 2014), or they cohabitate with professional 'unions' or syndicates (El Omari et al. 2013). Jurisdictional conflicts can be complicated by simultaneous *inter-* and *intra*-professional conflict (Evans and Honold 2007), closure may fail to establish a monopoly for the profession if the State fails to intervene, and boundary work may result in blurring distinctions instead of clarifying them.

In comparison with the ample historiography that exists on the influence of British (and to a lesser extent, American) accountancy around the world, the relations between centre and periphery have received much less attention in the case of non-Anglo-American colonial powers. The effects of French rule and influence are still pervasive in the organisation of professional accountancy and auditing in many African countries (Elad 2015). The case of Brazil is interesting because although it became independent from Portugal in 1822, it retained much of the socio-economic organisation of the former imperial power (Rodrigues et al. 2003). The State was instrumental in driving the professionalisation process (Lima Rodrigues and Sangster 2013), but in a way that favoured the emergence of accounting syndicates as part of the development of a corporatist society

(Lima Rodrigues et al. 2011). Using the work of Streeck and Schmitter on corporatism, Agrizzi and Sian (2015) have shown how the action of public authorities in Brazil laid the foundations for these syndicates to gain influence with the State and press for the recognition of a national professional organisation.

Beyond studies of national professional traditions in non-Anglo-American countries and their exportation to former colonies, a stream of research also looks at the encounter between these traditions and a model of professionalism that the large multinational accounting firms would epitomise. Encounters between national professional bodies and major Anglo-American firms have not always been peaceful (Dedoulis and Caramanis 2007; De Beelde et al. 2009; Ramirez 2010; Dedoulis 2016), but they have certainly influenced professional practices and the direction that accountancy and auditing has taken in these countries. In Greece for instance the organisation of auditors began as a post-war project by the State. In 1955 the Greek Parliament founded a body of auditors (its Greek name yields the initials SOL) to help collect tax revenues from privately owned companies. Caramanis (1999, 2002, 2005) and Ballas (1998, 1999) have analysed in detail the attempt during the 1990s to break down SOL's monopoly over statutory audit, establish a form of audit familiar to global capital and create space for international audit firms in an era of aggressive neo-liberalism in Greek political economy and culture. The application of political and economic pressure by America and the European Union was a major factor in SOL's eventual defeat by 2001.

Former planned economies

Former planned economies are also interesting sites for the study of the impact of deep social and economic transformations on the professionalisation of accounting and the effects of the importation of foreign professional models on the development of the national profession. China and Russia have been through successive episodes which saw a first wave of professionalisation, inspired directly or indirectly by Western models (in the case of China the indirect influence came through Japan), followed by a period during which the existence of professional accountancy was entirely subsumed under the communist state. As these countries were again opened to international economic and financial flows in the late twentieth century, Western professional practices settled in again, mainly under the aegis of the big multinational audit firms.

In spite of the existence from the end of the nineteenth century of accounting associations (both academic and professionally orientated) in major economic centres such as St Petersburg (Sokolov 2015), and the attempt to launch a professional project in the context of the New Economic Policy during the 1920s (Bailey 1992), accountancy and auditing never really took off as an independent profession in Russia until the end of the 1990s, when the first professional association (now the Institute of Professional Accountants and Auditors of Russia) was established. As was the case for other countries formerly behind the Iron Curtain (Seal et al. 1996) the opening of the country's economy proved a golden opportunity to advance professional projects given the rising pay and status of accountants and 'the renewed emphasis on monetary calculation' (ibid.: 486). These changes have not occurred without the necessity to adapt local institutions and practices to the new economic environment. The challenge to revise professionals' knowledge base, establish new functional categories and sort out relations between local associations has been partially met with the assistance of the large multinational audit firms. However, as Mennicken (2008) remarks in the case of the adoption by Russia of international auditing standards, change has been more than a mere diffusion of Western professionalism. Rather it has been a matter of 'translating' (in the Latourian sense of this word) international ideas and practices in order to accommodate them to Russian realities.

China, a world in itself, presents yet another unique pattern of professionalisation. Attempts to modernise Chinese accounting occurred in the first half of the twentieth century, driven mostly by bankers (many of them trained in Japan) rather than by accountants (Xu and Xu 2008), but, similar to the Russian experience, this modernisation did not result in a fully fledged accountancy profession that would be independent of the state. Chinese accountants had to wait until the gradual move, from 1978, from a planned to a 'socialist market economy' (Hao 1999: 291), to see the *re-emergence* of a practitioner community (Xu and Xu 2003), albeit one still constrained by government scrutiny and direction. Exercising its political and ideological leadership through a relationship akin to that between father and son (Yee 2009), the Chinese state has managed to mobilise accountants in the implementation of its economic agenda (Ezzamel and Xiao 2015).

Conclusion: one or several professions?

The accountancy professionalisation literature now includes a substantial number of historical, context-sensitive case studies of professional projects pursued across the world at various times. Examination of the establishment of accountancy as a profession has starkly highlighted the 'political' roots of professional development and the sustained efforts that accountants have made to achieve 'higher remuneration and prestige for their labour' (Willmott 1986: 559).

The literature reveals patterns, but they only go so far. Within the Anglo-American world Larson's notions of market dominance and collective social mobility have aided understandings of the efforts made to achieve more concrete goals. In other settings the role of the State has been seen as paramount to the facilitation (or the hampering) of the professional projects of accountants (including cases when public authorities have authored this project and led its development). Everywhere variations in tactics, allies, opponents and institutions faced by the leaders of professional projects have been noted, although the state-profession dynamic has been a persistent theme.

As the number of uncharted territories on the worldwide map of professionalisation has diminished (but has not been exhausted),[10] what then remains to be studied in the history of the professionalisation of accountants? First of all, it remains the case that several aspects of well-rehearsed professionalisation experiences require further exploration. We have referred to the need for a greater focus on women, ethnic minorities, rank and file professionals as opposed to white, male professional elites. There have also been calls for new theoretical perspectives beyond the 'professional project-social closure' diptych and the examination of its various components (usurpatory closure, exclusionary closure, etc.). Some scholars have even questioned the explanatory power of the concept of professional project, implying that, where there was already a structured community of accountancy specialists, the official recognition of professional bodies might represent just another episode in the history of professionalisation. On the basis of the use of resources such as censuses, and on the further investigation of pre-institutionalisation periods, the need to reconsider what seemed to be settled historiography has been revealed.

Fresh explorations of the times when the profession was in its infancy are also the occasion to think about the significance of the concept of professionalisation throughout the period of the professional project. We have mentioned how post-formation histories have investigated episodes such as successful or unsuccessful extensions of the privileges initially gained and jurisdictions initially won, and examples of how relations between the profession and the public authorities fluctuated over time. How can we interpret, from the point of view of the collective identity of the profession, the dynamics of what happens once the occupation has been institutionalised? What 'projects' follow the achievement of the initial 'professional project'?

In this respect, the evolution of the profession in the era of financial globalisation offers a fertile ground for research (Miranti 2014). The advent of the global firm, as analysed in Chapter 12, represents a challenge to the traditional occupational and territorial boundaries within which accountancy has prospered as a profession (Sonnerfeldt and Loft 2018). Such firms have not only outgrown the national professions from which they sprung; they also promote themselves as suppliers of business services rather than providers of accounting and auditing (Edwards and Anderson 2011). The advent of this new, big firm era, is often traced to the Enron scandal and the demise of Arthur Andersen, but the making of the global firm as a professional model (Cooper and Robson 2006) commenced decades before and has hardly been investigated otherwise than by in-house historians (Allen and McDermott 1993; Jones 1995). Returning to the evolution-metamorphosis distinction in tracking trajectories of professional change over time, it would be interesting to investigate whether the rise and power of the multinational firms represent a continuation in the history of the professionalisation of accounting or the birth of a new form of professionalism. Having observed different patterns of professionalisation it would be interesting to see whether the globalisation of the accountancy profession represents the exportation of a particular form of Anglo-American professionalisation or is an entirely new phenomenon resting on the advent of *sui generis* actors. From the perspective of the nationally orientated professional bodies, it would be equally interesting to analyse their efforts to retain their significance given the growth of global firms, especially in times of an increasing dispersion of professional identity (Ramirez 2009a).

Key works

The main text identifies major papers on specific episodes of professionalisation. The following are important reviews and general works.

Cooper and Robson (2006) provide a useful review linking professionalisation with regulation and also suggest new research foci (see also Chapter 12 of this volume).

Poullaos and Sian (2010) offer a comprehensive study of the influence of Britain on the development of the profession in its former colonies and dominions and on the emergence of an imperial accountancy arena.

West (1996) provides an alternative review of the professionalisation literature to that provided in this chapter.

Zeff (1988) provides a helpful collection of essays on a formative period in the history of the profession in the USA.

Notes

1 A term emphasising 'the coherence and consistency' of a particular course of action, even though 'the goals and strategies pursued by a given group are not entirely clear or deliberate for all members' (Larson 1977: 6, cited in Macdonald 1995: 10).

2 When interpreted critically, the increasing availability of electronic versions of census enumeration books (CEBs) for Canada, the UK and America offers opportunities for better understanding the history of occupations concerned with the performance of accounting functions; see Edwards and Walker (2007).
3 The discussion below is based on Macdonald (1984, 1985, 1987), Briston and Kedslie (1986), Kedslie (1990a, 1990b), Walker (1988, 1991, 1995, 1996), Shackleton (1995) and Lee (1996a, 1996b, 2000, 2006, 2011a, 2011b).
4 On the period prior to the formation of these bodies see Edwards et al. (2007). On their unification via the formation of the ICAEW see Walker (2004b). On the social origins of the founders of the ICAEW see Anderson and Walker (2009).
5 The numbers entering under the 1893 examination route declined quickly from 1900. By 1886 chartered accountants were dominating the audit market (Anderson et al. 1996).
6 While all these matters have received some attention, they have not been examined systematically utilising available archival sources (see Richardson 1993: 553). Creighton (1984), Richardson (1987) and Chua and Poullaos (2002) touch lightly on these various points. Richardson (1989a) and MacDonald and Richardson (2004) show that federation is still a factor in Canadian professional projects. American influence is noted in Neu and Saleem (1996) and Everett et al. (2005). Richardson (1997) provides an update to Macdonald (1985) applied to Canadian data.
7 Parker (2005) has mapped the spread of 'CA' and 'CPA' through the British Empire/Commonwealth from 1853 to 2003 by seeking patterns in the names given to accounting associations. While there is a limit to how much of a professionalisation dynamic can be read from the choice of a name, a range of future research sites has been identified. Briston and Kedslie (1997) have sketched the rise of the British-based Chartered Association of Certified Accountants (ACCA) as an examining body throughout the British Empire/Commonwealth and beyond to places where professional projects barely existed, local training did not suit the requirements of global capital, or the locals preferred an 'international' credential to a local one.
8 The SIAA added 'Incorporated' to its name in 1908. We have used the abbreviation 'SIAA' throughout.
9 Recent investigations exploit the 1880 census to assess the variety of profiles in the accountant community (Lee 2007) and, in particular, the role of women in accounting occupations (Roberts 2013).
10 Although we have attempted to cover a wide range of countries in our chapter, we are aware that there are zones of the world we have left aside, such as Latin America (with the exception of Brazil). Some countries have not been mentioned because of the uniqueness of their culture, society and political regime, which makes it difficult to allocate them to one of the more transversal professionalisation dynamics we have introduced (while, on the other hand, their uniqueness offers a good illustration of the contingency of professional projects). Belonging to this category, for instance, is the case of Saudi Arabia, which has been investigated by Mihret et al. (2017).

References

Abbott, A. (1988) *The System of Professions: An Essay on the Expert Division of Labor* (Chicago: University of Chicago Press).

Agrizzi, D. and Sian, S. (2015) Artificial corporatism: A portal to power for accountants in Brazil, *Critical Perspectives on Accounting*, 27: 56–72.

Allen, D.G. and McDermott, K. (1993) *Accounting for Success: A History of Price Waterhouse in America, 1890–1990* (Boston: Harvard Business School Press).

Altaher, N.A., Cadiz Dyball, M. and Evans, E. (2014) A study of the emergence of the Kuwaiti Association of Accountants and Auditors, *Accounting History*, 19 (2): 255–78.

Anderson, M., Edwards, J.R. and Chandler, R.A. (2005) Constructing the 'well qualified' chartered accountant in England and Wales, *Accounting Historians Journal*, 32 (2): 5–54.

Anderson, M., Edwards, J.R. and Matthews, D. (1996) A study of the quoted company audit market in 1886, *Accounting, Business & Financial History*, 6 (3): 363–87.

Anderson, M. and Walker, S.P. (2009) 'All sorts and conditions of men': The social origins of the founders of the ICAEW, *British Accounting Review*, 41 (1): 31–45.

Annisette, M. (1999) Importing accounting: The case of Trinidad and Tobago, *Accounting, Business & Financial History*, 9 (1): 103–33.

Annisette, M. (2000) Imperialism and the professions: The education and certification of accountants in Trinidad and Tobago, *Accounting, Organizations and Society*, 25 (7): 631–59.

Annisette, M. (2017) Discourse of the professions: The making, normalizing and taming of Ontario's "foreign-trained accountant", *Accounting, Organizations and Society*, 60: 37–61.

Bailey, D. (1992) The attempt to establish the Russian accounting profession 1875–1931, *Accounting, Business & Financial History*, 2 (1): 1–23.

Bakre, O.M. (2005) First attempt at localising imperial accountancy: The case of the Institute of Chartered Accountants of Jamaica (ICAJ) (1950s–1970s), *Critical Perspectives on Accounting*, 16 (8): 995–1018.

Bakre, O.M. (2006) Second attempt at localising imperial accountancy: The case of the Institute of Chartered Accountants of Jamaica (ICAJ) (1970s–1980s), *Critical Perspectives on Accounting*, 17 (1): 1–28.

Bakre, O.M. (2014) Imperialism and the integration of accountancy in the Commonwealth Caribbean, *Critical Perspectives on Accounting*, 25 (7): 558–75.

Ballas, A.A. (1998) The creation of the auditing profession in Greece, *Accounting, Organizations and Society*, 23 (8): 715–36.

Ballas, A.A. (1999) Privatising the statutory auditing services in Greece, *Accounting, Business & Financial History*, 9 (3): 349–73.

Baskerville, R.F. and Hay, D. (2010) The impact of globalization on professional accounting firms: Evidence from New Zealand, *Accounting History*, 15 (3): 285–308.

Bocqueraz, C. (2001) The development of professional associations: The experience of French accountants from the 1880s to the 1940s, *Accounting, Business & Financial History*, 11 (1): 7–27.

Briston, R.J. and Kedslie, M.J.M. (1986) Professional formation: The case of Scottish accountants-some corrections and further thoughts, *British Journal of Sociology*, 37 (1): 122–30.

Briston, R.J. and Kedslie, M.J.M. (1997) The internationalization of British professional accounting: The role of the examination exporting bodies, *Accounting, Business & Financial History*, 7 (2): 175–94.

Brown, R. (ed.) (1905) *A History of Accounting and Accountants* (Edinburgh: T. C. and E. C. Jack).

Burchell, S., Clubb, C., Hopwood, A., Hughes, J. and Nahapiet, J. (1980) The role of accounting in organizations and society, *Accounting, Organizations and Society*, 5 (1): 5–27.

Caramanis, C.V. (1999) International accounting firms versus indigenous auditors: Intra-professional competition in the Greek auditing profession, 1990–1993, *Critical Perspectives on Accounting*, 10 (2): 153–96.

Caramanis, C.V. (2002) The interplay between professional groups, the state and supranational agents: Pax Americana in the age of 'globalisation', *Accounting, Organizations and Society*, 27 (4): 379–409.

Caramanis, C.V. (2005) Rationalism, charisma and accounting professionalism, *Accounting, Organizations and Society*, 30 (2): 195–222.

Carnegie, G.D. (1993) The Australian Institute of Incorporate Accountants (1892–1938), *Accounting, Business & Financial History*, 3 (1): 61–80.

Carnegie, G.D. (2016) The accounting professional project and bank failures: The case of the early 1890s Australian banking crisis, *Journal of Management History*, 22 (4): 389–412.

Carnegie, G.D. and Edwards, J.R. (2001) The construction of the professional accountant: The case of the Incorporated Institute of Accountants, Victoria (1886), *Accounting, Organizations and Society*, 26 (4–5): 301–25.

Carnegie, G.D., Edwards, J.R. and West, B.P. (2003) Understanding the dynamics of the Australian accounting profession. A prosopographical study of the founding members of the Incorporated Institute of Accountants, Victoria, 1886 to 1908, *Accounting, Auditing & Accountability Journal*, 16 (5): 790–820.

Carnegie, G.D. and O'Connell, B.T. (2012) Understanding the responses of professional accounting bodies to crises: The case of the Australian profession in the 1960s, *Accounting, Auditing & Accountability Journal*, 25 (5): 835–75.

Carnegie, G.D. and Parker, R.H. (1999) Accountants and empire: The case of co-membership of Australian and UK accountancy bodies, 1885 to 1914, *Accounting, Business & Financial History*, 9 (1): 77–102.

Carrera, N. and Carmona, S. (2013) Educational reforms set professional boundaries: The Spanish audit function,1850–1988, *Abacus*, 49 (1): 99–137.

Chandler, R.A. (2017) Questions of ethics and etiquette in the Society of Accountants in Edinburgh, 1853–1951, *Accounting History*, 22 (2): 179–92.

Chua, W.-F. and Poullaos, C. (1993) Rethinking the profession-state dynamic: The case of the Victorian charter attempt, 1885–1906, *Accounting, Organizations and Society*, 18 (7–8): 691–728.

Chua, W.-F. and Poullaos, C. (1998) The dynamics of closure amidst the construction of market, profession, empire and nationhood: An historical analysis of an Australian accounting association, 1886–1903, *Accounting, Organizations and Society*, 23 (2): 155–88.

Chua, W.-F. and Poullaos, C. (2002) The Empire strikes back? An exploration of centre-periphery interaction between the ICAEW and accounting associations in the self-governing colonies of Australia, Canada and South Africa, 1880–1907, *Accounting, Organizations and Society*, 27 (4–5): 409–45.

Collard, E.A. (1980) *First in North America* (Montreal: Ordre des Comptables Agrees du Quebec).

Collins, R. (1990) Changing conceptions in the sociology of the professions, in R. Torstendahl and M. Burrage (eds.) *The Formation of Professions: Knowledge, State and Strategy*, pp. 11–23 (London: Sage).

Cooper, D., Puxty, T., Robson, K. and Willmott, H. (1996) Changes in the international regulation of auditors: (In)stalling the eighth directive in the UK, *Critical Perspectives on Accounting*, 7 (6): 589–613.

Cooper, D.J. and Robson, K. (2006) Accounting, professions and regulation: Locating the sites of professionalisation, *Accounting, Organizations and Society*, 31 (4–5): 415–44.

Coronella, S., Sargiacomo, M. and Walker, S.P. (2015) Unification and dual closure in the Italian accountancy profession, 1861–1906, *European Accounting Review*, 24 (1): 167–97.

Creighton, P. (1984) *A Sum of Yesterdays* (Toronto: ICAO).

De Beelde, I. (2002) Creating a profession 'out of nothing'? the case of the Belgian auditing profession, *Accounting, Organizations and Society*, 27 (4–5): 447–70.

De Beelde, I., Gonthier, N. and Mikol, A. (2009) Internationalizing the French auditing profession, *Accounting Historians Journal*, 36 (1): 29–59.

Dedoulis, E. (2016) Institutional formations and the Anglo-Americanization of local auditing practices: The case of Greece, *Accounting Forum*, 40 (1): 29–44.

Dedoulis, E. and Caramanis, C. (2007) Imperialism of influence and the state-profession relationship: The formation of the Greek auditing profession in the post-WWII era, *Critical Perspectives on Accounting*, 18 (4): 393–412.

Doron, M.E. (2013) The American Institute of Accountants and the professionalization of auditing: The campaign to end temporary audit staff and promote the natural business year, 1923–1960, *Accounting History*, 18 (2): 257–69.

Dyball, M., Chua, W.F. and Poullaos, C. (2006) Mediating between colonizer and colonized in the American empire: Accounting for government monies in the Philippines, *Accounting, Auditing & Accountability Journal*, 19 (1): 47–81.

Dyball, M., Poullaos, C. and Chua, W.-F. (2007) Accounting and empire: Professionalization as resistance – the case of the Philippines, *Critical Perspectives on Accounting*, 18 (4): 415–49.

Edwards, J.R. (2010) Researching the absence of professional organisation in Victorian England, *Accounting, Business & Financial History*, 20 (2): 177–208.

Edwards, J.R. and Anderson, M. (2011) Writing masters and accountants in England: A study of occupation, status and ambition in the early modern period, *Accounting, Auditing & Accountability Journal*, 24 (6): 685–717.

Edwards, J.R., Anderson, M. and Chandler, R.A. (2007) Claiming a jurisdiction for the 'Public Accountant' in England prior to organisational fusion, *Accounting, Organizations and Society*, 32 (1–2): 61–100.

Edwards, J.R. and Walker, S.P. (2007) Accountants in the British census, *Accounting Historians Journal*, 34 (2): 43–74.

Edwards, J.R. and Walker, S.P. (2008) Occupational differentiation and exclusion in early Canadian accountancy, *Accounting and Business Research*, 38 (5): 373–91.

El Omari, S., Rossignol, J.L. and Saboly, M. (2013) The search for unity in the French accountancy profession, 1969–1996, *Accounting History Review*, 23 (1): 85–105.

Elad, C. (2015) The development of accounting in the Franc zone countries in Africa, *The International Journal of Accounting*, 50 (1): 75–100.

Evans, L. (2018) Shifting strategies: The pursuit of closure and the 'Association of German Auditors', *European Accounting Review*, 27 (4): 683–712.

Evans, L. and Honold, K. (2007) The division of expert labour in the European audit market: The case of Germany, *Critical Perspectives on Accounting*, 18 (1): 61–88.

Everett, J., Green, D. and Neu, D. (2005) Independence, objectivity and the Canadian CA profession, *Critical Perspectives on Accounting*, 16 (4): 415–40.

Ezzamel, M. and Xiao, J.Z.J. (2015) The development of accounting regulations for foreign invested firms in China: The role of Chinese characteristics, *Accounting, Organizations and Society*, 44: 60–84.

Freidson, E. (1983) The theory of the professions: The state of the art, in R. Dingwall and P. Lewis (eds.) *The Sociology of the Professions: Lawyers Doctors and Others*, pp. 19–37 (London: Macmillan).

Freidson, E. (1994) *Professionalism Reborn: Theory, Prophecy, and Policy* (Cambridge: Polity Press).

Garrett, A.A. (1961) *History of the Society of Incorporated Accountants 1885–1957* (Oxford: Oxford University Press).

Habenstein, R. (1963) Critique of 'profession' as a sociological category, *Sociological Quarterly*, 4 (4): 291–300.

Hammond, T., Clayton, B.M. and Arnold, P.J. (2009) South Africa's transition from apartheid: The role of professional closure in the experiences of black chartered accountants, *Accounting, Organizations and Society*, 34 (6–7): 705–21.

Hammond, T., Clayton, B.M. and Arnold, P.J. (2012) An "unofficial" history of race relations in the South African accounting industry, 1968–2000: Perspectives of South Africa's first black chartered accountants, *Critical Perspectives on Accounting*, 23 (4–5): 332–50.

Hanlon, G. (1994) *The Commercialisation of Accountancy* (London: Macmillan).

Hanlon, G. (1996) 'Casino capitalism' and the rise of the commercialized service class – an examination of the accountant, *Critical Perspectives on Accounting*, 7 (3): 339–63.

Hanlon, G. (1997) Commercialising the service class and economic restructuring – a response to my critics, *Accounting, Organizations and Society*, 22 (8): 843–55.

Hao, Z.P. (1999) Regulation and organization of accountants in China, *Accounting, Auditing & Accountability Journal*, 12 (3): 286–302.

Johnson, T.J. (1972) *Professions and Power* (London: Macmillan).

Jones, E. (1995) *True and Fair: A History of Price Waterhouse* (London: Hamish Hamilton).

Kedslie, M.J.M. (1990a) Mutual self-interest- a unifying force: The dominance of societal closure over social background in the early professional accounting bodies, *Accounting Historians Journal*, 17 (2): 1–9.

Kedslie, M.J.M. (1990b) *Firm Foundations. The Development of Professional Accounting in Scotland* (Hull: Hull University Press).

Kimball, B.A. (1992) *The True Professional Ideal in America: A History* (Cambridge, MA: Blackwell).

Klegon, D. (1978) The sociology of the professions: An emerging perspective, *Sociology of Work and Occupations*, 5 (3): 259–83.

Larson, M.S. (1977) *The Rise of Professionalism: A Sociological Analysis* (Berkeley: University of California).

Lee, T. (1996a) Identifying the founding fathers of public accountancy: The formation of the Society of Accountants in Edinburgh, *Accounting, Business & Financial History*, 6 (3): 315–35.

Lee, T. (ed.) (1996b) *Shaping the Accountancy Profession: The Story of Three Scottish Pioneers* (New York and London: Garland).

Lee, T. (2000) A social network analysis of the founders of institutionalized public accountancy, *Accounting Historians Journal*, 27 (2): 1–48.

Lee, T. (2004) Economic class, social status and early Scottish chartered accountants, *Accounting Historians Journal*, 31 (2): 27–51.

Lee, T.A. (1997) The influence of Scottish accountants in the United States: The early case of the Society of Accountants in Edinburgh, *Accounting Historians Journal*, 24 (1): 117–41.

Lee, T.A. (2001) US public accountancy firms and the recruitment of UK immigrants: 1850–1914, *Accounting, Auditing & Accountability Journal*, 14 (5): 537–64.

Lee, T.A. (2002a) UK immigrants and the foundation of the US public accountancy profession, *Accounting, Business & Financial History*, 12 (1): 73–94.

Lee, T.A. (2002b) US public accountancy firms and the recruitment of UK immigrants: 1850–1914, *Accounting, Auditing & Accountability Journal*, 14 (5): 537–64.

Lee, T.A. (2006) Going where no accounting historian has gone before. A counterfactual history of the early institutionalization of modern public accountancy, *Accounting, Auditing & Accountability Journal*, 19 (6): 918–44.

Lee, T.A. (2007) American accountants in 1880, *Accounting, Business & Financial History*, 17 (3): 333–54.

Lee, T.A. (2009) Outliers in the professional project of Victorian public accountancy: David Souter Robertson, chartered accountant, *Accounting Historians Journal*, 36 (2): 75–92.

Lee, T.A. (2010a) Social closure and the incorporation of the Society of Accountants in Edinburgh in 1854, *Accounting, Business & Financial History*, 20 (1): 1–22.
Lee, T.A. (2010b) Consolidating the public accountancy profession: The case of the proposed Institute of Chartered Accountants of Great Britain, 1988–9, *Accounting History*, 15 (1): 7–39.
Lee, T.A. (2011a) Bankrupt accountants and lawyers: Transition in the rise of professionalism in Victorian Scotland, *Accounting, Auditing & Accountability Journal*, 24 (7): 879–903.
Lee, T.A. (2011b) Paul and Mackersy, accountants, 1818–34: Public accountancy in the early nineteenth century, *Accounting History Review*, 21 (3): 285–307.
Lee, T.A. (2015) 'A different army of the talented': Negative outliers in the rise of professionalism in Victorian public accountancy, *Accounting History Review*, 25 (2): 77–95.
Lima Rodrigues, L. and Sangster, A. (2013) The role of the state in the development of accounting in the Portuguese–Brazilian Empire, 1750–1822, *Accounting History Review*, 23 (2): 161–84.
Lima Rodrigues, L., Schmidt, P., Dos Santos, J.L. and Dutra Fonseca, P.C. (2011) A research note on accounting in Brazil in the context of political, economic and social transformations, 1860–1964, *Accounting History*, 16 (1): 111–23.
Loft, A. (1986) Towards a critical understanding of the accounting: The case of cost accounting in the U.K., 1914–1925, *Accounting, Organizations and Society*, 11 (2): 137–69.
Macdonald, K.M. (1984) Professional formation: The case of Scottish chartered accountants, *British Journal of Sociology*, 35 (2): 174–89.
Macdonald, K.M. (1985) Social closure and occupational registration, *Sociology*, 19 (4): 541–56.
Macdonald, K.M. (1987) Professional formation: A reply to Briston and Kedslie, *British Journal of Sociology*, 38 (1): 106–11.
Macdonald, K.M. (1995) *The Sociology of the Professions* (London, Thousand Oaks, CA and New Delhi: Sage).
MacDonald, L.D. and Richardson, A.J. (2004) Identity, appropriateness and the construction of regulatory space: The formation of the Public Accountant's Council of Ontario, *Accounting, Organizations and Society*, 29 (5–6): 489–524.
Matthews, D.R. (2017) Accountants and the professional project, *Accounting, Auditing & Accountability Journal*, 30 (2): 306–27.
McKinstry, S. (2014) From "colonial reciprocity" to international supremacy: Scottish chartered accountancy and its "discourse of superiority" in context, 1854 to the present, *Accounting History*, 19 (1–2): 77–96.
McMillan, K.P. (1999) The Institute of Accounts: A community of the competent, *Accounting, Business & Financial History*, 9 (1): 7–28.
Mihret, D.G., Alshareef, M.N. and Bazhair, A. (2017) Accounting professionalization and the state: The case of Saudi Arabia, *Critical Perspectives on Accounting*, 45: 29–47.
Mihret, D.G., James, K. and Bobe, B.J. (2014) Multiple informal imperial connections and the transfer of accountancy to Ethiopia (1905 to 2011), *Accounting History*, 19 (3): 309–31.
Mihret, D.G., James, K. and Mula, J.M. (2012) Accounting professionalization amidst alternating state ideology in Ethiopia, *Accounting, Auditing & Accountability Journal*, 25 (7): 1206–33.
Millerson, G. (1964) *The Qualifying Associations: A Study in Professionalisation* (London: Routledge & Kegan Paul).
Mills, P.A. and Young, J.J. (1999) From contract to speech: The courts and CPA licensing laws 1921–1996, *Accounting, Organizations and Society*, 24 (3): 243–62.
Miranti, P.J. (1986) Associationalism, statism, and professionalisation regulation: Public accountants and the reform of the financial markets, 1896–1940, *Business History Review*, 60 (3): 438–69.
Miranti, P.J. (1988) Professionalism and nativism: The competition in securing public accountancy legislation in New York during the 1890s, *Social Science Quarterly*, 60 (2): 361–82.
Miranti, P.J. (1990) *Accountancy Comes of Age: The Rise of an American Profession, 1886–1940* (Chapel Hill and London: University of North Carolina Press).
Miranti, P.J. (2014) The emergence of accounting as a global profession – an introduction, *Accounting History*, 19 (1–2): 3–11.
Neu, D. and Saleem, L. (1996) The Institute of Chartered Accountants of Ontario (ICAO) and the emergence of ethical codes, *Accounting Historians Journal*, 23 (2): 35–68.
Noguchi, M. and Edwards, J.R. (2004) Accounting principles, internal conflict and the state: The case of the ICAEW, 1948–1966, *Abacus*, 40 (3): 280–320.

Noguchi, M. and Edwards, J.R. (2008) Harmonising intergroup relations within a professional body: The case of the ICAEW, 1948–1966, *British Accounting Review*, 40 (2): 123–47.

Ohman, P. and Wallerstedt, E. (2012) Audit regulation and the development of the audit profession: The case of Sweden, *Accounting History*, 17 (2): 241–257.

O'Regan, P. (2008) 'Elevating the profession': The Institute of Chartered Accountants in Ireland and the implementation of social closure strategies 1888–1909, *Accounting, Business & Financial History*, 18 (1): 35–59.

O'Regan, P. (2013) Usurpationary closure and the professional project: The case of the Society of Incorporated Accountants and Auditors in Ireland, *Accounting History Review*, 23 (3): 253–71.

Parker, R.H. (1989) Importing and exporting accounting: The British experience, in A. Hopwood (ed.) *International Pressures for Accounting Change*, pp. 7–29 (Hertfordshire: Prentice-Hall International & ICAEW).

Parker, R.H. (2005) Naming and branding: Accountants and accountancy bodies in the British Empire and Commonwealth, 1853–2003, *Accounting History*, 10 (1): 7–46.

Parker, S. and Johnson, L.A. (2017) The development of internal auditing as a profession in the U.S. during the twentieth century, *Accounting Historians Journal*, 44 (2): 47–67.

Persson, M.E., Radcliffe, V.S. and Stein, M. (2018) Elmer G Beamer and the American Institute of Certified Public Accountants: The pursuit of a cognitive standard for the accounting profession, *Accounting History*, 23 (1–2): 71–92.

Poullaos, C. (1994) *Making the Australian Chartered Accountant* (New York and London: Garland).

Poullaos, C. (2009) Profession, race and empire: Keeping the centre pure, 1921–1927, *Accounting, Auditing & Accountability Journal*, 22 (3): 429–68.

Poullaos, C. (2016) Canada vs Britain in the imperial accountancy arena, 1908–1912: Symbolic capital, symbolic violence, *Accounting Organizations and Society*, 51: 47–63.

Poullaos, C. and Sian, S. (eds) (2010) *Accountancy and Empire: The British Legacy of Professional Organization* (New York: Routledge).

Praquin, N. (2012) Commercial legislation and the emergence of corporate auditing in France, 1856–1935, *Accounting History Review*, 22 (2): 161–89.

Preston, A.M., Cooper, D.J., Scarbrough, D.P. and Chilton, R.C. (1995) Changes in the code of ethics of the U.S. accounting profession, 1917 and 1988: The continual quest for legitimation, *Accounting, Organizations and Society*, 20 (6): 507–46.

Previts, G.J. and Merino, B.D. (1998) *A History of Accountancy in the United States: The Cultural Significance of Accounting*, 2nd edn (Columbus: Ohio State University Press).

Radcliffe, V., Cooper, D.J. and Robson, K. (1994) The management of professional enterprises and regulatory change: British accountancy and the Financial Services Act, 1986, *Accounting, Organizations and Society*, 19 (7): 601–28.

Ramirez, C. (2001) Understanding social closure in its cultural context: Accounting practitioners in France (1920–1939), *Accounting, Organizations and Society*, 26 (4–5): 391–418.

Ramirez, C. (2009a) Constructing the governable small practitioner: The changing nature of professional bodies and the management of professional accountants' identities in the UK, *Accounting, Organizations and Society*, 34 (3–4): 381–408.

Ramirez, C. (2009b) Reform or rebirth? the 1966 Companies Act and the problem of the modernisation of the audit profession in France, *Accounting, Business & Financial History*, 19 (2): 127–48.

Ramirez, C. (2010) Promoting transnational professionalism: Forays of the "Big Firm" accounting community into France, in S. Quack and M.L. Djelic (eds.) *Transnational Communities. Shaping Global Economic Governance*, pp. 271–302 (Cambridge: Cambridge University Press).

Ramirez, C. (2013) "We are being pilloried for something we did not even know we had done wrong!" quality control and orders of worth in the British audit profession, *Journal of Management Studies*, 50 (5): 845–69.

Richardson, A.J. (1987) Professionalization and intraprofessional competition in the Canadian accounting profession, *Work and Occupations*, 14 (4): 591–615.

Richardson, A.J. (1989a) Corporatism and intraprofessional hegemony: A study of regulation and internal social order, *Accounting, Organizations and Society*, 14 (5–6): 415–31.

Richardson, A.J. (1989b) Canada's accounting elite: 1880–1930, *Accounting Historians Journal*, 16 (1): 1–20.

Richardson, A.J. (1993) An interpretative chronology of the development of accounting associations in Canada: 1879–1979, in G.J. Murphy (ed.) *A History of Canadian Accounting Thought and Practice*, pp. 551–627 (New York and London: Garland).

Richardson, A.J. (1997) Social closure in dynamic markets: The incomplete professional project in accountancy, *Critical Perspectives on Accounting*, 8 (6): 635–53.

Richardson, A.J. (2002) Professional dominance: The relationship between financial accounting and management accounting, 1926–1986, *Accounting Historians Journal*, 29 (2): 91–122.

Roberts, D.H. (2013) Women in accounting occupations in the 1880 US Census, *Accounting History Review*, 23 (2): 141–60.

Roberts, D.H. (2015) Socialization of US novice accounting professionals through ethical discourse in 1931, *Accounting Historians Journal*, 42 (2): 63–90.

Robson, K., Willmott, H., Cooper, D. and Puxty, T. (1994) The ideology of professional regulation and the markets for accounting labour: Three episodes in the recent history of the UK accountancy profession, *Accounting, Organizations and Society*, 19 (6): 527–53.

Rodrigues, L.L., Gomes, D. and Craig, R. (2003) Corporatism, liberalism and the accounting profession in Portugal since 1755, *Accounting Historians Journal*, 30 (1): 95–127.

Roth, J. (1974) Professionalism: The sociologist's decoy, *Sociology of Work and Occupations*, 1 (1): 6–23.

Rueschemeyer, D. (1964) Doctors and lawyers: A commentary on the theory of the professions, *Canadian Review of Sociology and Anthropology*, 1 (1): 17–30.

Rueschemeyer, D. (1983) Professional autonomy and the social control of expertise, in Dingwall, R. and Lewis, P. (eds) *The Sociology of Professions: Lawyers, Doctors and Others*, pp. 38–58 (London: Macmillan).

Sakagami, M., Yoshimi, H. and Okano, H. (1999) Japanese accounting profession in transition, *Accounting, Auditing & Accountability Journal*, 12 (3): 340–57.

Saks, M. (1983) Removing the blinkers? a critique of recent contributions to the sociology of the professions, *Sociological Review*, 31 (1): 1–21.

Samsonova-Taddei, A. and Humphrey, C. (2014) Transnationalism and the transforming roles of professional accountancy bodies. Towards a research agenda, *Accounting, Auditing & Accountability Journal*, 27 (6): 903–32.

Schäffer, U., Schmidt, A. and Strauss, E. (2014) An old boys' club on the threshold to becoming a professional association: The emergence and development of the association of German controllers from 1975 to 1989, *Accounting History*, 19 (1–2): 133–69.

Seal, W., Sucher, P. and Zelenka, I. (1996) Post-socialist transition and the development of an accountancy profession in the Czech Republic, *Critical Perspectives on Accounting*, 7 (4): 485–508.

Shackleton, K. (1995) Scottish chartered accountants: Internal and external political relationships, 1853–1916, *Accounting, Auditing & Accountability Journal*, 8 (2): 18–46.

Sian, S. (2006) Inclusion, exclusion and control: The case of the Kenyan accounting professionalisation project, *Accounting, Organizations and Society*, 31 (3): 295–322.

Sian, S. (2007) Reversing exclusion: The Africanisation of accountancy in Kenya, 1963–1970, *Critical Perspectives on Accounting*, 18 (7): 831–72.

Sian, S. (2011) Operationalising closure in a colonial context: The Association of Accountants in East Africa, 1949–1963, *Accounting, Organizations and Society*, 36 (6): 363–81.

Sidhu, J. and West, B. (2014) The emergent Institute of Chartered Accountants of India: An upper-*caste* profession, *Accounting History*, 19 (1–2): 115–32.

Sikka, P. and Willmott, H. (1995) Illuminating the state-profession relationship: Accountants acting as Department of Trade and Industry investigators, *Critical Perspectives on Accounting*, 6 (4): 341–69.

Sokolov, V. (2015) A history of professional accounting societies in St Petersburg, *Accounting History*, 20 (3): 375–95.

Sonnerfeldt, A. and Loft, A. (2018) The changing face of ethics – developing a code of ethics for professional accountants from 1977 to 2006, *Accounting History*, 23 (4): 521–40.

Spence, C. and Brivot, M. (2011) 'No French, no more': Language-based exclusion in North America's first professional accounting association, 1879–1927, *Accounting History Review*, 21 (2): 163–84.

Stacey, N.A.H. (1954) *English Accountancy 1800–1954: A Study in Social and Economic History* (London: Gee & Co.).

Uche, C.U. (2002) Professional accounting development in Nigeria: Threats from the inside and outside, *Accounting, Organizations and Society*, 27 (4–5): 471–96.

Velayutham, S. (2003) The accounting profession's code of ethics: Is it a code of ethics or a code of quality assurance? *Critical Perspectives on Accounting*, 14 (4): 483–503.

Verhoef, G. (2013) Reluctant ally: The development of statutory regulation of the accountancy profession in South Africa, 1904–1951, *Accounting History*, 18 (2): 163–91.

Verhoef, G. (2014) Globalisation of knowledge but not opportunity: Closure strategies in the making of the South African accounting market, 1890s to 1958, *Accounting History*, 19 (1–2): 193–226.

Verma, S. (2015) Political, economic, social and imperial influences on the establishment of the Institute of Cost and Works Accountants in India post independence, *Critical Perspectives on Accounting*, 31: 5–22.

Verma, S. and Gray, S.J. (2006) The creation of the institute of Chartered Accountants of India: The first steps in the development of an indigenous accounting profession post-independence, *Accounting Historians Journal*, 33 (2): 131–56.

Walker, S.P. (1988) *The Society of Accountants in Edinburgh 1854–1914. A Study of Recruitment to A New Profession* (New York: Garland).

Walker, S.P. (1991) The defence of professional monopoly: Scottish chartered accountants and 'satellites in the accountancy firmament', *Accounting, Organizations and Society*, 16 (3): 257–83.

Walker, S.P. (1995) The genesis of professional organization in Scotland: A contextual analysis, *Accounting, Organizations and Society*, 20 (4): 285–310.

Walker, S.P. (1996) The criminal upperworld and the emergence of a disciplinary code in the early chartered accountancy profession, *Accounting History*, 1 (2): 7–36.

Walker, S.P. (2004a) The genesis of professional organisation in English accountancy, *Accounting, Organizations and Society*, 29 (2): 127–56.

Walker, S.P. (2004b) *Towards the 'Great Desideratum': The Unification of the Accountancy Bodies in England, 1870–1880* (Edinburgh: ICAS).

Walker, S.P. (2011) Professions and patriarchy revisited. Accountancy in England and Wales, 1887–1914, *Accounting History Review*, 21 (2): 185–225.

Walker, S.P. (2017) Accountants and the pursuit of the national interest: A study of role conflict during the First World War, *Critical Perspectives on Accounting*, 47: 8–25.

Walker, S.P. and Shackleton, K. (1995) Corporatism and structural change in the British accountancy profession, 1930–1957, *Accounting, Organizations and Society*, 20 (6): 467–503.

Walker, S.P. and Shackleton, K. (1998) A ring fence for the profession: Advancing the closure of British accountancy 1957–1970, *Accounting, Auditing & Accountability Journal*, 11 (1): 34–71.

Wallace, R.S.O. (1992) Growing pains of an indigenous accountancy profession: The Nigerian experience, *Accounting, Business & Financial History*, 2 (1): 25–53.

West, B.P. (1996) The professionalisation of accounting. A review of recent historical research and its implications, *Accounting History*, 1 (1): 77–102.

Wilenski, H.L. (1964) The professionalization of everyone? *American Journal of Sociology*, 70 (2): 137–58.

Willmott, H. (1986) Organising the profession: A theoretical and historical examination of the development of the major accountancy bodies in the U.K., *Accounting, Organizations and Society*, 11 (6): 555–80.

Willmott, H. and Sikka, P. (1997) On the commercialization of accountancy thesis: A review essay, *Accounting, Organizations and Society*, 22 (8): 831–42.

Xu, X. and Xu, X. (2003) Becoming professional: Chinese accountants in early 20th century China, *Accounting Historians Journal*, 30 (1): 129–53.

Xu, X. and Xu, X. (2008) Social actors, cultural capital, and the state: The standardization of bank accounting classification and terminology in early twentieth-century China, *Accounting, Organizations and Society*, 33 (1): 73–102.

Yee, H. (2009) The re-emergence of the public accounting profession in China: A hegemonic analysis, *Critical Perspectives on Accounting*, 20 (1): 71–92.

Zeff, S.A. (ed.) (1988) *The U.S. Accounting Profession in the 1890s and Early 1900s* (New York and London: Garland).

12
ACCOUNTING PRACTITIONERS, WORK AND ORGANISATIONS

David J. Cooper, Keith Robson and Chiara Bottausci[1]

Overview

In this chapter we focus on one crucial site of accounting practice: the multinational professional service firms (the Big 4), and the historical studies that have examined their emergence and development. We identify six characteristic contributions of these histories and point out their strengths and limitations. First, most histories serve as celebrations of individual firms, practitioners and the service of the audit function. Second, clients are presented as the motor force in the growth and characteristics of the multinational firms. The third theme is the contribution of elite practitioners to the development of the accounting profession. Fourth, histories recount the spread of practitioners and accounting knowledge across geographical space. The fifth theme is the account of the nature of the practice of accounting firms – from bankruptcy, to audit, to management consultancy. Lastly, the histories account for the formal organisational structures of the firms. Later in the chapter we offer several suggestions for further research on firm histories: histories as managed organisations, the experience and practices of work, the firms' role as cultural and political actors, and histories of firms as agents of imperialism.

Introduction

Several recent books have highlighted the power and significance of accounting firms. Notably, Gow and Kells (2018) offer an important analysis of the immense power of the international accounting firms (currently the Big 4, but more generically, the Big N) and the seriousness of their neglect of their traditional responsibilities. Brooks (2018) links these firms to the breakdown of capitalism. Insiders have discussed the 'uncertain future' of the Big 4 (Peterson 2015) and recent public policy debates, particularly in the UK, have talked of their break up (Bloomberg 2018). Such discussions all contextualise the present in relation to the history of these firms. This chapter takes their arguments further by examining the role of professional firms in both the development of the accounting profession and professional identity, as well as the development of practices that are now deemed to be part of accounting, but which can be seen as a threat to the claims about professional responsibilities that underlie the audit monopoly, if not capitalism itself. The nature of accounting practitioners, the work they do and the firms in which they trained, learned and practised their craft are important factors that have influenced accounting and society, and lead to concerns about the failures of professional responsibility.

Cooper and Robson (2006) argue that accounting research has tended to neglect the role of firms, particularly the larger organisations, and has instead concentrated on prominent accountants (both leaders of the professional bodies and innovators in accounting thought) and their professional associations. Much historical accounting research has assumed that these factors explain how and why accounting and accountants have become a powerful social and economic force.

In this chapter we focus on one crucial site of accounting practice: the multinational business ('professional') service firms (currently the Big 4), and the historical studies that have examined their emergence and development. From their origins in accountancy partnerships dating, in some cases, as far back as the mid-nineteenth century, mergers between founding accountancy partnerships and revenue growth have established the multinational accountancy firms as major global organisations.[2] Table 12.1 (drawn from Suddaby et al. 2007) indicates the size and scope of these firms. It is perhaps unsurprising that these firms audit almost all the publicly quoted companies in the major stock exchanges of the world, and are typically the preferred advisers to governments concerning economic and social reforms (from health care and education to tax policy and the management of government themselves). Accounting firms (even if the Big 4 no longer call themselves such) are everywhere, even advising regimes that present themselves as suspicious of capitalism (Catchpowle and Cooper 1999).

Who are these Big 4 firms and what are their antecedents? Since the mid-1980s Price Waterhouse and Coopers & Lybrand have combined to form PricewaterhouseCoopers; KPMG was the product of a merger between Peat Marwick and Kleinveld Main Goerdeler; Ernst & Whinney merged with Arthur Young to form Ernst & Young; Deloitte Haskins & Sells combined with Touche Ross; and Arthur Andersen would implode after the scandals of Enron, WorldCom and others. These firms featured in the largest 500 firms in the world, although they rarely appear on such lists because they are not required to publish audited statements of their own activities. Tracing their histories provides important insight into how accounting and accounting firms have been transformed in the last 150 years from minor actors to central figures on the world stage.

We acknowledge that the majority of professionally qualified accountants do not work in 'public practice', and certainly not in multinational accounting firms. But these firms are important locations where accounting and auditing practices emerge, become standardised and regulated, where accounting rules and standards are translated into practice, and where professional identities are formed, mediated and transformed. The alumni of such firms play a major role in the corporate accounting and finance function in many countries (Armstrong 1987; Fligstein 1993; Iyer 1998). And while there are historical studies of small accounting firms in earlier eras (e.g. Walker 1993; Habgood 1994), few studies exist of accountants and the work of smaller and regional firms (notable exceptions include Ramirez 2001, 2009). So, for reasons both of practicality and due to their importance in the development of accounting work and ideas, this chapter focuses on the histories of what have emerged as the global accounting firms.

The sources that we draw upon in this chapter show some diversity: historical overviews of firms have been produced or sponsored by the firms themselves (De Mond 1951; Cooper Bros & Co. 1954; Wise 1982; Falkus 1993; White 2003), many either commissioned

Table 12.1 Growth in scale of Big 8 (5, 4): 1980, 1999, 2017

1980 Big 8			*1999 Big 5*			*2017 Big 4*		
Firm	*Global Revenue* ($US millions)	*Number of* Employees	*Firm*	*Global Revenue* ($US billions)	*Number of* Employees	*Firm*	*Global Revenue* ($US billions)	*Number of* Employees
Arthur Andersen	645	15,500	Pricewaterhouse Coopers	17.3	155,000	Deloitte	38.8	263,900
Coopers & Lybrand	595	12,000	Arthur Andersen	16.21	135,000	Pricewaterhouse Coopers	37.7	236,235
Peat Marwick & Mitchell	586	14,000	Ernst & Young	12.58	97,800	Ernst & Young	31.4	247,570
Ernst & Whinney	500	14,000	KPMG	10.86	102,000	KPMG	26.4	197,263
Deloitte Haskins & Sells	450	10,000	Deloitte & Touche	10.6	90,000			
Arthur Young	400	15,000						
Touche Ross								
Price Waterhouse								

Source: Fortune, 1980; Public Accounting Report (1981, 2000), and Global Annual Reviews (2017).

(Richards 1950; Pollard 1975; Richards 1981; Marshall 1982; Coopers & Lybrand 1984; Jones 1981, 1995; Allen and McDermott 1993) or the work ('memoirs') of former partners (Kettle 1957; Spacek 1985; Benson 1989). Other studies follow biographical traditions of business research: the study of the professional elites (Howitt 1966; Richardson 1989; Persson et al. 2015), firm mergers (Boys 1988; Cypert 1991), or key individuals and their contributions to firm and professional development (Jones 1988; Persson et al. 2018). Some studies pursue journalistic themes or express insider accounts, perhaps written in response to event-specific crises or scandal (Stevens 1981; Squires et al. 2003; Toffler and Reingold 2003; Gow and Kells 2018). Yet other studies are not presented as accounting history but comment upon the professional firms and their practices in a historical context and in the light of other theoretical engagements (Loft 1986; Hanlon 1994; Poullaos 1994; Dirsmith et al. 1997; Gendron and Spira 2010; Brock et al. 2012; Malsch and Gendron 2013). Finally, our own research on professional service firms more generally informs our analysis of these secondary sources.

This chapter has a distinctly Anglo-American orientation, which reflects much of the research literature, but begs the question whether the concept of a profession is understood in the same way outside the Anglo-American world (Gietzmann and Quick 1998; Evans 2003; Poullaos and Uche 2012; Yee 2012; Gillis 2014; Belal et al. 2017), and whether these firms either did, or now do, operate in the way presented in these histories (Sluyterman 1998; Post et al. 1998; Kornberger et al. 2011). With this important caveat in mind, our main purposes are, first, to attend to the dominant themes within histories of accounting firms, and, second, to set out research issues that we consider have not been sufficiently addressed. Our review suggests that much of the literature on the major accounting firms has taken as its subject the lives and work of elite practitioners – those who founded the firms or succeeded to the position of senior partner. Indeed, many firm histories seem to be indistinguishable from biographies of the senior members (e.g. White 2003). Histories of their efforts in establishing and extending their firms have been complemented by accounts of the contributions of these senior figures to the growth of major professional associations.

The contributions of firm histories

In this section we identify six features of firm histories. First, many histories serve as celebrations of individual firms, practitioners and the service provided by the audit function. Second, clients, sometimes explicitly, but often indistinctly, are presented as the motor force in the growth and characteristics of the multinational firms and their predecessors. The third feature highlights the contribution of elite practitioners ('leaders' of the various firms) in the development of the accounting profession. Fourth, histories provide considerable detail about the spread of practitioners and accounting knowledge across geographical space, albeit with a UK focus. The fifth theme we identify is the changing service offerings of accounting firms, from bankruptcy, to audit and to management consultancy. Lastly, the histories offer an account of the formal structures and management controls of the firms themselves.

Celebratory histories

There has been a long tradition of historical studies of accounting firms. Consequently, it might be expected that there is a great deal to be learned from these studies. They might be expected to have mirrored mainstream economic and social histories of industrial and commercial firms (Chandler 1962; Pollard 1965; Best 1991; Useem 1996; Roy 1997), histories that have explored topics such as evolving conceptions of markets, industries, management practice, the spatial dimensions of economic activity, and shifting production technologies and the impact of firms on economic and social activity (Perrow 2002). Histories of railroads (Chandler 1965; Dobbin and Dowd 2000; Feeney 2013), textile companies (McGouldrick 1968), financial institutions (Chernow 1990) and so on have illuminated important aspects of the changing nature of the economy, international developments, the relationship between commercial and political life, industrial relations, and much else. Histories of accounting firms appear detached from these fundamental developments although they offer the potential to understand the development of accounting and audit work, changes in understandings of professionalism, and the relation between accounting, other professions, the economy and society.

Furthermore, with few exceptions, many accounting firm histories could be characterised as public relations documents that have been written for the firms themselves. Most histories of firms extol their virtues, celebrate their contributions and offer a functionalist and self-serving analysis of their activities (Robson and Cooper 1990). These histories are often expressed in chronological and dynastic terms, where one leader gives way to another in a parade of great men.

The prefaces of many firm histories highlight the celebratory nature of these works, which are often commissioned by the firms themselves to commemorate some significant moment in the firm's development. Indeed, the same motives can be seen in many histories of commercial organisations. The histories are often limited in terms of access to internal information about the operations and strategies of the firms, and many histories are quite explicit about confidentiality agreements with their firm subject.

In one sense, then, it would be churlish and redundant to complain about this uncritical and triumphant attribute, and there is no doubt that researching accounting firms has special challenges given the lack of public data and accessibility to firm data. Further, many of these histories may be seen as important elements in the formation of the identities and self-understanding of firms and the accountants who have been associated with them, and this indeed may be reason enough to study these histories. But they stand in marked contrast with Walker (2002; Anderson and Walker 2009) who shows the low status of those who called themselves accountants in England in the mid-nineteenth century.

However, the celebratory nature of these histories comes at a significant cost to the accounting researcher and historian. Absent from such histories is an analysis of employment and work practices of accountants or auditors, or a careful examination of relations with clients, the state and the economy. To learn about the sort of issues studied by modern economic and management historians, the accounting researcher has to infer a great deal. The life and achievements of the founding partners of the big firms may be interesting, but there is room for more focus upon the work of the professional firms, their development as organisations, and their expertise and work practices. So, this chapter is forced to make inferences from what has been written, and largely ignores the celebration of the achievements of the firms and senior partners. Instead, it considers issues that arise from reading between the lines of these texts.

Histories in the name of the client

Certain rhetorical themes are repeated throughout firm histories, and these themes offer insight into the implicit perspectives of their authors and the belief systems that permeate the accounting firms. The most prominent theme is 'in the name of the client', rhetoric used to justify many changes in organisation and activities. For example, conformity in dress is justified by the assumption that clients have a view of what an accountant should look like (Stevens 1981: 24).

Anderson-Gough et al. (2000) draw attention to how this theme endures in the current practices of accounting firms in the UK, as a form of internal discipline. Hammond (2002) indicates that assumptions about client expectations were a major reason offered by accounting firms in the US to exclude African-Americans for much of the twentieth century. In firm histories, 'the client' is used to justify the expansion of the firms; client pressures and needs are said to explain why individual partnerships have grown to be huge multinational enterprises. While large clients may often prefer large firms, this pressure does not seem to have operated to the same extent for other professional service firms (e.g. in law). We wonder why accounting firms studiously fail to explain their behaviours in terms of profit or growth (Previts and Merino 1988: 132). Haskins & Sells reportedly only realised the value of overseas operations when Barnum and Bailey's Circus ran into financial troubles while touring Europe, and thus merged with a London firm (Wootton et al. 2003). Price Waterhouse (PW) only opened their first office in the US in 1890 to investigate US breweries for British investors (Allen and McDermott 1993: xiii). PW opened their Pittsburgh office in 1902 to cater to their new client, US Steel (Jones 1995: 93). PW expanded to Liverpool in 1904 because of their existing work for shipping lines (Jones 1995: 89). Arthur Andersen apparently started to open overseas offices when they were appalled at the class-ridden treatment of clients offered by their London correspondence firm (Arthur Andersen nd). Jones reports that even in 1973, an influential paper presented to a PW partnership meeting declared 'excellence rather than size for its own sake should be our goal', but it went on to argue that:

> [n]evertheless, it is agreed that a certain size is inescapable to enable us to have a large enough base to provide a full range of external and internal services and in order to be able to attract the cream of the young men coming into the profession. In practice this means that we must aim to be broadly comparable in terms of size with our major competitors.
>
> *(Jones 1995: 258)*

Embedded in this quote is another motive for expansion – to provide partnership opportunities necessary for recruiting, which are themselves couched in terms of what is best for the client. Throughout Jones' (1995) history of PW, the tendency is to underplay commercial motivations for firm activities, such as concerns with staff recruiting, retention and promotion, and to interpret firm actions as client driven. In Jones' account, the development of PW is driven by clients and the market place, and in this sense, the history is not only functionalist but also determinist, curiously out of keeping with the otherwise individualist ethos of many histories. The history of PW is presented as great leaders responding to clients.

In examining the history of Lybrand, Ross Bros. & Montgomery, Chandar et al. (2014) argue that the evolution of accounting firms during the twentieth century followed the 'Chandlerian model of growth' in which increases in the size, scope and complexity of major clients provided strong incentives for the development of accounting firms. The growth in accounting firms' size, portfolio of services and network of local offices is seen as a response to the need to attract outstanding personnel and develop the economies of scope and knowledge specialisation required to serve large customers and the complex needs of diversified clients. However, while the study tends to position the great scale and scope of accounting firms as the result of horizontal integration and service diversification strategies that enabled a 'successful adaptation' of firms to changes in markets, professional knowledge, technology and regulation, it also suggests a more active role of firms in shaping their markets and the needs of their clients:

> The special acumen developed in giant enterprises qualified firms like Lybrand to participate in professional, business and governmental affairs to influence the direction of socioeconomic change. This enabled the firm to shape initiatives that influenced the interest of the firm, its clients and the profession.
>
> *(Chandar et al. 2014: 70)*

Generally, there has been little consideration to how accounting firms work to construct the market for their services and define the 'needs' of clients, as shown, for example, in accounts of the creation of 'needs' in cost accounting (Loft 1986), auditing (Power 1997) and public sector accounting (Gendron et al. 2007). However, in his study of the geographical expansion of PW, Lee (2014) notes how new client opportunities for the firm in the US were the result of the 'interested', active contribution of PW's partners in developing US accounting standards based on British practices. Jupe and Funnell (2015) stress the 'profit-seeking reasons' that motivated the active involvement of accounting consultants, especially large accounting firms, in the policy formulation and implementation of privatisation initiatives for the large-scale industries and utilities in the public sector. They note that, in seeking new opportunities for consultancy earnings, accounting firms contributed to construct governments' demands for their consultancy services.

Solsma and Flesher (2013) also attribute the growth of Haskins & Sells' professional services in the 1900s to the changing demands of clients. The expansion of the scope and size of the firm's operations is ascribed to the increasing size and complexity of clients' businesses, and clients' increasing demand for assistance in the recording, summarising and reporting of transactions for obtaining finance. They also highlight the growth of US capital investments and financial institutions, and investors' demands for auditing services to ascertain the financial condition and earnings of their customers or firms subjected to potential purchase. Echoing some of the current concerns with the Big 4, Solsma and Flesher (2013) also highlight concerns with white-collar crime, watered stocks, speculation and over-capitalisation problems.

The history of Ernst & Whinney (EW), a constituent of current Big 4 firm Ernst & Young (EY), portrays British accountancy as responding to the needs of clients (Jones 1981). An illustrative example is the claim that Whinney Murray began operating in continental Europe and the Middle East in the interwar period as British and US investment expanded there (Jones 1981: 174–6). The history of Cooper Brothers, written for the firm in 1954, is also written in terms of client needs:

> The policy originally laid down by the four Cooper brothers was that the business should be conducted only from the office in London. They felt that unless they could give personal supervision to the work of the firm they would not be able to maintain the standards that they felt to be important … Gradually, however, the necessity of providing services for clients with interests in other parts of the country and overseas and the improvement of communications caused this policy to be reversed.
>
> *(Cooper Brothers & Co. 1954: 37)*

In another house history, this time of Arthur Andersen, Duane Kullberg, head of Arthur Andersen in 1980, stated 'we are not seduced by size' but that growth was necessary to secure the firm's leadership in its field (Arthur Andersen nd: 171). Kullberg continues:

> We establish offices for one of two reasons – primarily to serve our existing or new clients as they expand geographically and secondarily to enter attractive new markets. Either way, we have always been committed to staffing our offices to meet client needs.
>
> *(Arthur Andersen nd: 177)*

This rationalising of growth for the purpose of benefiting the client rarely considers alternative motives, such as the desire to secure increased fee income, undermining competitors and profit for the partners. Allen and McDermott (1993) repeatedly stress that PW best serves its clients by protecting its own reputation – for example, claiming that PW's best reference were clients who fired them for being too scrupulous (ibid.: 144). A client-centred rhetoric seems like a boilerplate justification for almost any policy.

Yet, Cooper et al. (1998) point out the unanticipated effects of opening offices in new countries (in terms of serving previously unidentified local markets) that have little to do with the client-centred reasons Big 4 firms use to explain their original choice to enter new markets. History is often about reinventing the past. Further, as Pastra (2004) shows, the increasing internal leverage (where more and more employed accountants report to an individual partner) is an important explanation for the dramatic growth of the firms, particularly in the last thirty years. Others (e.g. Burrows and Black 1998) have shown that the internal profit sharing and promotion structures within accounting firms are important explanations for their growth, but such issues remain profoundly undeveloped in the firm history literature.

The firm as contributor to the profession

A dominant theme in many accounts of the history of Anglo-American based firms has been the role of their senior partners in the governance and development of professional associations. As noted earlier, most histories provide some insight into the social and cultural capital of the senior men (almost always men, except during war years – see Cooper Brothers & Co. 1954: 27; Jones 1995: 114–15) involved in the development of the firms and of the profession. And to be clear, the social, political, economic and cultural allegiances of early pioneers were very important in professional formation and legitimation (Fielding and Portwood 1980; Chua and Poullaos 1998; Richardson 2000; Persson et al. 2015, 2018). However, many histories provide limited direct analysis, treating them as of little importance in understanding the history of accounting practice and work.

Jones (1981) is an exception, devoting considerable space to the role of senior partners in Ernst & Whinney in establishing professional bodies. Turquand (of Turquand, Barton, Mayhew, later merged into Whinneys) was the first ICAEW president, and the third was Frederick Whinney. Similarly, Cooper Brothers & Co. (1954) starts with a quote from Ernest Cooper, describing the status of the early accountants in 1864, 'We could hardly, South of the Tweed, claim to be a profession … Our social position was not enviable' (1954: 4). The text goes on to indicate, that 'the concerted efforts of these two brothers (Ernest and Arthur Cooper) played a not inconsiderable part in the formation of the Institute' (ibid.: 6), each going on to be early presidents of the English Institute. The narrative continues, 'Ever since the Institute was formed, one or more of the partners of the firm have been a member of the Council' (ibid.: 6). The first twenty ICAEW Presidents also included William Deloitte, Edwin Waterhouse and William Peat, as well as partners of several firms later absorbed into the Big 4.

Jones' (1981) history of Ernst & Whinney examines the role and prominence of accountants in Scotland. Professional associations were incorporated in Edinburgh (1854), Glasgow (1855) and Aberdeen (1867), well before the English Institute (1880). Many Scottish accountants were also associated with the law, and indeed Sir Walter Scott in 1820 referred to accountancy as a branch of law, which aided its status and may explain Ernest Cooper's comments about the higher status north of the Tweed (also Edwards and Walker 2010). There have been several studies of Scottish pioneers (e.g. Walker 1988, 1993; Lee 1997) which tend to stress the connection to law, and that unlike English accountants, few were religious Nonconformists. Jones concludes by quoting a study of Glasgow chartered accountants:

> Almost the majority are the children of a tiny fraction of business and professional people. As in other professions, wealth and influence are as important in shaping the opportunities and interests of children as the ability with which they are endowed.
>
> *(Cairncross 1937: 374, cited in Jones 1981: 91)*

This characterisation would seem to apply to British accountants generally, and is unsurprising given that most firms required a 'premium' for those articling in the firm (£500 in 1945 – about £21,000 in 2017, according to Cooper Brothers & Co. 1954), and often didn't pay a salary until qualification.

More recent studies have usefully provided examples of the ways in which, through interaction with the state and government agencies, public accountants accomplished a process of transforming their public identity from a broad occupational group to expert professionals, and a transition from a semi- to a full professional status. Edwards (2016) remarked upon the significance of the contributions of two leading chartered accountants, Frederick Whinney (later Ernst & Whinney in 1979, and now Ernst & Young) and Edwin Waterhouse (later PwC) for the status of chartered accountants in late-Victorian Britain and government recognition of the significance of professional accountants as suppliers of consultancy services. Engaged by Parliament to examine the costing and accountability practices of the government's military manufacturing establishments, Whinney and Waterhouse's reports contributed to changes in government accounting practices and, by demonstrating the value of their consulting services to governmental bodies, were instrumental in the successful pursuit of claims to professional recognition. In general, Loft (1990) shows the importance of early practitioners in providing advice to government and Neu et al. (2006) indicate the continuing role of accounting advisers in implementing new public management in governments around the world.

Several historical studies note the contribution of Scottish and English chartered accountants, including, among others, Arthur Young, Arthur Lowes Dickinson and George O. May, to the evolution of US accounting and auditing practices (Previts and Merino 1988; Zeff 2003a; Solsma and Flesher 2013; Flesher and Previts 2016b; Watts and Zuo 2016). For example, Watts and Zuo (2016) examine the leadership role of George O. May, partner in Price Waterhouse in the US in 1902 and a senior partner in 1911, in the American Institute of Accountants (AIA), serving on two committees that were important to accounting standard setting: the Committee on Accounting Procedures (CAP) from 1937–1945, and the Committee on Terminology from 1939–1945. Solsma and Flesher (2013) document the involvement of Haskins in the establishment and advancement of the accounting profession in the US, serving as the first president of the New York Board of State Examiners of Public Accountants, President of the AAPA and participating in the founding of the School of Commerce, Accounts, and Finance of New York University. Flesher and Previts (2016b) provide evidence of the longstanding involvement of the partners of Haskins & Sells, as well as Price Waterhouse and Arthur Andersen & Company, in the development of the accounting profession in the US. Their prolific activities as authors and/or public speakers on accounting and business-related topics constituted a leading influence in the earliest days of the US public accounting profession.

While histories of US firms say less about the role of senior partners in professional development, Allen and McDermott's (1993) history of PW in the US devotes considerable space to the importance of George O. May in the AICPA and in negotiations surrounding the creation of the SEC (cf. Flesher and Previts 2016). Biographies of senior partners emphasise their role in professional developments. Benson (1989) is perhaps the most explicit, offering an account of a senior partner of Coopers who was highly influential in both the development of accounting standard setting in the UK and the setting up of the International Accounting Standards Committee.

Several studies highlight how accounting firms' practitioners traverse separate domains of activity, such as business and government arenas, academic and professional boundaries, to become agents of institutional, educational and technological change in the field of accounting, often through international lending agencies (Neu et al. 2006). This literature highlights the role of accountants and firms' partners in shaping the development of professional, academic and institutional discourses in the accounting discipline. Among the stories of prominent individuals/partners who have contributed to the academic field of accounting research, Persson et al. (2015) examine the role of Alvin R. Jennings (1905–1990), managing partner at Lybrand, Ross Bros. & Montgomery and President of the American Institute of Accountants' Committee on Auditing Procedure (1946–49) and the American Institute of Certified Public Accountants (1957–58), in advocating the establishment of a professional research programme into accounting and the work of accounting academics as a platform for financial reporting standard setting. Persson et al. (2018) trace the role of Elmer G. Beamer (1909–2000), a partner of Haskins & Sells, as an agent of institutional and educational change in the accounting discipline in the 1950s onward. That study highlights the significance of Beamer's involvement in the AICPA, in the codification of professional knowledge and the professionalisation of accounting as a discipline in the US.

Such studies reveal how accounting firms and practitioners, in traversing separate industries and/or business and governments became agents of accounting change, contributing to the standardisation, development, promotion and transfer of accounting technologies and knowledge from one sector or domain of activity to another (e.g. Feeney 2013; Black and Edwards 2016). Black and Edwards (2016) provide an account of an individual that exemplifies the processes earlier highlighted by Loft (1990). Their examination of the career of Henry William Sharp Whiffin (later PwC), and his colleague, James Charles Hurst, indicate how these individuals contributed to the reform of cost accounting and financial reporting practices within the British government's military manufacturing establishments by drawing upon knowledge and practices from private sector companies.

Focusing on the internal and external auditing practices within the railroad industry, Feeney (2013) reports on the extent to which the dominance and concentration of the Big 8 firms in the railroad industry contributed to the standardisation of accounting practices within the sector: virtually all the audits were performed by the Big 8 firms (with the three firms Haskins & Sells, Peat Marwick and Price Waterhouse together performing 91% of railroad audits), and specific firm audit reports were similarly worded and mentioned similar accounting issues, such as the treatment of depreciation and deferred income taxes (Feeney 2013: 28). The dominance of the Big 8 firms in the public accounting profession, coupled with their standardised auditing procedures, were likely to be directly responsible for certain shared accounting procedures and disclosures that were observed at the industry level:

> [t]hrough technical reviews as well as the adherence to certain specialized firm practices, a CPA firm would be expected to treat the financial statements of two companies in the same industry in the same way.
>
> *(Feeney 2013: 12).*

More generally, however, such histories tend to celebrate achievements and neglect the specific ways in which practitioners from the Big N shape the nature of the profession. Taken for granted, class, religion and national-based understandings of professions and trust are particularly evident in Preston et al.'s (1995) contrast between the notions of ethics and independence that informed US professional codes of ethics in 1917 and 1988. Further, firm histories say little about the role of gender, race or class in the development and concerns of the accounting profession. They neglect the tensions that have arisen in the professional associations' oversight and regulation of the professional coalition (Ramirez 2009). Although conflicts between the demands of larger firms and the interests of the small and medium practitioners (and between public practice and those in industry) have been a central component of professional heterogeneity since the 1970s (Robson et al. 1994), firm histories have little to say about the role of firms in the management of national and international professional associations, although it seems likely they are as central now as they were in the founding of the associations (Samsanova-Taddei and Humphrey 2014).

Geographical spread of firms and accounting practices

The expansion of the partnerships is a recurring theme in the firm histories and many discuss the internationalisation of the firm and the migration of accountants from one national jurisdiction to another. The case of Price Waterhouse's emergence in the US is an example. Jones (1995: ch. 4) shifts briskly from an account of the formation of regional offices in England to the development of US, European and Australian offices. Chandar et al. (2014) review the geographical expansion of Lybrand, Ross Bros. & Montgomery in the twentieth century. Their study traces the international spread of the firm from a network of small representative offices to its evolution via partnerships and acquisitions of established practices in overseas markets, and the later merger with Cooper Brothers, creating the global firm Coopers & Lybrand in 1957.

As indicated in a later section, in contrast to the motive stressed in the firm histories of 'responding to clients', Cooper et al. (1998) discuss different motivations for geographic spread, including perceptions of the potential profitability of regional and overseas markets, the geographical preferences of influential partners, a colonising spirit of bringing accounting to regions and nations that hadn't seen the benefits of accounting, and the pressures from international lending agencies for financial oversight from 'legitimate' audit firms.

The shift from a single office, often controlled by one or two patriarchs, is a recurrent theme in all the histories. Daniels et al. (1989) offer a path-breaking analysis of the international expansion of accounting firms, indicating that such expansion is often associated with shifts in the relation between the home firm and the overseas units. They discuss a range of associations between offices (from corresponding firms, to associations and federations (sometimes using an international name), to more or less integrated national firms to the 'world firms' of the Big 4) and track the patterns of expansion both geographically and historically. Their empirical analysis is now quite out of date reflecting the firms that existed in 1985, and is focused on UK-based firms. Moreover, their historical analysis seems largely based on the firm histories discussed in this chapter, categorising the period between 1890 and 1945 as 'guided by requirements of individual clients' (1989: 86), and the period since 1945 as 'heavily influenced by mergers at the international level' (ibid.), even when firms operated more or less independently under the same name. These explanations may reflect those offered in the firm histories, but Daniels et al. (1989) go on to examine the location of the offices of twenty UK firms between 1975 and 1985, showing that the major growth was actually in middle-sized accounting firms.

Table 12.2 shows the global expansion of the major multinational firms, indicating that some of the firms now have over 700 offices. While the story of global expansion may leave an impression of the diffusion of offices worldwide, it is important to appreciate that more than 50% of global fee revenue of the multinational accounting firms arises in North America, and that partners are concentrated in major financial centres, especially London and New York. Although we still know little about the local socio-economic effects of their location patterns, the studies reviewed by Boussebaa and Faulconbridge (2018) indicate that economic geographers have done quite a lot of work documenting and analysing the global spread of professional service firms, including accounting. But most of this work focuses on the recent period and is relatively mute about the socio-economic effects. We obtain some insight into these effects by examining the detailed firm histories. The history of Cooper Brothers, for example, discusses 'associated firms overseas' (Cooper Bros & Co. 1954: 37). It appears that the firm initially opened offices in Brussels (1921), New York (1926), Paris (1930), Johannesburg (1931) and Durban (1933), but no information is provided about the process of setting up and funding remote offices, the arrangements for referral and control of work, and any profit sharing. Evidence about the difficulties of setting up overseas operations is found in the case of establishing an overseas office in Moscow in the early 1990s (Cooper et al. 1998), where national stereotyping made the process of investing in an overseas office difficult. Yet in the official history of Coopers, there is no hint of the micro politics of organising an accounting firm, nor any reference to disagreements about strategies for producing and distributing profits.

A quarter of Cooper Bros & Co. (1954) describes the location of, and the chronology of setting up, overseas offices. What is noticeable, however, is the extensive coverage of offices located in the British Empire (as then was) and the dearth of information about European and US offices. From other, confidential, sources, we suspect that this emphasis on the British Empire reflects those offices where the UK firm had a direct ownership interest. The focus on British firms reflects which firms have an interest in accounting history, and in itself says something about the role of tradition and colonisation in these firms. Indeed, Jones (1981) explicitly thanks the 'history committee' of Ernst & Whinney.

The literature has begun to explore the organisational processes, strategies and tensions that underlie the geographical expansion of large accounting firms, and the intended and

Table 12.2 Global expansion of Big 8 (5, 4): 1982 to 1995, 2001 to 2017: change in total number of offices and partners

A. Number of offices worldwide

Global expansion of Big 8 (5): 1982 to 1995 *Twelve-year change in total number of offices*							*Global expansion of Big 4: 2001 to 2015* *Change in total number of offices*			
Firm	*1982*	*1988*	*1991*	*1992*	*1995*	*% growth*		*2001*	*2010*	*2015*
Arthur Andersen	155	217	289	392	454	109				
Coopers & Lybrand	424	565	737	805	814	44				
Deloitte Touche	697	986	722	757	781	−20	Deloitte	N/A	700*	674
Ernst & Young	530	796	777	812	803	1	Ernst & Young	670	684	700
KPMG	673	641	864	1,056	1,066	66	KPMG	754	700	900
Price Waterhouse	326	424	496	548	536	26	PricewaterhouseCoopers	814	766	756

Source: Centre for International Financial and Accounting Research (1994) Princeton, NJ: CIFAR Publishing, p. 283; Suddaby et al. (2007); Beaverstock (2007); *Company Reports, and International Accounting Bulletin (2011, 2017).

B. Number of partners worldwide

Global expansion of Big 8 (5): 1982 to 1995 Twelve-year change in total number of partners							*Global expansion of Big 4: 2001 to 2017* Total number of partners			
Firm	*1982*	*1988*	*1991*	*1992*	*1995*	*% growth*	*Firm*	*2001*	*2010*	*2017*
Arthur Andersen	1,438	2,133	2,478	2,507	4,294	101				
Coopers & Lybrand	2,282	3,341	5,152	5,373	5,528	65				
Deloitte Touche	3,831	5,137	4823	4,625	4,709	-8	Deloitte	N/A	9,538	11,378
Ernst & Young	3,439	5,283	5,700	6,059	6,452	22	Ernst & Young	5,777	8,603	11,480
KPMG	5,424	5,161	6,530	6,190	6,036	17	KPMG	6,655	7,921	10,147
Price Waterhouse	1,677	2,570	3,113	3,245	3,211	25	Price waterhouse-Coopers	9,219	8,625	11,181

Source: Centre for International Financial and Accounting Research (1994) Princeton, NJ: CIFAR Publishing, p. 283; Suddaby et al. (2007); Beaverstock (2007); International Accounting Bulletin (2011); and Global Annual Reviews (PwC website) (2017, 2018).

unintended consequences of their globalisation upon local firms, native accountants and the international transfer of accounting knowledge and standards (Baskerville and Hay 2010; Baskerville et al. 2014; Miranti 2014). Accounting scholars have highlighted the problems of 'embeddedness', acculturation and integration that accompanied, facilitated or retarded the geographical expansion of large accounting firms. Further, they have investigated the organisational strategies through which profit-seeking accounting firms have attempted to overcome local impediments and accommodate the diversity of professional, social, regulatory and economic factors that impinged upon their internationalisation processes. For example, Lee (2014) has explored the processes of assimilation and Americanisation that enabled the integration of the British-based firm of Price Waterhouse & Company in the US during the period 1890–1914, and how in turn the firm became an influential agency in the transfer of British-based professional values and practice in the US accounting arena. Lee's study is suggestive of the assimilation strategies and recruitment policies (accountants' professional qualification, participation in local professional associations, and professional profile in terms of citizenship, social class and experience) the firm developed and implemented in the attempt to Americanise. These adjustments related to restrictive access to professional markets for foreign accountants, local resistance to British professional ideals, and public antagonism towards immigrants that characterised the US political-economic context during the Progressive era. In documenting the way that the firm pursued Americanisation while maintaining a 'British identity', the study provides more detail on an observation made earlier by Previts and Merino (1988) that attempts by Price Waterhouse to transfer and apply British professional standards in the US context had to confront conflicting practices of local competitors, national stereotyping and expectations of US clients. However, while the study points to the significance of Price Waterhouse's partners in advocating the development of US accounting standards based on British practices, we are only starting to know about the role of large accounting firms in the globalisation of accountancy and their influence over the definition of accounting standards, norms and values in emerging professional contexts (Poullaos 1994; Chua and Poullaos 1998; Deng and Macve 2015; Belal et al. 2017).

Others have focused on the unintended and adverse consequences, and internal and external tensions that the globalisation and international expansion of large accounting firms might create for local actors and agencies, leading ultimately to disintegration and failure. Baskerville and Hay (2010) and Baskerville et al. (2014) analysed the effects and costs of the globalisation of the 'Big 8' international firms upon local firms and their partners, in terms of the de-institutionalisation of their local practices, loss of partnership and control, or firm failure. In their oral history study of partners in large New Zealand accounting firms in the 1980s, Baskerville and Hay (2010) noted how the survival of local accounting firms and the careers of their partners depended upon their ability to form and maintain affiliations with global firms: local firms with affiliations gained advantages from technology transfer, including both audit procedures and staff training, and national firms lacking or losing affiliation to a Big 8 firm disintegrated or reverted to small local firms. In their analysis of the historical formation and demise of KMG Kendons, a New Zealand-based accounting firm that failed following the affiliation with Peat Marwick Mitchell, Baskerville et al. (2014) highlighted the role of Big 8 firms as triggers of cultural and institutional tensions and 'de-institutionalisation' processes that challenge and destabilise the norms, professional values and practice cohesion of local firms, leading to their fragmentation as they eventually revert to a local status or are incorporated by different international firms.

In showing a trend for firms to move from the professional partnership model to a globally based managed professional business, these studies have also begun to highlight the shifting power distribution that accompanied the emergence of new professional business models: the loss of autonomy for small local firms, the strong position of the Big N firms relative to the local offices, and the Big N firms' strategies, 'greed' and 'cherry-picking' behaviour in selecting local firms as partners for transatlantic mergers. Greenwood and Empson (2003) discuss the partnership model in a contemporary and Anglo-American context, but there is a lack of research about the internal coordination practices, integration and control mechanisms that characterised firm business models and the management of local offices in different geographies and times.

Hanlon (1994) provides insight into accounting firms and the international division of labour. His analysis of the migration patterns and aspirations of Irish accountants within the global firms offers a valuable glimpse into the extent and effects of such movements and the crucial importance of global financial centres in affecting the offices in the semi-periphery. Published sources (e.g. White 2003) say little about the geographic spread of KPMG (which might be expected to have spread in a different manner given its combined Dutch, UK and US antecedents) or contrast their patterns with some of the multinational firms where the UK or US firm was more dominant. So, while we know quite a lot descriptively about the patterns of overseas expansion for UK firms, the firm histories in general have so far provided little insight into the conditions that shaped overseas expansion of the major accounting firms and the impact on firm management and practices.

Nature and scope of work in accounting firms

Firm histories provide some insight into the work of early accountants. Cooper Bros & Co. (1954: 4) summarises the nature of the UK business in the early years. Bankruptcy work was stimulated by the 1869 Bankruptcy Act but declined after the 1883 Act, and audit work started to increase after the Companies Acts of 1862, 1879 (the latter required the audit of banks) and 1900 (requiring audits of all companies). Jones (1995) also offers some detail on the early links to law and the importance of the railways in the early accounting work of Price Waterhouse.

That said, most firm histories focus on audit with only occasional reference to tax, bankruptcy and consulting work. White (2003: 113) offers a weak justification for this lack of attention by insisting that KPMG is distinctive in avoiding over-investment in non-audit activities. Jones (1995) offers six pages (out of 337) on the development of professional work and stresses the expansion into business services as a market-led phenomenon. He repeats the standard firm explanation: the stress is on the client and his or her 'value', not the motives that might require the firm's member to add value for themselves (insight into the current cultures of accounting firms is provided by Spence and Carter (2014); Spence et al. (2015), (2016), (2017)). An important (but often unacknowledged) background to the firm histories is the longstanding controversy about the scope of services provided by accounting firms. Jones usefully summarises the split in the occupation of professional staff in 1973, but offers no contemporary data. In particular, concern has been expressed over the provision of other services and whether such services compromise the independence of the external audit. Tables 12.3, 12.4 and 12.5 indicate the scope of work of the multinational accounting firms before the scope of their consulting work was restricted by legislation after Enron and the collapse of Arthur Andersen. The marked rise in income

Table 12.3 Revenue split for individual US Big 6 (5) firms: 1975 to 1999

	Audit %	*Tax* %	*Consulting* %
Arthur Andersen			
1975	66	18	16
1986	47	21	32
1994	33	18	49
1999	18	12	70
KPMG			
1975	70	20	10
1986	56	22	22
1994	49	21	30
1999	34	23	43
Deloitte Touche			
1975	68	17	5
1986	64	23	13
1994	52	22	25
1999	31	19	41
Ernst & Young			
1975	68	21	11
1986	56	26	18
1994	45	19	36
1999	38	25	37
Coopers & Lybrand			
1975	69	19	12
1986	60	21	19
1994	58	1	24
1999	34	19	34
Price Waterhouse			
1975	76	16	8
1986	58	24	18
1994	43	25	32
1999	34	19	34

Source: Suddaby et al. (2007).

from tax work, and even more so from management consulting, occurs in all the firms (see also Zeff 2003a and b). While management consulting accounted for 12% of aggregate fees among the Big 8 in 1979, this proportion had risen to 49% in 1999.

The histories of accounting firms shed some light on the historical evolution of the services provided by accounting firms and, indeed, what is regarded as proper work for accountants. In their examination of Haskins & Sells' (now Deloitte) engagement letters in the early twentieth century, Solsma and Flesher (2013) present evidence of the types of clients serviced and accounting services provided by accounting firms at a time when public accounting was expanding and becoming recognised as a legitimate profession. They report that 37% of the firm's business revolved around audit appointments (prepared for submission

Table 12.4 Revenue split for individual US Big 4 firms: 2004 to 2017

	Audit %	*Tax* %	*Consulting** %	*Other* %
KPMG				
2004	67	33	0	0
2011	43	26	31	0
2017	32	28	40	0
Deloitte				
2004	39	25	27	9
2011	32	20	44	4
2017	29	17	49	5
Ernst & Young				
2004	62	35	0	3
2011	40	31	23	6
2017	32	29	31	8
PricewaterhouseCoopers				
2004	62	33	5	0
2011	48	29	23	0
2017	42	25	33	0

Sources: *Accounting Today* (2004, 2012, 2018).
* Consulting % only includes Management Advisory Services.

Table 12.5 Proportional US revenue sources for Big 8 (5, 4) firms: 1975, 1990, 1999, 2011 and 2017

	1975 %	*1990* %	*1999* %	*2011* %	*2017* %
Audit	71	49	30	40	35
Tax	17	25	21	27	25
Consulting	12	26	49	33	40

Sources: Public Accounting Report, various years; *Fortune*; Suddaby et al. (2007); and adapted from *Accounting Today* (2012, 2018).

to stock exchanges, for stockholders' meetings, and detection of fraud and errors), 15% were requests for the evaluation of the efficiency of existing accounting systems and the set-up of new accounting systems; other services included examinations and consulting work. The study also documented the expansion of professional accountants' jurisdiction, and the shift in the primary audit objective, from fraud detection to an assurance of the quality of reported financial condition and earnings during this era.

One of the most interesting features of Jones' (1981) history of Ernst & Whinney is the careful attempt to trace the shifting work conducted within accounting firms. He analyses the fees for a series of predecessor firms from 1848, showing that 93% of fee income in

1858 was derived from bankruptcy work. He demonstrates that the fees of firms in the Victorian era were closely related to the state of the economy and various banking and other financial crises: 'accountants did particularly well in times of financial disaster and depression … they were the rich undertakers of the economic world' (1981: 45). Although the dominance of accountants in bankruptcy work declined after the 1883 Bankruptcy Act, audit was a small proportion of work till the 1890s, when it began to predominate. But auditing in the late Victorian era seems to have included general accounting work, including the compilation of financial statements and the detection of fraud.

Jones' analysis suggests that the work of accounting firms varied quite significantly over time and was largely affected by changing legislation and the state of the economy. Auditing was the major source of fees throughout the first half of the twentieth century, with insolvency work declining more or less consistently so that by 1935 the latter had become insignificant. Tax work only became significant after 1945 but was rarely above 10% of total fees up to 1960. As might be expected from an economic history commissioned and 'overseen' by the subject firm, Jones' (1981) history of Ernst & Whinney focuses on how the firm contributes to the economy. There is almost nothing about activities that may not be 'productive' – their involvement in scandals, frauds, money laundering, tax avoidance schemes, short-termism and so on, that are part of the less celebrated history of the accounting industry, and which lie behind many contemporary concerns (Sikka 2009; Sikka and Willmott 2010). Jones' Price Waterhouse history, however, provides an extensive discussion of the Royal Mail case, refers to Hary and Kreuger and the 1931 stock market crash, and the more recent Guinness and BCCI scandals. Jones (1995) mentions the firm's reluctance until the twentieth century to be associated with manufacturing, and its close allegiance to financial interests in the City of London, but offers no commentary on whether these were 'contributions' to the British economy.

Exploring the economic impact of the Great War on accounting practice and the profession, Flesher and Previts (2014) show the effects of the First World War on the activities, services and personnel of one of the largest US accounting firms at the time of the conflict, Haskins & Sells, now Deloitte (also Walker 2018). They show how the wartime effort led to the extension of the firm's geographical scope, the expansion of war – and post-war – related work (in particular, the increasing demand for taxation services and activities to support government operations), the employment of women in the accountancy profession, and formalisation of practices and standards of professionalism as a way to remind the firm's accountants of their role in attending to the public interest. The study also highlights the wartime role of public accounting firms and the contribution of their managing partners to the war effort, as well as the significance of the firm's collaboration with government and state agencies for the public affirmation of the accounting profession.

In retracing the evolution of Lybrand, Ross Bros. & Montgomery through the twentieth century, Chandar et al. (2014) show how the firm's growth resulted in a change from a CPA-centric conception of the firm to that of a diversified provider of knowledge-based services. They argue that changes in the services provided took the form of applying a common body of knowledge from auditing, to taxation and then management consulting. In turn, diversification enhanced the firm's reputation for technical proficiency and image of authority, as their members were perceived as leaders in defining how professional knowledge should be standardised. Concerning the establishment of the provision of consulting services during the post Second World War period, their study shows that, in the attempts of the accounting profession to legitimise the expansion into new product areas, and in particular management consulting, firms defined these new services as being within the domain of the existing profession. As they note: 'The Lybrand partners accomplished this by claiming that the new services were actually just a repackaging or leveraging of work already performed by the profession' (Chandar et al. 2014:

63). By the 1960s, though auditing and tax services were still the primary services, the firm began its transformation from an accounting firm to a professional services firm that offered audit, tax, IT, consulting, and pension and benefits services.

Chandar et al. (2014) also examine the change in organisational structure accompanying the geographical spread and diversification strategy of Lybrand, Ross Bros. & Montgomery, from its founding and a partnership formation in Philadelphia in 1898 through to the merger with Price Waterhouse in 1998. For most of the firm's history its leaders conceived it as a CPA practice in which local office practice was organised around auditing (tax and management consulting were ancillary services, and their timing and scope were a function of the basic audit plan), and each office had separate pyramidal hierarchies headed by a senior partner supported by a staff of managers and accountants. Each pyramidal group was assigned a particular mix of clients. The increase in the degree of diversification made the CPA organisation seemingly unmanageable: local office demand was often insufficient to support full-time personnel; the growth in the number of services increased the degree of administrative complexity; and the managerial protocols of new services were designed for regional rather than local markets. Under the knowledge-based services conception of the firm, the organisational structure developed around hub offices in charge of coordinating the different lines of practice on a regional basis. Service promotion moved to the pursuit of more lucrative non-audit services (IT reviews, valuation services, etc.).

The firm histories reveal that increased regulation and the use of computers led to decreased differentiation in how different firms produced audits (Arthur Andersen nd: 172; Jones 1981: 249; 1995: 288; Allen and McDermott 1995: 196–8, 213, 222). The need for personnel with specialised skills was resisted by older partners. For example, at PW America, it was only when the number of partners expanded, and as young recruits came to favour specialisation (it gave them a clearer sense of their role and a route for career progression), that resistance faded (Allen and McDermott 1993: 230–2). By the same token, Arthur Andersen cited a demand by consulting partners for a larger share of the profits as the motivation for creating a distinct consulting organisation in 1987. Consultants at AA felt that they were being held back by the outmoded attitudes of auditors, and thus sought greater organisational freedom (Stevens 1991: 116–19), eventually leading to the formation of Accenture in 1997 (Whitford 1997). Chandar et al. (2014) also shows how the rapid growth of IT in the 1980s changed the nature of auditing work, and increased the significance of computer auditing specialists and IT professionals within accounting firms.

The broadening of services resulted in substantial tensions within the firms in ways rarely discussed in firm histories, although other more recent studies have begun to highlight how the broadening of services resulted in substantial tensions within the firms, and in particular how the transformation of accounting firms into multidisciplinary practices generated internal tensions between consultants (high margin, high growth) and the audit partners (low margin and stable or declining revenues) (Gendron and Spira 2010; Greenwood et al. 2010; Cahan et al. 2011; Carson 2014). Chandar et al. (2014) provide evidence of firms' historical sensitivity to the possibility that certain services were incompatible with maintaining auditor independence, and concern about whether professional fees for non-audit services could grow so significantly as to undermine perceptions about firm independence. In their study of Coopers & Lybrand, they argue that resistance to consulting was clothed in terms of independence concerns, but often reflected animus towards consulting: 'There was a strong sense that auditing came first, formalised in firm policy bulletin E-20 that stated that the audit partner was to be the senior partner in all client relationships' (Chandar et al. 2014: 67).

This literature suggests that the growing emphasis on consulting and commercialisation undermined auditor professionalism and was one of the main causes of Andersen's demise and a general decline in audit quality since Enron, WorldCom and Parmalat. For example, Cahan et al. (2011) and Gendron and Spira (2010) note how the prolonged conflict between Andersen's auditing divisions and the consulting arm resulted in increasing competition among partners from auditing and consulting. Andersen audit partners were subjected to intense pressure to grow revenues and profitability in order to match the consulting division's profitability (Squires et al. 2003). Curiously, the split of Accenture from Andersen in 2000 seems to have increased the level of commercial pressure on Andersen partners in an attempt to replace Andersen Consulting's revenues.

The structure and organisation of firms

The expansion in the number of partners is associated with structural changes in the firms that reflected changes in what it means to be a partner (Greenwood and Empson 2003). All of the large accountancy firms began as partnerships where decisions could be made jointly and face-to-face. However, even in their earliest days, it was common for different partners to specialise in different activities, often with one partner performing most of the accounting work in the home office, while others sought primarily to build up the client list (Jones 1981: 95). Structures based on personal relationships lasted surprisingly long – into the 1960s in the cases of both PW and Whinney Smith and Whinney in the UK – but eventually the increase in the number of partners beyond a dozen or two, and the related increasing importance of non-auditing services, made these management structures unworkable. Partnerships had expanded until 'partners' came to be strangers to one another (Stevens 1981: 15, 1991: 102).

We learn comparatively little about the organisation and management of the firms from firm histories. Consistent with the dynastic approach that most of the histories exhibit, what can be gleaned are some of the power struggles over leadership (Cypert 1991; Stevens 1991; Squires et al. 2003; Toffler and Reingold 2003). These are typically expressed from the viewpoint of the victors. Histories may indicate organisation charts which depict the formal structures, but say little about the operation and management of the firms, especially given their tendency to use informal mentoring (Dirsmith and Covaleski 1985) and committees to manage work and relationships (Greenwood et al. 1990, 1999).

The general pattern was to have the partners choose an 'inner circle', often referred to as the Executive Committee, to lead the firm (Jones 1981: 214, 1995: 255). The level of democracy in these elections was time and firm dependent – for example, in the 1970s in the UK practice of PW, partners voted whether or not to accept the single nomination of a selection committee (Jones 1995: 252). However, even hand-picked choices could be rejected, as evidenced by the 'Battle of Boca Raton', where Peats partners rejected the reformist candidate selected by the previous leadership (Stevens 1981: 5). Cypert's (1991) book on the merger that created KPMG similarly illustrates the need to get support from a worldwide partnership with diverse priorities and national objectives.

Within the Executive Committee, divisions of responsibility only slowly became formalised. The firm histories also suggest that efforts were made to ensure a regional balance in senior management (Allen and McDermott 1993: 157; Jones 1981: 214), although Anglo-Americans still dominated. Most notably, the work of the Executive Committee tended to evolve into policy-making and strategic guidance, while another committee was made responsible for day-to-day oversight (Allen and McDermott 1993: 151).

Internal leadership tensions are suggested by the eventual creation (in the case of Whinney Murray, in 1973) of a 'national office' to handle the firm's coordination, instead of simply having a particular office (typically London or New York) as a first among equals (Allen and McDermott 1993: 96–8; Jones 1981: 233). As mentioned above, Arthur Andersen went further than other firms in restructuring their partnership as they expanded, by giving Andersen Consulting a distinct status loosely within the larger firm in 1987 (Squires et al. 2003; Toffler and Reingold 2003). In general, however, these firms say little about strategic, HR, marketing or control practices within the firms (although ethnographic studies of current firms such as Dirsmith et al. (1997), Barrett et al. (2005) and Carter and Spence (2014) are revealing in this respect).

Firm histories highlight the tensions that characterised the evolution of the organisational structure of accounting firms from semi-independent, geographically dispersed and self-contained local offices to transnational professional service firms. Greenwood et al. (2010: 174–6) show how firms' growth generated tensions in terms of coordination among multiple axes of differentiation, national and international considerations, conflicts and competition between lines of service (regarding professional independence, standards and norms of conduct) and the industry/market axes (which emphasise a more business-oriented perspective, commercial expertise and market growth). Moreover, they note how the potential antagonisms among senior professionals (partners) in charge of their respective national firms were reinforced by incentives that rewarded them on the basis of their client fees and client satisfaction (Greenwood et al. 2010). However, firm histories say little about the compensation mechanisms, organisational practices and arrangements that strengthened or managed these tensions within accounting firms.

The Chandar et al. (2014) history of Coopers & Lybrand provides evidence of the organisational changes that resulted from attempts to manage the increasing tensions and competition that emerged from the growth in the scale and scope of the firm. Early tensions between the distinct identities of the three founding firms initially resulted in a triumvirate to oversee activities in different geographic regions (Lybrand & Ross in the US, Latin America and Japan; Cooper Bros in Europe, Africa and the Middle and Far East; McDonald, Currie in Canada and the Caribbean), and a focus on the creation of shared knowledge and relationships rather than a blended enterprise: 'It was not intended that the international firm should itself practice accounting. Its function was to serve as the agency to coordinate the standards of the practice of the participating firms' (Jennings 1998: 27, cited in Chandar et al. 2014).

But diversification and bureaucratic structure created impediments for the execution of client-focused knowledge-based services, internal competition between regions and lines of business, and tensions in the consulting practice among accountants and those lacking an accounting background, who could not be admitted to the partnership. The organisational changes put in place to limit these tensions resulted in the creation of hub centres to coordinate multiple lines of service, serving as pockets around the country for the allocation of nationally managed and focused resources; the creation of the position of 'principal', routinely awarded to non-accounting personnel deemed otherwise worthy of a partnership position; the formation of a national consulting division separate from auditing; a rewording of firm policy to increase the role of consulting partners in defining client relationships; and the dissemination of standardised approaches to problem solving.

Firm histories: towards an expanded research agenda

In this section we offer an agenda for future work in order that firm histories contribute not simply to better understanding these major organisations and their impact, but also to permit theoretical developments related to organisational and management practices of professional service firms, processes of professionalisation, changing understandings of professions, and regulation. Our suggestions include explorations of the changing nature of firm work; the everyday practices and experiences of employees across time; the changing organisational control systems of the firms; their contributions to new forms of business knowledge, techniques and expertise; and the role of the large firms as social and political actors in regulatory fields.

Histories of firms as managed organisations

Historians of firms have taken the partnership model of ownership and control as the archetype for firm histories. Partners are the only actors that are deemed to 'count', and significant developments within firms are almost always only associated with the actions of senior partners. Since the founding of firms involves specific individuals, then of course the narrative of the firm is intimately related to their actions in establishing or merging their partnerships. However, this focus neglects a view of firms as managed and contested organisations (Clegg et al. 2015).

Information about firms' internal structures is often lacking and the concepts and practices of management control have little place in most firm histories, including the role of HR, marketing and other occupations in shaping management processes. Jones (1981, 1995) considers the problems of expansion, management and firm organisation, but even his discussion seems connected to the attitudes of senior partners, particularly towards expanding the number of partners. Certainly, Jones and others usefully emphasise the metropolitan bias of senior partners, as demonstrated by the reluctance for many years to sanction the appointment of partners in the provincial offices.

Later analyses of the firms are less specific as to the changes in organisational structures that firms have adopted. The (typically partnership) legal form that firms have adopted is one of the more visible aspects of their organisation. Yet, we know little about the organisational and ownership structures across national jurisdictions, or how these partnerships actually operate. For example, what are the decision rights related to being a partner, what are the actual practices of inclusion and exclusion, and how and why do these vary? In some countries, audit firms have been subsidiaries of other financial service corporations (e.g. banks). Others adopted limited liability in the late 1990s, but we do not know how such changes affect controls and behaviour within the firm (Sikka 2008).

The legal form of firms is a visible aspect of their organisation, but firm histories tell us little even about the organisational and ownership structures across national jurisdictions, and what their practices of co-ordination and control are within the context of their claims about global reach. It is now taken for granted that Arthur Andersen tried to operate with a global, 'one-firm' philosophy, whereas KPMG, for example, seemed to prefer operating a looser coalition of heterogeneous partnerships (Greenwood et al. 1999; White 2003: 113). The histories are silent on the degree to which such organisational rhetoric was matched by practical differences in organisation and control, although anecdotal evidence suggests that sensitivity to liability risks across jurisdictions have mitigated against tendencies to formal centralisation.

The partnership model would suggest that compensation for equity partners would reflect a profit-sharing arrangement (although firms historically have appointed some partners to salaried positions). Firm histories have little to say about governance, performance and compensation mechanisms. It is disappointing that little attention has been given to the firms' management control practices, and the implications of these mechanisms for behaviour. The groundbreaking work of Covaleski, Dirsmith and their associates (Dirsmith and Covaleski 1985; Dirsmith et al. 1997; Covaleski et al. 1998) in the US highlights some aspects of control systems. This work has inspired research elsewhere, typically focusing on recruiting, socialisation and career progression and their implications for the construction of professional identities (e.g. Anderson-Gough et al. 1998, 2002, 2005, 2006, 2016; Grey 1998; Kornberger et al. 2011; Carter and Spencer 2014; Lupu and Empson 2015). However, much more from a historical viewpoint could still be done to identify some of the identified features and understand the interaction between firm and professional identities. One announcement suggested that in response to past 'errors', the firms 'have changed, putting much greater emphasis on audit quality in all of our work and in our compensation systems' (CEOs of the international audit networks 2006: 7). This statement suggests that, at least in part, the firms accept the audit failures of the twenty-first century are connected to the consequences of compensation and management methods within the firms. Yet there exists little systematic historical study of firms' organisational controls, governance and compensation practices.

Studies have begun to explore the 'marketing and advertising practices' of large accounting firms (e.g. Chandar et al. 2014; Roberts 2015; Flesher and Previts 2016b). Flesher and Previts (2016b) have noted how Big 8 companies relied on their staff and partners' public written and oral communication of the firm's philosophy, leaderships and viewpoints as a way to reach the business, education and professional community and to gain recognition and status. For example, in 1955, Haskins & Sells formally chose to share the written thoughts of its leadership through annual publications. As Flesher and Previts (2016b: 334) note: 'The publications also could be considered an indirect marketing tool in an era when CPA firm advertising was prohibited'. They were certainly widely distributed to members of the firm, clients and university libraries. The scope and audience of these communications varied and broadened over time, and their historical development would offer insight into the firm's marketing and image.

Others have highlighted the tensions resulting from firms' marketing practices. Roberts (2015) notes how in the 1930s large accounting firms tended to deviate or disagreed with ethics rules of professional conduct that restricted solicitation and advertising. For example, in 1923, three partners in Ernst & Ernst were accused of violating the rules against solicitation and advertising. Chandar et al. (2014) notes how the tensions and problems of competition between the auditing and consulting areas of Coopers & Lybrand were exacerbated by the fact that, until the late 1970s, consultants were entirely dependent upon the auditing partners for marketing their services.

However, firm histories in general say little about the impact of marketing and advocacy on the public recognition of firms, internal tensions among divisions and lines of business, or recruiting. Flesher and Previts (2016b) call for studies about patterns of change for advocacy materials, both in terms of content and format of communication, such as via recruiting representatives to campuses and business leaders, or more immediate forms of marketing, such as position papers or brochures (Chatman 1991).

Other aspects of the firms as managed entities would include their role as sites of identity formation – both organisational and professional (Picard et al. 2014; cf. Zundel et al. 2016).

While the majority of firm histories extol the virtues of professionalism (but fail to articulate the meanings of the concept), debates about the commercialisation of accounting (and shifting historical and jurisdictional conceptions of the professional and commercial) are an important background to firm histories. Mitchell and Sikka (2004), Zeff (2003a, 2003b) and Wyatt (2004) claim that the commercialisation of the Big 4 went too far, and these claims emphasise the importance of not relying on the claims of professional associations and firm leaders. Researchers would also be well advised to go beyond the dualistic debates about commercialisation and professionalism, and examine what it means for the practices of accountants to talk in terms of commercialisation, being business-like, enterprising and modern (Hanlon 1996; Sikka and Willmott 1997). For example, it would be useful to examine whether claims to 'gentlemanly' and professional values might be a historically contingent strategy to be commercial. Appeals to such forms of social and cultural capital can be an effective strategy for accountants in developing their business and being profitable. Rather than reproducing a conception that commercialisation may be antithetical to professionalisation, studies of accounting and audit practices will benefit from examining the work practices and client relations of professional organisations (firms and associations).

Studies have started to uncover how the ascendency of commercialism within big accounting firms might create tensions and paradoxes within existing partnership structures. Scholars have seen the rise of multidisciplinary partnerships as one of the major shifts associated with the commercialisation of the profession (Greenwood and Suddaby 2006) and stress the internal tensions resulting from the coexistence of different professional domains, for instance differences among the accounting and legal profession concerning the rules regarding client confidentiality versus the duty to report (e.g. Richardson 2017). Gendron and Spira (2010) argue that the commercialisation of public accounting implies the corporatisation of partnership relationships, such that the relationships at the basis of professional partnerships are now similar to those within the management of corporate multinational organisations (Gendron and Spira 2010). Moreover, while extant studies have generally relied on the commercialisation thesis to highlight the tensions among a 'commercial logic' and 'professional logic', the accounting literature has at last started to question the idea of 'commercialism' and 'professionalism' as monolithic concepts, especially with reference to non-western countries such as China and Japan (Spence et al. 2017). Historical comparative studies could examine the work practices and values associated with different conceptions of professionalism and commercialism across countries, and their dialectics over time.

Histories of the practice and experience of work

Narratives of the work of accounting firms indicate that the early or founding years are characterised by insolvency work and the struggle to establish legitimacy and professional status within the (British) establishment. Firm histories then explore the growth of audit type functions in terms of client demands and regulatory changes. Little of the scope of the modern audit firm has been analysed by such narratives, except for the insider reports of the demise of Arthur Andersen (Squires et al. 2003; Toffler and Reingold 2003; Peterson 2015). These insider accounts emphasise the growth of non-audit services within Andersen during the 1990s and pressures on the firm's profit-sharing arrangements due to the comparative profitability of consulting. Some research has tried to explore the different experiences of professional training in different areas of work (Khalifa 2004), but such work is preliminary and has little historical dimension. One has to turn to novels (for example, W. Somerset Maugham (2002/1915) and Charles Dickens) and a few sociological studies (Montagna 1968, 1974; Hanlon 1994; Evans and Fraser 2012) to obtain historical insight into the work practices of accounting firms.

Hanlon (1994) discusses the implications of professionalisation for an analysis of power and the division of work in society. He suggests that many accountants are part of the service class and are often in marginalised activities which are threatened by automation and low wage competition. He argues that the accounting profession is segmented with a small elite of accountants who act as the agents of capital and who obtain very great rewards for their efforts, and the mass, comprising junior accountants, bookkeepers and others at the periphery (often women or new immigrants) who experience poor working conditions, for example low pay, oppressive control systems, threats of automation and increasing part-time work (see also Cooper and Taylor (2000); Tinker and Koutsaumadi (1997)). Hanlon's studies of human resource and work practices within the multinational accounting firms suggests that the internal dynamic of these firms explains how the elitist values of accountants (gentlemanly, aristocratic and paternalistic) are transformed into the commercial values of the large professional firm, in which profitability and contribution to the growth of capital are dominant. The mass of junior accountants consent to their position to the extent that they aspire to join the partnership elite through internal promotion.

With one or two exceptions, the experience of work and the transformation in audit technologies are absent from historical studies of accounting firms. Matthews' and Pirie's (2001) oral history of audit and auditing methods offers a valuable account of the development of audit methods and techniques. Dirsmith and associates (Carpenter and Dirsmith 1993; Dirsmith et al. 1997) consider the audit technologies and markets that firms develop as related to their activities as organisations and the contexts in which they are embedded. Other studies unpack the development of new audit techniques in ways that connect to the management of frontline audit staff, as efforts to control audit costs and mediate the impact of regulatory requirements (Power 1992, 2000, 2003). Barrett et al. (2005) analyse how the interpretation of standards, regulations and work manuals vary within the same, but dispersed geographically, firm. More recently, Knechel (2007), Curtis and Turley (2007) and Robson et al. (2007) have begun to explore the development of business risk audit methodologies, and show that they reflect internal tensions in the development of professional service firms. They do not merely serve markets, but accounting firms attempt through their techniques to construct new markets, re-order regulatory space and control the work of juniors.

Others have provided some evidence of the changing working techniques of accountants, linking the adoption of new audit procedures to the change in clients' demands, technological developments and shifting audit objectives. Solsma and Flesher (2013) document the shift in the primary objectives of Haskins & Sells from fraud detection to an assurance of the quality of reported financial condition and earnings, and the concomitant movement from detailed verifications (used to detect errors and fraud) towards audit techniques such as sampling, testing and/or obtaining outside appraisals and external verification:

> With fraud and error detection being the primary objectives of the audit, the focus on verifying all existing transactions was valid, yet undeniably imperfect. However, as businesses expanded and accounting services changed during the first decade of the twentieth century, audit objectives evolved … American accountants adjusted the primary audit objective to a focus on financial condition and earnings rather than fraud … This change of audit objective led to a transition from detailed verifications to sampling and testing.
>
> *(Solsma and Flesher 2013: 306)*

However, little is known about the reasons why firms developed particular techniques and procedures at particular times. Specifically, there is a lack of research about the ways accounting firms actively contributed to construct a market for their services (see Robson et al. 2007; O`Dwyer 2011).

Further historical work might start to address in a focused way how and why firms develop particular techniques at particular points in time, rather than treating all technical innovations as technological inventions with limited social and organisational implications. Power (1992) offers such a history of audit sampling, but much more can be done in other domains of accounting work, including the nature and focus of tax and management consulting.

Histories of firms as political and cultural actors

While it is clear that the superior histories of firms do address the impact of regulations and the involvement of key individuals in advising on new regulation (Jones 1995: 102–4, 143–56), little has been written on the role of firms as political actors on the stage of accounting and auditing regulation. Of course, there is a literature that looks at the development and work of regulatory agencies, both governmental and NGOs (e.g. Camfferman and Zeff 2007, 2015), but our point is that the practical relays and linkages between the studies of these bodies and the large audit firms are unexplored as an aspect of the history of the Big N.

It is now scarcely possible to discuss seriously accounting regulations without considering the complex of alliances, agreements and accords that exists between the Big Firms and agencies such as the IASB, IFAC, ASB, FASB, IOSCO or the EU on various accounting and auditing matters, and how these agreements and alliances affect implementation in specific jurisdictions (Graham and Neu 2003; Robson et al. 2005). While the importance of accounting regulations in the internationalisation of markets and policy regimes is now almost a cliché, many studies at the international level tend to focus on one particular 'international' institution or standard, and much less attention is given to the polycentric, networked or co-ordinated character of 'regulation work' and the complex of relations between accounting firms and national agencies (Caramanis 1999, 2002; Büthe and Mattli 2011).

The Big 4 firms are important in the establishment of policy, the staffing of these agencies, and the enactment and enforcement of international regulations, yet little research has examined whether the relationships of the Big Firms to NGOs and government networks continue to be mediated through the national professional associations, or whether these bodies are now effectively bypassed by the Big 4 (Suddaby et al. 2007). The work of accounting firms and associations, as well as 'non-accounting' institutions such as the OECD, WTO, World Bank and IMF, in the cultural normalisation and transmission of accounting and auditing practices needs to be examined. Accounting historians can provide important insight into the changing roles that the large firms have played in staffing these bodies, lobbying and advising on company regulation, and informing judgements on free trade and the regulation of professional services. Graham and Neu (2003) show how accounting and accounting firms are central in World Bank attempts to reform educational systems in Central America. Arnold (2005) examines the WTO and negotiations over regulations on practice rights of accountants across national jurisdictions and indicates the influence that accounting firms have as political actors.

Studies of the relationships between, for example, Big Firm partners, former partners, regulators' professional firm backgrounds and professional association administrators would help to examine the 'social' or informal backdrop to relationships between firms and regulatory agencies (Anderson-Gough et al. 2005). Social network analyses (Richardson 2009) or prosopographical approaches (Carnegie and Napier 1996) might help to further explore these interrelationships in the historical development of the firms and their burgeoning influence.

Among the histories that address the involvement of firms in advising on new regulations, Zeff (2016) documents the large and frequent presence of Price Waterhouse & Co., a premier public accounting firm in the US from the 1930s to the 1970s, in the US standard-setting arena. He explores its effects on the behaviour and deliberation outcomes of a succession of US standard-setting bodies. While the study provides no direct conclusions about the actual effects of Price Waterhouse & Co. in terms of coalitions and blocs in the voting patterns of standard-setting bodies, it points to many appointments of ex-firm partners and financial executives on their boards, leading to a strong 'communality in backgrounds' between standard-setter bodies and the firm. In their study of the historical evolution of Anglo-American accounting, auditing and corporate governance practices, Watts and Zuo (2016) note some of the influences and pressures exerted by Big 8 accounting firms on regulatory agencies. Those influences included the role of Colonel Arthur H. Carter (partner of Haskins & Sells) in persuading the Senate Committee on Banking and Currency to avoid a government takeover of auditing of publicly traded firms in the 1930s (see also Zeff 2003a: 192); the influence of Leonard Spacek (partner of Arthur Andersen & Co.) in opposing alternative accounting methods and accounting flexibility in the mid-1950s (Zeff 2001); and the formalisation of accounting firms' participation in the dialogue on accounting principles and issue pronouncement on GAAP, culminating in the 1960s with each Big 8 auditing firm having a representative on the APB Board. Ramanna (2015) offers a study of more recent interactions between firms and standard setters in the US.

Aside from the direct political influences and effects of Big Firm activities, we know little about the influences of accounting firms on modern society. For example, modern ways of thinking about the accountability and governance of all kinds of organisations (corporations, public sector, charities) are imbued with the accounting concepts and notions of audit that professional firms articulate and embed in social, political and cultural life. The very idea of organisational 'transparency' is seemingly inseparable from the production of financial statements. As Power notes (1997), the term audit has colonised all kinds of inspection and accountability practices that, although separate from traditional financial audit, are linked to the cultural influence and commercial activities of accounting firms. We are now accustomed to hearing of medical audit, efficiency audit, effectiveness audit, value-for-money audit, environmental audit, to name but a few, and it would be useful to understand the development of accounting firm service offerings in these areas. Although the character, methods, rationales and claims of these offerings may vary, financial audit is the model that has inspired the form of these administrative procedures and reforms (Pentland 2000). Many of the large accounting firms have been in the vanguard of consulting on these new audit technologies, and in so doing, important cognitive categories of everyday life (about accountability, transparency, responsibility, performance, management, etc.) have been shaped and transformed by them.

Moreover, the efforts of large firms to manage their environment and work may be subject to 'turf wars'. We know that the work domain of accountants vis-à-vis other occupations (e.g. lawyers, engineers, IT, actuaries, statisticians) varies according to national jurisdictions, yet the occupational and jurisdictional boundaries are never fixed (Walker 2004). Dezalay and Garth (2004) show the Big Firms have engaged in disputes concerning accounting and legal activities, the role of the multidisciplinary practice and the future organisation of, and interrelations between, the legal and accounting professions. Such issues have also been touched upon in the work of Cooper et al. (1996, 2000), Greenwood et al. (2002), Suddaby and Greenwood (2006), Brock et al. (2012), Morgan et al. (2001), Morgan and Quack (2006) and Halliday and Carruthers (2009). Many of these issues remain relevant to contemporary activities of the large firms (Empson 2001, 2004). Firm histories have yet to address this very significant theme – the role of firms in defining their tasks, structure and regulatory environment in relation to other occupations. Further, the challenges of managing multidisciplinary practices – of coordinating the work of professionals with quite different orientations, values and presuppositions – have yet to be addressed, but doing so would add insight into a range of theories relating, for example, to occupational competition and identity. The activities and practices of the large firms as political and cultural actors could usefully gather much more attention from historians.

Histories of firms as agents of imperialism

With large accounting firms outgrowing professional associations and entering the state/ profession dichotomy (Greenwood and Suddaby 2006; Suddaby et al. 2007), the accounting professionalisation project has been said to have 'entered a new phase – from one of local monopoly to that of building a global cartel' (Yee 2012: 428), in which large international accounting firms have emerged as key actors in processes of globalisation. Global accounting firms have been seen as powerful and influential 'interest groups' in extending their jurisdictions in a global market in a number of ways, particularly via their influence on national state regulators, membership of major international trade lobbies and collaboration with international actors (such as the WTO and OECD) in the globalisation of professional services (e.g. Arnold 2005; Hopper et al. 2017). Large accounting firms have been seen as the result of globalisation and, at the same time, as contributors in providing the latter with structures and arrangements that enable the operation of a global market (Ramirez et al. 2015). In addressing the relationship between globalisation and accounting firms, historical studies have generally tended to take an Anglo-American focus. Little is known about the role of large accounting firms in the shaping of the profession and the emergence of new accounting fields in non-western sites, such as Japan, India and China (Cooper and Robson 2006).

Contexts like Russia or China, in which the state has sought to control the foreign influence of international accounting firms, provide an interesting setting to explore the uneasy relationship between the state and the international accounting firms, as well as the impact of multinational accounting firms on the development of the public accounting profession (Yee 2012; Deng and Macve 2015). For example, in their study of the state-profession nexus in China, Ezzamel et al. (2018) have highlighted the power of the State to shape market dynamics and competition among local and Big 4 firms and in turn the strategies and forms of capital multinational accounting firms adopt to position and reposition themselves in the face of the different forms of State influence on the devolvement of the Chinese accounting field. However, these studies have little historical content.

While the literature has generally tended to explain the rise of the accounting profession as a response to the functional needs associated with the development of industrial societies, critical historical studies have seen the trajectory and development of processes of professionalisation as an expression of (or instrumental to) processes of empire, post-coloniality, domination and globalisation, and large accounting firms as a vehicle for the dissemination of accounting institutions and practices within colonialist and imperialist contexts (Annisette 2003). Within the framework of imperialism, this literature has examined the influence of statism, elites' strategies and social status struggles, and the self-interest and strategies of professional bodies on the development of the accounting profession in colonial contexts and the construction and maintenance of empire and imperialist project (e.g. Annisette 2000; Annisette and Neu 2004; Yapa et al. 2016; Hopper et al. 2017). However, scholars have also started to explore the role of large accounting firms in the enactment of imperialism and colonialism, and their impact on the nature and development of the field of accounting within the boundaries of imperial systems, in both developing (Chua and Poullaos 2002) and emerging countries (Annisette 2010; Altaher et al. 2014; Belal et al. 2017).

Focusing on the rise of accounting institutions within ex-British colonies in the pre-independence period, Poullaos and Uche (2012: 76) argue that the market for accounting services 'was dominated by British firms, fuelled by British capital, organised on British lines (for example, laws based on British exemplars), and served British interests', creating a local accounting space dominated by British accountants and their British-based notion of professionalism. In the context of Middle Eastern protectorates, Altaher et al. (2014) highlight the dominance of foreign accountants and British accounting firms in Kuwait in the period after the discovery of oil and Israel's invasion of Palestine, and their influence on the Kuwaiti accounting professionalisation project.

In examining the professionalisation-imperialism nexus in Trinidad and Tobago, Annisette (2000) shows the influence of large accounting firms upon the Institute of Chartered Accountants of Trinidad and Tobago to be the cause of an ideological shift from indigenisation to internationalisation, subverting the government's goal of indigenising accountancy training. In her study, the incorporation of local firms into the Anglo-American accounting conglomerates was seen as a means of achieving international standardisation, and large accounting firms as a medium for the worldwide standardisation of accounting practice.

Yapa et al. (2016) examines the nexus of internal and economic interests, class struggles, practices of state control, institutions and forces of colonisation and globalisation associated with the emergence of the field of accounting in Cambodia. The study highlights how the Cambodian accounting profession emerged from competition between local organisations concerned with maintaining local regulation and the influences of international institutions, including the globalisation effects of large accounting firms in modifying and redefining the growth of local institutions and practices of accounting.

Conclusion

This chapter has reviewed the histories of accounting firms and the key themes that emerge from them. Clearly some firms are better covered than others, and some have been well served by the scholarly celebrations offered by business historians. However, we find many firm histories 'Whiggish' in their perspectives and orientations. Much of the historical work on accounting firms focuses upon the professional elites – those that founded or led the firms through important periods of expansion – and what they enabled. Events are constructed as the accomplishment of key individuals leading their organisations in response to the demands of clients and the market; firms are presented as serving both their clients and professional ideals.

Much of the 'work' of accounting firms seems to be confined to the expansion of audit activities and the regulation that it has supported. The array of services that firms now offer seems to have merited little attention, except in the evaluations of recent years that was the starting point for this chapter. Yet at the same time such studies have little to say about the everyday experience of work, confining their attention to the actions of the senior partners of the firm. The practices and technologies of work are relatively uncharted.

It also worth stressing that most histories focus upon single firms, as if the story of each were independent and unique, despite the similarities of the underlying narratives. Few histories have attempted to address the organisational field of institutional activities in which firms practice or the common connections that exist in the audit field (Staubus 1996; Robson et al. 2007; Lounsbury 2008). Yet as the rise of various accounting and audit technologies shows, the adoption of similar technologies at the same time suggests that accounting firms are addressing a shared set of economic and institutional conditions.

Accounting is a heterogeneous profession in terms of the professional identity, size and global/local dimension of its actors, and yet the small accounting practice, despite being the most numerous part of the profession by number of firms, remains largely under-researched (Ramirez 2001, 2009). Little is known about the intra-professional relations between Big 4 accounting practices and small accounting firms, and their implications for the development of the accounting profession over time. As Ramirez et al. (2015: 1341) note, a profession is an institutionalised compromise among different professional segments that compete for status and power vis-à-vis other segments in the profession. In this respect, historical studies looking at small accounting firms have the potential to shed light on the professional struggles and power relations that exist between Big 4 firms and 'small practitioners' (Ramirez 2009), the basis and extent of their competition (Carter et al. 2015), and the consequences of this competition for professional hierarchies (Ramirez et al. 2015). Small firm histories could also provide scholars with a new perspective to study processes of globalisation as a transformation in the relationships and hierarchies between large and small firms, in which large organisations are becoming the most prominent figures in the profession, potentially leading to a redefinition of what counts as 'big' and what counts as 'small' in the accounting field (Ramirez et al. 2015). The recent work by Annisette and Trivedi (2013), Jeacle (2011) and Walker (2011) offers new ways of thinking about accounting labour, gender, immigration and reconstructions of accounting firms and practices.

Finally, we suggest that firm histories give more attention to the role of firms as actors in their field. Audit practices now extend beyond the accounting firms and their corporate clients (Power 1997), and the firms have actively sponsored developments in governments and the private sector (McSweeney 1994). They have been active in promoting new technologies of organisation, management and governance in the corporation, often through their consulting arms, and often in association with academics (Armstrong 2002; Jones and Dugdale 2002; Roberts et al. 2003; Roberts and Bobek 2004). The firms are significant cultural, economic and political actors, promoting and disseminating technologies of corporate and governmental performance across the globe. Accounting and accounting firms are seemingly everywhere. As we have argued, research will require access to firms' archives and their willingness to co-operate in studies that may question their own sense of identity. Yet it is time for historical research to catch up with the practice and influence of firms in ways that extend beyond individualist accounts of elite practitioners. Firm histories have the potential to address important theoretical issues of professionalisation, regulation and organisational management, and we encourage new studies that embrace multiple theoretical orientations.

Key works

Covaleski et al. (1998) is a seminal examination of management control and performance appraisal in large public accounting firms.

Jones (1995) is the pre-eminent firm history of its type: a business historian's study of the origins and growth of Price Waterhouse.

Sluyterman (1998) considers the dynamics of the internationalisation of audit firms.

Stevens (1991) presents a journalistic study of the power and politics of the Big 6 firms. Stevens offers a type of analysis not found in official histories.

Walker (1993) offers an historical analysis of the emergence of a Scottish CA practice in Edinburgh.

Notes

1 For example, one of the antecedent firms of PricewaterhouseCoopers, Price Waterhouse, dates from Stanley Price's London firm founded in 1849; Edwin Waterhouse and William Holyland joined in 1865. The other main component, Coopers & Lybrand, dates from William Cooper's London firm of 1854, and the firm of William Lybrand, Adam & Edward Ross, & Robert Montgomery, founded in 1898 in Philadelphia. William Deloitte founded his London firm in 1854 and the firm of Haskins and Sells dates from the New York firm of Haskins founded in 1898. Ernst & Young dates from 1849 when Frederick Whinney joined the London firm of Harding & Pullein, later Whinney, Smith & Whinney after Whinney became a partner in 1857, and the Cleveland firm of Ernst & Ernst founded in Cleveland in 1903. Arthur Young's firm was established in Chicago in 1898. KPMG's antecedents include William Peat, who joined the London firm of Robert Fletcher (founded in 1867) in 1870 and was made partner in 1877, and James Marwick's Glasgow firm, established in 1887.

2 Thanks to Stephen Walker, Chris Napier and Dick Edwards for their help and guidance, and to David Dolf for his excellent research assistance. David Cooper acknowledges the financial support of the Social Science and Humanities Research Council.

References

Accounting Today (2004) The 2004 Accounting Today Top 100 Firms. *Accounting Today*. Retrieved from www.accountingtoday.com

Accounting Today (2012) 2012 Top 100 Firms. *Accounting Today*. Retrieved from www.accountingtoday.com.

Accounting Today (2018) Special Report 2018 Top 100 Firms and Regional Leaders. *Accounting Today*. Retrieved from www.accountingtoday.com.

Allen, D.G. and McDermott, K. (1993) *Accounting for Success: A History of Price Waterhouse in America, 1890-1990* (Boston: Harvard Business School Press).

Altaher, N.A., Dyball, M.C., and Evans, E. (2014) A study of the emergence of the Kuwaiti Association of Accountants and Auditors, *Accounting History*, 19 (1-2): 255–78.

Anderson, M. and Walker, S.P. (2009) 'All sorts and conditions of men'. The social origins of the founders of the ICAEW, *British Accounting Review*, 41 (1): 31–45.

Anderson-Gough, F., Edgley, C., Robson, K., and Sharma, N. (2016) Professional identity and "the Enigma of Diversity": sensemaking and enacting hard and soft law in audit firms. HEC working paper.

Anderson-Gough, F., Grey, C., and Robson, K. (1998) *Making Up Accountants: The Organizational and Professional Socialization of Trainee Chartered Accountants* (Aldershot: Ashgate Publishing).

Anderson-Gough, F., Grey, C., and Robson, K. (2000) In the name of the client: the service ethic in two professional services firms, *Human Relations*, 53 (9): 1151–74.

Anderson-Gough, F., Grey, C., and Robson, K. (2002) Accounting professionals and the accounting profession: linking conduct and context, *Accounting and Business Research*, 32 (1): 41–56.

Anderson-Gough, F., Grey, C., and Robson, K. (2005) 'Helping them to Forget.': the organizational embedding of gender relations in two large audit firms, *Accounting, Organizations and Society*, 30 (5): 468–90.

Anderson-Gough, F., Grey, C., and Robson, K. (2006) The networked professional, in R. Greenwood and R. Suddaby (eds), *Professional Service Firms: Research in the Sociology of Organizations*, 24: 403–31.

Annisette, M. (2000) Imperialism and the professions: the education and certification of accountants in Trinidad and Tobago, *Accounting, Organizations and Society*, 25 (7): 631–59.

Annisette, M. (2003) The colour of accountancy: examining the salience of race in a professionalisation project, *Accounting, Organizations and Society*, 28 (7-8): 639–74.

Annisette, M. (2010) Maintaining empire: The practice link in Trinidad and Tobago, in C. Poullaos and S. Sian (eds), *Accountancy and Empire: The British Legacy of Professional Organization*, pp. 168–91 (London: Routledge).

Annisette, M. and Trivedi, V.U. (2013) Globalization, paradox and the (un) making of identities: immigrant chartered accountants of India in Canada, *Accounting, Organizations and Society*, 38 (1): 1–29.

Armstrong, P. (1987) The rise of accounting controls in British capitalist enterprises, *Accounting, Organizations and Society*, 12 (5): 415–36.

Armstrong, P. (2002) The cost of activity based costing, *Accounting, Organizations and Society*, 27 (1/2): 99–120.

Arnold, P.J. (2005) Disciplining domestic regulation: the World Trade Organization and the market for professional services, *Accounting, Organizations and Society*, 30 (4): 299–330.

Arthur Andersen. (nd) *Responding to New Challenges* (Chicago, IL: Arthur Andersen).

Barrett, M., Cooper, D.J., and Jamal, K. (2005) Globalization and the coordinating of work in multinational audits, *Accounting, Organizations and Society*, 30 (1): 1–24.

Baskerville, R.F., Bui, B., and Fowler, C.J. (2014) Voices within the winds of change: the demise of KMG Kendons, *Accounting History*, 19 (1-2): 31–52.

Baskerville, R.F. and Hay, D. (2010) The impact of globalization on professional accounting firms: evidence from New Zealand, *Accounting History*, 15 (3): 285–308.

Beaverstock, J.V. (2007) Transnational work: global professional labour markets in professional service accounting firms, in J. Bryson and P. Daniels (eds), *The Handbook of Service Industries*, pp. 409–31 (Cheltenham: Edward Elgar).

Belal, A., Spence, C., Carter, C., and Zhu, J. (2017) The Big 4 in Bangladesh: caught between the global and the local, *Accounting, Auditing & Accountability Journal*, 30 (1): 145–63.

Benson, H. (1989) *Accounting for Life* (London: Kogan Page).

Best, M. (1991) *The New Competition* (Cambridge: Cambridge University Press).

Black, J. and Edwards, J.R. (2016) Accounting careers traversing the separate spheres of business and government in Victorian Britain, *Accounting History*, 21 (2-3): 306–28.

Bloomberg (18 June 2018) Maybe the Big Four Auditing Firms Do Need to Be Broken Up. www.bloomberg.com/opinion/articles/2018-06-18/maybe-the-big-four-auditing-firms-do-need-breaking-up.

Boussebaa, M. and Faulconbridge, J.R. (2018) Professional service firms as agents of economic globalization: A political perspective, *Journal of Professions and Organization*, 6 (1): 72–90.

Boys, P. (1989) What's in a name – firms' simplified family trees, *Accountancy*, various issues.

Brock, D., Hinings, C.R., and Powell, M. (2012) *Restructuring the Professional Organization: Accounting, Health Care and Law* (London: Routledge).

Brooks, R. (2018) *Bean Counters: The Triumph of the Accountants and How They Broke Capitalism* (London: Atlantic Books).

Burrows, G. and Black, C. (1998) Profit sharing in Australian Big Six accounting firms: an exploratory study, *Accounting, Organizations and Society*, 23 (5/6): 517–30.

Büthe, T. and Mattli, W. (2011) *The New Global Rulers: The Privatization of Regulation in the World Economy* (Princeton, NJ: Princeton University Press).

Cahan, S., Zhang, W., and Veenman, D. (2011) Did the waste management audit failures signal lower firm-wide audit quality at Arthur Andersen? *Contemporary Accounting Research*, 28 (3): 859–91.

Cairncross, A. (1937) The social origins of accountants, *The Accountant*, 3276: 373–4.

Camfferman, K. and Zeff, S.A. (2007) *Financial Reporting and Global Capital Markets: A History of the International Accounting Standards Committee, 1973-2000* (Oxford: Oxford University Press).

Camfferman, K. and Zeff, S.A. (2015) *Aiming for Global Accounting Standards: The International Accounting Standards Board, 2001-2011* (Oxford: Oxford University Press).
Caramanis, C. V. (1999) International accounting firms versus indigenous auditors: intra-professional conflict in the Greek auditing profession 1990-1993, *Critical Perspectives on Accounting*, 10 (2): 153–96.
Caramanis, C.V. (2002) The interplay between professional groups, the state and supranational agents: pax Americana in the age of 'globalisation', *Accounting, Organizations and Society*, 27 (4-5): 379–409.
Carnegie, G. and Napier, C. (1996) Critical and interpretive histories: insights into accounting's present and future through its past, *Accounting, Auditing and Accountability Journal*, 9 (3): 7–39.
Carpenter, B. and Dirsmith, M. (1993) Sampling and the abstraction of knowledge in the auditing profession: an extended institutional theory perspective, *Accounting, Organizations and Society*, 11 (6): 41–63.
Carson, E. (2014) Globalization of auditing, in D. Hay, W.R. Knechel, and M. Willekens (eds), *The Routledge Companion to Auditing*, pp. 45–54 (London: Routledge).
Carter, C. and Spence, C. (2014) Being a successful professional: an exploration of who makes partner in the Big 4, *Contemporary Accounting Research*, 31 (4): 949–81.
Carter, C., Spence, C., and Muzio, D. (2015) Scoping an agenda for future research into the professions, *Accounting, Auditing & Accountability Journal*, 28 (8): 1198–216.
Catchpowle, L. and Cooper, C. (1999) No escaping the financial: the economic referent in South Africa, *Critical Perspectives on Accounting*, 10 (6): 711–46.
CEOs of the International Audit Networks (2006) *Global Capital Markets and the Global Economy: A Vision from the CEOs of the International Audit Networks*. Paris Symposium, November.
Chandar, N., Collier, D., and Miranti, P. (2014) Organizational evolution at Lybrand, Ross Bros. and Montgomery in the twentieth century, *Accounting History*, 19 (1-2): 53–76.
Chandler, A. (1962) *Strategy and Structure: Chapters in the History of the Industrial Enterprise* (Cambridge: MIT Press).
Chandler, A. (1965) *The Railroads: The Nations First Big Business* (New York: Harcourt Brace and World).
Chatman, J. A. (1991) Matching people and organizations: selection and socialization in public accounting firms, *Administrative Science Quarterly*, 36 (1): 459–84.
Chernow, R. (1990) *The House of Morgan: An American Banking Dynasty and the Rise of Modern Finance* (New York: Simon and Shuster).
Chua, W.F. and Poullaos, C. (1998) The dynamics of "closure" amidst the construction of market, profession, empire and nationhood: an historical analysis of an Australian accounting association, 1886-1903, *Accounting, Organizations and Society*, 23 (2): 155–87.
Chua, W.F. and Poullaos, C. (2002) The Empire Strikes Back? An exploration of centre–periphery interaction between the ICAEW and accounting associations in the self-governing colonies of Australia, Canada and South Africa, 1880-1907, *Accounting, Organizations and Society*, 27 (4-5): 409–45.
Clegg, S.R., Kornberger, M., and Pitsis, T. (2015) *Managing and Organizations: An Introduction to Theory and Practice* (London: Sage).
Coopers & Lybrand (1984) *The Early History of Coopers & Lybrand* (New York: Garland).
Cooper, C. and Taylor, P. (2000) From Taylorism to Ms Taylor: the transformation of the accounting craft, *Accounting, Organizations and Society*, 25 (6): 555–78.
Cooper, D.J., Greenwood, R., Hinings, B., and Brown, J.L. (1998) Globalisation and nationalism in a multinational accounting firm: the case of opening new markets in Eastern Europe, *Accounting, Organizations and Society*, 23 (5-6): 531–48.
Cooper, D.J., Hinings, B., Greenwood, R., and Brown, J.L. (1996) Sedimentation and transformation in organizational change: the case of Canadian law firms, *Organization Studies*, 17 (4): 623–47.
Cooper, D.J. and Robson, K. (2006) Accounting, professions and regulation: locating the sites of professionalization, *Accounting, Organizations and Society*, 31 (4-5): 415–44.
Cooper Brothers & Co. (1954) *A History of Cooper Brothers and Co., 1854 to 1954* (London: B.T. Batsford).
Covaleski, M.A., Dirsmith, M.W., Heian, J.B., and Samuel, S. (1998) The calculated and the avowed: techniques of discipline and struggles over identity in Big Six public accounting firms, *Administrative Science Quarterly*, 43 (June): 293–327.
Curtis, E. and Turley, S. (2007) The business risk audit – A longitudinal case study of an audit engagement, *Accounting, Organizations and Society*, 32 (4-5): 439–61.
Cypert, S.A. (1991) *Following the Money: The Inside Story of Accounting's First Mega-Merger* (New York: Amacom).

Daniels, P., Thrift, N., and Leyshon, A. (1989) Internationalization of professional producer services: accountancy conglomerates, In P. Enderwick (ed), *Multi-national Services Firms*, pp. 79–106 (London: Routledge).

De Mond, C.W. (1951) *Price, Waterhouse & Company in America* (New York, 1980: Reprinted by Arno Press).

Deng, S. and Macve, R. (2015) The development of China's auditing profession: globalizing translation meets self-determination in identity construction. Unpublished working paper, London School of Economics.

Dezalay, Y. and Garth, B.G. (2004) The confrontation between the Big Five and Big Law: turf battles and ethical debates as contests for professional credibility, *Law & Social Inquiry*, 29 (3): 615–38.

Dirsmith, M.W. and Covaleski, M.A. (1985) Informal communication, nonformal communications and mentoring in public accounting firms, *Accounting, Organizations and Society*, 10 (2): 149–69.

Dirsmith, M.W., Heian, J.B., and Covaleski, M.A. (1997) Structure and agency in an institutionalized setting: the application and social transformation of control in the big six, *Accounting, Organizations and Society*, 22 (1): 1–27.

Dobbin, F. and Dowd, T.J. (2000) The market that antitrust built: public policy, private coercion and railroad acquisitions, 1825 to 1922, *American Sociological Review*, 65 (Oct): 631–57.

Edwards, J.R. (2016) Whinney and Waterhouse's government assignment 1887-1888: a study of its significance, *Accounting Historians Journal*, 43 (1): 1–32.

Edwards, J.R. and Walker, S.P. (2010) Lifestyle, status and occupational differentiation in Victorian accountancy, *Accounting, Organizations and Society*, 35 (1): 2–22.

Empson, L. (2001) Fear of exploitation and fear of contamination: impediments to knowledge transfer in mergers between professional service firms, *Human Relations*, 54 (7): 839–62.

Empson, L. (2004) Organizational identity change: managerial regulation and member identification in an accounting firm acquisition, *Accounting, Organizations and Society*, 29 (8): 759–81.

Evans, L. (2003) Auditing and audit firms in Germany before 1931, *Accounting Historians Journal*, 30 (2): 29–65.

Evans, L. and Fraser, I. (2012) The accountant's social background and stereotype in popular culture, *Accounting, Auditing & Accountability Journal*, 25 (6): 964–1000.

Ezzamel, M., Spence, C., and Zhu, J. (2018) States of mind: the many forms of government influence on the accounting profession in China. Cardiff University Working Paper.

Falkus, M. (1993) *Called to Account. A History of Coopers and Lybrand in Australia* (St. Leonards, NSW: Allen & Unwin).

Feeney, K. (2013) Railroad audits: some arrived ahead of schedule, *Accounting Historians Journal*, 40 (1): 1–30.

Fielding, A. and Portwood, D. (1980) Professions and the state: towards a typology of bureaucratic professions, *Sociological Review*, 28 (1): 23–53.

Flesher, D.L., and Previts, G.J. (2014) Haskins & Sells during the First World War and its aftermath. *Accounting History Review*, 41 (1): 61–78.

Flesher, D.L. and Previts, G. J. (2016a) A historical episode of professional scepticism, *The CPA Journal*, 86 (7): 19.

Flesher, D.L. and Previts, G. J. (2016b) Haskins & Sells' selected papers - a profile in leadership thought (1955-1974), *Accounting History Review*, 26 (3): 333–50.

Fligstein, N. (1993) *The Transformation of Corporate Control* (Cambridge, MA: Harvard University Press).

Gendron, Y., Cooper, D. J., and Townley, B. (2007) The construction of auditing expertise in measuring government performance, *Accounting, Organizations and Society*, 32 (1-2): 101–29.

Gendron, Y. and Spira, L.F. (2010) Identity narratives under threat: A study of former members of Arthur Andersen, *Accounting, Organizations and Society*, 35 (3): 275–300.

Gietzmann, M. and Quick, R. (1998) Capping auditor liability: the German experience, *Accounting, Organizations and Society*, 23 (1): 81–104.

Gillis, P. L. (2014) *The Big Four and the Development of the Accounting Profession in China* (Somerville, MA: Emerald Publishing).

Gow, I.D. and Kells, S. (2018) *The Big Four: The Curious Past and Perilous Future of the Global Accounting Monopoly* (Oakland, CA: Berrett-Koehler Publishers).

Graham, C. and Neu, D. (2003) Accounting for globalization, *Accounting Forum*, 27 (4): 449–71.

Greenwood, R., Cooper, D.J., Rose, T., Hinings, C.R., and Brown, J. (1999) The global management of professional services: the example of accounting, in S. Clegg, E. Ibarra, and L. Bueno (eds), *Theories of the Management Process: Making Sense Through Difference*, pp. 9264–85 (Thousand Oaks, CA: Sage).

Greenwood, R. and Empson, L. (2003) The professional partnership: relic or exemplary form of governance? *Organization Studies*, 24 (6): 909–33.

Greenwood, R., Hinings, C.R., and Brown, J. (1990) P^2-form of strategic management: corporate practices in professional partnerships, *Academy of Management Journal*, 33 (4): 725–55.

Greenwood, R., Morris, T., Fairclough, S., and Boussebaa, M. (2010) The organizational design of transnational professional service firms, *Organizational Dynamics*, 39 (2): 173–83.

Greenwood, R. and Suddaby, R. (2006) Institutional entrepreneurship in mature fields: the Big Five accounting firms, *Academy of Management Journal*, 45 (1): 58–80.

Greenwood, R., Suddaby, R., and Hinings, C.R. (2002) Theorizing change: the role of professional associations in the transformation of institutionalized fields, *Academy of Management Journal*, 45 (1): 58–80.

Grey, C. (1998) On being a professional in a 'big six' firm, *Accounting, Organizations and Society*, 23 (5/6): 569–87.

Habgood, W. (ed.) (1994) *Chartered Accountants in England and Wales: A Guide to Historical Records* (Manchester: Manchester University Press).

Halliday, T. and Carruthers, B. (2009) *Bankrupt: Global Lawmaking and Systemic Financial Crisis* (Stanford, CA: Stanford University Press).

Hammond, T. (2002) *A White Collar Profession: African American Certified Public Accountants since 1921* (Chapel Hill, NC: University of North Carolina Press).

Hanlon, G. (1994) *The Commercialization of Accountancy: Flexible Accumulation and the Transformation of the Service Class* (New York: St Martins Press).

Hanlon, G. (1996) "Casino capitalism" and the rise of the "commercialised" service class-an examination of the accountant, *Critical Perspectives on Accounting*, 7 (3): 339–63.

Hopper, T., Lassou, P., and Soobaroyen, T. (2017) Globalisation, accounting and developing countries, *Critical Perspectives on Accounting*, 43: 125–48.

Howitt, H. (1966) *The History of The Institute of Chartered Accountants in England and Wales 1880-1965 and of Its Founder Accountancy Bodies 1870-1880* (London: Heinemann).

International Accounting Bulletin (2011) World Survey: emerging markets boost global growth. *International Accounting Bulletin* (IAB). January 2011, issue 481. Retrieved from www.internationalaccountingbulletin.com.

International Accounting Bulletin (2017) World Survey: what an uncertain world. *International Accounting Bulletin* (IAB). February 2017, issue 570. Retrieved from www.internationalaccountingbulletin.com.

Iyer, V.M.. (1998) Characteristics of accounting firm alumni who benefit their former firm, *Accounting Horizons*, 12 (1): 18–30.

Jeacle, I. (2011) A practice of her own: female career success beyond the accounting firm, *Critical Perspectives on Accounting*, 22 (3): 288–303.

Jennings, A.R. (1998) Firm History Notes for Business History Group, Box 7, folder 7. Pricewaterhouse-Cooper archives, Columbia University.

Jones, C. and Dugdale, D. (2002) The ABC bandwagon and the juggernaut of modernity, *Accounting, Organizations and Society*, 27 (1-2): 121–64.

Jones, E. (1981) *Accountancy and the British Economy, 1840-1980: The Evolution of Ernst & Whinney* (London: B.T. Batsford Ltd).

Jones, E. (1988) *The Memoirs of Edwin Waterhouse* (London: B.T. Batsford).

Jones, E. (1995) *True and Fair: A History of Price Waterhouse* (London: Hamish Hamilton).

Jupe, R. and Funnell, W. (2015) Neoliberalism, consultants and the privatisation of public policy formulation: the case of Britain's rail industry, *Critical Perspectives on Accounting*, 29: 65–85.

Kettle, Sir R. (1957) *Deloitte and Co. 1845-1956* (Oxford: Oxford University Press. Reprinted by Garland Publishing, New York, 1982).

Khalifa, R. (2004) *Gendered Divisions of Expert Labour: Professional Specialisms in UK Accountancy*, PhD Thesis, University of Manchester.

Knechel, W.R. (2007) The business risk audit: origins, obstacles and opportunities, *Accounting, Organizations and Society*, 32 (4-5): 383–408.

Kornberger, M., Justesen, L., and Mouritsen, J. (2011) "When you make manager, we put a big mountain in front of you": an ethnography of managers in a Big 4 accounting firm, *Accounting, Organizations and Society*, 36 (8): 514–33.

Lee, T.A. (Ed.) (1997) *Shaping the Accountancy Profession: The Story of Three Scottish Pioneers* (New York: Garland).

Lee, T.A. (2014) Assimilation and Americanisation in the Progressive Era: Price, Waterhouse & Company in the US, 1890-1914, *Accounting History*, 19 (1-2): 13–30.

Loft, A. (1986) Towards a critical understanding of accounting: the case of cost accounting in the UK, 1914-1925, *Accounting, Organizations and Society*, 11 (2): 137–60.

Loft, A. (1990) *Coming into the Light* (London: CIMA Publications).

Lounsbury, M. (2008) Institutional rationality and practice variation: new directions in the institutional analysis of practice, *Accounting, Organizations and Society*, 33 (4-5): 349–61.

Lupu, I. and Empson, L. (2015) Illusion and overwork: playing the game in the accounting field, *Accounting, Auditing & Accountability Journal*, 28 (8): 1310–40.

Malsch, B. and Gendron, Y. (2013) Re-theorizing change: institutional experimentation and the struggle for domination in the field of public accounting, *Journal of Management Studies*, 50 (5): 870–99.

Marshall, N.J. (1982) *Accounting for a Century: A History of the Antecedent Firms of Touche Ross & Co., Australia 1882-1982* (Australia: Touche Ross & Co).

Matthews, D. and Pirie, J. (2001) *The Auditors Talk: An Oral History of the Profession from the 1920's to the Present Day* (London: Routledge).

Maughan, W.S. (2002/1915) *Of Human Bondage* (London: Vintage Classics).

McGouldrick, P. (1968) *New England Textiles in the 19th Century: Profits and Investments* (Cambridge: Harvard University Press).

McSweeney, B. (1994) Management by Accounting, in A.G. Hopwood and P. Miller (eds), *Accounting as Social and Institutional Practice*, pp. 237–68 (Cambridge: Cambridge University Press).

Miranti, P. (2014) The emergence of accounting as a global profession–an introduction, *Accounting History*, 19 (1-2): 3–11.

Mitchell, A. and Sikka, P. (2004) Accountability of the accountancy bodies: the peculiarities of a British accountancy body, *British Accounting Review*, 36 (4): 395–414.

Montagna, P. (1968) Professionalization and bureaucratization in large professional organizations, *American Journal of Sociology*, 74 (2): 138–45.

Montagna, P. (1974) *Certified Public Accounting: A Sociological Analysis of a Profession in Change* (Houston, TX: Scholars Book Co).

Morgan, G., Kristensen, P.H., and Whitley, R. (eds) (2001) *The Multinational Firm* (Oxford: Oxford University Press).

Morgan, G. and Quack, S. (2006) The internationalization of professional service firms, in R. Greenwood and R. Suddaby (eds), *Professional Service Firms: Research in the Sociology of Organizations*, 24: 403–31.

Neu, D., Gomez, E.O., Graham, C., and Heincke, M. (2006) "Informing" technologies and the World Bank, *Accounting, Organizations and Society*, 31 (7): 635–62.

O'Dwyer, B. (2011) The case of sustainability assurance: constructing a new assurance service, *Contemporary Accounting Research*, 28 (4): 1230–66.

Pastra, Y. (2004) *A Descriptive Theory of the Big Accounting Firm*. Unpublished PhD dissertation, Strathclyde University.

Pentland, B. (2000) Will auditors take over the world? Program, technique and the verification of everything, *Accounting, Organizations and Society*, 25 (3): 307–12.

Perrow, C. (2002) *Organizing America: Wealth, Power and the Origins of Corporate Capitalism* (Princeton, NJ: Princeton University Press).

Persson, M.E., Radcliffe, V.S., and Stein, M. (2015) Alvin R. Jennings: managing partner, policy-maker, and institute president, *Accounting Historians Journal*, 42 (1): 85–104.

Persson, M.E., Radcliffe, V.S., and Stein, M. (2018) Elmer G Beamer and the American Institute of Certified Public Accountants: the pursuit of a cognitive standard for the accounting profession, *Accounting History*, 23 (1-2): 71–92.

Peterson, J. (2015) *Count Down: The Past, Present and Uncertain Future of the Big Four Accounting Firms* (Somerville, MA: Emerald Publishing Limited).

Picard, C.F., Durocher, S., and Gendron, Y. (2014) From meticulous professionals to superheroes of the business world: A historical portrait of a cultural change in the field of accountancy, *Accounting, Auditing & Accountability Journal*, 27 (1): 73–118.

Pollard, G.B. (1975) *A History of Price Waterhouse in Europe 1914-1969* (London: Price Waterhouse).

Pollard, S. (1965) *The Genesis of Modern Management* (Cambridge: Cambridge University Press).

Post, H., Wilderon, C., and Douma, S. (1998) Internationalization of Dutch accounting firms, *European Accounting Review*, 7 (4): 697–707.

Poullaos, C. (1994) *Making the Australian Chartered Accountant* (New York: Garland).

Poullaos, C. and Uche, C.U. (2012) Accounting professionalization in developing countries, in T. Hopper (ed), *Handbook of Accounting and Development*, pp. 74–94 (London: Edward Elgar).

Power, M. (1992) From common sense to expertise: the pre-history of audit sampling, *Accounting, Organizations and Society*, 17 (1): 37–62.

Power, M. (1997) *The Audit Society* (Oxford: Oxford University Press).

Power, M. (2000) *The Audit Implosion: Regulating Risk from the Inside* (London: ICAEW).

Power, M. (2003) Auditing and the production of legitimacy, *Accounting, Organizations and Society*, 28 (4): 379–94.

Preston, A.M., Cooper, D.J., Scarbrough, D.P., and Chilton, R.C. (1995) Changes in the code of ethics of the US accounting profession, 1917 and 1988: the continual quest for legitimation, *Accounting, Organizations and Society*, 20 (6): 507–46.

Previts, G.J. and Merino, B.D. (1988) *A History of Accountancy in the United States: The Cultural Significance of Accounting* (Columbus: Ohio State University Press).

Ramanna, K. (2015) *Political Standards: Corporate Interest, Ideology, and Leadership in the Shaping of Accounting Rules for the Market Economy* (Chicago: University of Chicago Press).

Ramirez, C. (2001) Understanding social closure in its cultural context: accounting practitioners in France (1920-1939), *Accounting, Organizations and Society*, 26 (4-5): 391–418.

Ramirez, C. (2009) Constructing the governable small practitioner: the changing nature of professional bodies and the management of professional accountants' identities in the UK, *Accounting, Organizations and Society*, 34 (3-4): 381–408.

Ramirez, C., Stringfellow, L., and Maclean, M. (2015) Beyond segments in movement: a 'small' agenda for research in the professions, *Accounting, Auditing & Accountability Journal*, 28 (8): 1341–72.

Richards, A.B. (1981) *Touche Ross & Co. 1899-1981* (London: Touche Ross).

Richards, G.E. (1950) *History of the Firm: The First Fifty Years, 1850-1900* (Price Waterhouse & Co, unpublished).

Richardson, A.J. (1989) Canada's accounting elite: 1880-1930, *Accounting Historians Journal*, 16 (1): 1–21.

Richardson, A.J. (2000) Building the Canadian Chartered accountancy profession: a biography of George Edwards, FCA, CBE, LLD, 1861-1947, *Accounting Historians Journal*, 27 (2): 87–116.

Richardson, A.J. (2009) Regulatory networks for accounting and auditing standards: A social network analysis of Canadian and international standard-setting, *Accounting, Organizations and Society*, 34 (5): 571–88.

Richardson, A.J. (2017) Professionalization and the accounting profession, in R. Roslender (ed), *The Routledge Companion to Critical Accounting*, pp. 127–42 (Abingdon: Routledge).

Roberts, D.H. (2015) Socialization of US novice accounting professionals through ethical discourse in 1931, *Accounting Historians Journal*, 42 (2): 63–89.

Roberts, R.W. and Bobek, D.D. (2004) The politics of tax accounting in the United States: evidence from the Taxpayer Relief Act of 1997, *Accounting, Organizations and Society*, 29 (5-6): 565–90.

Roberts, R. W., Dwyer, P. D., and Sweeney, J. T. (2003) Political strategies used by the US public accounting profession during auditor liability reform: the case of the Private Securities Litigation Reform, *Journal of Accounting and Public Policy*, 22 (5): 433–57.

Robson, K. and Cooper, D. J. (1990) Understanding the development of the accountancy profession in the UK, in D.J. Cooper and T. Hopper (eds), *Critical Accounts*, pp. 366–90 (London: Macmillan).

Robson, K., Humphrey, C., Khalifa, R., and Jones, J. (2007) Transforming audit technologies: business risk audit methodologies and the audit field, *Accounting, Organizations and Society*, 30 (1-3): 163–70.

Robson, K., Humphrey, C., and Loft, A. (2005) Globalizing Technologies of Performance: from National Jurisdictional Competition to Co-ordinated Network Governance. Paper presented at *Governance Without Government: New Forms of Governance in the Knowledge Economy and Society Conference*, Cardiff Business School, May.

Robson, K., Willmott, H., Cooper, D.J., and Puxty, A.G. (1994) The ideology of professional regulation and the markets for accounting labour: three episodes in the recent history of the UK accountancy profession, *Accounting, Organizations and Society*, 19 (6): 527–53.

Roy, W.G. (1997) *Socializing Capital: The Rise of the Large Industrial Corporation in America* (Princeton, NJ: Princeton University Press).

Samsonova-Taddei, A., and Humphrey, C. (2014) Transnationalism and the Transforming Roles of Professional Accountancy Bodies. Towards a Research Agenda, *Accounting, Auditing & Accountability Journal*, 27 (6): 903–932.

Sikka, P. (2008) Globalization and its discontents: accounting firms buy limited liability partnership legislation in Jersey, *Accounting, Auditing & Accountability Journal*, 21 (3): 398–426.

Sikka, P. (2009) Financial crisis and the silence of the auditors, *Accounting, Organizations and Society*, 34 (6-7): 868–73.

Sikka, P. and Willmott, H. (1997) On the commercialization of accountancy thesis, *Accounting, Organizations and Society*, 22 (8): 831–42.

Sikka, P. and Willmott, H. (2010) The dark side of transfer pricing: its role in tax avoidance and wealth retentiveness, *Critical Perspectives on Accounting*, 21 (4): 342–56.

Sluyterman, K.A. (1998) The internationalisation of Dutch accounting firms, *Business History*, 40 (2): 1–21.

Solsma, L.L. and Flesher, D.L. (2013) Exploring the clientele of an accounting firm in early twentieth century America, *Accounting History Review*, 23 (3): 295–315.

Spacek, L. (1985) *The Growth of Arthur Andersen and Company* (Chicago, IL: Arthur Andersen and Company).

Spence, C. and Carter, C. (2014) An exploration of the professional habitus in the Big 4 accounting firms, *Work, Employment and Society*, 28 (6): 946–62.

Spence, C., Carter, C., Belal, A., Husillos, J., Dambrin, C., and Archel, P. (2016) Tracking habitus across a transnational professional field, *Work, Employment and Society*, 30 (1): 3–20.

Spence, C., Dambrin, C., Carter, C., Husillos, J., and Archel, P. (2015) Global ends, local means: cross-national homogeneity in professional service firms, *Human Relations*, 68 (5): 765–88.

Spence, C., Zhu, J., Endo, T., and Matsubara, S. (2017) Money, honour and duty: global professional service firms in comparative perspective, *Accounting, Organizations and Society*, 62: 82–97.

Squires, S.E., Smith, C.J., McDougall, L., and Yeack, W.R. (2003) *Inside Arthur Andersen: Shifting Values, Unexpected Consequences* (Upper Saddle River, New Jersey: Pearson Education/Financial Times Prentice Hall).

Staubus, G. J. (1996) *Economic Influences on the Development of Accounting Firms* (New York: Garland).

Stevens, M. (1981) *The Big Eight* (New York: MacMillan Publishing Co).

Stevens, M. (1991) *The Big Six: The Selling Out of American's Top Accounting Firms* (Toronto: Simon and Schuster).

Suddaby, R., Cooper, D. J., and Greenwood, R. (2007) Transnational regulation of professional services: governance dynamics of field level organizational change, *Accounting, Organizations and Society*, 32 (4-5): 333–62.

Suddaby, R. and Greenwood, R. (2006) Introduction, *Research in the Sociology of Organizations*, 24: 1–16.

Tinker, T. and Koutsaumadi, A. (1997) A mind is a wonderful thing to waste: 'think like a commodity', become a CPA, *Accounting, Auditing & Accountability Journal*, 10 (3): 454–67.

Toffler, B.L. (with J. Reingold) (2003) *Final Accounting: Ambition, Greed and the Fall of Arthur Andersen* (New York: Broadway Books).

Useem, M. (1996) *Investor Capitalism: How Money Managers are Changing the Face of Corporate America* (NY: Basic Books).

Walker, S.P. (1988) *The Society of Accountants in Edinburgh 1854-1914. A Study of Recruitment to a New Profession* (New York: Garland).

Walker, S.P. (1993) Anatomy of a Scottish CA practice: Lindsay, Jamieson & Haldane 1818-1918, *Accounting, Business & Financial History*, 3 (2): 127–54.

Walker, S.P. (2002) 'Men of small standing'? Locating accountants in English society during the mid-nineteenth century, *European Accounting Review*, 11 (2): 377–99.

Walker, S.P. (2004) Conflict, collaboration, fuzzy jurisdictions and partial settlements. Accountants, lawyers and insolvency practice during the late 19th century, *Accounting and Business Research*, 34 (3): 247–65.

Walker, S.P. (2011) Ethel Ayres Purdie: critical practitioner and suffragist, *Critical Perspectives on Accounting*, 22 (1): 79–101.

Walker, S.P. (2018) War and organizational disruption in professional service firms, *Journal of Professions and Organization*, 5: 1–24.

Watts, R.L. and Zuo, L. (2016) Understanding practice and institutions: A historical perspective, *Accounting Horizons*, 30 (3): 409–23.

White, R. (2003) *Peats to KPMG – Gracious Family to Global Firm* (Wickford: Bradell Ltd).

Whitford, D. (1997) Arthur, Arthur … *Fortune*, November 10: 169–78.

Wise, T.A. (1982) *Peat, Marwick, Mitchell and Co. 85 Years* (New York: Peat, Marwick, Mitchell and Co).

Wootton, C.W., Wolk, C.M., and Normand, C. (2003) An historical perspective on mergers and acquisitions by major US accounting firms, *Accounting History*, 8 (1): 25–60.

Wyatt, A. (2004) Accounting professionalism: they just don't get it!, *Accounting Horizons*, 18 (1): 45–53.

Yapa, P., Jacobs, K., and Huot, B.C. (2016) The field of accounting: exploring the presence and absence of accounting in Cambodia, *Accounting, Auditing & Accountability Journal*, 29 (3): 401–27.

Yee, H. (2012) Analyzing the state-accounting profession dynamic: some insights from the professionalization experience in China, *Accounting, Organizations and Society*, 37 (6): 426–44.

Zeff, S.A. (2001) The work of the special committee on research program, *The Accounting Historians Journal*, 28 (2): 141–186.

Zeff, S.A. (2003a) How the U.S. accounting profession got where it is today: part I, *Accounting Horizons*, 17 (3): 189–205.

Zeff, S.A. (2003b) How the U.S. accounting profession got where it is today: part II, *Accounting Horizons*, 17 (4): 267–86.

Zeff, S.A. (2016) The influence of Price Waterhouse & Co. on the CAP, the APB, and in the early years on the FASB, *Accounting Historians Journal*, 43 (2): 129–40.

Zundel, M., Holt, R., and Popp, A. (2016) Using history in the creation of organizational identity, *Management & Organizational History*, 11 (2): 211–35.

13
EDUCATION

Carolyn Fowler

Overview

Accounting education is a two-sided coin; one side concerns education in accounting provided by a variety of organisations including schools, colleges, universities and commercial establishments; the other concerns the use of accounting in the administration and functioning of educational institutions. This chapter considers historical research on both sides of the coin. The first part of the chapter builds on Anderson-Gough's contribution to the first edition of the *Routledge Companion to Accounting History* by reviewing subsequent literature on accounting in education and broadening the temporal and spatial scope of the original chapter. The second part of the chapter considers historical research in an emerging area, the role and performance of accounting in educational institutions. While the chapter is broader in scope than its predecessor, there remain themes beyond its remit. These include coverage of the USA, where a significant body of historical literature exists (such as Van Wyhe 1994). Furthermore, it does not consider histories of textbooks, other educational materials, or the people that taught accounting (see Carnegie and Williams 2001; Clarke 2005, 2008; Edwards 2011; Anderson et al. 2014; Shelton and Jacobs 2015; Parker 2016; Zeff 2016).

Accounting education

Accounting education is simply the communication of accounting knowledge. Research in accounting education comprises around 2.5 per cent of research published in the specialist accounting history journals (Spraakman and Quinn 2018). Historical information about accounting education is located in published works on educational institutions, societies, professional bodies and firms. It also features in the literature on the professionalisation of accountants. Education has assumed something of a secondary status in the accounting field. It is often seen as simply following accounting, something that supports technical and professional agendas. It is rarely presented as a formative power that shapes the conditions of possibility of accounting (Hoskin and Macve 1986) and the individual and collective professional subjectivities of accountants (Anderson-Gough 2002).

Those researching in the accounting education arena have used a variety of theoretical lenses. For example, knowledge and education have been at the centre of the work on the professions since sociologists began to explore the phenomenon. Those using trait theories identify an abstract body of knowledge, formal education and the testing of competence as key characteristics of true professional status. Critical theorists examine the role of education and qualifications, and education as an ideology, in the pursuit of social closure. Symbolic interactionists examine the behaviours required to survive socialisation experiences. Foucauldian analyses have also been influential. Hoskin (1981, 1986, 1993) and Hoskin and Macve (1986, 1988) recognise the importance of understanding the formative aspects of the learning context and experience from which expertise in calculative functions has developed over time. In the area of accounting in educational institutions, discussed later in the chapter, neo-institutional sociology, stakeholder theory, accountability and institutional logics have all featured.

Early accounting education

Long before the modern accounting profession emerged, those educated and trained in institutions of religion, monarchy and empire to carry out administrative duties performed account keeping. In early medieval England, the Church was the source of literary education and educational practices. Latin was the language of Church administration and although local boys were taught Latin for a fee, the experience of the written, calculative and oral techniques that contemporary administration required was limited to a relatively exclusive body of men. Ensuring that there were sufficient clerics schooled in Latin to perform the everyday administrative and ecclesiastical work of the Church was central to its success and survival. Consequently, administrative expertise was shaped through the learning experiences of those who attended cathedral schools (such as Canterbury, Rochester, London, York and Winchester), which were established in the late sixth and early seventh centuries (Curtis 1963: 685). The difficulty of learning the alphanumeric techniques of administrative and organisational practice helped impart an elite status on such work during the medieval era. By the mid-thirteenth century, facilitated by, among other things, the growth of the *ars dictaminis*, the practice of writing, rewriting and ordering, spread. Among such practices was double-entry bookkeeping.

The value of a basic education subsequently gained wider recognition and methods for learning developed which engaged more students of differing levels of ability. During the sixteenth and seventeenth centuries, instruction in accounting was considered of value for those intending to pursue an apprenticeship (rather than attend university), particularly among the less wealthy classes and those aspiring to commercial occupations (Curtis 1963; Hunt 1996). There is evidence that bookkeeping (or casting) accounts was taught in English schools (Curtis 1963; Edwards 2009). Rather than being exclusive to the training of the administrative elite, accounting was increasingly linked to elementary reading and writing. Accounting learning and knowledge was therefore imparted in schools, businesses and families.

The teaching of accounting was also encouraged by increasing dissatisfaction with the content of grammar school and university curricula from the late seventeenth century, particularly among the mercantile class. Early university education offered limited vocational relevance as the utility of accounting knowledge extended beyond the administrative arena to the commercial sector (Lawson and Silver 1973). The growth of the printed media on accounting also facilitated learning practice in institutions and beyond (Hunt 1996).

Recently, Edwards (2009, 2011) explored the provision of accounting education in Britain from 1550 to 1800. This early-modern period was a time of 'rapid commercial growth and early industrialization' (2011: 37). Instruction in bookkeeping and accounting employed both oral delivery and the use of written texts. During the seventeenth and eighteenth centuries accounting education was part of an integrated commercial educational system targeted at young men who desired to enter a range occupations, such as public officials, merchants, lawyers, tradesmen, manufacturers, bankers and farmers. Other beneficiaries might include those seeking to augment their accounting knowledge or learn new techniques such as double-entry bookkeeping. Such subjects were seldom offered in the British education system until the eighteenth century.

Such developments in commercial education and the shift from solely on-the-job training also surfaced in Europe. In Portugal, from 1759, the state sponsored the teaching of commerce courses, including accounting, in institutions such as the newly founded Lisbon School of Commerce (Rodrigues et al. 2007, 2016) and the Rio de Janeiro School of Commerce in Brazil (Araújo et al. 2017). More than a century later, successive Italian governments (1890–1935) emphasised accounting education in schools as part of their attempts to transform the nation from a rural to an industrial economy (Lazzini et al. 2018). Historical research is now being conducted into the role of accounting education in the socio-economic transformation of other countries such Jordan (Alsharari 2017) and China (Zhang et al. 2014).

Modern accounting education: professionalisation and the growth of accounting knowledge

Therefore, by the nineteenth century, accounting, once associated with elite administration, now had (a socially dubious) association with commerce and trade. Universities offered learning of limited vocational relevance. The practice of undertaking learning outside schools and universities was becoming established (Morris 1993). The apprenticeship model also sited vocational learning beyond the classroom. This was the educational context in which the new profession of accountancy emerged.

Accountants (or those with similar occupational descriptions) appear in trade directories from the late eighteenth century (Matthews et al. 1998). The number of people occupied in the areas of bookkeeping, insolvency, audit and accounts preparation expanded greatly during the nineteenth century. It is difficult to generalise about the education and training of new entrants to accounting work prior to the formation of professional accountancy organisations, as the term 'accountant' was used to describe those performing a variety of functions (Walker 2002; Edwards and Walker 2007). Works on the early accounting profession reveal the interest of professional bodies in the establishment of qualifying examinations, the form and content of examinations, links between professional organisations and higher education, and the perceived relevance of examination to practice.

The first organisations of professional accountants in Britain were formed in educationally tumultuous Scotland during the 1850s. Historical insights into Scottish accounting education have been rigorously analysed within broader studies of professionalisation (Walker 1988; Kedslie 1990), a research trend that continues in multiple national contexts today. Walker (1988: 21) argues that formal examination was not initially a key concern of the Society of Accountants in Edinburgh (SAE). The original members of this body tended to be from professional families, would have had good secondary schooling and were instructed in the expert practices of the legal profession. The notion of learning through an apprenticeship was also well established. Some 53 per cent of early recruits also attended university classes (mainly in law) as part of their vocational training. However, lawyers, with their background in examination, criticised the lack of formal tests of knowledge in the SAE's constitution. Therefore, in 1858, an oral examination was introduced at the end of the indenture period.

A shift to written examinations occurred later in the century. In the 1890s, the local organisations of professional accountants in Scotland unified their examination arrangements and dispensed with oral examinations (Shackleton 1995). In 1873, the SAE adopted the increasingly popular three-stage structure consisting of a preliminary, intermediate and final examination. The Society of Accountants in Aberdeen also moved to more formal examination arrangements in 1889 (Kedslie 1990). Walker (1988) suggests the decision to adopt written tests reflected developments in other vocations and the increasing aspirations of middle class parents who had invested in the scholastic education of their male progeny with a view to their entrance into credentialed careers.

In England and Wales, the adoption of the written examination was a clear professionalisation strategy. The predecessor organisations of the Institute of Chartered Accountants in England and Wales (ICAEW) merged in 1880. The ICAEW immediately perceived that a comprehensive system of education and training was central to its efforts to distinguish the chartered from the non-chartered accountant and set its first written exams in 1882 (Anderson et al. 2005). These followed the Scottish profession's three-stage format. Passing the examinations and completing a period of articled clerkship (three or five years) became the norm. The Association of Chartered Certified Accountants (ACCA), formed in 1938, differed somewhat in its use of examinations. The ACCA ostensibly used written examinations in a manner aligned with its open access policy. Stafford (2002) has concluded that the ACCA's education strategy was key to its professionalisation project and the identity construction of its members.

Summaries of the syllabi of the professional bodies are found in a number of sources including Banyard (1985), Walker (1988), Kedslie (1990), Geddes (1995), Stafford (2002) and Anderson et al. (2005). Most writers allude to the changing way in which the accountancy specialisation has been assessed. When the older accounting bodies moved to three stage examinations, the preliminary exam was a test of general competence. Specialist occupational knowledge was assessed in later stage examinations. Over time, and reflecting shifts in the accountancy profession's jurisdiction, there was a move away from the heavy presence of law in the syllabus to the inclusion of tax and costing. In the 1960s, syllabi became more business-relevant and by the 1970s included economics, information systems and data processing, and financial decision-making. These changes were replicated in the educational programmes of accounting bodies in other Anglophone countries.

The precise role of examinations in professional training systems, where they should feature in the qualification regime and who should provide instruction, have a contested existence. In the USA, the fledgling profession turned to the universities for assistance in the learning and qualification aspects of professional expertise (Van Wyhe 1994). By the 1880s the value and acceptability of commercial education within the higher education sector in the USA was accepted. In Scotland, the universities were identified as useful suppliers of some of the knowledge necessary for professional expertise. In 1926, the SAE made attendance at university classes in accountancy compulsory and in 1960–1 the 'academic year' was introduced (Solomons 1974; Walker 1994). The higher education entry route helped establish the elite status of the accounting profession in Scotland (Gammie et al. 2018).

Interactions between professional bodies and universities also featured in many other Anglophone countries such as Australia, New Zealand and South Africa. For example, from the early 1900s, the examinations of the New Zealand Society of Accountants (NZSA) featured in the courses of the University of New Zealand's Bachelor of Commerce degree. Following the 1961 separation of the four University of New Zealand colleges into individual universities, the NZSA began its own examinations for those who did not attend university and offered exemptions from its professional examinations for those who completed a degree with an accountancy major. This changed in the late 1980s when the NZSA introduced a final qualifying exam, and began to accredit the universities' accounting degrees (Trow and Zeff 2010). In South Africa, from the nineteenth century to the present day, the Institute of Chartered Accountants and its predecessors exercised direct control over accounting education in universities, resulting in a technically focused curriculum (Verhoef and Samkin 2017).

England and Wales took a different path. Geddes (1995), using Abbott's (1988) model of jurisdictional competition between professions, explains how the provision of professional education there came to be dominated by private tutoring firms, and consequently how control of professional education was retained by practitioners. The ICAEW always regarded itself as an examining not a teaching body (Howitt 1966). Hence, the manner in which its students acquired knowledge was left open. Articled clerks had to rely on private sector tutors who offered correspondence courses. Tutor firms were, and continue to be, staffed by practitioners, and the aim of classes is to prepare students for the professional examinations. Nonetheless, the role that teachers in the private tutoring firms play has changed over time from being an autonomous mentor and guide to a deliverer of a commodified educational product (Gebreiter et al. 2018).

A key aspect qualification is the gaining of professional 'experience'. Hence in some countries such as the UK, experience became an essential component of the training of accountants. The combination of practical training and theoretical instruction has periodically aroused concerns about the relative roles of office training, classroom teaching and examination. An ICAEW policy document in the 1990s recognised the impossibility of achieving an easy relationship between examination content and what accountants do on a daily basis because 'practical experience … varies widely' (Geddes 1995: 154). The question of whether a general or specialist education should be provided also has a long lineage. The perceived differences between the role of 'education' and training have played out over time and continue today as a source of the power–knowledge dynamic affecting decisions about course content and delivery, location of study, and the identity and background of examiners. All professional bodies have faced such issues, not only because the nature of an accountant's work changes but also because the relationship of performance to competence is itself problematic (Anderson-Gough et al. 2011).

The universities

It should be recalled that accounting education has increasingly taken place beyond the realm of the professional bodies. For example, as accounting firms expanded, they developed their own formal in-house training programmes. By the early twentieth century, bookkeeping examinations were offered by local examination boards. Accounting and bookkeeping classes were also provided by numerous institutes and colleges, some of which attained university status.

The role of the universities themselves in the education of professional accountants has varied in different national contexts. Accounting was taught in Italian and US universities before the twentieth century. The teaching of modern accounting in Italian universities appears to have begun during the first half of the nineteenth century. In 1839 chairs in public accounting were established at Pavia and Padua (Zan 1994). Accounting's place in Italian academia is quite different from that in the Anglophone tradition. In Italy, accounting is one of several strands of the multidisciplinary and 'holistic' *Economia Aziendale* (Zan 1994: 288). Accounting education in US universities commenced in the 1880s and full professors were appointed at New York University in 1900 (Zeff 1997). Here, as elsewhere, accounting eventually became a distinguishable university specialism. The presence of accounting as a subject in British universities can be traced to the turn of the twentieth century (see Napier 2011), marginally later in Australian and New Zealand universities (c.1910s) and much later in developing countries. For example, accounting did not emerge as a university discipline in Fiji until 1972 (Sharma and Samkin, 2018).

In Britain, the universities were slow to offer expertise in commercial subjects. That UK accounting education did not primarily take place in a university did not prevent accountants from achieving professional status and identity. For the clients of those individuals and their firms, it was the credentialing offered by accountancy bodies that conferred the status of 'expert'. The introduction of accounting to British universities is often associated with demands from the late nineteenth century for the provision of commercial education in order to address concerns about a loss of industrial leadership and the fear that the country was falling behind in the production of experts in science and technology (Walker 1994). The lack of vocationally oriented education was seen as part of the problem. In England, the University of Birmingham established a Chair in Accounting in 1902. The London School of Economics followed in 1919 (Solomons 1974; Craner and Jones 1995: 39). However, the first full-time chairs of accounting in Britain were not appointed until 1947 (Parker 1995). In Ireland, a full-time chair was established at the University of Galway in 1914 (Zeff 1997; Clarke 2005). In Scotland, a Chair of Accounting and Business Method was instituted at Edinburgh University in 1919 (Walker 1994). In Australia, the first chair of accounting was established at Melbourne University in 1954 (Carnegie and Williams 2001). In contrast, the first full-time Chair in Accountancy in New Zealand was established at the University of Canterbury in 1961, followed by the University of Otago and Victoria University of Wellington in the same year (Trow and Zeff 2010).

These early accounting academics retained close links with the practitioner community, sometimes serving on the committees of accountancy bodies. Nonetheless, where chairs of accounting were established their holders often encountered a degree of 'academic disdain' from their colleagues in more established disciplines (Walker 1994; Napier 1996). Furthermore, until around the 1960s, there was no obvious academic home for the subject and accounting was often subsumed within economics departments, creating a problematic and potentially subordinate relationship with the related if 'higher' discipline (Solomons 1974; Stevenson et al. 2018).

During the 1960s and beyond, there was a considerable expansion of the university sector in the UK and other Anglophone countries. With this growth in mass higher education, an increasing proportion of recruits to the accounting profession were graduates, most with a degree in accounting or related 'relevant' subjects. The teaching of accounting in universities continued to be provided by a mix of accounting practitioners and specialist academics. Instruction continued to be oriented towards techniques and practices. However, as the 1970s and 1980s progressed (and into the 1990s in other countries), a quite different approach to academic accounting developed. The shortage of labour that accompanied the increased demand for accounting teaching (Nobes 1983: 78) resulted in more staff being recruited on the basis of a wider range of academic as opposed to purely accounting qualifications. This shaped the nature of accounting teaching and research in the UK (and elsewhere) and a more diverse community of academic accountants was created.

With an increasingly diverse mix of experts populating accounting academia, tension and fragmentation surfaced over issues such as theory versus practice and technical versus critical approaches to the subject. This increasing diversity also resulted in concentrations of specialist groups in Anglophone educational institutions, with some universities focusing on research driven by positivist theories and quantitative methodologies, and others specialising in more interpretive and critical approaches supported by qualitative methodologies. Such a separation has not proved conducive to conducting research into the history of accounting education in universities where the former approach prevails.

Other international trends include a growing divergence between academe and accounting practice. One potential source of this is the requirement for accounting academics to hold PhDs as opposed to professional qualifications. Comparatively few new generation accounting academics have experience of professional practice (Paisey and Paisey 2017). While the composition of accounting academe has changed, it is not so clear that accounting teaching has changed. The requirement to teach the subject in technically segregated compartments that match areas of practitioner work (financial accounting and reporting, management accounting, auditing, cost management systems, taxation, etc.), has persisted into the twenty-first century. Concerns have been raised that the university syllabus continues to be defined by the accounting profession that recruits accounting graduates as opposed to accounting academics. Periodically, resistance to increased collaboration between the accounting profession and academe has surfaced. This has manifested in a number of ways including shifting debates over professional accreditation requirements. With the growing demand for business education, accounting degrees have come to be seen by tertiary-level institutions as a revenue generator that can be used to support other parts of the university. In particular, high fee paying international students of accounting are often perceived as a commodity (Parker 2012).

Despite the relatively late development of accounting education in universities, the discipline clearly attained a presence and status in tertiary institutions by the end of the twentieth century. Accounting education itself is now established as a sub-discipline of accounting and a significant number of academics pursue it as a research specialism.

Accounting in educational institutions

Accounting is not only taught in educational institutions, it also features in their management. Such institutions may be privately run, or operated by the public sector. All will be subject to accounting rules, practices and processes and these have been the subject of accounting history research in certain temporal and spatial settings. This is a comparatively underdeveloped but emerging area. Researchers of accounting in educational institutions employ a variety of theoretical lenses including neo-institutional sociology, old institutional economics, stakeholder theory, accountability, institutional logics and Foucauldian concepts. This part of the chapter explores the use of accounting and accountability in primary (elementary) and pre-schools, and in secondary and tertiary-level institutions such as high schools, colleges and universities.

Accounting in primary schools

Accounting has long played a significant role in elementary educational institutions whether these were privately provided, community-supported, charitable institutions or publicly funded. This section mainly focuses on financing, accounting and accountability in primary-level educational institutions in New Zealand (Fowler 2008, 2009, 2010; Fowler and Cordery 2015) and the UK (Hoskin and Macve 1986; Connelly et al. 1995) during the nineteenth century. Accounting procedures, budgeting, performance management practices, auditing and accountability mechanisms are not static phenomena within schools. They shift over time, sometimes due to changes in governance structures and the dominant stakeholders. As the number of schools grows, school financing tends to shift from local community or benefactor support supplemented by pupil fees, to public funding, especially when the state assumes responsibility for elementary education.

Community-based schools were initially often funded by annual subscriptions, pupil fees, state grants, benefactor loans, cash and non-cash donations for specific items (such as books, equipment, land and buildings), and money raised from local fundraising events. Although these types of educational institutions were close to their communities, it was difficult for them to raise enough funds to be financially sustainable (Fowler and Cordery 2015). Once educational provision and associated school management were controlled by the state, funding came from revenue appropriations, the leasing of educational assets such as land, and in some cases, dedicated education taxes. For example, in New Zealand, the local authority in Nelson levied a householder-based education rate from the 1850s to 1870s that partially funded its public education system (Fowler 2008; Fowler and Cordery 2015).

In late nineteenth century Scotland universal parish-based education was financed by education boards that levied tax on the local community (at the rate of one penny per pound of rateable property value within the parish) and by charging pupil fees to supplement government grants (Connelly et al. 1995: 293). From the 1870s local school boards were elected to engender a sense of local accountability. However, in the 1900s, to achieve standardisation and increase the availability of educational expertise, these boards were centralised (Connelly et al. 1995; Fowler and Cordery 2015). Connelly et al. (1995: 304) conclude that these centralised education authorities lacked 'the local accountability, that had been provided largely as a result of the labours of the school board clerks and treasurers over the previous half century'.

Educational institutions have variously been required to keep accounting records, provide regular returns and audited financial statements, and to publish this information as part of their accountability to stakeholders and the communities that supported them. Internally, they used this accounting information for budgeting and performance management purposes (Connelly et al. 1995; Fowler 2009, 2010). The cash-based accounting records kept by non-profit schools recorded in a simple manner the funds received, what they were used for and any money owing to benefactors or other stakeholders. Types of financial records kept related to the cost of constructing school buildings and the amount and types of funding received such as pupil fees, donations and annual subscriptions. The amount and type of expenditures such as teachers' salaries were also recorded (Fowler 2010).

Under state (local or central) control the accounting records of schools in New Zealand and Scotland formed part of the cash-based government accounts and followed their format. Receipts and payments tended to be recorded in a Treasurer's Cash Book (Connelly et al. 1995; Fowler 2008). Other account books might include an 'Abstract of Disbursement Account', and 'Abstract of Revenue Account' for each financial year, as well as an 'Expenditure by Vote' book. Some of the accounting and auditing requirements were prescribed by educational statutes or dictated by other regulations. In New Zealand the local government accounting and reporting process began with the production of government estimates and ended with a form of variance analysis showing the difference between what was spent and amounts voted (Fowler 2008).

Educational and associated entities used these accounting records to inscribe funding received and monitor the costs of schooling. Many of the procedures used were common to both private and public sector education providers, such as the concept of the financial year, and the use of cash accounts (Fowler 2008). The accounting records were used for budgeting, performance management and to prepare the audited financial statements. Budgeting was often introduced in local education institutions when they were unable to support themselves financially from their community base and needed to obtain funding from governmental sources. Budgets enabled them to demonstrate the financial responsibility necessary to gain resources from the state. Such budgeting mimicked the public sector practice of producing estimates (Connelly et al. 1995; Fowler 2009). Once education was provided by the state, budgeting procedures became standardised and followed the public sector practices of the time. In New Zealand central education boards allocated money to the local education committees in charge of individual schools or school districts. The local committee had to justify its expenditure and was required to produce a budget of future needs, while the central board had to estimate planned expenditure for the forthcoming educational year. The estimates were also used to justify the need for extra money in the vote (Fowler 2009).

Both non-state and public educational authorities controlled schools via a system of inspection, performance measurement and reporting (Fowler 2009). In the New Zealand not-for-profit sector, inspections might be performed on a regular or irregular basis. The results of inspection visits were reported to inspection committees and sometimes to the wider community (Fowler 2009). Inspection systems were also instituted when schools fell under government control and resultant reports were published in official communications such as the *Government Gazette* and local newspapers. These reports included information such as the gender of pupils, number of days attended, and comparative returns of the ages and proficiency of pupils. The inspector also made recommendations for improvements in administrative practice, pupil attendance, curriculum development and teaching approaches. Some of the information contained in inspector's reports was included in a school's periodic returns and these were used to construct comparative measures of educational performance. Sanctions were imposed for the non-filing of school returns as well as for poor performance (Fowler 2009; Fowler and Cordery 2015). Financial and non-financial accounting information about educational institutions was also included in returns to other state bodies. Examples from New Zealand include statistical information about the number of schools and pupils, teachers and their salaries, types of school (free or fee paying), income sources and the amount of expenditure (Fowler 2009, 2010).

Accounting records were used to produce audited cash-based financial statements at a specified balance date. In one not-for-profit educational institution in New Zealand, the annual accounts were initially checked by a committee appointed for the purpose and then by two or more subscribers appointed prior to the annual meeting. The financial statements were subsequently presented to the annual meeting, and in some cases were published in local newspapers (Fowler 2010). State sector educational institutions were required by legislation to keep financial accounts, prepare a balance sheet and have these audited by a Board of Audit and later by a government auditor. The audited accounts were then published in the local newspapers (Connelly et al. 1995; Fowler and Cordery 2015). It was argued that this process would make it less likely that the local education committees would misappropriate funds.

Educational institutions were thus accountable to their funders, creditors and the wider community through the publication of audited accounts, the school inspection system and the production of various returns (Fowler 2010; Fowler and Cordery 2015). Annual meetings were also a key accountability mechanism. For example, private educational institutions in New Zealand held annual public meetings (AGMs) at which they elected committee members and presented annual reports. The reports contained information regarding the operation of the schools, including attendance, fees and other payments, the names of teachers, the condition of buildings as well as the audited financial statements. A list of subscribers or benefactors might also be presented. Discussion might ensue about funding, the school's financial situation, and new rules and regulations. The report of the AGM was reproduced in full in the local newspaper (Fowler 2010; Fowler and Cordery 2015).

With state control, schools in New Zealand fell within the orbit of the Central Board of Education and legislation required their accountability to local government and indirectly to the wider community. The Central Committee's half-yearly reports contained school inspector's comments, identified issues and discussed the progress of schools in the public education system. The central committee mandated the textbooks that the schools could use and required teachers to have an inspector-issued competency certificate. Local education committees followed similar accountability practices to the central committee. Once a year they held an annual meeting where the committee was elected and an oral report was presented (Fowler and Cordery 2015).

Another mechanism for demonstrating educational accountability to resource providers was through the public examination of pupils, a technique predominantly used by private institutions due to the need for accountability to the local users and subscribers. The oral examination of pupils in subjects such as reading, arithmetic, scripture and history was conducted by well-educated members of the community. These examinations were often scheduled for special occasions such as the Christmas assemblies of schools, and were open to the public and reported in local newspapers. For example, approximately one-third of the population of Nelson, New Zealand, attended the Christmas assembly of the local school in 1849 (Fowler 2010; Fowler and Cordery 2015). In state schools public examination was not required, even though its use was supported by the Central Education Committee. Some local school committees, especially those established under the previous not-for-profit system, continued with the public examination of their pupils, albeit on an irregular basis. Such practices of lateral accountability to local communities thus continued once control of education moved to the public sector (Fowler and Cordery 2015). Under the state education system, hierarchical accountability practices became more apparent as education legislation encouraged centralisation (Connelly et al. 1995).

Accounting in secondary- and tertiary-level educational institutions

The new public management (NPM) reforms of the 1980s and 1990s had a significant impact on accounting in educational institutions. Those impacts have primarily been explored in New Zealand (Tooley and Guthrie 2007a, 2007b) and the UK (Edwards et al. 1996, 2000; Ezzamel et al. 2012). These studies predominately focus on the decentralisation of budgeting and related performance management and reporting.

The English Education Act 1988 devolved the funding model and budgeting process to local educational authorities. Under this Act, school management was required to develop a comprehensive budget that took into account both past expenditure and perceived future educational needs. However, the budget funding formula preserved historical expenditure patterns (Edwards et al. 1996). The internal planning and budgeting systems were primarily designed for auditing and external compliance purposes. As a result, the coupling of budget expenditures and school strategic objectives was loose (Edwards et al. 2000). The concept of institutional logics was later utilised to examine prior research on the English educational reforms (Ezzamel et al. 2012: 281).

Research on secondary-level education, that is high schools or colleges, has focused on the NPM and post-NPM environments. For example, Tooley and Guthrie (2007a, 2007b) explored accounting in New Zealand secondary schools, following reforms of the 1980s onwards. As in England, these reforms devolved administration and financial management from government departments to the secondary schools themselves. Budgeting technologies, used in an economic-rationalist manner, also served unintended purposes; they became devices to legitimate the actions of school managers (Tooley and Guthrie 2007a). Furthermore, the annual reports of secondary schools, although compliant with legislation and other regulations, offered limited informational value in relation to performance data (Tooley and Guthrie 2007b). The use of accounting in secondary schools and colleges before the NPM reforms merits further investigation.

More historical attention has been given to accounting in tertiary institutions than secondary education. A particular focus has been on the types of costing and management control system used as well as their social implications. One of the earliest studies in this area was Jones (1991) who examined the accounting system used at Magdalen College, Oxford in 1812. The author offers an explanation of the system and provides examples of the accounting records kept and their relationship to each other. Jones reveals that the accounting was performed in a charge/discharge format. Evidence was also found to indicate that the 'duality of a transaction was not ignored' (Jones 1991: 154) and that an annual audit was conducted.

Accounting and accountability practices in tertiary education during periods of totalitarian rule are the subject of more recent historical research. Detzen and Hoffmann (2019) investigate changes in accountability in the *Handelshochschule*, Leipzig, during Nazi rule. The Nazi ideology impacted on the accountability of the educational institution and on academics who became politically accountable. Another perspective is offered by Papi et al. (2019). The authors examined the University of Ferrara under Italian Fascism and the manner in which accounting practices were used to justify the government's actions to restrict access to certain groups of students. The university resisted these actions by also utilising accounting practices. As a result, the Fascist government was required to employ different tactics to achieve its objectives, thus illustrating the power of accounting as a technology to resist an offensive political doctrine.

The NPM reforms of the 1980s and 1990s also impacted on tertiary education. These reforms resulted in the corporatisation of the university and were associated with the implementation of accounting and financial management practices and strategies that emphasised market-funded commercial operations (Christopher 2012; Parker 2012). Another impact of the reforms was a focus by the state on the research performance of universities and the implementation of measurement exercises such as the Research Assessment Exercise (RAE) and the Research Excellence Framework (REF) in the UK, Excellence for Research (ERA) in Australia and Performance Based Research Funding (PBRF) in New Zealand.

Historical studies of performance measures in tertiary education are beginning to surface. Narayan (2019) provides a 30-year history of performance measurement in tertiary education in New Zealand. The implementation of such measures had both intended and unintended consequences. The authors argue that PBRF achieved its intended objective of improving the quality and quantity of academic research and enhanced public accountability. However, its unintended consequences included a change in university culture towards imposed targets and performance measures that encouraged 'forms of creative compliance, manipulation and fabrication of results', as well as creating 'tensions, cynicism and complications' (Narayan, 2019). Similarly, Martin-Sardesai et al. (2019) investigated the history of research performance measurement in Australian higher education from 1987 to 2015. They highlight the use of management accounting technologies to support NPM dogma during 30 years of change. Given that governments in other countries, especially in Europe, are implementing such performance measurement regimes it is likely that the current body of knowledge on accounting in tertiary education organisations will be augmented in the future.

Conclusion

Tracing the history of accounting reveals enduring contests about the nature of the discipline, accounting expertise, the right to be called an 'expert' and jurisdictional claims based thereon. Disputes over the nature of accounting, the merits of abstraction versus specificity, theory versus practice, and academic versus practitioner, have featured throughout the history of accounting and accounting education, particularly in the modern age. The accounting knowledge base has been dynamically shaped by academics, practitioners, clients, students, citizens, governments, regulatory bodies, economic institutions and the media. Pedagogic practices, assumptions about knowledge and expertise, and the profession's relationship to its knowledge base have been impacted by the 'location' of education (Power 1991; Anderson-Gough 2002). The structure of educational provision and the style of delivery shape intellectual engagement with accounting. This has varied according to national context and prevailing power relations.

In her chapter in the first edition of the *Routledge Companion*, Anderson-Gough suggested that future research on the history of accounting education might usefully explore a number of themes. These included: a better understanding of the nature of expertise in different times through (comparative) studies of the professionalisation process and the form, content and location of learning; a detailed review of presentations of accounting theory and practice over time and space to reveal the dynamics of expertise and professional identity; and a more detailed knowledge of how the content and techniques of accounting education have changed. One decade on, these themes continue to be worthy of investigation.

As can be seen from the contents of this chapter, researchers have continued to explore accounting education in the British context. But here too there are significant gaps in our knowledge. As Edwards (2011: 37) notes, 'Education is not yet the subject of significant study by accounting historians, and this is particularly so for the period prior to the organization of examinations by the professional bodies'. In recent years studies of accounting education in continental Europe have begun to appear. For example, researchers in Italy have examined accounting and accountability in religious educational institutions such as at a girls' school (1785–1859) (*conservatorio*) and at a kindergarten from 1913 to 1926 (Sian et al. 2019; Sibilio and Vannini, 2019). Attention has also turned to the role of accounting education in the socio-economic transformation of countries such as Jordan and China.

However, there remain notable gaps in research beyond the Anglophone countries of New Zealand, the UK, the USA, Canada and Australia. There is little focus on gender, on accounting education prior to the mid-nineteenth century, and on accounting education in less formal, non-institutional settings. Evans and Paisey (2018) suggest three areas for future research. First, comparative studies that explore accounting as a global discipline and accounting education's role in the corporatisation of universities and the accounting profession. Second, investigating the history of accounting education in a wide range of settings, using a variety of theoretical lenses. Third, examining the global dominance of US academics in accounting teaching and research.

Likewise, there is scope for much more research on the use of accounting practices in educational institutions. As has been shown, accounting and accountability in schools are key, not only to their sound management and operation but also to their ability to achieve the stakeholder and community support (whether directly or via the state) necessary for survival. Historical research to date has explored accounting procedures, budgeting, performance management practices, auditing requirements and accountability mechanisms in educational institutions. Control over the primary school and its teachers and pupils was achieved by a system of inspection, oral examination and public reporting in the local media of the day, potentially rendering the people involved calculable. Previous to state control, education providers accounted to the local community to raise awareness of the education they provided and to justify the use of resources received. Under the public education system, different accountability and governance practices emerged. These too have hitherto been examined in predominantly Anglophone contexts.

The NPM reforms of the 1980s and 1990s had an impact on the way accounting was used in secondary and tertiary educational institutions. The accounting and accountability systems introduced had unintended consequences. As developing countries have implemented, or been 'asked' to implement, similar NPM reforms by organisations such as the World Bank and IMF, they become new research sites. The application of Foucauldian and institutional theory lenses offer scope for further comprehending the arguments that underpin these and other reforms, resistance to them, and the role and power of accounting in educational settings.

Given the continuing dearth of histories of accounting education and of accounting in education, it seems fair to assert that much more historical investigation in various times and places is to be welcomed. The more we know about how accounting and accountants were made in the past through education and other social processes, and the presence of accounting in the provision of education, the more we will also understand current contingencies and possibilities.

Key works

Edwards (2011) provides an overview of the nature and extent of accounting education in Britain between 1550 and 1800.

Fowler (2009, 2010) investigates the financing, budgeting, performance management, reporting and accountability practices of mid-nineteenth-century New Zealand primary educational organisations.

Geddes (1995) is a comprehensive study of accounting education and training in England analysed (using Abbott's framework of jurisdictional competition) from the nineteenth century to the 1980s.

Hoskin and Macve (1986) provide a comprehensive and theoretically informed review of medieval education practices and their relation to accounting.

References

Abbott, A. (1988) *The System of Professions: An Essay on the Division of Expert Labor* (Chicago, IL: University of Chicago Press).

Alsharari, N.M. (2017) The development of accounting education and practice in an environment of socio-economic transformation in the Middle East: The case of Jordan, *International Journal of Educational Management*, 31 (6): 736–51.

Anderson, M., Edwards, J.R. and Chandler, R.A. (2005) Constructing the 'well qualified' chartered accountant in England and Wales, *Accounting Historians Journal*, 32 (2): 5–54.

Anderson, R.H., Gaffikin, M.J.R. and Singh, G. (2014) The life and thought of Robert Keith Yorston: An advocate for accounting reform, *Accounting History*, 19 (4): 533–56.

Anderson-Gough, F. (2002) On becoming the new accounting expert: Between formal and informal learning, unpublished PhD thesis, University of Leeds.

Anderson-Gough, F., Chatterjee, P., Gough, M., Hoskin, K. and Lucas, U. (2011) *Between Workplace and Qualification: Engineering Integrative Learning* (London: ICAEW Centre for Business Performance Report).

Araújo, W.G., Rodrigues, L.L. and Craig, R. (2017) 'Empire as an imagination of the centre': The Rio de Janeiro school of commerce and the development of accounting education in Brazil, *Critical Perspectives on Accounting*, 46: 38–53.

Banyard, C.W. (1985) *The Institute of Cost and Management Accountants: A History* (London: Institute of Cost and Management Accountants).

Carnegie, G. and Williams, B.G. (2001) The first professors of accounting in Australia, *Accounting History*, 6 (1): 103–15.

Christopher, J. (2012) Tension between the corporate and collegial colleges of Australian public universities: The current status, *Critical Perspectives on Accounting*, 23 (7–8): 556–71.

Clarke, P. (2005) The story of Bernard F. Shields: The first professor of accountancy in the UK, *Accounting History*, 10 (2): 103–23.

Clarke, P. (2008) The teaching of bookkeeping in nineteenth century Ireland, *Accounting, Business & Financial History*, 18 (1): 21–33.

Connelly, P., Fletcher, M. and McKinstry, S. (1995) Educational accounting, accountability and accountants in the era of the 'Scotch' school boards, 1872–1918, *Accounting, Business & Financial History*, 5 (3): 289–307.

Craner, J. and Jones, R. (1995) *The First Fifty Years of the Professor of Accounting at the University of Birmingham* (Birmingham: The University of Birmingham).

Curtis, S.J. (1963) *History of Education in Great Britain* (London: University Tutorial Press Ltd).

Detzen, D. and Hoffmann, S. (2019) Accountability and ideology: The case of a German university under the Nazi regime, *Accounting History*. DOI: 10.1177/1032373219836301.

Edwards, J.R. (2009) A business education for 'middling sort of people' in mercantilist Britain, *British Accounting Review*, 41 (4): 240–55.

Edwards, J.R. (2011) Accounting education in Britain during the early modern period, *Accounting History Review*, 21 (1): 37–67.

Edwards, J.R. and Walker, S.P. (2007) Accountants in late nineteenth century Britain: A spatial, demographic and occupational profile, *Accounting and Business Research*, 37 (1): 63–89.

Edwards, P., Ezzamel, M. and McLean, C. (2000) Budgeting and strategy in schools: The elusive link, *Financial Accountability & Management*, 16 (4): 309–34.

Edwards, P., Ezzamel, M. and Robson, K. (1996) Comprehensive and incremental budgeting in education: The construction and management of formula funding in three English local education authorities, *Accounting, Auditing & Accountability Journal*, 9 (4): 4–37.

Evans, E. and Paisey, C. (2018) Histories of accounting education – an introduction, *Accounting History*, 23 (1–2): 3–13.

Ezzamel, M., Robson, K. and Stapleton, P. (2012) The logics of budgeting: Theorization and practice variation in the educational field, *Accounting, Organizations and Society*, 37 (5): 281–303.

Fowler, C. (2009) Performance management, budgeting, and legitimacy in primary educational organisations, *Journal of Accounting & Organizational Change*, 5 (2): 168–96.

Fowler, C. (2010) Financing, accounting and accountability in colonial New Zealand: The case of the Nelson School Society (1842–1852), *Accounting History*, 15 (3): 337–69.

Fowler, C.J. (2008) Financing, Accounting and Accountability in Social Institutions: Nelson Primary Education (1842–1859), unpublished PhD thesis, Victoria University of Wellington.

Fowler, C.J. and Cordery, C.J. (2015) From community to public ownership: A tale of changing accountabilities, *Accounting, Auditing & Accountability Journal*, 28 (1): 128–53.

Gammie, E., Allison, M. and Matson, M. (2018) Entry routes into the Institute of Chartered Accountants of Scotland training: Status versus sustainability, *Accounting History*, 23 (1–2): 14–43.

Gebreiter, F., Davies, M., Finley, S., Gee, L., Weaver, L. and Yates, D. (2018) From 'rock stars' to 'hygiene factors': Teachers at private accountancy tuition providers, *Accounting History*, 23 (1–2): 138–50.

Geddes, S.B. (1995) The development of accountancy education, training and research in England: A study of the relationships between professional education and training, academic education and research, and professional practice in English chartered accountancy, unpublished PhD thesis, University of Manchester.

Hoskin, K. (1981) The history of education and the history of writing, unpublished review, University of Warwick.

Hoskin, K. (1986) The professional in educational history, in J. Wilkes (ed.) *The Professional Teacher: Proceedings of the 1985 Annual Conference of the History of Education Society of Great Britain*, pp. 1–17 (London: History of Education Society).

Hoskin, K. (1993) Education and the genesis of disciplinarity: The unexpected reversal, in E. Messer-Davidow, D.R. Shumway and D.J. Sylvan (eds.) *Knowledges: Historical and Critical Studies in Disciplinarity*, pp. 271–304 (Charlottesville: The University Press of Virginia).

Hoskin, K.W. and Macve, R.H. (1986) Accounting and the examination: A genealogy of disciplinary power, *Accounting, Organizations and Society*, 11 (2): 105–36.

Hoskin, K.W. and Macve, R.H. (1988) The genesis of accountability: The West point connections, *Accounting, Organizations and Society*, 13 (1): 37–73.

Howitt, H. (1966) *The History of the Institute of Chartered Accountants in England and Wales* (London: Heinemann).

Hunt, M.R. (1996) *The Middling Sort: Commerce, Gender, and the Family in England, 1680–1780* (Berkeley, CA: University of California Press).

Jones, M.J. (1991) The accounting system of Magdalen College, Oxford, in 1812, *Accounting, Business & Financial History*, 1 (2): 141–62.

Kedslie, M.J.M. (1990) *Firm Foundations: The Development of Professional Accounting in Scotland 1850–1900* (Hull: Hull University Press).

Lawson, J. and Silver, H. (1973) *A Social History of Education in England* (London: Methuen & Co).

Lazzini, A., Iacoviello, G. and Ferraris Franceschi, R. (2018) Evolution of accounting education in Italy, 1890–1935, *Accounting History*, 23 (1–2): 44–70.

Martin-Sardesai, A., Guthrie, J., Tooley, S. and Chaplin, S. (2019) History of research performance measurement systems in the Australian higher education sector, *Accounting History*, 24 (1): 40–61.

Matthews, D., Anderson, M. and Edwards, J.R. (1998) *The Priesthood of Industry: The Rise of the Professional Accountant in British Management* (Oxford: Oxford University Press).

Morris, R.J. (1993) Clubs, societies and associations, in E.M.L. Thompson (ed.) *The Cambridge Social History of Britain 1750–1950*, vol. 3, pp. pp. 395–443 (Cambridge: Cambridge University Press).

Napier, C.J. (1996) Academic disdain? Economists and accounting in Britain, 1850–1950, *Accounting, Business & Financial History*, 6 (3): 427–50.

Napier, C.J. (2011) Accounting at the London School of Economics: Opportunity lost? *Accounting History*, 16 (2): 185–205.

Narayan, A.K. (2019) The development and use of performance measures in New Zealand tertiary education institutions, *Accounting History*. DOI: 10.1177/1032373219842383.

Nobes, C.W. (1983) *Becoming an Accountant* (Harlow: Longman).

Paisey, C. and Paisey, N. (2017) The decline of the professionally-qualified accounting academic: Recruitment into the accounting academic community, *Accounting Forum*, 41 (2): 57–76.

Papi, L., Bigoni, M., Gagliardo, E.D. and Funnell, W. (2019) Accounting for power and resistance: The University of Ferrara under the Fascist regime in Italy, *Critical Perspectives on Accounting*, 62: 54–76.

Parker, L.D. (2012) From privatised to hybrid corporatised higher education: A global financial management discourse, *Financial Accountability & Management*, 28 (3): 247–68.

Parker, R.H. (1995) David Solomons and British accounting, *Accounting and Business Research*, 25 (100): 311–14.

Parker, R.H. (2016) Thirteen not out: Nobes & Parker, comparative international accounting, 1981–2016, *Accounting History*, 21 (4): 512–21.

Power, M.K. (1991) Educating accountants: Towards a critical ethnography, *Accounting, Organizations and Society*, 16 (4): 333–53.

Rodrigues, L.L., Carqueja, H. and Ferreira, L.F. (2016) Double-entry bookkeeping and the manuscripts dictated in the Lisbon school of commerce, *Accounting History*, 21 (4): 489–511.

Rodrigues, L.L., Craig, R. and Gomes, D. (2007) State intervention in commercial education: The case of the Portuguese School of Commerce, 1759, *Accounting History*, 12 (1): 55–85.

Shackleton, K. (1995) Scottish chartered accountants: Internal and external political relationships, *Accounting, Auditing & Accountability Journal*, 8 (2): 18–46.

Sharma, U. and Samkin, G. (2018) Development of accounting in Fiji, 1801–2016, *Accounting History*. DOI: 10.1177/1032373218798645.

Shelton, W. and Jacobs, K. (2015) Allan Douglas Barton: A scholar who spanned theory and practice, *Accounting History*, 20 (1): 20–42.

Sian, S., Magli, F., Nobolo, A. and Guarini, E. (2019) Enacting accountability: The case of the *Asili di Carità*, 1913–1926, *Accounting History*. Doi:10.1177/1032373219845918.

Sibilio, B. and Vannini, I.E. (forthcoming) Development of the administrative-accounting system of the conservatorio S. M. delgi Angiolini in Florence from 1785 to 1859: Institutional changes and isomorphic pressures,*Accounting History*.

Solomons, S.D. (1974) *Prospectus for a Profession: The Report of the Long Range Enquiry into Education and Training for the Accountancy Profession* (London: Gee & Co).

Spraakman, G.P. and Quinn, M. (2018) Accounting history research topics – an analysis of leading journals, 2006–2015, *Accounting Historians Journal*, 45 (1): 101–14.

Stafford, A.P. (2002) Capitalising education: Exploring the development of professional identity in certified accountants through the role of education and training, unpublished PhD thesis, University of Warwick.

Stevenson, L., Power, D., Ferguson, J. and Collison, D. (2018) The development of accounting in UK universities: An oral history, *Accounting History*, 23 (1–2): 117–37.

Tooley, S. and Guthrie, J. (2007a) Budgeting in New Zealand secondary schools in a changing devolved financial management environment, *Journal of Accounting and Organizational Change*, 3 (1): 4–28.

Tooley, S. and Guthrie, J. (2007b) Reporting performance by New Zealand secondary schools: An analysis of disclosure, *Financial Accountability & Management*, 23 (4): 351–74.

Trow, D. and Zeff, S.A. (2010) *Accounting Education and the Profession in New Zealand* (Wellington, DC: New Zealand Institute of Chartered Accountants).

Van Wyhe, G. (1994) *The Struggle for Status: A History of Accounting Education* (New York: Garland Publishing Inc).

Verhoef, G. and Samkin, G. (2017) The accounting profession and education: The development of disengaged activity in accounting in South Africa, *Accounting Auditing & Accountability Journal*, 30 (6): 1370–98.

Walker, S.P. (1988) *The Society of Accountants in Edinburgh 1854–1914: A Study of Recruitment to A New Profession* (New York: Garland).

Walker, S.P. (1994) *Accountancy at the University of Edinburgh 1919–1994. The Emergence of a 'viable Academic Department'* (Edinburgh: ICAS).

Walker, S.P. (2002) 'Men of small standing'? Locating accountants in English society during the mid-nineteenth century, *European Accounting Review*, 11 (2): 377–99.

Zan, L. (1994) Toward a history of accounting histories: Perspectives from the Italian tradition, *European Accounting Review*, 3 (2): 255–307.

Zeff, S.A. (1997) The early years of the association of university teachers of accounting: 1947–1959, *British Accounting Review*, 29 (1/2, supplement): 3–39.

Zeff, S.A. (2016) Accounting textbooks as change agents: Finney's intermediate and Finney and Miller's intermediate from 1934–1958, *Accounting Historians Journal*, 43 (1): 59–78.

Zhang, G., Boyce, G. and Ahmed, K. (2014) Institutional changes in university accounting education in post-revolutionary China: From political orientation to internationalization, *Critical Perspectives on Accounting*, 25 (8): 819–43.

14
REGULATION

Alan J. Richardson and Eksa Kilfoyle

Overview

This chapter examines the interplay between general theories of regulation and histories of accounting regulation. We define regulation as the set of institutions, or 'rules of the game', that constrain and enable the practice of accounting. We identify five theoretical frames (public interest theory, regulatory capture theory, corporatist theory, negotiated order theories and cultural theories) and explore how these theories inform interpretations of the introduction, consequences, persistence and disappearance of regulation. These theories include teleological, evolutionary and naturalistic perspectives.

We focus on the contested interpretation of origin of the US Securities Acts 1933/34, and their impact on financial disclosure; topics that dominate the historical literature on accounting regulation. We also examine how these concerns are reflected in scholarship on the creation of the International Accounting Standards Committee (IASC) and the International Accounting Standards Board (IASB) and the diffusion of International Financial Reporting Standards (IFRS). We consider the impact of the common law, social norms and private regulatory initiatives on accounting regulation. This literature expands the concept of regulation beyond the intended action of the state on market actors to a more general concern with the rules, principles and social contexts of financial disclosure. This literature also provides insights into the emergence of regulation without assuming teleology. We conclude by identifying areas in which our understanding of accounting regulation can be advanced by a historical perspective.

Introduction

Accounting is both a technology of regulation in society and a highly regulated professional activity. The history of regulation in accounting is thus concerned with a three-way interaction between social processes (typically mediated by the state), regulatory bodies and those affected by regulation. Broadly speaking, we can identify three bodies of research in this area: the regulation of professional practice rights; the regulation of accounting and auditing technologies, particularly through formal standard-setting processes; and the use of accounting in the regulation of the economy.

Regulation is a common theme throughout this volume. The specific work of standard-setting agencies in relation to financial accounting theory and practice has been referred to in Chapters 7 and 8. The regulation of auditing is considered in Chapter 10 while the regulation of the profession is featured in Chapter 11. Accounting scandals emerging from regulatory failure, and the manner in which accounting in the public sector and the military have been regulated, are discussed in later chapters. Our main concern is to illustrate the interplay between histories of accounting regulation and theories of regulation. We focus on the regulation of financial reporting and the use of accounting to regulate publicly traded companies. In fact, the disclosure of information has become a key method of regulation in developed economies since Justice Brandeis (1914) extolled: 'Publicity is justly commended as a remedy for social and industrial disease. Sunlight is said to be the best disinfectant and electric light the most efficient policeman'. The rationale is that by releasing information, those affected will take action (Graham 2002; see also Chapter 24 on Bentham and publicity). The issues are to determine if disclosure must be regulated, and what information should be released to whom and in what form.

We bound our review of histories of regulation by distinguishing between inductive (or descriptive) histories of regulation and deductive (or theory informed) histories of regulation. We do not review descriptive histories of accounting regulation or regulatory bodies. These histories include insider accounts by regulators (Leach and Stamp 1981; Beresford 1998; O'Dell 2015), commissioned histories of regulatory bodies (Auditing Practices Board 1986; Dearing 1988; Camfferman and Zeff 2007), and general histories of regulatory processes (Zeff 1972; Walton 1995).

There is an active debate about forms of historical scholarship in accounting – this has typically been framed as a distinction between traditional and 'new' history (Miller et al. 1991; Funnell 1996; Carmona et al. 2006). For the most part, 'new accounting history' reinterprets events through macro-social lenses; for example, trying to understand the role of accounting in gender relations (see Chapter 21), race relations (Chapter 22), and imperialism (Chapter 23). Our approach is more of a 'mid-range' history of accounting regulation (inspired by Merton (1968: 39–73), but more in line with Laughlin (1995). We use theories of regulation to interrogate histories of accounting regulation and seek, modestly, to address the descriptive completeness of alternative theories of regulation. We review work that attempts to answer questions such as why regulations develop, who benefits from them, how they emerge from social practices and why they persist.

Defining regulation

The term 'regulation' typically connotes the intervention of the state in human affairs. But the state is neither the only nor necessarily the most effective, source of regulation in society. Human affairs are structured by 'institutions', which Douglas North (1990) has defined as 'the rules of the game' that may arise from within civil society or from political processes at sub-national, national, transnational and global levels. There has been a resurgence of interest in institutions in both economics and politics. This has been occasioned by two developments: one academic and one practical. On the practical side there have been a series of remarkable global experiments in *laissez faire* policies that have resulted in, at best, mixed results (Jordana and Levi-Faur 2004). The transition from planned to market economies, the liberalisation of capital markets, and the 2008 financial crisis provide vivid examples of how the success of economic markets is affected by the institutional framework within which transactions occur (Hodgson 2009).

On the academic side, institutional theorists such as Ronald Coase, Douglas North and Oliver Williamson (awarded the Nobel Prize in Economics 1991, 1993 and 2009, respectively) drew attention to the relationship between institutions and economic outcomes, and political institutionalists such as March and Olsen (1989) emphasised institutional design as a political choice. These developments fostered a new institutionalism that emphasises theory-building based on three contestable assumptions: (1) institutions affect economic outcomes, (2) institutions are endogenous rather than exogenous variables, and (3) the evolution of institutions is related to individual self-interest. The 'rules of the game' will vary over time and hence the emergence, persistence and change (or disappearance) of rules are phenomena to be explained.

These literatures support the repositioning of studies of regulation within a more general concern with 'governance', which 'comprises the traditions, institutions and processes that determine how power is exercised, how citizens are given a voice, and how decisions are made on issues of public concern' (PHAC 2007). By recasting regulation as a form of governance, neo-institutional theory recognises regulation as historically contingent achievements that reflect ongoing adjustments among actors within a framework of power and rights (Djelic and Sahlin-Andersson 2006).

Theoretical frames

Explanations for the emergence and persistence of and change in the institutions affecting market transactions can be clustered under five headings:

1. Public interest theory;
2. Regulatory capture theory;
3. Corporatist theory;
4. Negotiated order theories;
5. Cultural theories.

We briefly review each of these theories below and refer to these approaches as we review histories of accounting regulation.

Public interest theory

There are two variants of public interest theory. The classic version holds that markets are efficient resource allocation mechanisms but may fail due to factors such as information asymmetries or monopoly power. The state uses regulation to overcome market failure. Ronald Coase has demonstrated that where property rights are complete and transaction costs are zero, actors can negotiate efficient outcomes regardless of rules. This has refocused attention on market failures as incomplete property rights specifications and/or high transaction costs to the rearrangement of property rights rather than as an immutable characteristic of any situation. Williamson (1985) extends this insight to suggest that transactions are 'assigned' to alternative governance mechanisms – including the market and the state – to minimise costs.

Bozeman (2002) offers a variant on the market failure approach. He argued that regulation is used when public values are not realised by other means. This framework is relevant when state intervention is unrelated to the efficiency of markets (e.g. social versus economic regulation). For example, if the mechanisms for identifying social preferences fail, or if efficient markets result in a short-term focus at the expense of social goals, authoritative intervention may ensure that public values are realised. This concern reflects the fact that, while in a Coasian world economic efficiency can be achieved, the distribution of wealth is affected by the definition of property rights. Bozeman's concern is primarily with the distributional consequences of market outcomes.

Regulatory capture theory

Regulatory capture theory was developed by Stigler (1971) and Peltzman (1976). The basic premise is that regulation is an economic good subject to the forces of supply and demand. The demand for regulation arises because regulation can result in wealth transfers. Those who will benefit from regulation will lobby the state to enact a favourable law. Regulation is assumed to be instituted by elected legislators who gain utility from holding these positions. Their decision to regulate is based on the likelihood that votes gained from the lobbying group will be greater than votes lost from the group harmed by regulation. This is most likely when the benefits of regulation are concentrated and its costs are diffused across a large population. Peltzman (1976) generalised this result to allow for the effect of different elasticities of demand for the regulated product.

Corporatism

The concept of corporatism draws attention to the private sector bodies that implement state policy (Schmitter and Lehmbruch 1979; Richardson 1989). The theory suggests that the state enters into a bargain with private sector bodies providing them with access to state power and resources in return for their control of the regulated population. An important part of the corporatist bargain is that social conflicts are contained within functionally defined bodies (such as professional associations and regulatory bodies) rather than acting to disrupt broader social processes.

Negotiated order theory

The approaches described above assume that regulation is embedded in a rational social order characterised by a search for social benefit, or a game-theoretic search for equilibrium among competing interests. Several approaches to regulation eschew this model of social order and focus on the practical production of order in the face of uncertainty. In an uncertain environment the possibility of rational calculation disappears because the alternatives cannot be enumerated, costs and benefits are unknown, or preferences are unstable or unformed. In spite of these impediments to rational action, coordination among actors is still required. In these circumstances, a negotiated order may arise that allows successful interaction to occur. Negotiated order theories tend to be more focused on process than on teleology, that is, the question becomes *how* regulation is created and implemented rather than *why* regulation is created.

Cultural theories

Cultural theories of regulation are concerned with the interplay between institutions rather than focusing on a single institution at a time. Social groups develop core values and/or generic social mechanisms that are reflected across many institutions. These values are highly resistant to change because they are pre-cognitive from the perspective of participants, that is, they represent deeply socialised and taken-for-granted assumptions, and/or the mutual interdependence of institutions based on these values makes piecemeal adjustment of any single institution within society virtually impossible. These theories initially used the nation-state as a proxy for culture but may use mid-range levels such as the nature of the legal system (code law vs common law vs Sharia law).

Empirical frames

The historical study of accounting regulation has typically followed one of five empirical strategies. The first strategy is a simple description of regulation. The remaining four represent alternative 'periodization strategies' (Lieberman 2001) to explore possible causes and consequences of regulatory events. First, historians may explore the factors surrounding regulatory emergence (Merino and Mayper 2001). This requires a demarcation of pre- and post-regulatory periods. Second, historians identify 'exogenous shocks' and look for the impact of those events on continuing regulations and regulatory processes (for example, the impact on Japanese accounting institutions of the American occupation (Harrison and McKinnon 1986)). Third, historians look for regulatory changes and examine the motives and implications of the change (for example the effect of changes in the US accounting standard-setting process on the value relevance of accounting information (Ely and Waymire 1999)). Finally, historians compare cases (typically jurisdictions) or periods with variation in specific factors ('rival causes') thought to affect accounting regulation (Puxty et al. 1987; Ezzamel et al. 2007).

The study of regulatory history has largely focused on the United States although this is changing with the rise of the IASC/IASB and the diffusion of IFRS Standards (Meier-Schatz 1986; Camfferman and Zeff 2007, Nobes 2014; Camfferman and Zeff 2015). The role of the United States in regulatory innovation emerged during the inter-war depression. The New Deal policies of F. D. Roosevelt were implemented through agencies designed as 'rational' administrative structures with professional management, evidence-based decision-making and due process to control both the influence of special interests and the discretionary powers of administrators. The 1933/34 US Securities Acts and the creation of the Securities and Exchange Commission (SEC), in particular, are seen as innovations in the use of disclosure regulation to control corporate behaviour administered through an independent agency (Benston 1973; Vogel 1986).

The US Securities Acts 1933/34: a natural experiment

One of the longest running debates in the history of accounting regulation is whether or not the regulation of financial reporting is necessary. This debate involves two dimensions: first, what is the purpose of regulation; and second, has regulation achieved that purpose? The debate has been protracted largely because of disagreements over the purpose of regulation, which establishes the criterion used to judge success.

For many researchers the introduction of financial disclosure requirements in the Securities Act of 1933 and Securities Exchange Act of 1934 in the midst of the Great Depression provides a naturally occurring experiment for exploring the rationale for and effectiveness of regulation (Leuz and Wysocki 2016). The adoption process was relatively short and the change from the status quo was significant. The circumstances surrounding the creation of the Acts of 1933 and 1934 have been explored to understand the motivations for regulation, while the performance of the US stock market (particularly the New York Stock Exchange) before and after the legislation has been used to evaluate the effectiveness of regulation.

The debate focused on Benston (1969a, 1969b, 1973, 1975, 1982) who begins with the premise that the only rationale for financial disclosure regulation is to correct market failures. From his perspective, if there is no evidence of informational failures prior to regulation, and there is no difference in the performance of the stock markets before and after regulation, then there is no justification for regulation. This is a straightforward application of classical public interest theory to the regulation of financial reporting. Benston's work has been relied on by others and occasioned a response by the SEC (1977) disputing his claim that financial disclosure regulation is unnecessary.

Benston (1969a) argues that the common justification for the 1933/34 Acts – that financial disclosure prior to the Great Depression was often fraudulent – cannot be supported by the evidence. He bases this claim on a review of legislative records and secondary sources. These records show very few criminal convictions for securities fraud during this period. Okcabol and Tinker (1993) note this is a very narrow definition of investors' concerns; it is limited to acts of commission (fraud) to the exclusion of acts of omission (non-disclosure). Seligman (1983) provides evidence that the latter type of misrepresentation was more common, and Edwards (1989) presents evidence that the quality of financial statement disclosure declined during the 1920s.

Benston (1973) claims that voluntary disclosure prior to regulation was sufficient to support informed trading and stewardship. Further, he holds that the change in the information regime brought about by the Acts was inconsistent with the needs of informationally efficient markets. Information was released too late and was based on conservative accounting principles that were inconsistent with investment decision-making (a continuing theme, see Lev and Gu (2016)). The empirical results show no stock market reaction to the new information. Hence, Benston concludes that the information was not needed by investors. Finally, he argues that there are effective and efficient alternatives to monitor management and the capital and labour markets.

Contrary to this interpretation, Merino and Neimark (1982) question whether the disclosure of accounting numbers without the simultaneous disclosure of management assumptions and the basis for measurement would support investment decision-making either *before* or after the introduction of the Acts. They also document that companies were either unwilling or unable to provide data even under subpoena by the Federal Trade Commission (1928–32) investigating the financial disclosures of companies leading up to the stock market crash. They report contemporary concern with the quality of financial reporting, but neither Benston nor Merino and Neimark are able to provide a baseline for the level of financial misstatements during this period.

Davis (1999) examines Benston's claim that voluntary agreements between the stock exchanges and listing firms provided sufficient information to safeguard investors. He begins by noting that Benston's approach to data collection was unsound – he simply wrote to the exchanges and asked them whether disclosure requirements were in place. Davis (1999) examines the 'listing standards' of 34 US stock exchanges during the 1920s. He found that the listing agreements were highly varied, did not specify accounting standards where disclosure was required, and suffered from exemptions and lax enforcement. He further discovered that while these standards had evolved over time, the changes were due to government investigation of the exchanges rather than being initiated by firms or exchanges to achieve a comparative advantage in information transparency. The role of government in the emergence of stock exchange disclosure regulations raises doubts about the 'voluntary' nature of such rules, i.e. the potential for government intervention may be considered an effective and low cost form of regulation.

Focusing on econometric issues, Friend and Westerfield (1975) raise concerns about Benston's (1973) focus on the impact of a single change in disclosure (sales) on the market while the Acts had multiple effects. They also raise the concern that Benston found statistically significant results but discounted them in his conclusion as not being economically meaningful – hence allowing him to say that the disclosure requirements had no effect. Friend and Westerfield (1975) question whether or not Benston correctly identified the right 'event' on which to base his comparison. They suggest that while he focused on the 1934 Act, it was the 1933 Act that had the greatest impact on financial disclosure. They also point out that the tests used by Benston relate to market efficiency but not to distributional issues even though Benston uses the term 'market fairness' in reference to his tests. Benston (1975) provides a detailed response to these issues.

Benston's work is based on the reinterpretation of common knowledge rather than being designed to specifically test his hypotheses (see Okcabol and Tinker (1993) for critiques of Benston's data and methods). His model however has been examined by others such as Simon (1989), Daines and Jones (2012), and in studies by Waymire and colleagues. Ely and Waymire (1999), for example, examined the relevance of financial disclosures to New York Stock Exchange (NYSE) prices between 1927 and 1993. This study includes the pre-SEC period as well as regulation under the Committee on Accounting Procedure (1939–59), the Accounting Principles Board (1973–93) and the FASB (1973–93). They do not find improved correlation between earnings and stock prices over these periods. Ely and Waymire (1999) infer that regulation did not improve the information environment for investors but recognise that the correlation may be affected by changes in the economy and technology. They, of course, cannot compare their results to a counterfactual control where no regulation exists.

Gjerde et al. (2011) conducted a similar study to Ely and Waymire (1999), examining the value relevance of Norwegian financial statements from 1965 to 2004 after Norway changed their standards from a tax/creditor orientation to a market/investor orientation. Importantly Norway's standards emphasise the income statement rather than the balance sheet (so earnings relevance is more likely than under US and international accounting standards). They find a significant increase in earnings relevance over time but only when controls are included for market risk, industry composition and the proportion of companies reporting losses. Their study may indicate that regulation has a positive effect on the information environment depending on the nature of the regulation and the context in which it is introduced.

A common approach to demonstrating that regulation was not necessary is to show that firms were voluntarily using audits and disclosing the same financial information that was required by regulation (Benston 1973). These decisions may reflect a balancing of costs and benefits by management and shareholders. Regulation, it is suggested, requires an economically unsound use of resources to disclose information that is not required by the markets. Merino et al. (1994) correctly point out that to support this interpretation, alternative explanations must be eliminated and/or that the mechanism linking economic incentives to audit/disclosure decisions must be demonstrated. For example, the need for a monitoring/bonding mechanism does not imply which of many alternative mechanisms would be chosen or which would have been the most efficient in the circumstances.

Chow (1983) examined the period of the Securities Acts to determine if the regulations resulted in wealth transfers between shareholders and bondholders. His approach has elements of a regulatory capture model where the key premise is that the Acts had distributional effects among groups. His work has, however, been challenged by Merino et al. (1987) who identify problems in the definition of the event window, the separation of control and treatment samples, and biases in the interpretation of the consequences of the legislation for different stakeholders.

Recent work concerned with the social costs and benefits of regulation has taken a global perspective trying to generalise beyond the idiosyncrasies of the United States, and considering other measures of regulations' impact other than stock market outcomes. Waymire and Basu (2011), for example, examine the relationship between regulation and financial crises. They conclude that regulations might amplify crises and do not reduce future crises. Christensen et al. (2013) find that IFRS implementation across countries occurred with a coincident increase in enforcement activities. They suggest that market effects may be due to enforcement rather than a change in regulations per se. (Daines and Jones (2012) come to a similar conclusion about the 1933/34 US Securities Acts). Hail et al. (2018) examine the relationship between accounting scandals and regulation based on data from 26 countries between 1800 and 2015. They find that regulations are, on average, a reaction to scandals; that regulations are positively correlated with future scandals (regulations may facilitate identification of scandals); and, that the relationship between scandals and regulation is affected by culture and network effects (discussed later).

From 'market failure' to 'public value failure' and 'regulatory capture'

The tests of the value relevance of accounting information coincident with change in regulation presume that this was the intended purpose of regulation. The cliometrics (quantitative history based largely on neo-classical models) of Benston, Waymire and Hail are limited by the models used and the lack of attention given to the context in which events occurred (see North 1997). As Crafts (1987) concluded, following a review of the contributions of cliometrics to economic history, 'econometric methods need to be supplemented in historical work by other forms of evidence to obtain persuasive answers to historical questions'. This challenge was taken up by Merino and others who examined the debates leading up to the Securities Acts and the broader social context in which the legislation emerged.

Merino and Neimark (1982) argued that the Securities Acts were intended to maintain the US ideology of individualism and competition during a period of increased economic concentration. The US Constitution was designed as a series of checks-and-balances against the concentration of political power. The rise of trusts and cartels in the late nineteenth and early twentieth centuries, however, raised the spectre of a weak political structure facing a focused economic bloc. The debates in Congress and the press suggest that increased disclosure and widespread stock ownership were seen as a means of democratising the economy and maintaining the accountability of managers. The debates, however, did not assume that disclosures would be used directly by investors but rather by bankers, government agencies and a market for corporate control (takeovers to replace inept managements). The structure of the market envisioned was thus a 'two tier market structure' and 'moral regulation' by knowledgeable elites. Merino and Neimark (1982) challenge both the purpose of the Acts and the 'users' of the increased information. Merino et al. (2010) provide a similar analysis of the introduction of the Sarbanes-Oxley Act 2002 linking the required governance model to neo-liberal ideology.

Edwards and Chandler (2001) examine the introduction of accounting regulation on UK friendly societies (non-profit, mutual benefit organisations). This is an unusual setting where fraud or other crises were not the catalyst for regulation. Friendly societies were created for the UK working class and often associated with particular groups (such as Masons). These organisations were seen as reducing the demand on the state to alleviate the conditions of the working class but also posed a risk as bases for working class collaboration and radicalisation. State regulation of these organisations tended to precede the regulation of limited liability companies. Edwards and Chandler (2001) attribute this to the UK government's perception of these groups as less educated and less able to guard their own interests, hence a 'paternalistic' approach to regulation was adopted. This is similar to Merino and Mayper's view of US regulation.

Merino and Mayper (2001) continue the analysis of the symbolic role of regulation drawing on Edelman (1964). They examine private correspondence among 'New Dealers' and key members of the accounting profession. The analysis is consistent with the regulatory capture model that assumes that regulation will benefit small groups as opposed to larger groups over whom the costs of regulation are diffused. In the case of the Securities Acts 1933/34, Merino and Mayper (2001) see the laws as placating the public's demand for protection from systemic market failures without fundamentally changing business operating conditions. This was, in fact, Roosevelt's explicit intention: 'The purpose of the legislation I suggest is to protect the public with the least possible interference with honest business' (Woolley and Peters 2007).

The possibility that accounting regulation has been 'captured' has been widely examined (McQueen 2009). Mahoney (2001) notes that the required disclosures in the Securities Exchange Acts were selective and favoured investment bankers over other groups. Mezias and Chung (2006) focusing on standard-setting between 1973 and 1989, show that private interests affected 'non-substantive' rules but found that 'substantive' rules were independent of such interests, where 'substantive' rules represent fundamental changes in requirements while 'non-substantive' rules represent clarifications, implementation guidelines or applications to particular industries. Similar histories have been written about other jurisdictions. Maltby (1998), for example, argues that in the UK the disclosure provisions of the early companies' acts were more consistent with the interests of large investors than small investors. Walker (1987) raised concerns about the capture of the Australian Accounting Standards Board by auditors and their clients. Godfrey and Langfield-Smith (2005) examine potential regulatory capture at the IASB. Overall the evidence suggests that the economic consequences of financial disclosure regulation attracts lobbying pressure and may reflect the interests of a sub-set of society.

The impression that emerges from these studies is one of consensus on facts but significant disagreement on interpretation. The consensus is that, in general, the regulation of financial disclosure in the United States during the twentieth century, and globally over an extended period, has been ineffective in generating information that is more useful to investors than voluntary disclosures. It may have reduced the riskiness of stocks (Simon 1989) but has not generated information with greater relevance to stock valuation (Leuz and Wysocki 2016). Leuz and Wysocki (2016) conclude that evidence of the effect of regulations remains weak because of poor measurement of costs and benefits, failure to control for shifts in sample characteristics (e.g. riskier firms moving to unregulated markets), and failure to establish causal mechanisms for the effects hypothesised. In spite of the lack of evidence of benefits of accounting regulation, however, the authors note the persistence and diffusion of regulations suggesting that research is needed to explain this phenomenon.

Benston and others have concluded that regulation, with its attendant costs, could be reduced without ill-effect. Merino and others, by contrast, argue that disclosure regulation plays a symbolic role in maintaining the confidence of small investors and reducing the political pressure for intensive regulation of business. The purpose of the legislation was to protect private ownership and individual participation in the stock markets while reducing the opportunities for insider exploitation of uninformed traders. This suggests that the reduction of regulation is unlikely but that it could be used to monitor businesses independent of the market.

Searching for regulation

The periodisation used by Benston and others to judge the effect of the 1933/34 Securities Acts on US capital markets relies on the correct specification of the timing of a switch from an unregulated to a regulated environment. One criticism of Benston's characterisation of the pre-1933 period as unregulated is that the stock exchanges provided an authoritative standard of financial disclosure through their listing agreements. While this implies that some regulation existed during the 'unregulated' period, Davis (1999: 53) notes: 'although the stock exchanges were the clear leaders in setting national financial disclosure standards, the level of corporate disclosures through the stock exchanges prior to 1934 was inadequate'. This does not imply however that the level of regulation is determined solely by either the stock exchanges on which a firm is listed or the state regulations affecting that group of companies.

Walker and Mack (1998), in a reanalysis of the work of Whittred (1986) on the history of consolidated financial statements in Australia, shows that practice was influenced by regulations in other jurisdictions to which a company was exposed. For example, while the focus was on companies listed on the Sydney Stock Exchange, if the company had a subsidiary incorporated in a jurisdiction requiring consolidated statements, then that company was more likely to file consolidated statements in Australia voluntarily. The possibility of 'spill over' effects between jurisdictions is also noted by Hail et al. (2018) with respect to the effect of scandals on regulations. Walker and Mack (1998) also demonstrate that the likelihood of issuing consolidated statements increases as the authority of the standard increases. For example, a standard 'recommending' consolidation had less effect than a standard 'requiring' consolidation; a standard issued by government had more effect on behaviour than a standard issued by a professional association.

In addition to the effect of stock exchanges on financial disclosure there were also common law requirements. Mills (1993, see also 1990, 1994) provides a summary of the case law affecting accounting practices prior to the introduction of regulated financial disclosure. Her motivation is two-fold: to examine the claim that the only role of government/courts prior to regulation is to enforce contracts, and to examine conflicting accounts of the role of the courts with regard to accounting for depreciation and goodwill. She reports that, particularly in the UK, the courts played an active role in defining appropriate accounting – even overturning accounting methods specified in contracts. This approach in common law represents a change from the reliance of the courts on social norms and precedents to a focus on expressed agreements between consenting parties. The latter logic supported and fostered commercial interests. The evidence, however, shows a reluctance of US judges compared with UK judges to overturn contractual terms in favour of common meanings of accounting abstractions (Mills 1993). Mills' work thus shows that even in an 'unregulated' environment authoritative forces affected the development of financial measurement and disclosure, and that this unregulated environment, in spite of great similarities of institutions, varied across cultures (see Camfferman 2012).

It is also possible that accounting firms may have been a source of financial disclosure norms. Cooper and Robson (2006) suggest that the source of current practice standards is large firms rather than formal regulatory bodies. Although during the pre-1933 era the audit firms had not achieved their current level of market dominance, there is evidence that a small group of firms had established their presence and may have been able to exert influence on financial disclosure (see Richardson 2006). Bricker and Chandar (1998) identify investment bankers as another source of influence. These sources of regulation blur the boundaries between the market and regulatory bodies. A further complication is the rise of private transnational regulatory bodies such as the IASB, the Global Risk Institute in Financial Services, the International Integrated Reporting Council, etc. that exist outside any national legal context and rely on voluntary adoption by countries and companies for their success (Richardson and Eberlein 2011).

Negotiated order, regulatory 'progress' and cycles

The administrative agencies created by the New Deal were provided with unusual discretionary powers to restore the US economy after the Great Depression. This resulted in concern about agencies acting simultaneously in executive, legislative and judicial roles (Shepard 1996). The legislative role played by these agencies arose because the Acts creating them were incomplete and the agency (such as the SEC) was expected to create regulations (such as accounting standards) to implement the intent of the legislation. This, in turn, often resulted in regulations that allowed considerable flexibility of behaviour of the regulated. In other words, the creation of regulation provided a context in which the precise form would be negotiated but did not provide 'black letter' law. A persistent issue in US regulation has thus been the negotiation of the role of the regulatory body and the flexibility allowed under regulations.

The negotiation of accounting regulation is reflected in literature on lobbying standard-setting bodies (see Taylor and Turley 1986; Zeff 2006; Rutherford 2007; Cortese 2011). This literature is related to theories of regulatory capture but, while regulatory capture refers to control of the entire regulatory process, lobbying studies focus on specific events. There is little historical work on indirect lobbying of regulatory bodies in accounting. This probably reflects the lack of records concerning such activities. Direct lobbying, however, is captured in letters on exposure drafts and other formal due process opportunities. There is literature on lobbying for early UK regulation since hearings on the companies acts (in which financial disclosure regulation was embedded) occurred in public and lobbyists'/witnesses' comments are on record (Jones 1995; Jones and Aiken 1995; Walker 1996; Maltby 1998). The literature on lobbying regulators is also limited by a tendency to focus on individual issues. Saemann (1999) is an exception. She examines lobbying by four industry representative bodies across 20 controversial standards of the FASB and identifies consistencies in their lobbying patterns.

There is historical research on the form that accounting regulation takes. The contemporary debate on the form of regulation/standards in accounting is framed in terms of 'rules versus principles'. This has appeared in various guises in the literature such as concern with the degree of 'uniformity' in reporting practice (Mueller 1965). There is also a large literature on uniform costing systems. Jucius (1943), for example, traced the history of uniform accounting from 1875 to 1940. He attributes the rise of uniform accounting systems to the activities of trade associations who sought to provide members with a system to determine costs and thereby to end cut-throat price competition.

Merino and Coe (1978) discuss the history of 'uniformity' in accounting in the United States beginning with the Interstate Commerce Commission in 1887. The government demand for uniformity arises from the desire to have information to support policy analysis and rate regulation in certain industries (notably transportation). These systems were industry specific and allowed for variations among companies to reflect technological and scale differences. The demand for uniformity was generalised from these specific circumstances to corporate reporting. In general, Merino and Coe (1978) report a consistent reluctance of professional accounting associations to support uniformity in financial reporting. This arises from the recognition that accounting numbers (accruals) require judgements that cannot be reduced to simple rules.

The essence of the debate between rules versus principles is also reflected in the concept of 'true and fair' presentation (Alexander and Jermakowicz 2006). Under a rules-based system an auditor can give a 'clean' opinion if financial statements have been prepared according to Generally Accepted Accounting Principles (GAAP). GAAP may be further defined under law to refer to a specific set of documents, or to the standards that are produced by a particular organisation/standard-setting body. Under a principles-based system there is an additional requirement that the financial statements reflect a true and fair view of the financial position of the company even if the financial statements have been prepared according to GAAP. This additional requirement reflects a concern with the substance over the form of financial statements.

Chambers and Wolnizer (1991) provide a history of the concept of 'true and fair' based on legislative records and the charters of partnerships and companies that specified the quality of financial reports prior to formal regulations. They find that common usage of the term prior to its incorporation into British companies legislation in 1844 connoted two things: (1) that the financial statements contained no falsehoods; and (2) that assets were valued at selling prices (i.e. 'fair value') rather than cost. The charters that referred to the quality of financial information typically intended financial statements to have probative value in the event of the dissolution of the company or partnership. Maltby (2000) provides a related history of 'prudent' accounting.

Jones et al. (2000) compare the development of 'truth in advertising' and the rejection of 'true and fair' in US accounting/auditing standards during the Progressive era. They note the professional success of accountants who rejected 'truth' as a criterion for financial statements compared with the professional failure of marketers who succeeded in institutionalising 'truth in advertising'. The marketers' campaign resulted in legislation and criminal penalties based on the findings of the courts, while accountants were able to retain control over the definition of GAAP and hence with the standards that would be used to evaluate the adequacy of financial disclosures.

Macve (2015) compares the development of 'fair value' and 'conservatism' concepts in the longue durée. Fair value accounting represents a challenge to accounting based on transactions (Styhre 2018). It substitutes various 'market' values for transaction records based on the premise that market values provide better information for investment decision-making even if the market in question is fictive. The concept of 'fair value' is consistent with the valuation logic underlying 'true and fair' financial statements but formally ties the assessment of 'fairness' to documentable market values. This approach requires a history of regulation to also consider the history of markets (Fligstein and Calder 2015) and the relationship between market structures and accounting records (for example, the history of the 'lower of book or market value' for inventories may provide insights into these issues).

Hopwood (1987) raised concerns about the teleology of much accounting history. History was frequently interpreted as the inexorable movement towards 'better' accounting and auditing practice (see Napier (2001) on the concept of 'progress' in accounting history, and Sunder (2016) on the meaning of 'better' accounting). In many cases, however, historical work has shown that 'progress', regardless of how this is defined, is elusive. The debates surrounding 'rules vs principles', 'uniformity vs flexibility' and 'GAAP vs true and fair' have not achieved closure. Instead, the complex interplay of factors in the regulatory environment encourages symbolic changes without real change in the behaviour of firms, or a recycling of issues without resolution.

One approach to reconciling the continued existence of alternative approaches is to suggest that accounting regulation is subject to countervailing pressures that change in force over time, resulting in an oscillation between alternatives. Nobes (1991, 1992) for example, proposed a cyclical model of regulatory history to account for the dramatic swings in standards over time. This model has been used by some (Gordon and Morris 1996; Cooper and Deo 2005) but challenged by others (Skerratt and Whittington 1992).

The premise behind the cyclical model is that there are two opposing forces in the economy: for example, a force towards standardisation originating in the profession and governmental agencies, and a force opposed to standardisation originating in corporate management (Moran and Previts 1984); or changes in stakeholder concerns linked to the business cycle with standardisation following business downturns and benign neglect of regulatory standards during business booms (Clarke 2004). Baker and Quéré (2015) suggest that cyclicality may reflect tension between a nation exerting sovereignty vs seeking domestic social order. The trigger for a change in regulation may be a crisis or scandal in a particular industry or company that implicates the flexibility of accounting regulation in the problem (Walker 2000; Chapter 20 of this volume) or the enactment of an accounting standard in another country that is used as a benchmark. Regulation develops in a particular direction until countervailing forces reverse the process.

Byington and Sutton (1991) and Gaa (1991) suggest that accounting standard-setting activity is correlated with challenges to self-regulation of the profession. Gaa (1991) suggests that the relationship between the state and the profession can be modelled as a sequential game in which the state initiates a challenge to self-regulation, usually emerging out of crisis, and the profession responds to demonstrate that the crisis can be managed while maintaining self-regulation intact. Gaa (1991) suggests that this reflects a 'social contract' (or a corporatist bargain) between the profession and the state.

Byington and Sutton (1991) identify four events that they argue challenged self-regulation in the United States: the 1938 issuance of an accounting standard by the SEC; the 1971 US Revenue Act on accounting for tax credits; the Moss and Metcalfe hearings on the 'accounting establishment'; and the Dingell hearings on the 'expectations gap' in 1985. They find that the introduction of accounting and auditing standards in the United States increases during each of these episodes compared with other periods. They see regulation emerging out of a force to maintain self-regulation by the profession vs a desire by government to intervene directly during times of crisis.

This cyclical model highlights the negotiation process from which accounting standards emerge. One interpretation of the standard-setting process is that it is designed to create an 'arena' in which interests are defined and interact. This view of standard setting is reflected in several contributions to the literature.

Miranti (1989) traced the development of accounting by the Interstate Commerce Commission (ICC) as a by-product of their statistical department's attempt to define a model to allow them to monitor the railroad industry. The Commission was concerned to regulate rates to prevent abuse of monopoly power (overcharging consumers who had no options and undercharging to bankrupt competitive transportation modes). It was also concerned about watered stock and the potential bankruptcy of railroads. The accounting requirements grew out of the ICC's attempt to provide a context in which interests, including farmers, miners, individual state regulatory bodies and railroad associations, could negotiate; the accounting system reflected the information needs on which those relationships would be based.

Work by Robson (1991, 1992) developed the idea of 'constellations' to explain the development of reporting standards. This concept recognises that any proposed standard will affect various segments of society and become a site for the negotiations of interests. The constellation of forces that is activated will depend upon the particular standard and hence is not a regular and predictable feature of standard-setting processes. Young (1994) adopted the concept of a 'regulatory space' to capture these effects. Sivakumar and Waymire (2003) look at this issue in their exploration of the effect of accounting choice by managers facing both product market regulation and financial disclosure regulation.

King and Waymire (1994) provide a transaction cost theory of the evolution of US standard-setting processes. Their basic insight is that accounting standards are used in 'incomplete contracts', that is, contracts where, because of uncertainty or complexity, all future information needs cannot be specified. The parties to the agreement, however, agree to be bound to a set of standards emerging from a predefined process. The authors suggest that a successful standard-setter must: (1) respond quickly to emerging issues (e.g. new transactions for which there is no apparent authoritative accounting treatment), (2) be perceived as independent of the major interests affected by the contracts, (3) be capable of penalising deviations from the standards and (4) allow ex-post recontracting to deal with adverse effects from the standards that are set. The standard-setting process within this model is regarded as a super structure that arises from negotiations among interests and reflects the *a priori* agreement of parties to reduce *ex post* conflicts.

Culture and accounting regulation

The US experience of regulating financial disclosure should not be over-generalised. The creation of the SEC and mandatory financial disclosures arose during a stock market crash and a deep depression. The form that regulation took reflected an interaction between those conditions, the set of institutions upon which legislators could draw as models, and the culture in which regulation would be embedded. The histories of other countries show the influence of these variables on regulatory structures and the variety of possible reactions (Walton 1995; Ezzamel et al. 2007; Hail et al. 2018).

Merino and Neimark (1982) and Merino and Mayper (2001) emphasise that the concept of 'regulatory capitalism' in the United States grew out of the New Deal era and an attempt by reformers to enact the American Dream – a combination of communitarian ideals (equality of opportunity) and meritocracy. The initial shape of regulatory institutions was premised on the protection of private property rights subject to constraints on the 'unfair' accumulation of wealth (such as through trusts and the exercise of monopoly power). Within four years of the passage of the Securities Acts, however, the 'radical' version of the New Deal gave way to a philosophy that reaffirmed the role of the market over direct state intervention. The disclosure of financial information about corporate activities was seen as preserving individual investor opportunity (to make investment decisions, to evaluate management) without curtailing the same rights of management. Standardised disclosures provide a powerful image of equality within this rhetorical context.

The pattern identified by Merino and Mayper (2001) after the shock of the stock market crash of 1929 parallels the pattern observed by Harrison and McKinnon (1986) in Japan after the US occupation. Initially the reform of Japanese institutions followed the US model, but over time the operation of those institutions returned to the patterns embedded in Japanese culture. Fülbier and Klein (2015) show similar cultural path dependence in the use of IFRS Standards in Germany. In both cases the interaction of the institutions of financial disclosure regulation with other segments of society, including the courts and capital markets, resulted in a realignment of regulatory reforms to the broader social order in which these changes were embedded.

Baylin et al. (1996) trace the evolution of Canadian standard-setting structures over a 100-year period. They show the influence of colonial heritage (see Walton 1986 for further examples) and changing trading patterns on the models referenced by standard setters and the demands for harmonisation. They also emphasise the interplay between technical developments and the need to maintain the political legitimacy of the process. In spite of the close connection between the United States and Canada, and the similar experience of the Great Depression, Canada did not follow the United States in changing their approach to financial disclosure; instead Canada retained the UK tradition of specifying financial disclosure requirements through company legislation.

The US experience with accounting regulation has been contrasted with that of Europe. May (1939) observed that US intervention in financial markets has been concentrated around periods of economic downturn, while in the UK, France, Germany and the Netherlands regulation appears more measured, reflecting political philosophies rather than market dynamics. Hail et al. (2018) find national variation in the responsiveness of regulation to scandals to be associated with the form of legal system, with common law countries being more responsive. The form of regulation also differed with the United States establishing a formal administrative body (the SEC) that has no direct parallel in European systems of regulation.

May (1939) and Benston (1975) suggest that regulation in the United States has been 'explicit' while regulation in the UK has been 'implicit'. Explicit regulation was built into law and formal standard-setting bodies with enforcement. Implicit regulation occurs through social norms monitored and enforced informally by market participants. In the UK, the operation of informal regulation is facilitated by the physical concentration of financing activities in the City of London. May (1939) also notes that in Europe a greater reliance on criminal law to prosecute financial crimes rather than relying on the Companies Act or related regulations. This means that the bar for formal intervention by the state, i.e. criminal guilt, is higher than in countries using administrative mechanisms of enforcement. Matten and Moon (2008) also use the explicit/implicit distinction to explain differences in the regulation of corporate social responsibility between the United States and European Union.

Parker (1990) reviews the extent of the regulation of UK financial reporting after the Companies Act 1856 during a period regarded as typifying an 'unregulated economy'. He recognises that a large part of the UK economy was regulated under legislation specific to those industries (such as railroads, public utilities and banks). These industries are typically excluded from discussions of private economic activity because of their rather unusual technologies (natural monopolies and public safety issues) and long-term capital requirements. Initially each company had specific reporting requirements included in their acts of incorporation. Contrary to US tradition, British disclosure requirements typically opened the account books to inspection rather than just requiring the disclosure of financial statements. In the mid-nineteenth century, however, common clauses were consolidated (e.g. Companies Clauses Consolidation Act 1845) so that they could be incorporated into new legislation by reference. This approach encouraged the development of uniform financial reporting among companies within the same industries.

Bryer (1993) provides a more general perspective on this period arguing that financial disclosure requirements emerged out of shifts in the nature of capitalism from a focus on the individual investor to capitalism as a system. He emphasises the systematic departures of accounting measurements from neo-classic economic theory, focusing on depreciation as a key concept. Richard (2005) provides a similar analysis tracing the development of measurement bases (historic cost versus fair value) in European accounting practice as an outcome of conflicts between segments of the capitalist economy (such as bankers and the state versus entrepreneurs). Walker (2016) renews the call for greater attention to the relationship between accounting and the social.

The next wave of regulation: networked governance

The conception of regulation as a constraint imposed on the markets by the state tended to limit histories of regulation to events within national boundaries. As we argued at the beginning of this chapter, regulation theory has moved beyond this to consider the interconnections between regulators in multiple nations, transnationally and globally. This reconceptualisation of regulation highlights the need for accounting historians to examine the international (between nations), transnational (above nations) and global (beyond nations) process by which accounting and auditing are regulated (Botzem and Quack 2006), the connections between these levels (Richardson 2009), and the differences in process at each level of analysis (Richardson and Eberlein 2011).

There is, of course, a considerable literature on international differences in accounting regulation between countries and on the harmonisation/convergence of regulation among countries (Zeff 1972; Camfferman and Zeff 2015). Schoenfeld (1981) provided an early but brief history of the development of international accounting. He emphasised the information needs of multinational enterprises (MNEs) and the state regulatory bodies that tried to tax and control them. The material since his seminal survey is adequately captured in standard international accounting textbooks such as Nobes and Parker (2016).

Where more effort is needed is to develop theoretically informed histories of the key international and global bodies that now collectively set the direction for accounting regulation. This would include both formal bodies such as the World Bank (Arnold 2005), International Federation of Accountants (Loft et al. 2006), the IASC (Martinez-Diaz 2005; Camfferman and Zeff 2007), the IASB (Camfferman and Zeff 2015), as well as informal bodies such as the G4+1 (Street and Shaughnessy 1998) and G7/G20, and the relationships between them (Richardson 2009).

The networked regulation of accounting intersects with cultural issues at several levels including the interaction of legal systems (code, common and Sharia law), political ideologies (socialist vs capitalist) and linguistic differences. Evans et al. (2015), for example, point to the subtle ways that translation of IFRS into local languages allows cultural effects to be expressed. The diffusion of IFRS across distinct cultures raises still unresolved issues of implementation and enforcement.

Another lacunae in the history of regulation illustrated by the move to networked regulation is the role of technology (Lymer 1999). At a minimum, there is evidence that the technology of regulation must keep pace with the technology of financial reporting in order to detect and respond to issues (Arner et al. 2017). In addition, the creation of digital networks has layered a set of technological standards on IFRS Standards to allow these standards to be used in the flow of information between countries. Troshani et al. (2019) trace the process by which the concern for the content of accounting standards dominated the concern for technological compatibility under XBRL. The historical relationship between technology and accounting needs further work.

More generally, there has been increasing emphasis among students of regulation on the networks of regulators that coordinate actions in establishing accounting standards as an epistemic community. These bodies have been increasingly intertwined with the 'international financial architecture', a term that gained currency during the financial crises of the late 1980s to refer to the World Bank and International Monetary Fund (among others) that regulate currency flows and credit among sovereign nations. While there have been a small number of studies of particular aspects of this architecture, there needs to be better histories of the integration of accountants into this network (see Richardson and MacDonald 2002).

Conclusion: the three 'moments' of regulatory history

Histories of accounting regulation have struggled with three 'moments'[1] of regulation. The first moment concerns the existence of regulation; why did regulations arise? The second moment concerns what effects regulation has on those subjected to it. This moment also concerns the inherent ambiguities of implementation and the negotiation that occurs as a regulatory body establishes its place within an institutional order. The third moment concerns the persistence of regulations. As circumstances change, the original rationale for regulation may disappear, but the existence of regulation creates its own incentives and costs that activate interests. One of the fundamental problems facing this literature is that the logic of these moments may not be reducible to a single set of factors.

The reason for the introduction of financial disclosure regulation in the United States is still subject to debate. There have been two approaches to this question. The first is to identify a reason based on theory and test the implications of that theory. Benston's work and that of others who followed has taken this approach. Curiously, however, when the data is inconsistent with theory, the suggestion made is that the creation of financial disclosure regulation was a mistake rather than to search for alternative explanations (Leuz and Wysocki 2016). The second approach has been to work with the archival record around the origins of statutes and to identify a plausible historical explanation. This approach, however, is susceptible to criticism for inferential weaknesses – there are undoubtedly alternative explanations consistent with the historical record and the data may be biased and incomplete.

Our understanding of this 'first moment' in regulatory history has been advanced by international comparative studies that demonstrate that the US experience was conditioned by the institutional environment at that time. Other nations experiencing similar shocks to their economic systems relied more on 'implicit' regulation, that is, the functioning of social norms within a more closely knit community of financiers and companies. The literature has also broadened our conception of 'regulation' to include the influence of stock exchanges, common law and cross-jurisdiction factors. One of the gaps in the current regulatory literature is an understanding of the epistemic community of early regulators of financial disclosure. This type of analysis is implicit in Merino and Mayper's (2001) analysis of correspondence among key actors around the introduction of the Securities Acts, and Nobes (2014) examination of the development of consolidated reporting, but needs to be extended to understand, for example, the interplay between state and federal regulators in the United States,[2] and between them and other key trading partners at the time.

There is evidence that regulatory initiatives arise in times of crisis in the United States and may have substantial symbolic roles in managing public reactions to systemic issues. The political context of the creation of regulation opens research to a range of interest group phenomena and ties regulation into the problems of social order within the nation-state. Once regulation is established, however, the actors affected and able to play a role in the regulatory process change. This new context allows for implementation to drift from the trajectory established during the creation phase. In particular, the precise form that regulations take and the way they are implemented emerges from a complex negotiation among a 'constellation' of actors.

One perspective conspicuously absent from the histories of regulation has been the reaction of those subject to regulation. In part this is reflected in work concerned with lobbying, but, in addition, we need to understand the practical accommodations made to the changing regulatory regimes as they are implemented. The success of regulation ultimately requires the 'consent of the governed' (McCraw 1982) or the cost of enforcement will eradicate any possible benefit. But consent is never absolute and corporate archives may provide some insight into the impact of legislation on corporate behaviours. Several studies have suggested that changes in enforcement activity rather than changes in regulations account for much of the observed variance. We do not have histories of accounting enforcement to address these hypotheses. How have accounting regulations been enforced, by whom, with what intensity, and with what consequences?

The 'third moment' of regulatory history, the persistence and rare disappearance of accounting regulation, opens up additional questions and perspectives. The SEC in the United States, for example, is one of the few New Deal agencies that survived relatively unchanged after the 1930s. Its persistence may reflect its economic value-added, its capture by interests who continue to benefit from it, its integration within a network of other domestic and international standard setters, or other reasons. The continued existence of such a body, however, is not guaranteed and there are recurrent suggestions to modify the agency and the means by which it regulates financial disclosure (the key alternatives being to rely on private contracting or to allow competing standard-setting bodies).

The persistence of regulation (that is, explaining the lack of variation or isomorphism, rather than variation in a phenomenon) is the realm of institutional theory. The study of the effect of culture on regulation reflects some of these concerns. As the pressure for institutional isomorphism in regulation increases through the impact of international standard-setting bodies, the requirements of the World Trade Organization, and the entry criteria of regional trading blocs, it is important to illustrate and explicate how these processes unfold. These studies must be sensitive to the dual role of accounting as a subject of regulation and a technology of regulation.

The history of regulation is also in need of more genealogical work that examines the emergence, transformation, dispersion and disappearance of regulatory concepts. The concept of 'true and fair' has attracted some attention so that it is possible to understand the connection of this term to specific times and practices, its variations as it was disembedded and re-embedded in particular contexts, and the symbolic power that it attained within particular institutional and economic settings. Other concepts, for example 'moral regulation' and 'prudence', have fallen into disuse, but the history of such changes has not been written. The sets of regulatory concepts that currently receive widespread discussion are derived from neo-classical economic theory and may be enriched by developing our understanding of other regulatory concepts that have been used and abandoned.

Finally, the history of regulation should contribute to our understanding of the continued decentring of the nation-state (Richardson and MacDonald 2002). The regulation of accounting is becoming increasingly intertwined with the 'global financial architecture'. It has been identified as a key mechanism of international financial stability both through its ability to provide data for aggregate regulatory surveillance and to ensure that local decision-making reflects the risks of specific transactions. The way in which this regulatory network has emerged is still being written and must be carefully traced to avoid a view of the process being limited to commissioned histories and the records of the organisations that survived the tumultuous emergence of global regulation. In addition, the dispersed sites of regulation and their coordination across time and space suggest that a history of technology in accounting regulation may provide insights into the way that regulation is conceptualised and implemented.

Key works

Benston (1973) argues that there is no evidence that the Securities Exchange Act of 1934 was needed or desirable and that there are no measurable positive effects of the act on prices of securities traded on the NYSE.

Ely and Waymire (1999) offer a time series analysis which provides weak support for an increase in earnings relevance following the introduction of US standard-setting bodies.

Merino and Neimark (1982) interpret Securities Acts as an attempt to maintain the social and economic status quo while reconciling the contradictions between an individualistic market-based philosophy and the corporate dominance due to economic concentration.

Young (1994) comprises three studies which illustrate how accounting policy issues need to be constructed as a problem and assessed using the 'logic of appropriateness' to become an issue addressed by the standard setters within the regulatory space.

Notes

1 We use the term 'moment' in its mathematical sense as different dimensions of a distribution rather than a temporal sense of a moment in time.
2 F. D. Roosevelt explicitly refers to state regulators in some of his announcements on the Securities Acts.

References

Alexander, D. and Jermakowicz, E. (2006) A true-and-fair view of the principles/rules debate, *Abacus*, 42 (2): 132–64.

Arner, D.W., Barberis, J. and Buckley, R.P. (2017) *FinTech and RegTech in a Nutshell, and the Future in a Sandbox* (CFA Institute Research Foundation). https://www.cfainstitute.org/en/research/foundation/2017/fintech-and-regtech-in-a-nutshell-and-the-future-in-a-sandbox.

Arnold, P.A. (2005) Disciplining domestic regulation: The World Trade Organization and the market for professional services, *Accounting, Organizations and Society*, 30 (4): 299–330.

Auditing Practices Board. (1986) *APC: The First Ten Years* (London: APC).

Baker, C.R. and Quéré, B.P. (2015) Historical innovations in the regulation of business and accounting practices: A comparison of absolutism and liberal democracy, *Accounting History*, 20 (3): 250–65.

Baylin, G., MacDonald, L. and Richardson, A.J. (1996) Accounting standard-setting in Canada 1864-1992: A theoretical analysis of structural evolution, *Journal of International Accounting and Taxation*, 5 (1): 113–32.

Benston, G.J. (1969a) The effectiveness and effects of the SEC's accounting disclosure requirements, in H.G. Manne (ed.) *Economic Policy and the Regulation of Corporate Securities*, pp. 23–79 (Washington: The American Enterprise Institute).

Benston, G.J. (1969b) The value of the SEC's accounting disclosure requirements, *Accounting Review*, 44 (3): 515–32.

Benston, G.J. (1973) Required disclosure and the stock markets: An evaluation of the Securities Exchange Act of 1934, *American Economic Review*, 63 (1): 132–55.

Benston, G.J. (1975) Accounting standards in the United States and the United Kingdom: Their nature, causes and consequences, *Vanderbilt Law Review*, 28 (1): 235–68.

Benston, G.J. (1982) An analysis of the role of accounting standards for enhancing corporate governance and social responsibility, *Journal of Accounting and Public Policy*, 1 (1): 5–17.

Beresford, D.R. (1998) FASB's accomplishments to date: One participant's views, *Accounting Historians Journal*, 25 (2): 151–66.

Botzem, S. and Quack, S. (2006) Contested rules and shifting boundaries: International standard setting in accounting, in M.-L. Djelic and K. Sahlin-Andersson (eds.) *Transnational Governance: Institutional Dynamics of Regulation*, pp. 266–86 (Cambridge: Cambridge University Press).

Bozeman, B. (2002) Public-value failure: When efficient markets may not do, *Public Administration Review*, 62 (2): 134–51.

Brandeis, L. (1914) *Others People's Money - and How the Bankers Use It* (New York: Stokes).

Bricker, R. and Chandar, N. (1998) On applying agency theory in historical accounting research, *Business and Economic History*, 27 (2): 486–99.

Bryer, R.A. (1993) The late nineteenth-century revolution in financial reporting: Accounting for the rise of investor or managerial capitalism? *Accounting, Organizations and Society*, 18 (7/8): 649–90.

Byington, R. and Sutton, S. (1991) The self-regulating profession: An analysis of the political monopoly tendencies of the audit profession, *Critical Perspectives on Accounting*, 2 (4): 315–30.

Camfferman, K. (2012) A contract-law perspective on legal cases in financial reporting: The Netherlands, 1880–1970, *Accounting History*, 17 (2): 141–73.

Camfferman, K. and Zeff, S.A. (2007) *Financial Reporting and Global Capital Markets: A History of the International Accounting Standards Committee, 1973–2000* (Oxford: Oxford University Press).

Camfferman, K. and Zeff, S.A. (2015) *Aiming for Global Accounting Standards: The International Accounting Standards Board, 2001–2011* (New York: Oxford University Press).

Carmona, S., Ezzamel, M. and Gutiérrez, F. (2006) Accounting history research: Traditional and new accounting history perspectives, *De Computis-Revista Española De Historia De La Contabilidad*, 1 (1): 24–53.

Chambers, R.J. and Wolnizer, P.W. (1991) A true-and-fair view of position and results: The historical background, *Accounting, Business & Financial History*, 1 (2): 197–213.

Chow, C.W. (1983) The impacts of accounting regulation on bondholder and shareholder wealth: The case of the Securities Acts, *Accounting Review*, 58 (3): 485–520.

Christensen, H.B., Hail, L. and Leuz, C. (2013) Mandatory IFRS reporting and changes in enforcement, *Journal of Accounting and Economics*, 56 (2-3): 147–77.

Clarke, T. (2004) Cycles of crisis and regulation: The enduring agency and stewardship problems of corporate governance, *Corporate Governance: An International Review*, 12 (2): 153–61.

Cooper, D.J. and Robson, K. (2006) Accounting, professions and regulation: Locating the sites of professionalization, *Accounting, Organizations and Society*, 31 (4/5): 415–44.

Cooper, K. and Deo, H. (2005) Recurring cycle of Australian corporate reforms: A never ending story, *Journal of American Academy of Business*, 7 (2): 156–63.

Cortese, C. (2011) Standardizing oil and gas accounting in the US in the 1970s: Insights from the perspective of regulatory capture, *Accounting History*, 16 (4): 403–21.

Crafts, N.F.R. (1987) Cliometrics, 1971–1986: A survey, *Journal of Applied Econometrics*, 2 (3): 171–92.

Daines, R. and Jones, C.M. (2012) Truth or consequences: Mandatory disclosure and the impact of the 1934 Act, *Stanford Law Review*. Available at: www.law.stanford.edu/publications/truth-or-consequences-mandatory-disclosure-and-the-impact-of-the-1934-act (accessed June 2019).

Davis, J.E. (1999) Corporate disclosure through stock exchanges, working paper, Harvard law. Available HTTP: http://cyber.law.harvard.edu/rfi/papers/disclose.pdf (accessed February 2007).
Dearing, S.R. (1988) *The Making of Accounting Standards* (London: ICAEW).
Djelic, M.L. and Sahlin-Andersson, K. (eds.). (2006) *Transnational Governance: Institutional Dynamics of Regulation* (Cambridge: Cambridge University Press).
Edelman, M. (1964) *The Symbolic Uses of Politics* (London: University of Illinois Press).
Edwards, J.R. (1989) *A History of Financial Accounting* (London: Routledge).
Edwards, J.R. and Chandler, R. (2001) Contextualizing the process of accounting regulation: A study of nineteenth-century British friendly societies, *Abacus*, 37 (2): 188–216.
Ely, K. and Waymire, G. (1999) Accounting standard-setting organizations and earnings relevance: Longitudinal evidence from NYSE common stocks, 1927–93, *Journal of Accounting Research*, 37 (2): 293–317.
Evans, L., Baskerville, R. and Nara, K. (2015) Colliding worlds: Issues relating to language translation in accounting and some lessons from other disciplines, *Abacus*, 51 (1): 1–36.
Ezzamel, M., Xiao, J.Z. and Pan, A. (2007) Political ideology and accounting regulation in China, *Accounting, Organizations and Society*, 32 (7-8): 669–700.
Fligstein, N. and Calder, R. (2015) Architecture of markets, in R. Scott and S. Kosslyn (eds.) *Emerging Trends in the Social and Behavioral Sciences: An Interdisciplinary, Searchable, and Linkable Resource*, pp. 1–14 (New York: John Wiley).
Friend, I. and Westerfield, R. (1975) Required disclosure and the stock market: Comment, *American Economic Review*, 65 (3): 467–72.
Fülbier, R.U. and Klein, M. (2015) Balancing past and present: The impact of accounting internationalisation on German accounting regulations, *Accounting History*, 20 (3): 342–74.
Funnell, W. (1996) Preserving history in accounting: Seeking common ground between 'new' and 'old' accounting history, *Accounting, Auditing & Accountability Journal*, 9 (4): 38–64.
Gaa, J.C. (1991) The expectations game: Regulation of auditors by government and the profession, *Critical Perspectives on Accounting*, 2 (1): 83–107.
Gjerde, Ø., Knivsflå, K. and Sættem, F. (2011) The value relevance of financial reporting in Norway 1965–2004, *Scandinavian Journal of Management*, 27 (1): 113–28.
Godfrey, J.M. and Langfield-Smith, I.A. (2005) Regulatory capture in the globalisation of accounting standards, *Environment and Planning A*, 37 (11): 1975–93.
Gordon, I. and Morris, R.D. (1996) The equity accounting saga in Australia: Cyclical standard setting, *Abacus*, 32 (2): 153–77.
Graham, M. (2002) *Democracy by Disclosure: The Rise of Technopopulism* (Washington: Brookings/Governance Institute).
Hail, L., Tahoun, A. and Wang, C. (2018) Corporate scandals and regulation, *Journal of Accounting Research*, 56 (2): 617–71.
Harrison, G.L. and McKinnon, J.L. (1986) Culture and accounting change: A new perspective on corporate reporting regulation and accounting policy formulation, *Accounting, Organizations and Society*, 11 (3): 233–52.
Hodgson, G.M. (2009) The great crash of 2008 and the reform of economics, *Cambridge Journal of Economics*, 33 (6): 1205–21.
Hopwood, A.G. (1987) The archaeology of accounting systems, *Accounting, Organizations and Society*, 12 (3): 207–34.
Jones, D.G.B., Richardson, A.J. and Shearer, T. (2000) Truth and the evolution of the professions: A comparative study of "truth in advertising" and "true-and-fair" financial statements during the progressive Era in North America, *Journal of Macromarketing*, 20 (6): 23–35.
Jones, S. (1995) A cross-sectional analysis of recommendations for company financial disclosure and auditing by nineteenth-century parliamentary witnesses, *Accounting, Business & Financial History*, 5 (2): 159–86.
Jones, S. and Aiken, M. (1995) British companies legislation and social and political evolution during the nineteenth century, *British Accounting Review*, 27 (1): 61–82.
Jordana, J. and Levi-Faur, D. (2004) The politics of regulation in the age of governance, in J. Jordana and D. Levi-Faur (eds.) *The Politics of Regulation: Institutions and Regulatory Reforms for the Age of Governance*, pp. 1–27 (London: Edward Elgar Publishing).
Jucius, M.J. (1943) Historical development of uniform accounting, *Journal of Business of the University of Chicago*, 16 (4): 219–29.

King, R. and Waymire, G. (1994) Accounting standard-setting institutions and the governance of incomplete contracts, *Journal of Accounting, Auditing and Finance*, 9 (3): 579–605.

Laughlin, R. (1995) Empirical research in Accounting: Alternative approaches and a case for "middle-range" thinking, *Accounting, Auditing & Accountability Journal*, 8 (1): 63–87.

Leach, S.R. and Stamp, E. (eds). (1981) *British Accounting Standards: The First 10 Years* (Cambridge: Woodhead-Faulkner).

Leuz, C. and Wysocki, P.D. (2016) The economics of disclosure and financial reporting regulation: Evidence and suggestions for future research, *Journal of Accounting Research*, 54 (2): 525–622.

Lev, B. and Gu, F. (2016) *The End of Accounting and the Path Forward for Investors and Managers* (Hoboken, NJ:John Wiley & Sons).

Lieberman, E.S. (2001) Causal inference in historical institutional analysis: A specification of periodization strategies, *Comparative Political Studies*, 34 (9): 1011–35.

Loft, A., Humphrey, C. and Turley, S. (2006) In pursuit of global regulation changing governance and accountability structures at the International Federation of Accountants (IFAC), *Accounting, Auditing & Accountability Journal*, 19 (3): 428–51.

Lymer, A. (1999) Internet and the future of reporting in Europe, *European Accounting Review*, 8 (2): 289–301.

Macve, R.H. (2015) Fair value vs conservatism? Aspects of the history of accounting, auditing, business and finance from ancient Mesopotamia to modern China, *British Accounting Review*, 47 (2): 124–41.

Mahoney, P.G. (2001) The political economy of the Securities Act of 1933, *Journal of Legal Studies*, 30 (1): 1–31.

Maltby, J. (1998) UK joint stock companies legislation 1844-1900: Accounting publicity and 'mercantile caution', *Accounting History*, 3 (1): 9–32.

Maltby, J. (2000) The origins of prudence in accounting, *Critical Perspectives on Accounting*, 11 (1): 51–70.

March, J.G. and Olsen, J.P. (1989) *Rediscovering Institutions: The Organizational Basis of Politics* (New York: Free Press).

Martinez-Diaz, L. (2005) Strategic experts and improvising regulators: Explaining the IASC's rise to global influence, 1973-2001, *Business and Politics*, 7: 3. article 3. Available at HTTP: www.cambridge.org/core/journals/business-and-politics/article/strategic-experts-and-improvising-regulators-explaining-the-iascs-rise-to-global-influence-19732001/5DB73FDADA88CCDF093B4CA2C69B9419.

Matten, D. and Moon, J. (2008) "Implicit" and "explicit" CSR: A conceptual framework for a comparative understanding of corporate social responsibility, *Academy of Management Review*, 33 (2): 404–24.

May, A.W. (1939) Financial regulation abroad: The contrasts with American technique, *Journal of Political Economy*, 47 (4): 457–96.

McCraw, T.K. (1982) With consent of the governed: SEC's formative years, *Journal of Policy Analysis and Management*, 1 (3): 346–70.

McQueen, R. (2009) *A Social History of Company Law: Great Britain and the Australian Colonies 1854–1920* (Abingdon: Routledge).

Meier-Schatz, C.J. (1986) Disclosure rules in the U.S., Germany and Switzerland, *American Journal of Comparative Law*, 34 (2): 271–94.

Merino, B., Mayper, A. and Tolleson, T. (2010) Neoliberalism, deregulation and Sarbanes-Oxley: The legitimation of a failed corporate governance model, *Accounting, Auditing & Accountability Journal*, 23 (6): 774–92.

Merino, B.D. and Coe, L.T. (1978) Uniformity in accounting: A historical perspective, *Journal of Accountancy*, 146 (2): 62–69.

Merino, B.D., Koch, B.S. and MacRitchie, K.L. (1987) Historical analysis - A diagnostic tool for 'Events' studies: The impact of the Securities Act of 1933, *Accounting Review*, 62 (4): 748–62.

Merino, B.D. and Mayper, A.G. (2001) Securities legislation and the accounting profession in the 1930s: The rhetoric and reality of the American dream, *Critical Perspectives on Accounting*, 12 (4): 501–25.

Merino, B.D., Mayper, A.G. and Sriram, R.S. (1994) Voluntary audits in New York markets in 1927: A case study, *Journal of Business Finance & Accounting*, 21 (5): 619–42.

Merino, B.D. and Neimark, M.D. (1982) Disclosure regulation and public policy: A socio-historical reappraisal, *Journal of Accounting and Public Policy*, 1 (1): 33–57.

Merton, R. (1968) *Social Theory and Social Structure*, Enlarged (New York: The Free Press).

Mezias, S.J. and Chung, S. (2006) Regulatory capture, interest group theory, and institutional mediation: The regulatory politics of financial reporting rules, 1973–1987. Paper Presented at the First Annual Conference on Institutional Mechanisms for Industry Self-Regulation, Hanover, 24-25 February.

Miller, P., Hopper, T. and Laughlin, R. (1991) The new accounting history: An introduction, *Accounting, Organizations and Society*, 16 (5/6): 395–403.
Mills, P.A. (1990) Agency, auditing and the unregulated environment: Some further historical evidence, *Accounting, Auditing & Accountability Journal*, 3 (1): 54–66.
Mills, P.A. (1993) The courts, accounting evolution and freedom of contract: A comment on the case law research, *Accounting, Organizations and Society*, 18 (7/8): 765–81.
Mills, P.A. (1994) The adjudication of accounting-based compensation contracts in the pre-1934 period, *Accounting, Business & Financial History*, 4 (3): 385–402.
Miranti, P.J. (1989) The mind's eye of reform: The ICC's bureau of statistics and accounts and a vision of regulation, 1887-1940, *Business History Review*, 63 (3): 469–509.
Moran, M. and Previts, G.J. (1984) The SEC and the profession, 1934-84: The realities of self-regulation, *Journal of Accountancy*, 158 (1): 68–80.
Mueller, G.G. (1965) International experience with uniform accounting, *Law and Contemporary Problems*, 30 (4): 850–73.
Napier, C.W. (2001) Accounting history and accounting progress, *Accounting History*, 6 (2): 7–31.
Nobes, C. (2014) The development of national and transnational regulation on the scope of consolidation. *Accounting, Auditing & Accountability Journal*, 27 (6): 995–1025.
Nobes, C.W. (1991) Cycles in UK standard setting, *Accounting and Business Research*, 21 (83): 265–74.
Nobes, C.W. (1992) A political history of goodwill in the U.K.: An illustration of cyclical standard setting, *Abacus*, 28 (2): 142–67.
Nobes, C.W. and Parker, R. (2016) *Comparative International Accounting*, 13th (Harlow: Pearson Education).
North, D.C. (1990) *Institutions, Institutional Change, and Economic Performance* (Cambridge: Cambridge University Press).
North, D.C. (1997) Cliometrics-40 years later, *American Economic Review*, 87 (2): 412–14.
O'Dell, J.H. (2015) FASB and private company financial reporting: A story of institutional change, *Research in Accounting Regulation*, 1 (27): 88–95.
Okcabol, F. and Tinker, T. (1993) Dismantling financial disclosure regulations: Testing the stigler-benston hypothesis, *Accounting, Auditing & Accountability Journal*, 6 (1): 10–36.
Parker, R.H. (1990) Regulating British corporate financial reporting in the late nineteenth century, *Accounting, Business & Financial History*, 1 (1): 51–71.
Peltzman, S. (1976) Toward a more general theory of regulation, *Journal of Law and Economics*, 19 (2): 211–40.
PHAC. (2007) Glossary of terms. Available HTTP: www.canada.ca/en/public-health/services/public-health-practice/skills-online/glossary-terms.html (accessed 2 November 2007).
Puxty, A.G., Willmott, H., Cooper, D. and Lowe, T. (1987) Modes of regulation in advanced capitalism. Locating accountancy in four countries, *Accounting, Organizations and Society*, 12 (3): 273–92.
Richard, J. (2005) The concept of fair value in French and German accounting regulations from 1673 to 1914 and its consequences for the interpretation of the stages of development of capitalist accounting, *Critical Perspectives on Accounting*, 16 (6): 825–50.
Richardson, A.J. (1989) Corporatism and intraprofessional hegemony: A study of regulation and internal social order, *Accounting, Organizations and Society*, 14 (5/6): 415–31.
Richardson, A.J. (2006) Auditor switching and the great depression, *Accounting Historians Journal*, 33 (2): 39–62.
Richardson, A.J. (2009) Regulatory networks for accounting and auditing standards: A social network analysis of Canadian and international standard-setting, *Accounting, Organizations and Society*, 34 (5): 571–88.
Richardson, A.J. and Eberlein, B. (2011) Legitimating transnational standard-setting: The case of the international accounting standards board, *Journal of Business Ethics*, 98 (2): 217–45.
Richardson, A.J. and MacDonald, L.D. (2002) Linking international business theory to accounting history: Implications of the international evolution of the state and firm for accounting history research, *Accounting and Business Research*, 32 (2): 67–78.
Robson, K. (1991) On the arenas of accounting change: The process of translation, *Accounting, Organizations and Society*, 16 (5/6): 547–70.
Robson, K. (1992) Accounting numbers as inscription: Action at a distance and the development of accounting, *Accounting, Organizations and Society*, 17 (7): 685–708.
Rutherford, B.A. (2007) *Financial Reporting in UK: A History of the Accounting Standards Committee, 1969-1990* (London: Routledge).

Saemann, G. (1999) An examination of comment letters filed in the U.S. financial accounting standard-setting process by institutional interest groups, *Abacus*, 35 (1): 1–28.

Schmitter, P.C. and Lehmbruch, G. (eds). (1979) *Trends Toward Corporatist Intermediation* (London: Sage).

Schoenfeld, H.-M.W. (1981) International accounting: Development, issues, and future directions, *Journal of International Business Studies*, 12 (2): 83–100.

SEC (Securities and Exchange Commission) (1977) Report of the advisory committee on corporate disclosure to the securities and exchange commission, Committee Print 95-29, House Committee on Interstate and Foreign Commerce, 95th Cong., 1st sess., 3 November.

Seligman, J. (1983) The historical need for a mandatory corporate disclosure system, *Journal of Corporate Law*, 9 (1): 10–34.

Shepard, G.B. (1996) Fierce compromise: The Administrative Procedure Act emerges from New Deal politics, *Northwestern University Law Review*, 90 (4): 1557–683.

Simon, C.J. (1989) The effect of the 1933 Securities Act on investor information and the performance of new issues, *American Economic Review*, 79 (3): 295–318.

Sivakumar, K. and Waymire, G. (2003) Enforceable accounting rules and income measurement by early 20th century railroads, *Journal of Accounting Research*, 41 (2): 397–432.

Skerratt, L. and Whittington, G. (1992) Does the nobes cycle exist, and if so, what does it signify? *Accounting and Business Research*, 22 (86): 173–77.

Stigler, G.J. (1971) Theory of economic regulation, *Bell Journal of Economics and Management Science*, 2 (1): 3–21.

Street, D.L. and Shaughnessy, K.A. (1998) The evolution of the G4 + 1 and its impact on international harmonization of accounting standards, *Journal of International Accounting, Auditing and Taxation*, 7 (2): 131–61.

Styhre, A. (2018) Reforming corporate governance through new Accounting standards: The case of fair value accounting, *Academy of Management Proceedings*, 2018 (1): 102–53.

Sunder, S. (2016) Better financial reporting: Meanings and means, *Journal of Accounting and Public Policy*, 35 (3): 211–23.

Taylor, P. and Turley, S. (1986) *The Regulation of Accounting* (London: Blackwell).

Troshani, I., Locke, J. and Rowbottom, N. (2019) Transformation of accounting through digital standardisation: Tracing the construction of the IFRS taxonomy, *Accounting, Auditing & Accountability Journal*, 32 (1): 133–62.

Vogel, D. (1986) *National Styles of Regulation* (Ithaca: Cornell University Press).

Walker, R.G. (1987) Australia's ASRB. A case study of political activity and regulatory 'capture', *Accounting and Business Research*, 17 (67): 269–86.

Walker, R.G. and Mack, J. (1998) The influence of regulation on the publication of consolidated statements, *Abacus*, 34 (1): 48–74.

Walker, S.P. (1996) Laissez faire, collectivism and companies legislation in nineteenth-century Britain, *British Accounting Review*, 28 (4): 305–24.

Walker, S.P. (2000) Editorial, *Accounting History*, 5 (2): 5–12.

Walker, S.P. (2016) Revisiting the roles of accounting in society, *Accounting, Organizations and Society*, 49: 41–50.

Walton, P.J. (1986) The export of British accounting legislation to commonwealth countries, *Accounting and Business Research*, 16 (64): 353–57.

Walton, P.J. (1995) *European Financial Reporting: A History* (London: Academic Press).

Waymire, G. and Basu, S. (2011) Economic crisis and accounting evolution, *Accounting and Business Research*, 41 (3): 207–32.

Whittred, G. (1986) The evolution of consolidated financial reporting in Australia, *Abacus*, 22 (2): 103–20.

Williamson, O.E. (1985) *The Economic Institutions of Capitalism* (New York: The Free Press).

Woolley, J.T. and Peters, G. (2007) *The American presidency project*. Available at HTTP: www.presidency.ucsb.edu (accessed 2 November 2007).

Young, J. (1994) Outlining regulatory space: Agenda issues and the FASB, *Accounting, Organizations and Society*, 19 (1): 83–109.

Zeff, S.A. (1972) *Forging Accounting Principles in Five Countries: A History and an Analysis of Trends* (Champaign Ill: Stipes Publishing Company).

Zeff, S.A. (2006) Political lobbying on accounting standards - national and international experience, in C.W. Nobes and R. Parker (eds.) *Comparative International Accounting*, 9th edn, pp. 189–220 (London: Prentice Hall).

PART V

Economy

15
AGRICULTURE

Lisa Jack

Overview

Agricultural accounting history has to be pieced together from within the accounting discipline and from across a number of other disciplines. There is no defined group of historians who look at agricultural accounting, neither are there any books chronicling the history of accounting for agriculture over the millennia. Histories appear in economic history, farm management, rural sociology and food studies, accounting and, just occasionally, finance. Agriculture appears within other histories of accounting, and accounting appears in national histories of agriculture. Farms, as Giraudeau (2017: 211) sees it, are 'accounting laboratories' where:

> Agricultural accounting … stands at the intersection between multiple histories: the history of inscriptions; the history of capitalism; the history of science; the history of government and the history of business. At this intersection, accounting techniques of all sorts … have constantly crystallised and been manipulated, in diverse ways, by countless actors.

From there, Giraudeau (2017) pieces together the fragments of accounting history across thought lines but this overview of accounting in agriculture takes a more straightforward approach. Agricultural accounting practice is not 'one thing'. Like any other businesses, all areas of accounting are relevant and there are perhaps unexpected influences from agriculture on accounting practice in other areas of commerce and public accounting, such as fair value accounting for assets. For some, agricultural accounting is the forerunner of modern commercial management accounting practices (for example, Zell 1979; Scorgie 1997; Mussari and Magliacani 2007).

The history of farm accounts and record keeping emerges through two sources. First, there are the artefacts from farms and the histories that can be reconstructed through them. Second, there are numerous treatises in many languages over 2,000 years that provide normative advice on how to keep farm records, and polemics on the benefits of doing so for the farmer and for society. Model farm accounts include the many preprinted record keeping books for farmers, modern versions of which are still sold in hard copy or found as spreadsheets and other computer applications. The question of how farming can be profitable for the individual farm and the nation underpins both the historical narratives derived from farm records and the rationale for the mass of essentially educational materials. In many ways, this is a history of the giving of well-intentioned advice.

The limits of this review are that it largely excludes the accounting for agriculture included in the books of estates and larger manors, as this is discussed in Chapter 3 of the *Companion*. Similarly, discussions about the nature of capitalism and agriculture are kept brief as this overlaps with Chapter 17 on capitalism. Agricultural accounting in ancient times is covered in Chapter 4. There is little on the use that economic historians have made of farm accounting records, as the aim is to introduce readers to what can be claimed as agricultural accounting history. Deliberately, I have concentrated on the more modest landowning farmers and tenant farmers, the family farms that make up the majority of agricultural production over the last 600 years. There is also a limitation in that most of the literature in the English language relates to North America, Western Europe and Australasia. Exceptions are an overview of agricultural accounting by Doğan et al. (2013) that contains a brief account of Turkish agricultural accounting treatises from the late nineteenth century and Ji (2003) on ancient treatises in China.

The first section examines the artefacts that are available and the different types of case study that have been constructed from archival sources. The second section looks at studies concerning how farmers use – or are told how they ought to use – management accounting and control in their farm businesses over the centuries. These two areas cover most of the accounting history in agriculture available to us. The final section outlines all the missing areas and shows that the agricultural accounting history has opportunities to become a more comprehensive body of work.

Farm records as historical sources

Agricultural and social historians have used farm records for two purposes. The first is to try to construct aggregate economic histories through patterns of production, wealth and technological change (Rothenberg 1984; Turner et al. 1996). The second is to construct social histories of individual farm businesses and families in the context of social, political and technological change. Within the accounting discipline, there is a third purpose, which is to construct critical accounting narratives around capitalism, labour, power and the motives behind government initiatives to promote particular forms of farm accounting. Before reviewing each of these in turn, there are a few papers across disciplines that talk about the value of the artefacts in themselves to historians.

Rothenberg (1984) discusses the problems and possibilities in using farm account books. Economic historians have drawn heavily on probate inventories and other documents such as wills, to reconstruct economic trends in agriculture before 1700. However, as she points out, inventories are 'but the still life of an enterprise … Allocation, production, exchange, and distribution cannot be observed as unfolding in time, but only as the (perhaps inadvertent) consequences of interrupted processes' (ibid.: 106–7). They also take no account of hired, borrowed, shared or gifted labour and equipment in running the farm.

Finding actual day books, cashbooks and other records allows the researcher to enter into the day-to-day life of the farm, the transactions, prices paid and received and a whole mass of other detail. The economic historian might struggle in their attempts to find evidence of the interplay with markets and to establish trends. Rothenberg (1984) is particularly frustrated that her eighteenth-century Massachusetts farmers seem so little concerned with outputs, inputs and yields. Turner et al. (1996) try to find a way to bridge the gap between 1700 when the probate records become scarce, and the more plentiful farm account books from around 1790. They find some records and conclude that, for the economic historian, there is a possibility of carrying out productivity studies and also to assess the introduction of investment in new practices.

Accounting historians have different priorities. The concern is more with the systems of accounting used, their purposes and what external factors might explain the changes in how and why the books are kept. As social records, farm accounts can be fascinating – even simply in the who and what sense of historical investigation. Surviving farm records in archival collections range, as Jones and Collins (1965) show for the UK, from scribblings on scraps of paper to beautifully written, bound ledgers kept meticulously. Almanacs were often used to make notes in the eighteenth century, but from the mid-nineteenth century preprinted cashbooks begin to be evident. Jones and Collins (1965: 86–7) explain that:

> Farm record books vary considerably in their form and function. Most usual is the day book which records incoming and outgoing cash transactions although, particularly in the earlier period, there may be little real distinction between business, household and personal items. There are ledgers listing transactions by individual debtors and creditors, or receipts and expenditure entered in separate volumes, or books which distinguish rigidly between arable and livestock enterprises. Some record books concerned themselves with labour matters, cropping, yields, sheep, improvements or valuations, but more usually this sort of information was incorporated into the general account book.

Turning to the US, Rothenberg (1984: 109) enthuses:

> Massachusetts account books between 1750 and 1850 virtually recapitulate in their great variety six centuries of accounting and bookkeeping history, from the most primitive type of tally to full-fledged double entry bookkeeping with profit and loss accounting such as was not widely used even in industry until after the industrial revolution.

The changing pattern of accounting material is similar elsewhere. Carnegie (1993) shows transitions through memoranda to single-entry then to double-entry bookkeeping in Australia in the course of the nineteenth century. He links this to expanding education and the interest of professional accountants in pastoral stations as clients. Farm records were also subject early on in the 1960s to mass benchmarking and to computerisation (Jack 2005, 2009, 2015).

Given the number of farms, there is a relatively low number of surviving artefacts and it is only recently that farm records have been more carefully preserved in business and social archives. The creator of a list of the account books and diaries available at the Baker Library speculates 'that countless papers, manuscripts, and record books of importance to the economics and history of agriculture are stored away in unfrequented closets' (Harvard 1935: 60). From these records business historians and economists could be provided:

> [w]ith information on the trend of the rural standards of living, the influence of the competition of the various agricultural sections, the shifts and variations in crop acre- ages and livestock production, and the changes in systems of farm management … Much can also be found on yields, disease epidemics, and the dates of the introduction of new varieties and breeds, and new cultural practices.
>
> *(ibid.: 60)*

Jones and Collins (1965) make a plea for the collection and preservation of records. In the UK, the Museum of Rural Life (MERL) at the University of Reading has one of the largest archives and steps are now being taken to make this material available online. Others are found in local and national records offices and museums. The University of Guelph has a Rural Diary Archive and as Joly (2011) shows in her study of diaries (or agenda) in France, these record the everyday farming and social activities of farmers from the peasant and middle-classes rather than the nobility. Other collections that have been publicised include the Hocken Collection in Otago, New Zealand (Farquhar 2005).

From the existing archives, it is possible to see not only a wide variety in the type of records that survive but also in the people who kept those records. Jones and Collins (1965) identify four groups in Britain. There are the records of 'home farms' on estates, which were often model, hobby or training farms supplying the household, and the records tend to reflect the notion of how to run an efficient enterprise. Bailiffs accounts are short term, representing when the bailiff had to rescue a failing farm (as we would say nowadays) on behalf of a landlord. There is a potential history project here to examine these two types of record in context. More representative of farming practice are the records of 'larger owner occupiers and lesser gentry' (ibid.: 86) able to employ stewards and a large number of workers who had time to keep records and capital available from other sources to invest in improvements. Henry Best (Norcliffe 1857), discussed below, is one example of this type of gentleman farmer. The largest but least documented (or least curated in 1965) group comprises the 'farmers, tenants (and less often owner-occupiers) who largely relied on the profits of their holdings for their income' (Jones and Collins 1965: 86).

Hidden in these latter lists are many women. Miley and Read (2016) show how Lady Lisle was involved in the estate record keeping and correspondence with debtors on Lisle family manorial estates in dangerous political times (1533–40). There are very few other accounts of women being involved until the publication of findings by Walker (2014, 2015) and Jack (2004). Growing education for poorer, illiterate farm families from the mid-nineteenth century in Europe, North America and Australia often centred on farm record keeping as both a means and an end for encouraging reading, writing and arithmetic (see Carnegie 1993; Joly 2011; Walker 2014).

Case studies in farm accounting history

Historical case studies exist in which the account books, probate books, memoranda and diaries are simply presented together with a historical background as context for their creation. Zell (1979) presents one of the few surviving sets of accounts from the sixteenth century where the records are from a small- or medium-sized farm rather than an estate. The records for this farm from 1558 to 1560 probably survived because they featured in a rather salacious case brought before the Chancery courts involving allegations of inheritance fraud by a widowed mother and her new husband against the son from her first marriage. The accounts are used to both show the fact that the farm was doing well, but not as well as previously – yields and animal numbers were decreasing. Inventory valuations and lists of receipts and payments reveal both the extent of the manor and the range of its activities. The farm was returned to the boy and a court-appointed guardian.

Other studies deploy a historiography that uses the records to ask questions about how successful or otherwise farming was at certain times and places. These fall somewhere between being economic or accounting history. Zell cites Hoskins' (1963) *The Leicestershire Farmer in the Sixteenth Century* as an example, while Rothenberg (1984) on Massachusetts farmers also falls into this category. Another more recent example of this approach is a thesis by Heaton (2015), which is a detailed account of farming in the Midlands of England between 1919 and 1939 based on 35 sets of farm records. This provides a wealth of insight into the pressures farmers faced in a time of depression. However, the question that has stood since the time of Xenephon Oeconomia in 345 BC still stands – why is one farmer successful and another not? Accounting and good management techniques are only part of the answer despite the promotion both in textbooks, treatises and government interventions.

Most other studies by accounting academics that make use of farm books are critical-interpretative studies where 'An understanding of accounting in its local, time-specific contexts is dependent upon an exploration of the underlying environmental influences in order to provide probable explanations for the structure and usage of the accounting information examined' (Carnegie 1993: 9).

The earliest attempts to put accounting into its social and organisational context, where accounting is viewed not as a technique in itself but as one element of that context, are Carnegie's (1993, 1995) studies of pastoral farms in Victoria, Australia in the nineteenth century. Carnegie (1993) analyses the accounting and other farm records from the Jamieson station. These show that the initial records are a mix of farm, family and community information rather than any particular form of system. The station was the centre of a micro-community consisting of sometimes over 100 people including servants, station hands and boundary riders as well as itinerant shearers. By the end of the century, the books are kept using double-entry bookkeeping and formal sets of accounts are prepared. The culture of the community influenced the need to keep some form of record of people, stocks of animals and crops, transactions and events throughout, and especially to keep good workers in the community. From the 1890s, influences:

> [i]nclude the transfer of knowledge acquired at school by Robert Jamieson the younger, the impact of taxation legislation, the availability of specialist accounting skills in the region and the rapid economic development in the Colony together with the impact of a depression in the early 1890s.
>
> *(ibid.: 217)*

An extended version of this analysis is presented using data from other farms in Carnegie (1995). Around the 1890s, the promotion of double-entry bookkeeping in farms became promoted by professional accountancy practices, with immigrant accountants realising that their main client base would be mines and farms, particularly the large pastoral stations such as the Jamiesons. Carnegie et al. (2006) show how one pioneering Australian textbook, Vigars' *Station Accounting*, first published in 1900, promoted double-entry bookkeeping and facilitated the involvement of professional accountants in the industry. In the 1960s, Mallyon's *Principles and Practice of Farm Management Accounting* (1966) was an attempt to get professional accountants to offer value added services to farmers and to engage farmers in accounting for decision-making (Malcolm 1990; Jack 2015). Mallyon had an accounting practice in New South Wales for which most of his clients were in agriculture and also engaged with the academic farm management and economics community (Jack 2015). Although there are many textbooks across the world on farm accounting, the closest relationship between the accountancy profession and the development of accounting practices in the industry appear to be found in Australia and New Zealand. This provides the potential for a comparative project to test this notion across countries (Carnegie and Napier 2002).

Other critical-interpretative accounting researchers have drawn on social theory to understand the relevance of farm accounting in a wider political context. Another paper focusing on Australian agricultural history uses accounting data as just one source to reconstruct the historical biography or micro-history of George Best, who was transported from England to New South Wales in the early nineteenth century. He had been a farmer in England but the farm had failed and he turned eventually to burglary. He married a woman also transported for life and together they became sheep farmers, landowners and eventually respected members of the community. Bisman (2007) shows that the accounting records help to prove his worth as, first, an exemplary rehabilitated convict who should be given a chance, then as a successful farmer and trader, as an employer of other convict labour and as one whose performance was in line with the bourgeois hegemony encouraged in Australia by the English government:

> Best owned the means of production – important pastoral interests critical to the development of the colony, amassed the necessary capital to continue expansion of his interests, favoured the market economy, and had a ready supply of cheap labour (convict and free) to exploit in the pursuit of wealth and profit.
>
> *(ibid.: 11)*

Bisman tries out a number of social theories to help explain observed phenomena, including Marxian analysis (as is clear from the quote) to demonstrate how Best grasped and promoted a *laissez-faire* economy, using accounts and numbers to demonstrate how he had used the capital he amassed to make not only a profitable return on that capital but also a return on the social capital invested in him. Moreover, he fully embraced the use of convict labour and the social position that he gained to help establish a privileged capitalist class in the new colony. Using Foucault's notion of knowledge as power, Bisman also explains how accounting helped to elevate the Bests' and their children's roles in New South Wales.

Mussari and Magliacani (2007) reconstruct the financial affairs of the Rucellai Farm in Campi, Italy, in the nineteenth and early twentieth centuries based on books found in an antiques market and other sources about the family estates that they then searched out. The estate was leased out on a share-cropping arrangement which was common in Tuscany at the time and they examine the 'Pratello' Farm, which comprised part of the estate, in detail. They employ a diachronic technique to place the technical accounting in a precise moment in history, the period following the unification of Italy in 1870. They note that a number of the records used follow a format recommended by De Granges, a French writer whose 1857 treatise on agricultural accounting appears to have been influential in Italy. A number of detailed records, mainly using single-entry bookkeeping, demonstrate that rudimentary tools of cost accounting are used to assess the profit of each crop and the effectiveness of new systems of cultivation. In Britain, this form of management control became termed 'enterprise costing' (Jack 2005). Mussari and Magliacani (2007) is important for the extent to which they take each record and show how it is part of the time and place in which it is found. They attempt a light analysis to show how there is evidence of management control emerging in the nineteenth century, but this is less robust than the social and organisational contextual analysis that they provide.

In contrast, the work of Rob Bryer is important for providing a detailed and very careful analysis of how accounting can be used for a specific theoretical purpose. Bryer (2006: 369) states:

> [t]o explain the agricultural revolution, we must reconstruct the calculative mentalities of farmers, by analysing how they kept and used their accounts. It uses accounting ideas to define the capitalist mentality, and to explain Marx's theory of the agricultural revolution.

His papers (Bryer 1994, 2000a, 2000b) also provide a comprehensive historical record of the sources we have available to study agricultural accounting from the fifteenth century and illuminate how accounting historians such as Yamey used these same agricultural records to demonstrate the development of accounting practices in general in Britain.

Bryer looks at Marx's theory of transition from a feudal to a capitalist mentality (but not the next transition from a capitalist to a socialist one). There are scholars (for example, Zell 1979) who have argued that the application of double-entry bookkeeping is sufficient to show that farmers and merchants had a capitalist mentality. Bryer argues, however, that whereas double-entry bookkeeping is found in the sixteenth century, the accounting signature in agrarian-based records shows that rather than a return on capital, accounts demonstrate a feudal surplus rather than profit until well into the mid-seventeenth century. Elsewhere, he points out that 'In Marx's theory the commercial revolution culminates in the mid-seventeenth century bourgeois revolution in which the rate of return mentality overthrows the feudal surplus mentality' (2000b: 342). He puts forward a strong case that for agriculture, this mentality is not firmly evident until the nineteenth century. Oldroyd (2007), Depecker and Joly (2015) and others have argued that landowners who previously relied on the income from agriculture invested during the industrial revolution in the late eighteenth and early nineteenth centuries in mining, railways and other activities firmly bearing a capitalist imprint and that this then carried back into agriculture. Certainly, there is evidence that in the nineteenth century, some tenants and land-owning farmers demonstrate a more fluid discourse around investment in improving the land and their returns, as the treatise by Prout (1881), discussed later, shows.

There are disagreements with Bryer's interpretation of how accounting demonstrates the subsumption of agriculture into capitalism. Toms (2010) argues that the rationale of return on capital employed is linked more to the mentality of economic decision-makers than to accounting technique. The accounting signatures of profitability come later in the nineteenth and early twentieth centuries. I would also argue that it is not so sharply defined in agriculture. Talking to farmers, even in the early twenty-first century, reveals that few have a clear-cut capitalist mentality. Stewardship and survival tend to predominate over a profit-maximising, return on capital approach. The relationship of agriculture with markets and capital is more complex than might be expected despite the many economic historical and archival studies of production and wealth in farming. Beginning in the twentieth century, however, governments in many developed countries did encourage the use of accounting to make farming more business-like and productive for the good of the whole nation. Several critical historical case studies have been written about these schemes in Britain, the US and Italy.

Critical-interpretative case studies in agricultural accounting

More recent papers use social theory to assess these movements by governments in the twentieth century to make farmers more business-like, productive and independent. Jack (2005, 2006, 2007)) investigates how promises to deliver profitability in the UK Agriculture Act of 1947 led to the setting up of the National Agricultural Advisory Service (NAAS). Farm Management Liaison officers were appointed, and systems of farm recording and benchmarking were developed which could be used with and by small- and medium-sized farms with the help of these officials. Paper systems being cumbersome, computerised techniques were developed and, alongside this change, a method of management accounting known as 'gross margin accounting' was established and described as in 'almost universal' use by Nix (1979: 284), one of the leading writers in Britain on farm management.

Although an economics-based technique for establishing the optimal mix of enterprises on a farm, an unintended consequence was that gross margin accounting became institutionalised as a simplified form of comparative analysis and benchmarking. Jack (2005) uses structuration theory to show how the institution persists (it remains the basis of negotiation over farm gate prices and support payments some 60 years later) despite potentially harmful effects from its use – for example, few farms are mixed and overhead costs now exceed variable costs in most farm activities. Jack (2005) draws on notions of signification in Giddens (1985) to understand how rules and routines became a national structured behaviour. To complete the picture, the work of Stones (2005) on strong structuration theory is also used to examine the legitimation gross margin accounting gave to farm advisers and to consultants (Jack 2007), and the extent to which the practices enable the domination of corporate supply chain partners and constrain farmers' ability to act to achieve promised increased farm incomes (Jack 2009).

Gross margin accounting became widespread in Australia, introduced via the second edition of an influential textbook, Mallyon's (1966) *Principles and Practice of Farm Management Accounting*. Mallyon had discovered the technique through the work of Tony Giles, one of the Farm Management Liaison officers involved in the NAAS discussed by Jack (2005), published by the Ministry of Agriculture, Food and Fisheries in 1961. It became part of a government sponsored project to introduce standardised and computerised management accounting practices in Australia. The attempt, encapsulated in a book entitled *Accounting and Planning for Farm Management*, also known as 'The Blue Book' (QDPI 1971) is explored by Jack (2015) and interpreted using concepts of future time based on the work of the sociologist Barbara Adam. The management accounting schemes and computer programs were functional but the story of the future based on them failed to materialise, as more malleable and commercial comparative accounting practices took over the space that they were meant to occupy. As Bátiz-Lazo et al. (2014: 104) observe:

> [b]y discounting this general fascination with the future, historians may fail to appreciate the extent to which organizational adoption of technology, and particularly information technology, was based as much on imagined futures as it was on existing realities.

Critical-accounting researchers have also drawn on Marx, Foucault and Giddens to discuss structural change, institutionalisation and government agency. Walker (2015) examines US government initiatives to attach a requirement for smaller farmers to develop farm recording and planning as a condition for receiving 'supervised credit'. The underlying message was support for, and retention of, the American ideal of the family-owned farm as the heart of national identity. Analysing images used by government to publicise the desirability and success of the programme, Walker (2015: 1679) demonstrates that 'the photographs portray accounting as a technology for strengthening the economic foundations of the family farm'. Also, 'Accounting was often the subject-focus of these attempts to better integrate local farm families in the socio-political fabric and infuse a communitarian spirit' (ibid.: 1702). The photographs emphasise the companiate couple of the farmer and his wife as being together in planning the future of the farm, and their children as part of the process when the liaison officer came to coach the family in better farming, household and accounting techniques. They also show sociable gatherings where farmers could share successes and problems with other farmers, and work as a community alongside the officers, literally a picture of the productive rural industry and living that would provide sustenance for all America.

A companion paper (Walker 2014) uses Foucault and Gidden's social theory to investigate the use of power by the US government to achieve a New Deal for farmers following the Great Depression. In many ways, the initiative was successful. There were farms which received financial aid that became more effective and provided an income for the family. Women were brought more into farm management as they became part of farm planning and record keeping. Afro-American farmers in the South became more established and better supported. Literacy in rural areas increased as a result. The criticism of the government's intention to make farmers more governable lies in making credit and accounting government supervised and conditional activities.

Governmentality is also used by Sargiacomo et al. (2016) to analyse the influence of agricultural economist Arrigo Serpieri on Italian rural economic policy under Mussolini in the mid-twentieth century. The Serpieri laws governing the type of accounting and reporting systems that should be used, from government statistics down to farm cost-benefit analyses, are technologies of government to optimise the reclamation and productivity of land, the income from taxes and the overall welfare of peoples. Accounting was entwined in a discourse from which the overall power of the nation and its leaders is built on effective agriculture, industry and education. The importance of these last papers is that they evaluate the links between agricultural policy with day-to-day accounting practices, and the discourse of farming as a commercial enterprise that involves social capital as well as financial capital in shaping at least the rhetoric of what it means to be a nation state.

The purposes of farm records and accounting books

In Britain and the US, farm accounting is typically carried out (and still taught) as single-entry bookkeeping in a more or less extended cashbook, with debtors and creditors identified at the year end. There are examples of charge and discharge accounting up to the nineteenth century, particularly in the account books of landed estates (Edwards 2011), and some examples of complete double-entry bookkeeping from then on. Financial statements are relatively rare until the late nineteenth and twentieth centuries when governments began to introduce taxes on farm incomes. Adrian Bell (1930: 110), who learned farming as a profession in the 1920s, said that there is nothing as intricate as farm accounting. He was exaggerating for effect, but a mixed farm does create issues when you wish to examine the financial health of each enterprise on the farm rather than just the state of the bank balance or income tax obligations. An enterprise in this context means an individual crop or animal-based activity such as fattening cattle for beef, and there are internal transfers between the enterprises (e.g. feed, manure, young animals) as well as shared costs and overheads. In the twentieth century, a further form of recording was developed in the UK called 'enterprise accounting' in which the variable costs were assigned to headings, a gross margin calculated for each enterprise and then aggregated across the farm. Fixed costs were then deducted as a whole sum from the gross margin to calculate a net margin (Jack 2005).

How many farmers actually keep detailed management accounts for such purposes? Ball (1918: 153) states the following:

> No one knows better than the practical farmer that there is nothing of the cure-all in the keeping of accounts on the farm. The practice will not of itself turn a poor farm into a rich one, a poor farmer into a good one, or losses into profits. Farm records, if accurately kept and intelligently utilized, are an aid to a better understanding and insight into one's business affairs, and are worthwhile in exact proportion to the accuracy and completeness of their recording and the pertinence of the use that is made of them. These are facts well known to thousands of farmers who keep accurate accounts and make good use of them.

But writers since Xenephon in the fourth century BC have known exactly what the limitations are on that usefulness. In *Oeconomicus*, the narrator Critobulus comments that:

> [f]or my part I agree with all you [Socrates] say; only, one must face the fact that in agriculture nine matters out of ten are beyond man's calculation. Since at one-time hailstones and another frost, at another drought or a deluge of rain, or mildew, or other pest, will obliterate all the fair creations and designs of men; or behold, his fleecy flocks most fairly nurtured, then comes murrain, and the end most foul destruction.
>
> *(Xenephon 1890)*

The idea that record keeping and accounting will improve farm efficiency and performance persists – one recent example is Dervishi and Dervishi's (2017) application of the notion to contemporary vineyard production in Albania. There is a long history attached to persuading farmers to adopt innovations, including accounting, through treatises, textbooks, extension programmes and college education (see Williams 1968; Jack 2005, 2015). The main drift of all these approaches is to get farmers to analyse costs and profits and adopt better working practices to increase (or at least, make more secure) their income. In other words, the accounting innovations are primarily about management accounting in the form of cost accounting, budgeting and comparative analysis. However, it often took changes in tax law for farmers to even begin to keep books of account (Wyllie 1953).

Farming as profit-making

That farming should be profit-making and create a surplus goes back a long way with Xenephon, writing in the fourth century BC, drawing attention to the fact that armies, governments and other trades require farmers to feed more than themselves and their families (Xenephon 1890). Furthermore, as Karayiannis (2003) puts it: 'Xenophon, moreover, recognized that the entrepreneurial role in searching and exploiting the various profit opportunities could be exercised in agriculture as well'. There are further examples from the sixth century AD, and then from the fourteenth to the seventeenth century. Ji (2003: 69) demonstrates that, judging from the content of seventeenth-century Chinese agricultural treatises, 'it is clear that cost and management accounting concepts did exist in premodern China and were applied to agricultural production'. The earliest mentions of profit in farming are found in a text by Fan Sheng Zhi in the first century BC. Merchants and landlords had internal accounting structures in place by then and Ji argues that the same mentalities can be found in two key treatises from the seventeenth century. Essentially, the treatises contain many cost-benefit analyses of investing in different agricultural enterprises as a means of persuading farmers to adopt better agricultural methods. Although the possibility of a farmer ever making a decent and fair profit may have been challenged by Nix (1990), farm accounting as management control for better decisions and profit-making is still the main purpose in its promotion.

Rothenberg (1984: 110) uses the term 'accounting tools' to signify the transition 'from using accounting to control debt to using accounting to inform and direct the profitmaking activities of the enterprise'. She bases this observation of the books of Charles Phelps, in 1829, where she claims that there is a demonstration of a capitalist mindset in farming. The discussion between Bryer (2000a, 2000b) and Toms (2010) referred to above shows that these claims need to be approached cautiously, but the link between capitalism and the use of management accounting techniques is often easily (if perhaps a little carelessly) made by several authors.

In the next section, the review of management control practices in Britain follows a more or less chronological order without particularly getting involved in the accounting signatures of capitalism debate.

Early examples of management control in Britain

There are two types of paper or monograph in this area. There are biographies or micro-histories, and then more general overviews. Historians have produced biographies of the principal treatise writers and in one book I found in a second-hand bookshop, there is an intriguing autobiography of farming success presented through accounting (Prout 1881). The question, of course, is how representative they are of how farm accounting was done rather than how the writers thought it should be done.

John Freear's biographic account – *Robert Loder, Jacobean Management Accountant* – draws on a set of accounts dated 1610–20, an edited edition of which was published in 1936 by George Fussell, a well-known agricultural historian. The originals are held in Berkshire County Records office. Freear (1970: 25) points out that the accounts have been used extensively as a source for information about farm life in the seventeenth century and to provide illustrations of the early use of accounting techniques and concepts. Loder is praised for his application of what we would now term 'opportunity costing', for example. However, Freear also attempts to demonstrate 'that Loder made use of decision-making concepts and an information system which did not become officially recognized (i.e., in the governmental agricultural advisory services) as best practice until the 1960s'. He also claims that 'In this sense his techniques are superior to those contained in much nineteenth- and twentieth-century accounting literature' (ibid.: 25–6).

Loder's position as a small farm owner is a useful counter to a somewhat hazy perception that farmers (at least in the past) are either wealthy landowners, serfs or subsistence farmers. It takes us away from estate accounting to the middle range farmers as modest landowners or as tenants, whose activities are directly linked into the provision and trade in food and drink for larger, often urban, markets/populations. The other aim of this kind of study is to make it clear that farm accounting is complex, interesting and innovative. As an aside, the case of Robert Loder's farm in Berkshire shows that these are businesses that have lasted for centuries – a quick Internet search shows that Prince's Manor Farm still operates in 2018. The current owners are descendants of buyers in the early nineteenth century. 'Not losing the family farm and heritage' is the main reason I have been given in more contemporary studies of the industry for farmers engaging very seriously in management accounting.

Fussell (1936: x) wanted to show that:

> Loder's object in farming was to make his living from his estate. He wanted as large a financial return for his expenditure of capital, managerial work and manual work as he could get, and he did his utmost to obtain it.
>
> *(ibid.: xxiii)*

For Freear (1970) the key contribution by Loder to thinking in agricultural accounting was the development of enterprise costing and gross margin accounting. As noted above, this remained in fashion in the UK in the 1970s being promoted by government and consultants (see Jack 2005). Freear shows that the use Loder made of numbers demonstrates a decision-making process and management control based on clear objectives, opportunity cost and avoidable/unavoidable costs. Bryer (2000b), however, is cautious about classifying Loder, Henry Best and others as early capitalists, citing Zell (1979) as overstating the case. While such farmers exhibit some of the signatures of a calculative mentality that might be seen as concerned with a return on capital employed and a possible exploitation of labour, their notion of profit is more of a feudal surplus based on cash and inventory, as Bryer observes.

McLean (2009) examines the farm books of Henry Best of Yorkshire who left a comprehensive treatise for his son, written in 1642 and published by his descendant, Norcliffe (1857), distilling a lifetime's experience of managing labour and understanding the performance needed to achieve a profit. His memorandum book, like those reported in Joly (2011), Carnegie (1995) and the diaries in the University of Guelph archive are a mix of business, social and family details. On one page Best offers his advice on mowing (done by seasonal workers): 'Those that take corne to mowe by the acre are allsoe tyed to lye it [in] band, but not to bind and stooke it … they usually have 2*s* 6*d* per acre' (Norcliffe 1857: 114). On the next, the locations, nature and cost of board and lodgings of 'moore-folkes' (seasonal workers) and on the next 'concerninge our fashions att our country weddings' (ibid.: 115–16). There is also guidance on fields, crops, tasks based on a detailed understanding of the costs incurred and the time and effort required by the task in hand. This attention to human performance on the farm does not seem to have become widespread in Britain and, even in the 1950s, Wyllie (1953: 14) comments that not many farmers assess the cost of labour and when they do, the usual term 'man hours' might not reflect the many hours on the farm put in by women and children. However, Fleischman et al. (2004) and Oldroyd et al. (2008) show that disturbingly, on plantations in the West Indies and elsewhere, human performance was calculated to assess the value and price of slave labour, implicating accounting in the embedding of racism.

Like Freear (1970), McLean (2009) presents a biographical micro-history of Henry Best to illustrate how management control in the form of human performance measurement and management, evolved and had its precursors in agriculture. He shows that:

> The Farming Book incorporates a detailed plan of action and associated control mechanisms for the agricultural year: it explains when and how to raise and sell animals, crops, and agricultural products, let property, assess tax liabilities, deal with local communities, and it sets out detailed information on labour management. It is clear that Best operated in a developing market economy and understood the nature of market forces and their impact on costs and prices as he sought to find ways to manage his farm to the best advantage.
>
> *(McLean 2009: 64)*

There is probably still a wealth of case studies like those of Loder and Best waiting to be written. However, the most influential writer was Arthur Young, ironically a failed farmer, who turned to what we would now call travel and business writing, producing a prolific number of books that popularised new practices in farming during the English Agricultural Revolution in the early nineteenth century (Bryer 2000a). Juchau (2002) gives a detailed biographical sketch of Young and evaluates his considerable contribution to cost accounting in agriculture. In particular, Young recognised the problems of allocating overheads and shared costs between enterprises on mixed farms and devised a method of allocation so that 'the division was proportionate to the absorption of the expense' (ibid.: 376). He also advocated a form of exit-value accounting for assets at the year end.

Cost accounting in agriculture did not become as sophisticated or widespread as in manufacturing during the industrial revolution, but Young's importance is his influence on later thinkers rather than on contemporary farming practices. Juchau and Hill (1998) show that Young's work on costing influenced three economists – Daniel Hall, Charles Orwin and James Wyllie – from Wye College (now part of Imperial College London) in the period 1890–1950. Between them they developed full cost of production models and worked further on the problems of cost allocation in farming. Wyllie (1953), sensing that full costs of production models were not going to work effectively on the farm, laid the basis for the enterprise costing model that became established following the 1947 Agricultural Act in the UK (Jack 2005). What Young and 'the three men from Wye' (Juchau and Hill 1998; Juchau 2002) brought was the sense of the farm as a commercial business which required accounting innovation alongside scientific innovation, which has been the tension in farmer education and extension work throughout the twentieth century (Williams 1968).

Although Orwin and his colleagues were dismayed by the lack of cost accounting in Britain in the nineteenth and twentieth centuries, there is evidence that some farms were competent businesses and that farmers did keep detailed accounting records. Prout (1881) authored a short treatise which sets out to prove the value of his scientific method based on the use of artificial fertilisers for cultivating notoriously difficult London clay on the Hertfordshire-Essex border. Prout (1881: 8) uses accounting throughout the narrative to show that despite increasing imports from the British Empire he is 'confident that, in the present and prospective low markets, my system can still earn an adequate return for tenant's capital, and at the same time afford a satisfactory rent for the owner'. Prout's other purpose in writing his treatise was to show that the law was unfair because, in the event of his giving up the tenancy, the capital he had invested would not be recompensed and the landlord would benefit in terms of being able to charge a higher rent on the improved land from the next tenant.

Agricultural extension, farm management and benchmarking

Williams (1968: 6) defines agricultural extension as 'that part of the activities of State governments which provides farmers with technical advice' to enable them to improve their technical operations and economic decision-making. In the nineteenth century, farm accounting moved from being the subject of individual treatises and tracts on model farming (though new books containing formats and models for farm accounts are being published even today) to its promotion by government agents as a necessary activity for farmers. As Lampe and Sharp (2017) show, the model accounts of Arthur Young and the work of economists such as Aereboe (Hinrichs 1929) led to a desire to establish cost of production on farms. From there, the desire was to establish the economic contribution of agriculture to the nation and improve the economic efficiency of farming.

Agricultural education, as a way of improving the management of farms and thus the income of farmers (and following the introduction of taxation in farming, the national income), became more fully established along with the rise of public education (for example, Carnegie 1993; Joly 2011). In the US, the establishment of land-grant colleges and the development of extension services were specifically designed to make farmers use more scientific and economic methods of production (Williams 1968). Rogers (1995: 357) claims that the agricultural extension model is 'a set of assumptions, principles and organizational structures for diffusing the results of agricultural research to farmers in the United States ... [the US Department of Agriculture is] reported to be the world's most successful change agency'.

Increasing levels of taxation on farm incomes and the introduction of sales taxes affecting farm inputs and outputs required British farmers to produce or pay for financial statements for submission to the state along with their tax returns. Prior to 1941, farmers were taxed on land or on moveable property (Lymer and Oates 2015: 8, 12), and Wyllie (1953: 4–5) describes the shock when they were required, from that year onwards, to pay income tax:

> It is not suggested that farmers should not pay their fair share of the national taxation; merely that in so doing they were compelled to undertake a task which few of them had ever undertaken before – to keep systematic accounts of their yearly financial transactions.

In New Zealand, I was told by more than one interviewee that the imposition of a goods sales tax in the 1980s without any exemptions for farming (which is an unusual policy) led to all farmers keeping cashbooks, making the life of accountants and advisers much easier.

Various combinations at different times and places of cost of production economics, extensionism and financial reporting for taxation led to the conclusion at national level that farmers should be encouraged to keep accounts. Those accounts should be pooled into regional or national databases that could then be used to produce statistical analyses and 'yardsticks' against which farmers could measure their performance relative to other farmers, and governments could assess the efficiency and effectiveness of the agricultural industry. By the mid-twentieth century, agricultural economics had divided down two lines – there were economists who were using the data for production studies and those who used the data to advise farmers on the best modes of managing the farm. The latter coalesced into a new discipline, farm management, in the 1960s (Nix 1979). The benchmarking and comparative analysis techniques that were developed originally by economists in the field were adopted and commercialised by practising accountants and consultants hoping to offer management accounting alongside their financial and taxation services to farmers (Jack 2007).

There are few case studies based on individual twentieth-century farms, but the history of farm benchmarking has been constructed (for a more complete overview, see Jack 2009, chapter 2). Hinrichs (1929) provided one of the first historical accounts of how farm benchmarking evolved in Europe. He explains how in c.1898, Professor Ernst Laur, an economic adviser with the Swiss Department of Agriculture, wanted to extend the work of Freidrich Aereboe, a German economist widely regarded as a great innovator in farm practice. Aereboe and other economists had developed ways of calculating cost of production. Initially, a small group of farmers attended bookkeeping classes and were paid to maintain their books for one year. They then had to contribute their accounts to a pool kept by the Secretariat and the statistical analysis was published in an annual report. The government-sponsored programme had 487 single-entry systems and five double-entry systems by 1927, with between 8 and 20 people at the Secretariat processing the data. The annual statements were then used as the basis of statistical analyses. Laur insisted that 'agricultural economics could render no greater service to agriculture than actually to determine the true cost of production' and that the scheme allowed:

(a) A determination of Swiss agricultural incomes and their changes under the influences of natural and economic factors;
(b) Solutions to numerous farm management problems;
(c) A supply of statistical materials to farmers and agricultural schools for educational purposes;
(d) Evidence supporting demands for agricultural legislation;
(e) A dependable basis for land valuation, rental and inheritance purposes.

(Hinrichs 1929: 651)

Lampe and Sharp (2017) tell a similar story for the development of agricultural economists (in this case Albrecht Daniel Thaer in Germany and Carl Frederik Gyllembourg in Denmark, who both sought to establish systematic accounting practices among farmers to enable inter-farm comparative analysis. They hoped to uncover natural and market cost relations (ibid.: 92) and embed a more rational approach to agriculture. Their legacy is in the benchmarking systems still in use in both countries (Jack 2009; Pederson and Møllenberg 2015).

In the US, from around 1890, G.F. Warren (a prolific writer on farm management in the early twentieth century) surveyed orchards in Western New York using a statistical approach and published 'The income of 178 New York Farms' in 1909. This was the start of benchmarking in the US. S.W. Warren (1945: 19), who wrote a history of the survey method in the US, explains that the ethos behind the early surveys was that 'every farm is an experimental station and every farmer a director thereof'. The survey method was also seen as a means of gathering information from illiterate or semi-literate farmers: 'It means getting data by personal visits to farmers. A farmer may be able to answer questions from memory or from his records or both' (ibid.: 20). By the 1940s, there were over 40 surveys being conducted nationwide in the US. Inspired by G.F. Warren's early work, surveys were also conducted in Britain from the mid-1920s. Wyllie of Wye Agricultural College reported his first survey findings in 1925, and in 1934 the Agricultural Economics Research Institute in Oxford established the National Milk Costs Investigation Scheme (Juchau and Hill 1998). The University of Cambridge set up the Cambridge Food Recording Scheme in 1936, which later became the basis for the Farm Management Survey (now Farm Business Survey) in 1936.

S.M. Warren (1945: 23) summarises the problems that arose, however, in using farm data for mass participation benchmarking:

> Our big need for the future is to obtain groups of farm management records which are homogeneous, not only as to soil, climate, topography and markets, but also as to the education of the operator, acreage of the farm, and some other important factors. If we can eliminate these major factors by the sampling process we can then go ahead to study some of the minor factors affecting farmers' incomes.

Wyllie (1953) also made the case for standardised terms and benchmarks (or rather 'yardsticks') drawing upon tables of measures taken from his survey data over the period 1923–50 to demonstrate how management by farmers is changing and is differentiated. Like Prout (1881) it is an example where the accounting numbers become a clear part of the narrative, not just an illustration. Wyllie (1953: 55) concludes: 'there is far, greater scope for highly efficient management to-day than there was fifty years ago, and it is for this reason that the differences between good and bad management are much greater than they used to be', and that:

> [t]here are many small-scale farmers, working under difficult environmental conditions, who find it quite impossible to save all the capital they would like to have for development purposes, who never get the opportunity of showing the capacity for management which is latent in them.

For the pioneers of farm accounting in the seventeenth and eighteenth centuries (Loder, Best and Young, for example) the concern was to get farmers to understand the costs of running a farm and how to understand when one enterprise or another was profitable and worth pursuing. From the nineteenth century, farm accounting became the concern of agricultural economists and then farm management specialists (Malcolm 1990), and although some professional accountants promoted double-entry bookkeeping over single-entry or charge and discharge accounting (Carnegie 1995; Edwards 2011), it probably still holds that:

> Farm cost accounting has been developed as a method of economic research rather than as a matter of exact financial accounting. It is the result of efforts on the part of agricultural scientists and economists to assist farmers in establishing a method of analysing and improving the production and business management of their farms. It is the fruit of agricultural research rather than of business accounting.
>
> *(Boss 1930: 936)*

Missing histories

Agricultural accounting history has two narrative strands derived from archive-based case studies or micro-histories; explanations for the growth of management control and accounting; and more recent critical-interpretative studies that place, within social and political contexts, drives to make farmers more business-like through agricultural accounting. If there is a re-emergence of research at the interface of accounting and agriculture as Sargiacomo et al. (2016) claim, then there are many gaps to be filled.

There are few studies that explore accounting by farmers outside the written artefacts available, yet by its nature farming requires calculation, counting and an appreciation of time over seasons that may be outside the regulating effects of accounting and tax dates. Tallies and other evidence of calculative mentalities need to be investigated besides those from ancient cultures (see Chapter 4 of the *Companion*). Many other artefacts in non-Western cultures must exist that have not yet been fully explored. We know women have acted as bookkeepers and financial planners on farms as spouses, secretaries and, in fact, farmers. Women appear in several studies, such as Jack (2009), Joly (2011), Walker (2014, 2015) and Miley and Read (2016), but there are no feminist histories of women, accounting and agriculture. Similarly, Walker (2014) discusses the inclusion of Afro-American farmers as part of the New Deal accounting initiatives but there are no micro-histories of accounting on their farms. To my knowledge, there are no histories of indigenous peoples' use of accounting in their agricultural activities, whether traditional or as the result of colonial pressures that move hunter-gatherers into ranching or farming.

There are substantial gaps in the narratives. The emergence of the farm as a taxable entity and the need for financial reporting has not been examined except by Wyllie (1953) and Hooks and Stewart (2011) who look at the use of standard value accounting for livestock in the tax treatment of farmers in New Zealand. Sumner (2007) studies the impact of government support for agriculture in the US but, again, there is little or nothing on the historical connections between subsidisation of farming and accounting. Similarly, there is one single monograph on the links between agricultural finance and farm management, which relates mainly to the US (Barry and Stanton 2003). The relationships between the accounting profession, farmers and accounting techniques have been explored by Carnegie (1993, 1995) and Jack (2007, 2015) but this is based largely in one geographical location, Australia. There is a predominate interest in management accounting on farms, and the indicators of capitalism found within these activities, but agriculture as an industry requires all forms of accounting to be used. There is also room for an historical discussion on financial and food fraud in agriculture.

In a similar way, International Financial Reporting Standard 41 *Agriculture* (2000), which sets out fair value accounting for agricultural assets, has a longer history than that of the development of the standard. Both Australia and Canada had standards in progress when the discussions were going on inside the International Accounting Standards Board. Hooks and Stewart (2011) overlap this topic with their discussion of standard values and taxation. Juchau and Hill (2000) review the positions of four professional agencies between 1985 and 1999, just prior to the publication of the exposure draft for an international standard of accounting on agriculture. This analyses the policies proposed but not the history behind the discussions that led to the various proposals. There is therefore ample scope for more work on the relationship between agricultural accounting and policy at professional and national level.

Agricultural evaluators for inventory and bequests have been around for many centuries with Prout (1881) reproducing his farm valuation report in full. The basis of those valuations has not really been explored nor the impact that they have on accounting practice for inheritance, legal and taxation purposes. Again, attempts in the late twentieth century to set standards for farm accounting have not yet been fully explored, although the Farm Financial Standards Council in the US has attempted to achieve some cohesion over agricultural accounting practices, as has the New Zealand Society of Accountants (Juchau and Hill 2000, preface).

There are many biographies and micro-/meso-histories to be uncovered in the archives. There is also a rich stream of literature, largely autobiographical or semi-autobiographical, that could provide insight into the use of accounting and calculative mentalities in everyday farming life. Examples include Norcliffe (1857), Bell (1930), Street (1932) and Ingalls Wilder (1971). It would be interesting to know if there are more autobiographical treatises like that of Prout (1881) where accounting is used to tell the history of the farm and its improvements. What is also missing is any history of corporate farming. We need to know more about the role of farming in the growth of corporate farming in post-soviet Eastern Europe and Russia, and in socialist China, for example.

There are many other gaps in comparative accounting history (Carnegie and Napier 2002) for agriculture. Gross margin accounting can be found in Argentina and given that South America is a formidable part of the global food economy, there is a lack of writing (at least in English) about accounting from South American countries. While Alawattage and Wickramasinghe (2009) have provided case studies of plantation management in Sri Lanka that have some historical context, there is room for more historical accounts of planation management over time to sit alongside the work of Fleischman et al. (2004) and Oldroyd et al. (2008) on the valuation of slaves as assets and how accountants became complicit in institutionalised racism.

Finally, agriculture tends to be researched as if it is a separate, rather than integral, activity in the food supply chain. Economic historians look at the interplay of productivity, markets and incomes, but there is a need for the historical societal links between farms and their downstream customers, markets and consumers to be examined using accounting records. Developed countries have societies that now expect cheap food and abundant choice from a global market. Accounting has played a role in achieving this, and in making farming an ever more precarious industry, challenging the notion throughout history that good accounting can only make farming more secure and profitable. The historical and contemporary study of accounting in food and farming is still largely an open but vital field for researchers.

Key works

Bryer (2000b) provides an overview of the agricultural treatises and records available in his analysis of the transition from feudal to capitalist mentalities in nineteenth-century British agriculture.

Carnegie (1993) and Jack (2005) contain case studies in agricultural accounting practice that renewed accounting scholars' interests in farm accounting history through interpretative narratives.

Giraudeau (2017) provides an important guide to recent work on farm accounting.

Joly (2011) supplies another exemplary narrative on how farmers kept records and the role of education in improving farm accounting.

References

Alawattage, C. and Wickramasinghe, D. (2009) Weapons of the weak: subalterns' emancipatory accounting in Ceylon Tea, *Accounting, Auditing & Accountability Journal*, 22 (3): 379–404.

Ball, J.S. (1918) Value of records to the farmer, in: *The Yearbook of the Department of Agriculture*, pp. 153–68 (Washington, DC: US Department of Agriculture).

Barry, J. and Stanton, B.F. (2003) *Major Ideas in the History of Agricultural Finance and Farm Management* (Ithaca, NY: Department of Applied Economics and Management, Cornell University).

Bátiz-Lazo, B., Haigh, T. and Stearns, D.L. (2014) How the future shaped the past: the case of the cashless society, *Enterprise and Society*, 15 (1): 103–31.

Bell, A. (1930) *Corduroy* (London: Faber & Faber).

Bisman, J. (2007) Accounting concepts in the construction of social status and privilege: a microhistorical study of an early Australian convict, *Australasian Accounting, Business and Finance Journal*, 1 (4): 1–15.

Boss, A. (1930) Farm cost accounting in the USA, *Proceedings of the Second International Conference of Agricultural Economists held at Cornell University, Ithaca, New York*. Available HTTP: <https://econpapers.repec.org/paper/agsiaae30/209156.htm>.

Bryer, R.A. (1994) Accounting for the social relations of feudalism, *Accounting and Business Research*, 24 (95): 209–28.

Bryer, R.A. (2000a) The history of accounting and the transition to capitalism in England. Part one: theory, *Accounting, Organizations and Society*, 25 (2): 131–62.

Bryer, R.A. (2000b) The history of accounting and the transition to capitalism in England. Part two: evidence, *Accounting, Organizations and Society*, 25 (4–5): 327–81.

Bryer, R.A. (2006) The genesis of the capitalist farmer: towards a Marxist accounting history of the origins of the English agricultural revolution, *Critical Perspectives on Accounting*, 17 (4): 367–97.

Carnegie, G.D. (1993) Pastoral accounting in pre-federation Victoria: a case study on the Jamieson family, *Accounting and Business Research*, 23 (91): 204–18.

Carnegie, G.D. (1995) *Pastoral Accounting in Colonial Australia: A Case Study of Unregulated Accounting* (Abingdon: Routledge).

Carnegie, G.D., Foreman, P. and West, B.P. (2006) F.E. Vigars' *Station Book-Keeping*: a specialist Australian text enabling the adaptation and transfer of accounting technology, *Accounting Historians Journal*, 33 (2): 103–30.

Carnegie, G.D. and Napier, C.J. (2002) Exploring comparative international accounting history, *Accounting, Auditing & Accountability Journal*, 15 (5): 689–718.

Depecker, T. and Joly, N. (2015) Agronomists and accounting. The beginnings of capitalist rationalisation on the farm (1800–1850), *Historia Agraria: Revista De Agricultura E Historia Rural*, 65: 75–94.

Dervishi, S. and Dervishi, B. (2017) The evaluation of farm's economic effectiveness through the improvement of bookkeeping methods, *Albanian Journal of Agricultural Sciences*, Supplement: 413–19.

Doğan, Z., Arslan, S. and Köksal, A.G. (2013) Historical development of agricultural accounting and difficulties encountered in the implementation of agricultural accounting, *International Journal of Food and Agricultural Economics, Alanya*, 1 (2): 107–15.

Edwards, J.R. (2011) Accounting on English landed estates during the agricultural revolution – a textbook perspective, *Accounting Historians Journal*, 38 (2): 1–45.

Farquhar, I. (2005) Business series 1: farming, *Friends of the Hocken Collections Bulletin Number 50: July*. Available HTTP: <www.otago.ac.nz/library/pdf/hoc_fr_bulletins/Bull_50_Farming.pdf>.

Fleischman, R.K., Oldroyd, D. and Tyson, T.N. (2004) Monetising human life: slave valuations on US and British West Indian plantations, *Accounting History*, 9 (2): 35–62.

Freear, J. (1970) Robert Loder, Jacobean management accountant, *Abacus*, 6 (1): 25–38.

Fussell, G.E. (1936) *Robert Loder's Farm Accounts, 1610–1620* (London: Royal Historical Society of Great Britain).

Giddens, A. (1985) *The Constitution of Society* (Cambridge: Polity Press).

Giraudeau, M. (2017) The farm as an accounting laboratory: an essay on the history of accounting and agriculture, *Accounting History Review*, 27 (2): 201–15.

Harvard (1935) Agricultural records in the Baker Library, *Bulletin of the Business Historical Society*, 9 (4): 60–63. Available HTTP: <?macro tpmkset "webaddress1","Description","","*<www.jstor.org<www.jstor.org/stable/3111246>.

Heaton, M.W. (2015) *English Interwar Farming: A Study of the Financial Outcomes of Individual Farms, 1919–1939*, Unpublished thesis, University of Leicester.

Hinrichs, A.F. (1929) Swiss studies in farm accounting, *Journal of Farm Economics*, 11 (4): 648–51.

Hooks, J. and Stewart, R.E. (2011) Farmers, politics and accounting: The history of standard values, *Accounting Historians Journal*, 38 (2): 47–74.

Hoskins, W.G. (1963) The Leicestershire farmer in the seventeenth century, in W.G. Hoskins *Provincial England: Essays in Social and Economic History*, pp. 149–69 (London: Palgrave Macmillan).

Ingalls Wilder, L. (1971) *The First Four Years* (New York: Harper & Row).

Jack, L. (2004) *The Persistence of Post-war Accounting Practices in UK Agriculture* Unpublished thesis, University of Essex.

Jack, L. (2005) Stocks of knowledge, simplification and unintended consequences: the persistence of post-war accounting practices in UK agriculture, *Management Accounting Research*, 16 (1): 59–79.

Jack, L. (2006) Protecting agricultural accounting in the UK, *Accounting Forum*, 30 (3): 227–43.

Jack, L. (2007) Accounting, post-productivism and corporate power in the UK food and agriculture industry, *Critical Perspectives in Accounting*, 18 (8): 905–31.

Jack, L. (2009) *Benchmarking for Food and Farming: Creating Sustainable Change* (Aldershot: Ashgate).

Jack, L. (2015) Future making in farm management accounting: The Australian 'Blue Book', *Accounting History*, 20 (2): 158–82.

Ji, X.-D. (2003) Concepts of cost and profit in Chinese agricultural treatises: with special reference to Shengshi Nongshu and Pu Nongshu in the seventeenth century, *Accounting, Business & Financial History*, 13 (1): 69–81.

Joly, N. (2011) Shaping records on the farm: agricultural record keeping in France from the nineteenth century to the Liberation, *Agricultural History Review*, 59 (I): 61–80.

Jones, E.L. and Collins, E.J.T. (1965) The collection and analysis of farm record books, *Journal of the Society of Archivists*, 3 (2): 86–89.

Juchau, R. (2002) Early cost accounting ideas in agriculture: the contributions of Arthur Young, *Accounting, Business & Financial History*, 12 (3): 369–86.

Juchau, R. and Hill, P. (1998) Agricultural cost accounting development in Britain: The contributions of three men from Wye – a review note, *Accounting, Business & Financial History*, 8 (2): 165–74.

Juchau, R. and Hill, P. (2000) *Agricultural Accounting: Perspectives and Issues*, 2nd edn (Wye: University of London, Wye College).

Karayiannis, A.D. (2003) Entrepreneurial functions and characteristics in a proto-capitalist economy: the *Xenophonian entrepreneur, Wirtschaftspolitische Blätter*, 50 (4): 553–63.

Lampe, M. and Sharp, P. (2017) A quest for useful knowledge: The early development of agricultural accounting in Denmark and Northern Germany, *Accounting History Review*, 27 (1): 73–99.

Lymer, A. and Oates, L. (2015) *Taxation Policy and Practice*, 22nd edn (Birmingham: Fiscal Publications).

Malcolm, L.R. (1990) Fifty years of farm management in Australia: survey and review, *Review of Marketing and Agricultural Economics*, 58 (1): 24–55.

Mallyon, C.A. (1966) *Principles and Practice of Farm Management Accounting*, 2nd edn (Sydney: Law Book Co.).

McLean, T. (2009) The measurement and management of human performance in seventeenth century English farming: The case of Henry Best, *Accounting Forum*, 33 (1): 62–73.

Miley, F.M. and Read, A.F. (2016) Spies, debt and the well-spent penny: accounting and the Lisle agricultural estates 1533–1540, *Accounting History Review*, 26 (2): 83–105.

Mussari, R. and Magliacani, M. (2007) Agricultural accounting in the nineteenth and early twentieth centuries: the case of the Noble Rucellai family farm in Campi, *Accounting, Business & Financial History*, 17 (1): 87–103.

Nix, J. (1979) Farm management: the state of the art (or science), *Journal of Agricultural Economics*, 30 (3): 277–92.

Nix, J.S. (1990) Aspects of farm profitability: an outmoded concept? Presidential address, *Journal of Agricultural Economics*, 41 (3): 265–91.

Norcliffe, C.B. (1857) *Rural Economy in Yorkshire in 1641, Being the Farming and Account Books of Henry Best, of Elmswell, in the East Riding of the County of York, by Best, Henry, Died 1645* (London: Whitaker & Co.). Available HTTP: <https://archive.org/details/ruraleconomyinyo00bestrich/page/120>.

Oldroyd, D. (2007) *Estates, Enterprises and Investment at the Dawn of the Industrial Revolution: Estate Management and Accounting in the North-East of England, C.1700–1780* (Aldershot: Ashgate).

Oldroyd, D., Fleischman, R.K. and Tyson, T.N. (2008) The culpability of accounting practice in promoting slavery in the British Empire and antebellum United States, *Critical Perspectives on Accounting*, 19 (5): 764–84.

Pederson, H.B. and Møllenberg, S. (2015) *Agriculture and Danish Farm Returns through 100 Years 1916–2015* (Copenhagen: Statistics Denmark).

Prout, J. (1881) *Profitable Clay Farming under a Just System of Tenant Right* (London: Edward Stanford).

QDPI (1971) *Accounting and Planning for Farm Management ('The Blue Book')*, 2nd edn (Brisbane: QDPI).

Rogers, E.M. (1995) *Diffusion of Innovations*, 4th edn (New York: Free Press).

Rothenberg, W.B. (1984) Farm account books: problems and possibilities, *Agricultural History*, 58 (2): 106–12.

Sargiacomo, M., Ianni, L., D'Andreamatteo, A. and D'Amico, L. (2016) Accounting and the government of the agricultural economy: Arrigo Serpieri and the Reclamation Consortia, *Accounting History Review*, 26 (3): 307–31.

Scorgie, M.E. (1997) Progenitors of modern management accounting concepts and mensurations in pre-industrial England, *Accounting, Business & Financial History*, 7 (1): 31–59.

Stones, R. (2005) *Structuration Theory* (London: Palgrave).

Street, A.G. (1932) *Farmer's Glory* (London: Faber & Faber).

Sumner, D. (2007) *Farm Subsidy Tradition and Modern Agricultural realities, Paper Prepared for the American Enterprise Project on Agricultural Policy for the 2007 Farm Bill and Beyond* (Davis: University of California).

Toms, J.S. (2010) Calculating profit: a historical perspective on the development of capitalism, *Accounting, Organizations and Society*, 35 (2): 205–21.

Turner, M.E., Beckett, J.V. and Afton, B. (1996) Taking stock: farmers, farm records, and agricultural output in England, 1700–1850, *Agricultural History Review*, 44 (1): 21–34.

Vigars, F.E. (1900) *Station Book-keeping. A Treatise on Double Entry Book-keeping for Pastoralists*, 1st edn (Sydney: William Brooks).

Walker, S.P. (2014) Accounting and rural rehabilitation in New Deal America, *Accounting, Organizations and Society*, 39 (3): 208–35.

Walker, S.P. (2015) Accounting and preserving the American way of life, *Contemporary Accounting Research*, 32 (4): 1676–713.

Warren, S.W. (1945) Forty years of farm management surveys, *Journal of Farm Economics*, 27 (1): 18–23.

Williams, D.B. (1968) *Agricultural Extension: Farm Extension Services in australia, Britain and the United States* (London: Cambridge University Press).

Wyllie, J. (1953) *Researches in Farm Management, 1923–1950* (Wye: University of London Wye College).

Xenephon (1890) *The Economist*, translated by H.G. Dakyns. Available HTTP: <?macro tpmkset "webad dress3","Description","","★<www.gutenberg.org<www.gutenberg.org/files/1173/1173-h/1173-h .html>.

Zell, M. (1979) Accounts of a sheep and corn farm, 1558–60, *Agricultural History Review*, 27 (2): 122–28.

16
MERCANTILISM

Cheryl Susan McWatters

Overview

Mercantilism, in various guises, weaves itself through the fabric of accounting historiography. Rarely the central thread, it generally remains hidden under the surface of wider debates that have long captured the attention of accounting researchers. We need only look to the preoccupation in the accounting history literature with the development of double-entry bookkeeping and the emergence of capitalism.[1]

As a concept, mercantilism is controversial in terms of legitimacy, relevance and applicability. Claims of historicism feature with some prominence. In more recent historiography, mercantilism has become of renewed interest, particularly its translation across boundaries of space and time. We also see its reintroduction within current debates on globalisation, empire, political theory and government policy (Pettigrew 2013; Stern and Wennerlind 2013; Padgen 2015; Rhoden 2015; Gervais and McWatters 2017). The adoption of novel approaches and new questionings within other branches of history suggest room to reflect upon our own historiography. Doing so would contribute to fostering transdisciplinary approaches into the interface of accounting and mercantilism.

We begin the chapter with an elaboration of mercantilism and its interpretation as a historical concept. We then provide an overview of some recent work into mercantilism, particularly the translation of the concept across time and geography, followed by a short overview to ground and illustrate mercantilism in practice. Next, we examine a small selection of studies in accounting history where mercantilism appears more directly. We conclude with suggested research directions to re-examine the mercantilism–accounting interface.

What do we mean by mercantilism?[2]

Mercantilism has been debated and disputed for hundreds of years. Difficulties in analysing it begin with the opaqueness of the concept. For some economic theorists and historians, mercantilism did not exist at all. Rather it came into being retrospectively to provide a bridge to (or to demonstrate the superiority of) present-day economic theory and theoretical models. Recent literature has refocused debate by accepting that mercantilism cannot be grounded in one place and period but must be framed in terms of time and geography (Reinert 2011; Stern and Wennerlind 2013; Magnusson 2015). Heckscher's *Mercantilism* (1935/1994) demonstrates that while definitions of mercantilism prove elusive, it is possible to outline its characteristics. In his view (ibid.: 20), mercantilism is a unitary system of economic policy implemented variously at different points in time:

> Mercantilism never existed in the sense that Colbert or Cromwell existed. It is only an instrumental concept which, if aptly chosen, should enable us to understand a particular historical period more clearly than we otherwise might. Thus everybody must be free to give the term mercantilism the meaning and more particularly the scope that best harmonize with the special tasks he assigns himself. To this degree there can be no question of the right or wrong use of the word, but only of its greater or less appropriateness … the following exposition constitutes a return to the original meaning of the word-not in place of, but in addition to, the meaning that recent historians have wanted to give it.
>
> What mercantilism should be taken to stand for in this book may be stated in a few words: it is a phase in the history of economic policy.

Heckscher (1935/1994: 35–43) develops his interpretation and analysis of mercantilism by charting its course from the breakdown of universalism in the Middle Ages (due to the onset of particularism) – a breakdown fostered by many factors both social (including secularisation and the Reformation) and economic – to the rise of the nation-state. He underscores that the mercantilist system must be contextualised with respect to how it played itself out in various places at various times, primarily in Europe, politically, socially and economically. Moreover, Heckscher analyses mercantilism as ultimately a 'failed project' resurrected and 'saved' in the nineteenth century thanks to two conceptions which he terms 'revolution' and 'liberalism'. While arguing that revolutionary principles developed most clearly and quickly in France (see ibid.: 467–72), and borrowed in some fashion across the European Continent, it was England that first 'put its house in order' in terms of changing its institutions, championing and introducing new social ideals and conditions that were translated across geographic boundaries. France might have been the 'classic country' of formal revolution, yet England achieved more in that 'it created the *substance* of the new economic policy' – the policy of liberalism (ibid.: 468, 469). With its twin elements of *laissez-faire* and individualism, the victory of liberalism led to the dismissal of mercantilism – a shift from *raison d'état* and state intervention to political and economic policy grounded in individualism and unfettered markets.[3]

Heckscher remains a classic treatment of mercantilism, yet his arguments were challenged at the time and continue to be debated. Much of the criticism reflects wider discussions of historicism and theoretical arguments within economics and economic history. Magnusson (1994a), in an Introduction to the 1994 edition of Heckscher's book, provides a retrospective on how the work of Heckscher, along with that of other theorists and economic historians, cannot be disentangled from the context of the time, in that differences were not simply differences of opinion and interpretation but also differences of orthodoxy. Fay (1934) outlines a similar view in his analysis of the defeat of the mercantilist doctrine.

Operationalising mercantilism

In his Introduction to Heckscher (1935/1994), Magnusson offers a synthesis of the key elements of mercantilism à la Heckscher. This summary provides us with boundaries to operationalise the concept:

- a system of unification – a centralised regulatory space within nation-states;
- a system of power – policies to strengthen state power;
- a system of protection – a socio-psychological attitude presented as 'a fear of goods' rooted in the autarky of the medieval age;
- a monetary system – economic development incorporated wide circulation of money, yet money not equated with wealth; and lastly
- a conception of society – individual welfare giving sway to the regulatory state.

While Heckscher attempts to find common ground with Adam Smith and economic historicism, it never, according to Magnusson, crosses the divide of the invisible hand of the market. (Magnusson 1994a: xxxiv; see also Magnusson, 1994b: 32–6). He contends that many of the questions posed by Heckscher remain unanswered and argues for renewed efforts to examine them. Magnusson (1994b) takes up his own call in *Mercantilism: The Shaping of an Economic Language.* We briefly examine this volume to further our understanding of mercantilism.

Translating mercantilism across time and space

Magnusson's *Mercantilism* provides a rich synthesis of the literature and its history. Unlike Heckscher (and something for which Magnusson has been criticised), he restricts his focus to the seventeenth and eighteenth centuries.[4] His volume attempts to restore Heckscher and counter the 'relentless criticism'. With a nod to R.H. Tawney, Magnusson opens with the comment that:

> [m]ercantilism, like capitalism and feudalism, is one of those 'isms' that refuses stubbornly to die out. The reason for this is simple: mercantilism will not disappear merely by eschewing the word. The word is still useful in understanding the intellectual and political environment of the seventeenth and eighteenth centuries – so why not use it?
>
> *(Magnusson 1994b: vii)*

Magnusson sets out to treat mercantilism as discourse and to demonstrate that mercantilism and liberalism were not opposites, a view championed since the era of Adam Smith. He argues that mercantilism was part of the 'real world' via texts, books, tracts and pamphlets. Its discourse emerged within a national context – in his view, English – yet also travelled to be part of the discursive practices in other contexts. This emphasis on discourse potentially has much to offer accounting.[5]

This discourse travelled across political, cultural and institutional contexts. In the early seventeenth century, one sees the emergence of several principles that signalled a change in thinking within mercantilism about the most effective means to enhance state power and national economic wealth. Notwithstanding differences across time and space, several precepts emerge:

- increased recognition of the importance of the market mechanism;
- the economy perceived as a system operating in a law-like and predictable fashion;
- market processes linked together variables such as prices, wages, interest rates, monetary value and exchange rates;
- the economic realm regarded as independent from state and politics; and
- economic insights gained by practice and empirical evidence.

While debates have centred on mercantilism 'either as a folly or as a rationale for the state interest, only overcome by the enlightenment and Adam Smith', Magnusson argues that this interpretation neglects that it was this 'earlier revolution in the history of economic thought and discourse … which laid the foundation of modern economics' (Magnusson 1994b: 216).[6] While this emphasis on discourse potentially has much to offer accounting, it can overlook the real world of practice.[7]

Mercantilism as practice

In *Translating Empire: Emulations and the Origins of Political Economy*, Reinert (2011) offers a refreshing corrective to this discursive approach in his examination of political economy more generally. He argues against this research and researchers who devote their energies to the examination of a small number of canonical texts. By doing so, as historians (and as readers of history), we run the real risk of convincing ourselves of their representativeness. In his opinion, and one that would not be unfamiliar to many accounting historians, 'We must study the canon historically, not history canonically' (ibid.: 72). Moreover, Reinert (ibid.: 72) encourages the study of practice not 'canonical ideas' and the examination of how discourses were translated and 'emulated' as they travelled across Europe and the 'New World' to be further transmitted and reinterpreted.

Adopting Reinert's approach to mercantilism as practice provides a conduit to explore mercantilism in accounting through its administrative and bureaucratic mechanisms. To bring the strands of political economy and practice together, we further adopt the summary view of Winks and Kaiser (2004: xviii) in which 'Global commercialization evoked policies of "mercantilism," whereby princes sought to regulate and divert the anarchic flow of goods, labor, and money in ways that benefited themselves and the nations that they governed'. This definition incorporates bullionism (especially as practised by Philip II and Charles V of Spain), the cameralism of the Germanic States, *le colbertisme* of France and the commercial economy of roughly the mid-seventeenth to the mid-nineteenth century.[8] However diverse in implementation, mercantilism in practice relied on 'commerce, colonies, and sea power' (Winks and Kaiser 2004: 70). We turn to these categories of bullionism, cameralism, *le colbertisme* and commercialism to study the mercantilism–accounting interface.

Mercantilism–accounting interface

While an oversimplification, this four-fold classification reinforces the notion that mercantilism was not a static concept, but rather a complex system of theory, policies and practices transmitted and translated variously across time and space. This section uses a selection of accounting history research to demonstrate the mercantilism–accounting interface under those four headings.

Bullionism

It should come as no surprise that we first turn to Raymond de Roover given the breadth and depth of his scholarship and its boundary-spanning character. We often dip into de Roover's work related to double-entry bookkeeping, banking and bills of exchange, without expanding our horizons beyond topics familiar to us.[9]

In his analysis of the money market from the Middle Ages through to the modern era, de Roover examines these exchange processes, be they domestic or international. His studies underscore the role of the Church and Scholasticism. His interpretation of the place of the Scholastics reduces the frequent underestimation of their role and of what 'usury' meant in this context (de Roover 1955, 1958, 1967, 1971). Moreover, de Roover underscores the fact that usury was prohibited whereas speculation was not. Such speculation engaged accounting and was inherent in international transactions with fluctuating rates of currency exchange.

In his meticulous study of Gresham, de Roover (1949) examines the relationship between the early seventeenth-century depression in England and the power and position of the exchange dealers of Antwerp. Supple (1959) complements this analysis in terms of the overvaluation of English silver, debasement in continental Europe and the decreased demand for British cloth.[10] Moreover, de Roover provides an important clarification to the 'good money chases out bad' truism attributed to Gresham and the subject of erroneous understanding. As noted by de Roover and acknowledged by others, this expression arose only in the nineteenth century thanks to the work of a later economist H.D. MacLeod (1821–1902). What we do see in Gresham, however, is confirmation of the 'royal factor' or how monarchs and their agents controlled and affected exchange rates, be it the devaluation of the English currency relative to the Flemish or the stabilisation policy followed by Elizabeth I.

Those not familiar with de Roover's scholarship may have overlooked his engagement with the accounting evidence. For example, exchange required the extension of credit, the ability to work across currencies and internalise government policies. Exchange fluctuations affected all these factors given time lags and slow communications. Moreover, the 'self-regulatory mechanism of foreign exchange' operated in a period in which bills were not negotiable, not discounted and subject to usury prohibitions:

> 'Merchants' exchange' refers to the exchange by bills in which money was received in one place in order to be repaid in another place and in a different kind of currency. Prior to the Stuart revolution in England bills of exchange were always foreign bills and always involved an exchange transaction, whence the name of bill of 'exchange'. The nature of 'dry exchange' and of 'fictitious exchange' has given rise to a great deal of confusion; and to most people the meaning of these terms remains obscure.
>
> *(de Roover 1949: 250)*

To resolve this confusion, de Roover outlines the accounting mechanisms of merchant exchange and the impact of the balance of trade, while incorporating these processes within the underlying context of mercantilist thought. His study also demonstrates differences in the contemporary thinking on these matters, especially as debated in the work of Malynes, Mun and Savary (de Roover 1944b, 250–2).

Merchants and traders mitigated the possibility of fraud with exchange *(cambium)* contracts and standard time intervals, thus incorporating the extension of credit along with the exchange operations. De Roover frequently highlights the role of accounting – noting that economists (and likely accounting historians) have often paid less attention than necessary to these calculations and their meaning. Thus, his research ably combines the theoretical with the practical to enable others to delve into these sources appropriately.

In a series of articles (1935, 1942, 1944a, 1953, 1970, 1974) and in *Money, Banking and Credit in Medieval Bruges* (1948), de Roover outlines the decentralisation of the exchange, banking and credit markets that followed the decline of the medieval fairs, particularly those in Champagne, and the emergence of Bruges, London and Paris. He also demonstrates how these developments appeared later relative to those in the major cities of Italy and other regions of Europe. Moreover, these developments and the rise of one centre at the expense of others related to the underlying policies of states where cities remained within the orbit of other centres contingent on political circumstances and conflict.

Delving into de Roover is rewarding, notwithstanding the requisite effort to grasp the more technical aspects of his studies. These technical details open avenues to bring new questions to this literature, for example the role of social and cultural networks involved in the trade and accounting practices that he documents so meticulously. This comment is not meant to ignore alternative interpretations of de Roover, importantly that of Hoskin and Macve (1986) related to the late-medieval development of accounting technologies. De Roover worked at a time without digital records and data collection, an aspect to recognise and not quickly critique. His rich legacy, scope of analysis and extensive evidentiary detail are a critical resource on which to build novel investigations. Finally, de Roover's ability to cross-disciplinary and linguistic divides is exemplary in this era of transdisciplinary and transnational research.

Cameralism

Accounting history research into cameralism is limited. Similarly, it has not featured as prominently in other fields of history compared to the examination of mercantilism more generally. Renewed interest in mercantilism has motivated greater interest in these phenomena in non-Anglo-Saxon settings (Rössner 2016, 2018; Conti 2018). It would be fruitful to see this trend emerge in accounting.

Forrester (1990) examines cameralism with the focus on rational administration, accounting and control as taught to bureaucrats of the seventeenth and eighteenth centuries. The survey lacks coherence but, despite this weakness, does reveal how:

> The Cameralists dominated the teaching of bureaucrats who wished to serve the benevolent despots of the 17th and 18th century Enlightenment. They controlled the vaulted Treasuries or *Camera* of these princes. They initiated the teaching of administration and finance at universities. In a so-called Mercantilist era, they fostered trade, industry and agriculture with lofty goals.
>
> *(Forrester 1990: 285–6)*

Forrester offers illustrative examples of what he terms 'tactics' – especially the finance and accounting controls – used to deal with uncertainty of the time. Forrester contrasts the teaching of cameralism in universities to the training of merchants: the former influenced by paternalism and 'the happiness of one's subjects', and later by the ideas of Adam Smith and Emmanuel Kant; the latter based on knowledge and experience gained via family networks and merchant houses (ibid.: 289).

Drawing on the secondary literature, Forrester outlines how this 'science' of administration was introduced by Prussian rulers beginning with Frederick III and the founding of Halle University in 1694, an academy of arts in 1696 and the Royal Society of Sciences in 1700. Frederick William I supported other educational training including Chairs in administrative or Cameral Science at the universities of Halle and Frankfort-am Oder in 1727. Throughout the eighteenth century, imitation by other rulers led to similar posts across parts of Europe ensuring 'that administration was taught at one or more universities in his dominion' (Dorward 1971, 207ff; Maier 1966, as referenced by Forrester 1990, 289–90).

Teaching and the preparation of teaching materials were assigned to the 'Policey- or Cammer-collegium', individuals who privileged practical instruction over theory. Forrester (1990: 287) describes these cameralist professors as 'apologists for the benevolence, rationality and enlightened Polizei of their masters'. The Polizei reached its epitome under Napoleon, but the 'absolutist agenda was sharply reduced as a consequence of the teachings of Smith and Kant' (ibid.: 289; see also 292–3, 296, 301).

Forrester offsets limited use of primary sources by a rich application of secondary materials. Nevertheless, a presentism tendency exists in seeking parallels with modern management and practice, especially as the study proceeds ambitiously to examine the evolution of cameralism accounting of the current era. This 'case for cameralism' can also be found in research by Monsen (2002, 2006) which traces the history of cameralist accounting in Norway, Denmark and Sweden with a focus on its continued use and application in public-sector accounting.

In a strikingly different manner, Sánchez-Matamoros et al. (2005) utilise the Foucauldian framing of governmentality to investigate Enlightenment discourses in two contexts: the New Settlements of Sierra Morena and Andalucia (NSs) and the Royal Tobacco Factory of Seville (RTFS). The authors frame NSs as a 'social experiment' with a view to modernise agriculture and to reinforce the security of a *camino real* (royal highway) between Cadiz and Madrid. The RTFS was a tobacco production centre under the authority of the Tobacco Agency at Madrid that oversaw the production and distribution of tobacco and tax collection (ibid.: 182).

The study presents two competing yet complementary discourses – that of cameralism and that of agronomy. Cameralism focused on resources and management of the treasury whereas agronomy 'aimed at creating rich farmers who could pay taxes to maintain the state' (ibid.: 187). A strength of the research is its engagement with the archive, building on earlier studies in this context (Carmona et al. 1997, 1998, 2002; Álvarez et al. 2002; Álvarez-Dardet et al. 2002).[11] Yet, while arguing that accounting played a primary role in terms of 'accounting and control', it tends to play a secondary role in the study with its focus on governmentality. Framed around the tenets of space, rules and accounting, the focus on 'discourse' à la Foucault tends to shift the analysis in a direction that becomes its own discourse on governmentality. Nevertheless, the study does attempt to achieve a balance between theoretically driven versus theoretically informed analysis.

Le colbertisme

While the seeds of a centralised state and the *raison d'état* were sown under Louis XIII and Cardinal Richelieu, then continued under Mazarin, it was the administration of Louis XIV where divine-right rule and mercantilism 'flourished' (Winks and Kaiser 2004: 11–15). The Colbertian model of mercantilism emphasised a self-sustaining nation that sought to replace imports with domestic production and colonial commodities. The spillover effects of these policies included a growing emphasis on maritime trade, domestic manufacturing, the creation of monopoly trading firms, and centralised control of the nation and its colonies. While *le colbertisme* focused its energies on building a centralised nation-state, it also pursued foreign policies that overwhelmingly drained domestic resources.[12]

From an accounting perspective, this centralisation demanded a planning and control system and a bureaucracy.[13] Hoskin and Macve (2016) examine this topic empirically through the source documents and theoretically via the re-reading of two episodes,

Colbert's ordering of the finances of Louis XIV (Miller 1990; Soll 2009, 2014) and a similar attempt by the four Paris brothers for Louis XV (Lemarchand 1999; Soll 2014). The authors investigate the role of double-entry bookkeeping that 'has been identified as having played a significant role' in enabling the state to manage its finances. However, what is equally significant is their demonstration of 'what accounting could and could not do at the level of governing the "administrative" form of the state' (Hoskin and Macve 2016: 220). Their re-reading and critical analyses reveal that while the two cases depended on the deployment of double-entry bookkeeping, important differences exist between modern management and accounting and the 'government by inquiry' of Colbert. On the theoretical plane, Hoskin and Macve (2016: 240) call for recognition of the 'theoretical and historical limitations of the previous linkings of the Colbert episode to modern discourses of "governmentality" and of modern management' as presented by Miller (1990) and Soll (2009, 2014).

Moreover, the authors demonstrate the limits of the 'monopoly power' of an absolute monarch within an administrative state. The success of Colbert and of his use of accounting resulted from 'the ability to function as a single conduit through which all information generated by inquiry comes to one location where it can then be subjected to a unitary and "synoptic" critical reading of all the material turned into writing' (Hoskin and Macve 2016: 244). They (re)-introduce the principle as 'synoptic graphocentrism', which attempts to distinguish what is 'distinctive and new … but at the level of a form of "veridiction", a way of constituting statements that can then … be adjudged true or false' (ibid.: 244). While Colbert used this principle, it did not survive its dismantling upon his death when Louis XIV acted as his own principal amid a dispersed set of agents whose rivalries were once again fostered and permitted. The lack of strong and consistent leadership and a monarchy that had become 'so grandiose' meant that the systems in place were insufficient to maintain it (Winks and Kaiser 2004: 72).

Le colbertisme did not survive the social and economic challenges of the eighteenth century experienced in France and other parts of the globe. Hoskin and Macve provide important insights into the limitations of *le colbertisme* in terms of accounting and administrative systems. In some ways, we find echoes of their arguments in Beuve et al. (2017: 1170) with respect to the dynamic nature of such systems and the impetus for change:

> The broader lesson is that progress towards law-based, impersonal public administrations should not necessarily proceed top-down, that is, through broad changes in the political regime that then lead to redesigning the control mechanism of the state machinery as a whole. The experience examined here suggests that even under a classic absolutist monarchy, public administrations could be much more fluid, diverse, and open to experimentation than is often assumed. This may be in particular a defining feature of enlightened despotism.

Commercialism

The eighteenth century can be described summarily as one in which the old regimes were experiencing turbulent shifts from the dominant agrarian economy and society to ones in which the industrial revolution took hold. Within these economic and social changes were parallel political ruptures in terms of nations in their ascendancy and those in decline. Revolutions and political conflicts altered the balance of power domestically and internationally. It continued to be an era of commerce, sea power and colonies, one in which this trade played a significant part. The Age of the Enlightenment and its principles stood in dark contrast with the slave trade.

Yet within the history of accounting, the slave trade has not been studied intensively (compared to several analyses of slavery and slave plantations). The studies that have been undertaken focus primarily on the trade emanating from France and Spain. It may be that the extensive history of this topic in the Anglo-Saxon literature has reduced the motivation to examine it through an accounting lens. Our discussion of commercialism focuses on a number of these studies.[14]

Donoso (2002) examines the *Asiento*, a contract between the Spanish Crown and England giving the latter most-favoured nation status in trade as negotiated within the Treaty of Utrecht of 1713. This concession included the exclusive 30-year right of England to deliver slaves to the Spanish-American colonies. The English Crown granted an exclusive contract to the South Sea Company (SSC).

Interest in the accounting of the *Asiento* results from issues surrounding the lack of dividends and taxes paid by the SSC to the Spanish Crown. The inspection of the company's accounting records was a constant demand of the Spanish Crown. Donoso adopts a 'descriptive narrative' approach with the stated aim to introduce readers to this source without any 'theoretical embeddedness'. The study examines the contract of 1713–22 including ownership terms and the establishment of slave 'factories' in the Americas. The key element in this analysis is the lack of accountability of the SSC and how the accounting records were used to record economic events and to resolve conflicts between the Spanish Crown, the SSC and representatives in the Americas.[15] Donoso makes effective use of the accounts and related correspondence, but the examination remains highly descriptive. In terms of motivating study of the slave trade, it did produce that result, particularly research into the trade emanating from France.

Within the French context, McWatters and Lemarchand have undertaken a series of studies into the French slave trade,[16,17] firmly grounded within the precepts of mercantilism.

Privileging a neo-classical economics framework, McWatters (2008) analyses investment returns from the slave trade as part of a diversified portfolio, specifically in terms of investment behaviour and risk diversification including the assessment of liquidity and time frame. The research develops equally the context in which these investments took place – the mercantilist world of eighteenth-century France – and emphasises the limits of history and the role of historians to understand the logic of past systems of prior action. The results indicate that slave-trade investments held the *possibility* of above-average returns compared with other available investment opportunities. While reinforcing arguments in economic history, the study improves upon earlier work in this area given its direct examination of accounts and accounting data over a roughly 20-year period versus a theoretical reconstruction of market returns.

McWatters and Lemarchand have explored this mercantilist era in several studies focusing on the slave trade specifically or socio-economic relations of this milieu more broadly. Using the *Guide du commerce* of Gaignat de l'Aulnais as their backdrop, McWatters and Lemarchand (2006) investigate the extent to which this manual reflects real-world practice, thus representative of the socio-economic context of the period. The *Guide*, the only known work to present in a detailed manner the specialised accounting for slave-trade operations, includes a significant number of individuals intervening in diverse transactions who were actors of the period. Thus, it provides a realistic portrayal of the conditions and practices of the slave trade and of commerce more generally. The analysis reveals details about the trade's rationalisation processes including its systematisation to affect control over individuals and the mastery of an activity of eminent risk.

The authors further develop this angle in a cross-sectional analysis of ship owners, vessels, voyages and captains from several trading cities of eighteenth-century France (McWatters and Lemarchand 2009); see also Lemarchand and McWatters (2011). Situated within the broader context of social and trading networks and drawing upon insights from institutional economics, agency theory and organisational learning, the research demonstrates that the accounting for triangular trade exhibited the same rationalising tendencies as other forms of capitalism. While trade patterns differed across states and adapted to political, economic and social forces, McWatters and Lemarchand provide further evidence of how, within communities of practice, systems became routinised and refined as actors sought to obtain market returns and minimise risks. While the accounting system was based on procedures long established in maritime trade, the research demonstrates how these procedures were enhanced over time through the introduction of a wide variety of incentives and control mechanisms.

McWatters and Lemarchand (2010, 2013) shift the analysis from the slave trade to the broader examination of commercial relations and merchant networks. The first study introduces into the accounting history literature the arguments of Phillips (1995) which suggest that organisational analysis can be enriched by a greater interface with narrative fiction, along with those of Bottin (2001), who has argued that accounting manuals can be considered as source documents in the absence of primary materials. The authors re-examine the *Guide du commerce* along with a rich set of primary and secondary sources to illustrate accounting as narrative. The research also illustrates that the *Guide*, through its development of case studies and examples of actual accounting methods, provides insights into the strategic nature of the social and economic milieu in which commercial success might be achieved.

This research also reveals the place and pertinence of accounting manuals in the training of commercial traders and in knowledge transmission. The authors pose novel questions into accounting's utility within 'commerce' – as opposed to the more sustained focus of historical research on industrial cost accounting and financial reporting. It further demonstrates that double-entry accounting, if not indispensable, was particularly useful to monitor complex operations. However, rather than link double-entry's utility to the development of capitalism and decision making, McWatters and Lemarchand (2010: 48) argue that the value of accounting arose from

> its placing at the disposal of those involved in international commerce an immensely flexible technique to represent and control all manner of complex commercial relations … Importantly, in this international context, debit and credit accounts proved to be a sort of international economic language. This day-to-day operational role in the rise of merchant capitalism frequently has been underestimated relative to its potentially strategic one.

The interpretation of the accounting text as narrative enriches our understanding of how social and economic networks were developed and sustained.

McWatters and Lemarchand (2013) extend their research into the commercial world of the city of Nantes, its local and global actors to illustrate how accounting discourse was a crucial vector in merchant networks. Complementing the 2010 study, social network analyses reveal additional insights and more precise linkages on the networks of actors, the place and centrality of specific actors, and the ability of these networks to span space and time. Beyond information exchange, raising capital and credit, and knowledge transfer, the deep immersion into the accounting discourse confirms its criticality in networks of trust, reciprocity, kinship and social capital. At the methodological level, the novel use of social network analysis reinforces the value of combined qualitative–quantitative approaches to historical studies of accounting. The empirical results illustrate the place of social networks in fostering the growth of merchant capitalism.

Mercantilism and accounting: new directions and concluding comments

Accounting history has examined mercantilism in diverse settings but generally has kept mercantilism in the background while pursuing other discourses, especially those examining the 'social' rather than the 'economic'. Yet mercantilism demands that we do both and use our accounting tools to do so. One promising way to achieve this end would be research that recognises the value and necessity of cross-disciplinary boundaries and to embrace the archive *writ large* in innovative fashion.

McWatters (2019) is representative of such initiatives.[18] While grounded firmly in mercantilism, the individual studies in this volume emphasise the ways in which individuals across space and time navigated worldviews and cultural understandings. Moreover, transactions took place in a market captured within a global nexus of exchange that was transmitted and translated across contexts, as noted in the Introduction:

> In this spirit, we focus on this real world and how the mercantilist system did play out in various contexts. Moreover, we do view mercantilism as a system in which there was a market for goods, money and exchange, a market in which economic agents engaged in concrete actions to pursue their economic interests.
>
> *(McWatters 2019: 3)*

Within these networks of exchange, the authors focus on accounting as 'making account' – the practice of reckoning and providing an explanation of one's actions, often in the form of narrative descriptions. Some of these reckonings are sophisticated systems of accounting and control; others simple recordings of everyday transactions.

As noted earlier, nation-states promoted and fostered the commercialism of the sixteenth to eighteenth centuries including their establishment of chartered trading firms (e.g. the Dutch East India Company, la Compagnie des Indes, the Dutch West India Company, the Hudson's Bay Company [HBC] and the Russian American Company). Much research has been dedicated to these organisations that were granted charters to explore, trade, raise taxes, enlist private armies and, importantly, generate profits for their shareholders. In effect, they operated as quasi-states in a world of colonial expansion.

Accounting history has less frequently examined mercantilism from the perspective of those whose 'market model' did not equate with 'Western views' of rational behaviour. These studies emphasise the periphery in the periphery-core relationship and outcomes for those situated there. They also investigate how non-European trade actors reacted to the mercantilist system, especially in spatially-extended trade networks. Finally, the research recognises that the effects of changing political and economic policies established at the core affected the profitability and stability of operations in far-flung settings. Often these operations involved those characterised as bit players yet frequently key to smoothing exchange. McWatters (2019: 2) notes:

> For example, merchant companies competed with small traders, other Europeans who arrived in these settings along with traders and merchants, for example, missionaries, bankers and colonial agents. These actors included importantly local players who were the necessary ingredient to make these exchanges operate and function – players who equally were caught up in these economic and cultural exchanges through interaction with those who had sought and pursued global opportunities. All of these individuals together were part of and created this periphery-core relationship.

These studies favour contextual investigations anchored in their economic, social and cultural setting, as opposed to macro-level analyses and generalisations. The authors rely heavily on primary sources and archival material. The results exemplify a 'return to the archive' that can mitigate a tendency to neglect sound evidence for the sake of sophisticated theoretical musings.

Vermote (2019) utilises the account books of the seventeenth-century Jesuit missionary François de Rougemont to reveal his local interactions in China and his disconnection from the global economic networks of the Jesuits. Vermote illustrates how both copper and silver circulated in this local setting yet how the global economy also played out in terms of localised socio-economic relations. In his examination of New Netherlands and the Coastal Algonquians, Schmidt (2019) analyses differing understandings of money (perceived as a political problem by the Dutch colonists and as economic opportunity by the Coastal Algonquians). This research illustrates the effects of cross-cultural interaction in which mercantilist dogma conflicted with the market pragmatism of the Native Americans.

In Vorel (2019), accounting for the periphery-core relationship focuses on the markets for precious metals in the sixteenth-century Kingdom of Bohemia. Accounting for these precious metals is intertwined with the economic struggle for dominance in the mining and exporting sectors and parallel struggles for political control. McWatters and Lemarchand (2019) build upon their earlier research into the French slave trade with the investigation of the merchandise accounts of vessels sent to trade on the African coast. These accounts reveal the socio-economic relations between French traders, their African counterparts and intermediaries. Beyond the establishment of terms of trade and their negotiation over time and space, the research indicates how players reacted to a market for global commodities all the while operating within a local exchange dynamic.

Three studies also focus on Indigenous peoples. Parker (2019) examines consumption and production patterns of Indigenous peoples in the fur trade and whaling industries of North America and New Zealand respectively. Her analysis concludes that Indigenous actors were drawn into an increasingly colonial capitalist economy where adaptation resulted in dwindling self-sufficiency and growing dependency on colonial interests. Ray (2019) demonstrates how the introduction of district-level management records by the HBC enabled managers to assess the market and gather competitive intelligence. Beyond long-distance monitoring and control, from a quite different angle, the reports offer insights into the complex exchange relations in which Indigenous players and traders engaged. Through the meticulous examination of micro-level accounts of the HBC, Tough (2019) demonstrates how Indigenous trappers were connected to the fur markets of London and merchant goods. Consistent with McWatters and Lemarchand, he reinforces the view that 'periphery players were captured within increasingly globalised commodity chains where economic growth in the periphery was contingent on the consumption needs of the core' (McWatters 2019: 6).

In each of these studies, accounts and accounting underscore that mercantilism involves dynamic social and economic exchange. The studies reveal the interplay of social actors, shifting mercantilism from the theoretical abstract to the reality of exchange mechanisms.

We contend that recent research into accounting for mercantilism parallels the reimagining of mercantilism as expressed by Pincus (2012), Reinert (2011) and Stern and Wennerlind (2013), among others. Moreover, recent research underscores that future studies in accounting history must cross disciplinary divides, including actual engagement with researchers in sister disciplines. It also would be opportune to draw upon insights of earlier research to embrace mercantilism as practice and to explore the role of accounting therein. Only then can studies of the accounting–mercantilism interface reap the benefits – and deal with the many challenges – of navigating disciplinary norms and evidentiary standards. Such research requires us to reflect upon our own ontological and epistemological boundaries to move accounting history forward in innovative and captivating ways.

Key works

de Roover (1944a, 1994b) combines theoretical insights and practical analyses to illustrate the role of early market exchange anchored in the context of mercantilist thought.

Hoskin and Macve (2016) provide an in-depth investigation of *le colbertisme* within a provocative historical and theoretical examination of the limitations of modern discourses of governmentality and 'modern management'.

McWatters (2008) introduces empirical analyses of slave-trade investments and mercantilist precepts within a broader investigation of eighteenth-century social and commercial relations.

McWatters (2019) presents a set of investigations into mercantilism and accounting, underscoring the value of interdisciplinary approaches to examine mercantilism in practice across time and space.

Notes

1 This chapter does not examine double-entry bookkeeping and capitalism specifically, with these topics the subjects of Chapters 5 and 17 respectively.

2 We distinguish between 'mercantilist' and 'mercantile' to refer to mercantilism. In accounting history, the latter has been used as synonymous with commerce and trade, and in connection with double-entry bookkeeping (see for example, Edwards et al. 2002; Edwards and Greener 2003). Mercantile also has been utilised erroneously by Tyson (1998) to refer to costing methods of US textile firms of the eighteenth century.

3 Heckscher (1935/1994: 471) outlines further that the new and victorious methods were given 'free rein', and 'as a consequence they asserted themselves with a force unparalleled in previous history … it is undoubtedly true that their [English statesmen's] passivity influenced the nature and direction of the development'. 'And not the least reason for adherence to *laissez-faire* principles was the fact that they offered a very welcome pretext for doing nothing when nobody knew what to do' (ibid.: 472).

4 Magnusson has been criticised equally for his focus on specific geographies to the neglect of others. For example, Wachtel (2011), who focuses on mercantilist thought in Spain, notes that neither Heckscher nor Magnusson extend their horizons significantly beyond France and England.

5 Magnusson (1994b: vii) further contends that these arguments continue to be clothed in debates about the superiority of modern economics. Critics contend that he persists in a debate that has moved on. See Pincus (2012), Stern and Wennerlind (2013), McDiarmid (2016) and Conti (2018) for an overview of these criticisms including reaction to Magnusson (2015).

6 Wallerstein (1974; 1974/2011) offers a distinctive perspective on these developments in terms of historical sociology and world systems.
7 While provocative and stimulating, these disciplinary debates are not our present focus. Rather than summarise – inadequately – arguments that have continued for several decades, the interested reader is encouraged to engage Magnusson and related works directly.
8 This listing is not intended to discount developments in other settings including Sweden, Italy and Japan, along with the continued existence of mercantilist doctrine and policies well beyond this period.
9 Blomquist (1975) provides an excellent summary of de Roover's contributions.
10 However, de Roover (1960: 1054) notes that Supple supplements rather than extends other research and also criticises his analysis for its lack of recognition of researchers with whose ideas he disagrees.
11 Carmona (2005) reviews the (management) accounting history research of France, Italy, Portugal and Spain. Readers will find his synthesis and interpretation of 'mercantilism' in the eighteenth-century Spanish context most valuable. We do not duplicate this analysis in these pages.
12 Minard (1998) provides an excellent analysis of this period.
13 Although Beuve et al. (2017) focus on early eighteenth-century France, they offer important insights into the meaning of bureaucracy within the French context with a caution against overstating the 'modern character' of these bureaucracies.
14 This volume touches upon other areas of commercialism in terms of bookkeeping (Chapter 5), capitalism (Chapter 17) and colonialism (Chapter 23).
15 The British *Asiento* ended in 1750 with the Treaty of Madrid. Carmona et al. (2010) further analyse the *Asiento* focusing on its role as an instrument of treaty verification. They highlight the limited effectiveness of accounting for this purpose when no shared understanding existed regarding its purpose and interpretation.
16 The closing section introduces one additional study.
17 Pinto and West (2017) provide a recent study on the Portuguese case, but their focus is not mercantilism, but rather to contribute to the literature on 'the dark side of accounting'.
18 Another recent example of this transdisciplinary work is Gervais et al. (2014).

References

Álvarez, M., Gutiérrez, F. and Romero, D. (2002) Accounting and quality control in the Royal Tobacco Factory of Seville (1744–1790): an historical perspective, *Accounting Business & Financial History*, 12 (2): 253–74.

Álvarez-Dardet, C., Baños, J. and Carrasco, F. (2002) Accounting and control in the founding of the new settlements of Sierra Morena and Andalucia (1767–1772), *European Accounting Review*, 11 (2): 419–39.

Beuve, J., Brousseau, E. and Sgard, J. (2017) Mercantilism and bureaucratic modernization in early eighteenth-century France, *Economic History Review*, 70 (2): 529–58.

Blomquist, T.W. (1975) De Roover on business, banking, and economic thought, *Journal of Economic History*, 35 (4): 821–30.

Bottin, J. (2001) Entreprise et place de commerce dans quelques manuels de comptabilité français des XVIe et XVIIe siècles, in J. Hoock and P. Jeannin (eds) *Ars mercatoria. Handbücher und Traktate für den Gebrauch des Kaufmanns, 1470–1820, Vol III, Analysen 1470–1700*, pp. 131–56 (Paderborn: Schöningh).

Carmona, S. (2005) The history of management accounting in France, Italy, Portugal and Spain, IE Working Paper WP0530: 1–30.

Carmona, S., Donoso, R. and Walker, S.P. (2010) Accounting and international relations: Britain, Spain and the Asiento treaty, *Accounting, Organizations and Society*, 35 (2): 252–73.

Carmona, S., Ezzamel, M. and Gutiérrez, F. (1997) Control and cost accounting practices in the Spanish Royal Tobacco Factory, *Accounting, Organizations and Society*, 22 (5): 411–46.

Carmona, S., Ezzamel, M. and Gutiérrez, F. (1998) Towards an institutional analysis of accounting change in the Royal Tobacco Factory of Seville, *Accounting Historians Journal*, 25 (1): 115–47.

Carmona, S., Ezzamel, M. and Gutiérrez, F. (2002) The relationships between accounting and spatial practices in the factory, *Accounting, Organizations and Society*, 27 (3): 411–46.

Conti, T.V. (2018) Mercantilism: a materialist approach, *Scandinavian Economic History Review*, 66 (2): 186–200.

de Roover, R. (1935) Théories de la comptabilité dans les Provinces-Unies aux XVIIe et XVIIIe siècles, *Annales d'histoire économique et sociale*, 7 (34): 398–401.

de Roover, R. (1942) Money, banking, and credit in medieval Bruges, *Journal of Economic History*, 2 (Supplement: The tasks of economic history): 52–65.

de Roover, R. (1944a) Early accounting problems of foreign exchange, *Accounting Review*, 19 (4): 381–407.

de Roover, R. (1944b) What is dry exchange? A contribution to the study of English mercantilism, *Journal of Political Economy*, 52 (3): 250–66.

de Roover, R. (1948) *Money, Banking and Credit in Medieval Bruges* (Cambridge: Mediaeval Academy of America).

de Roover, R. (1949) *Gresham on Foreign Exchange: An Essay on Early English mercantilism, with the Text of Sir Thomas Gresham's Memorandum for the Understanding of the Exchange* (Cambridge, MA: Harvard University Press).

de Roover, R. (1953) *L'évolution de la lettre de change, XIV-XVIII siècles* (Paris: Armand Colin).

de Roover, R. (1955) Scholastic economics: survival and lasting influence from the sixteenth century to Adam Smith, *Quarterly Journal of Economics*, 69 (2): 161–90.

de Roover, R. (1958) The concept of the just price: theory and economic policy, *Journal of Economic History*, 18 (4): 418–34.

de Roover, R. (1960) Review of *Commercial Crisis and Change in England, 1600–1642* by B.E. Supple, *American Economic Review*, 50 (5): 1053–55.

de Roover, R. (1967) The scholastics, usury, and foreign exchange, *Business History Review*, 41 (3): 257–71.

de Roover, R. (1970) Le marché monétaire au Moyen Age et au début des temps modernes: problèmes et méthodes, *Revue historique*, 244 (495): 5–40.

de Roover, R. (1971) *La Pensée Économique des Scolastiques: Doctrines et Méthodes* (Montréal: Institut d'Études Médiévales).

de Roover, R. (1974) *Business, Banking and Economic Thought in Late Medieval and Early Modem Europe: Selected Studies of Raymond de Roover*, edited by J. Kirshner (Chicago, IL and London: University of Chicago Press).

Donoso, R.D.A. (2002) Accounting and slavery: the accounts of the English South Sea Company, 1713–22, *European Accounting Review*, 11 (2): 441–52.

Dorward, R.A. (1971) *The Prussian Welfare State before 1740* (Cambridge, MA: Harvard University Press).

Edwards, J.R., Coombs, H.M. and Greener, H.T. (2002) British central government and 'the mercantile system of double entry' bookkeeping: a study of ideological conflict, *Accounting, Organizations and Society*, 27 (7): 637–58.

Edwards, J.R. and Greener, H.T. (2003) Introducing 'mercantile' bookkeeping into British central government 1858–1844, *Accounting and Business Research*, 33 (1): 51–64.

Fay, C.R. (1934) Adam Smith, America, and the Doctrinal Defeat of the Mercantile System, *The Quarterly Journal of Economics*, 48 (2): 304–16.

Forrester, D.A.R. (1990) Rational administration, finance and control accounting: the experience of cameralism, *Critical Perspectives on Accounting*, 1: 285–317.

Gervais, P., Lemarchand, Y. and Margairaz, D. (eds) (2014) *Merchants and Profit in the Age of Commerce, 1680–1830* (London: Pickering & Chatto).

Gervais, P. and McWatters, C.S. (2017) Globalisation, in A. de Jong, S. Toms, J. Wilson and E. Buchnea (eds) *The Routledge Companion to Business History*, pp. 316–30 (London: Routledge/ Taylor & Francis).

Heckscher, E.F. (1935/1994) *Mercantilism*, vol. 1 (Abingdon: Routledge).

Hoskin, K. and Macve, R. (1986) Accounting and the examination: a genealogy of disciplinary power, *Accounting, Organizations and Society*, 11 (2): 105–36.

Hoskin, K. and Macve, R. (2016) 'L'État c'est moi' … ou quoi? On the Interrelations of accounting, managing and governing in the French 'administrative monarchy': revisiting the Colbert (1661–1683) and Paris Brothers (1712–1726) episodes, *Accounting History Review*, 26 (3): 219–57.

Lemarchand, Y. (1999) Introducing double-entry bookkeeping in public finance: a French experiment at the beginning of the eighteenth century, *Accounting, Business & Financial History*, 9 (2): 225–54.

Lemarchand, Y. and McWatters, C.S. (2011) Quelques aspects de la gestion de la traite négrière au XVIIIe siècle à travers l'exemple nantais, *Droits*, 51: 55–73.

Magnusson, L.G. (1994a) Eli Heckscher and mercantilism – an introduction, in E.F. Heckscher (ed) *Mercantilism*, vol. 1, pp. xi–xxxv (Abingdon: Routledge).

Magnusson, L.G. (1994b) *Mercantilism: The Shaping of an Economic Language* (London: Taylor & Francis).

Magnusson, L.G. (2015) *The Political Economy of Mercantilism* (Abingdon: Routledge).

Maier, H. (1966) *Die altere Deutsche Staats- und Verwaltungslehre-(Polizeiwissenschaft)* (Berlin: Luchterhand Literaturverlag).

McDiarmid, A. (2016) Review of *The Political Economy of Mercantilism*, *Reviews in History*. Available HTTP: <www.history.ac.uk/reviews/review/1993>.

McWatters, C.S. (2008) Investment returns and 'la traite négrière': evidence from eighteenth-century France, *Accounting, Business & Financial History*, 18 (2): 161–85.

McWatters, C.S. (2019) Introduction: mercantilism and accounting across space and time, in C. S. McWatters (ed) *Mercantilism, Account Keeping and the Periphery-Core Relationship*, pp. 1–7 (Abingdon: Routledge).

McWatters, C.S. and Lemarchand, Y. (2006) Accounting representation and the slave trade: the 'Guide du commerce' of Gaignat de l'Aulnais, *Accounting Historians Journal*, 33 (2): 1–37.

McWatters, C.S. and Lemarchand, Y. (2009) Accounting for triangular trade, *Accounting, Business & Financial History*, 19 (2): 189–212.

McWatters, C.S. and Lemarchand, Y. (2010) Accounting as story telling: merchant activities and commercial relations in 18th-century France, *Accounting, Auditing & Accountability Journal*, 23 (1): 14–54.

McWatters, C.S. and Lemarchand, Y. (2013) Merchant networks and accounting discourse: the role of accounting transactions in network relations, *Accounting History Review*, 23 (1): 49–83.

McWatters, C.S. and Lemarchand, Y. (2019) Trade, truck, custom and barter – glimpses from slave trade cargoes, in C.S. McWatters (ed) *Mercantilism, Account Keeping and the Periphery-Core Relationship*, pp. 61–87 (Abingdon: Routledge).

Miller, P. (1990) On the interrelations of accounting and the state, *Accounting, Organizations and Society*, 15 (4): 315–38.

Minard, P. (1998) *La fortune du colbertisme. Etat et industrie Dans La France des Lumières* (Paris: Fayard).

Monsen, N. (2002) The case for cameralism accounting, *Financial Accountability & Management Journal*, 18 (1): 39–72.

Monsen, N. (2006) Historical development of local government accounting in Norway, *Financial Accountability and Management Journal*, 22 (4): 359–80.

Padgen, A. (2015) *The Burdens of Empire: 1539 to the Present* (New York: Cambridge University Press).

Parker, L. (2019) Glimpses of an indigenous economy: patterns of consumption and production of indigenous peoples in the nineteenth-century fur trade and whaling industry, in C.S. McWatters (ed) *Mercantilism, Account Keeping and the Periphery-Core Relationship*, pp. 91–132 (Abingdon: Routledge).

Pettigrew, W.A. (2013) *Freedom's Debt: The Royal African Company and the Politics of the Atlantic Slave Trade, 1672–1752* (Chapel Hill, NC: University of North Carolina Press).

Phillips, N. (1995) Telling organizational tales, *Organization Studies*, 16 (4): 625–49.

Pincus, S. (2012) Rethinking mercantilism: political economy, the British Empire, and the Atlantic world in the seventeenth and eighteenth centuries, *William and Mary Quarterly*, 69 (1): 3–34.

Pinto, O. and West, B. (2017) Accounting, slavery and social history: the legacy of an eighteenth-century Portuguese chartered company, *Accounting History*, 22 (2): 141–66.

Ray, A.J. (2019) Economic intelligence and fur trade management by the Hudson's Bay Company: an examination of district reports in the nineteenth and early twentieth centuries, in C.S. McWatters (ed) *Mercantilism, Account Keeping and the Periphery-Core Relationship*, pp. 133–53 (Abingdon: Routledge).

Reinert, S.A. (2011) *Translating Empire: Emulation and the Origins of Political Economy* (Cambridge, MA: Harvard University Press).

Rhoden, N.L. (2015) Review of *Freedom's Debt: The Royal African Company and the Politics of the Atlantic Slave Trade, 1672–1752*, by W.A. Pettigrew, H-Albion, H-Net Reviews. Available HTTP: <www.h-net.org/reviews/showrev.php?id=40841>.

Rössner, P. (2016) New inroads into well-known territory? On the virtues of re-discovering pre-classical political economy, in P. Rössner (ed) *Economic Growth and the Origins of Modern Political Economy: Economic Reasons of State, 1500–2000*, pp. 3–24 (London: Routledge).

Rössner, P. (2018) Monetary theory and cameralist economic management, c. 1500–1900 A.D., *Journal of the History of Economic Thought*, 40 (1): 99–134.

Sánchez-Matamoros, J.B., Hidalgo, F.G., Espejo, C.Á. and Fenech, F.C. (2005) Govern(mentality) and accounting: the influence of different enlightenment discourses in two Spanish cases (1761–1777), *Abacus*, 41: 181–210.

Schmidt, M. (2019) 'But whatever were the honey in the mouth of that beast of trade, there was a deadly sting in the tail': New Netherland's monetary policy and the Coastal Algonquian pragmatic response during the seventeenth century, in C.S. McWatters (ed) *Mercantilism, Account Keeping and the Periphery-Core Relationship*, pp. 32–46 (Abingdon: Routledge).

Soll, J. (2009) *The Information Master: Jean-Baptiste Colbert's Secret State Intelligence System* (Ann Arbor, MI: University of Michigan Press).

Soll, J. (2014) *The Reckoning: Financial Accountability and the Rise and Fall of Nations* (New York: Basic Books).

Stern, P.J. and Wennerlind, C. (eds) (2013) *Mercantilism Reimagined. Political Economy in Early Modern Britain and Its Empire* (Oxford: Oxford University Press).

Supple, B.E. (1959) *Commercial Crisis and Change in England* (New York & Cambridge: Cambridge University Press).

Tough, F. (2019) Native labour and imperial consumption on the periphery of Empire as revealed by the York Factory account books of the Hudson's Bay Company, c. 1869–1870, in C. S. McWatters (ed) *Mercantilism, Account Keeping and the Periphery-Core Relationship*, pp. 154–79 (Abingdon: Routledge).

Tyson, T.N. (1998) Mercantilism, management accounting or managerialism? Cost accounting in early 19th century US textile mills, *Accounting, Business & Financial History*, 8 (2): 211–29.

Vermote, F. (2019) Jesuit account books and their role in connecting worlds, in C.S. McWatters (ed) *Mercantilism, Account Keeping and the Periphery-Core Relationship*, pp. 11–31 (Abingdon: Routledge).

Vorel, P. (2019) Encounters with the periphery: European merchant trading firms and the export of the precious metals from the Kingdom of Bohemia during the sixteenth century, in C.S. McWatters (ed) *Mercantilism, Account Keeping and the Periphery-Core Relationship*, pp. 49–60 (Abingdon: Routledge).

Wachtel, N. (2011) The 'Marrano' mercantilist theory of Duarte Gomes Solis, *Jewish Quarterly Review*, 101 (2): 164–88.

Wallerstein, I. (1974) The rise and future demise of the world capitalist system: concepts for comparative analysis, *Comparative Studies in Society and History*, 16 (4): 387–415.

Wallerstein, I. (1974/2011) *The Modern World-System I: Capitalist Agriculture and the Origins of the European World Economy in the Sixteenth Century* (Berkeley, CA: University of California Press).

Winks, R.W. and Kaiser, T.E. (2004) *Europe 1648–1815: From the Old Regime to the Age of Revolution* (New York & Oxford: Oxford University Press).

17
CAPITALISM

Steven Toms

Overview

It is difficult to imagine capitalist economic organisation without the techniques of double-entry bookkeeping. At the same time, capitalism is a system that constantly transforms economic organisation. It would be expected therefore that economic and social change contribute fundamentally to accounting change. Moreover, accounting itself may be an agent of such change. In short, accounting is fundamentally involved in all stages of the development of capitalism, in its different forms and its geographical variations.

Accounting is also thereby implicated in transformations in ownership, with war and social upheaval, and is also vital to our understanding of the more stable phases of capitalist development. Accounting enjoys a symbiotic relationship with social change, so that analysing social processes is necessary to our understanding of accounting, while accounting itself is a useful tool for historians and others for understanding those processes.

In this chapter, these relationships will be analysed using a critical framework, so that approaches from several research traditions can be acknowledged. Within this framework, the links between relevant literatures from various disciplines, particularly history, economics and politics, and commonly appreciated aspects of accounting theory and practice, will be explained.

The first main section of this chapter reviews the major literary contributions to each of the theoretical perspectives. These perspectives are then illustrated in the second main section, which studies a series of historical contexts in chronological order. These are first the transition from feudalism to capitalism, and how accounting was implicated in the transition, which has been the subject of debate for nearly 100 years. Second, the role of accounting in the upheavals of the industrial revolution is examined. Third, the rise of managerial capitalism and the associated development of accounting techniques are considered. Recent developments are then studied, with a focus on the Enron scandal. A concluding section sets out some future research directions and challenges.

Some theoretical contrasts

A common focus of accounting historians is the relative power of social groups especially managers and shareholders. Even so there are a larger number of interpretations of the relationships implied by differential power and the consequences for accounting. For example, accounting might be located in the social relations of production (Tinker 1980), or, alternatively, it may be incorporated into a legitimacy theory perspective (Gray et al. 1995). The former view implies a Marxist interpretation in which the accounting historian analyses how capital is created, accumulated and distributed. Because of the exploitation that underlies these processes, the corporation and capitalist accounting itself are seen as illegitimate. In the alternative view, the corporation's activities can be legitimised using accounting. To the extent that it is engaging in illegitimate activity, for example environmental degradation, accounting becomes a device to be used by managers to enable the firm to be rehabilitated in the public imagination, thereby justifying and continuing its activities. The legitimacy issue clearly separates these interpretations of the nature of the capitalist corporation. A further distinction is that, in the latter case, management uses accounting proactively, whereas in the former, managers and by implication accountants can make no difference to the systematic outcome, since power resides with the owners of capital. A method is needed to disentangle some of the competing approaches in a fashion helpful to the accounting historian.

Table 17.1 suggests a grouping with two dimensions. The first is the attitude of the researcher towards capitalism, which might be characterised as mainstream or radical:

> To be 'mainstream' is almost by definition to believe in, or at least to be open to, the legitimacy of the capitalist firm and the economic system in which it is embedded, while to be radical seems to require some display of hostility toward them.
>
> *(Putterman 1986: 25)*

The second dimension is the researcher's ontological perspective, which might be characterised as objective or subjective. Burrell and Morgan (1989) use a similar approach when considering research generally in the social sciences. The subjective view implies knowledge is grounded in individual experience and free will; the objective view implies a concrete reality where knowledge can be gained through observation. In accounting history research, the distinction has an important impact on the research focus as well as the method. A subjectivist accounting historian will focus on individuals and interpret their contribution using archival investigation. An objectivist accounting historian will more typically focus on institutions and markets and may for example compile numerical datasets to test hypotheses. In Table 17.1, the subjective-objective axis is shown horizontally and the mainstream-radical axis is shown vertically.[1] As a result there are four possible approaches in accounting history – managerialist and positivist are the mainstream approaches, and structuralist and post-modernist are the radical approaches.[2] Each is now discussed in turn, citing examples from the accounting history literature.

Table 17.1 Theoretical contrasts

		View of subject matter	
		Subjective	*Objective*
View of society	*Radical change*	Post-modernist	Structuralist
	Mainstream	Managerialist	Positivist

Mainstream approaches: managerialist accounting history

The managerialist approach gives primacy to the role of managers as independent and usually rational decision-makers. There is little explicit reliance on theory. Emphasis is placed on the empirical relationship between the emergence of managerial capitalism (Chandler 1977) and the development of modern accounting (Chatfield 1977; Edwards 1989).[3] For example, it has been argued that the *laissez faire* environment of the late nineteenth century implied a high degree of managerial choice, which became an important determinant of the financial reporting mechanism (Edwards 1989: 125; Baldwin 1994). Furthermore excess directors' power, reinforced by a lack of rules on disclosure, prevented the emergence of an efficient capital market (Kennedy 1987: 126). Even so, for this school of thought, managerial action is both rational and legitimate. An obvious criticism of the managerialist approach is that in separating the manager as an independent rational decision-maker, the governance issue, which lies at the centre of the positivist approach, is ignored. Accountability structures imposed by governance arrangements can significantly constrain managerial freedom of action.

Mainstream approaches: positivist accounting history

Unlike the empirical and atheoretical approach adopted by the managerialists, positive accounting has developed from two strands of theory in economics: transaction cost and principal agent theory. Transaction cost theory explains organisational forms in terms of governance costs and their minimisation, along with production costs, in conditions of managerial opportunism and asymmetric information (Coase 1937; Williamson 1975, 1981). Applying this approach to management accounting explains accounting innovation, for example arising from the expansion of the railroads (Williamson 1981; Johnson and Kaplan 1987). In similar vein, principal agent theory explains the consequences of asymmetric information in terms of monitoring costs incurred by principals to ensure managerial compliance with shareholder objectives (Jensen and Meckling 1976). Accounting information and processes are important in both theories for mitigating information asymmetry. For example, positivism suggests that management has an incentive to voluntarily submit to audit as a quality signal (Jensen and Meckling 1976; Watts and Zimmerman 1983; Edwards et al. 1997). An extension of the positivist methodology is the use of the event study, which in certain limited cases has been applied to historical data (Chow 1983; Sivakumar and Waymire 1993; Toms 2001). In the world of positivism, managerial attitudes are predetermined as rational and are therefore irrelevant. Because they respond rationally to market forces in the presence of information asymmetry and transaction cost, it is pointless for the historian or anyone else to consider their attitudes any further.

Although leading many positivist accountants to neglect history, such approaches may nonetheless provide a useful framework for the accounting historian. Edwards (2019: 16–17) notes the nature of managerial incentives, which while rational, are also ambiguous. On the one hand, managers are motivated to provide credible information to maintain investor confidence, but on the other, their own self-interest may lead to falsification and impression management. Recognition of these conflicts, as a function of the power of different groups in society, offers potential insight into long-run accounting change.

The positivist approach in general may nonetheless be problematic for several related reasons. First, it is often unsupported by historical analysis (Merino et al. 1987). Second, there is little empirical evidence on market efficiency in the periods analysed (Sivakumar and Waymire 1993: 88; Toms 2001). Third, from Ball and Brown (1968) onwards, studies of accounting earnings and share price relationship have taken informational market efficiency as descriptive (Watts and Zimmerman 1986: 37), notwithstanding the logical impossibility of market efficiency where transaction costs exist (Grossman and Stiglitz 1980). Consequently, empirical studies exclude from samples those companies whose stocks are likely to demonstrate attributes of inefficiency such as thin trading (for example, Sivakumar and Waymire 1993: 68).

Radical approaches: post-modern accounting history

The post-modernist perspective stresses the role of accounting, especially management accounting, in the control of labour. Ezzamel et al. (1990) attribute the rise of managerialism identified by Chandler (1977) to a genealogy of the disciplinary use of accounting controls traced to military training at West Point in the early nineteenth century. According to Hoskin and Macve (2000), in the coal, iron and other industries the accounting management used went beyond 'economic rationalism' and 'labour control' so that Foucault's 'disciplinary' power, exercised through continuous surveillance, forms the basis of human accountability essential to Chandler's (1977) 'visible hand' of administrative co-ordination. It has been this approach, characterised as the 'new accounting history', that has sought to increase accounting history's impact through broadening its methodologies so that it stands more centrally within the social sciences. Although this view implies attention to transformations in accounting knowledge, there is post-modernist-inspired scepticism towards the notions of progress and evolution (Miller et al. 1991).

Critics of the post-modernist interpretation in general and Hoskin and Macve in particular, have suggested that accounting cannot function as part of a continuous surveillance mechanism. Accounting by definition implies intermittent measurement. Moreover, surveillance also involves consideration of who does the surveillance and why and to whom such monitors are ultimately accountable (Toms and Fleischman 2015). Boyns and Edwards (2000) argue that the process of gathering archival evidence has scarcely begun and therefore it is dangerous to locate the origins of techniques so specifically and so definitively. As Tyson suggests (2000), over-reliance on theory can lead to denial of subsequent evidence where inconvenient.

Radical approaches: structuralist accounting history

The radical structuralist method is best exemplified by political economy approaches. The usual focus of political economy of accounting (PEA) is the relative power of social groups (Cooper and Sherer 1984: 218), especially managers and shareholders.[4] The radical structuralist approach, like the positivist, accordingly stresses the rise of the capital market, and underpins an alternative hypothesis of powerful shareholders and investor groups as the social instigators of modern accounting. Collective interests of capital dominate managers who assume the role of mere 'functionaries', as capital becomes 'socialised' (Bryer 1993a, 2000a, 2012). Consequently, modern accounting materialises as a response to the interests of collective capital. In these conditions, management is 'the eclectic pursuit of surplus value' (Bryer 2006a: 576). At the same time, the evolution of global capital market efficiency is evidence of the unexpended progressive tendencies of capitalism (Desai 2002). Accounting methods and their development reflect the interplay of the demands of capital markets and the characteristics of the fixed and working capital resources embedded in the firm (Toms

2010). Even so, PEA advocates rarely extol the virtues of markets, arguing that they are a poor description of the reality of scandal and corruption in resource allocation and distribution between labour and capital (Tinker et al. 1982: 171–2). Other variants of Marxism and radical structuralism tend to reify and even 'hypostatise' giant corporations, describing a form of capitalism without capitalists (Zeitlin 1989).

The main problem with the radical structuralist perspectives is their tendency to over-determine the evidence. In contrast to the post-modernists, they require everything to fit a grand narrative and unlike the mainstream approaches, they tend to look for single over-arching causes. Strands of radical structuralism are also fundamentally incompatible with one another. Are managers in large corporations powerful or not, for example? Or does power reside anonymously with 'capital'?

Contexts and debates

Each of the four perspectives introduced in the previous section surfaces to some extent in the major debates in accounting history that concern the relationship between accounting and capitalism. These are now dealt with chronologically, with examples of each of the four perspectives highlighted.

Accounting and the rise of capitalism

The debate on accounting and the rise of capitalism begins with Sombart (1916). The 'Sombart thesis' is based on six pages of *Der moderne Kapitalismus*, in which he suggests that it is impossible to envisage accounting without capitalism and impossible to envisage capitalism without accounting. For Sombart, double-entry bookkeeping is a sufficient condition for capitalism to exist, and he locates the origins of capitalism with double-entry bookkeeping in medieval and renaissance Catholic Italy. As double-entry bookkeeping replaced narrative accounts it brought order to the affairs of merchants. Specifically, it facilitated the process of valuing and accumulating capital, set out capital as a concept and allowed the business entity concept, or the separation of the business from its owner(s), to develop. Needless to say, the Sombart assertion has since enervated accounting history as an empirical project, as scholars have conducted extensive searches in the archives for falsifying examples.

As the Sombart hypothesis has been examined against the evidence, it has also been subject to refinement. Max Weber (1927) makes a far more specific claim. He makes no mention of the contribution of double-entry bookkeeping to the birth and development of capitalism, but more precisely equates the universal condition of capitalism with the development of the capital account. He attributes the original advocacy of the capital account to the Dutch Calvinist Simon Stevin in 1698, which post-dates Pacioli and double-entry bookkeeping by 200 years. In other words, for Weber at least, double-entry bookkeeping is a necessary but not sufficient condition for capitalism.

Bryer, as an illustration of the structuralist perspective, refines Sombart and Weber by a further stage, suggesting that the ability to calculate the rate of return on capital is the defining feature of capitalism. Such a calculation is impossible without Weber's capital account. However, Bryer's perspective differs in a fundamental respect, which is important for the accounting historian to recognise. His suggestion is that the historian should look for evidence of the calculations performed, not simply the existence of accounts of a certain type. These calculations are the 'accounting signatures' which encapsulate certain 'calculative mentalities'. Examples include the calculation of 'consumable surplus' by feudal landowners and profit calculations by capitalist farmers (Bryer 2004, 2006b), rate of return calculations by Italian merchants from the late fourteenth century (Bryer 1993b) and the calculation of return on capital employed by investing capitalists holding 'socialised' (i.e. collectively owned) capital (Bryer 2000a, 2000b, 2016).

The Sombart hypothesis has been subjected to considerable debate, refinement and empirical scrutiny. Gleeson-White (2011: 167) endorses Sombart and his argument that effectively states that double-entry bookkeeping 'gave birth to the entire modern scientific capitalist world'. Chiapello (2007) demonstrates that the idea or notion of accounting is important to the birth of the notion of capitalism, without conceding Sombart's more specific claim about the relationship between double-entry bookkeeping and capitalism. In the form of double-entry bookkeeping, according to Dean et al. (2016), accounting has recourse to intellectual foundations of perspective, harmony, order and balance.

In turn, double-entry bookkeeping encourages and makes possible the 'capitalist mentality', manifested as return on capital calculations. Such calculations are ruled out in the renaissance and early modern period by Bryer (2016), in the absence of socialised capital and associated investor demand for them, by Sangster (2015a, 2015b), who notes the concern of Italian merchants with individual transactions rather than overall consolidated business level financial position, and the overriding concern with custody and institutional scrutiny emphasised by Pacioli (Toms 2016). Toms (2010) notes that return on capital calculations are not an immutable feature of capitalism, and that the nature of such calculations varies considerably according to the stage of industrial and financial market development. Modern capitalism, across international jurisdictions, has incorporated capital calculation in very different ways (Richard 2015). In pre-industrial times, in the absence of substantial fixed capital, merchants and other capitalists were less concerned about business level profitability and its maximisation, reflecting instead feudal business norms or just price and prohibitions of usury (Toms 2010). As a consequence of the usury prohibition, Italian bankers and merchants kept accounts only recording debtors and creditors, without accounts recording cash or interest (Goldthwaite 2009; Sangster 2015a). The system facilitated book transfers and promoting credit creation and the commercial revolution, but business-level profitability calculations only emerged at a much later phase of capitalist development.

Accounting is, for Weber and others, a set of rational techniques which produce apparently objective and neutral results. In a long-run survey, Soll (2014) argues, in similar vein, that financial accountability is more effective when part of a moral and cultural framework. Rather than simply a matter of mechanical application, accounting should then be evaluated according to wider dimensions, including for example its rhetorical significance (Carruthers and Espeland 1991). These results provide symbolic legitimacy to the forms of business organisation adopting them. In other words, Carruthers and Espeland, like Bryer, are interested in how the objective content of accounts is subjectively determined. Unlike Bryer, they are concerned with a legitimation process at societal level and might therefore be classed as promoting a managerialist perspective, so that the advantages of double-entry bookkeeping from the point of view of the merchant can be appreciated. Aho (2005) broadly agrees with Sombart but challenges the aspects of Weber that link the rise of capitalism to Protestantism.[5] In contrast to Weber, Aho locates the origins of double-entry bookkeeping in the rhetoric and practice of the Roman Catholic Church. Medieval merchants used the rhetoric of double-entry bookkeeping to justify their behaviour in an age when business activity was likely to offend moral sensibilities. Aho therefore takes issue with Weber and, like Sombart, believes medieval Catholicism encouraged the pursuit of wealth and created the conditions for double-entry bookkeeping and the emergence of capitalism. The extent to which these general social forces and religious ideology determined capitalism and consequently the development of double-entry bookkeeping is a matter for debate within the structuralist school of thought.

In contrast to those scholars whose project is to refine the Sombart thesis, others have been more concerned with refuting it altogether. The most prominent of these is Yamey (1964, 2005). For Yamey, it is entirely possible to calculate the capital of a business without using double-entry bookkeeping, for example by valuing individual assets and adding the result. Accounts compiled using double-entry bookkeeping and rates of return calculations were in any case, he suggested, not very useful for decision-making purposes. He also challenges Sombart's argument, that only double-entry bookkeeping makes possible the separation of the business from its owners, by suggesting that partnership businesses predate double-entry bookkeeping. Period and context would appear to be important in assessing Yamey's general conclusion. In an extensive survey of treatises on double-entry bookkeeping written in the mercantilist period, Edwards et al. (2009) show that accounts created the means for establishing and monitoring changes in the value of an estate, encouraging decision-makers to act on the resulting financial information. However, further doubt is cast on the Sombart thesis by Funnell and Robertson (2011), using evidence from the Netherlands, which shows that until the late sixteenth century Dutch merchants used Hanseatic German factor accounting in preference to Pacioli's double-entry bookkeeping. Such methods suited the circumstances of merchants who needed to account for goods consigned to an agent or factor, in the form of venture specific and time limited sets of transactions. Lemarchand (1994) finds evidence in French businesses of relatively late evolution of double-entry bookkeeping, notwithstanding the earlier emergence of capitalistic organisations, providing further empirical evidence against the Sombart thesis. Although coming to different conclusions, like Carruthers and Espeland, these interpretations are essentially managerialist as they are concerned with evaluating the utility of double-entry bookkeeping for managerial decision-makers. Empirically, they expect to find double-entry bookkeeping where it has useful context.

To summarise all the debates, the Sombart thesis remains useful to the accounting historian for two reasons. First, it provides a framework for evaluating empirical research. The evidence from France alone suggests some very uneven patterns in the adoption of specific aspects of double-entry bookkeeping. So the more the Sombart thesis is refined the more focused the empirical project becomes. In turn this may encourage further refinement of the thesis. Second, therefore, through further historical accounting research, accounting historians can discover a good deal more about the process of transition from feudalism to capitalism.

The industrial revolution and nineteenth-century Britain

It is commonly accepted that Britain experienced an 'industrial revolution' between around 1760 and 1850 (Landes 1969). The industrial revolution and its associated developments in accounting methods have generated more interest among accounting historians than the Sombart thesis. A likely reason is that the operations of industrial companies provide a more obvious starting point for the discovery of early examples of the use of 'modern' accounting techniques. Ironically, one of the first major studies, carried out by Pollard (1965), found that accounting did nothing to aid entrepreneurial decision-making (Pollard 1965: 248). Since then revisionist, typically managerialist, historians have set out to discover evidence of good practice and in some cases have found it. For example, Edwards and Newell (1991) reject Pollard's pessimistic conclusions, and Fleischman and Parker (1991) conclude that accounting historians have by and large refuted Pollard's view of inadequate costing methods, but tend to agree with him on the inadequacy of financial accounting. Religious dissenters, as entrepreneurs operating through social networks of like-minded individuals, were particularly effective at developing and deploying cost accounting techniques (Funnell and Williams 2014).

While the managerialists have found plenty of examples of the evolution of managerial accounting techniques in the nineteenth century, positivists have advanced regulatory interpretations of nineteenth-century accounting developments. The effect has been to concentrate studies in particular industries to the exclusion of others. On the basis of such limited evidence, accounting change might be seen as a response to the demand for self-interested accounting choices, for example the development of depreciation accounting as a response to changes in taxation law (Watts and Zimmerman 1979: 293–5). For Parker (1990), accounting change in the late Victorian period was a response to increasing regulation, particularly in the banking sector (Parker 1990; Walker 1996) and railways and utilities (Edwards 1992). So when applied in a historical context, these authors suggest larger British firms tended to adopt professional auditors voluntarily. Therefore, they concluded, the unregulated free market was sufficient for adequate accountability (Edwards et al. 1997: 22), and that the emergence of a large capital market, and associated reductions in unit audit costs, was the prime determinant of the development of modern auditing (Watts and Zimmerman 1983: 630).

From a structuralist perspective, Bryer (2005) examines the accounting histories of the New Mills (Haddingtonshire, formed in 1681), the New Lanark Cotton Factory (1800 to 1812), and the Carron Company (formed in 1759), arguing that these cases show that the primary cause of variations in modern accounts were variations in the 'social relations of production'. He concludes that the published accounting evidence supports the theory that the industrial revolution was the victory of the capitalist mentality. Later, as the railways developed, the collective interests of capital dominate managers who assume the role of mere 'functionaries' as capital ownership became increasingly 'socialised' (Bryer 1993a). Recent evidence has tended to support Bryer's explanation of accounting calculation as the 'signature of capitalism' in relation to estate accounting (Oldroyd 2007) and canals in Britain (Arnold and McCartney 2008). Toms (2010) documents substantial variation in the use of return based measures as such signatures during the nineteenth century, reflecting the asset composition of capital as well as its social ownership. Bryer (2012, 2013) meanwhile has extended his analysis to explain the role of accounting in the rise of capitalism in the United States.

The post-modern perspective offers interesting new insights from an accounting history and social science perspective. These can be summarised as the necessity of context (Hopwood 1983), through the use of the Foucauldian notions of *archaeology*, or the emergence of forms of discourse and how they are configured in their non-discursive domains (for example, economic and institutional). *Genealogy*, on the other hand, looks at ruptures, or transitions leading to the adoption of new practices, which as a result achieve new significance in the revised context (Hopwood 1983: 230). Using the example of Josiah Wedgwood's pottery business, Hopwood explains how a financial crisis caused Wedgwood to set up an accounting system for the first time in order to investigate the situation. Although the system was used primarily for crisis management, by specifying costs, profit and profitability in relation to sales value it formed a crucial part of the strategy and decision-making process (McKendrick 1970). As Hopwood (1987: 213) suggests, organisational accounts are not merely a technical reflection of pre-given economic imperatives, but are actively constructed to create economic visibility as a powerful means for positively enabling the governance and economic control of the organisation.

As workers became concentrated in factories, accounting became a more important means of achieving these outcomes. Specifically, accounting provided management with a means of controlling human subjects. Hoskin and Macve (1994) trace the origins of such methods to the military academy at West Point and their application at Springfield Armory. By contrast, even the pioneering firms of the British industrial revolution, Boulton and Watt, Carron and Wedgwood, had significant limitations in their accounting. These conclusions are nonetheless contested (Boyns and Edwards 2013) with further empirical evidence demonstrating that Boulton and Watt made extensive use of accounting to control its workers and that by contrast Springfield Armory was riddled with corruption and production inefficiencies (Toms and Fleischman 2015).

As can be seen from this very brief review, the debates on the industrial revolution have concentrated on empirical sources, primarily with a view to finding evidence of managers using accounts to make rational decisions. In terms of debates, the industrial revolution, excepting some marginal contribution from the positivists, is primarily about structuralist and managerialist interpretations. Both have found plenty of evidence about 'rational decisions' and 'capitalist signatures'. Unfortunately it is easy to infer either conclusion from the same body of evidence and the attitude of the reader will have a strong influence on which view is believed. Meanwhile the new accounting history offers the possibility of further studies and new interpretations.

The rise of the managerial capitalism

Managerial capitalism is associated with the work of Chandler and his extensive research which documents the rise of the large business organisation in the United States from the late nineteenth century onwards. Accounting and managerial accounting techniques were important components of managerial capitalism. In contrast to the United States, where managerialism flourished, Britain in the Chandlerian view remained wedded to an increasingly out of date and uncompetitive system of personal capitalism. If the Chandler thesis is correct, then it is to the large US industrial firm that the accounting historian should direct attention. It might be expected therefore that this section is dominated by mainstream managerialism, but the other perspectives also offer important insights into the role of accounting in big business.

An influential application of transaction cost theory to management accounting history is Johnson and Kaplan's (1987) *Relevance Lost*. They examine the transition from a market environment where entrepreneurial instinct and centralised ownership prevailed, to decentralised business enterprises guided by accounting techniques that assisted in the reduction of transaction cost. Through this process, the vast majority of management accounting techniques in use today were developed by the 1920s and a period of stagnation ensued. According to their thesis, the stagnation was the result of the privileging of financial accounting by accountants and the failure of academics to go beyond simplified abstract questions.

If Johnson and Kaplan's approach can be characterised as positivist, there has been implicit or explicit criticism from all three alternative schools of thought in Table 17.1. Surveillance lies at the centre of post-modernist explanations of the genesis of accounting techniques. Hoskin and Macve's (2000) critique of Johnson and Kaplan suggested that 'managing it all by numbers' was a futile exercise for the purposes of controlling human activities and behaviour, and in any case accounting numbers could not capture economic magnitudes properly.

From the mainstream managerialist perspective, Chandler (1981, 1990) stresses the role of vertical integration and managerial co-ordination as the determinant of organisational efficiency rather than transaction cost. Hopper and Armstrong (1991), taking a radical structuralist perspective, assign similar importance to market power, which the transaction cost approach neglects, showing how budgeting was used to facilitate monopoly pricing at DuPont. Labour management and control of the labour process are also offered as important explanations for the development of twentieth-century budgeting techniques ignored by both Johnson and Kaplan's transaction cost and Chandler's managerialist perspectives. Using examples from the Boston district textile industry and US metals and arms manufacturers, Hopper and Armstrong show that techniques were adopted for the purposes of surveillance, workshop control and profit appropriation, even if such control was achieved at the expense of short-term efficiency. Bryer (2013) re-examines the accounting methods of the Boston textile mills and other industries to argue that their under-development in terms of depreciation and overhead absorption signalled the delayed arrival of US capitalism only by the 1920s. This conclusion has been challenged as counter intuitive and lacking sufficient empirical evidence (Oldroyd et al. 2015). There is good reason for scepticism. If certain accounting techniques are heralded as sufficient conditions for capitalism, such arguments, like the Sombart thesis in general, reduce to tautologies.

In summary, Johnson and Kaplan's work has been influential in the development of accounting history in part from the strength of its original thesis and also as a result of the robustness of the responses their thesis has provoked. Table 17.1 provides a useful mechanism for triangulating and contrasting these interpretations. If we accept their main argument, financial accounting remained dominant even during the managerial phase of capitalism, a dominance reinforced by the next and most recent phase of accounting and capitalist development.

'Financialisation' and the 'Enron' stage of capitalism

Since the 1980s, there is evidence that the rise of managerial capitalism has been reversed in Britain and the United States (Toms et al. 2015). Layered structures of management have been removed through downsizing and the scope of business activity has been reduced through refocusing. The accumulation of financial capital in the banking and shadow banking sector, and the search for financial returns increasingly through the development of risky financial products and speculation, led to the global financial crisis of 2007–09 (Boyer 2013). Accounting was perceived as deeply implicated in this disaster (Arnold 2009), and the financial scandals that preceded it, notably at Enron, WorldCom and other major US corporations in the early 2000s (Unerman and O'Dwyer 2004).[6] As a result, a research agenda has developed around the growth of financial capitalism and its boom–bust consequences.

The economic restructurings of recent decades have been characterised as a transition to capitalist post-modernisation, in which immaterial labour dominates the economy and immaterial assets dominate the balance sheets of firms. With these developments comes a 'new spirit of capitalism' (Boltanski and Chiapello 2007), in similar vein to Sombart and Weber, but now based on flat management structures, flexible workers and network co-ordination. With these developments also comes the associated problem of 'immeasurability' (Hardt and Negri 2001). In the global financial crisis, financial institutions, assisted by accounting, abandoned the order and proportionality of the Italian renaissance in favour of the asset inflation of securitised derivatives, underpinned by accounting valuation models (Dean et al. 2016).

Within organisations, the scientific management of the managerial capitalism era has been replaced by management rhetoric and teamwork. A leading example is the notion of the 'governable person' controlled through the language of 'economic citizenship' exemplified by the Caterpillar case (Miller and O'Leary 1987, 1994). In this account Miller (1986, 1991) also suggests that in the course of historical change, there are temporary and often fragile stabilities, or 'accounting complexes', which can be used to explain the adoption of accounting techniques, for example value added accounting, in the context of national economic objectives and political priorities. It is Caterpillar in particular that has attracted considerable criticism from other historians, particularly because of the way management rhetoric has been used as evidence, notwithstanding the difficulty of proving that the will of management altered actual events and practices on the shop floor (Armstrong 2006).

In addition to their critique of the post-modernists, the radical structuralists add perspectives of their own to these and other developments. Armstrong (1991) has called for a re-theorisation of and empirical investigation of the history of the agency relationship. Toms (2005: 648–9) attempts this, analysing the interaction of financial capital socialisation (efficient and globalised capital markets being the fullest expression of socialised or pooled capital), on the one hand, and the centralisation of physical capital, on the other. Historical variations along continua of socialisation and physical concentration jointly explain the relative power of managerial and ownership groups, which determine in turn the character of financial and management accounting. The period since 1945 has witnessed the rise of accountancy and finance specialists. Their dominance of the British boardroom was manifested in the solution of monitoring problems associated with diversification through the use of financial controls (Armstrong 1987: 415). Therefore, as Armstrong (1985: 137) suggests, the role of accountancy within the global function of capital has created a horizontal fission within the profession, whereby the activities of an elite have routinised, fragmented and deskilled the work of their nominal professional colleagues. These tendencies were if anything more pronounced for accounting workers outside of the accounting profession (Cooper and Taylor 2000). At the same time, the financialisation of the economy ahead of the global financial crisis can be explained in terms of the expansion of fictitious capital, aided by accounting, that developed valuation models which first legitimised and then destroyed capital (Cooper 2015).

In summary, as in previous stages of capitalism, accounting is deeply implicated. It has facilitated the development of financialisation, administered its processes and intermediated the dominant ownership and managerial groups. Revisiting Sombart, it is difficult to imagine present day financial capitalism without accounting.

Conclusion

Accounting history has made a move towards the centre stage of social sciences in the last 20 years. In doing so, it has focused on the question of 'accounting and capitalism', by placing accounting history in the appropriate context of the economic and political system in which it operates. Accordingly, accounting history has become a dynamic and polemical discipline, which has also begun to address debates among accounting researchers and future directions for accounting research as a whole.

This chapter has presented a conceptual framework and analysed the theoretical contributions on the relationship between accounting and capitalism into four principal schools of thought. None of these can be said to be truly dominant and they in any case only characterise a complex literature in a broad sense. Accounting history, where dominated by empiricism, almost by definition has little to say about the more fundamental aspects of the accounting and capitalism symbiosis discussed earlier, leaving the mainstream boxes in the grid relatively sparsely populated. On the radical side, the dominant events have been the rise of post-modern relativism and the decline of orthodox Marxism between 1968 and the recent financial crisis. These trends have themselves reflected changes in capitalism and the intellectual responses to those changes. The resurgence of neo-liberalism before and since the financial crisis has energised critical commentary from radical perspectives. Such criticisms have called into question the role of accounting as a rational arbitrator, as capitalism, through speculation, asset price bubbles and financial crashes demonstrates ever increasing irrationality. The global financial crisis represents a crisis of value and of the determination of value, and as such presents a challenge to accounting that it has thus far failed to respond to. If history teaches us anything, it is that accounting will be closely implicated in the next phase of capitalism. However this transpires, the relationship between accounting and capitalism will be crucial, and, as this chapter has demonstrated, continues to provide valuable theoretical perspective and social context for the study of accounting history.

Key works

Arnold (2009) discusses the role of accounting in the global financial crisis and how the gaps in accounting research revealed by the crisis can be addressed.

Bryer (2005) supplies, from a radical perspective, a comprehensive analysis of the relationship between the development of capitalism and the development of accounting.

Chiapello (2007) provides an intelligent overview of accounting and the rise of capitalism and useful summaries of the debates.

Soll (2014) Although subject to some criticism, mostly over its factual accuracy (Sangster 2015b), Soll's book provides an accessible long-run history of accounting through the different phases of capitalist development.

Toms (2010) covers the main debates and interprets the nature of capitalist accounting calculation over the long run.

Notes

1 The grid is adapted from Hopper and Powell (1995) who use a similar approach to define critical accounting. See also Bryer (1998) and Rowlinson et al. (2006).
2 A fifth category can be envisioned which avoids ideology and concentrates merely on the discovery of facts. For the purposes of this chapter such approaches are labelled 'antiquarian' and are not considered further.
3 For more detail on Chandler's influential perspective, see Chapter 9.
4 Political economy is the interplay of power, the goals of power wielders and the productive exchange system (Zald 1970), and is concerned with the origins and distribution of power in society (Jackson 1982).
5 For a more detailed discussion see Chapter 25, Religion.
6 For more on the role of accounting in these episodes see Chapter 20, Scandals.

References

Aho, J. (2005) *Confession and Bookkeeping: The Religious, Moral and Rhetorical Roots of Accounting* (Albany, NY: State University of New York Press).

Armstrong, P. (1985) Changing management control strategies: The role of competition between accountancy and other organisational professions, *Accounting, Organizations and Society*, 10 (2): 129–48.

Armstrong, P. (1987) The rise of accounting controls in British capitalist enterprises, *Accounting, Organizations and Society*, 12 (5): 415–36.

Armstrong, P. (1991) Contradiction and social dynamics in the capitalist agency relationship, *Accounting, Organizations and Society*, 16 (1): 1–25.

Armstrong, P. (2006) Ideology and the grammar of idealism: The Caterpillar controversy revisited, *Critical Perspectives on Accounting*, 17 (5): 529–48.

Arnold, A.J. and McCartney, S. (2008) The transition to financial capitalism and its implications for financial reporting: Evidence from the English canal companies, *Accounting, Auditing & Accountability Journal*, 21 (8): 1185–209.

Arnold, P.J. (2009) Global financial crisis: The challenge to accounting research, *Accounting, Organizations and Society*, 34 (6–7): 803–09.

Baldwin, T. (1994) Management aspiration and audit opinion: Fixed asset accounting at the Staveley Coal and Iron Company 1863–1883, *Accounting and Business Research*, 25 (97): 3–12.

Ball, R. and Brown, P. (1968) An empirical evaluation of accounting income numbers, *Journal of Accounting Research*, 6 (2): 159–78.

Boltanski, L. and Chiapello, E. (2007) *The New Spirit of Capitalism* (London: Verso).

Boyer, R. (2013) The global financial crisis in historical perspective: An economic analysis combining Minsky, Hayek, Fisher, Keynes and the regulation approach, *Accounting, Economics and Law*, 3 (3): 93–139.

Boyns, T. and Edwards, J.R. (2000) Pluralistic approaches to knowing more: A comment on Hoskin and Macve, *Accounting Historians Journal*, 27 (1): 151–58.

Boyns, T. and Edwards, J.R. (2013) *A History of Management Accounting: The British Experience* (New York: Routledge).

Bryer, R. (1993a) The late nineteenth century revolution in financial reporting: Accounting for the rise of investor or managerial capitalism, *Accounting, Organizations and Society*, 18 (7–8): 649–90.

Bryer, R. (1993b) Double-entry bookkeeping and the birth of capitalism: Accounting for the commercial revolution in medieval northern Italy, *Critical Perspectives on Accounting*, 4 (2): 113–40.

Bryer, R. (1998) The struggle to maturity in writing the history of accounting, and the promise – some reflections on Keenan's defence of 'traditional methodology', *Critical Perspectives on Accounting*, 9 (6): 669–81.

Bryer, R. (2000a) The history of accounting and the transition to capitalism in England. Part one: Theory, *Accounting, Organizations and Society*, 25 (2): 131–62.

Bryer, R. (2000b) The history of accounting and the transition to capitalism in England. Part two: Evidence, *Accounting, Organizations and Society*, 25 (4–5): 327–81.

Bryer, R. (2004) The roots of modern capitalism: A Marxist accounting history of the origins and consequences of capitalist landlords in England, *Accounting Historians Journal*, 31 (1): 1–56.

Bryer, R. (2005) A Marxist accounting history of the British industrial revolution: A review of the evidence and suggestions for research, *Accounting, Organizations and Society*, 30 (1): 25–65.

Bryer, R. (2006a) Accounting and control of the labour process, *Critical Perspectives on Accounting*, 17 (5): 551–98.

Bryer, R. (2006b) The genesis of the capitalist farmer: Towards a Marxist accounting history of the English agricultural revolution, *Critical Perspectives on Accounting*, 17 (4): 367–97.

Bryer, R. (2012) Americanism and financial accounting theory–part 1: Was America born capitalist? *Critical Perspectives on Accounting*, 23 (7–8): 511–55.

Bryer, R. (2013) Americanism and financial accounting theory–part 2: The 'modern business enterprise', America's transition to capitalism, and the genesis of management accounting, *Critical Perspectives on Accounting*, 24 (4–5): 273–318.

Bryer, R. (2016) Linking Pacioli's double-entry bookkeeping, algebra, and art: Accounting history or idle speculation? *Accounting History Review*, 26 (1): 33–40.

Burrell, G. and Morgan, G. (1989) *Sociological Paradigms and Organizational Analysis: Elements of the Sociology of Corporate Life* (London: Heinemann).

Carruthers, B.G. and Espeland, W.N. (1991) Accounting for rationality: Double-entry bookkeeping and the rhetoric of economic rationality, *American Journal of Sociology*, 97 (1): 31–69.
Chandler, A.D. (1977) *The Visible Hand: The Managerial Revolution in American Business* (Cambridge, MA & London: Belknap Press).
Chandler, A.D. (1981) Historical determinants of managerial hierarchies: A response to Perrow, in A. Van de Ven and W.F. Joyce (eds.) *Perspectives on Organisational Design and Behaviour*, pp. 391–412 (New York: Wiley).
Chandler, A.D. (1990) *Scale and Scope. The Dynamics of Industrial Capitalism* (Cambridge, MA & London: Belknap Press).
Chatfield, M. (1977) *A History of Accounting Thought* (Huntington, NY: Robert E. Krieger).
Chiapello, E. (2007) Accounting and the birth of the notion of capitalism, *Critical Perspectives on Accounting*, 18 (6): 263–96.
Chow, C.W. (1983) The impact of accounting regulation on bondholder and shareholder wealth: The case of the Securities Acts, *Accounting Review*, 58 (3): 485–520.
Coase, R. (1937) The nature of the firm, *Economica*, 4 (16): 386–405.
Cooper, C. (2015) Accounting for the fictitious: A Marxist contribution to understanding accounting's roles in the financial crisis, *Critical Perspectives on Accounting*, 30: 63–82.
Cooper, C. and Taylor, P. (2000) From Taylorism to Ms Taylor: The transformation of the accounting craft, *Accounting, Organizations and Society*, 25 (6): 555–78.
Cooper, D. and Sherer, M. (1984) The value of accounting reports: Arguments for a political economy of accounting, *Accounting, Organizations and Society*, 9 (3–4): 207–32.
Dean, G., Clarke, F. and Capalbo, F. (2016) Pacioli's double entry–part of an intellectual and social movement, *Accounting History Review*, 26 (1): 5–24.
Desai, M. (2002) *Marx's Revenge: The Resurgence of Capitalism and the Death of Statist Socialism* (London: Verso).
Edwards, J.R. (1989) *A History of Financial Accounting* (London: Routledge).
Edwards, J.R. (1992) Companies, corporations and accounting change, 1835–1933: A comparative study, *Accounting and Business Research*, 22 (89): 59–73.
Edwards, J.R. (2019) *A History of Corporate Financial Reporting in Britain* (New York: Routledge).
Edwards, J.R., Anderson, M. and Matthews, D. (1997) Accountability in a free-market economy: The British company audit, 1886, *Abacus*, 33 (1): 1–25.
Edwards, J.R., Dean, G. and Clarke, F. (2009) Merchants' accounts, performance assessment and decision making in mercantilist Britain, *Accounting, Organizations and Society*, 34 (5): 551–70.
Edwards, J.R. and Newell, E. (1991) The development of industrial cost and management accounting before 1850: A survey of the evidence, *Business History*, 33 (1): 35–57.
Ezzamel, M., Hoskin, K. and Macve, R. (1990) Managing it all by numbers: A review of Johnson and Kaplan's 'Relevance Lost', *Accounting and Business Research*, 20 (78): 153–66.
Fleischman, R.K. and Parker, L.D. (1991) British entrepreneurs and pre-industrial revolution evidence of cost management, *Accounting Review*, 66 (8): 361–75.
Funnell, W. and Robertson, J. (2011) Capitalist accounting in sixteenth century Holland: Hanseatic influences and the Sombart thesis, *Accounting, Auditing & Accountability Journal*, 24 (5): 560–86.
Funnell, W. and Williams, R. (2014) The religious imperative of cost accounting in the early industrial revolution, *Accounting, Auditing & Accountability Journal*, 27 (2): 357–81.
Gleeson-White, J. (2011) *Double Entry: How the Merchants of Venice Shaped the Modern World and How Their Invention Could Make or Break the Planet* (Sydney: Allen & Unwin).
Goldthwaite, R.A. (2009) *The Economy of Renaissance Florence* (Baltimore, MA: Johns Hopkins University Press).
Gray, R., Kouhy, R. and Lavers, S. (1995) Corporate social and environmental reporting: A review of the literature and a longitudinal study of UK disclosure, *Accounting, Auditing and Accountability Journal*, 8 (2): 47–77.
Grossman, S. and Stiglitz, J. (1980) On the impossibility of informationally efficient markets, *American Economic Review*, 70 (3): 393–408.
Hardt, M. and Negri, A. (2001) *Empire* (Cambridge, MA: Harvard University Press).
Hopper, T. and Armstrong, P. (1991) Cost accounting, controlling labour and the rise of conglomerates, *Accounting Organizations and Society*, 16 (5–6): 405–38.
Hopper, T. and Powell, A. (1995) Making sense of research into the organizational and social aspects of management accounting: A review of its underlying assumptions, *Journal of Management Studies*, 22 (5): 429–65.

Hopwood, A.G. (1983) On trying to study accounting in the contexts in which it operates, *Accounting Organizations and Society*, 8 (2–3): 287–305.
Hopwood, A.G. (1987) The archaeology of accounting systems, *Accounting, Organizations and Society*, 12 (3): 207–34.
Hoskin, K. and Macve, R. (1994) Reappraising the genesis of managerialism: A re-examination of the role of accounting at the Springfield Armory, 1815–1845, *Accounting, Auditing & Accountability Journal*, 7 (2): 4–29.
Hoskin, K. and Macve, R. (2000) Knowing more as knowing less? Alternative histories of cost and management accounting in the US and the UK, *Accounting Historians Journal*, 27 (1): 91–149.
Jackson, B. (1982) *The Political Economy of Bureaucracy* (Oxford: Oxford University Press).
Jensen, M. and Meckling, W. (1976) Theory of the firm: Managerial behaviour, agency costs and ownership structure, *Journal of Financial Economics*, 3 (4): 305–60.
Johnson, H.T. and Kaplan, R. (1987) *Relevance Lost. The Rise and Fall of Management Accounting* (Boston: Harvard Business School Press).
Kennedy, W. (1987) *Industrial Structure, Capital Markets and the Origin of British Economic Decline* (Cambridge: Cambridge University Press).
Landes, D. (1969) *The Unbound Prometheus* (Cambridge: Cambridge University Press).
Lemarchand, Y. (1994) Double entry versus charge and discharge accounting in eighteenth-century France, *Accounting, Business & Financial History*, 4 (1): 119–45.
McKendrick, N. (1970) Josiah Wedgwood and cost accounting in the Industrial Revolution, *Economic History Review*, 23 (1): 45–67.
Merino, B.D., Koch, B.S. and MacRitchie, K.L. (1987) Historical analysis – a diagnostic tool for event studies: The impact of the Securities Acts, 1933, *Accounting Review*, 62 (4): 748–62.
Miller, P. (1986) Accounting for progress – national accounting and planning in France: A review essay, *Accounting, Organizations and Society*, 11 (1): 83–104.
Miller, P. (1991) Accounting innovation beyond the enterprise: Problematizing investment decisions and programming economic growth in the UK in the 1960s, *Accounting, Organizations and Society*, 16 (8): 733–62.
Miller, P., Hopper, T. and Laughlin, R. (1991) The new accounting history, *Accounting, Organizations and Society*, 18 (7–8): 631–47.
Miller, P. and O'Leary, T. (1987) Accounting and the construction of the governable person, *Accounting, Organizations and Society*, 12 (3): 235–66.
Miller, P. and O'Leary, T. (1994) Accounting, 'economic citizenship' and the spatial reordering of manufacture, *Accounting, Organizations and Society*, 19 (1): 15–43.
Oldroyd, D. (2007) *Estates, Enterprise and Investment at the Dawn of the Industrial Revolution: Estate Management and Accounting in the North-East of England, C. 1700–1780* (Aldershot: Ashgate).
Oldroyd, D., Tyson, T.N. and Fleischman, R.K. (2015) American ideology, socialism and financial accounting theory: A counter view, *Critical Perspectives on Accounting*, 27: 209–18.
Parker, R.H. (1990) Regulating British corporate financial reporting in the late nineteenth century, *Accounting, Business & Financial History*, 1 (1): 51–71.
Pollard, S. (1965) *The Genesis of Modern Management* (London: Edward Arnold).
Putterman, L. (1986) The economic nature of the firm: Overview, in L. Putterman (ed.) *The Economic Nature of the Firm*, pp. 1–29 (Cambridge: Cambridge University Press).
Richard, J. (2015) The dangerous dynamics of modern capitalism (from static to IFRS' futuristic accounting), *Critical Perspectives on Accounting*, 30: 9–34.
Rowlinson, M., Toms, S. and Wilson, J.F. (2006) Legitimacy and the capitalist corporation: Cross-cutting perspectives on ownership and control, *Critical Perspectives on Accounting*, 17 (5): 681–702.
Sangster, A. (2015a) The genesis of double entry bookkeeping, *Accounting Review*, 91 (1): 299–315.
Sangster, A. (2015b) Jacob Soll: The reckoning: Financial accountability and the making and breaking of nations, *Accounting Historians Journal*, 42 (1): 139–56.
Sivakumar, K. and Waymire, G. (1993) The information content of earnings in a discretionary reporting environment: Evidence from NYSE industrials, 1905–1910, *Journal of Accounting Research*, 31 (1): 62–91.
Soll, J. (2014) *The Reckoning: Financial Accountability and the Rise and Fall of Nations* (New York: Basic Books).
Sombart, W. (1916) *Der Moderne Kapitalismus* (Leipzig: Duncker & Humbolt).

Tinker, T. (1980) Towards a political economy of accounting: An empirical illustration of the Cambridge controversies, *Accounting, Organizations and Society*, 5 (1): 147–60.
Tinker, T., Merino, B. and Neimark, M. (1982) The normative origins of positive theories: Ideology and accounting thought, *Accounting, Organizations and Society*, 7 (2): 167–200.
Toms, S. (2001) Information content of earnings announcements in an unregulated market: The co-operative Cotton Mills of Lancashire, 1880–1900, *Accounting and Business Research*, 31 (3): 175–90.
Toms, S. (2005) Financial control, managerial control and accountability: Evidence from the British cotton industry, 1700–2000, *Accounting, Organizations and Society*, 30 (7–8): 627–53.
Toms, S. (2010) Calculating profit: A historical perspective on the development of capitalism, *Accounting, Organizations and Society*, 35 (2): 205–21.
Toms, S. (2016) Double entry and the rise of capitalism: Keeping a sense of proportion? *Accounting History Review*, 26 (1): 25–31.
Toms, S. and Fleischman, R.K. (2015) Accounting fundamentals and accounting change: Boulton & Watt and the Springfield Armory, *Accounting, Organizations and Society*, 41 (1): 1–20.
Toms, S., Wilson, N. and Wright, M. (2015) The evolution of private equity: Corporate restructuring in the UK, c.1945–2010, *Business History*, 57 (7): 736–68.
Tyson, T. (2000) Accounting history and the emperor's new clothes: A response to knowing more as knowing less, *Accounting Historian's Journal*, 27 (1): 159–72.
Unerman, J. and O'Dwyer, B. (2004) Enron, WorldCom, Andersen et al.: A challenge to modernity, *Critical Perspectives on Accounting*, 15 (6–7): 971–93.
Walker, S.P. (1996) Laissez-faire, collectivism and companies legislation in nineteenth century Britain, *British Accounting Review*, 28 (4): 305–24.
Watts, R. and Zimmerman, J. (1979) The demand and supply of accounting theories: The market for excuses, *Accounting Review*, 54 (2): 273–305.
Watts, R. and Zimmerman, J. (1983) Agency problems, auditing, and the theory of the firm: Some evidence, *Journal of Law and Economics*, 26 (3): 613–34.
Watts, R.L. and Zimmerman, J.L. (1986) *Positive Accounting Theory* (Englewood Cliffs, NJ: Prentice-Hall).
Weber, M. (1927) *General Economic History*, trans. by F.H. Knight (London: Allen & Unwin).
Williamson, O.E. (1975) *Markets and Hierarchies* (London: Free Press).
Williamson, O.E. (1981) The modern corporation: Origins, evolution and attributes, *Journal of Economic Literature*, 19 (4): 1537–68.
Yamey, B.S. (1964) Accounting and the rise of capitalism: Further notes on a theme by Sombart, *Journal of Accounting Research*, 2 (2): 117–36.
Yamey, B.S. (2005) The historical significance of double entry bookkeeping: Some non-Sombartian claims, *Accounting, Business & Financial History*, 15 (1): 77–88.
Zald, M. (1970) Political economy: A framework for comparative analysis, in M. Zald (ed.) *Power in Organisations*, pp. 221–61 (Nashville: Vanderbilt University Press).
Zeitlin, M. (1989) *The Large Corporation and Contemporary Classes* (Cambridge: Polity Press).

18
RAILROADS

Dale L. Flesher and Gary J. Previts[1]

Overview

Railroads played a major role in the growth of the nineteenth-century US and British economies, and their contribution to the development of accounting and auditing has attracted considerable scholarly attention.[2] The first important aspect of railroad accounting is related to the way they were founded – as joint-stock companies, a type of business organization that created agency problems and the need for governance. Because railroads grew effectively and efficiently, they came to need accounting information and auditing services. Since accounting and auditing were unknown or little developed in the mid-1800s, the railroads had to devise effective practices to operate their businesses. Many of the procedures they developed were later adapted for use by industrial corporations. As a result, the railroad industry can be looked to for an explanation of the formulation of many accounting techniques.

Railroads utilised several innovative reporting practices: early use of cash flow statements, the identification of 'Net earnings', extensive socioeconomic reporting, and the development of the double account system. In the US, the Baltimore & Ohio Railroad Company (B&O) was an innovator with respect to governance and auditing, while the Mobile & Ohio Railroad Company (M&O) pioneered the use of accounting for the better determination of earnings power. At the same time, railway companies in both the US (including the M&O) and the UK published accounts that were the subject of 'nineteenth-century accounting error' (Brief 1965) – inaccuracy due to the omission of depreciation and other non-cash expenses and the failure to classify transactions correctly as capital or revenue. Nineteenth-century accounting error may be simply that – an error; alternatively, it may constitute 'bias' (ibid.: 12) reflecting management optimism, window dressing or even fraudulent behaviour when constructing published financial reports.

This chapter begins in the nineteenth century when issues of accounting, auditing and accountability came to the fore, were addressed, and to some extent resolved. Twentieth-century issues are then identified and discussed. But the railroads, particularly in the US, had matured by the end of the nineteenth century and faced new circumstances and context, due to their scale crossing the North American continent, and the political environment including public scrutiny of the perceived power of the industry to influence issues ranging from shipping costs to labour costs and community and business development. As a result practices evolved and regulation came into being as railroads were considered a distinctive part of the economy and therefore should be subject to more stringent disclosures and accounting practices than other industries. Given space constraints this chapter is confined to the US and, to a limited extent, the UK. The presentational approach highlights a review of the relevant literature augmented with some detailed case studies from US railroad history.

Introduction

As Chandler established in *The Visible Hand* (1977), railroad companies were America's first modern businesses. The B&O, formed in 1827, and based on a British concept, was the first major US railroad (Cleveland and Powell 1909: 61). In the UK, it was the success of the Stockton and Darlington Railway (1825) and the Liverpool and Manchester line (1830) that encouraged the start up of many similar operations (McCartney and Arnold 2000: 294). Although scores of other railroads were developed in the following decades throughout the US, the UK and continental Europe, the B&O was reputed to be the 'university' of railroad accounting and operations for a quarter of a century, i.e. a source of substantial technical, accounting and management innovation in railroading affairs. Then, in the early 1850s, a new railroading environment in the US led to the Illinois Central (IC) Railroad and the M&O becoming important industry leaders. An analysis of the accounting innovations of these three lines covers many important aspects of the first half century of railroading, although the chief financial officer of the Louisville and Nashville Railroad, Albert Fink, an alumnus of the B&O, is recognised as having made important contributions near the end of the period.

The broad history of railroading in the UK is similar to that in the US, but the environment was different. In the US, most early railroads were developmental enterprises whose profits were dependent on future geographic expansion. There were few opportunities for quick profits. In the UK, railroads had more in common with other business opportunities in that they were built to exploit existing trade channels. On both sides of the Atlantic, the need for vast capital outlays was the same, but an investment in a US railroad was a less economic-rational business decision than in the UK. As a result, US governmental entities, mostly state and local, assisted private investors by providing subsidies either in the form of direct investments or in the case of Federal subsidy, grants of various types including land-grants that could be sold subject to contractual conditions to provide incentives to help build the railroads. These subsidies introduced accounting questions that did not exist in the UK; for example, how does the road disclose the substantial acreage of raw land, with potential values undetermined, which were awarded as achieved incentives upon successful completion of land grant rail routes?

The first half century of railroad operations was essentially a growth phase and was followed by what has been called a regulatory phase. The detailed regulatory phase, beginning with state-based regimes such as the Massachusetts Railroad Law in 1846 (Neidert 1950: 34–6) and followed by the passage of the 1868 Regulation of Railways Act in the UK and the 1887 creation of the Federal Interstate Commerce Commission (ICC) in the US, signalled a period of controversy as railroads alternately responded to 'sunshine' regulation, i.e. requests for information that cast light on the financial and operating aspects of the roads, and also attempted to capture the regulatory mechanisms to achieve economic benefits of cartelisation (Kolko 1965).

The importance of 'sunshine' commissions, as the pre-Federal regulatory bodies, which were state based, were called, was that they had identified the concept of 'disclosure of information' as a means of achieving a remedy for society's 'railroad problem' – an expression used to identify the host of ills or disruptions associated with the dramatic changes brought about by these first 'natural monopolies' that dominated the economic and political landscape. Charles Francis Adams is seen in the writings of McCraw (1984: 8) as the best known proponent of the need for such a new apolitical institution. While earlier perfunctory reports were made to the various states, it is the work of the post-Civil War state railroad commissions that resulted in the first steps towards coordinated regulatory disclosures in filings and reports that were later adopted and adapted by the ICC. The ultimate focus was that the 'rate' to be charged needed to be sufficiently low to satisfy customers yet adequate to sustain a profitable enterprise. This political-economic issue became a central part of the regulatory genre and would continue throughout the ensuing century-long railroading epochs in the US. Accounting processes and information were inevitably embroiled in the perennial debate over the 'rate' issue.

This chapter is based on the work of many scholars who have studied railroad accounting over the years. The first important contributor in the UK was from Harold Pollins, who dealt primarily with the period prior to 1868 (Pollins 1952, 1954, 1956), although some might argue that Lardner's 1850 book was essentially a railroad history and analysis up to that early publication date. Many others in the UK have followed Pollins, including some who have attempted to clarify Pollins' work (such as Richards 1972). Edwards (1986, 2019) and the team of Arnold and McCartney (McCartney and Arnold 2000, 2002, 2003, 2012; Arnold and McCartney 2002, 2008) have also made important contributions. In the US, there are hundreds of original publications from the 1800s,[3] but the first real synthesis was undertaken by Neidert in 1950, although his work is strongest for the post-1887 period. More recently the work of Flesher, Previts and Sampson (Samson and Previts 1999; Flesher et al. 2000, 2003a, 2003b, 2006; Previts and Samson 2000; Samson et al. 2003) explores, in detail, the earlier period in the US. However, it should be noted that Brief (1965, 1976) made important contributions with respect to capital consumption allowances and that works by Miranti (1990), Heier (2000, 2006, 2009, 2010), Feeney (2005, 2013) and Thompson (2013, 2017) have expanded the scope and understanding of railroad accounting issues in the broader economic, investment and political context.

The economics and environment of the railroad industry

An attribute that established large railroads as modern businesses was the capital requirements of these natural monopolies, which were far in excess of those of other contemporary businesses and which, in turn, created barriers to competitive entry. Large capital requirements meant that external financing and public markets were needed to initiate or expand a railroad line. While most other contemporary businesses were owner-operated ventures, requiring local bank loans at most for seasonal financing, railroads, by contrast, required many individuals, including both debt and equity investors external to the railroad operations, to supply the required finance. This created new issues of how to communicate with external investors regarding the performance of the railroad and how to monitor the managers who were deemed to be stewards of the company's assets. These so-called 'agency' problems are still being addressed today, wherein the separation of the providers of capital from the management is fundamental to the control and communication structure, and to corporate governance.

The B&O was formed in 1827 as merchants of Baltimore, Maryland, sought to preserve their city's commercial advantage as a seaport link with the American interior. These merchants met and quickly seized on the railed-road idea (Dilts 1993: 38). The passage of similar incorporation acts in neighbouring Virginia and Pennsylvania soon followed. Some 30,000 shares of $100 stock were swiftly subscribed, as virtually every citizen of Baltimore supported the enterprise (Jacobs 1995: 13). City of Baltimore and State of Maryland funds also were invested and these entities received half the shares, making the B&O a quasi-public entity. The incorporation act specified that the Maryland legislature would set freight and passenger rates, but that no taxes would be paid by the B&O. An annual report (Statement of Affairs) issued by the corporation to its shareholders was required by the B&O corporate charter, although the contents of the annual report remained unspecified (Previts and Samson 2000: 5).

The growth of the B&O from the time of the initial public offering was staggering. The Erie Canal was a fully state-funded enterprise, and the cost of $8.8 million established a record for a US business project at the time of completion in 1825. The B&O started as a $3 million business and grew to a $30 million enterprise by the time it reached the Ohio River 25 years later. Railroads attracted large numbers of individual investors, outside the business and outside the region, who needed communication from management as the basis for exercising an element of control from a distance. The railroad management quickly evolved into a separate professional class, possessing only a small ownership interest but providing the expertise to run the operations. This early evolution would lead to agency relationships significant in the development of accounting, auditing, finance and business.

In accounting, the corporate annual report would evolve, becoming an essential financial communication device with management describing the company's performance and its role as stewards of shareholder assets. Their financial statements developed into an income statement, balance sheet and early cash flow report (ibid.: 18–30). Significantly, the compilation of financial statements became the prime object of accounting whereas, previously, record-keeping had been accounting's main goal (Chatfield 1974: 222). For external investors, the financial statements were the basis for assessing the earnings power of the enterprise as well as evaluating solvency and liquidity. Hence decision making, as well as control, became the end use of accounting. Ratios to assess railroad performance from period to period and from division to division and to compare the B&O versus other railroads were utilised early on (Previts and Samson 2000: 33–4). The track record of a railroad's ability to *pay* dividends led to the establishment of 'dividend value' as the basis for determining the worth of an equity share.

Path-breaking annual reports

The B&O published annual reports from its earliest years, primarily for the benefit of its existing investors, but it was the IC Railroad that took forward the concept of the annual report. From as early as the 1850s, the first years of its existence, the IC Railroad published annual reports that were aimed at both the general American public and the European capital markets, with the latter providing the majority of investors. The IC Railroad, because of its financing arrangements, had a greater responsibility to the general public than did most for-profit corporations. Its reporting practices provide a textbook example of duality reporting as the corporation's annual report appears to have satisfied the needs of both audiences.

At a time when patterns and expectations concerning the content of published annual reports were not well established, the IC Railroad's management took seriously its accounting obligations. In retrospect, it is probably fair to say that the European investors should have been able to obtain a reasonable understanding of the company's operations from the published reports. The stockholder report series began with a three-page document that covered activities from the founding of the company on 10 February 1851 through to 1 November 1852. A rudimentary receipts and expenditures statement and a budget statement are all that accompany the single-page letter of President Schuyler. This first report provided few clues about the capital formation and construction issues that would become highly important in the years that followed. The statements provided in the 1854 report are identified with the capital letters A, B, C and D, with A comprising a type of balance sheet, B a form of expenditures statement, C an Interest Fund statement and D a budget (Ways and Means) reporting the status of bonded indebtedness.

The alphabetic designation of reports was also a common practice at the B&O beginning shortly after its formation in 1827 (Previts and Samson 2000). However, the B&O statements are different in content, so it does not appear that the IC Railroad was simply following the pattern established by other railroads. More likely, the IC Railroad's management was responding to the information needs of its European creditors who were concerned with the integrity of their interest payments and the related principal. Although there was no external auditor, the statements for years after 1854 were examined and approved by a three-man audit committee of the board of directors. By the end of 1855, the first full year of operations, the IC Railroad's published report had expanded to over 50 pages of fine print.

Reporting regional economic development

Beginning in 1854, the tenor of the IC Railroad's annual reports began to change to incorporate information about the role and impact of the road on economic development. Page 1 of the report refers to the growth of new towns along the line and the financing by bankers of coal fields in the vicinity of the railroad. Economic development was following the path of the railroad.

When train operations began, management presented financial information in great detail, including revenues and costs, by month, for each depot along the line. Revenues, by depot, were also listed by the nature of the item shipped; the 1855 report included a spreadsheet with 32 columns for transportation of different types of commodities, including wheat, rye, hogs, whiskey, apples, butter, cheese and coal. Such detail, in ever-diminishing print size, continued throughout the pre-Civil War era; by 1860 the spreadsheet had 42 columns. The IC Railroad's management also provided extensive commentary on the economic environment within which the company operated. For instance, a table listed every station along the line, with columns for the population in 1850 and 1855, the number of houses in 1850 and 1855, and the number of churches, schools, stores, hotels, mills, factories and physicians.

The 1855 annual report also contained the Report of the Land Commissioner whose observations indicate that the accounts might have had public relations or marketing objectives – a feature not atypical of modern annual reports (Graves et al. 1996). The Land Commissioner noted that some of the company's land 'is rolling, undulating like the waves of the ocean under the influence of a gentle breeze' (IC Railroad's annual report 1855: 42). Other paragraphs note the fertility of the soil, the extensive deposits of coal and other minerals, and the fact that the lands were well watered. Their report concluded with an indication of the impact on economic development:

> In no other instance, probably, have such abundant benefits flowed from like causes. To the Government, the lands were comparatively valueless; to the State, they were in no way profitable; to the farmers, their productiveness was of no avail, while the quarries of stone and marble, and mines of coal with which the lands abound, were wholly undeveloped … This Company took these lands thus comparatively valueless … ,and by the expenditure of about twenty millions of dollars, imparted vitality to the whole matter by the construction and equipment of this road.
>
> *(IC Railroad's annual report 1855: 43–4)*

A full balance sheet appears for the first time for 1856. Each line of the balance sheet is keyed to supplementary abstracts (identified A through H) that provide details of the capital stock, the construction bonds, the free land bonds, and the other keyed lines on the balance sheet, for example, short-term debt ('scrip') and floating ('working capital') liabilities. The statement set concludes with a novel determination of net earnings that is then reconciled with the Interest Fund to assure the adequacy of that account. This latter statement was unique in that earnings were closed out to 'bondholders' equity', rather than to the traditional stockholders' equity. Statements for the next year end (1857) follow this pattern of reporting, and a resumé of cash transactions (a cash flow statement, in full particulars) is added. With minor exceptions, through to 1861, the form and content of the IC Railroad's financial statements remain substantially unchanged. A balance sheet focusing on the assets committed to the Interest Fund is the principal statement. Comparative columns are added in some instances detailing, for example, expenditures, so that trends between years, starting in 1852, can be studied. In fact, the reports are ideal benchmarking documents with many examples of five-year trends reported. They also contain numerous analyses of managerial decisions; for instance, the IC Railroad's annual report for 1859 (p. 6) includes a study of the advantage of burning coal over wood.

Did these accounts provide the information that investors needed? Certainly management thought so. The IC Railroad's 1857 annual report (p. 1) contains an opening statement, which seemingly recognises it as an extensive database for investors:

> The Directors submit herewith the Reports and Statements of the Officers of the Company in charge of the several Departments of its business, to which the careful examination of the Shareholders is invited, as affording sufficient data to enable each proprietor to form his own judgment as to the value of his investment and the details of its administration.

During the 1850s, the IC Railroad was more than a railroad; it was the change agent in a major social experiment – an attempt by government to foster economic development by using raw fertile land to motivate not only corporate management but also to attract a population. This experiment, as detailed in the narrative of the annual report to shareholders, proved successful; at least that is the conclusion reached based on the information provided by the IC Railroad's management.

Why such informative financial reports?

The IC Railroad's annual reports contained not only a financial report for the benefit of European capitalists who invested in the road but also a longitudinal view of the company's impact on the development of Illinois and the markets thereto related. Indicating investor appreciation of such reporting, an 1857 article in the *American Railroad Journal* stated that 'No other company enjoyed the unlimited confidence of money lenders of England and America to the same extent' (quoted in Sunderland 1955: 31). Further, the farmers and merchants, who were to be the principal customers and beneficiaries of the IC Railroad's services, were also interested in the information provided in the increasingly detailed annual reports. Why did the IC Railroad management publish the type and amount of information found in the 1851–61 annual reports? Such reports were not mandatory, neither were they common. Other railroads, including the Pennsylvania, which began in 1847, and the B&O produced quite different reports in terms of style, content and form. It appears that both the reporting obligations arising from the bond indenture entered into with European investors, who needed reassurance of the control that management had over the company's operations, and the desire to promote the sale of land granted to them by the government were addressed by the evolving form and content of the annual reports.

Ultimately, the IC Railroad was the source of many precedents. Later land-grant railroads adopted the IC Railroad's classification and appraisal system and its contract and credit systems. In addition, the IC Railroad's colonisation and advertising techniques were copied by other land-grant railroads (Decker 1964: 101). The IC Railroad utilised several reporting practices that had not heretofore been acknowledged. Examples are the early use of cash flow statements, the identification of 'Net earnings', and extensive socioeconomic reporting. These are not to be construed as 'firsts'. However, these early uses support an a priori belief that the corporate form of business, and the need to satisfy requirements of accountability to distant European investors, served to justify and cause such reporting practices to emerge.

We turn to Britain to engage with another significant nineteenth-century financial reporting innovation for which railway companies were responsible, the so-called double account system.

The double account system[4]

Although there were earlier important changes in financial reporting practices among canal companies, the development of the distinctive model, called the double account system, came to fruition among railway companies. In essence, the system divides the conventional balance sheet into two sections: the capital account, which sets out capital raised and expended, and the general balance sheet, which lists the remaining assets and liabilities of the enterprise as well as the balance of undistributed revenue and any under-spend or over-spend on the capital account. It appears that the capital account was designed to fulfil a stewardship function by providing a history of the application of money raised under statutory authority. In the early days, with accounts often wholly or substantially cash based, no general balance sheet was published – this emerged as receivables, payables, inventory, etc. were given recognition as railway managers began to embrace accruals accounting. The move towards accruals accounting was designed to achieve a higher level of accountability and to help counter defective practices. For example, the British accountant George Bott, writing in the *Railway Times* in 1843, demonstrated numerically how 'a railway in almost a bankrupt condition, may represent itself as a fair remunerative concern' by following the then popular practice of preparing accounts mainly on the cash basis (quoted in Edwards 2019: 100).

The earliest known example of the double account system was published by the London & Birmingham Railway for the half-year ending 31 December 1838. Then, and in the 1840s, most railway companies continued to publish only a capital account, and their continued failure to publish a general balance sheet was the subject of criticism. The importance of the general balance sheet was stressed in a letter to *Herepath's Journal* by a shareholder in the London, Brighton & South Coast Railway in 1850. In his view, its value:

> [t]o the shareholders cannot be sufficiently appreciated, unless Shareholders are aware of the borrowing and lending, the advances to forward other schemes, and the abuses which may be made of a trusteeship which gives no account of its assets and debts.
>
> *(quoted ibid.: 100)*

The profitability and financial position of railway companies also came under the microscope in the financial press of the late 1840s when criticism was fuelled by 'dissections of railway accounts' executed by the financial analyst Robert Lucas Nash (Odlyzko 2011: 320, 340–1). Shareholder confidence eventually plummeted and, between 1845 and 1848, the average fall in the prices of shares in 12 leading railway companies was 64 per cent. Growing concern encouraged companies to re-examine their accounting practices and the London & North Western Railway (LNWR),[5] which did not come under attack, provided leadership in devising improved means of financial communication. In October 1848 the directors took the unprecedented step of circulating to shareholders a statement of liabilities and a statement of estimated future expenditure and how it was to be financed. These practices were copied by other railway companies including the Great Western which, according to its chairman Charles Russell, used LNWR as a 'model' (quoted in Edwards 2019: 101). Also, more companies began to employ the accruals concept to recognise credit transactions when preparing their CFS, which increasingly included a general balance sheet. A contemporary observer (quoted in Odlyzko 2011: 312) summed things up as follows:

> [t]he reasonable demand made by the public has been for railway accounts such as they could understand; and aided by an eloquent press, they obtained from the directories, in October and November last, accounts at once explicit and clear, and then the clamour ceased.

A substantial recovery of share prices followed what Odlyzko (2011: 312) describes at this 'first [railway] accounting revolution'.

The number of companies preparing balance sheets in accordance with the double account system gradually increased due to shareholder demand for better information, the leadership provided by the LNWR company, the threat of legislation (c.1850) and the actions of public accountants. Adoption of the double account system became a statutory requirement for all railway companies in 1868, and for certain categories of public utilities in the years that followed. It was also adopted voluntarily in other sectors of the economy where the pattern of expenditure possessed similar characteristics, i.e. where a large initial investment was required to establish the infrastructure of the concern, followed by the need to finance only current operations, e.g. dock companies and companies working wasting assets such as mines and quarries. The companies required by law to use the double account system in the UK disappeared in the spate of nationalisation that followed World War II.

Nineteenth-century accounting error

Within the accounting history literature, the issue of 'error or bias' (Brief 1965: 12) in the published accounts of nineteenth-century railroads has been the subject of much debate.

For the period up to 1868, Pollins (1956: 354) has drawn attention to the fact that 'the basis for the allocation of certain important items between capital and revenue accounts was not the same in all companies, and that the allocation was not carried out in a consistent manner by any major company'. Edwards (2019: chs 6 and 14) has demonstrated major variation in methods of accounting for fixed assets both between railway companies and over time during much of the nineteenth century, with Brief (1965: 30) concluding that 'capital consumption charges were neglected or at least delayed by the accounting methods employed'. Whether such inconsistency, variation and neglect were intentional is a moot point. Pollins thinks that lack of experience may have been a factor early on, but later: 'It is more realistic to recognise that in practice the calculation of profits was often influenced by changing financial circumstances and the dictates of management policy' (Pollins 1956: 353).

In the remainder of this section, we focus on the US and consider the actions of the M&O, in the mid-1860s, as an illustration of how financial reports might be manipulated to communicate a particular message to stakeholders, and the kinds of issues that arose among railway companies, in both the US and the UK, concerning how to account for the fixed assets of these atypically capital-intensive nineteenth-century entities. The great debate existed not only among historians but in its own time drew from participants, both academic and practitioners. Henry Rand Hatfield, writing in the *Accounting Review* (1936), and George O. May, in the *Journal of Accountancy* (1936), studied in some depth the theories and practices which had evolved in this ongoing controversy.

Mobile & Ohio railroad: an exemplification

In April 1865, the M&O lay ravaged by the Civil War, and the burning question was how the company could overcome these obstacles, survive and eventually thrive. The 1866 annual report of the M&O is a 'case book' of how the accounting methods of the day were used to portray the capacity of the M&O to provide earnings, and thus attract capital, even as it faced a bleak situation. Looked at differently, these same financial statements contain prime examples of 'nineteenth-century accounting error' (Brief 1965).

As M&O's annual report for 1865 recounts, the Confederate Government took over operations of the railroad to transport men and supplies. The M&O was paid in Confederate notes and bonds with about $5 million owed to the company by the War's end. These receivables proved worthless as the Confederacy fell in April 1865. The loss was further magnified by the state of Alabama declaring its bonds (the company held $125,000 of these), issued for the purposes of War, to be void. Also, 50 slaves owned by the M&O were freed, causing another loss – $120,000, the cost of the slaves. Further, as described in the annual report, half of the railroad line had been destroyed by the Union troops as General Sherman swept across the Deep South on the way to Atlanta. Locomotives and cars had been seized by the Union such that only a quarter of the rolling stock remained with the M&O at the year's end, and the remaining equipment was in such poor condition that the railroad could not operate the portion of the track that was still open. The estimated loss due to War was more than $7 million.

With the Reconstruction Era commencing at the War's end and with the Federal troops occupying the South, the M&O was allowed to recommence operations with the reservation that the Federal Government might confiscate railroad assets. While this power of reservation seemed unlikely to be exercised by the government, it did prevent the M&O

from borrowing in order to get restarted; lenders naturally shied away from making loans when the government retained senior claim on assets.

The interesting aspects of the 1865 M&O annual report (published 17 April 1866) was not the recounting of the aforementioned current financial and operational problems; the railroad's condition was indeed bleak. The interesting issue is why such a bleak description of its financial position was presented. Perhaps it wished to be as forthright with investors as possible – to enhance trust that the management and directors were not attempting to paint a distorted picture of the railroad's condition. By portraying such a realistic image of the railway's operating condition, investors, particularly British investors, may have been persuaded to entrust the railroad management with new financing.

The second interesting feature of the 1865 M&O annual report was the detailing of both the 1864 and the 1865 operating results – because of the War, the 1864 annual report had not been published. The 1865 year, itself, was split into two periods: 1 January through 30 April (the War ended in April) and 1 May to 31 December. The 1 May breakpoint was used as the 'currency adjustment' point (i.e. the fall of the Confederacy). What is interesting is that on one dimension the 1864 and early 1865 periods of earnings were moot given that the Confederacy failed and the revenues were unpaid by the Confederacy prior to its demise. Yet, as Table 18.1 shows, the income numbers were presented in bold fashion:

Captured by these otherwise meaningless income statement numbers (because they were denominated in immeasurable and irrelevant Confederate dollars) is the essence that management was conveying to investors and potential investors: the earnings power of the railroad made its recovery viable and this earnings power would repay investors for their risk and patience.

Table 18.1 Income statements for war years

1864	
'Earnings' (i.e. Revenues)	$3,674,498.99
Expense*	2,281,596.38
Net 'revenue'	$1,392,902.61
1865 (1 January – 30 April)	
'Earnings'	$1,183,220.42
Expenses*	906,663.84
Net 'revenue'	$276,556.58
1865 (1 May – December 31)	
'Earnings'	$1,524,675.81
Expenses	699,898.14
Net 'revenue'§	$824,777.67

* 'The expenses during the periods referred to were greatly increased by the extraordinary repairs made necessary from injuries inflicted by the contending armies' (Annual accounts: 11).

§ 'This last statement is not a fair specimen of the *earnings power* of the road in times of peace, as we did not have the rolling stock necessary to meet the wants of the country' (Annual accounts: 11, *emphasis added*).

The annual report goes on to state that the M&O debt held by the State of Alabama, $300,000, and the State of Mississippi, $220,949, had been repaid as had $319,000 of income bonds that were due in 1862 and $168,000 of the income bonds due in 1865 and $103,000 of the second mortgage bonds. Thus, in this difficult period, the M&O had found a way to repay well over $1,000,000 of company debt. This, again, communicated to investors that the company should be able to do likewise on future loans.

The above disclosures set the stage for raising new capital. Because the 1864 and early 1865 data were denominated in valueless Confederate dollars, they had an 'as if' quality that required investors to gauge whether the M&O was a viable operating entity. Given the land holdings and, it seems, the demonstrated potential for 'earnings', capital providers were attracted. By the early 1870s, investors were rewarded as the company earnings were again annually at the $1,000,000 level, which the 'proforma' income numbers suggested. After the war, 8 per cent M&O bonds that had matured were exchanged for Sterling bonds. The unpaid interest on bonds was paid in kind by the issuances of '8% interest bonds' in exchange for the coupons on outstanding debt. Since the accounting records were maintained on a modified cash basis, the interest expense was not recorded when the interest notes were issued. Consequently, the above financial statements showed an overstated income. Similar stories can be told about other American railroads that were operating during the Civil War, such as the Louisville and Nashville (Heier 2010).

Accounting for fixed assets

With the accounts prepared mainly on the cash basis, the M&O did not record depreciation of its rails or rolling stock. This was not an uncommon practice, as pointed out by Brief (1965: 3) who concluded: 'reported profits and dividends were higher than they would have been if modern accounting practices prevailed. Thus, business investment, which is a function of reported profits, was over stimulated'. In Britain, by way of contrast, Arnold and McCartney (2002) point out that some railway companies did record depreciation in the 1830s and early 1840s. Edwards (1986: 253) reports that the London and Birmingham railway transferred £5,500 to 'a reserve Fund for the Depreciation of Stock' as soon as part of the line was opened in 1838. Others, including the Midland, followed suit (ibid.: 255–6). These practices appear to have received support from the Companies Clauses Consolidation Act of 1845, which stated that directors may 'if they think fit, set aside … such Sum as they may think proper to meet contingencies, or for enlarging, repairing, or improving the Works connected with the Undertaking, or any part thereof' (Pollins 1956: 343).

The early practice of charging depreciation by UK railway companies was abandoned for a range of reasons which include, according to Edwards (1986: 257), the desire to pay dividends when profits were low. Management's argument was that depreciation charges were unnecessary. By the 1850s, the railroads had procedures in place that served in lieu of depreciation accounting, namely 'replacement accounting' and 'repairs and renewals accounting', where the latter involved charging current expenditures on renewals and maintenance against revenue (Arnold and McCartney 2002: 206; Edwards 2019: ch. 14). Some recording of depreciation also occurred in the US in the late 1840s, perhaps because of the British influence, but the practice in the US was also short-lived. Again, as in Britain, it was believed that railway equipment kept in good repair would last forever.

Investors continued to provide funding based on replacement or betterment accounting models that deemed assets to have indefinite lives. But as long-lived assets expired, such models proved deficient, and over time appeared to overstate earnings and thereby exaggerate earnings power and income as a percentage of the cost of investment. Also, balance sheets were inflated because equipment was reported at cost without an offsetting provision for obsolescence or wear and tear. An 1879 article in the *North American Review* noted that even the venerable New York Central Railroad issued statements 'based, apparently, on improper book-keeping' (The mysteries 1879: 147).

Frauds

According to Edwards (2019: 147), 'Accounting history is littered with examples of financial information used as a means of deception', with events at Enron and WorldCom simply recent manifestations of managerial behaviour that is examined in detail in Chapter 20 of the *Companion*. In Britain, the period of intense speculation in railway shares – the 'railway mania',[6] which reached its zenith in 1846, played a major role in the general financial crisis of 1847, and was followed by investigations that showed railway company accounts to be deficient in important respects. As Wang (Edwards 1985: 26) put it, 'railway shareholders were so bewildered and mystified by cooked accounts, manipulated figures, partial statements, and delusive representations of railway property that they actually regarded the payment of dividend out of capital as a legitimate practice'. The accountants Quilter, Ball & Co., for example, were called in to examine the affairs of the Eastern Counties Railway – run by George Hudson known as the Railway King – which was revealed to have overstated income by £438,050 through debiting expenditure to capital rather than revenue, failing to record payables outstanding or write off bad debts, wrongly crediting significant amounts to revenue and charging interest to capital instead of the income account (Edwards 2019: 102, 149).

At the general level, Lee (1975: 21–2) argued that laxity in classification between capital and revenue expenditures during railway companies' early years led to wilful manipulation in the boom years of the 1840s to justify inflated dividends. McCartney and Arnold (2003) believe that the boom and slump of 1845–7 was the most important of the nineteenth-century railroad manias in terms of its effect on the economy as a whole. Although originally viewed as 'market irrationality', Bryer (1991) claims the mania was the result of deliberate and collusive actions by wealthy investors, aided by the central government, to 'swindle' middle-class investors. Accounting processes and distortions were critical to the success of this class-based fraud (ibid.). Regardless of the reason for the mania, Edwards (1986) observed that, thereafter, there was an increase in the quantity of accounting information provided to investors, and there was a move towards accrual-based reporting and away from cash-based reporting at large railway companies such as the LNWR. McCartney and Arnold (2002: 412) proved this observation with respect to the quantity of information provided, but were sceptical with respect to its quality. In a later publication, McCartney and Arnold (2003) also challenged Bryer's assertion that a fraud had been knowingly perpetrated. In their view, it was debateable whether the fact that wealthy investors ended up owning the railroads was indicative of a collusive fraud. They expressed doubts primarily because of their further observation that the railroads remained unprofitable. Thus, the middle-class who had given up their ownership were actually better off for having sold when they did (ibid.: 843). If a swindle, it certainly was not a successful one.

In the US context, early frauds were committed at the IC Railroad (1854–5) and the M&O (1856), but the most prominent railroad fraud involved the financing of the transcontinental railroad. Credit Mobilier was formed by Thomas Durant of the Union

Pacific Railroad to construct the transcontinental railroad, primarily because the creation of a separate corporation would allow Durant to 'line his pockets' without oversight from either the railroad company or Congress. President Abraham Lincoln was an avid proponent of the transcontinental project and provided unwavering support, but when he was assassinated in April 1865, before any tracks had yet been laid, Durant, and his successor, Oakes Ames, worried that Congress would vote to cut its losses and abandon the government contracts. The solution was to obtain support from Congressional leaders by selling them stock in the company at bargain prices (Heier 2009: 327).

A 4 September 1872 article in the influential *New York Sun* accused US Vice President Schuyler Colfax and other noted politicians of accepting stock in Credit Mobilier in exchange for the favourable exercise of their influence in Congress. Credit Mobilier was the construction company that built the transcontinental railroad on behalf of the Union Pacific Railroad. The objective of the bribes was to ensure that there would be no interference from Congress that would delay Federal money from being funnelled into railroad construction. To make matters worse, it is thought that one of the functions of Credit Mobilier, besides building the railroad, was to defraud the government by overcharging for construction of the tracks. Insiders at the Union Pacific Railroad had, therefore, created the construction company to enable them to pay themselves millions of dollars to build the railroad. Thus, Credit Mobilier was a scandal of unprecedented proportions (Ambrose 2000: 373–6).

The fraud investigation disclosed that Colfax had received 20 shares of stock in Credit Mobilier and dividends from that investment of $1,200. Colfax asserted that he had never owned any stock other than that which he had purchased. Similarly, he claimed never to have received the supposed $1,200 of dividends. However, the House Judiciary Committee determined that Colfax had indeed deposited $1,200 into his bank account just two days after the supposed dividend payment. After two weeks, Colfax explained that the deposit had been a campaign contribution from a friend who had since died. Even his strongest supporters doubted this story.

The impact of politics and regulation

In the UK, early railways were statutory companies with rights conferred by Parliament. The authorising statutes normally did not refer to matters of accounting, although there were exceptions; for instance, the Great Western Railway Act of 1835 required the company to prepare accounts twice a year and to make them available at meetings of shareholders and pay dividends out of 'clear Profits' (Lee 1975: 20). General acts were passed in 1844 (Railway Regulation Act) and 1845 (Companies Clauses Consolidation Act) that affected railroad accounting (Pollins 1956: 336–9). The 1845 act, which contained model clauses for statutory companies to adopt, included provisions for a bookkeeper to be appointed and the preparation of 'an exact balance sheet' giving 'a distinct view of the profit and loss' (ibid.: 338). Auditors, who were required to hold at least one share in the company, were to be appointed. The Regulation of Railways Act 1868 helped stabilise railway accounting in the UK (ibid.: 355). As was later to be true in the US, the Act of 1868 not only stabilised railway accounting, it also reduced innovation. That Act laid out a standard format for each of the 14 separate statements that railway companies were required to publish (Simmons and Biddle 1997: 6). Unfortunately, it did not address the way in which capital and revenue expenditures were to be defined. In 1911, the Railway Companies (Accounts and Returns) Act increased the amount of detail that companies had to provide in their accounts. The entire railway network was brought under government control during World War I, and the Railways Act 1921 gave the new Ministry of Transport licence to specify the form of railway accounts (Simmons and Biddle 1997: 6). Whereas the industry had long been an innovator in the development of accounting principles and practices, that was to decline with increased government regulation.

The nature of the transportation service was also acknowledged as making standardisation desirable in the US. Because freight and passengers were often transferred from one company to another, the problems of interline accounting became acute. The need for standardisation was first recognised at the state level with New England's Massachusetts Railroad Commission making appropriate provision as early as 1876 (Neidert 1950: 309–10). The move towards national provision gained momentum with the Second National Convention of Railroad Commissioners in Columbus, Ohio in November 1878 (*New York Times* 1878). Thereafter in June 1879 at the Third National Convention in Saratoga, New York, the main topic was uniformity of accounts prepared by railroads for the purpose of reporting to state regulators (Cullen 1926: 798). The theme of this conference is unsurprising, given that the leading Massachusetts state regulator involved was the influential Charles Francis Adams Jr. The presentations at the Convention were reported in *Railroad Gazette* and *Railway Age*, and this meeting of state railroad commissioners caused the Association of American Railway Accounting Officers – the voluntary organisation of railroad accountants that was formed to deal with inter-railroad billing practices – to take up the issue (ibid.).

The 1846 Massachusetts Railroad law initiative, referred to earlier, served as a model for 'sunshine' disclosure requirements when Federal involvement followed with the passage of legislation (1887) that established the ICC. Miranti's research in this area has assisted in providing an understanding of the features of the system initiated. It was instituted by Professor Henry Carter Adams, the first Statistician for the ICC, 1887–1911, who held a preference for 'rigidly uniform reporting formats and methods' (Miranti 1990: 183). About 20 years later, the Hepburn Act (1906) gave the ICC the power to set tariff and carrier rates. As noted earlier, the control over rates was a prime political and economic focus of all parties involved in the establishment of regulation. From 1906, therefore, in deliberating on such matters, the ICC could scrutinise railroads' financial records that had been prepared using a standardised accounting system. Along with the Elkins Act of 1903, the Hepburn Act fulfilled one of President Theodore Roosevelt's major goals, that of improving railroad regulation. The requirement for uniform accounting methods may not have been, for the most part, oppressive to railroads; despite the difficulties of obtaining agreement, the need for such practices had long been recognised by the railroads themselves.

Managerial accounting innovations

Albert Fink, famous for the design of iron bridges, began his distinctive railroad career at the B&O in December 1849. Galambos and Pratt (1986: 48) consider Fink to be worthy of the title, 'The father of cost accounting'. Much of the innovation for which Fink received credit, however, was in fact utilised by the B&O prior to his arrival. The B&O and other railroads were quick to integrate the data from bookkeeping sources into a system of information that managers employed to operate and measure business operations. The B&O's 'university' employees and 'alumni', including Fink, led the way in internal managerial reporting as they did with external financial reporting (Flesher et al. 2000: 115; Heier 2000).[7]

The early B&O annual reports reflect the existence of types of analysis that were also to provide efficient managerial information. To reflect the cost consciousness that management had in carrying out the building of the railroad, the quantity measures of progress contained not only physical measures but also per-dollar cost calculations including 'cost per mile' and 'cost per cubic yard'. With the coming of steam locomotives (early trains were pulled by horses), some costs began being measured in terms of 'cost per train', 'cost per round trip' and 'cost per train per day'. The next evolvement was to 'cost per ton of freight' and 'cost per passenger'. Given that most trains carried both freight and passengers, the breakdown by type of customer indicates that a rationale existed for joint cost allocation. A further refinement was to calculate 'cost per passenger mile' and 'cost per ton mile'. By 1833, the calculations were adjusted for differences in grade and curvature of tracks. Although first introduced at the B&O, these statistics were quickly adopted by other railroads and became standard for the industry (Knight and Latrobe 1838: 1–42). Such comparative displays were useful to convince legislators that the railroads were efficient, low cost providers of rail services. Such data also supported the case for rate increases to meet patterns of enhanced cost experienced at efficient levels of operation. Comparative data also included ratio analysis, whose use was evident in the B&O annual report from as early as 1831 (Flesher et al. 2000). Benchmarking occurred in the late 1840s, with the B&O's accounts reporting comparisons with other 'leading' railroads.

Cost-volume-profit analysis was also used early in the history of railroads. Solomons (1952) suggests that Fink may have learned to group cost accounts, based on behaviour, through reading Lardner's 1850 treatise entitled *Railway Economy*. However, analysis of the B&O's records again reveals that cost behaviour was understood by Fink's predecessors, including Benjamin Latrobe and W. Woodville. Indeed, Fink was Latrobe's understudy at the B&O. Woodville noted, in the 1831 B&O annual report, that some expenses increased as revenues increased while others remained the same regardless of the level of revenue. By 1833, expenses were being grouped as either fixed or proportional. Fink moved from the B&O to the Louisville and Nashville Railroad in 1857, and in 1875 wrote a treatise on cost behaviour (Fink 1875). In summary, transaction accounting numbers were developed to manage the railroad comparatively and in unit operating measures. Costs were reported by activity centre and by object. Comparison of costs helped managers to monitor performance. Cost behaviour and the relationship with revenue was understood early on and afforded better planning of both construction and operations. Whether Fink was the source is less relevant than the fact that little innovation came after his contributions. Writing in 1900, Woodlock (1900: 60) noted: 'The late Mr. Albert Fink, as far back as 1873, laid the lines upon which practically all scientific railroad thought has since proceeded'.

Given space limitations, the following review of relevant railroad accounting literature in the twentieth century is confined to the US experience.

Twentieth-century changes in railroad accounting

Years before the accounting profession devised an accounting framework for corporate financial reporting, generally, the ICC had in place a sophisticated standardised system of railroad accounting:

> The Commission was authorized by the original act [of 1887] to require from carriers' annual reports in the form prescribed by the Commission showing the amount of capital

> stock, funded and floating debt, interest paid, cost of property, number of employees and salaries paid, earnings and receipts, operating and other expenses, balance of profit and loss, annual balance sheet, rates and fares, and miscellaneous statistics.
>
> *(US Interstate Commerce Commission 1937: 105)*

The standardised system for railroad accounts, which was further extended following the Hepburn Act of 1906, was supposedly desirable for several reasons. Although the railroad industry was not an organised service unit in form, in substance it was highly standardised. The tendency towards a unified system was due partly to the nature of the industry. The use of joint facilities, employment of joint employees, the interchange of freight, and operations in connection with other railway lines led to uniformity of contracts and operating agreements. Inter-corporate, inter-divisional and inter-industrial transactions all contributed to the need for a uniform system of accounts (Adams 1918: 4–6). A standardised system of accounts was also necessary to enable the railway to comply with the provisions of Federal, state and municipal regulatory agencies. For the ICC to fulfil its mandate to regulate the railways and set rates, a standardised method of accounting was necessary. This comparability proved to be extremely helpful during World War I.

Some researchers, however, have argued that the ICC requirements reduced the quality of some railroad annual reports because the Federally-mandated reporting rules resulted in a 'dry, almost morbid' presentation. This was certainly noticeable at the IC Railroad, which had published lengthy, informative reports prior to the ICC requirements coming into force, whereas their reports of the early 1900s were shorter and less informative (Feeney 2005: 37–41). In sum, the financial statements for the IC Railroad were identical in appearance, organisation and format for a period of more than 25 years prior to the onset of World War II. For comparability purposes, these statements were models of clarity. Other elements of reporting innovation shown in the IC Railroad's annual reports included the move to consolidated financial statements in 1924, and examples of social reporting – particularly with respect to pensions and the great flood of 1927 (Quinn et al. 2012: 16).

One aspect of the ICC regulations that railroads initially welcomed was that conformity with its rules exempted publicly held railroads from the audit requirements of the Securities and Exchange Commission (SEC). However, following World War II, some railroads began subjecting themselves to audits and providing GAAP-type disclosures to their shareholders, all in the name of voluntary transparency. By 1956, about half of the US's publicly held railroads were audited. The remainder soon began to conform with what was becoming a standard industry practice. By 1976, when railroads were obliged to fully comply with the SEC's accounting and auditing requirements, due to Congress passing the Rail Revitalization and Regulatory Reform Act, the impact of requiring such audits was largely moot – almost all were already audited (Feeney 2013: 27). Additional aspects of this significant evolution in railroad reporting practices in the US are detailed below.

One of the most noteworthy events of the latter half of the twentieth century was the *Wreck of the Penn Central* (Daughen and Binzen 1999). The Pennsylvania Railroad had merged with the New York Central Railroad on 1 February 1968, and the New York, New Haven and Hartford Railroad had been added to the merger later in the year to create a transportation behemoth in the Northeastern United States. The new company filed for bankruptcy just two years later, after the merged companies proved to be even less profitable than their individual components; there was no synergy. At the time, it was the largest bankruptcy in US history. One of the main reasons for the bankruptcy was that the merged organisation could not make their three previous accounting systems compatible. As a result, trains were, at times, 'lost', and customers were never billed for services rendered (Stover 1997: 233). The lack of cash was at least partially due to the slowness with which billing occurred (Bowsher 2018). One consequence of the Penn Central bankruptcy was general recognition that regulation by the ICC was partially at fault. The Special Subcommittee on Investigations of the House Committee on Interstate and Foreign Commerce was highly critical of the failure of the ICC to protect the interest of investors:

> On June 24, 1970, a high-ranking official of the ICC testified that he was taken by surprise at the bankruptcy of the Penn Central Railroad. Certainly, a report-collecting regulator who is forced to make this admission either does not read the reports he elicits or having read them, does not comprehend their import. In either case, he is scarcely in a position to protect the interests of public investors who must rely upon the accuracy of those reports.
>
> *(US House of Representatives 1971: iv)*

This scathing comment marks the beginning of the end of the ICC. Clearly Congress had been told that the ICC's public policy position as the guardian of the information needs of investors was not well served. It would take another quarter of a century to unwind the ICC and disband it, replacing it with the Surface Transportation Board while creating a new public policy towards investor information.

The failure of Penn Central led to changes in the railroad reporting environment with new laws issued by Congress. In particular, the 1980 Staggers Rail Act was a US Federal law that deregulated the railroad industry, ending governance arrangements that had existed since the Interstate Commerce Act of 1887. The ICC had made it difficult for railroads to compete with the trucking industry, because of the regulator's outdated accounting rules and a complex system for setting shipping rates (Heier and Gurley 2007: 26). One of the rules that frustrated railroad accountants was the mandated use of Retirement-Replacement-Betterment accounting in lieu of recording an annual depreciation charge (Heier and Gurley 2007: 25; also see Heier 2006). Since the 1930s, the railroad industry had been declining; the passenger car had taken away much of the railroads' passenger traffic, and the creation of an extensive highway network, paid for by taxpayers, enabled truckers to compete favourably with the railroads.

One of the provisions of the Staggers Rail Act was the creation of the Railroad Accounting Principles Board (RAPB), which was eventually funded by Congress in 1984. The charge to the RAPB was to (1):

> [e]stablish a body of cost accounting principles to serve as the framework for implementing the regulatory provisions in which cost plays a vital role and (2) to make administrative and legislative recommendations it deems necessary to integrate the principles into the regulatory process.
>
> (Railroad Accounting Principles *1987: 2)*

The RAPB, under the leadership of Comptroller General of the United States, Charles Bowsher, issued its final report in September 1987 and its provisions remain valid today (Bowsher 2018).

The formation of the RAPB signalled a new awareness of the need for processes that could address both the political and economic issues related to the longstanding 'tug of war' over control of the rate setting of privately operated railroads. The subsequent abolition in

1995 of the ICC provided a further indicator that the processes of accounting and reporting involving regulated transportation entities were beginning to change. By the second decade of the twenty-first century the financial reporting processes of railroads in the US had continued a slow but steady movement away from government-mandated uniform standards and towards market-based generally accepted accounting financial reports. No longer subject to strict ICC uniformity requirements the major rail lines, represented by the Class I roads, now file their reports, as do other major capital enterprises, with the SEC in accordance with auditing standards of the Public Company Accounting Oversight Board. This realignment of the accounting principles and auditing standards to be in concert with the body of publicly traded companies who supply information to the capital markets under a private sector directed regime has resulted in a major transformation of railroad accounting and auditing. The lessons of accounting history and regulatory schemes are not always readily or easily identifiable, except perhaps one. The original focus of providing inexpensive transportation by involving uniform government regulation of accounts over a long period of time has led to an evolutionary return to a more market-based attributed system of accounting and auditing comparable to the current state of twenty-first-century capital market practices (Union Pacific Corporation Annual Report 2018: 45).

Whereas the US railroads tried to grow larger through consolidation in the latter half of the twentieth century, the opposite was occurring to some extent in the UK. The UK government, along with an array of private consultants, particularly accountants, pursued a policy which led to the 'flawed fragmentation and subsequent privatisation' of British Rail during the 1980s (Jupe and Funnell 2015: 65). A further UK initiative, mounted in the middle decades of the twentieth century, involved attempts to install modern methods of management accounting. This initiative, 'sponsored by the highest level of railway management', failed due to inability to overcome 'the railways' organisational structure and culture' (Quail 2006: 419).

Summary and conclusion

In the UK, railroads were built as modes of transportation to service a recognised market. In the US, railroads were initially constructed principally as change agents. The B&O was intended to keep Baltimore as a major seaport. The investors, many of them merchants of Baltimore, were less concerned with making money on the railroad and more preoccupied with achieving a return on their investment in local businesses. A generation later, the investors in the IC Railroad and the M&O did expect a return on their investments, but they were able to convince the Federal government that the railroads could help foster economic development. Thus, the government, with its land grants, was the majority investor. Perhaps Mitchell (1964: 333; see also May 1936) summed it up best when he explained that the railroads led to industrialisation in the US, but the UK was already industrialised when the railroads appeared. What was the same on both sides of the Atlantic was the impact on the need to create larger capital markets: 'the major influence of the coming of the railway was on the development of the capital market and on the level of savings' (Mitchell 1964: 333).

Because the railroads accomplished so many objectives, they grew, and with growth came the need for regular accounting and auditing. Since accounting and auditing were undeveloped in the mid-1800s, at the professional level, the railroads had to develop the practices needed to operate effectively their businesses. The principles of accounting and auditing that they formulated were later adopted by industrial corporations.

Railroads in the US utilised several innovative reporting practices such as cash flow statements, the identification of 'Net earnings', and extensive socioeconomic reporting; in the UK, the double account system was invented. In the US, the B&O was an innovator with respect to governance and auditing, while the M&O pioneered the use of accounting for determination of earnings power. At the same time, the accounts of many railroad companies, including the US's M&O and Britain's Eastern Counties Railway, contained early examples of what came to be known as 'nineteenth-century accounting error' – the inaccuracy of financial statements due to the omission of depreciation and other non-cash expenses and the failure to classify transactions accurately as capital or revenue.

Even the adverse features of railroad accounting, it could be argued, produced favourable consequences. The system of government oversight that arose when questionable accounting practices were revealed in the UK, in the mid-1860s, led to the passage of the widely acclaimed 1868 regulatory act. Similarly, in the US, the bankruptcies of the 1890s gave rise to a model for regulating natural monopolies in that country. That system relied on prescribed uniform accounting methods to inform investors and rate regulators. The ICC's uniformity rules differed markedly from the approaches followed by the SEC beginning in the 1930s. Not charged with the responsibility for regulating market competition, the SEC delegated responsibility for the financial reporting process to professional groups who standardised accounting information on the basis of generally accepted principles rather than uniform methods. Nevertheless, the regulatory system of prescribed accounting methods for the railroads lasted for over a century and was not forsaken until the passage of the Staggers Rail Act of 1980. The move towards deregulation was accelerated by the bankruptcy of the Penn Central Railroad – a bankruptcy that was accentuated by the weak accounting system at the railroad and the rules of the ICC. Nevertheless, the uniformity of the ICC rules did enable the Federal government to more easily manage the operation of the entire railroad industry during and immediately after World War I. Despite the ICC's requirements for uniformity, some railroads experimented with innovative reporting, such as the adoption of consolidated reporting and the inauguration of social reporting.

Future research needs in this area should be guided by a careful assessment of what has been outlined above, as to accounting and reporting, and further by the general developments in railroading history, using, for example, the review essay prepared by Churella (2006) on the variety of recent approaches to railroad history in the US. Also, as mentioned early in this chapter, there is great opportunity for research into the accounting contributions of other forms of transport, including canals (Forrester 1994; Russ et al. 2006), steamboats (Flesher and Soroosh 1987), trucking and horse tramways (Pollins 1991). Finally, study of railway accounting in the twentieth and twenty-first centuries has only just begun. It is hoped that this survey chapter will guide and encourage more research efforts focusing on that time period. An interesting set of topics, for example, would include the challenges faced during World War I and World War II.

Key works

Brief (1965) is the first major study of the impact of the failure to record depreciation in a capital-intensive industry.

Edwards (1986) discusses the depreciation accounting practices of early British railway companies and the impact of the Regulation of Railways Act 1868.

Pollins (1956) is the pioneer study of railroad accounting history and contains a good early overview of the subject.

Samson, Flesher and Previts (2003) present and analyse important examples of 'nineteenth-century accounting error' at a leading US railroad.

Notes

1 In spirit, if not in person, our departed colleague and co-author William D. Samson and his scholarship are reflected in this work.
2 There is also a limited literature on other early forms of transport such as canal companies (Kistler 1980; Edwards 1985; Forrester 1994; Russ et al. 2006; Arnold and McCartney 2008).
3 The Railway Accounting Officers Association published a 150-page bibliography on railway accounting in 1926–7 (Cullen 1926).
4 The material in this section is taken from Edwards (2019: ch. 6).
5 Created in 1846 from the merger of the Grand Junction Railway, the London and Birmingham Railway and the Manchester and Birmingham Railway.
6 A 'mania' can be defined as a situation wherein there is an excessive enthusiasm for an investment that is not supported by the underlying commercial elements of the investment itself.
7 See also Hoskin and Macve (1988) for comment on the contribution of railroads to the early developments in the control of multi-unit enterprises identified by Chandler.

References

Primary sources

Baltimore & Ohio Railroad Company, annual reports (1828–1840) Available at the Bruno Library at the University of Alabama, at the B&O Library and Museum in Baltimore, and on-line at Proquest Historical Annual Report Service.

Illinois Central (IC) Railroad Company, annual reports 1851–63 and 1917–27. Available at the National Library of the Accounting Profession at the University of Mississippi, the Newberry Library in Chicago, and on-line at Proquest Historical Annual Report Service.

Mobile & Ohio Railroad Company, annual reports (1850–76) Available at the University of South Alabama Library, and on-line at Proquest Historical Annual Report Service.

Other sources

Adams, H.C. (1918) *American Railway Accounting* (New York: Henry Holt).

Ambrose, S.E. (2000) *Nothing Like It in the World* (New York: Simon & Schuster).

Arnold, A.J. and McCartney, S. (2002) The beginnings of accounting for capital consumption: disclosure practices in the British railway industry, 1830–55, *Accounting and Business Research*, 32 (4): 195–208.

Arnold, A.J. and McCartney, S. (2008) The transition to financial capitalism and its implications for financial reporting: evidence from the English canal companies, *Accounting, Auditing & Accountability Journal*, 21 (8): 1185–209.

Bowsher, C. (2018) Interview by the authors, 12 March.

Brief, R.P. (1965) Nineteenth century accounting error, *Journal of Accounting Research*, 3 (1): 12–31.

Brief, R.P. (1976) *Nineteenth Century Capital Accounting and Business Investment* (New York: Arno Press).

Bryer, R.A. (1991) Accounting for the 'railway mania' of 1845 – a great railway swindle? *Accounting, Organizations and Society*, 16 (5–6): 439–86.

Chandler, A.D. (1977) *The Visible Hand: The Managerial Revolution in American Business* (Cambridge, MA and London: Belknap Press).

Chatfield, M. (1974) *A History of Accounting Thought* (Fort Worth, TX: Dryden Press).

Churella, A. (2006) Company, state, and region: three approaches to railroad history, *Enterprise & Society*, 7 (3): 581–91.

Cleveland, F.A. and Powell, W.F. (1909) *Railroad Promotion and Capitalization in the United States* (New York: Longmans, Green).

Cullen, E. (1926) *American Railway Accounting: A Bibliography* (Washington, DC: Railway Accounting Officers Association).

Daughen, J.R. and Binzen, P. (1999) *The Wreck of the Penn Central*, 2nd edn (Boston: Beard Books).

Decker, L.E. (1964) *Railroads, Lands, and Politics: The Taxation of the Railroad Land Grants, 1864–1897* (Providence, RI: Brown University Press).

Dilts, J.D. (1993) *The Great Road: The Building of the Baltimore & Ohio, the Nation's First Railroad, 1828–1853* (Stanford, CA: Stanford University Press).

Edwards, J.R. (1985) The origins and evolution of the double account system: an example of accounting innovation, *Abacus*, 21 (1): 19–43.

Edwards, J.R. (1986) Depreciation and fixed asset valuation in railway company accounts to 1911, *Accounting and Business Research*, 16 (63): 251–63.

Edwards, J.R. (2019) *A History of Corporate Financial Reporting in Britain* (New York & London: Routledge).

Feeney, K. (2005) A look at the Illinois Central Railroad through its annual reports: 1945–1962, *Green Diamond*, March: 37–41.

Feeney, K. (2013) Railroad audits: some arrived ahead of schedule, *Accounting Historians Journal*, 40 (1): 1–30.

Fink, A. (1875) *Cost of Railroad Transportation* (Louisville, KY: J.P. Morton).

Flesher, D.L. and Soroosh, J. (1987) Riverboat accounting and profitability: the Betsey Ann, *Journal of Mississippi History*, 49: 23–33.

Flesher, D.L., Previts, G.J. and Samson, W.D. (2000) Using accounting to manage: a case of railroad managerial accounting in the 1850's, *Accounting and History: A Selection of Papers Presented at the 8th World Congress of Accounting Historians*, pp. 91–126 Madrid: Asociacion Espanola de Compatabilided y Administracion de Empresas.

Flesher, D.L., Previts, G.J. and Samson, W.D. (2003a) The origins of value for money auditing: the Baltimore & Ohio Railroad 1827–1830, *Managerial Auditing Journal*, 18 (5): 374–86.

Flesher, D.L., Previts, G.J. and Samson, W.D. (2003b) Accounting, economic development and financial reporting: the case of three pre Civil War U.S. railroads, *Accounting History*, 8 (2): 61–78.

Flesher, D.L., Previts, G.J. and Samson, W.D. (2006) Early American corporate reporting and European capital markets: the case of the Illinois Central Railroad, 1851–1861, *Accounting Historians Journal*, 33 (1): 3–24.

Forrester, D.A.R. (1994) Early canal company accounts: financial and accounting aspects of the Forth and Clyde Navigation, 1768–1816, in R.H. Parker and B.S. Yamey (eds), *Accounting History: Some British Contributions*, pp. 297–326 (Oxford: University Press).

Galambos, L. and Pratt, J. (1986) *The Rise of the Corporate Commonwealth* (New York: Basic Books).

Graves, O.F., Flesher, D.L. and Jordan, R.E. (1996) Pictures and the bottom line: the television epistemology of US annual reports, *Accounting, Organizations and Society*, 21 (1): 57–88.

Hatfield, H.R. (1936) What they say about depreciation, *Accounting Review*, 11 (1): 18–26.

Heier, J.R. (2000) The foundations of modern cost management: the life and work of Albert Fink, *Accounting, Business & Financial History*, 10 (2): 213–43.

Heier, J.R. (2006) America's railroad depreciation debate, 1907 to 1913: a study of divergence in early 20th century accounting standards, *Accounting Historians Journal*, 33 (1): 89–124.

Heier, J.R. (2009) Building the Union Pacific Railroad: a study of mid-nineteenth-century railroad construction accounting and reporting practices, *Accounting, Business & Financial History*, 19 (3): 327–51.

Heier, J.R. (2010) Accounting for the ravages of war: corporate reporting at a troubled American railroad during the civil war, *Accounting History*, 15 (2): 199–228.

Heier, J.R. and Gurley, A.L. (2007) The end of betterment accounting: a study of the economic, professional, and regulatory factors that fostered standards convergence in the U.S. railroad industry, 1955–1983, *Accounting Historians Journal*, 34 (1): 25–55.

Hoskin, K. and Macve, R. (1988) The genesis of accountability: the West Point connections, *Accounting Organizations and Society*, 13 (1): 37–73.

Jacobs, T. (ed.). (1995) *The B&O: America's First Railroad* (New York: Smithmark).

Jupe, R. and Funnell, W. (2015) Neoliberalism, consultants and the privatisation of public policy formulation: the case of Britain's rail industry, *Critical Perspectives on Accounting* 29 (2): 65–85.

Kistler, L. (1980) Middlesex Canal – an analysis of its accounting and management, *Accounting Historians Journal*, 7 (1): 43–57.

Knight, J. and Latrobe, B.H. (1838) *Report upon the Locomotive Engines and the Policy and Management of Several Principal Railroads in the Northern and Middle States* (Baltimore: Lucas & Deaver).

Kolko, G. (1965) *Railroads and Regulation, 1877–1916* (New York: W.W. Norton).

Lardner, D. (1850) *Railway Economy* (New York: Harper).

Lee, G.A. (1975) The concept of profit in British accounting, 1760–1900, *Business History Review*, 49 (1): 6–36.

May, G.O. (1936) The influence of accounting on the development of an economy, *Journal of Accountancy*, 61 (1): 171–184.

McCartney, S. and Arnold, A.J. (2000) George Hudson's financial reporting practices: putting the Eastern Counties Railway in context, *Accounting, Business & Financial History*, 10 (3): 293–316.

McCartney, S. and Arnold, A.J. (2002) Financial reporting in the context of crisis: reconsidering the impact of the 'mania' on early railway accounting, *European Accounting Review*, 11 (2): 401–17.

McCartney, S. and Arnold, A.J. (2003) The railway mania of 1845–1847: market irrationality or collusive swindle based on accounting distortions, *Accounting, Auditing & Accountability Journal*, 16 (5): 821–52.

McCartney, S. and Arnold, A.J. (2012) Financial capitalism, incorporation and the emergence of financial reporting information. *Accounting, Auditing & Accountability Journal* 25 (8): 1290–316.

McCraw, T.K. (1984) *Prophets of Regulation* (Cambridge MA: Belknap).

Miranti, P.J. (1990) Measurement and organizational effectiveness: the ICC's Bureau of Statistics and Accounts and railroad regulation, 1887–1940, *Business & Economic History*, 19: 183–92.

Mitchell, B.R. (1964) The coming of the railway and United Kingdom economic growth, *Journal of Economic History*, 24 (3): 315–36.

Neidert, K. (1950) The development of railroad accounting as it relates to the general ledger and the financial statements, unpublished dissertation, Washington University.

New York Times (1878) Discussing railroad men's duties, November 13: 1.

Odlyzko, A. (2011) The collapse of the railway mania, the development of capital markets, and the forgotten role of Robert Lucas Nash, *Accounting History Review*, 21 (3): 309–45.

Pollins, H. (1952) The finances of the Liverpool and Manchester Railway, *Economic History Review*, 5 (1): 90–97.

Pollins, H. (1954) Marketing of railway shares in the first half of the nineteenth century, *Economic History Review*, 7 (2): 230–39.

Pollins, H. (1956) Aspects of railway accounting before 1868, in A.C. Littleton and B.S. Yamey (eds) *Studies in the History of Accounting*, pp. 332–55 (London: Sweet & Maxwell).

Pollins, H. (1991) British horse tramway company accounting practices, 1870–1914, *Accounting, Business & Financial History*, 1 (3): 279–302.

Previts, G.J. and Samson, W.D. (2000) Exploring the contents of the Baltimore & Ohio Railroad annual reports: 1827–1856, *Accounting Historians Journal*, 27 (1): 1–42.

Quail, J. (2006) Accounting's motive power—the vision and reality for management accounting on the nationalised railways to 1959, *Accounting, Business & Financial History*, 16 (3): 419–46.

Quinn, T., Flesher, T.K. and Flesher, D.L. (2012) The impact of environmental forces on the Illinois Central Railroad between 1915 and 1939: a financial statement perspective, *Journal of Business Administration Online*, 11 (2): 1–19.

Railroad Accounting Principles Board (1987) *Railroad Accounting Principles, Final Report* volume 1 (Washington, DC: Railroad Accounting Principles Board).

Richards, E.S. (1972) The finances of the Liverpool and Manchester Railway again, *Economic History Review*, 25 (2): 284–92.

Russ, R.W., Coffman, E.N. and Previts, G.J. (2006) The stockholder review committee of the Chesapeake and Ohio Canal Company (1828–1857): evidence of changes in financial reporting and corporate governance, *Accounting Historians Journal*, 33 (1): 125–44.

Samson, W.D. and Previts, G.J. (1999) Reporting for success: the Baltimore & Ohio Railroad and management information, 1827–1856, *Business and Economic History Journal*, 28 (2): 235–54.

Samson, W.D., Flesher, D.L. and Previts, G.J. (2003) Quality of earnings: the case of the Mobile & Ohio Railroad in the 19th Century, *Issues in Accounting Education*, 18 (4): 335–57.

Simmons, J. and Biddle, G. (1997) *The Oxford Companion to British Railway History: From 1603 to the 1990s* (Oxford: Oxford University Press).

Solomons, D. (1952) The historical development of costing, in D. Solomons (ed.) *Studies in Costing*, pp. 1–52 (London: Sweet & Maxwell).
Stover, J.F. (1997) *American Railroads*, 2nd edn (Chicago: University of Chicago Press).
Sunderland, E.S.S. (1955) *Abraham Lincoln and the Illinois Central Railroad* (New York: Pandick Press).
The mysteries of American railway accounting (1879) *North American Review*, 129 (267): 135–47.
Thompson, J.E. (2013) Railroad investing and the importance of financial accounting information in 1880s America, *Accounting Historians Journal*, 40 (2): 55–89.
Thompson, J.E. (2017) Selecting railway investments in 1890s America, *Accounting Historians Journal*, 44 (1): 77–93.
Union Pacific Corporation (2018) SEC 10-K filed 2 September. Report of the Independent Registered Public Accounting Firm. Available HTTP: <www.up.com/cs/groups/public/@uprr/@investor/documents/investordocuments/pdf_up_10k_02092018.pdf>.
US House of Representatives (1971) Committee on Interstate and Foreign Commerce, Staff Study for the Special Subcommittee on Investigations, 92nd Congress, July 27 (Washington D.C.: GPO).
US Interstate Commerce Commission (1937) *Interstate Commerce Commission Activities 1887–1937* (Washington, DC: GPO).
Woodlock, T.F. (1900) *The Anatomy of a Railroad Report and Ton-Mile Cost* (New York: S. A. Nelson).

19

NATIONAL ACCOUNTING

Ignace De Beelde

Overview

This chapter first defines national accounting and, next, briefly discusses early developments in estimating national income and the transition to national accounting. Systems of national accounts developed mainly after the Second World War. International harmonisation became stronger in the 1990s. More recent developments focus on attempts to integrate other types of capital in the national accounts, such as natural capital and human capital.

As national accounting provides macroeconomic information, it could be expected that there would be an interaction between economists and accountants. However, this interaction has been limited, and only from the 1940s are initiatives identified that brought together both professions. The current situation is characterised by an almost complete separation between these groups.

National accounting developed in different ways across different countries. To a large extent, this can be linked to the political aspects of national accounting and different opinions on the economic role of governments. Governments that directly control economic life have a considerable impact on the broad area of accounting, but also favour systems that directly link micro-level and macro-level accounting.

This leads us to exploring the relationship between both levels. Accounting traditions that favour the use of standardised charts of accounts make integration easier. However, differences in concepts and valuation frameworks continue to make this a difficult task. The chapter concludes with a number of suggestions for future research.

National accounting defined

National accounting is a key arena where economics and accounting meet. Attempts to account for the national economy have existed for a long time but, until the first half of the twentieth century, these remained isolated initiatives.[1] Only around the time of the Second World War did a literature on the measurement of national income become more systematic. Over time, terminology has changed and the subject of this chapter has been variously designated as national accounting, national income accounting, national economic accounting and social accounting. All refer to the same concept: measuring and reporting the effects of the activities of the economic actors within a nation. National accounting is not, therefore, the same as government budgeting. Both measure financial wealth but they have different conceptual frameworks and are implemented by different government institutions (Jones 2000a). National accounting – the label used in this chapter – also has a clear political aspect. As a specific type of 'governing by numbers' (Rose 1991: 673) it can be linked with the concept of democracy and the relationship between the state and individual economic entities.

Following the Second World War, the use of accounting in an economic context was apparently unproblematic, especially from the accountants' point of view. At the end of the 1940s, Everett Hagen described the analysis of national accounts in *The Accounting Review* as 'the application of accounting principles to an entire economic system' and stated that 'national income measurement is best thought of as double entry bookkeeping, involving the consolidation of the operating accounts of all productive enterprises in the economic system, including government' (Hagen 1949: 248). Mattesich (1959: 86) thought that the term 'national accounting' could be understood as a 'recognition that this area of economics actually is a kind of accounting' and argued that 'social accounting is distinct from business and other micro-accounting systems only by a higher degree of aggregation and a somewhat different technique in collecting and processing data'. Moonitz and Nelson considered the rapid development in national accounting theory and systems in the 1950s to be one of the major developments in accounting theory (Moonitz and Nelson 1960).

However, during the second half of the twentieth century, things have changed and the terminology itself has become controversial. Gradually, economists started speaking of 'national accounts' rather than 'national accounting', and even that term has now largely disappeared. For example, the *Journal of Economic Literature* no longer lists national accounts as a separate topic and most US universities no longer include it in the curriculum (Ruggles and Ruggles 1995; Jones 2000a).

This chapter highlights some key steps in the development of national accounting both in theory and in practice. The first section deals with the development of the national accounting frameworks under different social and economic systems, culminating in the United Nations' *System of National Accounts* issued in 1993 and updated in 2008 (Inter-Secretariat Working Group on National Accounts 1993; EU Commission, IMF, OECD, UN, World Bank 2009). A second section focuses on the role of Keynes and the interactions between accountants and economists in the 1940s. Literature dealing with developments in specific countries is referred to in the third section. As differences between ideologies with respect to state intervention have an impact on national accounting, some examples are discussed in the fourth section. The next section deals with the links between micro-accounting and the macro-level through the charts of accounts. The chapter ends by identifying issues for further research.

Before proceeding further, we need to acknowledge the difficulty of delineating what to include and what to exclude from this chapter, with a particular problem being the fact that national accounting lies at the crossroads of accounting and macroeconomics. The number of articles concerning national accounting from the macroeconomic perspective is huge. Some of them are included, but this chapter is not about how national accounts should optimally measure and represent the economy of a country. Consequently, most of the macroeconomic literature is omitted.[2] Napier (2006) observes that there have been few studies of the relationship between accounting and national income calculations (see also Suzuki 2003a). The number of research articles on the history of national accounting written from an accounting perspective is also extremely limited: the annual listings of accounting history publications in *Accounting, Business & Financial History*, *Accounting History Review* and *Accounting History* reveal few relevant articles published since 1991.

Developing national accounting frameworks

A starting point is the long history of the development of national income estimates, which has been discussed in Studenski (1958) and Vanoli (2005). Generally the origin of national income estimates is attributed to William Petty in England in the 1660s. Petty focused on the measurement of national wealth, consisting of land and labour. Money was only a part of national wealth; population numbers were a key item (Sy and Tinker 2014). With the exception of the work of Gregory King on the social accounts of England between 1688 and 1695, no links were made in the literature between estimates of national income and accounting for over 250 years (Vanoli 2010).

The main concerns of those preparing early national income estimates related to taxes and the assessment of the economic strength of a country (Vanoli 2005, 2014). Until the early nineteenth century, interest in preparing such estimations remained limited to a few countries and, even there, long periods without any notable work can be observed. The methods used to collect data were quite diverse, significantly reducing comparability between countries.

The idea of looking at the national economy from an accounting perspective became more widespread during the 1930s. It was present in the works of Irving Fisher, Morris E. Copeland and Robert F. Martin in the US, André Vincent in France and Ed van Cleeff in The Netherlands (Vanoli 2005, 2010). After the stock market crisis of 1929 and the Great Depression, interest further increased and more estimates were made, not only of income but also of expenditure. However, significant conceptual differences between these estimations persisted at that time (Jones 2000a).

The publication of Keynes' *General Theory* in 1936 was important as it provided a theoretical basis for the measurement of income, consumption, investment and saving (Keynes 1936). During the Second World War, in Britain, national accounting rose higher on the agenda of a government which needed measures to help coordinate the economy and to be able to assess better the financial implications of policy decisions (Tomlinson 1994). An example of this increased interest occurred in 1941 with the official publication of the White Book entitled: 'An analysis of the sources of war finance and estimate of the national income and expenditure in 1938 and 1940' (Vanoli 2005: 20). Similar developments were observed in the US, and accounting and calculation came to be seen as an essential prerequisite for governing a democratic society in the national interest (Rose 1991).

In June 1941, James Meade and Richard Stone published their accounting framework reporting net national income, net national output and net national expenditure (Meade and Stone 1941). Their tables were a systematic representation of macroeconomic aggregates showing the links between them. Stone also focused separately on the quality of measurement and the development of adjusting techniques by constructing variance matrices of measurement errors (Comim 2001).

At the end of the War, attempts to bring about the international harmonisation of national accounting became more prominent. In December 1945, a statistical subcommittee at the League of Nations adopted a number of recommendations based on a memorandum prepared by Stone in the same year. The system that Stone proposed was more elaborate than the one presented in 1941, and it recommended the aggregation of individual entities within five main sectors: productive enterprises, financial intermediaries, insurance and social security agencies, final consumers and the rest of the world (Vanoli 2005: 24). There were different accounts for operations, appropriation, revenue, capital and reserves. However, the recommendations were never officially endorsed by the League of Nations.

Following the War, international harmonisation was slow to develop with the framework constructed by Stone strongly opposed by Norwegian economists (Lie 2007). However, the US introduced its National Income and Product Accounts (NIPA) in 1947 and, in 1952, the UK had its National Income and Expenditure Accounts. Both bear a close resemblance to the first Standardized System of National Accounts, introduced by the Organisation for European Economic Co-operation in 1952. The Standardized System consisted of six national accounts and ten more detailed standard tables. The six national accounts were:

- a consolidated product and expenditure account, showing national income at factor cost, the other components of gross national product at market prices and the main types of expenditure;
- a breakdown of national income;
- an appropriation account for government;
- an appropriation account for households and private institutions;
- a consolidated capital transactions account;
- a consolidated account for the rest of the world.

Countries with centrally planned economies did not adopt this framework. Instead, they relied on the material product system (MPS), primarily because it was only the production of goods that was considered to create value. This resulted in a 'system of balances of the national economy' with essential contributions by P. Popov in 1926, T. Ryabushkin in 1950 and V. Sobol in 1960 (Vanoli 2005: 100–1). Although there are links to be made between the Soviet accounting system and German business economics traditions (see below), the national accounting systems of countries in the Soviet Union's sphere of influence in general developed separately from those in the West. Consequently, the introduction of the Standardized System should, in theory, have resulted in the existence of two main systems: the Anglo-Saxon and the Soviet models. However, within the Western world many differences continued to exist between individual countries as the 1952 Standardized System was not universally accepted. The French, for example, considered it to be both too aggregated and too confused. Consequently, they developed their own significantly different system (see Vanoli 2005 for full discussion).

The Organisation for European Economic Co-operation's 1952 Standardized System was adopted in 1953 by the United Nations' System of National Accounts (SNA). The harmonisation of accounting frameworks throughout much of the Western World was considered important because of its links with the operation of the Marshall Plan (Vanoli 2005). In the 1960s there was growing pressure on the United Nations standard setters to amend the 1953 SNA. In 1964, Vanoli proposed a national accounting framework that would harmonise reporting in Europe, and Stone suggested a model, rather closer to the French tradition and including the Social Accounting Matrix developed at Cambridge.[3] The negotiations that followed eventually led to a revision of the framework, published as the 1968 SNA by the United Nations and the 1970 European System of Integrated Economic Accounts (ESA) by the European Communities. Stone's influence on the 1968 SNA was quite obvious (Ward 2004). The new framework included input–output tables, sector accounts and financial tables. Its general structure adopted a matrix format with one column and one row for each account.

The 1968 SNA and 1970 ESA frameworks had considerable impact, although many countries failed to fully comply with their provisions (for a critical evaluation, see Vanoli 1969, 2014). The major exception to the implementation of the new frameworks was the

US, which continued to apply the NIPA it had developed (Carson 1975). The sophistication of the 1968 SNA made its application to the affairs of many developing countries difficult, although adoption of the accompanying Social Accounting Matrices proved feasible in countries such as Indonesia, Sri Lanka, Malaysia and Botswana. To a large extent, the problems in applying the 1968 SNA were a consequence of the economic importance in developing countries of a non-productive, non-market sector and the existence of inefficient state enterprises (Ward 2004). The lack of relevant data is another factor that reduced the reliability of national accounts in many developing countries.[4]

The SNA 1968 was eventually revised in 1993 (Jones 2000b). The main causes for this revision were the increasing complexity of economic and financial systems and rapid technological changes such as electronic transfer mechanisms, intellectual capital, financial services and other intangible activities (Ward 2004). Originally, the revision was intended to be of a limited character, but it turned out to be both revolutionary and fundamental. The new framework was supported by the United Nations, the European Economic Community, the International Monetary Fund, the World Bank and the Organization for Economic Cooperation and Development. The European involvement resulted in a high level of comparability between the 1993 SNA and the 1995 ESA, the successor to the 1970 ESA. This collaboration of leading international institutions significantly increased its impact and its potential to lead to far-reaching harmonisation. The new framework was more prescriptive and presented a complete accounting sequence, including current accounts, accumulation accounts and balance sheets. It introduced an integrated 'stock-flow' framework that allowed relating all transactions that took place within an accounting period to comprehensive opening and closing balance sheets (Jones 2000a; Ward 2004).

Following the collapse of the Soviet Union, countries that previously adopted the MPS replaced their systems with the SNA in the early 1990s. Hungary was a forerunner in this process as it had had experience of both MPS and SNA since 1968 (Ward 2006).[5] The compilation of long-term series of Gross Domestic Products (GDP) proved a complex process in many former MPS countries, as it required the retrospective construction of the SNA accounts. One method has been to use conversion keys to calculate GDP from the MPS. This was a difficult process because there are not only incidental differences between both systems but also differences in the fundamental underlying concepts and definitions (Ivanov 2006). Finally, the 2013 comprehensive revision of the US national income and product accounts further strengthened worldwide harmonisation of national accounting (McCulla et al. 2013).

Current debates focus on the usefulness of GDP, a key measure, and whether it should be replaced by indicators that measure social welfare, economic welfare and 'externalities' (World Bank 2011; Vanoli 2014; Hamilton and Hepburn 2017). The debate whether sustainability and the depletion of natural capital should be included has resulted in the development of the System of Environmental-Economic Accounting (SEEA) by the UN in 1993 (Obst 2015). Although a number of countries have decided to prepare national accounts adopting the SEEA framework, there still is extensive debate around how natural capital should be accounted for (e.g. Wackernagel et al. 1999; Cohen et al. 2017)

Keynes and the relationship between economists and accountants

There have always been strong links between national accounting and economic theory,[6] and many key persons in the development of national accounting were also important for the development of economic theory. Examples include Gregory King, William Petty, John

Hicks, Richard Stone and John Maynard Keynes in England; Simon Kuznets and Wassily Leontief in the US; and Ragnar Frisch in Norway (Bos 1997). Keynes played a key role in the development of macroeconomics and consequently also had a great impact on national accounting. An early example of the work of Keynes in this field is the pamphlet *How to Pay for the War*, written in the winter of 1939/40 in collaboration with the German economist and statistician, Erwin Rothbarth (Keynes 1940). Their pamphlet is important because it was the first development of double-entry based national accounts for the UK. Although quite rudimentary, the pamphlet predates the work of Meade and Stone and could be considered a 'first attempt' (Cuyvers 1983).

Suzuki (2003b; see also Tily 2009) also discusses early examples of attempts to present national accounts for the UK. The main interest of his paper is that it provides a detailed discussion of the relationship between the development of UK national accounting and macroeconomics, highlighting the role of Keynes, Stone, Meade and Frank Sewell Bray. The growth of national economic management (a macroeconomic issue) can be linked to the rise of a concern with productivity, which was itself linked to attempts to regulate companies in the endeavour to increase output and efficiency (a microeconomic problem) (Tomlinson 1994). In the 1940s' debates, issues that needed to be resolved included questions such as whether monetary units were suitable measurements for representing the affairs of a national economy, what was an appropriate accounting period, and how to define entities and sectors. Moreover, the relative importance of stock versus flow variables was discussed, as was the way the government sector should be included in the accounts. A further important issue was how to balance the accounts in the case of missing data: for instance, the practice of residual calculation was not accepted by all.

In the 1940s, accountants began to share the interest of economists in national accounting. In 1945–46, Stone and the accountant Frank Sewell Bray organised meetings between accountants and economists to discuss how company accounts could become more useful for macroeconomic management (Comim 2001; Suzuki 2003b; Vanoli 2010). Because the accountants and their professional bodies believed that the outcome of these discussions neglected the conventions of business accounting, the direct output was confined to an analysis of common terms and concepts, published as a report by the Institute of Chartered Accountants and the National Institute of Economic and Social Research, in February 1948, under the title *Terms and Concepts in Common Use* (Suzuki 2003b: 499).

The attempted collaboration between accountants and economists thus proved difficult. Moonitz and Nelson (1960), for example, thought that the developments of national accounting in the 1950s would bring accountants and economists together, leading to a theory of accounting that would not only cover the business enterprise but also embrace the national level, and result in financial statements that could be used more readily as inputs for the creation of national accounts. However, this did not happen. In the UK, for example, accountants often do not know much about economics, and economists are often perceived dismissive of accountants (Napier 1996a, 1996b). To an extent, the national income debate in the 1940s was an exception, in that accountants such as Bray worked together with economists (Parker 1980). In the following years, co-operation between 'the uncongenial twins' (Boulding 1977) evaporated. Bray continued to develop proposals to present statistical data in an accounting format (see, e.g. Bray 1951), but after Bray there is little evidence of the active involvement of accountants in the development of national accounting, and the 1993 SNA/1995 ESA were prepared by expert groups or officials that did not include accountants (Jones 2000b).

The next section discusses how the construction of national accounts interacted with economic policy.

Interactions between accounting and the state

Ideological positions had a significant impact on debates with respect to national accounting. In Western countries, ideas on national income calculation tended to be the subject of suspicion during an era when the ideology of laissez faire and non-intervention remained dominant. The opposite can be expected in countries with political regimes that actively intervene in economic life. The latter countries comprise two categories. The first is where new states are being created; the other where governments adopt an ideology of coordinating economic activity. Several papers have addressed the role of accounting in such circumstances.

During German unification in the 1870s, economic policy was a central item in the political debate (Gallhofer and Haslam 1991). Accounting practice in companies became strictly regulated by the state and linked with taxation. At the same time, intriguingly, accounting regulation accepted the practice of creating secret reserves and continued to do so after they had been outlawed in, for example, Britain in 1948. The widespread acceptance of accounting regulation was fostered by the economic success of state-led industrial policy. It came under pressure during the First World War, however, because of the tax regime relating to war profits and different views on the utility of secret reserves. The reporting of war profits gave accounting a conflict-enhancing role in German society during and after the War. Although secret reserve accounting continued to be an acceptable practice (Spoerer 1998), criticism appears to have been a stimulus to the development of uniform accounting as later adopted by the Nazis (see next section). Markus (1997) demonstrates how the accounting profession in Germany became increasingly integrated in the party and state under Nazism and how accounting was an important instrument in operating state-controlled industry.

Cinquini (2007) studied the relationships between business studies and accounting and the construction of the corporative economy in Italy in light of its fascist ideology in the 1930s. In so doing, he observed points of convergence between fascist ideology and accounting discourse. Economic sectors were to be organised within fascist corporations conceived as government instruments to regulate economic activities without the need to abolish the private sector. In fascist ideology, the objectives of firms became subordinate to 'national interests'. A number of authors proposed changes in accounting statements and valuations to make accounting data useful for the construction of 'enterprise statistical and accounting indexes'. These in turn would be used for the fascist corporations' purposes of coordination (Cinquini 2007). Within each industry, uniform accounting methods were to be used. Although individual firms were subordinated to national interests, however, the general intention was that the management within the firm would remain independent and autonomous.

These arrangements contrasted with those put in place by the Soviet Union. Although there was the continuing influence of German accountants (such as Schmalenbach) on accounting ideas in that country (Richard 1995a), the basic function of accounting was different. Whereas continental European tradition considered the individual enterprise as the focus of accounting, this was not the case in Soviet accounting. There, the accounting system was used by the central authorities to maintain control over the activities of the state enterprises (Bailey 1988). Bailey (1990) discusses the debate in the 1930s between 'bourgeois accountants' and 'Soviet accountants' and links it with the debates under Stalin on Marxism. Accounting had to be modernised to fit with the needs of an industrial society, as was the case in other countries. At the same time, business activities in the Soviet Union became focused on the enterprise's corporate plan, a component of the national economic plan. Accounting gradually changed into data keeping and the performance of enterprises was measured using physical and monetary (mainly cost) indicators. The accounting systems of individual enterprises were simplified and unified. In this way, the national economy became the accounting entity and enterprise accounting became more macro-oriented. At the same time, accounting procedures were standardised. Within enterprises, centralised accounting offices were oriented towards state control and the accountant became a state controller. A centralised perspective also existed in countries that were under Soviet influence. Arvay reports that in Hungary in 1974:

> [t]he reliability of national accounting is favourable in Hungary, as they are based mostly (92 percent) on the bookkeeping data of enterprises, cooperatives and institutions. The bookkeeping system is uniform in all economic organizations, in conformity with central regulations, and it takes into account the demand of computations for national accounting.
>
> *(Arvay 1974: 55)*

Linking the macro and micro perspectives: the use of charts of accounts

The previous section has demonstrated the linking of micro-level data to national aggregates. In many continental European countries (and countries in other parts of the world historically under their influence) standardised charts of accounts were considered to help in linking the macro and micro perspectives. However, a standardised chart of accounts does not solve the conceptual issues.

Although terminology is sometimes similar for national and business accounting, concepts and ways of operation are not always directly comparable (Vanoli 2010). In the 1940s, both systems used a different concept of double-entry bookkeeping (Jones 2000a; Suzuki 2003b). In business accounting, each transaction is recorded twice because it affects both assets or liabilities and income, or different types of balance sheet items. In national accounting, the double-entry aspect is that a transaction affects different entities in the economy. From the 1993 SNA onwards, national accounts have been based on the principle of quadruple entry, each transaction typically involving two accounting entities recorded twice within each entity.[7]

There also exist significant differences between business accounting and national accounting in valuation principles.[8] Both systems now generally follow accrual accounting principles, which has created more difficulties in national accounting because government accounts were (and still are in a number of countries) prepared essentially on a cash basis. Bray and Stone considered the change towards accrual accounting one of the major steps in the reform of governmental accounting (Bray and Stone 1948). However, national accounting never used the historical cost models that were (and still are) dominant in business accounting (Jones 2000b). Adoption of the fair-value perspective was easier to implement than the introduction of fair value at the individual company transaction level, due to the availability of price indices for national accounting aggregates.

In both systems, we have balance sheets and accumulation accounts or cash flow statements. Apart from disparities in valuation systems, the differences are quite limited. However, the differences are more important between income statements for businesses and current accounts in national accounting. Some items are not recorded in national accounts but have an impact on business income (e.g. bad debt provisions). More importantly, in national accounting, the emphasis is more on value added and output than on sales and profit (Vanoli 2010). The distance between both systems is especially significant if business income statements are prepared by function: income statements by nature of expense, as traditionally prepared by most companies in continental Europe, are much easier to link with national accounting.

On a global level, value added represents the value created by an economic system. At the level of an individual entity, such as a company, it shows the value created by that company exclusive of its consumption of items created by other economic entities. The issue is not widely discussed in the accounting literature in continental countries, probably because it is considered non-problematic. In the Anglo-Saxon literature, there has been some debate on this issue which, for the UK, Hopwood et al. (1994) locate essentially in the late 1970s. Disclosure of value added could be linked with payment for labour and profit sharing, but also with performance evaluation in British industry. The widespread debate on value added in the UK during the 1970s was related to, among other factors, incomes policies through value-added incentive payment schemes

The difference in concepts between business and national accounting raises the question of how to link them. The relationship between business accounting and national accounts is not always clear in Keynes' work. However, the system proposed by Stone in 1945 included the idea of aggregating national accounts from the accounts of individual entities (Vanoli 2010). This idea did not develop further in the UK, but the French example illustrates a country where data taken from business accounts was rearranged and served as inputs in national accounts through intermediate accounts (Vanoli 2005). The French model was adopted in a 2000 United Nations handbook on national accounting (United Nations 2000). However, not many countries have succeeded in using business accounts directly for the compilation of national accounts. Vanoli (2006) mentions two major difficulties in this respect: availability of company accounts and the lack of standardisation of company accounts. Postner (1986) reports two cases where micro-accounting data are used in modelling: a micro-to-macro model of the Swedish economy, and an econometric model of the UK economy developed at Cambridge. However, statistical inconsistencies remain an issue.[9]

As discussed above, the continental European tradition of standardised charts of accounts often prefers income statements classified by nature of expense. This tradition predates the national accounting debate of the twentieth century. In the nineteenth century, the development of company law resulted in the introduction of codified regulations of accounting and auditing in many continental countries.[10] The models that were used to regulate accounting can be traced from France to other countries such as Germany (Gallhofer and Haslam 1991). Although the level of regulation was not very detailed compared to current accounting and auditing standards, continental European countries often prescribed at least the minimum contents of financial statements.

In principle, countries that introduced standardised charts of accounts could more easily transfer business data into national accounts.[11] Most of these countries were located in continental Europe, which might explain why the (dominantly Anglo-Saxon) research literature has given little attention to this subject until recently. A first series of studies was published in the *European Accounting Review* in 1995. As well as a discussion of the development of accounting charts in different countries in the nineteenth and twentieth centuries (Richard 1995a), it included analyses of charts of accounts and their implementation in Spain (Chauveau 1995), Germany (Bechtel 1995), Russia and Romania

(Richard 1995b). Studies of other countries followed: Slovakia (Daniel et al. 2001), Poland (Jaruga and Szychta 1997) and Belgium (De Beelde 2003). There were important differences between the structure of these charts in different countries: Richard (1995a) distinguished between monistic and dualistic charts (depending on whether there is one or more than one type of valuation and a unity or distinction between financial and managerial accounting) and between charts that focus on the balance sheet and charts that follow the logic of an economic circuit.

There are two exceptions to the limited attention generally accorded by researchers, until recently, to charts of accounts: these involved the French *Plan Comptable Général* and (to a lesser extent) the corresponding developments in Germany. The developments in Germany were strongly influenced by the growing impact of Taylorism and a German business economics tradition that focused on economic circuits, including Rathenau and Schmalenbach (Richard 1995a). Discussion in Germany has focused to a large extent on the impact of Schmalenbach on the development of accounting charts that could be used to control an economy in its preparation for war (Forrester 1977). Schmalenbach wanted charts of accounts to be sufficiently flexible to allow decentralised decision making and at the same time include detailed cost accounts in the scheme, in order to improve the performance of German industry by allowing cost comparisons.

There is obviously a line from the German chart, introduced in 1937, to the first French *Plan comptable*, developed under German occupation in 1942 (Standish 1990). Following the Second World War, there was a greater acceptance in France of a significant state role in economic coordination, and the idea of a general chart of accounts was reintroduced in 1947. The *Plan comptable* has been studied extensively. Its development has to be seen in the context of post-war economic reconstruction and political modernisation (Miller 1986). The 1947 chart of accounts had different objectives: creating a control instrument for tax authorities and creditors, serving as legal evidence, but above all, providing information for economic statistics and national accounting (Hoarau 2003). It was an instrument to create a *Comptabilité Nationale* with industrial input-output charts similar to those that Leontieff developed for the US and the UK (Colasse and Durand 1994). As a consequence of European unification, the plan itself became gradually less central to French regulation.

The French state supervised all accounting regulation, on a micro-level via the Conseil National de Comptabilité (National Accounting Board) and on a macro-level through the Institut National de la Statistique et les Etudes Economiques (National Institute of Statistics and Economic Surveys). The Institut National is also present in micro-level accounting standard setting. Its impact is significant in the presentation of income statements that are organised by nature of expense and consequently show value-added or gross operating surplus: data that can be conveniently used in the compilation of national accounts. However, there still is no automatic reconciliation of French micro-accounting and national accounting. Adjustments have to be made in the aggregation process due to differences in valuation, recognition dates and classification (Lande 2000).

In Eastern European countries, charts of accounts were part of the centralised organisation of bookkeeping under Soviet influence. After the political changes in the 1990s, many countries maintained their chart-based systems. Examples include Poland, Hungary and the Czech Republic (King et al. 2001). In Russia, the structure of the new charts was strongly influenced by those used in the Soviet period, and it still adopts the 'circuit' principle that goes back to Schmalenbach (Richard 1995b). In Ukraine, on the contrary, the new charts were more influenced by French models (Golov 2006).

Issues for further research

National accounting is an area of accounting history that is largely unresearched. Historically, this can partly be attributed to a lack of data. Databases of national accounts or aggregates, such as those kept by the United Nations Statistics Division or Unesco, as well as more detailed data in individual countries, are now more easily available, however, so this should no longer be a significant obstacle. Another obvious explanation for its absence from scholarly journals is the lack of collaboration between accountants and economists demonstrated earlier. It led Suzuki (2003b: 505) to conclude that key questions – such as 'how did accounting affect the perception of the public sphere of the economy, the approach to economic problems and the policies adopted, and the consequences that may be desirable or undesirable in relation to the socio-economic welfare' – remain almost entirely unexplored.

Consequently, identifying future research possibilities is not difficult. The historical relationship between macroeconomics and accounting is one such possibility. Much of what is available deals with the UK. There is a need for an expansion of this focus to other countries such as the US, France, the Netherlands, Italy and Germany. Some of these countries used to have specific business economics traditions (e.g. the *economia aziendale* in Italy and the work of Limperg in the Netherlands), and one can expect that this interaction between economics and accounting was perceived differently compared with the UK. Such a study could include an analysis of the writings of leading theorists and scholars. Following the same line of thought, research into joint initiatives and working parties, such as those organised by Stone and Bray in the 1940s in the UK, could expand our understanding of the relationship between accounting and economics in other countries.

Most of the research has focused on Europe and the US. Only few examples can be given of research on the development of national accounting in the rest of the world. Speich (2011) is an exception, as he analyses how new methods of national income calculation met with difficulties when applied in a colonial context. More research is needed to investigate the effects of using Western economic aggregates on the relations between North and South.

The absence of work by the professional accounting bodies is also striking. At a time when these organised bodies commented on a wide range of issues, they apparently did not address, for example, the development of the SNA 1993. Further work on the evolution of the position of the organised accounting profession with respect to the developments in national accounting would be welcome. Again, it would be interesting to study a wider range of countries to see whether this lack of involvement in national accounting was universal.

Business accounting has been struggling with fair value concepts for many years. However, in macro-accounts, fair value has already been applied for a long time. It might be insightful to find out how these concepts were historically introduced, how fair values were measured and why these concepts apparently were not easily transferred to business accounting. Such work would also be of contemporary relevance in the current International Financial Reporting Standards context.

There are also a number of wider issues that are challenging for the future but that at the same time can be studied from a historical perspective. Very often they relate to what should be included in the national accounts (see Ward 2006). A typical example is the limited presence of households in national accounts and the related absence of unpaid household production (Froud et al. 2000; Walker and Llewellyn 2000). Many other issues have been discussed since the early twentieth century and they are also examined in the context of business accounting. Examples include accounting for human capital and reporting the social performance of companies. A number of countries (e.g. Belgium 1996) have introduced requirements for companies to prepare social balance sheets disclosing details on salaries, social expenses and training. It can be debated to what extent such social balance sheets actually measure human capital. It is also unclear how they could be linked with national accounts, where there is a growing consensus that human capital is becoming one of the major components of national capital (World Bank 2011). Another example relates to environmental issues. Sustainability reports and 'green accounting' are strongly debated issues in micro-accounting. However, there is also a growing literature on natural resource accounting, green national accounting and a green national product (e.g. Aaheim and Nyborg 1995; Harris and Fraser 2002; Asheim 2004). Are there links between these debates at the micro- and macro-levels? Should national accounts report welfare and, if so, how should this be measured? Are only items that can be expressed in monetary terms relevant? Again, how do you link this with business accounting, knowing that an optimal solution at a micro-level is not always optimal at the macro-level? Understanding how these questions were considered in the past might also be revealing for the future.

Key works

De Vries et al. (1993) contain a collection of essays on 50 years of national accounting in The Netherlands, not only discussing Dutch developments but also broader methodological issues.

Gilbert and Stone (1954) summarise the status of national accounting during a key period in its development – the 1930s to 1950s.

Studenski (1958) is an impressive study of the history and contemporary practice of national income calculation. It covers developments in a wide range of countries from the seventeenth through to the twentieth century and discusses the methodology for estimating national income.

Suzuki (2003b), focusing upon the Keynesian revolution from an accounting point of view, discusses a key period in the development of national accounting.

Vanoli (2005), written by a former director of the French Central Statistical Office, takes a look from the inside at the development of national accounting and supplies extensive discussion of historical developments, concepts and issues.

Notes

1 Examples include Canada (Baker and Rennie 2013) and Italy (Coronella et al. 2013). Broadberry et al. (2017) compare China and Europe.

2 For those interested in the evolution of technical and methodological issues in national accounting, the *Review of Income and Wealth* is the premier source. A historical analysis of developments in national accounting in the US is Perlman and Marietta (2005); their article also includes some discussion on Germany and the UK.

3 According to Ward (2004), the Social Accounting Matrices were pioneered by Thorbecke, Pyatt and Keuning in the Netherlands.

4 For a general discussion, see Barkay (1975); for individual cases, see Hardman (1986) on Papua New Guinea, Barkay (1982) on Nepal, Van der Eng (1999, 2005) on Indonesia and Sourrouille (1976) on Argentina.
5 Arvay (1969) analysed the differences between the two systems.
6 On the relationship between accounting and economics, see Suzuki (2003a).
7 There had been attempts in some countries to introduce double-entry bookkeeping in government agencies quite early. Edwards and Greener (2003) report on such initiatives in the UK between 1828 and 1844.
8 This does not mean that the concepts of value and income in national accounting are the same as those in economic theory. They are descriptive concepts that should be understood in their specific accounting framework (Bos 1997).
9 Postner (1988) gives a number of examples and refers at the same time to the French 'intermediate accounts' approach supported by the French *Plan Comptable Générale* as a solution.
10 Standardised accounts were not only found in continental Europe. In the UK and US, however, standardisation did not take place on an overall level but rather at an industry level. In the late nineteenth century, standardised accounts were introduced for certain industries in Britain such as the railways (Edwards 2019: ch. 11). In the 1930s, many UK and US industries used uniform systems of accounts and forms of financial statements (Lengyel 1949). Contrary to continental Europe, this standardisation was not based on a general chart and was often related to cost accounts.
11 Post-Second World War Japan is an interesting case where, in the context of macroeconomic data construction, 'the need for standardised corporate accounting and regulation came to be recognized as a micro-foundation of macro-data' (Suzuki 2007: 275).

References

Aaheim, A. and Nyborg, K. (1995) On the interpretation and applicability of a 'green national product', *Review of Income and Wealth*, 41 (1): 57–71.

Arvay, J. (1969) Development of the national accounting system in Hungary, *Review of Income and Wealth*, 15 (2): 185–95.

Arvay, J. (1974) Problems of determining and measuring the reliability of the national accounts: Hungary's experiences, *Review of Income and Wealth*, 20 (1): 55–69.

Asheim, G.B. (2004) Green national accounting with a changing population, *Economic Theory*, 23 (3): 601–19.

Bailey, D. (1988) *Accounting in Socialist Countries* (London: Routledge).

Bailey, D. (1990) Accounting in the shadow of Stalinism, *Accounting, Organizations and Society*, 15 (6): 513–25.

Baker, R. and Rennie, M.D. (2013) An institutional perspective on the development of Canada's first public accounts, *Accounting History*, 18 (1): 31–50.

Barkay, R.M. (1975) National accounting as planning tool in less developed countries: lessons of experience, *Review of Income and Wealth*, 21 (4): 349–69.

Barkay, R.M. (1982) National accounting with limited data: lessons from Nepal, *Review of Income and Wealth*, 28 (3): 305–23.

Bechtel, W. (1995) Charts of accounts in Germany, *European Accounting Review*, 4 (2): 283–304.

Bos, F. (1997) Value and income in the national accounts and economic theory, *Review of Income and Wealth*, 43 (2): 173–90.

Boulding, K.E. (1977) Economics and accounting: the uncongenial twins, in W.T. Baxter and S. Davidson (eds.) *Studies in Accounting Theory*, pp. 86–95 (London: ICAEW).

Bray, F.S. (1951) A national balance sheet, *Accounting Research*, 2 (3): 279–300.

Bray, F.S. and Stone, R. (1948) The presentation of the central government accounts, *Accounting Research*, 1 (1): 1–12.

Broadberry, S., Guan, H. and Daokui Li, D. (2017), China, Europe and the great divergence: a study in historical national accounting, 980-1850, *University of Warwick Working Paper Series 324*.

Carson, C.S. (1975) The history of the United States national income and product accounts, *Review of Income and Wealth*, 21 (2): 153–81.

Chauveau, B. (1995) The Spanish Plan General de Contabilidad: agent of development and innovation? *European Accounting Review*, 4 (1): 125–40.

Cinquini, L. (2007) Fascist corporative economy and accounting in Italy during the Thirties: exploring the relation between a totalitarian ideology and business studies, *Accounting, Business & Financial History*, 17 (2): 209–40.

Cohen, F., Hepburn, C. and Teytelboym, A. (2017) Can we stop depleting natural capital? A literature review on substituting it with other forms of capital, *INET Oxford Working Paper 2017-13*.

Colasse, B. and Durand, R. (1994) French accounting theorists of the twentieth century, in J.R. Edwards (ed.) *Twentieth-Century Accounting Thinkers*, pp. 41–59 (London: Routledge).

Comim, F. (2001) Richard Stone and measurement criteria for national accounts, *History of Political Economy*, 23 (annual supplement): 213–34.

Coronella, S., Lombrano, A. and Zanin, L. (2013) State accounting innovations in pre-unification Italy, *Accounting History Review*, 23 (1): 1–21.

Cuyvers, L. (1983) Keynes' collaboration with Erwin Rothbarth, *Economic Journal*, 93 (371): 629–36.

Daniel, P., Suranova, Z. and De Beelde, I. (2001) The development of accounting in Slovakia, *European Accounting Review*, 10 (2): 343–59.

De Beelde, I. (2003) The development of a Belgian accounting code during the first half of the 20th century, *Accounting Historians Journal*, 30 (2): 1–28.

de Vries, W., den Bakker, G., Gircour, M., Keuning, S. and Lenson, A. (1993) *The Value Added of National Accounting* (Amsterdam: Netherlands Central Bureau of Statistics).

Edwards, J.R. (2019) *A History of Corporate Financial Reporting in Britain* (London: Routledge).

Edwards, J.R. and Greener, H.T. (2003) Introducing 'mercantile' bookkeeping into British central government 1858–1844, *Accounting and Business Research*, 33 (1): 51–64.

EU Commission, IMF, OECD, UN, World Bank (2009) *System of National Accounts 2008* (New York: European Commission, IMF, OECD, UN, World Bank).

Forrester, D. (1977) *Schmalenbach and after – A Study in the Evolution of German Business Economics* (Strathclyde: Strathclyde Convergencies).

Froud, J., Haslam, C., Johal, S. and Williams, K. (2000) Representing the household: in and after national income accounting, *Accounting, Auditing & Accountability Journal*, 13 (4): 535–60.

Gallhofer, S. and Haslam, J. (1991) The aura of accounting in the context of a crisis: Germany and the First World War, *Accounting, Organizations and Society*, 16 (5–6): 487–520.

Gilbert, M. and Stone, R. (1954) Recent developments in national income and social accounting, *Accounting Research*, 5 (1): 1–31.

Golov, S. (2006) Development of chart of accounts in Ukraine and Russia since 1991. Paper presented at Annual Congress of the European Accounting Association, Dublin, 22-4 March.

Hagen, E. (1949) National accounting systems and the European recovery program, *Accounting Review*, 24 (3): 248–54.

Hamilton, K. and Hepburn, C. (eds) (2017) *National Wealth: What is Missing, Why It Matters* (Oxford: Oxford University Press).

Hardman, D.J. (1986) Paradigms of public financial administration in the evolution of Papua New Guinea, *Public Administration and Development*, 6 (2): 151–61.

Harris, M. and Fraser, I. (2002) Natural resource accounting in theory and practise: a critical assessment, *Australian Journal of Agricultural and Resource Economics*, 46 (2): 139–92.

Hoarau, C. (2003) Place et role de la normalisation comptable en France, *Revue Française de Gestion*, 29 (147): 33–47.

Hopwood, A.G., Burchell, S. and Clubb, C. (1994) Value-added accounting and national economic policy, in A.G. Hopwood and P. Miller (eds.) *Accounting as Social and Institutional Practice*, pp. 211–36 (Cambridge: Cambridge University Press).

Inter-Secretariat Working Group on National Accounts (1993) *System of National Accounts 1993* Prepared under the auspices of the Inter-Secretariat Working Group on National Accounts (Brussels: Office for Official Publications of the European Communities).

Ivanov, Y.N. (2006) On compilation of long term series of GDP for the former USSR Republics, *Hitotsubashi University Discussion Paper Series*,173:1–13.

Jaruga, A. and Szychta, A. (1997) The origin and evolution of charts of accounts in Poland, *European Accounting Review*, 6 (3): 509–26.

Jones, R. (2000a) National accounting, government budgeting and the accounting discipline, *Financial Accountability and Management*, 16 (2): 101–16.

Jones, R. (2000b) Public versus private: the empty definitions of national accounting, *Financial Accountability and Management*, 16 (2): 167–78.

Keynes, J.M. (1936) *The General Theory of Employment, Interest and Money* (London: Macmillan).

Keynes, J.M. (1940) *How to Pay for the War: A Radical Plan for the Chancellor of the Exchequer* (New York: Harcourt, Brace).

King, N., Beattie, A., Cristescu, A.M. and Weetman, P. (2001) Developing accounting and audit in a transition economy: the Romanian experience, *European Accounting Review*, 10 (1): 149–71.

Lande, E. (2000) Macro-accounting and micro-accounting relationships in France, *Financial Accountability & Management*, 16 (2): 151–65.

Lengyel, S.J. (1949) Standardised accountancy considered internationally, *Accounting Research*, 1 (2): 133–41.

Lie, E. (2007) The "Protestant" view: the Norwegian and Scandinavian approach to National Accounting in the postwar period, *History of Political Economy*, 39 (4): 713–14.

Markus, H.B. (1997) *The History of the German Public Accounting Profession* (New York: Garland Publishing).

Mattesich, R. (1959) Accounting reconsidered, *California Management Review*, 2 (1): 85–91.

McCulla, S.H., Holdren, A.E. and Smith, S. (2013) Improved estimates of the national income and product accounts. Results of the 2013 Comprehensive Revision, *Survey of Current Business*, 93 (9): 14–45.

Meade, J.E. and Stone, R. (1941) The construction of tables of national income, expenditure, savings and investment, *Economic Journal*, 51 (206-7): 216–33.

Miller, P. (1986) Accounting for progress – national accounting and planning in France: a review essay, *Accounting, Organizations and Society*, 11 (1): 83–104.

Moonitz, M.A. and Nelson, C.M. (1960) Recent developments in accounting theory, *Accounting Review*, 35 (2): 206–17.

Napier, C.J. (1996a) Accounting and the absence of a business economics tradition in the United Kingdom, *European Accounting Review*, 5 (3): 449–82.

Napier, C.J. (1996b) Academic disdain? Economists and accounting in Britain, 1850-1950, *Accounting, Business & Financial History*, 6 (3): 427–50.

Napier, C.J. (2006) Accounts of change: 30 years of historical accounting research, *Accounting, Organizations and Society*, 30 (4–5): 445–507.

Obst, C.G. (2015) Reflections on natural capital accounting at the national level, *Sustainability Accounting, Management and Policy Journal*, 6 (3): 315–39.

Parker, R.H. (1980) Memorial. Frank Sewell Bray 1906-1979, *Accounting Review*, 55 (2): 307–16.

Perlman, M. and Marietta, M. (2005) The politics of social accounting: public goals and the evolution of the national accounts in Germany, the United Kingdom and the United States, *Review of Political Economy*, 17 (2): 211–30.

Postner, H.H. (1986) Microbusiness accounting and macroeconomic accounting: the limits to consistency, *Review of Income and Wealth*, 32 (3): 217–44.

Postner, H.H. (1988) Linkages between macro and micro business accounts: implications for economic measurement, *Review of Income and Wealth*, 34 (3): 313–35.

Richard, J. (1995a) The evolution of accounting chart models in Europe from 1900 to 1945: some historical elements, *European Accounting Review*, 4 (1): 87–124.

Richard, J. (1995b) The evolution of the Romanian and Russian accounting charts after the collapse of the communist system, *European Accounting Review*, 5 (2): 305–24.

Rose, N. (1991) Governing by numbers: figuring out democracy, *Accounting, Organizations and Society*, 16 (7): 673–92.

Ruggles, R. and Ruggles, P. (1995) The value added of national accounting, *Review of Income and Wealth*, 41 (3): 367–71.

Sourrouille, J.V. (1976) The development of national accounts in Argentina, *Review of Income and Wealth*, 22 (4): 353–75.

Speich, D. (2011) The use of global abstractions: national income accounting in the period of imperial decline, *Journal of Global History*, 6: 7–28.

Spoerer, M. (1998) Window-dressing in German inter-war balance sheets, *Accounting, Business & Financial History*, 8 (3): 351–69.

Standish, P. (1990) Origins of the Plan Comptable Général: a study in cultural intrusion and reaction, *Accounting and Business Research*, 20 (80): 337–51.

Studenski, P. (1958) *The Income of Nations. Theory, Measurement and Analysis: Past and Present* (New York: New York University Press).

Suzuki, T. (2003a) The accounting figuration of business statistics as a foundation for the spread of economic ideas, *Accounting, Organizations and Society*, 28 (1): 65–95.

Suzuki, T. (2003b) The epistemology of macroeconomic reality: the Keynesian Revolution from an accounting point of view, *Accounting, Organizations and Society*, 28 (5): 471–517.

Suzuki, T. (2007) Accountics: impacts of internationally standardized accounting on the Japanese socio-economy, *Accounting, Organizations and Society*, 32 (3): 263–301.

Sy, A. and Tinker, T. (2014) Early European accounting theory: Sir William Petty's contributions to accounting, *International Journal of Critical Accounting*, 6 (3): 211–32.

Tily, G. (2009) John Maynard Keynes and the development of national accounts in Britain, 1895-1941, *Review of Income and Wealth*, 55 (2): 331–59.

Tomlinson, J. (1994) The politics of economic measurement: the rise of the 'productivity problem' in the 1940s, in A.G. Hopwood and P. Miller (eds) *Accounting as Social and Institutional Practice*, pp. 168–89 (Cambridge: Cambridge University Press).

United Nations (2000) *Studies in Methods. Handbook of National Accounting. Series F, n° 76, Links between Business Accounting and National Accounting* (New York: United Nations).

Van der Eng, P. (1999) Some obscurities in Indonesia's new national accounts, *Bulletin of Indonesian Economic Studies*, 35 (2): 91–106.

Van der Eng, P. (2005) Indonesia's new national accounts, *Bulletin of Indonesian Economic Studies*, 41 (2): 243–52.

Vanoli, A. (1969) Le système actuel de comptabilité nationale et la planification, *Review of Income and Wealth*, 15 (2): 171–84.

Vanoli, A. (2005) *A History of National Accounting* (Amsterdam: IOS Press).

Vanoli, A. (2006) Is national accounting accounting? National accounting between accounting, statistics and economics. Paper presented at Eleventh World Congress of Accounting Historians, Nantes, 19–22 July.

Vanoli, A. (2010) Is national accounting accounting? National accounting between accounting, statistics and economics, *Comptabilités*, 1: 1–29.

Vanoli, A. (2014) National accounting at the beginning of the 21th century: wherefrom? Whereto? *Eurona – Eurostat Review on National Accounts and Macroeconomic Indicators*, 2014 (1): 9–36.

Wackernagel, M., Onisto, L., Bello, P., Callejas Linares, A., Lopez Falfan, I.S., Méndez Garcia, J., Suarez Guerrero, A.I. and Suares Guerrero, M.G. (1999) National natural capital accounting with the ecological footprint concept, *Ecological Economics*, 29 (3): 375–90.

Walker, S.P. and Llewellyn, S. (2000) Accounting at home: some interdisciplinary perspectives, *Accounting, Auditing & Accountability Journal*, 13 (4): 425–49.

Ward, M.P. (2004) Some reflections on the 1968–93 SNA Revision, *Review of Income and Wealth*, 50 (2): 299–313.

Ward, M.P. (2006) An intellectual history of national accounting, *Review of Income and Wealth*, 52 (2): 327–40.

World Bank (2011) *The Changing Wealth of Nations. Measuring Sustainable Development in the New Millennium* (Washington, DC: World Bank).

20
SCANDALS

Thomas A. Lee, Frank L. Clarke and Graeme W. Dean

Overview

This chapter examines accounting scandals over approximately the last 175 years that threaten corporate financial reporting's credibility as a viable means of protecting stakeholders from corrupt senior managers. The first section addresses the effectiveness of accounting as a system of governance instrumentation. Corporate failures provide impetus for successive revisions of accounting standards intended to remove perceived malpractices. Paradoxically, however, they appear to have had the opposite effect. Instead of increasing the extent to which financial statements reveal wealth and financial progress, they have spawned greater problems thereby institutionalising tensions in the social function of accounting. The second main section examines recurring issues in corporate financial reporting which provide the basis for evaluating the effectiveness of auditing in detecting material fraud by dominant senior managers (DSM). Critical here is the extent to which management-prepared accounts fail to 'tell it as it is' – they fail to depict an entity's wealth at a point in time and the change in that wealth since it last reported. Instead they contain material accounting misstatement (MAM). We analyse the responses of the state and the public accountancy profession to accounting scandals over many decades and in several jurisdictions, examining the credibility of audit as a means of protecting stakeholders from corrupt senior managers. Through instances of fraudulent reporting, this chapter reveals auditors denying or limiting their responsibility to detect MAM by DSM upon whose honesty they rely. The peroration of this chapter recounts the two paradoxes of false expectations from the history of corporate financial reporting generally and accounting scandals in particular, specifically the paradox of accounting as a governance instrument, and the paradox of auditing as a fraud detector. Both result from unexpected outcomes. Both are inconvenient and unwanted. Both threaten the credibility of the reporting system.

Accounting as governance instrumentation

Autopsies of corporate failures have presaged the questioning of the usefulness of audited accounting data as effective instrumentation – whether it is a credible basis for regular and ongoing financial assessments and evaluations of a company's wealth and progress.[1] But that questioning has evoked little effective action to improve instrumentation. For at least 175 years, misleading financial statements have involved massaging expense and revenue data and the exploitation of complex organisational structures. It is what is now described euphemistically as 'aggressive' accounting. Repeatedly, corporate managers have argued that they are best able to assess their appropriateness in the circumstances. Incongruously, to the likes of Raymond Chambers, Abraham Briloff and Edward Stamp, corporate managers remain the scorekeepers. Despite intermittent governmental intervention, expectations that auditors will uncover accounting malpractices have been no better met in recent years than in the distant past.

Several episodes during the review period aptly illustrate the ineffectiveness of the responses by government and the public accountancy profession to corporate failure. An early major episode involving accounting and auditing irregularities culminated in reforms on two continents – a new Companies Act (belatedly in 1947) in the UK (Edwards 2019: 161–2) and Roosevelt's New Deal in the US that, *inter alia*, created the Securities and Exchange Commission (SEC). The triggers for these regulatory initiatives were the Royal Mail Case (1931) in the UK and, in the US, the stock market crash of 1929 that exposed many corporate financial statements 'full of water'. The second episode commenced in the early 1990s with the crashes of the Maxwell and Polly Peck empires in the UK and intensified in the US with the Enron and WorldCom affairs and numerous accounting restatement scandals a decade later. The spectre of corporate malpractice was fuelled further by Eliot Spitzer's enquiries into the analyst-merchant banker nexus, hedge funds' timing of trades, and reinsurance frauds. There were also Australian cases, such as Ansett, Harris Scarfe, HIH and One.Tel. The actions presaging those sagas spawned legislative reforms – the Sarbanes-Oxley Act 2002 in the US and *CLERP 9* (Commonwealth of Australia 2004/05) in Australia. A third episode studied here is associated with financial reporting malpractices during and after the global financial crisis (GFC), including: Royal Bank of Scotland and Northern Rock in the UK; Bear Sterns, Lehman Brothers and AIG in the US; and Babcock and Brown, Allco and several property-cum-finance companies in Australia.

MAM by companies with complex group structures, frequently controlled by DSM, characterised each scandal. The circumstances surrounding scandals around the time of Enron's demise provide a template for comparison with earlier events, accounting and auditing issues, and responses to them by the state and the public accountancy profession.

Enron and concurrent corporate failures

Immediately preceding Jeffrey Skilling's 24-year sentence in the Enron case, and following Kenneth Lay's sudden death, other notorious corporate managers were imprisoned in the US. Chief executive officer (CEO) Bernie Ebbers of WorldCom received a 25-year custodial sentence and Tyco's CEO Dennis Kozlowski a minimum eight-year gaol term. These were prestigious 'heads-on-poles' for regulators, but they did not answer questions about the need for fundamental and systemic reform of corporate financial reporting.

Dotcom collapses and related major failures were a catalyst for the Bush administration to push through its Sarbanes-Oxley legislation to 'clean up corporate America'. In retrospect, Enron's alleged devious accounting did not significantly exceed that of many other early 2000s alleged recalcitrants, e.g. Sunbeam, Cendant, Waste Management, Tyco, Adelphia, Qwest, WorldCom, Alhold, Fannie Mae, Freddie Mac and Vivendi – with their imposed downwards restatements of earlier quarterly earnings predictions. But Enron appears to have been the straw that broke the corporate camel's back. It was possibly too big and allegedly too well-connected with Capitol Hill and the Bush administration to ignore. Significantly, despite the prominence of alleged MAM in these corporate collapses and failures, governmental reaction focused on other matters, e.g. alleged audit failure and poor internal governance. Inevitably, an inference to be drawn is that, despite repeated MAM, regulators considered accounting was in good shape. The *problem* was not that there was anything wrong with accounting *per se*, but that the fraudulent manipulation of it by DSM was accepted by auditors lacking independence.

Although an explicit connection was typically not made, the focus on the influence of DSM on accounting practice and auditing implied a common-sense, causal link of managers behaving badly by manipulating otherwise sound accounting rules. Unsurprisingly in this climate, public comment on Enron usually implied that its accounting was grossly deviant due to managerial manipulation. Few commentators seemed to notice that a large part of Enron's accounting had been approved by the SEC and the Financial Accounting Standards Board (FASB). Although there was significant accounting malpractice at Enron, the oft-mentioned 'mark-to-model' techniques underpinning its 'front-end loading' of profits scheduled to be earned on its natural gas trading contracts had been approved by the SEC in 1992. Similarly, loading debt into its special-purpose entities (SPE) treated them as leverage instruments exactly as they had been designed. And, whereas dubious practices appear to have improperly nullified the SPE control and 3 per cent equity criteria (i.e. effectively placing the vehicles outside SPE status and, therefore, not subject to consolidation requirements), had they satisfied that criteria the financial statements of Enron would have been no less misleading and its debt no less masked in its consolidated statements.

Given the US response to corporate accounting malpractice, it is unsurprising that the Australian government pursued the issues of executive remuneration and, in particular, auditor independence when Australia's largest insurer HIH and high-flying telecommunications company One.Tel collapsed in 2001. Mimicking the US approach, the Australian federal government commissioned an inquiry that produced the Ramsay Report (*Independence of Australian Company Auditors: Review of Current Australian Requirements and Proposals for Reform*) in 2001. However, somewhat different from that of the US was Australia's commitment to the 2005 Australian version of International Financial Reporting Standards (IFRS® Standards). In Australia, capitulation to the IFRS Standards' push was already a *fait accompli*. By implication, whenever IFRS Standards differed from the national status quo, the Australian public accountancy profession declared the previous accounting standards deficient – what had been compliant and thus true and fair was, in fact, no longer so. Consistent with the US strategy, corrupt managers and allegedly insufficiently independent auditors were targeted as the major villains. Accounting *per se* was let off the hook.

Convictions and sentences related to HIH's Ray Williams and Rodney Adler (on charges not directly linked to HIH's collapse) were relatively minor compared to those in the US. They provide a background to the Australian corporate regulator's action to recover $92 million from One.Tel's Jodee Rich and Mark Silberman for overseeing alleged trading when it was insolvent. Revelations in court illustrate how accounting potentially can mask corporate insolvency. Meanwhile, public insights into the behaviour of non-executive directors are to be gleaned in that case from the revelations of witnesses Lachlan Murdoch and James Packer. Each of these non-executive directors was able to recall little of their involvement with One.Tel on many issues, other than being profoundly misled by disclosures to them of the company's financial performance and position leading up to its collapse. The One.Tel collapse cost the companies with which they were connected reportedly in the order of $900 million. Yet there was little suggestion publicly that One. Tel's accounting was other than basically compliant with existing Australian accounting standards.

At about the same time, Italian courts and regulators were busy untangling the Parmalat failure (Hamilton and Micklethwait 2006). The well-placed Tanzi family emerged as corporate malefactors. Their alleged deeds rivalled those in Italy a quarter of a century earlier perpetrated by 'God's bankers' (Michele Sindona and Roberto Calvi) at the Vatican Bank (Raw 1992). And in the US three-quarters of a century earlier, Ivar Krueger and Samuel Insull (and many others labelled financial rogues in decades in between) were household names (Clarke et al. 2003). The alleged acts of deception are similar. Significantly, neither time and the different legal framework underpinning (say) Parmalat's incorporation, and the different board structures it promotes, nor rules relating to auditor appointments of the kind under the Sarbanes-Oxley regime, negate that stark similarity. Indeed, they are similar to descriptions of malpractice in the US made in Ferdinand Pecora's 1930s Commission into the practices of financial intermediaries and investment trusts in the years preceding the Great Depression.

It is worth contemplating whether an expectation that the introduction of IFRS Standards will rectify accounting's failing to 'show it how it is', where such complexity is endemic, will be fulfilled. With respect to the insurance industry, for example, the initial signs are less than encouraging, even when side-letters do not exist. Two-thirds of respondents to a KPMG survey of Australian insurance companies perceived that the 'adoption of IFRS [Standards] had actually increased the risk of inaccuracy in financial reporting' (Johnston 2006). Some suggest that directors should report to shareholders in myriad ways, resulting in the 'annual report being less relevant' (Kitney and Buffini 2006). Others are concerned about the volatility in earnings associated with applying IFRS Standards (AIA 2006) or, more generally, with the empirical impact of the IFRS Standards (Clarke et al. 2003; Abacus 2006; Walker 2007).

Whereas the noting of accounting defaults and anomalies featuring in post-2000 reports might be taken as indicative of the *new* corporate governance mechanisms exposing corporate wrongdoing, arguably these episodes are little more than repeats of responses to embarrassing revelations concerning corporate behaviour that have occurred on numerous occasions over the past 175 years. Current regimes contain 'more of the same' rules prevailing over that long period. There is little reason to expect that the latest IFRS Standards would have prevented or disclosed the matters currently under judicial review. In a curious way, the plight of the victims of many unexpected corporate collapses in different jurisdictions in recent times has made it abundantly clear that the corporate structure (especially when group relationships are prevalent) is not sacred. At the end of the day, if a company structure no longer serves commerce in the way the UK Gladstone Committee intended when pressing the British Parliament to make incorporation readily available – which was done through the Joint Stock Companies Act of 1844 – it can and ought to be changed.

'Truth in securities' and earlier knee-jerk responses?

Around the time of the 1929 Wall Street Crash, a debate raged over corporate malpractices not dissimilar to that of the recent past. In the UK, Lord Kylsant's imprisonment following prosecution under the 1861 Larceny Act for his part in publication of the Royal Mail's misleading prospectus no doubt shocked the establishment. Criticism was levelled at the way in which corporate financial statements significantly misled and failed to depict the drifts in companies' financial affairs over time. In the US, there was the jiggery-pokery with group structures of the kind that Samuel Insull and Ivar Kreuger employed. Moreover, following the prescribed rules or everyday accounting conventions, even with the best of intentions, generally proved inadequate for the purpose of revealing a company's wealth and progress. Then, as now, the intention to mislead was an unnecessary condition for the creation of misleading financial statements.

Roosevelt's introduction of the 1933 Securities and 1934 Securities and Exchange Acts was promoted as injecting 'truth in securities' to mitigate the trust lost in corporate disclosures during the Great Crash fallout.[2] Compliance with accounting rules was tightened. This set the nation on the accounting rule-making path reflected today in FASB standards. Cleaning up accounting was to be achieved by more clearly articulating fundamental ideas both in the 1930s and, more recently, by a search for the principles underpinning accounting practices, financial reporting disclosure and monitoring mechanisms. In each ensuing decade, the drive appeared to be to protect an essentially co-regulatory mechanism, with the public accountancy profession's significant influence retained, alongside that of the SEC.

Ferdinand Percora as chair of the Senate's Banking and Currency Committee launched a scathing attack on accounting. But professional oratory by Price, Waterhouse & Co. partner George Oliver May cut the public accountancy profession in for its share of Roosevelt's New Deal measures designed to put 'truth in securities' – the ultimate corporate governance sentiment. The profession's self-regulatory status and its importance in the emerging co-regulatory regime (Zeff 1971; Chatov 1975) were the beneficiaries. Nonetheless threat of government regulation, were the profession to fail to inject financial statements with Roosevelt's 'truth', nurtured attempts to articulate the main principles underpinning accounting practice. The American Accounting Association's (AAA) *A Tentative Statement of Accounting Principles Underlying Corporate Financial Statements* in 1936 and Sanders, Hatfield and Moore's *A Statement of Accounting Principles* in 1938 indicate that US accounting *thinkers* were as much concerned with accounting practices as were its practitioners.

In more recent times, the impact of faulty accounting has fuelled attempts to purge corporate activity of its present ills. In this setting, what the principles ought to be, and any possible distinction compared with what are stated as rules, appear as uncertain as they were in the 1920s and 1930s (Ripley 1927; Chambers 1964, 1973; Staunton 2006; Walker 2007). As in the past, the profession's resolve to define the underpinnings of conventional practice, to search for *principles*,[3] diminishes once threats of unwelcome external intervention in its business dissipate (Chatov 1975; Clarke et al. 2003: particularly chs 2, 3, 6 and 10).

Juxtaposition of events post-1930 and those post-2000 places respectively Samuel Insull as the corporate poster bad-boy, similar to Kenneth Lay, Jeffrey Skilling and the Arthur Andersen firm of more recent years. For, in a curious twist, just as Enron's fall instigated Andersen's collapse, Roosevelt's New Deal edged Andersen into the auditing super-league: Roosevelt's appointment of the fledgling Andersen to unravel the wreckage of the Insull empire established it as the 'paragon of virtue' among public accountancy firms, and it is a status which may have been perfectly justified at that time.

Insull's corporate life was distinguished. Having previously headed up the Chicago-based Edison Company, he went it alone, establishing Insull Utility Investments in the 1920s to compete with Edison. Just as Lay and Skilling used the separate status claimed for Enron's

SPEs to shuffle assets through the group undetected and unaccounted for, Insull shuffled assets through the group's subsidiaries at ever-increasing amounts to pyramid their booked values. Group structures prevailed as an effective accounting manipulation *modus operandi*. Consolidation accounting's elimination of double-accounting Insull-like and debt-washing of the Enron-SPEs variety (Walker 1976; Clarke et al. 2014) does not ensure serviceable asset values are disclosed. Consolidation would have had little impact on either Insull's or Enron's exploitation of group structures. Misrepresenting that it does improve accountability effectively makes consolidation a potential accounting hazard. Like others since, Insull 'gilded the corporate lily'. When stocks generally fell in the 1929 Great Crash, his companies were found to be 'full of water', with grossly misleading accounting values ascribed to assets. Insolvent, brought to trial for suspected embezzlement in 1934, Insull was ultimately acquitted on all counts (Clarke and Dean 2007).[4]

The Insull affair (like the contiguous Royal Mail affair described below) demonstrated the frequent conflict between outcomes from applying the accounting rules of the day and the financial common-sense that non-accountants might draw upon in their reading of corporate financial statements. A considerable part of Insull's defence rested on the appeal of his financial common-sense rationale for his accounting practices and, by implication, the financial nonsense peddled in the conventional accounting wisdom. The contemporary rules prohibited treating stock dividends as income. The prosecution was unable to deny that the matter was controversial or that reputable accountants were divided on the issue. Similar to charges against WorldCom post-2000, the capitalisation of 'organisation expenditure' was allegedly improper – certainly contrary to the conventional wisdom. And questions as to the appropriate forms of infrastructure valuation and depreciation – contentious accounting areas where Insull again debunked conventional accounting wisdom – remain hotly debated more than three-quarters of a century later (Walker et al. 2000). Significantly, some of what Insull did is now accepted practice.

In the early 1930s, the general approach taken in the US was to specify accounting rules and pass them off as principles. The 'tick-box' mentality to accounting practice compliance has been pursued for the best part of 90 years. Comparability is claimed when each company consistently uses the same rules (Schipper 2003: 62–3). But variations between the outputs in financial statements prepared under the same input and processing rules demonstrate that the comparability expected by statement users is not guaranteed. The expectations gap remains.

Current concern over the serviceability of data reported in financial statements for determining wealth, progress and solvency differs little in its essential features from its counterparts of the best part of a century ago. Few commentators seem to recall that, in the 1920s in the UK, Royal Mail's undisclosed use of past profits to pay current dividends accorded with the rules of the day (conservatism was a virtue – as was secrecy).[5] The holding company's legal entity-based balance sheet was the Royal Mail's sole statutory financial disclosure document for an extremely complex group (Clarke et al. 2003 which drew on Brooks 1933; Green and Moss 1982). In that setting the company had maintained dividends of between 4 and 6 per cent during the period 1921 to 1927 by drawing upon secret reserves containing the top-up refunds of Excess Profits Duty and compensation for ships lost on World War I service.

A vague omnibus description masked the dividend source, inviting misleading inferences that the payments signified current profits were being earned. To the contrary the Royal Mail incurred trading losses over the period (Brooks 1933: Appendix). Drawing from so-called secret reserves was a common practice, but Lord Plender, former

President of the Institute of Chartered Accountants in England and Wales, agreed with Sir Patrick Hastings' suggestion that 'there might come a time' (Hastings 1949: 224) when disclosure was required for such material items – the forerunner of today's materiality concept. Sir William Jowitt, the Attorney-General, aptly noted that false impressions given though compliance with the rules meant that 'the accountants' profession has failed to carry out its primary and obvious duty ... to ensure ... a true and accurate account' (cited in Brooks 1933: 210).

Returning to more recent events, Enron's use of SPEs to hide debt was facilitated by a professionally prescribed ownership rule. Its 'mark-to-model' valuations bringing prospective profits into account had regulatory approval. WorldCom's expense capitalisation was arguably the product of the conventional accrual system (with a questionable twist) and differs little from the Australian case of Reid Murray and Stanley Korman's capitalisations of development expenditures in the 1960s (Clarke et al. 2003). Arguably, the devil is in the conventional view of capitalising expenditures *per se*.

WorldCom's expenditure capitalisation practice raises issues similar to those experienced in the fallout from the UK's Rolls-Royce episode in the 1970s – in particular, the capitalisation of development costs for its innovative RB-211 engine. Waste Management's alleged depreciation manipulation is associated as much with the accountants' claim that depreciation is an allocation of cost rather than a decrease in price as with any deviation from a reliable practice. US airline companies in the 1950s were embroiled in similar issues. 'Following the rules' therefore has emerged consistently to be a well-intentioned, though inherently deceitful, means of producing accounting numbers – a simulacrum of a quality mechanism.

GFC (2007–09) and currency crises (2010–11) – recurrence of DSM and MAM[6]

This subsection reveals that corporate commercial disorder, due to prescribed misinformation, persists both prior to and following the GFC. Accounting miscommunications of the kind that Chambers, Briloff, Stamp, Sterling and others sought to avoid, has re-emerged. Laux and Leuz (2009, 2010) criticised three types of GFC accounting practices, namely accounting for groups (especially the way banks accounted for their shadow banking activities), loan loss provisioning and fair value (mark-to-market) accounting. Of these three problem areas, mark-to-market accounting, especially in the US, is considered here. Clarke et al. (2014) suggest that the GFC episode provides evidence of the business community's strange penchant for shooting the messenger rather than resolving the problem. Cries of 'I told you so' emerged from politicians and commentators opposed to the introduction of the relevant accounting standards – Statements of Financial Accounting Standards (FAS) 157 (Fair Value Measurements) in the US and International Accounting Standard (IAS) 39 (Financial Instruments: Recognition and Measurement) in Europe. Academics soon followed (Katz 2008; Ryan 2008; Whalen 2008; Magnan 2009; Magnan and Markarian 2011). Camfferman and Zeff (2015, 2018) provide details of what occurred in the GFC mark-to-market (fair value) accounting saga.

Complaints from compliant financial institutions forced to make considerable write-downs as a result of mark-to-market accounting were common, as evident in the comments made by Standard and Poor's' Mark Zandi in *Financial Shock* (2009). There, he advocated a gradual writing-down process:

> The FAS 157 [mark-to-market] rules put pressure on institutions to quickly adjust the book value of their assets to market prices but I propose that, mark-downs … could be tweaked so that changing assets [read also liabilities] values could be phased in over time … Banks would still have to lower their holding as prices fell, but not as rapidly.
>
> *(Zandi 2009: 237–8)*

As Zandi's analysis suggests, even some US standards setters adopted the stance that current data of the fair value genre are essential for the effective and efficient operation of capital markets. By focusing on write downs at the time of the crisis, arguably attention was misdirected to its symptoms rather than its cause. The tensions between prudential and corporate regulators illustrate the problems this created.[7] While the level of transparency invoked by the mark-to-market rule drove prices down, it would only do so if those in the market accepted that the reduced prices better reflected what the securities were worth – to them. That, of course, is how markets work. When it is thought that securities are under-priced, buyers will move in and, ordinarily, prices will rise. So, whereas it is possibly true to say that the write-downs were major drivers of the loss in confidence underpinning the collapse of the world's stock markets and the related pessimism, marking-to-market did not 'cause' the initial loss in the worth of the securities, collateralised debt obligations and credit default swaps. Indeed several years earlier, some observers of stock market price movements had suggested the 'fantasy' nature underpinning those price changes.[8]

Principles-based accounting standards

The above review contains ample proof that rules of the kind known to have failed in the past are reinforced despite their dismal histories. Lack of transparency, misleading disclosure, arguably 'indecent disclosure', characterised the traumatic financial dilemmas of companies such as Enron, WorldCom, Tyco, Parmalat, HIH, Bear Stearns and AIG. Statements of financial performance and financial position have failed consistently to present reasonably reliable portrayals of companies' dated wealth and periodic progress. They are neither 'transparent' nor 'truthful'. The quest for 'truth in securities' has failed miserably.

Rules-based or principles-based accounting has become a major conundrum (AAA 2003; Schipper 2003). Regulators claim that rules are followed but, far too frequently, the intention underpinning them is not. Accounting rules are said to encourage financial engineering (FASB 2002: 2), but that criticism is not addressed by compelling argument about the soundness of the rules or their underlying principles. In contrast, those promoting principles-based accounting standards argue for adherence to a complete and internally consistent conceptual framework (FASB 2002: 6) rather than attempting to identify any undergirding primary principles drawn from commercial affairs. Indeed, Schipper (2003: 62–3), when advocating principles-based accounting standards, explicitly supports the conventional rules. Consistency in their application is her primary objective – to achieve numerical comparability. The consequences of fully following through on principles-based accounting standards have been exposed by Lee (2006b).Yet, principles do not seem to be on the regulators' radar whereas buttressing the conventional system is! Accounting's beauty therefore seems to be in the eye of the beholder.

That accounting ought to be principles-based rather than rules-based appears to be generally conceded by regulators. IFRS Standards are presented as principles-based and some suggest those of the FASB are too (Abacus 2006). Clearly the appeal of 'principles' is strong.

In virtually every domain outside accounting, the primary quality criterion of 'serviceability' or 'fitness for use' is embraced. Goods and services are universally recognised to be serviceable, meeting society's demands, when they can be employed to produce the desired outcomes in the uses ordinarily made of them. No good reasons to the contrary have emerged over the past 175 years to suggest that accounting data should be seen any differently. To that end, the PN119 statement by the UK's Financial Reporting Council (2005), that the true and fair criterion remains the 'cornerstone' of British accounting, might be taken as the necessary underlying primary principle. Few would disagree that corporate financial statements are true and fair when, overall, they show their wealth and financial progress, and are serviceable for deriving those companies' salient financial characteristics, i.e. rate of return, debt to equity, solvency, asset backing and the like. But the history of corporate financial reporting reveals that accounting has not developed in that fashion. The question is why?

Lee (2006a) identifies four contributing groups that have somehow engineered the state of reporting to be 'sidewardly mobile' over the last 175 years rather than improving or being upwardly mobile. These groups are financial statement preparers (predominantly senior corporate executives), auditors (the public accountancy profession), regulators (including bodies such as FASB, and the SEC) and academic accountants (the so-called conscience of the profession). Within this nexus of relationships, protecting the public interest by producing high quality financial statements has not characterised the annals of finance. Radically changing either accounting as business instrumentation or business structures has not been a primary objective. Instead, self-interest appears to have driven each group. Senior corporate executives have no incentive to change the conventional accounting model. It permits them to remain the scorekeepers. Their often short-term remuneration is dependent on accounting's poverty of principle. Neither do auditors have any incentive for change. Verifying bad accounting while pretending to seek better ways of instrumentation remains profitable. Were there no problems with corporate business structures and accounting, there would be no need for regulators. Academic accountants earn their reputations by observing and reporting participants' behaviour in the accounting 'game'. Without a refocusing to public interest protection, without a public awareness and censorship of the over-arching power of self-interest among the participants in corporate financial reporting, it is hard to see how the present state will change. The unwanted paradox will remain. Bad accounting will provoke responses that evoke further bad accounting.

Against this background of accounting as misinformation, the second main section of this chapter identifies recurring ineffectiveness of auditing in detecting material fraud by the DSM.

Auditing as detection

A parallel and equally unwanted paradox in auditing reinforces the parlous state of corporate financial reports. It reflects the same sequence of financial scandal followed by regulatory response evidenced in accounting. It concerns the repeated failure by auditors to detect MAM perpetrated by DSM. Through audit standards and other sources, public accountants articulate at best a limited responsibility for the detection of MAM by DSM. An over-riding instruction of dependence on managerial honesty prevails.

In these circumstances, auditing education and training appear to concentrate on the wrong target. Public accountants have emphasised reliance on internal control systems (frequently over-ridden by DSM) and compliance with prescribed accounting rules (that can be manipulated by DSM). This approach has been to the fore, rather than one that ensures auditors can identify and cope with DSM. Reviewing the history of governmental and professional responses to unexpected corporate auditing failures illustrates the paradox. Over many decades, several jurisdictions have maintained a persistent expectations gap between what audit beneficiaries desire and what audit practitioners provide by way of protection. The paradox threatens the credibility of audit as a means of protecting stakeholders from corrupt senior managers. The historical analysis draws upon a selection of significant legal cases of fraudulent reporting and subsequent public accountancy response, some of which have been examined in relation to accounting instrumentation. It reveals the persistent presence of MAM by DSM and equally persistent denial or limitation of responsibility of public accountants for detecting it.

Accounting misstatement and dominant managers

MAM by DSM occurs irrespective of the size of company, audit regulations or the skills of the auditor. Reflecting the willingness and capacity of senior managers to practice deceitful behaviour is closely associated with corporate failure and scandal. Despite the expectation of a reasonably careful, skilful and cautious auditor at work (Lee et al. 2008), it has created a model of excuses by public accountants that denies or limits their responsibility. History reveals public accountants remaining aloof from the audit standard-setting process until an advanced stage, and of appearing then to assume responsibility when, in effect, accepting very little. The consequence has been a permanent expectations gap between audit providers and preparers with respect to the detection of MAM by DSM. Paradoxically, as we reveal below, courts and the public accountancy profession have continually promoted the notion of auditors trusting the honesty of senior managers in relation to corporate financial reporting. Auditors can be trained to identify MAM. But this is irrelevant if they are not also trained to identify DSM. Unsurprisingly, the history of corporate reporting reveals numerous audit failures associated with MAM, DSM and unexpected corporate collapse.

The following analysis assumes that MAM occurs because of DSM and that the two are characteristic of a general condition in corporate financial reporting. MAM cannot exist without DSM. But the existence of DSM does not automatically signal MAM. The DSM motivation for MAM is irrelevant. Ultimately, its potential to damage any company and its stakeholders is the significance of the historical paradox.

Model for excuses

From 1844 to 1900 in Britain, the current limited audit responsibility for detecting MAM by DSM was forged from a model of excuses created not by public accountants but by lawyers. Accounting and auditing regulations emerged within a scenario of considerable state intervention in the regulation of corporate behaviour, and of numerous court cases addressing corrupt and deceitful practices by corporate managers. This regulatory basis underpinned professional accountants gradually becoming engaged in accounting and auditing services as they reduced their earlier focus on the provision of court-related and other services (Edwards et al. 2007). The public accountancy profession was newly institutionalised and primarily focused on securing and maintaining its legitimacy (Walker 1991).

Various Companies Acts from 1844 onwards in the UK introduced regulations involving incorporation, limited liability, balance sheet reports and compulsory (then voluntary and again compulsory) audit (Hein 1978). At first, auditors were shareholders (the amateur auditor) but, later, public accountants began to recognise a lucrative service market (Maltby 1999). However, public accountancy institutions made no attempt to influence or comment on these arrangements. By default, the field was left to lawyers without accounting education or training. Also at this time, partly due to the lack of adequate auditing, a number of corporate *causes célèbres* revealed the dangers associated with MAM by DSM. For example, in 1849, there was George Hudson, the 'Railway King' and CEO of the Eastern Counties Railway Company. As DSM, he falsified reported profits using insider information to manipulate the company's share price, and sold land the company did not own (Arnold and McCartney 2004). His case and another in 1866 led to legislation, in 1867 and 1868, as a governmental response to MAM by DSM in the railway industry. These acts required railway companies to publish an audited balance sheet conforming to a standardised format. In 1878, despite years of reported profitability, the City of Glasgow Bank collapsed, with a large deficit revealed (Couper 1879; French 1985). The entire board of directors was implicated and imprisoned because of falsification of several balance sheets involving fictitious accounting entries, manipulated valuations and coercion of employees. The Companies Act 1879 was the British government's response and required banks to publish audited balance sheets. Despite these interventions, by 1900 there was no overall regulation of companies in the UK and no consistent provision for financial statements audited by professionally qualified accountants. Neither had there been substantial comment by public accountancy institutions on reporting and auditing failures.

Legal comment from a succession of court decisions in the late nineteenth century filled the vacuum. A number of court decisions addressed the auditor's responsibility for detecting MAM: *Leeds Estate, Building and Investment Company* (1887), *London and General Bank* (1895) and *Kingston Cotton Mill* (1896).[9] These cases and individual public accountants' responses to criticism, created a model of excuses that persists to current times, i.e. a structure of credible excuses permitting public accountants to deny a primary responsibility for detecting MAM by DSM.[10] They ring-fenced accounting records and the balance sheet as the audit focus, and distanced auditors from senior managers – even where (as in *Leeds Estate, Building and Investment Company* and *Kingston Cotton Mill*) DSM were identified as facilitating MAM.

The ring-fence embraced several connected arguments. The auditor's duty was said to be checking the accounting records, not to question the honesty of senior managers. It was not the auditor's responsibility to tell senior managers how to manage the company. The auditor had to have his suspicions aroused, which depended on the circumstances, and was expected to audit with reasonable care, skill, caution and diligence. Taken together, these excuses ensured that the general standard by which auditors could be judged was to be decided on a case by case basis, creating flexibility with respect to responsibility for MAM detection. Consistent with the dictum in *London and General Bank*, they effectively signalled to the public that detecting MAM by DSM was not a matter reducible to the auditor following prescribed rules – the auditor was not an insurer against MAM.

The court cases relating to MAM in the late nineteenth century gave rise to regular criticism of the corporate auditor. In response, public accountants supplied excuses for their failure to detect MAM. These took various forms but captured judicial statements of the time. Most popular were complaints that audit fees were too small to provide for effective auditing, and that there was insufficient time to permit the detection of complex MAM, although some observed that the audit should not be restricted merely because the fee was inadequate. The comments about fees reinforced similar comments in court cases. They are also consistent with the 'low-balling' competitive nature arguments of current times. Also, public accountants have continued to protest their inability to assume detection of MAM as a primary audit objective because of cost and time factors (DeAngelo 1981).

The British professional publication, *The Accountant*, in the late nineteenth century also contained explicit excuses to limit the auditor's responsibilities. These related primarily to the relationship of auditors with senior corporate managers. Today, these are enshrined in legislative provision, e.g. management is responsible for accounting systems and therefore for preventing and detecting fraudulent activity through internal control systems. Practitioners also reflected on matters that appear just as apposite today, e.g. the difficulty of detecting management fraud because of senior managers' position of influence, the board of directors' influence over the audit appointment, the need to assume senior managers' honesty when relying on their representations, and avoiding audit functions that could be construed critical of management (see evidence in Chandler and Edwards 1994a). These excuses effectively created a long-standing paradox in corporate auditing, i.e. auditors denying or limiting responsibility for detecting MAM by DSM.

The principal driver in the construction by lawyers of a model of excuses for corporate auditors was the Court of Appeal, with *London and General Bank* and *Kingston Cotton Mill* as the major cases legitimising it (Teo and Cobbin 2005). *London and General Bank* contains many of the previously mentioned arguments; *Kingston Cotton Mill* reinforces them. The language of the two cases characterises the public accountancy profession's official position of limited responsibility. They contained common features – each had aspects that facilitated the MAM – a DSM who took advantage of complex corporate structures, boom economic conditions and related financing. In *London and General Bank*, its CEO, Jabez Balfour, was a leading businessman controlling a group including the bank. He orchestrated inter-company transfers to facilitate payment of dividends out of non-existent profits (Valance 1955). On appeal, the bank's auditor was found guilty of a breach of duty to the shareholders when not reporting the illegality of dividends. The profession's reaction emphasised the constraints to the audit function mentioned above rather than addressing the problem of a DSM who could override internal controls and employees to facilitate MAM within a complex corporate structure. Interestingly, in later company law reform inquiries (e.g. Davey Report 1895 and Greene Report 1926) there were consistent references to corporate businesses being managed in general by honest men. This view entrenched a tradition of auditors' reliance on assumed managerial honesty, obviously misplaced when there is MAM by DSM.

The 1896 *Kingston Cotton Mill* case involved overstating the value of assets for several years and dividends were declared on inflated profits. Inventory data were manipulated by the general manager and director William Jackson without deference to his fellow directors – 'to benefit the company, and bolster up its credit' (Chandler and Edwards 1994a: 152). On appeal, the auditor was found not guilty of negligence. The judgment used the same criteria about the boundaries of auditing as enunciated in *London and General Bank*, expanding on them in the context of the auditor as a 'watchdog rather than a bloodhound' (Teo and Cobbin 2005: 49). The case particularly emphasised the acceptability of relying on the honesty of senior managers but, as before, ignored the need for a solution to auditing in the presence of a DSM who facilitated MAM.

The *London and General Bank* and *Kingston Cotton Mill* cases popularised the audit mantra of 'reasonable care and skill in the circumstances' as the foundation for the model of excuses by corporate auditors regarding MAM detection. It was to be a further half century before public accountants formally included it in their guidance to auditors.

Mandated audits and co-regulation

The British Companies Act 1900 required publication of an audited balance sheet. It did not require professionally qualified auditors, although it is clear that professional audits were common by this time (Maltby 1999; see also Anderson et al. 1996: 363–88). The difficulty of detecting MAM continued to be discussed in the literature. Practitioners demanded and supplied excuses to support denials or limitations of responsibility (e.g. Wardhaugh 1908; Jenkinson 1913 in the UK; Montgomery 1912 in the US). Attention was turning to the burgeoning audit market in the US where, by the mid to late 1920s, there were out-of-control money markets, investment trusts and myriad corporate combinations.

As noted above, two of the most notorious US robber barons of the period were CEOs Samuel Insull and Ivar Kreuger, both of whom were well-known globally and found the doors of presidents, kings and high officials seemingly always open to them. McDonald (1962) provides a sympathetic account of Insull's corporate empire of utility monopolies organised in a labyrinth of hundreds of holding and subsidiary companies across the US. Funding and controls by several trusts sitting at the apex of the Insull Utility Investments' 'top heavy pyramid' obscured understanding of its operations (Valance 1955: 167–79). Issues of corporate governance relating to this corporate structure, asset valuation and other accounting practices emerged after Insull's death in 1938. Flesher and Flesher's (1986: 421–34) account of Kreuger's 'giant pyramid scheme' suggests the timing and scale of the fraud 'contributed significantly to the passage of the Securities Acts' in the early 1930s. Kreuger & Toll became one of the largest conglomerates and multinationals imaginable. However, when Kreuger died in 1932, the façade was revealed as a vehicle for deceiving millions of investors who received false financial statements over many years. Kreuger & Toll had the 'most widely-held securities in America (and also in the world) during the 1920s' (Flesher and Flesher 1986: 421). As later, with the likes of Enron and WorldCom, the market was shocked by revelations at Kreuger & Toll. Stoneman (1962: 936) attributes successful accounting manipulation to a combination of Kreuger's managerial dominance and the company's complex structure. His dominance was acknowledged by the investigating accountants Price, Waterhouse & Co. (May 1936: 110), who, even with hindsight and more evidence, were unable to determine the exact magnitude of the fraud due to Kreuger & Toll's organisational complexity.

The events at Insull Utility Investments and Kreuger & Toll demanded a strong regulatory response. It came with the creation of the SEC in 1934 and legislation such as the 1935 Public Utility Holding Company Act. Despite these responses, it soon became evident that the existing model of professional self-regulation (then co-regulation) would continue to be promoted (Chatov 1975). Limitations of audit responsibility characterised the post-Insull Utility Investments and Kreuger & Toll debate. When the American Institute of Accountants (AIA) published an audit guidance statement (AIA 1936) as a revision of earlier statements, scope limitation was repeated with respect to the detection of defalcation, understatement and manipulation. Company directors were stated to be assuming greater responsibility for accounting, detection of irregularities was deemed to require a special investigation, and reliance on internal controls and management representations became the foundations of the modern audit. Thus US public accountants formally started the model of excuses in 1936. The paradox for the auditor of MAM facilitated by trusted DSM became institutionalised.

The US position on audit responsibility was disrupted by the 1939 McKesson & Robbins case (Baxter 1999) involving a wholesale drug company which was, by 1937, one of the largest in the US. Its CEO Donald Coster had founded the business in 1923. However, much of the reported profitability and asset structure was false due to fictitious transactions in a fictional subsidiary. Price, Waterhouse & Co. failed to discover the deception. The SEC investigated and its report criticised the inadequacies of the audit, particularly the lack of scepticism of DSM representations. While these strictures were generally accepted at the time, within months the AIA issued standards on asset verification and reporting to counter criticisms. Nonetheless, AIA standards continued to limit auditor responsibility on the following grounds: the auditor is not an insurer or guarantor; the need for 'reasonable care and skill in the circumstances'; management is responsible for accounting and safeguarding assets; the discovery of defalcations is not a primary objective of auditing; and reliance on internal control and the integrity of management is acceptable in the absence of suspicions to the contrary.

In 1947, the AIA's *Tentative Statement of Auditing Standards: Their Generally Accepted Significance and Scope* clarified auditor responsibilities in the US. It gave guidance on general, fieldwork and reporting standards, and emphasised competence, independence and due care – a re-badging of the English legal concept of 'reasonable care and skill in the circumstances'. The discovery of errors and irregularities was mentioned only indirectly. MAM was mentioned only briefly. Thus, in 1947, the US limitation of responsibility to detect MAM remained. Indeed, four years later, the American Institute of Certified Public Accountants (AICPA) in its *Codification of Statements on Auditing Procedure* (AICPA 1951) reiterated the 1939 denial of a primary responsibility for detecting defalcations and other irregularities. In 1960, however, the AICPA (1960) *Statement of Auditing Procedure 30* appeared to modify the 1951 position, arguing responsibility where there was non-compliance with generally accepted auditing standards. Nevertheless, it restated the mantra of the auditor as neither an insurer nor guarantor and the expectation to act with due professional care and skill.

At approximately the same time, the Institute of Chartered Accountants in England and Wales (1961) adopted a similar position in *General Principles of Auditing*. The statement was expressed in terms of the 1896 dictum of the *Kingston Cotton Mill* case, i.e. reasonable care, skill and caution in particular circumstances, adopting a position and using the AICPA (1960) statement terminology. Denial of primary responsibility by major professional bodies thus continued. Detection of MAM was regarded as an additional service to the client. The approaches in the UK and US clearly drew on late nineteenth-century British judicial pronouncements.

1960s to present day

The 1960s saw little change to the position in the UK and US. MAM by DSM continued and the growing Australian commercial environment mirrored British and US characteristics. For example, the case of Reid Murray Holdings attracted considerable interest (Clarke et al. 2003: 55–65). One of Australia's largest retailers in the early 1960s, Reid Murray Holdings entered receivership in 1963. CEO Oswald O'Grady was a charismatic but dominant manager with a favourable reputation in the wider community. MAM included overstatement and misclassification of assets over several years. A government investigation found O'Grady not guilty of fraud. However, according to the inspectors, he was an 'inept manager' – an 'artless victim of his own incompetence'. As DSM, O'Grady had swept public investors along in his enthusiasm for property development.

In the US, in 1973, public scrutiny of the auditor's role intensified with respect to MAM (Seidler et al. 1977). Equity Funding Corporation of America specialised in innovative financial products combining life insurance with mutual fund investment. Its profits came from commission from mutual fund share sales and life insurance policies sold to re-insurance companies. With Stanley Goldblum as chairman in 1969, the company became one of the largest life insurance companies in the US. Goldblum appointed Fred Levin as vice-president of life insurance operations. Both were central to the fraud. Equity Funding Corporation collapsed when a whistleblower revealed a fraud of more than $60 million of inflated mutual fund assets and $80 million of other fictitious or inflated assets. Some $2 billion of life insurance policies were bogus due to Goldblum and Levin generating computerised documents, circumventing internal controls, pressuring employees and deceiving the auditors. Goldblum and Levin, and the audit engagement partner and two audit managers, were convicted of fraud and two audit firms paid a large out-of-court settlement.

The AICPA created a special committee to examine whether current audit standards were sufficient to cope with a situation such as Equity Funding Corporation (AICPA 1975). Also, other large corporate collapses of the time (including Penn Central, Stirling Homex and National Student Marketing) presaged establishment of the 1974 Cohen Commission on Auditors' Responsibilities to examine the role of the auditor and the adequacy of generally accepted auditing standards. The Commission reported that users were entitled to assume that corporate financial statements were reliable because the auditor gave reasonable assurance they were free of MAM (AICPA 1978). *Statement on Auditing Standards 16* (AICPA 1977) repeated the approach of limited acceptance of responsibility as enunciated in the 1960 AICPA statement, i.e. the auditor was neither an insurer nor guarantor, and that he should exercise due care in the application of generally accepted auditing standards. Little of substance changed in the 1970s in the US. MAM by DSM was not addressed.

The UK position was equally static. Humphrey et al. (1993) report on institutional activities in the 1980s concerning the detection of MAM. These culminated in an audit guideline from the Auditing Practices Committee (1990) maintaining a limited role for the auditor. Meantime, leading public accountancy firms offered fraud investigation as a separate service. The background to the 1990 statement was relatively clear. Research revealed perceptions of the auditor as responsible for the detection of fraud generally, and the guidance statement suggested auditors should plan to have a reasonable expectation of detecting MAM. However, following financial scandals in the 1980s (e.g. Johnson Matthey Bank) and UK government pressure for auditors to assume greater responsibility, the British professional bodies initiated two investigations. On fraud reporting, the recommendation was that auditors should communicate directly with relevant supervisory bodies rather than shareholders because of client confidentiality. With respect to fraud, both investigations supported the *status quo* of limited responsibility in the guidance statement. Humphrey et al. (1993) perceived little change in the British profession's lack of acceptance of responsibility for detecting MAM in the 1980s. British auditors appeared to claim an ability to detect MAM if this was a separate engagement involving a less litigious environment than the audit. Humphrey et al. (1993) particularly question in these circumstances what the audit was capable of detecting in relation to MAM by senior management.

An exemplar of DSM is Robert Maxwell who had an unusual career for a British businessman, having been a Member of Parliament and the subject of a 1973 Department of Trade and Industry report. It stated he was not to be relied on to exercise proper stewardship of a public company as he had used false information in his attempt, in 1969, to sell Pergamon Press to the Leasco Data Processing Equipment Corporation.[11] In 1974 Maxwell regained control of Pergamon Press and, by 1981, had also obtained control of the British Printing Corporation (renamed Maxwell Communications Corporation) in 1986. Two years earlier, a private company owned by Maxwell purchased Mirror Group Newspapers. Maxwell Communications collapsed sensationally and Maxwell's private companies filed for bankruptcy in 1992. Three years later, a Department of Trade and Industry report (Thomas and Turner 2001) stated that the primary responsibility for a massive fraud lay with Maxwell himself. Misappropriation of funds coupled with MAM were achieved through a complex private ownership of more than 400 companies intertwined in a public group (Clarke et al. 2003). The Mirror Group Newspapers' cash flow funded his other businesses, and its pension funds were raided to repay debt elsewhere in the group. In effect, all parts of Maxwell Communications, including its pension funds, were treated illegally by Maxwell as one entity.

In 1991, Bank of Credit and Commerce International (BCCI) closed with the discovery by its auditors Price Waterhouse of a fraud involving billions of dollars of lost or fictitious assets. It is estimated there were $13 billion of missing assets and claims of creditors totalling $16 billion. In 1998, Price Waterhouse paid a large out-of-court settlement without admitting liability. The most comprehensive account of the fraud is the US Senate report on BCCI in 1992 and what follows is a brief summary from that source (Kerry and Brown 1992).

Agha Hasan Abedi founded BCCI in 1972 and had worked in Indian and Pakistani banks. BCCI was based in Luxembourg and its activities from 1973 to 1991 became global. BCCI entered the US banking system through acquisition and became banker for governmental funds of many nations. It was alleged to be involved in money laundering, drugs and arms dealing, and trafficking, fraud, extortion, bribery involving fictitious loans and other transactions, imprudent lending and investment, stolen deposits and investments, and unrecorded deposits. Price Waterhouse became BCCI's sole auditors in 1987, having previously shared the audit with Ernst & Young. The US Senate report accused Price Waterhouse of failing to protect BCCI depositors and creditors when it had been aware of its accounting practices. The full story of BCCI may never be told, but it focuses on the existence of DSM in a multinational corporate structure of such complexity and depth that no individual jurisdiction was fully aware of what BCCI was doing. It was very much like events at Kreuger & Toll decades earlier.

Returning to Enron, the US energy, commodities and services company had been trading successfully in energy units since 1994 following deregulation of the industry. In reported profits terms, prior to the new millennium it was a global energy trading company that had reached 'Icarus' levels of reported performance. Arthur Andersen, which was not the auditor of the thousands of SPEs associated with it, would become enmeshed in its ultimate downfall. In 2001 Enron announced a large third-quarter loss and an even larger write-down of impaired assets connected to SPEs controlled by its chief financial officer Andrew Fastow (Sridharan et al. 2002). An SEC investigation into perceived conflicts of interest resulting from SPEs caused a downward restatement of its published earnings from 1997 to 2001 and it entered bankruptcy protection. A criminal investigation took place and Enron's auditors, Arthur Andersen, and its engagement partner, were found guilty of obstruction of justice. Arthur Andersen admitted shredding Enron audit working papers and was liquidated in 2003.

Enron shocked the global financial community with the scale of MAM in the presence of DSM and the auditors. However, as the facts of the Enron scandal emerged, another became headline news (Clarke et al. 2003). WorldCom was one of the largest US corporations in 2002 when it collapsed with an apparent $11 billion of MAM. WorldCom handled one-half of the world's email traffic and it was the second largest US long-distance phone carrier. The company entered bankruptcy protection in 2002 with $41 billion of debt. It was later renamed MCI and, by 2003, had returned to profitability. While investigations were ongoing, two reports were lodged with the Bankruptcy Court. These related to investigations by a former Chief of Enforcement at the SEC (on behalf of WorldCom) and a former US Attorney-General (on behalf of the Bankruptcy Court). Their findings were that the fraud was associated with DSM (including CEO Bernie Ebbers and chief financial officer Scott Sullivan), and there were two sets of accounting records, lax internal controls and poor oversight by the board of directors. The alleged MAM included inflated revenues, treating maintenance costs as capital expenditure and failure to write off bad debts. The company's auditor was again Arthur Andersen. Sullivan pleaded guilty to securities fraud, conspiracy and reporting false information to the SEC and was sentenced to gaol. He and Ebbers had unfettered control in the company. Other WorldCom accounting executives pled guilty to fraud charges.

Clarke et al. (2003) observe several largely unexpected failures in the 1980s and 1990s in Australia. For example, Bond Corporation, one of Australia's leading companies, with over 600 subsidiaries, suffered financial problems *circa* the 1987 stock market crash and was placed in provisional liquidation in the early 1990s. Founder Alan Bond was found guilty of Australia's largest corporate fraud, the so-called Bond Corporation/Bell Resources 'cash cow transaction'. Intermediaries were used to facilitate upstream transfers of more than $1 billion of cash funds from Bell Resources to other Bond Corporation subsidiaries and related parties. Both Bond Corporation and Bell Resources were listed holding companies and under the control of Alan Bond through direct holdings and by virtue of holdings through related parties. Because of the dominance of Alan Bond and other top-level Bond Corporation executives, information about Bond Corporation was released to shareholders and lower-level operational managers on a need-to-know basis. Mr Justice Sir Nicholas Browne noted regarding Alan Bond's 1980s failed attempt to take over Lonrho: 'It is a very remarkable phenomenon when you think that you have a company that had by that stage invested £360 million – odd that not a single piece of paper is available supporting that fact' (Haigh 1989: 41).

Then HIH, reportedly the second largest insurance company in Australia, suddenly became one of the country's largest corporate collapses with an estimated deficiency of more than $5 billion (Clarke et al. 2003). Interestingly, the HIH Royal Commission Report (HIHRC 2003: I, xiii) concluded that 'despite [myriad governance] mechanisms the corporate officers, auditors and regulators of HIH failed to see, remedy or report … [the] obvious'. This was a situation not assisted by the dominance of HIH CEO and founder Ray Williams who might be considered the epitome of the DSM genre.

At all times Williams played a dominant role at HIH (HIHRC 2003), with its board proving to be an ineffective monitor of his activities. The HIHRC (2003: III, paras 273–7) further details how two major and ultimately fatal transactions were allegedly actioned by Williams – the FAI acquisition by HIH and Allianz's purchase of a major part of HIH's cash flow base just before its ultimate collapse. Williams, with the absolute trust and confidence of his board, or possessing too much power for them to restrain him, was able to ensnare HIH in the FAI takeover without presenting an appropriate due diligence report. According to the HIHRC (2003: III, para. 273) 'Decisions … were often made by the Board on short notice with insufficient information and without adequate analysis … [The board accepted] views of management uncritically'. For the most part, the HIH board, and contestably perhaps the auditor, accepted virtually everything Williams put to them. His dominance overrode his sensitivity to the commercial reality of HIH's circumstances. However, whereas Arthur Andersen was subjected to some criticism in respect of its audit of HIH (primarily for what it did not detect), no charges were laid against the firm.

Fast forwarding to the end of the first decade of the new millennium, the GFC was marked by more of the same. In many countries the GFC had greater impacts on the survival of financial institutions than industrial or mining companies. And the effect was greater elsewhere than in Australia. But, even in Australia, financial sagas occurred at, for example, Babcock and Brown and Allco. One account of the GFC fallout suggests the Australian property and related financial sectors cost their shareholders billions of dollars (Kavanagh 2012).

Several recent books, including Clarke et al. (2014), Gow and Kells (2018) and Brooks (2018), suggest that criticism of the accountancy profession endures. Those works discuss corporate sagas (and, in some, related litigation settlements arising from audit failure to detect fraud – even though confidentiality clauses usually pertained), including events at the construction group Carillon, the Royal Bank of Scotland and Northern Rock in the UK, and at Colonial Bank, Lehman Brothers, Bear Stearns and AIG in the US. The mix of a DSM and MAM remains a major concern for users of accounts. Auditors were again faced with 'mission impossible' due to difficulties in attesting to managerial valuations in uncertain markets (when, as before and after the GFC, prices were rising and falling). The valuation of property (as security) for assets – such as collateralised debt obligations in financial institutions' accounts or investment asset balances in Real Estate Investment Trusts in the US – continues to cause auditors major headaches.

The above books also discuss official reports published in several countries during the second decade of the twenty-first century. They continue to criticise the increased concentration of audit fees within a few large audit firms and the potential conflict of interest arising from those firms also offering clients a range of financial services. This is especially so when conflicts are exacerbated by a DSM. The analyses presented in the above books therefore iterate Stevens' (1981) observations of the 1970s actions of the 'Big Eight' and the regulatory responses at that time (e.g. the US Moss and Metcalfe inquiries) following large unexpected corporate collapses.

Institutional responses of public accountants

Enron and WorldCom precipitated responses by the AICPA to the problem of the audit detection of MAM. First, the Private Securities Litigation Reform Act 1995 enshrined the dictum of auditors providing reasonable assurance that they would detect illegal acts having a material effect on financial statements. It therefore legitimated a credible legal excuse to limit responsibility. 'Reasonable assurance' has not been defined and is circumstantial in nature (Cullinan and Sutton 2002). Nevertheless, the AICPA continued to use it in *Statement on Auditing Standards 82* (AICPA 1997), which introduced two specific requirements for the auditor, i.e. the responsibility for assessing and judging the risk of MAM when designing the audit and documenting these assessments and judgments. *Statement 82* did not change the previous limited responsibility of US auditors, but it did make more explicit the need for them to think carefully about the risk of MAM in relation to audit procedures. *Statement 82* also provided an appendix containing examples of risk factors relating to MAM. These were categorised as incentives and pressures on management (e.g. economic threats, market expectations and compensation packages), opportunities (e.g. the nature of the business, monitoring of management, complex organisational structures and internal control systems), and attitudes and rationalisations of management. The need for auditors to emphasise even a limited responsibility for detecting MAM was made with more clarity in a report completed for the AICPA in 2001 (Beasley et al. 2001). The subsequent *Statement on Auditing Standards 99* (AICPA 2002) dealt with responsibility for the audit detection of MAM but it did not alter the previous acceptance of limited responsibility based on reasonable assurance. And it continued the tradition of excuses to justify this limitation.

Peroration on inconvenient outcomes

The previous sections identify two paradoxes from the history of corporate financial reporting generally and accounting scandals particularly. Both result from unexpected outcomes. Both are inconvenient and unwanted. Both threaten the credibility of the reporting system.

Paradox of false expectations: accounting as a governance instrument

Whereas the expectation that corporate financial statements will inform the public periodically about corporate wealth and progress appears eminently reasonable, they habitually fail to do so. This is highlighted when companies collapse unexpectedly. Those collapses that closely follow clean audit reports serve to increase tension between the public and accountants. That tension is manifest in complaints and criticism levelled at the profession as it stumbles time after time to deliver a product reasonably meeting the corporate information needs and expectations of investors and other interested parties.

Complaint has spawned the push for further means by which accountants can demonstrate their compliance with standards of the day. However, despite express and implied defence of past accounting practices, contemporary moves in the European Union, Australia, Canada and elsewhere to introduce IFRS Standards effectively refute the alleged technical propriety of these practices. Regulatory actions implying MAM is the product of deviating from accounting standards have been shown to be wrong. By implication, in many instances, compliance with previous standards was a means of producing misleading disclosure, albeit with the best of intentions in some cases.

Corporate collapses have possibly influenced adoption of IFRS Standards, although not in the US. Enron has become the exemplar for corporations behaving badly, however, and its collapse, followed by that of WorldCom, Global Crossing and Tyco, almost certainly was the catalyst for the corporate governance push post-2000 in the US. Spread of the corporate governance contagion was fuelled by similar events elsewhere. In Australia, for example, the push gathered momentum following the failures or financial dilemmas of HIH, Harris Scarfe and One.Tel.

The post-Enron resolve to clean up corporate America has a remarkable similarity to President Roosevelt's 'truth in securities' vow following the Great Crash of 1929. Likewise, the market impact of the enactment of the Sarbanes-Oxley Act 2002 bears a similarity to that of the passing of the 1933 Securities Act and the Securities and Exchange Act 1934.

In the first edition of the *Companion* we posited:

> Despite strong talk, legislation and litigation, little of substance appears to have been learned over the years. IFRS [Standards] are as likely to produce misleading financial information as not. There is no good reason to expect that FASB compliant data will any better disclose the wealth and progress of compliant companies in the future than in the past. Paradoxically, the push and the discussion may have allayed disquiet regarding the serviceability of accounting as instrumentation to the point of increasing false expectations of accounting's potential to disclose corporate wealth and progress.

Since that summary was written the world commercial system was placed under immense pressure from the fallout of the 2007–09 GFC. The financial system was close to meltdown. The above accounts reveal evidence of more of the same types of problems and failed resolutions by regulators and professional bodies during that period, and even more recently. Notwithstanding the advent of IFRS Standards and new regulatory and legislative regimes, such as the US Sarbanes-Oxley and Australia's CLERP legislation, fraudulent misrepresentations and difficulties in auditor attestations endure. The evidence suggests that little in the way of effective regulation and governance has occurred – importantly accounting is still a faulty instrumentation and auditors are still on 'mission impossible'.

Paradox of false expectations: auditing as fraud detector

Detection by corporate auditors of MAM by DSM is frustrated by a limited responsibility couched in ambiguous terms such as due care, proper scepticism, reasonable assurance and reliance on management. The reflective combination of court judgments and professional pronouncements portray corporate auditors as reasonably careful, skilful and cautious individuals responsible for an attested function with boundaries. More specifically, the current audit is paradoxical insofar as the auditor is expected to presume the honesty of senior managers when relying on their representations while concurrently recognising that DSM can use its position and authority to override internal controls, coerce junior managers and employees, and induce compliant external service providers to create the necessary conditions for MAM. Much is therefore left to the auditor's assessment of individual circumstances and, in that respect, the economic cost of MAM detection plays an important part in limiting the extent of audit procedures. Public expectations about corporate auditor responsibility, on the other hand, assume an unequivocal public duty to detect MAM by DSM irrespective of cost.

The history of this complex and potentially damaging situation has its genesis in mid- to late nineteenth-century court cases of fraudulent reporting in the UK. At that time, the institutions of public accountancy failed to set viable parameters for corporate audit responsibility and much was left to lawyers. Ambiguous and undefined legal terminology such as reasonable care and skill in the circumstances were invoked by public accountants later to create the reasonably careful, skilful and cautious image.

The historical evidence suggests that DSM is a sign of potential reporting difficulty. The extent of cause and effect is a matter of conjecture and research. The problem for the auditor is that, frequently, DSM features in successful companies. Perhaps the argument should be that, DSM makes a bad situation worse and corporate governance mechanisms less effective than they should be. More specifically, DSM coupled with any of a number of contributing factors such as boom economic conditions, lax internal controls, generous executive compensation packages and complex organisational and financial structures, may exacerbate the risk of MAM. Individual public accountants and their institutions over many decades have focused on symptoms of a disease (e.g. poor internal controls or manipulation of accounting standards) rather than the disease itself (i.e. DSM utilising complex organisational structures and financial engineering, tolerating weak controls and pressuring employees). Public accountants have consistently placed the major responsibility for detecting and preventing MAM on senior managers – the very individuals whose honesty they are expected to rely on.

The events reviewed here have had previous exposure in the literature. Professional responses have been fully debated and the expectations gap is a familiar topic. Ambiguity about the auditor's responsibility for detecting MAM is a subject of continuous professional reference and public concern. Bringing these matters together by connecting the pieces of the jigsaw, the historian 'bears witness' to decades of writing, comment and debate (Jordanova 2000: 204). It reveals an issue of public anxiety. The events recounted here *may* of course be exceptional, but they have been sufficiently high-profile affairs in their time to represent, arguably, the publicly visible tip of a much larger invisible iceberg. Identifying icebergs is a reasonable way of bearing witness for the accounting and auditing historian.

This enquiry indicates the need for further research into the DSM phenomenon and how audit firms react to it. Of particular interest might be in-detail enquiry into whether DSM is tolerated more or less according to the size of the audit firm – whether there is evidence of differences between the reactions to DSM by the Big 4, middle-tier firms and the remainder. Likewise, whether reactions differ according to the frequency of fee hikes and client size are obvious potential foci of enquiry with a view to better understanding how the DSM phenomena continue to prevail. The task for researchers in this area is to redirect attention to those icebergs, thereby providing further evidence showing regulators that the governance paths currently followed will not prevent more unexpected failures like Enron, Kreuger, Maxwell and HIH, again leading to criticisms of accounting and audit practices.

Key works

Chambers (1965) explains and illustrates the multiplicity of accounting numbers that can be generated when applying the conventional accounting standards of the 1960s. It illustrates the technical defect of claims that uniformity of method produces uniformity of outcomes that facilitate the making of valid inter-firm comparisons.

Clarke and Dean (2007) pursue the theme that misleading financial disclosures arise as much by virtue of compliance with the approved accounting standards than by dint of deviation from them with the intent to deceive. MAM of the kind discussed in this chapter are shown to be endemic of a seriously flawed (but approved) system of corporate group activity conducive to the relatively uncontrolled behaviour of DSM.

Clarke et al. (2014) build on Clarke and Dean (2007) to reveal recurring corporate sagas and their related accounting and auditing flaws.

Edwards (2019) contains significant discussion of accounting as misinformation in Britain with chapter 9 containing case studies of the railway mania of the 1840s, the demise of the City of Glasgow (1868) and the Royal Mail affair (1931).

Lee (2006b) examines recent attempts by the FASB to use a principles-based approach to accounting standards. In particular, it argues that the FASB and similar bodies are paying lip-service to the notion of representing socially constructed realities and, instead, are more concerned with traditional accounting conventions such as consistency and comparability.

Notes

1 This type of analysis has a long history and is well captured in Chambers (1965).
2 This section is a modification of Clarke and Dean (2003), which was based on Clarke et al. (2003: ch. 14). What follows here is limited to examining accounting and auditing reforms primarily.
3 Walker (2007) questions whether accounting ideas described as principles in the 1920s and 1930s really qualified for that title – as have many others including Chambers (1964), Sterling (1970), Staunton (2006) and Clarke and Dean (2007).
4 For accounts of the main disclosure and auditing issues and professional responses in the 1920s and 1930s, refer, *inter alia,* to Edwards (2019: chs 9 and 10), Manley (1973) and Walker (1977).
5 Green and Moss (1982: 141–2) support this claim, noting that the defence case made much of the auditor's use of the phrase 'after adjustment of taxation reserves' to justify the content of the 1926 and 1927 accounts. The defence was also able to plead successfully that, rightly or wrongly, the secret transfer of inner reserves was a fact of life in large conglomerate companies at that time.
6 This section is based primarily on Clarke et al. (2013, 2014) and Clarke and Dean (2014).
7 Davies (2010: 111) noted tensions between US and European politicians regarding accounting and between prudential and the corporate regulators – implying that, whereas the IASB promoted a set of international standards with a view to a 'convergence' with US GAAP, the SEC merely went along for the ride without any real commitment to achieve such an outcome.
8 Disconcertingly, some informed observers, such as Taleb (2001, 2007) and Mandelbrot and Hudson (2004), had been issuing warnings for over a decade.
9 These and other cases are discussed in several papers in Stamp et al. (1980).
10 This commentary is based on anthologies of court cases and contemporary contributions in *The Accountant* noted in Chandler and Edwards (1994a, 1994b) relating to the auditor and MAM and judicial parameters of responsibility set in the absence of public accountancy guidance or legislative mandate.
11 Stamp (1969), Stamp and Marley (1970) and Rutherford (1996) describe the events at Pergamon and contiguous concerns related to myriad takeovers that led to the development of accounting standards in the UK.

References

AAA. (1936) *A Tentative Statement of Accounting Principles Underlying Corporate Financial Statements* (Sarasota, FL: AAA).

AAA Financial Accounting Standards Committee. (2003) Evaluating concept-based vs rules-based approaches to standard setting, *Accounting Horizons*, 17 (1): 73–89.

Abacus. (2006) Special issues, 42 (3), 42 (4).

AIA. (1936) *Examination of Financial Statements by Independent Public Accountants* (New York, NY: AIA).

AIA. (1947) *Tentative Statement of Auditing Standards: Their Generally Accepted Significance and Scope* (New York, NY: AIA).

AIA. *Accountancy E-News* (2006) 27 October.

AICPA. (1951) *Codification of Statements on Auditing Procedure* (New York, NY: AICPA).

AICPA. (1960) Responsibilities and functions of the independent auditor in the examination of financial statements, *Statement of Auditing Procedure 30* (New York, NY: AICPA).

AICPA. (1975) The adequacy of auditing standards and procedures currently applied in the examination of financial statements, *Report of the Special Committee on Equity Funding* (New York, NY: AICPA).

AICPA. (1977) The independent auditor's responsibility for the detection of errors and irregularities, *Statement on Auditing Standards 16* (New York, NY: AICPA).

AICPA. (1978) *The Commission on Auditors' Responsibilities: Report, Conclusions, and Recommendations* (New York, NY: AICPA).

AICPA. (1997) Consideration of fraud in a financial statement audit, *Statement on Auditing Standards 82* (New York, NY: AICPA).

AICPA. (2002) Consideration of fraud in a financial statement audit, *Statement on Auditing Standards 99* (New York, NY: AICPA).

Anderson, M., Edwards, J.R., and Matthews, D. (1996) A study of the quoted company audit market in 1886, *Accounting, Business & Financial History*, 6 (3): 363–88.

Arnold, A.J. and McCartney, S. (2004) *George Hudson: The Rise and Fall of the Railway King* (London: Hambledon).

Auditing Practices Committee. (1990) *Auditor's Responsibility in Relation to Fraud, Other Irregularities, and Errors* (London: Auditing Practices Committee).

Baxter, W.T. (1999) McKesson & Robbins: a milestone in auditing, *Accounting, Business & Financial History*, 9 (2): 157–74.

Beasley, M.S., Carcello, J.V., and Hermanson, D.R. (2001) Top ten audit deficiencies, *Journal of Accountancy*, 177 (4): 63–66.

Brooks, C. (1933) *The Royal Mail Case* (London: Butterworth).

Brooks, R. (2018) *Bean Counters: The Triumph of the Accountants and How They Broke Capitalism* (London: Atlantic Books).

Camfferman, K. and Zeff, S.A. (2015) *Aiming for Global Accounting Standards: The International Accounting Standards Board, 2001–2011* (Oxford: Oxford University Press).

Camfferman, K. and Zeff, S.A. (2018) The challenge of setting standards for a worldwide constituency: research implications from the IASB's early history, *European Accounting Review*, 27 (2): 289–312.

Chambers, R.J. (1964) Conventions, doctrines and commonsense, *Accountants' Journal*, July: 182–87.

Chambers, R.J. (1965) Financial information and the securities market, *Abacus*, 1 (2): 3–30.

Chambers, R.J. (1973) *Securities and Obscurities: A Case for Reform of the Law of Company Accounts* (Melbourne: Gower).

Chandler, R.A. and Edwards, J.R. (1994a) *British Audit Practice 1884–1900: A Case Law Perspective* (New York, NY: Garland).

Chandler, R.A. and Edwards, J.R. (1994b) *Recurring Issues in Auditing: Professional Debate 1875–1900* (New York, NY: Garland).

Chatov, R. (1975) *Corporate Financial Reporting* (New York, NY: Free Press).

Clarke, F., Dean, G., and Edwards, J.R. (2013) An historical perspective from the work of Chambers, in L. Jack, J. Davison, and R. Craig (eds) *The Routledge Companion to Accounting Communication*, pp. 26–41 (London: Routledge).

Clarke, F.L., Dean, G, and Egan, M. (2014) *The Unaccountable & Ungovernable Corporation: Companies' Use-by-dates Close in* (London: Routledge).

Clarke, F.L. and Dean, G.W. (2003) An evolving conceptual framework? *Abacus*, 39 (3): 279–97.

Clarke, F.L. and Dean, G.W. (2007) *Indecent Disclosure: Gilding the Corporate Lily* (Cambridge: Cambridge University Press).

Clarke, F.L. and Dean, G.W. (2014) Corporate collapse: regulatory, accounting and ethical failure, in R. Di Pietra, S. McLeay, and J. Ronen (eds) *Accounting and Regulation: New Insights on Governance, Markets and Institutions*, pp. 9–29 (New York, Heidelberg, Dordrecht and London: Springer).

Clarke, F.L., Dean, G.W., and Oliver, K. (2003) *Corporate Collapse: Accounting, Regulatory, and Ethical Failure* (Cambridge: Cambridge University Press).

Commonwealth of Australia. (2004/05) Corporate Law and Economic Reform Program (Audit Reform and Disclosure) Act. (Canberra: AGPA).

Couper, C.T. (1879) *Report of the Trial of the City of Glasgow Bank Directors* (Edinburgh: Edinburgh Publishing).

Cullinan, C.P. and Sutton, S.G. (2002) Defrauding the public interest: a critical examination of reengineered audit processes and the likelihood of detecting fraud, *Critical Perspectives on Accounting*, 13 (3): 297–310.

Davies, H. (2010) *Financial Crisis: Who is to Blame?* (Maiden, MA: Polity Press).

DeAngelo, L.E. (1981) Auditor independence, 'low balling', and disclosure regulation, *Journal of Accounting and Economics*, 3 (2): 113–27.

Edwards, J.R. (2019) *A History of Corporate Financial Reporting in Britain* (London: Routledge).

Edwards, J.R., Anderson, M., and Chandler, R.A. (2007) Claiming a jurisdiction for the 'public accountant' in England prior to organisational fusion, *Accounting, Organizations and Society*, 32 (1–2): 61–100.

FASB. (2002) *Principles-Based Approach to US Standard Setting* (Stamford, CT: FASB).

Financial Reporting Council. (2005) *The Implications of New Accounting and Auditing Standards for the 'True and Fair View' and Auditors' Responsibilities*. Available HTTP: <www.accountingnet.ie/artman2/uploads/implications_20of_20new_20accounting_20and_20auditing_20standards5_1_.pdf>.

Flesher, D. and Flesher, T. (1986) Ivar Kreuger's contribution to US financial reporting, *Accounting Review*, 61 (3): 421–34.

French, E.A. (1985) *Unlimited Liability: The Case of the City of Glasgow Bank* (London: Certified Accountant Publications).

Gow, I.D. and Kells, S. (2018) *The Big Four: The Curious and Perilous Future of the Global Accounting Monopoly* (Carlton: La Trobe University Press).

Green, E. and Moss, M. (1982) *A Business of National Importance: The Royal Mail Shipping Group, 1902–1937* (London and New York: Methuen).

Haigh, G. (1989) UK judge chides Bond over lack of Bell records, *Sydney Morning Herald*, 22 (July): 41.

Hamilton, S. and Micklethwait, A. (2006) *Greed and Corporate Failure: The Lessons from Recent Failures* (London: Palgrave Macmillan).

Hastings, P. (1949) *Cases in Court* (London: Heinemann).

Hein, L.W. (1978) *The British Companies Acts and the Practice of Accountancy, 1844–1962* (New York, NY: Arno Press).

HIH Royal Commission Report (HIHRC). (2003) *The Failure of the HIH Insurance – Vol. III: Reasons, Circumstances and Responsibilities* (Canberra: Commonwealth of Australia).

Humphrey, C., Turley, S., and Moizer, P. (1993) Protecting against detection: the case of auditors and fraud, *Accounting, Auditing & Accountability Journal*, 6 (1): 39–62.

Institute of Chartered Accountants in England and Wales. (1961) *General Principles of Auditing* (London: Institute of Chartered Accountants in England and Wales).

Jenkinson, M.W. (1913) The audit of a public limited company, in *Glasgow CA Students' Society Transactions*, pp. 113–26 (Glasgow: Institute of Accountants and Actuaries of Glasgow).

Johnston, E. (2006) Disclosure proves toughest challenge for insurers, *Australian Financial Review*, 31 (July): 53.

Jordanova, L. (2000) *History in Practice* (London: Arnold).

Katz, I. (2008) SEC recommends keeping fair-value rule with changes, *Bloomberg*, December 30.

Kavanagh, J. (2012) After a period of shocking results property securities doing well, *SMH*, 29 August.

Kerry, J. and Brown, H. (1992) *The BCCI Affair* (Washington, DC: Committee on Foreign Relations of the United States Senate).

Kitney, D. and Buffini, F. (2006) ASIC offers reprieve on tough reporting rules, *Australian Financial Review*, 7 (August): 1, 11.

Laux, C. and Leuz, C. (2009) The crisis of fair-value accounting: making sense of the recent debate, *Accounting, Organizations and Society*, 34 (6/7): 826–34.

Laux, C. and Leuz, C. (2010) Did fair value contribute to the crisis? *Journal of Economic Perspectives*, 24 (1): 93–118.

Lee, T.A. (2006a) The war of the sidewardly mobile corporate financial report, *Critical Perspectives on Accounting*, 17 (4): 419–55.

Lee, T.A. (2006b) The FASB and accounting for economic reality, *Accounting in the Public Interest*, 6: 1–21.

Lee, T.A., Clarke, F.L., and Dean, G.W. (2008) The dominant corporate manager and the reasonably careful, skilful, and cautious auditor, *Critical Perspectives on Accounting*, 19 (5): 677–711.

Magnan, M. (2009) Fair value accounting and the financial crisis: messenger or contributor? Working Paper, CIRANO - Scientific Publications Paper No. 27.

Magnan, M. and Markarian, G. (2011) Accounting, governance and the crisis: is risk the missing link? *European Accounting Review*, 20 (2): 215–31.

Maltby, J. (1999) 'A sort of guide, philosopher and friend': the rise of the professional auditor in Britain, *Accounting, Business & Financial History*, 9 (1): 29–50.

Mandelbrot, B. and Hudson, R.L. (2004) *The Misbehavior of Markets: A Fractal View of Financial Turbulence* (New York, NY: Basic Books).

Manley, P.S. (1973) Gerard Lee Bevan and the City Equitable companies, *Abacus*, 9 (2): 107–15.

May, G.O. (1936) *Twenty-Five Years of Accounting Responsibility: 1911–1936* (New York, NY: Price, Waterhouse).

McDonald, F. (1962) *Insull* (Chicago, IL: Chicago University Press).

Montgomery, R. (1912) *Auditing: Theory and Practice* (New York, NY: Ronald Press).

Raw, C. (1992) *The Money Changers: How the Vatican Bank Enabled Roberto Calvi to Steal $250 million for the Heads of the P2 Masonic Lodge* (London: Harvill).

Ripley, W.Z. (1927) *Main Street and Wall Street* (Boston: Little Brown).

Rutherford, B.A. (1996) The AEI-GEC gap revisited, *Accounting, Business & Financial History*, 6 (2): 141–61.

Ryan, S. (2008) Accounting in and for the sub-prime crisis, *Accounting Review*, 83 (6): 1605–39.

Sanders, T.H., Hatfield, H.R., and Moore, U. (1938) *A Statement of Accounting Principles* (New York, NY: AIA).

Schipper, K. (2003) Principles-based accounting standards, *Accounting Horizons*, 17 (1): 61–72.

Seidler, L.J., Andrews, F., and Epstein, M.J. (1977) *The Equity Funding Papers: The Anatomy of a Fraud* (Santa Barbara, CA: Wiley).

Sridharan, U.V., Caines, W.R., McMillan, J., and Summers, S. (2002) Financial statement transparency and auditor responsibility: Enron and Andersen, *International Journal of Auditing*, 6 (2): 277–86.

Stamp, E. (1969) The public accountant and the public interest, *Journal of Business Finance*, 1 (1): 32–42.

Stamp, E., Dean, G.W., and Wolnizer, P.W. (eds) (1980) *Notable Financial Causes Célèbres* (New York, NY: Arno Press).

Stamp, E. and Marley, C. (1970) *Accounting Principles and the City Code: The Case for Reform* (London: Butterworths).

Staunton, J. (2006) Exiting intellectual grooves in the reporting of liabilities: an analysis of the reporting of liabilities under Chambers' continuously contemporary accounting, unpublished PhD thesis, University of Sydney.

Sterling, R.R. (1970) *Theory of the Measurement of Enterprise Income* (Lawrence, KS: University Press of Kansas).

Stevens, M. (1981) *The Big Eight* (New York, NY: Macmillan).

Stoneman, W.H. (1962) The matchless career of Ivar Kreuger – The match king, in *World of Business*, pp. 934–38 (New York, NY: Simon Schuster).

Taleb, N.N. (2001) *Fooled by Randomness: The Hidden Role of Chance in Life and in Markets* (New York, NY: Random House).

Taleb, N.N. (2007) *The Black Swan: The Impact of the Highly Improbable* (London: Penguin Books).

Teo, E. and Cobbin, P.E. (2005) A revisitation of the 'audit expectations gap': judicial and practitioner views on the role of the auditor in late-Victorian England, *Accounting History*, 10 (2): 35–66.

Thomas, R.J.L. and Turner, R.T. (2001) *Mirror Group Newspapers plc: Investigations under Sections 432 (2) and 442 of the Companies Act 1985* (London: Department of Trade and Industry).

Valance, A. (1955) *Very Private Enterprise* (London: Thames & Hudson).

Walker, R.G. (1976) *Consolidated Statements: A History and Analysis* (New York, NY: Arno Press).

Walker, R.G. (1977) The Hatry affair, *Abacus*, 13 (1): 78–82.

Walker, R.G. (2007) Reporting entity concept: a case study of the failure of principles-based regulation, *Abacus*, 43 (1): 49–75.

Walker, R.G., Clarke, F.L., and Dean, G.W. (2000) Infrastructure reporting options, *Abacus*, 36 (2): 123–59.

Walker, S.P. (1991) The defence of professional monopoly: Scottish chartered accountants and 'satellites in the accountancy firmament' 1854–1914, *Accounting, Organizations and Society*, 20 (4): 257–83.

Wardhaugh, J.B. (1908) The legal limitations of an auditor's duties and responsibilities, in *Transactions of the Chartered Accountants Students' Societies*, pp. 173–98 (Edinburgh, JK: Chartered Accountants Students' Society of Edinburgh).

Whalen, R.C. (2008) The subprime crisis: cause, effect and consequences, Networks Financial Institute Policy Brief No. 2008-PB-04. Available HTTP: <//ssrn.com/abstarct=1113888> (accessed 12 September 2011).

Zandi, M. (2009) *Financial Shock* (Upper Saddle River, NJ: FT Press).

Zeff, S.A. (1971) *Forging Accounting Principles in Five Countries* (Champaign, IL: Stipes).

PART VI

Society and culture

21
GENDER

Rihab Khalifa and Linda M. Kirkham

Overview

In this chapter a review of the literature on gender and accounting history is provided. The focus is on three principal themes. First, a review of the literature on gender and the accounting profession is presented. Second, there follows a discussion on gendered understandings of who counts as an accountant with a view to revealing how male-centric notions of who constituted an accountant has served to restrict and distort our understanding of accounting's past. Third, gendered concepts of accounting are highlighted and we discuss how their history has served to restrict where and when accounting historians have looked for evidence of accounting in the past. In the last section the focus shifts from the past accomplishments and disappointments of gender research in accounting history towards a vision for the future.

Introduction

Although it has long been accepted that gender processes and gendered understandings of the roles and identities of people, occupations, activities and institutions (Hines 1992) should be a prime focus of researchers, academic interest in the accounting history of gender only really began to emerge in the 1980s and did not become established until the 2000s. It is now a central feature of the accounting history research agenda. A recent survey of gender research in accounting between 2004–2014 revealed that historical research constitutes more than 25 per cent of papers published in top accounting journals (Hardies and Khalifa 2018). The survey also showed that research adopting archival and oral history methods perceives gender not as a mere 'dummy variable' but as a compelling conceptual lens through which the role and functioning of accounting can be better understood.

The early focus of the literature on the accounting history of gender was on examining the operation of discriminatory practices that excluded women from the accounting profession in Anglo-American contexts (Lehman 1992). More recently however, some writers have broadened the focus both temporally and spatially to include 'private' domains, non-professional occupational groups, non-Anglo-American contexts and pre-industrial periods. While still developing, the literature on gender and accounting history has opened up important new areas of research and provided compelling insights into accounting's past and present.

Gender and accounting history: the established link

Since occupations and activities have gendered identities that are not dependent on, but may be related to, the physical persons who practice them (Kirkham and Loft 1993), examining gender in accounting history involves more than an examination of the role and participation of women, important as this may be. Inspired by feminist writers who argue that male and female roles are both socially and historically constructed, not biologically determined, researchers have questioned the adequacy of our historical understanding of what counts as an accountant and an accounting task, and to challenge where we might look for evidence of accounting practices in the past.

Writers have examined how gendered discourses and practices have contributed to our understanding of what constitutes expert knowledge in accounting and the boundaries and legitimacy of accounting practices in the past. In particular, gender processes have been shown to be critical for the trajectory of the accounting profession in the US and the UK and have contributed to a reassessment of the factors that contributed to the profession's ascendancy (Lehman 1992; Kirkham and Loft 1993). Other work has identified the limitations of male-centric notions of what constitutes accounting in the past and what is and is not important to our appreciation of accounting history. This has been achieved through, for example, explorations of the gendered nature of accounting tasks, particularly bookkeeping, in the private and in the public domains (Walker 1998; Cooper and Taylor 2000). A further major contribution in this area has begun to emerge from the attention that writers such as Walker (1998, 2003a, 2003b) has given to alternative, marginalised locations for the performance of accounting tasks such as the home or small family businesses.

Accounting history was arguably alerted to the potential importance of gender with the publication of a special section of *Accounting Organizations and Society* in 1992. This contained a number of formative histories of the profession (Lehman 1992; Thane 1992) and a number of contributions that identified and explored the possibilities and imperatives of a gendered analysis of accounting history (Kirkham 1992; Loft 1992). Since then, the gender and accounting history literature has continued to centre on the professional accountant. In consequence, writers have invariably focused on the nineteenth and twentieth centuries and Anglo-American contexts (e.g. Kirkham and Loft 2001; Oldroyd 2003, 2004; Walker and Carnegie 2007), but there has also been an increasing tendency to venture into other temporal and spatial sites (e.g. Komori and Humphrey 2000; Carrera et al. 2001; McNicholas et al. 2004; Carmona and Gutiérrez 2003; Yapa 2006; Komori 2003, 2008).

A common theme in the literature covered here is the argument that gender should not be marginalised within accounting history research since, without an appreciation of the processes and influences of gender, accounting history is at best incomplete, and at worst, misleading (Kirkham and Loft 1993). By beginning the process of identifying the gendered nature of accounting knowledge, practices and institutions, early writers laid down a challenge to accounting historians to integrate a gender analysis into the mainstream questions of the discipline. In gauging the role that histories have played in advancing understandings of accounting and gender, Walker (2008) contended that there are a number of questions that accounting history scholarship has yet to address. Gender can be viewed as part of the 'new' accounting history which 'attempts to give voice to individuals and groups that traditional histories have tended to ignore' (Napier 2006: 459). Such an approach seeks to create new understandings of accounting history by probing and challenging the taken-for-granted understandings of what we know of accounting as a historical subject (Miller et al. 1991; Chua 1998; Merino 1998).

In the rest of this chapter the aim is to highlight some of the main gender themes, insights and arguments that have been introduced into the accounting history literature over the past few decades. However, while some writers claim that a 'substantial body of recent historical accounting literature emphasises gender as an important explanatory factor' (Napier 2006: 459), our review might suggest otherwise. Thus, when gender is understood to signify more than biological sex and is viewed as the social construction of what it means to be male or female, masculine or feminine, accounting histories that encompass a gender perspective remain disappointingly thin on the ground. When we extract the set of literature that simply accounts for women in accounting's past as a separate biological group, without questioning the distribution of the underlying power relationships or the sex-defined roles and identities assumed for such groups (Scott 1986), a much smaller but nevertheless significant body of literature remains.

Gender and the accounting profession

The majority of the gender literature in accounting history has been concerned with women's entry to, and their progression within, the accountancy profession (Cooper 2001). This is a limited focus given the potential range of issues that might be examined from a gender perspective (Walker 2008). This literature has followed a number of strands ranging from studies of pioneer women in the profession (Buckner and Slocum 1985; Reid et al. 1987) to studies that have adopted a historical framework to examine the ways in which the division of labour in accounting has been mediated and constituted by male dominated structures and unequal gender processes (Lehman 1992). In this section a brief overview of this literature is provided, with the aim of highlighting its contribution to understanding accounting history.

Pioneer women in accounting's history

Analyses of pioneer women remain a focal point for much of the historical gender research in accounting. Between the 1980s and 2005, the focus on women's history elicited a number of biographical studies of notable individuals in various branches of accounting and bookkeeping. Since 2005 more than 20 articles have been published in this area. Most of these biographical studies have examined the lives and contributions of pioneer women in the US (Buckner and Slocum 1985; Reid et al. 1987; Slocum 1994; Spruill and Wootton 1995, 1996; Slocum and Vangermeersch 1996; Vigilante 2005; Previts et al. 2007; Schultz 2008). More recently, studies have appeared which focus on pioneer women outside the US in periods such as the Ottoman Empire (Şensoy 2016), and places such as the Dead Sea (Bowlin and Reed 2016), Australia (Johns 2006; Hronsky et al. 2015), the South Seas (Carlos et al. 2006; Laurence 2006), Finland (Virtanen 2009) and Italy (Licini 2011). More studies have also shed light on women and gender within the English and Welsh contexts (Black 2006; Maltby and Rutterford 2006; Newton and Cottrell 2006; Rutterford and Maltby 2006, 2007; Wiskin 2006; Walker 2011b; Froide 2015).

While it should be recognised that some studies have explored the presence of women in accounting employments beyond the profession (Walker 2006, 2008), most of the 'pioneer' studies have been concerned with the struggle of 'heroic' women to gain entry to the professional bodies. An exception in the focus of those studies is Mitchell (2010), who showed how a pioneer woman devoted her income to charitable and religious causes, and this was reflected in the accounts she maintained. Also, Kirkham and Loft (1993) and Walker (2011a) noted how the work of some pioneer women accountants in the UK, such as Ethel Ayres Purdie, was bound together with their suffragism and other political activities. For other pioneer women success as accountants was facilitated by family and social connections and/or educational advantages (Mitchell 2010; Jeacle 2011). In 1931 in England and Wales, 12 years after women had been permitted by law to enter the profession, the census recorded just 119 women accountants. These pioneers however could not be considered to be representative of women in general or even of educated women of the period, as this observation in *The Accountant* illustrates:

> It is interesting to note that some of these new women Chartered Accountants bear names well known in the accountancy profession … Miss Christine Mosley represents the third generation of Chartered Accountants in her family … Miss M.C.B. Aston is the daughter of Mr. Hugh Aston head of the firm Aston, Wilde & Co, of Birmingham and is the second woman Chartered Accountant in that city.
>
> (The Accountant *23 August 1930, quoted in Kirkham and Loft 1993: 547)*

Biographies have helped make pioneer women and their achievements visible in accounting history. While such studies have examined the struggles and contributions of the individuals concerned, they have made a limited contribution to our understanding of the development of the division of labour within accounting more generally. Thus, while accounts of these women are important to the overall story of the profession, writers have argued that an over-emphasis on such pioneers risks obscuring and detracting from the majority of women who have acted as accounting functionaries throughout history. These pioneer women were by their very nature 'special', frequently privileged and by definition successful in their struggles. As such, their lives reveal little about the mass of women denied entry to, and progression within, the profession, and the structures of male domination and oppression that prevented their access. It is to the literature that attempts to shed light on these structures and processes that we now turn.

Pre 1990: gender and the profession remain hidden from view

By the 1980s, the critical accounting history literature had begun to explore many different aspects of professionalisation (for a summary, see Napier 2006: 464–466 and Chapter 11 of this volume) but had failed to link such histories to gender processes in any significant way. From the mid-1980s a number of studies appeared that examined the participation (or lack thereof) of women in the public accounting profession during the twentieth century. They examined the contribution of individual women and/or the overall participation of women in the US (Buckner and Slocum 1985; Reid et al. 1987; Pillsbury et al. 1989), the UK (Silverstone and Williams 1979; Ciancanelli et al. 1990) and Australia (Dando and Watson 1986). These studies served to highlight the presence of women in the accounting craft and emphasised their unequal and unfair treatment in the past.

However, as indicated above, these early studies of women in the profession rarely went beyond a celebration of the achievements of notable individuals or simply gave a brief overview of the multitude of factors that may have contributed to women's lack of inclusion and progression in the past. These factors included those pertaining to their own aspirations (Pillsbury et al. 1989), or those related to others resisting women's attempts to compete with men in the public domain (Cooper 2010). While differences between men and women were identified in such studies, gender as an analytical tool was invariably reduced to biological sex. Barriers to the advancement of women and modes of discrimination were identified, but the source and means of their production and reproduction were left unexplored. Such studies thus failed to trace the origins of the gendered division of labour and have contributed little to our understanding of the historical organisation of the profession more generally. They leave unexplored the lives of the masses of women who continued to be excluded from the profession even though they were undertaking accounting work and had aspirations to do so. By failing to engage with the broader gendered structures and processes that have mediated and helped determine the division of labour within accounting, extant histories of the professionalisation processes remained untouched and unchallenged. A notable exception to those studies, in focus and method, is Roberts (2013), who examined the characteristics of women who self-reported as accountants, bookkeepers or auditors in the 1880s. It is shown that before legal and credential barriers were constructed to prevent the entry to women, a number were drawn to the accounting profession. On the same theme of barriers confronting women in the profession, is the personal account of three women provided by Lightbody (2009). In the accounts of the three women, turnover decisions were the product of a complex interplay between structural as well as domestic factors.

The studies of the 1980s dealing with women's lives or gender issues rarely employed a feminist perspective and, where one could be discerned from the analysis, they invariably adopted a liberal feminist framework. One exception was the study by Tinker and Neimark (1987) that explored gender and class relations between 1917 and 1976 through a longitudinal study of General Motors' annual accounts and company archives. Adopting a largely socialist feminist framework, the authors suggested that the position of women altered with changes in the wider capitalist system. Focusing on the context of accounting work, they showed how in times of over-production and under-consumption, capitalism invented a consumerist role for women to help solve the crisis of surplus value.

In summary, very few pre-1990 studies in accounting shed light on the accounting history of gender. While the potential importance of adopting gender as an analytical category was highlighted in the 1980s, and the possible roles that gender may have played in the emergence and development of the accounting profession had begun to be acknowledged (Hopwood 1987), detailed historical analyses had yet to emerge. This was to change from the 1990s.

Post 1990: gender on the agenda – professionalisation, feminisation and accounting history

To some extent, the literature on gender and accounting history can take its reference point from a group of papers that appeared in a special edition of *Accounting, Organizations and Society* in 1992 (Kirkham 1992; Lehman 1992; Loft 1992; Roberts and Coutts 1992; Thane 1992). Although 1992 also saw a special edition of *Accounting, Auditing & Accountability Journal* devoted to gender issues, the papers published therein ventured little into accounting history, being more focused on critiques of accounting theory and the implications of feminist approaches for accounting practice.

With their focus on the historical division of labour the papers in *Accounting, Organizations and Society* began the process of revealing how accounting history may be (re)evaluated from a gender perspective. Lehman (1992) adopted a historical framework to examine gender issues in the context of the accounting profession in the Anglo-American context. She examined the first 80 years of women in the accounting profession and attempted to document some of the ways in which the profession has been implicated in the discrimination and oppression of women from the early 1900s to the 1980s. Lehman highlighted three levels of discrimination against women that the accounting profession has contributed to and promoted, to varying degrees, over the past century: economic deprivation, socio-economic hierarchies, and ideology. She concluded that practices detrimental to women are periodically re-established and continue, albeit in altered forms. Thane (1992) explored the gendered division of labour in accountancy in Britain from pre-industrial times and reflected on the discriminatory processes that had accompanied the development of the profession and restricted the access of women. By 1992, as these studies reveal, linkages between feminisation and the professionalisation of the accountant had begun to be established, especially in the Anglo-American context (Roberts and Coutts 1992).

Asserting a more comprehensive role for gender in recounting accounting history and commenting on Lehman's article, Kirkham (1992) emphasised the relevance of women's history and a gender analysis of accounting history. She argued that simply adding women to accounting history could be misleading. Rather, the challenge for accounting historians was to move towards a more integrated approach that placed gender at the centre of analyses of the accounting profession. Kirkham argued that any attempt to understand how the profession emerged and developed without an appreciation of the fundamentally gendered structures and processes which engulfed and facilitated change, may 'at best give us partial unsatisfactory understandings' and 'at worst, may result in misleading explanations which serve to perpetuate inequality and oppression' (ibid.: 295).

Following the theme of exploring the role of gender in understanding accounting history through a wider lens, Loft (1992) highlighted the importance of broadening the focus of enquiry beyond the profession and drew attention to the need to examine the role and development of other accounting functionaries, notably clerks and bookkeepers. Such an approach was manifest in the detailed historical study by Kirkham and Loft (1993) that established a crucial link between the rise of the male professional accountant and the fall of the increasingly female bookkeeper/clerk in the occupational hierarchy.

Accountancy in England and Wales emerged as an established profession between 1870 and 1930, in part, by elevating itself from related occupational groups like bookkeepers and clerks who were increasingly women (Kirkham and Loft 1993). Kirkham and Loft (1993) argued that the success of the professionalisation project 'was not simply a matter of establishing accountancy as a profession but involved creating and maintaining a masculine identity for the "professional accountant"' (ibid.: 552). By viewing the professionalisation process as fundamentally gendered, the authors revealed the important part played by developments in clerical work and a gendered discourse of professionalism in the 'construction of the professional accountant'. They claimed that by establishing the role of gender in the creation of the professional accountant, they also revealed how extant histories can be considered incomplete or even flawed.

Following these studies, which examined the formative years of the development of the profession, a number of writers have returned to the preoccupations of earlier contributions and focused on women's progression within the profession in the twentieth century. For example, Walker (2011b) revisited the theme of women's exclusion from the accounting profession in the UK in its early years. Although women were excluded from the membership of professional bodies until 1919, the employment of women in the offices of accountants in the UK became an issue during World War I as male accountants left to fight the war or work for the government (Loft 1986; Ikin et al. 2012). However these new opportunities for women to work in accounting disappeared as soon as the war ended and men went back to their former employments (Lehman 1992) even though women became eligible, in theory at least, for entry to the professional bodies. In 1919 the Sex Disqualification (Removal) Act was passed making it illegal to exclude women on the basis of their biological sex.

For some writers this early period marked the start of the progressive, although tokenist, entry of women to the profession (Shackleton 1999). Others have noted how, once the war ended, women's contribution within accountants' offices was once again limited and trivialised (Kirkham and Loft 1993). Indeed, women's progress and participation in the profession continued to be severely hampered until the 1970s (Ciancanelli et al. 1990). This lack of progress was noted despite women having (re)entered accountants' offices as substitute labour during World War II in the US (Wootton and Spruill 1994), the UK (Cooper 2001), and Australia and New Zealand (Linn 1996; Emery et al. 2002).

The increased representation of women in the accountancy profession since the 1970s has been taken by some as evidence of improving gender balance (French and Meredith 1994). However, researchers have also cautioned against measuring women's progress by looking only at their numerical representation, rather than their location within the profession (Khalifa 2004). Other studies have focused on the discursive and material mechanisms and practices that produce and reproduce inequalities in the recruitment and progression of women, especially the phenomena commonly known as the 'glass ceiling' (Ciancanelli et al. 1990; Barker and Monks 1998; McKeen and Richardson 1998; Shackleton 1999; Emery et al. 2002; Khalifa 2004). While the glass ceiling is well acknowledged in the accounting literature, another kind of barrier that operates at the horizontal level (i.e. in between specialisms within the profession) also demands attention. In her 2013 study, Khalifa demonstrated how the gendering of accounting specialisms serves to create the identities of those who practise them, as well as generating an intra-professional hierarchy within those gendered specialisms (Khalifa 2004). In that sense attention is now being given to studies of horizontal segregation as well as vertical segregation. Emery et al. (2002) showed how the accounting profession in New Zealand was male-dominated despite the lack of formal barriers to women's entry. Such studies have utilised archival and oral testimony to illustrate how discrimination and patriarchy are complex and are not overcome by simple number balancing. For example, Haynes (2008) has shown how social, institutional and cultural factors may play a role in restricting the ways in which identities are defined, particularity in the context where the identities of 'mothers' and 'accountants' are tangled. A similar line of enquiry focusing on women from ethnic minorities has examined the reasons why women struggle for acceptance and progression, despite decades of legislation that outlawed discriminatory practices against them (Fearfull and Kamenou 2006).

In summary, the 1990s alerted accounting historians to the potential for incorporating a gender analysis in any examination of the emergence and development of the profession. A few studies began to appear that demonstrated the centrality of patriarchal structures, discriminatory practices and gendered discourses of professionalism to the professionalisation process in accountancy. While such insights added new understandings to extant histories, they also established the need for accounting history to re-evaluate existing explanations and to reconsider the completeness and validity of the historical evidence upon which they are based.

Gendered understandings of what counts as accounting: bookkeepers and other accounting functionaries

The limited contribution made by accounting histories of women and the need to extend beyond a focus on the 'pioneer' was discussed by Walker (2008). Since the early 1990s, there has been a recognition of the need to study gender in accounting history by examining the accounting function as a whole and not simply the professional accountant (Loft 1992). Nearly a decade later, Cooper and Taylor (2000) noted the limited attention given to 'non-qualified' clerical workers who undertake routinised accounting tasks. This lacuna raises questions about taken-for-granted assumptions about what is understood and accepted as an accounting task and why such understandings arise. While these questions remain on the agenda, a few studies have examined developments in bookkeeping and clerical work in order to understand the relationship of these activities to professional accounting and the links between feminisation, professionalisation and deskilling (Kirkham and Loft 1993; Cooper and Taylor 2000; Emery et al. 2002; Walker 2003a; Khalifa 2013).

Kirkham and Loft (1993) showed that during the late nineteenth century, clerks and accountants in England and Wales were predominantly men. By 1931, however, women constituted 42.1 per cent of clerical labour and only 1 per cent of accountants. The authors demonstrated how these processes were inextricably linked such that the progressive feminisation and downgrading of bookkeeping was closely associated with the elevation of the professional accountant. Their gender analysis goes beyond a history of women in or on the margins of accounting and reveals how gendered discourses of professionalism served to separate different types of accounting work and classes of people. In this way, accounting tasks undertaken by men as well as women clerks came to be reconstituted as both 'menial' and 'women's work' (ibid.: 549). Similar processes were observed in New Zealand as women were slotted into routinised office and bookkeeping work under the title of clerk, thus 'reinforcing the male closure of the accounting profession' (Emery et al. 2002: 2).

In the US, the separation of the 'trade' of bookkeeping from 'professional' accounting and its feminisation is argued to have taken place between 1870 and 1930 (Wootton and Kemmerer 1996, 2000). Other studies have identified a range of factors involved in the feminisation of bookkeeping in the US, including the growth of cost accounting, the deskilling effects of mechanisation and the scientific management movement (Hedstrom 1988; Strom 1992). Komori (2008, 2012a, 2012b, 2013) has reflected on the experiences of women in the Japanese accounting profession, as well as how accounting has enabled the building of feminine identities and enhanced their political power as consumers.

Utilising a labour process framework, Cooper and Taylor (2000) attempted to provide a 'history of bookkeepers' in Britain from the mid-nineteenth century to the 1990s, focusing on the transformation of clerical labour during this period. This transformation is attributed in part to the impacts of mechanisation and computerisation that resulted in the deskilling and dehumanisation of bookkeeping. Using secondary sources, the authors note the gendered transformation that accompanied these processes and contend that during the late nineteenth and early twentieth centuries, bookkeeping clerks tended to be men, in contrast to the 1990s when women comprised nearly 80 per cent of the occupation (Cooper and Taylor 2000: 576).

While the evidence suggests that the majority of clerks in the latter part of the nineteenth century were men, the evidence pertaining to the gendered distribution of bookkeeping is less established. Although the feminisation of clerical work has invariably been conflated with the feminisation of bookkeeping temporally, Walker (2003b) provides evidence that woman bookkeepers were represented in large numbers in certain industries and geographical areas during the late nineteenth century. These women bookkeepers have remained hidden from view as historians traditionally focus on the role of women in 'large, bureaucratised organisations such as banks, insurance companies, railways and the postal and telegraph services' (ibid.: 630). Walker (2003b) uses data from the census enumerators' books and other documentary sources to bring these women bookkeepers into view. His study is revealing and suggestive of the need to trace the involvement of women as bookkeepers in smaller scale enterprises, crafts and the retailing sector.

Bookkeeping was promulgated as a male preserve until the early twentieth century when its feminisation was argued to have begun and been completed. However, these conclusions have been based on published census data that conflates bookkeepers with clerks (Strom 1987, 1992; Walker 2003b). Thus Walker (2003b: 631) reveals how, by the late nineteenth century, long before the introduction of office mechanisation, the majority of bookkeepers in the South of England were women. Other studies have begun to reveal women as bookkeepers and accounting functionaries in a variety of temporal and spatial settings where they were hitherto invisible – in state organisations during World War I (Black 2006), not-for-profit organisations in the nineteenth century (Walker 2006), genteel households in the eighteenth century (Kirkham and Loft 2001) and in their own businesses in the eighteenth and nineteenth centuries (Hunt 1996; Walker 2003b). Some studies, such as Beachy et al. (2006), have gone further by drawing on case studies throughout Europe to reveal that elite and middle-class women often manipulated financial resources in a highly sophisticated manner, contrary to contemporary beliefs about women's abilities.

Gender and the location of historical enquiry

The efforts of accounting historians to examine accounting within its broader contexts (spatial and temporal) were explored in a special issue edited by Annisette in 2007. In her editorial, Annisette (2007) reiterated the call for greater diversity in historical research in accounting:

> Sociological studies focus on the public, official, visible, and/or dramatic role players and definitions of situations; yet unofficial, supportive, less dramatic, private, and invisible spheres of social life and organisations may be equally important.
>
> *(Harding 1987: 32)*

This exhortation chimes with the call in 1991 for 'new accounting history', one that questions notions of natural progress and necessity in the development of accounting (Miller et al. 1991) and celebrates difference in the telling of historical stories (Chua 1998). Such an approach calls for the broadening of the 'conception of what counts as accounting and what counts as evidence' (Miller and Napier 1993: 645). Such appeals reflect and reinforce the demand for what has been referred to as the 'new history' (Gaffikin 1998) since both are concerned with views from 'below' rather than views from 'above' (Burke 1991). Covering a longer period and different localities, Czarniawska (2008) examined the changing perceptions of accounting using a combination of fiction and research findings from the eighteenth century to more modern times, in places such as Poland and Central Europe.

Despite seeking views from 'below' and arguing for difference to be recognised and celebrated, accounting histories have tended to focus on the dramatic role players: the large organisation, the successful entrepreneur and the public arena. Walker (1998), by contrast, drew attention to the paucity of gender research in accounting history on the home, household or small family business. The emphasis on the accounting practices of the 'male' merchant and male 'entrepreneur' have been questioned by Kirkham and Loft (2001) given that the genteel household could be larger than a small business and more women ran businesses than has been commonly thought (Hunt 1996). The household, family and small business provide arenas for examining accounting and gender in everyday life and culture (Hopwood 1994) and these themes have attracted the attention of some accounting historians.

Accounting in the home or household: gender in the 'private domain'

The limited emphasis on the home or household as a focus of accounting history has been, in part, attributed to its conceptualisation as a private domain in contrast to the public world of work. This conceptualisation has embodied the gendered notions of separate spheres that have dominated social and women's history (Davidoff and Hall 1987) and served to influence what is and isn't considered important in accounting history research (Walker 1998; Llewellyn and Walker 2000a, 2000b; Walker and Llewellyn 2000; Kirkham and Loft 2001).

Walker and Llewellyn (2000) suggest that the home has been construed as a trivial arena within accounting research and unworthy of academic study. Academic accountants have tended to establish their legitimacy by focusing on the 'public' nature of professional accounting and its importance to the workings of the modern economy. This has involved an emphasis on professional accountants in 'public' practice and their interaction with the 'owners and managers of large scale "visible" organizations' (ibid.: 443). The result has not only been a neglect of the home but also other less visible organisations. Additionally, the authors argue that the home has been marginalised due to its representation as a site of consumption rather than production. Such a representation has been questioned both in terms of its applicability to all historical periods (Kirkham and Loft 2001) and the underlying assumptions of productive labour that it embodies (Walker and Llewellyn 2000).

The identification of the home as a potential site for the exercise of male domination has inspired a number of historical studies that have explored the potentialities and actualities of household accounting as a technique of male domination (Walker and Llewellyn 2000). Walker (1998) was the first major study to explore accounting in the home. Through an analysis of instructional texts aimed predominantly at bourgeois families in Victorian England, Walker demonstrates how accounting assisted in the promotion and maintenance of patriarchy. While accounting provided women with responsibilities and opportunities for decision-making, these were confined to a narrow domestic sphere and were seen to constrain their horizons and limit their aspirations to within the boundaries of the stewardship of the household. Thus, domestic accounting systems operated to discipline and subjugate middle-class women in Victorian England and contributed to the maintenance of male-dominated social structures. Accounting in middle-class homes in the nineteenth century is shown to have been both repressive and disabling.

In a later study Walker (2003a) found further evidence of the repressive properties of household accounting. His study revealed how, in the early part of the twentieth century, in the wake of suffragism and scientific management, household accounting in the US and the UK served to divert the aspirations of women away from notions of career-building outside the home and reinforced the role of women as consumers.

The potentially repressive nature of household accounting has been observed in other contexts during post-industrial times, notably Australia. Ideological discourses and instructional texts on household accounting in Australia from the early nineteenth to the mid-twentieth century may have acted as instruments for restraining female consumption by attempting to contain female extravagance in matters of dress and fashion (Walker and Carnegie 2007). The budgetary earmarking ideology that was promoted served as a social process that was reflexive of gendered asymmetries of power in the home (ibid.).

Most of the extant research on accounting in the home has demonstrated how household accounting was associated with patriarchy and served as a potential source of inequality. However, studies of the accounting practices of genteel households in the eighteenth century suggest that accounting had the potential to empower and enable women in the management and control of their households (Kirkham and Loft 2001). Genteel household management during this period involved a more diverse set of tasks and responsibilities than commonly acknowledged. It involved both technical and managerial skills which were recognised and in demand from the male members of the household (Vickery 1998). In various aspects 'the household functioned like most eighteenth century commercial enterprises' (ibid.: 141) and genteel women were more akin to master or gentleman farmers than the ladies of leisure commonly portrayed in the literature. Such insights serve to problematise the meaning of private and public and to question the analytical frame of separate spheres during this period. Likewise, Day (2011) has studied household management as an empowering tool that enabled elite women in Yorkshire to exercise authority.

The gendered nature of concepts such as work and home, private and public, and separate spheres has been shown to be both historically and contextually constituted. While the literature has begun to explore the meaning of these concepts in relation to the interface of accounting and the home in post-industrial times, there have been very few studies of pre-industrial periods, although the potential for such work has been noted (Walker and Llewellyn 2000). Oldroyd (2003, 2004) began this endeavour by examining the performance and functioning of prehistoric calculation and counting functions in relation to gendered structures and relationships. Although the evidence is inconclusive it does suggest that calculation and counting functions were performed by women and helped sustain a matriarchal social structure (Oldroyd 2003).

The potentially enabling qualities of household accounting have been examined in other cultures, notably Japan (Komori and Humphrey 2000; Komori 2006, 2012a, 2013; Ramlugun et al. 2016). By viewing accounting practices through a non-Western lens, the authors claim that recent Japanese household accounting exhibited a number of positive and emancipatory qualities that have allowed women to improve their lives. In contrast to the revelations of other authors, Japanese accounting is claimed to be inclusive and co-operative. Nevertheless the authors acknowledge that at times accounting systems 'generally did not really challenge the essential underpinnings of the Japanese family system and its commitment to corporate Japan … but rather acted to accommodate or eliminate tensions' (ibid.: 467).

From the late nineteenth century onwards the role of Japanese women in household accounting was strongly linked to state savings drives which were designed to provide funds for corporate investment and to construct the social foundations necessary to achieve national goals (Komori 2006). Thus, in common with the observations relating to Anglo-Saxon countries during this period (Walker 1998; Walker and Carnegie 2007) accounting discourse and practice has served to contain Japanese women at home and limit their economic activities.

To summarise, the home or household has increasingly been revealed as an important site for the study of accounting and gender in pre-industrial and industrial societies. The studies that have emerged in the accounting history literature have demonstrated how accounting and accountabilities at home are implicated in gender relations, the ideology of the home and in maintaining a separation between the public world of work and the private realm of the home (Llewellyn and Walker 2000a).

Revealing accounting beyond and outside the male business enterprise

Accounting historians have traditionally tended to focus on the accounting practices of the male merchant and male entrepreneur (Parker and Yamey 1994) and the male manager of aristocratic estates (Napier 1991), rather than on the woman trader or woman household manager. Conceptualising accounting beyond professional practice has revealed women account keepers in a variety of domestic, business and financial settings (Hopwood 1994). Family trading or farming concerns constitute arenas where the boundary between public and private is more obscure and where business accounting might be performed by women (Cooper and Taylor 2000; Walker 2003b). Despite this recognition, there have been few detailed studies of women's involvement in the accounting practices of such organisations, and very little is known about those women who practised accounting prior to the formal establishment of the accounting profession (Broadbent et al. 1994; Llewellyn and Walker 2000b; Kirkham and Loft 2001).

As noted previously, the accounting history literature has begun to integrate women and gender perspectives into some of its central concerns, albeit in a limited way. Much of this literature has been concentrated on the modern period. Contributions relating to earlier periods present a story of the development and practice of accounting which, for the most part, excludes women. Before the nineteenth century, accounting was regarded as an essential skill for a merchant (Parker and Yamey 1994) and a recommended skill for the nobility and gentry on landed estates (Hunt 1996). However, it was also a skill acquired by some women during this period and historians have provided evidence of women's role as account keepers in a variety of trades and organisations (Vickery 1993, 1998; Hunt 1996; Dingwall 1999).

Historians have shown how women in seventeenth- and eighteenth-century Britain were prominent among renters, moneylenders and investors (Hunt 1996; Dingwall 1999). Wiskin (2006) conducted three case studies of English businesswomen during the eighteenth century. Her study suggested that both men and women maintained records and conducted business dealings on credit in similar ways, despite earlier studies suggesting that women's credit transactions were gendered 'feminine' and therefore different from those of men during this period.

Women participated in investment activities in the UK, Australia and other contexts in a variety of ways during the eighteenth and nineteenth centuries (Carlos et al. 2006; Freeman et al. 2006; Johns 2006; Laurence 2006; Newton and Cottrell 2006; Froide 2015). The group of papers published in a special issue of *Accounting, Business and Financial History* in 2006 revealed how women did not always behave in ways suggested by the separate spheres thesis. However, while the distinction between the private world of home and the public world of work were blurred, structural impediments prevented women's full participation as investors in the governance of joint stock companies (Freeman et al. 2006; Johns 2006). In Australia during the early nineteenth century, 31 per cent of shareholders in Australia's first bank were female, but women were prevented from exercising this power due to their being denied the right to vote directly or exercise proxy votes (Johns 2006). Such insights raise questions about how gendered inequalities have influenced the governance and development of large corporations. By the same token, legislative reforms related to married women's property as well as varying types of investments significantly changed the proportion of women owning stocks and shares (Rutterford et al. 2011).

Prior to the eighteenth century, women often contributed actively or independently as merchants and traders (Dingwall 1999). A recurrent role adopted by these women, with or without their husband's participation, was bookkeeping and handling money. Researchers have found evidence of women's participation in numerous industries and activities. For example, women in the brewing industry in Scotland during the 1500s were involved in the selling of ale, handling income and performing bookkeeping tasks while their husbands managed the practical side of the business (Mayhew 1995). Marshall (1983) suggests that such insights are not untypical and points to an abundance of printed and manuscript materials that provide evidence of women's active role in business and financial matters in Scotland over the past 150 years. She points to the existence of census reports, newspapers, government records, business archives and minute books of societies and organisations that reveal women's roles, not as pioneers or exceptions but as hitherto unrecognised participants in everyday life.

Walker (2006) draws attention to a(nother) previously 'hidden' group of women accountants in the nineteenth century whose philanthropic work involved them in a variety of accounting practices. Through a biographical study of Octavia Hill, the housing reformer, he explores the relationship between her accounting, prevailing notions of domesticity and gendered spheres, and illustrates the importance of accounting to her philanthropic endeavours. Few other studies have alluded to this group of women or the relationship of their work and activities to accounting.

Another trend relating to the inclusion of female voices in the history of accounting focused on questioning the taken-for-granted-ness of certain methodological and theoretical choices when delving into the historical accounts of female experiences. For example, 'oral history' as a method should be carefully used to liberate (rather than subjugate) women's historical accounts (Kim 2008; Haynes 2010; Adapa et al. 2016). Jeacle (2006) on studying the business of beauty during the period of 1930–1980, challenged the credibility of feminist rhetoric of exploitation and proposed a different way of looking at the history of gender and accounting.

Thus, a small but growing body of research has recognised the need for accounting historians to incorporate and assimilate accounts of accounting performed outside public practice: in the office, in the home in the philanthropic organisation, or in the small business or craft organisation (Loft 1992; Cooper and Taylor 2000; Walker and Llewellyn 2000; Walker 2003a, 2003b, 2006; Walker and Carnegie 2007). These hitherto marginalised domains have revealed new understandings of the development and functioning of the accounting craft and established the need for further research that questions taken-for-granted assumptions concerning where, how and why accounting was practised in the past.

Challenge and change: future avenues for gender and history

While this review has suggested that the literature on gender and accounting history has experienced a relatively slow development, it has also highlighted how gendered analyses have opened up new and important areas of research and provided fresh insights into accounting's past. Gender processes have been shown to be critical to explaining the trajectory of the accounting profession in the US, the UK and elsewhere and have contributed to a reassessment of the factors that contributed to the profession's ascendancy (Lehman 1992; Shackleton 1999; Kirkham and Loft 1993).

To conclude this chapter a shift of focus from the past accomplishments and disappointments of gender research in accounting history towards a vision for the future is offered. In particular, some suggestions are made about ways in which gender might be accorded a bigger role in accounting history. The potential for deploying a feminist methodology is highlighted, which involves listening to the 'female voice' and arguing for a general reassessment of the questions asked in the field. This is part of an attempt to reinforce and strengthen the voices of those who question the locations and boundaries of historical enquiry in accounting and advocate a move towards a broader, gendered appreciation of the practices and people who were involved in accounting's past.

Including the female voice: 'The gender of history'[1]

> It does make a difference who says what and when. When people speak from the opposite sides of power relations, the perspective from the lives of the less powerful can provide a more objective view than the perspective from the lives of the more powerful.
>
> *(Harding 1986: 26)*

Presently, most research in accounting history is told by men about men (Carnegie et al. 2003). Researchers who adopt 'feminist standpoint' theory challenge the taken-for- granted assumptions about neutrality and objectivity that underlie the sciences and their 'his-story' (Harding 1991). Hammond and Oakes (1992) trace the origins of this theoretical approach through the work of Hegel, arguing that 'the slave has a privileged perspective compared to that of the master. The slave can see social relations more clearly because he or she does not have an interest in distorting reality' (Hammond and Oakes 1992: 60). Standpoint theories have demonstrated the usefulness of moving away from 'adding' others' experiences to research, to 'starting' from those experiences to derive research questions, develop theories, collect data and interpret research findings (Harraway 1988; Harding 1991).

Writers have argued that research in accounting history could benefit from avoiding the 'add and stir' approach by adopting a more integrative approach (Hammond and Oakes 1992; Kirkham 1992). Harding suggests that history has been added to gender, and gender has been added to history without developing genuine insights into the 'other' gender's historical experience (Harding 1991). Women's subordination and accounting history are not independent of each other and simply adding women to accounting history could be misleading (Kirkham 1992; Kirkham and Loft 1993). Exclusionary and marginalising practices in the professions, which have adversely affected women, some men (e.g. working class clerks) and minority groups, were essential to the definition of expert knowledge in accounting and the development of professional legitimacy.

Simply adding women to accounting history is to construct women's experiences as 'supplementary' and risks foreclosing the option of alternative histories, leaving extant accounts unchallenged and unchanged. A feminist approach invites historians and researchers to look at and question the assumed and taken-for-granted 'truths' about accounting and to unpick the gendered identities of institutions, activities and occupations. In this way, it is argued, previously marginalised and hidden knowledge might be revealed and other forms of knowledge may emerge and perhaps change our understanding of what constitutes accounting history.

Gender, as an analytical category and a fresh perspective, can help challenge historical accounts of the profession of accountancy by probing into the process of knowledge and history production as we ask questions about the process of selecting research topics, gathering evidence and interpreting data. A good example of a study that went beyond the typical focus on the accounting profession and researched the life of women students and staff in accountancy is that by Lord and Robb (2010). The study reflected the lived experiences of female students and how they experienced discrimination in the business world.

Another area of feminist historiography is linked to methodological aspects of data gathering and interpretation. It urges historians to ask questions about the choice of substantive areas of historical inquiry, the delineation of the historical record that is deemed suitable for research, and the methods for interpreting data. It is suggested that male-centric notions of 'data' and 'evidence' have produced biased histories because the concerns of women and other oppressed groups are less likely to be represented in official public records. Their concerns were more likely to be expressed orally than in writing or were inscribed in domestic and personal documents. Assumptions about the definition and legitimacy of the 'public' domain militated against the inclusion of women in the written record. Only recently have historians begun to accept methods such as oral history as legitimate ways to gather evidence (Carnegie and Napier 1996). Through the adoption of such approaches in accounting history, women and other marginalised actors can emerge as new agents of knowledge.

Rethinking who and what constitutes an accountant

The professional identities represented in accounting history and in professionalisation studies are invariably masculine, incorporating prevailing gendered notions of what it means to be a man or a woman (Kirkham and Loft 1993). In turn, such masculine representations serve to perpetuate and reinforce the discriminatory practices and unequal power relations that they embed. By adopting a narrow conception of what it means to be a professional or an accountant, accounting historians have ignored important aspects of professional identity such as gender, race, sexuality and class. Although not entirely focused on identity, Matthews (2016) sought to trace the themes of social class, educational background and gender to understand the processes involved in the making of the professional accountant in the US.

While a less male-centric notion of the accountant has begun to be incorporated in some studies that explore aspects of race (Hammond and Streeter 1994; Hammond 2002; McNicholas et al. 2004; Smith 2005) as well as gender (Walker 1998, 2003b), the masculine identity continues to dominate accounting histories, old and new. By explicitly questioning the gender of the accountant (even in the visual representation of an accounting body, Page and Spira (2009)), researchers of accounting practices and institutions will challenge existing interpretations and reveal new understandings of who practised accounting in the past, and where and why it was practised.

This review has highlighted how historians have chosen to define accountants predominantly within the narrow confines of organised professions and large organisations and have left the underlying gendered structures of male domination and gendered processes of inequality largely unexamined. Such narrow accounts risk obscuring and distorting our understanding of 'the underlying processes and forces at work' (Hopwood 1987: 207). Histories which focus on the 'public' identity of the male accountant have neglected the contribution, not only of the myriad women who performed accounting tasks outside the 'public' but also the contribution of men who were also deemed 'outside' public accounting. By questioning, rather than accepting, gendered notions of expertise, skill, knowledge and practice, accounting historians will not only extend the focus of enquiry to include new locations and hidden contributions, they will also reveal altered understandings of accounting's past.

Conclusions

While historians in general have produced a substantial body of literature since the 1980s that has deployed feminist perspectives and explored women's lives in detail, this development has not been reflected in accounting history. Although a small body of literature has emerged which assimilates and incorporates accounts of accounting performed outside public practice, in the office, in the home, or in the small business or craft organisation (Loft 1992; Kirkham and Loft 1993; Cooper and Taylor 2000; Walker and Llewellyn 2000; Walker 2003a, 2003b; Walker and Carnegie 2007; Komori 2012a, 2013), the majority of accounting history continues to focus on the male accountant and the masculine location in which accounting is performed.

Despite the potential range of issues which might be examined from a gender perspective, until recently, the majority of the gender literature in accounting history has been concerned with women's entry to, and their progression within, the profession. While new areas of research in gender and accounting history have emerged, revealing new insights into accounting's past, this review would suggest claims that a 'substantial body of recent historical accounting literature emphasises gender as an important explanatory factor' (Napier 2006: 459), are premature. What is now required is for *all* accounting historians to accept that existing histories that fail to incorporate any consideration of gender are likely to be misleading or incomplete. Only when gender is accepted as integral to the subject itself will future research begin to cast light on *all* the people and practices involved in accounting's past.

Key works

Hardies and Khalifa (2018) provide a systematic review of gender research in accounting since the late 1980s.

Kirkham and Loft (1993) provides a major re-evaluation of the formative years of the accounting profession in England and Wales from a gender perspective and establishes a crucial link between the rise of the professional male accountant and the fall of the female bookkeeper/clerk in the occupational hierarchy.

Lehman (1992) represents a useful introductory article that outlines some basic feminist perspectives and examines the early years of the accountancy profession.

Scott (1986) is a seminal paper in gender studies that highlights research possibilities from a gender perspective. The paper calls for new ways to study history and to ask the old questions of history in new ways that includes consideration of the family and sexuality.

Walker (1998) is an excellent historical study of household accounting in Victorian Britain.

Note

1 The title 'the gender of history' was borrowed from the book by Bonnie G. Smith, *The Gender of History: Men, Women and Historical Practice* (Cambridge, MA: Harvard University Press, 1998).

References

Adapa, S., Rindfleish, J., and Sheridan, A. (2016) "Doing gender" in a regional context: Explaining women's absence from senior roles in regional accounting firms in Australia, *Critical Perspectives on Accounting*, 35: 100–10.

Annisette, M. (2007) Editorial: International perspectives on race and gender in accounting's past: An introduction, *Accounting History*, 12 (3): 245–51.

Barker, P.C. and Monks, K. (1998) Irish women accountants and career progression: A research note, *Accounting, Organizations and Society*, 23 (8): 813–23.

Beachy, A.O.R. and Craig, B., (eds) (2006) *Women, Business and Finance in Nineteenth-Century Europe: Rethinking Separate Spheres* (Oxford: Berg).

Black, J. (2006) War, women and accounting: Female staff in the UK Army Pay Department Offices, 1914–1920, *Accounting, Business & Financial History*, 16 (2): 195–218.

Bowlin, W.F. and Reed, S. (2016) Evidence of wealth management and financial planning by women in 2nd century CE: Contracts from Dead Sea Caves, *Accounting Historians Journal*, 43 (2): 1–38.

Broadbent, J., Laughlin, R., and Willig-Atherton, H. (1994) Financial control and schools: Accounting in 'public' and 'private' spheres, *British Accounting Review*, 26 (3): 487–507.

Buckner, K.C. and Slocum, E.L. (1985) Women CPAs – Pioneers in the first quarter of this century, *The Woman CPA*, 47 (October): 20–24.

Burke, P. (1991) History of events and the revival of narrative, in P. Burke (ed) *New Perspectives on Historical Writing*, pp. 1–23 (Cambridge: Polity Press).

Carlos, A., Maguire, K., and Neal, L. (2006) Financial acumen, women speculators, and the Royal African Company during the South Sea Bubble, *Accounting, Business & Financial History*, 16 (2): 219–43.

Carmona, S. and Gutiérrez, F. (2003) Outsourcing as compassion? The case of cigarette manufacturing by poor Catholic nuns (1817–1819), *Critical Perspectives on Accounting*, 16 (7): 875–903.

Carnegie, G.D., McWatters, C.S., and Potter, B.N. (2003) The development of the specialist accounting history literature in the English language. An analysis by gender, *Accounting, Auditing & Accountability Journal*, 16 (2): 186–207.

Carnegie, G.D. and Napier, C.J. (1996) Critical and interpretive histories: Insights into accounting's present and future through its past, *Accounting, Auditing & Accountability Journal*, 9 (3): 7–39.

Carrera, N., Gutiérrez, I., and Carmona, S. (2001) Gender, the state and the audit profession: Evidence from Spain (1942–88), *European Accounting Review*, 10 (4): 803–15.

Chua, W.F. (1998) Historical allegories: Let us have diversity, *Critical Perspectives on Accounting*, 9 (6): 617–30.

Ciancanelli, P., Gallhofer, S., Humphrey, C., and Kirkham, L. (1990) Gender and accountancy: Some evidence from the UK, *Critical Perspectives on Accounting*, 1 (2): 117–44.

Cooper, C. (2001) From women's liberation to feminism: Reflections in accounting academia, *Accounting Forum*, 25 (3): 214–45.

Cooper, C. and Taylor, P. (2000) From Taylorism to Ms Taylor: The transformation of the accounting craft, *Accounting, Organizations and Society*, 25 (6): 555–78.

Cooper, K. (2010) Accounting by women: Fear, favour and the path to professional recognition for Australian women accountants, *Accounting History*, 15 (3): 309–36.

Czarniawska, B. (2008) Accounting and gender across times and places: An excursion into fiction, *Accounting, Organizations and Society*, 33 (1): 33–47.

Dando, C. and Watson, R. (1986) Women in accounting, *Australian Accountant*, 56: 12–19.

Davidoff, L. and Hall, C. (1987) *Family Fortunes: Men and Women of the English Middle Class, 1780–1850* (Chicago, IL: University of Chicago Press).

Day, J. (2011) Household management as a method of authority for three eighteenth-century elite Yorkshire women, *Women's History Magazine*, 66 (Summer): 30–37.

Dingwall, H. (1999) The power behind the merchant? Women and the economy in the late 17th century, in E. Ewan and M. Meilke (eds) *Women in Scotland in the 11th Century – 1750*, pp. 152–62 (Edinburgh: Tuckwell Press).

Emery, M., Hooks, J., and Stewart, R. (2002) Born at the wrong time? An oral history of women professional accountants in New Zealand, *Accounting History*, 7 (2): 9–34.

Fearfull, A. and Kamenou, N. (2006) How do you account for it? A critical exploration of career opportunities or and experiences of ethnic minority women, *Critical Perspectives on Accounting*, 17 (7): 883–901.

Freeman, M., Pearson, R., and Taylor, J. (2006) 'A doe in the city': Women shareholders in eighteenth- and early nineteenth-century Britain, *Accounting, Business & Financial History*, 16 (2): 265–91.

French, S. and Meredith, V. (1994) Women in public accounting: Growth and advancement, *Critical Perspectives on Accounting*, 5 (3): 227–41.

Froide, A. (2015) Learning to invest: Women's education in arithmetic and accounting in early modern England, *Early Modern Women: An Interdisciplinary Journal*, 10 (1): 3–26.

Gaffikin, M. (1998) History is dead, long live history, *Critical Perspectives on Accounting*, 9 (6): 631–40.

Hammond, T. (2002) *A White-Collar Profession. African-American Certified Public Accountants since 1921* (Chapel Hill, NC: University of North Carolina Press).

Hammond, T. and Oakes, L.S. (1992) Some feminisms and their implications for accounting practice, *Accounting, Auditing & Accountability Journal*, 5 (3): 52–70.

Hammond, T. and Streeter, D.W. (1994) Overcoming barriers: Early African-American Certified Public Accountants, *Accounting, Organizations and Society*, 19 (3): 271–88.

Hardies, K. and Khalifa, R. (2018) Gender is not 'a dummy variable': A discussion of current gender research in accounting, *Qualitative Research in Accounting and Management*, 15 (3): 385–407.

Harding, S. (1986) *The Science Question in Feminism* (Ithaca, NY: Cornell University Press).

Harding, S. (ed) (1987) *Feminism and Methodology: Social Science Issues* (Bloomington, IN: Indiana University Press).

Harding, S. (1991) *Whose Science? Whose Knowledge? Thinking from Women's Lives* (Ithaca, NY: Cornell University Press).

Harraway, D. (1988) Situated knowledge: The science question in feminism as a site of discourse on the privilege of partial perspective, *Feminist Studies*, 14 (3): 575–99.

Haynes, K. (2008) Transforming identities: Accounting professionals and the transition to motherhood, *Critical Perspectives on Accounting*, 19 (5): 620–42.

Haynes, K. (2010) Other lives in accounting: Critical reflections on oral history methodology in action, *Critical Perspectives on Accounting*, 21 (3): 221–31.

Hedstrom, M.L. (1988) Beyond feminisation: Clerical workers in the United States from the 1920s through the 1960s, in G. Anderson (ed) *The White-blouse Revolution*, pp. 143–69 (Manchester: Manchester University Press).

Hines, R.D. (1992) Accounting: Filling the negative space, *Accounting, Organizations and Society*, 17 (3/4): 313–41.

Hopwood, A. (1987) Accounting and gender: An introduction, *Accounting, Organizations and Society*, 12 (1): 65–69.

Hopwood, A. (1994) Accounting and everyday life: An introduction, *Accounting, Organizations and Society*, 19 (3): 299–301.

Hronsky, J.J.F., Burrows, G.H., and Cobbin, P.E. (2015) A fine education but no 'bluestocking': Harriet Amies, pioneer female accounting professional, *Accounting History*, 20 (2): 118–37.

Hunt, M.R. (1996) *The Middling Sort: Commerce, Gender, and the Family in England 1680–1780* (Berkeley, CA: University of California Press).

Ikin, C., Johns, L., and Hayes, C. (2012) Field, capital and habitus: An oral history of women in accounting in Australia during World War II, *Accounting History*, 17 (2): 175–92.

Jeacle, I. (2006) Face facts: Accounting, feminism and the business of beauty, *Critical Perspectives on Accounting*, 17 (1): 87–108.

Jeacle, I. (2011) A practice of her own: Female career success beyond the accounting firm, *Critical Perspectives on Accounting*, 22 (3): 288–303.

Johns, L. (2006) The first female shareholders of the bank of New South Wales: Examination of shareholdings in Australia's first bank, 1817–1824, *Accounting, Business & Financial History*, 16 (2): 293–314.

Khalifa, R. (2004) Gendered Divisions of Expert Labour: Professional Specialisms in UK Accountancy, PhD Thesis, University of Manchester.

Khalifa, R. (2013) Intra-professional hierarchies: The gendering of accounting specialisms in UK accountancy, *Accounting, Auditing & Accountability Journal*, 26 (8): 1212–45.

Kim, S.M. (2008) Whose voice is it anyway?: Rethinking the oral history method on accounting research on race, ethnicity and gender, *Critical Perspectives on Accounting*, 18 (8): 1346–69.

Kirkham, L.M. (1992) Integrating *her*story and *his*tory in accountancy, *Accounting, Organizations and Society*, 17 (3/4): 287–97.

Kirkham, L.M. and Loft, A. (1993) Gender and the construction of the professional accountant, *Accounting, Organizations and Society*, 18 (6): 507–58.

Kirkham, L.M. and Loft, A. (2001) The lady and the accounts: Missing from accounting history, *Accounting Historians Journal*, 28 (1): 76–90.

Komori, N. (2003) The 'hidden' history of accounting in Japan: A historical examination of the relationship between Japanese women and accounting, *Accounting History*, 12 (3): 329–58.

Komori, N. (2006) Choosing to be Kyapi Yuapi or Gati Gati: The real life experiences of women in the accounting profession in Japan. Paper presented at the 8th Interdisciplinary Perspectives on Accounting, Cardiff.

Komori, N. (2008) Towards the feminization of accounting practice. Lessons from the experiences of Japanese women in the accounting profession, *Accounting, Auditing & Accountability Journal*, 21 (4): 507–38.

Komori, N. (2012a) Visualizing the negative space: Making feminine accounting practices visible by reference to Japanese women's household accounting practices, *Critical Perspectives on Accounting*, 23 (6): 451–67.

Komori, N. (2012b) Women as a driver for social change: Rethinking women's advancement in the accounting profession by reference to their experience in Japan, Paper presented at the 10th Interdisciplinary Perspectives on Accounting Conference, Cardiff.

Komori, N. (2013) From dressmakers to auditors: Restoring women in the history of accounting in Japan. Accounting History International Conference, Seville.

Komori, N. and Humphrey, C. (2000) From an envelope to a dream note and a computer. The award-winning experiences of post-war Japanese household accounting practices, *Accounting, Auditing & Accountability Journal*, 13 (4): 450–74.

Laurence, A. (2006) Women investors, 'That Nasty South Sea Affair' and the rage to speculate in early eighteenth-century England, *Accounting, Business & Financial History*, 16 (2): 245–64.

Lehman, C.R. (1992) Herstory in accounting: The first eighty years, *Accounting, Organizations and Society*, 17 (3/4): 261–85.

Licini, S. (2011) Assessing female wealth in nineteenth century Milan, Italy, *Accounting History*, 16 (1): 35–54.

Lightbody, M.G. (2009) Turnover decisions of women accountants: Using personal histories to understand the relative influence of domestic obligations, *Accounting History*, 14 (1/2): 55–78.

Linn, R. (1996) *Power, Progress & Profit. A History of the Australian Accounting Profession* (Blackwood: Historical Consultants Pty Ltd).

Llewellyn, S. and Walker, S.P. (2000a) Household accounting as an interface activity: The home, the economy and gender, *Critical Perspectives on Accounting*, 11 (4): 447–78.

Llewellyn, S. and Walker, S.P. (2000b) Accounting in the most basic of social and economic institutions – The home, *Accounting, Auditing & Accountability Journal*, 13 (4): 418–24.

Loft, A. (1986) Understanding accounting in its social and historical context: The case of cost accounting in the UK 1914–1925, *Accounting, Organizations and Society*, 11 (2): 137–69.

Loft, A. (1992) Accountancy and the gendered division of labour: A review essay, *Accounting, Organizations and Society*, 17 (3/4): 367–78.

Lord, B. and Robb, A. (2010) Women students and staff in accountancy: The Canterbury Tales, *Accounting History*, 15 (4): 529–58.

Maltby, J. and Rutterford, J. (2006) 'She Possessed Her Own Fortune': Women investors from the late nineteenth century to the early twentieth century, *Business History*, 48 (2): 220–53.

Marshall, R.K. (1983) *Virgins and Viragos – A History of Women in Scotland from 1080–1980* (Chicago, IL: Academy of Chicago Ltd).

Matthews, D. (2016) The social class, educational background, gender and recruitment of American CPAs: An historical profile, *Accounting Historians Journal*, 43 (1): 121–55.

Mayhew, N. (1995) The status of women and the brewing of ale in medieval Aberdeen, *Review of Scottish Culture*, 10: 16–22.

McKeen, C.A. and Richardson, A.J. (1998) Education, employment and certification: An oral history of the entry of women into the Canadian accounting profession, *Business and Economic History*, 27 (2): 500–21.

McNicholas, P., Humphries, M., and Gallhofer, S. (2004) Maintaining the empire: Maori women's experiences in the accountancy profession, *Critical Perspectives on Accounting*, 15 (1): 57–93.

Merino, B. (1998) Critical theory and accounting history: Challenges and opportunities, *Critical Perspectives on Accounting*, 9 (6): 603–16.

Miller, P., Hopper, T., and Laughlin, R. (1991) The new accounting history: An introduction, *Accounting, Organizations and Society*, 16 (5/6): 395–403.

Miller, P. and Napier, C. (1993) Genealogies of calculation, *Accounting, Organizations and Society*, 18 (7/8): 631–48.

Mitchell, C. (2010) Charlotte M. Younge's bank account: A rich new source of information on her work and her life, *Women's Writing*, 17 (2): 380–400.

Napier, C.J. (1991) Aristocratic accounting: The Bute estate in Glamorgan, 1814–1880, *Accounting and Business Research*, 21 (82): 163–74.

Napier, C.J. (2006) Accounts of change: 30 years of historical accounting research, *Accounting, Organizations and Society*, 31 (4/5): 445–507.

Newton, L. and Cottrell, P. (2006) Female investors in the first English and Welsh commercial joint-stock banks, *Accounting, Business & Financial History*, 16 (2): 315–40.

Oldroyd, D. (2003) Feminine context of prehistoric notation systems, *Accounting Historians Notebook*, 26 (2): 23–28.

Oldroyd, D. (2004) "Feminising" prehistory, *Accounting Historians Notebook*, 27 (2): 27–30.

Page, M. and Spira, L.F. (2009) Economia, or a woman in a man's world, *Accounting, Auditing & Accountability Journal*, 22 (1): 146–60.

Parker, R.H. and Yamey, B.S., (eds) (1994) *Accounting History: Some British Contributions* (Oxford: Clarendon Press).

Pillsbury, C.M., Capozzoli, L., and Ciampa, A. (1989) A synthesis of research studies regarding the upward mobility of women in public accounting, *Accounting Horizons*, 3 (1): 63–70.

Previts, G.J., Flesher, D.L., and Sharp, A.D. (2007) Eight special women in accounting, *Journal of Accountancy*, 204 (2): 61–63.

Ramlugun, V.G., Ramdhony, D., and Poornima, B. (2016) An evaluation of household accounting in Mauritius, *International Journal of Accounting and Financial Reporting*, 6 (2): 62–76.

Reid, G.E., Acken, B.T., and Jancura, E.G. (1987) An historical perspective on women in accounting, *Journal of Accountancy*, 163 (5): 338–55.

Roberts, D.H. (2013) Women in accounting occupations in the 1880 US Census, *Accounting History Review*, 23 (2): 141–60.

Roberts, J. and Coutts, J.A. (1992) Feminisation and professionalistion: A review of an emerging literature on the development of accounting in the United Kingdom, *Accounting, Organizations and Society*, 17 (3–4): 379–95.

Rutterford, J., Freen, D., Maltby, J., and Owens, A. (2011) Who comprised the nation of shareholders? Gender and investment in Great Britain, c.1870–1935, *Economic History Review*, 64 (1): 157–87.

Rutterford, J. and Maltby, J. (2006) Frank must marry money: Men, women, and property in Trollope's novels, *Accounting Historians Journal*, 33 (2): 169–99.

Rutterford, J. and Maltby, J. (2007) "The nesting instinct": Women and investment risk in a historical context, *Accounting History*, 12 (3): 305–27.

Schultz, S.M. (2008) The ledger of Ann DeWitt Bevier (1762–1834), early American estate manager and mother, *Accounting Historians Journal*, 35 (1): 135–66.

Scott, J.W. (1986) Gender: A useful category of historical analysis, *American Historical Review*, 91 (5): 1053–75.

Şensoy, F. (2016) The philanthropies of the Sultan's daughter Ayşe Sultan from the beginning of the 17th century, and her WAQF's accounting records, *Accounting & Financial History Research Journal*, 11: 125–68.

Shackleton, K. (1999) Gender segregation in Scottish chartered accountancy: The deployment of male concerns about the admission of women, 1900–25, *Accounting, Business & Financial History*, 9 (1): 135–56.

Silverstone, R. and Williams, A. (1979) Recruitment, training, employment and careers of women chartered accountants in England and Wales, *Accounting and Business Research*, 9 (34): 105–21.

Slocum, E. (1994) Women in accountancy: A reminder of a century past, *Accounting Historians Notebook*, 17 (2): 18–22.

Slocum, E.L. and Vangermeersch, R.G. (1996) A search for Lena E. Mendelsohn, *Accounting Historians Notebook*, 19 (1): 10–11, 22–27.

Smith, C.A. (2005) *Market Women: Black Women Entrepreneurs: Past, Present, and Future* (Westport, CT: Praeger).

Spruill, W.G. and Wootton, C.W. (1995) The struggle of women in accounting: The case of Jennie Palen, pioneer, accountant, historian and poet, *Critical Perspectives on Accounting*, 6 (4): 371–89.

Spruill, W.G. and Wootton, C.W. (1996) Jennie M. Palen, *CPA Journal*, 66 (6): 74–75.

Strom, S.H. (1987) Machines instead of clerks: Technology and the feminization of bookkeeping, 1910–1950, in H.I. Hartmannn (ed) *Computer Chips and Paper Clips: Technology and Women's Employment*, pp. 63–97 (Washington, DC: National Academy Press).

Strom, S.H. (1992) *Beyond the Typewriter: Gender, Class and the Origins of Modern American Office Work 1900–1930* (Urbana, IL: University of Illinois Press).

Thane, P. (1992) The history of the gender division of labour in Britain: Reflections on "'herstory' in accounting: The first eighty years, *Accounting, Organizations and Society*, 17 (3/4): 299–312.

Tinker, T. and Neimark, M. (1987) The role of annual reports in gender and class contradictions at General Motors, 1917–1976, *Accounting, Organizations and Society*, 12 (1): 71–88.

Vickery, A. (1993) Golden age to separate spheres? A review of the categories and chronology of English women's history, *The Historical Journal*, 36 (2): 383–414.

Vickery, A. (1998) *The Gentleman's Daughter: Women's Lives in Georgian England* (London: Yale University Press).

Vigilante, B. (2005) Women at full throttle, *Journal of Accountancy*, 2007 (4): 76–78.

Virtanen, A. (2009) Accounting, gender and history: The life of Minna Canth, *Accounting History*, 14 (1/2): 79–100.

Walker, S.P. (1998) How to secure your husband's esteem. Accounting and private patriarchy in the British middle class household during the nineteenth century, *Accounting, Organizations and Society*, 23 (5/6): 485–514.

Walker, S.P. (2003a) Professionalisation or incarceration? Household engineering, accounting and the domestic ideal, *Accounting, Organizations and Society*, 28 (8): 743–72.

Walker, S.P. (2003b) Identifying the woman behind the "railed-in desk". The proto-feminisation of bookkeeping in Britain, *Accounting, Auditing & Accountability Journal*, 16 (4): 606–39.

Walker, S.P. (2006) Philanthropic women and accounting. Octavia Hill and the exercise of 'quiet power and sympathy', *Accounting, Business & Financial History*, 16 (2): 163–94.

Walker, S.P. (2008) Accounting histories of women: Beyond recovery? *Accounting, Auditing & Accountability Journal*, 21 (4): 580–610.

Walker, S.P. (2011a) Ethel Ayres Purdie: Critical practitioner and suffragist, *Critical Perspectives on Accounting*, 22 (1): 79–101.

Walker, S.P. (2011b) Professions and patriarchy revisited: Accountancy in England and Wales, 1887–1914, *Accounting History Review*, 21 (2): 185–225.

Walker, S.P. and Carnegie, G.D. (2007) Budgetary earmarking and the control of the extravagant woman in Australia 1850–1920, *Critical Perspectives on Accounting*, 18 (2): 233–61.

Walker, S.P. and Llewellyn, S. (2000) Accounting at home: Some interdisciplinary perspectives, *Accounting, Auditing & Accountability Journal*, 13 (4): 425–49.

Wiskin, C. (2006) Businesswomen and financial management: Three eighteenth-century case studies, *Accounting, Business & Financial History*, 16 (2): 143–61.

Wootton, C.W. and Kemmerer, B.E. (1996) The changing genderization of bookkeeping in the United States, 1870–1930, *Business History Review*, 70 (4): 541–86.

Wootton, C.W. and Kemmerer, B.E. (2000) The changing genderization of the accounting workforce in the US, 1930-90, *Accounting, Business & Financial History*, 10 (2), 169–90.

Wootton, C.W. and Spruill, W.G. (1994) The role of women in major public accounting firms in the United States during World War II, *Business and Economic History*, 23 (1): 241–52.

Yapa, P. (2006) Cross-border competition and professionalization of accounting: The case of Sri Lanka, *Accounting History*, 11 (4): 447–73.

22
RACE AND ETHNICITY

Marcia Annisette

Introduction

The chapter gives a synopsis of the ways in which accounting historians have studied the complex interplay between accounting, race and ethnicity. A major objective of the chapter will be to critically assess accounting history's progress in the area, giving particular emphasis to assessing its overall contribution to the socio-scientific study of racial and ethnic phenomena. Motivated by the overall objective of identifying directions for future accounting history research, the chapter will also sketch the broad contours of racial and ethnic studies, highlighting the growing importance of historical research to the field. The chapter will be organised as follows. Its introductory section argues that the increasing salience of racial and ethnic phenomena throughout the modern world calls for greater scholarly attention to the manner in which race and ethnicity have been historically constituted, thereby reinforcing the critical and contemporary significance of historical studies in general and historical studies of racial and ethnic identity construction in particular. Also discussed here is the conceptual distinctiveness between race and ethnicity – two concepts that still are confusingly and interchangeably used by accounting historians. In the second section a review of the small universe of historical research in accounting that takes on race as its central theme is undertaken. The literature is structured around four themes and some of the underdeveloped lines of inquiry within each of these areas are identified. The final section addresses the narrowness of the field of inquiry of race and ethnicity in accounting and points to three shifts of focus which might yield fruitful research outcomes and so enhance accounting history's contribution to the wider study of race and ethnicity.

Race and ethnicity

Race and its conceptual twin ethnicity have without doubt emerged as the most potent of social forces of our times. The Rwandan Genocide of 1994, the 'ethnic cleansing' atrocities that plagued the Balkans during the 1990s, documented increases in anti-Semitism, xenophobia, anti-immigration sentiment and the rise of the extreme right wing and neo-fascist movements in Europe and the United States; the rise of Islamophobia; and a spectacular proliferation in social movements underpinned by the discourse of racial injustice such as the Million Man march, the *banlieues* riots in France and, the Black Lives Matter campaign, are all vivid reminders of the mobilising power of race and ethnic identity and their unquestionable salience as fundamental organising principles in the modern world. Indeed, it is hardly an overstatement to assert that 'almost every aspect of contemporary social and political relations is deeply inflected with a racial or ethnic dimension' (Bulmer and Solomos 1998: 823).

The increased salience of identity politics in modern social life has contributed to a meteoric rise in the prominence of race and ethnic issues in many branches of the academy. Initially confined to the disciplines of sociology, anthropology and history, current interest in race and ethnicity has extended to social geography, political science, political economy, social psychology, language studies, cultural studies, philosophy and archaeology (Bulmer and Solomos 1998: 820). This heightened academic interest in race and ethnic phenomena is not however reflected in historical research in accounting. To date, relatively few accounting historians have broached these topics, and so far, the range of inquiry has remained quite limited. As a consequence, accounting history has contributed little to our contemporary understanding of race and ethnicity. More critically, as explained later, given the very narrow focus of the subject to date, accounting history runs the risk of unintentionally propagating fixed, essentialist notions of race – notions long discredited by social and biological scientists.

The present-day dynamics of race and ethnicity are inextricably linked with historical forces. Sociologists of race and ethnicity point out that the forces associated with modernity and post-modernity – rationalisation, industrialisation, urbanisation, migration and globalisation – have shaped the context in which contemporary ethnic and racial identities are constructed and reconstructed (Bulmer and Solomos 1998: 824; Cornell and Hartmann 1998: xvii). Thus, it is firmly recognised that historical insight is *essential* to a sociological understanding of the racial and ethnic dramas of our times. To this end accounting historians have a vital role to play in illuminating accounting's involvement in the ongoing projects of race and ethnic identity construction.

The idea that race and ethnicity are socially fabricated identities whose construction involves dynamic, ongoing and unfinished projects has now taken root in the social scientific literature (Frankenberg 1993; Nagel 1994; Omi and Winant 1994; Bulmer and Solomos 1998; Cornell and Hartmann 1998; Kibria 1998) and has placed historical work centre stage of inquiry into race and ethnic phenomena. But this has not always been the case. History has not always been seen as central to such understandings. Indeed, it can be argued that for all of the nineteenth century and the early part of the twentieth, the prevailing Social Darwinist concept of race (which, at the time, was not analytically separate from ethnicity) rendered history quite irrelevant to the subject. By the 1920s, however, in what might be characterised as a 'cultural turn', ethnicity emerged as a theoretical construct distinct from race and replaced race as the explanation of human difference (Frankenberg 1993; Omi and Winant 1994). These new understandings stressed that it was culture and not some inherent genetic attribute that was the source of the widespread political and economic disparities between population groups. With its biological basis discredited, race was reconceptualised as a social category, subsumed under ethnicity; and it was ethnicity that drew scholarly attention and elaboration.

Based as it was on common heritage and descent, comprehending ethnicity required a measure of historical engagement. But history's role in shedding light on a sociological understanding of ethnicity remained somewhat limited, for dominating the early social scientific study of ethnicity were adherents to the US assimilation school of sociology whose primary focus was to explain why European immigrant groups (deemed ethnic) had a better assimilation experience in the US than other population groups (deemed racial). Arguing that the non-assimilation of the native African, Asian and Latin American population was a consequence of these groups respective cultures, the assimilation school nonetheless predicted their eventual integration into mainstream US society and the gradual melting away of their distinct racial and ethnic identities. The demise of the assimilation school in the 1960s, the failure of the American melting pot to materialise, as well as the emergence of newly independent post-colonial states with their own brand of post-colonial identity politics, all gave rise to a frenzied search for explanations of the resilience of race and ethnic identity (Nagel 1994; Omi and Winant 1994; Cornell and Hartmann 1998). This search led ultimately to the widespread recognition that history offered a reservoir of insight and understanding of current-day race and ethnic phenomena. There is now little disagreement with the view that answers to critical questions about the construction, maintenance and transformation of racial and ethnic boundaries and meanings cannot be comprehensively addressed without resort to history.

Accompanying the appreciation of history's indispensability to understanding race and ethnic phenomena has been greater conceptual clarity about the nature of race and ethnicity, and their analytical distinctiveness. Few now debate the ontological status of race. Race is variously described as a 'social', 'historical' or 'ideological' construct – a human creation – and not a biological fact. Race refers to a group of people socially defined on the basis of physical characteristics. Race is 'made' through a socially creative process since 'Determining which characteristics constitute the race – the selection of markers and therefore the constructions of racial categories itself is a choice human beings make. Neither markers nor categories are predetermined by any biological factors' (Cornell and Hartmann 1998: 24).

But race would be meaningless were it merely a human creative act. Race derives its social significance because it represents the fault line along which power, prestige and respect are distributed (Dalton 2005: 16). Race, therefore, is tightly fused with hierarchy and power, and as Cornell and Hartmann (1998: 27) remind us, it has been 'first and foremost a way of describing "others" of making clear that "they" are not "us"'. Important therefore to the conceptualisation of race is an understanding that racial categories reflect the externally imposed designations or assignments of dominant groups on others (Kibria 1998).

Sociologists of race have also come to recognise the continuing role of agency in race construction. That is, even though racial identities are initially imposed by dominant groups on subordinate ones, such identities can be inhabited, resisted, transformed or destroyed by the groups subjected to initial racialisation (Bulmer and Solomos 1998: 823; Cornell and Hartmann 1998: 24). This is the ongoing project of race – a process of continuous race making and the reconstitution of racial meanings. It is this final characteristic of race that brings it closer to ethnicity, thus giving rise to some scholarly fusing of the concepts.

Although in some contexts the outcomes of racial and ethnic phenomena are the same (e.g. inequality, conflict or genocide), there is general agreement that the two concepts are distinct. It is generally assumed that ethnicity is not based on *physical* characteristics. Rather, it is based on notions of common ancestry – memories of a shared past and common symbolic elements of culture, whether real or putative (Cornell and Hartmann 1998: 19). Further, in contradistinction to race, ethnicity is usually initiated as an act of 'self' assertion – the assertions of group members themselves. In short, while race is a way of *otherising*, ethnicity is a way of *asserting distinctiveness*.

Despite their conceptual dissimilarity, it is in the sphere of ongoing identity (re) construction that racial and ethnic processes overlap. Cornell and Hartmann (1998: 30) state:

> Ethnic and racial categories may be delineated first by others, but when groups begin to fill those categories with their own content, telling their own histories in their own ways and putting forth their own claims to what their identities signify, then they are engaged in a classics construction of ethnicity. When a racial group sets out to construct its own version of its identity, it makes itself both race and ethnic group at once.

Before turning to the following section it is important to summarise the fairly uncontested commonalities between race and ethnicity. First, is the widespread understanding that they are not natural phenomena but are 'made' by human beings. Second, is the recognition that they are shaped by agency as well as structure. That is, although social groups do participate in altering racial/ethnic boundaries and meanings, the choices open to the group are not infinite, but are structurally bounded (Bashi 1998: 962; Nagel 1994: 152). Third, as socially constructed identities, race and ethnicity are defined by historical and political struggles over meaning and can thus be seen as 'social and political resources used by both dominant and subordinate groups for the purposes of legitimizing and furthering their own social identities and interests' (Bulmer and Solomos 1998: 823).

Exploring accounting and race: general themes

Explorations of the interplay between race and accountancy are relatively recent and largely linked to the emergence and development of what is now widely known as the 'new accounting history' (Miller et al. 1991; Carmona et al. 2004; Napier 2006). The new accounting history is an approach which, among other things, seeks to understand accounting in the broader context in which it operates. Emanating from the call for more research on the interrelationships between race and accountancy (Hammond and Streeter 1994: 285), the historical studies that have so far been undertaken in accounting can be placed in five broad areas.[1] First, studies of accounting in settings characterised by racial oppression and exploitation; second, accounting and accountants in the context of genocide; third, racial processes in the accounting profession; fourth, studies of accounting in societies deeply structured by race; and fifth, historical studies that aim to make a methodological contribution to interrogating race. In what follows, the studies falling within these areas are introduced and their dominant themes discussed.

Accounting practice in settings characterised by racial oppression and exploitation

Much of the research falling in this area is associated with the work of Richard Fleischman and his co-authors, Thomas Tyson and David Oldroyd. Theirs has been a collaboration that departs from other historical accounting research which, though situated in settings characterised by extreme racial oppression and exploitation, makes no mention of, or value judgments about, the contexts within which accounting operates (Flesher and Flesher 1981; Razek 1985; Heier 1988; Cowton and O'Shaughnessy 1991; Barney and Flesher 1994; Donoso-Anes 2002; Vollmers 2003; McWatters 2008; McWatters and Lemarchand 2009; Newson 2013). Indeed, concerned as they are with the economics of slavery, the works cited above are completely silent on the issue of race and, consistent with what has come to be seen as a defining characteristic of traditional accounting history, depict an image of accounting as a value-free assemblage of techniques that contributes to the achievement of rational economic ends.[2]

In their inaugural attempt to break with this tradition, Fleischman and Tyson (2000: 10) suggested that 'an important facet of accounting history is to investigate the degree to which accounting records are reflective of the times'. Their aim therefore is to explore the social context surrounding slavery and other situations of racial exploitation by studying the historical traces left by accounting. Thus in their first paper, they explore the accounting–race nexus through an examination of the plantation records of a Hawaiian sugar plantation during the period 1835–1920. Staying true to their traditional accounting history roots, Fleischman and Tyson offer a rich descriptive account of the form and content of the plantation accounting books, giving much insight into the organisation of plantation labour. The accounting records reveal that plantation labour was classified by 'ethnic group rather than by occupational function, productivity or any other measuring calculus' (2000: 22) – an observation which becomes the central problematic of the paper. In their view the absence of accounting records on individual productivity indicates that it was 'ethnicity' rather than economic rationality which served as the primary measuring calculus for determining worker wages and wage differentials on the plantation. This claim immediately provoked a debate between the authors and Geoff Burrows (Burrows 2002; Fleischman and Tyson 2002), one that was also later taken up by Dyball and Rooney (2012) whose evidence elaborated and supported that of Burrows (2002) and questioned the interpretations of Fleischman and Tyson (2000, 2002).[3] Nonetheless, Fleischman and Tyson's pioneering attempt to interrogate accounting beyond the insights it could offer on the economics of slavery subsequently inspired a number of rich historical studies (Tyson et al. 2004; McWatters and Lemarchand 2006; Heier 2010; Hollister and Schultz 2010; Stewart 2010; Fleischman et al. 2011; Pinto and West 2017a, 2017b; Tyson and Oldroyd 2019; Baker 2019), which, based on the notion that accounting records are reflective of their times, have used such records to reveal the horrors of slavery and other forms of racial oppression and exploitation. One can also include within this group the investigations by Adams and McPhail (2004) and Hammond et al. (2017), both of which are longitudinal studies of corporate reporting practices that show how such practices reflected the broader sociopolitical context of the times, including changes in a state's approach to the race problematic and changing political discourses and ideologies about race in the UK (Adams and McPhail 2004) and apartheid South Africa (Hammond et al. 2017).

Fleischman and Tyson also pioneered another vein of research in settings characterised by racial exploitation and oppression, namely by going beyond the depiction of accounting as a passive reflector of 'the times' and instead take on a bolder, more critical stance which seeks to illustrate the supportive if not constitutive role played by accounting in extreme racial oppression and exploitation. In Fleischman and Tyson (2004) for instance they examine the records of a number of plantations in the antebellum South to discern the accounting representation of slaves and their activities during the mid-nineteenth century. Their extensive tracking of slave productivity records and careful analysis of slave valuations reveal much about plantation and slave life; but their overriding aim here is to expose accounting as an active participant in the enterprise of slavery. In summarising their archival investigation, the authors point out that 'slave workers were categorised, enumerated and valued with complete disregard for their humanity' (Fleischman and Tyson 2004: 393). This, they suggest, attests to accounting's complicity in bolstering slavery, for it was 'used to convert qualitative human attributes into a limited number of discrete categories (age, sex, colour) that could be differentiated and monetized in order to facilitate commercial slave trading' (Fleischman and Tyson 2004: 393).

Fleischman and Tyson subsequently collaborated with British accounting historian David Oldroyd and extended their investigation to include British West Indian plantations, thereby producing a comparative study of the reasons, processes and methodologies behind slave valuations on US and British West Indian plantations (Fleischman et al. 2004). Although at times they seem less confident in their indictment of accounting as a co-conspirator in slavery, the authors conclude that 'the further we delve into the archives and learn about particular accounting techniques like valuation, the more certain we become in asserting that accounting was instrumental in sustaining slavery's institutions and basic practices' (2004: 57). This theme of accounting's culpability in promoting and sustaining slavery has been recently picked up by Rodrigues and Craig (2018) and Rodrigues et al. (2015) who, focusing on Brazil, study government accounting and taxation practices as they related to slave transactions. The authors argue that such practices encouraged a structural inertia in Brazil, which in turn served to reify and institutionalise the practice of slavery in the country. On this score, Oldroyd et al. (2008) strike a more equivocal tone, suggesting that while accounting could be considered morally unjust in its support of slavery, it was to play a more positive role later on by facilitating the decision to abolish the institution in the British colonies. It did so, they argue, by establishing incentives for abolition, policing the process and implementing compensation schemes. They therefore argue for a more 'even handed' depiction of accounting, seeing it as a powerful tool of both racial exploitation/ oppression as well as emancipation and the liberation of racially oppressed peoples.[4]

Fleischman and his collaborators have also examined accounting in the immediate aftermath of racial slavery. In Fleischman et al. (2014) and Oldroyd et al. (2018), through an examination of the accounting functions of the Freedmen's Bureau, they consider whether accounting served the forces of racial oppression or worked against such forces during what they term the 'virginal period' of American Reconstruction (Fleischman et al. 2014: 76). In Tyson et al. (2005) they focus their attention on the 'apprenticeship period' (1834–1838) in the British West Indies. In the case of American Reconstruction, they provide evidence suggesting that accounting as it operated in the Freedmen's Bureau bore elements of both. This however seemed not to be the case in the British West Indies where 'apprenticeship' was a period of transition, marking the conversion of African slave labour into free waged labour. As the authors note, apprenticeship 'represented an attempt to sustain colonial plantation economies by getting freedmen accustomed to work for wages, to accept the practice as normal and to become willing waged workers' (Tyson et al. 2005: 204). The problem however was that given a choice, it was not clear that freed slaves would willingly offer their labour services to plantation owners. Indeed, there was a general belief that they would flee the plantations for the open lands. Tyson et al. suggest that in such a context, a punitive regime rather than one based on market incentives was needed to keep the former slaves on the plantations. And it was in the operation of such that accounting became central. Noting that 'the corporal punishment meted out on the basis of accounting evidence remained the ultimate deterrent for non-compliant work', Tyson et al. (2005: 227) conclude that accounting's functioning as a coercive weapon rested on the fact that it provided the documentary evidence to support the practice of the punitive regime. In a sense, therefore, the paper suggests that accounting was part and parcel of a new system of violence enacted on the former slaves. Whereas previously planters could use the whip to compel work effort, during apprenticeship the detailed records that were kept to document absences, work effort and contract violations, reflected a different but similarly effective regime of violence to ensure control and domination.

The strength of the studies produced by Fleischman, Tyson and their collaborators, as well as many of the subsequent studies patterned along these lines, is in their pioneering attempts to weld onto traditional accounting history the concerns of 'new' accounting historians. This strength is also its weakness, for these studies remain steadfastly committed to their traditional roots and fail to exploit the full potential for pursuing new accounting histories of these sites. Three principal criticisms may be identified. First, these studies are firmly grounded in the past – the past is seen as interesting for its own sake and there is no probing of how the insights gained connect to issues relevant to our times. Indeed, there is even a presumption that there is no such connection. In a 2004 reflection of his scholarly journey Fleischman (2004: 15) speculated that critical accountants have ignored slave plantation sites because 'slavery is too historical; that is it cannot be linked to a contemporary issue'.[5] However sociologists of race widely acknowledge the undeniable link between the current racial bases of US society and that country's experience with its 'peculiar institution'. So interrogating accounting in these sites does have the potential to provide deeper understanding of contemporary issues surrounding race and ethnicity. For instance, recognising that race is key to a system of cultural representation (Omi and Winant 1994), it becomes possible to interrogate how and the extent to which plantation accounting representations of African slave populations are linked to contemporary meanings/representations of the race, black or African. Further, one might interrogate the links between these slave valuation practices and other calculative practices involving the representation of human populations (such as the US census rule that required blacks be represented as three-fifths white for the purpose of representation), which in turn contribute to shared and enduring understandings of racial meanings.

A second criticism of these studies is that they remain firmly grounded in the notion of accounting as an agent of rational economic decision-making. There is an over-riding concern to explain the presence or absence of forms of accounting in economic rationalistic terms. But the focus of 'new' accounting historians is on the 'structure and uses of accounting information for control and even coercion, rather than as a mere input into a rational decision-making process' (Carnegie and Napier 1996: 9). Thus, in the context of racial slavery, where control/coercion of slave populations is guaranteed by authorised regimes of violence both at micro and macro levels, the potentially coercive/control role of plantation accounting is doubtlessly usurped, and understandably there is little on offer to new accounting historians in this respect. But while plantation records might not be particularly useful in rendering insight to accounting as an instrument of coercion/control, they may nonetheless provide informing glimpses into racialisation processes in context.

For instance, spatial variability in racial categorisation is well established. In Brazil race is primarily determined by appearance; in the US it is established by descent. As a result, whereas in Brazil a white person might have black ancestors (Bailey and Telles 2006: 76), in the US, the 'one drop' or *hypodescent* rule precludes this (Davis 1991; Kibria 1998: 941; Kolchin 2002). Moreover, it is well known that the criteria for racial designations follow no uniform logic – the *hypodescent* rule that applies to blacks in the US did not hold for Native Americans (James 2001) who were classified on the basis of percentage blood. This rule was probably devised to minimise land claims associated with native land treaty rights. Examples such as these point to a close relationship between asset management activities and the construction of racial boundaries and thus have the potential to reveal the impact of accounting and/or financial measures on racial construction.

A third criticism of traditional accounting history's exploration of the race–accounting nexus is its failure to engage with the theoretical literature on race. This failure, often reflected in the imprecise deployment of terms such as race, ethnicity and racism, has stymied the potential of such studies to better contribute to an understating of the resilience of racial phenomena in contemporary society. Crucial here is the tendency for these studies to treat race as a given. By ignoring the fact that race is not a fixed concept spatially or temporally, these studies have missed an important opportunity to expose the variety of roles that accounting might have played during racial slavery – the period generally accepted as formative for race making.[6]

Accounting and accountants in the context of genocide

Genocide, the systematic and deliberate destruction of a people, is the most tragic conclusion of a society's racialisation processes. The frequency and intensity of genocidal events became one of the most defining characteristics of the twentieth century and none has been subject to more scholarly enquiry than the Jewish Holocaust. Although a considerable amount of historical scholarship has focused attention on the enabling roles of the German professional class and expert knowledge systems in realising the diabolical Nazi dream, the culpability of accountants and accountancy long remained under-scrutinised. That was until the powerful and pioneering study by Funnell (1998) which set out to show that accounting was a potent weapon of the Nazi state bureaucracy for enacting what they termed 'the final solution of the Jewish question'. The study is primarily (though not exclusively) focused on the enabling power of accounting techniques in the service of the Holocaust. According to Funnell (1998), the Nazi annihilation of the Jewish people not only involved their physical extermination but also the alienation, appropriation and disposal of their wealth. Accounting and accountants were deeply implicated in all these activities.

By constructing the extermination of the Jews as an efficiency problem, the way was paved for enlisting accounting. As an enabling technology, accounting served to convert people into things and so ensured that millions of Jews were moved over great distances to their ultimate fate at the lowest cost possible. Accounting also acted to distance the acts of annihilation from those who made such acts possible. Accordingly, the aggregation, reductionism and anonymity of accounting numbers meant that:

> [p]eople who had no direct involvement in the murder of millions of Jews were able to divorce themselves from the objectives and consequences of their work … Jews passed the point where they were objectified to where they were *numerised*: they were numbers and little else.
>
> *(Funnell 1998: 437, 459)*

There was also an elaborate system of accounting procedures that accompanied the sequestration of Jewish property. In this regard accounting performed purifying and redemptive functions. As a purifier it served the dual roles of purging Jewish wealth of what the Nazis considered was its inherently corrupt nature. At the same time it cleansed the Nazi handlers of Jewish property of any 'impure motives' thus avoiding their contamination by the difficult tasks that the Jews had 'forced' upon them (Funnell 1998: 458). In its redemptive role, rigorous accounting procedures allowed the Nazi state to act with a clear conscience, for it demonstrated that the acts which produced the property were not guided by motives of avarice or material gain but instead were the outcome of the (ig)noble mission of purifying the 'German race'.

Funnell (1998) suggests that accounting can become captive to such horrendous regimes because it constitutes the core of functional reasoning. In addition, he suggests that it is the blend of two of accounting's acknowledged characteristics – its ability to render visibility and its inherent partiality – which makes it an enabling technology. By being inherently partial, accounting renders visibility to some things and invisibility to others – the latter, having at once been rendered invisible, runs the risk of becoming valueless. Such was the case with the humanity of the Jews. Accounting's utility and indeed its power in this context therefore rested on its ability to 'supplant the qualitative dimensions of the Jews as individuals by commodifying and dehumanizing them and therefore making them invisible as people' (Funnell 1998: 439). In short, through accounting, the Jews ceased to exist as human beings.

Turning to the culpability of German accounting practitioners, Funnell makes it clear that professional accounting expertise was essential to all stages of the extermination and wealth appropriation activities. Referring to Kohlberg's schema of morality he argues that accountants acted at the level of conventional morality. Funnell compares this with the highest level of morality – principled morality wherein persons are prepared to stand against laws and orders that contravene natural justice – and concludes that based on the evidence, such behaviour 'was not a feature of the practice of accounting in relation to the Jews throughout the Holocaust' (Funnell 1998: 437).

In their examination of Germany's slave labour operations, Lippmann and Wilson (2007) more directly tackle the issue of accountants' culpability in the Holocaust. They point out that during World War II, Nazi state-controlled enterprises and a number of prominent German companies made extensive use of prison slaves in their operations (among whom were Jews originally held in concentration camps). The practice was voluntary, widespread and yielded the highest returns to the enterprises involved, for, unlike ancient slaves who were treated in a manner to protect their value, 'German corporations and state controlled enterprises provided little to protect the concentration camp slaves' (Lippmann and Wilson 2007: 6). The authors reveal how accountants brought their knowledge and training to bear to ensure that these facilities were well run and that every aspect of Jewish internment and death was cost effective and profitable. In confronting the question of accountants' culpability, they note that the accountants involved in slave labour operations, as well as their peers in the wider society, were aware of the institutionalised discrimination and genocidal activities against the Jews.[7]

Indeed, one of the earliest casualties of Hitler's reign was the takeover of the German accountancy profession, which, in 1937, voluntarily relinquished its autonomy to become an arm of the Nazi state. Lippmann and Wilson (2007) argue that at this time the profession had just come into being and had not begun to grapple with ethical issues and standards. They raise the highly debatable issue of whether adherence to an ethical code is a sufficient basis for judging ethical behaviour and explore a number of logics to answer the question of accountants' culpability. Though not providing a clear answer, the authors suggest that it is worth considering the principle set forth by the rulings of the International Military Tribunal: participants in a system that make a crime possible are deemed as culpable as the perpetrators of the crime. By this standard it would seem likely that the answer to the question of accountants' culpability in what can only be considered to be the darkest episode of twentieth-century history is indisputably clear.

Whereas the above-mentioned studies indicate that by their acquiescence, German accountants acted only at the level of conventional morality and so contributed to the Jewish Holocaust, Walker's (2000) study reveals that this behaviour was not limited to accountants in Germany. In examining British accountants' relationship to the Nazi regime, Walker reveals that rather than rejecting the latter's advances, the British accounting elite acted in accordance with the UK government policy of appeasement. This posture inadvertently turned the most senior members of the British accounting establishment into effective propaganda machines for the Nazi regime (albeit briefly), as was evidenced by glowing tributes to the German state in all of the top professional journals of the time – *The Accountants' Magazine*, *The Accountant*, *Accountancy* and *The Certified Accountant*. Walker's study is a fascinating account of the propaganda effects of international events and how one such event in accounting – the Fifth International Congress on Accounting in Berlin, 1938 – could support the Nazi racist totalitarian state. As Walker points out, fascist regimes encourage international events for two reasons. First, to demonstrate their international credibility to domestic constituencies, and second, to proselytise their virtues to foreigners who would return home and proselytise on their behalf. With respect to meeting this second objective Walker's study reveals that the Nazi aspiration for the Fifth International Congress on Accounting was successfully achieved.

Walker (2000) shows that in the months immediately preceding the Congress there was increasing evidence that the mistreatment of Jews was escalating. But this did not feature in British accountants' deliberations about whether or not to attend the event. Instead it was only the fear of their personal safety that caused them to doubt. Walker could find no evidence of any 'principled stance against a regime that was clearly involved in morally reprehensible activities' (2000: 223). Thus with assurances that their personal safety was not at risk, the elite of the British accountancy establishment, comprising top functionaries of the professional institutes and practising firms, converged on Germany for the Fifth International Congress on Accounting with the overriding objective of appeasing and placating their Nazi hosts and thereby not jeopardising their expansionary projects in Europe.

Accountants played an even more direct role in the Highland clearances in Scotland during the mid-nineteenth century – a project aimed at purging the country of surplus population and dissolving the Gaelic traditional way of life. Walker's examination of the Highland clearances debunks the notion that the active agents in this episode of ethnic cleansing were 'absolutist landlords impatient to exploit the economic potential of their estates' (2003: 819). Instead, it was Edinburgh's most prominent accountants, acting in their roles as trustees on insolvent estates, who were the prime movers. In the face of overpopulation, falling agricultural prices and substantial rent arrears from tenants, many Highland estates became insolvent. Walker shows that with the single-minded pursuit of debt recovery, Edinburgh's accountants displayed no compunction in ordering the eviction of the most vulnerable members of the community. Those evicted faced extreme hardship and even death, yet the accountant-trustees remained impassive and unaffected by the accompanying human tragedy. Indeed it would seem that it was this aloofness that rendered the accountant appropriate for the job – an aloofness made more reprehensible when one considers that unlike German accountants, Edinburgh accountants had direct and personal contact with the victims of their actions.

In conclusion, therefore, the above studies reveal the moral bankruptcy of accountants and their institutions when confronted with matters involving social justice. To a large extent accounting institutions have been content to argue that they are powerless to bring about change in social ills as deep rooted as racism. They often argue that through their 'merit' based system of access and opportunity they represent some degree of moral progress over pre-existing racial orders. The following group of studies suggests the contrary – accounting institutions represent some of the most impregnable citadels of racial discrimination, bias and privilege.

Racial processes in the accounting profession

Appearing on the heels of a string of studies focusing on the exclusion of white women from the practice of accountancy, Hammond and Streeter (1994) broke new ground by extending the enquiry of those excluded from the profession to include racial groups. In presenting the oral histories of some of the first African Americans licensed as Certified Public Accountants (CPAs), Hammond and Streeter (1994) represented the first attempt to incorporate the theme of race into accounting history's research agenda. With opening lines revealing that in 1965 African Americans constituted 12 per cent of the American population yet only represented 0.1 per cent of the CPA population (then determined to be 100,000), Hammond and Streeter declared their purpose – to give visibility to a group whose history had, until then, not only been silenced and ignored but also seriously distorted. The group referred to were the minuscule number of African Americans who had succeeded in achieving their professional qualifications prior to the passage of the Civil Rights Act 1964 – the US law which outlawed racial discrimination in employment.

Based on a series of interviews with the surviving members of this group, Hammond and Streeter (1994) reveal the extraordinary measures taken by early pioneers to obtain their CPA status.[8] In various ways they succeeded in subverting a system deliberately designed to exclude African Americans from the opportunity to practise as accountants. Many state CPA societies debarred 'Negroes' from sitting the exam. Most required a prospective CPA to serve a period of apprenticeship with a licensed practitioner. And others, like Texas, restricted memberships 'to whites only'. All of the personal histories illustrate an admixture of unusual circumstances, extreme hardship and dogged persistence. Yet these were the histories of those who triumphed over harsh conditions and monumental obstacles 'despite the benefit of family wealth, academic excellence, light skin color, and mobility' (Hammond and Streeter 1994: 285). Hammond and Streeter speculate that others – the many who aspired to, but did not become CPAs – faced even more daunting obstacles.

Hammond and Streeter's work represents a powerful counterbalance to the many hagiographic accounts that celebrate the US profession as a historically positive force in a society deeply structured by race. But the setting of their paper is the pre-civil rights era – a time in which the US legal and institutional environment was still structured so as to exclude the African American from participating in wider American society; a period when white America and indeed the white world had still not arrived at the state of human enlightenment in which non-white others were seen to be equals. And so it could be argued that the obstacles constructed by the US accountancy profession and revealed in Hammond and Streeter (1994) were in fact a reflection of a wider state of ignorance and not of accountancy's inherent biases per se. Later studies (Hammond 1997; Annisette 2003; Kim 2004a, 2004b) would completely demolish this argument.

Hammond (1997) examines the profession's commitment to equal opportunity employment in the post-civil rights era. The study's focal period is 1965 (the year in which the Civil Rights Act 1964 became effective) to 1988 (the year in which the administration of President Ronald Reagan came to a close) and tests Edelman's thesis on the institutionalisation of organisational responses to public expectations. Hammond's insightful analysis shows that during the 1970s public accounting firms responded emphatically to changes in the legal environment, progressing from a policy of the complete exclusion of African Americans from the profession to making some visible efforts to recruit from this population. But she also shows how these efforts had waned dramatically by the 1980s. The American Institute of Certified Public Accountants de-emphasised many of the programmes it had adopted in the 1970s, recruitment and retention of African Americans (which had peaked in the 1970s) showed significant declines, and there was a drastic reduction in the number of articles discussing African Americans in the accounting industry's publications. Contrary to Edelman's predictions, Hammond (1997) thus concludes that the measures introduced by the profession in the 1970s did not proliferate or persist. Indeed, they appeared to be only token gestures aimed at giving the impression of change. Thus even though African American membership had climbed during the 1970s, by 1990 African Americans still only represented less than 1 per cent of the CPAs in the country – a statistic that according to Annisette et al. (2006) has remained relatively unchanged to date.

That the profession of accountancy in the US has historically taken on the character of a white-only space finds resonance with the case of British professional bodies during the era of the British Empire. Here, Poullaos (2009) shows how demands for entry into British professional bodies by racialised colonial subjects provoked a racist backlash from British accountants in the imperial centre. In particular, Poullaos shows that after explicit efforts were made to exclude non-whites from the profession, accountants in the imperial centre devised an implicit barrier that would navigate the contradiction of their racialist attitudes and their discourses of non-discrimination.

In contrast to the aforementioned studies which illustrate minority exclusion and under-representation in the profession, Annisette (2003) reveals majority exclusion and under-representation in the accountancy profession of Trinidad and Tobago (T&T) – a country in which the populations of African and East Indian descent represent 80 per cent of the total, yet only 33 per cent of partners of elite accounting practices represent these two groups (Annisette 2003: 640). The paper covers a 30-year trajectory of the development of the accountancy profession and culminates with the case of the ejection of the MSc Accounting credential from the Institute of Chartered Accountants of Trinidad and Tobago (ICATT) during the 1980s. For Annisette, it is the enduring legacy of racialism in the development of the profession that explains how race became enrolled in debates about accounting training.

According to Annisette, during T&T's colonial period, accountancy was associated with 'Britishness' and 'whiteness' (Annisette 2003: 651), reflecting a common-sense understanding in the country that linked race and ethnicity to different forms of work. By the 1950s only 6 of the country's 26 professionally qualified accountants were locals and none of these represented the country's two major population groups. The remaining 20 were British expatriates. Annisette demonstrates that exclusion from the profession was only *one* aspect of racialisation processes in accountancy. Others included the racialisation of accountancy credentials and the racialisation of accounting worksites. She argues that the tight coupling of race, worksite and accountancy credentials served to reinforce and widen existing status gaps between the dichotomous groups in the T&T profession, thus rendering race a powerful marker for status differentials within the practice of accountancy (Annisette 2003: 654). When the ICATT – an institution dominated by British expatriate accountants – failed to admit into its membership holders of the MSc Accounting credential (a credential exclusively held by Afro and Indo Trinidadians), this was seen as a racially motivated act. Annisette contrasts the ICATT's rejection of the MSc Accounting with its recognition of the Canadian-based Certified Management Accounting credential and concludes that the contrasting fates of these two credentials in the ICATT might not have been the outcome of racial processes. She argues, however, that because race so strongly coincides with credentials, worksite and professional status in the organisation of accountancy in T&T, the perceived role of race in the occupational dynamics of the profession is over-signified leading to the enlistment of race in what otherwise might be a technical issue.

Subsequent work which has examined exclusion and under-representation of the majority population in the profession include the insightful studies by Hammond and her collaborators which documents the exclusion of the native black population from the ranks of the South African profession (Hammond et al. 2009, 2012) and Sian's (2007) work on racial exclusion in the profession in Kenya.

Kim's (2004a, 2004b) studies of the experiences of Chinese accountants in the New Zealand profession attempts to broaden a literature that is overly focused on a black/white dichotomy. According to Kim the Chinese represent a unique racialised group in that they are often culturally different from both the indigenous population and members of the dominant group, thus forming 'a middle-man' class (Kim 2004a: 98, 126). In the case of New Zealand the Chinese were introduced to satisfy labour shortages in a society already structured on racial/ethnic lines. They thus suffered racial discrimination and hostility from both the dominant white population as well as the indigenous population. Based on interviews with 17 Chinese accountants in Auckland, Kim argues that whereas the accountancy profession seems to have been less exclusionary towards the Chinese than any other profession in New Zealand, the lack of upward mobility within professional practices created a situation where Chinese are 'clustered at the bottom of the hierarchy in the profession' (Kim 2004a: 111, 120). Although she does briefly mention some structural factors, Kim largely attributes the strong presence of Chinese in accountancy to cultural factors. In particular, 'Chinese culture places great emphasis on education' (Kim 2004a: 107) and, even more controversially, inherent attributes of 'Asian ethnicity that tend to have a logical mindset' (Kim 2004a: 107). Kim notes however that Chinese accountants in New Zealand experience the corporate glass ceiling and provides cultural explanations for this: 'quietness, prudence, humility, humbleness, or modesty' (Kim 2004a: 116). According to Kim, Chinese accept the glass ceiling as a fact of life 'Having been brought up to be submissive and servile to their superior White counterparts, they have learned to accept their second-class citizen status within society rather than challenging it' (2004a: 115). A similar theme of successful entry to the profession followed by limited upward mobility is articulated in Kim (2004b). This study is based on indepth interviews with five Chinese Auckland-based female accountants and analyses the intersection of race and gender in the profession. Relying less on essentialist and cultural explanations in this case, Kim's overall conclusion is that the Chinese have been constructed as different in New Zealand society and that the 'politics of difference' (Kim 2004b: 95–6) has been successfully used to keep them in their place.

While the above research focuses specifically on the enactment of racial phenomena in accountancy, other historical studies of the profession relating to Kenya (Sian 2006), Malaysia (Susela 1999) and Jamaica (Bakre 2005, 2006) point to a not insignificant racial dimension in the profession's development in those sites.

Studies of accounting in societies deeply structured by race

Apartheid South Africa represents the extreme case of a society structured by race and this is the context for Hammond et al.'s (2017) study. While their examination of 59 years of annual reports of the Anglo-American Corporation demonstrates how these reports reflected the dominant ideology of the times, the authors also highlight the complicity of annual reports in disguising oppression, defining annual reports in this context as 'weapons in ideological conflict' (Hammond et al. 2017: 1401). Importantly, their analysis draws attention to the paradox of accounting and accounting reports, namely that while their ideological underpinnings render them 'documents of disguise', at the same time, by being inscribed with the traces and priorities of capitalism, they represent a valuable resource for a critical interrogation and unmasking of corporations' diabolical racial pasts.

While apartheid South Africa stands out as the extreme case of a society deeply structured by race, there are other lesser-known instances of such countries. These are the many countries in where the legacies of British colonialism (and sugar production) have produced racially stratified societies in which the racialised groups 'mixed but did not combine' (Furnivall 1968). Having attained independence, the post-colonial states in these sites usually took an active role in refashioning the nature of racial interaction. Many such states have adopted strategies aimed at protecting or promoting certain groups who were perceived to have suffered prior economic, social and political disadvantage. But as Cornell and Hartmann (1998: 156–8) point out, regardless of the intent, these strategies often serve to heighten racial tension. Such has been the case in Fiji – a country deeply divided by race and where accounting has often been enrolled in racial projects. The legacy of colonialism and sugar has produced in Fiji a racial mosaic comprising native peoples (Fijians and Rotumans, collectively described in the studies below as Ethnic or indigenous Fijians), Indo-Fijians (descendants of East Indian indentured labourers) and a host of racial others including Chinese, Pacific Islanders and Europeans. Currently, Ethnic Fijians constitute 50 per cent of the island's population and Indo-Fijians represent 43 per cent. The focus of historical accounting research on this site concerns the use of accounting in affirmative action programmes that privilege Ethnic Fijians over Indo-Fijians.

For Nandan and Alam (2005) and Davie (2005), the notion that Ethnic Fijians – the group in whose interest affirmative action initiatives are directed – represent an economically disadvantaged group is contestable. However, indigenous privileging and protectionism governs almost every aspect of life in Fiji. For instance, it is evident in a constitutionally enshrined land tenure system that ensures that most of the country's land is owned by Fijians. It is also evident in a series of affirmative action programmes.

Race is therefore embroiled in almost every aspect of Fijian life, and in many instances, accounting is called upon to adjudicate the racial contests that often arise. Nandan and Alam (2005) assert that the accounting calculus used for determining rental income in the land tenure system 'is firmly implicated and intertwined in the process of wealth accumulation to promote the interests of the Fijian chiefly class' (2005: 19). In the Special Loans Division of the Fiji Development Bank, management accounting decision-making criteria were tweaked so as to provide a lower threshold of eligibility for Ethnic Fijian borrowers. And at the Ministry of Agriculture accounting procedures were installed to provide an aura of order and propriety over the inappropriate granting of loans to, and spending of money on, Ethnic Fijians (Nandan and Alam 2005).

Davie (2005: 557) labels these exclusionary practices as *development racism* – racist exclusion ostensibly for developmental purposes – and in her study of the restructuring of Fiji's pine industry identified three roles played by accounting in facilitating the development racism project. First, accounting expertise masked the political nature of indigenous privilege, giving it a semblance of neutrality. Second, accounting provided the means of acquiring a new knowledge base to facilitate discriminatory indigenous development. Third, accounting initiated a new way of expressing ethnic difference.

These studies make an important contribution to extant accounting history research on race and ethnicity in that they depart from the common black/white dichotomy that so overwhelms much of US research. In so doing, they affirm that there are a variety of bases over which racial politics are played out and suggest a need to broaden the scope of accounting history to incorporate this variety. In addition, these studies attempt to link historical processes of racialisation to contemporary racial and ethnic phenomena. Importantly, this research also serves to highlight the role of exclusionary practices in mobilising action, which in turn, ignites racial projects or reinforces racial boundaries. Unfortunately, these studies presume a certain pre-givenness of race or ethnicity and so fail to probe more comprehensively accounting's role in the processes in which racial and ethnic identities are reproduced and transformed. For instance, the lumping together of Fijians and Rotumans under the banner of 'Fijians' masks the constructed as well as the contested nature of 'Fijian' as ethnos.[9] What is lost therefore is the important role of these exclusionary practices (of which accounting is part) in (re)defining and (re)constituting the 'us' from the 'them'. That is, the function of rules of exclusion in constructing and solidifying the identity 'Indo-Fijian', and equally, the function of rules of inclusion in constructing and solidifying the boundary of who is 'Fijian'.

Studies on race with a methodological message

Because of the theoretically fraught nature of race, and in particular unsettled debates about who should study race, how it should be studied and indeed, whether the term itself should be deployed in research, studies of race and racialism in accounting history have been conducted with a view to making methodological contributions to the discipline. For example, because oral history has been touted as a powerful method to give voice to racialised others who have been silenced by hegemonic forces, some critical attention has been drawn to the limits of this method. Thus, in their analysis of the publication *Experiences in Transformation: Work in Progress* (published by a white-owned South African CA firm), Hammond et al. (2007) show how the firm portrayed a partial and fragmented account of the South African past which diminished the deep social and economic divisions that apartheid created. They highlight the potential of oral history in encouraging forgetting by selectively preserving memory, which according to Annisette et al. (2006) serves as a clear warning that oral history's much-celebrated potential to present the experiences of the marginalised and oppressed can be easily subverted when employed by oppressor groups to produce a distorted view of those experiences.

Kim's (2008) critique of the method goes even further, highlighting its potential for co-optation by dominant groups. Instead oral history has important implications for theory, practice and praxis by, first, pointing to its ethnocentric bias which, she argues, serves to perpetuate and reify Westocentric social categories such as race. Second, from a power perspective she argues that the method does nothing to confront the asymmetrical relationship between the privileged researcher and the disenfranchised racialised other. Finally, she suggests that because the method seeks to expose social injustices, it gives researchers a false sense of progress, absolving them of the responsibility to actually take those actions necessary to redress social injustice.[10]

While these works focus on the limits of oral history as a method for giving voice to marginalised and racialised groups, other studies have shown how racial biases and racist pasts are implicated in the practice of historical interpretation. Thus Funnell (2001) draws attention to the anti-Semitic views of German economic historian Werner Sombart and argues that Sombart's overly exaggerated claims about double-entry bookkeeping's contribution to capitalism were informed not by his enthusiasm for the technique, but by his intention to damn Jewish businessmen and Jews in general. Other studies in which the issue of race-inflected historical interpretation comes under scrutiny are those by Booth et al. (2007) and Detzen and Hoffmann (2018), both of which illustrate the potential of historical interpretation to justify a racist past and thus raise important methodological questions about the dilemmas of truth and relativism in representations of history.

Summary and the way forward

Accounting historians have examined the accounting–race interface from the standpoint of accounting's involvement in racial practices defined as discriminatory, oppressive/exploitative and genocidal. Not only has 'accounting as technique and practice' been interrogated but, as Table 22.1 illustrates, accounting historians have also examined the role of accountants and their elite institutions, as well as accounting academics in the enactment of these practices. These studies have added to the growing stock of literature aimed at exposing the myth of accounting as a passive, neutral and unbiased reflector of economic reality and so demonstrate accounting's deep involvement in political and ideological struggles (Arnold and Hammond 1994). The studies have also served to widen the arena of iniquitous, even nefarious, social practices in which accounting's partisanship has been observed. Importantly as well, studying race and racist practices in accounting history has

Table 22.1 Central focus of historical papers on accounting and race

Aspect of accounting examined	*Accounting and racial practices of:*		
	Discrimination	*Exploitation/Oppression*	*Genocide*
Accounting techniques and practices	Adams and McPhail (2004); Nandan and Alam (2005); Davie (2005)	Fleischman and Tyson (2000); Tyson et al. (2004, 2005); Fleischman et al. (2004, 2011, 2014); Rodrigues and Craig (2018); Oldroyd et al. (2008, 2018); Heier (2010); Stewart (2010); McWatters and Lemarchand (2006); Dyball and Rooney (2012); Oldroyd et al. (2018); Pinto and West (2017a, 2017b); Rodrigues et al. (2015); Hollister and Schultz (2010); Baker (2019); Hammond et al. (2017)	Funnell (1998); Lippmann and Wilson (2007); Lippman (2009)
Accountants, accounting academics and accounting institutions	Hammond and Streeter (1994); Hammond (1997, 2002); Annisette (2003); Kim (2004a, 2004b, 2008), Poullaos (2009); Hammond et al. (2007, 2009, 2012); Sian (2007)		Funnell (2001); Walker (2000, 2003); Booth et al. (2007); Detzen and Hoffmann (2018)

served to generate important methodological debates that have not only contributed to improving the study of the race–accounting nexus, but more broadly have contributed to historiography more generally.

This body of research however can only be described as an initial first step, albeit a promising one, to exploring the interaction between accounting and race. The research focus so far has been narrow. We have yet to probe accounting's involvement in some of the more critical questions posed by scholars interested in racial and ethnic phenomena. In other words, while there is a continued need to expose accounting's sponsorship of racially discriminatory exploitative and genocidal activities, to conceive of accounting's involvement in race exclusively in these terms is to limit our research impact in a number of ways. Below I discuss three shifts from our current focus that might serve to expand research on accounting and race in promising ways.

Shifting from fixed to fluid identities

There is a tendency in extant research in accounting history to treat identities as fixed. This largely reflects the fact that politics is usually conducted as *if* identities were fixed and people themselves present their identities *as* fixed (Dirks et al. 1994; Hall 1995: 66). But identities are fluid and are continuously being (re)fashioned. By disregarding this critical aspect of identity, we fail to explore the manner in which accounting is implicated in the social processes through which racial and ethnic identities are reproduced and transformed. In exploring this issue an obvious site for investigation is the state. In what she calls 'the political construction of ethnicity' Nagel (1986: 97–8) recognises the state's centrality to complex processes of racial formation. We have already seen the multifarious ways in which the totalitarian state has utilised accounting to operationalise, mask and sanitise discriminatory or genocidal acts (Davie 2005; Funnell 1998; Nandan and Alam 2005). Thus by situating accounting within the context of the racial state (Omi and Winant 1994) we can observe far wider impacts of accounting on identity, including its role in creating, reinforcing or altering racial or ethnic identities. Moreover, the political arena is but one 'construction site'. Cornell and Hartmann (1998: ch. 6) point to others: labour markets, residential spaces, social institutions and culture. These remain potentially fruitful arenas in which accounting's involvement in race and ethnic identity construction might be explored.

Shifting spatially and temporally

The tendency to see race and ethnicity as fixed also obscures from our vision the idea that these identities are variable, diverse and contingent. This in turn understates the perceived need for spatial and temporal variety in our research. Such variety is critical for a number of reasons. First, spatial variety will serve to dislodge the 'US folk concepts' (Wacquant 1997: 223) of racial categories such as 'blackness' and 'whiteness' that so dominate the literature.[11] Spatial variety will widen the situations in which accounting is being investigated beyond the common black/white or non-white/white binary dichotomy. Many recent episodes of racial and ethnic conflict manifest themselves along other lines. Fiji, as demonstrated by Nandan and Alam (2005) and Davie (2005), is a case in point, and there are a host of other situations of racial and ethnic conflict that move us away from the black/white bimodal perspective. These include, for example, British Guyana (African versus East Indian); Malaysia (Malay versus Chinese) and Sri Lanka (Sinhalese versus Tamil). This is not to render the binary black/white, non-white/white bifurcation irrelevant, but to assert that to overwhelmingly focus our efforts on this singular bi-racial order is to limit the potential to arrive at a more globally informed understanding of race and ethnic issues as they relate to accounting.

Furthermore, temporal variety in our historical research is called for in order to emphasise the continuing project of race/ethnic identity making. For instance Bonilla-Silva's (2002) 'Latin Americanization thesis' is suggestive of an emerging tri-racial order in the US and implies that the twentieth century also holds some promise for investigating the role of accounting in racial projects in the making.

Shifting from discrimination to privilege

The final shift that would enhance opportunities in race and accountancy research is a move away from the narrow focus on discrimination. Whiteness studies – a field which came into its own in the 1990s – recognises that a literature overly focused on discrimination and disadvantage masks the privileging that is created by systems of power (Wildman 2005). Research in this area, by rendering visible 'whiteness' as a position of power exposes its associated materiality rewards and privilege (Frankenberg 1993; Lipsitz 2005; Wildman 2005). The call for a shift away from an exclusive focus on discrimination to one that includes privilege is, therefore, a call which recognises that race is not something that only non-whites possess, but is a characteristic of whites as well, necessitating close scrutiny of whites' race and racial identity (Arnesen 2001).

Accordingly, for research in the area whiteness needs to be made 'strange', for as long as white people are not racially seen and named, they function as a human norm (Frankenberg 1993; Dyer 2005). Whiteness studies also aim at achieving hybridity. Dyer (2005: 10) asserts that 'the racing of whites will serve to dislodge them/us from the position of power by undercutting the authority with which they/we speak and act in, and on, the world'. Scholarship on whiteness and the professions is now an emerging field that offers some promise for historians of accountancy. Pearce (2005), for instance, has studied the meaning of whiteness in the US legal profession, but this is not a piece of historical research. Walker (2005), on the other hand, is an historical study which explores the meanings of whiteness and the opportunities this accorded white women in the South African medical profession during the period 1950–1990.

Although whiteness studies have been subject to critique (see for example, Arnesen 2001; Fields 2001; Kolchin 2002), there is a general acceptance that this work has helped to 'denaturalise' race. It has also encouraged closer scrutiny of white identity and has rendered visible whiteness's unmarked unnamed status in a number of fields including law, geography, education and film studies (Frankenberg 1993; Dyer 1997; Barrett 2001). Its incorporation into studies of accountancy and accounting history is therefore eagerly awaited.

Key works

Annisette (2003) presents a useful theoretical exposition on race and ethnicity and provides new insights into the various ways in which racial processes can unfold in professional accountancy.

Funnell (1998) is a classic paper that exposes accounting's ability to mask people's humanity and individuality. It provides a seminal explanation of how accounting technique can facilitate abhorrent practices involving human populations.

Hammond (2002) is an extensive study of racial discrimination in the US accountancy profession. The book is exceptional for the extensive coverage and the rich insights it offers into the challenges faced by African American CPAs during the period 1921–99.

Walker (2003) is a study that exposes the central role played by some of Edinburgh's most celebrated accountants in the lesser known 'ethnic cleansing' of Celtic communities in the Scottish Highlands during the mid-nineteenth century.

Notes

1 In identifying the studies I conducted a title and abstract search of the following words *race, racism, racial, racialization, apartheid, ethnic, ethnicity, genocide, holocaust, slave, slavery, Nazi* and *Nazism* in all accounting journals dedicated to historical research: *Accounting, Organizations and Society*; *Accounting History*; *Accounting Historian's Journal*; *Abacus*; *Accounting, Auditing & Accountability Journal*; *Critical Perspectives on Accounting*; *Accounting, Business & Financial History* and its successor journal *Accounting History Review*. From the articles identified, I then eliminated those which dealt with indigenous people (the subject of Chapter 23) as well as those which were not historical studies of race or ethnicity.

2 Indeed, in none of the studies cited is there any explicit mention of terms such as race, racism or racial exploitation.

3 Burrows (2002) provided a transaction cost explanation for the absence of individual productivity records and argued that this was not reflective of racism but was an industry characteristic. This argument was later supported by Dyball and Rooney (2012) who concluded that accounting was not complicit in the suppression of Filipinos' wages and job advancement.

4 This notion of accounting's capacity to serve contradictory social ends, particularly in the context of racial injustice, was revealed in Arnold and Hammond's (1994) historical study of the Sullivan principles and institutional divestment in apartheid South Africa. They illustrated how, as a technology that is ideologically inflected, accounting 'can serve either side of a political struggle' (1994: 124).

5 Tyson and Oldroyd (2007) later confirm this stance in their response to the Sy and Tinker (2005: 188) charge that their faithful adherence to the 'ideology of archivalist empiricism' has prevented them from critiquing present-day practices. They posit that 'We do not believe accounting historians have the authority or are well situated to address the problems in practice and theory today. That undertaking is better left to social activists, contemporary critics, and accounting regulators. Rather, historians should continue to examine, illuminate, and interpret, the past'.

6 Annisette and Prasad (2017), focusing on Dyball and Rooney's (2012) study, point to one of those missed opportunities, arguing that 'Whilst the authors conclude that "accounting does not appear to have been implicated in a concerted effort to repress Filipino workers' pay or conditions"' (2012: 222), they fail to consider the role of accounting in constructing the notion of the 'Filipino worker', and instead mobilize this construct as a taken for granted, uncontested category. In so doing these works have unwittingly reinforced rather than deconstructed the idea of race as essence (Annisette and Prasad 2017:10).

7 In illustrating the contemporary relevance of accounting history, Lippman (2009) developed a powerful instructional case out of this material. The student is presented with a financial statement prepared and used by the German Third Reich during World War II and is confronted with an ethical dilemma regarding 'the responsibilities of accountants and the actions that they should take when involved in accumulating and reporting information about immoral or illegal activities' (2009: 62).

8 Hammond later renders a more expansive account of the history of African Americans in the US profession in her book *A White Collar Profession* (2002).

9 Rotuman culture more closely resembles that of the Polynesian islands. Because of their Polynesian appearance and distinctive language, Rotumans now constitute a recognisable minority group within the Republic of Fiji. For electoral purposes Rotumans were formerly classified as Fijians, but when the constitution was revised in 1997–8, they were granted separate representation at their own request.

10 James (2010), however, adopting a neo-Marxist perspective, confronts the Kim critique about who should study race and how it should be studied. Using the case of musician Joe Strummer of the 1970s band The Clash, he argues that precluding members of the privileged race from studying racialised others establishes a false consciousness, which effectively prevents recognition of economic inequalities in society. He suggests that holding race over class as the primary social cleavage masks the insidiousness of income and wealth disparities that pattern and govern society.

11 An extreme example of international variability on the construction and meaning of these terms is reported in Kolchin (2002: 158), where the US rule that 'anyone with black blood is considered black', is contrasted with the Haitian rule that 'anyone with white blood is considered white', the latter leading Haitian dictator Papa Doc Duvalier to assert that the Haitian population is 98 per cent white.

References

Adams, C.A. and McPhail, K.J. (2004) Reporting and the politics of difference: (Non)disclosure on ethnic minorities, *Abacus*, 40 (3): 405–35.

Annisette, M. (2003) The colour of accountancy. Examining the salience of race in a professionalisation project, *Accounting, Organizations and Society*, 28 (7/8): 639–74.

Annisette, M. and Prasad, A. (2017) Critical accounting research in hyper-racial times, *Critical Perspectives on Accounting*, 43: 5–19.

Annisette, M., Ross, F., Wells, J., and Wood, L. (2006) The professional experiences of African-American Accountants (unpublished working paper).

Arnesen, E. (2001) Whiteness and the historians' imagination, *International Labor and Working-Class History*, 60 (Fall): 3–32.

Arnold, P. and Hammond, Y. (1994) The role of accounting in ideological conflict: Lessons from the South African divestment movement, *Accounting, Organizations and Society*, 19 (2): 111–26.

Bailey, S.R. and Telles, E.E. (2006) Multiracial versus collective black categories: Examining census classification debates in Brazil, *Ethnicities*, 6 (1): 74–101.

Baker, C.R. (2019) What can Thomas Jefferson's accounting records tell us about plantation management, slavery, and Enlightenment philosophy in colonial America? *Accounting History*, 24 (2): 236–52.

Bakre, O. (2005) The first attempt at localizing imperial accountancy: The case of The Institute of Chartered Accountants of Jamaica (ICAJ) (1950s-1970s), *Critical Perspectives on Accounting*, 16 (8): 995–1018.

Bakre, O. (2006) The second attempt at localizing imperial accountancy: The case of The Institute of Chartered Accountants of Jamaica (ICAJ) (1970s-1980s), *Critical Perspectives on Accounting*, 17 (1): 1–28.

Barney, D. and Flesher, D. (1994) Early nineteenth-century productivity accounting: The Locust Grove Plantation slave ledger, *Accounting Business & Financial History*, 4 (2): 275–94.

Barrett, J. (2001) Whiteness studies: anything here for the historians of the working class? *International Labor and Working-Class History*, 60 (Fall): 33–42.

Bashi, V. (1998) Racial categories matter because racial hierarchies matter: A commentary, *Ethnic and Racial Studies*, 21 (5): 959–68.

Bonilla-Silva, E. (2002) We are all Americans!: The Latin Americanization of racial stratification in the USA, *Race and Society*, 5 (1): 3–16.

Booth, C., Clark, P., Delahaye, A., Procter, S., and Rowlinson, M. (2007) Accounting for the dark side of corporate history: Organizational culture perspectives and the Bertelsmann case, *Critical Perspectives on Accounting*, 18 (6): 625–44.

Bulmer, M. and Solomos, J. (1998) Introduction: Re-thinking ethnic and racial studies, *Ethnic and Racial Studies*, 21 (5): 820–37.

Burrows, G. (2002) The interface of race and accounting: A comment and an extension, *Accounting History*, 7 (1): 101–10.

Carmona, S., Ezzamel, M., and Gutierréz, F. (2004) Accounting history research: Traditional and new accounting history perspectives, *De Computis, Revista Española de Historia de la Contabilidad*, 1: 24–53.

Carnegie, G. and Napier, C. (1996) Critical and interpretive histories: Insights into accounting's present and future though its past, *Accounting, Auditing & Accountability Journal*, 9 (3): 7–39.

Cornell, S. and Hartmann, D. (1998) *Ethnicity and Race: Making Identities in a Changing World* (California: Pine Forge Press).

Cowton, C. and O'Shaughnessy, A. (1991) Absentee control of sugar plantations in the British West Indies, *Accounting and Business Research*, 22 (85): 33–45.

Dalton, H. (2005) Failing to see, in: P.S. Rothenberg (ed) *White Privilege: Essential Readings on the Other Side of Racism*, pp. 15–18 (New York: Worth Publishers).

Davie, S.S.K. (2005) The politics of accounting, race and ethnicity: a story of a chiefly-based preferencing, *Critical Perspectives on Accounting*, 16 (5): 551–77.

Davis, J. (1991) *Who is Black? One Nation's Definition* (University Park PA: Penn State University Press).

Detzen, D. and Hoffmann, S. (2018) Stigma management and justifications of the self in denazification accounts, *Accounting, Auditing & Accountability Journal*, 31 (1): 141–65.

Dirks, N., Geoff, E., and Sherry, O. (eds) (1994) *Culture/Power/History: A Reader in Contemporary Social Theory* (Princeton, New Jersey: Princeton University Press).

Donoso-Anes, R. (2002) Accounting and slavery: The accounts of the South Sea Company 1713-1722, *European Accounting Review*, 11 (2): 441–52.

Dyball, M.C. and Rooney, J. (2012) Re-visiting the interface between race and accounting: Filipino workers at the Hamakua Mill Company, 1921-1939, *Accounting History*, 17 (2): 221–40.

Dyer, R. (1997) *White* (New York: New York University Press).

Dyer, R. (2005) The matter of whiteness, in: P.S. Rothenberg (ed) *White Privilege: Essential Readings on the Other Side of Racism*, pp. 9–14 (New York: Worth Publishers).

Fields, B.J. (2001) Whiteness, racism and identity, *International Labor and Working-Class History*, 60 (Fall): 48–56.

Fleischman, R., Tyson, T., and Oldroyd, D. (2014) The U.S. Freedmen's Bureau in post-civil war reconstruction, *Accounting Historians Journal*, 41 (2): 75–110.

Fleischman, R.K. (2004) Confronting moral issues from accounting's dark side, *Accounting History*, 9 (1): 7–23.

Fleischman, R.K., Oldroyd, D., and Tyson, T. N. (2004) Monetizing human life: Slave valuations on US and British West Indian plantations, *Accounting History*, 9 (2): 35–62.

Fleischman, R.K., Oldroyd, D., and Tyson, T.N. (2011) The efficacy/inefficacy of accounting in controlling labour during the transition from slavery in the United States and British West Indies, *Accounting, Auditing & Accountability Journal*, 24 (6): 751–80.

Fleischman, R.K. and Tyson, T.N. (2000) The interface of race and accounting: The case of Hawaiian sugar plantations, 1835-1920, *Accounting History*, 5 (1): 7–32.

Fleischman, R.K. and Tyson, T.N. (2002) The interface of race and accounting: A reply to Burrows, *Accounting History*, 7 (1): 115–21.

Fleischman, R.K. and Tyson, T.N. (2004) Accounting in service to racism: Monetizing slave property in the antebellum South, *Critical Perspectives on Accounting*, 15 (3): 376–99.

Flesher, D. and Flesher, T. (1981) Human resource accounting in Mississippi before 1865, *Journal of Accounting and Business Research*, 10 (supplement): 124–29.

Frankenberg, R. (1993) *The Social Construction of Whiteness: White Women Race Matters* (Minneapolis: University of Minnesota Press).

Funnell, W. (1998) Accounting in the service of the Holocaust, *Critical Perspectives on Accounting*, 9 (4): 435–64.

Funnell, W. (2001) Distortions of history, accounting and the Paradox of Werner Sombart, *Abacus*, 37 (1): 55–78.

Furnivall, J.S. (1968) *Colonial Policy and Practice* (Cambridge: Cambridge University Press).

Hall, S. (1995) Fantasy, identity, politics, in: E. Carter, J. Donald, and J. Squires (eds) *Cultural Remix: Theories of Politics and the Popular*, pp. 63–72 (London: Lawrence and Wishart).

Hammond, T. (1997) From complete exclusion to minimal inclusion: African Americans and the public accounting industry 1965-1988, *Accounting, Organizations and Society*, 22 (1): 29–53.

Hammond, T. (2002) *A White-Collar Profession: African-American Certified Public Accountants since 1921* (Chapel Hill: University of North Carolina Press).

Hammond, T., Arnold, P.J., and Clayton, B.M. (2007) Recounting a difficult past: A South African accounting firm's "experiences in transformation", *Accounting History*, 12 (3): 253–81.

Hammond, T., Clayton, B.M., and Arnold, P.J. (2009) South Africa's transition from apartheid: The role of professional closure in the experiences of black chartered accountants, *Accounting, Organizations and Society*, 34 (6-7): 705–21.

Hammond, T., Clayton, B.M., and Arnold, P.J. (2012) An "unofficial" history of race relations in the South African accounting industry, 1968-2000: Perspectives of South Africa's first black chartered accountants, *Critical Perspectives on Accounting*, 23 (4-5): 332–50.

Hammond, T., Cooper, C., and van Staden, G.J. (2017) Anglo American Corporation and the South African state: A contextual analysis of annual reports 1917-1975, *Accounting, Auditing & Accountability Journal*, 30 (6): 1399–423.

Hammond, T. and Streeter, D. (1994) Overcoming the barriers: Early African-American Certified Public Accountants, *Accounting, Organizations and Society*, 19 (3): 271–88.

Heier, J. (1988) A content comparison of antebellum plantation records and Thomas Affleck's accounting principles, *Accounting Historians Journal*, 15 (2): 131–50.

Heier, J. (2010) Accounting for the business of suffering: A study of the antebellum Richmond, Virginia, slave trade, *Abacus*, 46 (1): 60–83.

Hollister, J. and Schultz, S.M. (2010) Slavery and emancipation in rural New York: Evidence from nineteenth-century accounting records, *Accounting History*, 15 (3): 371–405.

James, A. (2001) Making sense of race and racial classification, *Race and Society*, 4 (2): 35–47.

James, K. (2010) Who am I? Where are we? Where do we go from here? Marxism, voice, representation, and synthesis, *Critical Perspectives on Accounting*, 21 (8): 696–710.

Kibria, N. (1998) The contested meanings of 'Asian American': Racial dilemmas in the contemporary US, *Ethnic and Racial Studies*, 21 (5): 939–58.

Kim, S. N. (2004a) Imperialism without empire: Silence in contemporary accounting research on race/ethnicity, *Critical Perspectives on Accounting*, 15 (1): 95–133.

Kim, S. N. (2004b) Racialized gendering of the accountancy profession: Towards an understanding of Chinese women's experiences in accountancy in New Zealand, *Critical Perspectives on Accounting*, 15 (3): 400–27.

Kim, S. N. (2008) Whose voice is it anyway? Rethinking the oral history method in accounting research on race, ethnicity and gender, *Critical Perspectives on Accounting*, 19 (8): 1346–69.

Kolchin, P. (2002) Whiteness studies: The new history of race in America, *The Journal of American History*, 89 (10): 154–73.

Lippman, E.J. (2009) Accountants' responsibility for the information they report: An historical case study of financial information, *Accounting Historians Journal*, 36 (1): 61–79.

Lippmann, E. and Wilson, P. (2007) The culpability of accounting in perpetuating the Holocaust, *Accounting History*, 12 (3): 283–303.

Lipsitz, G. (2005) The positive investment in whiteness, in P.S. Rothenberg (ed) *White Privilege: Essential Readings on the Other Side of Racism*, pp 67–85 (New York: Worth Publishers).

McWatters, C.S. (2008) Investment returns and la traite négrière: Evidence from eighteenth-century France, *Accounting, Business & Financial History*, 18 (2): 161–85.

McWatters, C.S. and Lemarchand, Y. (2006) Accounting representation and the slave trade: The guide du commerce of gaignat de l'aulnais, *Accounting Historians Journal*, 33 (2): 1–37.

McWatters, C.S. and Lemarchand, Y. (2009) Accounting for triangular trade, *Accounting, Business & Financial History*, 19 (2): 189–212.

Miller, P., Hopper, T., and Laughlin, R. (1991) The new accounting history: An introduction, *Accounting, Organizations and Society*, 16 (5/6): 395–403.

Nagel, J. (1986) The political construction of ethnicity, in: S. Olzak and J. Nagel (eds) *Competitive Ethnic Relations*, pp 93–112 (New York: Academic Press).

Nagel, J. (1994) Constructing ethnicity: Creating and recreating ethnic identity and culture, *Social Problems*, 41 (1): 152–76.

Nandan, R. K. and Alam, M. (2005) Accounting and the reproduction of race relations in Fiji: a discourse on race and accounting in colonial context, *Accounting, Business and the Public Interest*, 4 (1): 1–34.

Napier, C. (2006) Accounts of change: 30 years of historical accounting research, *Accounting, Organizations and Society*, 31 (4/5): 445–507.

Newson, L.A. (2013) The slave-trading accounts of Manoel Batista Peres, 1613-1619: Double-entry bookkeeping in cloth money, *Accounting History*, 18 (3): 343–65.

Oldroyd, D., Fleischman, R.K., and Tyson, T.N. (2008) The culpability of accounting practice in promoting slavery in the British Empire and antebellum United States, *Critical Perspectives on Accounting*, 19 (5): 764–84.

Oldroyd, D., Tyson, T., and Fleischman, R. (2018) Contracting, property rights and liberty: Accountability under the Freedmen's Bureau's labour-contract system, *Accounting, Auditing & Accountability Journal*, 31 (6): 1720–48.

Omi, M. and Winant, H. (1994) *Racial Formation in the United States: From 1960s to the 1980s* (New York: Routledge).

Pearce, R.G. (2005) White lawyering: Rethinking race, lawyer identity and rule of law, *Fordham Law Review*, 73: 2081–100.

Pinto, O. and West, B. (2017a) Accounting and the history of the everyday life of captains, sailors and common seamen in eighteenth-century Portuguese slave trading, *Accounting History*, 22 (3): 320–47.

Pinto, O. and West, B. (2017b) Accounting, slavery and social history: The legacy of an eighteenth-century Portuguese chartered company, *Accounting History*, 22 (2): 141–66.

Poullaos, C. (2009) Profession, race and empire: Keeping the centre pure, 1921-1927, *Accounting, Auditing & Accountability Journal*, 22 (3): 429–68.

Razek, J. (1985) Accounting on the old plantation, *Accounting Historians Journal*, 12 (1): 19–36.

Rodrigues, L.L. and Craig, R. (2018) The role of government accounting and taxation in the institutionalization of slavery in Brazil, *Critical Perspectives on Accounting*, 57: 21–38.

Rodrigues, L.L., Craig, R.J., Schmidt, P., and Santos, J.L. (2015) Documenting, monetising and taxing Brazilian slaves in the eighteenth and nineteenth centuries, *Accounting History Review*, 25 (1): 43–67.

Sian, S. (2006) Inclusion, exclusion and control: The case of the Kenyan accounting professionalisation project, *Accounting, Organizations and Society*, 31 (3): 295–322.

Sian, S. (2007) Patterns of prejudice: Social exclusion and racial demarcation in professional accountancy in Kenya, *Accounting Historians Journal*, 34 (2): 1–42.

Stewart, L.J. (2010) A contingency theory perspective on management control system design among U.S. ante-bellum slave plantations, *Accounting Historians Journal*, 37 (1): 91–120.

Susela, S.D. (1999) 'Interests' and accounting standard setting in Malaysia, *Accounting, Auditing & Accountability Journal*, 12 (3): 358–87.

Sy, A. and Tinker, T. (2005) Archival research and the lost worlds of accounting, *Accounting History*, 10 (1): 47–69.

Tyson, T.N., Fleischman, R.K., and Oldroyd, D. (2004) Theoretical perspectives on accounting for labor on slave plantations of the USA and British West Indies, *Accounting, Auditing & Accountability Journal*, 17 (5): 758–78.

Tyson, T.N. and Oldroyd, D. (2007) Straw men and old saws: An evidence-based response to Sy and Tinker's critique of accounting history, *Accounting Historians Journal*, 34 (1): 173–84.

Tyson, T.N. and Oldroyd, D. (2019) Accounting for slavery during the Enlightenment: Contradictions and interpretations, *Accounting History*, 24 (2): 212–35.

Tyson, T. N., Oldroyd, D., and Fleishman, R. (2005) Accounting, coercion and social control during apprenticeship: Converting slave workers to wage workers in the British West Indies, c.1834-1838, *Accounting Historians Journal*, 32 (2): 201–31.

Vollmers, G. (2003) Industrial slavery in the United States: The North Carolina turpentine industry 1849-61, *Accounting, Business & Financial History*, 13 (3): 369–92.

Wacquant, L. (1997) Towards an analytic of racial domination, *Political Power and Social Theory*, 11: 221–34.

Walker, L. (2005) The colour white: Racial and gendered closure in the South African medical profession, *Ethnic and Racial Studies*, 28 (2): 348–75.

Walker, S.P. (2000) Encounters with Nazism: British accountants and the fifth international congress on accounting, *Critical Perspectives on Accounting*, 11 (2): 215–45.

Walker, S.P. (2003) Agents of dispossession and acculturation. Edinburgh accountants and the Highland clearances, *Critical Perspectives on Accounting*, 14 (8): 813–53.

Wildman, S. (2005) Making systems of privilege visible, in: P.S. Rothenberg (ed) *White Privilege: Essential Readings on the Other Side of Racism*, pp 95–101 (New York: Worth Publishers).

23

COLONIALISM AND INDIGENOUS PEOPLES[1]

Lachlan McDonald-Kerr and Gordon Boyce

Overview

In seeking to understand the general relationship between accounting and colonialism, researchers have found clear connections between colonialist endeavours and accounting discourses and technologies. This work has explored how accounting has occupied a significant place in governing and controlling indigenous peoples, and instilled particular concepts and ways of thinking in both the colonised and their colonisers. The broader language and concepts implicit in this process, such as 'superiority' versus 'inferiority', are central to the practice of colonialism and are intertwined and infused with accounting language and concepts. They may be used to operationalise and legitimise colonial objectives, including through possession and/or dispossession.

This chapter provides an overview of research that considers how accounting discourses and technologies are intertwined with colonial practices and their particular impacts on indigenous peoples. The chapter examines the positioning of accounting within colonialism and indigenous–government relations, highlighting its historical and contemporary significance. In addition to discerning the place of accounting within colonialism as it affects indigenous peoples, we identify future research directions for further exploring this domain. The chapter seeks to make a timely contribution to understanding in this key area of historical and contemporary public debate around the world.

Introduction

It has long been recognised that accounting is not a neutral technology that involves the impartial recording and reporting of financial and economic activities. Rather, accounting is recognised as a powerful technology through which particular realities are created and recreated, and are commonly ascribed with the status of received 'truth' (Gill 2011). Crucially, accounting embodies a form of authority and expertise that may serve to mediate power relationships, such as those between governments and a range of social actors and constituencies. Thus, accounting is recognised to be, at least in part, a partisan practice (see for example, Rose 1991, 1993; Tinker 1991). In this regard, the use of accounting helps to legitimise or delegitimise particular forms of authority and particular kinds of decision-making.

A growing body of accounting research has examined indigenous–government relations in the context of colonialism. This work is typically interdisciplinary in nature, providing important insights into the way in which accounting is implicated in processes involving the extension and imposition of authority by one nation over another. Characteristically, 'the need for … colonies [was commonly] argued in economic terms' as a means for maintaining and furthering national financial wealth and prosperity (see Hoogvelt 1997: 19), but colonialism had profound implications for the lives of indigenous peoples. In this historical context, accounting had a central function as a technology that helped enable and legitimise colonial conquests. The ongoing and developing research agenda in this domain has provided a rich and evolving area for critical and interdisciplinary accounting history, albeit one that is yet to reach its full potential.

Researchers have examined how accounting and related ideas and technologies have functioned in processes of indigenous exclusion, alienation, dispossession and genocide (see for example, Neu 1999, 2000a, 2000b; Davie 2000, 2005a, 2005b; Gibson 2000; Neu and Therrien 2003; Annisette and Neu 2004; Neu and Graham 2004, 2006). This story of indigenous peoples and colonialism presents a notable part of the 'sinister' uses of a seemingly innocuous set of accounting technologies, which has been uncovered by critical histories that show 'accounting to be far more than a prosaic, neutral technical practice' (Fleischman et al. 2013: 1). A significant area of interest for these studies has been the role of accounting in the mediation of relations between colonial governments and indigenous peoples, especially in the furtherance of 'the late 19th century British imperialist project' (Annisette and Neu 2004: 1).[2] This research has documented the centrality of accounting language and technologies in the discourses and practices of imperialism and colonialism, showing how accounting has 'a pronounced and powerful moral dimension' (Fleischman et al. 2013: 1).[3] It has also explicated the role of accounting in the construction and application of a particular ideological vision of indigenous inferiority, which colonial governments used to justify hegemonic practices (Davie 2000, 2005b; Neu 2000b; Greer 2006).

In examining this research domain, we have organised the remainder of this chapter into four major subsections that outline key dimensions of accounting studies of colonialism and indigenous peoples. In the next section, we introduce the core underpinning concepts and outline the scope and focus of the chapter as it relates to the key concepts. Following this, we examine how a range of published research papers has made visible the connections between colonialism and accounting tools and technologies. The discussion is organised around the five geographical contexts that have formed the focus of the bulk of the extant body of research in this area. In the third major section of the chapter, we turn to elucidating several common themes that emerge from the body of prior work to discern key features of the contextual place of accounting. Finally, we bring the chapter to a close by suggesting possible directions for future research.

Indigenous peoples, colonialism and accounting

Indigenous peoples

Despite widespread usage of the term, extensive debate continues regarding the definition of 'indigenous peoples', with no universally accepted definition (even by the UN itself).[4] The most commonly accepted approach (Secretariat of the Permanent Forum on Indigenous Issues, 2004) defines indigenous peoples as members of present 'non-dominant sectors of society' (Martínez Cobo 1983: 50, para 379). This recognises that a country's Indigenous people have 'cultures and ways of life [that] differ considerably from the dominant society' (African Commission on Human and Peoples' Rights & International Work Group for Indigenous Affairs 2006: 9). They have 'a historical continuity with pre-invasion and pre-colonial societies that developed on their territories, [and] consider themselves distinct from other sectors of the societies now prevailing in those territories' (Martínez Cobo 1983: 50, para 379). The UN recognises that indigenous peoples:

> [a]re inheritors and practitioners of unique cultures and ways of relating to people and the environment. They have retained social, cultural, economic and political characteristics that are distinct from those of the dominant societies in which they live. Despite their cultural differences, indigenous peoples from around the world share common problems related to the protection of their rights as distinct peoples.[5]

Following accepted usage, the term 'Indigenous' is generally employed as a proper noun in this chapter when it refers to a particular group or groups of Indigenous people (including in relation to particular contexts or places) or any aspect of their culture, but as an ordinary noun when referring to indigenous populations in general. Similarly, we follow common usage by using the plural term 'peoples' throughout the chapter, in recognition of the fact that the singular term 'people' can serve to generate (mis)conceptions that Indigenous peoples belong to an 'amorphous cluster', rather than to many individualised, unique and distinct cultures (Pino Robles 2002: 139).

In delimiting the scope of the chapter, we focus on accounting studies that consider indigenous peoples as defined above. The particular scope of the chapter relates to the function of accounting in the causes, practices and consequences of the colonisation of Indigenous peoples and their lands. This generally excludes research that seeks to either examine the function and roles of accounting and the accounting profession within processes of colonisation, or colonial government in what are more broadly referred to as 'developing' or 'emerging' nations (Annisette 1999, 2000; Bush and Maltby 2004; Dyball et al. 2006, 2007). While such studies demonstrate the salience of accounting to the processes of colonialism in different contexts such as Trinidad and Tobago, the Philippines and West Africa, because they are not focused on Indigenous peoples and issues as defined above (see Sylvain 2017), they generally do not fall within the scope of this chapter.

Colonialism (and imperialism)

Colonialism and imperialism are related in theory and practice, sharing similarities including, importantly, that they both represent forms of domination. Colonialism broadly refers to 'the control by individuals or groups over the territory and/or behaviour of other individuals or groups' (Horvath 1972: 46), or, more specifically, 'the implanting of settlements on distant territory' (Said 1994: 9). Colonialism may be distinguished from imperialism by 'the presence or absence of significant numbers of permanent settlers in the colony from the colonizing power' (Horvath 1972: 47). Imperialism does not necessarily involve the establishment of settlements in colonised lands, and imperial rule may primarily occur at a distance (Said 1994). The distinction outlined here influences the scope of the chapter insofar as the focus is on colonialism as the *settlement* of distant territories.

Colonisation implies the exertion of control by an imperialist power over the original occupants of such territories. Colonial settlement is related to the imperialist endeavour, which Said (1994: 9) describes as the 'practice, the theory, and the attitudes of a dominating metropolitan centre ruling a distant territory'. The settlement of distant territories requires imperial powers to deal in some manner with existing Indigenous territorial owners and occupants. The related need to 'render the distant territory and its indigenous inhabitants "controllable"' is common to every colonial experience (Neu 2000b: 165). While colonialists have deployed different strategies to achieve their objectives, underpinning all colonial relationships with Indigenous peoples is 'a clear-cut and absolute hierarchical distinction ... between ruler and ruled' (Said 1994: 228).

As Loomba (2002: 2) notes: 'Colonialism was not an identical process in different parts of the world but everywhere it locked the original inhabitants and the newcomers into the most complex and traumatic relationships in human history'. Each historical instance of colonialism manifested three key aspects: the settlement of Indigenous lands by people from a distant territory; the exploitation of resources in and on those lands; and the subjugation of Indigenous peoples, 'supported and perhaps even impelled by impressive ideological formations' (Said 1994: 8) of inferiority. The construction of Indigenous peoples as 'inferior' was closely related to the ability of colonial authorities to intervene in, control and exploit indigenous territory, and to the ongoing perpetuation of unequal relations of power. Said (1994: 8) emphasised that the ideologies of imperialism and colonialism 'include notions that certain territories and people *require* and beseech domination, as well as forms of knowledge affiliated with domination' (original emphasis).

Colonial governments applied racial schemata that constructed indigenous peoples as 'lesser species' (Said 1994: 121). The received authority of colonialism faced 'no significant dissent' from Western art, science and expertise, wherein 'essentialist positions' were 'developed and accentuated ... proclaiming that Europeans should rule' (Said 1994: 120). Bhabha (1994: 70) highlighted how colonial discourse is 'an apparatus of power', arguing that its objective 'is to construe the colonized as a population of degenerate types on the basis of racial origin, in order to justify conquest and to establish systems of administration and instruction'. Thus, colonial discourse simultaneously constructs indigenous peoples as 'other' *while* producing them as 'entirely knowable and visible' (Bhabha 1994: 71). Thus, representations of European superiority and indigenous inferiority sustained relations of domination and control. Through discursive repetition, the inferiority of indigenous peoples came to assume the status of 'fact' on the basis of which governments formulated policies and practices to govern *over* the Indigenous peoples of colonial lands. The processes of government administration, in turn, made the discourses themselves seem appropriate and natural, thus forming an ideological circle of discourse and action, and reinforcing race-based discrimination (Neu and Graham 2006).

The ability of the colonial authorities to control Indigenous peoples depended on myriad technologies, among which a variety of accounting techniques were significant. This provides the focus of many accounting studies that examine how accounting ideas and practices were central to colonial government discourses, policies and actions.

The absence of consensus around issues relating to the classification of colonial endeavours, including on spatial and temporal dimensions (Horvath 1972; Loomba 2002) presents a challenge for researchers in this area. Choices relating to the inclusion or exclusion of particular geographical locations and periods may be contestable. In this chapter, we have largely avoided this issue by embracing a substantive, rather than formal, interpretation of colonialism. This results in the inclusion of literature that may be considered to relate to periods *after* the end of colonialism, but that nevertheless typifies how colonial ways of thinking and associated practices – the *substance* of colonialism – often continue beyond the formal (political) end of colonialism. Therefore, some research that is focused on periods after the formal end of the colonial era is considered in the chapter because it identifies rationalities of social engineering consistent with the colonial mentalities of government experienced in the colonisation of Indigenous peoples in various locations.[6] This research provides important insights into how governments translated colonial objectives into practices of modernity, demonstrating ways in which colonialism has a 'continuous legacy … for Indigenous peoples' (Pino Robles 2002: 140).

Accounting studies

Research into the role of accounting in the colonisation of Indigenous peoples has concentrated on five key sites of colonialism (and the Indigenous peoples affected):[7] Australia (Aboriginal and Torres Strait Islander peoples), Canada (First Nations peoples), Fiji (iTaukei peoples),[8] New Zealand (Māori peoples), and the USA (Native American peoples). This research examines the manner in which colonialism was a fundamental aspect of the modern history of each of these nations, and how accounting and accountability mechanisms were central to the power of colonial regimes.

Australia

Research into the Australian setting helps to highlight the central role of accounting systems in colonial discourses, and shows how they may function to mediate indigenous–government relations. Two recent historical studies (Greer and McNicholas 2017; Miley and Read 2018) provide important insights into the use of accounting in the context of the oppression, dispossession, alienation and disempowerment of Indigenous Australians.

Greer and McNicholas (2017) analysed the use of accounting technologies and information in the implementation and administration of 'apprenticeship programs' in New South Wales between 1883 and 1950. These programmes involved the forcible removal of Indigenous Australian children from their communities, for placement in government-led labour contracts. Using a theoretical framework that combined Foucauldian notions of governmentality and pastoral care, Greer and McNicholas found that accounting techniques and records helped to create economically focused accounts of programme participants. These 'individualised accounts' (1845) facilitated case-by-case management of children and, in turn, generated possibilities for their management as governable subjects across different institutionalised sites. Notably, Greer and McNicholas (2017) also contend that these accounts (and the information they contained) were not simply used as a bureaucratic box-ticking tool for purposes of organising and managing children across different institutionalised sites. Rather, they functioned as a means for realising what was regarded as the moral betterment of Indigenous children and monitoring 'the moral appropriateness of the actions of the employers and the apprentices themselves' (2017: 1861). By recording individual behaviours and transgressions, these accounts functioned more broadly as mediums that sought to recreate and reshape Indigenous children in accordance with norms of white Australian society.

Miley and Read (2018) investigated the case of Indigenous 'stolen wages' in Australia between 1897 and 1972 in order to study the nexus between accounting and stigma. This centred on the compulsory quarantining and controlling of Indigenous Australians' wages and savings in jurisdictional government-held trust accounts. Miley and Read found that systematic failures to sufficiently implement the regulatory framework surrounding the administration and management of these trust accounts – a crucial element of which was legislatively mandated accounting practices (such as auditing and maintenance of records) – helped to create circumstances that supported the stigmatisation of Indigenous Australians by the dominant white populace. While accounting was not seen to be the *cause* of stigmatisation, Miley and Read (2018) found that the breakdowns in accounting mechanisms helped to support stigmatisation by intensifying poverty. This, in turn, served to reinforce pervasive negative stereotypes of the Indigenous Australian population and provided justification for legitimising their ongoing need to be governed by (white) authorities.

Both of the above studies help to illuminate the often-hidden power of accounting as a technology that assists those with power to maintain and exercise their authority over non-dominant groups within a society. Distinctively, Miley and Read (2018) show how accounting and administrative failures help to further contribute to the impoverishment of Indigenous people, whereas Greer and McNicholas (2017: 1844) show how accounting practices were used in an attempt to 're-make and re-engineer' Indigenous Australian children in accordance with Western standards and norms. A unique and particularly valuable contribution from Greer and McNicholas (2017) arises from their approach to conceptualising an 'account' as being something that goes beyond the exclusive measure of financial information into a broad realm of 'scorekeeping' (which may include things such as behaviours).

A number of other studies have researched what may be characterised as the more general interface between accounting, Indigenous cultures and the governance of Indigenous populations in Australia in the period after colonialism (Chew and Greer 1997; Gibson 2000; Greer and Patel 2000). These studies have concentrated on cultural dimensions that relate to issues such as the use of accounting and related calculative measures to aid in the displacement of Aboriginal cultures, and the potential of Indigenous cultural values to inform new and innovative kinds of accounting practice.

Thinking about these historical studies from a contemporary vantage point, it is clear more studies are needed to investigate the Australian context. The relative paucity of contemporary studies in this area is surprising, considering the (at best) patchy history of Indigenous–government relations in Australia. More generally, much more work is required to render visible the extent of accounting's functioning in the domination and marginalisation of Indigenous peoples in a range of times and places.

Canada

In the accounting literature, the Canadian context is perhaps the most prominent setting for the investigation of the functioning of accounting in the colonisation of Indigenous peoples. Studies in this domain have generated detailed insights into the use of systems of accounting within Indigenous–government relationships (Neu 1999, 2000a, 2000b; Neu and Therrien 2003; Neu and Graham 2004, 2006; Neu and Heincke 2004). This research has helped to enhance understandings of accounting discourses and practices within the British colonial administration of the First Nations peoples of Canada, providing important insights into the historical antecedents of contemporary Indigenous–government relations in Canada.

Significant contributions have been made by Dean Neu and his colleagues, whose work has enhanced our understanding of important theoretical and practical dimensions such as Foucauldian notions of governmentality and the use of accounting as a technology of government. In so doing, these studies have added to our general understanding of how accounting may be used to transform indigenous peoples into governable subjects in a way that also legitimises dispossession, subjugation, exploitation and control.

Neu (1999) showed how a complex array of historical factors in the nineteenth century helped the British imperialist construction of Canada's First Nations peoples as governable subjects. Accounting technologies were already used to guide decision-making processes in the British Empire, helping to facilitate governance at a distance. After the process of 'discovering' the Indigenous population as governable subjects, accounting technologies emerged as a colonial technology of government and permeated the sphere of Indigenous–government relations.

Focusing on dispossession, Neu (2000b) contended that accounting played a pivotal role in legitimising the 'purchase' of land from First Nations peoples in the nineteenth century. Neu's detailed historical account of Indigenous–government relations surrounding landholdings in Canada shows how power asymmetries between parties meant that the First Nations people had little choice but to accept payment schemes proposed by the colonial government for the 'purchase' of Indigenous landholdings. This remained the case even where payment methods underpinning these arrangements were subsequently amended, such as changing payments from lump-sum to the payment of an interest component in perpetuity (Neu 2000b: 175).

The role of technologies of government in mediating Indigenous–government relationships in Canada was also examined by Neu and Heincke (2004), who considered two geographically separate groups of Indigenous peoples in North America (the Oka peoples of Canada and Chiapas peoples of Mexico). Their analysis shows how colonial governments in both settings used accounting technologies *alongside* other methods of control to govern subaltern people in the furtherance of certain administrative ends. These ends included the expropriation of lands and exclusion from certain economic activities. An important contribution of this work lies in the manner in which it examines how technologies of government, in the Foucauldian sense, may operate in conjunction with other methods – specifically techniques of force – in order to control indigenous peoples. Moreover, Neu and Heincke (2004) also suggested that subsequent resistances by the Oka and Chiapas peoples in more contemporary times (the Oka stand-off in 1990 and Chiapas conflict in 1994) were (in part) a long-term result of the imposition of these techniques of governing during colonial rule. The articulation of this linkage is a key contribution of this work, in that it helps to demonstrate a direct nexus between colonialist endeavours and contemporary issues relating to indigenous–government relations.

Neu and Graham (2004) employed a theoretical fusion of governmentality and modernity in order to investigate the use of accounting technologies by the Canadian Indian Department in the early twentieth century, under the leadership of a newly appointed Deputy Superintendent (himself a former accountant). The associated bureaucratic shift in management, alongside other administrative changes, meant that 'accounting solutions came to dominate the activities of the Indian Department' (2004: 595), both in terms of their internal process and (most importantly) their dealings with Indigenous peoples. Accounting technologies were a key element in the introduction of certain forms of rationality which, in turn, served to obscure moral dimensions of decision-making and encourage the governance of the Indigenous populations at a distance. One crucial contribution from this study is the focus on key *actors*, complementing the focus on institutions in a number of other studies.

Neu and Graham (2006) examined the use and role of accounting technologies in mediating the Canadian Government's dealings with the First Nations peoples. The key contribution of this study centres on its ability to 'analyze simultaneously the macro and micro aspects of governance processes' (2006: 49). In other words, it concurrently traced the role and positioning of accounting technologies in relation to different tiers of governance processes – from federal government legislation (macro), to its enactment and interpretation by the Indian Department, through to implementation by local agents (micro). In adopting this holistic approach, Neu and Graham (2006) showed how accounting technologies were intertwined through numerous tiers of governance processes *and* how accounting was instrumental in defining the limits of policy. Their analysis also shows how accounting technologies helped to facilitate governance at a distance, demonstrating how 'the agency of the aboriginal people was diminished by accounting, as disabling departmental programs and procedural requirements for the disposal of their own land circumscribed their agency, and helped engender a dependency on government' (2006: 74).

Significant insights from Neu and his co-authors relate to the functioning of accounting techniques in the context of the practices of a particular regime of colonial governance.[9] Key among the issues identified is the appropriation of Indigenous land and the measurement and/or representation of the values implicit within these transactions (Neu 1999; Neu and Therrien 2003). This work demonstrates how accounting technologies operated to 'shape, normalize and instrumentalize the conduct, thought, and decisions of the First Nations peoples in order to achieve governmental objectives aspirations' (Miller and Rose 1990: 8). Research from Neu and colleagues clearly positions accounting 'within the processes and practices that permit imperial powers to dominate distant territories and their inhabitants' (Annisette and Neu 2004: 1). Also making a unique contribution, their research utilises several themes from Foucault and the accounting governmentality literature: government as 'action at a distance'; the discursive character of governmentality; accounting as a 'technology of government'; and the optimistic but failing nature of technologies (see Boyce and Davids 2004).

This body of work drawing on the Canadian experience not only highlights 'accounting's mediative role in defining power relationships' (Neu and Therrien 2003: 6) and the pervasiveness of accounting within all levels of colonial governmentality (Neu and Graham 2006), but also exposes the role of accounting in the circumscription of Indigenous agency (Neu and Graham 2006). These studies also evoke theories from the colonialism, genocide and subaltern literatures to address both the structures and consequences of governance. Accounting was central to the targeting of Indigenous peoples as a governable population, and the measurement and fixture of the terms of exchange for land. In addition, accounting was important as a social engineering mechanism for the implementation of colonial policies, and as a discursive field in which the spoils of colonialism were represented, apportioned and rationalised. Accounting technologies facilitated the infiltration of government policies into the minutiae of Indigenous lives.

Fiji

The expansion of British imperial and colonial reach into the Fiji Islands in the latter parts of the nineteenth century relied on methods of rule that actively encompassed members of the colonised community. Rather than employing conventional methods for controlling the Indigenous population, such as suppression and alienation or segregation, the British strategy centred on the *construction* of hierarchical social structures and geographical regions that placed Indigenous chiefs at the pinnacle of their communities.[10] The British established control over the Indigenous Fijian population via the formation of alliances with chiefs, facilitating the *indirect* rule of the colonising power (Davie 2000, 2005a, 2005b, 2007; Alam et al. 2004).

Davie (2000) illuminated the central role of accounting in supporting imperialism and associated logics in the British colonisation of Fiji. Her work shows how the British imposed 'foreign' systems of accounting on Fijian chieftaincy (that is, those designated as elites by the colonialists). These accounting systems were used to create indirect systems of control, through which power was exerted and exploitation of the Indigenous peoples was legitimised, while benefiting a limited number of Indigenous chiefs.

The role of accounting in supporting British regimes of indirect control in Fiji was also examined by Davie (2005a). This study utilised theories of citizenship to highlight how the creation of class-based stratifications of the Indigenous population utilised accounting calculations and technologies (Davie 2005a).

The role of accounting in colonial endeavours in Fiji was revisited by Davie (2007), showing 'how the legislation of communal arrangements led to social structures based on exploitative and oppressive acts, while relying on accounting calculations to divert attention' (2007: 257). This study makes an important contribution to the accountability literature on colonialism, because it develops further understandings regarding 'accounting's complicity in Britain's social engineering efforts in Fiji' (2007: 273). In particular, it adds visibility to the value-laden nature of accounting – specifically, the propensity to *mis*perceive it as a neutral technology – and shows how it may serve to construct certain realities that mask issues of exploitation and coercion.

The *post*-colonial Fijian context formed the focus of a case study presented in Alam et al. (2004), which investigated the nexus between colonial accounting practices and present-day management accounting control systems in the Fiji Development Bank (FDB). Crucially, the authors found that 'historically constituted political, land, race and other customary Fijian structures are drawn upon, which in turn reproduces these structural components of the Fijian social system' (Alam et al. 2004: 154). In other words, features of colonialist rule permeated into modern-day accounting practices and served to manufacture an outlook that these conventions are indelibly Fijian. Alam et al. (2004) suggested that this, in turn, helped to legitimate colonially imposed constructions surrounding racial stratifications, and hindered nation-wide economic prosperity.[11]

The FDB also formed a locus of investigation for Irvine and Deo (2006). In this case, however, the impacts of theory selection in qualitative research was emphasised by the authors, considering alternative theoretical lenses (and levels of theorisation) as applied to the case study particulars. Irvine and Deo demonstrated how the same case study, when considered from alternative perspectives (here, Marxian and Weberian), may lead to alternative conceptions of the role of accounting. Specifically, the Marxian lens, as was employed by Alam et al. (2004), saw accounting as denoting an 'oppressive instrument of domination'; whereas a Weberian interpretation highlighted a 'conciliatory and facilitating role' (Irvine and Deo 2006: 223).

More recently, Davie and McLean (2017) investigated the role of accounting in disabling the agency of Indigenous peoples of Fiji under British colonial rule. They showed how the introduction of systems of accounting (purported under the semblance of a civilising policy) by the colonial power facilitated the 'cultural hybridisation' of Indigenous peoples by uprooting longstanding norms, traditions and habits, and demanding the reorganisation of systems of governance in accordance with Western standards of financial accountabilities. The imposition of colonial administrative systems of accounting was thus seen as the principal instruments for enabling control and domination over Indigenous peoples, and dismantling and alienating them from their antecedent identities.

The range of Fijian-focused studies illuminates the fundamental importance of understanding the historical social, political and economic contexts, and of taking account of both distinctive features of specific sites of investigation and the common threads occurring across different sites. British expansion into Fiji during the late nineteenth century depended on the (re)construction, collaboration and cooperation of a hierarchy of chiefs, rather than on traditional colonial practices of subjugation and exclusion of the Indigenous population (Davie 2000, 2005b). These studies reveal the multifaceted and strategic nature of colonial rule, and highlight the perpetration of colonial institutions and structurally racist practices that persisted in state-owned and controlled organisations, and in Fijian society generally, after the formal end of colonial rule.

Importantly, research on Fiji clearly demonstrates the centrality of accounting and accountability processes to colonial administration, used to justify programmes on various accounting-based criteria, including efficiency and cost minimisation. Thus, specific accounting practices and concepts may be central to ideological and political domination, and may be integrated into modern contexts. In the Fijian case, racial stratification by colonial powers exploited the chiefly system; laws and policies had a racial focus that not only ensured the cooperation of the Indigenous elite but also became embedded within modern Fijian governance practices. This became a colonially imposed 'system of socio-racial relations and ownership [that was] re-articulated and sustained in a capitalistic framework' (Davie 2005b: 553). Discourses and practices of accounting have facilitated the translation of race-based mentalities of governance, both colonial and modern, into 'an organising principle of a society's investment and development policies' (Davie 2005b: 573).

New Zealand

The colonisation of New Zealand followed a distinctly different pattern from that of the other countries considered in this chapter, because the significant influx of European (primarily British) settlers came *after* the signing of the Treaty of Waitangi in 1840.[12] The Treaty, agreed between British Crown representatives and a number of Māori chiefs, came to be regarded as New Zealand's founding document. Despite the existence of the Treaty, which recognised Māori rights and authority over land, sources of food and valued elements of culture, the overriding aim of the subsequent 'white' colonisation of New Zealand was to assimilate and '"Europeanise" Maori people' (McNicholas et al. 2004: 61). This was so successful that by the late twentieth century, Māori culture and way of life was under severe threat and 'it became apparent that the assimilation policy had proved to be highly destructive to Maori society' (ibid.). Māori people became more politically active, and the Treaty was resuscitated as an active and legally binding document under which Māori retained certain rights and authority, generating greater Māori social, cultural and political awareness.

This unique history in New Zealand provides a fascinating setting for a number of studies that have explored various aspects of the use of accounting in the processes of colonisation, dispossession and assimilation. More recently, accounting research has included important explorations of the potential for Westernised accounting to learn from aspects of Māori social, cultural and business practice.

Jacobs (2000) explored accountability obligations and practices pertaining to the Treaty of Waitangi. The analysis reveals that while certain obligations under the Treaty were auditable (and therefore offered mechanisms for adding visibilities to the concerns of Māori peoples), they were seen to offer a partial accountability as they focused on accountability *for* the Māori peoples, but largely ignored accountability *to* Māori peoples (Jacobs 2000: 376–7).

Hooper and Kearins (2008) investigated the role of accounting in the compulsory acquisition of Māori land by the New Zealand government in the late nineteenth and early twentieth centuries. Their work revealed how accounting expertise was embroiled in a broad political approach to governance via 'expertocracy'. More specifically, it showed how accountants and systems of accounting helped to legitimise the dispossession of Māori lands by creating an aura of expertise in the realms of political decision-making. This helped to create the perception that they were 'the purveyor of a supposedly objective truth' (2008: 1246) and that decision-making was removed from the contestable, political realm. Accounting and calculative processes enabled government to 'remain figuratively at a distance' (2008: 1252) from the mechanisms of exploitation and dispossession, albeit that they were responsible for those very same mechanisms. This paper is one of several important studies focused on the use of accounting in the creation of 'regimes of truth' that enabled the dispossession of Māori lands in New Zealand (Hooper and Pratt 1995; Hooper and Kearins 1997, 2004; Kearins and Hooper 2002).

McNicholas et al. (2004) researched the experiences of Māori women in the accountancy profession as a means of understanding the impacts of colonialism on their lives and, more generally, their culture. Interviews with Māori women offered a unique voice that highlighted numerous concerns regarding the persistent impacts of colonialism – in particular, issues surrounding the assimilation of Māori women into Western capitalist culture. McNicholas et al.'s analysis illuminates important challenges associated with incongruences between Māori culture and Western organisational culture, and how the former tends to be silenced by the 'mono-cultural staff systems and practices' (2004: 89) of many organisations and the accountancy profession more generally (cf. Chua 1996). The paper offers valuable insights by highlighting the enduring nature of colonialism and showing how the mentalities of these endeavours persist, albeit in a more nuanced way, in present-day settings.

Some recent studies have examined various aspects of contemporary accounting and business practice in New Zealand, focusing on attempts by Māori people to counter the impacts of colonialism and to recover important aspects of their culture. This work is solidly set against the backdrop of the historical effects of colonialism, but it also seeks to advance the accounting and related business agendas by considering how Indigenous values and approaches are today being recovered and renewed for the Māori people. Significantly, it further considers how aspects of Māori culture might be adopted and adapted in wider New Zealand society, in a way that enhances New Zealand life more generally.

Craig et al. (2012) examined the fundamental accounting concept of an asset by exploring how this idea may be understood by reference to *taonga* – the closest term to 'asset' in Māori language and culture (2012: 1026). The authors' critique of this taken-for-granted concept helps to lay bare the individualistic and economically centric approach to wealth and value enshrined in Western accounting systems and opens possibilities for alternative approaches and understandings of accounting concepts based on an alternative set of guiding principles. The paper presents an interesting exploration of Māori attempts to recover control over important aspects of their culture that were lost during colonisation, overcoming problems of cultural appropriation and misappropriation of Indigenous knowledge.

Accounting and accountability reports were problematised from an Indigenous vantage point by Craig et al. (2018). In this paper, the authors explored the annual reports of four Māori-controlled organisations to see how three core values seen to be central to Māori culture permeated accountability reports. These values are: *wairuatanga* and *tikanga* (spirituality and customary belief); *whakapapa* (inter-generationalism and restoration); and *mana* and *rangatiratanga* (governance, leadership and respect). Examining particular aspects of wider Māori attempts to recover lands and *mana* lost in colonisation, this work highlights the mono-cultural dimensions associated with Western accounting practices and illuminates the possibilities for accountability reporting guided by Indigenous values.

USA

Accounting and accountability research has also examined issues of colonialism in the context of the USA. This research, while often focused on culturally and geographically distinct Indigenous peoples, nevertheless illustrates commonalities by showing the central role that accounting may play in rendering possible acts of controlling and governing others.

Preston and Oakes (2001) investigated the US Government's use of accounting technologies in 1930s discourses and decision-making surrounding the case of the Navajo Reservation in the Southwest of the country. They found that surveyor reports centred on 'rationalized and scientific' (2001: 60) methods of reporting served to construct the 'realities' of this reserve, including the 'economic representation and construction of the Navajo' inhabitants (2001: 53). This approach to reporting was partial and devaluing as it served to silence the 'voice[s] of the Navajo' (Preston and Oakes 2001: 47). It also helped sanction and legitimise subsequent interventions and regulations by Government on this reserve.

The focus of Preston (2006) was also on the Navajo Reservation. In this study, the emphasis shifted away from the (re)presentation of the Indigenous peoples through a financial lens, towards an investigation of how accounts and accounting numbers may serve to legitimise actions and decisions – crucially, both at a distance *and* locally. Informed by Latour's work, this study demonstrated how accounts were returned to the (metropolitan) centre, rendering the Navajo lands and their occupants governable. These accounts were used to claim that Navajo livestock were detrimentally impacting a nearby Government project, providing the principal basis on which the US Federal Government decided to sanction a substantial livestock reduction programme on the Navajo Reservation. This action was seen to be permissible by the government because the accounts relied on market value for measuring the significance of livestock; but they overlooked the multifaceted social, spiritual and wellbeing values of livestock to the Navajo people (Preston 2006: 572). Perhaps most importantly, Preston (2006: 577) found that these accounts may also operate 'locally [in] securing acceptance' for this programme by many Navajo people, as well as representing mechanisms for 'shoring up and justifying the decision to take action when things go wrong'. This study provides important insights into how accounting representations were translated into actions, and economic accounts 'became entwined in other strategies' employed 'to ensure that action at a distance was taken, enacted locally and preserved' (Preston 2006: 560).

Holmes et al. (2005) examined colonial accounting practices in the context of Spanish dealings with the Coahuiltecan Indians in 'New Spain' (modern-day Texas) during the years 1718 to 1794. They contend that numerous missions controlled and managed by the colonising power imposed systems of accounting on the Coahuiltecan people. These served as means for both facilitating the dispossession of resources and indoctrinating Western standards and fiscal and economic practices aimed at shaping the 'mentalities and practices of the indigenous peoples' (Holmes et al. 2005: 134).

Thornburg and Roberts (2012) examined accounting practices in the context of Western colonialism in Alaska. Focusing on the US Government's enactment and application of the Alaska Native Claims Settlement Act, they found that this legislative mechanism helped to facilitate the economic assimilation of Native Alaskans, including via the dispossession of their lands. The key strategy was the establishment of corporate entities that vested stockholdings to Indigenous persons *only* when they relinquished rights to future land claims. Thornburg and Roberts (2012) suggested that the formation of these Alaska Native Corporations (ANCs) imposed corporate accounting and reporting requirements that, in turn, generated 'conflict in personal values … [as they] attempted to reconcile their cultural beliefs with their newly acquired interest in capitalist enterprise' (2012: 208). ANCs helped to create class divides among Native Alaskans and transformed 'the Alaska Native shareholder into an object with which the state and industrial interests can negotiate in order to commercialize the resources in Alaska and further the national interest of America' (Thornburg and Roberts 2012: 212). The US Government viewed the corporate form of land claim settlement with Alaskan Indigenous peoples as 'a technological improvement in American colonialism' (2012: 206).

These studies make an important contribution by identifying the role of accounting records in the construction and representation of indigenous peoples, and the consequences for their lives and wellbeing. This research also attests to the ongoing nature of colonial practices and accounting after the formal end of colonialism, providing insight into the historical lineage of practices that persist in contemporary settings. Thus, this work helps to situate our understanding of the present and provides a historical echo of current governmental approaches to indigenous peoples and other marginalised populations. For example, Preston and Oakes (2001) demonstrated how the construction of the Navajo as an 'economic problem' enabled the government to seek an economic solution to the poverty and social disadvantage of the Navajo people. This was 'an elaborate construction' (2001: 53), and financial accounts 'were the key element in the construction of an economic solution' (2001: 57). Although the ostensible intent of the Navajo documents was to save the 'Indian' (sic) from himself, by effecting a change in the Navajo lifestyle (put purely and simply: social engineering), this intervention proved disastrous for the Navajo people, and the effective result of the economisation of their existence was even greater financial disadvantage and increased dependency on government support.

Discerning the place of accounting

As the foregoing review indicates, accounting studies of colonialism and indigenous peoples provide a range of important and significant contextual insights into the social, political and cultural functions of accounting. Considering this work as a whole, we see three general themes that have significantly animated these studies and enhanced their insights into the place of accounting in this setting: (1) the discursive nature of accounting itself, and the infusion of accounting into wider discursive formations; (2) the way accounting has mediated and rationalised Indigenous–government relations under (and subsequent to) colonialism, with accounting technologies being central to key aspects of the processes of government itself; and (3) the implication of accounting in various contexts of power, such that accounting itself becomes a form of power. Under the aegis of each of these themes, we can discern how research brings to light the complex and multifaceted functions of accounting in relation to numerous elements of discourse, government and power.

Accounting and/as discourse

Foucault (1991b) identified the importance of *discourses* to our ability to understand the practices of government, because discourses are central to the constitution of subjects. Discourses 'found, justify and provide reasons and principles' for the practices of government (Foucault 1991b: 79). Building on this notion, Miller and Rose (1990) highlighted the importance of discursive frameworks to the practices of government, suggesting that it is through a wider discursive field, which includes accounting language and discourses, that governments are able to conceive of and articulate what come to be regarded as 'the proper ends and means of government' (1990: 5).

The importance of accounting language, as a part of wider discursive formations, to the practices of colonial government is borne out in a number of the accounting studies featured in this chapter. Research shows how, through language and discourses imbued with racial stereotypes, unequal power relations between particular Indigenous peoples and colonial powers were inscribed into reality. Discursive regimes actively constructed and maintained seemingly immutable hierarchies of race, upon which authorities premised colonial policies and practices. Studies show how authorities created and recreated racial inferiority through the normalisation of particular views of Indigenous (in)capacity that prioritised the interests of 'the "white" settlers sent to the colonies' (Neu 2000b: 167).

Studies also highlight the wider discursive formations at work in colonial contexts. As Neu (2000b: 167) notes, the construction of Indigenous peoples as 'inferior' and 'savages' was associated with a wider discursive formation centred on a notion of the 'right manner' for governing. The latter constituted particular Indigenous peoples as a problem for government, while simultaneously prioritising colonial interests. Initially, representations of indigenous inferiority encouraged the implementation of policies deemed appropriate for peoples for whom extinction was regarded as an 'inevitable destiny, decreed by God or by nature' (McGregor 1997: ix). However, the failure of Indigenous peoples to die out as expected did not result in a transition to more enlightened government policies, even with the decline of the 'doomed race theory' (McGregor 1997). Rather, the presumption of indigenous inferiority continued to dominate, albeit under the guise of a 'civilising mission', which itself was based on a presumption of innate inferiority of Indigenous cultures and lifestyles, and, thereby, peoples. Consistent with the civilising mission, social technologies such as accounting and law were, and continue to be, used to compel Indigenous peoples to conform to the dominant culture and economy (Bird 1987; Greer 2006; Greer and McNicholas 2017).

While accounting research is naturally concerned with the centrality of accounting discourses and techniques in the relations between colonisers and Indigenous peoples, a significant aspect of this discursive theme is the circularity of colonial frameworks. That is, the research shows that discursive frameworks of colonialism not only provided the *conditions of possibility* for the introduction of specific practices such as accounting to translate policies into practice; they also provided *rationalisations* for the impact of these same policies and thus the *justification* for further interventions. The notion of 'presents' used to describe payments for land to First Nations peoples in Canada (Neu 2000b) provides a clear example of this circularity of discourses, and the essential enmeshing of accounting discourse within the logic and practices of colonial systems of government. Neu (2000b) revealed the changing purposes served by accounting in the distribution of 'presents', including: the measurement of the terms of exchange over land; the practices for achieving these exchanges; and the rationalisation and justification for the values of exchange. Moreover, these exchanges were predicated on a wider discursive formation of Indigenous peoples as uncivilised and dependent on the government for support.

The role of accounting in creating justifications for initial and continued inventions in the lives of Indigenous peoples in the discursive practices of colonialism are not limited to one context. Accounting systems and information have been revealed to be instrumental in legitimising attempts to transform the economic behaviours of Indigenous peoples in Australia, ostensibly under a 'moral betterment' guise (Greer and McNicholas 2017). In the geographically distinct domain of the USA, Preston and Oakes (2001) showed how accounting technologies helped render an economic construction (that is, a representation) of the Navajo people, which in turn, created the possibilities for economic solutions (specifically, intervention) to issues on reservations, thus necessitating a situation whereby the 'Navajo were [needed] to be saved from themselves' (Preston and Oakes 2001: 40). Studies such as these show that accounting discourses, situated in the logic and practices of colonial systems of government, transcend both time and space.

The preceding discussion identifies two important aspects of accounting research on colonialism and indigenous peoples. The first of these relates to how the discursive social construction of particular Indigenous identities as inferior and non-citizens underpinned colonial systems of government. Particular representations of Indigenous peoples as a 'problem' requiring government action arose out of social and governmental practices rather than reflecting 'facts' (Boyce and Davids 2004; Bacchi 2009, 2013). These problematisations reflected particular attitudes towards Indigenous peoples and were essential to the ability of governments to intervene and control the populations in order to obtain control of Indigenous lands. Within the culture of colonialism, accounting discourses and practices helped structure and rationalise particular problematisations of Indigenous peoples, while facilitating the expropriation of the 'spoils of colonialism' (Neu 2000b: 182). This mode of representation of Indigenous peoples as a 'problem' was typically adopted by colonial governments, and continues to be used in contemporary settings as a precursor to particular kinds of government action, such as the 'intervention' into Indigenous communities in Australia (Calma 2010) and the invention of individualised regimes of responsibility and accountability (Watson 2004; Lawrence and Gibson 2007).

Preston and Oakes (2001) provide an example of the importance of particular representations of Indigenous peoples to Indigenous–government relations, and the resultant effects on the life experiences of Indigenous peoples (in this case, the Navajo people). They observe that, in order that 'the Navajo … be saved from themselves … A rationalized economy had to be constructed in terms of income and consumption and a new economic identity, namely that of a consumption unit, had to be forged for the Navajo' (2001: 60). The authorities sought an economic solution to the 'Navajo problem', and this necessitated an economic reconstruction of the Navajo people. Numbers, accounts and the like represented what came to be 'real', offering an economic 'window on the world of the Navajo' and substituting Anglo-American understandings for Indigenous ways of life and identities even as they claimed to 'reveal' the latter (ibid.).

The second aspect concerns the role of accounting as both discourse and technique. While governments used accounting discourse to *rationalise* policies, accounting techniques and calculations helped to *constitute* policies as well as *translate* policies into practice. In effect, policy 'ideas' depended on practices such as accounting to exist and these practices in turn 'shape[d] the possibilities of policy, and help construct the decision set of policy makers' (Neu and Graham 2006: 51).

Accounting and/as government

At the core of many of the papers reviewed in this chapter are conceptions of accounting as a technology of government, consistent with the notion of governmentality developed by Foucault (Neu 1999, 2000a, 2000b; Neu and Graham 2004, 2006; Neu and Heincke 2004; Greer and McNicholas 2017). Governmentality, according to Foucault (1991a: 102), broadly refers to an 'ensemble formed by the institutions, procedures, analyses and reflections, [and] the calculations and tactics that allow[s] the exercise of this very specific albeit complex form of power'. This perspective takes as its focus populations, attempting to ensure that 'the greatest possible quantity of wealth is produced, that the people are provided with sufficient means of subsistence, [and] that the population is enabled to multiply' (Foucault 1991a: 95). Yet for Foucault, as Neu and Graham (2006: 50) observe, the focus of government is not simply people, but rather 'a complex of people-and-things [such as customs and habits], a complex that must first be constructed by the technologies with which government represents the objects of governance'.

Miller and Rose (1990) used the term 'technologies of government' to describe the variety of techniques that governments rely on to represent the objects of government and to influence and shape the actions and conduct of subjects. Modes of calculation are central to 'acting upon individuals, entities and activities in conformity with a particular set of ideals' (Miller and O'Leary 1994: 99). This mode of analysis may be distinguished from that in which power is implicated in 'a simple and direct physical determination' of the objects of power (Boyce and Davids 2004: 7). While Rose and Miller (1992: 183) observe that the list of possible mechanisms available to authorities is both 'heterogeneous and in principle unlimited', figuring prominently on their list of technologies are the techniques and practices of accounting, and 'the inauguration of professional specialisms and vocabularies', which help make government possible.

Accounting studies of colonialism and indigenous peoples document how colonial authorities used accounting technologies at almost every step of the process: to institute government, to deploy programmes, to construct Indigenous peoples as the object of government, and to account for the financial consequences of government actions. In other words, the foregrounding of accounting as a technology of government in this frame of analysis has elucidated the salience of accounting language and techniques in the ability of colonial authorities both to *imagine* policies and translate them into *practice*.

This theme of governmentality also highlights the instrumentality of accounting in extending the dominion of colonial governments through a diverse group of agents. Neu (1999), for example, documents the importance of indirect agents such as religious organisations to the ability of colonial government to function in relation to Indigenous peoples.

Accounting and/as power

Extending the above, accounting research also illuminates important dimensions of the operation of power in colonial settings. This third theme, evident in studies of accounting and colonialism and indigenous peoples, renders visible the role of accounting as a mediating force and, in this context, its function in the disabling of Indigenous agency. In Foucauldian terms, power invokes the subjectivity of citizens and relations of power operate to 'invest the citizen with a set of goals and self-understandings' (Cruikshank 1999: 41). Notably, relationships of power are reproduced not only through institutions but also through practices of government. Thus, these studies provide insights into the way government seeks to shape human conduct and to structure the possible field of action of a subject population.

Neu and Graham (2006) provided evidence of the functioning of power relations within accounting-based governance processes related to the activities of the US Government's Indian agencies. Their examples of how accounting methods were used to help convert First Nations peoples into economic citizens documented how the enlistment and enabling of these agents often had 'the effect of disabling' (2006: 52) Indigenous agency. Moreover, this 'narrowed the domains in which indigenous peoples could exercise agency, and functioned as an ideological circle … that rationalized both the government's paternal attitudes and the need for further government control of indigenous affairs' (Neu and Graham 2006: 73). Their analysis also rendered visible the salience of accounting technologies to mutually sustaining webs of observation and discipline, enlisted, in this case, to teach the Indigenous peoples 'how to handle' money (2006: 63).

Conclusions and possibilities for future research

While the absolute number of studies investigating accounting and accountability issues relating to colonialism and indigenous peoples has increased since the publication of the first edition of the *Routledge Companion* in 2009, overall the amount of historical and contemporary research in this field remains limited. This is both unfortunate and surprising, given the importance and potential fruitfulness of this research agenda, the insights it has generated to date and the contemporary socio-political significance of the issues examined – for many settings and countries. Considerable opportunities for future research exist and many questions remain unexplored and unresolved. There is much more to understand about the relationship between accounting and indigenous peoples, in the context of colonialism as well as in other more contemporary contexts. To encourage further investigations we conclude the chapter by identifying key areas for both expanding and supplementing the research agenda.

Expanding the geographical gaze

The literature would benefit from research focused on non-British, non-Anglo colonialism (Walker 2008; Buhr 2011). For example, unique insights could be gained from an exploration of the accounting and accountability dimensions of the actions of other major European and Asian powers, such as Belgium (e.g. Congo); the Netherlands (e.g. Dutch East Indies); France (e.g. West Africa, Equatorial Africa and parts of Northern Africa); Italy (e.g. Libya and Eritrea); Spain (e.g. Morocco); and Japan (e.g. Korea and Taiwan).[13] New research investigating these contexts would not only address gaps in our present understandings, it would also create opportunities for comparisons and contrasts with existing literature on British colonialism. Furthermore, research into previously underexplored or overlooked sites may create opportunities for new authors to enter the field and therefore broaden the scope of contributors in the extant literature.

Cross-geographical comparisons could represent a particularly salient line of investigation, given that one theme emerging from the analysis in this chapter relates to the prevailing role of accounting in colonial discourses across space and time. Research investigating disparate contexts (such as Australia and Canada) illuminates noticeable commonalities in the mentalities and practices of colonial governments. Exploration of these consistencies has great research potential because it could help to show the pervasive and transcendent nature of accounting practices through processes of colonialism and the mediation of indigenous–government relationships more broadly. Cross-geographical comparisons would equally afford the possibility for examining differences and similarities in the manner in which authorities imagined Indigenous peoples as subjects of government, and in the practices enacted to achieve the government of the Indigenous peoples.[14]

Notwithstanding the benefits of research into previously overlooked geographical locations, the extant literature is also suggestive of the need to continue to explore particular sites of governance that have been considered to date. For example, the administration of Indigenous peoples in Australia has largely been the responsibility of different states and territories throughout much of the country's colonial history (see Greer 2009). Broader, deeper and more diverse studies into geographical settings already explored would enable us to obtain additional insights into specific and local manifestations of colonial mentalities, and inform the literature by highlighting contextual differences and transitioning away from a homogenous view of governance across different settings.

Diversifying theorisation

The adoption of any particular theoretical lens and associated assumptions about reality, society, human nature and knowledge (Burrell and Morgan 1979), has a profound impact on the interpretation of the subject matter under examination (Merino 1998; Baxter and Chua 2003; Irvine and Deo 2006; Broadbent and Unerman 2011). A prominent theoretical framing of the extant literature is Michel Foucault's work on governmentality. This approach has proven both productive and insightful in relation to the manner in which colonial authorities seek to shape the behaviours and activities of individuals. However, some key aspects of governmentality – such as space and spatial concepts – appear to have been largely overlooked in the research conducted so far. Introducing spatial thinking and methods of analysis could help with both physical (such as design configurations) and non-physical (spatio-temporal) understandings and interpretations of the social processes that constitute colonialism. This line of analysis could also benefit from recourse to the writings of other notable contributors to the sociology of space, such as Henri Lefebvre, Edward Soja and David Harvey.

Forms of power are central to Foucauldian analysis generally, but they represent particularly critical focal points of analysis under the particular theoretical conception of governmentality (Boyce and Davids 2004; Dean 2010; McKinlay and Pezet 2010; Spence and Rinaldi 2014). Given that (uneven) power dynamics are evidently at the heart of many problems in indigenous–government relationships, it is surprising that recourse has not yet been had to other important theoretical approaches to the analysis of power, such as the influential work of Steven Lukes or Stewart Clegg. Use of works such as Lukes' (2005) *Power: A Radical View* and Clegg's (1989) *Frameworks of Power* may present fertile avenues for further exploration, as they offer analytical frameworks that transcend particular theories for which power dimensions are important.

Alternative theoretical perspectives informed by the broader socio-political and political-economic realms also offer stimulating prospective avenues for future research. Marxist theories represent one such possibility for enhancing understandings of the junctures between accounting, colonialism and indigenous peoples. Although some prior work has embraced a Marxian analysis of imperialism or colonialism (see Hoogvelt and Tinker 1978; Fleischman et al. 2013), the broad theoretical strands of Marxian analysis remain largely overlooked and underexplored.

Marxian-*inspired* theoretical standpoints have also not featured to date. Future research may find it useful to draw on scholarly works that stem from the Critical Theory legacy of the Frankfurt School, such as the work of Max Horkheimer on 'reason' and Theodor Adorno on 'culture and homogenisation'. Antonio Gramsci's work on cultural hegemony and subaltern identity could also help to open up new avenues of critique and investigation. Overall, a more diverse set of critical theoretical lenses would create opportunities for new contributions that inform and extend present understandings in the extant literature.

Adoption of postcolonial theorisations such as those of Gayatri Chakravorty Spivak also offer opportunities to expand the consideration of the subaltern concept and generate further critical analysis – in particular, to show the doubly repressed nature of certain subaltern groups (for example, women may be oppressed by colonialism *and* discursive institutions). More generally, further consideration of manifestations of postcolonialism as the continuation of colonialism following its 'formal' (or political) end with the granting of self-rule may offer insights into how colonial subjugation can be transformed into a form of 'self-imposed' colonialism wherein former colonial subjects 'take on' the identities imposed upon them. The prior accounting literature on subalternity (Neu 2001; Neu and Heincke 2004; Graham 2009; Wickramasinghe and Alawattage 2009) points in this direction and may tie in nicely with developments in silent, shadow and counter accountings (Boyce 2014; McDonald-Kerr 2017) insofar as these may involve giving voice to the oppressed.

Methodological innovation

Alternative methodological dimensions represent another area that is ripe for future studies of the accounting history of colonialism and indigenous peoples. The contentions of Buhr (2011: 152) that there should be an increased focus on 'accounting "by" Indigenous peoples rather than accounting "for" Indigenous peoples' in the literature, continue to be relevant. While some recent research has started to address this lacuna (Lombardi 2016), this aspect of the literature nevertheless remains limited in both quantity and scope. More research along these lines has the potential to offer valuable insights because it would help to give 'voice' and 'visibility' to Indigenous persons, while transitioning away from the colonial-centric standpoint that dominates the existing literature.

This overarching research strategy broadly aligns with (and thus may be informed by) the emergent literature on silent, shadow and counter accounting, which seeks to shift and reorientate the analysis and production of accounts beyond traditional domains of powerful and dominant parties (Boyce 2014; McDonald-Kerr 2017). These types of analysis may help to create new 'spaces' of opposition and create alternative ways of 'speaking back', which may address questions of whether there were any attempts by indigenous peoples (or others) to resist or counter the hegemonic governmental forces focused on accounting.

It is interesting, but perhaps unsurprising, to observe that the extant literature has predominately focused on indigenous–government relationships in order to explore accounting and accountability issues. This is an obvious focus given the central role of governments in 'mediating' relationships between the colonialised and colonisers. There nevertheless remains substantial scope for enriching the extant literature by broadening these research forays into critical explorations of the roles of other key actors and private institutions, including corporations.

Some of the prior literature has already demonstrated the insights to be gained from research that shifts the focus away from specific organs of 'state government'. Neu and Graham (2004), for example, examined the key role of an individual player, Deputy Superintendent Scott in the Canadian Indian Department in the early twentieth century, and Hooper and Kearins (1997) focused on the activities, accounts and records of an early and wealthy New Zealand colonialist, Sir Donald McLean. This actor-centred mode of analysis has yielded interesting analytical insights that highlight the role of individual agency in colonial discourses, and there is further potential for more research endeavours along similar lines. It should, however, be noted that, while examination of individual (and collective) agency may help to cultivate further insights and understandings, this must remain just one element in the broader social, political, administrative contexts of colonial discourses.

Extending the above, there has also been limited research that focuses on the role of private corporations and other institutions as key actors in colonial discourses. It is clear that colonialism is far too complex a process to understand solely by reference to the discourse of governmental institutions, and although some research has ventured into this area (Thornburg and Roberts 2012), the quantum of studies remains limited.

Closing thoughts: rediscovering accountability

The overall lack of accountability theories and frameworks used in the literature on accounting and indigenous peoples and colonialism represents a particularly noteworthy lacuna. Perhaps this is because this notion is somewhat taken-for-granted in the broader accounting field, but there is value to be gained from examining, and perhaps problematising, the very notion of accountability (Roberts 1991; Gray 2006; Boyce 2014). More studies that adopt theoretical vantage points around the idea of 'accountability' are surely needed, because it is a *lack* of accountability that seems to be at the core of many issues raised in the literature.

There is also a noticeable lacuna in the literature pertaining to *pre-colonial* approaches to accounts and accountability (Annisette 2006; Walker 2008; Buhr 2011). A new research agenda in this area has the potential to better inform and enlighten existing and future accountability research examining colonialism, partly because it would help to create an improved vantage point from which existing research might be better understood and contextualised. Explorations into this arena have the potential to reveal pre-colonial approaches to record keeping, systems of accounting and understandings of accountability. This research would undoubtedly face challenges (including access to sources such as archival materials), yet, to the extent that these problems could be overcome, there is considerable potential to develop novel insights into antecedent systems of accounting by indigenous peoples. In addition, further studies along the lines of Craig et al. (2012, 2018) that examine attempts by indigenous peoples to recover and enhance key elements of their (pre-colonial) culture have the potential to inform the ongoing development of accounting in contemporary settings.[15]

Perhaps it is the pervasiveness and historical significance of colonialism itself that has brought us to a position where we know very little about pre-colonial Indigenous approaches to accounts, accounting and accountability. As we have observed, some recent studies have started to develop a contemporary research agenda in this area.

There is much to learn in relation to the history of the lands we currently inhabit and of their original peoples. Through their further study we are likely to find some energising and exciting ways to challenge our own sedimented styles of thinking about, and doing, 'accounting'.

Key works

Annisette and Neu (2004) is an editorial introduction to a special issue that brings together papers exploring the role of accounting in the furtherance of British imperialist endeavours.

Buhr (2011) provides a detailed overview of the accounting history literature pertaining to indigenous peoples.

Gallhofer and Chew (2000) is an editorial introduction to a special issue that contains a variety of articles introducing readers to the area.

Notes

1 We are very grateful to Susan Greer and Dean Neu, the authors of the chapter on 'Indigenous peoples and colonialism' that was included in the first edition of *The Routledge Companion to Accounting History* for permission to use their work as an initial basis for preparing this new chapter.

2 To date the majority of accounting research in this domain has concentrated on particular sites of *British* colonialism, but there were many other colonial powers. Said (1994: xxii), for example, identified several empires including (but not limited to) 'the Austro-Hungarian, the Russian, the Ottoman, and the Spanish and Portuguese', as well as the French and American.

3 The four themes that are used to organise Fleischman et al.'s book on *Critical Histories of Accounting* are all relevant to accounting research on colonialism and indigenous peoples: annihilation, subjugation, exploitation and exclusion.

4 'The prevailing view today is that no formal universal definition of the term is necessary' (Secretariat of the Permanent Forum on Indigenous Issues 2004: 4).

5 'Indigenous Peoples at the UN' (www.un.org/development/desa/indigenouspeoples/about-us.html Accessed December 2018).

6 In adopting this approach, we sidestep debates about the distinctions between colonialism, neo-colonialism and postcolonialism (see Loomba 1998). Rather, we focus on how accounting research has considered the effects of the 'encounter between peoples … of conquest and domination' (Loomba 1998: 2) and particularly on insights into the implication of accounting ideas and practices therein.

7 Considered here in alphabetical order. Included are the five countries on which most of the accounting research in this domain to date has focused. The scope of the chapter *excludes* work that has considered colonialism and its effects in developing and emerging country contexts, for example where the research focus is *not* on indigenous peoples (such as research set in India, Ghana, Kenya and the Caribbean, for example).

8 The inclusion of Fiji in this chapter might be somewhat contentious given our adoption of the definition of indigenous peoples as being members of present 'non-dominant sectors of society' (Martínez Cobo 1983: 50, para 379). This could be regarded as *precluding* studies set in the Fijian context, because Indigenous Fijians themselves occupied a dominant social sector. Indeed, rather than eschew the Indigenous customs of the original inhabitants, British colonial authorities incorporated many into the policies and structures of indirect rule, as well as enlisting the cooperation of the native chieftaincy to govern (Kaplan 1989; Davie 2005a, 2005b). Nevertheless, research in this area is included in the chapter because it represents a significant body of work that provides important insights into how specific accounting practices, laws and policies enabled colonial ideological and political domination, and because it exposes how accounting language and techniques facilitated the integration of these forms of domination into modern contexts.

9 The body of the research covers the period up to the date of Federalism in 1900 and is primarily concerned with the policies and practices of colonial governments.

10 Although they were embraced by the Indigenous populace, these structures did not exist before colonial rule (Davie 2007: 261). This approach was similar to that adopted by other colonial powers (Germany and then Belgium) in their rule in Rwanda – constructing a Hutu, Tutsi and Twa tribal divide (Eltringham 2006).

11 Echoing the findings of Davie's (2000) earlier work, Alam et al. (2004: 136) also referred to the power dimension of the cooperation of the chiefs: 'Fiji's annexation to the British Crown was mainly on the grounds of some influential chiefs (being) unable to maintain their power against their rivals and to control [a] considerable European settler population in the early 19th century'.

12 McNicholas et al. (2004: 59–63) provide a succinct but highly relevant overview of the colonial history of New Zealand, highlighting some of the significant elements that have been taken up in various accounting studies of this setting.

13 This suggestion may relate more to the accounting history literature on colonialism more broadly, rather than the specific focus of this chapter on colonialism and indigenous peoples. In relation to the latter, however, the Spanish and Portuguese Empires, for instance, had profound effects on Indigenous peoples in Latin America. Therefore, from a broad accounting history perspective, as well as from the perspective of colonialism and indigenous peoples, research that seeks to add to our understanding of the role of accounting in these contexts would be welcome.

14 There may also be interesting insights to be gained from examining how colonialism in countries such as Canada, New Zealand, Australia, wherein the English colonised (settled) and established their culture over time through the process of the British (and their descendants) becoming the *dominant people* of the country, differed (or not) from the experience in India, Nigeria and similar sites where colonial rule involved the forcible imposition of British institutions and norms on the majority population, with many of these norms persisting in the post-colonial era.

15 Gallhofer et al. (1997) and Greer and Patel (2000) also provide excellent explorations of this important domain.

References

Alam, M., Lawrence, S. and Nandan, R. (2004) Accounting for economic development in the context of post-colonialism: the Fijian experience, *Critical Perspectives on Accounting*, 15 (1): 135–57.

Annisette, M. (1999) Importing accounting: the case of Trinidad and Tobago, *Accounting, Business & Financial History*, 9 (1): 103–33.

Annisette, M. (2000) Imperialism and the professions: the education and certification of accountants in Trinidad and Tobago, *Accounting, Organizations and Society*, 25 (7): 631–59.

Annisette, M. (2006) People and periods untouched by accounting history: an ancient Yoruba practice, *Accounting History*, 11 (4): 399–417.

Annisette, M. and Neu, D. (2004) Accounting and empire: an introduction, *Critical Perspectives on Accounting*, 15 (1): 1–4.

Bacchi, C. (2009) *Analysing Policy: What's the Problem Represented to Be?* (Sydney: Pearson).

Bacchi, C. (2013) Why study problematizations? Making politics visible, *Open Journal of Political Science*, 2 (1): 1–8.

Baxter, J. and Chua, W.F. (2003) Alternative management accounting research-whence and whither, *Accounting, Organizations and Society*, 28 (2): 97–126.

Bhabha, H.K. (1994) *The Location of Culture* (London: Routledge).

Bird, G. (1987) *The 'Civilizing Mission': Race and the Construction of Crime* (Melbourne: Faculty of Law, Monash University).

Boyce, G. (2014) Professionalism, the public interest, and social accounting, in S. Mintz (ed.) *Accounting for the Public Interest: Perspectives on Accountability, Professionalism and Role in Society* (pp. 115–139) (Netherlands: Springer).

Boyce, G. and Davids, C. (2004) *The Dimensions of Governmentality Studies in Accounting: Complementary and Critical Potentials.* Paper presented at the Fourth Asia-Pacific Interdisciplinary Research in Accounting Conference, Singapore, Singapore Management University and APIRA.

Broadbent, J. and Unerman, J. (2011) Developing the relevance of the accounting academy: the importance of drawing from the diversity of research approaches, *Meditari Accountancy Research*, 19 (1/2): 7–21.

Buhr, N. (2011) Indigenous peoples in the accounting literature: time for a plot change and some Canadian suggestions, *Accounting History*, 16 (2): 139–60.

Burrell, G. and Morgan, G. (1979) *Sociological Paradigms and Organisational Analysis: Elements of the Sociology of Corporate Life* (Aldershot: Gower).

Bush, B. and Maltby, J. (2004) Taxation in West Africa: transforming the colonial subject into the "governable person", *Critical Perspectives on Accounting*, 15 (1): 5–34.

Calma, T. (2010) The Northern Territory intervention – it's not our dream, *Law in Context*, 27 (2): 14–41.

Chew, A. and Greer, S. (1997) Contrasting world views on accounting: accountability and Aboriginal culture. *Accounting, Auditing & Accountability Journal*, 10 (3): 276–98.

Chua, W.F. (1996) Teaching and learning only the language of numbers-monolingualism in a multilingual world, *Critical Perspectives on Accounting*, 7 (1): 129–56.

Clegg, S.R. (1989) *Frameworks of Power* (London: Sage Publications).

Craig, R., Taonui, R. and Wild, S. (2012) The concept of taonga in Māori culture: insights for accounting, *Accounting, Auditing & Accountability Journal*, 25 (6): 1025–47.

Craig, R., Taonui, R., Wild, S. and Rodrigues, L.L. (2018) Accountability reporting objectives of Māori organizations, *Pacific Accounting Review*, 30 (4): 433–43.

Cruikshank, B. (1999) *The Will to Empower: Democratic Citizens and Other Subjects* (New York: Cornell University Press).
Davie, S.S. and McLean, T. (2017) Accounting, cultural hybridisation and colonial globalisation: a case of British civilising mission in Fiji, *Accounting, Auditing & Accountability Journal*, 30 (4): 932–54.
Davie, S.S.K. (2000) Accounting for imperialism: a case of British-imposed indigenous collaboration, *Accounting, Auditing & Accountability Journal*, 13 (3): 330–59.
Davie, S.S.K. (2005a) Accounting's uses in exploitative human engineering: theorizing citizenship, indirect rule and Britain's imperial expansion, *Accounting Historians Journal*, 32 (2): 55–80.
Davie, S.S.K. (2005b) The politics of accounting, race and ethnicity: a story of a chiefly-based preferencing, *Critical Perspectives on Accounting*, 16 (5): 551–77.
Davie, S.S.K. (2007) A colonial "social experiment": accounting and a communal system in British-ruled Fiji, *Accounting Forum*, 31 (3): 255–76.
Dean, M. (2010) *Governmentality: Power and Rule in Modern Society* (2nd ed.) (London: Sage Publications).
Dyball, M.C., Chua, W.F. and Poullaos, C. (2006) Mediating between colonizer and colonized in the American empire: accounting for government moneys in the Philippines, *Accounting, Auditing & Accountability Journal*, 19 (1): 47–81.
Dyball, M.C., Poullaos, C. and Chua, W.F. (2007) Accounting and empire: professionalization-as-resistance, *Critical Perspectives on Accounting*, 18 (4): 415–49.
Eltringham, N. (2006) "Invaders who have stolen the country": the Hamitic hypothesis, race and the Rwandan Genocide, *Social Identities*, 12 (4): 425–46.
Fleischman, R.K., Funnell, W. and Walker, S.P. (eds.) (2013) *Critical Histories of Accounting: Sinister Inscriptions in the Modern Era* (New York: Routledge).
Foucault, M. (1991a) Governmentality, in G. Burchell, C. Gordon and P. Miller (eds.) *The Foucault Effect*, (pp. 87–104) (Chicago, IL: University of Chicago Press).
Foucault, M. (1991b) Questions of Method in G. Burchell, C. Gordon and P. Miller (eds.) *The Foucault Effect*, (pp. 73–86) (Chicago, IL: University of Chicago Press).
Gallhofer, S. and Chew, A. (2000) Introduction: accounting and indigenous peoples, *Accounting, Auditing & Accountability Journal*, 13 (3): 256–267.
Gallhofer, S., Gibson, K., Haslam, J., McNicholas, P. and Takiari, B. (1997) Developing environmental accounting: insights from indigenous cultures, *Accounting, Auditing and Accountability Journal*, 13 (3): 381–409.
Gibson, K. (2000) Accounting as a tool for Aboriginal dispossession: then and now, *Accounting, Auditing & Accountability Journal*, 13 (3): 289–306.
Gill, M. (2011) *Accountants' Truth: Knowledge and Ethics in the Financial World* (Oxford and New York: Oxford University Press).
Graham, C. (2009) Accounting and subalternity: enlarging a research space, *Accounting, Auditing & Accountability Journal*, 22 (3): 309–18.
Gray, R. (2006) Social, environmental and sustainability reporting and organisational value creation? Whose value? Whose creation? *Accounting, Auditing & Accountability Journal*, 19 (6): 793–819.
Greer, S. (2006) *Governing Indigenous Peoples: A History of Accounting Interventions in the New South Wales Aborigines Protection and Welfare Boards 1883-1969.* (Unpublished PhD Thesis), Macquarie University, Sydney, Australia.
Greer, S. (2009) "In the interests of the children": accounting in the control of Aboriginal family endowment payments, *Accounting History*, 14 (1-2): 166–91.
Greer, S. and McNicholas, P. (2017) Accounting for "moral betterment": pastoral power and indentured Aboriginal apprenticeship programs in New South Wales, *Accounting, Auditing & Accountability Journal*, 30 (8): 1843–66.
Greer, S. and Patel, C. (2000) The issue of Australian indigenous world views and accounting, *Accounting, Auditing & Accountability Journal*, 13 (3): 307–29.
Holmes, S.A., Welch, S.T. and Knudson, L.R. (2005) The role of accounting practices in the disempowerment of the Coahuiltecan Indians, *Accounting Historians Journal*, 32 (2): 105–43.
Hoogvelt, A. (1997) *Globalization and the Postcolonial World: The New Political Economy of Development* (London: Macmillan Press).
Hoogvelt, A. and Tinker, A.M. (1978) The rôle of colonial and post-colonial states in imperialism – a case-study of the Sierra Leone Development Company, *The Journal of Modern African Studies*, 16 (1): 67–79.

Hooper, K. and Kearins, K. (1997) "The excited and dangerous state of the natives of Hawkes Bay": a particular study of nineteenth century financial management, *Accounting, Organizations and Society*, 22 (3): 269–92.

Hooper, K. and Kearins, K. (2004) Financing New Zealand 1860-1880: Maori land and the wealth tax effect, *Accounting History*, 9 (2): 87–105.

Hooper, K. and Kearins, K. (2008) The walrus, carpenter and oysters: liberal reform, hypocrisy and expertocracy in Maori land loss in New Zealand 1885-1911, *Critical Perspectives on Accounting*, 19 (8): 1239–62.

Hooper, K. and Pratt, M. (1995) Discourse and rhetoric: the case of the New Zealand Native Land Company, *Accounting, Auditing & Accountability Journal*, 8 (1): 10–37.

Horvath, R.J. (1972) A definition of colonialism, *Current Anthropology*, 13 (1): 45–57.

Irvine, H. and Deo, H. (2006) The power of the lens: a comparative analysis of two views of the Fiji Development Bank, *Accounting, Auditing & Accountability Journal*, 19 (2): 205–27.

Jacobs, K. (2000) Evaluating accountability: finding a place for the Treaty of Waitangi in the New Zealand public sector, *Accounting, Auditing & Accountability Journal*, 13 (3): 360–80.

Kaplan, M. (1989) The "Dangerous and Disaffected Native" in Fiji: British colonial constructions of the Tuka Movement, *Social Analysis: The International Journal of Social and Cultural Practice*, (26): 22–45.

Kearins, K. and Hooper, K. (2002) Genealogical method and analysis, *Accounting, Auditing & Accountability Journal*, 15 (5): 733–57.

Lawrence, R. and Gibson, C. (2007) Obliging indigenous citizens, *Cultural Studies*, 21 (4/5): 650–71.

Lombardi, L. (2016) Disempowerment and empowerment of accounting: an Indigenous accounting context, *Accounting, Auditing & Accountability Journal*, 29 (8): 1320–41.

Loomba, A. (2002) *Colonialism/Postcolonialism* (New York: Routledge).

Lukes, S. (2005) *Power: A Radical View*, (2nd ed.) (London: Palgrave).

Martínez Cobo, J. (1983) *Study of the Problem of Discrimination against Indigenous Populations* (E/CN.4 Sub.2/1983/21/Add.8). New York: United Nations. Retrieved from www.un.org/development/desa/indigenouspeoples/publications/2014/09/martinez-cobo-study/.

McDonald-Kerr, L. (2017) Water, water, everywhere: using silent accounting to examine accountability for a desalination project, *Sustainability Accounting, Management and Policy Journal*, 8 (1): 43–76.

McGregor, R. (1997) *Imagined Destinies: Aboriginal Australians and the Doomed Race Theory, 1880-1939* (Melbourne: Melbourne University Press).

McKinlay, A. and Pezet, E. (2010) Accounting for Foucault, *Critical Perspectives on Accounting*, 21 (6): 486–95.

McNicholas, P., Humphries, M. and Gallhofer, S. (2004) Maintaining the empire: Maori women's experiences in the accountancy profession, *Critical Perspectives on Accounting*, 15 (1): 57–93.

Merino, B.D. (1998) Critical theory and accounting history: challenges and opportunities, *Critical Perspectives on Accounting*, 9 (6): 603–16.

Miley, F.M. and Read, A.F. (2018) "This degrading and stealthy practice": accounting, stigma and indigenous wages in Australia 1897-1972, *Accounting, Auditing & Accountability Journal*, 31 (2): 456–77.

Miller, P. and Rose, N. (1990) Governing economic life, *Economy and Society*, 19 (1): 1–31.

Miller, P. and O'Leary, T. (1994) Governing the calculable person in A.G. Hopwood and P. Miller (eds.) *Accounting as Social and Institutional Practice*, (pp. 98–115) (Cambridge: Cambridge University Press).

Neu, D. (1999) "Discovering" indigenous peoples: accounting and the machinery of empire, *Accounting Historians Journal*, 26 (1): 53–82.

Neu, D. (2000a) Accounting and accountability relations: colonization, genocide and Canada's first nations, *Accounting, Auditing & Accountability Journal*, 13 (3): 268–88.

Neu, D. (2000b) "Presents" for the "Indians": land, colonialism and accounting in Canada, *Accounting, Organizations and Society*, 25 (2): 163–84.

Neu, D. (2001) Banal accounts: subaltern voices, *Accounting Forum*, 25 (4): 319–33.

Neu, D. and Graham, C. (2004) Accounting and the holocausts of modernity, *Accounting, Auditing & Accountability Journal*, 17 (4): 578–603.

Neu, D. and Graham, C. (2006) The birth of a nation: accounting and Canada's First Nations, 1860-1900, *Accounting, Organizations and Society*, 31 (1): 47–76.

Neu, D. and Heincke, M. (2004) The subaltern speaks: financial relations and the limits of governmentality, *Critical Perspectives on Accounting*, 15 (1): 179–206.

Neu, D. and Therrien, R. (2003) *Accounting for Genocide: Canada's Bureaucratic Assault on Aboriginal People* (London: Zed Books Ltd).
Pino Robles, R. (2002) Colonialism: when will it end? *Ciencia Ergo Sum*, 9 (2): 139–50.
Preston, A. (2006) Enabling, enacting and maintaining action at a distance: an historical case study of the role of accounts in the reduction of the Navajo herds, *Accounting, Organizations and Society*, 31 (6): 559–78.
Preston, A. and Oakes, L. (2001) The Navajo documents: a study of the economic representation and construction of the Navajo, *Accounting, Organizations and Society*, 26 (1): 39–71.
Roberts, J. (1991) The possibilities of accountability, *Accounting, Organizations and Society*, 16 (4): 355–68.
Rose, N. (1991) Governing by numbers: figuring out democracy, *Accounting, Organizations and Society*, 16 (7): 673–92.
Rose, N. (1993) Government, authority and expertise in advanced liberalism, *Economy and Society*, 22 (3): 283–99.
Rose, N. and Miller, P. (1992) Political power beyond the State: problematics of government, *British Journal of Sociology*, 43 (2): 173–205.
Said, E.W. (1994) *Culture and Imperialism* (New York: Vintage Books).
Spence, L.J. and Rinaldi, L. (2014) Governmentality in accounting and accountability: a case study of embedding sustainability in a supply chain, *Accounting, Organizations and Society*, 39 (6): 433–52.
Sylvain, R. (2017) Indigenous Peoples in Africa in T. Spear (ed.) *Oxford Research Encyclopedia of African History* (Oxford: Oxford University Press). Retrived from http://oxfordre.com/africanhistory/view/10.1093/acrefore/9780190277734.001.0001/acrefore-9780190277734-e-263
Thornburg, S.W. and Roberts, R.W. (2012) "Incorporating" American colonialism: accounting and the Alaska Native Claims Settlement Act, *Behavioral Research in Accounting*, 24 (1): 203–14.
Tinker, T. (1991) The accountant as partisan, *Accounting, Organizations and Society*, 16 (3): 297–310.
Walker, S.P. (2008) Innovation, convergence and argument without end in accounting history, *Accounting, Auditing and Accountability Journal*, 21 (2): 296–322.
Watson, V. (2004) Liberalism and advanced liberalism in Australian indigenous affairs, *Alternatives: Global, Local, Political*, 29: 577–98.
Wickramasinghe, D. and Alawattage, C. (2009) Weapons of the weak: subalterns' emancipatory accounting in Ceylon Tea, *Accounting, Auditing & Accountability Journal*, 22 (3): 379–404.

24
EMANCIPATION

Sonja Gallhofer and Jim Haslam

Overview

This chapter is concerned to elaborate, promote and illustrate accounting history reflecting a critical theoretical approach. The particular approach, reflecting our work, is developed through engagement with postmodern, post-structuralist and post-Marxist orientation in theorising in the social sciences and humanities. The approach embraces the key elements of a critical approach. Reflexively, in this approach, the world is seen as problematic; the concern is to envisage a better world and seek to realise this vision. Rather than reduce to an unproblematic account of change as if narrative-free and transparently real, history is here aligned with and driven by a notion of emancipation – a concern to free from oppression/repression. Developments in the social sciences and humanities are drawn upon to refine the perspective.

The empirical and illustrative focuses here are on accounting in modern Britain, specifically in the context of the 'long nineteenth century'. The illustrative focuses are substantively writings on accounting by the English philosopher Jeremy Bentham (1748–1832), and accounting's actual (and threatened) mobilisation by socialistic agitators in the late nineteenth and early twentieth centuries.

Reflecting our critical theoretical approach, we begin by reviewing the concept of emancipation that here motivates historical analysis. We subsequently go on to explore, via our focuses, what is at stake in relating accounting, history and emancipation.

Questioning emancipation

Emancipation is a key concept of critical discourse. Yet, in theoretical debates of relatively recent times in the social sciences and humanities it has been deemed especially pertinent to ask 'what conceptions of emancipation are remaining or emerging?' (Doornbos 1992: 1). The very idea of emancipation has been questioned (Lather 1991; Doornbos 1992; Garnham 2000). In the process, a more reflexive and refined notion of emancipation has emerged which reflects the complexity and multi-faceted character of the concept as it has come to be appreciated.

Laclau and Mouffe (1987) articulate very key points here in relation to critical discourse and the impact upon it of philosophical currents that have influenced the social sciences and humanities. They stress that we have to take very seriously and reflexively the problematics of our contextual situatedness. If we do so, we can be less than confident about the notion of a pure progressive transformation out of that context. Moreover, we can be more deeply and reflexively appreciative of different, if progressive, interests, identities and projects for emancipation that are not straightforwardly aligned. In this context, a new pragmatism (Laclau and Mouffe 1987; Gallhofer and Haslam 2019) is merited in intervening for emancipation, and this extends into the domain of accounting history research (Gallhofer and Haslam 2019).

The Laclau and Mouffe view, which influences our own perspective, does not negate emancipation. In this view, emancipation remains a meaningful if altered concept. As Nederveen Pieterse (1992: 26) has argued, questioning of emancipation that tends to the extreme of rejecting the notion is suggestive of a contradictory position. If the overly simplifying promotion of emancipation is criticised as having even 'totalitarian' dimensions, the blanket rejection of it tends to the totalitarian itself (see Kellner 1988; Alvesson and Willmott 1992; Žižek 2001). Against the dangers of intervention in a complex field stand the problematics of overlooking social structure, not identifying with the (relatively) oppressed and not intervening (Leonard 1990; Alvesson and Willmott 1992; Benhabib 1992; Norris 1993; Squires 1993; Bronner 1994). Along with recognising that respect for difference is a universal principle (Calhoun 1995), we may appeal to values beyond scepticism, including politico-ethical solidarity, in seeking to justify intervention in the name of 'emancipation' (Rorty 1989; Alvesson and Willmott 1992; Benhabib 1992, 1994; Harvey 1993).

Concurrently, we need to acknowledge the intricate and ambivalent character of trajectories entailing emancipation in contexts where power functions within complex networks of relations (Aronowitz 1988; Doornbos 1992; Gabardi 2001). Emancipation is more than the overthrow of a single force. Myriad (mutable) progressive interests, projects and identities have to be aligned (Derrida 1978; Rorty 1989; Laclau 1990, 1992; Lather 1991; Alvesson and Willmott 1992; Weeks 1993; Gabardi 2001). We need to reflexively acknowledge our situated selves to avoid incompatible logical claims such as assuming that a pure emancipatory act may emerge from a problematic context. This requires a new pragmatism and more modest epistemology and eschatology.

Yet, this developed perspective, given the appreciation of the range of progressive interests, identities and projects, also opens up to new and deeper emancipatory possibilities (Laclau and Mouffe 1987; Laclau 1992; Gallhofer and Haslam 2003, 2019; Gallhofer et al. 2015).

Accounting, emancipation and the question of history

Critical historical analysis of accounting, driven by emancipatory concerns, properly reflects the above insights, reflecting cognisance of accounting complexity and ambivalence, and sensitivity to its multi-faceted character, instability, indeterminacy and transience (Nederveen Pieterse 1992: 26; Gallhofer and Haslam 2019). This approach surpasses crude conceptions of history as progress (Napier 2001). And it recognises that if modern accounting is emphatically repressive it also has emancipatory dimensions. A critical history illuminates trajectories of accounting in terms of both emancipatory and repressive dynamics, including dynamics whereby what was more repressive becomes more emancipatory, and vice-versa (see Prokhovnik 1999). In theorising accounting in relation to emancipation, emancipation is not seen in terms of a radical break. There is an appreciation of continuity as well as discontinuity. A more modest eschatology as well as epistemology is embraced (Gallhofer and Haslam 1996b; Gallhofer and Chew 2000).

At the same time, following the logic whereby emancipation is opened up to various possibilities across an array of identities, interests and projects, and acknowledging that emancipations are plural and mutable, one is drawn to a range of dimensions reflecting this in the historical analysis of accounting (Laclau and Mouffe 1987; Nederveen Pieterse 1992: 32–3; Laclau 1990, 1992, 1996).[1] The theoretical appreciation entails that there is no guarantee that a particular social class will substantively explain (or engender) change. We here need an analysis to better reflect the instability of categories and problematise overly simplifying constructions (Nederveen Pieterse 1992: 21–2; Laclau 2000: 297–301, 306, 316; Žižek 2000; cf. Derrida 1978; Gallhofer and Haslam 1995).

Concurrently, we should reiterate that a critical history remains concerned about praxis. And engagement with developments in the social sciences and humanities can import critical gains into praxis (Squires 1993: 1–2). These developments promote intervention for betterment, if reflexively and cautiously (Laclau 1990: 98, 216). The critique encourages intervention in and through accounting *more particularly*. The diverse agendas, the call for action and the building of a radical democracy to realise the potential of democratic forces (Laclau 1990; Nederveen Pieterse 1992: 26, 31) especially serve to stimulate the development of various emancipatory accountings: communication, information and accountability are key terms in democratic discourse (Bronner 1994).

Such theoretical developments are challenging. But we must meet the challenge to more positively align accounting and emancipation in the face of complexity, uncertainty, instability and contingency. This duly transforms how we may properly develop an understanding of accounting's emancipatory dimensions through contextual, including historical, analysis of accounting in action. Critical, contextual and interpretive analysis is further promoted by the challenging philosophical discourse that emphasises the case for paying attention to detail and reflecting awareness of the dangers of excessive and problematic dogmatism and universalism (Attridge et al. 1987).

Sensitivity to difference can engender new ways of seeing. And it can help develop a richer appreciation of the past as well as the present. There is thus a need to avoid excessive anachronism or 'chronocentrism' (Cousins 1987) in the contextual analysis of accounting: one can seek to gain critical insights from consideration of the past as different as well as similar.

Critical accounting history studies

While several analyses have theorised accounting as implicated in social struggle, they have tended to concentrate on accounting's repressiveness. Others have sought to address imbalance in analyses by recognising accounting's complex and multi-faceted character, including senses in which it may escape capture by any particular group or class, and recognise that it has emancipatory dimensions and possibilities. Although some have encouraged agency towards realising accounting's emancipatory potentialities (Tinker 1984, 1985; Gallhofer and Haslam 1996a, 2019; Sikka 2000), few have attended to radical activism implicating accounting in historical contexts. Here, we review some critical accounting history studies that do indicate emancipatory, including interventionist, possibilities for accounting.

The studies focus on the modern (Calinescu 1986, 1987; Gallhofer and Haslam 1995) British context within Hobsbawm's (1962, 1995, 1999) *lóng nineteenth century*.[2] This period especially merits our attention given that many modern-day institutions and practices were substantially shaped during this period (see Polanyi 1945; Hobsbawm 1962; Russell 1962;

Foucault 1977; Ignatieff 1984). The period witnessed key manifestations of State prescription and the formal professionalisation of accounting (Edwards 1989; Gallhofer and Haslam 1995). We here discuss several studies by Gallhofer and Haslam and the contribution of Arnold (1997) (the latter pursuing some similar themes to the former in relation to the same historical context). In particular, we explore Bentham's writings on accounting, considering these radical interventions with emancipatory intent. We proceed to discuss the campaigns, implicating accounting, of radical activists for labour and socialist change in the late nineteenth and early twentieth centuries (including a discussion of how a legal case implicating accounting was decided partly out of fear about how accounting could serve socialistic interests). Through these episodes insights are gained for praxis in relation to accounting.

Bentham on accounting

> From the art of Pauper Economy, studied with any attention, the transition is unavoidable to the ministering art of book-keeping … book-keeping was one of the arts which I should have to learn … the cries of the poor called aloud and accelerated the demands for it.
>
> *(UC, cliia: 33–4)*

> [p]ublicity is the very soul of justice. It is the keenest spur to exertion, the surest of all guards against improbity. It keeps the judge himself, while trying, under trial.
>
> *(Bentham, quoted in Harrison 1983: 131)*

Gallhofer and Haslam (1993, 1994a, 1994b, 1995, 1996b, 2003) analyse Bentham's writings on accounting as radical interventions with emancipatory intent. They elaborate how Bentham sought to change established, and promote unofficial, accountings to challenge the established order. The following summary relies especially on Gallhofer and Haslam (2003), where more detail is provided. Bentham wrote much on accounting, which he understood in broad terms and held in great esteem for its potential social benefits. Bentham was a radical, the great questioner of things established (Anonymous 1838; Hart 1982: 25–6; Boralevi 1984). He aimed to transform law and governance to the best state available, sought to liberate people from illusions and advocated pragmatic intervention. Despite his significance, Bentham is poorly appreciated. There remains limited knowledge of his writing and problematic understandings thereof (Gallhofer and Haslam 2003).[3]

Bentham promoted an extensive democracy and education, sought transformation in the lives of the poor and the oppressed – including women (Russell 1962: 742; Boralevi 1980, 1984: 4, 11), and sought to advance the happiness of the global community and its future generations (Mack 1962: 174, 397).[4] Boralevi (1984) articulates Bentham's concern for the oppressed explicitly in terms of emancipation. Bentham placed emphasis in this context on a more just and equal society: he wanted to introduce minimum wages, job security, pensions, health insurance and a welfare system. He stressed that wages were too low relative to other forms of income and sought ways to distribute inheritances to the community and excess profits to employees. His ideas thus continue to challenge today's socio-political order. He was enthusiastic about early socialistic experiments (Mack 1962: 178, 207–8, 427, 438; Boralevi 1984). Several writers point to Bentham's influence on later socialists (especially the Fabians). Some even point to a degree of affinity between Bentham and Marx (Mack 1962: 2, 196, 421; Russell 1962: 743; Letwin 1965; Hart 1982; Boralevi 1984).[5]

A critical theoretical reappraisal of Bentham's writings, requiring destruction and patient hermeneutic reconstruction (Critchley 2001: 47–8), is worthwhile given his significance and radicalism. And his radicalism extended to accounting, which he placed so prominently in his schema. Bentham sought to emancipate accounting so that it would better contribute to emancipatory social change. He was one of a number of writers of his time who perceived the significance of informed opinion and transparency for the progressive, emancipatory construction of social relations through rational communicative interaction (Habermas 1992: 102; Gallhofer and Haslam 1995).[6] Further, Bentham wrote at a time that was critical in the formation of many modern institutions and practices (*supra*) and before accountancy's formal professionalisation (Gallhofer and Haslam 2003).

Many emphasise Bentham's repressive side. Yet, reading critically, we may appraise his complexities and positive potential as well as the negative. Habermas encourages us to take a closer look at Bentham, including accounting, in that he gives emphasis to the positive radicalism and potentiality of Bentham in this respect (Habermas 1974, 1992; cf. Peters 1993). Focusing on Bentham's (1843) *Of Publicity*, Habermas (1992) portrays Bentham's concept of publicity in favourable terms, associating it with his own construct of the public sphere and seeing Bentham as an architect of that sphere (Habermas 1974, 1992; cf. Peters 1993; Gaonkar and McCarthey 1994). From this perspective, Bentham's publicity is a manifestation of, and facilitates, rational and critical discourse, engendering meaningful public opinion – Habermas' desiderata (Gaonkar and McCarthey 1994: 554; cf. Hume 1970). This is so long as there is no over-determining of opinion through publicity and where publicity challenging the official is possible (Bentham 1843; Mack 1962; Bronner 1994; Gallhofer and Haslam 2003). Bentham's concern to promote publicity parallels his concern to extend education (Mack 1962; Boralevi 1984).

Bentham saw accounting publicity[7] as fostering emancipation (cf. Boralevi 1984: 178) and wellbeing in a number of ways (cf. Hume 1970: 24–5). Publicity was seen as aiding the moral behaviour of those exposed – and Bentham gave some emphasis to exposing those in positions of power (Bentham 1843: 588; Harrison 1983: 131; Boralevi 1984: 191)[8] – enhancing an orientation towards sympathy, benevolence and the general wellbeing (Mack 1962; Boralevi 1984). Bentham explicitly linked his advocacy of a statistic/accounting society to the aim of 'promoting the condition of the labouring classes' (UC cxlix: 237). His accounting would serve the oppressed, partly by making the actions of the powerful more transparent (Bahmueller 1981: 190). In this respect, Bentham sought to give the oppressed a voice through accounting: in his poor houses, the poor were to be encouraged to write their observations about the poor house in a complaints book that would be open to the world. Managers were also to keep records of the state of health, meals, conduct and subject matter worked upon (Bowring 1843, vol. viii: 393; Gallhofer and Haslam 1993; cf. British Museum Manuscript MS 33,541: f. 203, note drafted by Bentham, 23/1/1791; UC, clii, 312; Bahmueller 1981: 192). Publicity was also envisaged as a system of informing in a more general sense, helping people steer their way through life and more substantively and meaningfully participating in a democracy. Accounting publicity is envisaged by Bentham as a key principle of management or governance.[9] As such, this principle of publicity is, for Bentham, second only to his broad-ranging Panopticon or Inspection Architecture principle of governance (Gallhofer and Haslam 1993; cf. Bentham 1812: 100–1; Bahmueller 1981: 91; Hume 1981; Harrison 1983; Gallhofer and Haslam 1996b, 2003: 47).

Bentham wanted to problematise and radically question accounting in order to foster its emancipatory potential. He wanted, as he put it, to rationalise accounting and extend it in its limits. Thus, accounting was to be shaped by its objects or ends rather than traditions

(Bentham 1816: 61–2; Bowring 1843, vol. viii: 393; Hume 1970: 27; 1981: 154–5). Bentham's accounting did not reflect a reduction to a narrow and abstracted economics. He struggled to articulate a relationship between a duty to achieve financial economic efficiency, or the *duty to economy*, and what he referred to as the *duty to humanity*. The latter is variously discussed in Bentham: there are dangers of seeing economics as separate and indeed abstracted, but there is a potential for a more holistic vision. In his pauper management and Panopticon projects, publicity was the chief device to, in his terms, expose moral behaviour, to better ensure that management was directed to fulfilling the duty to humanity and attending to the concerns of the oppressed. Bentham expressed the view that accounting publicity would be more effective in this moral sphere than it would be in the economic. Indeed, it was the most effective means of engendering moral behaviour (Harrison 1983: 130; Gallhofer and Haslam 1993).

Elsewhere, Bentham contended that this view of accounting's role was more generally applicable (Bahmueller 1981: 157; Hume 1981: 157; Gallhofer and Haslam 1993, 1994a, 1994b, 2003). The duty to humanity here is articulated as a duty towards those under the care of management. At times this extends to what we would today call a stakeholder approach (Gallhofer and Haslam 1993). Boralevi (1984) suggests, in a sympathetic reading, that the duty to economy is a 'means', whereas the duty to humanity is an 'end'. The more holistic accounting Bentham envisaged is expressed in the following quote:

> Pecuniary economy, usually regarded as the sole object of book-keeping, will here be but as one out of a number; for the system of book-keeping will be neither more nor less than the history of the system of management in all its points.
>
> *(Bentham 1812: 101; 1816: 61; UC, clii: 360; Hume 1981: 52; Hoskin and Macve 1986: 128)*

Subject to limits that may reasonably be placed on disclosure (Semple 1993), Bentham sought the recording of the widest range of potentially significant things, whose use might come to have a role in engendering wellbeing (Bentham 1812: 102–3; Bowring 1843, viii: 392; Bahmueller 1981: 192–3; Loft 1988). Hume (1970: 30) acknowledges that Bentham's notion of accounts included the financial but did not give primacy thereto. Information that would be disaggregated relative to common practice so as to render open to view the local effects of local activities was within the ambit of Bentham's vision (a vision more feasible today with developments in information technology) (Hume 1970: 28). Bentham sought to make visible individual as well as group activity (Gallhofer and Haslam 1993, 1994a, 1994b, 2003), and he sought to disclose to a very large audience consistent with his vision of democracy as well as what we might term stakeholders.

Consequently, accounting itself had to be a clear and comprehensive communication, that is, more accountable itself (UC, cl: 147, cliv: 33; cxxxiii: 61–2, 65; Bentham 1812: 105, 150, 1816: 61–4; Bowring 1843, vol. viii: 343; Goldberg 1957; Bahmueller 1981: 193; Hume 1981: 51, 155; Gallhofer and Haslam 1993; cf. Bentham 1830: 46). Bentham saw lack of clarity in accounting, and the use of fictitious entities, as a form of mystifying and problematic ideology that served particular rather than social interests, including an accounting expertocracy (UC, cxxxv; Bentham 1812: 106n; Goldberg 1957). Bentham also indicates a respect for particularity, difference and privacy, going beyond a crude universalism, in relation to his emphasis on publicity (Bentham 1812; Hume 1970, 1981; Rosen 1983). He explicitly cautioned against too much uniformity of disclosure and was concerned to respect and learn from difference (Boralevi 1984: 181; Gallhofer and Haslam 1993).

In summary, Bentham outlined a radical and progressive accounting for emancipation. A critical history, however, also explores the negative and problematic dimensions of Bentham's intervention and the Gallhofer and Haslam studies take up this challenge. One has to be especially sensitive to possible dangers in mobilising projects ostensibly informed by Bentham. One can envisage how such projects may come to accrue substantively problematic dimensions in their conception and application. In his enthusiasm for his projects and in his frustrations at their rejection by the established order, Bentham does overlook, at times, the imperfections in his schema.[10] He argues that the people should take control, but he wants to direct them first. Further, the practicalities involved in its implementation may tend towards a crude universalism. Sometimes he is impatient about the need to convince others of his plans and appears to think their logic or the case for them is self-evident (Letwin 1965). These things do not negate his philosophy – they are present in any philosophy implying intervention in the name of betterment, and Bentham acknowledged such tensions too (Letwin 1965), but they do suggest the need for caution and modesty in the application of his thinking and related thought.

A potentially crude universalism, or uniformity, and an insensitive dogmatism may be read into the following quote from Bentham:

> I have a machine put together … for answering all such questions … Panopticon or the Inspection-House … You had the goodness to offer me some papers relative to some of the establishments to which the idea promises to be applicable … Houses of Industry … Jails … Hospitals … Schools &c … Do you happen to want a plan of Education just now, or a plan of anything else? These are my amusements. One thing pretty much the same to me as another.
>
> *(Letter to the Right Hon John Parnell, Buxton, Derbyshire from Jeremy Bentham, 2 September 1790, British Museum Manuscript, MS 33541: f. 160; also Boyne 2000: 288–9)*

An issue here is that Bentham sees bookkeeping and his wider schema as a system of uniformity that will engender uniformity in behaviour: 'the general advantage depends on uniformity of which uniformity is productive … Refer to book-keeping' (UC, cliib: 363, see also 360n, 361; Bahmueller 1981: 188, 192; Hume 1981: 160–1).

This may equate to a forcing of order and uniformity onto a chaotic, disorderly, dynamic and threatening context, thus engendering a certainty that, whatever its benefits, may come to reassure and enhance prevailing hegemonic forces (see Bahmueller 1981: 93).

The excesses of Bentham's project may render its impact contradictory. Bentham advocates challenging expertise and seeks to ensure that expert practices are accountable to the people. Yet, ironically, his very own advocacy of accounting may fuse and be consistent with the notion of a scientific expertise distant from the public (Hume 1970, 1981; Bahmueller 1981; Gallhofer and Haslam 1994a: 269–70, n.39). Not unrelated to this, Bentham in some texts portrays accounting as uncontroversial and factual (Bentham 1816, 1817: table v; cf. Letwin 1965: 188).[11] His zeal may also engender a lack of trust in society so that mechanism would replace or be a substitute for substantive morality, which would give way to corruption and moral decay (Polanyi 1945; Himmelfarb 1968). A sympathiser might comment that Bentham's intervention is predicated on social experience – there are social problems partly because people have acted in corrupt and immoral ways – and would note that Bentham is especially concerned that one should distrust the relatively powerful in society. Nevertheless, diagnosis and prescription are complex and difficult: there are dangers in development trajectories inspired by Bentham, consistent with Himmelfarb's (1968) warnings and perspectives (also Bahmueller 1981).

There may be a failure to appreciate the flexibilities of Bentham's concepts, constructs and practices in their ostensibly progressive mobilisation. Letwin (1965), referring to Bentham's influence on policy, suggests that his 'colourless treatises were interpreted by disciples moved by different experiences and aims' to be problematic in various ways. In this respect Bentham's notions may be captured by powerful repressive forces and mobilised, for instance, for capitalistic aims (Hobsbawm 1962; Himmelfarb 1968; Hume 1981: 163). Bentham himself, in relation to capitalistic political economy, at times slipped into a narrow economicism that threatened to enhance such tendencies. In delineating a duty to economy separate from a duty to humanity – a separation paralleled in mainstream social accounting discourse of recent decades – Bentham ironically distances the economic from the social. One should surely regard a duty to economy as integral to a deeper duty to humanity (Bahmueller 1981: 193; Gallhofer and Haslam 1993).

The way forward here is to reflect on the tensions, complexities and ambiguities in projects inspired by Bentham. Such reflection would be consistent with seeing change as both progressive and regressive. In some ways this is to emphasise sensitivities and cautions professed by Bentham himself. There is also a need to deliberatively seek to communicate interactively with, and take guidance from, people. Related to this should be a determined attempt to listen to other voices of diversity and difference and to act upon them in terms of a differentiated universalism, thus constituting an appropriate extension of Bentham's local consideration principle. Further, one must be cognisant of the tendency for Bentham's endeavours to equate to capture by problematic hegemonic forces. One can learn from an analysis of the deficiencies of Bentham's accounting project, reflect on what can go wrong, and seek to develop his way of seeing in ways cognisant of more recent theoretical developments.

Gallhofer and Haslam's analyses of Bentham's writings on accounting bring out how accounting may be conceived of as an emancipatory force and how the emancipation of accounting itself may further the realisation of this potential. The analyses also illuminate how established accountings may be seen as serving the relatively powerful in the established political order, thus suggesting a political struggle. Concurrently, the analyses indicate the possibility that accounting forces will be transformed so as to better serve the weak. We can appreciate the longevity of notions of accountings in a variety of organisations that would serve organisational stakeholders and attempt to engender accountability for social justice, wellbeing and emancipation. It would be an unreasonable and prejudicial view that fails to see substantive congruence between Bentham's accounting proposals and progressive notions of social accounting for business organisations today (Gallhofer and Haslam 2005). If potentially radical projects today are reinforced, in and through accounting, the analyses of Bentham are also suggestive of new insights to, for example, the form and content of accounting. They also serve to encourage and inspire radical activism in and through accounting in the present. Gallhofer and Haslam's engagement with Bentham and accounting also offers cautions in respect of emancipatory projects involving accounting that have some affinity with Bentham. Gallhofer and Haslam (1995, 2003) indicate how much of Bentham's radicalism in relation to accounting may be displaced and problematically transformed in practice. Yet with appropriate sensitivity and awareness, mobilising Bentham's notion of accounting, as seen by Gallhofer and Haslam, may be consistent with a radical emancipatory project.

Accounting and socialistic agitators of the late nineteenth and early twentieth centuries

> In the case of the Match Girls … [publicity] … voiced their complaints, and forced them on the attention of the public, and what it has done for this one class of the oppressed it must do, one after the other for every such class.
>
> (The Link, *4 August 1888: 1)*

Gallhofer and Haslam (2003, 2006a) analyse the mobilisation of accounting by radical socialistic activists in the late nineteenth- and early twentieth-century British context. Arnold (1997) pursues themes overlapping their concerns in this period. In this section we précis the main points of these texts. A key theoretical insight shaping the analyses is that accounting has long been a focal point of conflicting objectives (Stiglitz 2002) that pulls it in different directions or puts it to different uses. Thus, for instance, governments and their agencies have seen accounting as a tool for gaining tax revenues, while shareholders and investors have taken it to indicate the dynamics of financial ownership interest. Conversely, labour interests have seen it as a way of achieving the distribution of a larger slice of the economic cake, and capitalistic interests see accounting as a means to maintaining or enhancing the value of capital. Some have effectively thought of accounting as enhancing or at least buttressing the socio-political order; others see it as facilitating radical progressive change. In this respect, from a critical perspective, even forms of accounting practice that have been manifest have had emancipatory dimensions and possibilities. Gallhofer and Haslam (2019) emphasise that at any moment accounting is both progressive and regressive, and its focus can shift over time. Given the dialectical and ambivalence-engendering character of the dynamic context, accounting can shift between substantively repressive and substantively progressive modes of functioning. Further, there is a role for engaged praxis in furthering accounting's emancipatory potential and responding to opportunities.

Accounting in context

Late-nineteenth-century Britain was shaped by crisis and conflict. An economic downturn set in from the early 1870s. In the 1880s, unemployment came to be recognised as a serious problem, alongside increasing poverty (Callaghan 1990: 4). Wages were low and work was long and intense (Daunton 2000). This was a decade of street riots and serious industrial unrest. Labour forces inched towards collective forms of action (Soldon 1978; Beaver 1985: 64; Callaghan 1990: 5). By the end of the 1880s there was considerable interest, including among the middle classes, in the plight of the poor and social problems (Hopkins 2000: 141). Efforts were made to expose poverty and labour experiences by numerous social investigators intent on engendering social change (Booth 1889–1903, 1890). A significant body of opinion now favoured more state intervention to tackle poverty and several government investigations of the problems were undertaken (Callaghan 1990: 5; Hopkins 2000: 138–41). Charitable activity and the social reform movement grew in relation to these concerns (Callaghan 1990: 4). Several organisations arose with distinct social and political missions. An example was Toynbee Hall, founded in the East End by the Reverend Barnett to establish a link between university and East End poor (Briggs and Macartney 1984). Beyond its educational mission, Toynbee Hall was keen to support labour in industrial disputes (Briggs and Macartney 1984: 45). The 1880s also saw enhanced concern about women's working and living conditions. The Women's Protective and Provident League fought for the establishment of women's trade unions (Bolt 1993).

More formally organised political movements seeking to improve the conditions of the poor and the working class grew. There was a revival of socialism in the 1880s. The Social Democratic Federation (SDF) under the leadership of H.M. Hyndman had a clear socialist objective. The Socialist League under the leadership of William Morris was more international and anti-state in orientation. The Fabian Society aimed to work for a reconstruction of the social system by placing wealth in the hands of the community. It opposed violent revolution, favoured gradual democratic reform and tried to influence existing political parties rather than pursue a strategy of forming a political party itself. All three of these bodies were established in 1884 (Tsuzuki 1961; Hopkins 2000). The strategies employed by these organisations and movements shared one striking similarity – a concern to make poverty and injustice visible through the publicity of 'facts'. This was to some extent inspired by the belief, a belief promoted by Bentham's philosophy and the nineteenth-century statistical movement (Cullen 1975), that such exposure would aid resolution of these issues by convincing reasonable people of the need to improve conditions. The Fabian Society in particular was much influenced by this thinking (Callaghan 1990: 39). The strong commitment to publicity indicates the influence of Bentham as well as Marx on the socialist movements of the time (Hulse 1970). In keeping with this philosophy, many socialist bodies had their own newspapers. Several of these were edited by H.H. Champion (*Christian Socialist, Common Sense, The Labour Elector* and the SDF's *Justice*) and two were edited by Annie Besant (*Our Corner* and *The Link*) (Callaghan 1990: 45).

By the 1880s, accountants were organised into recognised professional bodies and public accounting practice was substantively shaped by capitalistic interests. The regulation of accounting by the state and the profession was fairly minimalist with an emphasis on market forces, although a number of writers have indicated that there were forces at work providing incentives to attract capital, to enhance the image of business in the market place and to disclose accounting publicity (Parker 1990; Edwards 1992; Walker 1996). The profit figure was typically of great interest to late nineteenth-century shareholders because it often corresponded closely to the dividend (Gallhofer and Haslam 2003: 70; *The Labour Elector* 23/3/1889: 5). By the 1880s, auditors signing off accounts would often indicate their status as members of a formally organised profession. Companies would typically include provisions in their constitutions to publish accounts, provisions attaining a law like status.[12] And in addition to association with a profession and the law, accounts appear to have attained an aura of facticity even if many companies opted for as much flexibility over accounting disclosure as the law allowed (Edwards 1989, 1992; Parker 1990; Arnold 1997; cf. Marriner 1980; Gallhofer and Haslam 1991).[13]

The match girls

Champion and Besant's enthusiasm for publicity extended to a concern to make use of, and add to, accounting publicity. H.H. Champion was one of the most prominent socialist activists of the 1880s. The son of a major-general, Champion is understood to have turned to socialist activism after reading works by Marx and John Stuart Mill and having visited London's deprived areas (Tsuzuki 1961; Champion 1983). He initially rose to prominence in Christian Socialism and the SDF and worked closely with union and labour leaders on worker campaigns (Whitehead 1983: 17). He sought socialism through democracy and non-violence and was also involved in the Fabian Society (Tsuzuki 1961). In his own time, he was acknowledged to be an excellent communicator (Hyndman

1911). In Champion's *Common Sense,* not only was the Socialist emphasis clear but so too was the influence of Bentham's promotion of publicity[14] and the philosophy of the statistical movement with its emphasis on the power of 'undeniable facts' (*Common Sense* 15/5/1887). Champion was keen on contrasting experiences of rich and poor. The format of *Common Sense* was influenced by conventional financial accounting: the very first issue had national wealth in a distinct column on the left-hand side of the first page and national poverty on the right-hand side. Pursuing a similar theme, Champion contrasted high profits/dividends with poor wages/conditions, focusing on specific companies. In this respect he made use of accounting disclosures. The company mainly focused on in *Common Sense* was Bryant and May Limited.

Bryant and May was a notable match-making concern centred in East London. The company was incorporated and listed on the stock exchange in 1884 (MDM 12/6/1984).[15] It remained substantively a family firm and the remuneration of the directors, mainly drawn from the family, was linked to company profits (Gallhofer and Haslam 2003: 73). In the 1880s, the share price reflected the remarkable rise of the business. Dividends were 20–30% on the initial nominal value. There was a very close correspondence between accounting profit and dividends (*The Statist* 5/11/1887: 513–14; Gallhofer and Haslam 2003: 75). At the AGMs during the 1880s the firm was eulogised, making use of its accounting statements, which were certified by the auditor as 'a true statement of the Liabilities and Assets'.

Champion aimed to use the accounts to tell a different story for a different purpose. Most employees were East End women and match-making had long been associated with poor wages and poor working conditions (Collett 1893). Consistent with a politics of aggregation in accounting, the low wages, let alone the poor conditions, were not as visible in the accounts as the financial returns that generated so much pride among the directors. Investigative journalism was required to make the kind of contrast Champion sought. His first report on Bryant and May in *Common Sense* (15/5/1887: 11) set up a serialisation format style. The 1886 dividend of £80,000, or 20% of the nominal value of share capital, and the company's apparently high reserve fund, were highlighted as evidence of the company's high profit-making. The figures were taken from the accounts presented at the AGM. The article ends with a question to be answered in a future issue: 'What is the average wage of workers who produced this 20%?' On 15/6/1887 the paper reported that an investigator had 'made enquiries at Bow' to discover the very poor wages of a home worker employed by the company. Concurrently, the report indicates the difficulty of getting information from the factory workers who appear to have been intimidated against co-operating with the investigators. The report states that the journal considered advocating a boycott of Bryant and May's products.

Further, more information for exposure was sought: 'We shall be glad to have the name and address of any persons, known to be shareholders, profiting by this system of torture' (ibid.: 27). When *Common Sense* returned to the story (15/7/1887) more information on share ownership was forthcoming. The hypocrisy of Ministers of Religion owning shares was highlighted in the journal by a quotation from Proverbs, XXII, 1, 2: 'A good name is rather to be chosen than great riches and loving favour than silver and gold' and by the suggestion that they might preach a different version of the biblical text: 'Come unto us, ye who labour, and we will pay you three farthing an hour'. Fourteen ministers, to whom a copy of the journal was to be sent, were listed as sharing in the dividends (ibid.: 42). The attack on the capitalist financiers was strong and pointed to the immorality of profit-making:

> Judging them even by the conventional standards of fair dealing these gentlemen are sucking profit in a manner every bit as dirty as a money lender, who extorts 30% from the necessitous, or promoter of bubble companies. It is allowed by law, and they do not scruple to take advantage of the power they have to oppress the widow and orphan, in order to swell their dividends
>
> *(ibid.: 42)*

Champion referred to the Bryant and May case in a speech delivered to the annual Church (of England) Congress (5/10/1887). His speech received publicity in *The Record* and in *Common Sense* (5/10/1887). This not only enhanced publicity, it generated additional disclosures about the high rents paid by the workers (Gallhofer and Haslam 2003: 77–8). On these points, *The Christian* (28/10/1887: 12), which advocated ethical consumerism in a similar case (14/10/1887: 6–7), reported an extract from the *Birmingham Weekly Post*: 'If these assertions are not true, let … Bryant and May nail them to the counter … if they are facts, the time is come for another Wilberforce to emancipate another race of slaves'. *Common Sense* had earlier reported that the negative publicity was prompting something of an ethical investment movement (15/8/1887: 59). The secretary of Bryant and May recorded the publicity in his diary. He observed that several individuals had written to the company about it, seeking clarification and reassurance and referring to various moral issues. One shareholder had requested that the company calculate and disclose the average wage paid to the workers (SD, 1887–8, especially October and November, 1887).[16]

Champion brought the Fabian Society's attention to the campaign at a meeting on 15 June 1888. Prominent Fabian Annie Besant recalled that the meeting discussed issues of ethical consumerism and Champion's analysis of the significant rise in Bryant and May's share price, how this was built upon the exploitation of its labour, and his calling for a boycott (Besant 1938: 4). The resolution was passed and Besant, with Herbert Burrows, investigated the case further, managing to interview some of the factory girls. On 23 June 1888 Besant published an article in *The Link*.[17] In this article she called for an ethical consumerist boycott, and highlighted the contrast between the accounting profits/dividends and the poor deal for the match girls, including dangerous working conditions and the punitive system of fines and deductions. She declared that the factory girls were cheaper as labour than chattel slaves. Besant distributed her article to the workers as they left the factory (*The Link* 23/6/1888). She later advocated drawing up a blacklist of companies to boycott, published for each locality so that public opinion might call for greater honesty and fair dealing. She called for the comprehensive disclosure of wages and working conditions backed by law (3/6/1888: 1). In early July 1888, Besant and Burrows also wrote letters to the press, which referred to two workers being sacked for informing Besant (*Pall Mall Gazette* 3/7/1888–89). Bryant and May continued to monitor the publicity and the secretary's diary refers to Besant's article on 23 June as 'scurrilous' (SD 23/6/1888–89). The secretary sent letters the next day denying the allegations and claiming that the sackings had been for other reasons (SD 3,4/7/1888–89). The company later threatened legal action (*The Link* 7/7/1888: 3). The government also monitored developments. The Inspector of Factories visited the company as a result of the article in *The Link* (SD 27/6/1888).

The workers went on strike on 5 July 1888 (MDM 5/7/1888). According to some reports, the sackings occurred after the girls refused to call Besant's article a lie (*The Link* 7/7/1888: 3). The factory inspector asked the company to keep the Home Office informed of developments (Gallhofer and Haslam 2003: 82). Besant and Burrows agreed to the workers' request to support the strike. Publicity continued to be an important weapon through public meetings and *The Link*. The agitators continued to mobilise accounting in the dispute and Besant's articles were akin, in form and content, to those by Champion (*The Link* 14/7/1888: 1). Besant calculated returns of the company by adding capital gains to dividends and a giant matchbox was paraded at a public demonstration carrying the words '38%' dividend (Gallhofer and Haslam 2003: 83). In *St. James's Gazette* (9/7/1888: 11), Besant claimed 'to have stopped the fines inflicted on the girls by giving publicity to them'. An audience was secured with members of the House of Commons to discuss grievances (*The Star* 11/7/1888).

St. James's Gazette (12/7/1888: 4) reported on an investigation by Toynbee Hall. Toynbee Hall advocated ethical investment and repeated the contrast between the high dividends/profits and the poor wages/conditions of the workers and also referred to concerns about the poor state of employer–employee relations. The Toynbee Hall team elaborated on grievances specific to three categories of female worker, including effective reductions in pay resulting from technological change, fines and reductions (Gallhofer and Haslam 2003: 85). They called for more disaggregated wages accounting, adjusting for seasonal effects, excluding highly paid workers from and including the lower paid in the calculation so that the average would not be distorted. The Bryant and May directors felt the need to make counter claims. Yet Toynbee Hall continued to mobilise the publicity. Socialistic agitators saw value in emphasising the factual. Accounting's aura of facticity served them (Gallhofer and Haslam 2003: 86). *St. James's Gazette* called for the 'acknowledged facts' of the case to be respected: Bryant and May should pay its workers more (see *The Link* 28/7/1888: 1).

The strike ended on 19 July 1888 (SD 19/7/1888). The London Trades Council had, unusually, seen fit to negotiate on behalf of female unskilled labour. The workers had a number of victories, apparently small, but labour historians see them as significant. The sacked were reinstated, the fines system withdrawn. Small wage increases were granted. A canteen was eventually provided and a Matchmakers' Union established with Besant as first secretary (Gallhofer and Haslam 2003: 87).[18] The *Liberal Radical* (28/7/1888), in praising Besant's advocacy of the match-girls' case, declared: 'The emancipation of the workers is no party question ... All praise to those who dare to be *practical* as well as theoretical'.[19]

Besant had been encouraged in her view that the publicity of 'facts' could help rectify social injustices. Her article in *Pall Mall Gazette* (23/2/1889) praises statistical reporting and notes that 'nothing but good can come from throwing on the many problems of our social system the dry, cold light of facts' (also *The Link* 4/8/1888: 1).

Brunner, Mond

Champion also focused on Brunner, Mond and Co., a major listed chemical company (later a major part of ICI) located in Northwich, Cheshire. The founder and continuing head of the company, John Tomlinson Brunner, was the Liberal MP for Northwich. To expose what he saw as unjust practices, Champion again sought to analyse the publicly available accounting disclosures that were conventionally understood to be of interest only to shareholders and potential investors.[20] In introducing his case, Champion declared:

> He who remembers and repeats what will be here recorded will be furnished with the most complete answer possible to many a hackneyed argument used against the emancipation of Labour from the thraldom of Capital.
>
> (The Labour Elector *1/11/1888: 1–2)*

Champion outlined the dramatic increase in the price of the shares owned by Brunner and the enormous dividends the 'millionaire MP' received. He calculated how long a worker would need to save to accumulate the same amount as Brunner accrued over eight years. He conservatively estimated this at just over 7,692 years (*The Labour Elector* 15/11/1888: 4–5). Champion reported the sacking of union members who had asked for a pay rise. By contrast, Brunner used the annual accounts as a vehicle for praising company success (*The Labour Elector* 16/2/1889: 4). Champion analysed the accounts to show how much equity had been increasing despite the high dividend distribution. He later explicitly suggested that amounts were transferred to reserves to avoid the publicity of high profits/dividends (*The Labour Elector* 26/1/1889: 9), and argued that Brunner (and Mond) benefited hugely from the conversion to a limited company (*The Labour Elector* 15/12/1888: 13).

The story spread and criticism was made of the company in Parliament (*The Labour Elector* 15/12/1888: 14). As with Bryant and May, Champion contrasted accounting profits with poor working conditions. He analysed the case for introducing the eight-hour day pointing out that the shareholders would scarcely notice the reduced profit (*The Labour Elector* 5/1/1889: 7).[21] On 19 January 1889, the half-yearly accounts to 31 December 1882 of Brunner, Mond were substantively discussed and an attempt was made to calculate the surplus made by capital from labour (ibid.: 8–10). Aside from transfers to reserves, Brunner was accused of operating a device for hiding profits. Champion attempted to negotiate with Brunner through his article, urging him to introduce an eight-hour day in return for Champion keeping silent about the device (26/1/1889: 10). As Brunner did not respond to this, the next issue of *The Labour Elector* brought up the dilution of share capital via a bonus issue to reduce the apparent dividend as a percentage of the nominal value of shares issued (2/2/1889: 1–4). Champion analysed the accounts to show that before the bonus issue, the amount 'earned' by Brunner was 56% of nominal capital (2/3/1889: 5). He criticised an accounting practice of aggregation, which he suggested was aligned to the capitalists' concern to disclose minimal information. He also implicated the accounting profession in support of his argument:

> This practice of including two separate things in one item may be, for the Directors, a convenient system of account keeping but we are surprised at its receiving the sanction of any auditor who signs himself a chartered accountant.
>
> (The Labour Elector *9/3/1889: 5)*

Champion compounded his exposure by pointing out that Brunner, Mond & Co polluted a river by pumping it with brine (*The Labour Elector* 26/1/1889). By 19 January 1889, Champion must have felt that he was winning the publicity campaign, encouraging him to disclose even more (ibid.: 10, 27/4/1889: 3).[22,23] His paper received many commentaries on the 'villainies of capitalism'.

Champion considered that it was important to 'select those cases [for publicity] in which exposure, besides relieving the condition of the workers, teaches a great political lesson and economic truth' (*The Labour Elector* 26/1/1889). He tended to publish counter claims by Brunner but then proceeded to counter these, encouraging suspicions about the company's accounting statements. Champion was threatened with legal action by Brunner. His immediate response was to continue his campaign. However, he eventually departed for Melbourne, disillusioned with political activism in Britain. He had successfully contributed to a critical questioning of the socio-political order through accounting publicity.

Newton v. Birmingham small arms

Arnold's (1997) study, again focused on Britain, indicates how accounting was controversial and featured in socio-political conflicts in the years leading up to the First World War. Not only was more attention being given to the disclosure of profit (or loss) through accounts in a developing capital market but also accounting was being seen as potentially increasing tensions between capital and labour. For Arnold (1997: 163) 'company profits and their disclosure were matters of considerable, class-based public concern'. He pointed out that: 'The process of informing those who make financial investments in public limited companies, whether as shareholders, lenders or creditors, was bound to provide information to organized labour relevant to bargaining on wages and employment conditions' (ibid.: 164).

A key legal case in this context was *Newton versus Birmingham Small Arms Company Limited* [1906 2 Ch. 378]. The case was decided in favour of shareholder and director discretions and contained references to tensions between labour and capitalistic interests (Arnold 1997). The company's defence included the view, not substantively challenged by the government or the accountancy profession, that in the event of a contested disclosure 'great injury may be done to the business [as] difficulties may be caused between rival traders or between capital and labour'. Mr. Justice Buckley, in substantively supporting this position, referred to publicity as being potentially injurious to business for a number of reasons including 'complications sometimes arising from the strained relations between capital and labour' (Arnold 1997: 164–5).

Forward

Gallhofer and Haslam (2006a) elaborate a critical historical analysis of accounting's mobilisation in the radical media during the crisis context of the First World War and its aftermath. The main focus is on how accounting is mobilised in *Forward*, an important radical weekly newspaper. The authors cite the emphasis given by Gramsci, Althusser and Hall on the significance of the media as a hegemonic organ of public opinion (ibid.: 226).[24] The location of the study is 'Red Clydeside' (Glasgow and the Clyde region of Scotland), a centre for counter-hegemonic and socialist activities (Foster 1990). The aim is to bring out, through historical analysis, accounting's potential and the realisation of this potential.

Economic pressures exacerbated tensions between capital and labour during the early twentieth century. Socialistic political parties and movements strengthened. The possibilities of global socialistic development appeared to be enhanced and was encouraged by the Russian Revolution of 1917[25](Arnold 1997). 'Red Clydeside', as the name suggests, was a hotbed of radical socialist activity that experienced serious industrial unrest between 1914 and 1919 (Foster 1990). The workers were concerned about wages and working conditions and more generally about food and coal prices, poor housing, increases in rent and unemployment. In this environment, radical socialist parties gained significant support (ibid.).

During the nineteenth century corporate accounting was barely regulated by the state (Edwards 1992; Arnold 1997). Consequently, flexibility was possible in terms of aggregation, profit concealment and secret reserve accounting (Marriner 1980; Edwards 1989; Arnold 1997). However, there was a step in the direction of greater state regulation during the first decade of the twentieth century. The Companies Act 1900, for instance, required all limited companies to produce an audited balance sheet for the shareholders attending an AGM, and the auditors were to be appointed by the shareholders and report on whether the balance sheet gave a 'true and correct' view (Edwards 1989; Gallhofer and Haslam 2006a).[26] In practice, accounting statements did not disclose great detail, common financial accounting principles were occasionally overlooked and auditors rarely qualified the accounts (Edwards 1989). Prior to 1914, Arnold (1997) suggests that serious financial statement manipulation was uncommon and published accounts reflected internal book equivalents reasonably well. Many companies produced some sort of profit and loss account. However, manipulation of accounts to create impressions became more common around the time of the First World War (Arnold 1997; cf. Edwards 1989, 1992; Gallhofer and Haslam 2006a).

Forward was founded in 1906 by socialist Thomas Johnston and some of his Fabian friends. Johnston had worked as a clerk and inherited a printing works from a distant relative. He held the view that the key to change lay in educating workers to their class interests, primarily through making visible the 'facts' of injustice and oppression. For example, an article on the poor state of Glasgow's housing was published under the title 'Some Official Figures for Propagandists' (*Forward* 9/5/1914: 1). Among the paper's focuses was war-time profiteering and corporate profits. The paper was actually censored for a brief period in 1915.

Accounts were mobilised as integral to the socialist critique presented in *Forward*. There were two main usages. Firstly, accounts were mobilised – often appearing on the front page – as akin to straightforward facts. The data was taken from annual company reports, *The Stock Exchange Yearbook*, *The Economist* and *The Times* (Gallhofer and Haslam 2006a: 236). If *The Economist* utilised accounts in a way supportive of the existing socio-political order, *Forward* mobilised what it portrayed as accounting facts in a way consistent with a labour-orientated, socialistic and counter-hegemonic intervention. It emphasised excessive profits (using the figures a company disclosed itself) and substantial directors' fees (*Forward* 28/4/1917: 2).

Secondly, *Forward* stressed the manipulative character of capitalistic accounting representation. This approach, which was not as commonly pursued, still hung on to the view that there were facts to be had beneath the manipulation. The manifestation and trajectory of the First World War gave new significance and thematic emphasis to the mobilisation of accounting information. Under pressure, the government introduced an excess profits duty, albeit that this created an incentive to overstate profits made prior to the War (Marriner 1980; Arnold 1997, 2014).

Gallhofer and Haslam (2006a) suggest that in particular contexts, including in media sites such as a particular newspaper, accounting takes on a new meaning. In a context substantively characterised by hegemonic norms, beliefs and values, a text or an accounting may be encoded to reflect these characteristics and align with a hegemonic position. Oppositional reading may decode messages in a contrasting way (Hall 1980). As Gallhofer and Haslam (2003) point out, for Hall (1980: 138):

> One of the most significant political moments … is the point when events which are normally signified and decoded in a negotiated way begin to be given an oppositional reading. Here the 'politics of signification' – the struggle in discourse – is joined.[27]

Gallhofer and Haslam (2003) suggest in their historical analyses that at any given moment in a problematic socio-political order accounting functions in both emancipatory and repressive ways. The repressive tendency may dominate, but repressive forces never absolutely control accounting's functioning. Accounting has the potential, realised by radical activism, to function so that emancipatory effects come to dominate the repressive. If accounting is mobilised by repressive forces, it also engenders countervailing forces, and radical activism may have a role in contributing to currents of resistance and counter hegemony. Gallhofer and Haslam (2003: 102) suggest that if 'the inextricable positioning of accounting in the field of tension of its wider context, no matter how non-controversial the practice may come to appear'. They suggest that if accounting is to change in terms of its functioning and consequences, one or more of its elements (they highlight form, content, aura or usage) needs to change (in interaction with their context). Gallhofer and Haslam's (2003: 104) analysis indicate the potential of accounting to offer critical reflection on the socio-political order.

Reflections

The studies by Gallhofer and Haslam and Arnold reviewed in this chapter illuminate accounting as a focus of conflict, as an ambivalent phenomenon reflective of social tensions. Gallhofer and Haslam (2003: 102) note 'the inextricable positioning of accounting in the field of tension of its … context, no matter how non-controversial the practice may … appear'. At any moment in the problematic socio-political order, accounting functions as both emancipatory and repressive (Gallhofer et al. 2015; Gallhofer and Haslam 2019). As indicated above, if accounting is to change in its functioning and consequences, one or more of its elements (form, content, aura or usage) in interaction with the wider dynamic context must also change. It matters what understanding of accounting is reached, who grasps it and what they do with it.

Gallhofer and Haslam elaborate accounting's mobilisation in relation to a relatively repressed social body by focusing on Bentham's general articulation of accounting for wellbeing, social progress, and socialistic and labour campaigns, giving some emphasis to the position of women in the workforce. Existing and new accountings were mobilised. New, including disaggregated accountings were campaigned for. The trajectories of these struggles underscored accounting's emancipatory potential. Even when it substantively serves the established order, accounting as a form of openness becomes an awkward phenomenon for the powerful to control. Powerful forces meet with resistance in and through accounting. Repressive forces may be influential but never absolutely control accounting's functioning. Accounting has potential, the realisation of which may be furthered by activism, to function so that emancipatory effects may dominate the repressive. Where accounting is mobilised by repressive forces, countervailing forces may be engendered as activists are provided with opportunities to respond and contribute.

Gallhofer and Haslam's historical analyses also remind us that accounting has been shaped by struggles, helping us to appreciate its problematic dimensions today. Their studies alert us to the continuing emancipatory potentialities of accounting in interaction with the contextual dynamics of which they are a part. Gallhofer and Haslam indicate accounting's potential to offer deeper critical reflection on the socio-political order. The studies also hint at the value of the alignment of different progressive perspectives in relation to accounting's emancipatory potentiality. We may also reflect on how the power of facticity, trust in accounts and perceptions of accounts have changed. Further, one may theorise negative dimensions of radical activism that invokes 'factual' accounts. Analysis points to how accounting has been mobilised by activists and this may inspire and strengthen emancipatory struggle in the present.

Conclusion

In this chapter we have reviewed a number of critical historical studies that have attempted to advance emancipation in and through accounting and furnish analyses of accounting's mobilisation and location in projects of radical activism with emancipatory intent. The studies reviewed have focused on the socio-political context of modern Britain, up until the First World War. They have suggested insights of relevance to emancipatory projects today. Comparatively few historical studies have been performed in this area even though they have potential significance to the wider critical project in accounting (Gallhofer and Haslam 2006a). There is then considerable scope for further work that promises to add further insight. The mobilising of accounting in projects of radical activists with emancipatory intent has continued to manifest in the years since 1918, and there have been a number of studies in the accounting literature that have given some attention to this. Gallhofer and Haslam (2003, ch. 4) discuss instances of 'counter accounting' in the British context from the 1970s, whereby pressure groups have mobilised accounting to come to the service of radical campaigns. They give attention to the work of such bodies as Counter Information Services and Social Audit Ltd in the 1970s and more recently the work of pressure groups such as Corporate Watch. Gallhofer et al. (2006) explore how the Web is variously facilitating and impeding such counter accounting activity. Technological changes are understood as changing the form and dissemination of counter accountings in a context where the intertwining of accounting and radical activism continues and has enhanced pertinence (Gallhofer and Haslam 2003, chs. 1, 4; 2006b). Gallhofer and Haslam (2019) and Gallhofer et al. (2015) emphasised the need for more socio-historical analyses focusing upon the plurality and mutability of progressive interests, identities and projects in relation to accounting. The complex trajectory of accounting and its ambivalence suggest the case for pragmatism. The insights from the studies considered here have helped to provide new insights, but they continue to suggest that there is much still to discover. Further critical historical research of this genre is strongly encouraged.

Key works

Arnold (1997) addresses themes similar to those elaborated by Gallhofer and Haslam in theorising accounting's emancipatory potential.

Bentham (1843) Bentham's writings in general incorporate reflections on accounting publicity, but readers may find 'Of publicity' particularly well focused on the ideas elaborated in this chapter.

Gallhofer and Haslam (2003) espouse a critical theoretical position on accounting and emancipation as refined by engagement with developments in the social sciences and humanities. It includes analysis of Bentham's accounting writings and the mobilisation of accounting by radical agitators and activists in the late nineteenth and early twentieth centuries.

Gallhofer et al. (2015) and Gallhofer and Haslam (2019) are helpful refinements of a theory of emancipatory/repressive or progressive/regressive accounting.

Notes

1 The move beyond dichotomous thinking impacts upon accounting's delineation. Accounting opens up towards broader conceptions of its possibilities from notions of narrow financial economistic representations (*basically* consistent with a mainstream financial economics, see Tinker 1985), to forms of calculation (see Miller and Napier 1993; Napier 2001), to (broadly conceived) systems

of informing for control. Gallhofer et al. (2015) indicate the value of analysing a variety of particular accountings but point to the need to clarify the accounting one is focusing on: when we discuss accounting, including in historical analysis, our different understandings may leave us talking past each other in significant ways.

2 This is understood to begin with the French Revolution and ends with the First World War and its immediate aftermath (Hobsbawm 1962, 1995).

3 Bentham kept numerous writings from public view in his own severely repressive context (Boralevi 1980, 1984; Foot 1984; cf. Russell 1962: 742; Harrison 1983: 131). Much of his work has only recently been published.

4 Happiness (for the giver) was to be advanced through the act of benevolence, the key word, for Mack (1962: 310), in Bentham's moral dictionary. Bentham was in the tradition of seeing virtue as wisdom (Mack 1962: 249, 323; Critchley 2001).

5 Bentham had links with active early socialists including William Thompson and Robert Owen (Russell 1962: 747; Boralevi 1984: 37). Mack (1962) notes that some of Bentham's work was admired by Trotsky.

6 For us, Bentham's treatment of accounting in itself is significant. He is more typically deemed significant, however, as a key philosopher of 'utilitarianism', which has been translated into concerns for the poor (Russell 1962; Gallhofer and Haslam 1993; Schofield 2006).

7 The construct 'accounting publicity' was not confined to Bentham (Gallhofer and Haslam 1995). Bentham used the terms accounting, publicity and indeed bookkeeping interchangeably (Gallhofer and Haslam 2003: 45). The terms, including bookkeeping, had a quite unrestricted scope in principle and Bentham's 'book-keeping at large' went well beyond conventional financial accounting: his proposals amounted to a kind of 'social accounting' (Gallhofer and Haslam 1993, 1996b). Reference to publicity or something similar has been apparent in the accounting laws of some continental European countries, such as Germany and Sweden (Lowe et al. 1991).

8 Bentham (1843: 589) asked 'Whom ought we to distrust, if not those to whom is committed great authority, with great temptations to abuse?' (see also his advocacy of unofficial systems of accounting to challenge the powerful (1843: 583)).

9 Alternative names Bentham gave to his publicity principle were: the 'open-management-principle', 'transparent-management-principle' and the 'all-above-board-principle' (Gallhofer and Haslam 1994a: 256).

10 These reflect contextual imperfections. The socio-political context of Bentham's time was a poor one for the establishment of effective democratic practice. It was a repressive society where one could make a case for suggesting that Bentham's faith in the possibilities of democracy were naively optimistic (Foot 1984).

11 Here, Bentham may ironically contribute to displacing alternative accountings that were less restricted in terms of form and content and were relatively more emancipated (see Edwards (1989), on the varieties of form in the historical context).

12 This aspect was enhanced by the then still operational Companies Act of 1862, which contained model articles specifying that companies were to present a balance sheet and an income and expenditure account in prescribed form to the AGM, to open their books to inspection by members and to undergo an annual audit by an auditor appointed by the members who would report on whether the balance sheet was 'full and fair' and gave a 'true and correct view' of the firm's state (Edwards 1989: 182).

13 Some companies apparently took things to extremes by going against the law's spirit by filing the same balance sheet every year (Edwards 1989: 136).

14 The journal was not formally an organ of any particular political association although it contained advertisements for the SDF, the Socialist League, the Fabian Society and the Land Restoration League (see *Common Sense* 15/7/1887: 56).

15 MDM refers to the Minutes of Directors' Meetings at Bryant and May Limited held in the Hackney Archive Department.

16 SD here denotes the Secretary's Diary, Bryant and May, Hackney Archives Department.

17 On 30/6/1888 *The Link* contained the following quotation: 'comfortable people object to the veil being torn off the putrefying wounds of society'. *The Link*'s motto, from Victor Hugo, reflected a proactive concern to transform negative into positive environments through making things visible and known. It further stated: 'I will be the word of the people … I will say everything' (*The Link* 30/6/1888: 1).

18 Perhaps the directors preferred negotiation with the union behind closed doors to the trial by publicity that had manifested. The directors were still feeling the need to counter adverse publicity at the next AGM (Gallhofer and Haslam 2003: 88).
19 The success of the prior accounting publicity did encourage the usage of more, and Champion, in *The Labour Elector*, the paper he edited after *Common Sense*, attacked the level of directors' pay at Bryant and May (24/8/1889).
20 Champion was frustrated that, as a partnership during the first eight years of its existence, Brunner, Mond had no published accounts during this period (*The Labour Elector* 15/11/1888: 4).
21 This position contrasts with that of the Trades Unions who were worried about the economic effects of any reduction in working hours. Champion repeated his analysis for many industries, engendering a similar message (*The Labour Elector* 15/6/1889: 6). One reader thought Champion's analysis too generous to the employer (22/6/1889).
22 Per *The Labour Elector* (27/4/1889: 3), *The Star* was correct in saying that a newspaper 'can bring to bear the force of public opinion on natures that would otherwise defy with impunity every power, human and divine'.
23 For Champion: 'since our exposure of the atrocious system maintained at Mr. BRUNNER's works, many improvements have been made in the conditions of labour to which the workmen are subjected' (*The Labour Elector* 25/5/1889: 1; Gallhofer and Haslam 2003: 98–9).
24 Newspapers were the dominant form of media and *Forward* reached a substantial readership in this context (Gallhofer and Haslam 2006a).
25 A socialist revolution almost succeeded in Germany (Gallhofer and Haslam 1991, 2006a).
26 Further, the government and the profession secured something of a greater alignment towards the end of the nineteenth century and endorsed a preference for substantive corporate financial secrecy (Edwards 1989; Arnold 1997).
27 Gallhofer and Haslam (1991) is in part a related study focused on the German context. It discusses the mobilisation of accounting in socialist media in Germany during the First World War and its aftermath.

References

Alvesson, M. and Willmott, H. (1992) On the idea of emancipation in management and organization studies, *Academy of Management Review*, 17 (3): 432–64.

Anonymous (1838) Article XI, The works of Jeremy Bentham: now first collected under the superintendence of his executor John Bowring, Parts 1-4, *London and Westminster Review*, April-August (Edinburgh: Tate).

Arnold, A.J. (1997) Publishing your private affairs to the world: corporate financial disclosures in the UK, 1900-24, *Accounting, Business & Financial History*, 7 (2): 143–73.

Arnold, A.J. (2014) 'A paradise for profiteers'? The importance and treatment of profits during the First World War, *Accounting History Review*, 24 (2-3): 61–81.

Aronowitz, S. (1988) Postmodernism and politics, in A. Ross (ed.), *Universal Abandon? The Politics of Postmodernism*, pp. 46–62 (Edinburgh: Edinburgh University Press).

Attridge, D., Bennington, G., and Young, R. (1987) (eds.) *Post-structuralism and the Question of History* (Cambridge: Cambridge University Press).

Bahmueller, C. (1981) *The National Charity Company: Jeremy Bentham's Silent Revolution* (Berkeley, CA: University of California).

Beaver, P. (1985) *The Match Makers* (London: Henry Melland).

Benhabib, S. (1992) *Situating the Self: Gender, Community and Postmodernism in Contemporary Ethics* (Cambridge: Polity Press, in association with Oxford: Blackwell).

Benhabib, S. (1994) In defence of universalism – yet again! A response to critics of Situating the Self, *New German Critique*, 62 (Spring/Summer): 173–89.

Bentham, J. (1790) Letter to Right Hon John Parnell, 2 September 1790, *British Museum Manuscript*, MS 33541: f.160.

Bentham, J. (1812) *Pauper Management Improved: Particularly by Means of an Application of the Panopticon Principle of Construction* (London: Robert Baldwin & James Ridgeway), first published 1797 in Arthur Young's Annals of Agriculture.

Bentham, J. (1816) *Chrestomathia* (London: Payne & Foss and R. Hunter).

Bentham, J. (1817) *Chrestomathia, Part II* (London: Payne & Foss).

Bentham, J. (1843) Of Publicity, in An Essay on Political Tactics, in J. Bowring (ed.), *The Works of Jeremy Bentham*, Vol. 2, pp. 310–15 (Edinburgh: Simpkin, Marshall & Co.).

Bentham, S. (1830) *Financial Reform Scrutinised in a Letter to Sir Henry Parnell, Bart, MP* (London: Hatchard & Son).

Besant, A. (1938) *An Autobiography*, 2nd. (London: Fisher Unwin).

Bolt, C. (1993) *The Women's Movement in the United States and Britain from the 1790s to the 1920s* (New York: Harvester Weatsheaf).

Booth, C. (1889-1903) *Life and Labour of the People of London*, Vol. 17, (London: Macmillan & Co).

Booth, W. (1890) *In Darkest England and the Way Out* (London: Salvation Army).

Boralevi, C. (1980) In defence of a myth, *The Bentham Newsletter*, 4 (May): 33–46.

Boralevi, C. (1984) *Bentham and the Oppressed* (Berlin: Mouton de Gruyter).

Bowring, J. (ed.) (1843) *The Works of Jeremy Bentham* (Edinburgh: Simpkin, Marshall & Co.).

Boyne, R. (2000) Post-panopticism, *Economy and Society*, 29 (2): 285–307.

Briggs, A. and Macartney, A. (1984) *Toynbee Hall: The First Hundred Years* (London: Routledge & Kegan Paul).

Bronner, S.E. (1994) *Of Critical Theory and Its Theorists* (Oxford: Blackwell).

Bryant and May, Minutes of Directors, Records of Bryant & May (Ref D/B/BRY), Hackney Archives, London.

Bryant and May, Secretary's Diary, Records of Bryant & May (Ref D/B/BRY), Hackney Archives, London.

Calhoun, C. (1995) *Critical Social Theory: Culture, History and the Challenge of Difference* (Oxford: Blackwell).

Calinescu, M. (1986) Naming and difference: reflections on 'Modernism versus Postmodernism' in literature, in D. Fokkema and H. Beretens (eds), *Approaching Postmodernism: Papers Presented at a Workshop on Postmodernism*, pp. 21–23 September, 1984, (Utrecht: University of Utrecht).

Calinescu, M. (1987) *Five Faces of Modernity* (Durham, NC: Duke University Press).

Callaghan, J. (1990) *Socialism in Britain since 1884* (Oxford: Blackwell).

Champion, H. (1983) Quorum pars fui: an unconventional autobiography, *Bulletin of the Society for the Study of Labour History*, 47: 17–35.

The Christian (1887).

Collett, C. (1893) Women's work, in C. Booth (ed.), *Life and Labour of the People in London, First Series: Poverty IV, The Trades of East London Connected with Poverty*, pp. 256–327 (London: Macmillan and Co.).

Common Sense (1887).

Cousins, M. (1987) The practice of historical investigation, in D. Attridge, G. Bennington and R. Young (eds), *Post-structuralism and the Question of History*, pp. 126–38 (Cambridge: Cambridge University Press).

Critchley, S. (2001) *Continental Philosophy: A Very Short Introduction* (Oxford: Oxford University Press).

Cullen, M. (1975) *The Statistical Movement in Early Victorian Britain: The Foundation of Empirical Social Research* (Hassocks: Harvester Press).

Daunton, M. (2000) Society and economic life, in C. Matthew (ed.), *The Nineteenth Century, The British Isles: 1815-1901*, pp. 40–82 (Oxford: Oxford University Press).

Derrida, J. (1978) Violence and metaphysics: an essay on the thought of Emmanuel Levinas, in J. Derrida (ed.), *Writing and Difference*, pp. 79–153, trans. by Alan Bass (Chicago, IL: University of Chicago Press).

Doornbos, M. (1992) Foreword, *Development and Change*, 23 (3): 1–4.

Edwards, J.R. (1989) *A History of Financial Accounting* (London: Routledge).

Edwards, J.R. (1992) Companies, corporations and accounting change, 1835-1933: a comparative study, *Accounting and Business Research*, 23 (89): 59–73.

Foot, P. (1984) *Red Shelley* (London: Bookmarks).

Forward (1914, 1917).

Foster, J. (1990) Strike action and working-class politics on Clydeside 1914-1919, *International Review of Social History*, 35: 33–70.

Foucault, M. (1977) *Discipline and Punish: The Birth of the Prison* (Harmondsworth: Penguin).

Gabardi, W. (2001) *Negotiating Postmodernism* (Minneapolis, MN: University of Minnesota Press).

Gallhofer, S. and Chew, A. (2000) Accounting and indigenous peoples, *Accounting, Auditing & Accountability Journal*, 13 (3): 256–67.

Gallhofer, S. and Haslam, J. (1991) The aura of accounting in the context of a crisis situation: Germany and the First World War, *Accounting, Organizations and Society*, 16 (5/6): 487–520.

Gallhofer, S. and Haslam, J. (1993) Approaching corporate accountability: fragments from the past, *Accounting and Business Research*, 23 (91a): 320–30.

Gallhofer, S. and Haslam, J. (1994a) Accounting and the Benthams: accounting as negation, *Accounting, Business & Financial History*, 4 (2): 239–73.

Gallhofer, S. and Haslam, J. (1994b) Accounting and the Benthams: or, accounting's potentialities, *Accounting, Business & Financial History*, 4 (3): 431–60.

Gallhofer, S. and Haslam, J. (1995) Accounting and modernity, in C. R. Lehman (ed.), *Advances in Public Interest Accounting*, Vol. 6, pp. 203–32 (Greenwich, CT: JAI Press).

Gallhofer, S. and Haslam, J. (1996a) Accounting/art and the emancipatory project: some reflections, *Accounting, Auditing & Accountability Journal*, 9 (5): 23–44.

Gallhofer, S. and Haslam, J. (1996b) Analysis of Bentham's Chrestomathia: or towards a critique of accounting education, *Critical Perspectives on Accounting*, 7 (1/2): 13–31.

Gallhofer, S. and Haslam, J. (2003) *Accounting and Emancipation: Some Critical Interventions* (London and New York: Routledge).

Gallhofer, S. and Haslam, J. (2005) Social accounting: an historical perspective, in C. Clubb (ed.), *Blackwell Encyclopaedia of Accounting*, pp. 388–93 (Oxford: Blackwell).

Gallhofer, S. and Haslam, J. (2006a) Mobilising accounting in the radical media during the First World War and its aftermath: the case of *Forward* in the context of Red Clydeside, *Critical Perspectives on Accounting*, 17 (2/3): 224–52.

Gallhofer, S. and Haslam, J. (2006b) The accounting-globalisation interrelation: an overview with some reflections on the neglected dimension of emancipatory potentiality, *Critical Perspectives on Accounting*, 17 (7): 903–34.

Gallhofer, S. and Haslam, J. (2019) Some reflections on the construct of emancipatory accounting: shifting meaning and the possibilities of a new pragmatism, *Critical Perspectives on Accounting*, 63: https://doi.org/10.1016/j.cpa2017.01.004

Gallhofer, S., Haslam, J., Monk, E., and Roberts, C. (2006) The emancipatory potential of online reporting: the case of counter accounting, *Accounting, Auditing & Accountability Journal*, 19 (5): 681–718.

Gallhofer, S., Haslam, J., and Yonekura, A. (2015) Accounting as differentiated universal for emancipatory praxis: Accounting delineation and mobilisation for emancipation(s) recognizing democracy and difference, *Accounting, Auditing & Accountability Journal*, 28 (5): 846–74.

Gaonkar, D. and McCarthey, R. (1994) Panopticism and publicity: Bentham's quest for transparency, *Public Culture*, 6 (3): 547–75.

Garnham, N. (2000) *Emancipation, the Media and Modernity: Arguments about the Media and Social Theory* (Oxford: Oxford University Press).

Goldberg, L. (1957) Jeremy Bentham: critic of accounting method, *Accounting Research*, 8: 218–45.

Habermas, J. (1974) The public sphere, trans. S. Lennox and F. Lennox, *New German Critique*, 1(3): 49–55.

Habermas, J. (1992) *The Structural Transformation of the Public Sphere: An Inquiry into a Category of Bourgeois Society*, trans. T. Burger with F. Lawrence (Cambridge, MA: The MIT Press).

Hall, S. (1980) Encoding/decoding, in D. Hall, A. Hobson, D. Lowe, and P. Willis (eds), *Culture, Media, Language: Working Papers in Cultural Studies, 1972-1979*, pp. 128–38 (London: Hutchinson).

Harrison, R. (1983) *Bentham* (London: Routledge & Kegan Paul).

Hart, H. (1982) *Essays on Bentham's Jurisprudence and Political Theory* (Oxford: Oxford University Press).

Harvey, D. (1993) Class relations, social justice and the politics of difference, in J. Squires (ed.), *Principled Positions: Postmodernism and the Rediscovery of Value*, pp. 85–120 (London: Lawrence and Wishart).

Himmelfarb, G. (1968) The haunted house of Jeremy Bentham, in G. Himmelfarb (ed.), *Victorian Minds*, pp. 32–81 (New York: Knopf).

Hobsbawm, E. (1962) *The Age of Revolution: Europe 1789-1848* (London: Weidenfeld and Nicholson).

Hobsbawm, E. (1995) *Age of Extremes: The Short Twentieth Century, 1914-91* (London: Abacus).

Hobsbawm, E. (1999) *Industry and Empire: From 1750 to the Present Day* (Harmondsworth: Penguin).

Hopkins, E. (2000) *Industrialisation and Society: A Social History, 1830-1951* (London: Routledge).

Hoskin, K. and Macve, R. (1986) Accounting and the examination: a genealogy of disciplinary power, *Accounting, Organizations and Society*, 11 (2): 105–36.

Hulse, J. (1970) *Revolutionists in London: A Study of Five Unorthodox Socialists* (Oxford: Clarendon Press).

Hume, L. (1970) The development of industrial accounting: the Benthams' contribution, *Journal of Accounting Research*, 8 (1): 21–33.

Hume, L. (1981) *Bentham and Bureaucracy* (Cambridge: Cambridge University Press).

Hyndman, H. (1911) *The Record of an Adventurous Life* (London: Macmillan).

Ignatieff, M. (1984) *A Just Measure of Pain: The Penitentiary in the Industrial Revolution, 1750-1850* (London: London University Publishing).

Kellner, D. (1988) Postmodernism as social theory: some challenges and problems, *Theory, Culture and Society*, 5 (3): 239–69.

Laclau, E. (1990) *New Reflections on the Revolution of Our Time* (London: Verso).

Laclau, E. (1992) Beyond emancipation, *Development and Change*, 23 (3): 121–37.

Laclau, E. (1996) *Emancipation(s)* (London: Verso).

Laclau, E. (2000) Constructing universality, in J. Butler, E. Laclau, and S. Žižek (eds), *Contingency, Hegemony, Universality: Contemporary Dialogues on the Left*, pp. 281–307 (London: Verso).

Laclau, E. and Mouffe, C. (1987) Post-Marxism without apologies, *New Left Review*, 169: 34–61.

Lather, P. (1991) *Getting Smart: Feminist Research and Pedagogy With/In the Postmodern* (London: Routledge).

Leonard, S.T. (1990) *Critical Theory in Political Practice* (Princeton, NJ: Princeton University Press).

Letwin, S. (1965) *The Pursuit of Certainty: David Hume, Jeremy Bentham, John Stuart Mill, Beatrice Webb* (Cambridge: Cambridge University Press).

Liberal Radical (1888).

The Link (1888).

Loft, A. (1988) *Understanding Accounting in its Social and Historical Context: The Case of Cost Accounting in Britain, 1914-25* (New York: Garland).

Lowe, E., Gallhofer, S., and Haslam, J. (1991) Theorising accounting regulation in a global context: Insights from a study of accounting in the Federal Republic of Germany, *Advances in Public Interest Accounting*, 4: 143–77.

Mack, M. (1962) *Jeremy Bentham: An Odyssey of Ideas, 1748-1792* (London: Heinemann).

Marriner, S. (1980) Company financial statements as source material for business historians, *Business History*, 22 (3): 203–35.

Miller, P. and Napier, C. (1993) Genealogies of calculation, *Accounting, Organizations and Society*, 18 (7/8): 631–47.

Napier, C. (2001) Accounting history and accounting progress, *Accounting History*, 6 (2): 7–31.

Nederveen Pieterse, J. (1992) Emancipations, modern and postmodern, *Development and Change*, 23 (3): 5–41.

Norris, C. (1993) Old themes for new times: postmodernism, theory and cultural politics, in J. Squires (ed.), *Principled Positions: Postmodernism and the Rediscovery of Value*, pp. 151–88 (London: Lawrence and Wishart).

Pall Mall Gazette (1888-89).

Parker, R. (1990) Regulating British corporate financial reporting in the late nineteenth century, *Accounting, Business & Financial History*, 1 (1): 51–71.

Peters, J. (1993) Distrust of representation: Habermas on the public sphere, *Media, Culture and Society*, 15 (4): 541–71.

Polanyi, K. (1945) *Origins of Our Time: The Great Transformation* (London: Victor Gollancz).

Prokhovnik, R. (1999) *Rational Woman: A Feminist Critique of Dichotomy* (London: Routledge).

Rorty, R. (1989) *Contingency, Irony and Solidarity* (Cambridge: Cambridge University Press).

Rosen, F. (1983) *Jeremy Bentham and Representative Democracy: A Study of the Constitutional Code* (Oxford: Clarendon Press).

Russell, B. (1962) *History of Western Philosophy and its Connection with Political and Social Circumstances from the Earliest Times to the Present Day* (London: Allen and Unwin).

Schofield, T.P. (2006) *Utility and Democracy: The Political Thought of Jeremy Bentham* (Oxford: Oxford University Press).

Semple, J. (1993) *Bentham's Prison: A Study of the Panopticon Penitentiary* (New York: Oxford University Press).

Sikka, P. (2000) From the politics of fear to the politics of emancipation, *Critical Perspectives on Accounting*, 11 (3): 369–80.

Soldon, N. (1978) *Women in British Trade Unions: 1874-1976* (Dublin: Totowa).

Squires, J. (1993) Introduction, in J. Squires (ed.), *Principled Positions: Postmodernism and the Rediscovery of Value*, pp. 1–13 (London: Lawrence and Wishart).
St James's Gazette (1888).
Star (1888).
Stiglitz, J. (2002) *Economics*, 3rd. (London and New York: Norton).
Tinker, T. (1984) Accounting for unequal exchange: wealth accumulation versus wealth appropriation, in T. Tinker (ed.), *Social Accounting for Corporations: Private Enterprise versus the Public Interest*, pp. 137–203 (New York: Marcus Wiener).
Tinker, T. (1985) *Paper Prophets: A Social Critique of Accounting* (London: Holt, Rinehart and Winston).
Tsuzuki, C. (1961) *H.M. Hyndman and British Socialism* (London: Oxford University Press).
UC, Bentham (Jeremy) Papers, University College London.
Walker, S.P. (1996) Laissez-faire, collectivism and companies legislation in nineteenth-century Britain, *British Accounting Review*, 28 (4): 305–24.
Weeks, J. (1993) Rediscovering values, in J. Squires (ed.), *Principled Positions: Postmodernism and the Rediscovery of Value*, pp. 189–211 (London: Lawrence and Wishart).
Whitehead, A. (1983) Champion, Henry Hyde, in J. Bellamy and J. Saville (eds), *Dictionary of Labour Biography*, Vol. 8, pp. 24–32 (London: Macmillan).
Žižek, S. (2000) Class struggle or postmodernism? Yes, please!, in J. Butler, E. Laclau, and S. Žižek (eds), *Contingency, Hegemony, Universality: Contemporary Dialogues on the Left*, pp. 90–136 (London: Verso).
Žižek, S. (2001) *Did Somebody Say Totalitarianism? Five Interventions in the (Misuse) of a Notion* (London: Verso).

25
RELIGION

Salvador Carmona and Mahmoud Ezzamel

Overview

This chapter provides a synthesis of the literature on the relationship between accounting and religion. It is organised around micro and macro perspectives. The micro perspective addresses the role of accounting in religious organisations, such as temples and religious orders. In particular, it reviews the so-called sacred–secular divide as well as the technical aspects of the implementation of accounting systems in religious organisations. The macro perspective examines the distinctive role of religious beliefs in shaping wider, social understandings of accounting and business.

Proponents of the sacred–secular divide contend that accounting is part of the secular world and, as such, its use in religious organisations is viewed as an unwanted intrusion in the domain of the sacred. Our analysis indicates that such a dichotomy is not universally relevant to all forms of religious institutions, and is problematical even in the Christian religion where this distinction was initially drawn.

Our analysis also shows that religious beliefs exerted lasting influences on business activities and society. This is especialy evident in the prohibition of lending money at interest (usury) and how accounting and cost calculations endowed profit with meanings objectionable in some Roman Catholic circles. We show that accounting had a major impact on societies with a religious worldview, even though religious values were not necessarily mirrored in financial statements. The chapter also discusses how religious and cultural beliefs in China have had a major impact on promoting an understanding of accounting as irrelevant to decision-making, and as an occupation unworthy of elevated social classes.

Religious beliefs in accounting and business practice

The role of religion in the history of humankind can hardly be overstated (Smith 1979). Religious beliefs exert a major and lasting influence on human behaviour as well as on the constitutive elements of social activities and institutions (Durkheim 1976). Religion is widely regarded as one of the earliest forms of human knowledge (Armstrong 1993; Zubiri 1993). At the macro level, religious thoughts have permeated almost every sphere of social life, ranging from political systems to international relations (Suárez 2004).[1] Furthermore, religious beliefs mediate micro-spaces and professional activities such as architecture (Kubler 1982; Ezzamel 2012) and banking by being inscribed onto such spaces and activities (Karim 1990).

It is a widely recognised view that accounting has a major and enduring impact on individuals, institutions and social life in general (Burchell et al. 1980), hence, an examination of the relationship between accounting and religion is a key research area for students of history. Given the rich diversity of religious experience across time and space, such an examination has the potential to contribute to our understanding of the role that accounting has played in a variety of organisational and societal settings. It also promises to yield rich insights that could provide a better theorising of the accounting craft.

The literature on the relationship between accounting and religion has a number of salient characteristics. It draws on a plurality of epistemological perspectives and research sites within a given system of religious beliefs. Examples include accounting in a sixteenth-century Benedictine monastery (Sargiacomo 2001), the links between accounting and comparative spirituality (Laughlin 1988), and management accounting practices in a German-American religious commune (Flesher and Flesher 1979). Investigations also cover a broad canvass of religious regimes, ranging from the influence of Confucianism on Chinese accounting (Guo 1988) to the impact of shifting religious beliefs on accounting during the transition from a Hindu to an Islamic administration in Indonesia (Sukoharsono 1998).

Previous research has, in the main, been Christian-centric (Tinker 2004; Cordery 2015: 433; Kaluvilla 2017), drawing on beliefs and organisations in Christian societies to the relative neglect of other religions and forms of spirituality such as Islam and Buddhism. Moreover, with few exceptions (e.g. Ezzamel 2002), extant research has overwhelmingly focused on a short time-frame, in particular, the nineteenth and early twentieth centuries. To partly compensate for this limitation, our review also refers to 'histories of the present', that is, those studies which examine the relationship between accounting and religion in contemporary societies. Such investigations of the modern age, we argue, are likely to produce many useful insights.

The extant research on accounting and religion is a far cry from the Kuhnian notion of 'normal science' (Kuhn 1962). Generally speaking, accounting historians do not work within a single, agreed-upon paradigm. Instead, the literature is disparate and addresses issues that tend to be only marginally interrelated. In saying this, we are not advocating the idea that better accounting history research is likely to emerge if its production is constrained within a single paradigm. Rather, the diversity of theoretical perspectives in the literature is, we argue, a source of strength. We only allude to the difficulty of synthesising research that is informed by theoretical variety, a difficulty exacerbated by the weak interconnections between the issues examined. Essentially, this chapter reviews an area of accounting history that has not been extensively researched and it identifies several areas for future investigation.

The chapter is organised around the micro and macro perspectives of accounting and religion suggested above. From a micro perspective, our aim is to address the role of accounting in religious organisations, such as temples and religious orders. From a macro point of view, we examine the distinctive role of religious beliefs in shaping wider, social understandings of accounting and business. Further, we explore the views of religious texts on the functioning of accounting in organisations and society.

The remainder of the chapter is organised as follows. In the following section, we survey the literature on accounting in religious organisations, with an emphasis on two major themes. First, the so-called sacred–secular divide, where our analysis spans accounting practice in ancient societies, particularly that of ancient Egypt, medieval times, the proto-industrial period, the Enlightenment and nineteenth-century Europe, and contemporary religious institutions in Christianity and Islam. The second major theme relates to the technical aspects of accounting practice used in Christian religious institutions. In a separate section, we deal with the literature concerned with the influence of religious thought on accounting and business practice, paying special attention to how concepts such as interest, usury, prices and profit (earnings) were defined across different religious beliefs and over time. We pay attention to such influence in relation to the Middle Ages, the Renaissance and Protestantism but also extend our discussion to the teachings of other religions such as Islam and Confucianism. In the penultimate section, we examine some of the literature which discusses how accounting is treated in sacred religious texts, including the Quran, the Old Testament and the New Testament. The chapter concludes with a summary and suggestions for future research.

Accounting in religious organisations

Research using a micro perspective on the role of accounting in religious organisations is analysed here around two key themes. First, examination of the sacred–secular divide. In this context, accounting has been perceived by some as part of the secular world and, as such, its use in religious organisations has been viewed as an unwanted intervention into the sacred domain (Laughlin 1988; Booth 1993).[2] Others have rejected this duality (Quattrone 2004; García Marí and Martínez Soto 2016). Overall, and as noted by McKernan and Kosmala (2007), the accounting debate on the sacred–secular divide has been very promising, 'having the potential to instill religion into accounting' (see Joannidès and Berland 2013: 525). Second, we look at research that has focused on the implementation of double-entry bookkeeping in religions institutions before the Industrial Revolution (Hernández Esteve 2001).

Accounting and the sacred–secular divide

The debate on the sacred–secular divide has drawn on conceptual frameworks borrowed from the social sciences (Joannidès and Berland 2013). Durkheim (1976: 37) has pointed out that the modelling of the world by religious belief divides the world into two: 'the one containing all that is sacred, the other all that is profane'. Therefore, the profane is treated as something fundamentally different, and separate from, the sacred. Laughlin (1988, 1990) drew on aspects of Habermas' critical theory and research on comparative spirituality (Eliade 1959) to examine the functioning of accounting systems in the Church of England. He noted how, initially, the state acted as a 'resource supplier' for the Church and for the dioceses and parishes. However, when the resource suppliers no longer required the guidance of the Church of England, this institution internalised the resourcing problem. It was in this new context that the accounting system of the Church of England was located. Laughlin (1988: 38) argues that accounting systems 'are legitimate aids to this resourcing problem, but they are not part of the sacred agenda and should not interfere with more important endeavors of the Church of England'. Thus, Laughlin argues, accounting did not play a role in the functioning of the sacred elements of the Church of England.

In his examination of the Australian Uniting Church, Booth (1993) emphasises the sacred–secular divide. In particular, Booth argues that the dichotomy helped to differentiate the 'legitimate' part of religious organisations from support activities, the latter entering the domain of the secular. Booth asserts that the secular plays a secondary role in religious institutions and that accounting constitutes an integral part of the domain of the secular. In spite of this subordinate role, Booth reports that accounting did not necessarily face resistance in religious organisations and that its role 'can be highly prominent within Churches' (Booth 1993: 41).

Some studies in accounting have questioned the sacred–secular divide. For example, Hardy and Ballis (2005: 25–6) argued that 'The sacred and secular model remains problematic: it consists of general arguments that oversimplify religious organizations, on the one hand, and on the other, the role of professionals in these organizations'. In a similar vein, recent research has suggested that the sacred–secular dichotomy is time–space specific and may not be applicable to religious institutions except perhaps those of contemporary Christian Western cultures (Carmona and Ezzamel 2006). This is shown by Banos Sanchez-Matamoros and Funnell (2015) in their study of a Catholic order that managed military hospitals in eighteenth-century Spain. Similarly, Dobie (2015a) conducted a study of accounting, financial and management controls in Benedictine monasteries in England during 1214–1444. He found that the leadership of the Benedictine Order enforced procedures to restrict the authority of the abbot and required accountability, and even consent, for decisions related to transactions such as leases or loans. Furthermore, the status of these monasteries required the periodic accountability of monks serving in an office in order to justify their stewardship and had not broken their vow of poverty. Overall, Dobie (2015a: 15) concludes that 'there is not a natural sacred-secular divide with spiritual practice on the one side and accounting on the other … [as] accounting and accountability was an essential part of the life of a medieval Benedictine monastery'. Likewise, Bigoni et al. (2013) examined accounting and accountability practices in the Diocese of Ferrara (1431–1457), that is, during the period that witnessed substantial reforms to restore the moral authority of the Catholic Church as well as to enhance the role of accounting and financial practices to guarantee the success of the reforms. Bigoni et al. found that accounting practices were complementary to the Church's religious mission and, hence, did not find support for the sacred–secular divide.

Given the importance of context-embeddedness for an informed understanding of the sacred–secular divide, we will follow the chronological development of the relevant literature. As shown below, some of these studies do not explicitly address the sacred–secular dichotomy, but the richness of their evidence provides insights to this issue.

Ancient societies

Ezzamel (2005, 2009, 2012) examined the role of accounting practices in the functioning of funerary temples during the Old Kingdom (2700–2181 BCE) in ancient Egypt as well as the link between accounting and order in the New Kingdom (1552–1080 BCE). In his examination of funerary Ezzamel (2005, 2012) noted that accounting in these institutions provided different types of visibility: organisational, technical and dependency. The temple ensured organisational visibility through recording an inventory of items using a combination of black and red ink in a tabular format. Further, the enumeration of quantities of inventory tools drew on a flexible categorisation that made it easy for the scribe to signal damaged items as well as the nature of the damage. These entries were then audited by a foreman who made entries in the inventory list to that effect. Taken together, these practices provided a form of technical visibility of inventory items. Dependency visibility was evident in how accounting entries shed light on the intricate relationships between economic institutions that provided daily supplies to the funerary temple. In turn, such entries were aggregated in monthly income statements that indicated theoretical (expected) deliveries, actual deliveries and any balances outstanding, day by day. Ezzamel (2005: 48) concluded, 'this complex and detailed range of accounting intervention in the activities of the temple neither signals accounting as "irrelevant", nor as highly "rudimentary" nor as an unwanted, profane inconvenience'.

Concerning the role of accounting numbers in the creation and promotion of 'order', Ezzamel (2009, 2012) argues that accounting was conceptualised as an integral part of the assemblage that formed the heavenly order deemed by the ancient Egyptians to underpin their world. This assemblage produced a fragile equilibrium between the gods in the sky, the Pharaohs, their living subjects and the dead. Importantly, any disruption of this order was deemed catastrophic. Accounting constituted a performative ritual that enforced order in the cosmos, on earth and in the netherworld. Further, accounting numbers combined with linguistic texts and pictorial scenes in architecture to produce a monumental discourse that made possible the construction and perpetuation of this orderly schema. In ancient Egypt, Ezzamel (2012) notes, rather than being a marginal, profane practice accounting was intertwined with the sacred activities of the temple and the religious understandings of society. This was consistent with the religious ideology of ancient Egypt that drew no clear demarcations between what was sacred and what was secular.

Other investigations of the sacred–secular divide in ancient societies include Fonfeder et al. (2003) who investigated the Hebrew Talmud's account of internal controls in the ancient Temple of Jerusalem (*c.* 823 BCE to CE 70). The authors state (2003: 75) 'the Talmud was so concerned with preventing any suspicion of financial malfeasance, that controls were designed to prevent even any appearance of theft', thus enhancing the fiscal credibility of the Temple in the eyes of its congregants. Talmudic sources enforced the use of extensive internal control processes over the Temple Treasury, including the collections of biblically mandated half-shekel donations, withdrawals from the Treasury, and distributed offerings, all premised on the idea that public confidence in the workings of the Temple was sacrosanct. Fonfeder et al. (2003: 90) contend that 'the Talmud's extended discussion of internal controls indicates that systems of accountability formed an integral portion of the Temple's rituals', thereby indicating that accounting was not a secular activity at odds with the Temple's mission.

Medieval times

Monastic orders played a fundamental role in the Middle Ages. As noted by De Vaujany (2010), this period is called the 'age of monks' and monastic orders contributed significantly to the emergence of bureaucratic organisations. The Order of the Temple was created after the First Crusade in 1096, to protect pilgrims on their way to Jerusalem. The Temple combined military and religious activities and, as such, its members were a disciplined force who performed the double role of monks and soldiers. The Temple grew in social and political importance during Medieval times until its sudden demise in 1314. De la Torre's (2004) study of the role of the Order of the Temple in the origins of banking is of particular interest to our analysis. De la Torre argues that the Knights Templar engaged in banking in relation to donations received from pilgrims in acknowledgement of their protection on their round trip to Jerusalem. In turn, these funds were deployed in supporting the wars against the Arab Muslims. More importantly, the Temple became heavily engaged in public banking, that is, lending money to European monarchs, especially to the Kingdom of France.

Banking became essential to the mission of the Knights Templar and a sophisticated accounting system was deployed to record the web of transactions and transfers of funding across the Order's sites in different countries and regions. Although De la Torre did not address the sacred–secular divide explicitly, the variety of financial activities performed by the Templars is suggestive of the intertwining of the sacred and secular. Accounting systems did not constitute an external, detached activity, but facilitated the ventures pursued by the Order.

Dobie (2015b) examined accounting, management and control practices at Durham Cathedral Priory. While the Cathedral was growing in size, and despite the *Rule* that accounting and administrative duties had to be performed by the abbot and the cellarer, thereby making no clear distinction between what is sacred and what is profane, such activities were delegated to officers, which might hint at a distinction between the sacred and profane in practice. The system was complex in its management, as it had to enforce mechanisms that ensured the delegation of activities and control techniques. In a similar vein, the system was technically advanced; for example, it used an accrual system to monitor unpaid rents.

The proto-industrial period

In 1503, the City of Seville was granted the monopoly of Spanish trading with Spain's Latin American colonies and, as a result, became one of the most important trading centres in Europe. In this context, the Cathedral of Seville became a major social, economic and political organisation, and the scale of its activity is indicated by the 9,000 accounting books catalogued in the Cathedral's archive from the fifteenth to the nineteenth centuries.

The accounting system of the Cathedral of Seville has been examined by Hernández Borreguero (2016) for the years 1625–50. During that period, the Cathedral kept 630 accounting books, that is, more than 25 per year. This wealth of accounting records reveals an intricate web of transactions indicative of the Cathedral's aim to secure funds from the city's businesses and enhance its own political and social standing. In pursuing this objective, the Cathedral of Seville engaged in transactions banned by the doctrine of the Catholic Church. Hernández Borreguero discusses evidence of lending activities at an interest rate that was regarded as usury by the Catholic Church and, hence, banned, but the Cathedral drew on the skills of its accountants to mask these transactions. The expertise of its accountants also proved instrumental in resolving disputes between parties in different areas of business activity. Although Hernández Borreguero's study did not address the sacred–secular divide directly, his evidence suggests that accounting played a fundamental role in the organisation of the Cathedral's activities.

Other investigations have addressed the role of accounting in religious organisations before the Industrial Revolution. Quattrone's (2004) analysis of accounting and accountability in the Society of Jesus is particularly significant in this regard. Quattrone provides a detailed description of the internal organisation of the Jesuits amid the ideas of the Counter-Reformation enforced at the Council of Trento, 1545–63. As in the case of the Order of the Temple, the Jesuits also adopted a hierarchical, disciplinary structure, calling themselves 'soldiers of Jesus'. Quattrone (2004: 654) notes that the Jesuits 'were animated by an activism previously unknown in the Catholic Church, where monastic organisations were devoted to contemplation and isolation'. In their pursuit of the salvation of souls, the Jesuits engaged in missionary, educational and economic activities.

The Society of Jesus offered teaching and religious services free of charge. In this respect, the Colleges – the primary unit of the Jesuit organisation and the venue for conducting its activities – were instrumental. These activities required substantial financial resources and sophisticated accounting systems. In fact, accounting became central to the pursuit of the Society's mission. Quattrone (2004) argues that the accounting systems excelled in their sophistication and accuracy. The systems concerned different sources of income generation: legacies and annuity payments, farms and rents. In keeping these records, the Jesuits were inspired by the ideas enshrined in the *Trattato del modo di tenere il libro doppio domestico col suo essemplare*, which presented the double-entry method as an effective combination of analysis and synthesis. In addition to accounting for economic activities, Quattrone shows that the Jesuits engaged in other ideologically embedded accountings such as accounting for sins and accounting for the soul. Therefore, and as Quattrone (2015) demonstrates, the Jesuit Order focused on two practices (spiritual self-accountability and administrative accounting and recordkeeping), which did not assume any external ordering principle, but were founded on continuous interrogations. This unfolding Jesuit rationality led to individuals and the community at large developing actions that were not anchored in a substantive logic but conformed to the specifics of their wider social and organisational contexts.

In addition to its written and calculative practices, the Society of Jesus also enforced a practice of oral accounting – the *Account of Conscience* (Bento da Silva et al. 2017). This practice was developed to facilitate human resource management and obedience mediation and, according to Bento da Silva et al. (2017), it persists largely unchanged to the present day. The Account of Conscience is local in character and is grounded in the Christian pastorate and produced practices that are not written, with the aim of managing a dispersed population of Jesuits. As noted by Bento da Silva et al. (2017), such oral accounts take priority over textual-visual accounts of individual character and performance sent to the senior hierarchy of the Jesuits, in Rome, and are critical vis-à-vis decisions about where to place each individual member of the Society. Bento da Silva et al. (2017) found the sacred–secular divide problematic. However, in contrast to Quattrone (2004), who observed that accounting techniques 'travelled' from the secular world of commerce to the sacred context of the Church, Bento da Silva et al. (2017: 54) found a movement in the other direction – 'a sacred technique (the confession) is transformed into a technique of governance'.

The Enlightenment and the nineteenth century

In contrast to the absolutist ideology enforced by the Council of Trento, the Enlightenment provided a more relaxed environment for the development of religious activities. However, it also led to a conflict between the State and the Catholic Church. Álvarez-Dardet et al. (2006) examined the regulation of brotherhoods during the period 1768–75 and found that they had a perception of the sacred that differed significantly from that of 'enlightened' people. The brotherhoods supported a popular view of religiousness that included elements which 'champions' of the Enlightenment deemed secular. Furthermore, the Bishop of Ciudad Rodrigo supported the views of the enlightened and considered that most of the activities of the brotherhoods were far removed from the sacred sphere. From this perspective, the brotherhoods had to be accountable to the religious hierarchy and also to civil power. In such contexts, accounting played a secondary role because the government mainly sought the compliance of the brotherhoods with prior regulations concerning the approval of their activities.

Baños Sanchez-Matamoros and Funnell (2015) also address this time–space intersection in their investigation of the management of military hospitals by the St John's Order. At that time, the military enforced major reforms to simplify and enhance the management of military hospitals. Their study shows that accounting was critical to ensuring successful commercial relations between the Order and the State. Furthermore, the accountability practices of the Order to the State were not regarded as secular and antithetical to their religious beliefs – the Order provided the military with low cost essential care for injured soldiers and this accountability process was essential to overcoming the resistance of the State to the Church's influence in secular matters. The case of brotherhoods operating in eighteenth-century Spain suggests that no distinction was drawn between the sacred and the secular in relation to the intervention of accounting in religious matters.

Mutch (2012) focused on Scottish Presbyterianism to examine the organising practices that are implemented to put belief into action. In particular, he investigated the extent to which the Scottish pre-eminence in accounting texts during the eighteenth century was influenced by religion. He found that the culture of systemic accountability and record-keeping cultivated by Scottish Presbyterianism, along with Scottish economic practices, became an important contributor to the production of accounting texts.

Research on accounting in religious institutions has overwhelmingly focused on organisations inhabited by men. In one of the few studies addressing female institutions, Oliveira and Brandao (2005) examined accounting practices in the Cistercian Monastery of Arouca during the period 1786–1825. As with the Order of the Temple, the Society of Jesus and the brotherhoods discussed above, the Cistercian congregation was organised in a hierarchical fashion, an organisational form that impacted on the accounting systems of the monastery. According to the rules of the Cistercians, the Monastery of Arouca had to report to the Congregation of Alcobaça on its financial performance and adhere to the Congregation's rule of maintaining a charge and discharge accounting system. Accounting was crucial for the activities of the Monastery of Arouca. Oliveira and Brandao (2005) provide evidence on the use of accounting data to produce estimates of revenues and expenses. Such information was compared to the numbers living in the monastery to produce estimates of the population of Arouca in future years. Such information, Oliveira and Brandao argue, was crucial in making decisions about the number of nuns that the monastery could admit in the future and the amount of long-term investments that could be funded. As with some other studies already referred to, Oliveira and Brandao did not focus explicitly on the sacred–secular divide. However, their evidence suggests that accounting played a central role in the activities of the monastery and thus throws doubt on the validity of this dichotomy.

Accounting also played a significant role in the activities of Wesleyan Methodist missionaries in New Zealand during the period 1814–40. John Wesley preached that followers should 'gain all you can, save all you can and give all you can' (Cordery 2006). Cordery found that the Methodists' letters and diaries included records about the exchange of barter goods and ledger accounts. Consequently, the Methodist missionaries were 'totally familiar with the need for accounting for the mission' (Cordery 2006: 214).

Moving the focus to England, Irvine (2002) examined the role of accounting in the Salvation Army, 1865–92. This organisation, which heavily relied on external funds to survive, was engaged in an intense accounting exercise aimed at garnering legitimacy from the users of financial statements. The Salvation Army used accounting to convey a public image of sound financial responsibility with a view to securing the survival of the organisation in the longer term. Irvine's investigation demonstrated that accounting played a key role in the 'sacred' mission of the Salvation Army.

Contemporary organisations

Some studies have examined the sacred–secular divide in contemporary religious organisations. Jacobs and Walker (2004) drew on a combination of interviews and historical documents to explore accounting and accountability practices in an organisation associated with the Church of Scotland, the Iona Community. They show how the members 'are committed to a Rule of daily prayer and Bible study, sharing and accounting for their use of time and money' (ibid.: 363). Practices of financial accounting were deeply embedded in the central religious observances of the Iona Community. The findings challenge the suggestion that accounting was of marginal significance in sacred settings. Jacobs and Walker also found that structures of individualising accountability were subject to resistance, while structures of socialising accountability had the potential to function as forms of internalised surveillance and domination.

Similarly, Jacobs (2005) examined the sacred–secular divide by drawing on the ideas of Christian thinkers critical of the dichotomy. He argued that accounting and financial issues do not necessarily conflict with religious values. Based on the interviews conducted in the Church of Scotland, Jacobs demonstrates that the categorisation of accounting practices as secular is too simplistic. One interviewee revealed that 'the control and management of money within the Church was the responsibility of the clergy rather than the accountants' (Jacobs 2005: 206). Jacobs' study indicates that while there was some resistance to the incursion of accountants, accounting played an important role in the activities of the Church of Scotland. Therefore, and as noted by Joannidès and Berland (2013: 524), Jacobs rejected a structural approach to accounting and religion, which saw religion as inherently sacred and accounting as inherently secular.

In contrast to the foregoing emphasis on Christian religion, Abdul-Rahman and Goddard (1998) focused on two contemporary Islamic organisations established in Malaysia that collected and disbursed the *Zakah*, that is, the annual payment which Muslims with a minimum wealth are compelled to make to the poor. Abdul-Rahman and Goddard examined modes of thought (such as the dichotomy between secular-accounting and sacred-religious activities, level of professionalism and the existence of power elites) and the modes of action (the processes and structures of accountability and organisational processes). They reported that the accountants in both organisations agreed that the accounting system was not alien to or separate from the religious domain. Accounting was considered part of the support activities of the organisation; hence there is no clear separation between sacred and secular activities. Abdul-Rahman and Goddard (ibid.: 197–8) concluded that 'The world-view of Islam encompasses both sacred and secular aspects and the secular must be related in a profound and inseparable way to the sacred' (see also Basri and Khalid 2012).

Hardy (2008) and Hardy and Ballis (2013) examined the accounting practices of the Sanitarium Health Food Company (SHF), a food manufacturing business owned and operated by the Seventh Day Adventist Church. Given this ownership structure, the SHF company did not need to comply with accounting requirements and accountability practices. The study suggests that the SHF company adopted low profile, formal reporting practices while also using a sophisticated system of social accountability that promoted the activities of the company to the Seventh Day Adventist Church as well as to the public. Finally, Fernandez-Roca (2010) examined the Benedictines of Montserrat (Spain) during 1900–36, that is, the period following the confiscation of the property of religious orders by the Spanish government. In order to conceal their estates from the Spanish government, the Benedictines created a fictitious organisation in the form of a legal limited liability company, which was more opaque and more successful in protecting the Benedictine's estates when compared to companies created by other religious orders.

Overall, the sacred–secular divide has been the subject of debate and discussion and has attracted research on accounting and religion, an area that had been widely neglected until the early work by Laughlin (1988, 1990). However, research shows that the divine–secular divide is too rigid and at best is time–space dependent.

Technical aspects of accounting in religious institutions

In contrast to studies addressing the sacred–secular divide, several investigations have examined the level of sophistication of accounting techniques used in religious organisations. A particular focus of these studies is to test the idea that accounting practices in religious institutions are rudimentary or outdated. A related theme is to assess the extent to which these institutions were early adopters of double-entry bookkeeping. These studies have also examined how accounting practices in religious organisations are context embedded.

In the Kingdoms of Aragon and Catalonia during the fourteenth century, wealth was concentrated in the hands of the nobility, with the majority of the population living in impoverished conditions. Charity was crucial to ensuring the survival of the poor, with the Roman Catholic Church playing a prominent role in this connection. Charitable activities were performed by the almoner who was accountable to the state for his management of funds. In a decree dated 18 May 1370, the King of Aragon granted the Abbot of the Monastery of Poblet the privilege of Royal Almoner. This decree stipulated detailed rules for the management of charitable activities and covered receipts, management of cash assets and the delivery of funds to the poor. Monclús Guitart (2005) compared the sophistication of these records with those kept by the contemporary *Taula de Canvis*, a banking institution. Monclús Guitart found that apart from differences in the frequency of record keeping (which was conducted daily in *Taula* and monthly in the monastery), both the structure and the method of keeping accounts were identical. The study showed that practices of accounting and accountability were not only present in religious institutions of the Middle Ages, but they were similar to those of specialised, private institutions, such as banks.

Paisey and Paisey (2011) examined financial management in a pre-Reformation church in Aberdeen (Scotland) during 1488–1514, within the term of Bishop William Elphinstone. This period witnessed corruption in the church, amid greed and nepotism. Furthermore, the interplay between church, state and society resulted in the medieval church operating as an actual 'state' – the church enacted its own laws, taxes and enforced discipline. Consequently, at the turn of the sixteenth century, the church was among the wealthiest institutions; the parishes supplied much of the income to the cathedral, which deployed an administrative machinery that offered education, health, welfare and religious services. However, the cathedral was not accountable either to the people who provided its funds nor to the metropolitan cathedrals that comprised the next layer in the hierarchy of the Catholic Church. Overall, accounting was central to the functioning of the church and the records were important for proper financial management practices. As noted by Paisey and Paisey (2011: 601), 'the excesses of the Pre-Reformation church show that a lack of what would now be recognized as accountability was a contributory factor in rising discontent'. Paisey and Paisey also considered that the notion of the sacred–secular divide was too rigid.

In sixteenth-century Spain, the Archbishop of Toledo collected the highest rents in the country (Fernández Alvarez 2004) and had considerable economic and religious influence. This prompted Villaluenga de Gracia (2005) to challenge the findings of Futcher and Phillips (1986), who argued that religious institutions constituted the last pocket of resistance against the implementation of innovative accounting and managerial techniques. In her analysis of accounting practices at the Cathedral of Toledo during the period 1533–39, Villaluenga de Gracia undertook an extensive examination of the accounting books kept to track the flow of rents. In particular, she focused on the design and implementation of a double-entry system at this relatively early stage in the history of the technique. She argues that the double-entry system provided timely information on the Cathedral's properties and their contribution to the generation of wealth and shows that such information was crucial to the long-term survival of the institution.

The Benedictine Monastery of Silos constituted a major Spanish spiritual centre. Prieto Moreno et al. (2006) examined Benedictine procedures and accounting records to explore the extent to which accounting served accountability and decision-making purposes during the seventeenth and eighteenth centuries. The authors reported that accounting records were subject to strict and comprehensive scrutiny 69 times per year. The system of accountability consisted of quadrennial statements delivered by the 45 monasteries to the Congregation. In turn, the Congregation used this information to demand further financial contributions from the state. The Congregation aggregated monasteries' reports and provided the state with a detailed breakdown of expenditure (salaries, building works, lawsuits, transport and rents) incurred by the monasteries for the management of their patrimony; for the upkeep of their monks and servants; for the material and spiritual needs of marginalised social classes (alms, gratuities); and for maintaining financial details relating to other strata of civil and ecclesiastical society (donations to the Crown and quinquenniums to the Holy See).

Interestingly, the reports issued by the monasteries included data on expenditure per monk, a calculation that went beyond 'expenses on upkeep and clothing'. Such information was crucial for decision-making and control purposes at the monastery. Prieto Moreno et al. (2006) also reported that the Monastery of Silos implemented an early form of accrual-based accounting for revenues. The accounting system of the Monastery of Silos combined elements from both the charge and discharge system and the double-entry method enforced by the Cathedral of Toledo (see Villaluenga de Gracia 2005).

As well as examining accounting books kept by religious institutions (e.g. Bisaschi 2003), some researchers have explored the impact of religious practice on the development of accounting techniques. In particular, Aho (2005) makes a connection between the development of double-entry bookkeeping and the Catholic confessional, with double-entry being the worldly counterpart of the spiritual giving of account. Aho (2005: 28) notes, 'It is … difficult to appreciate that originally there might have been something more than just a figurative parallel between business chronicling and moral confession'. Aho argues that as commerce fell under the jurisdiction of the medieval church, merchants and bankers sought to demonstrate their high moral standards. Business narrative began to assume an apologetic, justificatory style akin to that used in confessions. This style was reflected in the manner in which transactions were recorded under double-entry bookkeeping: 'Who took part in the transaction? What goods or services were involved? Where did it take place? When? Why? And how much money was involved?' (Aho 2005: 29).

Confession, Aho argues, encouraged businessmen to record transactions on a daily, even hourly, basis. Every detail was to be entered not once, but twice to demonstrate their impeccability. The author contends:

> Once sacramental confession became routinised into a weekly habit of self-reflection and divulgence, it began to insinuate itself into other realms, serving as a standard for a plethora of accounting practices that appeared in the decades immediately after the Fourth Lateran Council.
>
> *(ibid.: 84)*

Indeed, Aho suggests that in order to address the moral anxiety implied by lending at interest despite the religious ban on usury in medieval Christendom, double-entry bookkeeping was the most potent weapon businessmen could deploy to demonstrate their morality. For Aho, the development of double-entry was one of the key manifestations of the emergence of modern Christian consciousness, which was born out of sacramental confession.

Aho's arguments are certainly stimulating and provocative. The connections he makes between confession and the development and dissemination of double-entry bookkeeping are worthy of serious scholarly reflection. Urton (2009: 805) qualifies the chronology suggested by Aho concerning the relationship between confession and double-entry bookkeeping. Drawing on past research, Urton notices that a well-developed version of the double-entry method was used in the Scriba cartulary papers from 1154 to 1164 and, hence, 'the causal connection asserted by Aho between the 1215 introduction of compulsory confession and the appearance of double entry cannot be sustained'. However, Urton agrees that there was a clear case of the intensification of accountability after the imposition of auricular confession. Therefore, Aho's arguments invite the attention of scholars with an intimate knowledge of Catholic theology to subject it to scrutiny. It would also be useful to explore more deeply what specific attributes of double-entry (which is one of several techniques for recording transactions) render it the logical outcome of sacramental confession.

In his investigation, Urton (2009) emphasises the differences between the understandings of sin by the Spaniards and by the Inca at the time of the Spanish invasion of the Inca Empire during the first half of the sixteenth century. While the Spanish notion of sin (*pecado*) referred to discipline at the level of the individual, the Inca concept (*hucha*) had a social underpinning and focused on the extent to which the individual had performed her/his commitments to the community. Thus, the record-keeping method brought by the Spaniards to Latin America aimed at keeping track of transgressive actions against the community. Future researchers might seek to explain the spread of double-entry bookkeeping into places with religious ideologies radically different from Catholicism.

The work of Aho also suggests that double-entry bookkeeping partly addressed concerns about the profit-seeking spirit in Catholic settings during the Renaissance. Further, he shows that double-entry draws heavily on the notion of balance because 'genuine double-entry did emerge in paragraph form' (2005: 592) and is closely linked to a history of writing (Hoskin and Macve 1986). Within this stream of research, Thompson (1991) examined the rhetoric of double-entry with respect to three institutional mechanisms: the Church, the educational apparatus and the printing/publishing regime. Thompson (1991: 595) notes that 'Pacioli was writing at the peak of the power and security of the Church', and that this impacted on his presentation of double-entry. According to Sangster (2018), Pacioli was part of a 200-year Franciscan tradition of theologian-mathematicians. Furthermore, *Abaco* mathematics was the primary focus of Pacioli's *Summa Arithmetica*, and, in addition to Pacioli's background as a mathematician, such an approach was motivated by Pacioli's understanding of mathematics as the most fundamental and divine science. He believed that it revealed the secrets of the universe and his humanist belief. By being given the opportunity to learn and understand mathematics humans too could access these secrets and improve their standing in the eyes of God.

Research on the role of accounting in religious institutions suggests that the divide between the sacred and the profane was blurred in different eras and in different religions. This review also indicates that accounting practices and techniques in religious institutions were far from rudimentary. Sophisticated accounting techniques were implemented by religious institutions for the purposes of decision-making and control. It is perhaps not too far-fetched to argue that the development and use of refined accounting techniques was one of the key factors that underpinned not only the functioning but also the survival of many religious institutions. Accounting could hardly be considered a marginal, low-status practice resented by the clergy as an unwanted intervention in the sacred domain.

Charities and brotherhoods

The design and implementation of the accounting and accountability practices of the Jesuits were inspired by the absolutist ideology of the Roman Catholic doctrine during the Counter-Reformation. This ideology exerted a distinctive influence on other organisations related to the Roman Catholic Church. For example, the Council of Trento promoted religious brotherhoods. Under the dictates of the Council, the brotherhoods would become a conduit for ensuring the indoctrination of the populace (López Manjón et al. 2007). In pursuing such aims, the brotherhoods provided members with educational, entertainment and religious services. Ultimately, the brotherhoods were formed by groups of secular people and aimed at underpinning social cohesion around religious beliefs (Sánchez Herrero 1985). Although accounting was supposed to be used by the brotherhoods to handle their relationships with the religious and civil powers, this system of accountability was enforced through government regulation.

López Manjón et al. (2007) focused on the accounting practices of the religious brotherhoods established in the wider region of Seville during the period 1563–1604. The governance structure of the brotherhoods was set in their 'rules', which were detailed in various documents. López Manjón et al. argue that the brotherhoods' rules established a multifaceted understanding of accounting. First, according to the provisions of the Council of Trento, the brotherhoods were subject to a strict system of accountability before the Archbishop of Seville and his representatives. If deemed necessary by the Archbishop, the brotherhoods were audited, during which time their officers were temporarily removed and administrative matters were managed by the representatives of the Archbishop. Second, the brotherhood's management was held accountable before its members. The general meetings of the brotherhoods were formative events where members decided on long- and short-term plans and management was obliged to report on the financial condition of the institution. Furthermore, accounting played a fundamental role when new officers were appointed. Outgoing officers had to deliver a comprehensive inventory of items owned by the brotherhoods and this was subject to internal audit. Furthermore, accounting played a fundamental role in the day-to-day activities of the brotherhoods. In addition to accounting for sundry activities, ranging from leisure to education, the accounting books contained records of all waste and consumption that occurred in relation to religious activities (such as religious dress and ornaments, and the consumption of wax). Drawing on the sacred–secular framework, López Manjón et al. (2007) thus reveal how accounting was a powerful instrument for exerting strict internal and external control over the management of the brotherhoods. The authors show how accounting played an active role in the daily activities of the brotherhoods and was consistently used to evaluate past actions. Far from being associated with the secular, accounting mediated the core, 'sacred' aspects of these religious institutions.

In Florence, during the early Renaissance, the republic established a partnership with a charity organisation, the Confraternita of Misericordia, to manage the plagues (Manetti et al. 2017). The Misericordia was the outcome of social and religious traditions of citizenry – it dispensed charity and offered services such as the management of hospitals and burying the dead. In this time–space intersection and during the plague epidemics, the Misericordia implemented a system of accountability that was capable of measuring, managing and allocating resources in order to comply with religious values. As noted by Manetti et al. (2017: 526), this resulted in a complex and innovative accounting system which aimed at complying 'not only with external calls for efficiency and transparency but also to comply with the religious values that inspired it'.

The full implications of accounting practices in securing material provision for the poor have been examined in Victorian England and Wales. Walker's (2004) research on poor relief demonstrates the roles that accounting can play in constituting the poor. He documents how the church/parish administered relief and how this was accounted for in detail by church officers. In particular, Walker shows how accounting was used to manage the cost and financing of relief and also contributed to the social and moral control of its recipients. Walker examines detailed accounting records on paupers and how the publication of the names of relief recipients provided local officials with a potent device for monitoring and governing the poor and facilitating community surveillance.

The influence of religious thought on accounting and business practice

The above discussion demonstrates how, and to what extent, accounting has influenced the functioning of religious institutions. At the same time, religious thought has exerted a pervasive influence on multiple spheres of organisational, business and social life (Homza 2000). In this section, we focus on usury, interest and earnings, and also examine the impact of religion on accounting and business. The main concern of the extant literature has been to articulate the position taken by different religions, and indeed different varieties of the same religion, or even differences within a stream of religious thought across time, towards concepts such as interest, usury, prices and profits. Absent in most of the literature is any direct engagement with how accounting as a technology of measurement and valuation might have mediated the articulation of these concepts. Similarly, there are lacunae concerning the examination of accounting entries or reports related to these concepts within particular contexts. This is clearly one area that future researchers could turn their attention to.

Interest, usury and earnings[3]

The case of usury illustrates how religious beliefs mediated social and business values. In the present-day, usury is understood as the lending of money at a disproportionately high rate of interest. Historically, usury involved lending money at interest (Ali Jafri and Margolis 1999). The Holy Scriptures of major religions including Judaism (Deuteronomy 23: 20–1), Christianity (Luke 6: 35) and Islam (Quran 2: 275 and 278–80) banned the practice of usury. For Christians, usury was tied to the capital sin of greed and considered the same as robbery, lying, violence and harassment (Soll 2014: 35). The treatment of usury in the Quran explains much about the nature of financial systems used in Islamic countries until very recently. The prohibition against *riba* in commercial loans rested on the central belief that one should not gain profit where one has also not taken on risk (Taylor and Evans 1987: 21) or exerted effort. Religious doctrine and the risk of severe financial and personal sanctions (e.g. the Third Lateran Council of 1179 denied Christian burial to usurers) did not prevent the practice of usury, but the desire to avoid these sanctions encouraged the pursuit of ways to circumvent the ethical concerns regarding usury (e.g. currency exchange), including attempts to render it a legitimate practice (Aho 2005: 85).

In the Middle Ages, the notions of usury and profiting were closely related. The Schoolmen, those who developed the ideas of Scholasticism, considered that speculation was to 'sin most gravely'. Drawing on the moral philosophy of Aristotle, the Schoolmen stated that trading should involve charging a 'just price' (Wren 2000) as an antidote to avarice and gluttony. However, there was no general agreement on what a 'just price' should be (de Roover 1967: 421). For some, it meant the amount that allowed a person to maintain his/her social status. For others, it was the cost of production, or it could be set at a maximum or minimum level by legal authorities.

These ideas set the stage for the promulgation of the laws of profit and usury. The exchange of property, argued St Thomas Aquinas (1952, 10: 328) in the thirteenth century, such as by a businessman trading commodities or money, is natural and necessary when it is done in order to satisfy the needs of life. In contrast, the exchange of commodities or money, 'not on account of the necessities of life, but for profit … is justly deserving of blame … it satisfies the greed for gain which knows no limit and tends to infinity'. Profiting by itself is not sinful. It is lawful if intended for the upkeep of one's household, for assisting the needy, or for fulfilling a clear and present need of one's country. In such cases, seeking gain is not an aim in itself. It is a person's 'payment for a person's labour'. Such profiting accords with *natural* law.

Given that the notion of competition was neglected in the writings of Scholastics until the end of the sixteenth century (Wren 2000), attention was paid to the role of the state in price setting. St Thomas Aquinas (1952, 10: 320, 323) pointed out: 'those who govern the state must determine the just measure of things saleable … it is not lawful to disregard such measures as are established by public authority or custom'. A higher price, however, could be asked if the seller 'has changed something for the better … or because the value has changed with the change of place or time … [or] on account of the danger incurred in bringing the object to the market' (Aquinas 1952, 10: 328). Exclusion from price should refer to disguised usury, that is, charging more for an object with payment to follow at a later date. Terms such as 'just measure', changing a product 'for the better', changes in value over time, and the 'danger incurred in bringing the object to the market' have accounting implications given its major role in identifying and costing such elements. Yet, these considerations have not featured in the accounting history literature. They merit investigation.

In Florence, as noted by Sangster (2018), double-entry bookkeeping had been in use at all levels of society two centuries before the publication of Pacioli's *Summa Arithmetica*. Soll (2014) reports the case of a Florentine merchant and banker, Datini, who did business during 1380–1410 and had the papacy as one of his clients. Datini was knowledgeable for using double-entry bookkeeping and having well-preserved archives containing 124,540 letters and 573 account books. Each ledger had a religious formula: 'In the name of the Holy Trinity and all the Saints and Angels of Paradise'. He imposed a one *soldo* fine on employees who failed to keep proper accounts and considered that, after ten punishments, they would become reliable. As noted by Soll (2014: 34), 'this punishment had a religious, penitential aspect'. One major set of entries listed Datini's expensive, illuminated prayer books, his very generous gifts to the church and his alms to the poor. As summarised by Soll (2014: 41), 'Datini's account books not only measured his profit but also what he had to pay back to God for his sins'.

The Renaissance and Protestantism

In its criticism of the doctrines of the Roman Catholic Church, the Reformation changed understandings of business profits. Some versions of the Reformation argued that individuals should engage in secular vocations and invest their money in business rather than using it for charity or luxurious consumption (Weber 2001). Such religious beliefs were particularly prominent in Calvinism. Calvin noted that church leaders engaged in luxurious ostentation and perhaps the pursuit of personal wealth (Tawney 1954). Concerning the debate on earnings and usury, Luther pointed out that money lent on specified commodities must conform to interest rates in keeping with reason and charity, a limit of 4–6 per cent per year (Barnett 1961). This made the charging of interest and the notion of profit socially acceptable.

In a similar vein, Calvin departed radically from the position of the Greek philosophers and the earlier Church teachings by proclaiming that money was not sterile and unable to yield its own fruits (Homer and Sylla 1991: 80), especially where loans were used for productive purposes (Divine 1967: 499). Calvin stated that Scripture only prohibited 'biting' usury (Homer and Sylla 1991: 80). He pointed out that capital and credit were indispensable and that the financier was not a pariah, but a useful member of society (Tawney 1954: 95–6). The Calvinist approach to earnings was summarised as follows: 'What reason is there why the income from a business should not be larger than that from land-owning? Whence do the merchant's profits come, except from his own diligence and industry' (ibid.: 93).

Shifts towards the spirit of profit in Roman Catholic settings

The case of the Royal Soap Factory of Seville illustrates the increasing tolerance of business profit during the Renaissance and proto-industrial periods in Roman Catholic settings. In 1423, the King of Castile granted the Duke of Alcalá a monopoly over the production and supply of soap to the city of Seville (Carmona and Donoso 2004). The royal decree granting the monopoly established that the price of soap was to be set by the local government of Seville. Such policy of granting monopolies was typical in Spain during the Middle Ages and, ultimately, complied with the doctrine of St Thomas Aquinas of entrusting the state with the final pricing decision. The local government and the Duke of Alcalá had continuous conflicts over determining the just price of a pound of soap. These conflicts were resolved through the deployment of tests that reproduced the soap production process and tracked the corresponding costs using sophisticated calculations. To endow the tests with the aura of neutrality, the parties engaged the services of soap experts from outside Seville. The tests were also monitored by a local judge and the minutes were written by an accountant of the Catholic Church to ensure compliance with its doctrine.

The cost calculation of a pound of soap illustrates prevailing notions of earnings and public service in sixteenth-century Spain. In calculating the cost of a pound of soap, the parties estimated expected annual production, which amounted to 417,000 pounds in 1525. It was agreed that non-production costs amounted to 171,175 *maravedíes* (0.41 *maravedís/* pound). However, the parties faced insurmountable problems in handling decimals, which led to a difference of 14,900 *maravedíes* (171,275–156,275). The final report of the test stated: 'the remaining 14,900 *maravedíes* are for the people [of Seville] because there is no way to allocate this amount to the pounds [of soap], and ultimately, this amount is consumed and are consumed [*sic*] by the people of Seville'. This rounding down of the decimals to benefit the people of Seville shows compliance with Scholastics who gave permission for a 'just price' but not for earnings. During the rest of the sixteenth and seventeenth centuries the parties continued their disputes over the constitutive elements of the cost of soap. However, it was not until 1692 that the Duke of Alcalá first claimed his right to 'earnings as a constitutive part or price'. He argued (Carmona and Donoso 2004):

> [The local government] does not admit any earning to me as a purveyor, as it has done in the past, and as it is currently done in the cities of Cádiz and Xerez. Further, it has recognized an additional 8 per cent to prevent the deterioration of the materials and the stored soap. *The contention that spreads throughout the City is that if such expense is considered, then there will be no allowance for earnings. This lacks support [because] what is expense is not earnings, and earnings cannot be denied to the purveyor. Moreover, the privilege will be useless if I cannot profit from it.*
>
> *(emphasis added)*

This claim to receive earnings was in sharp contrast to the claim following the 1525 test that the monopoly for soap production and distribution was intended to provide a service to the people of Seville.

Cost accounting and the concepts of stewardship and prudence

Funnell and Williams (2014) examined the influence of the teachings of the Dissenting Protestant churches on the development of accounting practices in the factory. In a context where religious teachings dominated people's lives and where the middle classes could only make progress through 'innovativeness, self-discipline and hard work' (ibid.: 375), they implemented innovative managerial and accounting practices to cope with changing demands and to enforce discipline in the workforce. To tackle social discontent arising from the implementation of disciplinary practices, these businessmen drew upon the teachings of the dissenting churches.

Religious Evangelicalism exerted a strong influence over the middle classes in industrialising Britain. As noted by Soll (2014: 129–37), a manifestation of British industrial power was that it had become the centre of accounting culture and education; there was a market for accounting manuals for gentlemen and merchants who wanted to manage their own businesses. By the second half of the eighteenth century, accounting and double-entry bookkeeping had become common in English society. Many accounting academies were led by Dissenters and Puritans, who had been excluded from the Anglican Church for refusing to renounce their religious beliefs and were forbidden to hold public office. Josiah Wedgwood stands out of all the Dissenters. He excelled as an industrial innovator as well as in his use of cost accounting to manage production costs, labour and pricing. In Industrial Britain (see Hopwood 1987), bookkeeping became a way of thinking about 'happiness, well-being, and individual worth beyond the bottom line … Holy industriousness could bring both pleasure and pain' (ibid.: 143).

Of special importance for our purposes is the impact of evangelical ideas on stewardship and prudence. Stewardship has long been associated with accounting that arises when an agent is held accountable to the owner of the assets he manages. This notion was strong in Evangelicalism. Evangelicals sought new ways of securing a rationalised and ordered existence to secure personal salvation through assiduousness and moral rectitude (Walker 1998: 488; Davidoff and Hall 1987: 87). As noted by Maltby (2000: 58), 'Evangelicals saw the economy as an area of moral struggle, in which the good would eventually be rewarded and the wicked punished'. In turn, such ideals brought about the enforcement of techniques of measurement, estimation and classification (Walker 1998: 488). Furthermore, individuals were accountable to God for every waking moment and their use of earthly resources. This emphasised the notion of stewardship, 'men held property in trust from God and were accountable for the proper administration of His wealth' (ibid.; Gartnett 1987: 352).

Similarly, Maltby (2000) examined the (accounting) notion of prudence as one of the four cardinal virtues under Evangelism. In eighteenth-century Britain, Evangelicals considered business failure to be the consequence of imprudent behaviour rather than the outcome of market forces. The notion of prudence was at the core of business management and exerted a major influence on a number of key aspects of economic life, such as notions of time-short-termism, which was regarded as detrimental to business performance.

Accounting and business in settings with a religious worldview

The ideas of the Enlightenment that pervaded some Christian countries enforced a dichotomy between the secular and the non-secular (Tinker 2004). As noted above, these notions had hardly any influence in countries with religious worldviews on human and societal activities that perceive no such dichotomy (Hamid et al. 1993; Napier and Haniffa 2011). Such contexts, we argue, feature a number of distinctive characteristics that are relevant to any project seeking to shed light on the intertwining of accounting and religion at the macro, societal level. In this section, we examine the role of religion in accounting and business practices in Islamic countries (Haniffa and Hudaib 2010), and the influence of religion on understandings of accounting and the accounting profession in China.

An Islamic perspective on accounting and business practice

Since early studies by Abdel-Magid (1981) and Gambling and Karim (1986) on Islamic banking and social accounting, respectively, there have been several investigations of accounting practices in contemporary Islamic organisations (e.g. Karim 1990). As Napier (2009) notes, the term 'Islamic accounting' groups together quite disparate accounting practices and ideas. For example, 'Islamic accounting' could be understood in a religious sense as well as from a time–space perspective. In the main, studies on Islamic accounting explore the extent to which accounting and business practice reflect Islamic beliefs (e.g. limited liability is not recognised in Islamic contexts, as businesses are considered extensions of their owners), and how such beliefs were communicated to organisational stakeholders. The *Sharia* is the Islamic law or code of practice for individuals and communities, and financial transactions and business. Furthermore, as Afifuddin and Siti-Nabiha (2010: 1143) note, from an Islamic point of view, those in charge of economic resources must present an account of the execution of stewardship, irrespective of whether the transactions and resources are those of government, business or non-profit organisations.

In the main, studies in this area have focused on Islamic banks. As demonstrated by Maali et al. (2006), countries with a strong Islamic focus such as Pakistan and the Sudan have completely changed their banking systems to make them compatible with the *Sharia*. In the case of Pakistan, the banking system was privatised in 1991 and a dual banking industry now operates (Rammal and Parker 2013). Under the *Sharia*, banks have a clear social focus. Maali et al. (2006) examined the social disclosures of 29 banks operating in 16 countries according to Islamic principles. Social disclosure benchmarks were identified against which actual reporting was compared. Given the assumption that banks are expected to comply with the social norms established in the *Sharia*, the results indicate that the sample of banks fell short of the standards for social reporting. Moreover, the study reported that the banks used financial statements selectively to convey to stakeholders positive news about their image but refrained from reporting adverse information.

The independence of religious and external auditors in Islamic banks is important because the credibility of an organisation's financial reports is at stake; full disclosure is a central demand, as a consequence of the importance of the community, or *umma* (see Lewis 2001). Karim (1990), has shown that Islamic banks have in-house boards of religious advisers commonly known as the Sharia Supervisory Board which oversees compliance with the *Sharia*. For example, the *Sharia* prohibits the payment and receipt of *riba*, which is technically usury but can be interpreted as interest. Karim (ibid.: 43) argues:

If religious auditors report any misrepresentation in the bank's financial statements that are due to a violation of Islamic principles, then the consumers of these statements are likely to react in a manner which could be detrimental to the bank's management.

By contrast, external auditors are guided by economic concerns.

Accounting in Buddhist and Confucian settings

Traditionally, religion has exerted an important influence on Chinese society (Guo 1988). Gao and Handley-Schachler (2003) examined the impact of Confucianism, Feng Shui and Buddhism on the history of accounting in China. Confucianism perceives individuals as being part of various overlapping social networks. Obligations and rights are attached to the relative position of an individual in such networks (Guo 1988: 44). Feng Shui refers to the Chinese science and art of creating harmony between inhabitants and their environment. The essence of Buddhism is reflected in its Four Noble Truths: life is painful, the origin of pain is desire, the cessation of pain is to be sought by ending desire, and the way to this goal is through his Noble Eightfold Path (Guo 1988: 48). Furthermore, as Hong (2014) suggests, Buddhist temples located along the Silk Route provided people with board and lodging and, importantly, played a key role in attracting merchants to Buddhism.

Gao and Handley-Schachler (2003) examined the influence of these philosophical and religious beliefs on bookkeeping methods, accounting information, accounting regulation, government accounting, private accounting, and accountants and the accounting profession. The authors reported that economic factors constituted the most influential forces underpinning the evolution of Chinese accounting, particularly the emergence of double-entry methods in the Ming and Qing dynasties. They also show how the concomitant effects of the concepts of Yin (dark swirl, associated with shadows and femininity) and Yang (light swirl, representing brightness, passion and growth), Feng Shui belief, Buddhism and Confucianism have exerted a strong influence on the views held of accounting in China. For example, the influence of Feng Shui teachings has meant that the potential benefit of accounting information as an aid for control and decision-making has been neglected. The status of accountants and their profession was not advanced by the fact that under Confucianism accounting was not considered a suitable activity for noblemen and other educated people (Guo 1988: 60). Kuasirikun and Constable (2010) examined the indigenous accounts of mid-nineteenth-century Siam/Thailand and found that accounting was heavily influenced by the interaction of socio-religious, economic and political practices. The resulting accounting practices had a multifaceted role. Accounting played a critical role in the substantive elements of the economy, social structure, political governance and wider Buddhist cosmology.

Our review of research on the impact of religious beliefs on business activities and society in general indicates that this influence extended to different domains of public life. The ban against lending money at interest, in particular, usury, resulted in the development of alternative ways to exploit loopholes and circumvent concerns about morality so that businessmen could continue to advance loans at high interest. We have observed the importance of accounting and cost calculations in endowing profit with a meaning that was unacceptable in some conservative, Roman Catholic settings. We have indicated the religious underpinnings of key accounting concepts such as prudence and stewardship. The literature reviewed suggests that accounting had a major constitutive impact on societies with a religious worldview, even though such religious values were not necessarily mirrored in financial statements. Finally, our review has shown that certain religious and cultural beliefs in China have had a major impact on promoting an understanding of accounting as irrelevant to decision-making, and as an occupation unworthy of respected social classes.

Accounting in sacred and religious texts

Research examining accounting and business practice in sacred and religious texts and in holy books has addressed a variety of topics, ranging from episodes of accounting and accountability to the emergence of modern management. In this section, we examine the relatively sparse literature in this area.

The Holy Quran supports a worldview in which sacred and secular activities are not separate. Among monotheistic texts, the Quran provides the most comprehensive perspective on accounting and business practice. Muturza (2004) examined the doctoral dissertation by Charles Torrey on 'The Commercial-Theological Terms in the Koran' at the University of Strasbourg in 1892 to reflect on the use of business terminology in Islam. In particular, Muturza analysed ten concepts related to business practice contained in the Quran: reckoning, weights and measures, payments, wages, loss, fraud, buying and selling, profit, loans and security. Muturza argued that the worldview of the Quran is wide-ranging, as it does not only refer to the Divine reckoning of human behaviour but also to interactions between human beings. Furthermore, there are concerns in the Quran regarding accountability as well as the pursuit and use of wealth. Muturza argues that the use of a secular vocabulary to refer to theological concepts underscores the point that 'one ought not to compartmentalize the sacred and the secular', and observes that there is a long-standing tradition in Islam that governs accountability and equitable behaviour.

Other research has focused on Biblical episodes of accountability. Barlev (2006) examined the statement of accountability presented by Moses to the Israelites following the exodus from Egypt. Barlev argues that being invested by God as their leader, Moses was not obliged to render accounts of his activities to the Israelites. Yet, Moses issued a statement of accountability on the collection and use of silver for the Holy Sanctuary, detailing the materials used in the erection of the Sanctuary, its furnishings and vessels. Drawing on the Pentateuch and, particularly, on the Book of Exodus, Barlev argues that this statement of accountability was intended for educational purposes. Moses aimed to provide his people with an example of appropriate behaviour and to demonstrate to them that he was above suspicion.

Baker (2006) explored the genealogy of wealth through an examination of changes in its meaning in the Old and New Testaments. In the Old Testament, Abraham's wealth was praised because it derived from God. Conversely, in emphasising that the only way to Heaven was through the rejection of wealth, the New Testament portrayed Abraham as a protector of the poor. Baker elaborated a number of possible explanations for these changes in the treatment of wealth in the Bible. He speculates that Paul could have been influential in this change of view inasmuch as he usually addressed audiences of the poor. Echoing Nietzsche, Baker elaborated the possibility that the will to power was repressed by the emergence of Christian morality. Baker also drew on Foucault to suggest that these self-forming activities facilitated the creation of docile bodies so that powerful entities could better control populations. Finally, he argues that discourses about wealth may be seen as implicated in regimes of truth and modalities of power in that the transformation in the discourse about wealth was related to the emergence of the Church as the successor to the Roman Empire.

Conclusion

As Walker (2008) argues, religion is a re-emerging area in accounting history research (see also Baños Sánchez-Matamoros and Gutiérrez Hidalgo 2011). In this chapter we have reviewed the literature devoted to examining the relationship between accounting and religion. In the main, the literature reviewed has a Christian-centric focus and covers events of the nineteenth and twentieth centuries. The literature examines a variety of issues motivated by different paradigms and rich theoretical variety rather than being constrained within a single, dominant paradigm in the image of 'normal science' (Kuhn 1962).

Our review of the literature has been organised around micro and macro aspects of accounting. With respect to the micro focus, we have analysed the role of accounting in religious organisations and, especially, the debate on the sacred–secular divide and the degree of sophistication of accounting techniques used in religious institutions. From the macro perspective, we have examined the extent to which religious beliefs have mediated business and societal values, and addressed religious treatments of interest, usury and earnings, themes that are relevant to accounting, even though the extant literature has barely begun to address them. Furthermore, we have examined the extent to which religious beliefs have impacted the roles of accounting. Finally, we reviewed accounting and business treatment in some sacred and religious texts.

Our analysis of research on the sacred–secular divide indicates that such a dichotomy is not universally relevant to all forms of religious institutions, and is problematic even in the Christian religion from where this distinction was initially drawn. According to the sacred–secular divide, accounting operates in the domain of the secular (Laughlin 1988; Booth 1993) and it is viewed as incompatible with sacred religious values and activities. Our review has shown that such a dichotomy is, at best, time–space specific. Institutions operating across different times, countries and systems of religious thought did not function on the assumption of a clear divide between the spheres of the sacred and the secular. It is clear that many religious institutions excelled at business and financial activities. Indeed, some commentators consider that the subsequent demise of such institutions can be attributed to their failure to deal adequately with financial and monetary concerns. Moreover, our review indicates that notions of the sacred and secular are fluid, mutable concepts. Thus 'accounting has the potential to be sacred, to be secular or to be both sacred and secular', depending upon the context (Jacobs 2005: 193).

Our review indicates that accounting systems in religious organisations were far from rudimentary. As some commentators have noted, religious institutions of the Roman Catholic Church constituted the main repositories of human knowledge during Medieval and Renaissance times. That knowledge included accounting (the *Summa* was written by a monk of the Roman Catholic Church). We have observed how the Monastery of Poblet, which played a major role in charitable activities in medieval Spain, implemented highly sophisticated accounting systems that were comparable with those used by contemporary merchant banks (Monclús Guitart 2005). Similarly, the Cathedral of Toledo, a major spiritual and economic centre of the Spanish Renaissance, implemented a sophisticated double-entry system in the 1530s, well in advance of similar developments in private and state-owned organisations (Villaluenga de Gracia 2005).

Our examination of research on the impact of religion on the notions of interest, usury and earnings suggests that this is a potentially fruitful area for conducting comparative research. Extant studies indicate that early positions on the nature of interest and usury were quite similar across Judaism, Christianity and Islam. Future research in this area could shed light on the conditions that led subsequently to charges of interest on loans becoming acceptable in some religions, and why this change did not occur in others. Similarly, future researchers could explore the extent to which religious beliefs exerted influence over understandings of accounting and the way accounting numbers were reported to organisational stakeholders (Maali et al. 2006). Perhaps more importantly, future researchers could examine the extent to which the definitions of terms such as interest, usury, prices and profits were mediated via the intervention of accounting as a technology of measurement, valuation and recording, and how the emergence of these terms and technologies was contextually embedded.

Similarly, our review suggests that comparative research on the religious underpinnings of key accounting notions such as prudence and stewardship holds much promise, particularly in advancing the theorisation of accounting. Research on accounting in sacred and religious texts is sparse and fragmented. There is considerable potential to explore such texts in relation to a variety of accounting themes (such as accountability, governance and wealth).

Perhaps unsurprisingly, this review has revealed that some topics have been extensively researched – in particular, the micro focus, while others have been sparsely explored – in particular, the macro perspective on the interrelationship between accounting and religion and how accounting is presented in religious texts. There remain other unexplored areas whose study has the potential to contribute significantly to the histories of accounting and religion. For example, Rothstein and Broms (2013) suggest that a relationship exists between practices of accountability and sources of funding in religious organisations. They argue that institutions that are financed 'from below' (e.g. believers) are more transparent and accountable than those financed 'from above' (e.g. the state). Future, comparative accounting research could provide further evidence in relation to this contention.

Furthermore, as noted in our review, gendered dimensions of accounting in religious institutions, such as the construction of masculinity and femininity, and power relations within the institution and with external parties (Araújo and Gomes 2014), have yet to be explored fully (see Carmona and Ezzamel 2016). In a similar vein, research to date has devoted little attention to examining how the impact of religious beliefs on societal values has been mediated by accounting. Future research could examine the extent to which accounting and religion mediated processes of secular organisations through the deployment of systems of human accountability. Additionally, and as noted by Jacobs (2005), religious organisations are particularly complex and may feature either accountability (Hardy and Ballis 2013) or secrecy (Robbins and Lapsley 2015). Further research examining the underpinnings of such practices would add to our knowledge in this area.

Finally, the connection between accounting, religion and ethics/liberation/enlightenment has so far received very little attention (Carmona and Ezzamel 2006). How do notions of ethics in different religious contexts intertwine with accounting as a calculative technology and a discourse? What role, if any, does accounting play in rendering such notions of ethics applicable in practice or collude against their implementation? How are concepts of liberation constituted in different religious settings, and how is accounting implicated in this process? Is enlightenment the aim of religious ideologies, and if so what role does accounting play in underpinning, even constructing, or impeding such an ideal? If religion is about creating and enforcing some notion of social order, how does accounting help shape and secure this notion of order? What attributes of accounting render it a desirable and malleable technology for intervening in religious organisations?

Key works

Carmona and Ezzamel (2006) is a special issue providing a wide-ranging set of articles on accounting and religion. The introductory piece posits some suggestions for future research in this area.

Cordery (2015) reviews the literature on accounting history and religion and posits some suggestions for future research in this area.

Laughlin (1988) embraces the argument that accounting does not constitute an integral part of the sacred agenda in religious organisations.

Quattrone (2004) examines the ideological underpinnings of accounting and accountability systems in religious organisations.

Notes

1 For example, Pope Alexander VI issued the *Bula Inter-Coetera* in 1493 to 'donate' the Latin-American continent to Spain. As a papal donation of a continent to another country, this 'gift' was accorded religious legitimacy and sanctioned by sacred beliefs, at least in the eyes of the receiver if not always in the eyes of those whose territories had been 'donated'.

2 The sacred–secular divide phrasing was first used by Booth (1993). However, Booth attributes the notion to Laughlin (see Joannidès and Berland 2013: 520).

3 This section is based on Carmona and Macintosh (2002); see also Visser and MacIntosh (1998).

References

Abdel-Magid, M.F. (1981) The theory of Islamic banking: accounting implications, *International Journal of Accounting*, 17 (1): 79–102.

Abdul-Rahman, A.R. and Goddard, A. (1998) An interpretive inquiry of accounting practices in religious organisations, *Financial Accountability & Management*, 14 (3): 183–201.

Afifuddin, H.B. and Siti-Nabiha, A.K. (2010) Towards good accountability: the role of accounting in Islamic religious organisations, *World Academy of science, Engineering and Technology*, 66: 1133–39.

Aho, J. (2005) *Confession and Bookkeeping* (Albany, NY: State University of New York Press).

Ali Jafri, S.H. and Margolis, L.S. (1999) The treatment of usury in the Holy Scriptures, *Thunderbird International Business Review*, 41 (4/5): 371–79.

Álvarez-Dardet, C., Baños Sánchez-Matamoros, J. and López Manjón, J.D. (2006) Accounting at the boundaries of the sacred: the regulation of the Spanish brotherhoods in the 18th century, *Accounting History*, 11 (2): 129–50.

Aquinas, St. T. (1952) *Summa Theologica* (Chicago, IL: Fathers of the English Dominican Province).

Araújo, D. and Gomes, D. (2014) Accounting for Religion or Accounting for Women: the case of the Monastery of Santa Ana of Viana do Castelo (1701-1895). Paper presented at the 7° Encontro de História da Contabilidade da OTOC, Lisboa.

Armstrong, K. (1993) *A History of God* (New York: Ballantine Press).

Baker, C.R. (2006) Towards a genealogy of wealth through an analysis of biblical discourses, *Accounting History*, 11 (2): 151–71.

Baños Sanchez-Matamoros, J. and Funnell, W. (2015) War or the business of God, *Accounting, Auditing & Accountability Journal*, 28 (3): 434–59.
Baños Sánchez-Matamoros, J. and Gutiérrez Hidalgo, F. (2011) Publishing patterns of accounting history research in generalist journals: lessons from the past, *Accounting History*, 16 (3): 331–42.
Barlev, B. (2006) A biblical statement of accountability, *Accounting History*, 11 (2): 173–97.
Barnett, H.H. (1961) *Introducing Christian Ethics* (Nashville, TN: Broadman Books Inc).
Basri, H. and Khalid, S.N.A. (2012) Examining accounting and accountability issues in religious context: insights from literature, *Aceh International Journal of Social Science*, 1 (1): 27–35.
Bento da Silva, J., Llewellyn, N. and Anderson-Gough, F. (2017) Oral-aural accounting and the management of the Jesuit corpus, *Accounting, Organizations and Society*, 59: 44–57.
Bigoni, M., Deidda Gagliardo, E. and Funnell, W. (2013) Rethinking the sacred and secular divide. Accounting and accountability practices in the Diocese of Ferrara (1431-457), *Accounting, Auditing & Accountability Journal*, 26 (4): 567–94.
Bisaschi, A. (2003) The accounting system of the Venerable Society of the Living and the Dead of Parma in medieval times, *Accounting History*, 8 (1): 89–111.
Booth, P. (1993) Accounting in churches: a research framework and agenda, *Accounting, Auditing & Accountability Journal*, 5 (4): 37–67.
Burchell, S., Clubb, C., Hopwood, A.G., Hughes, J. and Nahapiet, J. (1980) The roles of accounting in organizations and society, *Accounting, Organizations and Society*, 5 (1): 5–28.
Carmona, S. and Donoso, R. (2004) Cost accounting in early regulated markets: the case of the royal soap factory of Seville (1525–1692), *Journal of Accounting and Public Policy*, 23 (2): 129–57.
Carmona, S. and Ezzamel, M. (2006) Accounting and religion: a historical perspective, *Accounting History*, 11 (2): 117–27.
Carmona, S. and Ezzamel, M. (2016) Accounting and lived experience in the gendered workplace, *Accounting, Organizations and Society*, 49: 1–8.
Carmona, S. and Macintosh, N. (2002) Earnings, interest and usury: a genealogical approach. Paper presented at the First Symposium on Management Control, Queen's University, Canada.
Cordery, C. (2006) Hallowed treasures: sacred, secular and the Wesleyan Methodists in New Zealand (1819–1840), *Accounting History*, 11 (2): 199–220.
Cordery, C. (2015) Accounting history and religion: A review of studies and a research agenda, *Accounting History*, 20 (4): 430–63.
Davidoff, L. and Hall, C. (1987) *Family Fortunes: Men and Women of the English Middle Class, 1780–1850* (London: Routledge).
de Gracia, V. (2005) La aparición de la partida doble en la iglesia: el diario y mayores de la Catedral de Toledo (1533–1539), *De Computis*, 3: 147–216.
De la Torre, I. (2004) *Los Templarios Y El Origen De La Banca* (Madrid: Dilema).
de Roover, R. (1967) The scholastics, usury, and foreign trade, *Business History Review*, XLI, 3: 257–71.
De Vaujany, F.X. (2010) A new perspective on the genealogy of collective action through the history of religious organizations, *Management & Organizational History*, 5 (1): 65–78.
Divine, T.F. (1967) Usury, in Most Rev. W. J. McDonald (ed.) *New Catholic Encyclopedia*, pp. 498–500 (New York: McGraw-Hill).
Dobie, A. (2015a) The role of the general and provincial chapters in improving and enforcing accounting, financial and management controls in Benedictine monasteries in England 1215-1444, *British Accounting Review*, 47 (2): 142–58.
Dobie, A. (2015b) *Accounting at Durham Cathedral Priory: Management and Control of a Major Corporation, 1983-1539* (New York: Palgrave Macmillan).
Durkheim, E. (1976) *The Elementary Forms of Religious Life* (London: George Allen and Unwin).
Eliade, M. (1959) *The Sacred and the Profane: The Nature of Religion* (New York: Harcourt, Brace and World).
Ezzamel, M. (2002) Accounting and redistribution: the palace and mortuary cult in the Middle Kingdom, ancient Egypt, *Accounting Historians Journal*, 29 (1): 61–103.
Ezzamel, M. (2005) Accounting for the activities of funerary temples: the intertwining of the sacred and the profane, *Accounting and Business Research*, 35 (1): 29–51.
Ezzamel, M. (2009) Order and accounting as a performative ritual: evidence from ancient Egypt, *Accounting, Organizations and Society*, 34 (3-4): 348–80.
Ezzamel, M. (2012) *Accounting and Order* (Abingdon: Routledge).
Fernández Alvarez, M. (2004) *Sombras Y Luces De La España Imperial* (Madrid: Espasa).

Fernández-Roca, J. (2010) Monks and businessmen in Catalonia: the Benedictines of Montserrat (1900-1936), *Enterprise & Society*, 11 (2): 242–74.
Flesher, T.K. and Flesher, D.L. (1979) Managerial accounting in an early 19th century German-American religious commune, *Accounting, Organizations and Society*, 4 (4): 297–304.
Fonfeder, R., Holtzman, M.P. and Maccarrone, E. (2003) Internal controls in the Talmud: the Jerusalem Temple, *Accounting Historians Journal*, 30 (1): 73–93.
Funnell, W. and Williams, R. (2014) The religious imperative of cost accounting in the early industrial revolution, *Accounting, Auditing & Accountability Journal*, 27 (2): 357–81.
Futcher, T. and Phillips, T. (1986) Church budgeting: a secular approach, *The National Public Accountant*, 31 (9): 28–39.
Gambling, T.E. and Karim, R.A.A. (1986) Islam and 'social accounting', *Journal of Business Finance and Accounting*, 13 (1): 39–50.
Gao, S. and Handley-Schachler, M. (2003) The influences of Confucianism, Feng shui and Buddhism in Chinese accounting history, *Accounting, Business & Financial History*, 13 (1): 41–68.
García Marí, J.H. and Martínez Soto, S. (2016) La contabilidad de la Real e Ilustre Cofradía de Nuestro Padre Jesús Nazareno de Cartagena durante el segundo tercio del Siglo XX, *De Computis-Revista Española De Historia De La Contabilidad*, 12 (23): 92–109.
Gartnett, J. (1987) Gold and gospel: systematic beneficence in mid-nineteenth England, in W.J. Sheils and D. Wood (eds.), *The Church and Wealth*, pp. 347–58 (Oxford: Basil Blackwell).
Guo, D. (1988) Confucius and accounting, *Accounting Historians Notebook*, 11 (1): 8–10.
Hamid, S., Craig, R. and Clarke, F. (1993) Religion: a confounding cultural element in the international harmonization of accounting, *Abacus*, 29 (2): 131–48.
Haniffa, R. and Hudaib, M. (2010) The two Ws of Islamic accounting research, *Journal of Islamic Accounting and Business Research*, 1 (1): 5–9.
Hardy, L. and Ballis, H. (2005) Does one size fit all? The sacred and secular divide revisited with insights from Niebuhr's typology of social action, *Accounting, Auditing & Accountability Journal*, 18 (2): 238–54.
Hardy, L. and Ballis, H. (2013) Accountability and giving accounts: informal reporting practices in a religious corporation, *Accounting, Auditing & Accountability Journal*, 26 (4): 539–66.
Hardy, L.H. (2008) *Socialising Accountability for the Sacred: A Study of the Sanitarium Health Food Company* (Doctoral dissertation). University of Adelaide.
Hernández Borreguero, J.J.H. (2016) La contaduría mayor del cabildo catedral de Sevilla en la era moderna: gestión y censura, *De Computis-Revista Española De Historia De La Contabilidad*, 8 (14): 99–120.
Hernández Esteve, E. (2001) Contabilidad monástica y empresa, *Revista De AECA*, 56: 26–30.
Homer, S. and Sylla, R. (1991) *A History of Interest Rates* (New Brunswick, NJ: Rutgers University Press).
Homza, L.A. (2000) *Religious Authority in the Spanish Renaissance* (Baltimore, MD: The Johns Hopkins University Press).
Hong, M.Y. (2014) The influence of Buddhism in Accounting and control in medieval China. PhD thesis. University of Wollongong.
Hopwood, A. (1987) The archeology of accounting systems, *Accounting, Organizations and Society*, 12 (3): 207–34.
Hoskin, K.W. and Macve, R.H. (1986) Accounting and the examination: a genealogy of disciplinary power, *Accounting, Organizations and Society*, 11 (2): 105–36.
Irvine, H. (2002) The legitimizing power of financial statements in the Salvation Army in England, 1865–1892, *Accounting Historians Journal*, 29 (1): 1–36.
Jacobs, K. (2005) The sacred and the secular: examining the role of accounting in the religious context, *Accounting, Auditing & Accountability Journal*, 18 (2): 189–210.
Jacobs, K. and Walker, S.P. (2004) Accounting and accountability in the Iona Community, *Accounting, Auditing & Accountability Journal*, 17 (3): 361–81.
Joannidès, V. and Berland, N. (2013) Constructing a research network: accounting knowledge in production, *Accounting, Auditing & Accountability Journal*, 26 (4): 512–38.
Kaluvilla, B.B. (2017) Understanding Accounting in Christian organisations and the influence of culture on accounting practices: A literature review, *Ushus-Journal of Business Management*, 12 (1): 1–16.
Karim, R. (1990) The independence of religious and external auditors: the case of Islamic banks, *Accounting, Auditing & Accountability Journal*, 3 (3): 34–44.
Kuasirikun, N. and Constable, P. (2010) The cosmology of accounting in mid 19th-century Thailand, *Accounting, Organizations and Society*, 35 (6): 596–627.

Kubler, G. (1982) *Building the Escorial* (Princeton, NJ: Princeton University Press).
Kuhn, T. (1962) *The Structure of Scientific Revolutions* (Chicago, IL: The University of Chicago Press).
Laughlin, R.C. (1988) Accounting in its social context: an analysis of the accounting systems of the Church of England, *Accounting, Auditing & Accountability Journal*, 1 (2): 19–42.
Laughlin, R.C. (1990) A model of financial accountability and the Church of England, *Financial Accountability & Management*, 6 (2): 93–114.
Lewis, M. (2001) Islam and accounting, *Accounting Forum*, 25 (2): 103–27.
López Manjón, J.D., Baños Sánchez-Matamoros, J. and Álvarez-Dardet Espejo, C. (2007) Rendering of accounts and transfer of accounting knowledge at religious organizations: the case of the brotherhoods of Seville (1563–1604). Paper presented at the XII Workshop on Management Accounting and Control, Raymond Konopka Memorial, Almería.
Maali, B., Casson, P. and Napier, C. (2006) Social reporting by Islamic banks, *Abacus*, 42 (2): 266–89.
Maltby, J. (2000) The origins of prudence in accounting, *Critical Perspectives on Accounting*, 11 (1): 51–70.
Manetti, G., Bellucci, M. and Bagnoli, L. (2017) The management of the plague in Florence at the beginning of the Renaissance: the role of the partnership between the Republic and the Confraternita of Misericordia, *Accounting History*, 22 (4): 510–29.
McKernan, J.F. and Kosmala, K. (2007) Doing the truth: religion-deconstruction-justice, and accounting, *Accounting, Auditing & Accountability Journal*, 20 (5): 729–64.
Monclús Guitart, R. (2005) El abad del monasterio de Poblet como Limosnero Real y su rendición de cuentas (S.XIV), *De Computis*, 2: 154–80.
Mutch, A. (2012) Theology, accountability and management: exploring the contributions of Scottish Presbyterianism, *Organization*, 19 (3): 363–79.
Muturza, A. (2004) Quranic use of 'commercial' vocabulary and its implications, working paper, Seton Hall University.
Napier, C. (2009) Defining Islamic accounting: current issues, past roots, *Accounting History*, 14 (1-2): 121–44.
Napier, C. and Haniffa, R. (2011) *Islamic Accounting* (Cheltenham: Edward Elgar Publishing).
Oliveira, J. and Brandao, M. (2005) Monastic accounting in Portugal: the case of the Cistercian monastery of Arouca, 1786–1825. Paper presented at the 4th Accounting History International Conference, Braga.
Paisey, C. and Paisey, N.J. (2011) Visibility, governance and social context: financial management in the Pre-Reformation Scottish church, *Accounting, Auditing & Accountability Journal*, 24 (5): 587–621.
Prieto Moreno, B., Maté Sadornil, L. and Tua Pereda, J. (2006) The accounting records of the monastery of Silos throughout the XVIII century: the accumulation and management of its patrimony in the light of its accounts books, *Accounting History*, 11 (2): 221–56.
Quattrone, P. (2004) Accounting for God: accounting and accountability practices in the Society of Jesus (Italy, XVI–XVII centuries), *Accounting, Organizations and Society*, 29 (7): 647–83.
Quattrone, P. (2015) Governing social orders, unfolding rationality, and Jesuit accounting practices: A procedural approach to institutional logics, *Administrative Science Quarterly*, 60 (3): 411–45.
Rammal, H.G. and Parker, L.D. (2013) Islamic banking in Pakistan: A history of emergent accountability and regulation, *Accounting History*, 18 (1): 5–29.
Robbins, G. and Lapsley, I. (2015) From secrecy to transparency: accounting and the transition from religious charity to publicly-owned hospital, *British Accounting Review*, 47 (1): 19–32.
Rothstein, B. and Broms, R. (2013) Governing religion: the long-term effects of sacred financing, *Journal of Institutional Economics*, 9 (4): 69–90.
Sánchez Herrero, J. (1985) Las cofradías de Sevilla: los Comienzos, in Colección Cultura Viva (ed.), *Las Cofradías De Sevilla: Historia, antropología, Arte*, pp. 9–34 (Seville: Servicio de Publicaciones de la Universidad de Sevilla).
Sangster, A. (2018) Pacioli's Lens: God, humanism, Euclid, and the rhetoric of double entry, *The Accounting Review*, 93 (2): 299–314.
Sargiacomo, M. (2001) Pro & contro delle procedure contabili dei Monaci Benedettini nell XVI Secolo. Paper presented at the VI Convegno Nazionale – Società Italiana di Storia della Ragioneria, Caserta.
Smith, W.C. (1979) *Faith and Belief* (Princeton, NJ: Princeton University Press).
Soll, J. (2014) *The Reckoning: Financial Accountability and the Rise and Fall of Nations* (New York: Basic Books).
Suárez, L. (2004) *Los Reyes Católicos* (Ariel: Barcelona).

Sukoharsono, E.G. (1998) Accounting in a historical transition: a shifting dominant belief from Hindu to Islamic administration in Indonesia. Paper presented at the APIRA Conference, Osaka.

Tawney, R.H. (1954) *Religion and the Rise of Capitalism* (New York: Mentor Books).

Taylor, T.W. and Evans, J.W. (1987) Islamic banking and the prohibition of usury in western economic thought, *National Westminster Bank Quarterly Review*, 9 (4): 15–27.

Thompson, G. (1991) Is accounting rhetorical? Methodology, Luca Pacioli and printing, *Accounting, Organizations and Society*, 16 (5-6): 572–99.

Tinker, T. (2004) The Enlightenment and its discontents: antinomies of Christianity, Islam and the calculative sciences, *Accounting, Auditing & Accountability Journal*, 17 (3): 442–75.

Urton, G. (2009) Sin, confession, and the arts of book-and cord-keeping: an intercontinental and transcultural exploration of accounting and governmentality, *Comparative Studies in Society and History*, 51 (4): 801–31.

Visser, W.A.M. and MacIntosh, A. (1998) A short review of the historical critique of usury, *Accounting, Business & Financial History*, 8 (2): 175–89.

Walker, S.P. (1998) How to secure your husband's esteem: accounting and private patriarchy in the British middle class household during the nineteenth century, *Accounting, Organizations and Society*, 23 (6): 485–514.

Walker, S.P. (2004) Expense, social and moral control: accounting and the administration of the old poor law in England and Wales, *Journal of Accounting and Public Policy*, 23 (2): 85–127.

Walker, S.P. (2008) Innovation, convergence and argument without end in accounting history, *Accounting, Auditing & Accountability Journal*, 21 (2): 296–322.

Weber, M. (2001 [1930]) *The Protestant Ethic and the Spirit of Capitalism*, translated by Talcott Parsons (London: Routledge Classics, 2001).

Wren, D.A. (2000) Medieval or modern? A scholastic's view of business ethics circa 1430, *Journal of Business Ethics*, 8 (2): 109–19.

Zubiri, X. (1993) *El Problema Filosófico De La Historia De Las Religiones* (Madrid: Alianza Editorial).

26
CREATIVE ARTS

Sam McKinstry

Overview

This chapter examines studies in accounting history which involve the creative arts of architecture, literature, fine art, the graphic arts and film. It begins with a summary of the various ways in which such studies can, and have, shed light on accounting practice and the social and cultural aspects of accountancy, as well as upon the practice of the creative arts themselves and the motivation of those who carry them out. There then follows a review of the accounting history literature relating to architecture, which begins with a summary of papers and books dealing with buildings and the professionalisation of accountancy. Studies examining architectural motivation and accounting practices are also reviewed. Accounting history studies involving literature are next examined, more or less in the chronological order of the literature concerned. These reveal a wide range of facets of accounting, from the place it has occupied in society to its role in the home, as well as shedding fresh light on the literary figures whose practices and attitudes have been uncovered. The centrepiece of the chapter's next section, which deals with fine art, is a summary of Basil Yamey's (1989) *Art and Accounting*, a review of works of art which have depicted accounting and accountancy from the late-medieval period onwards. In the next section, on accounting history and the graphic arts, papers which discuss 'ways of seeing' annual reports and their potential for manipulation are summarised. Accounting history and film come next, and the medium's ability to reflect and shape public attitudes to accounting is examined. The chapter concludes by suggesting and speculating upon possible future trajectories for accounting history studies concerning the creative arts.

Accounting history and the creative arts

Accounting history can be seen at its interdisciplinary and erudite best as it explores the interaction of the world of accounting with the creative spheres of architecture, art, literature, the graphic arts and film.

Several types of insight can be gained from the study of this interaction. First, the creative pursuits we are concerned with have often depicted or described accountants, accountancy and related practices in images or words. This can provide useful evidence as to what accountants actually did in the past, in terms of activities, techniques and tools, as well as yield information on how accounting has been perceived from outside itself, for instance, as a social phenomenon. The depiction of accounting and accountants may, in turn, have influenced the attitudes of the general public towards them, and this too is of interest to accounting historians.

Where the creative discipline concerned has itself been brought into play through the commissioning or acquisition of work by accountancy bodies, historical study can also reveal how the profession has perceived itself, or sought to depict or describe itself, as it has attempted to foster favourable impressions in the eyes of the public. The creative packaging of accounting in annual reports can also yield historical insights into the impression management techniques employed by firms through the designers and other creative individuals whom they have engaged for this purpose, and the political and economic climates in which these practices have taken place.

A related set of insights regarding the impact of accountancy upon society at large, in terms of the ways in which it has affected attitudes to aspects of life, may also be gained from what is depicted or represented by creative writers or artists, who may not always be complimentary in what they say.

A further valuable set of insights, little explored so far, relates to the motivation of the artists who design, paint, write or otherwise produce creative work. Their motivation has found its reflection, betimes, in their attitudes to their own accounting, financial and business practices, such as the pricing of work and the drawing of salaries or capital. Studies in this area have the potential to set the economist's 'black box' model of firms and the individuals who set them by the ears, as it is discovered that not all business entities are there to maximise profit or personal wealth as a first priority. Although economists have for some time written on the economics of culture in organs such as *The Journal of Cultural Economics*, they have tended to consider it as just another 'good', subject to the forces of supply, demand or price, or examined the public policy implications of arts funding. One exception has been the work of Klamer (1997), an economist who has sought to explore the relationship between creativity and the business/financial dimension. It is, however, only through the detailed examination of financial practices and records that we can see with precision how creative individuals have actually balanced profitability and creativity.

Also of interest are the detailed accounting practices which have been employed within the creative professions themselves. How, for example, have creative individuals or businesses carried out their accounting, or had it carried out for them? How have they dealt with overheads in pricing, the valuation of work-in-progress, or the monitoring of costs? An additional benefit available from the accounting records of creative individuals is the light that they can shed on their private lives and the interpretation of their work, of interest to scholars within the relevant creative disciplines.

Thus, there are many insights to be gained from the work of accounting historians in the general area of the arts, and multiple opportunities for historians to explore and analyse broad societal, political, philosophical and aesthetic questions affecting accounting in ways that may, or may not, be critical.

This chapter will proceed by undertaking reviews of accounting history studies which have examined the interaction of accountancy with the creative disciplines with which we are concerned, in many of the ways outlined above. It will begin with a review of studies related to accounting and architecture, for no other reason than that architecture has always been regarded as 'the mistress art', since it is in buildings that the other arts are practised or their fruits stored and enjoyed. Historical studies related to accounting and literature will then be considered, after which studies of accounting and fine art will follow. The chapter will conclude with reviews of studies which feature histories of the interactions between accounting and the graphic arts, and finally, accounting and film. In each case, recommendations and speculations affecting future research activities will be made.

Architecture

A seminal study of the role of professional headquarters buildings in the acquisition of status for the bodies which erected or owned them, authored by Macdonald (1989), was published in the sociology literature. In spite of a somewhat tortuous methodological approach to assessing the, necessarily subjective, architectural quality of the buildings concerned, Macdonald's paper successfully demonstrated that professional bodies utilised their headquarters buildings to enhance their respectability, as an integral part of the 'professional project' to increase their power and influence in society. Salient in Macdonald's study were the professional headquarters buildings of the Institute of Chartered Accountants of England and Wales (ICAEW) and the (then) Association of Certified Accountants. While the ICAEW created what Macdonald considered the archetypal, paradigmatic professional headquarters building and was highly successful in utilising it to enhance its status, he notes that the certified accountants, in contrast, squandered the architectural opportunity to build their status in this manner, a reflection of their comparative lack of success, generally, as compared with the ICAEW, in promoting themselves.

The ICAEW has always been conscious of its architectural heritage at Moorgate, London, especially the first phase (1889–93), designed in competition by John Belcher. A number of descriptive works celebrating its sheer visual distinction have appeared, including Squire (1937), Boys (1990), ICAEW (2002) and Pile (2004). Useful and informative as these may be in their own way, their analysis is not intended to be penetrating.

A study by McKinstry (1997) utilises an analysis of the connotative power of architectural style to explain, how, in detail, the architectural symbolism of the ICAEW's Hall, as erected to Belcher's designs, actually works, locating it in the stylistic context of the period. It sets the building's baroque detailing in the context of the buildings of the older professions, such as medicine and the law, which the fledgling ICAEW was anxious to emulate, as well as in the City world of banking premises, gentlemen's clubs and even the adjacent, much revered, buildings of Sir Christopher Wren. The study interprets the iconography of the building's sculptural frieze as a piece of aspirational rhetoric, intended to evoke chartered accountancy's associations with the legal profession and to suggest (misleadingly at the time) that the business of the empire revolved around chartered accountancy. It points out that the ICAEW building's style was much emulated in the styling of the next generation of government offices, symbolically, if perhaps unintentionally, suggesting alignment between the aims of government and the ICAEW through the creation of an establishment architecture, referred to today as 'the Grand Manner', or 'Edwardian Baroque' (Service 1977).

Macdonald's (1989) study of professional buildings made no distinction between their older parts and the many extensions made to them, or even their wholesale replacement by new buildings, at a stage when the status of the professional body owning them was well established. McKinstry (2008) examines the 1970 Brutalist extension to Chartered Accountants' Hall, London, explaining its deliberate use by the ICAEW to adjust public perceptions of the profession, which at the time, carried great prestige, but still had a grey, 'subfusc', image, related to the (necessarily) backward-looking auditing function.

The new extension, by Sir William Whitfield, connoted in its *avant garde*, 'with it' styling that the Institute now wished to be associated with the more recently developed, forward-looking functions of accountancy, such as forecasting and business planning, with which it could assist senior management in taking businesses forward into a future of economic prosperity, which the nation required. Whitfield's extension to Belcher's original Hall, in the Belcher style, added in parallel to the new, Brutalist extension, was part of the programme of works completed in 1970, and is often mistaken for original Belcher work. As well as paying homage to Belcher, Whitfield was deliberately forging in this section of the building a metaphorical homage to accounting's venerable past, turning the Hall, as revised, into a Janus-like structure which embraced the future while revering and claiming links with accountancy's long history.

McKinstry's (2008) paper also adds to MacDonald's insights by explaining that the key factors in maximising the potential of architecture to advertise a profession's prestige are the architect's individual creative gifts and the presence in a professional institute of a senior, powerful, committee member personally attuned to the nuances of architectural style and its potential for the communication of prestige. That key individual, in the case of the ICAEW's 1970 extension, was Sir Charles Peat, President of the Institute and himself a wealthy patron of architecture who had previously employed Whitfield on domestic work. This confirms the insights of Lee (1996), who stated that the involvement of key individuals in the professionalisation project was often crucial to success.

In a study of the headquarters building of the Institute of Chartered Accountants of Scotland, its suitability as a status-enhancing home was examined (McKinstry 2000). When it was first occupied by the Society of Accountants in Edinburgh, the oldest of Scotland's bodies of chartered accountants, in 1891, a refurbished classical house in Queen Street, in the prestigious New Town of Edinburgh, was acquired to accommodate a library, examination rooms and committee rooms. Given the relative smallness of the Society (which had received its Royal Charter in 1854), it selected and fitted out a well-sited building of appropriate *gravitas* on a restricted budget, thus demonstrating that, even if funds were limited, status could still be projected.

Studies of the financial and business histories of firms engaged in the creative profession of architecture are few and far between. In an analysis of the business strategy of Arcop, a large firm of Canadian architects, by Mintzberg et al. (1986), the authors revealed that its design direction was driven by the individual design interests of the partners, the dominant influence in the business. Unsurprisingly, perhaps, the partners felt from time to time that the firm's success was not reflected in sufficient levels of profit and that the firm 'should be making more money'. It is clear that the prime motivation for the practice of architecture lay elsewhere.

A study of the business, financial and accounting history of Scottish provincial architects, Cullen, Lochhead and Brown (McKinstry and Wallace 2004) reached the conclusion, also, that money was not a prime motivator. Among these, the tendency to make small or no charges for preliminary or incidental work, restraint in personal drawings and sparing no effort to complete jobs to the highest standards, even where they had been under-priced, were discovered. The maintenance of detailed job costs highlighted such instances, but did not change the firm's attitude.

The potential for further study in this area of accounting history depends on the availability of suitable records. In common with other professional firms, architectural practices have tended not to preserve client-related records or financial details. In the case of architects, what have mainly been preserved are the various design and working drawings produced by practices, which are clearly seen within the profession as of the highest importance. Another matter which has tended to militate against the retention of financial and cognate records relates to retrospective liability claims for defective buildings. Architects are reluctant to preserve evidence of how deep their pockets are. In recent years the practice records of a major UK architectural firm, amounting to some 40,000 items, have been deposited in a national archive, leaving out the financial records for this reason. Where financial evidence has managed to survive, further analyses of how accounting and financial record keeping reflect the motivation of firms will add to the store of case studies from which reliable generalisations can flow.

One area which would reward study by accounting historians is the degree to which status-building by non-UK professional bodies has involved architecture and the associated arts of sculpture and painting. Is the UK unique in this respect, or are there other variable factors, such as the lack of an entrenched, time-honoured class system, that make what has happened beyond the UK different? Of interest also are studies, national or international, which examine the architecture of the offices of accountancy practices.

Another area, potentially of vast interest, is the degree to which financial constraints and associated accounting systems have affected what has been built. Has Mammon, and its erstwhile servant, accounting, been to blame for a deteriorating built environment? Has short-termism, or the drive for improvements in the bottom line and associated executive remuneration, affected our aesthetic experiences of buildings through under-investment in architecture, or has the desire for corporate image and associated branding still been enough to ensure aesthetic quality has been sought and paid for? Willis (1995) suggests that, to a large extent, 'Form Follows Finance', as exemplified by the skyscrapers of Chicago and New York. This author notes that, 'Skyscrapers are the ultimate architecture of capitalism. The first blue print for every tall building is a balance sheet of estimated costs and returns' (Willis 1995: 182). Excusing the accounting solecism, is Willis right, and what accounting systems have supported such building programmes? The accounting historian is well placed, subject to the existence of records, to find out. And what effects have the Public/Private Partnership and Private Finance Initiative programmes, or international equivalents, had on architectural quality in Britain? Adverse, one would suspect, but work needs to be done by historians in the future to confirm or deny, including investigation of the accounting systems which have supported these programmes.

Another angle on the relationship between accounting and architecture was explored by Jeacle (2003), who attempted to show that the plethora of trade price guides to building costs, which were published in the eighteenth century, had a material bearing on cost control in the creation of the Georgian house, the styling of which appeared to lend itself to standardisation. She held that this could be seen in Foucauldian terms as builders coming to possess documentary tools for human accountability. There is evidence to the contrary. In a substantial study of the costs of country house building in the UK from 1660–1880, Wilson and Mackley (1999: 448) quote the architect and builder Thomas Rawlins, who in 1769 noted that it was impossible to provide a uniformly acceptable set of estimates for his designs 'because the prices and methods of building varied considerably across England'. Wilson and Mackley's paper is of considerable interest, also, for the references it makes to extant building accounts associated with the construction of large country houses, which have yet to be examined from an accounting point of view.

In a more nuanced paper, Jeacle (2005) was able to argue more successfully and from a stronger evidential base that published price guides covering the labour costs of producing Georgian furniture did indeed have a role in the negotiation of prices for furniture work, and that this may be seen as Foucauldian.

A study by Mussari and Mussari (2006) operates at a more fundamental level in terms of the interface between accounting history and the history of architecture. Their description of the book-keeping systems in use in building the sixteenth-century Castello of Crotone, in Calabria, Italy, drew attention to the usefulness of the records for tracing the architectural transformation, over time, of a defensive structure which by its nature was subject to periodic change. Such records are capable of revealing chronology, types of materials used, which workmen were involved, and even such small matters as the purchase of string for measuring purposes.

In a similar but more comprehensive vein, Wissel's fascinating study of 2013 carried out an extensive examination of the stelae (stone tablets) of Buddhist temples in nineteenth-century (late-Qing dynasty) south China and Taiwan, analysing with the help of pictures the accounting and financial material which was inscribed upon them. This disclosed detailed building costs as well as names of donors of the necessary funds, together with the identities of builders and other contractors who had carried out the work, in order to make public and honour their generosity, skill and accountability to God. The paper also reveals details of contemporary Chinese accounting methods. It highlights the fact that, contrary to what had been previously thought about the existence of tensions between religion and money in China, by the nineteenth century these had been reconciled.

McKinstry and Ding's (2015) study examined the 'hybridised' system of accounting used in the pricing and cost control systems supporting architectural commissions in the Victorian period, as exemplified in the work of Sir George Gilbert Scott in rebuilding Glasgow University from 1865 to 1878. It was discovered that the sophisticated system of bills of quantities to aid contractors with fixed pricing employed in this case had come into widespread use in the UK across the early Victorian period, remaining in use to the present day. The new system superseded earlier systems which did not give a carefully pre-computed detailed estimate of costs in advance of the completion of buildings, leading, at times, to clients being unpleasantly surprised at the final costs. This study also examines how costs were accumulatively tracked during the progress of buildings, under the new system. This was done by 'measurers' (later called surveyors) who were originally on the architect's staff, in hybrid control systems devised in collaboration with the client. The individuals who carried out this type of accounting work later came to practise as part of the chartered surveying profession, in independent firms separate from architects. The study ends by exploring why this type of accounting work was not taken up by the young accounting profession, remaining in the surveying domain until the present day.

Literature

Thus far, a number of major figures in English literature have been investigated by accounting historians. The paper by Parker (1999; see also Buckmaster and Buckmaster 1999) on accounting in Chaucer's *Canterbury Tales* demonstrates that Chaucer, a customs officer and an accountant, was well versed in accounting and mercantile finance and the securing of loans by personal 'bonds'. Parker's paper shows how Chaucer enriches and enlivens his at times bawdy narrative with details of everyday life from his business experiences. In the same paper, Parker suggests that Chaucer may have used accounting more subtly in *The Shipman's Tale*, as an allegory of creative bookkeeping. Readers of Parker's work, and of Chaucer, are also able to acquire an otherwise unobtainable feeling for the day-to-day commerce of the medieval period, together with the reassurance that, in essentials, and notwithstanding the absence of double-entry, little changes over time.

In his introduction to accounting in Chaucer, Parker (1999) notes that Defoe, author of *Robinson Crusoe* (1719), has a knowledge of bookkeeping, expressed in a later work, *The Complete English Tradesman* (1725–7), but states that this knowledge 'appears to be limited', a matter surely worthy of further investigation. Defoe's *Moll Flanders* (1722) and the authoress Aphra Benn's short story *The Fair Jilt* (1688) are examined by Connor (2004) in a major work concerned with the narrative and metaphorical use of bookkeeping in these novels, substantial proof of the degree to which accounting had penetrated society's consciousness by this time. In Benn, accounting concepts are used beneath the surface to 'tell' the narrative, while in Defoe, accounting and individual responses to wealth are used throughout for characterisation. Connor's work is also valuable for its survey of contemporary women's guides to accounting, and for its detailed description of the evolution of money and credit up to the time in which the novels are set. Connor notices Defoe's anachronistic references to the (as yet uncreated) Bank of England in *Moll Flanders*, a warning to accounting historians that care must be exercised in utilising novels as factual evidence, and that authorial licence must be taken into account.

A paper by Boys (1995) on the personal accounts kept by Samuel Pepys, the seventeenth-century diarist, reveals that the Pepys' methodical nature was also expressed through his careful attention to financial matters. The records kept by Pepys show that he counted his personal wealth by comparing his assets and liabilities at periodic intervals. Boys also reveals that Mrs Pepys was expected to account to her husband for household expenditures, confirming the widespread use of domestic accounting in genteel households at this date. The study both sheds more light on the character of a notable literary figure and on his personal circumstances, as well as providing insights into contemporary domestic accounting, which, in the case of Pepys, did not as yet manifest itself in the form of double-entry.

Sir Walter Scott, the world's first literary giant, kept personal account books throughout much of his life, and these are examined in a study by McKinstry and Fletcher (2002). Scott attended with more diligence to these in the earlier part of his career, but, even later, in the midst of a hectic life, performed intermittent reconciliations of his income and expenditure and his assets and liabilities. Scott was adept in accountancy as a result of his studies at the Royal High School of Edinburgh, his training in his father's law office, his sheriffship of Selkirkshire and his post as a clerk to the Court of Session, a senior legal position at the highest civil court in Scotland. The paper points out that Scott's personal accountancy conformed to the norms of genteel households at the time, with his wife running the home and he in overall control. The opportunity is also taken to examine Scott's frequent business and financial difficulties towards the end of his life and, in particular, the accusation that he was financially reckless, greedy and wrote only for money. The study takes the view, from an examination of his accountancy knowledge and other circumstances, that such claims are implausible.

A different type of study of Byron, a contemporary and admirer of Scott, was authored by Moore (1974), who utilised the papers of Zambelli, Byron's secretary, to examine details of his income and expenditure in order to shed fresh light on his personality and circumstances. Moore observes that, if Zambelli had been consulted, 'the accusation of avarice could never have been sustained, or at the worst, he [Byron] would have been recognised as a man, who having great kindness greatly abused, tries to build up defences' (Moore 1974: 4). Moore's book also gives a real sense of immediacy as it refers to Byron's tastes in expensive clothing and personal effects. Apart from what it reveals about Byron, the study also gives, as a by-product, a picture of the accounting work undertaken by

Zambelli, secretary to an aristocratic celebrity, as Byron was, and how such matters as transactions in various currencies were recorded, namely, in parallel columns in sterling and local currency.

A paper on Dickens' *Hard Times* (1854) by Fraser et al. (2006) discloses an affinity between the social critique in Dickens' novel and the anti-utilitarian writings of Carlyle. The novel, set in the industrial north, paints a negative picture of exploitative and demeaning factory work and its dispiriting effect on those who carried it out. Here, the novelist attacks an over-zealous and misplaced reliance on statistical 'facts' by management, and thus, by implication, criticises aspects of industrial accounting, in the sense of performance indicators, and perhaps also, by implication, cost accounting. From the same era, a study by Maltby and Rutterford (2006) argues for Trollope's novels as a reliable source of information on the social and financial implications of marriage for women in Victorian Britain.

Looking beyond Britain, Maltby's (1999) paper on Freytag's immensely popular German novel, *Soll und Haben* (debit and credit) reveals how double-entry accounting, ubiquitous in nineteenth-century Germany, had come to embody and act as a symbol of middle-class morality. Work on the German novelist E.M. Remarque by Evans (2005) suggests that, post-1918, accounting in Germany had lost its moral overtones and its aura of authority, being seen as the symbol of a decadent and failed capitalism. Further international perspectives have been provided by Czarniavska (2008), who analyses the role of women in accounting through the lens of nineteenth-century Polish novels and through the work of the twentieth-century US author, Douglas Adams. She concludes from these sources that accounting was seen in Poland as lowly 'women's work', whereas today it is seen as highly paid men's work.

A later work by Czarniavska (2012) provides a study of the detective novels of US CPA David Dodge, written in the 1940s, initially reflecting on alternative ways of reading novels in the light of the reader's experience, as against the straightforward suspension of disbelief normally practised. The novels involve CPAs as heroes, contrary to the common stereotypes of unadventurous CPAs, which are discussed in the novels but also controverted by the characters in them. For example, Dodge's heroes have a sense of humour, are often younger and more physically attractive than expected to be and have a different dress sense, while remaining on the right side of justice and the law. Czarniavska concludes by asking, from this example, 'can accounting scholars do something to change the stereotype of accountants in popular culture?' (2012: 669).

Evans and Fraser, in their 2012 study of the novels of a Scottish CA, Alexander Clark Smith, written in the 1950s, attempt to use these works to explore the social origins of Scottish chartered accountants, as well as to examine the accounting stereotype applying at the time. Smith was not a typical CA. Coming from a skilled working class background, he was interested in the philosophy of David Hume and was an author of detective novels, retiring from the profession in his mid-50s. His career path involved internal auditing and his knowledge of this area is used in the novels, the hero of which was Nicky Mahoun, a fictional chartered accountant from the Gorbals, then a socially deprived area of Glasgow. Mahoun is unconventional, anti-elitist and is a hero-figure involved in the exposure of corruption and fraud. Evans and Fraser (2012) discuss the 'outsider' status of Mahoun within accountancy, noting that this would normally result in limited opportunities to rise to the top of the profession. They conclude that his depiction in the novels is not untypical of how accountants of the period were portrayed across the field of popular literature, leading to the conclusion that the notion of a standard accounting stereotype may be ill-founded.

Literature has also been a source of insights into contemporary perceptions of accountants and their work. A short paper by Walker (1995) notes that in a little-known novel of 1894, *The Accountant* by F.H. Mel, a London accountant is depicted as a hero, raising questions as to the degree to which any single novel or novelist can be taken in isolation as proof of the way in which accounting or accountants may be understood at a given time and place. Studies of twentieth-century novels include an examination of accounting in the work of Somerset Maugham, who was at one time a chartered accountancy trainee (Boys 1994). A picture of early twentieth-century accountancy training, involving much copying and casting of columns of figures, emerges from the work of Maugham, but as Boys points out, the impression of the rather dull and introverted chartered accountant that it paints may have been appropriate in the earlier part of the twentieth century, but would be misleading today. West's study of 1930s auditing in Marshall's *The Bank Audit* (2001) provides literary evidence that the profession's status was already rising at this point.

Napier's (2017) analysis of Shute's novel of 1938, *Ruined City*, also casts light on the auditing profession as it operated in conjunction with financial and banking institutions in the 1930s. After reflecting on some aspects of literary theory which suggest that fiction may be close to 'factual' history, and on Shute's biography, Napier outlines the plot. Warren, a wealthy executive in his family's bank, while recovering from a failed marriage, visits the northern town of Sharples, where the shipyard has all but collapsed for lack of work. Warren arranges through unscrupulous intermediaries for an oil company in an eastern state to buy ships from the shipyard then arranges to expand its capital to carry out the order and save jobs. The prospectus forecasts profitable business, which Warren knows is fraudulent, and he ends up in jail for three years. In his absence, the shipyard is saved and he returns a hero to start a new life. Napier notes the failure of the standard models of fraud to explain it when it is morally motivated, emphasising the veracity of the accounting and financial techniques described in the novel, based on Shute's experience in industry. He concludes by reflecting on the use of 'big bath' provisions and the auditing profession's involvement in them, thus using the novel for moral reflection.

An entirely different proposition is the paper on Johnson's 1972 novel, *Christie Malry's Own Double Entry* (McKinstry 2007). The analysis points to the left-leaning political tendencies of the author, who in a savage triumph of black humour, attacks in the novel the tendency of accountancy to focus on the gains of proprietors, monetise everything and completely ignore the human dimension. The hero uses double-entry accounting to record all the 'aggravations' and 'recompense' in his life which are ignored by accountancy. Johnson's attack on capitalism is set in the context of the rising political unrest of the 1960s and 1970s, and is interpreted as a contribution, through satire, to the power-dominated discourse (in a Foucauldian sense) surrounding accountancy and business during the period.

Accounting history studies involving literature can, as has been shown, shed light on accountancy in a multitude of ways, not always complimentary, and there remains much for accounting historians of all nations to do.

Fine art

Yamey's (1989) *Art and Accounting* is the principal work published to date whose purpose is to shed light on accounting history through a study of paintings and other pictorial illustrations of accounting.

Even if only treated as a coffee table book, *Art and Accounting* would stand on its own by reason of its lavish colour plates, included among which are Hogarth's *Shortly After the*

Marriage, painted in 1743. This work, a piece of biting social criticism, was part of Hogarth's *Marriage à la Mode* series of the same date, and one of two pictures in that series containing account books. An unhappily married earl, beside his uninterested wife, watches his steward leaving the scene with ledger and accounts, disgusted at the master's refusal to be consulted on the parlous state of the household finances. This slice of everyday life in mid-eighteenth-century Britain is hugely entertaining.

Yamey also deals with portraits of businessmen. The images of Renaissance Italian bankers, Netherlandish merchants and occasionally their wives make an appearance, many created by the finest artists of the day. For example, the Barings, vigilantly posed over a ledger, in Sir Thomas Lawrence's Augustan conversation piece of 1806, peruse their account with Hope & Co, of Amsterdam, a Quaker bank with which they had a long and profitable association. While dealing with the portraits, Yamey discusses everything from the significance of the books depicted in them (often not clear) to the techniques employed by the portraitists.

Yamey also deals with Bible illustrations involving books which are at least possibly account books, including a number of versions of *Joseph Distributing Corn in Egypt*, notable among which is a sumptuous Caravaggio. Not mentioned is the fact that such books are in codex rather than scroll format, and thus reflect contemporary life rather than that of Biblical times.

While dealing with allegories, symbols and emblems, Yamey wrestles with the interpretation of pictures where, often, supporting evidence of the artist's programme, or intention, has been lost. In the case of a work by Koninck, entitled *The Gold-Weigher*, there is considerable doubt, such that Yamey asks, 'Is every seventeenth-century Dutch portrayal of an aged gold-weigher or money-changer to be read as symbolic of avarice?' Clearly not. Equally difficult, sometimes, is the identification of the exact purpose of the account books depicted.

Much more clear and rewarding to the observer are the *vanitas* still life paintings which are also studied by Yamey. This type of work was intended, through the depiction of groups of objects, to symbolise, from a Christian perspective, the brevity of earthly life and the temporary and ultimately futile nature of its pursuits. In these pictures, account books are occasionally found, and Yamey has included a selection of such works. Here, he describes one by Lourens in considerable detail, and as a by-product, readers learn about the merchants' marks which adorned account books of the period, a tribute to the power of the visual in accounting history, as well as to Yamey's erudition.

Yamey's book devotes much study to the *Allegory of Commerce*, a large, single-sheet woodcut of 1585 by Jost Amman, a Swiss artist working in Nuremberg. Based on the work of Johann Neudorfer the elder, a teacher of commerce and bookkeeping, the work depicts mercantile trade taking place around the prosperous port of Antwerp, with, beneath, a suite of offices in the classical style, where bookkeeping is in progress on every hand. There are allegories of profit, capital and cash flow, testifying to the universal prevalence of double-entry accounting by this time.

Yamey also provides a detailed treatment of various paintings in which Luca Pacioli features. Of special note is his inclusion of Pope-Hennessy's praise for the superiority of Piero Della Francesca's portrait of Pacioli in his Brera altarpiece. It shows an 'unerring grasp of the structure of the face, the delicate shading of the corners of the mouth, the sense of intellectual eminence which colors [*sic*] the whole image [and] makes this one of the peaks of quattrocento portraiture' (Yamey 1989: 133). It is, in all probability, the closest we can come today to apprehending the personality of such a seminal figure as

Pacioli. Yamey's book is a tremendous scholarly endeavour as well as a source of visual lessons in what the accountants of the late-medieval, renaissance and enlightenment periods actually did.

In contrast with the studies based on the historical interpretation of works of art by Yamey, Coslor and Spaenjers (2016) have analysed the financialisation of the art market, over time, in a welcome if theory-heavy paper. Utilising an 'epistemic cultures approach' which employs a variety of research methods, including the extensive use of interviews, their paper studies the relative growth of art markets and the much later development of financial tools and investment vehicles to transform them into part of the financial market. Early signs of the convergence of the two types of market were visible from the early 1960s, when graphs of stock market versus art market performance were produced, showing superior returns for sales of art works. Over the 1970s, art indices were developed and institutional investors took a major stake in works of art. Then in the 1980s, dedicated art investment funds came into existence. These grew in scale and scope, fuelled by developments in the analytics field such that, by the 2000s, we were in the era of 'Monet, Manet, money' (Coslor and Spaenjers 2016: 61), but not quite ready for art derivatives. The authors note that much of the foregoing change was based on trial and error and specialist art knowledge, including the discovery that some art sales were distorted by the behaviour of auctioneers.

The graphic arts

A number of accounting history studies involving the graphic arts have focused on annual report design. Setting itself in a historical context, Preston et al.'s (1996) study, 'Imag(in)ing Annual Reports', concentrates on different 'ways of seeing' annual reports, which are, of course, designed objects.

Preston et al. examine three approaches to the interpretation of annual reports, the first one involving the commonly understood 'way of seeing' that underpins practical annual report design. That is, the approach which takes for granted that 'images are a transparent medium of communication through which corporations send messages to investors and the public' (Preston et al. 1996: 115). To explore this, the authors examine some of the design techniques commonly used to carry corporate messages, including visual photographic metaphor. As an example, they cite the use of a Sumo wrestler as a symbol of brand 'power' (by Pepsico). The use of visually pleasing, brightly coloured photographic images is another common technique employed in annual reports, and they cite as an example the 'dreamy' depiction of marine life (by Texaco), used to highlight positive environmental achievements the company claimed to have implemented. Another technique discussed is the use of black and white pictures and grey colouring to reinforce an admission of poor performance. The authors note that annual reports using these 'reader-friendly' techniques, as well as being read as intended, may also be read sceptically in order to expose attempts at manipulation.

The second 'way of seeing' that Preston et al. discuss involves a more systematic way of 'looking beneath the surface' (1996: 119). As an example of this Marxist-informed approach, the photographic content of Northern Telecom's 1989 annual report is analysed, first, in terms of what its producers intended it to *denote*, namely, the company's advanced technological capability and its worldwide reach. This is conveyed with the aid of photographs of scientists or technicians in white coats, in settings which feature the electronic components which the firm uses, against architectural backgrounds with an international feel. However, this imagery may also be read in terms of what is excluded, that is, in terms of what the images *connote.* It may be seen as symbolic of the exclusion of the 'full- and part-time employees with readily available clerical, secretarial and routine manual skills', who are cheap to hire, easily disposable, low-paid and on whom the firm depends. These are 'the missing faces in annual reports'. Such a reading places the images in 'a wider sociocultural context in which more profound [i.e. ideological] significances may be read' (Preston et al. 1996: 122).

The third 'way of seeing' is the 'postmodern'. Postmodern art and graphic techniques and their interpretation allow the formation of new meanings in the mind of the beholder through the subversion and amendment of historical images. One example cited is the alteration of a painting of a woman by Klimt in the 1989 annual report of Talbrands. Her bare breast has been edited out and the word 'woman' has been superimposed, as in other images in the report. Klimt has been subverted in order to portray one of Talbrands' markets, 'western woman'.

However, it is a logical extension of the views of postmodern writers, such as Baudrillard, that an annual report can be infused with any meaning ascribed by the reader, and that it can take on a life of its own quite apart from the meanings it was intended to convey. Baudrillard states that: 'As simulacra, images precede the real to the extent that they invert the causal and logical order of the real'. Readers are entitled to ignore intended meanings and substitute their own subjective responses to text and images. Such relativistic approaches, the authors admit, 'are sometimes seen as an extreme view' (Preston et al. 1996: 128).

Examining the Marxist critique of postmodern interpretations, Preston et al. (1996: 129) note that 'For neo-Marxists, the decentered, allegorical and appropriated images that increasingly characterise contemporary sign production are seen to mute the possibility of critique', since, for Marxists, the underlying socio-economic realities remain.

Two contemporaneous, historically rooted, studies of annual report design expand on the first 'way of seeing' discussed by Preston et al., scrutinising in different ways the deliberate use of persuasive visual and textual techniques to attempt to influence readers. The first of these, by Graves et al. (1996), examines the 'television epistemology of US annual reports'. Building on the contention by Postman (1985) that public discourse in America has been dominated for some time by televisual techniques inextricably bound up with notions of legitimacy, these authors provide many examples of 'the rhetorical nature of visual design in annual reports' (Graves et al. 1996: 59), and the role of 'Pictures … [in relation to the] … Bottom Line'. The essence of their study is the rather uncomplimentary but at least partly true assertion that the average US 'reader' of annual reports has a short attention span which has grown out of a diet of television and television-borne 'show business'. The paper asserts that this has affected the epistemologies in use in US culture generally, as well as leading, in the case of annual reports, to concern with the 'headlines' only, such as total profit.

A printed culture, accessed by reading, has given way to a visual one. This means that if a message 'does not appear in an amusing or attractive format or if the message is not instantaneous, that is, if it does not come packaged in the rhetoric of television, it will not be attended' (Graves et al. 1996: 65). Visual images from annual reports 'as if framed by a television screen' are discussed in this study, including the Sumo wrestler already highlighted in Preston et al.'s (1996) analysis referred to above. The use of this example in two slightly different ways by two sets of writers looking at the deliberate intentions of annual report designers underscores the subjectivity involved in visual interpretation.

Nevertheless, the insight afforded by drawing attention to the 'epistemology of television' utilised in the past memorably enhances our understanding of the techniques of impression management employed today. This is especially worth bearing in mind in an age of internet annual reports, which allow users random access to visual material in an unprecedentedly convenient way while having the potential to subject them to the show business techniques of television and associated visual rhetoric, especially since they are accessed by that extremely televisual framing device, the personal computer screen.

The study by McKinstry (1996), traces the progress of British annual report design through the lens of Burton PLC's annual reports, produced over the period 1930–94. It highlights the influence of US advertising firms in the UK, and their British emulators and counterparts in developing annual report design. It was US advertising firms that first offered public relations services and devised notions such as 'corporate identity', importing these into annual reports and enlisting the advancing technologies of paper production, photolithography and typography in order to do so. This happened in Britain slightly later than in America. Guided by UK-based full-service advertising firms, Burton and some other key UK public companies turned, in the 1970s, to making annual reports, at least in part, corporate communications tools, as opposed to the basic tables of financial accounts and minimal textual information of which they had previously consisted.

McKinstry's study links the specific visual imagery used by Burton, especially from the 1980s onwards, with impression management geared towards shareholder support for the takeover of Debenhams, a large High Street retail chain, and the approval of extravagant remuneration packages for directors, who had been borne along on the economic upswing of the Thatcher years. When an economic downswing came, dramatic changes of design approach and indeed, designer, were implemented, as the new top management denigrated their predecessors and the falling profits associated with them. Burtons' iconic and visually stunning fashion-related annual reports gave way to sackcloth-and-ashes grey, together with the reduced and muted use of photographic images as the firm rebuilt itself in the early 1990s.

The Burton study concludes with the caveat that limited attention is paid by city analysts to the visual content of annual reports, and that there is a case for some form of control on annual report design to ensure that the more gullible reader is not misled. It advocates that design briefs for annual reports should be geared towards the interpretation of accounts rather than the aggrandisement of senior management, as it then was and may still be.

There is, in annual report design, a fertile field for the accounting historian as economic cycles come and go, as graphic and information technologies move on and as cultures, their manufacturing technologies and associated political priorities, not to mention art movements, change.

Rarely studied in the accounting history literature, cartoons feature in the paper by Miley and Read (2014), who examine the humorous drawings of Bruce Bairnsfather, a British front-line military officer during World War 1. Accounting scholars have discovered that the British Army's accounting systems supporting its military efforts were deficient in failing to record and feed back detailed usage and distribution problems suffered by those in the trenches to those in ultimate charge. Miley and Read show that Bairnsfather's cartoons humorously pointed this out to soldiers in the field through his widely circulated and ironic illustrations of the embarrassments faced stoically by the troops. While the authors claim that the cartoons, as artefacts of popular culture, can become accounting in themselves by, in this case, highlighting the human consequences of the failing accounting system to those who ought to know about it, this can only be true at a metaphorical level, useful though this appears to have been.

Film

Of all the creative arts which have some relevance to accounting history, film is undoubtedly one of the least-studied. One of the few treatments of film having a bearing on accounting history is Beard's (1994) paper on 'Popular Culture and Professional Identity: Accountants in the Movies'. As this author notes, 'what occurs on film … is almost by definition, culturally significant' (Beard 1994: 303). In an analysis of films produced since 1957, Beard identifies 16 popular films in which accountants have appeared as central characters, including such successful ones as *The Producers* (1968) and *Ghostbusters* (1984).

In an analysis of the narrative capacities in which the accountants operate in the films analysed, Beard notes three roles: as stock comic characters who manifest stereotypes of the members of the accounting profession; as complex personalities whose identity as accountants is an integral part of their characters; and as intermediaries whose identities are necessary to develop and resolve the plot (Beard 1994: 307). Beard observes that producers of films, who are in the entertainment business, have no obligation to truthfulness in their portrayal of accountants. However, the study implies that, in general, what has been portrayed is consistent with the improving image that accountants created over the last 50 years of the twentieth century. The comedic figures portrayed in *The Producers*, Monty Python's *The Meaning of Life* or *Ghostbusters* tend to give way in later films to characters 'who emerge from their stereotype' (Beard 1994: 309).

In the earlier films, too, accountants tended to be portrayed as joyless, lonely or dysfunctional, whereas, in the middle period examined, accountants 'begin the transition from a kind of programmed rigidity to a more complex emotional maturity'. The final period sees them portrayed as average men and women 'who just happen to be accountants' (Beard 1994: 309). An improving image for accountants was also found in a study of films released in North America in the twentieth century, with CPAs or CAs the most likely types to be depicted as 'heroes' (Dimnik and Felton 2006).

While accounting historians might welcome the retreat from stereotyping in films that the above papers disclose, few would deny having laughed at the ludicrous depictions of Monty Python or *The Producers* and the pleasurable departure they represented, in their time, from the quotidian experience of accountancy and its pedagogy.

Another rare work of relevance to the world of film was Amernic and Craig's (2000) 'Accountability and Rhetoric during a Crisis: Walt Disney's 1940 Letter to Shareholders'. These authors analysed, through close reading, a communication made by Disney to his shareholders in order to make a case for the injection of extra capital at a time of heavy losses for the company. A framework of rhetoric and metaphor was selected in order to examine how Disney put his arguments. Amernic and Craig concluded that it was 'fitting that Disney the storyteller would incorporate narrative into his CEO discourse' (Amernic and Craig 2000: 63), shedding fresh light on the, at times, enigmatic personality that created and drove forward an organisation in which there was 'a curiously seamless fusion of cinematic art and consumerism' (Amernic and Craig 2000: 57). The marketing of specially designed merchandise was part and parcel of the strategy for maximising revenues from new productions and the new characters they featured. At a technical level, the paper revealed that Disney's extremely prudent depreciation policy involved 'writing off the entire cost of the picture against the first revenues received', as in the case of *Snow White and the Seven Dwarfs* (Amernic and Craig 2000: 65).

Turning the focus away from profits and the accounting of those who make and market films for cinemas and the public, Jeacle's (2009) paper on 'Going to the Movies' examines the public experience of movies and aspects of accounting in a major Edinburgh picture house. Her analysis is based on the fortuitous survival of a complete run of the Edinburgh Playhouse's 'box office ledgers' for the years 1930–72. The paper produces graphs of turnover, costs, profits and cinema-going numbers over time, showing the generally downward trend that applied until the end of the period, together with commentary on the most popular movie themes and titles over the years, an index of changing tastes and thus an important social insight. Of special note was the Playhouse's recording in its ledger of two indirect but relevant explanatory factors for fluctuating attendances and profits: the state of local competition in other local cinemas and also the weather, which affected attendance numbers. The use of these factors as early as 1930 presages later developments in strategic management accounting and also 'new' techniques, such as the balanced scorecard, by introducing external factors into the analysis of results many decades earlier than these 'innovations'.

The filmic genre moves on. In 2001, *Christie Malry's Own Double Entry* was turned into a film which was not put on general release but won the British Independent Film of the Year Award. A new production of *The Producers* was distributed in 2005, coinciding with its relaunch as a musical play. *The Accountant*, starring Ben Affleck, whose previous roles have included Batman, was released in 2016. The eponymous accountant in the film is an autistic CPA, whose highly developed forensic accountancy skills and martial arts prowess landed him on the wrong side of the law. After imprisonment, he hid himself in small town America where he took on legitimate forensic assignments and tried to do good, but his violent past catches up with him as the Mafia try (in vain) to stop him. How his complex, un-stereotypical character works out is not fully revealed, and at the time of writing, a sequel is in production which seems likely to provide some answers.

Given the objective distance required of events before they can be researched as history, these and like developments are building up a future archive of potential interest to accounting historians of the future. It is also noteworthy that, so far, historical studies of accounting and film have been restricted to western film, leaving an open door for researchers from non-western cultures.

Coda and concluding remarks

Perhaps surprisingly, the world of music has as yet received little attention from accounting historians, and so it has not been given a separate treatment in this chapter. One rare exception is the paper by Zan (2004), in which he analyses the structure of an 'unorthodox music historiography' as a potential model for the writing of accounting and management history. The musical history analysed began with a history of the present, proceeding backwards in time instead of forwards, a treatment of the theoretical underpinnings of the music concerned, an emphasis on non-linear development, a social history, a pluralist view of genres and a multi-geographical focus. From this one example, Zan attempted (somewhat tenuously, if articulately) to argue the benefits of such an open-minded approach to accounting history.

That study apart, the accountancy arrangements of musicians, musical combines, retailers, wholesalers and promoters of music remain largely untouched by historians. One possible reason is the lack of relevant archival materials, in the absence of which, speculation is necessary, as is shown by De Loo and Davis (2003) in their not wholly satisfactory study of the demise of Black Swan records in America in the early 1920s. Musicians and musical impresarios, like architectural practices, are quite likely to view their creative work, that is, the music they have composed, arranged or played, as of first importance when it comes to record retention, and other items such as business books are probably seen as less worthy of preservation.

A perusal of the lists of archives presented in the scholarly *New Grove Dictionary of Jazz*, for example, reveals the existence of very few financial records among the many collections listed (Kernfield 1994: 698–708). Using the listing provided in *Grove*, the writer of this chapter undertook a preliminary examination of the archives of the Casa Loma Orchestra, a famous swing orchestra active from the 1920s to the 1950s, which are located in Northeastern University, Boston. Somewhat exceptionally, he found notebooks containing salary records and other financial details which might reward further study. On the other hand, disappointingly, queries addressed to Tulane University's William Ransom Hogan Jazz archive, in New Orleans, revealed that it contains little of interest to the accounting historian. This does not rule out the possibility, of course, that other musical genres and institutions may have suitable archives as yet undiscovered.

An overview of what has been written to date in the field is perhaps now in order. The studies that have appeared seem to have been driven either by the arts-based proclivities or educational backgrounds of the accounting scholars who wrote them. This is a fruitful characteristic, for it enables readers and scholars to see accountancy in a wider setting, where the norms of industrial or commercial practice do not always apply.

In terms of the sustained commitment of scholars to this field, it is true in some cases that the pieces of research which have been undertaken are single ventures, not followed up in further studies, sometimes even 'retirement' ventures. It is to be hoped that this is not because of a perception that such studies are of inferior value to, say, a piece of research on a new accounting standard. These studies require, and promote, a commendable breadth of view, and need, betimes, vast amounts of work, when compared with some areas of more mainstream accounting research. Value may be found in the accumulation of case studies, and in this respect, the work of those who specialise in accounting histories of the creative arts may be of significance for the synthesis of findings and the making of wider generalisations.

The barriers which confront scholars of the interface between accounting and the arts are a reflection of the nature of the work. Journals that welcome such studies need to find suitable referees and associated processes which reflect the width of scholarship within a paper. This lends itself to the forging of cross-disciplinary alliances with academics and specialists in the creative arts.

Furthermore, much more high quality illustration than that presently seen in journals is required for the visual material in papers examining the interface between accounting and the creative world. Since the text being studied is often the artefact itself, good illustration is required in order to reflect the visual richness involved, which frequently transcends full interpretation. A picture may indeed paint a thousand words, but not if it is badly reproduced. Publishers must be prepared for further expense if they are to support the work properly, and editors should be prepared to argue the case.

Research trajectories for the future have been suggested above, *en passant*. To these may be added the question of the involvement of senior, successful accountants in arts and arts funding bodies. To what extent does this reflect their 'establishment' social position, attempts to enhance socio-cultural capital, and to what extent is it meritocratic, reflecting a genuine love of the arts? What unique contribution do these individuals have to make, if any? Are there among us today accountants with a love of the arts such as Edwin

Waterhouse, a pioneer of the English profession (Jones 1988)? Or does success and affluence enable the most senior accountants to patronise the arts, and by so doing, nurture an interest in them that was previously lacking? We would like to know.

Although studies of the world of art markets and valuations are beginning to emerge, as we have shown above, further aspects of the art field remain to be explored. Paintings by artists such as Vincent van Gogh, who lived a life of poverty, sell today for prices that beggar the imagination. But what happens to the work of artists who enjoyed fame in their lifetimes? To what extent is their work rationed by agents in order to ensure high prices, and what other factors are at work? How do the purchasers of such work, such as corporations, value these in their accounts? We look forward to future ventures in these areas by accounting historians.

As we enjoy a more leisured lifestyle in the developed world, and as our affluence grows, we have more time in our lives and more resources both to enjoy the creativity of others and to practise what creative gifts we ourselves may have. In these circumstances, the accounting and financial dimensions of creativity, and their histories, can only be of increasing interest.

Key works

Connor (2004) represents a major study on the use of accounting and accounting concepts by Daniel Defoe and Arpha Benn in their late seventeenth-/early eighteenth-century novels. The book also includes a review of contemporary bookkeeping guides for women and a summary of the forms of money in use in the wider economy.

Graves et al. (1996) examines the effects of television and show-business on the concentration span of the American public, and how it has influenced the design of annual reports of US corporations, in their desire to communicate the messages they wish to emphasise.

McKinstry (1997) examines the status-building intentions of the fledgling ICAEW as it erected its magnificent 'Hall'. The paper offers an art-historical explanation of the building's stylistic connotations, the iconography of its sculpture and how these furthered the aims of a foremost professional body.

Yamey (1989) is a major work, lavishly illustrated, which examines depictions of accountancy, accountants and account books in western art from the late-medieval period onwards. The book sheds new light on various aspects of accountancy, as well as on art history.

References

Amernic, J.H. and Craig, R. (2000) Accountability and rhetoric during a crisis: Walt Disney's 1940 letter to shareholders, *Accounting Historians Journal*, 27 (2): 49–86.

Beard, V. (1994) Popular culture and professional identity: accountants in the movies, *Accounting, Organizations and Society*, 19 (3): 303–18.

Boys, P. (1990) *Chartered Accountants' Hall: The First Hundred Years* (London: ICAEW).

Boys, P. (1994) A source of accounting history: Somerset Maugham, *Accounting Historian's Notebook*, 17 (2): 9, 24.

Boys, P. (1995) Samuel Pepys' personal accounts, *Accounting, Business & Financial History*, 5 (3): 308–20.

Buckmaster, D. and Buckmaster, E. (1999) Studies of accounting and commerce in Chaucer's Shipman's Tale, *Accounting, Auditing & Accountability Journal*, 12 (1): 113–28.

Connor, R. (2004) *Women, Accounting and Narrative: Keeping Books in Eighteenth Century England* (London: Routledge).

Coslor, E. and Spaenjers, J. (2016) Organisational and epistemic change: the growth of the art investment field, *Accounting, Organizations and Society*, 55: 48–62.

Czarniavska, B. (2008) Accounting and gender across times and places: an excursion into fiction, *Accounting, Organizations and Society*, 33 (1): 33–47.

Czarniavska, B. (2012) Accounting and detective stories: an excursion to the USA in the 1940s, *Accounting, Auditing & Accountability Journal*, 25 (4): 659–72.

De Loo, I. and Davis, D. (2003) Black Swan records, 1921 to 1924: from a Swanky Swan to a Dead Duck, *Accounting History*, 8 (2): 35–57.

Dimnik, T. and Felton, S. (2006) Accountant stereotypes in movies distributed in North America in the twentieth century, *Accounting, Organizations and Society*, 31 (2): 129–55.

Evans, L. (2005) Brothels, tombstones and morality: a literary look at offbeat perspectives on accounting and finance, paper presented at British Accounting Association Annual Congress, Heriot-Watt University, Edinburgh.

Evans, L. and Fraser, I. (2012) The accountant's social background and stereotype in popular culture: the novels of Alexander Clark Smith, *Accounting, Auditing & Accountability Journal*, 25 (6): 964–1000.

Fraser, I., Gallhofer, S., Haslam, J., and Sydserff, R. (2006) *Hard Times*: Carlyle and Dickens on accounting in the name of social progress, paper presented at Interdisciplinary Perspectives on Accounting Conference, Cardiff, July.

Graves, O.F., Flesher, D.L., and Jordan, R.E. (1996) Pictures and the bottom line: the television epistemology of U.S. annual reports, *Accounting, Organizations and Society*, 21 (1): 57–88.

ICAEW (2002) *Chartered Accountants' Hall: An Illustrated Tour* (London: ICAEW).

Jeacle, I. (2003) Accounting and the construction of the standard house, *Accounting, Auditing & Accountability Journal*, 16 (4): 582–605.

Jeacle, I. (2005) Accounting and the construction of taste: standard costs and the Georgian cabinetmaker, *Abacus*, 41 (2): 117–37.

Jeacle, I. (2009) Going to the movies: accounting and twentieth century cinema, *Accounting, Auditing & Accountability Journal*, 22 (5): 677–708.

Jones, E. (1988) *The Memoirs of Edwin Waterhouse* (London: Batsford).

Kernfield, B. (ed.) (1994) *The New Grove Dictionary of Jazz* (London: Macmillan).

Klamer, A. (ed.) (1997) *The Value of Culture: On the Relationship Between Economics and the Arts* (Amsterdam: University of Amsterdam Press).

Lee, T.A. (1996) The influence of the individual in the professionalisation of accountancy: the case of Richard Brown and the Society of Accountants in Edinburgh, in C.W. Nobes and T. Cooke (eds) *The Development of Accounting in an International Context*, pp. 31–48 (London: Routledge).

Macdonald, K. (1989) Building respectability, *Sociology*, 23 (1): 55–80.

Maltby, J. (1999) Accounting and the soul of the middle class: Gustav Freytag's, *Soll und Haben, Accounting, Organizations and Society*, 22 (1): 69–87.

Maltby, J. and Rutterford, J. (2006) Frank must marry money: men, women and property in Trollope's novels, *Accounting Historians Journal*, 33 (2): 169–200.

McKinstry, S. (1996) Designing the annual reports of Burton plc from 1930 to 1994, *Accounting, Organizations and Society*, 21 (1): 89–111.

McKinstry, S. (1997) Status building: some reflections on the architectural history of Chartered Accountants' Hall, London, 1889–1893, *Accounting, Organizations and Society*, 22 (8): 779–98.

McKinstry, S. (2000) *Twenty Seven Queen Street, Edinburgh: Home of Scottish Chartered Accountants, 1891–2000* (Edinburgh: ICAS).

McKinstry, S. (2007) Christie Malry's own double entry, by B. S. Johnson: an interpretation as Foucauldian discourse, *Critical Perspectives on Accounting*, 18 (8): 975–91.

McKinstry, S. (2008) Reframing a "Subfusc" institute: building on the past for the future at Chartered Accountants' Hall, London, 1965–1970, *Critical Perspectives on Accounting*, 19 (8): 1384–413.

McKinstry, S. and Ding, Y.Y. (2015) "Hybridised" financial control in the Victorian construction industry: George Gilbert Scott's rebuilding of Glasgow University, 1864–1872, *Accounting History*, 20 (2): 206–227.

McKinstry, S. and Fletcher, M. (2002) The personal account books of Sir Walter Scott, *Accounting Historians Journal*, 29 (2): 59–89.

McKinstry, S. and Wallace, K. (2004) Cullen, Lochhead and Brown, architects: the business, financial and accounting history of a non-profit maximising firm, 1902–2002, *Accounting, Business & Financial History*, 14 (2): 183–207.

Miley, F. and Read, A.F. (2014) Cartoons as alternative accounting: front-line supply in the First World War, *Accounting History Review*, 24 (2–3): 161–89.
Mintzberg, H., Otis, S., Shamsie, J., and Waters, J. (1986) Strategy of design: a study of architects in co-partnership, in J. Grant (ed.) *Strategic Management Frontiers*, pp. 311–59 (Greenwich, CT: JAI Press).
Moore, D.L. (1974) *Lord Byron Accounts Rendered* (London: John Murray).
Mussari, R. and Mussari, B. (2006) Book-keeping in the sixteenth century building yard of the Castello of Crotone: an accountancy and architectural analysis, *Accounting History*, 11 (3): 319–56.
Napier, C.J. (2017) The good fraud: accounting finance and banking in a 1930s English novel, *Contabilita e Cultura Aziendale*, 2: 43–70.
Parker, R.H. (1999) Accounting in Chaucer's, *Canterbury Tales, Accounting, Auditing & Accountability Journal*, 12 (1): 92–112.
Pile, L. (2004) A building of distinction, *Accountancy*, February: 41–43.
Postman, N. (1985) *Amusing Ourselves to Death: Public Discourse in the Age of Show Business* (New York: Viking).
Preston, A.M., Wright, C., and Young, J.M. (1996) Imag(in)ing annual reports, *Accounting, Organizations and Society*, 21 (1): 113–37.
Service, A. (1977) *Edwardian Architecture: A Handbook to Building Design in Britain 1890–1914* (London: Thames and Hudson).
Squire, J. (1937) *The Hall of the Institute of Chartered Accountants in England and Wales* (London: ICAEW).
Walker, S.P. (1995) An early challenge to the accountant stereotype? The accountant as hero in late-Victorian romantic fiction, *Accounting Historian's Notebook*, 18 (2): 13–14, 32.
West, B.P. (2001) On the social history of accounting: *The Bank Audit* by Bruce Marshall, *Accounting History*, 6 (1): 11–30.
Willis, C. (1995) *Form Follows Finance: Skyscrapers and Skylines in New York and Chicago* (Princeton, NJ: Architectural Press).
Wilson, R.G. and Mackley, A.L. (1999) How much did the English country house cost to build, 1660–1880? *Economic History Review*, 52 (3): 436–68.
Wissler, T.E. (2013) Accounting for eternal glory: financial statements on temple stelae in nineteenth-century South China, *Accounting History*, 18 (2): 229–55.
Yamey, B. (1989) *Art and Accounting* (New Haven, CT: Yale University Press).
Zan, L. (2004) Writing accounting and management history: insights from unorthodox music historiography, *Accounting Historians Journal*, 31 (2): 171–92.

PART VII

Polity

27
THE STATE

Philip Colquhoun

Overview

This chapter discusses histories of the intertwining of accounting and the state, focusing on entities that make up the state. A central theme in any discussion of the relationship between the state and accounting, in both the historical and contemporary accounting literature and in wider public discourse, is accountability. Various notions of accountability are applied to this relationship including constitutional, hierarchical and stewardship accountability. Accountability relationships are evident from the earliest records of ancient civilisations where individuals were accountable to the state and the state was accountable to individuals. During different periods of history, accounting practices are shown to mediate aspects of the accountability relationships between the legislative and executive branches of government; between the elected, their officials and the electorate; and between entities within the state. While accounting technology is a constant, the nature of the technology changes. It is suggested that changes in the nature of accountability are often driven by philosophical and ideological shifts.

The chapter pays particular attention to the long-running debates on the technical issues surrounding the introduction of double-entry bookkeeping, the utility of replacing traditional cash-based with accrual-based accounting systems, and the discourses surrounding changes to the mandate of government auditors. Historical research on the new public management reforms of the later twentieth century are discussed, both as technical and political reforms. The use of accounting by the state in social institutions is addressed in relation to both their financial management and the control of individuals who populate them. The chapter concludes by indicating the potential for future historical research on accounting and the state.

Introduction

The activities of the state and accounting practices are intertwined in numerous ways (Miller 1990). A great deal of accounting undertaken by or for individuals has elements controlled, managed or sanctioned by the state. A significant amount of commercial activity, and hence its accounting, is controlled through state regulatory regimes. The regulation, ostensibly in the public interest, of private sector monopolies is activated in large part through accounting processes. The authority of financial reporting standards is derived through mandates from the state. The accounting profession itself obtains much of its power, prestige and viability from the sanction it receives from the state.

This chapter focuses on where this intertwining of accounting and the state is at its most direct, that is, state entities that use accounting for management, control, accountability and/or record keeping. Such entities range from institutions of central government and sub-national government units, to individual trading operations, autonomous public bodies and organisations established in the pursuit of social policy and the management of misfortune. Discussion of the relationship between accounting and these entities in historical contexts ranges from the technical and managerial to the political and social. Literature on specific technical issues relate to issues such as the introduction of double-entry bookkeeping and accrual-based accounting. Literature on social and political issues relates to the philosophical choices and ideological debates behind the introduction of new accounting and auditing technologies and the presumed intentional impacts of accounting on individuals and various social groups.

A dominant theme in the literature on accounting and the state is accountability. The manner in which this concept is understood differs among authors. For example, Funnell (2007) views the accountability provided by accounting in the context of constitutional rights, freedoms and protections provided by liberal democratic states. In consequence, Funnell (1994, 1998, 2004) locates debates surrounding accounting, auditing and the state in relation to notions of constitutional accountability. Alternative understandings of accountability focus on its vertical and hierarchical nature and the processes that are often combined with notions of stewardship and individual responsibility.

However, accountability is not the only framework within which the relationship between accounting and the state is understood. Theoretical frameworks employed to analyse this relationship include those based on neo-classical economics, critical analysis (especially governmentality and the work of Foucault), and institutional theory. One of the most common approaches focuses on agency – in particular, identifying and narrating the contribution of individual actors and groups in the debates surrounding continuity and change in accounting and audit practice.

The chapter is structured by selected themes discussed in published histories of accounting and the state. The themes focus on chronological development, technical issues, agents for change and entity types. The first two sections are chronological and address the development of accounting for the state in ancient and classical civilisations, and the period from the Middle Ages to the eighteenth century. The following sections discuss technical issues on accounting and the state. The first issue relates to the basis of reporting in government – cash or accrual accounting and the use of double-entry bookkeeping. The following two sections look at institutions or movements involved in promoting change to accounting in the state. The first discusses various agents of change, predominantly professional or accounting bodies, which have led the movement for change in accounting for the state. The second discusses changes sought to accounting practices since the late 1970s under the banner of new public management. In the section that follows, conflicts over assurance and value for money audits are discussed, including those from the period of new public management. The role of accounting in social and other institutions, and in hospitals, under the auspices of the state is discussed on two levels – where accounting techniques are used in the financial management of organisations, and where accounting is used as a tool to control the individuals who inhabit them. The chapter concludes with a brief overview of comparative studies, accounting at the moment of the creation of new states, and studies that cover nations that are poorly represented in the literature to date.

Ancient and classical civilisations

The surviving records of accounting systems in ancient civilisations, as discussed in Chapter 4 of this volume, provide insights into accounting for and by both private individuals and the state. Carmona and Ezzamel (2007) conceptualise three spheres of accountability relationships in ancient Mesopotamia and Egypt: individual to individual, individual to state and state to individual. It is the latter two that are of interest in this chapter. The individual to state sphere provides an example of hierarchical accountability, while the state to individual sphere is concerned with honouring commitments to subjects.

Sources from ancient Babylonia, Egypt, Greece and Rome discuss how various states, republics and empires managed and accounted for their resources. Much of the impetus for this accounting stemmed from the need to account for the collection of taxation, especially in the more expansive empires. Accounting records were used as an accountability mechanism for tax and tribute collectors. In line with the political structures of states, accountability was generally hierarchical to the ruler; often mediated through a series of governors, superintendents and other officials. The Athenian state c.410 BC provides an early example of democratic notions of public accountability for financial management. Receipts and disbursements were recorded on marble stones and displayed in public (Boyd 1968; Ezzamel 2002b).

The scale of the Roman Empire necessitated the creation of accounting records, especially when regular taxes were collected, and regular payments were required to be made, such as for army personnel. Accounting was part of a much larger system of management of the Empire, with controls, reviews and a hierarchy of officers and officials leading to Rome. At times the Roman financial management system included a form of yearly budgeting, although this appears to have been an appropriation for expenditure rather than a decision-making tool (Boyd 1968).

While the purpose of most financial management systems in ancient times was the accountability of officials for the taxes they collected and the review of expenditure, there are instances of what could be labelled 'information for decision-making'. The Middle Kingdom in Ancient Egypt c.2000 BC provides an example of accounting by the state for the purposes of accountability and decision usefulness. The accounting system recorded the inflow of taxes, generally received as grain, and thus ensured the accountability of the officials responsible for their collection. An equally important function of the accounting system was accounting for the outflow of grain and other material collected. The taxation was applied to the redistribution of wealth according to predetermined ratios and the accounting system facilitated this redistribution (Ezzamel 2002a, 2002b).

Middle Ages to the eighteenth century

Moving forward three millennia, but several centuries before the publication of Pacioli's celebrated work on double-entry bookkeeping in 1494, an important treatise appeared in England on accounting by the state. The *Dialogus de Scaccario* (the Course of the Exchequer) was written around the late 1170s by Richard fitz Neal. As its title suggests, the work is presented in the form of a dialogue (which took place on the banks of the River Thames) between a junior and a senior employed in the English Exchequer. Richard fitz Neal was Treasurer for the King, a position that his father purchased for him and which he held between c.1158 and 1198. The *Dialogus* provided a comprehensive account on how the Exchequer was to be managed and offered detailed explanations of associated practices. No doubt influenced by the author's other position, namely Bishop of London, there are strong moral overtones in the instructions given to the junior official. The *Dialogus* reflects the accountability function of the Exchequer in dealing with the King's revenue and expenditure. Central to the treatise are instructions to ensure that the correct taxation is collected and recorded systematically, together with the importance of the accountability of the officials. The *Dialogus* provides insights into the operation of the English Treasury and thus the thinking behind much of the subsequent development of accounting by the English state, especially the focus on the accountability of the individuals in its service (Richardson 1928a, 1928b; Johnson 1983).

At the heart of the development of the Exchequer was providing assistance for the collection of taxation (Jones 2010). Although the management and effective governance of the King's dispersed estates was a feature of the Exchequer, aiding the collection of taxes was central. Using Mann's sources of power model, Jones (2010) explains accounting and the Exchequer in terms of political, economic and ideological power and its enforcement in twelfth-century England. Also on the theme of the importance of accounting for taxation, Baker (2013) provides a discussion of the administrative and accounting practices of the Byzantine Empire. This discussion focuses on the key role of accounting in the collection of taxes, duties and tolls and the associated administration. The paper uses the lens of governmentality to view the accounting and administrative tools used.

With the development of double-entry bookkeeping in medieval Italy, an alternative to the existing single-entry methods of accounting was provided for use in the state and private sectors. The single-entry system, often in the form of charge and discharge, allowed for a record of monies collected by an official on behalf of the ruler or the public, and in separate books, the payments (or discharges) made from the public money by that official. According to Jones (1985), these accounts were concerned with ensuring the accountability of the individual – they were a way for the agent to provide an account of his stewardship of money and/or other resources. As such, charge and discharge did not deal with the use of assets other than (at times) debtors and (even more rarely) inventories. Its shortcomings included:

> [t]he possibility of leaving blank spaces, the ability to modify past entries and of inserting sheets. Furthermore, the system used too many separate books and note-books for registering transactions. But possibility the most important shortcoming was that it failed to provide an administrative link between income and expend-iture and, therefore it was impossible to present an overall balance.
>
> *(Jurado-Sanchez 2002: 167)*

As the analysis in Chapter 5 suggests, the private sector embraced double-entry bookkeeping in various forms relatively quickly. The first known use of double-entry by a European central government was in the Spanish Royal Treasury in 1592. The introduction of double-entry bookkeeping arose from a period of financial crisis and was part of the wider reform of state administration. In contrast, parts of the Spanish commercial sector were compelled to adopt double-entry bookkeeping 43 years prior to its requirement in the Royal Treasury (ibid.).

The literature on the adoption of double-entry bookkeeping by European governments has identified the important role played by individuals in the process. For example, in the Netherlands, Stevin's 1608 text and his earlier work in the royal domains were pivotal to the introduction of double-entry bookkeeping in the upper level of Dutch central government. Stevin argued against applying double-entry bookkeeping in the lower levels of central government due to the difficulty of training all officials in the technique. The Dutch merchant, Cabiljau, was responsible for the introduction of double-entry to the Swedish government in 1623 (Gomes et al. 2006). Double-entry bookkeeping was applied to public finances in France in 1716, the result of the work of four brothers, Antoine, Claude, Joseph and Jean Paris. The Paris brothers were leading financiers of the period and the introduction of double-entry bookkeeping was part of an overhaul of the collection of money by the Treasury, aimed at providing better information on revenue and thereby decreasing interest paid by the Treasury (Lemarchand 1999). The French reforms were halted in 1726 but double-entry bookkeeping was reintroduced in the early nineteenth century as part of a larger reform of government accounting. These reforms in France were linked to the later introduction of double-entry bookkeeping in England through the involvement of Count Mollien (Nikitin 2001).

Double-entry bookkeeping and cash vs. accrual accounting

The study by Edwards et al. (2002) on the discourses leading to the introduction of double-entry bookkeeping in British central government in the 1830s also draws attention to the importance of individual actors. The design of the double-entry bookkeeping system for British central government was allocated to a committee comprising two senior civil servants and Peter Harris Abbott, a 'leading public accountant of the day' (ibid.: 643). The committee was unanimous on the advisability of introducing double-entry bookkeeping. However, there was debate over its form. Abbott advocated 'the universal adoption of the mercantile system in the various departments of the Government' (ibid.: 648), while the two civil servants argued for a form of double-entry bookkeeping that was consistent with the traditional stewardship function of accounting in British government. Edwards et al. (2002) frame this episode as an ideological contest. The professional accountant advocated full double-entry bookkeeping to bring about a more business-like approach to government financial management. The civil servants, in contrast, wanted to maintain the personal accountability and stewardship of individual officials, which was central to the charge and discharge system. Another feature of the debate was the use of the cash or accrual basis of accounting. Abbott's mercantile system included accrual accounting, while the stewardship model was based on maintaining the use of a cash-based system. The advantage of the latter was that flows of public money could be traced to the individual responsible for its collection or disbursement. The arguments of the government officials won the argument and a cash-based form of double-entry bookkeeping was to be introduced to British central government. However, as Edwards et al. (2002: 638) note, whether it was introduced 'in substance or in form, awaits the location and study of relevant archival records'. Mann et al. (2016) contest Edwards et al.'s (2002) analysis, suggesting that rather than the ideological differences of class alone, it was 'a complex amalgam of class interest, ideology, personal antipathy, profession intolerance and ambition' that underpinned the difference of opinion on the form of double-entry bookkeeping (ibid.: 739). While accepting that class was one factor in the introduction of double-entry bookkeeping, Mann et al. (2016) suggest that the desire for stringent economy in government was the driving force behind its ultimate introduction. Similar to Edwards et al. (2002), Mann et al. (2016) identified two men as champions in the introduction of double-entry bookkeeping – the naval officer, John Deas Thomson, and the aristocrat, Sir James Graham. The difference between the analysis in Mann et al. (2016) and Edwards et al. (2002) can be, at least in part, attributed to the different archival sources used.

The argument over cash versus accrual in early nineteenth-century England is illustrative of numerous and still ongoing debates surrounding the use of the cash or accrual basis of accounting. This has been a major controversy in government accounting and a widely studied feature of the history of accounting by the state. With the focus historically on tracking the receipt of taxation and/or to ensuring correct approval for the expenditure of public money via an appropriation or other legal authority, a cash basis of recording and reporting suited the demands for government accountability. Regardless of whether the accounting technique involved tally sticks, single-entry charge/discharge or double-entry bookkeeping, a system for recording the cash received and disbursed was traditionally deemed sufficient.

At times, the cash versus accrual issue was part of a wider debate about the financial management of the state, as in the above-mentioned debate over double-entry bookkeeping. More recently, discussion of the introduction of accrual accounting has been associated with the reforms that began in the late 1970s, frequently referred to as new public management or new public financial management. The adoption of accrual accounting is a common feature of new public management reforms. The issue of accrual accounting in recent times is discussed in a later section of this chapter. Literature on the cash versus accrual accounting debates, outside the new public management period, has arisen most frequently in relation to accounting by municipalities and here the principal foci of historical investigation has been on the UK, the USA and New Zealand.

Coombs and Edwards' (1995) study, based on the archives of five large municipal corporations in Britain, indicates that the movement from cash to full accrual accounting occurred between 1852 and 1922. Their paper argues that accounting innovation was supply-driven rather than demand-led. The impetus for change from cash to accrual was driven by those involved in the accounting process rather than those for whom the accounts were prepared. The agents of change were specific local authorities and officials, and the professional associations that represented council treasurers and accountants. Coombs and Edwards' study supports Jones' (1986, 1992) observation that the costs to individuals engaging in debates over municipal accounting outweighed any benefits. However, as noted in the following section on agents of change, there have been situations where civic groups have engaged in accounting policy debates with state and local government.

Potts (1976, 1978, 1982) discusses changes to municipal accounting, predominantly in the USA in the first third of the twentieth century. Based on published works, the author compares the arguments advanced on the cash versus accrual debate by various authorities. Two phases in the development of municipal accounting are identified. The first was 1900–20 when discussion focused on similarities to commercial accounting. The second was 1920–35 when the dissimilarities between municipalities and commercial activities, and thus the accounting that emanated therefrom, were highlighted. In the earlier period, the intention was to introduce commercial accounting and especially accrual accounting to municipal authorities, while in the later period, arguments against introducing accrual accounting were dominant in the professional literature. For Potts, the evolution of municipal accounting was not random or disorganised, but reflected the opinions of prominent accountants at the time. Discussions on the possibility of introducing accrual accounting were always connected with related issues including accounting for capital, permanent property and the associated recording of depreciation, and the notion of going concern as used in the private sector. According to Potts, this debate had run its course by 1935 with the conclusion that permanent property should not be recorded in the accounts, and that the focus of municipal accounts should be on the liquidity of the authority. A cash basis was considered the best and most efficient way of revealing liquidity.

In New Zealand, full accrual accounting was introduced to local government as part of the new public management reforms of the late twentieth century. However, a number of specific activities such as local government trading enterprises and harbour boards had a long-standing obligation to use accrual accounting as the basis of their reporting. Pressure for the introduction of accrual accounting by municipal government began in the 1930s, predominantly driven by the government auditor and, on occasion, from within the sector's professional administration and accounting bodies. The accounting profession more widely rarely demonstrated any interest in government accounting until the 1980s and the commencement of the new public management reforms. Opposition to the numerous earlier attempts to introduce accrual accounting was based on a combination of technical and implementation concerns. The demarcation lines of the debates over cash versus accrual in New Zealand were not drawn around the interested groups, but rather around individuals within each interested group. At the technical level, many of those involved in municipal accounting viewed cash as the preferred approach as it provided for accountability per legal requirements and was in accord with the tradition of government accountability. The standard argument against the introduction of accrual accounting was the lack of available expertise to prepare accrual-based accounts across the sector. Arguments for the use of accrual accounting were based on the benefits of recording fixed assets, deprecation and other non-financial transactions, removing 'creative' cash accounting based on managing the timing of cash payments and receipts, and a belief that the accounting technology employed in the private sector would be an improvement on that used in the public sector (Colquhoun 2005).

There are a number of studies on the use of accrual accounting in other countries. Carpenter and Feroz (2001) discuss the introduction of generally accepted accounting principles (GAAP), including accrual accounting, in four states of the USA from the 1970s to the 1990s. The authors use institutional and resource dependency theories to frame their history. The study identifies a number of factors that led to the adoption of GAAP and accrual accounting: the impact of individuals (in this case elected government officials), the fiscal condition of the state, the potential to change power relations in the state government, the participation of the state's key accounting bureaucrats in their professional associations, and the nature and strength of the organisational process used to maintain non-GAAP practices including cash accounting (organisational imprinting).

Scott et al. (2003) provide an interpretative history using stakeholder theory on the use of cash and accrual systems in two Australian hospitals from 1857 to 1975. The paper traces the shift from a cash to an accrual basis followed by a reversion to a cash basis over the period studied. The government is identified as the stakeholder responsible for the change back to the cash basis in 1975, when the state became the primary funder of hospitals. The paper charts the introduction of accrual accounting in both hospitals, noting that while company legislation was the reason for its introduction in one hospital, in the other, a not-for-profit entity, no definitive reasons could be identified.

Yamamoto and Noguchi (2013) examine how the Japanese local government sector converted from a cash-based system to an accrual-based accounting system in the 1990s. The authors deploy new institutional sociology and the concept of coercive isomorphism to explain the widespread use of a modified form of accrual accounting in Japan following the recommendation of the Ministry of Internal Affairs and Communications. Yamamoto and Noguchi note that adoption generated external legitimacy for funding from national government, yet the system provided little valuable information for financial management.

Agents of change

This section examines institutions that have been important in the adoption of new accounting technologies in various countries. Of particular importance in the USA were the nineteenth-century reform movements and the role of the Government Accounting Standards Board. The first promoters of change in government accounting in the USA responded to the perception that municipal government was inefficient, dishonest and corrupt. Reform was associated with the Progressive Era, the 1890s to the 1920s. The National Municipal League (NML) formed in 1894, as well as municipal research bureaus, proposed improvements to the management of various cities in the USA. The bureaus suggested accounting reforms designed to create uniform reporting practices by cities and improved accounting and management processes. Although it had no formal authority, the NML could claim significant success by 1908, when it reported that half of large cities in the USA had adopted their uniform accounting methods (Fleischman and Marquette 1986: 72). The introduction of budgeting to municipalities, which, according to Fleischman and Marquette, had not been transported to the USA from the English public sector where it was central to the financial management system, was a major achievement of the reforms during the Progressive Era.

Since the 1930s, a number of bodies have been involved in promoting standards and offering guidance in relation to municipal accounting in the USA. These bodies had a common parent or sponsoring organisation in the Municipal Finance Officers Association. Their focus continued to be on the production by municipal authorities of comparable financial data. In later years they also broadened their interests to issues such as revenue recognition, reporting objectives and disclosure practices. The accounting profession only became involved in providing assistance and guidance to the public sector in the USA in 1974 when the American Institute of Certified Public Accountants issued an audit guide for state and local government units (Remis 1982).

The most important single instigator of change in US public sector accounting has been the Government Accounting Standards Board (GASB), organised in 1984. The GASB mandate covers financial reporting standards for state and local governments. Roybark et al. (2012a, 2012b) provide a comprehensive review of the work undertaken by GASB in its first 20 years. They also provide an analysis of its operational history. One of the first issues to be addressed by the GASB was accounting for staff post-employment benefits. In a forerunner of future debates, the GASB required that these benefits be accounted for on an accrual basis. In June 1999, the GASB issued Statement 34, which dealt with significant financial reporting issues including the accrual basis and reporting of both short- and long-term assets and liabilities. The introduction of such changes did not diminish the importance attached to budgeting information, and comparison between budget and actual was maintained. The reporting of non-financial or service efforts and accomplishments was encouraged but not required (Patton and Freeman 2005). Kinnersley (2016) examines a specific aspect of Statement 34, namely the totals columns in summarised financial statements for assets, liabilities and equity.

In the UK, the devising of standards and the introduction of changes to the accounting practices of municipalities followed a pattern analogous to the USA. Professional bodies for municipal officials, especially the Corporate Treasurers and Accountants Institute formed in 1885 (later the Chartered Institute of Public Finance and Accountancy), took the lead in suggesting change. During the 1880s the Institute requested the Local Government Board exercise its statutory power and make changes to the way municipalities prepared their accounts. Even after the introduction of statutory regulation in the 1930s the Minister responsible for municipalities would not promulgate accounting changes until they had been agreed by the professional associations in local government (Coombs and Edwards 1993).

On occasion, civic and citizen associations have also been agents for change in government accounting. Pridgen and Flesher (2013) outlined the role of the Tennessee Taxpayers Association (TTA) in the development of requirements that increased the level of accountability of local and state governments in the 1930s. The TTA produced reports on the performance of governments. In 1953 legislation was passed in Tennessee that required governments to report on performance – an accounting change partly due to the work of the TTA. Colquhoun (2011) similarly identified the impact of a ratepayer group on accounting for fixed assets by local government in early twentieth-century New Zealand. At the heart of the debate was a conflict over reporting that ensured inter-generational equity or expanding the colony through current ratepayers fully funding capital growth. Following engagement in the political and legislative process by the local ratepayer's association, changes were made to the accounting requirements of the city council. Both Pridgen and Flesher, and Colquhoun, thus provide relatively unusual examples of 'users' as change agents.

New public management

The reforms of the public sector that began internationally in the late 1970s are often grouped together under the title of new public management. The reforms are normally characterised as introducing markets to the public sector, financial performance measures, decentralisation and a focus on results or outcomes rather than inputs. New public management is also associated with performance or value for money audits and accrual accounting. However, it is important to note that the extent to which new public management reforms were introduced varies between countries (Humphrey et al. 2005). Buhr (2012) provides an overview of practices over a 30-year period (1980–2010) and focuses on the government adoption of accrual accounting in five Anglo-American sites.

The introduction of accrual accounting in Australia has been the subject of a number of historical studies. Ryan (1998) focuses on the adoption of accrual accounting by federal and state governments. Using an agenda-setting framework, Ryan examines the factors that led to the introduction of accrual accounting, separating the factors into political and policy agendas. Her analysis chronicles the emergence of accrual accounting as a potential issue in the early 1970s to its implementation as policy in the late 1990s. The key political agenda setters were the Auditors-General, parliamentarians and the accounting profession. The key policy agenda setters were the Public Sector Accounting Standards Board and government officials from the treasury and finance ministries. Ryan concludes that the introduction of accrual accounting cannot be attributed to one act or event, but rather rose 'onto [the] agenda due to several factors coming together at a given point in time' (ibid.: 533). Davis (2017) uses institutional theory to understand the changes in the annual report of one Australian Commonwealth Government agency. The institutional pressures were aligned to ensure that the agency adhered to a new form and format for accounting as part of the new public management ethos.

Christensen (2002, 2003) provides insights into the discussions concerning the introduction of accrual accounting in the late 1980s by the New South Wales (NSW) state government. Both his papers pay particular attention to the role of partners in accounting firms acting as consultants to the government and a number of senior politicians who were identified as users of the accounting information. Christensen (2002) uses contingency theory to locate the agents of change who promoted the adoption of accrual accounting in NSW. Christensen (2003) uses institutional theory to explain how the accountant–consultants were able to convince public sector officials to introduce accrual accounting to the state government.

Turning to the USA, Watkins and Arrington (2007) discuss the increasing importance and power of accounting in the public sector during the period of new public management reforms. In particular, they focus on the National Performance Review programme of the Clinton Presidency. Drawing on the work of political theorists Wolin and Connolly, the authors discuss the extent to which political discourse has come to be written as a language of accounting. Accounting fills the void left by the demise of political foundationalism. Costs, calculations, benefits and performance have become the language of government. The economic justification of all things political, which is central to the new public management reform agenda, requires the deployment not only of accounting techniques but also its language.

Newberry and Pallot (2004) examine the use of incentives in the financial management regime of the New Zealand central government. Based on extensive archival documents, the paper traces the development of the incentives and their impact on government departments. Focusing in particular on the capital charge, chief executive's performance contracts and the ability of departments to retain any surpluses generated, Newberry and Pallot argue that the impact of accounting-based incentives is detrimental to the public sector and counter to the stated aims of new public management reforms. They argue that the accounting technologies and incentives they generate have resulted in a loss of capability to deliver within the public sector and are likely to cause declining morale in departments. The authors question the intentionality of such outcomes of the financial management reforms.

Goddard (2005) examines changes to UK local government accounting, governance and accountability requirements within a broader framework on the nature of institutional structures. The study reviews accounting and financial management changes in historical, economic and social contexts. Using regulation theory, Goddard argues that the financial management reforms undertaken in the name of new public management since the mid-1970s represent a shift from the traditional or 'Fordist' regime to a post-Fordist regime. This shift is part of a new ideology that emphasises the merits of private sector structures and practices.

Audit

Two areas dominate studies on auditing and the state in the accounting history literature: i) the introduction of value for money/operational auditing and ii) the right to undertake and/or control probity and assurance audits of state entities. The literature focuses for both areas, on the contested nature of decisions about what and who to audit. A number of papers have discussed state audits in terms of the ongoing conflicts between the executive and legislative branches of government. Such conflict is presented as almost inevitable given that the executive seeks to maintain or (re)gain as much freedom from the oversight of the legislature as possible, while the legislature seeks to exercise its rights and obligations in relation to the oversight of public money. Much of this oversight is performed by an auditor on behalf of the legislature.

Funnell (1994) discusses the battle for an independent state auditor in Britain, which culminated in the passing of the Exchequer and Audit Departments Act 1866. The Act is portrayed as the result of more than a century of development commencing with haphazard auditing, moving to executive-controlled audits, and culminating in the emergence of parliamentary controlled audits. The 1866 Act represented a major *de jure* shift in the emphasis and control of the audit function from the interest of the executive to the interest of Parliament. The response of the executive to this shift was to support the 'independence' discourse surrounding the newly created position of Comptroller General of the Receipt and Issue of Her Majesty's Exchequer and Auditor General of Public Accounts (C&AG). Yet the executive continued to maintain *de facto* control over the state audit through its control of the audit department's finance and the appointment of the C&AG. This ensured that the independence enacted by Parliament and, superficially supported by the executive, was severely limited in practice. Elsewhere Funnell (1997) traces the content of the 1866 Act to earlier issues, particularly the long-standing concern of the British Parliament with uncontrolled and unauthorised expenditure by the military. These issues are dealt with in Chapter 28.

The theme of struggle over the control of audit also features in Coombs and Edwards' (2004) study of the audit of municipal corporations in Britain during the period 1835–1935. While the constitutional issues identified by Funnell were not present, the provision of audits became a three-way struggle between the accounting profession, the locally elected auditors, and central government-controlled district auditors. During the 1880s, the accounting profession looked to municipal audit as a source of business for its members. The newly organised profession raised its profile by publicly criticising the existing system of elected auditors and made much of the fraud in municipal corporations that the elected auditors had failed to detect. At the same time, the District Audit Board continued to press for legislative changes that would augment its responsibilities in relation to the accounts of municipal corporations. Despite the efforts of all three parties, none received any significant increase in responsibility or powers relating to the auditing of municipal corporations, although the members of the accounting profession did gain the right to be appointed auditor. Indeed, in practice, increasing numbers of municipal corporations engaged professional accountants as their auditors in preference to either the elected auditors or the District Audit Board.

Colquhoun (2013) uses concepts of political and organisational legitimacy to explain how two attempts by the New Zealand Auditor-General to increase his mandate as local government auditor had different outcomes. The first attempt, to gain the sole mandate as local government's auditor was successful, while the second attempt, to increase his powers as local government auditor, was unsuccessful. The failure to gain the enhanced powers sought in the second attempt was due to a perceived lack of trust in the Auditor-General himself, a key element of political legitimacy.

As a relatively recent technology value for money audits (or operational audits) have been contentious and contested. Value for money audits developed from the early 1940s in the USA but failed to transfer to other countries until the 1970s, especially to government bodies. While traditional government auditing has focused on probity, compliance and the accuracy of the financial records, the focus of value for money auditing has been on the activities undertaken by the government entity. Those activities are reviewed as to either their efficiency or results, or both. Radcliffe (1998), Funnell (1998) and Guthrie and Parker (1999) have all authored histories of the early days of value for money audits. Radcliffe's study concerns the Canadian province of Alberta while Funnell (1998) and Guthrie and Parker (1999) focused on the Australian Commonwealth Audit Office. Using the Foucauldian concept of governmentality, Radcliffe (1998) discusses the development and operation of efficiency audits in the 1970s, emphasising the importance of various discourses during their development. The parties that featured large in this discourse were politicians and providers of expert knowledge. The paper discusses how the discourses of political actors and expert actors engaged with those of their own professional and social networks.

Both Guthrie and Parker (1999) and Funnell (1998) focus on the contested nature of Australian federal audits. The former draw on the analogy of masque to discuss the events that occurred during the development of performance auditing between 1973 and 1998 and the personnel involved. The analogy is used to provide insight to 'the malleability and subjectivity of performance auditing concepts' (Guthrie and Parker 1999: 303). Funnell identifies the debate between 1978 and 1984 as one engaging the value for money auditor, as an agent of the Parliament, and the executive, whose policy and activity might be subject to audit. Given their highly subjective nature, efficiency audits are shown to be more threatening to the executive than financial audits. The latter places greater reliance on well-defined standards of practice and the results are more predictable. The outcomes of efficiency audits are less predictable and therefore less politically manageable. The paper concludes by identifying how little independence the state auditor has when in conflict with executive government departments.

Funnell (2004) returns to the theme of the conflict between the legislature and the executive in his response to Flesher and Zarzeski (2002). Flesher and Zarzeski provide a history of the development of value for money/operational audits in English-speaking countries. Value for money auditing was developed from the mid-1940s in the USA, especially in relation to public sector bodies. However, it was not until the 1970s that such audits began to be undertaken in English-speaking countries outside the USA. Flesher and Zarzeski conclude their paper with a question: given the development of value for money auditing in the USA, why didn't other Anglophone countries such as the UK, Australia, Canada and New Zealand quickly emulate the American practice of value for money audits in the public sector? Funnell's (2004) answer relates to an essential difference between the US and Westminster forms of government. Under the Westminster system, the executive is also part of the legislature. Therefore, the lines and nature of accountability are significantly different from the USA where there is a strict separation of powers between the executive and legislative branches of government. Under the Westminster system, the state auditor is intended to be a 'watchdog' rather than a 'bloodhound', as the executive has the right 'to govern without the intrusion of parliament once monies are appropriated' (ibid.: 220). In the USA, the legislature and its agencies, including the audit function, have a stronger 'bloodhound' mentality. According to Funnell, this discouraged the introduction of value for money audits in countries following the Westminster system until the later twentieth century.

English and Guthrie (2000) discuss the struggle for control over the functioning of the state auditor in the Australian Commonwealth from the mid-1970s to the 1990s. In this episode, the government had undertaken a number of actions aimed at reducing the effectiveness of the auditor. In particular, the executive was unwilling to introduce legislation to update the Audit Act 1901 under which the state auditor operated. English and Guthrie argue that this unwillingness reflected the government's view regarding the necessity of the state having a government auditor. The executive considered that the work of both the state auditor and the audit department could and should be undertaken by professional accounting firms through a series of tenders and contracts. This is consistent with the new public management reform agenda that was pursued by the Australian government at the time.

Bunn and Gilchrist's (2013) study of the Swan River Colony provides a different perspective on public sector auditing. While most literature on auditing focuses on independence and professionalism and the distance of the auditor from the auditee, Bunn and Gilchrist (2013) document a situation of where only a few men held all the senior positions in the new Colony's administration. Rather than this leading to poor management in the colony, the lack of separation of duties resulted in effective financial management as values of honour and reputation ensured that the 'few good men' responsible for managing the colony remained 'good men'.

Social and other institutions

The apparatus of the state extends beyond the institutions of central and local government. The state has coercive powers for taxation, imprisonment and regulating societies, and may assume a moral responsibility to care for those unable to care for themselves, such as the sick and the poor. The state may also establish or control existing economic entities. Histories of the role and functioning of accounting in organisations associated with crime and punishment, welfare, and medical provision are an area of increasing scholarly interest in accounting history.

Walker (2004, 2008) provides an analysis of the use of accounting in the English system of poor relief before and after the formative Poor Law Amendment Act 1834. Using official reports into the reform of the Poor Laws and reviewing records of the relief provided, Walker focuses on how the 1834 Amendment Act was used as a device for the social control of the poor. The accounting system was used to monitor recipients of relief and deter claimants. The disclosure in public places of the names of those receiving relief allowed for checks on eligibility and contributed to the stigmatisation of the poor. Care (2011) examines the financial reporting and bookkeeping introduced by the Poor Law Amendment Act 1834. The statute was aimed at improving the efficiency and administration of poor relief, specifically through centrally directed administration. As mentioned above, at the time of these reforms there was considerable debate about the adoption of the mercantile system of double-entry bookkeeping. The Poor Law, and its associated Amended Order of 1836, however, saw 'an immediate and generally smooth switch to accruals-based' double-entry bookkeeping for the administration of poor relief by most unions (ibid.: 138). Adoption appears to be based on clerks mimicking the model records provided in the Order. These studies provide examples of how the same accounting can be interrogated through different lenses to provide alternative and not mutually exclusive insights.

Other areas of state involvement in areas of human misery included in the literature are the Irish famine and New Zealand's earthquakes. O'Regan's (2010) study of the responses to the Irish famine (1846–1847) focused on the relief measures and their associated 'vast accounting architecture and culture underpinned by several hundred imported and native accountants and bookkeepers' (ibid.: 416). Accounting tools were used to control and govern the Irish from a distance, namely from London. O'Regan shows how the accounting system introduced was imbued with notions of paternalism, racial stereotyping and the moral improvement of those impacted by the famine. It also applied pressure to the Anglo-Irish landlords to follow diktats from London. In similar vein to Walker (2004, 2008), the accounting system and accountability mechanisms for famine relief served more than administration. It allowed the government to exert greater control on both those suffering from the famine and the local landowners. The role of accounting as a form of social control in such contexts is apparent (Walker 2016).

Miley and Read (2013) and Vosslamber (2015) seek to understand the role of local government and central government in response to three earthquakes in New Zealand's history: those in Hawke's Bay, Murchison and Christchurch. These two articles came to different conclusions on the importance of the state versus private sector in responding to earthquakes based on the evidence they viewed. The role of the state and accounting in the management of natural disasters, both in the past and present, is an emerging theme in accounting research (Sargiacomo 2014).

An example of a study of public sector commercial activity is the study by Carmona et al. (1997). Their paper is also noteworthy because unlike most histories of accounting in governmental settings that focus on either ex ante or ex post reporting and auditing, this study concerns management accounting. Carmona et al. analysed the cost accounting system operating in the Spanish Royal Tobacco Factory in 1773. While the paper relates to a factory, it treats the site as a social as well as a productive arena. Following Foucault, the authors analyse cost accounting practices operating as part of a strong disciplinary regime founded on instructions issued for the management of the factory. The instructions covered the factory's physical situation, production patterns (including rates and mixes of the resources to be used), as well as monetary controls. The purposes of the control system within the state-owned factory are to minimise the theft of tobacco and maintain factory discipline. The regime of calculability facilitated the surveillance and discipline of individuals working in the factory. Carmona et al. provide an alternative to the management accounting literature that focuses on economic rationalist catalysts for the implementation of cost accounting systems. In this case of a state-run monopoly, the cost accounting system was shaped by the need for revenue collection and the construction of national identity: the factory being a 'symbol of the organisation and industrial prestige of eighteenth-century Spain' (ibid.: 443).

Accounting and health care

The history of accounting in state operated and/or funded hospitals has provided a fertile ground for accounting history research (Gebreiter and Jackson 2015). Robson (2003) outlined attempts at 'accountingisation' in UK hospitals. These commenced with uniform systems of annual accounts from 1893 to their proposed replacement by departmental costing and budgeting between 1948 and 1956 with the advent of the National Health Service. Using Porter's six elements of abstraction – individual, group, institution, conceptual, forces and universals – Robson identifies various forces that contributed to the systems introduced in 1893 and the rejection, in 1956, of changes proposed over the previous decade.

Gebreiter (2015) draws on Foucault and various medical discourses to examine how clinical medicine has been conceptualised during the post-war era in the UK National Health Service, and what that has meant for accounting. During this period cost accounting was only relevant to the administrative and hotel functions of hospitals. Its use within the clinical functions was rejected due to the perceived uniqueness of patients, disease and clinical practice, as well as the autonomy of the medical profession. Gebreiter (2015) shows that specific context is key when understanding the development of accounting in hospital settings. In this case, medical discourses were key as opposed to economic, political and institutional factors.

Again using Foucault, Ferry and Scarparo (2015) examine the use of performance measures in the UK National Health Service over the 13 years to 2010. These financial and operation performance measures were centrally imposed as part of the disciplining process deemed necessary to control the health sector and address a crisis facing the NHS. The paper concluded that, although the use of the performance measures extended the use of neo-liberal ideas in the health sector, they didn't solve the problems it faced.

Gebreiter (2016) also focused on the use of accounting tools in the British health sector during the 1980s and indicated that accounting reforms had a significant role in clinical practice. The notion of 'care pathways' resulted in standardised models of clinical practice being introduced as a quality tool. Although sold as a clinical device, care pathways represented an application of the logic that lay behind new public management. It was closely connected to accounting concepts of variance, costs and monitoring. Gebreiter argues that although there was not a direct link between accounting and medical work, there was an indirect link during the new public management reforms.

Jones and Mellett (2007) provide an expansive longitudinal study of British hospitals over the period 1800–2000. Drawing on a social forces model, the paper examines the relationship between accounting and institutional and organisational changes in hospitals over the two centuries concerned. The history of hospital organisation is described in terms of three principles: communitarian, etatist and market. The associated roles for accounting under each principle are discussed. Communitarian principles dominated during the early years studied. With most of the hospitals being independent and self-governing, accounting focused on stewardship and internal checks. The subsequent appearance of etatist principles and their association with government control through centralisation and bureaucracy were reflected in an accounting that emphasised hierarchical control and standardisation aimed at maintaining efficiency. In more recent times, market principles associated with competition and profit-making were in evidence. In this context, accounting was characterised by adherence to private sector models, external audits and providing information for decision-making. With the change from a dominant communitarian principle through etatist to market principles, both the form and role of accounting have altered. When communitarian principles prevailed, accounting assumed a supportive role; under etatism it had an informing decisions function; and, under the quasi market system, accounting not only supported and assisted but also became an essential requirement for the operation of markets. As with several of the authors discussed above, Jones and Mellett also note the importance of key personnel and outside agencies in achieving accounting change in hospitals.

Comparative studies

In this section some historical studies that have adopted a comparative approach are briefly discussed. Comparisons have been drawn in relation to specific accounting issues in the public and private sectors or in relation to the accounting practices deployed in different nations.

Hill (2000) provides an example of a comparison of management accounting practices in private, public and not-for-profit sectors. The study looks at the adoption of new costing systems in US hospitals between 1980 and 1990. While the research is more aligned to positive accounting research and quantitative history than narrative and archival-based history, it provides insights into similarities between sectors. Key factors discussed are changes to revenue reimbursement procedures, increases in competition and the organisational structure of the hospital. In determining if a new costing system was to be developed, changes to revenue reimbursement procedures and increases in competition were identified as important. Organisational factors, such as whether the entity was a government, not-for-profit or profit-based organisation, seemed to have little impact. The study found that government hospitals were less likely to introduce new costing systems than other categories of hospitals. This was explained as a result of government hospitals having less access to discretionary resources for investment in new accounting systems.

Edwards (1992) provided a comparison of financial reporting in non-regulated companies, public utility companies and municipal corporations in the UK between 1835 and 1933. Having reviewed a number of key aspects of financial reporting, Edwards concluded that innovation in accounting was not driven by one sector. Rather, different sectors were 'ahead' in applying new technology relevant to the particular issues they faced. Municipal corporations were early in their use of consolidated accounts, requirements for the standardisation of accounts, and the provision of greater detail and graphical presentation in financial reports. Companies were quicker to introduce double-entry bookkeeping, profit and loss accounts, accrual accounting and the balance sheet. Public utility companies first used the double account system with its separation of capital raised and spent and other balance sheet items. This technology was later transferred to municipal corporations. Edwards notes that the often-implied assumption of the superiority of the private sector in accounting innovation is not historically accurate.

Coronella et al. (2013) provide a comparison of accounting by five states in pre-unification Italy between 1815 and 1861. The comparison alerts us to a range of innovative accounting practices across the five sites. Coronella et al. link variation in innovations to regime change and the political structures and power relations in each of the states. However, many of the innovations introduced in four of the states were lost following unification when the Kingdom of Sardinia's accounting model was adopted for the new Italian state.

Accounting and state building

The search for continuities and discontinuities in the history of accounting for the state are likely to be most apparent during the creation of a new state, be that as a result of war, political mergers or splits, colonisation, or gaining independence from colonising powers. This section reviews historical studies that look at accounting at the start of modern states.

Baker and Rennie (2012a, 2013) examine the creation of the Dominion of Canada in 1867. At the time little attention was paid to the creation of an accounting system for the new Dominion, which resulted in the adoption of the system of one of the pre-confederation provinces. Using institutional theory, Baker and Rennie (2013) suggest that the chaos of confederation, including the lack of clarity around designing or adopting a new accounting regime, meant that using the disestablished Province of Canada's system provided stability to the new Dominion. This stability 'may well have helped facilitate the smooth transition to nationhood (ibid.: 46).

Gatti and Poli (2014) examine accounting for the state and accounting for religion in their discussion of the role of accounting in the rise of the Papal States. The accounting system established in the *Pro commissa* Bull of 15 August 1592 provided the technology that contributed to the absolutism of the Papal States. At the heart of the accounting technology was both ex ante and ex post control through reporting by each community to the central Congregation, primarily in the form of receipts and payments. Although based on a decentralised system of actions, control through reporting 'allowed the central government (through the Congregation) to extend, concentrate and centralise its power' (ibid.: 491).

Beyond the Anglo-American

Numerous review articles have highlighted the focus of accounting history on English speaking countries, and especially during the period 1850 and 1940 (Carmona and Zan 2002; Carmona 2004). The preceding sections of this chapter have included a number of papers that confirm this dominant focus but also suggestions of increasing attention to sites beyond it. This section reviews five further studies that indicate broadening focus and which fall outside the section headings used above. These studies enhance our understanding of the history of accounting and the state and can indicate areas of future research.

Changes in the Chinese economy and political spheres over the 30 years to 2008 have been substantial, and have included changes to the rules for accounting in the public sector. Xue and Zan (2012) describe this change as 'crossing the river by touching stones' or more incremental than linear (ibid.: 217). They identified four phases in public sector accounting over this period of change: i) restoration, when accounting practices from before the cultural revolution were restored, ii) revision, when only minor changes were made, with financial reports not including notions of surplus or loss, iii) innovation, which saw the introduction of double-entry bookkeeping, and iv) maintenance, when further but minor changes occurred.

Nistor et al. (2015) and Nistor and Deaconu (2016) provide historical accounts of change in Romanian public sector accounting. Nistor et al. (2015) discuss developments between 1831 and 2011, which they separate into seven phases. For each of these phases the importance of a number of environmental factors is assessed for their impact on public sector accounting. The cluster analysis shows the political system as having most impact on public sector accounting. Nistor and Deaconu (2016) specifically look at the post-communist period. Their paper describes the changing nature of public sector accounting with the introduction of accrual-based accounting systems and the adoption of international public sector accounting standards. A key factor in generating change was gaining international loans, a condition of which was ensuring that financial statements be prepared according to IPSAS.

Yayla (2011) adds to the literature using Foucault with an analysis of accounting changes in the Ottoman Empire in 1826. He shows that the accounting rules were intertwined with the state, facilitating central control over the vast distances of the Ottoman Empire, and thereby creating a compact disciplinary mechanism. Accounting, its calculations and its language were used to manage and control how the population responded to the central Ottoman government. In a similar vein Gomes et al. (2014) used Foucauldian analysis, alongside Snooks' theory of practical drift, to show how accounting was used in the Portuguese Empire to exercise control from a distance during the eighteenth century. Such control ensured that individuals were captured in the enforcement regimes of the dispersed empire.

Conclusion

A number of reviews of accounting history research have lamented the relative lack of attention devoted to accounting and the state (Anderson 2002; Walker 2005; Funnell 2007). Whereas public sector accounting in modern-day settings has been the focus of considerable research activity, its history has not attracted the same level of interest. There is scope for much more research into all areas of this field. Funnell (2007: 266) argues that the history of public sector accounting deserves the attention of researchers if for no other reason than to illuminate accounting's role in the accountability and oversight of the executive. Accounting is a tool in the protection of liberty. The accounting historian entering a state archive ventures into 'arsenals of democratic accountability and continuity' (Eastwood 1993: 36) and thus becomes a contributor to the process of holding the executive to account and protecting liberty.

The existence of state archives and the relative ease of access to them might encourage the greater use of primary source material for researching the intertwining of accounting and the state. Many of the studies discussed in this chapter represent examples of the value of re-entering the archive. In addition to further investigation of the subjects covered in the preceding sections there are also hitherto unexplored territories. Almost every issue covered elsewhere in this *Routledge Companion* can be researched from the perspective of the state.

The 'dearth of research' in public sector accounting referred to at the start of the twenty-first century (Carnegie and Potter 2000: 194) suggests that there are many areas open for further scholarship. However, three forms of accounting history remain particularly underrepresented in the current literature – longitudinal and comparative studies and investigations of accounting in social and economic institutions operated under the auspices of the state. Further, a great deal of the existing literature focuses on relatively short periods and single issues. While such studies are important, greater emphasis needs to be placed on the larger context. Rarely do debates in accounting merely concern narrow technical issues. Debates about accounting technologies are invariably conducted in relation to the economic, ideological and political (see Edwards et al. (2002) and Mann et al. (2016). Furthermore, these debates are seldom resolved in a particular period; they often resurface in later times and in different places (see Potts 1976, 1978, 1982; Colquhoun 2005). Longitudinal studies will provide a richer understanding of accounting and the state. Similarly, given that accounting change rarely takes place in the jurisdictional isolation of particular nation-states, the benefits of international comparative histories become obvious. The international spread of new public management is one area where international comparative studies would be fruitful (see Buhr 2012). Historical studies of accounting in socio-economic institutions are necessary when it is recalled that the modern state is not only about law making and tax raising but comprises a series of apparatuses that extend into numerous arenas.

Accounting research assists understandings of the coercive activities of the state and the manner in which the state may establish and maintain unequal power relations. States are replete with institutions that seek to manage these relationships. The recording and dissemination of accounting information by state officials provide insights into state processes and ideologies and the wider economic and social structures with which they engage.

With the passage of time more and more public archives and records relating to the new public management reform era are available to the research community. This research may take a variety of forms including those mentioned earlier; namely comparisons between public and other sectors, international comparative history and longitudinal studies of accounting in individual countries and individual entities. Furthermore, as the reforms were part of an international trend, supported by governments and organisations such as the International Monetary Fund, international historical comparisons offer scope for insights into their adoption, integration and subsequent acceptance across nations and cultures. Investigations of past accounting change, its successes and failures, may also contribute to future policy-making in public sector accounting, both social and technical.

Key works

Edwards et al. (2002) and Mann et al. (2016) identify the contest of ideologies which lay behind technical debates over the introduction of double-entry bookkeeping in British central government. Using different archival sources, they arrive at different conclusions, providing evidence of the value of revisiting extant historical research.

Funnell (2007) locates English state accounting within a framework of historical constitutional accountability.

Newberry and Pallot (2004) is an archival study on selected aspects of new public management reforms.

Walker (2004) provides a compelling insight into the social consequences of accounting in a field regulated by the state, while Care (2011) provides an analysis of the same historical situation from the perspective of the technical.

References

Anderson, M. (2002) An analysis of the first ten volumes of research in Accounting, Business & Financial History, *Accounting, Business & Financial History*, 12 (1): 1–24.

Baker, C.R. (2013) Administrative and accounting practices in the Byzantine Empire, *Accounting History*, 18 (2): 211–27.

Baker, R. and Rennie, M.D. (2012) Accounting for a nation's beginnings: challenges arising from the formation of the Dominion of Canada, *Accounting History*, 17 (3–4): 415–35.

Baker, R. and Rennie, M.D. (2013) An institutional perspective on the development of Canada's first public accounts, *Accounting History*, 18 (1): 31–50.

Boyd, E. (1968) Ancient systems of accounting, in R. Brown (ed.) *A History of Accounting and Accountants*, pp. 16–40 (London: Frank Cass & Co. Ltd).

Buhr, N. (2012) Accrual accounting by Anglo-American governments: motivations, developments, and some tensions over the last 30 years, *Accounting History*, 17 (3–4): 287–309.

Bunn, M. and Gilchrist, D.J. (2013) "A few good men": public sector audit in the Swan River Colony, 1828–1835, *Accounting History*, 18 (2): 193–209.

Care, V. (2011) The significance of a 'correct and uniform system of accounts' to the administration of the Poor Law Amendment Act, 1834, *Accounting History Review*, 21 (2): 121–42.

Carmona, S. (2004) Accounting history research and its diffusion in an international context, *Accounting History*, 9 (3): 7–23.

Carmona, S. and Ezzamel, M. (2007) Accounting and accountability in ancient civilizations: Mesopotamia and ancient Egypt, *Accounting, Auditing & Accountability Journal*, 20 (2): 177–209.

Carmona, S., Ezzamel, M. and Gutierrez, F. (1997) Control and cost accounting practices in the Spanish Royal Tobacco Factory, *Accounting Organizations and Society*, 22 (5): 411–66.

Carmona, S. and Zan, L. (2002) Mapping variety in the history of accounting and management practices, *European Accounting Review*, 11 (2): 291–304.

Carnegie, G.D. and Potter, B.N. (2000) Publishing patterns in specialist accounting history journals in the English Language 1996–1999, *Accounting Historians Journal*, 27 (2): 177–98.

Carpenter, V.L. and Feroz, E.H. (2001) Institutional theory and accounting rule choice: an analysis of four US state governments' decisions to adopt generally accepted accounting principles, *Accounting, Organizations and Society*, 26 (7/8): 565–96.

Christensen, M. (2002) Accrual accounting in the public sector: the case of the New South Wales government, *Accounting History*, 7 (2): 93–124.

Christensen, M. (2003) Without 'Reinventing the Wheel': business accounting applied to the public sector, *Australian Accounting Review*, 13 (2): 22–27.

Colquhoun, P. (2011) Intergenerational equity in municipal accounting: New Zealand in the early 20th century, *Accounting History Review*, 21 (2): 143–61.

Colquhoun, P. (2013) Political and organizational legitimacy of public sector auditing in New Zealand local government, *Accounting History*, 18 (4): 473–89.

Colquhoun, P.M. (2005) A history of New Zealand Municipal Accounting and Auditing 1976 to 1988, unpublished PhD thesis, University of Canterbury.

Coombs, H.M. and Edwards, J.R. (1993) The accountability of municipal corporations, *Abacus*, 29 (1): 27–51.

Coombs, H.M. and Edwards, J.R. (1995) The financial reporting practices of British municipal corporations 1835–1933: a study in accounting innovation, *Accounting and Business Research*, 25 (98): 93–105.

Coombs, H.M. and Edwards, J.R. (2004) The audit of municipal corporations – a quest for professional dominance, *Managerial Auditing Journal*, 19 (1): 68–83.

Coronella, S., Lombrano, A. and Zanin, L. (2013) State accounting innovations in pre-unification Italy, *Accounting History Review*, 23 (1): 1–21.

Davis, N. (2017) The annual reporting practices of an Australian Commonwealth Government department: an instance of deinstitutionalisation, *Accounting History*, 22 (4): 425–49.

Eastwood, T.M. (1993) Reflections on the development of archives in Canada and Australia, in S. McKenmmis and F. Upward (eds.) *Archival Documents: Providing Accountability through Recordkeeping*, pp. 27–39 (Melbourne: Ancora Press).

Edwards, J.R. (1992) Companies, corporations and accounting change 1835–1933: a comparative study, *Accounting and Business Research*, 23 (89): 59–73.

Edwards, J.R., Coombs, H.M. and Greener, H.T. (2002) British central government and 'the mercantile system of double entry' bookkeeping: a study of ideological conflict, *Accounting, Organizations and Society*, 27 (7): 637–58.

English, L. and Guthrie, J. (2000) Mandate, independence and funding: resolution of a protracted struggle between parliament and the executive over the powers of the Australian Auditor-General, *Australian Journal of Public Administration*, 59 (1): 98–114.

Ezzamel, M. (2002a) Accounting and redistribution the palace and mortuary cult in the Middle Kingdom, Ancient Egypt, *Accounting Historians Journal*, 29 (1): 61–103.

Ezzamel, M. (2002b) Accounting working for the state: tax assessment and collection during the New Kingdom, Ancient Egypt, *Accounting and Business Research*, 32 (1): 17–39.

Ferry, L. and Scarparo, S. (2015) An era of governance through performance management–New Labour's National Health Service from 1997 to 2010, *Accounting History Review*, 25 (3): 219–38.

Fleischman, R.K. and Marquette, R.P. (1986) The origins of public budgeting: municipal reformers during the Progressive Era, *Public Budgeting Finance*, 6 (1): 71–77.

Flesher, D.L. and Zarzeski, M. (2002) The roots of the operational (value for money) auditing in English-speaking nations, *Accounting and Business Research*, 32 (2): 93–104.

Funnell, W. (1994) Independence and the state auditor in Britain: a constitutional keystone or a case of reified imagery? *Abacus*, 30 (2): 175–95.

Funnell, W. (1997) Military influences on the evolution of public sector audit and accounting 1830–1880, *Accounting History*, 2 (2): 9–29.

Funnell, W. (1998) Executive coercion and state audit – a processual analysis of the responses of the Australian audit office to the dilemmas of efficiency auditing 1978–84, *Accounting, Auditing & Accountability Journal*, 11 (4): 436–58.

Funnell, W. (2004) Further evidence on the roots of public sector operational (value-for-money) auditing: a response to Flesher and Zarzeski, *Accounting and Business Research*, 34 (3): 215–22.

Funnell, W. (2007) The reason why: the English Constitution and the latent promise of liberty in the history of accounting, *Accounting, Business & Financial History*, 17 (2): 265–83.

Gatti, M. and Poli, S. (2014) Accounting and the Papal States: the influence of the Pro commissa Bull (1592) on the rise of an early modern state, *Accounting History*, 19 (4): 475–506.

Gebreiter, F. (2015) Hospital accounting and the history of health-care rationing, *Accounting History Review*, 25 (3): 183–99.

Gebreiter, F. (2016) "Comparing the incomparable": hospital costing and the art of medicine in post-war Britain, *British Accounting Review*, 48 (2): 257–68.

Gebreiter, F. and Jackson, W.J. (2015) Fertile ground: the history of accounting in hospitals, *Accounting History Review*, 25 (3): 177–82.

Goddard, A. (2005) Reform as regulation – accounting, governance and accountability in UK local government, *Journal of Accounting & Organisational Change*, 1 (1): 27–44.

Gomes, D., Carnegie, G.D. and Rodrigues, L.L. (2006) Accounting change in central government: the adoption of double entry bookkeeping at the Portuguese Royal Treasury (1761). *Paper presented at the 11th World Congress of Accounting Historians*, Nantes. July.

Gomes, D., Carnegie, G.D. and Rodrigues, L.L. (2014) Accounting as a technology of government in the Portuguese empire: the development, application and enforcement of accounting rules during the Pombaline era (1761–1777), *European Accounting Review*, 23 (1): 87–115.

Guthrie, J. and Parker, L.D. (1999) A quarter of a century of performance auditing in the Australian federal public sector: a malleable masque, *Abacus*, 35 (3): 302–32.

Hill, N.T. (2000) Adoption of costing systems in US hospitals: an event history analysis 1980–1990, *Accounting and Public Policy*, 19 (1): 41–71.

Humphrey, C., Guthrie, J., Jones, L.R. and Olson, O. (2005) The dynamics of public financial management change in an international context, in J. Guthrie, C. Humphrey, L.R. Jones and O. Olson (eds.) *International Public Financial Management Reforms: Progress, Contradictions and Challenges*, pp. 1–22 (Greenwich: Information Age Publishing).

Johnson, C. (ed.) (1983) *Dialogus De Scaccario. The Course of the Exchequer by Richard, Fitz Nigel* (Oxford: Clarendon Press).

Jones, M.J. (2010) Sources of power and infrastructural conditions in medieval governmental accounting, *Accounting, Organizations and Society*, 35 (1): 81–94.

Jones, M.J. and Mellett, H.J. (2007) Determinants of changes in accounting practices: accounting and the UK Health Service, *Critical Perspectives on Accounting*, 18 (1): 91–121.

Jones, R. (1985) Accounting in English local government: from the Middle Ages to c.1835, *Accounting and Business Research*, 15 (59): 197–210.

Jones, R.H. (1986) The financial control function of local government accounting, unpublished PhD thesis, Lancaster University.

Jones, R.H. (1992) *The History of the Financial Control Function of Local Government Accounting in the United Kingdom* (New York: Garland).

Jurado-Sanchez, J. (2002) Mechanisms for controlling expenditure in the Spanish royal household, c.1561–1808, *Accounting, Business & Financial History*, 12 (2): 157–85.

Kinnersley, R.L. (2016) The development of the totals column on the combined balance sheet for state and local government in the United States during the 20th century, *Accounting Historians Journal*, 43 (1): 35–58.

Lemarchand, Y. (1999) Introducing double-entry bookkeeping in public finance: a French experiment at the beginning of the eighteenth century, *Accounting, Business Financial History*, 9 (2): 225–54.

Mann, I., Funnell, W. and Jupe, R. (2016) The liberal contest for double-entry bookkeeping in British Government, *Accounting, Auditing & Accountability Journal*, 29 (5): 739–66.

Miley, F. and Read, A. (2013) After the quake: the complex dance of local government, national government and accounting, *Accounting History*, 18 (4): 447–71.

Miller, P. (1990) On the relationship between accounting and the state, *Accounting, Organizations and Society*, 15 (4): 315–38.

Newberry, S. and Pallot, J. (2004) Freedom or coercion? NPM incentives in New Zealand central government departments, *Management Accounting Research*, 15 (3): 247–66.

Nikitin, M. (2001) The birth of modern public sector accounting systems in France and Britain and the influence of Count Mollien, *Accounting History*, 6 (1): 75–101.

Nistor, C.S. and Deaconu, A. (2016) Public accounting history in post-communist Romania, *Economic research-Ekonomska Istraživanja*, 29 (1): 623–42.

Nistor, C.S., Deaconu, A. and Mare, C. (2015) Influence of environmental factors on the evolution of Romanian public accounting, *Journal of Business Economics and Management*, 16 (6): 1154–69.

O'Regan, P. (2010) 'A dense mass of petty accountability': accounting in the service of cultural imperialism during the Irish Famine, 1846–1847, *Accounting, Organizations and Society*, 35 (4): 416–30.

Patton, T.K. and Freeman, R.J. (2005) Government accounting standards come of age: highlights from the first 20 years, *Government Finance Review*, 21 (2): 16–20.

Potts, J.H. (1976) An analysis of the evolution of municipal accounting to 1935 with primary emphasis on developments in the United States, unpublished PhD thesis, University of Alabama.

Potts, J.H. (1978) The evolution of municipal accounting in the United States, 1900–1935, *Business History Review*, 52 (4): 518–36.

Potts, J.H. (1982) A brief history of property and depreciation accounting in municipal accounting, *Accounting Historians Journal*, 9 (1): 25–37.

Pridgen, A. and Flesher, D.L. (2013) Improving accounting and accountability in local governments: the case of the Tennessee Taxpayers Association, *Accounting History*, 18 (4): 507–28.

Radcliffe, V.S. (1998) Efficiency audit: an assembly of rationalities and programmes, *Accounting Organizations and Society*, 23 (4): 377–410.

Remis, J.S. (1982) An historical perspective on setting governmental accounting standards, *Governmental Finance*, 11 (2): 3–9.

Richardson, H.G. (1928a) Richard fitz Neal and the Dialogus de Scaccario, *The English Historical Review*, 43 (170): 161–71.

Richardson, H.G. (1928b) Richard fitz Neal and the Dialogus de Scaccario (continued), *The English Historical Review*, 43 (171): 321–40.

Robson, N. (2003) From voluntary to state control and the emergence of the department in UK hospital accounting, *Accounting, Business & Financial History*, 13 (2): 99–123.

Roybark, H.M., Coffman, E.N. and Previts, G.J. (2012a) The first quarter century of the GASB (1984–2009): A perspective on standard setting (Part One), *Abacus*, 48 (1): 1–30.

Roybark, H.M., Coffman, E.N. and Previts, G.J. (2012b) The first quarter century of the GASB (1984–2009): A perspective on standard setting (Part Two), *Abacus*, 48 (2): 147–98.

Ryan, C. (1998) The introduction of accrual reporting policy in the Australian public sector: an agenda setting explanation, *Accounting, Auditing & Accountability Journal*, 11 (5): 518–39.

Sargiacomo, M. (2014) Accounting for natural disasters and humanitarian interventions, *Critical Perspectives on Accounting*, 25 (7): 576–78.

Scott, J.E.M., McKinnon, J.L. and Harrison, G.L. (2003) Cash to accrual and cash to accrual: a case study of financial reporting in two NSW hospitals 1857 to post 1975, *Accounting, Auditing & Accountability Journal*, 16 (1): 104–40.

Vosslamber, R. (2015) After the earth moved: accounting and accountability for earthquake relief and recovery in early twentieth-century New Zealand, *Accounting History*, 20 (4): 518–35.

Walker, S.P. (2004) Expense, social and moral control: accounting and the administration of the old Poor Law in England and Wales, *Journal of Accounting and Public Policy*, 23 (2): 85–127.

Walker, S.P. (2005) Accounting in history, *Accounting Historians Journal*, 32 (2): 223–59.

Walker, S.P. (2008) Accounting, paper shadows and the stigmatised poor, *Accounting, Organizations and Society*, 33 (4/5): 453–87.

Walker, S.P. (2016) Revisiting the roles of accounting in society, *Accounting, Organizations and Society*, 49 (2): 41–50.

Watkins, A.L. and Arrington, C.E. (2007) Accounting, new public management and American politics: theoretical insights into the National Performance Review, *Critical Perspectives on Accounting*, 18 (1): 33–58.

Xue, Q. and Zan, L. (2012) Opening the door to accounting change. Transformations in Chinese public sector accounting, *Accounting History Review*, 22 (3): 269–99.

Yamamoto, K. and Noguchi, M. (2013) Different scenarios for accounting reform in non-Anglophone contexts: the case of Japanese local governments since the 1990s, *Accounting History*, 18 (4): 529–49.

Yayla, H.E. (2011) Operating regimes of the government: accounting and accountability changes in the Sultan Süleyman Waqf of the Ottoman Empire (The 1826 Experience), *Accounting History*, 16 (1): 5–34.

28

MILITARY

Warwick Funnell and Stephen P. Walker

Overview

The study of the military and their accounting has reflected the essential political nature and purpose of armies. Accounting historians have had a particular interest in the political protections provided by accounting in Britain after the constitutionally fraught seventeenth century when the supremacy of Parliament had been compromised by military intervention. Until the twentieth century, accounting for military expenditures was determined almost entirely by the need to ensure that Parliament had effective control over how much the military spent; it was not intended to enhance military performance.

Accounting historians have suggested that the circumstance of war and military culture have played a role in the evolution of cost accounting. Indeed war, but especially World War I, has been a significant impetus to the evolution and professionalisation of cost accounting in the early twentieth century. Particularly influential was the greater intervention required of government during the war in the affairs of business through the regulation of production and prices.

Military themes in accounting history

There is a persistent contradiction in the accounting history literature – although war and the methods of prosecuting war have dominated the history of human kind, and the financial needs of armies and navies until well into the twentieth century dwarfed all other government spending, until very recently this resonating historical significance has not found a proportionate response in the study of military accounting (Funnell and Chwastiak 2010). Among the limited, but expanding volume of research, Britain and the USA during the nineteenth and twentieth centuries have figured most prominently. While the recent commemoration of the centenary of World War I was accompanied by increased interest in the role of accounting in total war (Gallhofer and Haslam 1991; Funnell and Walker 2014), it remains the case that military accounting during major twentieth-century conflicts has yet to be accorded the recognition in accounting history that the importance of these conflagrations warrants. In the USA there has been a recent increase in studies of accounting and finance in the Civil War and more recent conflicts in Vietnam and Iraq.

Beyond Anglophone countries there are increasing excursions into European and Asian sites. However, there remains considerable scope for further extensions of the spatial and temporal scope of research in this field. Indeed, there remain 'many conflicts in modern and pre-modern times which have yet to attract the attention of accounting historians' (Funnell and Walker 2014).

Given that Britain has figured most prominently in military accounting research, reference in this chapter will be primarily to Britain and its army. For the most part, discussion will be concerned with the control of armies and the act of war and not the industries that supply armies.

Governments, whatever their form, have the ominous ability to dominate the lives of individuals through the forces of violence that they inevitably control and, often, rely upon to maintain power. Ultimately, the liberty of individuals requires that governments be held accountable for the exercise of this power and that they have under their authority sufficient controls to ensure that the military is never in a position to overcome the state. Howard (1957: 11) has suggested that 'no community of any degree of complexity has succeeded in existing without force, and the manner in which that force is organized and controlled will largely determine the political structure of the state'.

Recognising the pervasive, malevolent presence of military force throughout history and the consequences of the exercise of this force, extant accounting histories with the military as their subject are preoccupied with the political motives and alarms which have determined military accounting practices and the consequences of these for military performance (see Funnell 1988, 1997). Thus, the main military interest by accounting historians has been the nexus between the military and the British constitution, most importantly from the seventeenth century when the consistent and abiding concern of governments was the strengthening of protections against threats from the military to the supremacy of Parliament and to the liberty of individuals. These histories have established that accounting has been an essential means of providing protection to the state from the threat of military power. Accordingly, accounting by and for the military until well into the twentieth century was fundamentally a means of ensuring control of the military through financial accountability to their civilian masters in Parliament. However, a number of studies have shown how this control of military finances by civilians for the sake of political security had prejudiced, for centuries, the performance of the soldiers whose activities were pointedly hobbled by the institutions and practices of financial control. These controls were exercised first and foremost in the interests of civilians, not to promote military efficiency (Funnell 1990, 2005).

Ever since the constitutional settlements of the late seventeenth century provided essential guarantees of Parliament's ascendancy and the military's subservience to Parliament, accounting practised by the British military (and on behalf of the military by civilians at the War Office and the Treasury) was never predicated on promoting the interests and wellbeing of the military by enhancing the military's ability to prosecute wars. Rather, this would have been regarded as a dangerous constitutional innovation. Consequently, until well into the twentieth century the British military had little or no influence over its finances and accounting practices. Thus, the dispensing, management and accounting for military finances would be the sacred responsibility of civilians. This largely unquestioned constitutional identity between civilians, accounting and liberty was, however, unable to withstand unscathed the pressures for the reform of military finances and administration prompted by the failures of the South African War (1899–1902) and the deluge of World War I.

Although a constitutional theme in military accounting is given particular prominence in this chapter, also recognised is a widening interest that goes beyond the constitutional imperative. Researchers interested in the evolution of business accounting have also sought to establish the origins and uses of accounting techniques that were to become the precursors of modern management accounting. Particularly prominent have been studies that demonstrate the influence of a military culture on the evolution of management accounting and studies that have examined the impetus provided by World War I for the spread and acceptance of cost accounting by the private sector, which, as a by-product, also advanced the professionalisation of cost accounting. Thus, scholars seeking to map the evolution of cost and management accounting have exposed a military legacy with studies of the British Ministry of Munitions (which had been created during World War I to coordinate the production of the implements of war (Loft 1986; Marriner 1994)) and, in the USA, cost accounting practices which are said to have developed at the Springfield Armory in the mid-nineteenth century by graduates of the West Point military academy (Hoskin and Macve 1988, 1994, 2000; Tyson 1990, 1993). While these studies are purported to have detected a military legacy in the history of cost accounting, absent from these studies is evidence of the adoption of business accounting practices, in particular cost accounting, by the military.

The penultimate section of the chapter reveals the increasing connectedness between accounting histories of the military and armed conflict and numerous other themes explored in the chapters of this volume. As the research agenda becomes more expansive interfaces are being revealed between military accounting and topics such as auditing, fraud and scandals, the profession, gender and culture.

In the next section the concern is the nexus between the military, accounting and the British constitution, which has proved so attractive to accounting historians. Later in the chapter the political servitude of military accounting across the centuries is shown to have had significant adverse consequences for the military's preparedness for war and for its performance in the field, especially throughout the nineteenth century, leading, finally, to limited reforms in the early twentieth century after the South African War.

The military and the state

The constitutional force and the power of the purse

The proven uncertain allegiances of military forces throughout history and the terrible consequences of the use of military force to oppress fellow citizens requires that the relationship between the military and the citizenry is something with which all societies have to deal effectively. Societies, suggests Howard (1957: 12):

> [a]re orderly and peaceable only in so far as they have solved this double problem, of the subordination of the military force to the political government, and of control of a government in possession of such a force by legal restraint and the popular will.

Thus, in the case of the English Government and its people after the constitutional crises in the seventeenth century the question confronting them, notes Howard (1957: 12), was 'how can the armed forces necessary for external security be prevented from crushing internal liberties'. The British Parliament determined that this problem was best solved by adhering to strict limits on the size of the army and by ensuring that the state always had under its authority sufficient controls to preclude the possibility that the military was in a position to overcome the state.

The unavoidable intimidating presence of an army and its interventions in matters of state in the seventeenth century ensured that the British Parliament was determined to keep the army small, unprepared if necessary for war and kept in its place. The army, as the object of suspicion and apprehension, would be kept starved of funds. Professional armies even at the beginning of the nineteenth century were believed to constitute an abiding political danger, to be inherently inefficient and mostly unnecessary (Howard 1957: 15). This enduring antipathy towards the army, especially in times of peace, allowed the House of Commons after the seventeenth century to 'escape from their constitutional dilemmas by denying to the Crown the powers and the funds necessary to maintain a really effective army' (Howard 1957: 13–14).

Although control over the number of soldiers provided some measure of protection, the prominent role it played during civil war (from 1642) and revolution (in 1688) demonstrated that this was neither a complete nor a certain protection in the absence of other controls. These controls included legitimate political authority, as established through historical understandings and constitutional formulations, and the controls that were auxiliary to or emanated from the political controls. Of the latter, the most important was the sole and supreme authority of the state in matters of finance related to the military and the accounting processes upon which these powers depended for their efficacy. The defenders of Parliament were determined to implement mechanisms to ensure that military spending would only occur in the future with the approval of Parliament and would be administered entirely by civilians (Funnell 1988).

The authority of Parliament in all matters of military finance subsequent to the revolutionary settlement in 1689 effectively meant that only Parliament could raise an army. The inglorious role of the army in perpetuating Cromwell's dictatorship (1653–8) at the expense of Parliament was not to be readily forgotten. The Mutiny Act reinforced the constitutional protections of annual appropriations by stipulating that each year the Crown was required to reaffirm its allegiance to the principle of parliamentary control of the army as enunciated in the Bill of Rights (1689 1 William and Mary c. 5 and 6, S.R.55). Soon after leaving office as Chancellor of the Exchequer in 1886 Lord Randolph Churchill confirmed that 'the control of Parliament, the interference of Parliament, the jealousy of Parliament for its rights and privileges, these are the arguments in favour of an adherence to the main lines of our present system of naval and military administration' (Royal Commission into the Civil and Professional Administration of the Navy and Military Departments, 1890: 15).

Similar concerns to those expressed in Britain were present across the Atlantic nearly 200 years later when accounting changes were introduced in the US military by Robert McNamara as Secretary of Defense (1961–1968) during the Vietnam War. Chwastiak (1999, 2001, 2006) has shown that accounting's ability to mediate the relationship between the military and its civilian political masters continued to be enduring and fundamental to the control of military forces in democratic states. In one especially provocative paper, Chwastiak (2001) argued that accounting was used by McNamara and the Department of Defense to shift the balance of power in military affairs from the more technically knowledgeable, but recklessly spendthrift, military to the financially powerful and financially literate civilians in the Department of Defense. This was achieved by McNamara by introducing the technique of Planning, Programming and Budgeting (PPB) in order to:

> [r]edefine the normative and cognitive facets of the defense political process in such a way that military expertise (something that McNamara lacked) was discredited while quantitative rationality (a trait that McNamara excelled at) was elevated to the status of authority and legitimacy.
>
> *(Chwastiak 2001: 501)*

As a result of McNamara's determination to introduce into the US military the financial disciplines and accountabilities common in business he was able to supplant military control with his own authority in defence acquisition. When McNamara was appointed Secretary of Defense at the height of the Cold War there were few limits on military spending and, in a dangerous, nuclear-armed world, even less resolve by governments and the military to rein in spending. According to Chwastiak (2001: 507), the introduction of PPB required that rationality, manifesting itself in cost-benefit analysis, be given pre-eminence over military expertise and experience, with the result that control over the military became increasingly centralised in McNamara and the Department of Defense. After the introduction of PPB the military was forced to argue their case for increased spending on McNamara's terms and in his language. In the process PPB and its discourse of rationality and cost-benefit came to dominate defence decision-making.

War was now conceptualised as a problem of resource management amenable to the discipline of accounting under civilian control. Only those aspects of the war that could be quantified according to the procedures of PPB would be accorded visibility. The effect was that the quantification of war required by PPB transformed political debate into an objective discourse where numbers were the determinant of decisions and not people or their welfare (for example, the number of the enemy killed and the resources required to achieve this result) (Chwastiak 2006: 32). Truth was now equated with that which could be counted, thereby precluding a 'moral vocabulary' for war. PPB allowed nuclear war to be 'normalised' and the achievement of victory in Vietnam to be conceived solely in terms of prosecuting the war in an economically rational manner, thereby transforming it into a series of problems framed in such a manner as to be amenable to solution by the rational instrumentality of accounting (Chwastiak 2006: 40, 43). Those who managed the war in the Department of Defense 'believed they could increase the productivity of the troops by using techniques derived from the managerial control systems of corporations, such as incentives, standards, performance evaluations, appraisals of efficiency and monitoring' (Chwastiak 2006: 43).

While McNamara's attitude towards the military reflected his faith in the salvation afforded by rational management practices, of which accounting stands supreme, it also recognised the historical antipathy since the seventeenth century between civilians suspicious of the military's spending habits and its uncertain political allegiances which had the potential to threaten the liberty of individuals.

The costly reassurances of accounting

From the eighteenth century the civilians who controlled British military finances worked in a multitude of pettifogging offices at the War Office from which emanated a plethora of regulations to cover every conceivable situation including trivial amounts of spending by the military. The result, it was widely agreed, was a system of administrative control that served only to prejudice the military's ability to prepare itself for war and to prosecute war in an efficient and, most importantly, victorious manner, much to the ongoing frustration and humiliation of the military (Wright 1956: 464). An enduring tension arose during the seventeenth century between military efficiency and control of the military to ensure political security, with Britain's naval superiority allowing the former always to be sacrificed. Even into the twentieth century the War Office (Reconstitution) Committee (hereafter the Esher Committee) (1904: 131) complained that the army was 'tied and bound in the coils of excessively complex and minute regulations drawn up without regard to the essential requirements of modern war'.

From the late seventeenth century the sole object of accounting for British military expenditures was to check that departmental financial procedures had been followed, that all expenditures were correctly authorised and that total spending had not exceeded the total amount appropriated by Parliament and issued by the Exchequer. At the end of the nineteenth century, the apparent indifference of successive parliaments to the benefits of an accounting system that would provide information to enhance the management of military operations still betrayed a lingering antipathy to the military. Most importantly, this ensured that Parliament was prepared to forego the uncertain, uncorroborated benefits of alternative accounting systems used by business in the pursuit of efficient operations and thereby retain the proven constitutional protections of an accounting system determined by the process and conventions of appropriation.

Regardless of the extent of the financial burden placed by the army on the nation, until the twentieth century there was only a spasmodic appreciation by British governments of the potential for accounting practices used in the management of large businesses to enhance military operations in the field. Thus, the long-standing constitutional purpose of military accounting quarantined the army from accounting developments in the business world. This calculated indifference irrevocably altered as a consequence of the serious deficiencies in military preparations and performance in battle that were exposed during the Crimean War (1854–1856) and the South African War (1899–1902) (Funnell 2005).

Accounting for military performance

Not unlike business, the provision of everything necessary for the combatant to live and fight, upon which success in battle hinges, is ultimately a matter of money and the way in which it is managed (see *Edinburgh Review*, Vol. CXXXIII, January to April 1871: 233). Financial arrangements and controls exercised over military spending assume a crucial role in military performance. As a critical component in the good management of the financial resources upon which the very existence of the military depended, any deficiencies in accounting had the ability to magnify other weaknesses (Funnell 2006).

Recognising the constitutional intent of accounting for military expenditures, developments in military accounting until the twentieth century consistently focused on preserving narrow fiduciary purposes, which thereby denied a wider management role to military accounting. Befitting an accounting and audit regime which was preoccupied with constitutional protections, the concern was with the 'subjects' of expenditure, that is broad types of expenditure, such as salaries, munitions and transport, and not with what was achieved with this expenditure. As a consequence, with accounts and estimates based on subjects of expenditure it was not possible to ascertain the total cost of the various aspects of military spending. Not surprisingly, army officials responsible for military accounting and civilians at the War Office who controlled military finances regarded army accounts as 'valueless' for the purpose of financial control (as understood by businesses) and incapable of ensuring an efficient and economic army administration (Grimwood 1919). However, it proved to be politically difficult to supplant the constitutional equivalence that had been created between an inefficient army and political safety: an inefficient, unprepared army was no threat.

From the latter decades of the nineteenth century the demands of modern war on military forces, but especially on the preparedness necessary to engage enemies which now possessed the capabilities to move men and arms much more quickly and to use the vast lethal power of new armaments to deliver potentially decisive blows in the early, critical phases of war, made previous understandings which had governed the affairs of military administration seem more untenable. Thus, all aspects of military administration, in particular the fundamental premises upon which it was grounded and from which its structures and practices were derived, were increasingly questioned during the second half of the nineteenth century. Prompted by the criticisms of military administrators in the Crimean War, accounting was increasingly viewed by more enlightened military administrators in the War Office less as a constitutional protection and more as a management tool to ensure the most efficient and effective use of resources.

Sir Charles Harris, widely recognised as the foremost expert in military finances in the decades that spanned the beginning of the twentieth century, confessed that the army had no idea of the use of accounts for management purposes (Harris 1911: 64). Leo Amery (1902, Vol. 2: 41), who, as a *Times* correspondent, had witnessed the humiliation of the British Army in the South African War, referred to the whole system of parliamentary financial control as anachronistic, consisting of 'cumbrous (accounting) safeguards'. Indeed, the inability of army administrators to control their own finances in peace prevented them from assuming financial responsibility in war, thereby suppressing any initiative, the extravagant consequences of which were entirely predictable in war. More seriously, Harris believed that the army's accounting system would continue to subvert attempts to give it greater autonomy from civilian financial control and, crucially, jeopardise the certainty of victory in modern wars (Select Committee on National Expenditure 1918, Report: 391). His long association with military finances had convinced him that reliable accounting systems could become a matter of life and death in war through their role in allocating scarce resources. Long after the management failings of the British Army had been revealed in the South African War, the Lawrence Committee in 1924 (Committee of Administration of, and Accounting for, Army Expenditure, Report: para. 5) belatedly warned that without 'a proper system of accounting it is impossible to obtain the best and most economical administration results', upon which victory would depend.

These silences in army accounts were entirely consistent with the very narrow range of visibilities permitted by the cash-based appropriation accounting designed to serve constitutional, not management, purposes (Loft 1986: 140). Harris, who expressed his views forcefully before and after World War I, wanted to see cost accounts become the main means of ensuring efficient and effective military administration, while at the same time meeting the needs of parliamentary control (Select Committee on National Expenditure 1918, Minutes of Evidence, Questions 220 and 248: 334–6). If economy of operation were to be made the concern of individuals in the army, then accounts would have to identify the cost of operations under each individual's control. These accounts would enable:

> [r]esponsibility to be delegated to those subordinates who know the details and who alone can adjust them to actual requirements. By means of the account you can allow a free hand and judge by results. The delegation of power which … accounting makes possible develops those invaluable human qualities of enterprise and resource.
>
> *(Sir John Keane quoted in Grimwood 1919: 158)*

Cost accounts would promote military efficiency and also reassure the nation, from which the army gained its financial sustenance, that its taxes were not being needlessly squandered. Unfortunately, irrespective of the arguments advanced in favour of the replacement of existing systems of accounting and augmenting the purposes that they served, the constitutional imperative long entrenched in military accounting proved a formidable barrier to reform. Until after World War I, Parliament remained unable to free itself from the consequences of much earlier constitutional alarms and to broaden the aims of public sector audit and accounting to encompass improved management practices.

According to the Treasury (see comments by Sir Charles Harris, Public Accounts Committee 1924–1925, Question 6708), cost accounting could not hope to provide the level of constitutional assurance provided by existing accounting systems. In 1924 the Secretary of State for War, Sir Herbert Creedy, also expressed his concern that to move to a new system of cost accounting in preference to existing systems of accounting predicated on categories of appropriation approvals would require the reorganisation of all levels of army administration, from the War Office down, which were presently organised on a 'subject basis' (Public Accounts Committee 1924–1925, Minutes of Evidence: Questions 6839, 6884, 6887). This would not only be prohibitively costly and highly uncertain in its benefits but certain to dilute the ability of Parliament to control military spending. Doubts were also expressed about whether, in the heat of battle, matters of economy and efficiency would be uppermost in the minds of military leaders for, above all else, victory was the expectation, irrespective of financial cost. Others, however, believed that military success depended upon financially literate officers in the field who were attuned to the advantages of economy. The financial ignorance which the system of constitutionally constrained financial administration forced upon army administrators, army commanders and army personnel responsible for supplying the army with its material needs, became only too obvious during the ferment of war, as did the need for reform (Funnell 2005).

Accounting reform and the stimulus of war

Nineteenth-century wars and accounting reform

The disruptions of war can incite the reform of governmental accounting. For example, Funnell (2008: 8) has shown how the political and economic crisis incited by the calamitous American War of Independence (1776–1783) revealed the defects of government accounting in Britain and engendered changes that laid the foundations for public sector audit reforms in the nineteenth century.

In Britain war had its greatest impact on the evolution of military accounting. Most important in convincing governments of the need for accounting reform were the Crimean War, the South African War and World War I. The Crimean and South African Wars have attracted the most concerted interest of accounting historians. Although World War I has figured prominently in several seminal accounting history papers, most notably those by Loft (1986), Fleischman and Tyson (2000) and Marriner (1994), and is attracting increasing attention (Funnell and Walker 2014), few studies have examined accounting as practised by the military in the field.

War mercilessly exposed deficiencies in military preparedness and the ability of military administrators to prosecute war decisively and efficiently. Shortcomings in preparation, leadership or management of the war effort by civilians and the military very quickly became obvious in the face of better prepared, and better led, foes. Consequently, it was usual in nineteenth-century Britain that after each military failure there was 'an outcry in Parliament and the press and distress at court; new ministers are drafted in, and commissions of inquiry set up. The public interest wanes and the whole cycle begins again' (Hanham 1969: 356). The Esher Committee (1904 Part I, page 8) reported with dismay that investigations of army administration had been, unfortunately, so numerous and 'great changes have been so frequent … (that) stability of administration has never been attained'. Most influential in the substantive reorganisation of the administration of the army in the nineteenth century were the Cardwell Reforms of 1868–74, precipitated by the administrative failings of the Crimean War (Funnell 1990).

The seriousness of the situation and public anger at the government's incompetence during the Crimean War forced the government to appoint a commission of inquiry while the conflict was still in progress. Of particular interest to the controversial McNeil-Tulloch Royal Commission was the performance of the Treasury-controlled commissariat, which supplied the army with food, clothing and other material needs. Among their duties the Commissioners were required to examine the effect on the wellbeing of the army of the accounting system required of the commissariat. According to the letters patent issued in 1855 the McNeil-Tulloch Royal Commission (First Report 1856: 3) was charged with examining 'the mode of accounting, and if the system be in your opinion unnecessarily complicated for a period of actual warfare, you will suggest such means of simplification as may occur to you'. The Commission soon found that all accounting practice in the commissariat was subordinated to parliamentary needs and handicapped the army's ability to conduct war successfully.

The Commissioners discovered that an immense number of financial and store regulations governed every aspect of the commissariat's work, requiring pettifogging attention to the documentation required to complete accounts at the expense of other concerns of more relevance to the performance and wellbeing of the army. Financial and accounting regulations were meant solely to be the servants of the Treasury as the agent of parliament. The accounting procedures drilled into the men responsible for supplies encouraged unthinking application of rigid regulations designed to ensure control over the minutest matters connected with stores and cash. Given the accountability requirements of Parliament the commissariat perceived the purpose of accounting records in terms of surveillance and accountability rather than the means to facilitate military victory. Indeed, as previously established, military accounts were never intended to ensure the efficient management of military campaigns. Further, the evaluation of the performance of commissariat officers did not consider anything outside that which could be disclosed in reports stipulated by Treasury regulations.

Unfortunately, despite the numerous administrative reforms enacted in the army after the Crimean War, the effect was piecemeal and deceptive, providing apparent assurances that the more blatant weaknesses had been addressed. Not until the South African War (1899–1902) were the fundamental causes of military administrative problems addressed, namely national neglect born out of suspicion and selfish parsimony and the military's managerial incompetence, the certain outcome of keeping the military financially ignorant and dependent upon civilians for sustenance. So important were the administrative reforms arising from the army's experiences in the South African War that it is generally regarded by military historians as a watershed in military administration and the reason why the British Army was so well prepared at the outbreak of World War I (Watt 1988: 156). Not until after the South African War was the British Government prepared to consider, through the reforms of Richard Haldane as Secretary of State for War, the organic changes urged for half a century by the army and its supporters which were required to ensure that the army would be able to manage its own finances (Funnell 2005, 2006).

Financial and accounting arrangements at the time of the South African War offered no facility for military views to be accorded any prominence in matters of finance, thereby compounding the isolation of the military from control of its finances. This was subsequently revealed to be a potent source of military failures. According to the War Stores Commission (Royal Commission 1906, Appendix 50: 336–9), in a scathing judgement which proved decisive for attempts to reform military accounting, the shortcomings of the Accountant-General's Department at the War Office had jeopardised the prospect of a decisive victory, contributed unnecessarily to the pressures under which the generals operated and to the 'unreasonable' cost of the war. The Esher Committee (1904: 139) was also scathing about the army's financial preparedness and its accounting systems. In particular, the Committee criticised Treasury regulations for being too prone to interfere in the military actions of officers commanding troops in the field. The intrusions from London were so overbearing that they were deemed 'intolerable, and they *fully* account for the administrative inefficiency of the War Office' (Esher Committee 1904: 139, *emphasis added*). 'The whole army', lamented Amery (1902: 141):

> [s]pent the greater part of its existence in checking its accounts … (E)very item of daily accounts was checked and rechecked and copied out in duplicate and triplicate … *It was accountancy run mad.* The object of it all was to prevent defalcations. The object was obtained but at a ruinous cost.
>
> (emphasis added, *see also the War Office Cost Accounting Committee 1918: 2)*

According to the Esher Committee (1904: 137) the War Office's financial system was:

> [b]ased upon the assumption that all military officers are necessarily spendthrifts and that their actions must be controlled in gross and in detail by civilians … This theory is largely responsible for the unreadiness for war which has been exhibited, as well as for reckless and wasteful expenditure … The department of the Accountant-General has become a huge and costly machine which is supposed to control expenditure by the aid of involved regulations which serve to aggrandize its power over the military branches.

Army accounting systems in South Africa could not cope with the turmoil and unpredictability of war, resulting in accounting information which was so incomplete as to be unreliable for decision-making purposes. Amery (1909: 461–2) described accounting in the field 'resolving itself into utter chaos … ludicrous … (and) hopelessly inadequate in war'. Yet it was not to be unexpected, warned the Esher Committee (1904: 138), that a financial system in which officers in peace were not given any financial responsibility would be anything other than 'futile in peace … (and) ruinous in war'.

The results of the South African War also sharpened awareness that in a world of recurring international political unease, a pronounced feature of the late 1880s and the 1890s, the financial demands of the army could probably be checked only temporarily. While the money spent on the army in peace seemed to be an annoying and fruitless drain on national finances which had to be closely monitored, during the urgency of war the army could hold the country to financial ransom knowing that demands for money couched in anxiety for the nation's safety would prove an irresistible lever on the nation's purse.

Thus, no matter what lip service the army paid to parliament's control of military finance in peacetime, the perpetuation of a financially unsophisticated army ruled by minute accounting requirements superintended by civilians was a case of being 'penny wise and pounds foolish'. The extravagant expenditure committed by Britain through its army to even a small war could soon outweigh any short-sighted peacetime savings procured through a policy which propagated financial ignorance among soldiers and encouraged their unpreparedness by restricting access to finance.

Accounting for the business of war

The South African War had made it very clear that it was essential for a modern army to have the financial skills and the freedom to manage its affairs. It was also very obvious that it was from the management practices and principles of business enterprises that military administrators and officers should seek the means of their financial salvation. Successful armies in the twentieth century would have to be run on similar principles to business enterprises. Sir Charles Harris was convinced that modern commercial accounting systems offered the best means to military success by promoting economy and efficiency in military spending, something not possible by using the plethora of regulations emanating from the War Office governing every procedure for the sake of procedure, and relying upon outmoded constitutional administrative niceties (Harris 1911). Success in modern war demanded that accounting could no longer be valued solely as a constitutional protection but as a tool for the efficient management of military forces. Accordingly, when, as a consequence of wartime failings at the turn of the twentieth century, the military again began to reconsider its management and accounting practices, any innovations to promote efficiency in the field of battle were entirely reliant upon innovations in the private sector, especially its use of cost accounting.

After the South African War the army was increasingly conceived in terms of the language and principles of business: efficient management of resources and the equivalence of military success to a profitable business (Funnell 2005). War had become a 'commercial enterprise' that required the expertise of the 'soldier businessman' (Mackinder 1907: 5). Army administration needed 'to be as nearly as possible on all fours with the business arrangements which are understood in civil life' (Secretary of State for War Richard Haldane quoted in Watt 1988: 1580). If the army's administrative departments were to be operated in the best interests of military efficiency they must be led by those who were trained in business and had the values of businessmen (Young 1906: 1284). Economy of operation, as measured by the amount of money spent, and efficiency, as measured by the achievement of military objectives for the least practical financial cost, were only compatible and achievable aims with the support of a financially experienced and sophisticated military.

Early tentative steps towards the transformation of military accounting in the image of business after the South African War admitted the possibility that cost accounting practised in the private sector might serve similar purposes in the military, most importantly to allow the military to cost its work and to manage these costs. However, despite much support for reform within and outside Parliament in the first decade of the twentieth century, attempts at the systemic reform of military accounting through the introduction of cost accounting would have to wait until after World War I. Until then military accounting, especially in the field of battle, remained largely immune to accounting developments in the private sector. When compared to the accounts of even small businesses, the army's accounts were widely regarded by experienced administrators as nothing but rudimentary and mechanical, despite the acknowledged complexity of British Army administration.

The first significant attempt to inculcate business methods and principles in military officers, which was initiated after the South African War, allowed selected officers from the supply and administrative branches of the army to attend classes in business at the London School of Economics (LSE). The course known as the Army Class was run by the renowned and much published accountant Lawrence Dicksee between 1907 and 1932, with interruptions during and after World War I (LSE 1906–7; Funnell 2006). Haldane, Secretary of State for War, regarded the Army Class at the LSE as the means of getting the army on 'a sound business footing' (Haldane quoted in Watt 1988: 159). At the opening ceremony of the new class in January 1907 the head of the LSE, Halford Mackinder (1907: 5, 7, 10), emphasised the importance of understanding the ways of 'civilian business and … working the people according to their habits … We wish to obtain for you the experience of practical business men'. At the same time that the Army Class was recommenced after World War I, the army was allowed to embark upon an experiment with a new cost accounting system.

Although budgetary reforms in the Royal Navy during the 1880s may have anticipated it (Cobbin and Burrows 2010), the army cost accounting experiment arose most immediately out of the financial extravagance of World War I that had shocked the nation and followed closely an earlier pilot exercise in developing cost accounts in a small number of British military units (Black 2001, 2006). The experiment was expected to initiate a revolution in military accounting and, thereafter, the accounting of all government departments (Grimwood 1919). At the commencement of the new scheme the War Office Cost Accounting Committee (1918: 2) praised cost accounts for the way in which they would 'fix responsibility … and secure economy … while increasing efficiency'. Towards the end of the experiment, Sir Charles Harris emphasised the way in which a cost accounting system would allow officers:

> [t]o manage expenditure properly. It is the difference between a system of account which is designed to control expenditures and a system of account that has nothing to do … with seeing whether the Public Services are being carried on efficiently and administered with reasonable care for economy. The present system has nothing to do with that question at all … This new system is intended, in particular, to take into account the psychological factor and produce economy … by showing people the results of their actions and appealing to their reason.
>
> *(Public Accounts Committee 1924–1925, Minutes of Evidence, Question 7206; see also Grimwood 1919)*

Unfortunately, the still insistent dictates of a rigid interpretation of the constitutional function of government accounting effectively precluded the adoption of cost accounting not only in the army but throughout departments of state until the latter decades of the twentieth century. Cost accounting, as portrayed by the Treasury, was considered unable to provide a similar level of constitutional assurance to the existing appropriation system of accounting. Any contribution which cost accounting might make to improved economy in the army, while certainly recognised as a benefit, was never sufficient of itself to convince the British Government that the technique and the ways of business were either necessary or constitutionally appropriate, even though the army was one of the two largest spending departments.

Curiously, although the British Government was not prepared to allow cost accounting to be institutionalised within the military after World War I, during the war it had been quick to grasp the importance of the protections and assurances that cost accounting could provide to the government in its dealings with private sector firms contracted to supply the military and to ensure victory. Cost accounting was quickly recognised as being essential to the economical and efficient prosecution of the war. This resulted in the British Government playing, unexpectedly, a highly significant role in promoting the adoption of cost accounting by lethargic businesses during World War I. In this regard, neglect of cost accounting by the British Army was little different at the time from similar neglect by the private sector. Loft (1986: 146, 148) describes most manufacturers at the outbreak of World War I as ignorant of the cost of their products. According to *The Accountant* (1 March 1919: 150) many manufacturers at the outbreak of war would have regarded the need for cost accounts as 'ridiculous'. One contributor to *The Accountant* in 1900 (30 June: 600) complained that it was 'surprising how many manufacturers pay little attention' to cost accounts. During World War I Dicksee (1915: 19) also criticised senior business managers for being 'quite ignorant of the uses that accounts might have'.

Business accounting and the military influence

According to Marriner (1994) and Loft (1986) significant developments during World War I in the use of cost accounting and the subsequent professionalisation of cost accountants were driven by the British Ministry of Munitions, which had been created in 1915 to coordinate war production. In the first year of World War I when many military supplies were short of requirements, and market prices for these were unavailable, the British Government had to contend with extensive profiteering (Arnold 2014). Without 'fair market prices' as a basis for setting contract prices the advantage in contract negotiations at a time of great national peril was initially with profiteering suppliers. This determined the government to revise the Defence of the Realm Act, which provided the state with extensive powers to wage war and to allow contract prices to be set not by reference to market prices, but on the basis of 'the cost of production of the output so requisitioned' (quoted in Loft 1986: 144). Neither was the government prepared to accept the cost figures provided by the suppliers and manufacturers, providing instead that these may be required to be verified on behalf of the government by appointed cost investigators.

The effect of the new legislation prompted by the peril of World War I, suggests Loft, was to force many firms to consider seriously, often for the first time, how they might determine the cost of their products, thereby providing a strong incentive for the spread of cost accounting throughout British industry. The 'new interest in cost accounting went hand in hand with a general transformation of industry' and, as an unintended consequence of the legislated costing requirements, raised the public profile of accountants and accelerated their professionalisation (Loft 1986: 146). The establishment of the Institute of Cost and Works Accountants in 1919 was especially notable. Fleischman and Tyson (2000) identified a similar phenomenon in the USA whereby the demands of World War I on cost accounting precipitated the professionalisation of that specialism. Boyns and Edwards (2007), however, have contested the importance given to the impact of World War I on business accounting practices in Britain. The authors point to the raised awareness and utility in wartime of extant costing techniques and suggest that studies of individual companies provides 'little support for the view that the First World War had a major impact on either the cost estimating procedures used or the nature of cost statements produced' (Boyns and Edwards 2013: 191–2).

Although the extent to which cost accounting pervaded government relationships with the world of business escalated during World War I, the benefits of sophisticated costing had long been appreciated in government ordnance factories. Supply failures during the Crimean War had encouraged accounting reforms in British government establishments for the manufacture of small arms, cannons, gunpowder and ammunition with a view to identifying 'real true cost' of production (Edwards 2015). The managers of these establishments were potentially at the forefront of costing innovation during the Victorian period. Foreman and Tyson (1998) and Foreman (2001) also identified a pre-World War 1 appreciation of cost accounting in government military manufacturing establishments in Australia. Here, factories operated by the Department of Defence were the first public sector enterprises to use modern cost accounting practices borrowed from commercial firms.

Costing techniques have also long been deployed in the shipbuilding establishments of naval powers. At the Venice Arsenal during the late sixteenth and early seventeenth centuries, Zambon and Zan (2007) found strong evidence that the notion of costs and costing emerged unexpectedly from the efforts of the Venetian Senate to introduce tighter forms of financial control over the operation of the city's arsenal. They concluded that accounting at the arsenal had been 'transformed from a mere tool of inspection and control, into an instrument for understanding and managing complex organisations' (Zambon and Zan 2007: 121). Cost accounting was also practised on ships at sea. McBride et al. (2016) contend that the accounting required of pursers in the British Royal Navy represented a nascent form of standard costing and inventory control in the pre-industrial age.

The extent to which accounting innovations flowed from the military to business organisations, or vice versa, is a source of controversy in accounting history. The possibility of an influence on business accounting by the military prompted a contentious debate between Tyson (1990, 1993), a 'traditional' historian, and the Foucauldian accounting historians Hoskin and Macve (1988, 1994). According to Hoskin and Macve (1988), and also Ezzamel et al. (1990), accounting practices of the Springfield Armory in the USA during the middle decades of the nineteenth century were highly influential in the development of modern cost accounting and the marriage of cost accounting and managerialism. The Armory's accounting systems, which Chandler (1977: 74) has described as 'the most sophisticated used in any American industrial establishment before the 1840s', are said to have incorporated a set of standard costs upon which the piece rate system of payment used in the Armory was based. These standard costs were used to exert, in Foucauldian terms, 'disciplinary power' over the workforce, possibly for the first time anywhere, suggest Hoskin and Macve (1988). Further, and most important for their thesis, they argue that the development of these standards of performance, measured by accounting, can be traced to the behaviour and mentality induced in West Point graduates by the system of meticulous educational assessment developed by Sylvanus Thayer at the US Military Academy after 1817.

At the West Point academy students were placed under a strict disciplinary regime whereby, across all subjects, each day their performance was assessed and numerically graded. These results formed the basis of weekly reports of progress upon which students would be rewarded. This finely tabulated system, argue Hoskin and Macve (1988), rendered 'calculable men' – cadets whose performance was intimately knowable and in whom, in Foucauldian terms, the system of disciplinary control was internalised. Subsequently, the performance culture engendered by the obsessive reliance upon examinations to monitor and assess performance was transmitted to business establishments through West Point's engineering graduates when they later transferred to the Springfield Armory. Thus, when graduates such as Daniel Tyler were appointed to senior positions in the Ordnance Corps, which was responsible for the Springfield Armory, the disciplinary regimes and management discourses of West Point followed. After 1841 West Point graduates, a new brand of 'men-managers' (Ezzamel et al. 1990: 158), took over the superintendency of the Armory, with some finding their way to influential positions in several railway companies. It has been suggested that the accounting practices and principles taught at West Point informed the sophisticated costing systems deployed by the Union Army during the American Civil War. When the war was won the officers who practised costing entered the managerial hierarchies of business organisations and disseminated the technologies taught at West Point (King et al. 2009). Edwards (2018) suggests that certain practices used at the Springfield Armory were also imported to government military manufacturing establishments in Britain during the 1850s.

Tyson (1990), however, rejects the proposition that West Point education and management training had a significant impact on the evolution of accounting practices. Instead, he concludes that:

> West Point training and discipline probably helped managers perform their work, but this particular background should not be given undue credit for increasing productivity and bringing fundamental change to accounting and accountability systems. Economic and social forces appear to be far more significant.
>
> *(Tyson 1990: 57)*

Tyson (1993) disputed not only the conclusions of Hoskin and Macve and Ezzamel et al. but also questioned the quality of their historical research. According to Tyson (1993: 13), these authors in their eagerness to 'substantiate a particular social theory', required them to be less constrained by the facts and, thus, they had grossly overstated the importance of the contributions of the Armory's accounting systems to the development of modern managerialism. Tyson was particularly critical of Hoskin and Macve's characterisation of Tyler's work as 'unique' at the time. In a scathing assessment of Hoskin and Macve's work, Tyson (1993: 10) claims that Hoskin and Macve even 'go beyond factual embellishment by attributing a singular motive to Tyler's 1832 piece-rate activities, without qualification and without supporting evidence'. At one point Tyson (1993: 10) argues that a report in 1841 provides no support for the contention by Hoskin and Macve that 'managerialism was invented at the Armory'. Indeed, this allegedly hyperbolic assessment by Hoskin and Macve, concludes Tyson, was but one example of the way in which they and Ezzamel et al. had been prepared to overstate some aspects of the management practices at the Springfield Armory and overlook others so that the evidence would fit the specifications of the Foucauldian perspective to which they subscribe. After an extensive investigation of the historical material, Tyson (1993: 12) argues that 'there is no corroborating evidence to indicate that normalizing judgements or performance evaluations were ever based on accounting numbers … (at the Armory). In fact, there is strong evidence to the contrary'. Neither were variances from norms of performance ever computed or the workers turned into 'calculable men'.

Calls for further studies of the influence of the military on business accounting have encouraged investigations in new spatial and temporal sites. Noguchi et al. (2015), for example, reveal a two-way interaction between the military authorities and private enterprises in devising costing regulations in Japan during World War II.

Interdisciplinary ventures

Reflecting the importance of the military and war as arenas for accounting history research, and the increasing interdisciplinarity of the field, a number of recent studies connect with diverse other foci in the current volume, beyond the most obvious interrelationship between the history of military accounting and the state. For example, the deficiencies of auditing as a mode of increasing transparency have been revealed in the context of reconstruction following the Iraq War. Here, Chwastiak (2013) contends that audit reporting contributed to the institutionalisation of fraud. In relation to the same conflict, Cooper and Catchpowle (2009) point to the dire consequences for the Iraqi people of the failure to institute proper accounting controls in the post-war environment. Studies of the Italian experience during World War 1 also point to the scope for fraud, embezzlement and scandal when powerful networks of politicians and industrialists control the procurement of military equipment (Vollmers et al. 2016). Where such power elites exist in wartime, accountability and accounting transparency are deprioritised in the name of the more pressing need to address the national emergency (Antonelli et al. 2014).

Where accounting controls and systems are established, they may come under considerable pressure during rapidly escalating conflicts. During World War II the accounting procedures used to supply the Australian Army with military equipment and personal requisites were inadequate (Miley and Read 2014). However, in the American Civil War internal controls proved sufficiently robust to prevent large-scale fraud in the procurement of supplies (Lippman and McMahon 2017). The disruptive impact of war on the operations of corporations has also been shown to have implications for their financial and management accounting practices (Fleischman and Marquette 2003; Heier 2010; Quinn and Jackson 2014). Maltby (2005) contends that contemporary innovations such as corporate social reporting have antecedents in the World War I. Military emergencies may accelerate the implementation of new accounting techniques and regulations (Djatej and Sarikas 2009).

We have seen that World War I has been implicated in the professionalisation of cost accountants in the UK and USA. Such total wars also impact on accounting firms and practitioners. They may disrupt fee income but also generate new sources of work, especially as a result of increases in the burden of taxation necessary to finance the conflict (Jones 1981, 1995; Flesher and Previts 2014). The mobilisation of mass armies can cause staff depletion crises in accounting firms and ideological conflicts for professionals and the organisations that represent them. In wartime accountants and accountancy bodies have to decide whether to prioritise acting in the public and national interest or the interests of their firms and members (Walker 2017, 2018). The deployment of the reserve of female labour in the accounting function during total wars has had significant implications for women's work and claims for access to the accountancy profession (Kirkham and Loft 1993; Shackleton 1999; Black 2006; Ikin et al. 2012). The credentials of the accountants enlisted by government departments to help resolve wartime problems offer important insights into perceived status hierarchies in the accountancy profession (Cobbin 2009).

Other interfaces include: military hospitals as the scene for the historical exploration of the relationship between accounting and religion (Sanchez-Metamoros and Funnell 2015); the role of accounting classification in determining entitlement to disablement pensions among those who sustained injury on military service (Miley and Read 2017); the relationship between defence budgets, social policy priorities and military accounting change (Funnell 2011); accounting calculation and the increased burden of taxation in the financing of wars (Giroux 2012; Arnold 2014; Billings and Oats 2014; Rutterford and Walton 2014);

and, in relation to popular culture, wartime cartoons as an alternative form of 'accounting' for deficiencies in securing supplies to the front line (Miley and Read 2014). Finally, predicated on the desirability of emancipatory forms of accounting, there have been calls for new accountings for the costs of war – accounts that extend beyond the measurement and disclosure of the short-term financial outlays necessary for the prosecution of war and the rendering visible of the long-term human, social and environmental costs of armed conflict (Chwastiak 2008; Chwastiak and Lehman 2008).

Conclusions

This survey of accounting history in which military forces have a presence highlights both research opportunities and the urgent need for a more concerted engagement by accounting historians with the military past, especially given the numerous situations in which armies have been involved over many centuries and the social, political and economic consequences of war. Among the topics which hold particular promise for accounting historians are further investigations of how accounting developments in the military reflected the evolution of cost accounting practices in the private sector, the influences that the military might have had on business accounting, the opportunities that war created for women to work as accountants, both in private practice and in government agencies such as the Army Pay Corps in Britain, and the contribution of accounting to the operational success of armies. With each major military conflagration producing its own war management problems and calls for remedial action, there is a vast repertoire of possible accounting histories, with the last two centuries especially fecund in this regard. Accounting historians outside the USA and Britain continue to be encouraged to consider the opportunities that this research provides in non-Anglophone settings. This will allow the introduction of a far greater diversity of government forms and constitutional practices than that which presently pervades the study of accounting and the military.

Unavoidably, and necessarily, the political identity of armies cannot but dominate much of military accounting research. Armies are the manifestation of political will and power; they exist for political purposes, having no identity beyond the exercise of violence in the interests of a political body, usually the state. Recognising that military accounting is ultimately derived from the need to serve a political body and thus have a political purpose, the consequences of military accounting will be necessarily assessed in terms of their contributions to the performance of the military in the achievement of these purposes. However, while the political overlays the study of military accounting, this does not mean that all accounting histories which have the military as their subject need be dominated by the heavy presence of political theory. Rather, this chapter has demonstrated how the details of the practice and effects of military accounting can direct discussion to the level of specific accounting practices and technologies and their contributions to military performance and management.

Key works

Chwastiak (2006) is a particularly innovative examination of the role of accounting in an attempt to transform the prosecution of the Vietnam War into an exercise in efficient management and the political consequences of this for Secretary of Defense McNamara.

Funnell (2005) provides an extensive examination of the events that proved to be a watershed in the history of the financial control of the British Army. The South African

War was a key development in the acceptance of the benefits of systems of financial control and accounting used by businesses.

Funnell and Chwastiak (2015) provide an impressive collection of studies on the functioning of accounting in wars during the modern age. They emphasise the politicised nature of military financing and accounting.

Funnell and Walker (2014) provide an introduction to a journal special issue devoted to the role of accounting in the First World War.

References

Amery, L. (1902) *The Times History of the War in South Africa*, Vols. 1 and 2 (London: Sampson Low & Co).

Amery, L. (1909) *The Times History of the War in South Africa*, Vol. 7 (London: Sampson Low & Co).

Antonelli, V., D'Alessio, R., and Rossi, R. (2014) Budgetary practices in the Ministry of War and the Ministry of Munitions in Italy, 1915–1918, *Accounting History Review*, 24 (2–3): 139–60.

Arnold, A.J. (2014) 'A paradise for profiteers'? The importance and treatment of profits during the First World War, *Accounting History Review*, 24 (2–3): 61–81.

Billings, M. and Oats, L. (2014) Innovation and pragmatism in tax design: Excess Profits Duty in the UK during the First World War, *Accounting History Review*, 24 (2–3): 83–102.

Black, J. (2001) Full circle: the cost accounting experiment in the British Army 1917–25 and the Corps of Military Accountants, *Journal of the Society for Army Historical Research*, 79 (318): 145–63.

Black, J. (2006) War, women and accounting, the pioneering role played by women in the Army Pay Department during the First World War, *Accounting, Business & Finance History*, 16 (2): 195–218.

Boyns, T. and Edwards, J.R. (2007) The development of cost and management accounting in Britain, in: C. Chapman, A. Hopwood and M. Sheilds (eds.) *History of Management Accounting Research*, Vol. 2, pp. 969–1034 (London: Elsevier).

Boyns, T. and Edwards, J.R. (2013) *A History of Management Accounting: The British Experience* (Abingdon: Routledge).

Chandler, A.D. (1977) *The Visible Hand* (Cambridge, MA: Harvard University Press).

Chwastiak, M. (1999) Accounting and the Cold War: the transformation of waste into riches, *Critical Perspectives on Accounting*, 10 (6): 747–71.

Chwastiak, M. (2001) Taming the untamable: planning, programming and budgeting and the normalization of war, *Accounting, Organizations and Society*, 26 (6): 501–19.

Chwastiak, M. (2006) Rationality, performance measures and representations of reality: planning, programming and budgeting and the Vietnam War, *Critical Perspectives on Accounting*, 17 (1): 29–55.

Chwastiak, M. (2008) Rendering death and destruction visible: counting the costs of war, *Critical Perspectives on Accounting*, 19: 573–90.

Chwastiak, M. (2013) Profiting from destruction: The Iraq reconstruction, auditing and the management of fraud, *Critical Perspectives on Accounting*, 24: 32–43.

Chwastiak, M. and Lehman, G. (2008) Accounting for war, *Accounting Forum*, 32: 313–26.

Cobbin, P.E. (2009) "The best brains of the public accountancy world": the restricted membership of the Army Accountancy Advisory Panel, 1942–1945, *Accounting Historians Journal*, 36 (2): 1–29.

Cobbin, P.E. and Burrows, G.H. (2010) The British navy's 1888 budgetary reforms, *Accounting History*, 15 (2): 153–72.

Committee of Administration of, and Accounting for, Army Expenditure (Lawrence Committee) (1924) *British Parliamentary Papers*, (Cmd. 2073) VII: 707.

Cooper, C. and Catchpowle, L. (2009) US imperialism in action. An audit-based appraisal of the Coalition Provisional Authority in Iraq, *Critical Perspectives on Accounting*, 20: 716–34.

Dicksee, L. (1915) *Business Methods and the War* (Cambridge: Cambridge University Press).

Djatej, A. and Sarikas, R. (2009) The Second World War and Soviet accounting, *Accounting History*, 14 (1–2): 35–54.

Edinburgh Review (1871).

Edwards, J.R. (2015) Accounting for fair competition between private and public sector armaments manufacturers in Victorian Britain, *Abacus*, 51 (3): 412–36.

Edwards, J.R. (2018) Towards constructing the governable worker in nineteenth-century Britain, *Critical Perspectives on Accounting*, 50: 36–55.
Ezzamel, M., Hoskin, K. and Macve, R. (1990) Managing it all by numbers: A review of Johnson & Kaplan's Relevance Lost, *Accounting and Business Research*, 20 (78): 153–66.
Fleischman, R. and Marquette, R. (2003) The impact of World War II on cost accounting at the Sperry Corporation, *Accounting Historians Journal*, 30 (2): 67–104.
Fleischman, R. and Tyson, T. (2000) Parallels between US and UK cost accountancy in the World War I era, *Accounting, Business & Financial History*, 10 (2): 191–212.
Flesher, D.L. and Previts, G.J. (2014) Haskins & Sells during the First World War and its aftermath, *Accounting History Review*, 24 (2–3): 211–25.
Foreman, P. (2001) The transfer of accounting technology: A study of the Commonwealth of Australia Government Factories, *Accounting History*, 6 (1): 31–59.
Foreman, P. and Tyson, T. (1998) Accounting, accountability and cost efficiency at the Commonwealth of Australia Clothing Factory, 1911–18, *Accounting History*, 3 (2): 7–36.
Funnell, W. (1988) The guardians of liberty: The role of civilians in British military finance 1850–99, *War and Society*, 6 (2): 32–57.
Funnell, W. (1990) Pathological responses to accounting controls: The British Commissariat in the Crimea 1854–6, *Critical Perspectives on Accounting*, 1 (4): 319–35.
Funnell, W. (1997) Military influences on public sector accounting and auditing 1830–1880, *Accounting History*, 2 (2): 9–31.
Funnell, W. (2005) Accounting on the frontline: Military efficiency and the South African War, *Accounting and Business Research*, 35 (4): 307–26.
Funnell, W. (2006) National efficiency, military accounting and the business of war, *Critical Perspectives on Accounting*, 17 (6): 719–51.
Funnell, W. (2008) The "proper trust of liberty": Economical reform, the English constitution and the protections of accounting during the American War of Independence, *Accounting History*, 13 (1): 7–32.
Funnell, W. (2011) Social reform, military accounting and the pursuit of economy during the liberal apotheosis, 1906–1912, *Accounting History Review*, 21 (1): 69–93.
Funnell, W. and Chwastiak, M. (2010) Editorial: accounting and the military, *Accounting History*, 15 (2): 147–52.
Funnell, W. and Chwastiak, M. (2015) *Accounting at War. The Politics of Military Finance* (Abingdon: Routledge).
Funnell, W. and Walker, S.P. (2014) Accounting for victory, *Accounting History Review*, 24 (2–3): 57–60.
Gallhofer, S. and Haslam, J. (1991) The aura of accounting in the context of a crisis: Germany and the First World War, *Accounting, Organizations and Society*, 16 (5/6): 487–520.
Giroux, G. (2012) Financing the American Civil War: developing new tax, *Accounting History*, 17 (1): 83–104.
Grimwood, J. (Lieut-Col.) (1919) Costing in relation to government control, efficiency and economy, *The Incorporated Accountants Journal*, March: 114–20; April: 133–38; May: 156–61.
Hanham, H. (1969) *The Nineteenth Century Constitution 1815–1914* (Cambridge: Cambridge University Press).
Harris, C. (1911) Army finance, *Army Review*, 1 (July): 55–76.
Heier, J.R. (2010) Accounting for the ravages of war: corporate reporting at a troubled American railroad during the Civil War, *Accounting History*, 15 (2): 199–228.
Hoskin, K. and Macve, R. (1988) The genesis of accountability: the West Point connections, *Accounting, Organizations and Society*, 13 (1): 37–73.
Hoskin, K. and Macve, R. (1994) Reappraising the genesis of managerialism: a re-examination of the role of accounting at the Springfield Armory, 1815–1914, *Accounting, Auditing & Accountability Journal*, 7 (2): 4–29.
Hoskin, K. and Macve, R. (2000) Knowing more as knowing less? Alternative histories of cost and management accounting in the U.S. and the U.K., *Accounting Historians Journal*, 27 (1): 91–149.
Howard, M. (ed.) (1957) *Soldiers and Governments* (London: Eyre & Spottiswoode).
Ikin, C., Johns, L., and Hayes, C. (2012) Field, capital and habitus: an oral history of women in accounting in Australia during World War II, *Accounting History*, 17 (2): 175–92.
Jones, E. (1981) *Accountancy and the British Economy 1840–1980. The Evolution of Ernst & Whinney* (London: B.T. Batsford Ltd).

Jones, E. (1995) *True and Fair. A History of Price Waterhouse* (London: Hamish Hamilton).

King, D.L., Premo, K.M., and Case, C.J. (2009) Historical influences on modern cost accounting practices, *Academy of Accounting and Financial Studies Journal*, 13 (4): 21–39.

Kirkham, L. and Loft, A. (1993) Gender and the construction of the professional accountant, *Accounting, Organizations and Society*, 18 (6): 507–58.

Lippman, E. and McMahon, M. (2017) Professionalism and politics in the procurement process: United States Civil War early years, *Accounting Historians Journal*, 44 (1): 63–76.

Loft, A. (1986) Towards a critical understanding of accounting: the case of cost accounting in the U.K., 1914–1925, *Accounting, Organizations and Society*, 11 (2): 137–69.

LSE 1906–7, Notes on the Course established at the LSE in the Session 1906–7 for the Training of Officers for the higher administrative appointments on the Administrative Staff for the Army and for the charge of Departmental Services, LSE Archives, File 232/C.

Mackinder, H. (1907) *Address Delivered on the 10th january, 1907, on the Occasion of the Opening of the Class for the Administrative Training of Army Officers* (London: HSO).

Maltby, J. (2005) Showing a strong front: corporate social reporting and the 'business case' in Britain 1914–1919, *Accounting Historians Journal*, 32 (2): 145–71.

Marriner, S. (1994) The Ministry of Munitions 1915–1919 and government accounting procedures, in: R. Parker and B. Yamey (eds.) *Accounting History: Some British Contributions*, pp. 450–72 (Oxford: Clarendon Press).

McBride, K., Hines, T., and Craig, R. (2016) A rum deal: the purser's measure and accounting control of materials in the Royal Navy, 1665–1832, *Business History*, 58 (6): 925–46.

Miley, F. and Read, A. (2014) The implications of supply accounting deficiencies in the Australian Army during the Second World War, *Accounting History Review*, 22 (1): 73–91.

Miley, F. and Read, A. (2017) The purgatorial shadows of war: accounting, blame and shell shock pensions, 1914–1923, *Accounting History*, 22 (1): 5–21.

Noguchi, M., Nakamura, T., and Shimizu, Y. (2015) Accounting control and interorganisational relations with the military under the wartime regime: the case of Mitsubishi Heavy Industry's Nagoya Engine Factory, *British Accounting Review*, 47: 204–23.

Public Accounts Committee (1924–5) First and Second Reports with Proceedings, Evidence, Appendices and Index, *British Parliamentary Papers*, (33, 138), Vol. 1.

Quinn, M. and Jackson, W.J. (2014) Accounting for war risk costs: management accounting change at Guinness during the First World War, *Accounting History Review*, 24 (2–3): 191–209.

Royal Commission into the Supplies of the British Army in the Crimea (McNeil-Tulloch Commission) (1856) *British Parliamentary Papers*, First Report, Vol. XX, including Appendix: 497.

Royal Commission on War Stores in South Africa (1906) Report with Appendices of Messrs. Annan, Kirby, Dexter & Co., Chartered Accountants, *British Parliamentary Papers*, (Cd. 3130) LVIII: 1, 73.

Royal Commission to Enquire into the Civil and Professional Administration of the Naval and Military Departments (1890) *British Parliamentary Papers*, Report, Vol. XIX, Appendix VI: 85.

Rutterford, J. and Walton, P. (2014) The war, taxation and the Blackpool Tower Company, *Accounting History Review*, 24 (2–3): 103–18.

Sanchez-Metamoros, J.B. and Funnell, W. (2015) War or the business of God: sacred mission, accounting and Spanish military hospitals in the 18th century, *Accounting, Auditing & Accountability Journal*, 28 (3): 434–59.

Select Committee on National Expenditure. (1918) *British Parliamentary Papers*, (23, 30, 59, 80, 92, 97, 98, 111, 121, 132) IV, First to Tenth Reports: 95.

Shackleton, K. (1999) Gender segregation in Scottish Chartered Accountancy: The deployment of male concerns about the admission of women, 1900–1925, *Accounting, Business & Financial History*, 9 (1): 135–56.

Tyson, T. (1990) Accounting for labor in the early 19th Century: The U.S. arms making experience, *Accounting Historians Journal*, 17 (1): 47–59.

Tyson, T. (1993) Keeping the record straight: Foucauldian revisionism and nineteenth century US cost accounting history, *Accounting, Auditing & Accountability Journal*, 6 (2): 4–16.

Vollmers, G., Antonelli, V., D'Alessio, R., and Rossi, R. (2016) Cost accounting for war: contracting procedures and cost-plus pricing in WWI industrial mobilization in Italy, *European Accounting Review*, 25 (4): 735–69.

Walker, S.P. (2017) Accountants and the pursuit of the national interest: A study of role conflict during the First World War, *Critical Perspectives on Accounting*, 47: 8–25.

Walker, S.P. (2018) War and organizational disruption in professional service firms, *Journal of Professions and Organization*, 5: 206–29.
War Office (Reconstitution) Committee (Esher Committee) (1904) *British Parliamentary Papers*, Part I (Cd. 1932) VIII: 102, Part II (Cd. 1968) VIII, Part III (Cd. 2002) VIII: 121.
War Office Cost Accounting Committee. (1918) *Instructions Relating to Experimental Cost Accounting in Selected Units* (London: War Office).
Watt, D. (1988) The London University class for military administrators, 1906–31: a study of British approach to civil-military relations, *LSE Quarterly*, 2 (2): 155–71.
Wright, F. (1956) The British Army cost accounting experiment 1919–1925, *The Australian Accountant*, 26 (November): 463–70.
Young, H. (Captain) (1906) Practical economy in the army, *Journal of the Royal United Services Institute*, L: 1281–85.
Zambon, S. and Zan, L. (2007) Controlling expenditure, or the slow emergence of costing at the Venice Arsenal, 1586–1633, *Accounting, Business & Financial History*, 17 (1): 105–28.

29
TAXATION

Margaret Lamb and Lynne Oats

Overview

The histories of taxation and accounting are intertwined. Taxation requires accounting to record the taking from those taxed and the giving to those on whose behalf tax is levied. Accounting becomes a matter of public concern and requires consistency, truth and fairness when tax appropriations occur in political systems where rulers are accountable to citizens.

The aim of this chapter is to explore the interrelationships between accounting and taxation with a view to framing research questions that bring taxation clearly into view in accounting history scholarship. The chapter traces taxation themes through several strands of accounting history scholarship and through scholarly publications in which taxation is sometimes, but not always, the explicit research focus. The exercise consists of a review of how accounting historians study taxation and how the historical influences on taxation are addressed by accounting scholars with more contemporary concerns. Concluding comments focus on challenges facing the accounting historian of taxation. These include strengthening connections between historical questions of taxation and other fields of accounting history, and linking such research to histories of taxation by historians operating in other sub-fields. The chapter emphasises US and British tax accounting history. This is a practical, not a principled matter. While research on other parts of the world will be discussed, the authors focus on work published in English.

Taxation research themes in accounting history

Taxation stretches far back in time and covers the globe. Egyptian pharaohs of the first dynasty of the Old Kingdom (3000–2800 BC) collected taxes in a systematic way. In Ancient Greece and Rome taxation shaped political institutions, social life, culture, philosophy and religion. Experiments with income taxation both reflected and shaped political philosophy and practice in many parts of Europe from the early Middle Ages to the nineteenth century. New institutional figures and accounting practices emerged through innovative tax impositions, such as those introduced during Louis XIV's reign in seventeenth-century France. The introduction of income tax in 1799 to fund Britain's war with Napoleon represents a milestone in the development of taxation as we understand it today. The adoption of income tax on a continuous basis in the nineteenth and twentieth centuries, and following the constitutional amendment of 1913 in the US, were important events in the linked histories of tax and accounting. The subsequent extension of income taxation to the masses – living individuals, as well as other legal persons – gave taxation the ubiquity and calculative forms that are still recognisable today. Other modern forms of taxation, including the value added-type taxes – introduced in France in 1954, the European Union (EU) as a whole by 1974, and many other parts of the world – overlay their own complexity on pre-existing tax regimes.

Accounting historians tend to start thinking about taxation by focusing on puzzling or important tax matters that relate to accounting. Questions are concerned with taxation as specialised accounting practice. Where and why did ambiguities and difficulties of calculation arise? How was tax calculation embedded in the financial routines of businesses? Other questions probe deeper into the ways that accounting has changed over time. What did taxation have to do with the origins of accounting? How did taxation help clarify important accounting concepts like 'income', 'profit', 'depreciation' and 'entity'? Some accounting historians look to taxation for clues about how persistent tensions in accounting emerged. How was discipline achieved in reporting assessable values for taxation? How were tax returns audited? Which features of regulation improved the accuracy and consistency of financial reporting? How did tax work become embedded as part of the work of the accountancy profession?

Most tax history written in an accounting context focuses on the rules and practices of particular taxes. The complexity and importance of taxation as an area of professional practice mean that many researchers are preoccupied with understanding the nuts and bolts of tax. Further, interpretation and application in practice often depend on legal and procedural precedent, thus creating an essential historical element. Beyond the focus on the nuts and bolts, accounting histories of tax can be divided into two types: explorations of tax history for better understandings of accounting theory, practice and institutions; and explorations of tax history to understand accounting in its broader social, political and economic context. Such themes feature in the following sections.

Taxation rules and practice

The tax rules and practice literature includes many histories of particular taxes or of the features of taxes in particular times and places. Among the more substantial pieces of research by scholars who have explored the historical accounting dimensions of tax rules and practices in Britain are the following. Oats and Sadler (2004, 2007) and Sadler and Oats (2002) focus on contextualised studies of stamp duties from the eighteenth century. On the nineteenth century Edwards (1976) examines the tax treatment of capital expenditure and profit measurement; and Lamb (1996, 2002) looks at business tax practices and profit measurement for tax purposes. On the twentieth century Casson (1996) explores share options, imputation tax credits on dividends (1998) and employee share ownership plans (2004); Noguchi (2005) discusses tax accounting for stock in trade; and Stopforth (2004, 2005a, 2007) addresses capital gains tax and tax avoidance legislation (1992, 1999, 2005b).

For the US, the following scholars have researched particular taxation rules and practices in the nineteenth and twentieth centuries and make connections to the wider historical context. Cataldo (1995) explored earned income tax credit; Wells and Flesher (1999) focused on consumption taxes; Kern (2000) looked at interactions between tax and accounting depreciation rules and conventions; Pincus (1989) examined the background to legislative recognition of the LIFO principle; Sadler and Oats (2013) consider the interaction between stamp duty and freedom of speech; and various authors have discussed the antecedents of modern US taxes (Crum 1982; Kozub 1983; Samson 1985; Mehrotra 2010, 2013, 2017).

In addition to these publications, accounting historians interested in taxation are advised to utilise contemporary literature, particularly periodicals which catered for practitioner and scholarly audiences. For example, *The Accountant* (published in London from 1874) was an important journal in the Anglophone world. It published well-researched, authoritative articles on taxation. Contributors in the late 1930s and 1940s include senior practitioners (such as George O. May (1938), senior partner in Price Waterhouse) and leading academics (such as T.H. Sanders (1939), Professor of Accounting, Harvard Business School). Taxation represented almost one-third of articles published in *The Accountant's Magazine* (published in Scotland from 1897) in the years 1942–52 (Lee 2006: 30–1). In the second half of the twentieth century more specialist journals emerged that were intended for tax practitioners and also addressed recent tax history. Many such journals relied on contributions from both accountants and lawyers.

The tradition of authoritative scholarship on the links between accounting practice and taxation policy and law continued in more recent times. The leading weekly journal on US tax policy, *Tax Notes* (published since 1972), has provided an important medium for academic and practising accountants and lawyers. *The British Tax Review* (published since 1956) provides authoritative analyses of matters of current interest to practitioners and academics, but it is also the leading interdisciplinary source of tax commentary and assumes a broad scope and long view. Among the early contributors to tax research written from an accounting perspective was Professor Harold Edey (1956) of the London School of Economics. Both *Tax Notes* and *British Tax Review* publish work by authors from both practice and academe.

The National Tax Journal (*NTJ*) (published from 1948) also provided venues for scholarly analyses of US tax rules and practice by practitioners and accounting and finance academics, as well as by fiscal economists. In the early years of *NTJ* articles such as those by Mills (1955) on the influence of taxation on accounting profit measurement, and Troop Smith (1953) on the tax effects of corporate financing costs, provide historical starting points for exploring questions that continue to puzzle accounting researchers.

Tax historical research and better understandings of accounting

Challenges for accounting historians interested in taxation include the research and study of detailed taxation rules and practices and finding references to taxation in works with a primary focus on accounting theory, practice and development. Tracing such fragments is essential to understanding how taxation is intertwined with accounting. Lamb (2003, 2004) analyses why taxation studies in an accounting context are relatively underdeveloped and suggests methods for exposing and studying the historical connections between the two subjects.

Taxation and the origins of accounting

Historians of the origins of accounting have often encountered taxation as a site for the use and development of the technique. Jose and Moore (1998) studied taxation in the Biblical age and explored aspects of accounting (counting, measurement and computation).

Ezzamel's studies (2002, 2012) of ancient Egyptian tax assessment and collection, and Oldroyd's (1995) work on Roman governmental accounting, are fine examples of how historical work by accounting historians may be critically grounded in the general historical scholarship of the time and place. Macve's (1994) work on Greek and Roman accounting and taxation engages with the work of a specialist historian of the period, Geoffrey de Ste Croix. Mena (2016) studies the influence of the Aztecs, Incas and Mayas on pre-Columbian accounting. The functioning of taxation in ancient economies and its implications for accounting practice are also considered in Chapter 4 of this volume.

For later periods, scholars have sought to locate the antecedents and narrate transitions to modern concepts and forms of accounting. McDonald (2002, 2012) used the Domesday Book (1086) of Norman England as an evidential base for exploring the taxation of income, wealth and estates. Jones (2010: 89) explores Exchequer accounting observing that 'the need to monitor the collection of taxation was the main motive for the emergence of a written accounting system'. Thompson (2013) considers early income taxes in the context of political arithmetic in the long eighteenth century. Treisch (2005) examines the tax exemption of basic, or subsistence, income and traces the emergence of the principle to the theories of human rights in German natural law during the seventeenth to nineteenth centuries. Accounting technologies essential to state-building are studied by Vogeler (2005: 236) in medieval German territorial states. As oral accounting for taxation gave way to paper accounting for taxation from the thirteenth to the sixteenth century, tax came to be used as 'a symbol of the fact that everyone belongs to the state' (ibid.). For a later period in France, Miller (1990) studied the formative interrelations between practices of accounting, taxation and the institutions of state when Louis XIV's government extended controls deep into the provinces and businesses.

Taxation and the emergence of 'modern' accounting theory

Debates concerning taxation and the emergence of accounting theory from the nineteenth century onwards have revolved around various questions. Is tax just another cost to be accounted for? Is tax a discipline that is separate from accounting? Is tax a process that is linked to and influences accounting?

Representation of tax costs

In Anglo-American accounting, academics tend to address taxation as a cost that requires appropriate treatment. In financial reporting 'accounting for tax costs' encompasses the measurement and presentation techniques developed to represent tax expenses, tax liabilities and tax cash flows in published accounts. Techniques of accounting for tax costs were developed to reflect the fact that taxation systems may recognise economic events in a manner that differs from the 'true and fair view' of accounting and to reflect the fact that the underlying tax system has a changing set of interrelationships with accounting. Some differences between accounting conventions for recognising profits and their tax counterparts are created by statute (for example, certain categories of income are tax exempt and certain categories of expense are not deductible for tax purposes). Other differences arise through the application of different tax principles. Differences between accounting depreciation and tax depreciation ('capital allowances' in the UK) are created by statute and represent a prominent category of difference between tax and accounting profit calculations. 'Deferred tax' refers to the collection of techniques developed to account for these sorts of timing differences.

One strand of historical research on the representation of tax costs in financial reporting supports an analysis of standard setting as a political process (Horngren 1973; Solomons 1978, 1983). Here the economic consequences of accounting policy choice shape the positions adopted by lobbyists (Zeff 1978; Watts and Zimmerman 1979; see also Chapter 14 of this volume). Schultz and Johnson's (1998) research on deferred taxation theory and practice is integrated into the history of US financial reporting. In a British context, Hope and Briggs (1982) identify issues 'at the heart of the deferred tax debate' and, based on their historical analysis, argue that accounting standard setters were influenced by political lobbying when drafting a standard for deferred tax accounting. Arnold and Webb (1989) found that Statement of Standard Accounting Practice 15 on deferred tax was inconsistent with the concepts of other UK accounting standards. Based on their evaluation of the economic effects of partial provision for deferred tax versus the (hypothetical) economic effects of full provision, they found 'evidence of major deficiencies in the accounting standards process' and that full provision deferred tax accounting (abandoned in 1978) 'was a convenient "scapegoat"' (ibid.: 49–50). They argue 'that the rationale for partial deferral was constructed to fit the political need to avoid an embarrassing level of non-compliance with accounting standards' (ibid.: 50). Nurnberg (2009) examines the conceptual nature of corporate income tax for accounting purposes in a US setting. Zeff (2007) documents the tussle between the US Securities and Exchange Commission and the Accounting Principles Board in relation to deferred tax. Morton (2019) uses a constructivist lens to discern the factors contributing to the legitimisation of a norm of tax effect accounting in Australia.

Tax influence in an accounting context

'Tax influence' on accounting is a recurrent observation in the academic literature, especially in Anglo-American accounting history and comparative international accounting. Most 'tax influence' research focuses on the impact of tax law on company financial reporting law and practice, and on measurement differences between tax and financial reporting.

By the mid-nineteenth century income taxation was effectively permanent in Britain. According to Parker (1986: 5), its introduction was one of four significant factors in the development of British accountancy. The others were the growth of large-scale organisations, especially the railroads; the development of limited liability; and the high rate of insolvency. Parker (1986: 39) argues that World War I 'brought to the fore' tax services which had been 'slowly developing', but devotes little space to discussion of pre-World War I tax or to changes that occurred after the military crisis. We return to the taxation developments triggered by World War I later.

Watts and Zimmerman (1979) argue forcefully – but with limited exposition of detail – that taxation caused accounting theories. Looking at relevant US and UK history, the authors find a range of evidence to support their argument that accounting theories emerge to strengthen governmental actions following particular interventions. For example, the introduction of a British income tax law of depreciation prompted, they say, the development of the relevant accounting theory. Watts and Zimmerman focus on governmental intervention in the form of a new income tax statute and the direct impact this had on changing accounting principles and the subsequent production of prescriptive literature by writers on accounting. Watts and Zimmerman observe that income tax law increased pedagogic, information and justification-based demands for accounting theories. The implied medium of change was a coalescence of individual desires to be better off by transforming accounting theory to take advantage of the tax change. An accounting theory would, they argue, 'buttress preconceived notions' (1979: 23, quoting Zeff 1972: 177) and has the character of an economic good that is subject to market forces of supply and demand. A demand for a particular accounting theory is a demand for a 'rationale' or 'excuse'.

Some authors refute Watts and Zimmerman's argument that changes to British income tax law impacted the development of related accounting theories. Bryer (1993), for example, finds evidence of the development of an accounting theory of depreciation that predates the relevant income tax law. Relatedly, Edwards (1976: 313) argued: 'If there is a relationship between tax law and accounting practice it remains, nevertheless, difficult to trace the cause and effect'. Edwards' purpose was to study tax influence on the development of depreciation and other aspects of fixed asset accounting. He stated that 'in the absence of any readily available figure for business profit, the tax authorities were obliged to introduce their own rules' (ibid.: 302). Relatedly, Lang and Heier (2013) explore how accountants in the US grappled with accounting concepts such as depreciation following the introduction of federal income tax in 1913.

Citing Edwards (1976), Napier (1996: 452) argues that the main principles to emerge from an early period of interaction between tax and accounting in practice concerned 'the identification and treatment of capital expenditure ... where tax law did not permit a deduction in determining profits'. Napier argues that this phenomenon in accounting was probably related to 'an unreflective adoption by businessmen of a capital/revenue distinction articulated originally in the context of British aristocratic estates'. Tax law and practice, therefore, reinforced an accounting distinction that was a residue of an earlier age. Napier implies that tax was one of the reasons why theoretical work on accounting emerged slowly.

Lamb (2002) analyses British tax cases in the late nineteenth century and makes clear that officials representing tax agencies struggled to devise effective concepts and techniques of accounting just as businessmen and their accountant advisers did. Her work traces interrelationships between business profit measurement techniques and the emerging treatment of depreciation. The give and take between tax and commercial accounting practices is highlighted, as is the way in which practitioners with different perspectives attempted to grapple with the impact of new technologies in industry, commerce and finance. From a different perspective, Koowattanatianchai et al. (2019) trace the history of accelerated depreciation and identify three social discourses justifying its use as a form of investment incentive.

Watts and Zimmerman (1979: 44) take it for granted that tax is a negative influence on accounting. They argue that where accounting theories are developed in response to a governmental need for justification, high political or transaction costs can lead to the adoption of a less-than-'best' accounting theory (ibid.: 34–5). Further, they say that tax depreciation techniques were based on historic cost rather than periodic valuation and on an annual allowance equal to 'an arbitrary proportion of historical cost' because such techniques reduced the cost of administering tax laws (ibid.: 45). Not only did this process of rationalisation influence depreciation accounting but 'the demand for a rationalization of this procedure and other accruals under the tax law eventually resulted in the concept of income based on matching and the realization concept' (ibid.). Edwards (1976: 310), too, argues that 'the detailed provisions of income tax legislation had an unfavourable influence on accounting practices'. In the area of capital accounting 'early tax law and practice retarded the development of accounting theory' (ibid.: 314).

Many accounting historians appear to accept that by the late nineteenth century taxation and accounting in Britain operated under separate principles and rules of profit measurement. Edwards (1976: 300) treats the fact that 'profits' have a different meaning for tax and financial reporting purposes as self-evident from the different measurement principles assumed by tax authorities and the users of financial accounts. In an argument similar to that of the legal scholar Judith Freedman (1987), Edwards (1976: 317) argues:

> The figure for taxable income is designed to fulfil a function quite different from that performed by the balance reported as accounting profit and any attempt to produce one figure to do both jobs might well result in it doing neither job properly.

This is, therefore, a normative argument that tax and accounting measurement of profit *should* be kept separate in a contemporary sense. Edwards (1976) makes a related argument that tax reform can only follow not precede accounting developments. This offers an interesting contrast to the argument put forward by Watts and Zimmerman in 1979.

Edwards explains the separation between accounting and tax calculation as the result of the fact that UK income tax was introduced before commercial accounting practice had developed widespread reliability and consistency. The timing of the introduction of income tax forced relevant authorities to develop their own rules, and thereafter 'recognition of the essential difference between taxable and accounting profit' ensured the separate and distinct nature of tax and accounting approaches to profit measurement (1976: 300–1). Freedman (1997: 32) argues that a 'culture was created in which a divergence of taxable profits from accounting profits could evolve without causing any great surprise'. Divergence between tax and accounting profit calculations, thereby, became 'natural'. Lamb (2002) argues that such divergence was *constructed* over a long period by interacting institutions and practices. For much of the nineteenth century many income tax authorities sought consistency with commercial principles to represent transactions and balances. Oats and Sadler (2013) explore a curious Australian case where the interaction between tax law and accounting practice led to peculiar results in the case of dividend distributions.

World War I gave rise to innovations in taxation that linked closely to the notion of profit, and thereby accounting. In the UK, as in other countries, an excess profits duty emerged which entailed developing notions of a baseline profit from which an excess could be derived. The UK experience spawned considerable creativity, as explored by Billings and Oats (2014). In the same context, Arnold (2014) examines the politicisation of the concept of 'profit' and the difficult question of profiteering. Other World War I innovations include the entertainments tax discussed by Rutterford and Walton (2014) in their study of its impact, together with the excess profits duty, on the Blackpool Tower Company. The US Civil War had also acted as a catalyst for innovation in taxation (Giroux 2012). The relationship between war and taxes in the US is explored more generally by Bank et al. (2008). Xu and Xu (2016) discuss how the Chinese Civil War and the Sino-Japanese War both influenced the new tax regime as an expression of state power.

In a comparative study of the historical influence of tax on accounting, Lamb et al. (1998) recognise the distinctiveness of tax and accounting rules during the late twentieth century. They assume that this distinctiveness does *not* follow from the fact that income tax predates modern financial reporting. Instead, they argue that the separation is counter-intuitive and requires explanation. A more intuitive result would have been for UK financial reporting to follow income tax rules more closely because compliance with tax rules would have created a reason for preparing accounts. Such a rationale appears to have been influential in maintaining a close link between tax and accounting profit measurement rules in several countries of continental European. Lamb et al. (1998) argue that from the late nineteenth century British capital market requirements provided a competing purpose that was stronger than any tax reason for preparing accounts. The accounting requirements of capital markets thus diverged from the accounting requirements of the tax authorities. UK financial reporting acquired a capital market orientation and tax computations were prepared as a substantially separate exercise using distinctive computational rules and principles.

'Tax influence' research in comparative international accounting

National regimes have been distinguished by the degree of 'tax influence' on the development or operation of financial reporting rules (Nobes 1983, 1984, 1992, 1991, 1995; Nobes and Schwencke 2006; Nobes and Parker 2016). Various terms describe this relationship: 'dependence/independence' (Hoogendoorn 1996); 'congruence/reverse congruence' (Haller 1992); 'authoritativeness/reverse authoritativeness' (Ordelheide and Pfaff 1994); and 'bindingness' (von Wysocki 1984). The degree of current, or 'operational influence', is closely linked to the patterns of 'historical influence' established in particular countries (Lamb et al. 1998). Some research in comparative international accounting has considered the tax/accounting link in its historical, national and institutional contexts (see Hoogendoorn 1996).

According to Choi and Mueller (1992: 30), there are 'two thrusts that characterize basic thinking in the international accounting field': classification and development. Both influenced the way in which we think about interrelations between accounting and taxation and their historical development. A third area, harmonisation studies, also concerns tax/accounting interrelations. A fourth area, the comparative study of the tax/accounting relationship, is less concerned with convergence and accounting commonalities than with deepening understanding of such relationships in their particular national contexts.

Mueller (1967) classifies national accounting systems into four patterns: 'macroeconomic', 'microeconomic', 'independent discipline' and 'uniform accounting'. Uniform accounting (as in France, Germany, Sweden and Switzerland) creates a strong link between accounting and taxation. In discussing Mueller's classification Nobes (1991: 41–2) suggests that 'we might expect' the macroeconomic pattern 'to be equivalent to tax accounting', meaning that there is equivalence in accounting practices used and reports produced for financial reporting and reporting to taxation authorities.

In a study that focuses on the financial reporting measurement practices of public companies Nobes (1983, 1984) adds a hierarchical dimension to international accounting classification. The importance of tax rules in accounting measurements is a differentiating factor between corporate reporting systems. Using an analytical method borrowed from biological taxonomy, 'tax-based' systems are a 'family' of the 'Continental: government' 'sub-class', which in turn is part of the 'class' 'macro-uniform'. In Nobes' hierarchy the 'tax-based' 'species' – Spain, France, Belgium and Italy – are very 'distant' from the UK-Irish species. In a later version of the hierarchical classification, Nobes (1991: 48–9; 1992: 96) redefines his two 'classes' as 'micro-fair-judgmental/commercially-driven' and 'macro-uniform/government-driven/tax-dominated'.

Several empirical classification studies (Da Costa et al. 1978; Frank 1979; Nair and Frank 1980) group countries according to the accounting practices actually used. This literature, which bases differentiation on such observed practices as deferred taxation provision and measurement, helps confirm that countries can be differentiated according to patterns of accounting/tax interrelations. The studies are significant for having introduced the idea that a financial reporting *representation* of the tax/accounting link should be used as a proxy for examining the nature of the links themselves in international accounting classification. The focus on the representation of interrelationships as opposed to underlying patterns has contributed to an exaggeration of the degrees of independence or dependence between tax and accounting in some countries.

For Choi and Mueller (1992) development is the second defining thrust in international accounting thinking. Many scholars have identified factors that influence the development of accounting. However, development factors are defined in different ways. For example, Radebaugh and Gray (1993) emphasise the cultural level while others describe multiple levels of interpretation. Taxation is only examined in detail as an explicit factor in the work by Nobes and Parker (2016).

In his own classification studies (Nobes 1983, 1984 and when writing with Parker (Nobes and Parker 2016: chs 1, 2, 5), Nobes has explored the influence of taxation on accounting. It is possible to distinguish between 'creditor/insider' countries where tax considerations dominate accounting rules, and 'equity/outsider' countries where the accounting rules are separated from taxation (Nobes and Parker 2016: 37). The degree to which taxation determines accounting measurements 'is seen by studying deferred taxation' (ibid.: 38).

Nobes and Parker (2016) discuss the 'separation' of accounting and taxation. This notion is manifest in the 'separation' and 'independence' of the calculation of depreciation for accounting purposes and UK tax (capital allowances) purposes in the twentieth century. (By the early twenty-first century, tax and accounting depreciation calculations had begun to converge in some significant respects.) They write that 'separation' permits 'a complete lack of subjectivity in tax allowances, but full room for judgment in financial depreciation charges' (ibid.: 38). By contrast 'in countries like Germany, the tax regulations lay down the depreciation rates to be used for particular assets' (ibid.). The continental approach to the accounting/tax link is explained in a historical sense as 'perhaps due partly to the persuasive influence of codification in law and partly to the predominance of taxation as a cause of accounting' (ibid.: 39).

The alternative, Anglo-Saxon approach is implied to have origins in 'an older tradition of published accounting, where commercial rules have come [before tax rules]' but where a capital markets orientation has been strong since the late nineteenth and early twentieth centuries (ibid.). Within this Anglo-Saxon approach, Nobes and Parker (2016: 39) observe that 'taxation authorities have to adjust the commercial accounts for their own purposes'. This is not the same as saying that taxation is unimportant for financial reporting in the US and UK. We know from Freedman (1987, 1993, 1995) and others that accounting reports are (and have been historically) 'the basis', in the sense of starting place, for taxable profit calculation in the UK. A broadly similar relationship exists in the US (see Lamb et al. 1998).

Many studies of accounting harmonisation draw on the 'classification' and 'development' themes in international accounting research. Different national systems of taxation represent obstacles to harmonisation. Tax/accounting differences create complex patterns of variation in financial reporting by multinational enterprises and thereby reduce comparability.

Another approach to the tax/accounting angle of accounting harmonisation is to analyse the reverberations caused by one country's reactions to harmonising proposals that (potentially) alter the domestic tax/accounting relationship. Haller (1992) argues that taxation may be a bar to accounting harmonisation in the European Union. In Germany, for example, the congruence required by law between accounting and taxation principles and calculative practices for individual companies is effectively a drag on Germany's ability (or desire) to respond to harmonising calls from the EU. Hoogendoorn (1996: 783–4) notes that the mutual dependence between tax and accounting has 'often been considered to be the main obstacle to accounting harmonization', but he asserts that the greater emphasis on shareholder value concepts and corporate governance has loosened the relationship of dependence.

In some cases the international accounting literature focuses on whether or not taxation is a causal influence on patterns of accounting change. Such studies have tended to be based on broad generalisation rather than detailed review of accounting/tax interrelations in particular national contexts. They also tend to focus on the representation of taxation in published accounts and then move, in a limited way, to consideration of the patterns of interaction between the underlying tax system and accounting. A number of authors have been critical of this approach (including Walton 1992, 1993; Hopwood 1997).

Comparative international accounting research based on surveys of national practices or focusing on the identification of broad environmental factors influencing accounting development is also criticised in various quarters. Some commentators prefer detailed country studies undertaken within a broad comparative framework (Walton 1993). A *European Accounting Review* Supplement in 1996 considered the accounting/tax link in historical and contemporary contexts in 13 European countries. The 'research forum' contained detailed case studies organised around a common set of questions. Each article analysed a problem using the same broad analytical structure, while an overview article (Hoogendoorn 1996) summarised themes and comparative findings. The results suggest that the 'dependence/independence' dichotomy referred to earlier represents two ends of a continuum that never feature in practice. Instead the tax/accounting relationship falls somewhere in between, is not necessarily stable and is likely to change over time. Although some contributors of country-based cases have extended their research on the past, there remains an opportunity for tax/accounting historians to pursue these histories more deeply.

Lamb et al. (1998) tackle the question of 'tax influence' more directly than earlier work in this field. Their paper is a comparative study of the 'historical' and 'operational' influence of taxation on financial reporting in France, Germany, the UK and the US. It tests the claim of a clear distinction between the degree of tax influence on accounting in Anglo-Saxon countries and in some continental European countries. 'Operational influence' (or otherwise) is identified through the recognition of connections (or disconnections) between tax and accounting in the application of key measurement rules. The study found some support for the distinction between Anglo-Saxon and continental European models of tax influence. More importantly, the study found a complex and changing pattern of reciprocal influence between tax and accounting practices (similar to Hoogendoorn (1996). The classificatory method adopted in the study is proposed as one that could be used to measure the changing strength of tax influence over time and in other countries. The approach has since been extended historically and applied to the European Union (Cuzdriorean and Matis 2012), France (Barbe et al. 2014), Germany (Gee et al. 2010), Italy (Gavana et al. 2013), Norway (Nobes and Schwencke 2006), Romania (Deaconu 2012) and Spain (Oliveras and Puig 2007).

Lamb (1995) considers relationships between accounting and tax in EU concepts of group recognition – a relationship at the level of principles with implications for (differences in) calculative techniques. This study adopts a historical-legal approach to examine the interplay of the national and supranational factors behind the adoption of group concepts in law. One pattern of influence tentatively recognised in the study is not *tax* influence on accounting, but *accounting* influence on tax, and here 'accounting concepts of groups, especially *de facto* control, appear to have been influential in shaping modern concepts of tax groups for anti-avoidance purposes' (ibid.: 52).

Tax accounting in its social, political and legal contexts

We catch glimpses of tax practice and its interrelationships with accounting from accounting research that adopts a sociological perspective and which recognises that accounts are: 'the medium and outcome of relations of power through which the boundaries of social reality are defined and legitimized, and resources are differentially distributed' (Gilmore and Willmott 1992: 161). From this perspective accounting is not regarded as acting as an accurate mirror of the facts of economic reality (Knights and Collinson 1987). Instead, accounting 'has come to be regarded as a social and institutional practice, one that is intrinsic to, and constitutive of social relations' (Miller 1994: 1). The sociological approach moves beyond the study of methods and techniques and recognises the political processes that condition accounting and through which accounting is transformed (Gilmore and Willmott 1992: 164). Historical research forms an essential element of this approach. Research into 'accounting in motion' has become a method for comprehending how accounting is implicated in the construction of organisational and social orders (Hopwood 1987).

Investigations of the interrelationship between accounting and the state are well developed in the accounting literature (Hopwood and Johnson 1986; Loft 1986, 1994; Hopwood et al. 1994). Scholars have brought taxation practice into the analysis. Preston (1989) studied the interactions of a taxpayer (a small record company) and the Inland Revenue in the UK. In their study of US tax audit Pentland and Carlile (1996) adopt an 'expression game' framework to analyse interactions between the taxpayer and Internal Revenue Service agents. In a study of cost accounting in the UK during and after World War I, Loft (1986, 1994) considers the impact of wartime taxation and the increasing burden of general taxation on costing techniques and related accounting issues.

Miller (1990) deals more directly than many writers with the relationship between accounting and the taxation apparatus of the state. In a paper intended to develop ways of conceptualising the linkages between accounting and the state, he illustrates accounting and state practices in France during the 'Colbert period' of Louis XIV's reign, 1661–83. Through studying this period of 'concurrent developments within accounting and the state', Miller was able to 'explore how changes in the constitutive components of one complex make possible the emergence, articulation or transformation of the other' (ibid.: 316). Likhovski (2012) considers the cultural history of tax by reference to the transplantation of British income tax into Palestine in the early twentieth century at the interface between law and culture. Mehrotra (2010) considers the introduction of income tax in the US set against transformations in the economy and the concentration of economic power in corporations, linking to the rise of rational calculation. For a broad sweep, see Soll (2014), and for a more light-hearted look at the US, see Starkman (2008).

Eden et al. (2001) examine international transfer pricing policy and practice in the US, Mexico and Canada. Using a socio-historical model derived from institutional theory, the authors provide an important example of how accounting and tax practices link and were diffused across national borders in the last three decades of the twentieth century. Other scholars have examined the taxation apparatus of the state from the perspectives of groups of taxpayers and the individual. Hooper and Kearins (2003) study how capital taxation in mid-nineteenth-century New Zealand and the prevailing models of public finance were linked to the disenfranchisement of the Maori. Boden et al. (1995) examine the treatment of women in UK tax and national insurance from the mid-twentieth century and Boden (1999) considers taxation and the self-employed in the late twentieth century. Lamb (2001) explores the taxation apparatus of the state from the perspective of the individual. The study examines the social context for the income taxation of profits and the associated processes of accountability in mid-nineteenth-century Britain. The paper exposes how local tax authorities employed sovereign powers as the basis for regulatory control, and traces the conditions of possibility that existed for Inland Revenue powers based on disciplinary practices. The complex relationship between taxation and slavery has been explored in the case of Brazil (Rodrigues et al. 2015; Rodrigues and Craig 2018). See also Einhorn (2006) for the US.

While the natural inclination is to see the linkages between taxation and accounting in the context of taxes on incomes or profits, other forms of taxation bring accounting to the fore in other domains. Studies of such taxes include medieval knights' fees (Frecknall-Hughes and Oats 2007; Brayson 2016), the window tax (Glantz 2008; Oates and Schwab 2015), and head taxes as discriminatory forms of coercion (Heaman 2013; Wohl et al. 2013).

The politics of taxation also resonates with the politics of accounting. Vosslamber (2012) traces the passage of New Zealand's first income tax through Parliament and finds echoes of modern debates about legitimacy and progression. Barney and Flesher (2008) explore the influences of the agricultural sector on the passage of tax laws in the US. The role of the Tennessee Taxpayers' Association in holding the local governments to account is examined by Pridgen and Flesher (2013). Also in the context of US state financing, Covaleski et al. (2005) trace the emergence of tax incremental financing (TIF) as a social process, analysing the power plays involved in the institutionalisation of the TIF programme.

Tax practice in an accounting context involves both tax compliance work (preparation and submission of returns; applications of other rules and procedures) and tax planning. Here the ethical tensions of accounting are evident and the overlap in practice with law creates a rich area for interdisciplinary research. In the US context, Broden and Loeb (1983) have taken a historical look at accountants' professional ethics in relation to tax practice. Samson (1998) uses tax history as a case study to convey the ethical tensions in tax planning as a component of accounting practice. Walker (2011) discusses the role of Ethel Ayres Purdie, accountant and suffragist, in the Women's Tax Resistance League in the UK. Donohoe et al. (2014) examine the recent history of corporate tax planning in the US by reference to the transformation from compliance through profit enhancement to risk management (see also Rostain and Regan (2014) in this regard). Frecknall-Hughes and McKerchar (2013) trace the emergence of the tax profession in Australia and the UK.

Tax planning also attracts interest from legal scholars and accounting researchers in the UK. Collaborative research between lawyers and accountants has taken a historical approach (Freedman and Power 1992; McBarnet and Whelan 1992). Interpretation of the dialectical process of tax avoidance and anti-avoidance is often the historical focus. The legal scholar Picciotto (1992a, 1992b) wrote an influential historical work on international business taxation that emphasised this dialectic. An accounting academic, Shah (1996) explored the process of 'creative compliance' using the example of complex convertible securities issued by UK listed companies in the late 1980s. This research into the mechanisms of creative compliance reveals interactions between representatives of the finance, legal and accountancy professions in crafting hybrid securities designed for their tax planning and financial reporting advantages. Tax regulatory changes were important drivers in what Shah (1996: 24–5) refers to as a 'game' of creative compliance. Shah shows that close collaboration between auditors, lawyers and tax specialists is a prerequisite of the successful implementation of tax avoidance innovation, and that specialist innovators often devise new schemes as products for marketing by their firms (ibid.: 29–30). He also finds support for McBarnet and Whelan's (1992: 105) thesis that powerful economic elites 'may be beyond legal control'.

The importance of a historical analysis of how accounting and the law intertwine is emphasised in several studies (Bromwich and Hopwood 1992; Gilmore and Willmott 1992; Miller and Power 1992; Napier and Noke 1992; Edgley 2010). A historical approach develops the idea that the forms of this relationship are time and culturally specific and that the 'residues' of ways of thinking or ways of relating can endure. For example, Napier and Noke (1992) see tax as a residue of an older legal-based accountancy practice. They describe tax practice as 'legalistic'. Anecdotal sources tell us that tax is perceived by members of accounting and audit departments as 'narrow'. These descriptions may be nothing more than a reflection of an epistemological difference.

Miller and Power (1992: 246) use tax planning as their primary example of 'creativity' and describe it as 'one of the purest instances where law and economic calculation meet'. Tax law is dependent on accounting practice in two senses: first, 'it must appropriate calculative practices in a dialectical process of counter creativity'; and second, it depends on accounting practice to provide a basis on which to charge tax (ibid.: 248).

Conclusions: future directions and challenges to researchers

One of the authors has argued elsewhere that:

> The accounting historian who wishes to tackle a taxation subject has two primary obligations when framing … research questions… First, the contribution to accounting history must be clear … what is it about the research that extends our historical understanding of accounting theory, practices, or institutions? Second, the links to a more general, but relevant, history of taxation must be clear.
>
> *(Lamb 2003: 176)*

This chapter has reviewed research in tax accounting history and highlighted the themes that link the endeavour to accounting history broadly defined. Scholars attracted to study tax accounting histories in the future are urged to frame their research questions in ways that make the contribution to accounting history clear and strong. Researchers also face a number of other challenges.

Challenge 1: linking the accounting history of taxation to general histories

Tax accounting history is strengthened when it builds strong bridges to other sub-disciplines such as political, economic and social history. Particular research questions may be concerned with the philosophy and policy of taxation or with the history of tax practices in particular spatial and temporal frames. Set out below are some starting places for making relevant connections with historians working in other fields.

Theories and philosophies of taxation

Underlying all systems of taxation are theories and philosophies of what taxation should and should not do. Tax research is enriched by an understanding of the aims and ideals that precede the compromises and tax policies adopted by governments and advocated by particular policymakers. A starting place is Groves' (1974) *Tax Philosophers: Two Hundred Years of Thought in Great Britain and the United States.* Equally important to the tax researcher is a broad overview of the history of taxation from the earliest times to the modern age in an internationally comparative, social science framework. Webber and Wildavsky's (1986) *A History of Taxation and Expenditure in the Western World* remains the best critical overview of this sort.

Taxation in the UK

Accounting historians with a focus on taxation must be familiar with administrative and professional tax practice, as well as theory and policy. For the UK, five works provide inspiration for research projects as well as insights into thinking about taxation at particular times. The earliest (originally published in 1884) is the multivolume work by a former tax administrator, Dowell's (1965) *A History of Taxation and Taxes.* The next work, Sabine's (1966) *A History of Income Tax*, was also produced by a tax administrator. Kay and King (both fine academic and practising economists) produced an influential short work in 1978, *The British Tax System*, last updated in 1990. Although this should not be read as a comprehensive or detailed history of British taxation prior to the 1960s, it is an excellent encapsulation of influential taxation policy in late twentieth-century Britain. The two-volume history of British income taxation written by Cambridge historian Martin Daunton, *Trusting Leviathan* (2001) and *Just Taxes* (2002), set the bar high for those intending to contribute to historical scholarship on UK taxation.

Taxation in the US

Books by five authors serve similar purposes for the US. Seligman's (1914) *The Income Tax: A Study of the History, Theory and Practice of Income Taxation at Home and Abroad*, authored by an economist, is a good starting place. Brownlee's (1996) *Federal Taxation in America: A Short History* offers a broad but concise history. A trio of books introduce historical researchers to works which have shaken received wisdom and understandings of tax attitudes and practices in the US: Stanley's (1993) *Dimensions of Law in the Service of Order* examines the social and political underpinnings of the federal income tax laws; Weisman's (2002) *The Great Tax Wars* offers a readable survey and synthesis by a financial and political journalist; and Einhorn's (2006) *American Taxation, American Slavery* (2006) traces the ways in which slavery and slave-owning influenced US politics and its systems of taxation. In addition to these, Martin et al.'s (2011) book *The New Fiscal Sociology* brings together a collection of papers by authors who explore tax from a variety of sociological perspectives.

The Centre for Tax Law at the University of Cambridge has produced a series of books flowing from a biennial conference, *Studies in the History of Tax Law* edited by Professor John Tiley until his untimely death in 2013 when Peter Harris and Dominic de Cogan assumed the role. These volumes include work by accountants, lawyers and tax practitioners and others spanning a wide range in time and space, offering sources of both historical reference and inspiration.

Challenge 2: interpretation of evidence in taxation research

The privacy of tax returns and problems of access to relevant records limit how far the researcher can draw conclusions at a disaggregated level. Recourse must be made to statements of policy and practice and sources of aggregated data. As with other aspects of accounting, there is always a 'presentation' problem in tax matters – taxpayers are inclined to present their transactions and asset summaries in the best possible light (that is, consistent with tax savings). On rare occasions access to tax returns is possible. For a fascinating study of the use of an archive of private income tax returns to explore the lives of an immigrant couple in Canada, see Bujaki et al. (2016). In terms of the bigger picture, some argue (Weisman 2002) that private interests concerning tax policy and practice are hidden behind *all* public policy discourse on taxation. Thus, statements by politicians and administrators about tax require careful interpretation as to meaning. The perpetual shifts in balance and compromise over tax policy mean that histories of policy and practice must be interpreted with care. The considerable challenges of interpretation (and endless possibilities of interpretation) leave most areas of tax accounting history open to fresh, insightful research.

Challenge 3: complexity in taxation research

Taxation is connected to accounting, politics, economics, social relations, law etc. – seemingly anything and everything. Where then does one draw boundaries and frame manageable research problems? A clue for the accounting historian is to identify where accounting and tax issues are in the frame at the same time. Another type of complexity arises from the ways in which different types of tax complement each other – a tax system works because it is a system, not a collection of unconnected parts. The researcher faces the challenge of how to isolate the discussion of one tax from others and keep the research focused when the phenomenon under examination is part of a shifting and complex puzzle.

Challenge 4: prepare to be surprised and to set aside understandings based on the contemporary world

The distinguished US historian Robert Stanley talks of the need to remove the spectacles through which we view the contemporary world. At the outset of his study of the development of US income tax legislation, Stanley (1993) hypothesised that taxation would provide a powerful lens through which to see how structures of wealth and opportunity developed between the Civil War and World War I. He saw matters differently once his research had been completed:

> I began my historical research by focusing on statutes and court decisions relating to income taxation, intending to look for factors which determined their form and timing … I expected to find the traditional panoply of interest groups, party alignments, and ideologies, the tax fitting congenially within these categories that our society finds familiar.
>
> Preliminary research led instead to a far murkier view … I began to realize that my difficulty lay less in the data itself than in the attitude with which I was interpreting the data … The meaning of the early tax remained hidden from view … because of the spectacles I had learned to use …

> The lenses which finally revealed the meaning of early income taxation – composed of assumptions about society, the state, law, and history which depart from the dominant progressive and pluralist view – generated a likewise untraditional interpretation of the meaning of law in society.
>
> *Stanley (1993: viii)*

Meeting the challenges

As a means to producing valuable contributions to the accounting history of taxation researchers are advised to keep their focus on themes of relevance to accounting history. These may include transformational policy, theory and ways of thinking; the translation of tax policy and practices in new settings (international research especially); the translation of accounting policy and practices in taxation settings, and *vice versa*; and the intended and unintended effects of tax policy and practice changes. A focus on questions of relevance to historians in other fields is also encouraged. Dispelling some of the myths about taxation has been a concern of some influential historians such as Daunton (2001, 2002) on public trust in taxation; Einhorn (2006) on US taxation and slavery; and Stanley (1993) on the origins of the US federal income tax. These historians understand taxation as a site of social tension and as a catalyst of change in social, economic and political arenas. Accounting historians should perceive taxation in the same way.

Key works

Daunton (2001) is an important source for understanding how the general social and economic history of a nation, the UK, may be articulated through a close analysis of the administrative and calculative routines of taxation.

Eden et al. (2001) provide an excellent example of how the interrelations between accounting and taxation at the policy level can be analysed within a socio-historical framework.

Lamb (2003) discusses how accounting historians of taxation may clear two hurdles of research quality.

Martin et al. (2011) state their aim of 'bringing taxation back in' to the social sciences, challenging tax scholars to probe the world diachronically and to explore how tax intertwines with other aspects of social life.

Miller (1990) conceptualises linkages between accounting and the state and locates taxation prominently among state-building practices. The paper is a fine example of the application of theory to accounting research (through Foucauldian analysis).

References

Arnold, A.J. (2014) 'A paradise for profiteers?' The importance and treatment of profits during the First World War, *Accounting History Review*, 24 (2-3): 61–81.

Arnold, A.J. and Webb, B.J. (1989) *The Financial Reporting and Policy Effects of Partial Deferred Tax Accounting* (London: The Institute of Chartered Accountants in England and Wales Research Board).

Bank, S.A., Stark, K.J. and Thorndike, J (2008) *War and Taxes* (Washington, DC: Urban Institute Press).

Barbe, O., Didelot, L. and Ashta, A. (2014) From disconnected to integrated tax and financial systems: A post-IFRS evaluation of evolution of tax and financial reporting relationships based on the French case, *Research in Accounting Regulation*, 26: 242–256.

Barney, D.K. and Flesher, T.K. (2008) A study of impact of special interest groups on major tax reform: Agriculture and the 1913 Income Tax law, *Accounting Historians Journal*, 35 (2): 71–100.

Billings, M. and Oats, L. (2014) Innovation and pragmatism in tax design: Excess Profits Duty in the UK during the First World War, *Accounting History Review*, 24 (2–3): 83–101.

Boden, R. (1999) Figure it out yourself: Financial reporting, accountability and the self-employed, *Critical Perspectives on Accounting*, 10 (1): 37–62.

Boden, R., Childs, M. and Wild, W. (1995) Pride and prejudice: Women, tax and citizenship, *Critical Perspectives on Accounting*, 6 (2): 125–148.

Brayson, A. (2016) 'The English Parishes and Knights' Fees Tax of 1428: A study in fiscal politics and administration, *Historical Research*, 89 (246): 651–672.

Broden, B. and Loeb, S. (1983) Professional ethics of CPAs in tax practice: An historical perspective, *Accounting Historians Journal*, 10 (2): 81–97.

Bromwich, M. and Hopwood, A.G. (1992) The intertwining of accounting and the law, in M. Bromwich and A.G. Hopwood (eds) *Accounting and the Law*, pp. 1–14 (London: Prentice Hall).

Brownlee, W.E. (1996) *Federal Taxation in America: A Short History* (Cambridge: Cambridge University Press).

Bryer, R.A. (1993) The late nineteenth-century revolution in financial reporting: Accounting for the rise of investor or managerial capitalism? *Accounting, Organizations and Society*, 18 (7/8): 649–690.

Bujaki, M.L., Gaudet, S. and Iuliano, R.M. (2016) Governmentality and identity construction through 50 years of personal income tax returns: The case of an immigrant couple in Canada, *Critical Perspectives on Accounting*, 46: 54–74.

Casson, P.D. (1996) The taxation of executive share options – Lessons from the past: A note on the 1966 Finance Bill. *British Tax Review*, 4: 431–437.

Casson, P.D. (1998) International aspects of the UK imputation system of corporate taxation, *British Tax Review*, 5: 493–507.

Casson, P.D. (2004) The evolution of UK tax legislation for employee share ownership plans, in J. Tiley (ed) *Studies in the History of Tax Law*, pp. 147–176 (Oxford: Hart Publishing).

Cataldo, A.J.I.I. (1995) The earned income credit: Historical predecessors and contemporary evolution, *Accounting Historians Journal*, 22 (1): 57–79.

Choi, F.D.S. and Mueller, G.G. (1992) *International Accounting*, 2nd (Englewood Cliffs, NJ: Prentice-Hall International).

Covaleski, M.A., Dirsmith, M.W. and Mantzke, K. (2005) Institutional destablilization and the new public management: The case of tax incremental financing, *International Journal of Public Policy*, 1: 122–146.

Crum, R.P. (1982) Value-added taxation: The roots run deep into colonial and early America, *Accounting Historians Journal*, 9 (2): 25–42.

Cuzdriorean, D.D. and Matis, D. (2012) The relationship between accounting and taxation insight (sic) the European Union: The influence of the International Accounting Regulation, *Annales Universitatis Apenlensis Series Oeconomica*, 14 (1): 28–43.

Da Costa, R.C., Bourgeois, J.C. and Lawson, W.M. (1978) A classification of international financial accounting practices, *International Journal of Accounting*, 13 (2): 73–85.

Daunton, M. (2001) *Trusting Leviathan: The Politics of Taxation in Britain, 1799–1914* (Cambridge: Cambridge University Press).

Daunton, M. (2002) *Just Taxes: The Politics of Taxation in Britain, 1914–1979* (Cambridge: Cambridge University Press).

Deaconu, A. (2012) Accounting models and influential factors in post-communist Romania, *International Journal of Critical Accounting*, 4 (2): 194–216.

Donohoe, M.P., McGill, G.A. and Outslay, E. (2014) Risky business: The prosopography of corporate tax planning, *National Tax Journal*, 67 (4): 851–874.

Dowell, S. (1965) *A History of Taxation and Taxes in England*, 3rd (London: Frank Cass and Co. Ltd).

Eden, L., Dacin, M.T. and Wan, W.P. (2001) Standards across borders: Crossborder diffusion of the arm's length standard in North America, *Accounting, Organizations and Society*, 26 (1): 1–23.

Edey, H.C. (1956) Valuation of stock in trade for income tax purposes, *British Tax Review*, 1: 23–37.

Edgley, C.R.P. (2010) Backstage in legal theatre: A Foucauldian interpretation of 'Rationes Decidendi' on the question of taxable business profits, *Critical Perspectives on Accounting*, 21: 560–572.

Edwards, J.R. (1976) Tax treatment of capital expenditure and the measurement of accounting profit, *British Tax Review*, 5: 300–319.

Einhorn, R.L. (2006) *American Taxation, American Slavery* (Chicago, IL: University of Chicago Press).
Ezzamel, M. (2002) Accounting working for the state: Tax assessment and collection during the New Kingdom, Ancient Egypt, *Accounting and Business Research*, 32 (1): 17–39.
Ezzamel, M. (2012) *Accounting and Order* (Abingdon: Routledge).
Frank, W.G. (1979) An empirical analysis of international accounting principles, *Journal of Accounting Research*, 17 (2): 593–605.
Frecknall-Hughes, J. and McKerchar, M. (2013) Historical perspectives on the emergence of the tax profession: Australia and the UK, *Australian Tax Forum*, 28 (2): 275–288.
Frecknall-Hughes, J. and Oats, L. (2007) King John's tax innovations – Extortion, resistance, and the establishment of the principle of taxation by consent, *Accounting Historians Journal*, 34 (2): 75–107.
Freedman, J. (1987) Profit and prophets – Law and accountancy practice on the timing of receipts – Recognition under the earnings basis (Schedule D, Cases I & II), *British Tax Review*, 2: 61–79. (3): 104–33.
Freedman, J. (1993) Ordinary principles of commercial accounting – Clear guidance or a mystery tour?, *British Tax Review*, 6: 468–478.
Freedman, J. (1995) Defining taxable profit in a changing accounting environment, *British Tax Review*, 5: 433–524.
Freedman, J. (1997) The role of realisation: Accounting, company law and taxation, in International Fiscal Association (ed.) *The Influence of Corporate Law and Accounting Principles in Determining Taxable Income*, Vol. 21b, pp. 29–48 (The Hague: Kluwer Law International, IFA Congress Seminar Series).
Freedman, J. and Power, M. (1992) Law and accounting: Transition and transformation, in J. Freedman and M. Power (eds) *Law and Accountancy: Conflict and Co-operation in the 1990s*, pp. 1–23 (London: Paul Chapman).
Gavana, G., Guggioloa, G. and Marenzi, A. (2013) Evolving connections between tax and financial reporting in Italy, *Accounting in Europe*, 10 (1): 43–70.
Gee, M., Haller, A. and Nobes, C. (2010) The influence of tax on IFRS consolidated statements: The convergence of Germany and the UK, *Accounting in Europe*, 7 (1): 97–122.
Gilmore, C. and Willmott, H. (1992) Company law and financial reporting: A sociological history of the UK experience, in M. Bromwich and A.G. Hopwood (eds) *Accounting and the Law*, pp. 159–190 (London: Prentice Hall).
Giroux, G. (2012) Financing the American Civil War: Developing new tax sources, *Accounting History*, 17 (1): 83–104.
Glantz, A.E. (2008) A tax on light and air: Impact of the Window Duty on tax administration and architecture, 1696–1851, *Penn History Review*, 15 (2): 18–40.
Groves, H.M. (1974) *Tax Philosophers: Two Hundred Years of Thought in Great Britain and the United States* (Madison, WI: University of Wisconsin Press).
Haller, A. (1992) The relationship of financial and tax accounting in Germany: A major reason for accounting disharmony in Europe, *International Journal of Accounting*, 4: 310–323.
Heaman, E. (2013) "The Whites are Wild about It": Taxation and racialization in mid-Victorian British Columbia, *The Journal of Policy History*, 25 (3): 354–384.
Hoogendoorn, M.N. (1996) Accounting and taxation in Europe – A comparative overview, *European Accounting Review*, 5 (Supplement): 783–794.
Hooper, K.C. and Kearins, K. (2003) Substance but not form: Capital taxation and public finance in New Zealand, 1840–1859, *Accounting History*, 8 (2): 101–119.
Hope, T. and Briggs, J. (1982) Accounting policy making – Some lessons from the deferred taxation debate, *Accounting and Business Research*, 12 (46): 83–96.
Hopwood, A.G. (1987) The archaeology of accounting systems, *Accounting, Organizations and Society*, 12 (3): 207–234.
Hopwood, A.G. (1997) Internationalising international accounting research, *Accounting, Organizations and Society*, 22 (6): iii–iv.
Hopwood, A.G., Burchell, S. and Clubb, C. (1994) Value-added accounting and national economic policy, in: A.G. Hopwood and P. Miller (eds) *Accounting as Social and Institutional Practice*, pp. 211–236 (Cambridge: Cambridge University Press).
Hopwood, A.G. and Johnson, H.T. (1986) Accounting history's claim to legitimacy, *International Journal of Accounting*, 21 (2): 37–46.
Horngren, C.T. (1973) The marketing of accounting standards, *Journal of Accountancy*, 136 (4): 61–66.
Jones, M.J. (2010) Sources of power and infrastructural conditions in medieval governmental accounting, *Accounting, Organizations and Society*, 35: 81–94.

Jose, M. and Moore, C. (1998) The development of taxation in the Bible: Improvements in counting, measurement, and computation in the Ancient Middle East, *Accounting Historians Journal*, 25 (2): 63–80.

Kay, J. and King, M (1990) *The British Tax System*, 2nd (Oxford: Oxford University Press).

Kern, B.B. (2000) The role of depreciation and the investment tax credit in tax policy and their influence on financial reporting during the 20th century, *Accounting Historians Journal*, 27 (2): 145–164.

Knights, D. and Collinson, D. (1987) Disciplining the shopfloor: A comparison of the disciplinary effects of managerial psychology and financial accounting, *Accounting, Organizations and Society*, 12 (5): 457–477.

Koowattanatianchai, N., Charles, M.B. and Eddie, I. (2019) Incentivising investment through accelerated depreciation: Wartime use, economic stimulus and encouraging green technologies, *Accounting History*, 24 (1): 115–137.

Kozub, R. (1983) Antecedents of the income tax in Colonial America, *Accounting Historians Journal*, 10 (2): 99–116.

Lamb, M. (1995) When is a group a group? Convergence of concepts of 'group' in European Union Corporate Tax, *European Accounting Review*, 4 (1): 33–78.

Lamb, M. (1996) The relationship between accounting and taxation: The United Kingdom, *European Accounting Review*, 5 (Supplement): 933–949.

Lamb, M. (2001) 'Horrid appealing': Accounting for taxable profits in mid-nineteenth century England, *Accounting, Organizations and Society*, 26 (3): 271–298.

Lamb, M. (2002) Defining "profits" for British income tax purposes: A contextual study of the depreciation cases, 1875–1897, *Accounting Historians Journal*, 29 (1): 105–172.

Lamb, M. (2003) Questions of taxation framed as accounting historical research: A suggested approach, *Accounting Historians Journal*, 30 (2): 175–196.

Lamb, M. (2004) Taxation research as accounting research, in M. Lamb, A. Lymer, J. Freedman and S. James (eds) *Interdisciplinary Perspectives on Taxation Research*, pp. 55–84 (Oxford: Oxford University Press).

Lamb, M., Nobes, C. and Roberts, A. (1998) International variations in the connections between tax and financial reporting, *Accounting and Business Research*, 28 (3): 173–188.

Lang, T.K. and Heier, J.R. (2013) The AIA's special bulletin series and its early guidance on tax issues related to depreciation, 1920–1929, *Accounting Historians Journal*, 40 (1): 51–78.

Lee, T.A. (2006) The professional journal as a signal of movement to occupational ascendancy and as legitimation of a professional project: The early history of *The Accountant's Magazine* 1897–1951, *Accounting History*, 11 (1): 7–40.

Likhovski, A. (2012) Chasing ghosts: On writing cultural histories of tax law, *Irvine Law Review*, 1: 843–892.

Loft, A. (1986) Towards a critical understanding of accounting: The case of cost accounting in the UK, 1914–1925, *Accounting, Organizations and Society*, 11 (2): 137–169.

Loft, A. (1994) Accountancy and the First World War, in A.G. Hopwood and P. Miller (eds) *Accounting as Social and Institutional Practice*, pp. 116–137 (Cambridge: Cambridge University Press).

Macve, R.H. (1994) Some glosses on Greek and Roman accounting, in R.H. Parker and B.S. Yamey (eds) *Accounting History: Some British Contributions*, pp. 57–87 (Oxford: Clarendon Press).

Martin, I.W., Mehrota, A.K. and Prasad, M. (2011) *The New Fiscal Sociology: Taxation in Comparative and Historical Perspective* (Cambridge: Cambridge University Press).

May, G.O. (1938) The consequences of increasing taxes, *Accountant Tax Supplement*, 13 (8): 383–385.

McBarnet, D. and Whelan, C. (1992) The elusive spirit of the law: Formalism and the struggle for legal control, in J. Freedman and M. Power (eds) *Law and Accountancy: Conflict and Co-operation in the 1990s*, pp. 80–105 (London: Paul Chapman).

McDonald, J. (2002) Tax fairness in eleventh century England, *Accounting Historians Journal*, 29 (1): 173–193.

McDonald, J. (2012) Investigating tax fairness in eleventh century England: Evidence from Wiltshire estates, *Journal of Accounting and Taxation*, 3 (6): 140–146.

Mehrotra, A.K. (2010) American economic development, managerial corporate capitalism, and the institutional foundations of the modern income tax, *Law and Contemporary Problems*, 73: 25–61.

Mehrotra, A.K. (2013) *Making the Modern American Fiscal State: Law, Politics and the Rise of Progressive Taxation, 1877–1929* (New York: Cambridge University Press).

Mehrotra, A.K. (2017) Fiscal forearms: Taxation as the lifeblood of the modern liberal state, in K. Morgan and A. Orloff (eds) *The Many Hands of the State: Theorizing the Complexities of Political Authority and Social Control*, pp. 284–305 (New York: Cambridge University Press).

Mena, R.F. (2016) From the Aztecs their tax systems; of the Incas their accounts, and of the Mayas their scripture; the outcome is the pre-Columbian accounting, *Accounting & Financial History Research Journal*, 10: 181–244.
Miller, P. (1990) On the interrelations between accounting and the state, *Accounting, Organizations and Society*, 15 (4): 315–338.
Miller, P. (1994) Accounting as social and institutional practice: An introduction, in A.G. Hopwood and P. Miller (eds) *Accounting as Social and Institutional Practice*, pp. 1–39 (Cambridge: Cambridge University Press).
Miller, P. and Power, M. (1992) Accounting, law and economic calculation, in M. Bromwich and A. G. Hopwood (eds) *Accounting and the Law*, pp. 230–253 (London: Prentice Hall).
Mills, L. (1955) Tax accounting and business accounting, present status and remaining differences, *National Tax Journal*, 8 (1): 69–80.
Morton, E.F. (2019) A historical review of the rise of tax effect accounting as a financial reporting norm accounting history, *Accounting History*, 24 (4): 562–90.
Mueller, G.G. (1967) *International Accounting* (New York: Macmillan).
Nair, R.D. and Frank, W.G. (1980) The impact of disclosure and measurement practices on international accounting classifications, *Accounting Review*, 55 (3): 426–450.
Napier, C.J. (1996) Accounting and the absence of a business economics tradition in the United Kingdom, *European Accounting Review*, 5 (3): 449–481.
Napier, C.J. and Noke, C. (1992) Accounting and law: An historical overview of an uneasy relationship, in M. Bromwich and A.G. Hopwood (eds) *Accounting and the Law*, pp. 30–54 (London: Prentice Hall).
Nobes, C. and Schwencke, H. (2006) Modelling the links between tax and financial reporting: A longitudinal examination of Norway over 30 years up to IFRS adoption, *European Accounting Review*, 15 (1): 63–87.
Nobes, C.W. (1983) A judgmental international classification of financial reporting practices, *Journal of business, Finance and Accounting*, 10 (1): 1–19.
Nobes, C.W. (1984) *International Classification of Financial Reporting* (London: Croom Helm).
Nobes, C.W. (1991) International classification of financial reporting, in C.W. Nobes and R. Parker (eds) *Comparative International Accounting*, 3rd, pp. 38–51 (London and New York: Prentice Hall).
Nobes, C.W. (1992) *International Classification of Financial Reporting* (London: Routledge).
Nobes, C. W. (1995) *International Classification of Financial Reporting* (London: Routledge).
Nobes, C.W. and Parker, R. (eds) (2016) *Comparative International Accounting*, 13th (Harlow: Pearson Education).
Noguchi, M. (2005) Interaction between tax and accounting practice: Accounting for stock-in-trade, *Accounting, Business & Financial History*, 15 (1): 1–34.
Nurnberg, H. (2009) Conceptual nature of corporate income tax, *Accounting Historians Journal*, 36 (2): 31–74.
Oates, W.E. and Schwab, R.M. (2015) The Window Tax: A case study in excess burden, *Journal of Economic Perspectives*, 29 (1): 163–180.
Oats, L. and Sadler, P. (2004) Political suppression or revenue raising? Taxing newspapers during the French Revolutionary Wars, *Accounting Historians Journal*, 31 (1): 93–128.
Oats, L. and Sadler, P. (2007) Securing the repeal of a tax on the material of thought, *Accounting, Business & Financial History*, 17 (3): 355–373.
Oats, L. and Sadler, P. (2013) The Stamp Duty on newspapers – The unseen hand in the First Amendment, *British Tax Review*, 13: 345–366.
Oldroyd, D.A. (1995) The role of accounting in public expenditure and monetary policy in the first century AD Roman Empire, *Accounting Historians Journal*, 22 (2): 117–129.
Oliveras, E. and Puig, X. (2007) The changing relationship between tax and financial reporting in Spain, *Accounting in Europe*, 2 (1): 195–207.
Ordelheide, D. and Pfaff, D. (1994) *European Financial Reporting: Germany* (London: Routledge).
Parker, R.H. (1986) *The Development of the Accountancy Profession in Britain to the Early Twentieth Century*, Monograph No. 5 (San Antonio, Texas: The Academy of Accounting Historians).
Pentland, B.T. and Carlile, P. (1996) Audit the taxpayer, not the return: Tax auditing as an expression game, *Accounting, Organizations and Society*, 21 (2/3): 269–287.
Picciotto, S. (1992a) *International Business Taxation: A Study in the Internationalization of Business Regulation* (London: Weidenfeld and Nicolson).

Picciotto, S. (1992b) International taxation and intrafirm pricing in transnational corporate groups, *Accounting, Organizations and Society*, 17 (8): 759–792.
Pincus, M. (1989) Legislative history of the allowance of LIFO for tax purposes, *Accounting Historians Journal*, 16 (1): 23–55.
Preston, A.M. (1989) The taxman cometh: Some observations on the interrelationship between accounting and Inland Revenue practice, *Accounting, Organizations and Society*, 14 (5/6): 389–413.
Pridgen, A. and Flesher, D.L. (2013) Improving accounting and accountability in local governments: The case of the Tennessee Taxpayers Association, *Accounting History*, 18 (4): 507–528.
Radebaugh, L.H. and Gray, S.J. (1993) *International Accounting and Multinational Enterprises* New York: John Wiley & Sons.
Rodrigues, L.L. and Craig, R. (2018) The role of government accounting and taxation in the institutionalisation of slavery in Brazil, *Critical Perspectives on Accounting*, 57: 21–38.
Rodrigues, L.L., Craig, R.J., Schmidt, P. and Santos, J.L. (2015) Documenting, monetising and taxing Brazilian slaves in the eighteenth and nineteenth centuries, *Accounting History Review*, 25 (1): 43–67.
Rostain, T. and Regan, M.C. (2014) *Confidence Games: Lawyers, Accountants and the Tax Shelter Industry* (Cambridge, MA: MIT Press).
Rutterford, J. and Walton, P. (2014) The war, taxation and the Blackpool Tower Company, *Accounting History Review*, 24 (2/3): 103–117.
Sabine, B.E.V. (1966) *A History of Income Tax* (London: George Allen & Unwin).
Sadler, P. and Oats, L. (2002) This great crisis in the republick of letters: The introduction in 1712 of stamp duties on newspapers and pamphlets, *British Tax Review*, 4: 353–366.
Sadler, P. and Oats, L. (2013) The stamp duty on newspapers – The unseen hand in the first amendment, *British Tax Review*, 3: 345–366.
Samson, W. (1985) The nineteenth century income tax in the South, *Accounting Historians Journal*, 12 (1): 37–52.
Samson, W.D. (1998) Instructional resource: Using tax history to teach the concepts of tax planning, *Issues in Accounting Education*, 13 (3): 655–692.
Sanders, T.H. (1939) Speech reproduced, *Accountant*, 22 (4): 523.
Schultz, S.M. and Johnson, R.T. (1998) Income tax allocation: The continuing controversy in historical perspective, *Accounting Historians Journal*, 25 (2): 81–111.
Seligman, E.R.A. (1914) *The Income Tax: A Study of the History, Theory and Practice of Income Taxation at Home and Abroad* (New York: Macmillan).
Shah, A.K. (1996) Creative compliance in financial reporting, *Accounting, Organizations and Society*, 21 (1): 23–39.
Soll, J. (2014) *The Reckoning: Financial Accountability and the Rise and Fall of Nations* (New York: Basic Books).
Solomons, D. (1978) The politicization of accounting, *Journal of Accountancy*, 146 (5): 65–72.
Solomons, D. (1983) The political implications of accounting and accounting standard setting, *Accounting and Business Research*, 13 (50): 107–118.
Stanley, R. (1993) *Dimensions of Law in the Service of Order: Origins of the Federal Income Tax, 1861–1913* (New York and Oxford: Oxford University Press).
Starkman (2008) *The Sex of A Hippopotamus: A Unique History of Taxes and Accounting* (Atlanta, GAUSA: Twinset Inc).
Stopforth, D.P. (1992) 1922–36: Halcyon days for the tax avoider. *British Tax Review*, 2: 88–105.
Stopforth, D.P. (1999) Creating Anti-avoidance legislation, *British Tax Review*, 2: 106–113.
Stopforth, D.P. (2004) Deliberations over taxing capital gains – The position up to 1955, in: J. Tiley (ed) *Studies in the History of Tax Law*, Vol. 1, pp. 133–145 (Oxford: Hart Publishing).
Stopforth, D.P. (2005a) Birth of capital gains tax – The official view, *British Tax Review*, 6: 584–608.
Stopforth, D.P. (2005b) Getting tough on avoidance – Blocking revenue annuities, *British Tax Review*, 5: 557–567.
Stopforth, D.P. (2007) Official deliberations on capital gains tax: 1955–1960, in J. Tiley (ed) *Studies in the History of Tax Law*, Vol. 2, pp. 119–135 (Oxford: Hart Publishing).
Thompson, S.J. (2013) The first income tax, political arithmetic, and the measurement of economic growth, *Economic History Review*, 66 (3): 873–894.
Treisch, C. (2005) Taxable treatment of the subsistence level of income in German natural law, *Accounting, Business & Financial History*, 15 (3): 255–278.

Troop Smith, D. (1953) Corporate taxation and common stock financing, *National Tax Journal*, 6 (3): 209–225.

Vogeler, G. (2005) Tax accounting in the late medieval German territorial states, *Accounting, Business & Financial History*, 15 (3): 235–254.

von Wysocki, K. (1984) The Fourth Directive and Germany, in S.J. Gray and A.G. Coenenberg (eds) *EEC Accounting Harmonisation: Implementation and Impact of the Fourth Directive*, pp. pp. 55–61 (Amsterdam: North Holland).

Vosslamber, R. (2012) Taxation for New Zealand's future: The introduction of New Zealand's progressive income tax in 1891, *Accounting History*, 17 (1): 105–122.

Walker, S.P. (2011) Ethel Ayres Purdie: Critical practitioner and suffragist, *Critical Perspectives on Accounting*, 22 (1): 79–101.

Walton, P. (1992) Les liens entre la comptabilité financière et la fiscalité au Royaume Uni: l'exploration d'un mythe, *Revue Française De La Comptabilité*, 235: 48–50.

Walton, P. (1993) Company law and accounting in nineteenth-century Europe: Introduction, *European Accounting Review*, 2 (2): 286–291.

Watts, R.L. and Zimmerman, J.L. (1979) The demand for and supply of accounting theories: The market for excuses, *Accounting Review*, 54 (2): 273–305.

Webber, C. and Wildavsky, A. (1986) *A History of Taxation and Expenditure in the Western World* (New York: Simon & Schuster).

Weisman, S.R. (2002) *The Great Tax Wars: Lincoln to Wilson – The Fierce Battles over Money and Power that Transformed the Nation* (New York: Simon & Schuster).

Wells, S.C. and Flesher, T.K. (1999) Lessons for policy makers from the history of consumption taxes, *Accounting Historians Journal*, 26 (1): 103–126.

Wohl, M.J., Matheson, K., Branscome, N.R. and Anisman, H. (2013) Victim and perpetrator groups' responses to the Canadian Government's apology for the Head Tax on Chinese immigrants and the moderating influence of collective guilt, *Political Psychology*, 34 (5): 713–729.

Xu, Y. and Xu, X. (2016) Taxation and state-building: The tax reform under the nationalist government in China, 1928–1949, *Accounting, Organizations and Society*, 48: 17–30.

Zeff, S.A. (1972) *Forging Accounting Principles in Five Countries: A History and an Analysis of Trends* (Champaign, IL: Stipes Publishing Co).

Zeff, S.A. (1978) The rise of "economic consequences", *Journal of Accountancy*, 146 (6): 56–63.

Zeff, S.A. (2007) The SEC pre-empts the accounting principles board in 1965: The classification of the deferred tax credit relating to installment sales, *Accounting Historians Journal*, 34 (1): 1–23.

INDEX

Printed in the United States
by Baker & Taylor Publisher Services

Printed in the United States
by Baker & Taylor Publisher Services